# JEAN RHYS

# CAROLE ANGIER

# JEAN RHYS

## Life and Work

Little, Brown and Company

*Boston   Toronto   London*

FIRST U.S. EDITION

ISBN 0-316-04263-3
Library of Congress Cataloging-in-Publication information is available.

10  9  8  7  6  5  4  3  2  1

MV-PA

Printed in the United States of America

*For my parents*

# CONTENTS

    After *Voyage in the Dark* – Dominica –
    Paultons Square – Good Morning, Midnight

6   Good Morning, Midnight                                          377

PART THREE: **THE LOST YEARS, 1939–1966**

1   War, 1939–1945                                                  411
    Norfolk – Breakdown – The Gower Peninsula –
    John and Maryvonne – Leslie's death

2   Max, 1945–1957                                                  400
    Seven years' bad luck: 1945–1952 – Maidstone:
    1950–1952 – The Ropemakers Diary – London:
    1952–1955 – Bude: 1955–1957

3   The Writing of Wide Sargasso Sea, 1957–1966                     475
    Cornwall – Cheriton Fitzpaine

4   Wide Sargasso Sea                                               525

PART FOUR: **THE LAST YEARS, 1966–1979**

1   Life, 1966–1975                                                 571

2   Death, 1976–1979                                                627

3   Jean                                                            655

    Notes                                                           659

    Bibliography                                                    737

    Index                                                           747

# LIST OF ILLUSTRATIONS

1   *Top*: Roseau, Dominica, at the turn of the century.
*Bottom*: The Administrator of Dominica, Sir Henry Hesketh Bell, with the Legislative Council in 1901. Dr Rees Williams is third from the right in the second row down. (By courtesy of the Royal Commonwealth Society.)

2   *Top*: At Geneva: Granny Woodcock and Great-Aunt Jane, with an unidentified woman. (By courtesy of the Royal Commonwealth Society.)
*Bottom left*: Jean's sister Brenda, at school in England.
*Bottom right*: Brenda Lockhart, Jean's Auntie B.

3   Minna Rees Williams, Jean's mother.

4   *Top*: The Rees Williams' house on Cork Street, Roseau; lacking its verandah, which has been enclosed, and the garden at the back, which has been built over.
*Bottom*: All that was left of the Geneva garden when Jean revisited Dominica in 1936.

5   From a group photograph of the Perse School staff in 1908. Kind Miss Street is in black, with fierce Miss Osborn, in a spotted dress, on her right. (By courtesy of Perse School for Girls, Cambridge.)

6   Lancelot Grey Hugh Smith, the love of Jean's life, in 1912 or '13.

7   Jean (on the right) in *Chanteclair*, 1910.

8   *Top*: Julian Martin Smith, Lancelot's cousin, the original of Vincent in *Voyage in the Dark*.
*Bottom*: Philip Heseltine, the original of Julian in 'Till September, Petronella', in 1915, on the verandah of the cottage described in the story.

1   To the Crabtree Club: an illustration by Dorothea St-John George for *London's Latin Quarter* by Kenneth Hare (The Bodley Head, 1926).

I wish to thank the following people for sending me photographs: Mrs Jean Beck for Jean's sister Brenda; Mr Lennox Honychurch for Dominica at the turn of the century; Mr Julian Martin Smith for Julian Martin Smith; Mrs Helen Mather for Max Hamer; Diana Melly for Jean in Venice; Madame Maryvonne Moerman for Jean and John in Vienna; Group Captain L.E. Robins for Lancelot Hugh Smith; Mr Malcolm Rudland for Philip Heseltine; Mr Hubert Sturges for Mrs Adam; Mrs Pauline Thomas for Mr and Mrs Greenslade; Mrs Mary Woodard for the Rev. Alwynne Woodard.

Unacknowledged photographs are from the Estate of Jean Rhys.

# AUTHOR'S NOTE

When this book began, as a critical study with one biographical chapter, it also contained two chapters on Jean Rhys's short stories. But the more I learned the more I realised that Jean's work was even more about her life, and her life even more about her work, than we already knew. The only form adequate to explore and express this was the one the reader will find, in which life and work are almost equally balanced. But with eighty-nine years and five novels this made a long book, however hard I tried to emulate Jean's economy. In the end, therefore, I adopted her other solution, and cut the short story chapters altogether. Her stories are absent, in other words, for reasons of space only, not because I think them less good or important than her novels. In fact some of them ('Till September Petronella', for instance, 'Let Them Call It Jazz', and 'I Used to Live Here Once') seem to me as great as her greatest novels, and in the same characteristic way: distilling truth out of evasion and art out of pain.

# ACKNOWLEDGEMENTS

First and foremost I wish to thank Francis Wyndham, Jean Rhys's literary executor, for his unfailing trust, patience and generosity over the last six years. The result is entirely my own responsibility, but owes everything to him.

Secondly I wish to thank Diana Athill, Jean's editor and mine, for her equally patient support, hard work and invaluable advice; and Diana Melly, co-editor of Jean's letters and friend of her last years, for all her help from the beginning.

Thirdly I would like to thank Jean Rhys's daughter, Maryvonne Moerman-Lenglet, for her personal expression of support to me, despite the fact that she felt unable to answer any more questions after 1985. This book, therefore, has been written without her further participation.

Fourthly I would like to record my special thanks to two members of Jean's family: her brother Owen's widow, Dorothy Rees Williams, who was my main source of information about the family and Jean's relation to it; and her second husband's daughter, Anne Smyser, who was my main source of information about Leslie Tilden Smith and Jean's life with him in the nineteen thirties. To my sorrow, Anne died before the book could be finished.

Fifthly I would like to express my debt to two Dutch scholars. Emile van der Wilk wrote *Ed. de Nève*, his biography of Jean's first husband, Jean Lenglet (published in Holland in 1989) at the same time as I was writing *Jean Rhys*, and generously shared all his discoveries with me. Even more generously, Martien Kappers den Hollander translated for me, in detail, over many hours, the contents of his book and of Lenglet's novels, all but one available only in Dutch; and shared with me her ideas and discoveries, even though she is still working on her own book about Jean Rhys's Dutch connection. Almost all the information about Jean Lenglet's life and work here comes from Martien Kappers and Emile van der Wilk.

As well as these, the following people were extremely generous with their time and energy, submitting to long interviews, writing long letters, and sometimes undertaking researches of their own to help me: *Part One, Chapter One* Especially Daphne Agar, Jean Beck, Lennox Honychurch, John Rees Williams and Ena Williams. Also Eva Abraham, Megs Frampton, Elsie Gale, Emma Gale, Joe Hone, Professor Louis James, Polly Pattullo, Rosalind Smith, Nicole Stott and Elizabeth Varvill. *Chapter Two* For the Perse School, especially Miss Gwen Neal; also Mrs Nancy Barrett, Mrs Clare Myers, Miss Marjorie Pye and Mrs Mary Russell, all Old Perseans; Miss M.R. Bateman, Headmistress; Miss Heather Cubitt, Head of History and Archivist; Mrs Margaret Chamberlain, Registrar, the Old Persean Guild. For the Academy of Dramatic Art, Richard O'Donoghue, Administrator-Registrar, the Royal Academy of Dramatic Art. For the chorus, Tristram Powell. For Lancelot Hugh Smith and Julian Martin Smith, especially Aubrey Baring, Julian Martin Smith and Group Captain L.E. Robins, CBE; and Oliver Baring, Bill Corney, Lady Alethea Eliot, Maude Ehrenstein, Jocelyn Hambro, Faith Raven and Fortune Stanley. *Chapter Three* For Maxwell Henry Hayes Macartney, Dr Barbara Coventry and Miss S. Maberly Smith. For Arthur Henry Fox Strangways, Mark Baker, Tony Gould and Professor Mary Lago. For Philip Heseltine, Malcolm Rudland, Secretary, the Peter Warlock Society. For Adrian Allinson, Michael Holroyd, Lee & Pemberton, Solicitors, Joan Seay, Peyton Skipwith. For Sir William Orpen, his biographer Bruce Arnold. *Chapter Four* For translating part of her father's *Ed. de Nève*, Hester van der Wilk. *Chapter Five* For Ford, Dr Max Saunders. For Mrs Adam, Hubert M. Sturges. *Part Two, Chapters One, Three and Five* For Jean and Leslie: Phyllis Shand Allfrey; Eliot Bliss; Rosamond Lehmann; Hamish Hamilton (through Diana Petre); Muriel (Sue) Ramsay, formerly Tilden Smith; Robin Waterfield. For Simon Segal: M. Alain Bouret and Mme. Mireille Kocher, Editions Ides et Calendes, Neuchâtel, Switzerland. *Part Three, Chapter One* Barbara Campbell, Margaret Feast and Rev. Eric Griffiths. *Chapter Two* Sue Brown, Christopher Hamer and Helen Mather. *Chapter Three* Especially Mrs Mary Woodard; and Janet Bridger, Joan Butler, Helen Howitt, Joan Lee and Pauline Thomas. For Mr Woodard, also Basil Handford. *Part Four, Chapters One and Two* Al Alvarez, Larry Cole, Joan Forman, Antonia Fraser, Michael Henshaw, Jo Hill, George Melly, Diana Petre, David Plante, Herbert Ronson, Michael Schwab, Madeleine Slade, Oliver and Mollie Stoner, Jan van Houts, Esther Whitby. Also David Perry, Senior Producer of Talks and Documentaries, BBC Radio, for the transcript of Paul Bailey's 'Jean Rhys', broadcast on 15 August 1981; and Isabelle Yhuel of Radio France, for the tape recording of her programme on Jean Rhys, broadcast 15 January 1987. *Chapter Three* Hansi Kennedy, Principal Child Psychotherapist, Anna Freud Centre,

London; Susan Baxt, M.Ed., M.A. and Dr Jack Klein, Canada; Dr Joan Schachter and Jan Wiener, M.S.A.P., London.

I am also indebted to many institutions, especially libraries, and their staffs. First, to the Special Collections of the McFarlin Library, University of Tulsa, to its Curator, Sidney F. Huttner, and to its Curator of Literary Manuscripts and Art when I visited in 1985, Caroline S. Swinson; to the British Library, London Library and Library of the Army Museum, London; and to the Bodleian, Taylorean and Rhodes House Libraries, Oxford. And to the following libraries, archives and institutions:

*Part One, Chapter One* Library of the Royal Commonwealth Society, London; Library of the University of Edinburgh; Royal College of Surgeons of England; St George's Hospital Medical School; University of Manchester Medical School. *Chapter Two* The Theatre Museum; Library of Trinity College, Cambridge. *Chapter Three* Wellington College Archive, Heather Tomlinson, Archivist; *The Times* Archive, Clare Handley, Archivist (1985) and Melanie Aspey, Archivist (1990); Marylebone Library. *Chapter Four* Centre de documentation juive, Paris; Chambre de Commerce et d'Industrie de Paris; Direction des Services d'Archives, Préfecture de Paris, M. Phillippe Grand, Director; French Embassy, London; Institut français du Royaume-uni, London; Maison Française, Oxford; Manchester City Art Gallery; National Diet Library, Tokyo, Azusa Tanaka, Director of Interlibrary Services Division. *Part Two, Chapters One, Three and Five* Greater London Record Office and History Library; Library of the Royal Air Force Museum, Peter Elliot, Librarian; Ministry of Defence, RAF Personnel Management Centre. *Part Three* Central Library, London Borough of Bromley, Miss Silverthorne, Librarian; Library of Jesus College, Cambridge; Records Section, Lord Chancellor's Department, London.

Finally, I would like to thank Helen Burnett for typing this big book so well; and Southern Arts for awarding me a bursary in 1986.

Because Jean Rhys was nearly ninety when she died in 1979, and I didn't start work until five years later, many of my informants were already very old when I began. Anne Smyser was not the only one to die before the book was finished. I'd like to list their names, in memory.

| | |
|---|---|
| Phyllis Shand Allfrey | Rosamond Lehmann |
| Aubrey Baring | Gwen Neal |
| Maude Ehrenstein | Mary Russell |
| Megs Frampton | Anne Smyser |
| Elsie Gale | Oliver Stoner |
| Hamish Hamilton | |

# PART ONE

---

# LIFE
# 1890-1927

# CHAPTER ONE

# Dominica, 1890–1907

*The island — The family — Childhood — Mr Howard's house —
Missy — Leaving Dominica*

Nothing brings violence and death closer than an extreme abundance
of life and beauty. And nowhere on earth are life and beauty more
abundant than on the island of Dominica where Jean Rhys was born.
In her last novel, which is set there (though she called it Jamaica),
she wrote: 'Our garden was large and beautiful as that garden in the
Bible — the tree of life grew there. But it had gone wild.'

The rain forest of Dominica is so dense and wild it is still mostly
unexplored. More mountains and more rivers (three hundred and
sixty-five, they say, one for each day of the year) crowd more closely
together here than almost anywhere else in the world. (A famous
Dominica story says that when Queen Isabella asked Christopher
Columbus to describe the island he had discovered, he crumpled up
a piece of parchment in his hand and threw it on the table.)

The sun shines hotter and the moon brighter here than anywhere
in Europe. Rain falls more suddenly and night comes more quickly.
Colours are brighter, smells stronger; trees and flowers and insects
grow bigger. So much grows so quickly that almost everything has
a parasite, even people. Species overflow, individuals don't count.

All this careless, cannibal life is beautiful, but also sinister. 'Beauty
and violence, beauty and decay: that was the island,' wrote another
Dominican novelist, Phyllis Shand Allfrey. Nothing lasts; everything
decays as fast as it grows. The guava blossom, the orchids, the night-
flowering lilies smell so sweet and strong it's like the smell of death.
'Twice a year the octopus orchid flowered,' Jean wrote in *Wide
Sargasso Sea.* 'It was a bell-shaped mass of white, mauve, deep purple,
wonderful to see.... I never went near it.'

The beauty is mainly on the surface, the violence beneath. Huge
interior forces buckled the Antilles out of the ocean floor, and
Dominica is still close to its volcanic birth. Hundreds of hot springs
push up through the ground; near them you only have to poke the
soft grey surface with a stick and boiling water gushes out. Halfway

across the island from Roseau, where Jean was born, is the Valley of Desolation, where sulphur fumes have a made a black hole in the green forest. In the middle of this valley is the Abomination of Desolation, the huge crater of a semi-active volcano, its summit three thousand feet above the sea. A grey mist always hangs over it; the sulphur fumes that rise from it are so strong that silver coins turn black in the air. Twice a day fountains of scalding water, steam and smoke burst up through the grey sand at the bottom and make the inner crater a boiling cauldron, hundreds of feet across.

Violence lurks also − lurks especially − in Dominica's history. Five hundred years before the first European arrived the fierce Caribs drove out the Arawaks, who were so gentle and innocent they are supposed to have been the originals of the noble savage. For two hundred and fifty years the Caribs killed and (it was said) ate any European who tried to settle on the island. Finally the French won. Then there came fifty years of white war, until in 1805 Dominica became British. But the greater violence of slavery had arrived with the French in the 1750s, and lasted through French and British domination alike for nearly a hundred years.

Even after slavery was abolished in 1834 the violence didn't end. Only a few years before Jean was born the sober imperialist J.A. Froude wrote that the black people of Dominica were 'poor creatures whom the law calls human, but who to [the white people] are only mechanical tools, not so manageable as tools ought to be.' In *Wide Sargasso Sea* the black nurse, Christophine, says: 'No more slavery! She had to laugh! "These new ones have Letter of the Law. Same thing.... New ones worse than old ones − more cunning, that's all".'

On top of violence and excess Dominica has always had ineradicable poverty and plain bad luck. It has always been hard to work here: the interior repels all effort; the air is so damp that salt dissolves, glued furniture falls apart, and people have to change their clothes three times a day. It has often seemed pointless to try. 'There are places which are supposed to be hostile to human beings,' Jean Rhys wrote.

When I was a child it used to be said that this island was one of them. You are getting along fine and then a hurricane comes, or a disease of the crops that nobody can cure, and there you are − more West Indian ruins and labour lost. It has been going on for more than three hundred years.

Nothing ever gets done here, everything always goes wrong. It's a bit like this on all West Indian islands, but none as bad as Dominica. 'Typical Dominica', people on the other islands say, with 'affectionate, fraternal mockery'. Plague, flood, fire, hurricanes are all typical Dominica. There was a hurricane a few years before Jean was born, several close together just before she came back on a visit; a few months after she died another devastated the island and destroyed most of Roseau. There was coffee blight in the nineteenth century and lime blight in the twentieth; when she was a child the Dominican sugar trade ended, and another generation of planters was ruined. Coconut, cocoa, rubber, most recently tourists, have all been tried, without much success. It's all been 'typical Dominica'. Jean's island is both an earthly paradise and almost uninhabitable. 'Life was like that,' she would write: 'Here you are, it said, and then immediately afterwards, Where are you?'

All this has very similar effects upon most people, black and white. It induces both fear and fatalism: the grandeur of nature dwarfs you, its voracity and caprice defeat you, but its fecundity allows you to survive anyway. Black people express their fear in *obeah,* the black magic of the islands. White people, at least the English people of Jean's time, had their own magic, which was to pretend that they were not afraid. There they were, marooned on a tiny hostile island, its total population 30,000 souls, and only 300 of them white. It was too frightening to think of, so they didn't think of it. Instead they lived in a little England, and thought always of England, not *here,* as home. Even after many generations they brought their clothes and food, their books, newspapers and ideas out from England; they went back to England themselves to rest or retire, and sent their children back there to school. If they had any money they often sent that back to England too.

And it showed. Dominica was owned by England, but it was not English. English clergymen preached austere, educated English sermons which no one understood; French priests had preached in *patois,* and ever since their day the black people have spoken *patois* and been Catholics. Under French rule the streets of Roseau had been paved, and a road built right across the island; when Jean was born grass was growing between the paving stones, and the road across the island had reverted to forest. During her childhood the energetic administrator Sir Henry Hesketh Bell tried to rebuild it, indeed in general to rebuild Dominica. But Parliament never provided enough money, and he failed. England needed and exploited Dominica, but didn't love her; and Dominica resented England. It remained gloriously beautiful, and desperately poor; it remains relatively so today. 'The people who live behind God's back,' the Dominicans call themselves; and their island, self-mockingly, 'the Cinderella of the West Indies', 'the third world's third world'.

Perhaps it goes back to the original, defeated Arawaks, who as they died or fled were said to have put a curse on the island: the Caribs could capture it, but never conquer it. Each time it was captured it was unconquered. For hundreds of years it has given its different masters the same experiences and the same feelings: the promise of beauty and plenty, and the reality of poverty and isolation; the promise of everything and the reality of nothing.

This elusiveness, this siren-like beckoning, creates the characteristic Antillean atmosphere: beauty, gaiety and longing, and underneath menace, cruelty and fear. Everyone feels it, especially Englishmen. It is 'a kind of lovesick sloth', they say, 'a heavy languishing drowsiness', an 'alternation between lassitude and gaiety'; gaiety on the surface, and beneath 'an almost desperate defeatism'. Dominica is so green, they say, the mountains shut you in; it feels evil, especially at nightfall. Everyone goes crazy there, they say, many commit suicide. And yet ... Dominica has 'something'. Despite squalor and failure, fear and hate, it haunts them; it won't leave them alone. They don't want to leave it; if they do, they want to come back. The French recognise this, for they call Martinique, Dominica's sister island, *l'île des revenants:* 'not the island of ghosts, but the island to which strangers inevitably return.'

★   ★   ★

Like so many 'English' colonial families, Jean's was not English, but Welsh, Irish and Scottish.

On both sides family knowledge went back three generations. On her father's side her great-grandfather was Griffith Rees Williams of Cardiganshire in South Wales. Her Welsh grandfather, William Rees Williams, was the eldest of his twelve children, born in Llanarth in 1815. William went to Cambridge, where his great friend was an Irishman, Robert Potts, who became a famous mathematician. William married Robert's sister Sophia; Jean's Aunt Jeanette, whom she visited from school in Cambridge, was Robert's wife. (Professor and Mrs Potts were the Beauty and the Beast of family legend, whose story Jean put into both *Smile Please* and *Voyage in the Dark*.)

William went as deacon to a parish in South London, where his first two children were born: Clarice Mary in 1847 and Neville in 1849. For two years the family lived in Cornwall, where William was headmaster of Bodmin Grammar School. Then in 1853 they moved back to Wales: to Carnarvon, where William became principal of the Training College, and where Jean's father was born in 1853. He was christened William Potts, after both his father and mother. In 1865 the family moved again, to the village of Bodelwyddan, where William became rector of the famous marble church. Their last move was to Gyfylliog near Ruthin, where he was rector for nearly twenty-five years.

From this side of the family came the connection to two important places in Jean's life: Cambridge, where she was sent to school, and Wales, her father's home. Her middle name was Welsh — Gwendoline, which meant 'white'; and her father taught her a few Welsh words, including *hiraeth* which meant 'grief'. Her home in Roseau was called 'Bod Gwilym'; on its walls hung a picture of Betwys-y-coed, and a photograph of her Welsh grandfather.

On her mother's side Jean's great-grandfather was a Scot: James Potter Lockhart, a cousin of Sir Walter Scott's biographer. According to family lore James had come to Dominica towards the end of the eighteenth century to manage a sugar plantation. In 1824 he bought it: 'Genever' or 'Geneva' Plantation at Grand Bay, an estate of 1,200 acres and 258 slaves. For ten years he was a prosperous sugar-merchant and slave-owner, with many mistresses and children amongst his slaves, like old Cosway in *Wide Sargasso Sea*. Like old Cosway too, he married a young wife from another island. Then in 1834 slavery was swept away. Only three years later James died, leaving his young widow to run the estate with an overseer. In 1844 a rumour spread that slavery was about to return: there was a riot, and the labourers at Geneva attacked the estate house and burned it down.

This great-grandmother of Jean's, James's widow, was called Jean Maxwell: and though Maxwell sounds just as Scottish as Lockhart, the family story was that she was Spanish, or had some Spanish connection, and had come from Cuba. She had dark hair, like Antoinette's mother in *Wide Sargasso Sea;* so dark that, like Anna's mother in *Voyage in the Dark*, people might say she was coloured. The Lockharts were proud of their 'pure English descent', and Jean Maxwell's darkness disturbed them. For this reason, perhaps, and also because she was pretty, lively and a lapsed Catholic, Jean was drawn to her Lockhart great-grandmother. She tried to find out all she could about her, though she was too shy or incurious to ask about anyone else, even her parents. She based Antoinette's mother, Annette, on her, and the fire at Coulibri on the fire at Geneva which had nearly killed her.

When her husband died Jean Maxwell Lockhart was left with four children, two boys and two girls. Family history doesn't say what happened to the girls, except that Cora married, Sophia did not, and neither had children.* The eldest son, Richard, disappeared: one

*But Jean used both names in her fiction: Sophia for her oldest heroine, and Cora for Antoinette's only loving relative in *Wide Sargasso Sea*. She also wrote (in a draft which never became a finished story) of an 'Aunt Clara' who was 'peculiar', and 'shut away'.

story was that he'd been disinherited for beating a slave, another that
he ran off with the family silver. The second son, Edward, became
a magistrate. He married as his second wife Julia Matilda Woodcock,
Jean's grandmother: and it was she who took over the running of
Geneva Estate in about 1850.

She and Edward rebuilt the estate house and had six children. The
first, Ella, died at the age of thirteen. Then came twins, Minna and
Brenda — Jean's mother and Auntie B — born in 1853; Edith, born
in 1854; Norman in 1856, and Acton, probably in 1858. Then, like
a repetition of a pattern, Edward died while he was still quite a young
man; and Julia Matilda was left alone with five children.

This was in a bad time, when the price of sugar was going down
and down, and Geneva Estate had become run down, almost derelict.
(So Jean drew on her grandmother as well as her great-grandmother
for Annette at Coulibri.) But Julia Matilda carried it on until her son
Acton took over, probably in the early 1880s. When William Rees
Williams arrived in Dominica in 1881 Julia Matilda was still the
moving spirit of Geneva.

What made a young Welshman from a disciplined, intellectual
home want to strike out to the wilds of Dominica? No doubt it was
that very discipline and intellectuality, represented and required by
his father. One day Jean saw him shake his fist and curse at the
picture of her Welsh grandfather. Her mother explained: 'The old
man grudged every penny spent on Willie. Everything must go to
the eldest son, his favourite.' (And this favoured elder brother Jean
gave to Rochester in *Wide Sargasso Sea*.) The eldest son, Neville, had
followed their father to Cambridge, and set out on a conventional
and distinguished medical career. William Rees Williams's progress
through life would be much less smooth. His own two sons would
repeat the pattern: Edward, the elder, progressing steadily from
school to university to the Indian Medical Service; Owen, the
younger, trying job after job, some of them wild (like joining the
Canadian Mounties) and never training himself to anything properly.
'I think my father lacked diligence and deep down suffered from his
failure for the remainder of his life,' his son John says. So did Jean;
and her father understood her. I think she and Owen got their
natures from him: dreamy, rebellious, and longing for adventure.

At fourteen — he told his daughter — he ran away to sea, because
people were unkind to him and he couldn't bear it. At Cardiff he
was caught and taken home. But he still longed to be a sailor; and
in the end he was allowed to join HMS *Conway* and HMS *Worcester*,
training ships for the merchant navy. At twenty he qualified as a
First Mate, and for some years he sailed the world. But on one
voyage the captain ill-treated him ('I'll teach you to think you're a

gentleman,' he said); on another they met a hurricane and icebergs, and his mother begged him to give up the sea. If his father loved his brother, his mother loved William, and he loved her. To please her he agreed. Like his brother, then, he turned to medicine: not at Cambridge, but at a small new training college in Manchester, Owens College. (Perhaps because, as Jean said in *Smile Please,* his mother paid for it.)

From Manchester he followed his brother to St George's Hospital Medical School in London, getting his medical qualifications in 1879 and 1880. His mother must have been happy; but he was evidently unable to settle to a safe and respectable life in Victorian England even for her. In 1881 he answered an advertisement in *The Times,* and was appointed Medical Officer to the Stowe District of Dominica.

Stowe is only three miles from Geneva, and when William arrived by canoe from Roseau he was met by the two elder Miss Lockharts: the twins, Minna and Brenda. They took him to Mitcham, the Geneva estate house, and gave him tea; then they led him along the road to Stowe, so close to the cliff edge that sometimes they had to ride through the sea.

William worked for a year at Stowe. Jean's Aunt Clarice, his sister, told her that during this time he fell ill with fever and was nursed back to health by the twins; and 'as soon as he recovered he married my mother.' This may or may not have been true; in any case Jean again made it part of Rochester's story in *Wide Sargasso Sea.*

Minna was the younger and smaller twin: 'Miss Petit', the servants called her. William thought her 'the more angelic of the two – a beautiful sweet nature'. She was also quieter and (Jean said) less serene. After dinner they sat out on the *glacis* at Mitcham and William played the flute: 'Oh don't play that again, it is too sad,' Minna would say. 'Play something gay.'

William and Minna were married on January 10, 1882. They went to live in the town, where William had now been made Medical Officer and Health Officer to the Port of Roseau. Their first house was on the last street near the river, Hillsborough Street – as it was called in the *patois,* la rue Hillsborough Street. Here their first three children were born: William Edward in 1883, Owen Lockhart in 1885, and Minna Sophia in 1886. In their second, bigger house across the street the last two were born: Ella Gwendoline – that is, Jean – in 1890, and Brenda Clarice in 1895. Some time later they moved into their last Roseau home, 'Bod Gwilym'. It was a large wood house on the corner of Cork and Queen Mary Streets: from it they could look straight down Cork Street to the jetty and the sea.

★     ★     ★

Much later, in the 1930s, Jean began to write about her childhood in Dominica. Some of these memories she used in *Voyage in the Dark*, some in *Wide Sargasso Sea*, some in short stories like 'Pioneers, Oh, Pioneers' and 'Goodbye Marcus, Goodbye Rose'. At the very end of her life she got out her autobiographical writings, and set herself to remember more; and wrote her autobiography, *Smile Please*.

Her childhood as she tells it in *Smile Please* is like Antoinette's in *Wide Sargasso Sea*: almost all loneliness and rejection from the beginning, lit only by rare flashes of peace and happiness: the tragedy of her later life, like Antoinette's, almost over-determined. She was a writer of fiction, and chose carefully what to tell of her later life: can we trust her at all about her childhood?

Not completely, of course. She left out a great deal, both happy and unhappy. But that is what she always did, in *Smile Please* as in her fiction, and in her conversation too: she cut, she left out, she kept silent. Unless it was absolutely necessary she didn't lie.

But did she not unconsciously distort? Did she not see the child in the shadow of the woman, and always look for explanations, even justifications, of what she'd become? Yes, she did. But it went the other way too; it went the other way more. For what became of her, as for what became of Antoinette − of all the heroines − only something deep in her childhood could account ('the girl must have had some tragedy in her life which she cannot forget,' she wrote of Antoinette. 'As a child. I have got that.') It was, rather, the child who threw her shadow forward. Jean always remained a child, and the reason must have gone back to the beginning.

In 'Heat', about the eruption of Mont Pelée on Martinique in 1902, Jean mentions a famous event of the year before, when a young Englishman had been killed by the sulphur fumes of the Boiling Lake. He was buried in the Anglican cemetery, she says: under a large marble headstone, 'quite near the grave of my little sister.'

She never mentioned this little sister anywhere else. Dominican birth and death records have almost all been lost in a fire (typical Dominica), so that we cannot be absolutely sure when she died. But nearly.

Brenda Gwenith Maxwell Rees Williams was born just before Jean, probably in early 1889, when she was baptised. But then (again almost though not quite certainly) in November 1889, when she was nine months old, there was a dysentery epidemic in Roseau: and she and Minna caught the disease. Owen, who tells this story, says that the baby 'hovered at death's door'; but that by Christmas both girls were better, and 'all was well'. But he had set out in his account to lighten 'the tragedies which have always dogged this beautiful Island';

and probably he did so here. For certainly the infant Brenda Gwenith died; and the likeliest occasion was this attack of dysentery.

Jean was born exactly nine months after November 1889. When a baby dies doctors often say that the mother should have another child straight away, to staunch her grief. And that is often the mother's desire too. Jean's father was a doctor, and her mother loved babies: I think Jean was the baby they had to assuage their grief over the loss of her little sister.

Often, perhaps mostly, this works, and pulls the mother back into life. But sometimes it doesn't. Then there is a phenomenon which doctors also recognise: what can happen to a child with a mourning mother. It can be left with a lifelong sense of loss and emptiness, of being wanted by no one and belonging nowhere; of being nothing, not really existing at all.

Like her heroines Jean often felt like a ghost, and from childhood she felt that she'd been fated. She also felt that names matter ('like when he wouldn't call me Antoinette' she wrote in *Wide Sargasso Sea*, 'and I saw Antoinette drifting out of the window with her scents, her pretty clothes and her looking-glass.' But she never said that her own names, *Ella* and *Gwen*, were both the names of dead girls, her mother's sister and her mother's baby daughter. Perhaps she didn't know; perhaps she had forgotten.

★　　★　　★

In her earliest memories both she and her mother are pretty, happy and young. In the very first one she is still a baby, 'for I was,' she wrote

> *... in a crib*
> *when she bent*
> *down & kissed me*
> *smelling sweet*
> *In a low cut black*
> *dress*
>
> *I remember*
> *I remember*
> *& the other baby not yet born.*

In the next one she was five, her last birthday before her sister was born. The family was at beautiful Bona Vista, her father's estate in the hills. Her hair was curly, her cheeks dimpled, she wore a pretty white dress and a wreath of frangipani in her hair. She sat, 'crowned, bursting with pride and importance, safe, protected, sitting in a large armchair, my father on one side, my mother on the other, my shiny shoes a long way off the ground.'

Four months later Brenda was born, and soon (Jean felt) everything changed. Up to then she had loved her mother, like her heroines Julia and Antoinette. 'Her mother had been the warm centre of the world. You loved to watch her brushing her long hair....' But suddenly she was 'entirely wrapped up in the new baby,' Jean wrote of Julia's mother; and of her own she said 'My mother didn't like me after Brenda was born.'

By the time she was eight or nine she felt changed. She was no longer that proud little girl 'without doubt without fear.' She felt 'singled out' from her brothers and sisters, for they were all dark and sturdy, while she was pale and thin and fair. And she was wearing an ugly brown school uniform; she was no longer pretty. Brenda was the pretty one now, the one with the dimples in her cheeks and the curly hair; Brenda was the baby. She was left 'aching with the difference between what you want to be and what you are.' 'It was the first time I was aware of time, change and the longing for the past.'

After her mother turned to the new baby, or even before, she had a nurse, a *da*. And that was the next step on the road, for Meta was not like Christophine in *Wide Sargasso Sea*. Christophine is warm and loving to Antoinette, and makes up to her (if anything can) for the loss of her mother. Meta, as Jean remembered her, was the opposite. She never smiled; she 'always seemed to be brooding over some terrible, unforgettable wrong.' And Jean felt that she 'couldn't bear the sight of me.'

Meta played tricks on her. Several times she pretended Jean's friend Willie was waiting for her, so that she flew downstairs long before she was ready — to find no Willie, and Meta laughing loudly. And once, when she was seven or eight, the maid called her into the kitchen, and there was Meta in a carnival mask, talking in a high soprano voice. The child hung back, giggling with fear. Then suddenly Meta stuck her tongue out through the mouth of the mask. 'When I saw the long tongue protruding idiotically under the blank eyes, I went into a fit of hysterics and had to be put to bed and pacified by a handkerchief saturated with eau-de-cologne tied round my head.' ('*A pretty useful mask that white one*,' she wrote in *Voyage in the Dark*, '*watch it and the slobbering tongue of an idiot will stick out — a mask Father said with an idiot behind it I believe the whole damned business is like that — .*')

Meta taught her to fear many things — zombies and loups-garoux (werewolves) and soucriants, who came at night and sucked your blood; centipedes and scorpions, and lizards who would drop down on you from the ceiling and fasten on your face, and cockroaches (especially cockroaches), who would fly in when you were asleep and bite your mouth, and 'the bite would never heal.' Meta wasn't allowed to hit her, but she would put her hard hands on her shoulders and shake her violently. Then Jean would scream at her 'Black Devil! Black Devil! Black Devil!' And Meta would threaten her with 'tears of blood'. It was her favourite phrase. 'If you don't keep your nails clean you going to weep tears of blood. If you don't do this that or the other you going to weep tears of blood.' 'One day I'm going to weep tears of blood,' Jean wrote. 'I had that fixed in my head this tears of blood business.'

She never complained to her mother about Meta, but just waited for the fear to end. One day Meta left, or was sent away, and she was very relieved. But the fear didn't end. 'It was too late,' she wrote in *Smile Please*. 'Meta had shown me a world of fear and distrust, and I am still in that world.'

Whether it was Meta's doing or not she was afraid, and unable to hide her fear. Often she screamed, cried, collapsed with terror. Over the horrible mask, for instance; or over 'God knew what scenes of lust or cruelty' told her by an old man had been born a slave. The first day she was to go to school she 'shrieked, clung to my mother and kicked up such a fuss that I didn't go.' ('The first day I had to go to the convent, I clung to Aunt Cora as you would cling to life if you loved it,' she wrote in *Wide Sargasso Sea*.) Once a friend of her father's who was hugely tall and had a long red beard took her on his knee. In an 'agony of terror' she screamed again, and was taken away in disgrace. And once a boy who was always teasing her about cockroaches actually put one down her back. She 'went nearly mad with horror and disgust,' until she got fever and was ill.

She already had complicated feelings about black people. On the one hand she admired and envied them for their gaiety and ease, which she saw especially in a little brown girl of the household called Tite Francine. This girl became Francine in *Voyage in the Dark* ('The thing about Francine was that when I was with her I was happy'), and Tia in *Wide Sargasso Sea* ('fires always lit for her, sharp stones did not hurt her bare feet, I never saw her cry'). Black people 'were more alive, more part of the place than we were'; and she wanted to be like them. ('I wanted to be black,' says Anna in *Voyage in the Dark*, 'I always wanted to be black .... Being black is warm and gay, being white is cold and sad.')

On the other hand there had been the Riot. One night her mother had woken her and Brenda and told them to come downstairs. When they got there Jean heard 'a strange noise like animals howling but I knew it wasn't animals, it was people.' Her father had said 'They're perfectly harmless'; but her mother had replied 'That's what you think.' ('They wouldn't hurt a fly,' Mr Mason says in *Wide Sargasso Sea*; 'Unhappily children do hurt flies,' Aunt Cora replies.) The black people whom she knew well were individuals whom she liked or disliked. But about the others after that she became wary. 'Did they like us as much as all that? Did they like us at all?'

And there was one group of people about whom she had no doubt: *they hated.* These were the coloured people, the betwixt and between, whom no one wanted and everyone could despise. Later she would put one into her short story 'The Day They Burned the Books': Mrs Sawyer, whose white husband despises her, and whose eyes go 'wicked, like a soucriant's eyes.' 'And as for Mrs Sawyer,' Jean wrote ' – well, I knew bad temper (I had often seen it), I knew rage, but this was hate. I recognised the difference at once.' She felt exactly the same about a beautiful coloured girl at school with whom she longed to be friendly. 'I tried, shyly at first, then more boldly, to talk to my beautiful neighbour,' she wrote.

> Finally, without speaking, she turned and looked at me. I knew irritation, bad temper, the 'Oh, go away' look; this was different. This was hatred – impersonal, implacable hatred. I recognised it at once and if you think that a child cannot recognise hatred and remember it for life you are most damnably mistaken.
> I never tried to be friendly with any of the coloured girls again. I was polite and that was all.
> They hate us. We are hated.
> Not possible.
> Yes it is possible and it is so.

She knew why. She knew it was because, like Mrs Sawyer, they had been hated. That is why Daniel in *Wide Sargasso Sea* hates too, and why he does what he does to Antoinette. She understood it, all too well. But she also feared it.

On one side her fears closed in; on the other Brenda was now the pretty one, and 'did all she was expected to do and nothing that she wasn't.' There wasn't much left for her but defiance, and a kind of perverse pride. She hated herself, for instance, with her stockings falling around her ankles; but her mother wouldn't let her wear tight garters around her knees. So she decided that if she had to be untidy she would be *very* untidy, and she became untidier every day. Then she felt an outcast, or more of an outcast; but when another outcast tried to befriend her she refused. 'I preferred being an outcast by myself,' she wrote in *Smile Please.* That would be one of her heroines' struggles too: no matter how lonely they are, they refuse to relieve their loneliness with other lonely people.

This perversity — this pride which was also self-punishment — started very soon. Before she was ten two dolls arrived from England, one dark and one fair. As soon as she saw the dark doll Jean 'wanted her as I had never wanted anything in my life before.' But her little sister wanted the dark doll too, and her mother made her give it up to the baby, as mothers do. Jean walked into the garden, into the shadow of the big mango tree.

> I laid the fair doll down. Her eyes were shut. Then I searched for a big stone, brought it down with all my force on her face and heard the smashing sound with delight.

There was a terrible fuss about this. Why had she done such a wilful, such a really wicked thing? She didn't know: but she had had to do it. And she had felt very vividly 'the satisfaction of being wicked. The guilt that was half triumph.'

She would remain addicted to the delights of wilfulness and 'wickedness'. But it was more than that. For when she wanted the dark doll and not the fair one so badly she was surely wanting more than a doll. She was wanting to be black and not fair herself, to fit in to her family and her island. And when she destroyed the fair doll so violently she was surely wanting to destroy her 'fair', her outcast self. When her last heroine, Antoinette, destroys herself it is a similar triumph: a revenge on the rejecting world, and an escape from loneliness and madness.

But there were always pleasures too, not just perverse ones. Until she was about ten there were two very important ones: Geneva and Great-Aunt Jane.

Her mother thought that Great-Aunt Jane spoiled her, encouraged her in her wilfulness, but she felt that only Great-Aunt Jane restored her. She was 'the one person who loved me exclusively and really.' She encouraged instead of discouraged her; so to her alone the child could talk about what she really felt. (' "They are always expecting me to do things I don't want to do and I won't. I won't. I won't...." She said, "Don't think about it any more." ') 'She let me sit on her knee, put her arms around me and kissed me,' and in return Jean adored her. 'I loved Great-Aunt Jane better than anyone else in the world. Far better than my mother, even better than my father.'

Jean would suffer all her life from an inability to express her love and gratitude (or her anger and hatred) directly to the person for whom she felt them. Because she was shy? Because she was lazy? (That would be her own explanation.) Because she was afraid? So now 'I never returned this love (outwardly) and when I left for

England I never wrote to her.' But all her life she would put her love into her books instead. So Great-Aunt Jane became Aunt Cora of *Wide Sargasso Sea*, who is brave and kind and wise. And Jean wrote a story about her (though it was never published) called 'The Cardboard Doll's House'. 'She wore her hair in six little white ringlets,' she wrote, 'and her hands were long, slim and covered with enormous brown freckles.' She came from St Kitts, and talked about beaux and belles instead of ladies and gentlemen; she remembered the slave days, and had once had a maid given to her as a birthday present. She sang Jean the old songs her mother had taught her, like 'Charlie over the water,' ('A Benky foot and a Benky leg, for Charlie over the water,' Antoinette sings when she is drunk.) She made her the cardboard house and paper dolls; she told her fairy tales; she even sang her to sleep sometimes. With 'her soft kindness and her dear, lazy West Indian drawl,' Jean wrote, 'she was utterly and entirely satisfying.'

Great-Aunt Jane belonged to Geneva, and especially to the Geneva garden. These were happy places for Jean. It was cool in the garden even on the hottest day. 'Tall tree ferns grew there, and clumps of bamboo, and beds of hibiscus.' There were oleanders and crotons and a frangipani tree, and great masses of 'English flowers', roses and honeysuckle. There were steps down to the lawn, and in the middle of it two huge mango trees and the shaddock, the 'tree of life'. Behind the house were more bamboos, and then the end of the estate, marked by a deep ravine. And in the garden were old walls covered in moss and creepers, or the remains of pavement: for the old estate house had stood where the garden was, before it was burnt down in that first, long-ago riot. 'One ruined room for roses, one for orchids, one for tree ferns,' Jean wrote in *Voyage in the Dark*.

Not only the garden in the ruins but all of Geneva had a very strong atmosphere of 'melancholy and adventure', and she drew on it for *Voyage in the Dark* and *Wide Sargasso Sea*. The gardener, who may have been called Godfrey, and who had been born ('rumour said') on a slave-ship, became Godfrey of *Wide Sargasso Sea*. Jean's grandmother's parrot became Annette's: "*Qui est là?*" he would say in a cracked and shrewish voice. And answer himself: "*Chère cocotte. Chère cocotte*".' ('Our parrot was called Coco ... he could say *Qui est là? Qui est là?* and answer himself *Ché Coco, Ché Coco*'.) And Great-Aunt Jane became Aunt Cora. Cora's kindness, her memories of slavery, her patchwork quilt, her dying, are all Great-Aunt Jane's. At the end of 'The Cardboard Doll's House' she is very ill. The girl, who is leaving for England, kisses her goodbye: then the old lady 'turns away her head. "But it's no use," she said, "for the Lord has quite forgotten me".'

★     ★     ★

At about ten Jean moved on to a new stage of her life. It happened because her Uncle Acton, who ran Geneva Estate, fell in love and married a girl from St Lucia, where the wedding took place. Jean was bridesmaid, and spent three happy months in St Lucia. It was her first time away from dowdy English Roseau, in exciting French Castries, and she felt '*I like this place, I wish I could stay here forever.*' Acton's pretty bride Evelina liked her, her red-haired brother liked her. There was a young Englishman, Mr Kennaway, who (she was sure) didn't think her pretty, but 'I needn't think about him....' The stay in Castries was 'a definite stage' in her life: 'I no longer thought of myself as an outcast.'

Several other things happened at about this time. First Jean's family became smaller. Her elder sister, Minna, had already disappeared years ago, probably before Jean was five. She'd gone to live with their Aunt Edith and Uncle John Spencer Churchill, who'd come as an Acting Administrator to Dominica, and later became Colonial Secretary of the Bahamas.* Now her elder brothers disappeared too, to school in England. For the next two years at least she was left alone with her younger sister, as the oldest child in the family.

And at much the same time, when she was about ten, there was a family upheaval. Uncle Acton's new wife and his sister, who 'had always ruled supreme at Geneva', didn't like each other, as Jean had instantly known in St Lucia. They had a serious quarrel; and Auntie B left Geneva and came to live in Roseau. Thus Jean lost the two great comforts of her early childhood, Great-Aunt Jane and Geneva, for her father took Auntie B's side, and she was no longer allowed to go there. She got Auntie B instead: an unhappy exchange, for Great-Aunt Jane loved her and Auntie B didn't. Auntie B was brave and calm and practical and she wasn't; she was the opposite. Auntie B, she was sure, disliked her. But her aunt and her mother were twins; there was a link, an understanding between them. They would look at each other and laugh quietly. Her father would say 'Oh I

---

*Minna remained with the Spencer Churchills; she was evidently, as Jean says, 'adopted but not in any formal way.' When they remet in England John Spencer Churchill (who was nearly twenty years older than his wife) was dead; but Minna lived with 'Auntie Mackie' (as Edith was called) for the rest of her life.

This 'adoption' is unexplained. But the Rees Williamses were not well off: Dr Rees Williams wouldn't take any payment from his poor patients, and at the same time had a 'reckless, throw-away attitude' to money. And the Spencer Churchills had no children of their own. No doubt this seemed the best solution to both problems. But one can't help wondering what they all felt about it – not least Jean, who saw a daughter given away, and she was next in line.

do like to see them laugh like that.' 'But I, watching, was uneasy. Could they possibly be laughing at me?'

At Bod Gwilym from now on there were two Brendas, both of whom her mother preferred to her. And at the same time St Lucia had taken away her feeling of being an 'outcast', and she was no longer afraid at school. She began to spend much of her time away from home.

Whatever Mr Kennaway thought, she was pretty. She was more than pretty: she was someone who 'attracted people to her.' Although she was sometimes frightened and sad she could also be lively and gay. She loved riding, she loved music, she loved pleasure and excitment. So as she got older 'life was often exciting'. She began to have friends — lots of friends. She went to children's parties, she went riding and swimming and on picnics, and in all these activities she was no mere follower in the background. She was the ringleader and organiser; when it was mischief she was the instigator. She was very vivacious and carefree, 'keen on outdoor things,' 'a thoroughly outgoing person.' Later she felt that it was her sister who was the 'extrovert' and had many friends; perhaps she even felt it at the time, for 'the friends I played with' (she wrote in *Smile Please*) 'weren't really important to me.' And it was true that Brenda would be considered the greater beauty, and would be still more popular. But Jean was more adventurous, naughtier, wilder.

As she grew older she moved away from her mother and towards her father. Her mother (perhaps backed by Auntie B) watched her, disapproved of her, tried to change her. She tried to make her English. She banished mangoes from the breakfast table and made her eat porridge; she made her wear porridge-coloured woollen vests because 'wool next the skin is healthy' ('you feel the perspiration trickling down under your arms ... a disgusting and a disgraceful thing to happen to a lady'). But her father said *Leave her alone.* He stopped the hated plate of porridge, he let her stop her extra lessons in mathematics; he taught her, she said, that if you cannot bear something it is all right to run away. He told her that she played the piano splendidly, that she mixed his evening drink better than anyone else. He was different, like her — so different that some of the more respectable white people thought he didn't behave as a white man should. When he was Chairman of the Town Board he refused to wear his ceremonial uniform. He played cards and golf with anyone, rich or poor; he treated black people and white people exactly the same; he even liked the French ('You don't mean you're backing up that damned French monkey?' someone says in *Voyage in the Dark*; 'I've met some Englishmen,' Anna's father replies, 'who were monkeys too'). He was talkative, excitable, gay; but sometimes also melancholy, with a sudden fierce temper. Then it would take 'two strong cocktails, a glass or two of wine [at dinner] & a whisky & soda after' before he was himself again. In *Voyage in the Dark* Anna remembers how one day she 'was crying about nothing,' and her father hugged her close and said, 'I believe you're going to be like me, you poor little devil.'

Now that Jean was older she no longer had such wild terrors. The red-bearded man, for example, was no longer an ogre; he was a nice man who made her laugh, with his song about the man whose wife had a wooden leg: '*She was a great surprise to me, Half a woman and half a tree....*' But instead of terrors there were worries. She worried about marriage: girls were supposed to marry, at least white girls were, and what if no one asked her?

> *If no one ever marries me*
> *And I don't see why they should*
> *For nurse says I'm not pretty*
> *And I'm seldom very good ...*

'That was it exactly,' says Phoebe in 'Goodbye Marcus, Goodbye Rose'.

She also worried about the business of ladies and gentlemen. In one of her books she read that a farmer is not a gentleman, and wasn't a planter — like her great-grandfather — a farmer? But then she thought that 'only ladies and gentlemen have butlers, and we have a butler. And a groom, too....' But the English children she met said that colonials couldn't be ladies and gentlemen. They weren't English either — only British, which was quite different. And they had an awful accent. 'I never liked their voices any more than they liked mine,' Jean wrote. 'I'm glad to remember I slapped one little English girl good and hard once.'

Then, of course, there was the worry about girls and boys. There was one boy in particular — Willie, whom Meta had teased her about so unkindly. This was Willie Nicholls, youngest son of Dr Nicholls, the senior doctor on the island. When they were small she and her brothers, Willie and his sisters had all splashed together in the stone bath as big as a room, in the damp green darkness of their bathroom. At first she hadn't noticed that the little boys were any different. But one day she slithered down from the edge into the bath with a conscious grace; and 'that,' she wrote, 'was the day you began to be a woman.'

That was before she was ten. Afterwards Willie disappeared to school, and she saw him only on fine afternoons, when their little group of boys and girls was taken to the Botanical Gardens to play.

Now her favourite game was 'Looby Li'. 'Looby Li' was 'about the game of love and chance'; and after each verse 'we'd try to act out the enigmatic, scarcely understood words we'd sung.' But one day her mother said that it was a wicked game and she must never play it again. 'Who started it?' she asked. 'Who taught you the words?' Jean answered truthfully that she didn't know; but immediately added 'Perhaps it was Willie.' Then she was very miserable. 'Why had I said it was Willie when it wasn't Willie?' For it was Willie she liked... But of course that was why his name had come into her head. She had had her first glimpse of the connection between love and guilt, desire and punishment.

At the edge of adolescence her differences were becoming confirmed. She wouldn't think what she was supposed to think; 'my opinion was generally insufferable.' She noticed, for instance, that white people had all the money and black people did all the work, and whenever she thought about this she felt '*Not fair, not fair*'. But when she said it people just laughed, or called her 'Socialist Gwen'. She tried to help Victoria the housemaid with the washing-up, but Victoria only looked at her suspiciously: ' "What's this trap now?" her eyes said.' Then she tried to help John, her father's overseer at Amalia Estate, to learn to read and write. But John's wife was angry and suspicious, and the lessons had to stop. She'd managed to teach John to write his name, however; and soon afterwards his friend Emile came to her mother and asked for her hand in marriage. He promised her mother in return the present of a large yam. 'I never heard the last of that yam,' Jean wrote. ' "You're only worth a yam," they would say, shrieking with mirth.'

She had tried to help people, and all she'd got had been ridicule. So she soon stopped trying. She concentrated her pity now on imaginary people; when it was still for real ones it remained locked inside her.

After the 'socialist fit' came the 'religious fit'. This was connected to her convent school, and especially to its Superior, Mother Mount Calvary. All the girls loved the Good Mother, as she was called, and here at least Jean felt the same as the others. Mother Mount Calvary came from St Kitts, like Great-Aunt Jane; she spoke beautiful French and was wonderfully kind, and Jean loved her. 'Well the end of all this of course was that I became religious'; and not only religious but Catholic. The Catholic Cathedral was more beautiful than the Anglican Church, she thought; there were more black people in it, and they sat among the whites, not just in the last few pews. 'Protestants believed that when you were dead, you were dead'; but in the Catholic cemetery people lit candles in front of the graves, and covered them in flowers, and wrote letters to the dead people.

And though it was too much to hope for heaven, you needn't fear hell either. 'Children,' said Mother St Anthony, 'it is an article of faith that there is a hell. It is not an article of faith that there is anybody in it.'

Jean told Mother Mount Calvary she wanted to be a nun: not a teaching nun, but a contemplative ('I would contemplate the Five Glorious and the Five Sorrowful Mysteries'). Mother Mount Calvary laughed her out of this idea, but she remained religious. She wept for the death of Jesus and put stones in her shoes to share his suffering. She felt a 'certainty that you were upheld, protected'; and she was happy.

> ... The sky came nearer. The sun was not a terrible god it was only the sun and did as it was told. So did the moon the stars the wind and the sea. So would I. Everything is easy.

Of course it wasn't *quite* easy, because this fit too was disapproved of. 'Don't tease her, she'll grow out of it,' her father said; but she could feel her mother watching, waiting for it to go away. And after two months or so it did. One night she prayed 'with less ecstasy and certainty. The next morning mechanically. And the next day not at all.' Soon 'the whole thing was like a dream.'

It had been, she wrote 'the happiest time in my life.' And yet she was not altogether sad that it was over. 'The sky receded. The sun was again God. Terror came back into my world. And also life. I was glad – I'd missed it.'

She lived in books and in her imagination now, and she was wildly romantic. All the books she read were English, so England became her dream of glamour and excitement. She imagined it as great houses and parks, or else as wild heaths and fells, over which strode brilliant figures – Heathcliff, Sherlock Holmes, Rob Roy. London was beautiful rosy-cheeked ladies, fog and blazing coal fires, splendid theatres and shops, strawberries and cream.... She was attracted not just to grandeur and glory but to danger and death. She was thrilled by lovely Nina Rodriguez, the Only Girl Who Works Without a Net, defying death a dozen times a night. And when she realised on the night of the Riot that the mob might kill them she thought: *Kill us!* And she wasn't frightened, but excited.

Words were important to her, especially their sounds. Some she hated, like 'mountain' (No, not mountain, Antoinette tells Rochester, *morne*. 'Mountain is an ugly word – for them'). Many words she loved, lovely ones like *wisteria*, sad ones like 'pain', 'shame', 'sea', 'silence'. This love of beautiful words came especially from Mother Sacred Heart, a new nun who'd come out from

England to teach the literature class. She read English poetry aloud, with her ironic wit and her beautiful voice; and Jean loved poetry for life. At the same time Mother Mount Calvary introduced her to French poetry, which thrilled her even more. 'The Bishop who visits the convent every year says they are lax. Very lax,' Antoinette says, and no doubt they were. One of the French poems was Victor Hugo's.

> *Partons, c'est la fin du jour*
> *Mon cheval sera la joie*
> *Ton cheval sera l'amour.*

Probably Good Mother thought it was an allegory, Jean said.

By the time she was twelve or thirteen her nature and course were almost set. She was the difficult daughter. She could be so shy and awkward that people thought her rude. ('Overcome with shyness I turned my head away and pretended not to see him'; 'Why were you so rude?' her mother said. 'He said that you cut him dead.') She was distant and dreamy, and that seemed rude too. ('I am speaking to you; do you not hear? You have such an absent-minded expression. Try not to look vague. . . . So rude!') Her ideas and enthusiasms were odd and embarrassing, and she clung to them for dear life, until they suddenly disappeared. If criticised or denied, she became stubborn, sulky, perverse. She was jealous of her little sister, and sometimes cruel to her: once, for example, she had made her sit on the piano, and then played louder and louder until Brenda cried with fear. She was 'lackadaisical' and 'mooned around' at home, but went for recklessly long rides and walks for her own pleasure. She was morbidly sensitive and fiercely proud. Sometimes she hated her family's slave-owning past so much it made her 'sick with shame'; sometimes she thought with pride of her great-grandfather's rich estate, and longed to have lived in that fabulous time, full of splendour and cruelty. But no – the end of her thoughts was always the same: 'to be identified once and for all with the other side, which of course was impossible.' She felt akin to them, but they didn't like white people. 'White cockroaches they called us'; and she didn't blame them.

She wanted even more to be identified with this beautiful mysterious place. Once, 'regardless of the ants,' she lay down and kissed the earth and thought, 'Mine, mine.' But really she wanted to belong to *it*, 'to identify with it, to lose myself in it.' Sometimes she came near it, 'this identification or annihilation that I longed for.' But it eluded her; and the place eluded her, 'it turned its head away, indifferent.' She was miserable when she heard other people, especially English visitors, say that *they* loved it, that they saw its beauty. At least she knew that you couldn't say 'mine, mine' to this place, she thought. It broke her heart to know it, but she knew it.

Her family didn't understand any of this, she felt; and she was right, they didn't. It was unhealthy, exaggerated; it was showing off and pretending. 'It was so intolerable, this longing, this sadness I got from the shapes of the mountains, the sound of the rain the moment after sunset, that one day I spoke of it to my mother': but all her mother could give her, she wrote, was 'a large dose of castor oil.' (Perhaps that was more image than reality; but if so it was an image of reality.)

But one day she discovered a way of working her sadness off by herself. She got an exercise book; on the cover she wrote *My Secret Poems*, and underneath 'I unlock locked hearts,' which was the motto of the Lockharts. 'I had found out that writing poetry took away sadness, doubled joy and calmed the anxious questioning feeling that tormented me then.' She also wrote other things in her secret poems book that she couldn't tell anyone. (About a male visitor, for instance: 'After lunch he sat in a long armchair. He was so beautiful that I thought I'd faint.') Her poems were full of a sense of doom and fatedness; but after she had written them she was happier.

There were only a few other things that 'formed me, made me as I am.' One of them marked the end of her childhood. It happened, she said (like starting to write poetry) when she was about twelve.

'Most of all,' she wrote when she was nearly fifty, 'I was afraid of being disapproved of.' But it was always happening. Often she was 'bewildered', 'not knowing what it was that I was supposed to have done' ('That's always my trouble,' she added, ' – I never know what it is I'm supposed to have done'). Her behaviour was disapproved of, her thoughts were disapproved of, her feelings (especially her feelings) were disapproved of. Her mother was brave, like Auntie B, and she wasn't. 'You're not my daughter if you're afraid of a horse,' Jean wrote in a short story.

> ... You're not my daughter if you're afraid of being seasick.
> You're not my daughter if you're afraid of the shape of a hill,
> or the moon when it is growing old. In fact you're not my
> daughter.

Now Mrs Rees Williams was a kind woman, sweet-natured (as her husband had said) and devoted to her children: Jean knew this herself. Perhaps she didn't say these things out loud, or the other cruel things Jean makes her say in stories ('Captain Greig thinks you are an ugly little girl and it's Audrey whom he likes.') On the other hand perhaps she did, for she was a simple woman, and may have thought like the mother in the story that 'it was my duty to speak to her.' But whether she said them or not, Jean knew that she thought them. And despite her claim to be 'bewildered', she knew exactly why her mother punished her. It was because she was 'worried', as she wrote in *After Leaving Mr Mackenzie*: because she was worried about *her*. 'She must have seen something alien in me which would devour me and make me unhappy,' Jean wrote, 'and she was trying to root it out at all costs.'

In *Mackenzie* Julia's mother only slaps her ('for no reason that you knew'). Between Antoinette and her mother in *Wide Sargasso Sea* things are much worse. Annette wants only her son; to her daughter she says 'Let me alone' and turns away, and after the fire she pushes her away violently, crying 'No no no.' But what really happened to Jean she gave to none of her heroines; only to pretty, sentimental Lise in *Good Morning, Midnight*:

> ... She is afraid of her mother. Her mother beat her. 'For anything, for nothing. You don't know...'

We cannot know, of course, how often this happened or how bad it was. Perhaps Jean exaggerated (as people always felt she did) when she said 'my mother beat me,' even 'whipped me,' and when she makes Lise say 'She hates me.' For she was also fond of her mother, and proud of her. But that her mother did punish her, at least sometimes physically, is almost certainly true. For her account of how these punishments ended is terribly vivid. It is the thing that ended her childhood.

> As for the punishments for I seldom knew what — they also stopped abruptly, when one day, to my great surprise, I heard myself shrieking 'God curse you, if you touch me I'll kill you.' She gave me a curious look — a long, sad look. Ha, you're growing up then.... She said 'I've done my best, it's no use. You'll never learn to be like other people.'
>
> There you are, there it was. I had always suspected it, but now I knew. That went straight as an arrow to the heart, straight as the truth. I saw the long road of isolation and loneliness stretching in front of me as far as the eye could see, and further. I collapsed and cried as heartbrokenly as my worst enemy could wish.

From May to December 1904 Dr Rees Williams was given his first long leave in nearly twenty-five years, and he and his wife went to England. Brenda, who was now nine years old, was left with friends or relatives, probably Auntie B; Jean went as a boarder to her convent.

'This convent was my refuge,' Antoinette says in *Wide Sargasso Sea,* and Jean wrote of herself: 'I was quite happy at the idea of becoming a boarder at the convent.' Perhaps her mother was too. It was a safe place, a good place. The nuns taught 'kindness to God's poor' (perfunctorily), and order and chastity, that 'most precious possession', that 'flawless crystal that, once broken, can never be mended.' Antoinette learns a religious modesty there — never to be naked, never to let her body be seen when she washes or dresses, even by herself. At first she thinks 'is there no happiness?' But soon — 'oh happiness of course, happiness, well.' And Jean learned something very comforting: thoughts are not sins, for they may be sent by the devil. As long as you drive them away at once they are not sins. You make the sign of the cross on your breast and say 'Lord save me, I perish'; and you go and work very hard at something, which is the best way to drive out the devil.

Besides, happiness was not quite forgotten, because three of the boarders were her friends. They were sisters from a South American country, whose father only visited them very rarely. Jean put them into *Wide Sargasso Sea* as Hélène, Germaine and Louise de Plana (and Louise into *Voyage in the Dark* and 'The Bishop's Feast' too). Hélène has perfect hair and Germaine perfect deportment, but Antoinette's favourite is Louise. Louise is her connection to happiness. She is dark and very pretty, she has a high sweet voice, and she is quite untamed. 'It is easy to imagine what happened to the other two,' Jean wrote for Antoinette. 'Ah but Louise!... Anything might have happened to you, Louise, anything at all.'

The trip to England was not a success. Jean's mother missed her beautiful island, which she may never have left before. And her father almost certainly felt like Anna's father in *Voyage in the Dark*: it cost too much, and he didn't really enjoy it. His beloved mother was dead, and so was his father; only his sister and brother were left. His sister was fond of him, but then she came out to Dominica several times; England really meant his brother Neville, his father's favourite. 'I've got nobody there who cares a damn about me,' Anna's father says. 'The place stinks of hypocrites if you've got a nose. I don't care if I never see it again.'

For both Anna and Antoinette their months of boarding at the convent are a watershed in their lives. Anna's father returns from England with a new wife; and Antoinette is only sent to the convent after her mother has 'really' died. On one side of the convent is childhood, however anxious and lonely; on the other side is the cold outside world, an English stepmother, an English stepfather, a waiting English lover.

This feeling about the convent (like all the other feelings) came straight from Jean's own life. Before the convent her relationship with her mother had been bad enough (and Anna's mother in *Voyage in the Dark* dies young, Antoinette's in *Wide Sargasso Sea* rejects her); but after the convent it was over. Before it she'd been a child, however difficult, different, secretive; after it she was an openly defiant adolescent.

★　　　★　　　★

One day her father said that she was old enough to have a dress allowance. It wasn't very large, but she bought a red tam o'shanter, and she began to feel quite grown-up. She still had her black moods sometimes ('The sadness which swooped and took possession so suddenly after sunset,' she wrote in *Smile Please*; and in *Wide Sargasso Sea* Antoinette says 'I was always happy in the morning, not always in the afternoon and never after sunset, for after sunset the house was haunted, some places are'). But then she had her secret poems book to turn to. 'And sometimes weeks, months would go by happily no black moods nothing going wrong'; and she couldn't think of any place in the world where you could be happier.

There was, however, one way in which she hadn't wanted to grow up, ever since she'd told that strange, guilty lie about Willie and 'Looby Li'. Whenever she saw a group of older girls talking in lowered voices she 'drifted away'; once when she saw some diagrams of a woman having a baby she refused to believe them. Her mother told her nothing, and she was glad; she didn't want to know.

But now this was changing. A boy sent her a letter, 'You are as slender as Solomon's Pillar,' and she kept it. She wrote that note in her secret book — 'He was so beautiful that I was afraid I'd faint ...' She dreamed, vaguely, of marriage ('the dark moustache and perfectly creased trousers'); she made secret lists of her trousseau ('One pink dress, four blue dresses, six white dresses.... Six pairs of long white gloves'). She knelt at her open window, no longer praying, but 'wondering what my life would be like now that God and the Devil were far away. And the sea, sometimes so calm and blue and beautiful but underneath the calm — what?'

In 'Goodbye Marcus, Goodbye Rose' Captain Cardew is a 'calm, unruffled man', very handsome and very old, like 'some aged but ageless god'. In Jean's 'record of facts' he is called Mr Howard (though this was probably not his name either). In the short story, as always, the details are removed, and all that is left is the essence. But the 'record of facts' in her Black Exercise Book is twenty pages long and very vivid. ('I shut away at the back of my mind any sexual experiences,' she wrote in *Smile Please*, 'not knowing that this would cause me to remember them in detail all the rest of my life.')

Mr Howard was tall, upright and soldierly, with a white moustache and one glass eye. He was about seventy, and 'had fought bravely in some long-ago war.' He was an old friend of her mother's. He and his wife were on their way back to England, and broke their journey in Dominica.

Jean had already heard a great deal about him; he was 'an almost fabulous person', 'the hero of numberless adventures', and she longed to meet him. He didn't disappoint her. He was 'an English gentleman with a capital G'. He was brave and calm, he walked with long strides, he 'spoke, looked and moved as though everything and everybody in the whole world belonged to him.' And he spoke very politely to her, he included her in the conversation, he treated her 'with deference, exactly as if I were grown-up.' 'I was captivated,' she wrote. 'And I went on being captivated.' When he asked her to show him the town she was very pleased.

They walked in the Botanical Gardens, the pride of Roseau, and sat down on a bench. She chatted to him in the most grown-up way she could. He asked her how old she was. 'I'm fourteen,' she said (or twelve or thirteen, in different versions of the story). 'Fourteen,' he said. 'Quite old enough to have a lover.' And suddenly she felt his hand on her breast. 'It travelled downwards, a cool, masterful hand, until stopped by the tight waist belt.' She sat very still ('everything would be worse if I moved,' Antoinette thinks, and Anna: 'It won't hurt until I move'). 'This is a mistake,' she thought, 'a mistake. . . . If I sit quite still & don't move he'll take his hand away & won't realise that he has touched me.' Then there were voices, and a couple came round the corner. Calmly, with dignity, he withdrew his hand. 'All the way home he talked of indifferent things.' But she was in a tumult, 'dreadfully attracted, dreadfully repelled.'

That was how it began. She felt that it lasted for weeks, even months; in any case she saw him again many times. The second time she said she didn't want to go, but her mother told her not to be rude. And after that he won her over. He found out what sweets she liked and bought them for her, he asked her questions about herself and listened to the answers. 'Mostly he talked about me, me, me. It was intoxicating . . . irresistible.'

He never touched her again. But one day he said, 'Your mother dresses you hideously. If you belonged to me I'd dress you quite differently. Would you like to belong to me?' 'I don't know,' she said. 'I'd seldom allow you to wear clothes at all,' he said.

Then it really began. Mr Howard told her a story about herself which shocked, fascinated, hypnotised her. And 'After two or three doses of this drug' she no longer struggled.

In his story he abducted her and took her to his beautiful house on another island. She could smell the flowers that decorated its large rooms, hear the blinds flap at the windows, see the bats that flew out at sunset.

> ... My arms were covered with bracelets and my hands with rings. I laughed and danced but I was not happy or unhappy. I was waiting.... My bracelets tinkled when I moved and sometimes quite naked I waited on the guests.

Sometimes he talked of other things — London, India, the war in which he had lost his eye. But always he would return to his story, and to the same themes: submission, punishment, cruelty. That was love, he told her, that was making love: not kindness, but violence and cruelty. She would only be allowed to rebel enough to make it more fun to force her to submit. She would have to obey his will. And always in the end she would have to be punished.

Part of her felt that Mr Howard's story was a crude and second-rate fantasy. But part of her 'lapped it up & asked for more.' For what he said seemed to find an echo in her; something in her said 'Yes that's true. Pain humiliation submission — that is for me.' 'It fitted in with all I knew of life, with all I'd ever felt.'

At the start she hadn't dreamed of telling her mother: 'It was not a thing you could possibly talk about.' She wouldn't believe her, or if she did she would blame her. Then later, perhaps, her mother suspected, for she became cold to Mr Howard, and once she questioned Jean. By then she was completely under his spell and she lied fluently. But Mr Howard's wife knew. She didn't interfere; but she began to look at Jean, and say sarcastic things, and hate her. One day when they were alone she said, 'You are a wicked girl. And you will be punished' ('Punished — whichever way I turned I met that word.')

By now, of course, she believed that she deserved it even more. 'I only struggled feebly. What he had seen in me was there.' He had known at once that she would never tell anybody, and that she would make no effort to stop him talking. 'That could only mean that he'd seen at once that she was not a good girl — who would object — but a wicked one — who would listen. He must know. He knew. It was so.'

'Now what was the end of this story?' Jean wrote. 'Did Mr Howard go potty, the little *saleté* that I was go from bad to worse?'

'Not at all,' she answered herself. Simply, Mr and Mrs Howard left for England. For the last week there were no more walks. 'I knew that he was going and was very sad ... all the time I hoped that before he left he would say something to me that would make it all right and as if I had not been wicked.' But he never did. Her only revenge was not to go and see him off. Everybody went down to the jetty, her father and mother even went on board the steamer. 'But I didn't go. I said I had a headache and didn't go.'

Mr Howard 'died an easy death at the age of nearly eighty, respected and loved by all,' Jean wrote. 'And I? What happened was that I forgot it.' 'I became very good at blotting things out, refusing to think about them'; and 'It went out of my memory like a stone.'

Does that sound extraordinary? Yet I am sure it was true. This capacity to hide and forget was at the heart of her nature. It allowed her to survive as a woman; and it gave her her task as a writer, which was to stop hiding and to remember. So her adolescent dream of Mr Howard sank below the surface of her conscious mind. It struggled up for a moment in *Voyage in the Dark*, when Anna identifies with the slave girl Maillotte Boyd as she lies in her lover's bed: *Maillotte Boyd, aged eighteen. Maillotte Boyd, aged eighteen.... 'But I like it like this. I don't want it any other way but this.'* Then Jean reclaimed it in her Black Exercise Book a few years later, painfully and tenaciously. And from its twenty pages she distilled just one charged, enigmatic paragraph for *Good Morning, Midnight*:

> I am in a little whitewashed room. The sun is hot outside. A man is standing with his back to me, whistling that tune and cleaning his shoes. I am wearing a black dress, very short, and heel-less slippers. My legs are bare. I am watching for the expression on the man's face when he turns around. Now he ill-treats me, now he betrays me. He often brings home other women and I have to wait on them, and I don't like that. But as long as he is alive and near me I am not unhappy. If he were to die I should kill myself.

★　　　★　　　★

Jean's brother Owen had stayed at Wellingborough School until 1902, and had then come home. At some point he had his brief flirtation with the Canadian Mounted Police. But he was probably on the island most of the time from 1903 until about 1907, when he had a liaison with a black woman and was 'spirited out of Dominica.'*

---

* His daughter Ena Williams was born of this affair. Later he returned for long enough to have two more half-caste children. He left Dominica for good in around 1914, to join the British Army and fight in the First World War. While he was back home he worked at Bath Estate, the lime plantation owned by the British company of L. Rose and Sons, and on Geneva and Amalia Estates. This gave him his training, and he became an orchardist.

In his last years, when he was housebound with bronchitis, he wrote a book about his family, lightly fictionalised and with the names slightly changed. In it he devoted a whole chapter to the sister who is clearly Jean. She is called 'Missy'; and it's clear (though only said indirectly) that she is just turning sixteen.

'Missy had grown up and was a young lady in a world of her own,' Owen wrote. She still went daily to the convent, but 'lessons had long ceased to interest her.' She 'preferred her own company to that of the other young girls of her age', and she still had her different ideas ('I would like to carry a load on my head like the native girls. That is what gives them their beautiful carriage and figures'). With her mother she was hostile, defensive, as though she were always thinking *Why are you prying into my mind?* And if her mother asked her directly where she was going she was rude. 'That is no concern of yours,' she would say. No one really cared what she thought and felt; these questions were only attempts to control her, and she would not be controlled.

They 'couldn't get Gwennie to do anything' was the family's version. She was lazy and indolent, she did nothing but lie in the hammock and read all day.... 'Lying in the hammock, swinging cautiously for the ropes creaked, one dreamt,' Jean wrote; and in *Smile Please* 'I'd take no notice of the shouts of "Stop that, the ropes are creaking!"' 'So does one learn the bitter lesson that humanity is never content just to differ from you and let it go at that. Never. They must interfere, actively and grimly, between your thoughts and yourself.'

She did only two things with intensity and dedication. The first was to read. She blotted out the real world and plunged into the world of books, which she thought more real. She liked books about prostitutes, especially one called *The Sands of Pleasure*, about an Englishman's affair with a demi-mondaine in Paris. So beside her picture of England as snow and fires there now rose other pictures: the streets of Paris, lost women forced to abase themselves for money. She herself 'flirted', and had 'a mild love affair – several,' she wrote in her Black Exercise Book. But they were childish, unimportant. 'I never liked being kissed,' she wrote. 'All or nothing had been driven deep in.'

The other thing she did was play the piano. Every day she had a lesson with Mother Mount Calvary, and practised for long hours. Her family thought her indolent, she *was* indolent. But when she wanted to she could work very hard. Her father thought she was so good that he wanted to send her to the Royal College of Music in London. She would become a great pianist, she would take London by storm.... I expect that her mother (and Auntie B) felt he was spoiling her, encouraging her to think she was different. But in any case Jean wouldn't go. 'I much prefer to remain,' she said (in Owen's awkward prose) 'in this tragic but beautiful Island.' The real reason, Owen wrote, 'she kept a profound secret, buried in the depth of her soul.'

Missy's secret is a love affair. Not a 'mental seduction' by an old man; but a passionate affair with a young lover. 'A lover — a lover is tall and beautiful and strong,' Jean had thought when Mr Howard first said the word to her; and sometimes listening to his story she had imagined such a lover, 'Young dark and splendid,' she wrote, 'like — the man in Quo Vadis.' Owen gives him to her. His name is Anthony, he is twenty-one, and he is all the things she has dreamt of. But he is not white. He is half white and half Carib, with a touch of black; and he has been taken into the family — almost adopted, like Heathcliff — by the doctor and his wife.

Anthony and Missy met in secret. For a time they only kiss and cuddle. But finally, quite alone at the distant Falls, they become lovers. Afterwards Missy says — 'Oh, Anthony, what peace, what happiness, what a love is ours. There are many, many, who would say it is a sin. Yes it is, but oh ...!' She covers her face and eyes. Then she paces round, seizes her clothes and dresses. 'I am dying for a cup of tea,' she says. 'I wish I could swallow it and it would kill me. We will never know such love and such happiness again, it is all over....'

A month passes or two, and Anthony begins to be tormented by guilt. Love can be happiness, he thinks; but when it is 'wrong and sinful' it is a 'terrible malady'. He and Missy go on meeting, but 'their world had altered.'

> 'What a fool you are,' she said, 'making such a fuss over nothing. It has happened before many times and it will happen again. The world will drift along just the same.'
>
> Her ideas were abhorrent to him.
>
> 'Have you no shame?' he said. 'You are different from me. I feel I can never look your parents in the face again.... I am going to run away, to disappear, you won't see me again...'
>
> With that she changed her attitude, clung to him, kissed him and hugged him and begged him to think more of her.
>
> 'I love you so madly,' she said. 'You are my life and my all. What could I do if you went away? It is not like you to say such beastly hurtful things.'

They resolve nothing; finally it is resolved for them. One evening in the Botanical Gardens Mrs Potts and the Mother Superior, strolling there together, come upon them. 'It had to come,' Anthony says. 'We might have kept it secret in London, Paris or New York. This Island is too small.'

'Damn them all,' she said. 'Why the hell did they want to walk this way?'

'What an enigma you are,' he said. 'A conglomeration of sweetness and wit, at the same time a devil incarnate ....'

'The events which followed were terrible in their anguish,' Owen wrote. Anthony goes to Mrs Potts and asks for her pardon. He says he will take Missy far away to Martinique. 'As long as I go with you we can go to Hell together,' Missy says. In the middle of the night she meets him, and they ride together across the island towards Soufrière. But when they get to the sea Anthony says:

'You know, when my ancestors used to be all over the island and before the slaves came from Africa, if there was a young girl or a woman who had done anything wrong, deceitful or immoral in the eyes of the tribe, she was tried by the Heads. The wrong doer would be taken to the top of this mountain and flung into the sea. To my mind and in my way of thinking we have done wrong; there is no alternative, we must suffer the penalty for our sins....'

She seemed to have no argument, no reasoning left. She just looked at him and followed him obediently without a murmur....

They arrived at the top of the mountain, a sheer drop of five to six hundred feet. Below was the calm sea in the still and silent darkness....

'Anthony,' she said, 'take me up in your arms, squeeze the life out of me, kiss me as you did at the Falls. Kiss my eyes, hold me tight, tight, tighter.'

Anthony does as she asks, and with her in his arms he jumps into the sea.

'If I could die. Now, when I am happy,' Antoinette says; and Annette: 'That would have been a better fate. To die and be forgotten and at peace. Not to know that one is abandoned, lied about, helpless....' Did something like this happen − except that Jean didn't die?

If it did happen someone would have heard about it − on that island everyone would have heard about it, it would have been (as Rochester says) 'gossiped about, sung about (... they make up songs about everything, everybody ...).' But no one has heard of it; there is no song. Owen has an explanation − 'The people were discreet out of the very great respect and love which they had for their Doctor and his wife.' Dr Rees Williams *was* loved; but I don't believe that would have been enough.

Where did this story come from? How did Owen know so well what Jean would say and do in love? Why is this the only part of his book with any sense of shape and drama? Was it perhaps just a fantasy, which she told to the only person in the family who wouldn't condemn her, but would sympathise? . . . It's too late; we'll never know. But there was *something* behind it; even if it was only in Jean's mind, and even if she forgot it afterwards still more thoroughly than she forgot Mr Howard. For it did leave a few traces. She planned to write a novel called *Wedding in the Carib Quarter,* but never did: and on the plan for it she wrote *No playing around with ME.* And there are one or two notes she scrawled when she was drunk and depressed − 'This feeling I have about the Caribs & the Carib Quarter is very old & very complicated . . . When I try to explain the feeling I find I cannot or do not wish to. . . .' And finally, there is Antoinette's love for her half-caste cousin Sandi in *Wide Sargasso Sea*: 'We had often kissed before but not like that. That was the life and death kiss, and you only know a long time afterwards what it is, the life and death kiss.'

Of affairs like this one Jean wrote: 'in those days, a *terrible* thing for a white girl to do. Not to be forgiven. The men did as they liked. The women − *never*.' Even just to think of it, certainly to show it, to speak of it, would be enough to make you feel as she did for the rest of her life: beyond the pale.

She had just over eighteen months at home after boarding at the convent. Then it was arranged that she should go, not to the Royal College of Music, but to school in England. This was quite normal; most white girls as well as boys finished their schooling in England. Her sister Brenda would soon follow her (though not to the same school). But Jean was chilled and afraid. There was something 'unexpected & strange' about the decision, something *wrong* about it; she felt she was not going to England but 'being sent to England, a different thing after all.' It felt like another attempt to change her − and no doubt it was. (Even her father said 'Well, you are a bit of a savage, you know. That's why you're going to England.' But then he put his arms around her and hugged her.)

He told her on a hot silent July afternoon. That night she went to her room early and sat out on the flat roof outside her window. She wrote a poem about leaving:

*I am going to England*
*What shall I find there?*
*'No matter what*
*Not what I sought' said Byron.*

*Not what I sought,*
*Not what I seek.*

After that she felt cooler and more confident, as she always did when she'd written down her fears.

Soon she began to feel excited, then very excited. Her father gave farewell picnics for her, and finally even a farewell dance, a 'coming out dance' especially for her. He hired a band — concertina, triangle and shak-shak — and they played lovely waltzes, English ones like the Antigua Waltz, and French ones too ('one two three one two three *pourquoi ne pas aimer bonheur suprème*' ...). She drank rum punch, and talked to her dancing partners about the glorious world she was about to enter. ('What is a *fille de joie*?' she asked one. 'What?' he said. 'You don't mind my giving you a word of advice? Don't talk like that when you get to England.')

Her Aunt Clarice was taking her, and it was Aunt Clarice she would stay with in her holidays. That was part of the trouble, because she was afraid of her English aunt. She was so clever and decided, so controlled, so cool. 'Clarice doesn't wear her heart on her sleeve,' her father said, 'take a bit of trouble, try to make her fond of you.' 'Yes,' Jean said, but she didn't mean it. She felt that her aunt disliked her; and that would be that. She was too proud to 'make someone fond of her,' and she didn't know how.

Her mother didn't come to Bridgetown in Barbados, where their boat left from. She'd been ill, perhaps she wasn't well enough yet to travel; and I'm sure she had her own doubts and fears about this new plan for her unruly daughter. Jean must have said goodbye to her at home. She'd always thought of her mother as her English parent, the one who set high standards, and who didn't love her because she failed them. But now this role would be taken on more and more by her Aunt Clarice. Her mother would move away in her mind from Englishness, and closer to her own grandmother, Jean's pretty, lively, dark great-grandmother Jean Maxwell. Clarice would become the wicked stepmother of *Voyage in the Dark*; her own mother would go into Antoinette's mother in *Wide Sargasso Sea*: rejecting but beautiful, and suffering Antoinette's fate of cruelty, madness and death before her.

Jean's father, however, did come to see her off. He loved her; even she knew it. 'When we said goodbye at Barbados he hugged me so tight that a coral brooch I wore was squashed. "Take care of yourself," he said in a strangled voice. . . .' But she said 'Goodbye, goodbye' very cheerfully, because she was only going for a year or two, and at last she would see England. Later she wrote of Anna that when the ship pulled away she knew she was going, and she cried. But of herself she wrote that she went down to her cabin and put away the coral brooch 'without any particular feeling.' 'Already my childhood, the West Indies, my father and mother had been left behind; I was forgetting them. They were the past.'

# First Steps, 1907–1912

*To England — The Perse School, 1907-1909 — Tree's School, 1909
— The Chorus, 1909-1910 — Lancelot*

All her life Jean loved departures and new beginnings. And all her
life her feelings were as lavish and intense as Dominican weather. So
now she was 'nearly wild with delight.' It was hot, the sea was
smooth, even Aunt Clarice was enjoying herself. The orchestra
playing at meals enchanted Jean. They gave a concert and she sang;
the audience clapped warmly. She thought 'When I get to London
I'll go straight on to the stage.' At the concert she made friends with
two young men on the way home from Rio, and with 'a dark lady'
who sang a haunting song. When she was over seventy she still
remembered how it began: '*It is all in vain to entreat me* ...'

But her moods changed as fast as Dominican weather too. Quite
suddenly, it seemed to her, the sky went from blue to grey, the ship's
officers exchanged their tropical whites for heavy dark uniforms, the
sea grew rough and the air cold. Aunt Clarice was seasick and
snapped at her; she couldn't stop shivering no matter how many rugs
they piled on her. Her delight was forgotten as though it had never
been; instead she was 'nearly sick with doubt and anxiety.' When the
ship docked at Southampton and she looked through the porthole
at the dirty grey water she felt heavy, weighted down. 'I knew for
one instant all that would happen to me,' she wrote forty-odd years
later. 'I swear I did.'

The bewildering world of England closed round her, where she was
expected to know so many things. In Dominica there had been no
trains, no buses or cars or bicycles, no indoor plumbing. One by one
these things — and then many others — would trip her up, and the
pale blue eyes, the pale white faces, would turn and watch as she fell
over.

It started with the train. She was expecting something brightly
coloured, red, green and blue like toy trains, not this dingy, tiny,
brown room. Then they'd hardly started when they were plunged
into blackness. *What was happening?* When at last it was light again

she asked faintly, 'Was that a railway accident?' She'd never imagined a tunnel.

At home she was used to getting up by half past six because the early morning was the best part of the day. So on her first London morning she did the same. She got up very early and went out to see what London looked like. Soon she felt hungry and a little disappointed, and she turned round. Back at the boarding house she thought it would be lovely to have a bath, so she ran one and got in. She felt happier now; she turned up the hot tap and began to sing. But suddenly a voice shouted at her to turn off the water at once. It was very angry ... what had she done? Her aunt explained that she had taken all the hot water. But it had never occurred to her that the supply was limited. 'I've already noticed that you are quite incapable of thinking about anyone but yourself,' her aunt said, and wouldn't speak to her all morning. When she finally spoke it was only to say 'You shouldn't go out like that in the morning, without telling me. It's a most peculiar thing to do.'

Over the next few days Aunt Clarice tried to show this strange and silent girl the sights of London. It was a disaster. Jean tried to hide it, but she was bitterly disappointed. Westminster Abbey was crowded. St Paul's was bare and dull, the theatre was nothing like Auntie B's passionate descriptions.... Worst of all was the zoo. Aunt Clarice took her specially to see the Dominica parrot, so old no one knew his real age: but 'Poor bird,' was all Jean could say. The parrot, the lion, the hummingbirds gave her such an impression of misery she could hardly bear to look at them. Their colours were dim, their eyes sad, they seemed to her only longing to escape.

She was at her most difficult, withdrawn, contrary, impossible to please. She asked for impossible things like iced water, she yawned, she lagged behind – she even disappeared, and Aunt Clarice was furious when she found her at last, asleep on a bench. But Clarice had spent three winters in Dominica, she should have known how strange everything would be to Jean. And she must have had some idea of her nature. But she didn't notice, Jean wrote, 'that I needed reassuring or comforting, felt strange or sad.' Or (more likely) if she noticed she couldn't help; she could only disapprove.

So it began straight away, Jean's feeling about England: it had disappointed her (and she had disappointed it). She had had such high hopes, such romantic dreams; but now she was homesick, unhappy, she trailed around London 'in a state of complete disappointment which almost amounted to hatred.' Nothing was *grand*, nothing was beautiful or exciting, as she'd been so sure it would be. The streets were narrow, the people were ordinary, the whole city was shabby and grey. The women especially looked so ugly, and so *poor*. 'I

couldn't get used to the idea that white women could look like that.'
She couldn't get used to it, and it frightened her. In England she had
thought to find the small glories of white West Indian life grown to
fairytale greatness. Instead she saw that where everyone was white
the beggars were white too.

Still, she hoped; she'd go on hoping for a long time. 'Of course
this isn't England,' she told herself, it couldn't be. That must lie just
round the corner – at any moment she would see it, quite suddenly,
the real England. . . . And sometimes she did see it, she tantalisingly
glimpsed it. A few very pretty girls in shops, a few actresses on
posters outside the theatres, seemed to hold out the promise she'd
made herself. And once 'a very pretty lady' in a park, who was just
as she'd imagined English ladies would be: rich, respected,
protected. . . . Her dream was really a dream of riches. It was 'a little
bourgeois dream', and looking back she knew it. But for a long time
it didn't change. For ten, even twenty years she tried to make it come
true, to become the actress on the poster, the lady in the park. But
the poverty of the Bloomsbury streets turned out to be her real
England after all.

★    ★    ★

The first thing that Jean remembered about going to the Perse School
for Girls in Cambridge was shopping for school clothes in London.
Her aunt took her to Swan and Edgar's; they bought blouses,
woollen combinations, all very sensible. But there would have to be
a suit too. Now Jean saw her chance for something lovely, something
that would give her the courage to face Cambridge: a beautiful wine-
red costume, with an elegant three-quarter length coat and a grey
fur collar. 'Oh do let me have it,' she pleaded – but silently,
inwardly. 'I will be so different if you do, you'll like me better, oh
I must have one pretty thing . . . .' But the price ticket said twenty-
five guineas. 'Not at all suitable,' Aunt Clarice said; and chose one
for four guineas instead, blue and hairy with brass buttons. Jean said
nothing, but she was heartbroken. How could she appear before a
lot of strange girls in such a hideous thing? 'They're bound to dislike
me,' she thought. She'd made up her mind to that before she ever
got there, having to leave behind in Swan and Edgar's the girl she
wanted to be – grown-up, expensive, not at all suitable.

In 1907 the Perse School was a small, sedate, old-fashioned school.
Miss Street, who had founded it in 1881, was still headmistress. She
had fought hard for twenty-five years to make the Perse accepted in
Cambridge. She'd succeeded magnificently, but now she was tired. In
1909 a new headmistress, the famous Miss Kennett, would take over.

She was a Girton mathematician and a strict disciplinarian; under her the Perse became much more modern, much more academic. Jean had arrived at probably the sleepiest ebb in the history of the school – luckily for her.

But the Perse was sleepy only compared to what it soon became. Compared to many other schools – and compared especially to Jean's convent – it was a formidable place. The mistresses, especially in the upper school, were high-minded and strict, teaching methods were old-fashioned, standards of behaviour high. There would be no French poetry here. The English mistress, Miss Umfreville Wilkinson, taught grammar and bowdlerised Shakespeare; in History Miss Luard dictated endless pages of notes. In Miss Kennett's time girls were not allowed to speak between lessons; they were forbidden to run or walk abreast in the school, or to go anywhere without hat or gloves outside it; they could not walk to school with another girl unless they had written permission. The rules may have been less strict under Miss Street, but not very much. Jean had come from a lazy corner of the tropics straight into a stronghold of correctness. It was a shock she would never forget. Ever after England seemed to her cold and unwelcoming, full of clever, critical, respectable people. Ever after it seemed to her like a prison, where you could never be free, never be yourself, without breaking dozens of incomprehensible and arbitrary rules. 'The school part of my life explains so much,' she wrote sixty years later. And in *Wide Sargasso Sea* she gave Antoinette's attic the dark corridors and red curtains of her memories of the Perse School.

What really happened there, to make her so unhappy? Sometimes she suggests she was already 'a dead girl ... a drowned girl' by the time she got there, just as Antoinette was destroyed by her mother, by her whole childhood, long before she was seventeen. And we know now that that was partly true. But Jean was never more than half destroyed, even when she was old – half of her always fought back, and went on hoping and working. And so it did now. She remembered mostly the doomed and driven things; but other things happened too.

What she remembered most was feeling out of place, and ignorant of the simplest things which everyone else took for granted. She couldn't play hockey, she couldn't ride a bicycle, she couldn't talk properly ('What a really nasty voice you've got,' one of the girls said). 'Is it "honey don't try so hard" or "honey don't cry so hard"?' they'd ask. 'How should I know?' she'd reply. 'Well, it's a coon song,' they'd say, winking at each other, 'you ought to know.' ('That awful sing-song voice you had!' Hester says in *Voyage in the Dark*.

'Exactly like a nigger you talked — and still do.') In revenge she made up wild stories of volcanoes and hurricanes, of brave governors subduing dangerous natives — and these fantastic lies, she found, they would believe. They simply didn't understand her world, and she didn't understand theirs. The dark, the cold, the icy wind, the hopeless grey-yellow sky — they were used to them, and they expected her to get used to them too. But she couldn't. She thought — 'What on earth am I doing here? ... I'm hopeless — I'm caught — I will always be lonely, I will never get away....' Then she would feel so weak and ill that Miss Street would let her go to bed with extra blankets and a cup of hot milk, and Miss Street's personal maid would bring her her own hot water bottle.

Miss Street was calm and kind, and Jean did remember that. But she remembered the others more. Miss Paterson, the classics mistress, for instance, whom she calls 'Miss Patey' in 'Overture and Beginners Please'. (She calls Miss Street — characteristically — 'Miss Rode'.) Miss Paterson was young and attractive and I expect Jean would have liked to please her, but she didn't succeed. Miss Paterson tried to teach her to ride a bicycle, which wasn't a success ('She always skimmed gracefully ahead as though she had nothing to do with me and I followed her, wobbling dangerously from side to side'). Miss Paterson was in charge of the school's architectural society, the Pelican Studio, which in the summer term of 1908 visited Ely Cathedral. Jean was so excited and moved by the cathedral's beauty that she began to tremble. Then they went to tea with the Kennetts, family of the future headmistress; and Jean's hands were still trembling so badly that she dropped her cup, smashing it to pieces on the flagstones. Miss Paterson, she learned, could be even more sarcastic than Aunt Clarice.

But far far worse — Jean's worst memory of the Perse — was Miss Osborn ('Miss Born' of 'Overture and Beginners Please'). Miss Osborn was Miss Street's companion and assistant. She didn't teach, except occasionally Scripture. She was Miss Street's dark and silent shadow. She was prim, pious and alarming; she had a grey face, grey hair and sharp black eyes. People said she was 'a great asset to the school': 'she represents breeding and culture'. Myrtle Newton, who was a bit of a rebel too, said she was a snob.

Unluckily, Jean was one of the small group of boarders who lived with Miss Street and Miss Osborn in the main school building. She remembered especially one Christmas holiday, when she and another girl were left alone in the school with the headmistress and her companion, in Jean's case because Aunt Clarice was ill. ('*She says!*' said the other girl; and in a draft Jean wrote: 'I'd wondered the same thing myself.') In the evenings the two ladies and the two young girls sat in the small dining room by the fire, and Jean had to read out loud from a novel by Charlotte M. Yonge. Miss Street sat placidly, hardly listening; but Jean felt Miss Osborn's sharp black eyes fixed on her face. That always made her uneasy. And sure enough, Miss Osborn would wince. 'Your voice,' she would say. 'Drop it. An octave at least.' And soon: 'That will do, don't go on. I really can't bear any more tonight.'

Miss Osborn nearly spoiled the one happy part of Jean's school life. In her first term the fifth and sixth forms put on 'Scenes from *The Winter's Tale*', and Miss Street offered her the part of Autolycus. 'What is Autolycus?' Jean asked. 'He's a rogue,' Miss Osborn answered, 'an admirable part for you.' Then of course Jean said she wouldn't take it. But Miss Street the peacemaker said quickly, 'Autolycus can be a most charming rogue,' and played the songs that he would sing. Jean was won over. She dressed like Rosalind in *As You Like It* − green tights, brown boots, a cap with a feather, and burnt cork on her eyebrows. She sang well, and the applause of the assembled parents was 'a splendid sound'. Only now Miss Osborn's disapproval turned to active dislike.

Still, Autolycus had given her confidence, for the next term she took part in a school debate. The motion was 'That the popularity of modern literature, to the exclusion of standard works, is unreasonable and deplorable.' She couldn't resist. Did these stuffy snobs despise modern novels? Well then, *she* would defend them. And in front of a large audience of girls and parents − well over a hundred people − she stood up and spoke in her own voice, however high. There were two other girls on the side of modern literature. Margaret Kellett would soon be Head Girl, and I imagine she gave a clever, controlled speech, smiling in all the right places to show that she didn't mean it. But Jean and Myrtle Newton were both disapproved of by *The Persean Magazine*. Jean was both 'flippant' and extreme ('she expressed her views fearlessly'). *The Persean's* final verdict foreshadowed every damning, dampening English criticism to come. 'Daring and originality are always welcome in a speech,' it said, 'but they must not be confused with exaggeration.'

At the end of her first year she sat the Oxford and Cambridge Higher Certificate in English Literature and Roman History. She wasn't expected to do well in History; but Miss Wilkinson had high hopes for her (and for Myrtle Newton too) in English Literature. But Jean was always contrary. When the results arrived she had done poorly in English − and extraordinarily well in Roman History. She always remembered Miss Wilkinson's sad face as she said 'I was so sure of you'; and pretty, popular Miss Luard smiling: 'I'm very pleased, dear child, but surprised.'

Jean's explanation of both results was typical. In English she'd chosen as her favourite book a 'modern' novel, *The Garden of Allah,* by Robert Hichens: 'That explains it!' Miss Wilkinson said, throwing up her hands in despair.*

And in History? She hadn't remembered a word of Miss Luard's lessons, she said; she'd got it all from reading *Quo Vadis*.... The History examiners were evidently more imaginative than Literature's; they were much impressed by her detailed knowledge of 'Nero and his emerald eyeglass and Petronius cutting his veins in a lovely bath made of a seashell.' On the next Speech Day *The Persean* had to record that the History Prize was given by W.L. Mollison, Esq to 'G. Rees Williams'.

She'd now come back for a second and last year of English schooling. Presumably she took up some other subjects, French probably, or Classics with Miss Paterson; or perhaps she was meant to concentrate on piano lessons with Miss Evans, in pursuit of the Royal College of Music. (But when she told Miss Evans that her father thought she might be 'a professional' Miss Evans laughed. 'It's the only time I've ever seen her laugh,' Jean wrote.) And now something happened which changed everything.

First, she was in another play. This was quite different from *The Winter's Tale,* which had been only a few scenes on Speech Day, squeezed between speeches and prizes. *She Stoops to Conquer* was given in full, and Jean was the star. She played the main role, Tony Lumpkin; and according to *The Persean Magazine* itself 'Gwen Williams as Tony carried off the palm'; 'Tony was a triumph.'

She never mentioned this, surely the greatest success of her school career, nor did she ever mention the literature debate. Success didn't fit her feeling of rejection, and had to be explained away (like her success in Roman History) or forgotten. And there was another reason: to do, again, with Miss Osborn.

In 'Overture and Beginners Please' Jean remembers the end of the evenings in Miss Street's sitting-room. 'Goodnight Miss Rode,' she would say.

> ... 'Goodnight, dear child,' said Miss Rode, who was wearing her purple, always a good sign. 'Goodnight Miss Born.' Miss Born inclined her head very slightly, and as I went out remarked, 'Why did you insist on that girl playing Autolycus? Tony Lumpkin in person.'
> 'Not in person, surely,' said Miss Rode mildly.
> 'In manner then, in manner,' said Miss Born.

*According to Jean, Myrtle did badly too, perhaps for the same reason.

She'd always known that Miss Osborn thought her rude, clumsy, ignorant. Now she'd put a name to it: Tony Lumpkin. And all the pleasure of playing Tony so well would drain away, leaving him only as the image of everything Miss Osborn thought her, and everything she didn't want to be.

*She Stoops to Conquer* was presented in early December 1908. During this term Myrtle Newton left the Perse, and Jean got a letter from her. When she told the story fifty years later she'd forgotten Myrtle; but she remembered her letter. She'd kept it until it fell to pieces, because it had changed her life. 'Dear West Indies,' Myrtle wrote,

> I have been thinking about you a lot since I came to Switzerland, perhaps because my mother is getting divorced. I see now what a lot of silly fools we were about everything that matters and I don't think you are. It was all those words in *The Winter's Tale* that Miss Born wanted to blue pencil, you rolled them out as though you knew what they meant. My mother said you made the other girls look like waxworks and when you dropped your cap you picked it up so naturally, like a born actress. She says that you ought to go on the stage and why don't you? . . .

'Suddenly,' Jean wrote, 'like an illumination, I knew exactly what I wanted to do. Next day I wrote to my father. I told him that I longed to be an actress and that I wanted to go to the Academy of Dramatic Art in Gower Street.'

Since she'd left home her happiest moments had been on stage, listening to the audience applaud; and she had often dreamed of being an actress. Sometimes she wrote that it had been 'my greatest wish as long as I could remember.' But all this was now forgotten, and it seemed to her that Myrtle ('a girl I hardly knew'), and not her own desire or decision, was responsible for her new direction. She would always be like this, as a person and as a writer: passive, unconscious, feeling (needing to feel) 'less a chooser than a being chosen.' There would be many more moments in her life like this one of Myrtle's letter.

'When the answer arrived it was yes,' Jean wrote. She doesn't seem to have been surprised that her family's plans for her – a proper girls' school, then home – were given up so quickly. Well, her father supported her in everything she did, and was as unorthodox as she was; perhaps he was as happy to imagine her a great actress as a great pianist. As for her mother and Auntie B, perhaps they were relieved: the difficult daughter had found something she wanted to do. And the legitimate stage, after all, was beginning to be respectable.

'I was happier than I'd ever been in my life,' Jean wrote in

'Overture and Beginners Please'. Of course she wanted to start straight away. But now her father insisted on caution. There was after all an entrance examination; she must stay out the term, and have extra lessons in elocution and singing. For once Jean didn't mind. She was so happy nothing could touch her, 'not praise nor blame'. 'All that term I walked on air.'

Her lessons were as decorous and prim as Cambridge could make them. A clergyman came from one of the Colleges to teach her elocution. The first words he said were 'Now, we'll have that smile off, please.' After that his lessons were stiff and solemn affairs. 'Why do you want to go on the stage?' he asked her. 'Because I love the sound of words.' 'And?' he pursued. 'Out with it!' 'I like it when the audience claps and I adore everything to do with the stage.' He sighed. 'Well, we'll do our best,' he said.

He taught her 'The Bells', 'Once more into the breach dear friends'; and something in which she had to pretend to be American (perhaps to suit her accent). But he cannot have been very encouraging. By the time the examination arrived Jean was nervous. The girls all said 'You won't pass it'; she said 'Yes I will,' but she didn't believe it. She managed to recite 'The Bells' to 'two sarcastic gentlemen' and a lady, but they seemed very bored, stopped her before she'd finished and didn't want to hear any more. She was astonished when she heard she'd passed. ('The place was not royal then,' she said, and perhaps 'it wasn't so choosy.')

Miss Wilkinson and Miss Luard were distant, the French mistress raised her eyebrows, the girls either envied or laughed at her. But 'Nobody could touch me,' she wrote. 'My course was set.' At the end of 1908 she left school 'without a qualm'.

★    ★    ★

Aunt Clarice strongly disapproved of 'the whole business', and perhaps Dr Rees Williams didn't send her enough money. Not enough for Jean, anyway. 'All my clothes were hideous,' she wrote, 'for my aunt's one idea had been to fit me out as cheaply as possible.' They bought some cheap furs, and a cotton dress for ten shillings. The dress was too big, the skirt far too long even for 1909. But Aunt Clarice said it would be too expensive to have it altered, Jean must just tuck it up at the waist: 'You're so thin no one will notice.' This is what she must have done, however much she hated it; she never thought of getting needle and thread and turning up the hem. Clarice installed her in a boarding house in Bedford Place, around the corner from Gower Street, and went back to Wales.

Tree's School, as The Academy of Dramatic Art was called (after its founder, Sir Herbert Beerbohm Tree) had opened five years before. It was divided into A's, B's and C's — first, second and third year students. When Jean entered it on 16 January, 1909, there were thirty-four other A's. In Miss Gertrude's acting class they were taught to laugh (by singing down the doh-re-mi-fa-so-la-ti-doh very quickly) and to cry, and how to fall when they were stabbed: forward when you were stabbed in the back, backward when you were stabbed in the front, and straight down when you stabbed yourself. Jean felt that none of the teachers approved of her very much, and I don't suppose they did. In fencing class she soon realised it would be a long time before she'd be able to fight a duel, and lost interest; the only thing she took away from the ballet class was a beautiful new word, *arabesque*. Only acting in well-known scenes for Miss Gertrude came close to what she'd imagined, especially when she played romantic roles — Juliet in *Romeo and Juliet*, Celia in *As You Like It*, Francesca in *Paolo and Francesca*; even once Lady Macbeth, which one of her fellow students praised. But there were no triumphs such as she'd had at school. Those had been a brief flowering: a sign, like her piano playing, that she would be very good at something, but hadn't yet discovered what it was. Among dozens of jostling talents Jean's gifts as an actress began to appear to her teachers, and probably to herself, as small.

But Tree's School was much better than the Perse for making friends. She soon got caught up in a small group of students. There were two other girls, one Australian and one half Turkish, and two men — which was a full quarter of the male A's. Evidently Jean already felt happier with foreign women than with English women, and with men than with any women at all. None the less, the person she liked best at Tree's School was a girl: and a very English girl indeed.

Her name was Honor Grove. Her father was a baronet, her mother a famous society beauty, and she lived in a grand house in Bedford Square. Through Honor Jean learned that snobbery did not stop with girls at school, but pervaded the grown-up world as well.

The lesson turned on a question always very important in England, especially (perhaps) in Edwardian England: the proper pronunciation of a word. From its foundation until well into the 1960s, the Academy of Dramatic Art insisted that the King's English, the language of the ruling class, was the only possible speech for the stage. Jean had been told by English people from her childhood on that she had an 'accent', a nasty, sing-song nigger's voice; it was part of her reason for wanting to come to the school of acting ('They'll teach me how to drop my voice and everything'). The question was, therefore, not an abstract one to her.

On this occasion the pupil, Honor Grove, had a more upper-class accent than the elocution master. The class was reciting a poem in which the word 'froth' occurred. The master said 'Froth', Honor said 'Frawth'. Neither would give in. Honor's face grew white, his red.

> For a long time they shouted at each other: 'Froth' − 'Frawth' − 'Froth' − 'Frawth'. At last Honor said: 'I refuse to pro-nounce the word "froth". "Froth" is cockney, and I'm not here to learn cockney.'

She was made to leave the class, and very soon she left the school. The elocution master was dismissed or left. (As there was no other acting school in London in 1909 that was probably the end of his career.) Honor returned to Bedford Square, and two years later married an officer of the Imperial Russian General Staff. 'Froth' had sunk without a trace; 'Frawth' was safe.

It went far beyond *froth*, of course; just how far Jean also learned from Honor Grove. For the main authority in Edwardian London on this matter of pronunciation was Honor's own mother, Lady Agnes Grove. She'd published essays on it in fashionable magazines such as the *Cornhill* and the *Westminster Review*; in 1907 she'd published a book on it, *The Social Fetich*.* She intended 'to amuse, not seriously to instruct,' she said, but no one was deceived by that. The more lightly the English spoke the more deeply they felt. With her instinct for what was hidden, I'm sure Jean very quickly understood that.

In *The Social Fetich* Lady Grove, like her daughter, especially condemned cockney for torturing and murdering English to the 'refined and cultivated' ear. She condemned 'couch', 'mirror' and 'mantel', insisting on 'sofa', 'looking glass' and 'chimney piece'. She abominated abbreviations ('piano' for pianoforte, 'port' for port wine),† and all objects 'reserved solely for the use of middle classdom' − napkin rings, tea cosies, fish knives. Anyone saying *reely* or *gurl* was 'beyond the pale': 'Believe me, my friends, there are those of us with whom this does for you.'

All these prohibitions, possible false steps and self-betrayals pressed around Jean like walls. They gave her her 'first insight,' she said (for-getting the English children in Dominica, the stuck-up girls at the Perse, Miss Osborn) 'into the snobbishness and unkindness that went on.'

---

* *The Social Fetich* by Lady Agnes Grove, Smith, Elder & Co., London 1907.

† Abbreviations show haste, and 'Any sign of undue haste,' Nancy Mitford wrote in *Noblesse Oblige* in 1956, 'is bound to be non-U.' According to *Noblesse Oblige*, in 1956 *gurl* was still 'unthinkable', and *mirror* still non-U (I believe it still is today).

She said it as though all her sympathy was with the poor elocution master, but really it was more complicated than that. 'And yet it was true that Honor was the only girl who was nice to me,' she'd added.* 'People whom you're supposed not to like seem always to me to be very nice and kind.' These English people could be cruel and snobbish and put you beyond the pale; but they could also be kind and take you in. It was just that you had to get over those walls; you had to learn the rules. Jean never managed that, but she tried. To the end of her life she too said 'chimney piece' and 'looking glass', never 'mantel' or 'mirror'; to the end of her life she too hated the sound of cockney.

And during her first term at Tree's School she nearly leapt over the walls into an English marriage. 'Having a proposal made me feel as if I had passed an examination,' she said. It came from one of the men in her group: Harry Bewes, whose family were Devonshire gentry. His father was a Plymouth solicitor, and he would come into his own money when he was twenty-one. When she stood up to some conceited and snobbish B students one day ('You're always trying to make a big envious thing of a small mean thing,' she said) Harry Bewes said 'Hear, hear!' loudly and bought her a cup of coffee. Jean decided she liked him because he 'didn't care a damn' about anything or anybody. She also liked his suggestion of crossing Africa from the Cape to Cairo on their honeymoon. But that was all. She declined his proposal 'solemnly', saying that her only wish was to be a great actress. ('After some thought I crossed out *great* and put *good*.') Harry never mentioned it again. At the end of the term he told her he'd given up the stage and was going to travel in Africa. The Academy entered the same reason for his early departure as Honor's: illness.

Jean always started things eagerly, then storm clouds gathered. She'd started at the acting school like this — 'very excited and anxious to do my best', but most of what she wrote about it belonged to the first term. The second is a blank.

Later Jean said that in her summer holiday after this second term she went to visit her uncle Neville Williams, her father's and Clarice's older brother, in Harrogate. There she heard the news that her father had died suddenly. And as if that were not bad enough her mother added that 'she could not afford to keep me at the Academy and that I must return to Dominica.' That's why, she

*Lady Grove too was no mere society snob. Before *The Social Fetich* she'd written *Seventy-One Days' Camping in Morocco*; after it she became a leader in liberal and feminist causes, in the Union of Women's Suffrage Societies, for instance, and the Anti-Vivisection League.

suggests, her time at acting school ended; and why, determined not to go back, she took the next step of her life, into the touring chorus.

It wasn't true. It wasn't her mother who said she couldn't continue at the Academy. It must have been her father, because he hadn't died.

At the end of the first term Aunt Clarice had asked for a report on the progress of her niece, 'Miss Gwendolen Williams'. The Administrator of the Academy had replied: 'I write to say that although she is painstaking, we consider that her accent will stand very much in her way in stage work. She might in the course of a long training be able to conquer it or improve it greatly, but we would not like to speak with any certainty on this point. Taking all the circumstances mentioned in your letter into consideration I do not think I should be justified in advising Miss Williams to hope for real success upon the professional stage.'

No doubt the 'circumstances' in Aunt Clarice's letter included money. Still, Jean had returned for the second term. But a few weeks before its end the Administrator wrote again, this time to her father.

Dear Sir,

In answer to your letter of June 13th I write to say that your daughter is slow to improve with her accent which in my frank opinion would seriously affect her chances of success in Drama. I fear it would take her a considerable time to overcome this accent which in my judgement would only fit her for certain parts and those perhaps few and far between.

Believe me, dear Sir,
Yours faithfully,
George P. Bancroft.

No reason was entered on the Register for the withdrawal of 'Gwendolen Williams' from the Academy of Dramatic Art after only two terms. But it was clearly this. Her father must have accepted the judgement of her teachers, and he couldn't afford the 'considerable time' it would take to change it. *That* was the news Jean received at her Uncle Neville's.

When she heard of her father's death I'm sure that she cried inconsolably, as she describes in 'Overture and Beginners Please'. But that was the next year, in June 1910. In the summer of 1909, at her uncle's house in Harrogate, what made her cry was disappointment and frustration. Soon she was 'packed off,' she wrote, to her aunt in Wales — packed off sooner and with less sympathy, very likely, than if her tears had been for her father. It's the only time she ever mentions seeing her Uncle Neville, and when he appears in her fiction he is not sympathetic. Probably he wasn't, and this encounter was one reason why.

The 'social fetich' had defeated her, she'd fallen at the first wall. When she wrote about the Academy sixty years later it was bitterly: 'I learnt nothing at the school of acting except the exact meaning of the word snob.'

It was her voice, her 'nasty nigger's voice', that had let her down. For some time longer she would be defiant about it, or unable to change it. But when she was a famous old lady people could hardly hear her she spoke so softly, in a 'little child's voice'; she almost whispered. And she'd done this since at least her thirties. She'd learned to hide.

For days now she was immured in Aunt Clarice's house in St Asaph, brooding on her failure. She would have to go home unchanged, with nothing to show but a history prize and a bad mark in English literature. Everyone in Roseau would know that she'd failed at the Academy of Dramatic Art, and got nowhere near the College of Music. And she would never be like the lovely women on the posters now... She couldn't bear it, she wouldn't go. 'But you'll have to,' Clarice said. 'I won't,' said Jean.

Clarice was really a kind woman, as Jean secretly knew, and she was also a clever one. If the story Jean told now is true, her aunt was still cleverer and kinder than she admitted. For trying to distract her she said: 'Why don't you try to write? I've always thought that you ought to write. Have you never written anything?'

Jean's first thought was that Clarice had looked at her secret book of poems. But she hadn't written a word since she'd been in England. 'Oh dear no,' her aunt said. 'I meant a story. Something you can sell.' 'I'm too miserable,' Jean said. 'The nightingale sings sweetest when its breast is pierced by a thorn,' said Clarice.

Jean replied 'I don't believe it'; but when her aunt left her alone in the house she sat down and wrote a short story. It was a West Indian story, about a young white man who makes love to a coloured girl and then leaves her and her island without a word. Aunt Clarice was sceptical about the plot, but she said 'I like the bit about the flowers and the music,' and sent it to a magazine. Very soon it came back with a long list of criticisms, headed by 'Very unlikely'. 'What a pity,' Clarice said. Jean wanted to tear it up and throw it into the River Afon, but her aunt wouldn't let her. 'I'm going to keep this,' she said. 'Out of the ashes of your failure on the stage will arise the phoenix of a great novel' ('she talked like that,' Jean said).

Would she have invented this — a deep understanding and appreciation from the aunt she felt had no sympathy for her at all?

Surely not; something like it, I think, must have happened. But Jean cut it out of *Smile Please* and 'Overture and Beginners Please'. And part of it — the line 'After this we became friendly' — she scored out in her draft too.

If they did become friendly it was only briefly and on the surface. For Clarice was planning to ship Jean home, and Jean was planning not to go. They went up to London to buy her tropical clothes: and one day, while her aunt was visiting friends or doing her own shopping, Jean went secretly to Blackmore's agency and got a job in the chorus of a musical comedy.

'Marya had longed to play a glittering part — she was nineteen then — against the sombre and wonderful background of London,' Jean wrote in *Quartet*.

> ... She had visited a theatrical agent; she had sung — something — anything — in a quavering voice, and the agent, a stout and weary gentleman, had run his eyes upwards and downwards and remarked in a hopeless voice: 'Well, you're no Tetrazzini, are you, deary? Never mind, do a few steps.'
> She had done a few steps. The stout gentleman had glanced at another gentleman standing behind the piano.... Both nodded slightly. A contract was produced. The thing was done.

Clarice must have been appalled. She was responsible for this child; how could she tell her brother what had happened? Then she was furious. Jean had behaved deceitfully, outrageously, she said. She was under twenty-one, her contract was illegal, she would stop her from going.... 'A heated argument followed.' Finally poor Clarice threw up her hands in despair. 'It's unfair to expect me to deal with you,' she said. 'You're too much for me altogether.' She would write to Jean's parents; they would have to decide.

In Jean's account, of course, her father was already dead, and it was her mother to whom Aunt Clarice wrote. When the reply came, she said, 'it was very vague.' Her mother 'didn't approve, neither did she altogether disapprove. It seemed as if what with her grief for my father and her worry about money she was relieved that I'd be earning my own living in England....' But it cannot have been like this. Her father was alive, he was the head of the family, Clarice was his sister. It must have been he who wrote. And he must have given his permission. For Clarice saw Jean through rehearsals; and she can't have been merely frosty and grudging, for the other girls approved of her enthusiastically ('Is that your auntie? Oh, isn't she nice'). They continued to meet; and she even sent Jean telegrams wishing her luck on several of her opening performances. It was only as time went on and 'I refused to give up my precious job' that their meetings became fewer, and finally ended. Or perhaps (like Hester with Anna in *Voyage in the Dark*) the last straw for Clarice was Jean's becoming a 'kept woman', after just over a year in the chorus.

'Sometimes she would reflect that the way she had been left to all this was astonishing, even alarming,' Jean wrote about her first heroine, Marya, in *Quartet*.

> ... When she had pointed out that, without expensive pre-liminaries, she would be earning her own living, everybody had stopped protesting and had agreed that this was a good argument. For Marya's relatives, though respectable people, presentable people (one might even go so far as to say quite good people) were poverty-stricken and poverty is the cause of many compromises.

Perhaps this *was* part of the reason why Jean was allowed to go on to the musical comedy stage. For it's true that it was surprising. The Lockharts and Rees Williamses were so conventional and respectable, still so Victorian. And though girls from good families could become 'Ladies of the chorus' in the fashionable London theatres, and from there (if they were very beautiful) marry younger sons of the aristocracy, the life of an ordinary chorus girl in a second or third-rate touring company was a very different thing (as Jean would soon discover). If her father had really died, and it had been up to her mother, I don't think it would have happened: she would have been made (and surely she *could* have been made) to come home. I think her father took her side again; I think he let her (and perhaps himself) go on dreaming. Jean was not abandoned to the chorus, like Marya; against all sense and advice she was allowed to have her own way.

Surely this was why she lied about this time of her life, why she pretended that her father was already dead in the summer of 1909. Incidentally it allowed her to hide her failure as an actress; but that didn't really matter — she freely admitted that she was 'no good on the stage.' No: what she really wanted to hide was that when she took the first step out of her sheltered childhood into the demi-monde beyond the pale *it was her own choice and her own doing.* When she defied her family, when she deceitfully, obstinately insisted on becoming a chorus girl, it wasn't because her mother didn't want her back, and was relieved she'd be earning her own living: it was because she wanted to, and her father let her.

She wanted to forget that she'd chosen her own course; and she wanted to forget that to do so she'd had to defy and persuade not her mother and her aunts, but her father. So she pretended he was already dead. But then of course she couldn't thank him for once again having taken her side. So instead of reducing her secret guilt towards him, she increased it.

'I was astonished when Aunt Clarice told me that I'd behaved outrageously, deceitfully,' she wrote in 'Overture and Beginners Please'. And at the end: 'The man who engaged me at the agent's was at one rehearsal. He came up to me and said in a low voice: "Don't tell the other girls that you were at Tree's School. They mightn't like it." I hadn't any idea what he meant.' Can she really not have realised what her aunt would feel? Can she really not have understood the immense gulf between the Academy and the chorus?

Well: she was young and naive, and cut off in her own world of fantasy. Perhaps there *were* many things that puzzled and defeated her (as she'd said about trains, plumbing, bicycles, hockey). But on the other hand she was hypersensitive and quick, with a 'needle-sharp intelligence'. Half of her knew perfectly well what she was doing, and what other people would think and feel. Much of her bewilderment and incomprehension was a smokescreen, behind which she hid — from herself even more than from other people — the fact that she was guilty. It was something she'd do more and more; until she would seem sometimes like a sleep-walker, trying not to wake.

But not yet. Now she was excited and happy. She had won her chance, and she was in the chorus of *Our Miss Gibbs*. She didn't miss a single rehearsal. Several of the other girls were dreading the tour up north in the winter; one of the boys showed her a sketch he'd done of a street in a northern town, which he'd called *Why we drink*. But once again nothing could touch her. She still thought of freedom and safety as 'twins', 'inseparable'. 'It was a long time before I learnt that when you are safe you are very rarely free. That when you are free you are very rarely safe.'

Jean joined the chorus in 1909, in the heyday of the English stage. People flocked to melodramas, to comedies, especially to the great musical comedies of the Gaiety years. Gaiety stars like Gertie Millar and Lily Elsie were the darlings of the popular press, just as film stars are today. So many companies toured the provinces with productions of the great London hits that the chorus girls told jokes about two railway men talking:

'What have you got there, Bill?'
'Fish and actors.'
'Oh, shove them in a siding.'

*Our Miss Gibbs* was one of the most successful musical comedies of all in these halcyon years. It had opened at the Gaiety in January, with George Grossmith and Gertie Millar: 'the best and brightest Gaiety show we have had for five or six years,' said the *Daily Chronicle*, 'a dream of splendour and beauty.' By 1910 there were three productions of it touring the country, crisscrossing and competing with the other great hits of the day, such as *Floradora*, *The King of Cadonia* and *Cingalee*.

The story of *Our Miss Gibbs* was very silly and very seductive. Mary Gibbs is a proud and honest Yorkshire lass who comes to work at 'Garrods' store. There she falls in love with a young bank clerk – only to discover that he is really Lord Eynsford, son and heir of the Earl of St Ives. He is engaged to Lady Betty Thanet, and Mary despairs. But Lady Betty wants to marry the Hon Hughie Pierrepoint instead; and after much singing and dancing, all ends happily. On tour in 1909 and 1910 *Our Miss Gibbs* met dozens of imitators, with titles like *The Earl and the Girl*, *The Prince and the Beggarmaid*, *From Shop Girl to Duchess* and *From Mill Girl to Millionairess*.

The melodramas told the same story, but with a different ending. Their theme was the terrible punishment that awaits the girl if the prince finally fails to offer marriage. *Our Miss Gibbs* met many of these on tour too: *Her Road to Ruin*, for instance, *The Woman Pays* and *Men Were Deceivers Ever*; countless variations on the theme of *The Girl Who Went Astray*. From nineteen to twenty Jean lived with this shining hope and this ghastly warning held always before her, dressed in beautiful costumes, sung in sweetly memorable music.

Of course she hoped. 'Chorus-Girl Marries Peer's Son,' said the headlines, and half the girls would think: 'It happens all the time and why not to me?' There was Rosie Boote, who rose from the Gaiety chorus to become a star, and who had married the Marquess of Headfort in 1901. There was beautiful Lily Elsie, who married the Hon Ian Bullough in 1911 – straight from *The Count of Luxembourg*, while Jean was probably in its chorus. Even in her own touring company of *Our Miss Gibbs* there was Nancy Erwin, who became Lady Dalrymple-Champneys. Jean followed Nancy's career through the *Tatler* and the *Sketch* for the rest of their lives. She was a fatalistic loser of possessions, but at her death, among the dozen photographs of herself, her daughter, and two or three friends, a portrait of the chorus girl turned Lady was still there.

The summer tour of Sir George Dance's Number Two company

of *Our Miss Gibbs* began in Ramsgate at the end of August. Somewhere between the Pavilion, Ramsgate, and the Royal, Worthing, Jean had her nineteenth birthday.

In *Voyage in the Dark* Anna says that she was all right her first winter: 'They say it's always like that — it takes a year before the cold really gets you.' This was probably true of Jean's first tour. She says nothing about it, though it lasted until November, and October and November must have been cold. It was overshadowed by what came after.

First she had to get through December somehow, without her thirty-five shillings and extra for matinées. Perhaps she went to the 'Cats' Home', the chorus girls' hostel in London; perhaps she stayed with Aunt Clarice in Wales or in London. Then in January 1910 the winter tour began, which the others had tried to warn her about, but which in her newness and eagerness she had looked forward to so carelessly.

In *Quartet* Marya is a member of 'Albert Prance's Number One touring company,' and sometimes Jean said that she moved up to George Dance's Number One company herself. But if so it wasn't until her third tour. In the first half of 1910 she was almost certainly still in the Number Two touring company of *Our Miss Gibbs*, playing (as she says in *Smile Please*) 'small towns in the north': Doncaster, Grimsby, Accrington, Rochdale, Wigan, Dewsbury, Barnsley, Darlington, Wolverhampton, Wakefield, Derby, Hanley....

At best the company moved once a week, usually every three days. Jean's trunk was a theatrical basket which went ahead with the scenery, leaving her only a small suitcase for travel — 'washing things, toothbrush and very minimal make-up.' There was 'perpetual manicuring of one's nails in the Sunday train,' then arriving at one's lodgings to a tough joint of beef. 'On Monday we had it warmed up. On Tuesday minced. On Wednesday shepherd's pie or stew....'

Then it was moving on again, and it was just like the sketch the boy had shown her, *Why we drink*: 'There was always a little grey street leading to the stage door of the theatre and another little grey street where your lodgings were, and rows of houses with chimneys like the funnels of dummy steamers and smoke the same colour as the sky.'

There were good theatrical lodgings, but they were always taken. Jean dated her hatred of landladies from this year. They were morose and mean, prim and disapproving; or if they weren't it was suspicious. When their landlady says 'Good morning' to Anna and Maudie in *Voyage in the Dark*, Maudie says 'She's very smarmy. What's the matter with her? I bet she puts that down on the bill. For saying "Good Morning", half a crown.' At thirty-five shillings a week extras on the bill were the last straw. Once there were so many that the total was three times what Jean and 'Billie' (as she calls the real girl she was living with) were expecting. Billie said 'There's only one thing to do about this,' and they jumped out of the window. It wasn't quite as romantic as the Wild Irish Girls Jean had read about when she was a child, 'escaping to freedom and life' by climbing down the wisteria. But it was just as exciting.

On this winter tour of the north, however, she suffered terribly from the cold — '*I got used to everything except the cold and that the towns we went to always looked so exactly alike*' — '*Cold, cold, cold.*' Her bedroom was often icy, the chorus dressing room was always the coldest. She 'coughed and wheezed' her way along; once she got pleurisy, like Anna, and had to be left behind, ill and alone. But she never stopped being buoyed up by the certainty that there would be something else for her, soon. One night a fortune teller came into the dressing room and looked at her hand for a long time. 'I see something great in your hand,' she said at last, 'something noble.' 'I was pleased but not surprised,' Jean wrote in *Smile Please*. She'd felt it all through that horrible tour: 'Something is going to happen that will change my life. I know it, it's Kismet.'

But it didn't happen yet. The winter tour of *Our Miss Gibbs* ended in the first week of May, and a great gap yawned: three whole months before the next summer tour started. Most of the girls went home; those who had no home, or who needed the money, looked for jobs in the music hall sketches that went on all year round.

A man called Joe Peterman produced such sketches — several, in the summer of 1910. One was called 'Chanteclair or Hi Cockalorum', a 'Feathered Fantasy in Three Fits'. It was an imitation of the great Paris hit of the year, *Chanteclair* by Edmond Rostand, the famous author of *Cyrano de Bergerac*. Rostand's *Chanteclair* had lovely music; and it was wonderful to look at, with gorgeous feathered costumes and sets so huge the actors really seemed the size of birds. Joe Peterman's wasn't the only imitation in the music halls of England that summer.

Jean never said how she got into *Chanteclair*, but during it she belonged to a group of girls called Liska's Troupe, who did a dance of their own. She kept two photographs of Liska's Troupe. In one they are dancing, dressed in rustic costume appropriate to *Chanteclair's* farmyard. But in the other they are acting out a scene, two dressed as gentlemen in top hats and tails, three — including Jean — in little dresses with puffy sleeves and flowers pinned on the front. Perhaps this was also in *Chanteclair*; but if so Joe Peterman had changed the story a great deal. Perhaps, rather, Liska's Troupe was already forming in *Our Miss Gibbs*: and *that* was how Jean got her job in *Chanteclair*. For as a chorus girl she used the stage name Gray: Vivien, Emma, or (perhaps usually, for it was her real name) Ella Gray. And briefly (she always said) she was taken out of the chorus and given a line, but she always fluffed it.... Now, in *Our Miss Gibbs* there were several parts just above the chorus, among them 'Three Irish Colleens', who did their own bit of singing and dancing. During Jean's first tour they were played by 'Nina Terri, Norah Neile and Mollie Cole'; but on her second tour they became 'Mollie Cole, Norah Neile and Olga Gray'. Perhaps this was Jean, in her short dress and puffy sleeves; and perhaps Mollie and Norah went with her to *Chanteclair*.

According to Jean, Peterman's *Chanteclair* was 'appalling'. It was hardly rehearsed, she said; its biggest joke was 'a girl in tights walking across the stage, dropping an egg and clucking loudly.' She seems to have been right about the jokes: '*Chanteclair* [one critic wrote] is not wildly funny.... But,' he went on, 'the music is worth hearing, and the dresses should be the talk of London.... A more elaborate production has not been seen on the variety stage.' Others even called it 'a beautiful, animated production' and 'an unmistakable and emphatic success.'

What happened, I think, was that Jean remembered only her own failure, and it spread to cover the whole of *Chanteclair*. For when they opened in a northern town she was waiting in the wings with the rest of Liska's Troupe, shivering with cold although it was early summer, and suddenly she heard a loud tramping noise: the gallery was walking out.

> As soon as we began I felt the mockery and scorn coming up from the audience like smoke. I was at the end of the line, near the wings, and after a bit of this I simply left the line and went off stage.

Before she left she looked at the girl next to her. 'She felt it as much as I did but bravely she went on dancing....' She felt very unhappy at being so cowardly. 'There is something as unstable as water in me, and when things get tough I go away. I haven't got what the English call "guts".' She determined to go back the next day and stick it out, no matter what the audience did.

But Joe Peterman wouldn't let her. The next day he called her into his office and fired her. Why, he demanded, had she walked out? Was she ill? No, Jean said, she was frightened. Frightened of what? Frightened of the audience. 'And what the hell are you doing on the stage,' Peterman said, 'if you are frightened of an audience?'

Jean always knew the truth when she met it, and I'm sure she recognised it now. But she wasn't going to admit it to him. 'As always when I am desperate,' she said, 'I was able to fight'; and she threatened to report Peterman to the Society for the Protection of Chorus Girls if he didn't pay her fare back to London. 'I had never before heard a man growl like a dog,' she said, 'but he did.' Still, she got her fare to London. She sat up all night, afraid of missing the train. The next day, dirty, pale and exhausted, she appeared at Aunt Clarice's flat in London.

'I have forgotten how I got over the rest of the gap,' she wrote in *Smile Please.* 'I suppose my aunt helped me.' Perhaps they went back to St Asaph together. But now, on 19 June, her father really died. Probably Clarice once again tried to persuade her to give up her 'precious job' and go home. But Jean refused. She'd fought so hard for this, she wasn't going to give it up after less than a year. She closed her mind to Joe Peterman's words ringing in her ears, and went back to *Our Miss Gibbs.*

Aunt Clarice was not thinking only of the danger to Jean's health when she tried to persuade her to give up the stage. Everyone knew that for chorus girls the real hope, and the real danger, came from men. There was the 'casting couch' in the agent's office, there were the 'mashers' in the stalls and at the stage door. The Rees Williamses didn't talk about such things ('some things must be ignored, some things I refuse to be mixed up with I refuse to think about even,' Hester says in *Voyage in the Dark*). But when Jean argued with her aunt about the chorus it was this unspoken accusation she answered. 'Chorus girls aren't bad,' she said, 'they're very good. Because they want to marry rich men and rich men don't marry second-hand goods.'

This was the hope, the intention; but of course you had to get to know the rich men in order to marry them. Success, she knew, was being asked out for a drive, or to supper after the show. 'Invitations to the Trocadero or Frascati weren't much thought of. The Savoy and Romano's were worth thinking about. The Carlton and still more the Ritz really meant something. . . .' She was still an innocent; she was secretly shocked at the chorus's jokes and stories. But she was also reckless. She didn't like the ambitious, careful girls. She liked the brave, gay, wicked ones; she liked the tarts.

In fact, she already had an admirer: a Colonel Mainwaring. He came to see her several times; he gave her a bracelet for her birthday. But this was still a curiously innocent affair. 'Sometimes he kissed me, but very gently,' Jean said; and he wanted not to marry but to adopt her. Perhaps this soothed her for a while for the loss of her father, but it wasn't what she wanted. When she found that, she pawned the bracelet and stopped answering the colonel's letters.

She wouldn't have been able to afford the expensive fur stoles and matching muffs of the very smartest chorus girls, like Nancy Erwin, but she would have looked as chic as she could. Her hat would have been as wide as her shoulders, the brim turned up at the front and hanging down to touch her back. Her dress would have been as short as she dared to wear it — in 1910, just above her ankles. Her stockings would have been the most open of openwork; her high shoes would have been laced with the widest ribbon she could get through the eyelet holes. And whenever she entered or left the theatre the cabmen and the mashers would crane their necks in admiration.

Chorus girls were her first friends in England. They weren't snobs; they couldn't be. They were the opposite, poor and exploited. Yet at the same time they were self-sufficient, mysteriously privileged. They were like the black servants at home: 'a secret society that I'd like to join.'

She was fascinated by them: by their cheeky little girls' names, like Daisie and Maudie, little boys' names like Laurie and Billie, exotic foreign names like Gaby and Yetta; by their talk, their secret-society slang — 'I could blow you out the window,' 'One word to you,' 'The more you swank the better.' She was shocked by their gossip 'in an ascending scale' (beginning with 'She's a tart of course,' and ending with 'every known and unknown vice'), but she was also soothed by it, and by their laziness, their amorality, their love of pleasure. Her family had made her feel she was the only wicked girl in the world; well, she wasn't.

Besides, they weren't just wicked: they were brave. Under their tough talk they were just as frightened as she was — like the girl beside her in *Chanteclair*, who went on dancing. She learned from them, if not to *be* brave, at least to sound it: to speak — and to write — in their defiant, self-mocking, careless tone.

She learned other things from them too, or already shared them: their love of pretty clothes, rich men, romantic music; their fear of boredom, of losing one's looks, of age. She shared their reliance on mascots, superstitions, lucky charms. Above all she shared their simple division of the sexes. Men were either protectors or exploiters; women were either winners or losers, and what they won or lost was men.

But she wasn't happy. This wasn't really what she had imagined. Her lodgings were squalid and so were the theatres. The orchestras were amateurish and under-rehearsed. The stages were dirty and dimly lit, the costumes were getting old. 'A vague procession of towns all exactly alike,' she wrote in *Quartet*,

A vague procession of men also exactly alike. One can drift like that for a long time, she found, carefully hiding the fact that this wasn't what one had expected from life. Not in the very least.

Marya learned 'to talk like a chorus girl, to dress like a chorus girl and to think like a chorus girl – up to a point. Beyond that point she remained apart, lonely, frightened of her loneliness....' Of herself Jean wrote: 'The other girls don't like me much.'

The chorus gossiped, told stories, sang popular songs, talked endlessly about men. But they didn't read. So she didn't read either. But there was one book (she said) which they all read. It was a great romantic hit of the day called *The Forest Lovers*, by Maurice Hewlett. It was set in the Middle Ages, and was about 'a man and a girl who loved each other very much,' but who 'always slept with a sword between them.' ('The conversation about the sword was endless. "What did they have to do that for? Why? Besides you could easily get over the sword." "No you couldn't, you'd get cut." "Of course you wouldn't." ')

In *The Forest Lovers* a highborn girl called Isoult la Desirous is thrown into the depths of degradation – called a witch, made to endure 'scorn, shame, bleeding, stripes, blindness and the swoon like death'. In the end she is raised up again by a young knight, Prosper, whom she has loved since he saved her from the falcon which pecked her heart when she was a child, leaving her with an unhealable wound.

*The Forest Lovers* is a bad book, but every word of it, like every word of *Our Miss Gibbs*, spoke to Jean.

> 'Dost thou desire death, child?' cried he, 'and is this why thou art called La Desirous?'
> 'I desire to be what I am not, my lord, and to have that which I have never had,' she answered, and her lip trembled.
> 'And what is that which you are not, Isoult?'
> She answered him 'Clean.'
> 'And what is that which you have never had, my child?'
> 'Peace,' said Isoult, and wept bitterly.

'I got sick of being in *Our Miss Gibbs*,' Jean wrote in *Smile Please*, 'sick of wearing old Gaiety dresses cleaned.' So she left *Our Miss Gibbs* at last.

It was December, and she got a job in the chorus of a London pantomime. It was *Cinderella*. There were ten lavish sets, from Cinderella's kitchen to the Prince's palace, 'Dreamland' and 'Fairyland'. The second act opened in a zoo, and live monkeys, giraffes, even lions filled the stage; Cinderella's crystal coach was drawn by six Shetland ponies, black in a white harness. The other girls told her that there were rats in the dressing room, but she didn't see them. For she had entered her own Dreamland, her own *Forest Lovers*. The thing she had been waiting for had happened.

★    ★    ★

In *Voyage in the Dark* Walter Jeffries picks Anna up in the street in Southsea, where she is on tour. Jean probably met the love of her life while she was on tour at Southsea too: but much more decorously, at a supper party after the show, just as it was meant to happen.

The first thing Anna notices is the way Walter walks. Jean's love walked as Mr Howard had walked: easily, swinging his shoulders ('as if everything and everybody in the whole world belonged to him'). But Anna doesn't like Walter at first, nor did Jean like this man. She wrote in *Voyage in the Dark*:

> ... He didn't look at my breasts or my legs, as they usually do. Not that I saw. He looked straight at me and listened to everything I said with a polite and attentive expression.

That was just like Mr Howard too. But she added: 'and then he looked away and smiled as if he had sized me up,' 'as if he were laughing at me.'

In *Voyage in the Dark* Maudie asks the other man his name.

> 'Jones,' the tall man said. 'Jones is my name.'
> 'Go on,' Maudie said.
> He looked annoyed.
> 'That's rather funny,' Walter said, starting to laugh.
> 'What's funny?' I said.
> 'You see, Jones is his name.'
> 'Oh, is it?' I said.

Perhaps she and her lover had this conversation themselves. Perhaps it was she who said, assuming the cynicism of the chorus: 'Go on.' For part of her lover's name was Smith.

But that was only the formal part, the part for everybody. The rest was for her. His first name was Lancelot, as though he were a real knight. His middle name was Grey — which was the name she'd chosen for herself (as if, she must have thought, she'd known). She called him Lancey.

Soon all her cynicism and all her reserve had dropped away, and she worshipped him. Lancelot Grey Hugh Smith was twice her age.

('How old do you think I am?' Walter says in *Voyage in the Dark*. 'Never mind. Tottering, I expect you would say if you knew.') He wasn't handsome. But he was elegant and distinguished, beautifully dressed, and looked 'just right — always.' He smelled just right too, of 'leather and cigars and men's clothes'. She loved his voice, his walk, the way he teased her ('You've got a hairpin sticking out this side, spoiling your otherwise perfect appearance'). She loved his house near Berkeley Square, with its beautiful furniture, its blazing fires, its warmth and space and comfort. He was a dream come true. He was like all the men in all the books she'd ever read about England.

And he really was. His father was rich and his mother was a lady. His family was related by blood, marriage or friendship to many of the great banking families of England: Smith, Baring, Hambro, Rothschild. His father, Colin Hugh Smith, had founded Hay's Wharf in the City of London, and was for two years Governor of the Bank of England. Of his brothers, Vivian, the eldest, became Lord Bicester and Chairman of Morgan Grenfell, Owen took over Hay's Wharf from their father, and John became a Managing Director of Hambro's Bank.* The two other non-banking brothers, Aubrey and Humphrey, became admirals; Aubrey was also a KBE, and had commanded the guard at Queen Victoria's funeral. Of his sisters, Olive was married to a Baring, and Mildred to Lord Buxton, who became Governor of South Africa during the First War. Olive was dim and gentle; but Mildred was the other clever one of the family, and wrote a book about her time in South Africa.

Lancelot was the third son. He was born in 1870, at his family's beautiful Georgian house, Mount Clare, set in thirty-five acres of park and farmland in Roehampton. He went to Eton, like his father and brothers, and to Trinity, where he read History. He went down without a degree, having gone to Cambridge, like most of his set, simply to enjoy himself. But he did enjoy himself; he loved Cambridge for the rest of his life, and history too.

His father wanted an orthodox financial career for him. He took him in to Hay's Wharf, then placed him in Smith's Bank in Derby. But Lancelot was not (quite) orthodox. He wanted to go onto the

---

*John, the youngest, was the intellectual of the family. He got a double First in History from Trinity, Cambridge (Vivian and Lancelot didn't take degrees at all, and Owen's was undistinguished). He had literary tastes too, becoming friend and correspondent, for instance, of the American novelist Edith Wharton. (His full name was Arnold John, and he signed his letters 'A. John Hugh Smith.' 'You aren't *a* John Hugh Smith, you are *the* John Hugh Smith,' she wrote to him.)

Stock Exchange. His father was against it, because 'no Smith had ever been a stockbroker'; but his elder brother Vivian supported him. He held out; and in the mid-1890s he entered the Stock Exchange.

In 1898, when he was twenty-eight, he joined a small new firm called Rowe and Pitman. George Rowe and Frederick Pitman were celebrated oarsmen, one from Oxford and one from Cambridge; and the story is that they chose Lancelot because he wasn't a wet-bob but a dry-bob, and could hold the fort over Henley Week and the Boat Race. But Lancelot began to transform Rowe and Pitman. He was clever, decisive, and rarely wrong. Above all, he tactfully but single-mindedly used his family and social connections to bring in the rich private clients who were still the main owners of wealth in Europe. Over the next forty years he made Rowe and Pitman into the leading 'old boy brokers' of the City: a hugely powerful firm, built on whom, even more than what, Lancelot and his partners knew. By the time his reign was over Rowe and Pitman's clients included the biggest companies and the richest aristocracy of England, including its Queen.

By 1910 this process was well under way. Lancelot was rich and getting richer. He lived at Mount Clare with his mother and unmarried brothers; he had his house on Charles Street near Berkeley Square. And he was still unmarried.

Four or five years before he had very much wanted to marry Violet Hambro, daughter of his father's friend Sir Everard Hambro. His cousin Everard Martin Smith was also wooing her, but allowed him to hope. Then, just as he was about to propose, Violet's engagement to Everard was announced. The family has believed ever since that Lancelot's desire to marry Violet was merely social and dynastic, but Lancelot himself said that he had been deeply in love with her, and that the sudden announcement of her engagement to Everard had been a cruel shock to him.

Whether it was love or ambition (or both) which Violet Hambro had thwarted, he hadn't tried again. Instead he'd settled to an Edwardian routine of restaurants and parties with rich men friends and their *demi-monde* women. He had had girlfriends like Jean before; he may even have been quite well known for it. In *Triple Sec* (her first version of the affair and its aftermath), Daisie warns 'Suzy' about her lover: he only keeps a woman for six months. 'That sort of man thinks women are just put into the world for his amusement. Make him give you money, but don't love him!'

In *Voyage in the Dark*, when at last Anna allows herself to be led to Walter's bed ('Come on, be brave,' he says) she feels warmth coming from him, and it's as if she's remembering something she's always known, and yet utterly forgotten. She thinks 'anything you like, any way you like'; she thinks *'But I like it like this. I don't want it any other way but this.'* She loves 'Dressing to go and meet him and coming out of the restaurant and the lights in the street and getting into a taxi and when he kissed you in the taxi going there....' She loves being kissed, she loves being made love to. ('You shut the door and you pull the curtains over the windows and then it's as long as a thousand years and yet so soon ended.') She is 'hopeless, resigned, utterly happy.'

In *Triple Sec* 'Tony' (but once Jean forgot and called him Lancey) says 'Come here at once, Miss Gray, and say good morning nicely.' Suzy laughs — 'no, no' — and hides under the sheet. He pulls it away and catches her, saying 'You'll be eaten up, so look out....' He says 'Kitten, if people went about without their clothes you'd have a *succès fou*'; he says 'Kitten, your eyes are shining like stars, by Jove!' Walter says, 'You're lovely from this angle.' 'Not from every angle?' Anna asks. 'Certainly not, conceited child,' he says. 'But from this angle you're perfectly satisfactory.' 'Well, let's go upstairs,' he says, 'you rum child, you rum little devil.'

And Lancelot was so kind to her, patient and kind. He asked her about Dominica, about the flowers and the birds, and he listened to her answers. And once, when she thought he would be angry because she didn't want to go to Hendon with his friends, he wasn't. 'I don't want to see it with them, or anything with them,' she said. And instead of being angry he put his hand out and squeezed hers. She thought: 'I have not only a lover, but a friend. How lucky I am.' He understood her.

And he loved her. Briefly, reluctantly, confusedly: but he did. He was jealous if another man flirted with her, his heart hammered when he held her. He said she was so sweet, she was his darling and his dear, he said she gave so generously, like a princess. He wrote that he loved her ('Shy Anna, I love you so much. Always, Walter'); he said that he loved her. And she knew he did, not because of anything he said or wrote, but by the way he looked at her and by the feel of his arms.

Freedom and safety were twins, were inseparable.

These were the years of Edward VII, in which a few vastly rich families (including the Hambros) entertained the King on their great estates, and everyone else tried to imitate them. Lancelot had been born on the edge of this glittering world. The Hugh Smiths were not as rich as their cousins the Martin Smiths or their friends the Hambros, but they held to the same creed of money and achievement. Lancelot had been taught ambition and conformity, he had been taught to respect and desire worldly and social success. He did respect and desire them. He pursued them all his life, never missing a smart party in youth or a chance to cultivate the nobility in age. And he achieved them: money, position, conformity. He belonged to the right school, university and clubs, he had the best tailor and shirtmaker, he lived in the best streets and squares. He wasn't *very* rich until he was old, and perhaps he wasn't quite as successful as his most successful brothers. But he had the life he wanted, and he lived it with style.

Yet he was not quite happy, not quite at ease. He wanted what they had, but did he want what they wanted? He learned to hide his uncertainty and dissent ('How old was I when I learned to hide what I felt?' Rochester says in *Wide Sargasso Sea*. 'A very small boy. Five, six, even earlier. It was necessary, I was told, and that view I have always accepted.') But he continued to feel them. He lived his successful, desired life with effort and strain; 'and always' (Jean wrote) 'the battle was going on in him between what he had been taught and what he felt.'

As time went on this would get worse. He loved what his success brought him, his houses, his beautiful furniture and pictures. He loved his family, his friends, lively people around him. But inside he remained uncertain and unsatisfied. He became more and more demanding and despotic on the outside, and more and more lonely and isolated on the inside. He never married. He had several close and warm women friends, but no one could see him as a lover. He became neutral, avuncular. He surrounded himself in age with charming and handsome young men rather than charming and pretty young women. To these young cousins, nephews and husbands of nieces he was charming and affectionate; to the few personal servants on whom he relied he was affable and generous. ('I owe them more than I can express,' he wrote in his will. And one of his favourite stories was of his chauffeur, Herbert Street: 'Afraid your shares have gone down today, Herbert,' he said; 'I'm very sorry, sir,' Street replied, 'I'll have to change my broker.') But increasingly he was fastidious, irritable, quickly tired of the company he'd eagerly sought. He was always hypochondriac ('I shouldn't wonder if I got ill with all this worry,' Walter says in *Voyage in the Dark*); he became insomniac. He was 'terribly nervous,' older people say; 'neurotic,' say the younger ones. He had a bell in his room so that he could summon Leggatt the butler in the middle of the night, or one of his young cousins or nephews, perhaps Oliver Martin Smith or Aubrey Baring. They would find him upright, rigidly tense, his fist clenched on the counterpane. They would sit with him for ten or fifteen minutes, not saying anything. They would just put a hand on his arm; and very slowly he relaxed. ('The touch of the human hand,' Jean would write in *Good Morning, Midnight*, 'I'd forgotten what it was like, the touch of the human hand.')

When she knew him, of course, he was in his prime. His exterior was firmly in place, he was in control. But he was the same man. And so he was drawn to her. 'My dear Anna,' Walter writes, in the letter which will begin their affair, 'I wish I could tell you how sweet you are. I'm worried about you. Will you buy yourself some stockings with this? And don't look anxious when you are buying them, please ....' 'Shy Anna,' he says; 'You mustn't be sad, you mustn't worry'; 'Look happy .... Be happy. I want you to be happy.' Jean was nervous and shy and uncertain, and underneath his elegant exterior so was Lancelot. She didn't fit in, and nor, secretly, did he. She was lonely and longing for love; and so, I am sure, was he.

He hadn't been taught only to compete with other men and win. He'd also been taught to lay his victory at the feet of a chaste, rich woman of his own class and kind. At this he had failed. But I think he had accepted the code of chivalry as much as the other. More robust natures were content with hypocrisy: but Lancelot was a dreamer, like Jean, and took seriously the ideals of service, charity, and the obligations of power. He could rescue and raise her, he could treat her like a child, a goddess and a slave. And there was Jean, longing to be rescued and raised, petted and pitied, worshipped and desired. Their dreams fitted so perfectly that for a time even he forgot that their real lives didn't fit at all.

Like real dreams this one happened mostly at night. During the day Lancelot worked in the City; at the weekend he disappeared to Mount Clare. So in the daytime Jean waited. She went to the singing and dancing lessons he wanted her to have, she had the dresses made he wanted her to wear. She waited for his letters and telegrams, she waited to be fetched in his car. She waited for the night, as Rochester does in *Wide Sargasso Sea*, as Mary had done in *Our Miss Gibbs*:

> *All day long I'm just as good as gold*
> *Always doing everything I'm told!*
> *But as soon as the sun's in bed*
> *Well, it's then I've such a flighty little, foolish little head....*

At night she would spend hours dressing for him. Sometimes she would be a little girl, in a short white frock with a black velvet bow in her hair. Sometimes she would be a lady, in a black velvet dress and a little black hat with a white osprey's feather. And sometimes she would be a woman, in a dark blue dress so long and tight that when she moved she saw the shape of her thighs. Then the taxi would come and she would go to Charles Street for a party, or to a restaurant alone with him, which she liked better. Afterwards they would go back to Charles Street and go upstairs. She would stay until it was just getting light and her landlady would be getting up in an hour or two. They would walk to Park Lane or the Ritz, past the men who were coming out to water the streets, and get a taxi. And she would be back in her room, waiting for the next night of pleasure and love.

At the height of her affair, in May 1911, *The Count of Luxembourg* opened at Daly's, the Gaiety's sister theatre: and I think she was in the chorus. Lancelot wanted her to 'get on', and he'd probably pulled some strings for her. Now her evenings were a dream too, 'a voluptuous dream of luscious music and dazzling light.' *The Count of Luxembourg* starred the beautiful, the magical Lily Elsie, who played – once again – a commoner who loves and marries a count. In the middle of the run life imitated art, and Lily Elsie left to marry the Hon Ian Bullough. An Irish actress called Daisie Irving (who'd been playing Lily's part on tour) took over: Jean's friend Daisie of 'Before the Deluge', and no doubt the Daisie who warned her not to love Lancelot.

By now of course it was far too late. She loved him desperately. She was lonely away from him, she did everything for him; 'He is my life – I'm not exaggerating – it's just true.' If he were to stop loving her she would die. But he wouldn't stop loving her. Perhaps he might even marry her, like Lily Elsie.... Why not? She was beautiful too. She was a Rees Williams, and related to the Spencer Churchills, she'd had servants and carriages, the young English officers had queued up to dance with her.... They must have talked about Lily Elsie; they did talk about Rosie Boote. But Lancelot said that Rosie Boote had been an exception. The other chorus girls had never really been accepted. She asked why, but he couldn't explain.

All her life Jean could half-know, could not-know. Twenty years later her first husband would write about her: 'When she wishes to do a foolish thing she sees quite clearly in front of her what is going to happen. Not that that stops her from doing it.... She disdains consequences. She sacrifices everybody who may suffer, starting with herself.'

So it was now. In the middle of laughing, of giggling, she would suddenly cry — she didn't know why. Sometimes Lancelot would be moody or 'cynical'; once when she said she didn't want to do anything but be with him, he looked away and said 'You'll soon be bored with me.' Sometimes he would say things like 'Kitten, you make my heart ache sometimes, I tell you'; or 'Oh my dear, my dear, you are so sweet — you're much too sweet for this sort of thing. . . .' Sometimes he said 'Don't you see — you make me hate myself?' But she didn't see. 'What do you mean?' she asked. 'It doesn't matter,' he said. And then — 'By God, I'll never let you regret it — by God, I'll always be good to you.' 'I'm getting used now to this horrible stab of unhappiness I get sometimes,' she wrote. 'I only looked at him. I don't understand — I won't.'

But of course she did. 'When it was sad was when you woke up at night and thought about being alone and that everybody says the man's bound to get tired,' she wrote in *Voyage in the Dark*. And in *Triple Sec* — 'I wake up at night and think of it' — 'It's like a shadow. . . .' The girls on tour said it, books said it, Daisie said it. Lancelot's men friends didn't say it, but they looked it. So she hated them.

She didn't meet Lancelot's cousin Julian for a long time, though he was her lover's 'greatest friend'. But one night she did. 'He really is very handsome,' she wrote in *Triple Sec*; and in *Voyage in the Dark*: 'He had blue eyes with curled-up eyelashes like a girl's, and black hair and a brown face and broad shoulders and slim hips — the whole bag of tricks, in fact.' 'He likes you,' Walter tells Anna. 'He thinks you're a darling.' 'Oh does he?' Anna says. 'I thought he didn't, somehow.' In *Voyage in the Dark* 'Vincent' says, 'Well, how's the child? How's my infantile Anna?'; in *Triple Sec* 'Guy' says 'Well, how's the kitten?' And Jean wrote: 'Somehow the way he said it made me curl up inside. I don't believe I like him.'

Julian Martin Smith was Everard's younger half-brother, and at least fifteen years younger than Lancelot. And he was exactly as Jean described him: handsome, charming, 'not a bit spoilt', the golden boy of his generation. She hated him, of course, because she thought that he destroyed her affair. But she also hated him for his effortless belonging; and she hated him, I think, because Lancelot loved him.

Julian was brave, modest, good at games; he was full of charm and gaiety, grace and ease. Women loved him and men admired him. He was everything Lancelot would have liked to be: the perfect English boy. Lancelot had recently taken him in to Rowe and Pitman; in 1913 he would make him a partner. But barely a year later Julian was dead, one of the very first to be killed in the War. That set the seal on his perfection, as it did on Rupert Brooke's, or on his

Desborough cousin Julian Grenfell's. 'For a long time the sun went out of my life,' Lancelot wrote, 'and out of many others.' When Everard and Violet had a son in 1915 they called him Julian; and the story goes that thirty and forty years later, when old ladies met the young Julian Martin Smith they still frowned in disappointment that he was not his uncle.

Lancelot did not need anyone to tell him that Jean was unsuitable, but he needed someone to stiffen his resolve, and to do the dirty work for him. And Jean was right: it was Julian. Many years later Lancelot told Aubrey Baring that 'a cousin' once said to him: 'That girl is getting too fond of you.'

The summer of 1912 was very hot. In *Voyage in the Dark* Walter takes Anna to the Savernake Forest. It is a hot, blue day; Anna says 'I didn't know England could be so beautiful.' 'I was thinking how happy I was, and then I didn't think anything — not even how happy I was,' Jean wrote. And 'It's unlucky to know you're happy, it's unlucky to say you're happy. Touch wood. Cross my fingers. Spit.'

Some time after this Lancelot told her that he was going to New York on business. (In *Triple Sec* Tony says for six weeks, in *Voyage in the Dark* Walter says for 'a couple of months at the outside.') They had a last night together at Charles Street. First they sat by the fire in a little downstairs room. One of Lancelot's *objets d'art* was there, Houdin's famous bust of Voltaire, with its tired, sceptical smile. Jean hated it. 'Who is that horrid, sneering old woman?' she said.

Anna is afraid. 'Afraid of what?' she thinks. But in *Triple Sec* Suzy knows: 'I'm so frightened of myself,' she says, 'and the way I love Tony.' They both say: 'Don't forget me, don't forget me ever,' and Walter and Tony both reply, 'No, I won't ever, I tell you.' Then both Walter and Tony mention money, and suddenly both Anna and Suzy are breathless, sick and sweating. 'I'm all right,' they say, and go to the door. For one last moment he holds them back — 'Are you sure you're all right?' he says, pulling them into the little room downstairs. 'Take care of yourself,' he says, 'Bless you,' and over them all the time 'there was that damn bust smiling away.'

According to both *Voyage in the Dark* and *Triple Sec*, Julian went to America with Lancelot. In *Triple Sec* Tony tells her that Guy said goodbye to his girlfriend yesterday — 'floods of tears, I believe.' Suzy writes 'the sweetest letter I can that will reach him before he sails,' and says: 'Guy won't be able to say "Tony said goodbye to the kitten yesterday — floods of tears, I believe."' She tells herself that she's being absurd — he's often been away before. And according to both *Voyage in the Dark* and *Triple Sec*, Jean now went away herself, to the seaside.

In *Voyage in the Dark* Walter writes to Anna after only three weeks and says that he may be back sooner than he expected, that he is very fond of her and wants to see her very much. So at last she stops worrying. 'It's always like that,' her friend Laurie says. 'They always do it that way.' ('Life was like that,' Jean wrote in *Quartet*: 'Here you are, it said, and then immediately afterwards, Where are you?')

'Letter from Guy to Suzy,' Jean wrote in *Triple Sec*: 'My dear kitten — This is a very difficult letter to write — for I shall hate hurting you....' In *Voyage in the Dark* Jean made Julian's letter — for of course it must have been Julian's letter — into a classic of glib carelessness. *I'm quite sure you are a nice girl and that you will be understanding about this,* 'Vincent' writes; and *You are young and youth as everybody says is the great thing, the greatest gift of all* ('And that's what terrifies you about them,' Jean would write in *Good Morning, Midnight*. 'It isn't their cruelty, it isn't even their shrewdness — it's their extraordinary naiveté. Everything in their whole bloody world is a cliché.... And they believe in the clichés — there's no hope.') 'My dear Infant,' Vincent says, 'I am writing this in the country, and I can assure you that when you get into a garden and smell the flowers and all that all this rather beastly sort of love simply doesn't matter.'

'I'm so damn sorry about it all, Kitten,' Guy writes in *Triple Sec*. 'I'm very fond of you and terribly sorry and I do hope you won't hate me too much.' But of course she did.

Jean saw Lancelot once more. I think she thought, like Anna, *'He won't be able to, he won't be able to,'* when she looked in the glass. But he did. So she ran away. Lancelot and Julian thought she'd wait to hear about money, did they? Well, she wouldn't. 'All I wanted was to get right away and never see him again. Never, never, never,' she wrote in *Triple Sec*. And in *Voyage in the Dark*: 'Anywhere will do, so long as it's somewhere that nobody knows.'

# CHAPTER THREE

# The Interval, 1913–1919

*The real death — The Crabtree Club — Petronella —
The end of the second affair — John*

It was as though a mortal illness had struck her that night in Charles Street in 1912, and all through 1913 she was dying. At the end of it she made up her mind to kill herself. She didn't: but she felt ever after that she should have, she might as well have, for she was really dead. (*There are always two deaths ... that would have been a better fate ....*)

She had always been shy and secretly lonely, a dreamer, uncertain in the real world. But youth and ignorance and a thirst for happiness had rushed her into life. She had been more than brave, more than daring. Afraid of solitude, she had cut herself off from everything and everyone she knew. Afraid of the audience, she had spent a year and more on the stage. Afraid of people, she had put her life in the hands of her lover without reserve. For two years she'd lived like a gambler, staking all on one wild throw.

But now it was over. She was all in, *kaput, fichue*. 'Tired — something gone,' Suzy says in *Triple Sec*. 'I'll always be tired now.' And Jean was. From now on her passivity was like death, or a wish for it, her indolence a huge unbanishable fatigue. From the end of her affair she belonged nowhere. 'The whole earth,' Francis Wyndham says, 'had become inhospitable to her after the shock of that humdrum betrayal.'

She had already been so weak, half her heart pecked away, like Isoult La Desirous. In Lancelot she had found not only a lover but a father and friend. So she really had given her life up to him ('*J'ai mis toute ma vie aux mains de mon amant*,' Roseau quotes in 'La Grosse Fifi'). It was as though after that she could receive life only from him, as though she'd gone back to being an infant, as they all called her, a kitten, unsteady on its feet, still blind. And then he'd taken it all away, love, life itself. Soon she would write: 'My life from seventeen to twenty-two is responsible for my damned weakness.' And later: 'She came to England as a girl of seventeen, she died at twenty-three.'

Now she wrote hundreds of pleading, threatening letters, very
quickly, crossing most of them out and never sending them. And a
poem:

> *I didn't know*
> *I didn't know*
> *I didn't know.*

In the boarding-house they've run to, Anna (in *Voyage in the Dark*)
and Suzy (in *Triple Sec*) meet a short fat woman called Ethel. She
says she is a trained nurse and is setting up as a 'Swedish masseuse'
in a flat near Oxford Street: Number 4 Branch Street in *Triple Sec*,
Number 227 Bird Street in *Voyage in the Dark*. She invites each of
them to come and work there as a manicurist.

There is no real Branch Street, and no real Number 227 Bird Street.
But starting on 9 November 1912, there was a new advertisement
in the 'Medical' column of the *Daily Telegraph*:

> Manicure, Face Massage, Chiropody, Sciatica, Rheumatism,
> Swedish treatment. Royal and medical references. Mme Faber S.
> from Ostende and Nice. Hours ten to eight and Sundays. – 4,
> Bird-street, Oxford-St., W.

Ethel, of course, is English; she's already English in *Triple Sec*.
Perhaps Jean made Madame Faber English because she fitted her
feeling about England, but not her feeling about France. Or perhaps
'Madame Faber' *was* English, and her foreignness was just a pose, a
sexual signal (like the chorus girls who called themselves Gaby or
Yetta). Jean added Ethel's xenophobia only later, when she wrote
*Voyage in the Dark* in the thirties, and her feeling about England had
grown more bitter. I think she even made a little secret joke about
it. For in *Voyage in the Dark* Ethel talks all the time about how respectable she is, and says: 'That Madame Fernande, for instance –
well, the things I've heard about her and the girls she's got at her
place....' In reality Madame Faber was soon calling herself *Madame
Hermine.*

So Jean was now falling down into a life the respectable world saw
as only a step away from the stage. In fact it was two or three steps;
but she took them quickly.

First, she went to stay with a girl who'd been in the chorus with
her, and whom she met one day on Oxford Street. This is the girl
she calls Laurie in *Voyage in the Dark*, and Alison in *Triple Sec* (her
real name was probably Shirley). 'Laurie' was, Jean said later, a 'call

girl'; Joe Adler in *Voyage in the Dark* says baldly that she's a tart. So for several weeks Jean saw a tart's life. Indeed she lived a tart's life, except that she did not sleep with the men. ('Suzy' lets them kiss her, but that's all. 'If kisses marked one,' she says, 'how scarred and hideous I'd be!') They got up at ten and dressed at twelve. They hardly ever ate alone, or paid for their own meals. There was the same round as in the chorus: shops and taxis and restaurants, and often motoring somewhere to tea ('I like that,' Suzy says). They met Germans, Dutchmen, Americans, Jews – and, of course, Englishmen, who were the worst of all. They were 'at the same time sly and insolent – leering and ashamed.'

One night Laurie and Joe take Anna to an hotel, make her drunk and undress her. In the end she disarms Joe, who is basically kind, and escapes. But after this she takes the next step. Ethel's flat is ready; and she goes there.

Once again Jean half knew and half refused to know what she was doing. Suzy says 'I don't know what to say – I really don't – or quite what to think.' The flat was clean and pretty, with white wallpaper and white furniture and chintz covers on the armchairs. Ethel wore a white overall and had references and certificates and talked all the time about being quite different from the other masseuses. (But when Jean told Shirley this she laughed.) Ethel said that the men had the wrong idea, and a living could be made out of that, without going further ('if people do things thinking that they're going to get something that they don't get, what's it matter to you or me or anybody else?') But she also says Anna must be 'a bit nice' to them; and Suzy has to let them kiss her, 'otherwise they wouldn't pay'. There is something funny here, something beastly (something interesting, Alison says, something exciting). 'On the surface everything is all right – underneath one glimpses all sorts of horrors.'

Jean was a real slave now. She had to wait on strange ugly men, and on Madame Hermine, who made her fetch and carry, and even dress her hair. The slavery she had dreamt of, and lived, had been exaltation and abasement, the life and death kiss. This – this furtive barter of sex for money – was the reality. At least in England. 'Love is a stern virtue in England,' she would write in *Good Morning, Midnight*: 'Usually a matter of hygiene, my dear. The indecent necessity....' 'Men are horrible,' Suzy says; 'Terrible things are usual to me now.'

And yet Jean stayed. Probably for several months, from November 1912 to February or March 1913. Why did she – how could she? Well (she wrote in *Triple Sec*), she had no money. Couldn't she have gone back to the stage? But she didn't want to. To Aunt Clarice?

No, impossible. Because she was indifferent, then, because she felt, like Suzy, 'What does it matter? – nothing matters?' But she was only trying to be indifferent, and failing ('I shouldn't have boasted about not feeling and being peaceful, for, after all, I do feel often and am very unhappy' ....)

That was why. She stayed because she was too miserable to go. She was plunged so deep into grief and longing for Lancelot that she wanted not to think, not to move. She wanted to sleep, as though she were dead. Drink helped ('I'm finding out what a useful thing drink is'). Also, finally, because she had a plan, for which Madame Hermine's was as good a place as any – in fact, very good. 'How I loathe men and only want to make use of them,' she wrote in *Triple Sec*. On the surface, to get money ('It must be someone rich'); but underneath, to cure herself of her longing for Lancelot.

> Only one way to cure myself ... the next man who wants me, I swear....
> I'll drink a lot so that my head sings, and I'll shut my eyes and put my arm over them so that I can't see. – Then, what's it matter who it is or what he does?

That too would reappear in *Good Morning, Midnight*, twenty-five years later.

In both *Triple Sec* and *Voyage in the Dark* he is an American called Carl. Carl is not nervous or furtive. He is big and dark and forceful. When he kisses her she feels it, for the first time since she lost her lover. She asks him to stop and he does; he only looks at her mouth and throat 'with such a queer look.' Finally Suzy writes:

> Well, it is Carl.
> It is Carl.

'When he touched me I knew that he was quite sure I would,' Anna says. 'I thought, "All right then, I will".'

Carl is ugly and hairy and his brutal love-making revolts Suzy. He is cruel and jealous, and says he will thrash her if he catches her with another man. Then he smiles and says he'll thrash her anyway, 'just hard enough to show you who's boss.' But he says, 'Now, Suzy, you belong to me, so you've not to worry,' and he gives her money so that she needn't work any more. She pays Ethel more rent, and another girl comes in to manicure.

Jean's situation now was a squalid parody of her life with Lancelot. Once again a man was keeping her; and once again he was more infatuated than such men usually are. Again, therefore, her mind is a battleground of hopes and fears.

Imagining God knows what. Imagining Carl would say, 'When I leave London, I'm going to take you with me.' And imagining it although his eyes had that look — this is just for while I'm here, and I hope you get me.

'I picked up a girl in London and she.... Last night I slept with a girl....' That was me.

Not 'girl' perhaps. Some other word perhaps. Never mind.

In *Triple Sec* we see only Carl, but Ethel says that Suzy has other men, and calls her a prostitute. In *Voyage in the Dark* Anna allows other men to pick her up after Carl leaves. And Jean did too, at some time or times after her first affair.

> I would allow myself to be picked up, sometimes in the street, sometimes in a park. I decided very quickly who I would allow to speak to me and who I wouldn't. I only had one qualification: did he, by his voice, his clothes, his walk, in any way whatsoever remind me of the one I thought I loved so much?

Either by Carl (like Suzy) or by one of the others (like Anna), in around February 1913 she became pregnant.

In her ignorance Suzy doesn't realise she's going to have a baby until Ethel tells her. They have a dreadful row ('the names she called me — and the names I called her ...'), and Suzy runs away with nothing but the clothes on her back. 'Thinking desperately and quite clearly' she goes to 'Jan', a fat, pink, gentle man, who takes her in. She lies in the sun that comes into the flat and thinks of her island so intensely that one day 'I could have sworn I smelt stephanotis — that's the flower for the dead.' She makes no plans, but she hopes she will die when her baby is born. 'I wish for nothingness,' she says, 'and that is, I believe, what will come to me.'

In *Voyage in the Dark* Anna sometimes wants to have her baby, but mostly she wants to get rid of it. ('The Abbé Sebastian's pills, primrose label, one guinea a box, daffodil label, two guineas, orange label, three guineas. No eyes, perhaps .... No arms, perhaps .... Pull yourself together.') Finally she takes Laurie's advice and writes for help to Walter. He sends it, but only through Vincent, and she never sees him again. But in *Triple Sec* Suzy has sent her address to Ethel, so that her things can be sent after her. And Ethel, instead of writing her 'peach of a letter' to Laurie, as in *Voyage in the Dark*, writes it to Suzy's lover: and one afternoon there is a knock at the door, and it is Tony.

That is what really happened. Jean cried, and Lancelot cried ('I simply didn't believe that men ever cried'). He had been desperately worried, he thought that she'd killed herself. He said, 'Kitten —

forget it – don't talk of it – My darling, it's over now – I can't bear to hear of it.'

He wouldn't hear of an abortion. He arranged for her to go into the country to have her baby. Jean thought 'Poor little baby! Perhaps I will love it, if it is a little girl,' and she half-pretended it was his. She was not at all unhappy. Her longing had worked, and pulled Lancelot back to her. He was there, and that was all she wanted.

But this dream-happiness, this pretend-happiness, was very brief. Soon she noticed that he was looking ill, he was sad and restless, and she had a 'ghastly thought': 'I believe I am making him unhappy.' And of course she was. She could close off her mind to 'afterwards', but he could not. His relief at finding her alive, his real feeling for her, his kindness and his cowardliness had put him into a more impossible position than ever. So now he did what he often did when he was under strain: he fell ill. He sent Jean a Persian kitten, a rose plant, and flowers every day, but for the second time Julian took over; and for the second time everything changed.

The moment Julian appeared he said 'My dear Kitten, you simply can't have the kid – it would be an awful mistake, I think – I've told Lancey so from the first. Why, Good Lord – ....' ('looking so boyish and so handsome standing there, hands in pockets ...'). And suddenly she realised that she'd only been pretending her baby was Lancelot's. And suddenly she was desperate not to have it.

By now she must have been four or even five months' pregnant. The doctor warned her that the operation would be dangerous, and she prepared to die. She had nothing to leave, but she burned Lancelot's letters. Julian sent the money in gold, sewn up in a little canvas bag. He came to see her every afternoon and was 'extraordinarily kind and gentle'. But underneath his kindness she felt 'a fixed determination' that her affair with Lancelot should be over for ever; and of course she was quite right.

Anna gets only a glass of brandy, but Suzy has chloroform. The doctor and the chloroform doctor both kiss her, and Guy's doctor says she won't be able to do without love now.

Afterwards Jean was very weak and thin. Julian carried her into the sitting room and said she weighed only an ounce. He took charge of everything. He provided money ('enormous sums') and a daily woman; he too sent her flowers.

At last she was a little better, and so was Lancelot. He came to see her; he said, 'It's the ghost of my kitten.' He said she must go to the seaside. Julian's doctor came for the last time and talked of the future. 'My future!' she wrote in *Triple Sec.* 'As if I can think of that!'

At this time Jean had a friend, an artist's model called Mabel

Hampshire. Now Mabel went with her to Ramsgate. At first she was still so weak Mabel had to push her in a Bath chair; but very soon she could walk, leaning on Mabel's arm. And soon she was so much better that they went on outings to Margate, and to restaurants for supper, and 'laughed and giggled like kids.'

One day, as they sat by the sea in the sun pretending to read the books that Lancelot sent, Jean saw Mabel looking at her curiously. She asked her why. And Mabel said, 'I don't know — you seem such an absolute kid. I believe you've forgotten everything already.' Then Jean thought: 'It's time for me to face things now.'

Her love affair was over. There was no love left, only pity, and she wouldn't live on his pity. She would make a fresh start. She would go back to London, she would get some money somehow, and she would go right away, to America. She'd find a chorus job to take her there, or Lancelot would help. Her mind was made up.

But on her first night back in London she saw him, and when he mentioned money she couldn't do it. Again she felt sick and cold. And then he said that rather than put money in her bank, Julian had suggested that his solicitors — she didn't hear any more. She felt as if he had hit her. The room got misty and he seemed very far away. 'I can't explain this,' she wrote in *Triple Sec*; and in *Smile Please*: 'It was completely illogical.' But in *Smile Please* she went on:

> It seems to me now that the whole business of money and sex is mixed up with something very primitive and deep. When you take money directly from someone you love it becomes not money but a symbol.... I am sure the woman's deep-down feeling is 'I belong to this man, I want to belong to him completely.' It is at once humiliating and exciting.

Even when Julian brought the money she had known it was Lancelot's, and he was still there. But 'To get money through a lawyer, stating please acknowledge receipt and oblige, was a very different matter.' It was distant and impersonal. It made the money not a symbol but merely money. It made her not a slave, but merely a servant.

She saw the look in his eye — 'the hard, cold look men always get when they're dreading a scene' — and with an enormous effort she didn't make one.

Now came the worst time. She was so thin and hollow-cheeked that none of Mabel's artists would want her. She went back to

Blackmore's and got one or two jobs as a film extra, but it was winter now, and so icy in the Alexandra Palace that under her make-up the leading lady was blue with cold. Jean lasted only a few hours. Then — just as in *Chanteclair* — she gave up and ran away.

Now she did nothing. She had 'a complete conviction that I was a useless person.' She felt hopeless and horribly tired. All day she sat and stared in front of her, or walked for hours 'like a demon'. All night she moaned and cried. She lost interest in her appearance and never picked up anyone. When one lonely man spoke to her in a restaurant she saw his lips move, but didn't hear a word he said. She was appallingly lonely but she wanted to see no one, and she wanted no one to see her. Soon she could sleep fifteen hours a day, without dreaming. And she accepted Lancelot's money. 'I got quite used to changing that cheque, because you can get used to anything. You think: I'll never do that; and you find yourself doing it.'

It grew colder, and then it was Christmas. On Christmas morning her landlord brought in a Christmas tree. There was no letter, only a card and some money; but of course she knew the handwriting. It was a very beautiful Christmas tree, everything a Christmas tree should be, with candles and little silver and gold parcels and a big silver star at the top. She looked at it, and she thought: 'Even when I was a child I had this feeling that it was all a mistake, that I didn't belong. But perhaps in England I'd find what I wanted, I'd think.' But now she knew that that was a mistake too. *'I don't belong here any more than I belong there.'*

> ... I would never belong anywhere, and I knew it, and all my life would be the same, trying to belong and failing. Always something would go wrong. I am a stranger and I always will be, and after all I didn't really care.

She ate the Christmas dinner the landlord brought her, and then she went out and got rid of the tree. She never remembered afterwards what she'd done with it (taken it to the Hospital for Sick Children? Given it to the taxi driver?) There was a blank: and then she was back in her room, and she knew what to do. She would wait until the house was empty and then she would drink a whole bottle of gin and jump out of the window. 'I knew what I wanted. I wanted nothing.'

Then there was a knock at the door, and in came Mabel, carrying a pair of red Turkish slippers for her and saying 'Happy Christmas!' 'Are you giving a party tonight?' she asked when she saw the gin bottle. 'Not a party exactly,' Jean said. And it came out what she meant to do. 'But, my dear,' Mabel said, 'this isn't the right house. Oh no, it isn't high enough. If you jumped out of that window you wouldn't kill yourself. You'd just smash yourself up, and then you'd have to live smashed up and how would you like that?'

So Jean didn't jump. Instead they drank the gin together, and soon they were both giggling. Mabel said she should move to Chelsea, she'd find a room for her; and Jean promised she wouldn't jump out of the window, at least not until she'd tried Chelsea. 'I'm always like that,' she wrote, 'the least hope and I shoot up.' But underneath she hadn't changed. She thought she should have died then, and she despised herself for clinging on to 'mean, silly life.' 'Oh God,' she wrote in one of her early stories, 'what a fool I was — what a fool!'

1913 was 'a lovely year,' she said once, but 'a bit bewildering for me.' Many people have a superstitious dread of the number thirteen, but she took it to extraordinary lengths. For the rest of her life she would never do anything or go anywhere on a thirteenth; and her first book, *Triple Sec*, has no page thirteen.

The room Mabel got Jean was at the far edge of Chelsea. 'World's End', it said on the buses. She only stayed in World's End for a short time; but there she made a new beginning.

On her very first day (she said) she went out for lunch to a restaurant on the King's Road. Afterwards she walked along, looking into shop windows. In a stationer's window she saw some coloured quill pens, red, blue, green and yellow. They would look pretty, she thought, in a glass on her table. She went in and bought a dozen. Then she noticed some exercise books on the counter, generously thick, with stiff shiny black covers and red spines and edges. She bought several, 'I didn't know why, just because I liked the look of them.' Then she bought a pen, nibs, a bottle of ink, an inkstand. 'Now that old table won't look so bare,' she thought.

It was after supper that night (as usual a glass of milk and some bread and cheese) that it happened.

> .... My fingers tingled, and the palms of my hands. I pulled a chair up to the table, opened an exercise book, and wrote *This is my Diary*. But it wasn't a diary. I remembered everything that had happened to me in the last year and a half. I remembered what he'd said, what I felt. I wrote on until late in the night, till I was so tired that I couldn't go on, and I fell into bed and slept.

For a week or ten days she walked up and down her room all day and most of the night, crying and laughing and pouring the bitter memories into the black and red books. She forgot to eat, she forgot to be afraid of the landlady, though she took her shoes off and tried to laugh and cry quietly so that she wouldn't be turned out. She filled three exercise books and half another; and then she felt she'd said what she wanted to say. She pushed the exercise books to the bottom of her suitcase and moved back to Bloomsbury, where after all she felt more at home. For the next ten years she never looked at the exercise books again. But wherever she went she took them with her, hidden under her make-up and her dresses.

This is such a *Jean* story, in its deep passivity and unconsciousness, which I'm sure were true. And in the rest, which I think was not. For she'd been writing out her sadness in poems since she was a child; she'd probably been writing it out in a sporadic diary for years. She went on doing this for ten more years; indeed, for all her life. I believe her when she says she didn't keep a diary, and only wrote in 'spurts'. But there'd been spurts before, I'm sure; this one, in the first days of 1914, was only the longest.

Yet it was the most important: and that is what this story of the pens and the notebooks is about. It is an image of her real death and her real life. On Christmas Day, 1913, although she had not jumped, the girl who could have become a woman, with a husband and children and an ordinary happiness, really had died. The Jean who made a new beginning was the writer. She would die again, several times; but each time she would write about it, and start again.

Now she sat for Mabel's artists after all. She posed in the nude for Sir Edward Poynter, and didn't mind because he was so old. Then Tonks of the Slade introduced her to another, younger artist, and when she had to stand before him naked she began to cry. But he was so kind to her she went back. Soon she was posing for him regularly. He called her a nymph, he told her she was beautiful and sent her a beautiful blue chiffon dress; he said he was in love with her. She wasn't at all attracted to him, but she liked him. He was rich, sensitive, and he made her laugh; and she let him take her out to dinner several times.

This painter and would-be lover of Jean's is most likely to have been Sir William Orpen. In *Triple Sec* she calls him 'Tommie', and Orpen was known as 'Billie'. 'Tommie' is small and neat, quite unlike the other artists Jean had met, who were bohemianly dirty — and Orpen was small and 'perfectly turned out' too. And what amused Jean about him above all was his extraordinary energy and love of dancing: in the middle of painting her he would suddenly put on the gramophone and dance a Highland fling or a tango — '"La-di-diddle-da" he sings and flies around feet twinkling ...' That was just like Orpen, who used to enter dancing competitions and win (especially at the tango). And it was just like Jean too — to captivate one of the top society painters of the day, and despite her brave fantasies to take no advantage of it at all.

Well, she did try, just once. For even with Lancelot's cheque and her model's wages she was very poor now, and she hated that. Her mind went round and round the problem — 'I must make some money — I must — I must.' But how? Sell herself? Ask Lancelot? She couldn't bear to do either. And then she met 'Harry Benson'. That, at least, is what she called him in *Triple Sec.*

'Harry' had been an officer and a gentleman. He still had rich friends, a military bearing, a beautiful voice and good clothes. But when she looked closer his clothes were shabby and his eyes furtive. He was an adventurer and 'a bad lot'; and she rather liked him.

Harry (like Lancelot) is not 'a ladies' man', but he desires Suzy. He picks her up in his arms, 'so easily', and Suzy feels 'tired and weak', 'as I always do when men hold me in their arms.' He says 'How pale you are — how pale you are! Like a lily,' and he kisses her. But as soon as he kisses her Suzy wakes up. She doesn't care for him; and he is as poor as she is, 'he can be no earthly good to me.' So she pushes him away. But Harry is in love with her, and he promises not to 'misbehave' again. So they are friends; and soon, perhaps, partners. Suzy suggests, half-jokingly, that they start a gambling club; and Harry takes her seriously. She will lure the men in, and he will run it. 'I'm going to make money,' he says. 'Then you'll smile sweetly at me — and let me kiss you, won't you — you little devil!'

Harry actually starts the club 'in a small way' in a Soho alley. Suzy is 'bitten with the excitement of it,' and with the hope that it will bring her 'life and a fight and a chance.' But Jean's men were never any good at making money. Soon the club begins to founder. And that's when Suzy thinks of the only rich man she knows: Tommie.

She rings him up and asks to see him straight away. Then she puts on a little black and white dress she'd bought when she was with Carl. And suddenly she is excited, suddenly she feels alive again, for the first time in so long. When Tommie sees her he says she looks different — more beautiful than ever — and in the taxi he 'kissed and kissed me.' At last she asks him for money — and sees by his look of surprise and relief that he expected her to want more. ('I must remember that — it's silly wanting a little'.) He gives her a cheque; then he pushes her on to the sofa and starts to tear off her dress. But once again she could stop him — 'You're making me *hate* you,' she says, and he stops. She takes the cheque to Harry. But her pleasure is quite gone. 'I know now that I have a certain power,' she tells herself, 'and yet — how mean, how mean.'

★　　　★　　　★

In Suzy's Bloomsbury boarding-house she meets a boy she calls 'Mark James', who is a journalist 'on a Daily'. He is handsome and amusing, and she enjoys his company. This boy's real name was Alan Bott; he was twenty-one, and a sub-editor on the *Daily Chronicle*. He and Jean became friends, and in April he did something very important: he introduced her to the Crabtree Club.

Anything went at the Crabtree. It was started by Augustus John and a few others as a club for artists, poets and musicians. Alan Bott took Jean there on the night it opened (so that she thought he and his friends had started it). That first night no one came, and they left feeling very glum. But the next night people began to arrive, and soon it was packed every night.

The Crabtree was up four flights of narrow wooden stairs over a shop in Greek Street. It was really just a large room with a raised platform at one end and a tiny piano. But it was the first of the great bohemian night clubs. John and his friends had intended it to be 'a very democratic affair', and it was. Soon it was crowded not just with artists and writers — John himself, Epstein, Gaudier-Brzeska, Compton Mackenzie — but with all sorts of people. There were Fleet Street journalists like Alan, there were West End actresses and dancers, and students and models from the Slade. And there were smart young men about town, and *cocottes,* and Jewish shopkeepers from the East End.

The platform at the end could be many things. Sometimes it was a dancing stage, with the Destiny Waltz thumped out on the piano. Sometimes the club's stars, the actress-models Betty May and Lilliane Shelley, stood up on it and sang. Sometimes someone gave recitals of the most modern music or poetry on it; and sometimes the piano was taken off, and there were boxing matches for the men.

The Crabtree was a raffishly intellectual place, where you could talk and argue till dawn. And it was a glamorously, self-mockingly decadent place, full of 'weedy youths drinking absinthe,' Jean said, 'trying hard to be vicious and hoping they looked French — girls in trousers, you see the place — .' If people arrived in evening dress they were taxed a shilling. One young artist strode around in dancing pumps and exquisite clothes, fixing everyone with burning eyes and offering them a pinch of his cocaine.

'A bad imitation of Montmartre, one is supposed to say,' Jean wrote — and she loved it. Lilliane Shelley (who had red lips and black hair and was supposed to be a gypsy) she thought especially beautiful. As the night wore on and the atmosphere grew more extravagant Lilliane and the others would start throwing bottles around the room — and Jean would secretly admire that too. The Crabtree was shabby and gay, careless and shocking, and it suited her perfectly. She went there nearly every night for many months; she almost lived there. She arrived at midnight, stayed till dawn and ate sausages for breakfast. Then she went home and slept all day, waking just in time to go there again. She never forgot the Crabtree; she talked about it often. Its feeling of 'tense tedium and relaxed excitement' exactly matched her own. It was the only place in England that ever did.

But now she did a strange and typical thing. In the Crabtree Club, full of wild young men, she got engaged to one who was neither wild not even young. He was ten years older than her, and slightly stiff and severe; slightly — to her — dull.

In *Triple Sec* she called him 'Ronald'. 'Ronald by force of contrast,' she wrote, 'looked very nice the night I met him there. His hair was black and ruffled, his eyes very blue, his voice charming, and his manner just shy enough, just formal enough, to be very attractive at the Crabtree, where shyness and formality were rare....' Partly it was because she was looking for someone like Lancelot; partly it was because she was looking for someone rich. But mostly it was just because she was divided against herself, split in two. Wherever she was half of her wanted to be somewhere else. Wherever she was, half of her had to go against it.

'Ronald' *was* rather like Lancelot. He was, Jean wrote in *Triple Sec*, 'a gentleman'; upper-class, well educated, old fashioned. 'I didn't dream you put any paint on,' he says severely; and when Suzy airs her 'hard won cynicism' he says, 'It is perfectly awful — a child like you talking like that ... it's all arrant nonsense, I assure you.' He asks her to his flat in the Temple and gives her an old-fashioned nursery tea — 'large slabs of buttered toast and strawberry jam', and Fuller's walnut cake. He has a small iron bedstead and a large tin bath ('no sybarite Ronald,' Suzy says). There are pictures of his family and his home, a big sketch of G.K. Chesterton and several photographs of George Bernard Shaw; and lots of books, from the Dialogues of Plato to Hardy and Shaw. Suzy loves the flat, and the tea; and she likes Ronald. Smiling, and 'looking very tall and large', he points at two big cupboards in the hall: 'Those are to lock you up in when you don't behave nicely,' he says. And she thinks, 'Really I do like this man.' 'Funny how at five o'clock I thought "This man is a dear — but dull" — And at half past six "What a darling tweed suit, how nice it smells — love tweed — How lovely to be taken care of ...."'

And then, in the middle of tea, it happened: he asked her to marry him. By now (she wrote) her distrust of people had bitten deep, and she was sure he didn't mean it — it was only a trick for grabbing at her. So she was angry, cynical, cruel. She told him the worst things she could about her life — 'Be disgusted,' Suzy thinks fiercely — 'Idiot!' But to her surprise he is not disgusted, he is gentle and pitying. So she sobs out all her misery of the last two years; and when he takes her home they are engaged.

Suzy lies awake making resolutions.

> To get up early in the morning — To stop putting black on my eyes —
> To take only one hour to dress....

And two more:

> To be awfully good.
> To be a wonderful wife.

Jean hardly ever talked about this engagement in later life and never used it in her fiction. Her silence may be a measure of her disappointment. For the real 'Ronald' was everything he seems in *Triple Sec,* and more. His name was Maxwell Henry Hayes Macartney. When Jean met him he was a journalist with *The Times*. He was well-bred and well-spoken; a gentleman and a scholar.

She must have felt miraculously lucky and reprieved. Just as she'd given up all hope of ordinary happiness, in the most unlikely of places she'd found it — or it had found her — again. Perhaps she could even live her secret dream of Rosie Boote, of Nancy Erwin, after all.... She was happy and grateful to Maxwell Macartney. She carried out her resolutions. 'I stopped sleeping all day and sitting in the Crabtree all night,' 'I made up less, drank less, ate more.' She gave up her *louche* friends, and went to tea at the Temple every afternoon with some women friends of Max's who were very nice to her. 'He did me a lot of good,' she wrote in *Triple Sec.* She grew less lonely, more normal; she grew happy and eager to please him. She prepared to carry out her other resolutions too: to be awfully good, to be a wonderful wife.

But ... of course there was a but. 'It was an odd, up-and-down engagement,' is all she says in *Smile Please*. But *Triple Sec* fills in this mysterious code: they started to quarrel.

First they were silly quarrels. She continued to 'air her cynicism,' and he continued to disagree: 'My dear Suzy, you're simply morbid.' Then they became more serious: 'I will *not* stand your looking at men like that.' When she realised that 'submission made him worse' she became 'distrustful, obstinate, sulky.' 'Marriage is dull,' she said. 'All the girls on the stage say so.' 'I wish to *God*,' he exploded, 'you'd stop quoting the girls on the stage....'

Their real lives were emerging and clashing, just as had happened with Lancelot. When she'd lashed out at him so angrily at the start, and told and showed him the very worst about herself, she'd probably hoped to lose or secure him straight away. She hadn't lost him. But she didn't understand (because she didn't want to) the slow, English battle in him between what he would want to feel — pity and protection — and what increasingly he did feel — distrust and dismay. He couldn't forget what she'd said when he asked her to marry him: 'I felt as if you'd smashed me in the face,' he would say at the end. And she was a flirt always — a charming and light-hearted flirt when she was happy, a reckless and compulsive one when she wasn't. She would have begun as the first sort; but under his jealous, possessive gaze she'd become the second.

She had several men friends during her engagement. There was Alan Bott, who may have introduced them at the Crabtree; soon there was a young painter called Adrian Allinson, whom she also first saw there. Later there was someone she called 'Alastair' in *Triple Sec*, and someone called Freddy who lived in the Temple. She would be very fond of 'Alastair'; and with Adrian Allinson she would have, during one of the 'down' times in her engagement, a 'semi-demi love affair'. Probably Max was jealous of all of these. Then there was another man, who must have seemed the least important to a young lover. Yet — given Jean's strange and perverse nature — he was probably the most important.

He too worked for *The Times* and lived in the Temple. Perhaps, therefore, Max introduced him to Jean; or perhaps she met him at the Crabtree, which he would certainly have known. His name was Arthur Henry Fox Strangways.

Fox Strangways would have seemed safe to Max, but was really dangerous, for the same reason: he was old. When Jean knew him she was in her mid-twenties, and he was in his mid-fifties. He was also an intellectual, an idealist, and a confirmed bachelor. For several years he had been Secretary of the India Society, and Rabindranath Tagore's unpaid literary agent in England; in 1914 he had published *The Music of Hindostan*, which has since become a classic. Before that he had been a public school master for twenty-five years. During much of his life he had probably rarely spoken to a young woman.

And indeed his relationship with Jean was probably entirely decorous and gallant. He was *The Times*' music critic; and what he did was take her to concerts. 'I had never been to any opera,' Petronella thinks in 'Till September Petronella': 'it must happen quickly or it will be too late.' Jean knew she was ignorant and uncultured even in music, despite her father's fond illusions. Fox Strangways was a scholar and a teacher, and for a while during the War he much improved her musical education.

But Jean was Jean, and perhaps it didn't stop there. In fact, of course, she had a weakness for older men, and they for her. Fox Strangways was close to the ideal Englishman of her dream — in some ways closer than Lancelot had been. His family was nobler and more military. He himself was tall, handsome and authoritative, inspiring respect even in that most anarchic of creatures, the schoolboy ('Nobody every ragged Foxie; if anyone tried, Foxie had only to *look.*') At the same time he hid a core of irascibility and unhappiness; he'd left Wellington because (though one didn't say so openly in those days) he'd clearly had two nervous breakdowns. This combination of social confidence and inner conflict was just what had drawn Jean to her first lover, and was drawing her now to Maxwell Macartney.

As to Fox Strangways, he was just the sort of man who fell in love with Jean most easily and deeply: naive, sensitive, inexperienced with women and perhaps a little afraid of them, like Lancelot, like 'Harry Benson'. They needn't see her as a women, or even a girl: she was a child, a lily, a nymph. ('I believe you're a nymph really come to see what it's like being a girl,' 'Tommie' had said.) No woman's name was ever associated with Fox Strangways'. But one of the friends who knew him best and longest wrote of him when he died: 'There were touches of tenderness in him at all times, of knowledge of the human heart which this schoolmaster-critic-recluse could only have acquired by intuition. Or had he known more but preferred to leave it unpursued ...?'

Perhaps, then, Max became jealous of Fox Strangways too. Whatever happened, or didn't happen, he should have. For in later life Jean rarely spoke of her fiancé; she tried to forget him. But she often spoke of Arthur Henry Fox Strangways, with admiration and also with tenderness. He was linked in her mind with her father, as a true, old-fashioned gentleman. She couldn't pay a man a higher tribute than to link him with her father. When she spoke of them together towards the end of her life her eyes would fill with tears.

Now, after a gap of several years, Jean briefly took a job on the stage. This was — perhaps to mollify Max — a mixture of respectability and daring. Daring, because the play, *Monna Vanna,* had actually been banned: the story turned on the visit of the heroine to the enemy general's tent, clad only in a cape.... But respectable, because the cape was so long and full that 'one couldn't imagine anything more decent.' And also because it starred Constance Collier; and there were only a few performances, none at night.

*Monna Vanna* played in the last two weeks of July 1914. On 28 June Jean had seen the news on the placards in Leicester Square: ARCHDUKE ASSASSINATED AT SARAJEVO. Max had said: 'That means war.' Now the girls in the dressing room echoed England's innocence: 'It'll all be over by Christmas.' Only one girl, a Hungarian, said, 'Oh no, it won't be over by Christmas, don't you make any mistake.' But Jean didn't believe in the war at all, until she went to the Crabtree one night and found a notice posted up:

## CLOSED FOR THE DURATION

On 24 August, her twenty-fourth birthday, her old enemy Julian Martin Smith fought in his first battle. She wouldn't have been pleased to know that he was very brave. A day or two later a piece of shrapnel hit him in the spine, and he was dead.

★    ★    ★

'The man I was supposed to be engaged to' (Jean wrote but didn't keep for *Smile Please*) 'thought of nothing else [but the war]. He volunteered and came back very angry because they'd turned him down as he was over age. He didn't rest until he was sent to France for his newspaper. Our engagement and everything else was completely forgotten.'

Maxwell Macartney began sending despatches to *The Times* from the Western Front in late 1914. In *Triple Sec* Ronald leaves for France in about November. Feeling sad but excited, Suzy helps him to pack. 'One pair of exceedingly ancient trousers' are surely too old to wear, she says. But Ronald says that 'one got news more easily in old clothes,' and they are his favourites. '"Damn good trousers," said Ronald the conservative.'

Suzy spends the next six months 'reading *The Times* for the first time in my life.' 'I remember reading one of my fiancé's despatches,' Jean wrote, 'and thinking, it's dull....' None the less Suzy writes Ronald long letters. But she gets 'colder and colder' answers. 'Brooding....'

'I hated the war,' she says. 'I grew unbearably depressed that first horrible winter, when it rained every day.' And Jean wrote for *Smile Please* that the whole war was 'most horribly dull. Everyone seemed to vanish. All the men I knew volunteered or were conscientious objectors.... Nearly all the girls I knew melted away too. One joined the WACS, another went to be a landgirl on a farm....' More than anything she would always hate being alone. Much of the horror of both wars for her was loneliness.

What could she do with herself, alone in London? She didn't need to work: she still had Lancelot's allowance (what had she told Max about that, I wonder?). It had allowed her to live on the fringe of the leisured classes, and it continued to do so. She spent the war doing what many middle- and upper-class girls and women did: volunteer work for the war. She heard of a club for soldiers' wives, and a canteen near Euston Station for troops on their way to France. Soon the club fizzled out ('so dull that the soldiers' wives, poor dears, couldn't be persuaded to come'). But she worked at the canteen until the middle of 1917.

'The younger men often looked excited,' she wrote. 'The older men were more thoughtful and silent; they knew what they were going to do.' She knew too. One day a young soldier came into the kitchen and asked if they would straighten the strap that fixed his kit. Jean did it, and he winked and thanked her. 'I prayed for him every night,' she said, 'but I don't suppose it did much good.'

In the early summer of 1915 Suzy gets 'a specially horrible' letter from Ronald and decides 'to think no more of him.' Instead she plunges into the war atmosphere, into 'What's anything matter — we may be dead tomorrow' flirtations ('Of course I'll dine with you — of course I'll kiss you ...'). And into 'a sort of semi-demi love affair with a young artist called Hebertson trying to pretend I liked him — .'

Adrian Allinson was exactly her age. He was a thin young man with sloping shoulders, a long face and wavy brown hair. He was strongly pacifist, but also suffered from 'a chronic gastric weakness', and was declared unfit for military service. 'Not incarceration but social ostracism was my lot,' he wrote in his autobiography. At his army examination the Medical Officer took one look at him and asked 'Are you a poet?' No, he was a painter, Allinson replied. 'Same thing, same thing,' the Medical Officer said. His mother was German Jewish (his original first names were Alfred Pulvermacher), and his father an ultra-rationalist, vegetarian teetotaller, who had named his children in alphabetical order (after Alfred/Adrian came Bertrand, Cyril, Dulcie and Enid). Allinson had always felt 'something of a freak and misfit'; in wartime he stood out more than ever. 'It was no good,' he wrote, 'freak I was, and freak I would have to remain.'

But he was clever, very talented, and not at all shy. He played the piano extremely well, and sometimes got up and played at the Crabtree. He was very romantic, and 'always in difficulties with an endless succession of girlfriends.' Jean had noticed him at the Crabtree; then in May they were both at a studio party in Chelsea.

Now it was Allinson who noticed 'Ella, a fair young Englishwoman born in the West Indies.' He was 'instantly struck' (he wrote) by her 'tender loveliness,' and by her 'remarkable resemblance to the famous Renaissance beauty' who was one of Botticelli's favourite models. He wanted to paint her as Botticelli had painted his model, as the embodiment of spring. He asked her to sit for him.

Allinson conceived his picture of Jean 'amid the dappled sunshine and shadow of some vernal spot.' So he painted her outside, 'among the blossoming but soot-laden trees of Manchester Square' ('I'm going to paint you out in the opulent square,' Marston says in 'Till September Petronella'). But the soot, or the city, destroyed the 'Arcadian mood' he had in mind, and he was dissatisfied with his painting. Then he saw a solution.

A year or so before he had met an extraordinary young man, a composer, music scholar and now music critic, though he was just down from Oxford and not yet twenty-one. He too was both a conscientious objector and medically unfit for service; and he and Allinson became firm friends. His name was Philip Heseltine.

Recently, in the Café Royal, Heseltine had been smitten by a Chelsea model called Bobby Channing. Allinson had introduced them, and they'd begun a violent love affair. In July Heseltine suggested that Allinson join him and 'Puma' (as he called the dark, catlike Bobby) in a cottage on Crickley Hill near Cheltenham. Allinson glimpsed his Arcadia, and asked Jean to join them in August.

This was, perhaps, unwise. Allinson didn't know Jean well yet, but he did know Heseltine. And Jean had made conditions. Their 'semi-demi love affair' was, so far, platonic; and it was to continue so. Allinson was in love with her beauty, but not (yet) with her; and what he was really thinking of was his picture. He agreed.

When Marston asks Petronella to come to the country she is happy, because she's been very lonely. And in *Triple Sec* Suzy is happy too. 'I thought I should love it that first evening,' she says. 'It was so peaceful after London — everything smelt so good and Hebertson had put a big bunch of flowers in my bedroom.' ('I walked miles to get you that honeysuckle this morning,' Marston says. 'I thought about you all the time I was picking it.') After supper they turned the lamp out, so that only moonlight lit the room. It was very still, very warm; and Heseltine began to whistle.

He was a marvellous whistler; he would often compose whistling, sitting at the piano. Now he whistled the love duet from *Tristan*. It was 'the sweetest truest sound,' and the loveliest music Jean had ever heard. It made her want to cry. It made her want to be kissed, and she let Allinson kiss her. But all the time he kissed her she watched Heseltine whistling.

That night — no doubt emboldened by those permitted kisses — Allinson came to her room. He gazed at her and 'breathed extremely hard.' Jean said, 'Adrian dear, I love it here,' but she did not relent. She said she was tired; and 'firmly' she said goodnight.

That was the end of peace for all of them. The next day Allinson was sulky and sad, and Heseltine was angry. Jean pretended not to know why ('Why, I couldn't make out'); so did Allinson, calling her an 'unoffending girl'. But according to him 'Philip and "Puma" took so instantaneous and violent an aversion to Ella' that they 'refused point-blank even to eat in the same room' with her, and 'could not be even decently civil to her.' According to Jean, they had an open and violent quarrel. Heseltine accused her of making an artist suffer: 'You've been laughing at him for weeks,' Julian says in 'Till September Petronella', ' — the best painter in this damnable island, the only one in my opinion....' Allinson didn't defend her, or defended her only feebly; and suddenly she did something 'indefensible'. 'I find you both ridiculous,' Suzy says, 'why aren't you at the war anyway?' And in another version, to 'Phil': 'If you were a man you wouldn't be here, you'd be fighting.' 'Marvellous,' Phil says, 'I've been waiting for that remark for several days....' 'Oh look here she doesn't mean it,' says 'Adrian', 'she is not as bad as all that....'

After this terrible row in 'Till September Petronella' Petronella leaves immediately. In *Triple Sec* Suzy tries to leave too, but has to wait for a few days for money to come from London. According to Adrian Allinson, Jean didn't leave at all. 'With a streak of hard determination oddly at variance with her outer frailty,' he wrote, 'she insisted ... on taking full advantage of my offer of a holiday in the country.' She could not face the return to an empty London; and he, 'obsessed with the thought of my picture, ... hoped that the situation would improve.'

It didn't. The 'ensuing weeks' were 'sheer hell' (Allinson), 'nerve-shattering' (Heseltine), a 'funny time' (Jean). Heseltine hated her more every day; Allinson, on the contrary, fell in love with her. Heseltine and Puma made noisy scenes of sado-masochistic love; Jean said Allinson could be her lover if he would 'do his bit for King and Country.' With all this strain he had a bad attack of gastritis. 'When the situation had reached breaking point,' two gentle and tactful Indian friends arrived and resolved it. Heseltine and Puma apologised. Heseltine went to Oxford with his friends; and Jean finally returned to London.

Jean Rhys and Peter Warlock — for Philip Heseltine became Peter Warlock: it's extraordinary to think of these two narrow but deep artists meeting in their artistic infancy, and having such a cataclysmic effect on each other.

When they met Heseltine was only twenty, Jean just turning twenty-five. He was tall, pale, blond, green-eyed. A 'strange derisive smile played forever about his handsome features,' said Augustus John. He was clever, witty and erudite, and an extreme iconoclast, ridiculing all the cultural icons of the day and praising only people no one had ever heard of. He was extremely charming and entertaining. 'He had that rarest quality in human beings' (said another friend) 'that when you were with him you were never dull.'

Outwardly he was everything Jean was not, and everything she would admire and envy. But underneath *he was like her*; and that was even more, I think, what drew her to him. For like her he was hypersensitive, uncertain and shy, and tried to hide it. He devised, for protection and show, a wild, extrovert, swaggering side, for which he would soon take the name Peter Warlock. Armed with his Warlock cover he would drink and whore and behave outrageously – now, for instance, racing his motorcycle through the village streets at midnight, stark naked. ('Fight?' says Julian in 'Till September Petronella'. 'I never fight. I'm frightened ... I'm never rude, either. I'm far too frightened ever to be rude.')

As he grew older his Warlock moods grew more savage and cruel, his secret Heseltine self more and more melancholy. He had cultivated the Warlock legend himself, but in the end it imprisoned him. To a few close friends he could still be simple and sincere, but to others he was ferociously cruel and aggressive, as he'd been to Jean, and his career was littered with violent quarrels and vendettas. To the end he was magnetic and fascinating; no one who met him ever forgot him. But he hated himself; and much more thoroughly than Jean ever could he changed and destroyed himself. In his mid-thirties, convinced that his creative powers were over, he committed suicide.

Heseltine had the 'gift of personality', and Jean was not the only novelist who wrote about him. Lawrence put him into *Women in Love* as Halliday (which ended *that* friendship); Aldous Huxley put him into *Antic Hay* as Coleman. After his death he reappeared as Giles Revelstoke in Robertson Davies' *A Mixture of Frailties*, and in several other, less well-known novels, including one by Osbert Sitwell. But Jean had met him first; and Julian Oakes of 'Till September Petronella' is his youngest literary incarnation.

His effect on her is clear in that story, and she often talked about it later. She fell for him, she desired him. And he, I think, desired her. Everyone did, when she was young; and you didn't have to like her for it to happen, as poor Adrian Allinson discovered. What else could the explosion between Marston and Julian mean? 'You're letting your jealousy run away with you,' says Marston: 'Jealousy?' Julian shrieks. 'Jealous of what?' And he is 'unrecognisable. His beautiful eyes were little, mean pits and you looked down them into nothingness. . . .' Heseltine was in love with Puma; the next winter he would marry her. If at the same time he was attracted to this girl, who belonged (or ought to belong) to his friend – well, he would become wild and cruel, as wild and cruel as in fact he was.

I think they felt the same complicated, dangerous things about one another: desire, hatred and fear. Jean was certainly afraid of Heseltine. In 'Till September Petronella' Petronella kisses the mouth of a Greek statue, and is suddenly very afraid. Later she writes a letter she never sends: 'Julian, I kissed you once, but you didn't know. . . .' Heseltine looked like a Greek statue; and later many people would feel something sinister about him. With her acute sensitivity made still sharper by desire, Jean was being (as she often was) almost clairvoyant.

This short, horrible summer holiday suddenly reveals Jean at twenty-five, like a photograph that's lain forgotten in a drawer for most of a century. And what it shows is that she was formed now, she would never change. This disaster was like all the disasters to come, in which she would hurt and be hurt, and which she would try to face and forget by turning them into fiction. She would always be as much a sexual manipulator of men who wanted her as a sexual victim of men she wanted. At the end of her weakness she would always show a 'streak of hard determination'; and she would often stay somewhere where she hated and was hated, because she was more afraid to go.

In other ways too Adrian Allinson's description of Ella in 1915 shows Jean just as she was twenty, forty, sixty years later. Despite her resolutions of a few months before, she spent 'hours', he said, in front of a mirror, 'combing out her lovely hair and playing with a make-up box filled with a variety of unguents, powders and lipsticks.' And the schoolgirl who had been such a 'keen outdoor person', who'd loved to ride and swim and go on picnics, was quite gone. Was it her unhappiness, her 'illegal operation', her life in bed-sitting rooms and night clubs, drinking too much and eating too little ('You must have one good meal a day,' Estelle says in 'Petronella', 'it is *necessary*')? Whatever it was, already Allinson's 'proposals of tough walks among the hills, bathes in streams or jaunts further afield on my motor-cycle with her riding pillion, alike filled Ella with horror,' he wrote. 'A gentle ten minutes' totter down the lane seemed the limit to which her slender legs could carry her.'

One last thing Allinson can tell us: what was wrong with Jean's voice. It wasn't her fault, he said, but her voice 'offended our musical ears beyond endurance.' It was 'of a most unfortunate timbre, something between a high-pitched pipe and a nasal whine peculiar to certain transatlantic regions.' Very likely her voice was one of the things Heseltine was rude to her about ('I think, I rather think, Marston, that I hear a female pipe down there,' Julian says in 'Petronella'). Perhaps it was now that she began to whisper.

★     ★     ★

Petronella returns to London so empty that she cannot bear to go back to her empty room. She lets a young man pick her up; she lets him think she is a tart. Jean's heroines always let strange men have them when their lovers have rejected them. She'd done it herself before, she'd do it again. Perhaps she did it now. And then went back to her soldiers' canteen, which at least kept her busy all day, and made her so tired she could sleep at night.

By the spring of 1917 Jean was 'on terms of cool (very cool) friendship' with Max, and hadn't 'heard or written for months.' But now she suddenly got a letter from him asking if she would like to go and live in his flat in the Temple. She was so delighted that she accepted enthusiastically, without wondering why he'd asked, or whether it was 'a very dignified thing to do.'

She always said that for years after she came to England she didn't read at all. But now something important happened. She wasn't well; and she spent 'hours, whole days, curled up on the sofa,' reading Max's books. She couldn't understand Plato, and at first she found Galsworthy dull and sad. But 'suddenly a sentence gripped me'; and for the first time in her life, she said, she read a novel 'slowly, carefully, stopping to think it over.' She was 'completely caught and fascinated.' She read all the Galsworthys Max had. She tried Conrad but didn't like him; she read all the Hardys, all the Shaws. Friends came to see her; she spent 'many afternoons watching pigeons,' and reading, reading, reading. She'd found, or rather refound, the second great haven of her childhood.

She felt a pain in her side for weeks; suddenly she was very ill, and had to have 'a slight operation'. It sounds like appendicitis. She spent three weeks in an expensive nursing home (paid for, I imagine, by Lancelot). When she returned to the Temple, pale and ghostly, she briefly glimpsed another haven. For Max's sister said: 'Now listen, I'm going to arrange everything. I've told Lady P about you and we're going to pack you off into the country to a farm near my home.'

'After three days on the farm my entire outlook on life had changed,' Suzy says in *Triple Sec*. She met 'nice people, kind people,' especially one called Lady Marjorie, whom 'I'll always love.' She lay under the tall pine trees, listening to the sound they made in the wind: 'the nature note', her singing teacher had called it. She drank milk, she ate eggs; and she was much, much better. She made up her mind to 'buck up' — 'I will — the stage . . . that must be the way. *This time to stick to it.*' And she went back to the Temple 'chock full of good intentions.'

Jean's 'odd' engagement was on again now. Just before she'd got ill Max had suddenly appeared at the flat. First he had tried to kiss her, and they'd quarrelled. Why had he asked her to come there? Why had he pretended to love her when he didn't, why had he written her 'rotten letters', and then started all over again? . . . He looked thin and white and 'much much older'. He said he'd meant to make her marry him, then he'd started thinking . . . but he couldn't bear not to see her again either. 'You look like a child today,' he said. 'Please forget all I've said — I adore you. . . .' And then there'd been more good resolutions. The stage — hard work — eternal friendship; 'a ridiculous pact of eternal friendship which I believed in with all my idiotic heart.'

'All my life I've caught tantalising glimpses of peace and calm or of happiness and companionship,' Jean wrote in *Triple Sec*. 'I stretch out my hands to grasp — and there's nothing there.' When she got back from the country, doubly determined to carry out her optimistic plan, she had a letter from Max. And it was not at all friendly. It was sarcastic, it was 'brutal'.

> 'Generous offer of your friendship' —
> 'Ridiculous situation that must stop'
> 'Your numerous men friends'
> And then the brutality —
> 'I object exceedingly to your bringing them up to the flat late at night as you apparently do — though I oughtn't perhaps to be surprised' — etc etc —

Suzy cannot understand it, she cannot believe it ('for after all Ronald is a gentleman'). Then she feels 'the blood run into my face and my heart begin to thud with rage.'

> I thought 'How dare you, how *dare* you insult me like that? Cruel, cruel and stupid . . .'
> Then,
> 'God, if he was here I'd kill him for writing that.'
> This was fact not hyperbole.

She starts to write Ronald a furious letter. Then she does what Jean will do in her novels. She cuts back her rage to coldness; then she cuts it back to nothing. She doesn't write the letter at all.

Jean's rage had been growing for years. She had bitten it back with Lancelot, though she had almost fainted with the effort. But it had burst out with 'Ethel', and with poor fat 'Jan'. It had flared out at 'Tommie' when he gave her the money she'd asked for, and then tried to make love to her; it had flared out at Max himself when he'd 'grabbed' at her, and at Philip Heseltine when he'd attacked her. Often — with 'Jan', for instance, and with Heseltine — she knew she was being cruel and unfair. But it had grown out of her control. Now it nearly suffocated her. Suzy thinks 'If I go on feeling like this I shall have some sort of fit — Stupid to die of a fit of rage —'.... Then she doesn't remember any more, until she is out of the flat and far away, in Piccadilly Circus.

For a week Suzy is too ill to leave the Temple. But finally she does, still without a word to Ronald. She simply disappears, as she did after 'Guy's' letter four years before.

That was the end of Jean's first engagement.

Maxwell Macartney broke off several more engagements. Finally he married, twice. He worked as a Times foreign correspondent all his life and became an expert on Italy. He was extremely clever, says someone who remembers him: and; she adds, 'very difficult'.

★     ★     ★

After Suzy's new rage at Ronald's dismissal had come something that was already old: fear.

> My old fear — of the world — of the extraordinary hardness of the most unlikely people — I'm one of the weak ones and I'll always be hurt — always I saw it with extraordinary clarity — and I can't I can't any more bear it....

As always when Jean was unhappy she was 'horribly tired', indifferent, thin and plain. Everything seemed ridiculous — her fuss over Max, her ambitions to go back to the stage....

> Ridiculous to imagine that I could ever do anything — ever be anything —
> Lay thinking of nothing at all — just tired.
> Self confidence blown out like a candle.

But then someone lifted her up again. She remet an acquaintance, a French doctor. He stopped her endless crying ('You must stop, my dear, you will hurt yourself'); he brought her peaches and wine; he coaxed and caressed, teased and flattered her. He showed her 'the Latin worship of women': 'La Femme — the mainspring of everything, the greatest joy, the greatest pleasure, the most beautiful thing in the world — the most powerful.' And he told her that it was 'fatal to be afraid,' that 'everyone respects arrogance,' that a French girl would not sit and cry — '*use* what you have,' he said, 'use it....' 'He influenced me enormously,' Jean wrote. When Suzy leaves the Temple it is with 'an extraordinary excitement burning me up — A longing to get my own back. Somehow — anyhow.'

There are air-raids every night, but they only excite her. Like Sasha — but twenty years earlier — she seeks her revenge ... on men, of course. She lets them wine and dine her, then she refuses to let them touch her. Some accept it; one (who was old) even seems to understand it. But finally (of course) one doesn't. She 'smacked his face hard.' She was lucky, he only attacked her in words. He told her 'home truths': 'from A to Z he told me exactly what he thought, loudly and clearly.'

Suzy doesn't accept what he says. But 'Fate' does. That's how she puts it to herself; that's how she does things. 'Certainly it was Fate,' she says. 'Why otherwise should I for once in my life have made up my mind quickly and acted at once, almost as if someone else was doing it for me?'

She goes to a producer who has offered her work before and asks for a job. He has nothing for her in London until the spring, he says, but he sends her to a dancing teacher, who agrees to train her for one of her troupes. Then she goes back to Bloomsbury and looks for the very cheapest boarding house she can find. She finds one in Torrington Square: so cheap that it rented rooms by the hour, and cabs and policemen followed one another to its door.

Torrington Square has long since been swallowed up by the University of London, but in 1917 it had a seedy charm. It was full of trees. Its terraced houses had once been fine; now they held a colourful population of Slade students and artists, poor Londoners and even poorer foreigners.

Jean paid thirty shillings a week for her room, breakfast and supper, plus sixpence a day for lunch, 'an enormous plate of soup and a chunk of bread'. There were hairs in the soup, there was rationing and the cooking was bad, but she was eating regularly. And she was working. She worked so hard that Madame Zara gave her a contract; she even said 'If you'd come to me earlier I could have made an acrobatic dancer of you.' And this was the girl who could hardly totter down the lane for ten minutes in Gloucestershire.... It was because she was eating, and not drinking; because she was working, because she was happy. 'To be happy one must work,' Suzy says. It was one of the many things Jean would always know, but always forget.

The house in Torrington Square was draughty, dirty and disreputable, but somehow it was also comfortable, warm, *fun*. The boarders were Greek, Italian, South American; Jean was the only English ('or pseudo-English') person there. She made great friends with a Signorina who taught Italian, and even greater friends with a man: a Belgian refugee called Camille.

She never forgot Camille. He was 'my first friend,' she wrote nearly fifty years later, 'when I was very lonely ... and young and kind of bewildered.' He wasn't young. He had grey hair, and very blue eyes behind pince-nez. He was a great talker and a great reader; indeed he was a scholar, who'd been at a Belgian university before the war and was writing a book on the Japanese No theatre. Now he was a temporary cashier at the Banque Congo-Belge, and lucky to have the job. He had a family: a wife rather older than himself and two grown-up stepdaughters. Jean liked his wife too, who was pretty, and had made a miraculously warm, comfortable home out of their dingy room. 'Wonderful woman!' Suzy says. If she were a man she would choose a woman like that, 'and leave far, far, away, as far away as possible, haggard, nervous, hysterical females who talk like blazes [but] can neither cook, sew, nor do anything else useful....' But luckily Camille didn't stay away from her. He befriended her, he defended her; he talked to her of books and pictures. And he was fun too. He'd been a sailor, he said; he hinted that he'd known pirates, even been one.... One day he said he could easily 'grab the cash' from the Banque Congo-Belge, 'and would I light out with him if he did.' 'He was not serious – but what a darling man.'

Then one day there was a new person at Torrington Square: a slim young man with very quick brown eyes. He looked at her very intently, very sharply, but his manner when he spoke to her was modest, even a little shy. Camille seemed to know him; he said he was a French journalist. His name was Jean Lenglet.

The next day, or perhaps the next, he asked her to lunch with him. Before lunch was over she knew (she wrote in *Triple Sec*) many things:

That he was certainly a personality –
That I didn't understand him –
That he probably understood me –

After lunch he took her to a shop called Bichara and bought her flowers, a bottle of scent, a hundred scented cigarettes, and a glass

bottle of dark and glittering kohl. Then he took her to Madame
Zara's in a taxi. Now, of course, he'll want to kiss me, she thought
– but he didn't. Instead he turned away to look at the buildings,
and asked her what each one was, 'always preserving the same
manner of formal distant respect.' About Madame Zara he looked
dubious; it was not a good life for her, he said. 'Why not?' she asked,
piqued. 'Because,' he answered calmly, 'I zink you will never be a
great artiste, and otherwise it is not worth.' She was astonished,
annoyed, and very interested.

Night after night after that she and Camille and John (she would
always call him John) went to the Café Royal and argued. She
insisted that London was 'splendid', 'tremendous' – 'Beautiful,
hideous, romantic London'. *'Mais le brouillard,'* John said. It was just
the fog and mist that *were* London, she cried, they were just what
she loved – anything could happen in a fog. Camille looked severely
at her over his pince-nez. 'It shows a sad mental attitude to love the
dark,' he said. 'Young people should love the sun.' 'I love the fog
and the rain,' she said stubbornly. *'Pour un coeur qui s'ennuie, oh le
chant de la pluie,'* John said. 'What's that?' she asked, and he recited
Verlaine's *Il pleut dans mon coeur* for her:

> *C'est bien la pire peine*
> *De ne savoir pourquoi*
> *Sans amour et sans haine*
> *Mon coeur a tant de peine*

*That's me, that's me,* she thought.

He must be poor, or he wouldn't stay in Torrington Square. And
yet he was so generous – crazily, recklessly generous. He was 'quick
as lightning' in repartee, and instantly crushed anyone who tried to
joke about her. He was used to women, to pretty women, to women
who were petted. And he was completely sincere and natural, because
he didn't give a damn about ordinary standards.

Marya [Jean wrote in *Quartet*,] told herself that this stranger and
alien was probably a bad lot. But she felt strangely peaceful
when she was with him, as if life were not such an extraordinary
muddle after all, as if he were telling her: 'Now then, look here,
I know all about you. I know you far better than you know
yourself. I know why you aren't happy. I can make you happy.'

And he was so sure of himself, so definite, with such a clean-
cut mind. It was a hard mind, perhaps, disconcertingly and
disquietingly sceptical .... But, good or bad, there [he] was.
Definite. A person. He criticised her clothes with authority and
this enchanted her. He told her that her arms were too thin,

that she had a Slav type and a pretty silhouette, that if she were happy and petted she would become charming. Happy, petted, charming — these are magical words. And the man knew what he was talking about, Marya could see that.

A few weeks later it was Christmas. The landlady gave a fancy-dress party; Jean wore a pierrette costume. The boarding house was actually two or three houses with cobblestone passages between them. At midnight, standing in one of the passages with a huge moon overhead, John asked her to marry him. '*Tu viendras à Paris?*' he said, '*ma jolie petite Pierrette....*' He was quiet, his eyes were melancholy, he didn't try to kiss or touch her. When she said yes he still didn't kiss her. She wrote in *Triple Sec*: 'I loved that.'

Almost immediately he left London; he had overstayed his time already, he said. He wrote to her from Holland and she replied. But now their engagement was under siege. By the whole world, for the war would keep them apart for a year. And especially by her family.

She never mentions her family, she hasn't mentioned them for years. Her silence (and her novels) suggest that she'd been quite out of touch with them since her chorus days, six or seven years before. Yet they did know about her engagement: perhaps she'd imagined they would be pleased, and had told them. But of course they weren't pleased; only Jean could have thought they would be. The man was a foreigner, she'd known him only a few weeks, she knew nothing about him, and now he'd disappeared.... And how *did* he travel around like that in wartime? 'Someone who I knew didn't care if I lived or died' wrote a three-page letter, warning her of the dire fate that awaited her if she insisted (again) on such a mad, such an 'idiotic' thing. For 'someone' she'd first written 'my sister.'

But she held out, for a whole year, and she married John Lenglet. Three things had decided her. The first was simply himself — the attraction of his personality and his life, which she knew wouldn't be dull. But that was absent now, and it was the other two that sustained her through this long year: so that when she remembered her engagement in *Smile Please* they seemed even more important. One was the chance of escape he offered, the chance she'd been waiting for for so long. And the other was the support of Camille. He was her friend, he wanted her to be happy: and he approved, he laughed at all the prophecies of disaster. So she laughed too, and waited.

She'd been meant to start in Madame Zara's troupe at Christmas, and Christmas had come and gone. Perhaps she'd taken John's words to heart; or perhaps she'd decided that she had her escape route now, and it was no longer necessary. In any case there was no more talk of dancing, no more talk of the stage. In the spring Camille suggested that she try for an ordinary job, at the Ministry of Pensions. She'd never thought of an ordinary job — quite literally, I think, the idea had never entered her head. But she got it 'surprisingly easily....' Well, of course she was more than presentable, she was intelligent, and labour was very short. But she was right, really; she wasn't cut out for this sort of thing. None the less she seems to have escaped the sack, and stuck at the job for the rest of the year.

In November the Armistice was signed, and at last the war was over. But it was early 1919 before she could book a passage to Holland.

'A week before I sailed I wrote and told the man who had been supporting me for so long that the lawyer's cheque would no longer be necessary,' Jean wrote in *Smile Please*. 'No one can imagine the acute pleasure with which I wrote this.' The next day she had a letter from him. 'Can you meet me at the Piccadilly Grill tomorrow for lunch? Important.'

Lancelot had had a good if not a glorious war. He'd been too old to fight — forty-four at the beginning, forty-eight at the end. Instead he'd offered his financial talents to the government. In 1915 he'd headed a British Mission to Sweden, which successfully persuaded the Swedes to give free passage to British goods to Russia and stop their re-export to Germany. For the rest of the war he'd done a series of such jobs for the Board of Trade, all of which sounded thoroughly inglorious, but were in fact very important. (The 'Norwegian Fish Purchase Committee', for example, had a budget of five million pounds with which to buy up most of the Norwegian fish harvest of 1916, and so keep it away from Germany.) It sounded boring; but it had brought Lancelot even closer to real power. He'd become a member of the Prime Minister's circle; in 1917 he'd been made one of the first CBEs for his war service. And through all these activities, and those of his brothers, cousins and friends, he knew a good deal about the secret workings of the war.

This was, curiously, why he wanted to speak to Jean now. He wanted to tell her that John Lenglet was 'not a suitable person' for her to marry. 'But you don't know anything about him,' Jean said. 'Well,' he replied, 'as it happens I do.' He told her that when John got to Holland 'he was watched'; that he associated with 'very questionable people', several of whom had been arrested; that in fact he was 'under grave suspicion of being a spy.' 'If you marry him you'll be taking a very big risk,' he said.

He should have known her better. She said: 'I like taking big risks, don't you know that?' He nodded. Outside he said, 'If anything goes wrong, will you write to me?' and she promised she would. Then he got into one taxi and she got into another; and 'it was only in the taxi that I began to cry.'

At last, at last, she was leaving England. She 'hadn't quite paid' the dressmaker who was making a new dress for her, and in revenge the woman kept not only the dress but the big trunk that held most of her clothes. She went to Gravesend with only a small suitcase and her coat over her arm. Only 'one man' came to see her off; she doesn't name him, but surely it was Camille. He nearly burst into tears; but she could only be wildly happy. When she landed in Holland she knelt down and thanked God for letting her escape at last. She vowed to herself that she would never go back: 'Whatever happened, whatever happened whatsoever.'

# CHAPTER FOUR

# John, 1919–1924

*John — Paris — Vienna and Budapest — The flight — Paris again*

Willem Johan Marie Lenglet, journalist, married Ella Gwendoline Rees Williams, without profession, on 30 April, 1919, in The Hague. Jean gave her age as twenty-four, cutting four years off the truth. John gave his real age, twenty-nine; but he cut several rather more important things. The main one was that he wasn't really free to marry her at all, because he was still married to someone else.

John Lenglet had been born in Tilburg in the south of Holland on 7 June 1889. That is certain; not a great deal else is. For he was an adventurer and a novelist; and he invented, embroidered and hid even more of his life story than Jean.

His mother was Dutch; her name was Johanna Petronella Nooteboom. John always said that his father, Jean, was French. The name was French; and John's elder brother had a French name too: Edouard. But the truth seems to be that their father was Dutch too, though his family had been Walloon: French-speaking Belgian. And he seems to have been Catholic; John sometimes said he went to school in Holland, sometimes in France, but wherever it was it was always a Jesuit school.

The Lenglets were, like the Rees Williamses, 'good people', 'respectable people' — and the south of Holland was a very respectable place indeed. They didn't have the skin-deep grandeur which West Indian servants and estates had lent the Rees Williamses, but they were probably better off. (John told his daughter later that his father had owned two wool factories, one in France and one in Holland.) So his early experience was not unlike Jean's: middle-class, fairly privileged, with an awareness of difference — part-Walloon among the Dutch, part-Catholic among Calvinists.

As he grew older he became even more like her: he too became the rebel and the black sheep of the family. At seventeen — so he always said, and it seems to be true — he ran away from his Jesuit school to Paris. There he became an art student and occasional journalist by day; and by night a *chansonnier,* scraping a living by singing in the Montmartre nightclubs, Le Chat Noir and Le Lapin Agile.

From seventeen to twenty-five, therefore, he lived a life almost exactly like Jean's from nineteen to twenty-nine: alone in a huge, exciting, dangerous city; living on his wits and his looks (for 'The Chevalier of the Place Blanche' was his story, and the Chevalier was himself), among artists and riff-raff, as far from good bourgeois Tilburg as he could get.

By the time they met, therefore, his view of the world was an articulate version of hers. Life was a gamble and a life-and-death struggle; conventional morality was hypocrisy and the bourgeoisie fair game, but courage, humour and loyalty to one's friends were sacred. He never managed to pass on to her his more general social and political ideas (though she was once 'a G.K. Chesterton sort of socialist,' she said, 'a cow and an acre of land for every man,' and that was probably under his influence). But her philosophy, in so far as she had one, was his. As she knew. He'd influenced her 'tremendously,' she wrote after he died, 'greatly and for keeps': 'Far more than anyone else.'

John's story even of his early years is, at the very least, selective. He didn't spend all his time in Paris, for example: for in 1910, when he was twenty-one, he was in Antwerp. Here he met a nineteen-year-old girl called Maria Staudenmayer, and in September he married her. It was evidently a marriage of necessity rather than choice, for in January 1911 a son was born, and in 1912 John left for The Hague and then Paris. In early 1913 he was divorced, by proxy, for adultery.

Now he *was* in Paris: for there, in April 1913, he married again. His bride was once again nineteen; her name was Marie Léonie Pollart, and John was living with her and her widowed mother in Montmartre.

Though there were no children, this marriage was an important one. First because — judging from what he wrote* and said about it later — it was in several ways a rehearsal for his marriage to Jean. Marie was probably an actress; she probably had a 'past' she was afraid to tell him; and he probably lost her through a combination of absence and suspicion — perhaps even, as he would lose Jean, to a richer and more powerful 'patron'. And secondly because this was the marriage that was still valid in 1919. John was not divorced from Marie Pollart when he married Jean; in fact he was not divorced from her until 1925.

*There is a portrait of this marriage in John's third novel, *Muziek Voorop.*

According to Dutch law, this did not make Jean's marriage invalid, *so long as no one challenged it*. No one ever did, so it never ceased to be perfectly legal; but of course someone *could* have challenged it, for six whole years. Lancelot had told her she would be taking a big risk when she married John, but I don't think even Lancelot knew about this one.

Did *she* know? I doubt it very much. Like Stephan Zelli, John was secretive and a good liar; like Marya, Jean didn't ask questions. And it wouldn't occur to her to ask this one; why should it? John never mentioned either of his first two marriages to anyone until many years later, or his first child either. I'm sure Jean didn't know; at least not at this stage.

A year after he married Marie Pollart the war broke out. Perhaps the marriage was already as unhappy at it is in *Muziek Voorop*; in any case, John volunteered immediately. As a Dutch citizen he couldn't join the French Army, but he was devoted to France and felt it was his home. On 22 August 1914, he joined the French Foreign Legion '*pour la durée de la guerre*'.

This was a characteristically quixotic and rash gesture, which had endless appalling consequences. For he hadn't – of course – bothered to get official Dutch permission to serve in a foreign army, so he lost his Dutch citizenship; and for eight or nine years after the war he was a stateless person. This would make terrible trouble for him and Jean, when they already had far more than they could manage.

For this sacrifice, John told everyone, he had had the privilege of fighting the Germans as a second lieutenant, and of being so badly gassed that he suffered from choking fits for the rest of his life. But the truth was rather different, and worse. A month after he'd joined the Legion '*pour la durée de la guerre*' he was declared unfit, and removed from the list. He never fought; and he lost his nationality not for years of active service at the front, but for one month's preliminary training in the middle of France.

What happened now is obscure. Presumably he was sent for treatment for the disease he'd been discovered to have, and which was the real cause of the ill health which dogged him for the rest of his life. Then, when he was declared fit, he was drafted into French intelligence. He wasn't allowed to say much about this, and he didn't. But he seems to have been smuggled in to Germany several times, and returned via the Netherlands and London back to Paris. It was on one of these hazardous journeys that he met Jean.

This was the man she'd known for a few weeks, and waited a year to marry. He was brave, clever and quiet; I expect he made a good spy. Altogether he was good in war, when his instincts for freedom, lawlessness and survival were just what was needed. For peacetime he would be too reckless, too anarchic, too careless.

Sasha in *Good Morning, Midnight* doesn't like The Hague very much. 'Narrow streets, with the people walking up one way and down the other. So tidily. In the park, the Haagsche Bosch, the trees upside down in the green water....' The Jensens stay with a couple who own a chemist's shop. Sasha likes the wife; but she hates the husband, who looks cruel. His name is Hans Steen, which means 'stone'. The Steens come to their wedding at the town hall; afterwards they have a drink with them, and with a Frenchman who sings English songs and calls himself Dickson. Sasha doesn't feel warm or happy until she's had her fifth glass of port. She says 'You won't ever leave me, will you?' '*Allons, allons*, a little gaiety,' Enno replies.

I think it was almost exactly like this. Jean didn't like The Hague either. The two witnesses to her marriage were Jacques Proot, a chemist, and Ennemond Bousquet, a singer. The end of April in Holland is just as she describes it in *Good Morning, Midnight*, cold and rainy, with vases of tulips on the tables. She would have thought, like Sasha, 'I've got away from all that, anyhow'; like Sasha she would have been a bit drunk when they took the train to Amsterdam.

Sasha and Enno both long for Paris, but stay first in Amsterdam, then in Brussels, in order, it seems, to raise money. It feels quite a short time, but it is long enough for Sasha to guess before they leave Belgium that she is pregnant.

Jean must have got pregnant straight away, perhaps before their wedding day, for her first baby was born at the end of December. She and John didn't get to Paris for six months. Perhaps they too were trying to raise money. And they had another worry, which Jean left out of *Good Morning, Midnight*. She had her British passport; but John had nothing. And it was just their luck — before the war no one had needed a passport, now you couldn't move in Europe without one.

Sasha cries at the station before they go to Calais because the idea of having a baby frightens her. But this is what Jean wrote in her diary-like draft:

> ... Don't cry any more will you he said & the next time I cried was in the lavatory at the station when all at once it came over me again that here I was without money & without a passport & going to have a baby. Going without a passport to cross from Belgium to France. How? Just by walking over the frontier. By walking along the road between rows of poplar trees at night.

A quiet night with a moon up. Walking along until you get past the sentry & finding yourself in Dunkirk in the early morning so tired so tired....

And the fear.... Because just as we were going to sleep in the train a soldier came up & asked for our passports.... I looked down at the ground. I didn't want to look at him or hear what he'd say. But when I looked up again he was making the gesture of passing us on.

I said What did you show him? I showed your English passport. And for yourself what did you show him? I showed him my paper calling me up. I showed it to him without any hope at all. Just a wild hope because he looked so stupid he might pass you on any paper with your name on it.... And there we were in France without passports or money & me going to have a baby.

It was a man at the station in Belgium who'd told them you could simply walk across. He was a waiter who lived in Calais, and he told them to come and see him when they got there. So they did. They walked about in the grey day; they sat and drank absinthe in the waiter's house. Jean saw herself in the glass over the sideboard. She looked thin and dirty and haggard, and she thought 'Fancy having to go to Paris looking like that....' The absinthe made her feel quarrelsome, and she imagined herself shouting at them all to shut up. But she didn't. That night they ate with the waiter and his wife and he lent them twenty francs. Then they got on the train to Paris.

★     ★     ★

'All my life I'd thought about Paris & here I was in Paris looking awful & awful & dirty oh my Lord,' Jean wrote. But in *Good Morning, Midnight* Enno has said 'You'll see, when we get to Paris it'll be all right.' And it was. She fell in love with Paris that first brief time they were there, in late 1919 and early 1920, and she remained in love with it all her life. 'I've been very faithful and never really loved any other city,' she wrote when she was old.

It was a very beautiful autumn morning when they arrived. They went to a café, and everything was clean and bright. Some men were having a glass of wine before they went to work. She waited there while John went to arrange things. In *Good Morning, Midnight* Sasha waits one hour, two, three and a half.... But as soon as Enno returns she sees from his face that he has got some money. Jean never forgot that moment, eating and drinking in the sun in Paris.

I've never been so happy in my life. I'm alive, eating ravioli and drinking wine. I've escaped. A door has opened and let me out into the sun. What more do I want? Anything might happen.

She'd escaped England, she'd got out of prison – that was one wonderful thing. The other was Paris itself. London was harsh and sombre, but Paris was romantic, feminine, seductive. London was grey, but Paris was pink – 'The light is quite pink,' she said, 'there's nothing like it anywhere else.' Paris lifted her up, as drink lifted her up; Sasha will even say, self-mockingly, that the two are connected. ('I can only marvel at the effect this place has on me. I expect it is because the drink is so much better.') London 'tells you all the time, "Get money, get money, get money, or be for ever damned," ' Julia will think in *After Leaving Mr Mackenzie*: but 'Paris tells you to forget, forget, let yourself go.'

This love was one that she'd been waiting for, that she'd been fated to. When the English had beaten the French and taken Dominica away from them, long before she was born, it had been settled that her adolescent dreams would be of England. But really all the time she'd loved the defeated French instead – their more romantic language and religion, their kinder morality. Her francophile father, her Good Mother, Francine and the others chatting and singing in patois, had all turned her towards France long before she got there. And she felt this: in 'an unexplainable way,' she said, Paris, the whole of continental Europe, was 'a *known* world – a *déjà vu* world' when she got there, though she'd never thought of Paris in all the long years of planning her escape from London. It was another of the things which she'd always known, yet always forgotten. England had disappointed her; Paris didn't. Here she felt what she never felt there: 'This is beautiful, this is grand, this is what I hoped for, longed for.'

John was different in Paris too. She had guessed from the start that he was poor; but in London he'd been so generous, he clearly had a great gift for conjuring money out of nothing. This gift had failed him in the first six months of their marriage; but in Paris he was at home, he had friends, his optimism and confidence returned. He borrowed enough money to get them a hotel room in the rue Lamartine, near the Gare du Nord. He said that more money was owing to him for a song he'd written called 'La Charme de la Femme'. It went –

> *C'est un rien*
> *Plus leger que le vent*
> *Ce charme....*

She never knew if that money came. She didn't care, because she was so happy. Once again nothing could touch her. Even when they woke up that night and the walls of their room were crawling with bugs she didn't mind. John was furious, and determined to get their month's rent in advance back from the *patronne*. But Jean just lay down again under the dirty pink eiderdown and went to sleep, 'and when I slept I dreamt of flowers which is my lucky dream.' The next day the landlady argued ('I expect you brought them'); but in the end she agreed to fumigate the room, and they could stay. Jean was glad. The room had its own running water, which was strange and luxurious to her; soon it had a *flamme bleue* (from one of John's friends), and pictures of Gaby Deslys and Huguette Duflos pinned on the walls. It was on the top floor, and outside was a little iron balcony. 'You could stand and lean your arms on the cool iron and look down at the street'; and in the evenings they would sit out on the balcony with friends and drink white wine.

John found a job. She didn't know what it was; he was vague about it, and she soon stopped questioning him. Whatever it was it can't have made much money, for, despite the fact that she was now six months' pregnant, she got a job too.

She went to the Rotonde, where the newspapers hung on sticks on the wall in the continental fashion, and where, also in the continental fashion, she could sit as long as she liked over one cup of coffee. Finally, in *Le Figaro*, she found an advertisement for a young woman to speak English to children. Surely, she thought, even she could speak English to children. She went to the address: Number 3 rue Rabelais, a large old house behind a high wall, very close to the Champs Elysées. The concierge directed her to the first floor; upstairs a manservant in a striped apron opened the door. Mademoiselle would be with her soon, he said.

As soon as Jean saw Germaine Richelot she knew that this was someone even more nervous than she was, 'more shy, more delicate'. And despite her shabby black suit, her protruding stomach, she felt at ease. Mademoiselle Richelot said straight away she was sure Jean was what they wanted. Then her sister came in, the mother of two of the children. She was more business-like; but she was kind too, and smiled at Jean. The job was hers.

It was October. She would work for the Richelots for nearly three months. She and John had hardly any money, she had no idea how they were going to manage when the baby arrived. But this lovely autumn of 1919 was one of the happiest times in her life.

She would wake at half-past seven or eight at the rue Lamartine. John would make two delicious cups of chocolate on the *flamme bleue*. Then she would take the tram as far as the church of St Augustin, and walk the little way to the rue Rabelais. On the tram people were kind to her — '*Passe, Femme Sacrée....*' In the morning she would read to the children and take them for a walk in the Champs Elysées. There were four of them: Jacqueline and Jacques, the children of Germaine's second sister, Madame Lemierre; and Georges and Pierrot, the children of the eldest sister, Madame Bragadier, whom she had met on her first day. They all spoke English perfectly well, and were always sweet, kind and obedient. Very soon they started to take care of *her*, 'steering me about, telling me where to go, in fact being rather patronising, as most people who know me are. "Now sit here, Mrs Ella," the oldest one, Jacqueline, would say.'

After this they would return to the rue Rabelais for an enormous lunch. Jean listened to their conversation, amazed; she had never known a family like this before. They spoke in English or German instead of their usual French, about grammar, words and books; and they would become very passionate and excited. They were extremely civilised and extremely modest. The flat was full of beautiful things collected by Professor Richelot and Germaine — rare smiling Madonnas, beautiful tapestries, little china and pottery horses. It was also full of books and music, of governesses and music teachers. Madame Richelot, the elderly Jewish matriarch, had taught herself to speak beautiful, pure English by reading aloud. Professor Richelot was President of the Academy of Medicine and wore the little rosette of the Légion d'Honneur in his buttonhole; but he was so silent, gentle and vague that Jean at first thought he must be a tutor. Every morning the daughters would go in to their mother's room and kiss her hand; the old Professor didn't know for a long time who Jean was, but he always smiled and bowed when he met her on the stairs. 'I had never seen manners like theirs before,' Jean wrote. 'I didn't know they existed.'

After lunch she was still more amazed: they insisted she must rest, because she was pregnant. Germaine made her lie down on a chaise longue, covered her with a rug, and gave her a Dickens novel. 'Now try to sleep,' she said. But Jean couldn't sleep, she was too happy. She lay looking out at the light and the trees, and thought that she hadn't known such peace for years. Later she would get up and take the children for an afternoon walk; at six o'clock she would have a small, healthy supper in the studio. Then it was time to return to John and the rue Lamartine.

She loved and admired all the Richelots, but most of all she loved Germaine, 'my real friend, the only friend I've ever had, I think.' Germaine was thin and dark and anxious, with a soft voice and a very gentle expression. The Richelots were rich, but Germaine gave away all she had. She wore only cheap cotton gloves and plain dresses, and she employed 'a tribe of girls' to do things she didn't need because she wanted to help them. She hated being rich. 'How I hate the Daimler,' she would say. Instead she preferred to take a tram or a bus — 'or perhaps,' she would say shyly, 'a motor-bike — I would like that.' She'd never married; her father had arranged a marriage for her, but she disliked the idea (she told Jean) and he dropped the plan. She was nervous and shy, but never gauche. Indeed, she was elegant. She knew about clothes, though she didn't bother about them; and she knew all the *gens du monde*, though she didn't bother about them either. She was, quite simply, good. When you looked into her eyes, Jean said, you saw 'the pure spring of goodness untainted.'

Freedom and safety had long since stopped being inseparable. But Jean still needed both: and briefly, now, she had them. 'I was happy,' she wrote in *Smile Please*, 'because both sides of me were satisfied — the side of me which wanted to be protected ... and the side which wanted adventure, strangeness, even risk.' Too much of either was too much for her. Her days with the Richelots and her nights with John — that was perfect. The Richelots were too erudite, too honest, too good. They wore no scent, no make-up.... 'I remember how gladly I would dart out of the iron gate into my warm subtle Paris,' Jean wrote. 'Back to my room on the fifth floor of the hotel and iced wine and women whose faces were properly dressed — not naked....'

She could never have a simple, undivided feeling about any human being. But the Richelots' house she could uncomplicatedly love. She could imagine it wasn't a house at all, she said, 'but a person, restful and protective.' She loved its high protective wall; she loved its sound, the sound of Madame Bragadier playing Bach on a distant piano. The Richelots' house, she wrote, was 'the real Paris' to her. It was her real happiness, even more than Germaine (whose goodness went also to other needy girls). 'It was the quiet, safe house with the piano in the distance ... you'd think it would never be, could never be, knocked down.'

But soon it was impossible for her to go to the Richelots any more. She always remembered the last time she took the children for a walk on the Champs Elysées. She sat down on a bench; someone smiled at her, and she smiled back. Suddenly she was utterly happy, like an apotheosis of all her happiness of the last three months. When she thought about that moment later she wondered if it wasn't a trick nature played on all pregnant women: 'just as your hair gets thicker, your eyes get brighter, your skin gets nice — all a trick.'

Sasha has her baby in 'a place for poor people' on the Boulevard Magenta. When she first goes there in the morning her room is not ready, and she is told to come back between five and six. 'Has anybody ever had to do this before?' she thinks. 'Of course, lots of people – poor people. Oh, I see, of course, poor people....' Then there is a long night, an interminable night, and no chloroform.

When her baby is born in the *Left Bank* story 'Learning to be a Mother', the narrator says at first: 'I did not like him. I had been too much hurt.' But the midwife assures her that maternal feeling will come, that it is always so in the beginning. And indeed one night the baby looks at her with his eyes 'set slantwise' like hers; and she imagines they look sad. She thinks, 'Perhaps that is why he looks so sad – because his mother has never kissed him'; and suddenly she wants to. In *Good Morning, Midnight* Sasha says 'Do I love him? Poor little devil, I don't know if I love him. But the thought that they will crush him because we have no money – that is torture.'

Jean took him home to the rue Lamartine. They had a little basket or cradle for him, which they put near the door to the balcony. John seemed fascinated by him, and sat for hours smoking pipe after pipe and gazing at him. They called him William Owen, after (presumably) his father, his grandfather and both of his mother's brothers.

He was a very pretty baby, and very quiet. In *Good Morning, Midnight*, Sasha is worried by his silence ('Ought a baby to be as pretty as this, as silent as this? The other babies yell from morning to night ...'). But Jean and John noticed nothing wrong; and perhaps this was hindsight. Until one morning something *was* wrong. 'This damned baby, poor thing, has gone a strange colour and won't eat,' Jean thought – 'and I don't know what to do, I'm no good at this.' The *sage femme* came, and then a doctor, and the baby was taken to the Pasteur. But they had no money; so he was moved to the Hospice des Enfants Assistés. The next day they had a *pneumatique* from there to say that he was very ill with pneumonia.

At first Jean had been (she wrote later) not so much sad for her baby as 'tremendously sorry for him.' Now she became extremely anxious that he should be christened, in case he died. John, who was an atheist, said he wouldn't consent to such hocus-pocus. But Jean, who had imagined she was an atheist too, found that she had returned to everything she had learned in her convent. That her baby should be christened suddenly seemed 'the most important thing in the world', and she began to cry. John ran out to buy a bottle of champagne to cheer her up; he returned with two bottles, and a friend called Colette. Soon Jean felt better. 'By the time the first bottle was finished,' she wrote, 'we were all laughing.'

The next day they learned that the baby had died the night before: at half-past seven in the evening, just when they had been drinking champagne and laughing. Jean ran to the hospital and asked the nun, 'Did you baptise him before he died?' The nun said yes, they baptised all babies brought to the hospital. 'When I cried,' Jean wrote, 'it was half with relief.'

When she told this story fifty years later she would have tears in her eyes. But otherwise she told it as she'd learned to tell all her stories: without excuse or explanation. She knew that people would wonder. Should she have let a new-born baby lie close to a window in January? Shouldn't she have noticed something sooner? *Did she really want this baby?*

I think the death of her first child was one of the sorrows of her life; but most of her sorrows were part guilt, and so was this one. Though she was nearly thirty she was still a child herself, because she always would be. 'I must have done something wrong,' was her own explanation. 'I was never a good mother.' She was extra-ordinarily passive and hopelessly incompetent all her life. She had no one to help her but John, who'd had little if anything to do with the baby he'd had nine years before, and who would certainly expect children to be her responsibility. And they'd only been married a few months, they'd had so little time alone, so little time for love and pleasure.... Out of all the things she knew of her, and all the things she said, a close friend of her old age made this summary: 'She didn't want the child to die.... When it did she saw that life was as cruel as she had always believed, but it did become less difficult.'

William Owen died on 19 January, 1920, when he was three weeks old. 'And then you rush round trying to raise money enough to bury him,' Julia says in *After Leaving Mr Mackenzie.* He was buried in the cemetery at Bagneux, south of Paris. It cost 130 francs, sixty centimes, for a carriage, small coffin and temporary cross. Jean kept the receipt all her life.

But now this catastrophe changed their luck. Jean's friends the Richelots were *'désolés et peinés pour elle,'* and they stepped in with their *savoir faire,* their power and position. The Interallied Commission, which was overseeing the disarmament process in Austro-Hungary, was advertising for staff in the Paris newspapers. John was an excellent linguist, with perfect French, very good (if accented) English, and probably good German too. The Richelots recommended him for one of the posts of secretary-interpreter. At the same time they solved (at least temporarily) his passport problem. Germaine enlisted the help of an aunt who knew *'quelqu'un d'influent à la Préfecture de police:' 'elle obtiendra sûrement,'* she wrote to John, *'ce que vous seriez encore peut-être des mois à demander.'* It all happened very quickly — *'j'ai agi le plus rapidement possible,'*

*Germaine said, 'les mots ne sont rien.'* In the very same week their
baby died they learned that John had got the job. He was to be
secretary to one of the Japanese members of the Commission,
Lieutenant Colonel Miyake.

The Commission left for Vienna some time in early 1920. Wives
and dependants weren't allowed to go with them straight away, and
Jean had a short time alone in Paris. Once she said months, but it
was probably only a week or two; she went, she said, 'long before
I was supposed to.' Once again Germaine came her rescue. 'She told
me that she knew how nervous and lonely I must be,' Jean wrote.
She came to see her every day, she took her to lunch and to the
cinema, she lent her money to buy dresses. The last time they
lunched together she ordered champagne. As Jean drank it Germaine
lectured her in her soft, precise voice on the evils of alcohol. ('But
all the same, it looks nice,' she said. '*Allez*, give me some.')

Then they were at the station, and Jean was stepping on to the
Orient Express. Both Germaine and lovely Madame Bragadier had
come to see her off. They were as kind and generous as ever. They
gave her money for a couchette, and Madame Bragadier whispered,
'I don't like those two men. Be careful if they speak to you.' 'Goodbye,' they said, 'Good-bye,' and Jean saw that they both had tears
in their eyes. She was sad too to be leaving lovely Paris; but she was
too excited to cry. She loved them, she would never forget them,
but *she was going to Vienna.* She climbed into the little bed and slept
to the sound of the train. When she woke up she was in another
country.

★　　　★　　　★

Jean arrived in Vienna in April, 1920. It was an extraordinary time:
the end of an empire that had lasted more than a thousand years.
All that Vienna had left now was its past, its cunning and its pretty
women. It smelt, Jean said, 'of lilacs, of drains and of the past,' 'very
strongly of the past.' 'Gone the "*Aristokraten*",' she wrote in
'Vienne': 'They sat at home rather hungry, while their women did
the washing.'

The atmosphere she stepped into was hectic and abandoned.
Hidden away in the city people were starving, but the ones she met
were making fortunes out of inflation and the black market. She and
John and the others were the conquerors, with foreign currency and
dinners at the Sacher. The pretty Viennese girls (and boys) lined up
to please them and to take their money. John, of course, had to work
during the day: to translate everything into French for Colonel
Miyake, and to help him (Jean said) to be tactful and always vote

with the majority. But in the evenings and weekends their life in Vienna was a round of suppers and parties, night clubs and music halls, restaurants and hotels. It was exciting, happy, alive, 'fantastic'. Jean loved Vienna; she felt strongly while she was there that she was 'seeing the last of something lovely.'

When she arrived the Commission found them a flat: the top floor of a house in the Favoritenstrasse, in the elegant Fourth District. It was an old flat, with large rooms and polished wooden floors; double windows with fat bolsters between them in the winter; a big picture of Emperor Franz Joseph, and smaller ones of the owners. Jean disliked the sitting room, which was too 'gloomy and whiskery and antimacassary'; but she loved the bedroom, with its piano, its Bohemian glass and its little low tables for coffee.

The house belonged to the von Heuskes (who went into 'Vienne' and 'Temps Perdi' as the von Markens). General von Heuske was 'short and sharp' and wore a monocle; Madame von Heuske, fat and smooth-faced, did menial things for them with the 'far-away air' of a lady. There was a son, Wolf; and a daughter, Blanca, who was very young, but engaged to 'a horrible old man' because he was rich and a baron. Jean's feelings about the von Heuskes were like her feelings about their flat. Sometimes they were like the sitting room, gloomy and disapproving (like the time Madame complained about an Apache dancer they'd brought home); but sometimes they were like the bedroom, dignified and charming, with beautiful old-fashioned manners. It didn't occur to her that these were two sides of the same thing. She was too romantic, too lazy, and she could never accept that something she loved or admired could have a dark side too. It would have to be one thing or the other. She would break off the dark side and tell herself that it was something else, not part of the thing she loved at all. She did that with the von Heuskes; she would do it, more dangerously, with herself.

They stayed at the Favoritenstrasse for a year. Part of that time they shared it with someone else: André, secretary to another member of the Japanese delegation.* André was a Parisian, a dandy and a satyr. (It was he who was responsible for the Apache dancer.) He was obsessed with women; he'd stiffen all over like a dog, Jean said, when he saw a pretty girl. 'He lived for women; his father had died of women and so would he. *Voilà tout.*' This combination of love and death, gambling and obsession, appealed to Jean immensely. And when André in 'Vienne' becomes enslaved to Tillie who torments and tricks him, 'Frances's' heart goes out to him. 'I could

---

*André was his real name. His signature was stylishly illegible, but his surname looks like Burnot.

have shaken his hand and said: "Hail, brother Doormat, in a world of Boots."' I'm sure Jean felt just the same about the real André. She saw him very clearly with her novelist's eye, and in 'Vienne' he sounds weak, naive and vain. But she makes you feel his charm; she makes you say, with her, 'Poor André!', and hope that he has better luck next time.

That first year went extraordinarily well. The gay round of entertainment reached its peak on her thirtieth birthday in August, when the Japanese delegation gave a lavish supper party in her honour. She hadn't changed from the little girl who'd sat between her parents, 'bursting with importance,' on her sixth birthday; she loved and remembered this one just as much. They had soup *and* hors d'oeuvres, veal *and* pheasant; ices, cheese, coffee, liqueurs. Afterwards everyone signed her menu, which she kept. At the top are their names, Ella and John; then dozens of illegible signatures, including André's. But proud and perfectly legible are three of the Japanese officers: Lieutenant Colonel Miyake; Lieutenant Colonel Oyaizu; Capitaine Oshima. Jean made Mitsujiro Miyake into Matsijiri in 'Vienne' and Lieutenant Colonel Matsu in 'Temps Perdi': she evidently found him sympathetic, saying in 'Temps Perdi' that he had 'music in him somewhere,' and that on a visit to London he'd spent 'a whole day ... lost in the Inner Circle.' Lieutenant Colonel Oyaizu became Captain Oyazu in 'Temps Perdi', who is also quite harmless. But Yoshi in 'Temps Perdi' and Ishima in 'Vienne' are a different matter. They are cruel to women; and already they are great admirers of the Germans. Jean wouldn't have been surprised by what happened to the real man, Hiroshi Oshima: he became Japanese Ambassador to Germany throughout World War Two, and was sentenced to life imprisonment as a war criminal after it. (It wouldn't have surprised her either that he got off after only a few years).

In the spring of 1921 Frances in 'Vienne' notices that Pierre seems to have more and more money: so much that people are becoming quite 'deferential'. One day they leave their flat for a suite in the Hotel Imperial. Soon they have a car, a chauffeur, a maid; Frances has flowers, dresses and rings. It is 'The Spending Phase'.

Jean didn't like to talk about her own 'Spending Phase', and she refused to write about it in *Smile Please*. 'I am determined not to write about Vienna and what happened there,' she said. This was mostly because she didn't want to 'tell tales' against John; but also, I think, because she couldn't bear to relive one of her greatest disappointments.

It all happened just as it does in 'Vienne' − the Hotel Imperial, Vienna's most luxurious after the Sacher (for which you had to have *old* money); the chauffeur, the maid (who was called Dini), the dresses and rings.... John was doing what 'everyone was doing' in Vienna: making money 'on the 'change'. That is to say, he was selling foreign currency illegally, on the black market: francs and crowns, shillings and yen. In the hyper-inflation of postwar Austria this was hugely profitable. Only a little longer, Pierre says in 'Vienne', and he will 'pull it quite off and we will be rich, rich....'

They'd been poor for so long, separately and together. Of course they both longed to be rich – not to have to worry or borrow, not to have to send another child to a charity hospital. But by now Jean especially had a passion for money, an obsession, almost a worship. Perhaps it had begun that day in her childhood when her mother had cried, and her 'comfortable certainty' about money had ended. Everything in her life since had made it grow and grow, until like Anna's fear in *Voyage in the Dark* 'it filled her and it filled the whole world.' Now at last she had money; and she was as happy as a child, as humble as a lover.

Nice to have lots of money – nice, nice. Good to have a car, a chauffeur, rings, and as many frocks as I liked.

Good to have money, money. All the flowers I wanted. All the compliments I wanted. Everything, everything.

Oh, great god money – you make possible all that's nice in life. Youth and beauty, the envy of women, and the love of men.

Even the luxury of a soul, a character and thoughts of one's own you give, and only you. To look in the glass and think I've got what I wanted.

I gambled when I married and I won.

'I was cracky with joy of life that summer of 1921,' she wrote in 'Vienne'. It was pretty women, music, heat; and 'Poverty gone, the dread of it – going.' As often as she liked she could go for a massage, or to have her face made up like a doll's: and drops in her eyes to make the pupils big and black. It worked. Men gazed at her, they called her '*la poupée de porcelaine de saxe*'. And she had lovely lovely dresses, as many as she wanted. She had two feather-light muslin dresses, one blue and one white, covered with frills. A striped taffeta dress with a tight waistband, a white satin dress and a black one, with three flounces, bordered with green. A dirndl, a check dress, a blue serge dress with a wide skirt and sleeves, and a long loose dress in yellow and blue to lie down in when she was tired. The white satin was the prettiest, and also the cheapest. But her favourites were the muslins, fresh as daisies ... or perhaps, after all, the yellow and blue. 'It was like cornfields and the sky, and looking at it made you feel happy, made you feel free.'

★      ★      ★

Well: almost happy, almost free. She knew that John was taking chances. *All the pretty people with doubtful husbands or no husbands, or husbands in jail,* she wrote in 'Vienne', (*lots of men went to jail — I don't wonder. Every day new laws about the exchange ...* ). Frances has presentiments of disaster. She makes wild plans — to change her life completely, to end it. But she knows that she won't do either of these things. She doesn't *want* to change her life — to work, to wear ugly clothes; she knows 'I could never be poor again with courage or dignity.' 'I've compensations,' she thinks. 'Oh yes, compensations — moments.' And she goes on seizing them. 'Spending and spending. And there was always more.'

In the high summer of 1921 the Commission moved to Budapest. Budapest had a smell too: just drains, without the lilac. But Jean loved it even more than Vienna. It was fascinating, exciting, 'theatrically lovely'. They lived the life she loved, a night life of hotels, restaurants, dancing places. They would dine outside Buda, then drive back to the city in their car, to listen to tzigane orchestras and watch the dancers at the Orpheum. The girls were even lovelier than the Viennese, the gypsy music even more melancholy, like 'the wind over the plain, the hungry cry of the human heart.' To her Budapest was the music, the scented vicious girls, the heat, 'the moon like a white bird in the afternoon sky.' And still spending, spending, spending.

There was so much money that in the autumn Jean went on a visit to London. Perhaps she still had her forebodings, and wanted to escape them; or more likely John did, and wanted her out of the way while he made a last throw at averting a crisis. Or perhaps she just went for fun.

And she had it. This was, she said, 'the only time she liked London.' It was the only time she was rich enough to live in the London of her imagination, 'splendid and tremendous'. She stayed at the Berkeley Hotel opposite the Ritz. There she discovered that she was pregnant again, and was very happy.

What did she do? I think she probably went to see Lancelot, and to show him: the big risk she'd taken had paid off. John wasn't so unsuitable after all. He was rich, she was pregnant, and all was well — wonderfully well. She was about to grasp her dream of the happy woman after all.

And she may have gone to show her family too. For some time in the early 1920s Mrs Rees Williams, Brenda and Auntie B left Dominica for England. There they joined Minna and Auntie Mackie; and together the two generations of women settled in Ealing, in West London. This was the sister who'd predicted disaster for her marriage, the mother who'd predicted disaster for her whole life. If they were already there I'm sure she would have gone to see them. It would have been hard to resist the victory; and there was always a side of her that still wanted to please them.

From 'Vienne':
There was a hard, elegant little sofa in our room, covered with striped, yellow silk — sky-blue cushions. I spent long afternoons lying on that sofa plunged in a placid dream of maternity.

I felt a calm sense of power lying in that dark, cool room, as though I could inevitably and certainly draw to myself all I had ever wished for in life — as though I were mysteriously irresistible, a magnet, a *Femme Sacrée*.

One can become absorbed ... exalted ... lost as it were, when one is going to have a baby, and one is extremely pleased about it.

'I was very happy all the time I was going to have you,' Jean wrote to this child fifty years later. 'I never doubted that everything would be all right.'

'Vienne' again:
One afternoon Pierre said: 'If anyone comes here from the Allgemeine Verkehrsbank you must say that I'm not in and that you don't know when I'll be back.'

Someone called from the Bank — a fat, short man, insisting, becoming rude in bad French. He would see Monsieur. He must see Monsieur. Madame could not say when Monsieur would be back. '*Très bien — très bien.*' He would go to Monsieur's office to make inquiries.

He departed. His back looked square, revengeful — catastrophic — that's the word. I believe that looking at the man's back I guessed everything, foresaw everything.

Ten days later she finds Pierre sitting hunched up on the striped yellow sofa, staring at a revolver in his hand.

In the first version of 'Vienne', published in Ford Madox Ford's *transatlantic review* in 1924, Frances and Pierre are called Ella and John, and Ford has noted: 'From novel called *Triple Sec*.' And in everything they do and say John is utterly John, Ella utterly Ella — utterly Jean. Now she cries, she says 'Oh, put that thing away! How horribly unkind you are to frighten me!' 'Looking rather like a schoolboy,' he tells her that he has 'lost money — other people's money — the Commission's money;' he had tried everything, but it's no good. He has saved four thousand francs for her, and she has her rings; he wants her to save herself, and leave him to put a bullet in his head. He won't wait to be arrested, he won't go to jail in Budapest. He hasn't a chance, he is *fichu*.

'You aren't,' she says. 'Why can't you be a man and fight?' She says that he must not kill himself and leave her alone — 'that I was frightened — that I did not want to die — that somehow I would find the money to pay his debts'..... 'Let's go, let's get away,' she says — her old remedy, escape.

> '... and shut up about killing yourself. If you kill yourself you know what will happen to me?'
> We stared at each other.
> 'You know damn well,' I told him.
> He dropped his eyes and muttered: 'All right — all right! ...'

They plan their escape, speaking in whispers. They have dinner in their room ('paprika, canard sauvage, two bottles of Pommery'). And suddenly he's full of fight again, in one of those quick, complete changes of mood for which she loved him. '*Allons*, Ella, cheer up, he says. '*Au mauvais jeu il faut faire bonne mine.*'

Even so she was so frightened that she drank most of the Pommery, and nearly turned to an English friend for help. 'I've always liked those big men with rather hard blue eyes,' she says. 'I trust them instinctively — and probably wrongly. I opened my mouth to say: "Haughton, this and that is the matter.... I'm frightened to death, really.... What am I to do?" And as I was hesitating John came back.'

In the middle of the night they packed, making as little noise as possible. And at half-past six in the morning they got into their car and drove away.

★ ★ ★

As soon as they were moving she was better. 'There is no doubt that running away on a fresh, blue morning can be exhilarating,' Ella thinks. She begins to plan her 'triumphant return to Hungary with money to pay John's debts. I saw myself sitting at the head of a long table handing little packets of notes to everyone concerned, with the stern countenance of a born business woman: "Will you sign this, please?"'

But now came the first check: an 'unexpected fuss' at the Czech frontier. This time it wasn't passports; John had a Japanese *laissez-passer* from the Commission, and evoked its magic name

('*Kommission* – Kurrier'). What was it, then? 'It was horrible waiting there in the night for what seemed hours, my eyes shut, wondering what jail would be like.' When John came back he was still arguing. He said '*Je m'en fiche*' and yelled to the chauffeur – and they sped into Czechoslovakia illegally. 'I imagined for one thrilling moment that we would be fired on, and the nape of my neck curled itself up.'

But the guards weren't interested in them, the whole thing had had nothing to do with them at all. The frontier had been closed – they learned when they got to Prague – because the ex-emperor, King Charles, was trying to return to Hungary, and Czechoslovakia was mobilising. So we know when John and Ella's flight began: on or just after 20 October 1921.

'Listen, Ella, it's just the best of luck for us, that business of [King] Karl,' John says. 'Nobody will worry about me just now.' And gaily he gives her a present, a pearl necklace in a long box.

> 'John!'
> 'Nice, hé?'
> 'Where did you get them?'
> He did not answer.
> I looked from the pearls to his dark, amused face, and then
> I blushed – blushed terribly, all over my face and neck.

A minute later she clasps the pearls around her neck: 'If we're going the whole hog, let's go it.' But at four o'clock in the morning she lies awake, crying, and won't let him comfort her. 'He had suddenly became a dark stranger who was dragging me over the edge of a precipice.'

'Vienne' ends in Prague, with John and Ella planning to go to Warsaw, London, Liège. Perhaps they did go to Warsaw: there's a stamp saying *Destination Varsovie* on the *passeport à l'étranger* Jean had got in 1920. But she never said anything about the last six months of her pregnancy and flight. We know only the end of it. Around May 1922 they'd planned to be in Italy, but instead found themselves in Belgium. On the twenty-second her baby was born in Ukkel, near Brussels.

It was a little girl, which was what she'd wanted the first time she was pregnant ('Perhaps I will love it if it is a little girl'). But of course what life gave you with one hand it took away with the other. She'd dreamed that it would be so different this time – and it wasn't, it was the same, or even worse. All she could think of was money. When Maryvonne was two weeks old she left her in a clinic and went straight to London to borrow money 'from the only person who, as usual, would give it.' Then she rejoined John at Ostend, and they went to Knokke to rest and recover. They sent money to the clinic so that Maryvonne could stay a little longer. They had no work, nowhere to live, nowhere to keep a baby. There was only one place that might help them.

★      ★      ★

When Jean and John returned to Paris in July or August 1922 they went back to Montmartre, and soon back to their hotel at 10 rue Lamartine. 'She felt that her life had moved in a circle,' Jean would write of Julia. 'She was a defiant flame shooting upwards.... Then the flame sank down again, useless, having reached nothing....' 'That's the way it is,' she would write in *Good Morning, Midnight*, 'that's the way it goes, that's the way it went.... A room. A nice room. A beautiful room.... Up to the dizzy heights of the suite.... Swing high.... Now, slowly, down. A beautiful room.... A nice room. A room.'

They hadn't even fallen back to the point where they'd begun, they'd fallen below it. Jean had a baby she couldn't keep, and John was a fugitive from the law. The only papers he had were the ones supplied by the Japanese – but to be identified as *John Lenglet, secretary to the Interallied Commission* was exactly what he could not afford. With papers or without he was equally in trouble.

Jean knew that the Hungarian police were looking for him. But she didn't know – perhaps John didn't know himself – that the French civil courts were looking for him too. Marie Pollart wanted a divorce.

On 17 October 1922, a process-server called at the rue Lamartine and officially summoned him to '*réintegrer le domicile conjugal*'. John officially declined, saying that he'd been separated from his wife for more than four years; and the divorce process could begin.

The questions, of course, crowd in. Was Jean at home? ... Why hadn't *John* sued for divorce four years before, which if Francine in *Muziek Voorop* is anything like a fair portrait he could easily have done? Why would he still let the whole thing drag on for another three years? Perhaps it was a form of revenge; or just an extreme example of his carelessness and refusal to be bound by the rules.

We'll never know. Jean never said a word about this particular complication in her life. She also said she couldn't remember why John now left Paris, perhaps for Amsterdam. Probably he was having trouble finding work, because of the business of his papers; and he 'always went to Holland when he didn't have a job, didn't know what to do.' And perhaps this *contretemps* of the process-server was the last straw.

He left her, I think, in the care of two friends. One was her old and best friend, Germaine Richelot. What on earth did they tell Germaine about the job with the Commission, which she'd helped John to get? Not the truth, anyway. But here they were back in Paris, and now Germaine would help them very much once more.

But Jean couldn't stay at the rue Rabelais, it seems; in any case she didn't. She went to stay with the second friend instead: Mrs Adam.

Mrs Adam is a familiar name in Jean's story. She was — Jean wrote in *Smile Please* — the wife of *The Times* correspondent in Paris; and the person who, by introducing her to Ford Madox Ford, began her literary career. Now, all this part of Jean's story is full of confusion and misdating — even more than usual. It's because she was trying to cover up so much — John's arrest, and perhaps his divorce; and (most of all, perhaps) the true facts of Maryvonne's early childhood. She succeeded, and it's all still far from clear. But through her smokescreen (and John's) we can see the main outlines.

H. Pearl Adam was a journalist and a writer herself.* Jean had first met her 'at a tea party in London' long ago, just before the War. Then I think they'd met again during the Lenglets' first, brief stay in Paris. John was a journalist, whenever he could get a job; throughout his life journalism was his aim and his profession. Both the Adams were prominent Paris journalists, whom he'd be likely to meet. Then Jean and Mrs Adam would remember having met before — and perhaps John and George Adam too, for Adam had been a correspondent in Paris since 1912, when John had been starting out in journalism there. Indeed I'm sure Jean had known the Adams her first time in Paris, and not only her second, for she always said that George Adam was *The Times* correspondent in Paris: *and this was true only up to 1921.* In January 1921 he left *The Times,* and after

---

*She was the daughter of one of the very first women journalists in England, Mrs C.E. Humphry, who wrote as 'Madge' of *Truth.* Mrs Adam was eight years older than Jean, and had been a journalist since the age of seventeen. She had married George Adam in 1909. Both worked as journalists in Paris during the First War, and Mrs Adam wrote a book about it (*Paris Sees It Through: A Diary 1914*–19). She later worked for the *Evening Standard, Observer* and *Sunday Times,* and for many magazines. She was a hard-working professional, producing commissioned books on subjects like wartime cookery and the British leather industry as well as her regular journalism. She also wrote two books together with her husband. He wrote, apart from his journalism, a biography of Clemenceau (*Consult the Tiger,* 1929) and articles on French subjects for the *Encyclopedia Britannica.*

George Adam died in Paris in 1930 at the early age of forty-seven. Mrs Adam returned to England, and died there in 1957.

that worked mostly for American newspapers. If Jean had only remet Mrs Adam in late 1922 (or even 1924, as her story of the 'diary' implies), she wouldn't have been introduced to him, or therefore thought of him, that way.

When John went to Holland in late 1922, then, Jean went to stay with Mrs Adam. And one day in around November she went to the clinic in Brussels and fetched her daughter. Someone took a photograph of her on the balcony of the Adams' flat on the rue Taitbout, looking happy, with Maryvonne wrapped in a blanket in her arms.

But now what? She had no money left – 'Absolutely none. Not a sou' – and an absent, fugitive husband. What *could* she do? Only accept help. And I think it came from Germaine Richelot. Jean always said that when John was sent to prison Germaine found 'a place' for Maryvonne. But that was two years later, at the end of 1924. Again Jean put up a smokescreen of silence and confusion, because – I think – she didn't want her daughter to know that she'd been forced to give her up long before that final disaster. (But Maryvonne knew anyway.) The truth almost certainly was that Germaine found (and probably helped to pay for) Maryvonne's place now, in late 1922 or early '23.

The rest of what Jean said about this time, however, I think was true. She wouldn't part with her daughter, she said, 'not definitely'; 'I simply said no I will *not* – I don't care what *anybody* says.' 'I stuck to her like glue when she was a baby and refused all "sensible" alternatives.' The main sensible alternative was adoption: 'People had been wanting to adopt her,' Jean said (perhaps that was Germaine, or one of her married sisters, too). Even John thought this a good thing; but she refused. Later he would be very grateful for this; but he was practical, he would see that adoption (especially if it was by rich, kind friends) was a better prospect for his daughter than an endless vista of clinics and absent, penniless parents. Jean was not practical. It was (she said herself) 'partly obstinacy and partly instinct,' but she refused to take the final step of adoption. She preferred the hope of the clinic. She would have to hope for several years.

When she talked about this second stay in Paris she always moved straight from her return after Maryvonne's birth to its two main events, her meeting Ford through Mrs Adam, and John's arrest. But this left out almost two years: all of 1923 and most of 1924. She had to do this, because of Maryvonne – because of pretending, in order to protect them all, that Maryvonne had only had to go into a clinic because John was in prison. And it helped to suggest that that happened soon too. For she always said, in order to protect John, that his arrest was very different from Stephan Zelli's in *Quartet*. Stephan's offence is plain theft, '*escroquerie*'; John's was only to have entered France illegally (and what else could he do, without papers?), and to have partaken in those currency dealings in Vienna (which 'everyone was doing'). And this was much more probable if he were arrested very soon: only say (for Jean was never very clear about it) some months later. Even for 'currency offences' two years was a long time for the police to have kept looking; for 'illegal entry' it was highly unlikely. And in fact John never was caught for his currency dealings in Vienna; he got away with those. What he was arrested for in Paris was very close to Stephan's crime after all.

In 1923 and '24 Jean must have done almost all her Paris jobs — the jobs Sasha remembers in *Good Morning, Midnight*. The first time she came to Paris she'd been six months' pregnant, and only stayed for six months; she only mentions working for the Richelots then,* and I'm sure that was right. From 1925 until she returned to England she was embroiled first with Ford and then with writing, and was in no shape to do a job. She may have worked for the Richelots again, as we shall see; and at that stage she probably did Sasha's job, being a receptionist in a smart dress shop near the Avenue Marigny. But that is about all she could have managed after the débâcle with Ford.

Sasha is not much more successful even in her earlier jobs, and I don't suppose Jean was either. As a saleswoman in an English shop Sasha lasts exactly a week, as an American Express guide exactly a day (and Jean said that an English person 'wouldn't know the prices or anything,' and got hopelessly lost in the Parc Monceau). Sasha gives 'farcical' English lessons; the only ones she suggests aren't farcical are to someone who 'speaks English just as well as I do....' Much of this, of course, is Jean's black humour. But she was anxious, impatient, and really no good at anything but one thing, which she hadn't discovered yet. She exaggerated, I'm sure, as usual; but as usual, I'm sure, she didn't invent very much.

There was only one kind of job (apart from the one she hadn't yet discovered) that she was any good at. That was anything to do with beauty and being looked at: what Al Alvarez has called 'the muse business'. She'd already been an artist's model; and there was (especially in Paris) dress modelling too: being a *mannequin*.

In *After Leaving Mr Mackenzie* Julia has been both an artist's model and a mannequin. 'We stayed at a little place called Coq-sur-Mer, near Ostend,' she says. 'And then I came along to Paris by myself. And

* And one other disaster as a *gouvernante*, which lasted only a day.

then after a while I met this woman, and I started sitting for her.'
She sits for a sculptress called Ruth: and I think Jean sat for a
sculptress too. When *Quartet* came out a picture was published of
a portrait bust of her: *Jean Rhys, a new novelist*, by 'Dreschfelt'. And
'Dreschfelt' was Violet Dreschfeld, an English sculptress who
exhibited in Paris from 1929.

There are several women artists in Jean's Paris novels and stories,
and I think they're all based on Violet Dreschfeld. 'Dreschfeld' is a
(German) Jewish name; 'Ruth' is a Jewish name too, and Miss Esther
De Solla in *Quartet*, who is a painter, *is* Jewish. They are both
English and sensible — as Miss Bruce of 'Illusion' is as well, though
her name isn't Jewish. And they are both 'a bit fanatical', Miss De
Solla 'ascetic to the point of fanaticism,' Ruth with 'something of
the real artist in her,' 'so, of course she was fanatical'. Miss Bruce
and Miss De Solla are similar in other ways too — both tall and
gaunt and masculine, both called 'Mademoiselle', both with sudden
bouts of illness.... And Ruth and Esther De Solla both seem to
promise comfort to the heroine. Marya runs to Miss De Solla when
Stephan is arrested ('Her mind clung desperately to the thought of
Miss De Solla's calm, her deep and masculine voice'); Julia tells her
story to Ruth, wanting her to understand. But in the end both let
the heroine down. Ruth doesn't believe Julia; when Marya tells Miss
De Solla she's living with the Heidlers she looks 'uneasy', and says
'I must be getting along.' All this, I am sure, went on (or seemed
to Jean to go on) between her and Violet Dreschfeld in 1923
and '24.

Being a mannequin was probably her best job in these years. Sasha
worked 'at the Maison Chose in the Place Vendôme'; Anna in the
*Left Bank* story 'Mannequin' works '*chez* Jeanne Veron, Place
Vendôme'. Jean's shop wouldn't have been very far away. Anna gets
the job because of her legs ('It was to her legs that she owed this
dazzling, this incredible opportunity'); and Jean had very lovely,
slender legs. But really all of her was lovely — Lancelot had said so,
and 'Tommie'. She was proud of her body; and as long as she was
young, wearing a beautiful dress, and didn't have to speak, she was
happy, even eager, to be looked at. Later, when she was old and
shabby (or thought she was) it would be a nightmare, just because
when she was young it was such a happy dream. At *déjeuner* in
'Mannequin' the saleswomen and sewing girls secretly watch Anna
and the others, 'with their sensual, blatant charms and their painted
faces,' where they sit 'envied and apart'. Just for once — as so briefly
in Vienna and Budapest — Jean was among the privileged, among the
possessors of what everybody wanted.

And the 'atmosphere of slimness and beauty' suited her. Here everyone worshipped money, artifice and feminine beauty; here everyone sat in front of the mirror for hours, and took hours to make up and dress. Here was the same poignant mixture of romance and tawdriness as in the musical comedies of long ago, and in the popular songs which haunted her, 'Valse Bleue', 'La Vie en Rose'. Here was, perhaps, the life conjured up for her by those mysterious words *fille de joie* when she was sixteen. Just this combination had thrilled her then – the fantasy of worship for *La Femme*, 'the most beautiful thing in the world and the most powerful'; and the reality of her powerlessness, her being a plaything, bought for money. It had also frightened and repelled her; but the fear and repulsion were part of the excitement, as they had been in her long dream of Mr Howard.

And the language of the place had a poetry for her. It made her think of poetry, it made her write poetry. The mannequins' types, for instance: the *gamine*, the *garconne*, the *femme fatale*, the *jolie laide* with the 'chic of the devil'; and Anna's own type, the *jeune fille*, the innocent, vulnerable girl. 'There is, of course, an English manne-quin,' she wrote in *Good Morning, Midnight*, '"kind, kind and gentle is she" – and that's another damned lie. But she is very beautiful – "*belle comme une fleur de verre*". And the other one, the little French one whom I like so much, she is "*Belle comme une fleur de terre* ...".'

Even this job, though, Sasha keeps for only three months; 'I got bored,' she says. And Anna thinks: 'I won't be able to stick it.' She is exhausted; the white and gold walls seem to close in on her. She has to fight 'an intense desire to rush away. Anywhere!' But she sticks it, at least for her first day. And at six o'clock she is 'out in the rue de la Paix':

> ... Her fatigue forgotten, the feeling that now she really belonged to the great, maddening city possessed her and she was happy in her beautifully cut tailor-made and a beret.
> Georgette passed her and smiled; Babette was in a fur coat.
> All up the street the mannequins were coming out of the shops, pausing on the pavements a moment, making them as gay and as beautiful as beds of flowers before they walked swiftly away and the Paris night swallowed them up.

And what about John – where was he? Julia comes to Paris alone, having been divorced and lost her child. Enno is with Sasha, except when he leaves her for two days; but there is a prospect of her having her baby alone, because a job may take him away. Then after the baby is born and dies he too leaves her for good.

In reality John had probably not left Jean even for a few days during their first stay in Paris; and they were still together now. Nevertheless this idea that the heroines are alone in Paris may be based on something real in the Lenglets' second stay. John went away for some unknown time towards the end of 1922, as we know. Then he came back again: but still he may have spent a good deal of time out of Paris. For he probably worked, for part of the time at least, for a paper called *Le Petit Parisien,* as their correspondent for 'mid-France'. I expect he was pleased, for it was a job, and a job in journalism. But perhaps he was worried too. For he knew Jean very well by now; and she'd already warned him what would happen if he left her alone. At the end of *Quartet* Marya says to Stephan: 'You left me all alone without any money. And you didn't care a bit what happened to me. Not really, not deep down, you didn't.' In the novel she can only be referring to his imprisonment, and it makes her seem very cruel. But perhaps John did leave Jean alone in Paris with little or no money sometimes, or often, in 1923 and '24. Perhaps that's why Julia and Sasha feel so alone; perhaps it's why Marya was so ready to turn to Heidler, and Jean so ready to turn to Ford.

# CHAPTER FIVE

# Ford, 1924–1927

*The meeting — The start of the affair — The Chateau Juan-les-Pins
— The end of the affair — Afterwards*

Whatever their jobs, and however long they kept them, they did not make enough money. John got very depressed, Jean said, 'but I persisted in being hopeful. I notice that when things go very badly, I invariably am.' So one day she thought of a new idea: John should write some articles, she'd translate them into English, and they'd try to sell them to some English paper or magazine.

John wrote three articles: 'My House', about (she said) 'a house in the country where he longed to live'; 'The Chevalier of the Place Blanche'; and a piece called 'The Poet'. I wonder what Jean thought as she translated this last one. For 'The Poet' is about an outcast and vagabond who was once a celebrated poet, but who ever after falling in love has been unable to write a word. He's an old man now, and begs a living by selling to passers-by the book he wrote when he was young. The narrator buys a copy. When he opens it he sees a couplet on the first page:

ADVICE TO BACHELORS
*If you'd be happy all your lives
See that you take to yourselves no wives.*

'The other pages,' John wrote, 'were blank.'

'I had brought one pretty dress from Vienna,' Jean says in *Smile Please*. 'I put this on and took the articles to the Continental *Daily Mail*.' But the *Daily Mail* weren't interested; so 'Then,' she said, 'I thought of Mrs Adam.'

It seems odd that she hadn't thought of her before, rather than braving strange people in a strange office. And it also seems odd that sometimes she left out the Continental *Daily Mail* altogether, and said only that she went to Mrs Adam. The reason for the oddness is that she wasn't telling the truth. Whichever way she told the story she left out the main thing, which was that she'd remet Mrs Adam not now, but two years before. She had to leave this out, as part of her cover-up for Maryvonne; but it made the story hard to remember, and rather implausible. The idea of Jean bearding strangers when not absolutely necessary is implausible enough; but the next part of the story is worse. Mrs Adam, she wrote, said she'd try to help with John's articles, but didn't hold out much hope; and then she asked: 'Have you ever written anything yourself?' That is surely an odd question to ask a near-stranger who's merely translated some not very sellable articles of her husband's. But if in fact you have known the woman for several years, if she's lived in your house, you might easily know that she sometimes writes obsessively in a diary; and you might easily say, 'But what about that diary of yours?'

However it happened, Mrs Adam did now ask to see Jean's diary, or diary-novel. Jean hesitated; and again not quite as she tells it in *Smile Please*. For she didn't have just the three and a half exercise books she'd written in 1914, but everything she'd written since — about Vienna, probably about Budapest, possibly right up to the present day. 'I told myself not to be such a fool, all that was finished,' she says in *Smile Please*. But it wasn't finished; perhaps it would even be dangerous to John to show parts of it to people. And perhaps Jean removed those parts before she did. Then she left the notebooks with the concierge, instead of taking them up herself. 'I thought,' she said, 'that Mrs Adam probably got a lot of manuscripts and letters, and if mine was forgotten, well, that would be fate and would have nothing to do with me.' More likely she thought that if hers was *remembered* it would be fate, and have nothing to do with her.

And hers was remembered. More than that: Mrs Adam liked it. That was the real intercession of her fate, for it wasn't very likely. Even the *Triple Sec* we have now, edited by Mrs Adam herself, is pretty formless, its grammar and punctuation wild, its expression — as Mrs Adam noticed — naive. And its content was (as one of the first people to see it would say) 'unpublishably sordid'. Mrs Adam was a down-to-earth woman and a journalist; but on the other hand her own life was sheltered, her own style solid, conventional and slow. And yet she did see through its hasty, artless surface and dubious content to the gifted writer beneath.... In fact, sensible, very English Mrs Adam must have had a secret taste for romance. She was forty-two, and childless; a stout, round-faced woman who often wished she were thinner and prettier. Instead she mothered thin and pretty young girls. She'd already mothered Jean herself, when she'd taken her into the rue Taitbout. And she was *au fait*, she knew about the *avant garde*. She knew exactly where to take such racy, daring stuff: to Ford Madox Ford, famous editor of *The English Review*, discoverer and champion of such wild and shocking young men as D.H. Lawrence and Wyndham Lewis.

Jean had never heard of Ford, and Mrs Adam had to explain. He was famous for helping young expatriate writers, she said. Jean thought: 'Expatriate? Expatriate from where?' But she agreed. Mrs Adam cut and edited the notebooks; she divided the story into Parts and Chapters, each headed with a man's name. She gave the result a title: *Suzy Tells*. Then she sent it to Ford.

In April Ford had published *Some Do Not*, the first in his great tetralogy, *Parade's End*. Since then he'd poured all his energies into *the transatlantic review*. The *review* published everyone – Joyce, Pound, Hemingway, Gertrude Stein, Dorothy Richardson, Djuna Barnes, Paul Valéry, Philippe Soupault, and dozens of others, all *avant garde*, almost all young, most quite unknown. Ford loved it; but everything that could go practically and financially wrong with it did. By October it was already dying.

Stella Bowen, the Australian painter who lived with Ford, wrote that after 'any big creative effort' he needed 'refreshment'. In particular he needed 'to exercise his sentimental talents from time to time upon a new object. It keeps him young. It refreshes his ego. It restores his belief in his powers.' He met Jean in the autumn, probably in October; at the end of that month he began *No More Parades*.

It was Beauty and the Beast. Jean was thirty-four and looked twenty; she was slender and delicate, *la jeune fille*. Ford was fifty, fat and wheezing. He looked like Humpty Dumpty, someone said – a walrus, said Gertrude Stein, Falstaff (Robert McAlmon), an 'animated adenoid' (Norman Douglas). But he had no trouble with women, as Joyce noticed.

> *O Father O'Ford you've a masterful way with you,*
> *Maid, wife and widow are wild to make hay with you....*

In fact Ford was exactly the sort of man Jean always fell for. He was just like Haughton in 'Vienne' ('I've always liked those big men with rather hard blue eyes. I trust them instinctively – and probably wrongly'); just like Mr Sims in 'Let Them Call it Jazz': '*Some men when they are there you don't worry so much.*' 'He was a rock of a man with his big shoulders and his quiet voice,' she wrote of Heidler in *Quartet*. And if underneath there was someone who could be as anxious, as lonely, as neurasthenic as she – then she was really lost, as she'd been with Lancelot. It was Ford's extraordinary sensitivity and understanding that really caught her: his sensitivity like a woman's (like Germaine's), his understanding like a novelist's. Marya feels 'passionately grateful' to Heidler at their first meeting because he alone sees she's ill and close to tears. And when finally he takes her in his arms, she whispers that he doesn't understand. 'Oh, yes, I do, my dear,' he says. 'Oh, yes, I do.'

He was older than her; he was calm, authoritative, sympathetic. And he was an English gentleman. Well: not quite, not really. Really he was middle-class, half-German, with a shifting, troubled, far from respectable past. In fact he was something more dangerous to her than a real English gentleman: a believer, like her, in the myth of one. His greatest literary creation was the ideal Englishman, the brave, selfless, honourable Good Soldier. And he tried to create the Good Soldier in himself as well. He failed, badly (as in the end his heroes Edward Ashburnham and Christopher Tietjens fail too). But he loved the fantasy, and so did Jean. It was like her dream-life with Lancelot, all over again: except that Ford was an artist, and briefly he must have made it seem even more perfect and more beautiful than the real thing.

No wonder she believed in fate; no wonder she felt that her life went in a circle, or endlessly up and down, reaching nothing. For she always fell in love with men like Ford; and he always fell in love with girls like her. Just as much as she — perhaps even more — Ford had 'an emotional programme that he was driven to act out many times.' ('I'm sick of myself,' Heidler says. 'One knows that the whole damn thing's idiotic, futile, not even pleasant, but one goes on. One's caught in a sort of trap, I suppose.')

Ford would need, and find, a strong, intelligent, capable woman, often an artist in her own right. Then, as soon as he 'had someone to lean on, he would sally forth in search of someone who needed to lean on *him*'. He'd done it long before the War, for example, when he was supposed to marry Violet Hunt, and at the same time invited a girl called Gertrud Schlabowsky to live with him 'and be respectable'. And 'he always said' (Violet Hunt wrote) 'that she was the thirteenth to whom he had made the proposition.'*

Gertrud Schlabowsky could almost have been Jean. She was a 'poor pathetic victim of life' whom he wanted to rescue and make happy. She was 'faint', silent and shy, and also 'bored, pining and discontented'. She was 'a lazy Slav type' who wanted 'luxury, gaiety, new clothes'; she didn't do the housework Ford gave her, but spent all day manicuring her nails. She looked like a beautiful pale Russian

---

*Violet Hunt (1862-1942) was a novelist herself, daughter of the artist Alfred William Hunt. She met Ford in 1908, when he was the editor of *The English Review*, and their affair lasted till 1910. She wrote a book, *The Flurried Years*, which is largely about Ford (published in 1926–7). Her portrait of him is very like Stella Bowen's in *her* book, *Drawn From Life*.

princess, with a white moonface, a wide red mouth and a 'short Calmuck nose.' Marya too is a 'Slav type'; and in *Quartet* Heidler suddenly sees her face upside down, so that her cheekbones look 'higher and more prominent, the nostrils wider, the lips thicker. A strange little Kalmuck face.' 'Kalmuck' must have been Ford's word; and for a moment he himself saw how he kept picking the same girl.

Ten years before his affair with Jean (but five years after the one with Gertrud Schlabowsky) Ford wrote his greatest novel, *The Good Soldier*; and it was the anatomy of their affair laid bare, predicted, understood. Edward Ashburnham is married to Leonora, who is strong and beautiful, and who alone saves him from squandering the inheritance he loves. But he does not love her, 'because she was never mournful; what really made him feel good in life was to comfort somebody who would be darkly and mysteriously mournful.' Instead he loves a series of mournful girls, each time with the 'intense, optimistic belief that she was the one he was destined, at last, to be eternally constant to.' He loves a servant girl, a Spanish dancer, a brother officer's wife; and poor little Maisie Maidan, who dies young, smiling in the light of the mortuary candles. ('A man always liked a woman to be slightly ailing,' Ford told Stella, 'so that she might be the more dependent upon his protection.')

Then at last comes the great passion of his life: a girl just out of convent school, his wife's ward, whom has has brought up as his daughter since the age of thirteen. She is the child of a violent father and an alcoholic mother. She is vivid, upright, full of gaiety; but she is also afraid, tormented by dreadful dreams, and she has a 'tortured mouth' and 'agonised eyes'. Against every law of their world and the whole force of their wills, Edward and Nancy fall desperately in love. But they obey law and will, and resist. In the end Edward kills himself; and Nancy, like Jean's Antoinette Cosway, lies in his beautiful English house, quite mad.

Ford's first Leonora was his wife, Elsie Martindale. But that had ended long ago. By 1924 he'd been with the next one, Stella Bowen, for six years. She was just what he needed — young, strong, practical, and utterly dedicated to him, with a small inheritance she was very willing to put into their life together. But six years was a long time for Ford, who never started a book or a love affair (said Violet Hunt) 'that he did not lose interest in before he came to *finis*.'

'Of the question of the sex instinct,' says Dowell, the narrator of *The Good Soldier*, 'I know very little and I do not think that it counts for very much in a truly great passion.' ('A cold, patient man, without fire,' wrote Violet Hunt; 'He wasn't a good lover, of course,' Marya says, 'He didn't really like women.')

... But the real fierceness of desire, the real heat of a passion long continued and withering up the soul of a man is the craving for identity with the woman that he loves.... For, whatever may be said of the relation of the sexes, there is no man who loves a woman that does not desire to come to her for the renewal of his courage, for the cutting asunder of his difficulties. And that will be the mainspring of his desire for her. We are all so afraid, we are all so alone, we all so need from the outside the assurance of our own worthiness to exist.

So, for a time, if such a passion come to fruition, the man will get what he wants. He will get the moral support, the encouragement, the relief from the sense of loneliness, the assurance of his own worth. But these things pass away; inevitably they pass away as the shadows pass across sundials. It is sad, but it is so. The pages of the book will become familiar; the beautiful corner of the road will have been turned too many times. Well, this is the saddest story.

There is one thing *Quartet* leaves out of the meeting between Marya and Heidler, though it was the thing that had brought Jean and Ford together: *Suzy Tells*. It was a lot to leave out; it was almost everything. For writing was Ford's real passion, and because of him it became hers.

Jean wasn't just another melancholy girl to Ford, because he saw straight away that she was a natural, completely original writer, and he set himself to help her. And Ford wasn't just another powerful protector, or even just another understanding lover, to Jean. '*Men have spoilt me — always disdaining my mind and concentrating on my body*,' she wrote in 'Vienne'. That was true even of Lancelot. But not of Ford. He did concentrate on her body — she would have been very worried and mortified if he hadn't. But he concentrated on her mind too. He talked to her, he taught her, he took her seriously. He was the first man since her father who told her that she was good at something. And unlike her father he showed her, at last, what it really was.

★   ★   ★

Ford set her to write short stories. At first they had (she said) 'melodramatic endings': 'Ford stopped that and told me to write about what I knew.' He taught her to cut; he taught her never to tell, only to show. He made her read French novels. He told her if she wasn't sure of a passage to translate it into French: 'If it looked utterly silly one got rid of it.' He pushed her, he gave her a discipline.

If a story wasn't working, he said, put it away — but write another.

'I can't think of any,' I said sulkily.
'Then try to translate one of my books into French. It will be very good practice for you.'
'I don't know French well enough to translate one of your books,' I said.
'Then try *La Maison de Claudine*. Bring me the first chapter tomorrow.'

By the time Jean met him *the transatlantic review* was sinking fast, and he'd begun to lose interest in it. He wrote, as always, for several solid hours every day; the rest of the time he gave to social life. This too he made Jean share. She came to drink in the Dôme, the Deux Magots, the Closerie des Lilas; she came to eat in the Nègre de Toulouse, where M. and Mme Lavigne kept a little back room for Ford and his friends. Every Thursday Stella gave a tea party at the *review*'s offices on the Quai d'Anjou; every Friday Ford gave a party at a *bal musette* on the rue du Cardinal Lemoine, 'a steep and twisting old street behind the Panthéon'. Marya isn't happy at Lois's Thursdays, and no doubt Jean disliked Stella's. But she should have liked the Bal du Printemps. It was like the Crabtree Club, with rough tables and wooden benches painted scarlet, 'and the walls round the dance floor were set with mirrors and painted pink, with garlands'. On a small gallery sat the accordion player, working up a rhythm (said Stella Bowen) 'that positively lifts you off the floor'.
Stella thought it very daring. You had conversations like this: '"I love an accordion," you say. He, "So do I. I have a beauty at home, in carved ivory and pink silk. My wife gave it to me the first time she was unfaithful to me."' But Jean said 'The Bal du Printemps is a family ball. If you want something *louche* you walk further on'....
Stella said it was 'a public spot' and you never knew who would be there; but really the owner was tipped 'to give preferential treatment to the friends of Monsieur Ford'. So it was the same crowd — 'Mr Rolls and Mr Boyes', as Jean said in *Quartet*, 'Swansea Grettle', 'Miss Lola Hewitt'....
Ford said he wanted his 'painfully shy' writers to 'be drawn from their shells and establish contacts' with each other. But he underestimated Jean's shyness. She would never in her life 'establish contacts', especially with other writers: not in Paris in the twenties, and not in London in the thirties either. Now she came to Ford's parties, she went with him to meet Hemingway, Gertrude Stein and Alice B. Toklas. But she was so shy she hardly ever spoke: a bit to

Alice Toklas, but not at all (she said) to Hemingway.* 'Ford's girl,'
Nina Hamnett said: 'Good-looking girl. She didn't speak much.' She
was so shy people hardly noticed her. But she noticed them all right.
'Everything — even sin — was an affair of principle and uplift if you
were American, and of proving conclusively that you belonged to
the upper classes, but were nevertheless an anarchist, if you were
English.' In the end Ford's *bal musette* was killed, Stella said, by
people who came to gape at it, especially by 'English women in
evening dress, who thought it fun to go slumming in Paris'. But to
Jean that described Ford's friends themselves; and most of all Stella.

Yet Stella's life and opinions were surprisingly like Jean's. She'd
grown up in Australia when it was still 'a suburb of England'. She
had been equally full of romantic expectations and equally
disappointed. She too found London dismal and cruel; she too loved
Paris, with its 'quick and brilliant life', its knowledge of how to live,
its real understanding and admiration for women. She too felt
insecure. Ford never had any money, and was always giving away
what he had; and though she was known as 'Mrs Ford' they weren't
married. She'd broken away from bourgeois life too; and she too was
an artist.

And yet she was completely different. She had her own bit of
money. She could keep her daughter, even have someone to help take
care of her. Unfortunately for her, she was sensible and strong, and

---

*People say that Cairn in *Quartet* is Hemingway, but this is quite wrong.
Cairn is clearly a friend of Marya's, while Jean scarcely knew Hemingway.
Cairn was someone else altogether: Ivan Bede, a young American writer
of short stories, and Ford's assistant on the *transatlantic review* after Basil
Bunting. Jean actually calls Cairn 'a writer of short stories'. He is an
'imaginative and slightly sentimental young man' in 'horn spectacles'; Ivan
Bede, according to Ford, 'wore large, myopic spectacles in front of
immense dark eyes,... and boasted of his Indian blood and the severe
vastnesses that had enveloped his childhood' (he was a Middle Westerner
from Nebraska). In an unpublished fragment called 'And Paris, Sinister'
Jean writes of being in a restaurant with 'Beede', who says of Paris 'It
gets you too much. It's too sweet, too poignant.' Cairn finds Marya 'the
type he liked', and makes several impulsive gestures of sympathy and
generosity towards her, including an offer to borrow 500 francs for her.
In the end he is too 'calm', 'clever' and 'cautious', or Marya thinks he
is, and she withdraws from him ('There he was, incapable of helping.
Before she had walked three steps from the Closerie des Lilas she had
forgotten all about him'). When Heidler says she must 'cut him out' she
agrees without a fight. But Ivan Bede went on knowing Jean until the
thirties. He was, I think, quite an important friend to her during the affair
with Ford, and I am glad to have rescued him from the confusion with
Hemingway.

no one ever 'showed the slightest disposition to allow me to be helpless'. And though she thought she had emancipated herself from the 'inhibitions of Adelaide' she hadn't really. Jean's world was a revelation to her. She tried to be fair to it; she *was* fair to it. She accepted much of what Jean taught her: 'You can't have self-respect without money. You can't even have the luxury of a personality. To expect people who are destitute to be governed by any considerations whatever but money considerations is just hypocrisy.' But Jean would only hate her more for this English fairness, this English intelligence which stopped far short of sympathy. For of course it did stop short of sympathy. A 'period of lawlessness is almost a necessity if you want to qualify as an adult human being,' Stella said; but 'a good many of the weaker brethren stay in the gutter far too long.' And the virtues of the gutter, daring and gallantry, were 'more attractive..., no doubt, than patience or honesty or fortitude'; but really they were 'a rather feeble and egotistical kind of anarchism'. Stella was intelligent and generous; but she was not soft, and not patient. 'Lois was extremely intelligent,' Jean wrote in *Quartet*. 'And, in spite of all this, or because of it, she gave a definite impression of being insensitive to the point of stupidity – or was it insensitive to the point of cruelty? Which? That was the question.'

Earlier in the year the Fords' lease on their studio in the Boulevard Arago had expired, and they had moved into a small apartment on the rue Denfert-Rochereau. Then that had had to be given up too, and for the next year they seem to have camped in Stella's painting studio. This must have been where Jean came to live with them: 'a big, high-ceilinged room, sparsely furnished, dimly lit,' she wrote in *Quartet* . At the same time Stella had found a cottage in the country, an hour away from Paris, where she installed her daughter Julie and her nanny. Every week-end Ford and Stella, or sometimes Stella alone, went to the cottage at Guermantes to visit Julie.

This was the cottage at 'Brunoy' in *Quartet*, where Marya has her fight with Heidler at the turning point of their affair. It was a small stone labourer's cottage in a little orchard. It had only four rooms; but soon Stella rented 'a primitive kind of annexe' too, with a beamed ceiling and an open fireplace, which became Ford's study. 'Nearly every weekend the Heidlers went down to a country cottage they had found near Brunoy on the way to Fontainebleau,' Jean wrote in *Quartet*. 'Twice Marya went with them.'

In December the twelfth and last number of *the transatlantic review* appeared. It had poems by Tristan Tzara and Havelock Ellis; prose by Ford, Hemingway, Gertrude Stein, Nathan Asch, Robert McAlmon and Ivan Bede; and six pages (up to the end of 'The

Spending Phase') of 'Vienne'. Ford had changed the title of the 'novel' from which it was taken from *Suzy Tells* to *Triple Sec*, and the author's name from Ella Lenglet to Jean Rhys. She was a published writer.

Jean was free to become a writer in the autumn of 1924 because John had a job. Whenever he couldn't get a newspaper job he used his language skills, to be spy, secretary to Colonel Miyake, tutor, travel guide. Now he got a job with a travel agency called Exprinter, on the rue de Scribe, near the Opéra.

In 'The Chevalier of the Place Blanche' the Chevalier too works in a 'Tourist Office'.* 'I cheat Americans before they have time to cheat me,' he says. But he's not really joking. 'He had waited his opportunity there for three long months,' the narrator tells us; and finally it had come.

.... A cheque for thirty thousand francs had disappeared to be converted, as he knew only too well, into a couple of Impressionist pictures fabricated by a friend of his, and several new suits of clothes.

But something has gone wrong. 'He had not resold the pictures as profitably as he had hoped and he would have to give an account of the cheque much sooner than he had expected,' says the narrator of 'The Chevalier'. The hero of John's novel *Sous les Verrous* has taken 20,000 francs, and he too knows *'C'est fini. Je l'ai su pendant des semaines.'* He doesn't tell his wife. *'J'ai été seul à porter cette crainte,'* he says, *'ne voulant pas en parler à Stania.'*

On 28 December John was arrested at their hotel, 20 rue de l'Arrivée. Exprinter accused him of having stolen 23,421 francs, which he'd been given for transactions on their behalf. This was *abus de confiance*, a 'premeditated felony' for which the French penal code laid down a minimum sentence of two months and a maximum of two years.

In *Quartet* Marya is out when Stephan is arrested, and the police do not let him leave a message for her. In *Sous les Verrous* Jan is arrested when he comes in, and the police do not let him go upstairs to tell Stania. In both novels the husband and wife are unable to reach each other for several days. Marya thinks, 'I haven't much

---

*Jean said that this was one of the 'articles' John wrote for her to translate and sell before she met Ford. The story of the Chevalier's crime must therefore have been added later – no doubt by Jean ('a much-adapted translation'), in a characteristic effort to tell the truth, and to write out a terrible experience, in fiction.

money, either. This is a beautiful muddle I'm in.' Jan feels neither worry about his future nor remorse about his past. '*Toute ma misère est dans la pensée de ce que va faire Stania, de ce qu'elle va devenir.*'

All four participants wrote about what happened during the next two years. Jean wrote *Quartet*. John wrote *Sous les Verrous*. (Later Jean translated, cut and edited this to become *Barred*, which is in effect, therefore, by both of them.) Ford wrote a novel called *When the Wicked Man*. And Stella wrote an autobiography called *Drawn from Life*, which naturally includes an account of the end of her life with Ford.

Everyone blamed everyone else, and saw himself or herself as the main victim. Jean blamed the Fords, especially Stella: like Marya she didn't want to go and live with them, but like Lois Stella insisted. And in *Quartet* at least she blamed John, making Stephan say 'You must go, Mado; it seems to me so much the best thing for you to do. Look here, you must go.' In *Sous les Verrous* John also blames Madame as much as Monsieur 'Hübner', warning Stania against both from the start, saying that Madame Hübner will deliver Stania up to her husband in order to keep him, and writing bitterly about her '*complaisance horrible*'. And of course he blames Stania, with her '*indolence constante*', her '*indécision chronique*' and her '*passivité inébranlable*': '*une seule semaine de misère peut suffir à perdre Stania*'. Ford's novel is one of his failures, so bad that it's hard to tell what he wants to achieve. He also complicates things by adding a fifth character, another woman. But in his portrait of the vampiric, alcoholic Creole journalist Lola Porter he is clearly blaming (and taking cruel revenge on) Jean. Stella, of course, agrees.

Now Ford, Jean and John were all three novelists, fantasists and sometimes plain liars. And Ford and Jean were perhaps the two greatest artists of self-pity in English fiction, never more so than in *When the Wicked Man* and *Quartet*. Stella was the only one who was not a novelist; and the only one who claimed, at least, not to be writing fiction but the truth. She was an interested party; but she was also a fair and honest person, and everyone who has studied this tangled affair* agrees that she is its most reliable witness. But the

*First Thomas C. Moser in *The Life in the Work of Ford Madox Ford*, Princeton 1980. Then, more fully, Paul Delany in 'Jean Rhys and Ford Madox Ford: What "Really" Happened?' in *Mosaic*, Fall 1983. Most recently and most fully, Martien Kappers den Hollander in 'A Gloomy Child and its Devoted Godmother', *Autobiographical and Biographical Writing in the Commonwealth*, 1984, and 'Measure for Measure: *Quartet* and *When the Wicked Man*', in the *Jean Rhys Review*, Spring 1988.

trouble is that she deals with it only briefly and generally; and only with character and feeling, not at all with events. For those we have to go back to the novels. That is a risky business; but we do have something to help us. John was a journalist, not an artist like Jean and Ford. He lacked their creative imagination, and their passion (especially Jean's) for form and flow, which ruthlessly eliminated any mere fact unless it 'fitted'. He was angry and bitter, but he cared about facts. He often stuck to them — giving Jan exactly his sentence for exactly his offence, for instance; he stuck to them, I think, even when they were awkward, so that Jan's moves after prison are complicated because (probably) his were. As a result *Sous les Verrous* is often cumbrous and confusing — while *Barred*, in which Jean once again brings facts to heel, is a smoother, clearer, better novel. But the less good novel is probably a better guide to what really happened.

What happens in *Sous les Verrous* is that Stania's rich friend Mathilde Dubar comes to her rescue first, renting a room for her in a hotel, and taking her for a rest to her villa outside Paris. The Hübners raise money for her; but so far that's all.

Surely this happened: for surely 'Mathilde Dubar' was Germaine Richelot. It's impossible to imagine Germaine *not* helping Jean now. And Ford and Stella may have been away at the start: they left Paris for the south of France during the next two winters, and may have done so briefly during this one. For the first month John was in the Santé, on the Boulevard Arago; perhaps, then, Jean visited him there from Germaine's hotel. Then on 10 February, 1925, he was tried, convicted and sentenced to eight months' imprisonment, and moved to the prison at Fresnes, just outside Paris.

In *Sous les Verrous* Stania simply tells Jan just before he leaves for Fresnes that Hübner has raised some money for her, and *'Alors, je vais habiter chez lui.'* In *Quartet* Lois comes to see Marya a few days after Stephan's arrest; she issues the invitation, and says 'I want to help you. I'll be awfully disappointed and hurt if you don't allow me to.' In *When the Wicked Man* Lola Porter's husband doesn't go to jail: he commits suicide, because Notterdam, the hero and Ford-figure, has withdrawn an ill-advised, practically lifelong contract to publish his books. Therefore Notterdam feels guilty from the start. Then Lola begs for help 'in her soft stealthy voice'. She shows him that they have no food in their squalid flat, and hardly any clothes 'except for their dress things'; she clings to his arm, she shivers, her teeth chatter, she catches one of his hands and kisses it 'continuously', 'as if she had been a slave'. Notterdam has already been fascinated by her ('He wondered with increasing curiosity what could be behind that smile ... How could you find out? ... no doubt by making love to her'). The thought that 'this beautiful, flashing little creature was actually starving' makes a 'shuddering' impression on him; and he finds he has 'actually promised to take her home and have his wife look after her'.

According to Stella, Jean was 'very pretty and gifted', but 'on the other side of the balance were bad health, destitution, shattered nerves, an undesirable husband, lack of nationality, and a complete absence of any desire for independence ... She was down to her last three francs and she was sick.' Stella doesn't say how or why; simply 'She lived with us for many weeks whilst we tried to set her on her feet.'

For the first many days, perhaps weeks, everyone was quiet, careful, distant. Heidler never looks at Marya; his 'cautious glances' slide over her, he is 'the remote impersonal male of the establishment.' Lola Porter keeps to her bedroom, or lies quietly on a chaise longue in the sun; at dinner she is 'as limp as if her limbs were of India rubber'; after it she immediately returns to her room for the night. In *Quartet* Marya models for Lois, and spends 'long, calm afternoons' listening to her talking about 'Love, Childbirth (especially childbirth, for the subject fascinated her), Complexes, Paris, Men, Prostitution, and Sensitiveness, which she thought an unmitigated nuisance.' In *When the Wicked Man* Notterdam suggests that Lola should get out and 'take a little air and day-time exercise', but his wife tells him that she 'dared not shew herself by day, for her daytime clothes were mere rags'. 'Ford gave her invaluable help with her writing', Stella wrote in *Drawn From Life*, 'and I tried to help her with her clothes.'

They continue to go around Montparnasse together. In *Sous les Verrous* Stania is so busy with the Hübners that she rarely writes to Jan, just '*quelques nouvelles vagues*' on the cheap lined paper of the '*petits bars de Montparnasse*'. When she comes to see him she says that the Hübners are both '*très gentils pour moi*', and Jan smiles bitterly. In *Quartet* Marya says to Cairn 'They've been nice to me, you know, wonderfully nice.' Cairn flashes her 'a quick, curious look'; 'Ah, Marya mia ...,' he says. 'Well, that's all right, then.' 'When she wishes to do a foolish thing she sees quite clearly in front of her what is going to happen,' John wrote in *Sous les Verrous*, and Jean translated for *Barred*. '[But she] disdains consequences. She sacrifices everybody who may suffer, starting with herself.'

The fifth character in *When the Wicked Man* is Henrietta Felise, who becomes Notterdam's real love. No one has paid much attention to her, because Lola Porter is so clearly Ford's vengeful version of Jean. Henrietta Felise may be partly based on Ford's next (and equally brief) love, René Wright; in any case she is once again that recurring ideal of his own imagination, the fragile, mournful, mysterious girl. *But of course Jean had been that too*: indeed for a time she must have been it more perfectly than most, or Ford wouldn't have risked (and lost) Stella for her. In *The Good Soldier* he'd divided himself into ideal and reality — Edward Ashburnham, the tragically idealistic Englishman, and John Dowell, the bumbling, cowardly observer. In *When the Wicked Man* he divides his dream of love in the same way: into the ideal of the sweet and mournful girl, and the reality of the grasping woman. And I think he put Jean into both.

Henrietta Felise is like Jean when Ford first loved her: 'a tiny tender thing' with 'infinitely tiny bones', 'a soft, cool voice', perfumed hair, and 'deep shadowed Southern eyes', 'extremely large-pupilled', with a 'mournful and puzzled expression' ('above all ... puzzled. Puzzled about you, about life, about her own self ...'). When she is afraid she touches her hand to her side and draws a little breath; she pants a little, her lips wide apart and her eyes agonised. When Notterdam has met her only once he longs to exclaim to his 'absolutely admirable' wife: 'I love Henrietta Felise to madness ... I mean to make her mine.'

In *Quartet* Heidler sounds just like Edward Ashburnham, and Ford: *'I'm dying with love for you, burnt up with it, tortured with it....'* And in *When the Wicked Man* Henrietta Felise sounds just like Marya, and Jean: *'My dearest ... Now I have found you I can't go ... You must take care of me ... You must never leave me ... You don't know how sick at heart ... You don't know how I long....'*

Immediately, in *When the Wicked Man*, both Notterdam and Henrietta have desperate doubts. Notterdam is revolted at her abandoned sexuality. He has the impression that she expects him 'to fall upon her immediately'; when they leave he nearly tells her to 'dress herself' because her dress is too revealing; he gives her a lot to drink, and she is 'all over him' ... 'I knew that I could have you by putting my hand out, and I kept off you,' Heidler says in *Quartet*. '[But] I've been watching you; I watched you tonight and now I know that somebody else will get you if I don't. You're that sort.' 'He was horribly afraid,' the narrator says in *When the Wicked Man*. 'That was what made him speak brutally.'

And Henrietta too alternates between saying she loves him, and little screams of repulsion because she has sold herself to him: '"Poor father ... He would understand ... isn't it a pretty market to have brought his flesh to? Isn't it a pretty market?" She was speaking with extreme bitterness. She exclaimed: "Why don't you take me? Now? For God's sake get it over or I shall go mad."'

★

But now came peace, happiness, safety. 'I want to make you happy,' Heidler says. 'It's my justification that I want to.' And 'I want to comfort you. I want to hold you tight — and safe — d'you see. Safe!...' And he does. Marya thinks 'How gentle he is. I was lost before I knew him. All my life before I knew him was like being lost on a cold, dark night.'

.... She was absorbed, happy, without thought for perhaps the first time in her life. No past. No future. Nothing but the present: the flowers on the table, the taste of wine in her mouth. She glanced at the rough texture of Heidler's coatsleeve and longed to lay her face against it.

'"Of course," she told herself, "I ought to clear out." But when she thought of life without Heidler her heart turned over in her side and she felt sick.'

Jean was the centre of Ford's attention, his admired pupil and adored mistress. Ford paraded the first, and that hid the second. He read her stories aloud, sometimes in front of Stella, putting on a special solemn voice if he liked them, shouting 'Cliché! Cliché!' if he didn't. 'I was singularly slow at discovering that she and Ford were in love,' Stella said. Marya seems to have no more than a few hours of unclouded peace and happiness. But Jean must have had many days, perhaps weeks.

But of course Stella did discover it. In *When the Wicked Man* Lola and Notterdam's wife Elspeth become more and more polite to each other, until the atmosphere is electric with politeness. In *Quartet* Lois sends Marya on little errands; she says cruel things indirectly, to Heidler. Stella was 'patronising', Jean said, she 'laid down the law', she gossiped maliciously with her friends. 'She hates me,' Marya says to Cairn. 'Of course she hates you,' Cairn replies. 'She'd be a very unnatural woman if she didn't.' 'But I don't mind her hating me,' Marya says. 'What I mind is that she pretends she doesn't.'

'Life with Ford had always felt pretty insecure,' Stella wrote:

... Yet here I was cast for the role of the fortunate wife who held all the cards, and the girl for that of the poor, brave and desperate beggar who was doomed to be let down by the bourgeoisie. I learnt what a powerful weapon lies in weakness and pathos and how strong is the position of the person who has nothing to lose, and I simply hated my role.

Peace and happiness were over, for all of them. Stella was unhappy because she still loved Ford, and Ford was in love with Jean. Ford was unhappy because he knew he was going to leave both of them, and because Jean fought him. ('I'm as unhappy as you are,' Heidler says, and he looks it. 'I love you; I can't help it. It's not your fault; it's not my fault ... Why can't you just accept it instead of straining against it all the time?') And Jean was unhappy because Ford was forcing her to share him, because he was treating her like a servant, 'to be made love to every time the mistress's back is turned'; because she had to trail around Montparnasse with them, although she knew what everyone was saying. ('And there she was,' she wrote of Carlo in 'The Blue Bird', ' − the tragedy of Montparnasse − called "Poor Carlo" by the charitable, and "that awful woman" by the others ....') 'They say that Lois picked me up when I was starving and that the moment I got into her house I tried to get hold of you,' Marya tells Heidler; and I'm sure that this was true. Jean's passivity *was* manipulative, designed to make Ford fall in love with her, Stella take care of her, and nobody blame her. But it only achieved the first two aims briefly, and the third not at all. Ford was much better at that game than she was, as Marya knows. His egotism, and his capacity for self-deception and evasion, were even greater than hers ('I'm awfully drunk,' Heidler says after their violent fight at Brunoy, 'I shan't remember a thing about all this tomorrow morning.') And though Stella was the opposite, and really was cast for a thankless role by both Ford and Jean, I'm sure she did have *tout Montparnasse* behind her. When Jean wrote 'But of course it wasn't a love affair. It was a fight. A ruthless, merciless, three-cornered fight. And from the first Marya, as was right and proper, had no chance of victory', she was right. Except that it was a *four*-cornered fight, and the worst loser of all was John.

When Heidler puts his hand on hers, peace descends on Marya, 'and to that peace,' Jean wrote, 'she was ready to sacrifice... anybody or anything.' Even in *Quartet* it is clear that what she sacrifices is her husband. She goes to see him every weekend − but when Heidler asks her not to she doesn't, and poor Stephan goes mad waiting for her. When she's there she cannot comfort him, and often says the wrong thing because 'her brain isn't working properly'. She even fails to go to his trial. There are excuses − Stephan doesn't want her there; she is ill. But she doesn't go.

*Sous les Verrous* tells the same story, but much, much worse. Stania abandons Jan almost with alacrity. In his first month, at the Santé, she only writes those vague notes from Montparnasse bars, saying '*Je suis tellement fatiguée*'. He asks her to fetch some letters from his office which he's sure will clear him, and she fails to. She doesn't come to his preliminary hearing or his trial, though she has promised she will, though he longs for her to be there, and though his lawyer suggests that a pretty, weeping wife might help him. Once he's in

Fresnes it's even worse. He writes her passionate letters; often she replies sharply. She won't promise to visit him often; and sometimes she comes only once a fortnight, although there are visiting days twice a week. When she does come she defers all her plans, present and future, to Hübner; and when Jan objects she is bitterly angry and offended. '*Ne suis-je pas libre de faire ce que je veux?*' she says: '*Est-ce que toi, tu fais quelque chose pour moi?*' And '*tu m'ennuis avec toutes tes questions. Si tu veux que je ne viens plus, tu n'as qu'à continuer. Je suis déjà assez bien ennuyée sans que tu me harcèles de tes soupçons...*'

Well: John felt betrayed, cuckolded and let down, and he was angry... But Jean did betray him, cuckold him and let him down; and she knew it. It's clear even in *Quartet*; it's still clearer in *Barred. For Jean left in almost all these accusations and exchanges.* She cut some of the worst of Stania's indifference and cruelty to her husband, which struck her as 'too unfair' – the business of the letters which might have saved him, for instance (which in any case John probably invented). But it's extraordinary how much she left in – almost all Stania's indolence and doll-like passivity, her self-pity and 'tiredness', her unreliability, her flaunting of Hübner and other men, her anger and cruelty when questioned... In fact the largest changes she made protect not herself but the Fords. She removed John's cruellest descriptions of 'Hübner'; and she removed all reference to 'Madame Hübner', and with it all suggestion – so central and strong in *Quartet* – of Stella's *complaisance horrible.* She gave what was left of her role to Mathilde Dubar, causing infelicities in the text which must have hurt her... Why? She translated *Sous les Verrous* only four years after writing *Quartet*; what had happened? I doubt she'd forgiven Ford (though no doubt she was a little calmer); she certainly hadn't forgiven Stella. There had been a fuss about *Quartet* libelling Ford, and probably she wanted to avoid a repetition of that. But I don't believe it was only this. I think it was like her translating, with (in her words) 'rage, fury and devotion', almost everything John had written against her: a way of admitting her guilt, towards him and towards Stella, behind the double mask of someone else's fiction.

In *Quartet* Marya goes to live in a hotel months before Stephan's release; in *Sous les Verrous* Stania stays on in the Hübners' house for some time after Jan has left prison and been deported. Again *Sous les Verrous* was probably closer to reality. Jean never left any company for solitude until she had to, however unwelcome and unhappy she was. Still less would she leave Ford's now, for he and she were still in love.

John left Fresnes on June 18th. Normally he would have been

deported that day or the next; but *Quartet* and *Sous les Verrous* agree
that he managed to stay in Paris for several days. Marya and Stania
both take hotel rooms for their husbands. Marya feels guilty; and
briefly, irrationally, secure ('He ... waited on her with anxious
gentleness ... It was extraordinary, but there it was. This was the
only human being with whom she had ever felt safe or happy'). But
this doesn't last. Really he seems a stranger to her, and pitiful: 'She
remembered Stephan calm, silent and self-contained; now it was as
if prison had broken him up.' ('I have lost my prestige with Stania,'
Jan thinks. 'If we were to stay for years together she would never
be able to forget that she had seen me shiver when a warder spoke.')
When they meet the Heidlers at the Taverne Panthéon Marya at first
leaves with them. But then she returns to Stephan at his hotel,
knowing that she will lose Heidler forever. ('I've never shared a
woman in my life,' he says, 'and I'm not going to start now.') 'You
don't love me any more,' Stephan says. 'You stiffen when I touch
you.' 'I'm awfully tired,' Marya says, 'and awfully sad. Will you just
be kind to me for a little? And don't let's think about love at all.'

In *Sous les Verrous* Stania has gone out for lunch when Jan arrives
at the hotel. She returns, very pretty in a sleeveless beige flannel dress
with a sailor blouse and a big orange bow; and Jan is caught again
by '*toute sa délicieuse jeunesse, toute sa frèle beauté*'. She cries and
strokes his hair; but that is all. She treats him with pity and impatience, as one would treat a puppy. Her eyes are '*tristes et fatigués*',
but also '*un peu heureux*'. She lies about two love marks on her arm.
She tells him that she will spend as much of the day as she can with
him (though not all of it, because she must work with Hübner); but
not the night, because unless she is separated from him she will be
deported too. He feels dishonoured, bitter, utterly miserable, but he
cannot give her up. He drinks to dull himself: '*Tout comme
Stania ... Car elle aussi, elle boit, plus vite que moi et des choses plus
fortes. Cela se voit qu'elle a eu de l'entraînement pendant mon absence.*'

On their last evening Marya and Stephan dine 'recklessly'; Jan
makes Stania very drunk. In the taxi to the station Marya turns to
Stephan to say 'Stephan, don't leave me here. For God's sake, take
me with you.' But he is already speaking, making his plans, and the
moment has passed. 'I'm not going to wait to see your train out,'
Marya says. 'It's unlucky.' Stania says the same thing — she will not
wait until the train goes, '*Ça porte malheur.*' But Hübner is there;
and she smiles up at him, '*de son sourire plein de soumission et
d'admiration.*' And, Jan says, '*si elle pleure en me disant au revoir, c'est
peut-être que sa pitié, pour un bref instant, dépasse son bonheur d'être
toute à Hübner désormais.*'

Jan goes to Belgium (helped by money from Hübner); Stephan goes to Amsterdam. John was probably expelled to Holland, for he'd given his nationality as Dutch. Both *Sous les Verrous* and his next novel, *Kerels*, suggest that he spent most of the next two years tramping around Europe, being a sandwich man in Lucerne, selling newspapers in Berlin, carrying books for publishers in Frankfurt; and when he couldn't get even such lowly jobs, passing round his hat as a street musician.

In *Quartet* Marya is now brutally dropped by Heidler, but in reality this didn't happen for another year. Jean's and Ford's affair went on.

But she couldn't live with him any longer. 'A friend of an American lady came to Montparnasse searching for someone cheap to help her write a book,' Jean said, and 'Ford and Stella both did their best to help me get this job.' Ford wrote an article on eighteenth-century English furniture, and then a 'Serbian folk story', both of which he passed off as Jean's; and Stella talked 'very persuasively about how nice I was and how the American lady would be sure to like me.' Clearly Stella was desperate to get rid of her by now, and Ford desperate to separate them. Even Jean 'quite agreed it was high time I got away from Montparnasse.' She got the job; and in July she set off for Juan-les-Pins.

This would be an extraordinary interlude, both ridiculous and pleasant. She left it out of *Quartet*, she said later, 'because it did not fit into the novel's shape'. Marya's movement must be straight down to abandonment and annihilation. There was no room in it for fun. But life isn't like that, especially not Jean's life. She had interludes of fun right up to the end, and despite everything she had fun now — and saw that it was funny too. That's why this episode fitted instead into the black comedy of *Good Morning, Midnight*.

The American lady believed in reincarnation, and that if you dressed and furnished your home in the style of your previous lives you would be happy. This theory was the subject of the book Jean was to help her write — though of course Jean knew no more about ancient Persia or Egypt than she did, or about any other period in history. Nor could she type or take shorthand. In fact the lady couldn't write, and her new assistant couldn't assist her. None the less their undertaking grew more instead of less ambitious.

> ... She would come into my room [Sasha says] very early in the morning in her dressing-gown, her hair hanging down in two plaits, looking rather sweet, I must say. 'Are you awake,

Mrs Jansen? I've just thought of a story' ... 'Once upon a time there was a cactus —' Or a white rose or a yellow rose or a red rose, as the case might be. All this, mind you, at six-thirty in the morning ... 'This story,' she would say, looking anxious, 'is an allegory. You understand that, don't you?' 'Yes, I understand.' But she was never very explicit about the allegory. 'Could you make it a Persian garden?' 'I don't see why not.' 'Oh, and there's something I want to speak to you about, Mrs Jansen. I'm afraid Samuel didn't like the last story you wrote.' Oh God, this awful sinking of the heart — like going down in a lift. I knew this job was too good to be true. 'Didn't he? I'm sorry. What didn't he like about it?' 'Well, I'm afraid he doesn't like the way you write. What he actually said was that, considering the cost of these stories, he thinks it strange that you should write them in words of one syllable. He says it gets monotonous, and don't you know any long words, and if you do, would you please use them.'....

Sitting at a large desk, a white sheet of paper in front of me and outside the sun and the blue Mediterranean ... Persian garden. Long words. Chiaroscuro? Translucent? I bet he'd like cataclysmal action and centrifugal flux, but the point is how can I get them into a Persian garden? ... Well, I might. Stranger things have happened.

The lady isn't named in *Good Morning, Midnight*. In Jean's early story 'At the Villa d'Or' she's called Mrs Robert B. Valentine, and her husband is 'Robert B. Valentine, the Boot-Lace King'. Really Mr and Mrs Robert Valentine were Mr and Mrs Richard Hudnut, of the huge American cosmetics firm. Their daughter was married to Rudolf Valentino, which probably gave Jean their name; they were extremely rich, quite absurd, and very kind.

The Chateau Juan-les-Pins had been built by a rich Russian before the Revolution. It was excessively, extravagantly luxurious, 'like walking into a movie', and everyone in Montparnasse laughed at it. But Jean didn't laugh at it: she liked it, and she immediately became used to it. She had a beautiful bedroom and her own bathroom. In the morning she swam in the fresh blue sea ('coming out of it one would be fresh, purified from how many desecrating touches'). During the day she sat at her desk listening to Mrs Hudnut ('I believe in survival after death. I've had personal proof of it. And we'll find out dear, familiar bodies on the other side'), and taking dictation: 'The piano must be very Egyptian in feeling ...'. And in the evening there was delicious food; 'coffee, peace, optimism.'

For the first time since John had been arrested Jean was happy, even extremely happy. She'd got away from the three-cornered fight, and people cutting her dead on the Boulevard Montparnasse; yet Ford was still her lover, protector and patron. Though she was earning very little she could keep it all, and soon she felt quite rich. Mrs Hudnut talked of friends who would employ her when her job at the Chateau Juan-les-Pins was over. Jean saw her future on the beautiful Riviera, ghosting dozens of books on improbable subjects for rich Americans. She found a flat; she made plans to fetch Maryvonne. 'She sighed with pleasure at the glimpse of her white, virginal bathroom through the open door — the bath-salts, the scents, the crystal bottles.' Sasha still dreams of these bottles years later. Jean remembered it all very fondly — the cabinets with jade and the cabinets with china; the double circular staircase; the little room where Mr Hudnut kept his essential oils, and a pile of linen handker-chiefs and a rose. And when she told stories about it in old age she laughed until she wept.

She stayed at the Chateau Juan-les-Pins for a long time, probably several months. She got very brown; she relaxed. She wrote to Ford and Stella to say how much she loved the south of France, and how happy she was with the job they'd found her, which now included taking down fairy tales as well. And nearly every Sunday she went with Mr Hudnut to the Casino at Monte Carlo. When she lost he insisted on paying; and when he kissed her 'on the way there and on the way back' she let him. He was old, and 'I didn't see any harm in it,' she said. 'It never occurred to me that the chauffeur was staring at us in the driving mirror and could see everything.' It didn't matter to her if Mr Hudnut kissed her; so she couldn't imagine it would matter to anyone else.

But then one day Mrs Hudnut came into her room, 'not smiling as usual'. She said 'I've had a most extraordinary letter from Mr Ford,' and gave it to Jean to read. It accused her of exploiting Jean disgracefully, of paying her 'less than a housemaid in New York', of trying to get two books out of her for the price of one. It was an extremely rude letter, and Mrs Hudnut was very angry. Jean tried to say that she didn't know why Ford had written like that, that she knew nothing about it. But Mrs Hudnut said, 'You must have written complaining.' Obviously Jean would prefer not to be exploited any further, and to return to her friends the Fords the very next day. And she swept out of the room, 'followed by all her six Pekinese.'

Jean was devastated. All her happiness, all her wild hopes, had been swept away, so cavalierly, so high-handedly.... When she asked Ford later why he'd done it he said that she didn't understand the literary world: Mrs Hudnut was exploiting her, a protest had to be made. Jean hadn't felt exploited, and she never did understand why he'd sent that letter. But in fact the whole episode was typical Ford. He imagined himself — he *was* — the champion of the poor writer; he was always attacking publishers, agents and all other literary parasites, and always using just this lofty, superior tone. And underneath, perhaps, he wanted Jean back. He'd got her the job; now he took it away again.

Jean behaved entirely typically too. She didn't leave the next day; although 'things were made very uncomfortable for me' she stayed for several, perhaps many, days more. Mrs Hudnut said her work had to be typed, so she found a girl in a newspaper office in Nice who typed it for nothing. But this must have taken some time. Mr Hudnut was angry and didn't speak to her at all; the maid who did her room glared at her; 'Meals were especially uncomfortable'.... 'Then of course the story came up from the chauffeur that I'd let Mr [Hudnut] kiss me all the way to Monte Carlo and back again. Soon I was looking out of the window at the lovely view for the last time.'

Mrs Hudnut was a kind woman, and very likely Jean's childlike bewilderment and genuine distress convinced her that the men in the case were more to blame. She 'thawed towards the end': she and Jean travelled up to Paris together, talking quite affably, and later she even came to visit Jean in her hotel. But she cut Ford dead on the platform in Paris. And Mr Hudnut had remained 'cold and aloof to the last'. I expect Mrs Hudnut had showed him her displeasure too; and of course, Jean said, he had 'stumped up for the book, perhaps unwillingly.'

Jean was back with Ford, but she wasn't happy. Paris was grey and cold, and she longed without ceasing for the warmth and sun of the Riviera. Ford and Stella had moved to the studio on the rue Notre Dame des Champs, but they wouldn't have her there. Instead Ford had found a room for her in a hotel near the Gare Montparnasse. When she saw it she couldn't bear the contrast to her beautiful room at the Chateau Juan-les-Pins, and she burst into tears. It smelt of drains and stale scent; it looked out not on the blue Mediterranean, but on the smoking, clanking trains.

Now, Jean said, the trouble started.

★     ★     ★

John was gone, her plans for having Maryvonne with her were destroyed. And Ford no longer really wanted her. This is when Marya says of Heidler: 'He wasn't a good lover, of course.' He is clumsy and heavy, his eyes are 'sad and cold like ashes'. But he is determined that he will play out his role — and that Marya will play out hers. 'Despising, almost disliking, love, he was forcing her to be nothing but the little woman who lived in the Hôtel du Bosphore for the express purpose of being made love to.'

But now that Jean felt her power over Ford waning, with characteristic masochism and perversity she felt his over her growing. He 'seemed her only friend. She fell for him.' Marya, 'miserable weakling that she was, found herself trying to live up to his idea of her.' She loves Heidler, she knows that she will never be able 'even to pretend to fight him again.' But he always hurries the end of his dressing, as if longing to escape; he always says 'Well, look here, my dear one, I must go,' and 'I'd better leave some money, hadn't I?' The endless repetition of these words, these acts, becomes a torture; but she thinks 'I must get used to this,' and fixes a smile on her lips.

Heidler also repeats that Marya must come to lunch and to tea with Lois, that Lois is very fond if her, that they cannot let Lois down. 'Everybody knows that you were staying with us,' he says, 'and if there's a definite split it will give the whole show away.' Everybody knows already, Marya says; and Lois hates her and only wants to tear her to bits with her friends. But Heidler insists that she must keep up appearances, she must play the game; and so she does. She goes to Lois's tea parties. Lois greets her with a gleam of triumph in her eyes; she orders Heidler about, and is spiteful to Marya as soon as he is out of earshot. Marya cannot even fight Lois any more. She is crushed, borne down; she feels as though she has fallen down a precipice.

This went on till Christmas. Then there was a break in the round of hope and fear, love and hate. The year before Ford had decided that winter in Paris was bad for his chest, and that he couldn't write there. Now he was wanting to write again — and perhaps to escape the round of love and hate too. At the end of December he and Stella and Julie left for Toulon. They stayed there for three months; and Ford began *A Man Could Stand Up*.

And Jean? She wouldn't want to stay alone in Paris for long, and I don't think she did. Ford had withdrawn into the world of books; and I think he encouraged and helped her to do the same. He had already sent some of her *Left Bank* stories and sketches to an agent in London, and recommended her work to Edward Garnett, the best known publisher's reader in England. Now, with money he had given her, she probably went to England to find a publisher.

All of this, of course, she cut out of *Quartet* (and out of the stories too). Not just the time (most of 1926) and the move to another place.

But the main thing: the fact that she was writing, that she was a writer.

And this wasn't just a literary device — because, for example, she thought it boring or pretentious to make her heroine a writer. It was because she did not think of herself as really, voluntarily, a writer. She wrote; she'd written since she was a child. But only for herself. She wrote to get rid of her sadness, to understand it and to make something good out of it. But she didn't think of readers; she didn't think of publishing. Left to herself, she said, she probably never would have. Two things pushed her into it: the need for money, and Ford. The need for money had led her to Ford in the first place. He had published her first story, 'Vienne'. And now both, I'm sure, were behind this effort to publish the others, which left to herself she would never have made.

Jean cut her behaviour as a writer out of the way she spoke of this part of her life, too, so we don't know whether she met Edward Garnett (though she wrote to him); we don't know whether it was he, or the agent, or Ford, or even Jean herself who sent *The Left Bank* to Jonathan Cape. But Cape published it the next spring, and it may well have been now that he accepted it.

She stayed in London for a few weeks at least, perhaps a few months. When Ford returned to Paris in March she was probably still there. But some time in the spring she returned to Paris.

She moved back into her hotel, or perhaps into another one. This was the room which had 'huge and fantastically shaped mauve, green and yellow flowers on a black background' all over the walls ('*maladroitement peint*,' John said, by '*quelque artiste du quartier*'). In *After Leaving Mr Mackenzie* this has grown even more grotesque, and sprouted sinister bird-like creatures, 'fungus and queerly shaped leaves and fruit' ... It has become Jean's nightmare room, her 'bedroom in hell'; because in it the final scenes of her affair were played out.

In the spring of 1926 Ford and Stella gave more parties than ever in the studio at the rue Notre Dame des Champs. But in *Quartet* Marya is no longer invited to them. Instead she stands outside in the street, looking up at the lit windows.

Jean knew it was all over, but she couldn't let go. She could never let go of anyone if the alternative was solitude; and Ford was not just anyone. He was (almost) what Lancelot had been — lover, father and friend; and teacher and patron too. She had let herself depend on him utterly; and when she did that she was like an infant: the person she depended on would be life itself to her, if he left her she would feel that she was dying. *The thing is that you don't understand,*

Anna imagines herself saying in *Voyage in the Dark*. *You think I want more than I do. I only want to see you sometimes, but if I never see you again I'll die. I'm dying now really....*

Jean was desperate, and she was no longer nineteen, like Anna. 'When you were nineteen, and it was the first time you had been let down, you did not make scenes,' she would write in *After Leaving Mr Mackenzie*. 'That started later on, when the same thing had happened five or six times over, and you were supposed to be getting used to it.' It started now.

It's all in *Quartet*, even though *Quartet* is the least honest and the most self-excusing of Jean's novels. Marya 'fought wildly', she wrote, 'with tears, with futile rages, with extravagant abandon.' '"What's the matter with you?" she would ask herself. "Why are you like this? Why can't you be clever?" Uselessly. "No self control," [she thought]. "That's what's the matter with me. No training."' She becomes abusive, although she sees that it is making Heidler hate her. 'Why should I be a butt for Lois and her friends?' she says excitedly. 'She wants me there so that she can watch out for the right moment to put her enormous foot down.'

> She began to laugh loudly. There was a coarse sound in her laughter. Heidler looked at her sideways. He disliked her when she laughed like that.
>
> He told her coldly: 'You talk the most awful nonsense sometimes, don't you?'
>
> 'What?' said Marya, 'Aren't Lois's feet enormous? Well, I think they are. You didn't exactly look for *fines attaches* when you married, did you?'

When she cries ('quietly, all soft and quivering'), he thinks, 'I'm still fond of her. If only she'd leave it at that.'

> But no. She took her hands away from her face and started to talk again. What a bore! Now, of course, she was quite incoherent.
>
> 'The most utter nonsense,' thought Heidler. Utter nonsense about (of all things) the visiting cards stuck into the looking glass over Lois's damned mantelpiece, about Lois's damned smug pictures and Lois's damned smug voice....
>
> Heidler was stung and interrupted coldly: 'It's extraordinary that you don't see how unintelligent it is of you to abuse Lois.'
>
> But she didn't take the slightest notice. She just went on talking.

Jean had struggled against rage ever since Lancelot. It had burst out before — with 'Ethel', with Max, with Philip Heseltine. Now it was engulfing her. Roseau in 'La Grosse Fifi' feels 'suspended over a dark and terrible abyss — the abyss of absolute loss of self-control.' Jean fell in.

The main reason was drink. Even before Stephan is arrested Marya thinks 'It was astonishing how significant, coherent and understandable it all became after a glass of wine on an empty stomach.' When Jan returns from prison in *Sous les Verrous* he notices that Stania's drinking has got worse. And in *Quartet* now Marya drinks until she is dazed, to deaden the pain. And thinks: 'Well, there she was. In a bad way. Hard hit. All in. And a drunkard into the bargain.'

Drink did deaden Jean's pain; it must have, or she wouldn't have turned to it more and more. But only sometimes, and only for a moment. At other times it did what the absinthe does to Sasha in Calais: it made her feel quarrelsome. It let out the rage inside her.

That is what happens to Marya. When she pours out her abuse of Lois she is probably drunk: Jean doesn't say so, but Heidler thinks 'She drank so much that she was getting hoarse as a crow.' And at first she only imagines letting violence and murderousness out as well. ('One of these days,' she thinks, 'I'll smash a wine bottle in her face,' and 'she would imagine the sound of the glass breaking, the sight of the blood streaming ... she imagined it, breathing quickly, and then she would tell herself, horrified, "My God, I'm going mad!"') But soon after the 'torrent of nonsense' violence breaks out of her too. One day, she says to Heidler, 'I'll walk into your studio and strangle your cad of a Lois — kill her, d'you see? Get my hands around her thick throat and squeeze ...'. And Heidler says calmly: 'I know. As a matter of fact, I've thought several times that you might try some nonsense of that sort. So has she.'

All this — drunkenness, violence and loss of control — Ford gave to Lola Porter in *When the Wicked Man*. He hoped to shock and frighten everyone with this portrait of Jean, as much as he'd been shocked and frightened by her. But he was *too* frightened, and too furious: he portrayed Lola so badly that he defeated his own purpose. No one can believe in her, so no one can believe that she is a fair portrait of Jean. And of course she isn't; for the other half of Jean is in Henrietta Felise. But of the dark, desperate half Lola is a cruel, but not an inaccurate portrait. Cut away the phony American slang, and there is Jean at her worst moments. She hinted at it herself in *Quartet*; Stella hinted at it in *Drawn from Life*, saying she was 'a doomed soul, violent and demoralised', who 'showed us an underworld of darkness and disorder'. Only Ford, ironically, managed to hide the truth, by burying it in a novel so bad that few people ever read it, and those few didn't believe it.

From the beginning Lola's relation to drink is just what Jean's will be a few years later. She doesn't drink all the time, and when she is sober she is 'delicate', 'languidly fastidious', 'charming in a stand-offish way and terribly concerned for her reputation'. And 'quite a star journalist', from whose writing about her husband Notterdam gets 'astonishing flashes' of his personality ('his caustic humour, his fantastic pride,' just like John's). But when she does drink she becomes 'terrible', 'abandoned'. That is why she cannot keep a job. Her drunken times last only a day or two, but during them she destroys everything. ('It would have been better,' says Henrietta Felise, 'if she had soaked solid for a month and kept away from the office.')

That is at the beginning. By the end of the novel Lola is drinking heavily, and when she is drunk she makes violent scenes. After 'two to three cocktails she became almost madly obscene and furious'; after 'a few more she might become either lachrymose or singularly reasonable.' At her worst she is 'pallid and almost insensible all day'; then begins 'to drink wine by the two or three bottles at dinner', and by one in the morning is 'stark insensible'. She rings Notterdam up and pours abuse on him, followed by 'a cascade of obscenities, of sheer, filthy, old-fashioned English schoolboy words ... well, that was drink.' (So Antoinette, drunk, will curse Rochester, 'shouting obscenities' at him. 'Your *doudou* certainly knows some filthy language,' he will say to Christophine). Then the next day she is ashamed, or sulky, or 'mournfully well-behaved. Compliant.' Or else she is 'in one of her halting, india-rubber Creole moods. As if her hips were limp,' and asks him 'to take no notice of what she had said the previous afternoon. She had been feeling lonely and wretched'.... Or she simply says that she doesn't remember. (That, of course, is exactly the technique that Jean gives to Heidler.)

Lola's behaviour is incomprehensible, because although he is deeply disturbed and tempted by her, Notterdam is not her lover. But she cries that he has made her love him, he has ruined her. She makes 'suicidal and enigmatic remarks'; she makes 'the most fantastic offers of herself' ('Listen: I know things... oh, from the tropics...'). She begs and pleads with him, on her knees, kissing his hand. ('I love you, I love you, I love you,' Marya says. 'Oh, please be nice to me. Oh, please say something nice to me. I love you.' And she is 'quivering and abject in his arms, like some unfortunate dog abasing itself before its master.') Then she tries to blackmail him instead. She threatens him with her gangster friends, she threatens him herself – 'I will smash everything in this room. I'll set fire to your damned snobbish Jacobean curtains ... I'll slit your rotten contemporary – God, it makes me want to vomit – portrait of Cromwell ...'.

Notterdam admits only the vaguest guilt towards Lola ('If this

woman was in earnest hadn't he perhaps ... misled her?'); he only
feels guilty towards her husband, who was 'by way of being an
English gentleman', and whose suicide he'd caused. What he feels
towards her at the end is revulsion and terror. Underneath her
'Creole nonchalance', her fastidiousness and beauty, he sees a tiger,
a witch, a whore, a murderess. He calls her a 'blackamoor'; he feels
she practises voodoo on him. He hears, and believes, that she was
'notoriously unfaithful' to her husband, who killed himself (he now
thinks) because of her 'misconduct with members of the underworld'. He feels that she is 'infernal', 'a virulent cloud', 'a malignity';
but that Destiny has fixed her around his neck with a strong
grip ... He feels, in other words, just as Rochester feels about
Antoinette at the end of *Wide Sargasso Sea*.

'Are you vexed with me?' Marya asks Heidler.
  'Not at all,' answered Heidler. He cleared his throat. 'My dear
Mado ...' He began to talk dispassionately and deliberately. He
spoke with dignity and with a certain relief, as though he were
saying something which he had often longed to say. Towards
the end of his explanation he became definite, even brutal,
though not to excess....
  Then she said: 'But, H.J., I — I love you.'
  'You haven't behaved as though you did,' answered Heidler.
'And it's too late now.' He began to talk again — more
emphatically, as if her presence irritated him.
  She couldn't see his face clearly. There was a mist around
it....
  [He] was saying in a low voice: 'I have a horror of you. When
I think of you I feel sick.'

Usually falling out of love is losing someone else, and that is painful
enough; but for Ford and Jean falling out of love was losing themselves. Each had a dream of his or her self, in which for a time the
other believed. So, for a time, it was real. But then the other stopped
believing, and it was lost. Then they became their nightmare selves
instead, Ford cowardly and brutal, Jean violent and hysterical. I
think that Ford *was* first like Edward Ashburnham to Jean, and then
like Heidler; and that Jean *was* first like Marya (and Henrietta) to
him, and then like Lola. Ford had been like Heidler before (to Violet
Hunt, for instance); and Jean would be like Lola more and more in
the future. Her second heroine, Julia, will say that the end of her
affair with Mr Mackenzie 'had destroyed some necessary illusions
about herself'. The end of her affair with Ford did the same to Jean.

★

Marya's affair ends in an August and September, when Stephan comes out of prison. Heidler says, 'If you go back to your husband I can't see you again.' And when she does it's over.

Jean's ended in an August and September too: August and September 1926. And in much the same way.

John had in fact left prison, and then the country, the summer before, but at some point before early August of this year he had returned — illegally, like Jan in *Sous les Verrous*. And like Jan he went to live in the suburb of Clamart. Jan goes to see Stania, and once or twice she goes to see him. She denies that she is Hübner's mistress, or that he is about to drop her. But Jan sees that she is very unhappy. Her eyes are red with crying; she is silent, as though in a dream. When he presses her they have a huge, raging quarrel.

'And sooner or later he'll probably try to get back to Paris,' Heidler says to Marya. 'That's what they all do, it seems. They come back to Paris and hide till they're arrested again. I mean, I'm not going to be mixed up in all that sort of thing. I can't be. I can't afford to be.' In *Sous les Verrous* Hübner reports Jan to the police, and he's back in the Santé. And in reality John was arrested on 4 August, 1926, for breaking his expulsion order, spent six days back in the Santé, and was expelled again.

Jan now finds a lawyer, begins to fight for the return of his nationality, and gets a month's legal residence permit in France. But John regained his Dutch citizenship only six months later, and got no such legal permit. Instead, I think, he simply turned round and went straight back to Paris.

Jan finds Stania in her hotel room with fantastically shaped flowers on the wall. She is nervous and anxious, she doesn't seem to hear him.

> . . . . *Elle m'écoute d'une façon distraite, le regard fixé sur un point quelconque du mur . . . Quand j'ai fini son regard se porte sur moi. Je vois ses pauvres yeux battus qui sont prêts à verser leur larmes. Elle a du beaucoup pleurer ces derniers jours, beaucoup veiller et beaucoup boire.*

Stania denies that Hübner has dropped her — but she says '*Si tu n'étais pas venu déranger tout, j'aurais pu être heureuse*'; and she accuses Jan of being jealous '*du bonheur, du bien-être que je pourrais avoir avec Hübner.*' Despite everything Jan still wants her, and still wants to help her. He takes a job, and goes to see her every night. But he is like 'a collector who is in possession of the broken bits of a beautiful vase which he cannot piece together and yet cannot throw away.' Stania is plunged into a '*tristesse profonde*'. She is silent, she sighs, she can think of nothing but Hübner. And when

Jan says so, when he tries to 'open her eyes', she turns on him. '*Qu'est-ce que cela peut te faire?*' she says. And '*Si tu m'aimais comme tu le dis, tu parlerais autrement. Tu es un mesquin, un jaloux. Je me demande ce que tu viens faire ici tous les soirs*'.... She treats him '*avec un dédain froid qu'elle n'essaie même pas de dissimuler*'. But love makes him a coward, and he submits to everything.

It was probably late August by now, even early September. Perhaps Jean wanted to get away from John; perhaps Ford wanted to get her away from him, or away from himself. He gave her money to go to the Hôtel des Oliviers in Crus de Cagnes.

In the Hôtel des Palmiers in Cannes Marya hits rock-bottom. After she's visited by Lois's friend Miss Nicolson, inquisitive and patronising, she drinks so much, and on top of it takes so much sleeping-draught, that she has a terrible drunken night of panic and sickness.

Roseau in 'La Grosse Fifi' is also in a hotel on the Riviera, having been dismissed by her lover; she too is tired, bruised and aching, with 'no house, no friends, no money, no nothing'. She too drinks several glasses of wine, and takes several cachets of veronal; she too wakes in the middle of the night. Like Marya she is very dizzy; she staggers against a table, loud enough to wake Fifi.... Both Marya and Roseau stay in bed next day. They both look ill; but Marya knows that she wasn't ill, she was drunk.

Marya is alone in Cannes; she sees no one but Miss Nicolson. Everything has been cut away but her drunkenness and her despair. But Roseau does and feels a bit more. She meets and very much likes (but also fears) Fifi; she meets and clearly dislikes Mark and Peggy Olsen, the American Mrs Ward, and the businessman Mr Wheeler. Jean herself did more, like Roseau. 'Mr Wheeler' is probably based on Mr Hudnut, and so on a memory of the previous summer; but Mark Olsen is based on the artist Paul Nash, whom she really met now.* (And didn't like, for Paul Nash was only a half-bohemian, like Mark. To him her beloved Crabtree Club was a 'most disgusting place ... A place of utter coarseness and dull unrelieved monotony') Like Roseau, she went to the Casino at Monte Carlo. And − like Roseau too − she was working.

'I'll move,' Roseau says, 'when I've finished some work I'm doing.' She never says what it is, and we never see her doing it; indeed we can't imagine Roseau doing anything, and Jean should have cut this as ruthlessly as she cut everything that didn't fit desperate, drowning Marya. But reality, of course, is full of facts that don't fit − especially

---

*Paul Nash (1889-1946) was a well-known painter of poetic and surreal landscapes. He was a member of the New English Art Club and a war artist in both World Wars.

the reality of Jean's personality. Since at least 1914 she'd written down 'everything that had happened' — 'what he'd said, what I'd felt'; since 1924 she'd learned to cut it, hone it, turn it into art. From now on, the more painful something was the more it would insist on this transformation; and the more quickly, very often, she would begin it. Now she must have written 'La Grosse Fifi' more or less as it was happening, for six months later it was in *The Left Bank*. In the story Roseau has 'a queer smile — a little sideways smile. Mark wasn't quite sure that he liked it.' Lola Porter has it too. I bet Jean smiled that smile when Paul Nash took her back to her hotel, and she went upstairs to turn him into Mark Olsen. ('How rum some English people are! They ask to be shocked and long to be shocked and hope to be shocked, but if you really shock them ... how shocked they are!')

In *Quartet* the weather suddenly changes, and Marya gets a letter from Stephan. He is coming to Paris ('Don't be afraid; ... as long as nobody actually denounces me to the police, I am all right.') He wants to see her; and he sends her 400 francs for the journey. 'Come as quickly as you can,' he says.

Jean said she got a letter just like this from John. Perhaps she did; or perhaps she was (as she said a moment later) 'confusing the novel and what actually happened'. It's more likely John was already in Paris. For what happened now was the opposite: in the middle of September he was caught, sent to the Santé, and expelled for a second time. I think that his letter probably came from prison (which Jean wouldn't want to say); and that he said that this time he couldn't return, he'd stay in Holland and fight for his citizenship, and if she wanted to talk about going with him she'd better come quickly. Roseau packs her bags; Marya feels 'a faint stirring of hope'; and Jean went straight to Paris.

When Marya gets there she finds Stephan much more like his old self. He is active again, making plans — not very realistic ones, but still plans. 'Stephan is a clever boy and energetic,' says his Santé friend Jacques Bernadet. 'He won't stay long in *la misère*.' Marya decides she wants to go with him, and this time she manages to tell him so. But Stephan promises nothing; again he may not even have heard her.

John's story, of course, is different. During Jan's last days in Paris Stania is morose, silent, withdrawn. She does not agree to come with him now, but only when he can offer her a home. '*Quelle prudence dans cette réponse*,' he thinks bitterly.

Of herself Jean said: 'because she didn't know what else to do, didn't want to stay in Paris, hated Ford, she accepted her husband's offer to go to Amsterdam.... They went almost immediately.' But

I don't think this was true. She would have waited until John had somewhere for her to come to, as Stania says. For once both novels now tell very much the same story, and the best reason I can think of for this is that it was true.

Marya is 'so unhappy that I think I'm going to die of it'; Stania sobs terribly for ages. For each the breaking point has been a letter from her lover about money. Stania's is brutal and straightforward: she will receive money from now on through a lawyer, and if her husband menaces him Hübner will lay charges against her. Marya's is kinder, and says nothing about a lawyer. 'I'm worried about you,' Heidler writes, 'I am only too anxious to do all I can to help you...'. But Marya imagines their meeting, Heidler cool, impatient, in control. '"Of course you want money," he would be thinking. "Naturally. How much? I'm willing to give the traditional sum ... and no more."' And she is as broken as Stania. 'I can't any more,' she thinks. 'I can't. I must be comforted. I can't any more. I can't any more. Can't go on. Can't....'

Both Stephan and Jan leap to the idea of revenge. Stephan pulls out a revolver; Jan determines to go after Hübner. (And John too wanted to kill Ford; he even told his next wife that that is what he was arrested for — not embezzlement, but attempting to kill Ford.) But Marya and Stania bar the door to their angry husbands. Both threaten to call the police; both cry that they love Heidler/Hübner, and hate Stephan/Jan. Suddenly Stephan becomes 'the symbol of everything that all her life had baffled and tortured' Marya, and her 'only idea [is] to find words that would hurt him — vile words to scream at him'. Stania screams '*Salaud, c'est toi! et un voleur, et un maquereau! Hübner est un gentleman!*' Stephan catches Marya's wrist to swing her aside, and she fights him 'wildly, with frenzy'. Jan grasps hold of Stania, and '*comme une panthère elle se jette sur moi, s'accroche et me mord en pleine poitrine.*' Stephan pushes Marya with all his force, Jan punches Stania '*d'un vigoreux coup de poing.*' And both heroines fall unconscious to the floor.

Both Stephan and Jan leave them there. Stephan, of course, goes off with Mademoiselle Chardin. Jan sets out on a new life alone. And John too almost certainly left Paris alone. During the last months of 1926 he seems to have returned to his life of tramping around Germany and Holland.

★    ★    ★

At the end of *Sous les Verrous* Stania hears that she is to receive money through Hübner's lawyer. And when we open *After Leaving Mr Mackenzie*, Julia is receiving a weekly allowance of 300 francs — the same sum Heidler had given Marya — through Mackenzie's lawyer.

Now Jean always insisted that Ford had never made her an allowance: Lancelot had, but Ford hadn't. And it was true that he hadn't made her a regular allowance, for years and years. But he did send her money now, probably until the end of 1926; and probably through a lawyer. For Hübner's lawyer is called Maître Petit, Mackenzie's Maître Legros; and *the transatlantic review*'s lawyer was a Maître Legrand. Maître Legros bullies Julia, calls an *agent*, and talks about the *police des moeurs*; he 'perfectly represent[s] organised society' to her, and she is very much afraid of him. Maître Legrand froze even Ford. He was (Ford wrote) 'an inflexible, hard-fleshed, silent man,' with 'a perfectly elegant figure, perfectly manicured hands, perfectly fitting clothes and a perfectly implacable manner.' Like Julia, and like Stania too, I'm sure Jean not only had letters from him but met him.

Her life went in circles, through the same scenes, the same patterns, but each time worse. Once again she was pensioned off; once again it was *acknowledge receipt and oblige*. But now she was being treated as a criminal as well.... She'd refused at first to take Lancelot's money; and I think she refused at first to take Ford's. I think she now had a time like the one Sasha remembers in *Good Morning, Midnight*; a time when she starved, slept (again) 'fifteen hours out of the twenty-four', and thought again of suicide.

'That was the high point,' Sasha says, 'when I had nothing to eat for three weeks, except coffee and a croissant in the morning.'

> Twice I said I was ill, and they sent me up soup with meat in it from downstairs, and I could get an occasional bottle of wine on tick from the shop around the corner. It wasn't starvation at all when you come to think of it. Still, I'm not saying that there weren't some curious moments.

'After the first week I made up my mind to kill myself,' she says. But she doesn't. 'Next week, or next month, or next year I'll kill myself. But I might as well last out my month's rent, which has been paid up [so perhaps Jean had let Ford pay that, at least], and my credit for breakfast in the morning'.... She lets a man pick her up and buy her a drink ('And, of course, vlung — first breath of fresh air and I'm so drunk I can't walk'). She writes to England to borrow some money; they keep her waiting a long time for an answer, and she starts to eat at a convent 'where the nuns supply very cheap meals for destitute girls.'

As always, however, Jean left something out of *Good Morning, Midnight*: the fact that she not only starved and slept and thought of suicide, like Sasha, but sat as she had in Cagnes and wrote it all down. For several of the stories of *The Left Bank* were probably written now, in the last months of 1926. 'Hunger' perhaps, though that may have been earlier ('I have never gone without food for longer than five days, so I cannot amuse you any longer'). 'A Night', and 'Discourse of a Lady Standing a Dinner to a Down-and-Out Friend'; and perhaps 'In the Rue de l'Arrivée'. 'I don't belong here. I don't belong here,' the narrator of 'A Night' thinks, just as Jean had thought during her 'sad Christmas' of 1913. 'I must get out — must get out ... Well, then.... what? Make a hole in the water?...'

> Shoot oneself?...
> I'd sit down. No: lie down. And open my mouth ... That's the place: against the roof of mouth ... And pull the trigger.*

But she doesn't do it either. And Dolly Dufreyne, the heroine of 'In the Rue de l'Arrivée', gets drunk instead.

> ... For it was her deplorable habit, when she felt very blue indeed, to proceed slowly up the right hand side of the Boulevard, taking a *fine à l'eau* — that is to say a brandy and soda — at every second café she passed....
>
> She sat ... to all outer appearances calm, respectable, and mistress of her fate. But over the unseen, the real Dorothy Dufreyne, a tiny shrinking thing in a vast, empty space, flowed red waves of despair, black waves of fatigue....
>
> Sharp urgings to some violent deed, some inevitable fated end, and craven fear of life, and utter helpless, childish loneliness. Never before had drink, which usually warmed and uplifted her, had this effect on her. Perhaps it was because that afternoon she had passed a gentleman whom she knew intimately — very intimately indeed — and behold the gentleman had turned his head aside, and coughing nervously, pretended not to see her.

In September Ford and Stella had a holiday in Avignon; then in October Ford left Paris for a lecture tour of America. If Jean still had any idea of staying near him, in order to attack or appeal to him, that was the end of it. And perhaps John wrote to say that he had somewhere for her to come to. By mid-December I think she had joined him in Holland.

---

*Compare this to *Good Morning, Midnight*: '"Why didn't you drown yourself," the old devil said, "in the Seine?... Why didn't you make a hole in the water?"' '"If you really want to die you must put [the revolver] into your mouth — up to the roof of your mouth."' A confirmation that the time Sasha is remembering is the one these stories describe?

She had already, she said later, begun to write *Quartet* in Paris, and in Amsterdam she finished it. But she was using the title loosely. It took her some time to dare the novel. She wrote several other versions before it: a 'record of facts' — that is, a spurt of her diary; a short story; and a play. All or some of these were what she'd begun in Paris; and it was the play, I think, that she finished in Holland at the end of 1926.

Jean said later that she lost this play. She lost many things; but not work, unless she meant to. It was 'a literary play, meant to be read not acted,' she said. This means that it wasn't very good: that it wasn't really a play, but the dialogue of a novel. In fact it was an early stab at the novel; and when she got the novel she let it go. But it is very characteristic that it had come to her in this way. Her first approach, her 'record of facts', was always largely 'what he'd said, what I'd felt': inner and outer dialogue. Much of her writing was voices.

We have one other glimpse of *Quartet* as a play: from Mrs Adam. Jean couldn't, of course, discuss *Quartet* in any of its forms with Ford. Probably she discussed it with John; but she must have wanted another opinion. So she sent it to Mrs Adam. Mrs Adam said '[We] are both struck with how well it is written'; but she had one major criticism: 'the wife is a very obscure character.' It may have been Jean's artistic grappling with this remark as much as her hatred of Stella which made her think so carefully about Lois's motivation that she put it, finally, at the very centre of the novel.

'Houdia', the short story from which, as Jean put it, '*Quartet* started', she hung on to much longer. It too finally disappeared; but not before John had made (and published) a Dutch adaptation. Houdia is a sculptress — one of Jean's very few artist heroines, all of them early (Dolly Dufreyne is a 'fashion artist', Sara in 'At the Villa d'Or' a singer). She is caught in a *ménage à trois* with a couple called Steiner, and is making a sculpture of the husband. 'Houdia' is not only written in anger and revenge, like *Quartet*; it is *about* anger and revenge, like Ford's *When the Wicked Man*. Houdia stabs her sculpture of Steiner in the eyes — and in a voodoo-like way Steiner has eye trouble; then Houdia tries to shoot him in the street.

'A bit melodramatic,' Jean said later, and denied that any of it had happened. And of course it didn't — I'm sure she didn't stab a sculpture of Ford, or try to shoot him. But 'Houdia' confirms the atmosphere of voodoo and violence at the end of *When the Wicked Man*, of violence and anger at the end of *Quartet* and *Sous les Verrous* (and in 'In the Rue de l'Arrivée' too — 'Sharp urgings to some violent deed, some inevitable fated end . . .'). At the very least Jean *imagined* violent revenge on Ford at the end of their affair; and he felt it.

None the less he still wanted to help her. In early January 1927 he tried to find her, to tell her two things: his American publisher was showing some interest in *The Left Bank*, and he had a translation job for her to do. Germaine Richelot put them in touch, and Jean did the translation of *Perversité*, by Francis Carco. She took it back to Holland, probably in January, to get John's help with the Parisian *argot*; then she worked on it herself, probably in Paris.

This last kindness Ford had done her ended no better than the others: for when *Perversity* was published in 1928, the translation was credited not to Jean but to Ford. She was angry and upset about this for a long time, convinced that once again he had deliberately exploited and betrayed her. In fact, in this affair she hadn't been Ford's victim but that of the publisher, Pascal Covici. Ford had clearly named her as translator from the start, both to Covici and to others; but Covici had evidently decided that the book would sell better with Ford's name on it.

By the time this new trouble arose between them Jean and Ford were no longer in touch, but Ford must have guessed she would be angry. Then in October *Quartet* appeared; and the next spring he had letters from her about *Perversity*. So as he worked on *When the Wicked Man* he knew that he wasn't forgiven, that she accused him of betrayal both personal and professional.... I'm sure this business of *Perversity* increased the sense of injustice which so unbalances *When the Wicked Man*. It's true that Ford was extraordinarily generous to young writers, who were often ungrateful to him afterwards. 'H.J.'s always rescuing some young genius or the other,' Lois says to Marya in *Quartet*. 'And they invariably hate us bitterly afterwards. Never mind! Perhaps you'll be the brilliant exception.' Ford himself put it in his best Eeyore fashion. 'I am a halfway house between the unpublishable young and real money,' he said, 'a sort of green baize door to kick on entering and leaving, both ways.'

Jean, of course, saw no 'real money', now or later. But she had a little in the spring of 1927, thanks to Ford: £250 for *Perversity* (half of which, he claimed, came out of his own pocket, because Covici never sent the second half of the fee). In March *The Left Bank* appeared with an introduction, again, by Ford; and for a first collection it was quite widely and well reviewed. But none of this made any difference to Jean's feeling that he had exploited and betrayed her. She forgot that he went on helping her work, and so had not rejected her entirely; instead she remembered that he had rejected her as a mistress, and told herself that therefore he could not really have cared for her work either.

In the meantime John had hit rock bottom, and as often happens there his luck had changed. In the first week of February he went back to The Hague. He was down and out, and determined to stop running and settle in Holland for good. And suddenly his long years as a stateless fugitive were over, so easily. The Registry in The Hague rang the Foreign Office, and John heard the decision just like that, over the telephone: the Foreign Legion was not strictly a foreign army, so he need not forfeit his Dutch citizenship after all. It makes one wonder if he had ever actually asked the right authorities before. It would have been very like him not to bother; so that heart-breakingly, infuriatingly, this part of his war with half the police of Europe may have been unnecessary, for some or even all of the last long years.

Now that he was, after all, a Dutch citizen, he was also entitled to state assistance; and he entered an asylum for the poor.

It was like being back in Fresnes, with destitution imprisoning people as effectively as locks and bars. In *Sous les Verrous* Jan saves his sanity by helping the other prisoners, running the library and writing their letters. Now John did the same. Soon he was no longer an inmate, but manager of the asylum; and he set to work with messianic and utopian energy to improve it.

In his second novel, *Kerels*, Jan too is manager of a poorhouse. Stania, he says, 'has not had the courage to share his fate,' but has stayed in Paris. He still thinks obsessively about her. He doesn't mention a lover any more; but he is jealous of her friends, and worried about how she can live. Then she writes to him: she has received a small legacy, and will come to visit him.

Jan hopes that she will stay with him now, but once again he is disappointed. When she arrives she does not even kiss him, but goes straight to her room. Then she stays only two weeks before dis-appearing again. She visits friends; she spends money on clothes and at a Casino. Jan is caught again by her delicacy and fragility, her soft voice, her 'slow, indolent gestures'. He abases himself before her; he feels 'cowardly, servile, characterless'. But she remains cool and distant; she doesn't let him make love to her. One evening he gives a party for the inmates, and asks Stania not to dress elaborately in front of such poor people. But she doesn't listen. She appears like a princess among the paupers, in a beautiful evening dress and golden slippers. And Jan was wrong — the men are not angry, but delighted.

I don't think we can doubt that Jean paid John a brief visit like this one some time in 1927, most likely when she got her *Perversity* money in the spring. For the rest of the year she was probably in Paris, writing *Quartet*.

She was as unreliable about the writing of her novels as about any other fact. Once they were done she felt she'd written them more quickly and easily than she had — certainly more quickly and easily than the one she was writing now.... So she often said she'd written *Quartet* in two quick bursts, with a time of despair in between when she couldn't get the ending; but sometimes she said she'd worked away at it for 'a long dreary time', a year or even two. I expect she worked at it whenever she could during 1927 and early '28; part of the time at least in a 'depressing' hotel in the rue Vavin, near the Luxembourg Gardens.

Now Jan's question about Stania arises: how did Jean manage to live? There could be no money from John, and there was no longer any from Ford. The answer, I think, is that she worked, at least sometimes; and that the person who helped her (for of course someone helped her) was no longer Ford but Germaine Richelot.

In fact Germaine had been helping all along. She'd helped with Jean's work, acting as her go-between with Ford, and sending her *Left Bank* sketches to possible patrons. And even more, of course, she'd helped with Jean's daughter. She'd found Maryvonne's place in the clinic; I'm sure she'd been paying for it, or helping to pay for it, for the last four years. Then in July 1926 she'd done more. Perhaps Maryvonne was getting too old for the clinic; in any case, she needed to be moved. But Jean, plunged into the *tristesse profonde* of the end of her affair, couldn't do everything, or perhaps could do nothing. It was Germaine who wrote to boarding schools and convents near Paris, looking for a place for a *'fillette de quatre ans'*. And I expect it was Germaine who found one; who helped Jean (or John, if he was in Paris at the time) to move Maryvonne there; and who went on paying for Maryvonne, or helping to. And on top of all this she now gave Jean money; and may have found her a job as well.

In Jean's story 'Susan and Suzanne',* the heroine, Susan Helder,† has exactly the same job as Sasha once had: *dame de réception* at a *couturier* near the Avenue de Marigny. Susan is English; she has had

---

*Like 'Houdia', never published. Jean said it was 'a very early effort and I'm not proud of it'. Just once, in the 1950s, she tried to do something with both these stories; she sent them to a friend, and both were lost. (Except for Part III of 'Susan and Suzanne', which is in the British Library). But once again John had made, and published, a Dutch version; so at least the main lines of the story were preserved. Martien Kappers den Hollander very kindly told me in detail the contents of both 'Houdia' and 'Susan and Suzanne'.

†'Helder' is so close to 'Heidler', just as (Marya) 'Hughes' is so close to 'Hugh', Heidler's Christian name.... It's as though both heroines are still Hugh's, still Heidler's.

a French husband, but the year before he committed suicide. She is still in a state of shock; her face is expressionless, she feels numb and apathetic. She has a small daughter, Suzanne, whom she visits every Sunday at her *nourrice* in Versailles. This is not a happy arrangement. The little girl is sickly, and will never embrace her mother; the *nourrice* thinks that Susan lacks real maternal feeling, and resents being underpaid.

Susan goes to her employer, Monsieur Brega, and asks for a rise in salary. He suggests that she come as English governess to his daughter Jacqueline; and his wife agrees, in order to help Susan.

Madame Brega is an ambivalent character. She is (as though to sum this up) half French and half English. On the one hand she is genuinely good-hearted, generous and kind. On the other, she is proud of her charity, and flattered when people praise it. And she has touches of the worst qualities anyone can have in Jean's world: condescension, snobbery, and impatience with 'sentimentality'.

She urges Susan to put her daughter in a sanatorium for children, run by some women friends of hers as a charitable, or half charitable, institution. It is called *Le Nid* ('The Nest'), and is at Melun near Paris.

Suszanne comes to stay with her mother for a fortnight before she goes to the sanatorium, and Madame Brega is kind to her and her mother. But then she is sent to Melun, where Susan can only visit her once a month. On her first visit Susan is terribly upset, because the little girl looked so frightened, and because they had shorn off her hair, which was her only really attractive feature. That night Susan makes up her mind to steal Madame Brega's pearl necklace. At around midnight she goes stealthily to Madame Brega's room.

Madame Brega wakes up to see a dark figure — but it is not Susan. It is a man with a black handkerchief over his face. He threatens her with a revolver and she gives him the key to her jewellery box. But as he is about to make off with the pearls, Susan enters: and he shoots her.

The burglar escapes, Madame Brega regains her pearls, and the Bregas adopt little Suzanne. Madame Brega writes to the Directrice of Le Nid, Melun: Suzanne Helder is now legally theirs, and 'the undersigned' will come and fetch her. The story ends: '"Some people are just lucky," was the opinion of Madame la Directrice.'

'A bit melodramatic,' as Jean said of the other story, 'Houdia'; she was right not to be proud of it. But it is perfect example of her worst view of the world, all the clearer because her art has failed to smooth its edges. Susan is the essential Jean Rhys heroine: alone, abandoned by her protector; numb and paralysed, unable to cope with life. She struggles to recognise kindness, but in even the best case she sees charity and condescension, without real understanding. In the extremity of her poverty and need she plans a violent act, which will both save her and revenge her on the world of comfort and power. But fate itself conspires against her, crushes and kills her. Then the world of power, and particularly legal power, robs her of her child, even after death. She is left with nothing at all. Everyone wins but her; everyone lives but her.

This is what will happen, literally or metaphorically, to all the heroines (except Anna, the youngest, who does not yet fight back): oppression, revenge, failure, death. The story will remain the same; what will change is Jean's way of telling it. Susan will become Marya, Julia, Sasha, finally Antoinette; and out of each one's story she will burn more pity for herself and blame for others, until, in the last two especially, she will achieve both truth and great art.

But 'Susan and Suzanne', like all Jean's stories, also reflects her life at a particular moment or moments. Suzanne's move from the *nourrice* to the sanatorium reflects, I'm certain, a move of Mary-vonne's, probably from her clinic to a children's home or boarding school, and probably in 1926. For among the places Germaine considered then was one with a horribly coy name very like 'The Nest': *Le Berceau*, 'The Cradle'.

And Madame Brega, I think, reflects Germaine herself, and probably one of her sisters. The combination of wealth and kindness – but a little less kindness than Germaine's – sounds like the elder sister, Madame Bragadier: and of course the name sounds like her as well. Perhaps the other sister, Madame Lemierre, contributed her daughter, Jacqueline. Monsieur Lemierre was a doctor; but Monsieur Bragadier (who was, Jean said, Romanian) could have been a *couturier*.... Or perhaps, of course, the job near the Avenue de Marigny was quite separate. But that Jean often thought of jobs with children when she needed money is certain. The lady in 'Discourse of a Lady....' proposes it for her down-and-out friend; Julia has done it before Mr Mackenzie, and tries to do it again after him. Jean did it before Ford, with the Richelots; and now that she was poor and alone after him, what more natural than that her rich, kind friends should employ her again? Madame Brega gives Susan her job more out of charity than because she really needs her; and if Madame Brega was really Germaine's sister, or perhaps one of her friends, then that, too, would have reflected reality.

But Madame Brega was also Germaine herself. Germaine was Jean's best friend: perhaps the only real friend, she said, she'd ever had. But she could never wholly love and trust anyone for long. In the end Germaine was too safe, too rich; she was even too kind. I think Jean came to feel that her kindness was too much like pity. That part of Madame Brega was Germaine, even if it was someone else as well.

In the final version of *Quartet* Marya has no kind friend like Germaine; and when Jean translated *Sous les Verrous* she made Mathilde Dubar even more of a villain than John had. There were artistic reasons in the case of *Quartet*, but none in *Barred*; quite the contrary. No, there was something else behind this: the resentment that Susan feels for Madame Brega's charity. During the summer of 1927 Jean's own similar resentment built up. Germaine was being kind only because she wanted thanks — she was giving Jean money in order to enslave her.... Finally she burst out in rage and bitterness against her friend.

'My dear Ella,' Germaine wrote sadly afterwards, in her careful, imperfect English,

> ... I see you still have much bitterness against me. Perhaps, later, much later, you will understand how unjust you have been and understand then that I have loved you. Had you loved me, had *you* had a real friendship for me, you would not have been so sore about this awful money question, and hurt me as you did. You say 'I wanted your friendship and not your money.' Well, *because* I gave you the first and you needed the second, I gave it to you ...
> My dear Ella, I have nothing to forgive (had I anything to forgive, you would be forgiven long ago, as you are unhappy, and because I did love you). But I have nothing to forgive: although I think that exaggerated pride (I would say in French 'amour-propre mal placé') is a fault and can only cause harm. I believe that I have understood you better than you think, *because* I loved you. And may be, if you had loved me too, you would have understood me, and all this bitterness would have been 'epargnée' to both of us.

Happily, they made up this first quarrel. But it is unlikely that Jean ever really changed her mind, or rather her feelings, about Germaine's charity. It was her maddest point, this one about money: her weak point, like something which, having once been broken, will very easily break again in the same place. All her friendships, if they survived everything else, would be wrecked on this rock of money.

There are two other things wrong between Susan and Madame Brega, which probably also reflected reality. One is Susan's resentment, or the story's resentment, at Madame Brega's 'legally adopting' her daughter ('*Some people are just lucky*'). That is, Jean's resentment against comfortable and powerful people who could afford, as she couldn't, to bring up Maryvonne: and Germaine, I've guessed, or her whole family, were among those people. And the second was Susan's unhappiness with Le Nid. I think that Jean was similarly unhappy with Le Berceau, or the Maison Ste Marie, or whichever institution it was that Germaine had chosen. For in September 1927 Germaine was once more looking for 'somewhere good for Maryvonne'. If Jean wanted to keep her in France, she said, the Princesse de Poix was willing to help; and so of course was she, 'though I said that I would no more interfere'. But Jean could no longer accept anything from Germaine or her friends. In early October she took Maryvonne out of her home and went with her to the other person who loved them: John.

This was a desperate, perverse and stubborn move. It was always a desperate move for Jean to leave Paris; but never as desperate as this. For she had left Maryvonne in other people's care all these years because she and John were too poor and too estranged to have her. Now at last she had fetched her: *but nothing had changed*. There was no *rapprochement* between husband and wife; and John's situation was worse than ever.

He was in trouble again, like the repetition of a nightmare. He had been accused of embezzlement and slung out of the asylum.

He tells the story in *Kerels*. For months Jan champions the criminals, beggars and drunkards of the poorhouse against the director. He makes the place clean and decent; he serves coffee to the men as though they were guests in a hotel. He lifts them up, and they love him. But doing it swallows up his budget, and his own salary, and still there is not enough.... The governors send in an accountant, and he cannot account for six hundred guilders. The men fight for him, threaten the governors, go wild; but all in vain. They form a ragged guard of honour for him as he is kicked out into the gutter.

It is a self-serving account, only saved by the fact that John's fierce indignation is even more for the derelicts of the poorhouse than for Jan. But it seems to have been true that he spent the money on the asylum rather than on himself. In Vienna he'd gambled and stolen for his wife and himself, in Paris for his whole family, now for his down-and-outs. He saw himself each time as a defender of the have-nots in his care against the haves; and he was. But he also saw himself as above the law: and that, of course, he wasn't.

He was thrown out of the asylum on 12 September, penniless, perhaps threatened with prosecution, certainly without a reference or recommendation.... At the end of *Kerels* Jan has some hope of returning to journalism, but for John this was surely wishful thinking. It must have been very unclear how, even whether, he could possibly survive. It was on the same day, 12 September, that Germaine wrote to Jean offering her help and the Princesse de Poix's, and Jean chose to turn them down and fall back on John. It was just her luck, and just her defiance of reality. As she said later, such comic mistiming was '*exactly* me. It would happen just that way and no other.'

From October 1927 to early 1928 John, Jean and Maryvonne lived together in Esdoorn Street in The Hague. Maryvonne was five and a half; it was almost certainly the first time she had lived with both her parents, and certainly the last. Not surprisingly, she remembers these months well. But they must have been hard ones. No one knows how John earned a living, or what Jean was doing: perhaps working on *Quartet*. He had never forgiven her for Ford; and she still withheld herself from him. It was a stop-gap, a huddling together out of habit, and for the sake of their daughter. Their marriage was over.

'Did I love Enno at the end? Did he ever love me? I don't know,' Sasha says in *Good Morning, Midnight*. But Jean tried to tell the truth about this in that book, as about everything. 'Because I wanted to escape from London I fastened myself on him, and I am dragging him down,' Sasha says. 'All the gaiety is going and now he is thin and anxious.' But it is when she sees him thin and anxious that she is suddenly sure she loves him.

> ... I saw him in the street below, standing by a lamp-post, looking up at our window, looking for me. He seemed very thin and small and I saw the expression on his face quite plainly. Anxious, he was....
> When I saw him looking up like that I knew that I loved him, and that it was for always.

It wasn't for always, but that was how Jean loved John at moments, and how she liked him always: not for his strength but for his weakness, like hers. Her love for him was always a kind of pity; and a loyalty and protectiveness for the two of them against the world. So in the one story in which he becomes a romantic lover he is also persecuted, mad and finally dead. This is 'The Blue Bird', in which he is Carlo's lover, Paul.

Montparnasse calls Paul the Bad Man, and says he takes all Carlo's money. He doesn't live with her, and he disappears for weeks at a time, and worries her. But to her he is 'one of those people whom one adores and whom one is never sure of because they seem marked out ... fated.' Paul is wanted by the police, and one day he wires to her to join him. His eyes look desperate, childish, quite mad. But suddenly she feels so happy with him that she wants to die, then, at the height of their love ... But she draws back, frightened; and Paul kills himself alone.

*John needed her*, that was the key. So did her last husband, Max. She loved them both for this, with perhaps her best, most generous love. But she could never feel it for long. She was too weak; she wanted a man to lean on, not to lean on her. In the end it frightened her to be needed, because she knew she would fail him. As she did.

*Did he ever love me?* Yes: and hated her too. He felt rejected, betrayed, deeply wounded in his masculine pride. And not just because of Ford. She had had those moments of real love for him: but she was never in love with him. Sexual attraction, romantic love, she felt only for those big calm Englishmen she trusted so instinctively and so wrongly. In this way she never really gave herself to John, but hurt him long before Ford. '*Lorsque je m'approchais pour la prendre dans mes bras,*' Jan says, '*combien de fois a-t-elle prévenu mon baiser en me disant "Je suis tellement fatiguée!"*' Stania responds with '*froideur*', with '*manque d'enthousiasme dans les heures intimes*'.

> *Etait-ce pudeur, raisons de santé, crainte? Je ne sais. Toujours est*
> *il que là nous ne nous sommes pas compris comme il le fallait.*

At the same time, Jan says, 'she pretended that she disdained everything physical; she would even say that she attached no importance whatever to the act of love. She was like that when I first met her, and she remained like that.'

> *....Souvent [m'a-t-elle] exaspéré par une imprudence effroyable.*
> *Adepte convaincue de la doctrine de la libre disposition de soi-*
> *même, elle n'a jamais réfléchi aux risques qu'elle courait par la*
> *fréquentation d'amis, voire d'hommes recontrés au hasard.*

So Jan sometimes leaves her alone in the night, '*anxieuse de mon absence et vaguement jalouse*', while he seeks solace elsewhere. ('You don't know how to make love,' Enno tells Sasha in *Good Morning, Midnight*. 'You're too passive, you're lazy, you bore me. Good-bye', and he leaves her for several days.)

'*Que j'ai grimacé de fois derrière ce masque joyeux du rire depuis que je connais Stania!*' Jan says. Yet to the end he loves her beauty, '*exquise, lasse et triste*'. To the end he feels that underneath everything she is '*loyale, fidèle*', and that 'without her charm, her *beau naturel*, her manners of a great lady, without her prettiness and, above all, without her generosity of thought, I am nothing.' John would go on feeling this, angrily, obsessively, for at least five years.

★     ★     ★

Ford's and Stella's life together was over too, at almost exactly the same time. In early 1927 Ford told her he was in love with René

Wright. He wanted to have both René and Stella, as he'd had both Jean and Stella; but this time Stella objected. René Wright was less tractable too, refusing to become his mistress, only his wife. So in the end this came to nothing; and Ford had to wait until 1930 for his last love, Janice Biala. Jean would replace him much more quickly.

Did they ever see one another again? Ford was in Paris for much of 1927, and so was Jean. She'd imagined revenge in stories, in 'Houdia' and in 'The Spiritualist'; she was writing *Quartet* in anger and revenge. And in *After Leaving Mr Mackenzie* she would write that six months after the end of their affair, Julia follows Mr Mackenzie into a restaurant and slaps him in the face with her glove. Montparnasse gossip said almost exactly the same: that six months after their affair had ended Jean saw Ford, 'walked straight up to him and slapped him hard in the face.'

When she read Ford's biography in the 1970s Jean was furiously angry, and insisted that this and everything else about her was lies, 'obvious lies'. Some of it — that she had had a child by Ford, for instance — was; but some of it — for instance that he had given her money until the end of 1926 — wasn't. And this? Well, despite her denial, she could easily have done it. Thinking only of Ford's personal, not his literary treatment, of her, I rather hope she did.

But then they may have met again later, when Jean had begun her new life. For this happens to Notterdam with Lola in *When the Wicked Man*; and his description of her then is just like Jean. She lived in the present, like a child, and could cut herself off from the past in an instant. She'd done it with her parents, her Great-Aunt Jane, the Richelots when she left for Vienna; and perhaps she did it, or pretended to do it, with Ford. For Lola remarries, and she and her husband plan to start a chicken farm in Sussex. That was not at all like Jean; rather it was one of Ford's own romantic ideas, which he'd tried (with pigs instead of chickens) with Stella. Of course it had failed. ('He's such a good writer,' Stella said, 'and such a bad farmer!') But to Ford it still meant happiness, and so victory for Lola. And he wrote: 'You might have thought that she had never done anything else than start chicken farms all her life. Her eyes rested on Notterdam with complete aloofness.'

Towards the end of her life Jean tried to set the record straight (or sometimes to tip it in her direction) about Ford. First of all, she acknowledged her debt to him as a writer. 'Ford helped me more than anybody else,' she said; 'he was the most kind and generous man', to her as to so many young writers. This was certainly true, and especially of Jean. Ford discovered her, encouraged her, published her, wrote the introduction to her first book. He discovered and encouraged so many young writers then and later — Robert Lowell and William Carlos Williams, Allen Tate and Caroline Gordon, Djuna Barnes and Katherine Anne Porter.... But for none of them can he have played as vital a role as he did for Jean, for none of them can have needed as much encouragement as she did. She didn't think of a career; she didn't think, as she said, of publishing at all. Without Ford she wouldn't have known how, and she wouldn't have dared. It's quite possible that we owe to Ford, not that she wrote her novels, but that we can read them.

She gave him still more credit. 'He told me what to do, what not to do,' she said, and 'I learnt a good deal from him.' And this too must have been true, for as writers they are often similar. Allen Tate called Ford a French writer who wrote in English, and that was even truer of Jean. Ford loved economy, clarity and strong emotion in writing, and so did she; he hated moral and political preaching, and so did she. He brooded for hours on a sentence or a paragraph before writing them down; and so did she. But all these were things that found echoes in her, that were in her already. When he suggested something that wasn't, she rejected it. He tried very hard, he said, to get her 'to introduce some topography of [the] region, bit by bit, into her sketches.... But would she do it? No! With cold deliberation, once her attention was called to the matter, she eliminated even such two or three words of descriptive matter as had crept into her work...' No: the one thing Jean was sure about was writing. She followed her instinct; and no one, not even Ford, could teach her very much.

She generously acknowledged his importance to her as a writer; but his importance to her as a lover she denied. She often insisted he was not Mr Mackenzie (though at least once she said he was). And she said that what had really hurt her at the end of their affair was not the idea that Ford had rejected her, but that he had rejected her writing.

> ... That was what hurt most: she had imagined she had been a bit in love with Ford, but she wasn't, and she didn't think he was ever in love with her, but only [with] her writing, and he was, finally, false to that, because she couldn't believe he could behave as he had and still be sincere about her work.

But this wasn't true. She *had* been in love with Ford, and he with her. From this point on writing became the most important thing to her: but only because she had to give up her dream of being a happy woman. And it was Ford himself who made her give that up, finally and forever: Ford who was, therefore, the turning point, as Mackenzie is for Julia. Like Mackenzie with Julia, he had 'destroyed some necessary illusions about herself'. In *When the Wicked Man* he drew her as selfish and violent, a drunkard and a harlot, whose abject submission was just another means of getting her own way. When he dropped her I'm sure he thought these things of her. Perhaps he said them ('Towards the end of his explanation he became definite, even brutal, though not to excess'). But he didn't need to say them, because she already thought them herself. At that moment she had to give up the illusion that she might still be an ordinary happy woman; she had to ask herself if what Ford thought of her was true. That is what she spent the rest of her life doing. In this way too it was Ford who made her into a writer.

# CHAPTER SIX

# *Quartet*

When *Postures* — that is, *Quartet*\* — appeared in England in September 1928, then in America in early 1929, the critics reacted strongly. The worst reviews said what Jean's bad reviews would always say: that 'for its sordidness, lack of a redeeming feature either as literature or possessing a moral, [*Quartet*] seems unsurpassed.' The good ones said what the good ones would always say: that it was 'a very remarkable and powerful piece of work.' And most said what most would always say: that *Quartet* must enter your literary pantheon — '*if* you don't mind the plot and do care for style.'

Some of this reaction was specific to the time. During the 1920s *avant garde* writers had taken the bit of modernism in their teeth and galloped away from the ordinary reader so hard that by now Paris, where most of them seemed to live, was as far from England and America as another planet. Like Hemingway, or like Fitzgerald, Jean was writing about drink and dissipation, adultery and violence. But it was even more shocking when she did it, because she was a woman, writing about a woman. And because hers was a harsher, uglier world: she described not just vice and immorality, but poverty, prison and crime. Anglo-Saxon readers had always been shy and shockable: less prepared to face ultimate questions about the meaning of life in their reading than the Russians or Germans, less prepared to face the realities of sex and money than the French. Jean forced them to do both, and they didn't like it.

Now we are more used to it. That doesn't mean, however, that people can't continue to find her sordid in some deeper sense: and they are reacting to something real in her work when they do. First, there is very little morality in it. She is not interested in right and

\*Jean's first title for this novel was *Quartet*. For its 1928 publication the title was changed to *Postures* (in England, not in the USA). The original title was restored when it was reissued in 1969.

wrong, but only in what people say and do; sometimes (as in *Quartet*) she goes further, and sees morality as Marx saw religion — as an instrument of control, one more way the powerful have of oppressing the weak. And second, her whole aim as a writer was to cut through the polite and pretty surface of things, and reveal the reality she saw beneath: cruelty, egotism, lack of any decency, sympathy or imagination. Perhaps we are no longer so shocked by promiscuity, drunkenness and crime; but a vision of human nature as black as Jean's — especially in *Quartet* — must always upset and depress us.

And finally, she wrote for the underdog and the slave. She had so often felt trapped and oppressed, used and discarded; in writing — especially in *Quartet* — she wanted not only to understand how this could have happened, but to imagine and express her revenge. Who is master and who is slave changes; one day it may be black men oppressing white, women men, or children grown-ups. But Jean will always speak for the slave, expressing the slave's humiliation and sense of worthlessness, the slave's smouldering anger and rebellion. And any master who reads her will still feel, uneasily, that she is 'sordid'.

Yet what most readers feel now, and felt in 1928 too, is Jean's power and energy. *Quartet* drives forward, or downward, without a wasted moment: each stage of Marya's fall is drawn in a few rapid, accurate strokes, and we drop instantly and inevitably to the next — or the next but one, skipping whatever we do not absolutely need to know.* The plot is inevitable — long before Stephan is arrested we know from Heidler's hand on Marya's knee that he will pursue her; and we know from the first moment that she sees him again, and feels so happy and secure, that he will not pursue her in vain. The dialogue is brilliantly natural, the imagery hypnotic, the atmosphere unique. *Quartet* has its faults: I want to understand Jean's growth as a writer, and in this chapter I may seem to concentrate on them. So I should say right away that I agree with most of *Quartet*'s contemporary critics: it is extraordinarily well written, for a first or indeed any novel. What she describes is depressing, but how she describes it is exhilarating. *She* sees no excellence; but we do. And so we come away from *Quartet* as we do from all Jean's novels:

*E.g. the ten days Marya spends alone and ill, when the Heidlers are in Brunoy, before Stephan's trial; her first days at the Heidlers — when we join her there, there is already a routine; where she met Cairn, or how long she's known him; the first days or weeks or even months (the next we know it's April and Stephan was arrested in October) of the affair, before Marya first says she can't go on; how long she stays at the Bosphore, or at the Palmiers . . .

disturbed and distressed, and yet excited, feeling — like the heroine herself — against all the odds, hopeful.

★     ★     ★

*The Quartet*: The key to all Jean's novels is the heroine. We begin with her, and we follow her throughout: sometimes we hear what the others think and feel too, but mostly it is the heroine's point of view we inhabit. For the book to succeed we must be able to do so, if not happily at least with understanding and sympathy. Otherwise we will not care; we will even become impatient with her, as practical and strong-minded readers often do. At times we may not quite believe her; and at the end we may blame her for her fate much more than the novel itself seems to do. This is a problem which Jean will come nearer to solving with each heroine; though only the last two, Sasha and Antoinette, will in their different ways quite overcome it. With Marya, her first heroine, it is at its most acute. Why is she so melancholy, so lonely, so 'strangely pathetic', aimlessly wandering sordid streets in a strange part of a foreign city? Though she is married she seems to be mostly alone. She has few friends. When her husband is arrested her first thought is to turn to Miss De Solla, who is clearly little more than an acquaintance — but who is large and calm, a woman with a deep voice, both mother- and father-figure. Then throughout the time her husband is in prison she is inert, passive, given up to her fate. The Heidlers think of jobs for her; Stephan tells her to write to her family for money, but Marya has already decided that 'they haven't got any to send' and torn up her letter. After that, apart from selling her dresses, she never thinks of doing anything at all. She never thinks of survival in terms of managing her physical, practical life, but only her feelings: she must learn to be hard, to face hardness, she tells Lois, and to do this she must remain indifferent and not care what becomes of her. These negative and inner decisions are the only sort she ever makes — and she cannot act on these either. Going to the Heidlers, leaving them, abandoning Stephan, returning to him — none of these things does she clearly decide to do; in all of them she gives in to the wish of the strongest personality, or to her own strongest momentary feeling. Though her first thought about Heidler is 'I bet that man is a bit of a brute sometimes,' she falls into his clutches immediately; and when he takes her into his arms she thinks: 'I was lost before I knew him. All my life before I knew him was like being lost in a cold, dark night.' Even when Stephan met her four or so years before, she was already the same, with 'an air of fatigue, disillusion and extreme youth ... shadowed eyes, ... pathetic and unconscious lapses into helplessness.' She is a victim, an *'enfant perdu'*, a neurasthenic; from the start she has a 'fear complex', and needs 'a glass of wine on an empty stomach' before life seems to her 'significant, coherent and understandable'.

Now this is a striking character, not quite like anyone we've ever met before. We are intrigued; like the gigolo with Sasha in *Good Morning, Midnight*, we wonder what has happened to make her so afraid. But in *Quartet* we never know. We only dip very briefly into Marya's past. We know that before she met Stephan she was a chorus girl for five years, and increasingly lonely and unhappy; we know that her family is respectable but poor, that they therefore left her to earn her own living from the age of nineteen, and that (according to Stephan) 'they didn't seem to care in the least what became of her.' That is the beginning of a story which might help us to understand Marya, but it is not enough.

As Marya suffers more and more, in her unhappy affair, our sympathy should grow. But it may not. Instead many of us will feel that we understand her still less, or even not at all. Her happiness is so brief, and so negative — merely a peacefulness, an absence of thought and worry. And for that brief peace she pays so dearly — tormented by her love of Heidler, her hatred of Lois, her guilt towards Stephan, her ostracism by the whole of Montparnasse. Can we understand, can we even believe, that she would stay like this, for so many months in Heidler's house, for so many more in her sordid hotel? Well, such things happen. She is obsessed; her husband is in jail; she has no money, no family, no friends, nowhere to go.... But though we may accept it, we cannot feel that this is just an unhappy love affair: a story that can tell us about love, about ourselves. There is something much sadder and sicker about it — and not just in Heidler's behaviour, but in Marya's. She cannot simply be a victim of others, as Jean tells us. There must be more — a self-destructiveness, a masochism, a *need* for what she blames others for inflicting on her. And there is, in fact, some evidence for that.

For consider Marya when we first meet her. She wanders down the rue Vaugirard, 'which was a very respectable thoroughfare on the whole. But, if you went far enough....' She *wants* to 'go far enough', to escape 'the soul-destroying middle'. Her marriage is risky and haphazard; her husband pets her but tells her nothing; he lies to her and treats her like a dependent child. Yet this, Marya tells us twice, makes her happy: she is 'very near to being happy', for the first time in her life. We can only feel that just this risk, and just this being desired, yet treated like a child, is what she wants out of life. And this is, of course, what she gets with Heidler. It goes wrong, and hurts her more than she foresaw; but that is not simply Heidler's fault. It is because her love of risk and of utter passive dependence is a dangerous and self-destructive desire. Heidler destroys her; but she has half-desired destruction all along.

From the start, then, we suspect that Marya is more responsible for her own unhappiness than Jean realises. And as her affair develops, the gap between what Jean wants to tell us and what we suspect is true grows wider. For Jean's whole effort is to show the Heidlers as powerful, cruel and in control, Marya as weak, abused, unable to 'play the game'. But in the end she makes the Heidlers too evil, and Marya too innocent, to be believed.

Perhaps not both the Heidlers. Lois is the most active villain of the piece, yet the problem is not there. For one thing, Jean lets us see that she suffers too: she loves Heidler, who treats her badly; she accepts her suffering, and waits 'like a well trained domestic animal' until it is over. *Of course* she hates Marya, as Cairn says; and we are quite prepared to believe that she might snipe at Marya, and sneer at her with her friends. I think we are prepared, too, to believe that she would prefer to permit and control the affair, rather than fight with Marya's 'bad weapons' — tears and rages — and risk losing Heidler altogether. She's done it all before, she says, and I think we can believe that too. She is the one who is really in control — inviting Marya to dine after their first meeting, visiting her, inviting her to stay, deliberately leaving her alone with Heidler, refusing her offer to leave ... and of course it works; that is believable too. With Lois Jean has achieved what she set out to do.

The problem is with Heidler. For we really can't understand, I think, what Marya can love or want in him, except the illusion of safety — and the reality of danger; nor can we understand what he really wants from her. He is simply a monster. He is cold and sadistic. He uses the language of love and desire, but he is cruel and contemptuous to Marya throughout. At the beginning he says, 'I know that somebody else will get you if I don't. You're that sort'; and at the end, 'I have a horror of you. When I think of you I feel sick.' He forces her to live with him like a maid, 'to be made love to every time the mistress's back is turned.' He forces her to give up Cairn, and finally to give up her husband. And for all this he never gives her one moment of loyalty, or of the protection she craves; he is always Lois's husband more than Marya's lover. We see no lightness or pleasure or kindness in his love; the best we could do would be to invent some, in the time they have together which Jean doesn't describe. In everything we do see, from his heavy hand on Marya's knee to his clumsy caresses in the Hôtel de Bosphore, he is cold, gross and overbearing. We understand all too well why Marya does not like or trust him; we cannot understand how she could love him.

As for him, at first we guess that he is chasing Marya for sex: that is what Jean Rhys's men usually want, and what they offer the heroines in place of love. This is what Heidler says: that he is tortured by desire for Marya, that he is tortured by love. But it is a twisted, reluctant desire. At the beginning he says, 'One knows the whole damn thing's idiotic, futile, not even pleasant, but one goes on. One's caught in a sort of trap, I suppose.' And at the end he says that sex is ferocious, 'terrible and pitiful and futile' — 'And a nuisance too.' As soon as he touched her, Jean writes, Marya knew that 'he didn't really like women . . . . No, not a lover of women, he could say what he liked . . . .' Heidler doesn't *enjoy* this love affair, any more than Marya; it is just as hard to understand why he goes on with it as why she does.

In fact, as we know, Ford was most of all needing to refresh his ego, to find new energy and new material for his artistic imagination. But this literary motivation Jean left out of *Quartet*, as she left out her own. In the absence of this explanation — or any other — we can only guess at what impels Heidler. Without real pleasure, or real tenderness, what is left, I think, is power. Heidler simply needs to bend others to his will, to have everyone to himself, even if he doesn't really want them. He insists on having both Lois and Marya, though he no longer wants Lois at all, and doesn't really want Marya either. He forces her to give up everyone else and dedicate herself completely to him, even though their affair gives him no pleasure. Cairn, the calm clever outsider, sees through Heidler even before the affair begins. When he and Marya first meet he says, 'I thought you weren't coming . . . . I thought Heidler would stop you.' Marya asks why he should stop her, and Cairn replies: 'Because he is a . . . oh, well, doesn't matter.' He never says what Heidler is, except a 'humbug'. But a few months later Heidler *does* ask Marya to stop seeing him; and not to go and see poor Stephan that weekend either. They have just been in a church: Marya says 'God's quite a pal of yours?' 'Yes,' replies Heidler. That is the clue. Heidler is trying to play God. *That* is what he wants, rather than sex or love: absolute dominion. The only time he shows any tenderness to Marya is when she has given it to him, and abased herself before him completely.

The only thing that can be said in Heidler's defence is that he is not happy either. He has had a nervous breakdown, we hear, and those early words of his to Marya — 'One's caught in a sort of trap, I suppose' — suggest that he is as much the victim of a self-destructive obsession as she. But that is to make excuses for him which in its final effect *Quartet* does not make. There is one moment in Brunoy when he looks 'white and lined', and says 'I'm so miserable that I wish I were dead.' But otherwise he remains as Marya first sees him:

fresh, sturdy, arrogant, brutal. 'He looked as if nothing would break him down,' and nothing does. When Marya is utterly destroyed he is flattered and impatient; in his last letter he speaks more coolly and smugly than ever, still as though he were God, or Marya a maid.

Now this portrait of Heidler as unloving and inhuman, a cruel despot who wants to impose his will for its own sake, without real pleasure or desire, is what Jean set out to achieve. For the thesis of *Quartet* is that 'life is cruel and horrible to unprotected people': that (as the little sculptor puts it) 'Victims are necessary so that the strong may exercise their will and become more strong.' Marya is a victim, and all her life she has been afraid that this would be her fate: that life held 'something cruel and stupid that had caught her and would never let her go.' Heidler is simply the final embodiment of the thing that Marya had feared. He is the embodiment of the novel's thesis that life and people devour the unprotected, to increase their own security and power, or just because they want to. That is clear at the end, when Monsieur Bernadet warns Marya that someone is likely to betray Stephan. 'People are *vache*,' he says. 'People play dirty tricks for no reason at all.' 'Perhaps it makes them feel warm and comfortable,' Marya says. 'What?' replies Monsieur Bernadet. 'Well, it's no use making philosophy about these things. Nearly everybody will be *vache* if you give them a chance; the best way is not to give them a chance. That's life.'

Heidler's gratuitous evil is, therefore, part of Jean's plan; it is even the heart of it. Yet it is also the heart of the novel's failure. For we might accept her thesis in the abstract: but embodied in these characters it no longer rings quite true. Heidler is too horrible to attract and attach anyone, too unreal to be really interesting. The worst happens, and we begin to doubt Jean's word. We begin to doubt her thesis, that people and life are cruel, stupid, gratuitously evil. We begin to protest that this is not a true, if dark, portrait of the world, but a portrait of one pathological relationship: and that the sickness is not all on Heidler's side. And in her description of Marya, especially in her relationship to Stephan, Jean gives us — usually without intending to — all the material we need for another, more believable story.

If Heidler wants to enslave anyone and everyone, at whatever cost, Marya wants to be a slave, on the same terms. She is drawn to Stephan in the first place because he is sure of himself, definite, self-contained. But once he is in prison he becomes broken and afraid: and immediately Marya is impelled to find another protector, another lover into whose hands she can give her life, and be happy. Her need not to 'think', to find peace and rest, is the main one, more than her desire for pleasure; that is why she can stay with Heidler for so long after all pleasure has gone. Victims are necessary to Heidler, so that he may exercise his will and feel strong: but equally a master is necessary to Marya, so that she may surrender her will, and feel weak.

Marya needs to feel this — that she is helpless, that her own will has nothing to do with what happens. But it is not true. Her behaviour is self-destructive; but it is as selfish as everyone else's, if not more. She tells Stephan that she loves him, but he does not believe her ('*C'est vrai?* Well, perhaps.') And nor do we. As soon as he is gone she becomes obsessed with another man, and hardly ever thinks of him from one end of the book to the other. When she does remember and regret him it is because of what he gave her: kindness and fun, youth and gaiety. It is because, as she says herself, 'He represented her vanished youth — her youth, her gaiety, her joy in life.' The 'passion of tenderness and protection' she suddenly feels for the idea of him, therefore, is more a passion for her lost self; and she only feels it when she is afraid of losing Heidler. For the real, broken Stephan she feels only pity. She knows she has failed him, and feels guilty. When he tells her about the loyalty of the other men's girls, she cannot meet his eyes. Jean tries hard to excuse her: when she misses Stephan's trial it is because she is ill, and he didn't want her there anyway; when she says the wrong thing to him it is because 'her brain wasn't working properly'; when she fails to visit him it is because Heidler kept her away; when she fails to assure him of her love, or of her desire to stay with him, it is because he is 'unreachable', withdrawn into his own pain or his own plans. All this is perfectly likely; and we do sympathise with Marya, left alone and penniless in a strange city. Yet we cannot help but wonder if it is the whole story. We notice how, when Stephan tries to explain to her what happened, it is she who withdraws: 'She had suddenly ceased to be able to understand French,' and 'he had become strangely remote.' And we notice how what she wants from people is help: if they cannot help her, they cease to exist for her. Miss De Solla cannot help, so she disappears; Jean sends her to Florence, and she drops out of the story. Cairn cannot help, so 'Before Marya had walked three steps ... she had forgotten all about him.' While Stephan is in prison *he* cannot help, and so she nearly forgets all about him too. Four days after he has left Paris she reads his letter 'indifferently, almost impatiently', because he cannot help her over Heidler; and when he returns, that help is all she wants from him.

From the moment that Stephan comes out of prison, and Marya must lose one of her protectors, her selfish need to keep the stronger one and sacrifice her husband ('to that peace she was ready to sacrifice anybody or anything') becomes more and more obvious. She cannot, in the end, stay with Heidler while Stephan is in Paris: but that is her real desire, and at first she acts on it. It is very hard to imagine what Stephan says that day, when she returns to their hotel; and Jean doesn't try. But we must feel a gap there, a problem which is never solved; and we must be surprised that even after this Stephan still does not suspect that there is anything between his wife and Heidler. Especially as he does notice that she stiffens when he touches her; and there is a strong suggestion each time we see them alone together that she no longer lets him make love to her, or even kiss her. Our feeling of her selfishness grows; and so does our sense that the story is breaking down under the strain of not facing up to it. So far Stephan's role has been believable in the same way as Lois's, which it resembles: he loves Marya as Lois loves Heidler, and he waits out the uncertainties and disappointments she causes him because he is afraid to lose her altogether.* But he is no fool, and he suspects she doesn't love him: his unexplained silence now, therefore, is another strain on our belief in the truth of this story.

In their last dreadful battle it cracks wide open, and not even the most sympathetic reader can any longer ignore Marya's quite pathological self-obsession. At the beginning she does half-recognise her guilt towards Stephan, but only to reject it violently: 'Nothing to kneel about. How perfectly ridiculous!' From then on she behaves as we have seen her do before, with Cairn, and with Stephan himself on Stephan's return from prison: 'I'm awfully tired,' said Marya, 'and awfully sad. Will you just be kind to me for a little? And don't let's think about love at all....' She treats him only as a source of comfort, not as a person, and certainly not as her husband; she speaks only to relieve herself, and never imagines what effect her words may have on him. She speaks, in fact, to herself: in a voice, Jean writes, 'of someone talking aloud in an empty room.' When he asks questions she answers impatiently, vaguely, fretfully. When she hears the anger and jealousy in his voice she withdraws even further: 'What am I doing here with this man?' she thinks. 'This foreigner with his ugly voice?' And when he pursues her, out of his own pain ('You

---

*Interestingly, however, we have to guess at this explanation. We hardly get inside Stephan at all, less than we get inside Lois, or even Heidler. We only share Stephan's thoughts at the very beginning, in the past, and at the end when he leaves; what he actually thinks and feels during the main action of the book we are not shown. It seems at first odd that Jean should have found it more possible to enter her enemies' minds than her own husband's: but the explanation lies of course in Marya's guilt and selfishness. Jean had only to avoid *some* of the Heidlers' thoughts and feelings about Marya, to preserve the picture of her innocence; with poor Stephan there was no alternative but to avoid them all.

mean to say that all the time you used to come and see me in jail you were Heidler's mistress? ... When you went to the hotel Heidler came to see you?') she says that it doesn't matter – because it doesn't matter to *her*. She tells him the simple, selfish truth: that she longed to see him when he came out of jail 'because I thought it would help me.' And when he tries to take her in his arms she shrinks away: 'No, don't touch me,' she says. 'Don't kiss me. That isn't what I want.' What *does* she want? She wants him 'to be good to me, to be kind to me': to take care of her, like a nurse or a parent, with no demands or even existence of his own, as though he were (as Stephan says) Jesus Christ. But of course Stephan isn't Jesus Christ; and he reacts as Marya must have known he would, if she had spared him a single thought. He is angry and jealous, and he determines to take revenge on Heidler. That is, he refuses to be turned into a nurse or a saint: he remains, simply, *another human being*. But for Marya that makes him 'the symbol of everything that all her life had baffled and tortured her.' She screams at him that she loves Heidler and hates him – that he left her alone without any money, and didn't really care what happened to her; she laughs insultingly and screams 'vile words' at him, she says she will call the police.... Finally Stephan catches her shoulders and pushes her out of the way 'with all his force'. She strikes her forehead on the table, falls and lies still: certainly unconscious, possibly dead. '*Voilà pour toi*,' says Stephan, and walks away. A moment later he disappears, heading for the Gare de Lyon (and perhaps Argentina) with Mademoiselle Chardin.

This ending is shocking and confusing. It bares the real reason why Marya finds people so cruel and inhuman: not necessarily because they are, but because she wants and expects them to be *super*human. The lack of imagination, the cruelty and exploitation, which she and the other heroines see in other people are often there – we do believe that; but they are also, perhaps even more, in her. 'Eat or be eaten is the inexorable law of life,' Jean had written in '*Vienne*': and Marya now takes her turn as eater.

That is the shock, and it is a bad one. All along we've been asked to sympathise with Marya: by her situation, by Jean's assurances that she is a weak and passive victim, above all by the simple fact of the narration's being overwhelmingly from her point of view. Our identification with her has already been weakened: but now we must lose it altogether. And that is disturbing, at the end of the book. But even worse is our confusion. For it is not at all clear that we are being *invited* to condemn Marya, to see that the cruelty she fears is as much in her as in the world. If that is what Jean is doing, it is confusing enough, when all the rest of *Quartet* has argued the opposite. But *is* she doing that? Is she asking us to change our allegiance suddenly at the end, and to go off, like Mademoiselle Chardin, with Stephan? ... Some things suggest that the answer is yes. For it is Jean who tells us everything we know – that Marya speaks as though Stephan isn't there, and is full of hate for him, while Stephan speaks gently, and even after all her revelations still feels sorry for her. And yet ... It may be that his move to put his arms around her seems to Jean just what it does to Marya: an invasion; it may be that she tells us all this as Marya tells it to Stephan – thinking it will *gain*, not lose, our sympathy. For the narrative does just what Marya herself does: it tells us only what happens to her, and is not interested in what is going on inside Stephan. However badly she behaves, we know why – she screams at Stephan because he has become a symbol; she fights him with such frenzy because she is afraid of being left alone in the sinister room. We never understand Stephan in this way: and the effect of this is to keep us (or at least try to keep us) on Marya's side. True, at the very end we follow Stephan, and enter *his* feelings. But what he does and feels is clearly not meant to seduce us to his side: quite the contrary. He hurts Marya badly, perhaps even kills her; and this time he really does leave her all alone, and not care a bit. Our last impression, therefore, is not of her violence but of his; and our last picture, of her lying 'crumpled up and ... still', while he sets off for a new life with Mademoiselle Chardin, can only be meant to attach us firmly to Marya, the victim and the loser after all. It may fail: we may feel that she deserves it. But the way that Jean has told the whole story, and the way she tells these last two pages, makes it clear that she doesn't feel that. She has been as honest as she can about Marya, as fair as she can to Stephan; but in the end she's only and entirely on Marya's side. Her honesty and fairness are still very incomplete: and they leave *Quartet* almost worse off than if she hadn't tried. For they make us see Marya more clearly than she does: so that at the end of the novel we are left with dislike for its heroine, and dissent from its author.

*Themes*: The problem of our disagreement with Jean about her heroine is very serious. It doesn't only affect our relationship to Marya herself, though that is bad enough. It affects our relationship to the whole book. For the question Jean asks about Marya and the answer she gives are the main point of *Quartet*. The question Jean asks about Marya is the question she will ask about all the heroines: *why do such terrible things happen to them?* Why are they unloved, abandoned, destroyed? And the answer she gives in *Quartet* is: because they are soft and unprotected people, and 'life is cruel and horrible to unprotected people.' 'People are *vache* and play dirty tricks for no reason at all. That's life.' Heidler is like this, pursuing her and then dropping her for no reason at all, for a whim. Life is senseless ('Here you are, it said, and then immediately afterwards, Where are you?'), and Marya has never been able to understand it without a glass of wine. In the end she gives up trying; it's just fate.

> ... And what was there to catch on to in life but that same idea of fate? A dark river that swept you on to you didn't know where — nobody knew where. What was the use of worrying anyway? *Nitchevo*!

This is a dark doctrine, pessimistic and nihilistic. And it is applied not only to Marya: life is cruel to all unprotected people, to everyone without money or power. It is cruel to Stephan, to all the men in prison and all the women waiting outside. It is cruel to exiles, to the 'internationalists' in Marya's hotel, 'who invariably got into trouble sooner or later.' And it is cruel to artists, whose rich patrons pick them up and drop them again carelessly, as Heidler picks up Marya. To these people — convicts, prostitutes, exiles, poor artists — Marya extends her passion and her sympathy. Like the homeless cats she sees in the street, they too are unprotected and dependent; and in all such 'thin vagabonds' she sees reflected the world's cruelty to herself.

*Quartet*'s harsh view of life is, therefore, also sentimental, and above all it absolves Marya of any responsibility. People are cruel, and she has no money or power; so she is exploited. *That* is why the terrible things happen. Beyond that it is simply fate, and no one knows where we are going....

You need a certain sort of courage to go on living, if that is what you believe, and Jean's heroines all have it: the gallantry of gamblers who know they are going to lose. But this is an easy courage, compared to the permanent and unglamorous burden of respon-sibility for one's actions. When Jean wrote *Quartet* she found it easier to be a romantic pessimist, in black despair about the whole of human nature, than to think that Marya might have brought her suffering upon herself, because of something in her own nature. *Quartet* is Jean's blackest book about the world and about other people, because it is the least black about the heroine.

This is what made people feel that *Quartet* was 'sordid'. It wasn't just the fact that the Heidlers were unprincipled Bohemians, Stephan a thief and a liar, Marya an adulteress, almost a prostitute. It was also because they felt that *Quartet*'s whole view of life, its central theme, was 'sordid'. And if 'sordid' means low, reductive, without any hope of redemption, they were right.

The book has another theme which is 'sordid' too: the idea that law and morality are mere 'humbug', just something society uses to control the weak, just another excuse people have to be cruel. Marya states this idea very clearly, immediately after Stephan has been arrested. What if he *is* a 'bad lot', she thinks. He has been kind to her, a good friend. 'Humbug it all was,' she thinks:

> ...The rotten things that people did. The mean things they got away with — sailed away with — smirking. Nobody caring a bit ... But, of course, anything to do with money was swooped on and punished ferociously.
> 'Humbug!' she said aloud.

Heidler will destroy her, Lois will abet him, and they will get away with it, 'smirking'. Stephan steals to stay alive, and he goes to prison. That is the rule of law — the haves keeping out the have-nots; and that's all. That is morality too. Later, when Marya has become Heidler's mistress, she and the Heidlers go to dine at Lefranc's restaurant. Monsieur Lefranc is heavily disapproving. Madame Lefranc has more imagination; she says 'Life is very droll. One never knows, Josef, one never knows.' But Monsieur Lefranc judges his female clients (only the females, we note) 'with severity'. As always, we see this from Marya's point of view: we feel that Madame is kind, Monsieur mean and cruel. But it is Monsieur whom Jean calls, in ironic brackets, 'a very moral man'. And so she suggests — as she did in calling Stephan 'a bad lot' — that the world has these things the wrong way round. 'Morality' is just meanness. 'Lois is a good woman and you are are bad one,' Marya imagines Heidler saying, 'it's quite simple. These things are. That's what is meant by having principles.' And 'principles' only apply to 'good' people, not to 'bad' ones. 'Nobody owes a prostitute a fair deal,' Heidler's imagined voice continues. 'It isn't done. My dear girl, what would become of things if it were? ... Intact or not intact, that's the first question. An income or not an income, that's the second.' It is all a question of money.

Nor are the poor and unprotected allowed to have any principles themselves. Lois carefully destroys Marya's feeble effort to hang on to any notion of right and wrong and to go away before the affair can begin. This is what Marya remembers most bitterly about her, and repeats many times: 'Lois said: "What's the matter with you is that you are too virtuous."' 'Virtue' in a have-not is ridiculous and a nuisance, because it stops the haves from doing what they want with them. Again morality is simply a question of power: haves display it to haves, but it has nothing to do with the others.

This rejection of morality and law as false, as merely devices which the wicked use to control the weak, is confirmed by everything in the book. The most powerful people, the Heidlers, are the most immoral; the most decent, Stephan, goes to jail. Marya herself never judges anyone on ordinary moral grounds, and the narrator never suggests that she should. Stephan lies to her: that has no effect on Marya except to make her stop questioning him, and be happy. When he acquires 'Napoleon's sabre' from (he says) the son of an old French family who are now very poor, Marya is 'vaguely uneasy'. 'He probably has no right to sell it without his mother's consent,' she says in an 'unhappy' voice. But Stephan silences her objections, and Marya drops them immediately. She 'never knew what became of the sabre'; and Jean repeats that 'Marya stopped questioning and was happy.' She does not suggest that Marya was wrong − or even foolish − to do this. On the contrary, the narration is firmly on her side. It goes on immediately to say how gentle Stephan is, and how Marya likes him: it drops the question of his lying and his crooked dealing as quickly as Marya does. Indeed it goes further, and makes a joke of the whole business. We have to laugh at Marya's reaction to the news that the object 'lying naked and astonishing on her bed' is Napoleon's sabre: 'one of his sabres, she supposed. He must have had several of them, of course. A man like Napoleon. . . .' We don't often laugh in *Quartet*; it is clever of Jean to make us do so here, so that we are disarmed by Marya's amorality, and complicitous from the beginning.

Her amorality continues, through Stephan's arrest − where she contrasts its unfairness to the *really* 'rotten things that people did' − to his imprisonment − where she says to him no more than, 'My poor boy, what rotten luck.' Even when Lois argues cynically that she must 'cut loose' from Stephan if she wants to save herself, Marya's reaction seems to have no moral content. She says violently 'I can't. I don't think about things that way.' But when we hear what she thinks it is nothing to do with any love or loyalty she owes her husband. She only thinks, 'You don't understand'; and what Lois fails to understand is not a moral imperative but the imperatives of pain. It's just possible she means Stephan's pain , but she doesn't say so. Rather she seems to mean her own; and that she cannot leave Stephan now, however likely he is to drag her down, because he is still the only person who really cares for her.

Later on, however, there are some signs that Marya does not live in a complete moral vacuum. Once she tells Cairn that she is 'horribly sorry' for Lois, 'conscience-stricken about her'. And twice she shows that she feels conscience-stricken about Stephan − first when he talks about the other prisoners' girls, and again at the end, when she rejects with such guilty violence any need to kneel before him. Deep in Marya therefore — and deep in Jean, or she wouldn't bring out this side of her heroine — there are still some 'ordinary' principles, an 'ordinary' moral code: the idea, for example, that one shouldn't hurt other people — steal their husbands, or cuckold one's own; and that if one must do so one should at least have a bad conscience about it.

Like all subversive writers, Jean walks a delicate tightrope here: for though she wants to unmask 'principles' and reject them, yet she wants us to condemn her villains and pity her heroine, and this we must do on some principle or another. 'Principles', accordingly, creep back in, and her struggle must be to restrict them to ones which will damn the Heidlers without equally damning Marya and Stephan. If the Heidlers lie and dissemble, so does Stephan: if Heidler uses Marya, so does Marya use Heidler, for protection. Jean gives these shared failures different weights, by making the Zellis so much weaker: their poverty and dependence give them an excuse, while the rich and secure Heidlers have none. But she does something else too, to present the Zellis as the more moral pair: she substitutes a morality of thought and feeling for the usual morality of outward behaviour. Thus, the Zellis at least feel pity and remorse towards each other, even (in Marya's case) towards Lois: while the worst thing about the Heidlers is their utter smugness, their ability to behave appallingly and never feel they've been anything less than perfectly reasonable, perfectly 'good people'. This is what will distinguish the damnable from the pitiable throughout Jean's work: not what they do, since to survive they must behave as badly as everyone else, or worse; but what they *feel*. So in *After Leaving Mr Mackenzie* Julia will say to Norah:

> '... What do you know about me, or care? Not a damned thing! Listen. When I saw that you'd changed and that you looked older, as if you'd had a rotten time, I cried, d'you see? I cried about you. Have you ever cried one tear for me?'

And Norah hasn't. She feels moments of compunction, and she tries to stop herself being cruel to Julia; but her real feelings towards her sister are indifference and envy. Julia, at least, has *felt* for Norah, and tried to *imagine* what her life is like. More and more that will be the heroine's — and Jean's — harshest judgement on 'good people': that they have no feeling and no imagination. That is what allows them to dismiss and condemn other people. The beginning of this elevation of imagination to a moral principle is here in *Quartet*, with the contrast between Monsieur and Madame Lefranc. Monsieur is cruel and judgemental; Madame, who is imaginatively alive to the difficulties of understanding other people's lives, is unbiased and kind. She is the only person in the book who looks kindly on Marya – except for Cairn. And Jean uses the word 'imaginative' about him twice on the same page ('imaginative and slightly sentimental').

Imagination and kindness produce tolerance: especially tolerance of failure to live up to the requirements of principles and laws. Tolerance is thus a moral value which has room for immorality – and one therefore which has room for the Jean Rhys heroine. In this it is like forgiveness, which the heroine will also increasingly crave. She will find both more often in religion, especially in Catholicism, than in people: and this is already so in *Quartet*. At the peak of their affair Marya and Heidler meet in a church, St Julien le Pauvre: 'Marya stood for a long time staring at the tall Virgin and wondered why she suggested not holiness but rather a large and peaceful tolerance of sin. . . .' Holiness is like 'principle', that's why; something which can cast out and keep out the unholy. But 'a large and peaceful tolerance of sin': that can include Marya. And interestingly, she immediately remembers Heidler saying something which suggests that he too tolerates sin: 'A little more or a little less, a dirty glass or a very dirty glass, as Heidler would say. . . .' Once again Heidler is like a god, and this time like the god Marya desires. Indeed, on the very next page he destroys her religion ('I'll never be able to pray again now that I've seen him do that'), and *becomes her religion himself*. All the complete submission she might give to God, all the peace she might get from him, she gives to and (briefly) gets from Heidler. Her 'God's quite a pal of yours?' and his 'Yes' mean this too.

Of course, in taking Heidler as her god Marya is making a dreadful mistake: for Heidler has only his absolute power, none of his love and forgiveness. But these remain Jean's moral ideals. People who judge, condemn and 'sneer' are always her worst villains; the few who try to understand and sympathise come closest to goodness. And since 'good' people are the quickest to condemn, her morality neatly stands the conventional sort upon its head.

*Quartet*'s answer to the question of Marya's suffering, then, is that life is simply like that. The strong exercise their wills on unprotected people, cynically manipulating morality and law to do so. That is the true nature of reality, whatever 'good' people pretend.

Those last words are important. For 'good' people always pretend. The whole world pretends: that is the other important point that Jean wants to make in *Quartet* (and in her other novels too). Life and people are cruel and despicable: that is the real truth. But that real truth is always hidden. This is the 'cruel and stupid' thing which has always hunted Marya, and in *Quartet* finds her. 'She had always known it was there,' Jean writes, 'hidden under the more or less pleasant surface of things.' People *say* that they want to help you, like Lois, or that they love you, like Heidler; but underneath they hate you, and just want to control you for their own ends. They pretend to fairness, kindness, love: but underneath they hold the knife ready to plunge into your back.

This idea of pretence is in fact the first that *Quartet* introduces us to, long before Marya begins to see what is lurking beneath it. Like her, and with her, therefore, we have the sense that something bad is waiting, hidden, before we know what it is. Only three pages into the book Marya and Miss De Solla talk about English people. Miss De Solla says there is 'something unreal' about them: 'They're pretending about something all the time. Pretending quite nice and decent things, of course. But still....' And Marya thinks: 'French people pretend every bit as much, only about different things'; in fact, 'Everyone pretends.' And that is exactly what we will discover. The Heidlers, who are English, will pretend 'nice and decent things': that Lois does not hate Marya, that Heidler is not in love with her, that they are merely helping a poor girl whose husband is in prison. There are no important French characters in the book:* but if we take 'French' as Jean Rhys shorthand for 'not English', and especially for 'not respectable', then this is true too: underdogs also pretend, but about different things.

Respectable people pretend about ugly realities, especially their own: they hide away their lower motives and acts, as they hide away — Marya notices — embarrassing necessities like prisons and drains, 'their little arrangements', tucked away where nobody can see. And this is just what the Heidlers do: they tuck away their own 'little arrangement' with Marya, and what they care about most is that nobody should see. Heidler says this over and over again to Marya

---

*The French are merely in the background — like the Hautchamps, the *patrons* of Marya's hotel, the Lefrancs in the restaurant; the lawyers and officials in the Palais de Justice, the warders in the Santé and Fresnes, and Stephan's prison acquaintance Jacques Bernadet and his girlfriend, Mademoiselle Chardin. This is, of course, like all 'Anglo-Saxon' literature set in France in the twenties. Jean liked to think that her unprotected and poverty-stricken life there took her out of the narrow and in-turned world of the 'Anglo-Saxons of Montparnasse', and into something much closer to the real Paris. It did take her to John's prison, and introduced her to his French friends, from prison and before: experience which set her outside and against the English Montparnos, but did not really take her into the lives of French people, or indeed of any others. It took her deeper into her own life, that's all: *that* is what she tells us about, not France, or Paris.

— 'Lois doesn't want anybody to know, and I assure you that that's all she cares about.' It isn't *all*: Lois says she loves Heidler, and she is certainly desperate not to lose him, however badly he treats her. But it is extremely important to her. After the scene at Brunoy, for example, she says to Marya, 'You're not going to talk to anybody in Paris about all this, are you?' And of course Heidler is partly using Lois as an excuse; he doesn't want the affair to be known about either. He already has a bad reputation — Cairn suggests this early on, and Marya herself implies it at the end ('Shall I tell you what else they say,' she taunts Heidler, 'the ones who have lived there long enough?'); he doesn't want it to get worse. He is terrified that Mme Guillot next door will hear Marya screaming; he is terrified of getting mixed up with Stephan and the police. 'I can't be,' he says to Marya. 'I can't afford to be.' He will protect his respectability at all costs — that is to say, of course, at Marya's.

This is the top line of *Quartet*'s motif of hiding and pretence, which continues its central critique of 'respectable' English people. But it has that lower line too, the idea that French people also pretend, 'Everybody pretends.' This line is more hidden and muted; but it pervades the novel even more. By 'French' people, I've suggested, Jean doesn't always mean the real French: she means everyone she can identify with, everyone who isn't 'English' and respectable, everyone, in fact, who is 'utterly unlike the Heidlers'. This usually includes the real French; and so it does here. Jacques Bernadet, for instance, does not pretend that he and his friends are incapable of meanness, as 'respectable' people do. He warns Marya that Stephan is likely to be betrayed, and that he will not lift a finger to help him — and Marya likes him better for his honesty. The haves pretend to be good; this humbug the have-nots are free of. But their lives are sordid and dangerous: and what they pretend to is insouciance, courage, self-sufficiency. And prime among these pretenders is Marya.

Jean never explicitly says that Marya puts on a falsely brave front during the time of *Quartet*, but she does say that in the past, as a chorus girl, Marya has covered up her doubts and fears and shown a brave face to the world. ('She learned, after long and painstaking effort, to talk like a chorus girl, to dress like a chorus girl and to think like a chorus girl — up to a point. Beyond that point she remained apart, lonely, frightened of her loneliness, resenting it passionately...') And now, when things go wrong, we can see that she tries to do it again. For as long as she can — until almost the end of the book — she tries to maintain a fiction of independence, even though Stephan had already noticed her helplessness before the story began. She maintains this fiction in front of Stephan himself,

pretending to him that she will be all right, and hiding her vast
dependent love of Heidler from him until nearly the last page. But
she maintains it even more with Lois and Heidler. She tries to
respond to Heidler's advances with hard decision – though a
moment later she cannot hide her weakness and desolation. She tries
to tell Lois, and Heidler, and herself, that she will go 'right off'; she
doesn't, of course, but she goes on from time to time trying to resist,
to stop, to withdraw. She longs above all to give in to him entirely:
'To give in and have a little peace,' to say 'Heidler save me. I'm
afraid. Save me' – 'Just like that.' But she doesn't. Instead she keeps
trying to hit back, to kick back, to rebel like the 'savage' and
'bolshevist' he accuses her of being. Once, in the climactic scene at
Brunoy, she actually hits him. After her long humiliation in the
Hôtel Bosphore she feels that there is 'not a kick left in her'; even
so she makes herself defy Heidler a last time and returns briefly to
Stephan. It is only after Heidler finally rejects her brutally and
completely ('When I think of you I feel sick') that she can no longer
even pretend to fight him any more. The only thing she can kick
is her own hat, lying on the floor. After that she is (as she writes
to Heidler) 'nothing at all. Nothing. Nothing.'

Marya is torn, it is clear, between a longing to give herself up, to
belong – to the chorus, to Heidler – and the need to resist their
requirements and retain her own individuality. The burden of
responsibility and loneliness is unbearable to her: but the surrender
of her separate self is just as bad. To this dilemma her solution is
pretence. In the chorus she held herself back, but outwardly
pretended to conform; now she inwardly surrenders to Heidler from
very early on, but pretends to him – and to herself – that she hasn't
done so. It is as Ford wrote about Lola Porter: 'when she suffered
from one appetite she superimposed over it the pretence of another.'

This idea, that 'everybody pretends', was, I think, originally a more
important theme in Jean's mind than it became in the finished novel.
Her first two titles, *Masquerade* and *Postures*, suggest this very
strongly; and so does her choice of Richard Cheever Dunning's poem
as a motto:

> *... Beware*
> *Of good Samaritans – walk to the right*
> *Or hide thee by the roadside out of sight*
> *Or greet them with the smile that villains wear.*

'Beware of good Samaritans' warns of the deceptiveness of others
– the Heidlers, of course, with their pretence of disinterested
helpfulness, and their reality of selfish exploitation. But the rest
evokes Marya's defence, which is also deceptiveness: hiding, and

wearing a false smile to disguise her real feelings. This suggests, of course, that what is false about Marya is her submission, and what is real is some hidden villainous intent. And Jean does occasionally suggest that what Marya hides is such an intent. Once, when she looks at Lois, there is 'something very like a menace in her long eyes'; and when they quarrel about fate and weakness, Marya says suddenly 'Weak, weak, how does anybody really know who's weak and who isn't? You don't need to be a fine bouncing girl to stab anybody, either. The will to stab would be the chief thing, I should think....' As she becomes more desperate her 'will to stab' grows. She imagines smashing a bottle in Lois's face; finally she even bursts out to Heidler: 'One day I'll walk into your studio and strangle your cad of a Lois — kill her, d'you see?' But the moments when the hidden villain breaks through her smile are her very worst ones. When she pictures 'the glass breaking', 'the blood streaming', she is horrified and thinks she is going mad; when she says she will kill Lois Heidler responds with his coldest contempt, and it is Marya who almost dies. She goes red, then white, and cold, and collapses, 'breathing loudly and quickly as if she had been running.' Afterwards she is 'quivering and abject', 'Like some unfortunate dog abasing itself before its master.'

Marya must hide her 'will to stab', because it means to her madness and rejection. So *whatever* she feels she cannot act on, but must try to hide. When she longs to submit completely, she holds back, and pretends that she can still 'kick'; when she has been beaten down so far that she longs for violent revenge, she is afraid to admit to it. It is not surprising that she takes refuge from this *impasse* in complete passivity: doing nothing, just lying for hours in her room.*

---

*Dunning's poem was called 'The Hermit', and appeared in the issue of *the transatlantic review* before 'Vienne'. This is its whole first verse:

> *Bleed, O my heart, bleed slowly but take care*
> *That no one hear thy bleeding. In the night*
> *Let not thy bedfellow divine thy plight.*
> *Bleed softly, O my heart, and in the glare*
> *And heavy silence of high noon, beware*
> *Of good Samaritans — walk to the right*
> *Or hide thee by the roadside out of sight*
> *Or greet them with the smile that villains wear.*

The reference to not letting 'thy bedfellow divine thy plight' is interesting: I wonder if it reminded Jean of how much she hid and held back from her husband. That of course touches on the sorest spot in *Quartet*; it's not surprising she left it out.

This, then, is what Jean wanted to say on the theme of 'postures' or pretence. Mostly she wanted to explode the pretence of the 'good Samaritans', the Heidlers, and to show the cruel exploitativeness beneath. And then she also wanted to show how Marya must adopt a pretence of her own in self-defence, and hide her real need and her real anger. At the end of her life she remembered all this quite well. 'I called the book *Masquerade*,' she wrote, 'for already it had dawned on me that the whole thing was a pretence. Stella was pretending to be a "sport", I was pretending to be quite reckless, not to care what I did, but underneath I was lonely and afraid....' But outside fiction she could not admit for long that she might share anything – particularly 'pretending' – with Stella Bowen. So for most of the time she claimed that *Postures* was 'a meaningless title', and that she couldn't remember why on earth she'd chosen it.

★      ★      ★

*Techniques:* Jean's aim in *Quartet* is to convey her fear of life and people; but though this fear paralyses Marya, it does not paralyse *her*. On the contrary it galvanises her; and this is why this dark and angry novel is not debilitating to read. 'When I say afraid,' Sasha says in *Good Morning, Midnight*, 'what I really mean is that I hate.' Jean's fear of the Fords was also hate. She longed to 'stab' them as much as Marya longed to stab the Heidlers; and unlike Marya she was able to – with *Quartet*. *Quartet* is driven by her hate and anger. They unbalance it, shifting all the guilt on to her enemies; but they also give it its intensity, its urgent power, which everyone has always felt.*

This is the 'terrific', 'almost lurid', passion for the underdog which Ford picked out in his introduction to *The Left Bank*. But on its own, of course, it wouldn't be enough. Hate can unfocus as easily as focus; fanatics can maunder and bore. But Jean never does that: for now Ford's other observation about her style comes in, her 'singular instinct for form.' That is the real explanation of *Quartet*'s power and achievement. As it must be, in the end, about any work of art, the explanation is technical. *Quartet* grips you and drives you on because, first of all, it is so spare. The rhythm of the chapters is short and stabbing: some are only one page long, none is more than nine or ten, even two- or three-page ones are broken into still shorter sections by asterisks or spaces. During all the spaces between chapters

*Thus, even an early reviewer who didn't know *Quartet* was a *roman à clef* guessed that 'Miss Rhys' hated and feared the person upon whom she based Lois Heidler.

and sections time passes, and we must imagine for ourselves what has happened. Think, for example, of how we learn about Marya's past, in Chapter Two. Her whole life up to this moment in Paris, when she is twenty-eight years old, is sketched in for us in under seven pages. Stephan's impulsiveness, Marya's passivity, the recklessness and risk of their marriage, are all conveyed as much by what is left out (the courtship, Marya's acceptance) as by what is written. It all seems to happen very quickly – again because so much is left out. Then Jean cuts out more time, and all the space, between London and Paris, and gives us only their arrival, 'on a June afternoon, heavy with heat.' Two and a half pages sum up the four years since then. The chapter ends with a mysterious intuition into the 'value of an illusion', the idea that 'the shadow can be more important than the substance.' We have no more time than Marya to ask ourselves what this means. But then we find out: the real world breaks in, and we learn about Stephan's arrest as cruelly as she does, on the first page of Chapter Three.

Economy and pace would always be Jean's great strengths: the ability to evoke a complex mood and story with a few accurate seen and felt details, leaving us to imagine their connections and explanations. She would work extraordinarily hard to get the details right, to make us tell ourselves the story she wanted; but after that she left it to us. That is a very hard thing to do. The writer's impulse is almost always to over-control the reader – and how much more in Jean's case, who set out in her writing to justify her life? Her first outpouring was often (certainly in *Quartet*) 'a jumble of facts' in which she obsessively tried to remember exactly what happened, and to explain to herself exactly why. But then she would ruthlessly cut and distil, removing much more than she left in, and especially taking out almost all the explanation. She would leave only the most essential, significant landmarks: bits of dialogue, the heroine's feelings, the sensual details of her inner and outer world. Even before we know that she did this we can feel around her words on the page a mysterious dark space, where she has cut away so much description, so much explanation. Her novels work like poems, evoking enormously much more than they actually say.

The only thing Jean does not yet have under control in *Quartet* is her pity for the heroine, and her anger against the world. In every other way she is already, in this first novel, in possession of her mature technique. The shape of *Quartet*, for instance, is as perfect as the shape of all her novels. The peak of Marya's affair, the plateau of her peace and surrender to Heidler, is almost exactly halfway through the book: the moment in the church of St Julien le Pauvre, when Heidler becomes her god and she agrees to sacrifice Cairn,

Stephan, everything for him (Chapter 13 out of twenty-three). After this Marya has a moment of lucidity, seeing the three of them detachedly – Lois formidable, Heidler cold, herself 'burnt up by longing'. She waits for 'the violent reaction that might free her,' and – again immediately, in the telling – it comes. Heidler is brutal; she hits him; he sends her back to Paris, to the Hôtel de Bosphore. And the last phase, the rapid downward spiral, begins.

The handling of the plot is not only shapely but subtle. Neither Marya nor we know what will happen – and yet we both do. For the end of her affair is implicit from the beginning. It is there when she first meets Heidler, in his speaking so sharply to Lois that she winces, in his hand on Marya's knee, huge, possessive, 'heavy as lead'. And in Marya's reaction: 'Ridiculous sort of thing to do. Ridiculous, not frightening. Why frightening?' This *half-knowing what will happen* is always there. It gives us a permanent sense of menace, of half-apprehended doom.

Thus, Marya feels 'extraordinary dismay' at the idea of living with the Heidlers, and melancholy fills her when she has agreed – though she tells both herself and Lois that she is grateful. Then Jean tells us that it is spring, and Marya feels 'excited, strangely expectant' – but she doesn't say what Marya expects. Heidler talks too – of feeling sick of himself, of being caught in a trap – without saying why, or what the trap is: but he has just said to Marya, 'Don't rush off....' So Jean builds up the inevitable attraction between Marya and Heidler, without naming it; and so too she builds up our sense of its menace and danger, without naming *them*. She hints at Heidler's reputation for exploitation through Miss De Solla, and through Cairn. She hints at Lois's role through a casual aside: 'I always give way to H.J. I give him what he wants until his mood changes. I found out long ago that that was the only way to manage him.' And she hints at Heidler's motivation, just after he has first declared himself to Marya: through her memory of the little sculptor's words, 'Victims are necessary so that the strong may exercise their will.'

Here Jean is taking one of Marya's – and her own – most self-destructive weaknesses, and turning it into art. I mean what John called her ability to 'disdain consequences', to refuse to recognise what she really knows will happen. This half-knowledge Jean describes with great accuracy in Marya, and also reproduces in her own prose: and so she creates that sense of doom and mystery which is her unique atmosphere. Marya does not let herself think of what will happen, but underneath she really knows: so her knowledge breaks through as fear, melancholy, expectation – that is, as an irrational sense of doom. This feeling of hers surrounds and infects

us. And then we too half-foresee the real machinery of Marya's affair
in Lois's remark about 'managing' Heidler; we too half-foresee his
cruelty in De Solla's and Cairn's distrust of him, and in the little
sculptor's enigmatic saying. Like Marya, we don't *know*, but we fear.
Jean not only shows us a heroine who inhabits a world of hidden,
waiting danger, therefore: she also creates it for the reader by the way
she tells the story. And that is why even rational and practical
readers, who want to resist her description of the world, are drawn
in. Jean's enigmatic, hinting, glancing style is the technical correlative
of the truth she wants to convey about the hidden dangerousness of
the world. It is, therefore, a perfect style for her purpose, a perfect
match for her meaning: her medium mirrors her message, as it does
in all great writing.

This hinting, haunting effect is achieved in many ways: principally
through cutting. But Jean has one other main technique of
indirection, which brings her writing closer to poetry than prose.
That is her use of imagery. Her novels are almost *made* of imagery;
their meanings, their feelings, even the movement of their plots, are
expressed most fully in compressed and powerful images. And this
main technique too is as fully formed, as perfect, in this first novel
as her other skills of shaping and pacing her story.

*Quartet*'s imagery, like the other novels', is so pervasive that it is
hard to know where to begin. Perhaps with the most general: its
image for life as a whole.

One of the strongest feelings Jean had always, and which she gave
to her heroines, was that she didn't fit in the world, that life was
a game she had never learned how to play. And this is the first of
*Quartet*'s dominant images: the game which Marya cannot play.
When she tries to find out what has happened to Stephan, she cannot
find her way around the Palais de Justice; when at last a man helps
her, 'Marya, hastening after him, began to feel as though she were
playing some intricate game of which she did not understand the
rules.' This is a foretaste of her main experience in the book, because
her affair too is a game of which she does not understand the rules.
Whenever she tries to escape from it Heidler says the same thing:
that she is not playing the game, that she must play the game. This
is a very English phrase: 'playing the game' is what English people
do. But Marya isn't English. The very first thing Heidler says to her
is 'But you are English — or aren't you?' Marya says she is, but she
isn't: she's Welsh (judging by 'Hughes'), and married to a Pole. So
she cannot play the English game. She says so herself: 'It's all a game
I can't play, that I don't know how to play.'

But as the game goes on we see that this isn't quite right. It's not
so much that Marya doesn't know how to play, as that she doesn't

want to. For really she understands the rules perfectly well: the point is that they are designed to destroy her. Thus she says fiercely to Heidler 'What game? Your game? Lois's game? Why should I play Lois's game?'; and she insists that it is Heidler, not she, who has failed to understand, or rather to admit what the real game is:

> Lois simply wants me around so that she can tear me to bits and get her friends to help her to tear me to bits. . . . They'll tear me up and show you the bits. That's what will happen, and you won't see it. A Frenchman would see the game at once, but you won't see it, or you pretend not to.

Marya is right, of course: Heidler has made the rules of this game, and she can only lose. One of his rules, for instance, is that he will not share Marya with Stephan, though she must share him with Lois. When Marya briefly breaks this rule, the game is over.

This image of love (or the whole of life) as a game whose rules are drawn up against the heroine is a very precise picture of Jean's view of things. It captures her idea of Marya as an innocent victim, cast for a losing role from the start. It captures her sense that people are not just cruel, but pointlessly and capriciously cruel – playing a game with Marya and her kind, like cats with mice (which is also Jean's image for Lois). And it captures the hiddenness of this truth, that life is a cruel game: for first Marya doesn't see it, and when she does see it Heidler says it isn't so.

*Quartet*'s second image of life is connected to the funfair. When Stephan has been sentenced to a whole year in prison, Marya suddenly feels excited instead of afraid. 'What's the use of worrying about things?' she thinks. 'I don't care. I'm sick of being sad.' And she stands and looks at the Lion de Belfort fair – the booths, the swings, the crowds, the merry-go-rounds. Then again after her next visit to Stephan, she sees a merry-go-round:

> . . . Children were being hoisted on to the backs of the gaily painted wooden horses. Then the music started to clank '*Je vous aime*'. And the horses pranced around, pawing the air in a mettlesome way.
>
> Marya stayed there for a long time watching a little frail, blonde girl, who careered past, holding tightly on to the neck of her steed, her face tense and strained with delight. The merry-go-round made her feel more normal, less like a grey ghost walking in a vague, shadowy world.

These glimpses of funfairs and of merry-go-rounds are set in deliberate contrast to the dark, defeated sadness of prison: to Stephan becoming hunted and broken, to Marya having to face life alone and

penniless. They are images of excitement, of sadness banished and
hope renewed. The merry-go-rounds especially are gay and bright,
full of energy and promise, with children riding the prancing horses
to music about love. They are 'all the fun and sweetness of life', the
joy Marya longs for, but which is always just out of her reach. The
little blonde girl whom she watches for so long is an image of her
own childish self, the innocent adventurous, pleasure-loving girl she
still longs to be, but whom life and Heidler will crush. *But now Jean
does a wonderful thing*: she pictures that destruction through the same
image, a funfair. The night after her affair has begun she is for one
moment 'absorbed, happy, without thought for perhaps the first time
in her life.' But Lois, of course, is desperately unhappy; and she says:
'Let's go to Luna Park after dinner. We'll put Mado on the joy wheel,
and watch her being banged about a bit. Well, she ought to amuse
us sometimes; she ought to sing for her supper; that's what she's here
for, isn't it?'

Suddenly the idea of the funfair is turned upside down. It is no
longer the opposite of a prison, but a prison too. The 'joy wheel'
is the perfectly compressed image of this sinister transformation. Joy
is what Marya longs for; but the wheel on which the Heidlers fix
her is only *called* 'joy'. Really it is an instrument of torture, a wheel
on which she is strapped and torn to pieces. Once again the 'game'
is not a game at all, but a cruel machine for breaking the heroine,
to the amusement of her enemies. The gaiety and hope of the funfair
is just another illusion, another deception; the little blonde girl grows
up to be Marya.

When Ford tried to persuade Jean to introduce 'topography of the
region' into the stories of *The Left Bank*, she refused, he said, because
she wanted to concentrate on 'passion, hardship, emotions'. In
*Quartet* Jean does describe the Montparnasse background: but only
in order to express these same things. However accurate and redolent
of real places her descriptions are, she only ever puts them in for
that reason. They are, in other words, not 'topography' at all, but
*imagery*: images of the heroine's emotions. Thus, for example, Marya
endlessly wanders the streets to escape from her fear, loneliness, or
pity for Stephan. These streets are described: but they are always the
same. Dark pavements glisten like water, reflecting red and yellow
light; on either side loom tall dark houses, shuttered against her. This
is not Paris, it is Marya's isolation and fear. She sees these streets and
lights when Stephan has been arrested, and when he has been
sentenced; she sees them when Heidler declares his intention to 'get'
her, and when she is drawn back from her hotel to his flat, and stands
outside looking up at the windows. The streets are dark and
glistening like water because she feels she is drowning in her fear as

though in water. Soon after Stephan's arrest she stands looking into the Seine, and red and yellow lights wink up at her just as they do from the streets. Later, when she feels 'quite dead', the streets seem to her to *be* water, in which she has drowned: 'As she walked back to the hotel after her meal Marya would have the strange sensation that she was walking under water.'

Jean would repeatedly use drowning as an image of emotional death, from Anna's 'letting go and falling back into water' when Walter rejects her (*Voyage in the Dark*) to Sasha's living death, 'Saved, rescued, fished-up, half-drowned, out of the deep dark river' (*Good Morning, Midnight*). Sasha too identifies the streets with the river of fear and isolation in which she once drowned ('Now I have forgotten about dark streets, dark rivers, the pain, the struggle and the drowning'); she too associates lights, especially red lights, with danger. 'Our luck has changed and the lights are red' she says, after her son has died. In her degradation after Heidler has dismissed her, Marya is afraid of light, and seeks only darkness: 'Surely at the end of this long and glaring row of lamps she would find it, the friendly dark where she could lie and let her heart burst.' And in *Wide Sargasso Sea* Antoinette, right at the end, feels the same: it is light which frightens her, night and darkness where she belongs. All through Jean's work these same images haunt her imagination: the dark river of death, the merciless searching light of exposure to other people. The first culminates in her short story 'The Sound of the River', where the heroine's husband lies in bed beside her, and she hears death swooping down on him, like the sound of a river. The second culminates in *Good Morning, Midnight*, which is full of lights and eyes, and which ends with the image of 'all that is left in the world': an enormous machine bearing lights and eyes.

The novels all use music, too, in the same way. They are especially full of popular songs: real, contemporary songs, but again not there to evoke (say) Paris in the twenties, but to distil for us what the heroine is feeling. So here the merry-go-round music is 'Je vous aime': love is the adventure Marya hoped for as a child, and still seeks with Heidler. But during her affair the song we hear is the little Spanish dancer's, with its 'atmosphere of fate and terror', and its story of stabbing a lover. *That* is what Marya feels, instead of the peace and happiness she'd longed for: fate, terror and 'the will to stab'. And as the affair ends the music echoes Marya's loss and despair: the pipe of the goatherd, 'dwindling away in the distance, persistent as the hope of happiness'; 'I want to be happy', played by her neighbour in the Hôtel du Bosphore; 'Laugh, Pagliacci, for your love is ended', as she sits in the Panthéon with the Heidlers and Stephan; and 'Par Pitié', the last song she hears with her husband. As Heidler delivers his 'explanation' the sound of jazz reaches them only faintly, 'from the farther side of the café'; finally, when Marya goes to a café by herself that evening a fussy, bespectacled pianist plays only bits of classical music, lugubriously, 'Jazz ... very far from her well-ordered mind.'

*Every detail* of Jean's description is like this — not outer but inner, not object but emotion. Take the little boat, for instance, which we see when Marya lies like a ghost on the beach at Cannes: it is called *Je m'en fous*. But boats are not so typical of Jean: clothes are more so. In *Quartet* she uses clothes brilliantly to render mood and character. What could be more revealing of Marya's nature than the episode in which she tries to sell her dresses? Not just because they seem to be all she has to sell (except herself, which in effect she sells next, to the Heidlers), but because of what Madame Hautchamp tells us. They will be hard to sell, she says, because they are all like the *robe de soirée*: not practical. 'Who would buy it? Nobody. Except a woman *qui fait la noce* ... it's a fantasy, one may say.' And she has summed up Marya. Someone not practical; someone who lives in a fantasy, and a fantasy of pleasure, beauty, frivolity. Then at the end, when her fantasy lies shattered, Marya expresses her fury and despair indirectly, through her clothes. Heidler is trying to persuade her to go away to Cannes, but she says 'I won't go':

> Her felt hat was lying on the floor and she gave it a violent kick.
> 'Leave me alone!'

Is she kicking Heidler through the hat, or herself? Or just the idea of going? All of these: as Heidler, in picking the hat up, smoothing it, and putting it on the table, also indirectly expresses a complex of desires — to smooth away Marya's anger and his own distress — to rescue the idea of Marya's leaving from her stamping on it, and — as we actually say — put it back on the table. All this Jean distils in the image of Marya's felt hat. And Heidler wins, of course: we guess that through the hat too, before we see Marya in Cannes. For as the chapter ends Heidler is persuading her to put on the hat, and we feel that she will obey.

This isn't the only time Jean uses a hat to reveal character and feelings in *Quartet*. When Heidler decides to begin their affair he looks different. 'He had tilted his hat to the back of his head.... He looked much younger, she thought, and extraordinarily hard.' And when he has evidently decided to end it, he looks different again: 'To begin with, he wore a bowler hat. When they were seated in the Restaurant de Versailles she was still thinking uneasily about the hat, because it seemed symbolical of a new attitude.' He stills looks 'rakish', but now 'self-possessed, respectable': and he begins to insist that Marya come to lunch and to tea with Lois. He is moving back to respectability, to Englishness; and he signals it — or rather Jean does — by donning an English bowler. The changes in Stephan, too, as prison breaks him down, emerge not only in his thinness, his nervousness, his rusty voice, but in a kind of hat: a piece of coarse sacking which he wears on his head. Nothing could be further from Heidler's hard expensive bowler than this cheap and shapeless piece of material, which was never meant for a human head. Nothing could more neatly contrast Heidler's invulnerability to Stephan's degradation.

Of course, all these things were very likely quite real — convicts may well have worn sacking over their heads, and Ford probably did have a bowler. But Jean's use of them is like her use of every other event, word, place in her fiction, real or invented: she includes them for their emotional colour, for the inner truth they reveal or evoke. All we see of Heidler's clothes is a dressing gown, a rough (tweed?) jacket, and that bowler hat. Very English; very masterful and paternal. That is what we need to understand: and that is what these few, cunning details tell us. In her own life, of course, Jean was fascinated by hats, and by all clothes. Her own dresses, coats, hats lifted her up or cast her down; they seemed to have for her almost magical properties of affecting not just her appearance but her real identity. This is the feeling she draws on here: so that *all* her characters have her own quality of having their identity displayed by their clothes. That is typical of Jean in so many ways. First, that one of her most characteristic literary techniques should come, initially, from a natural and unconsidered habit of her mind.* Second, that she should construct a view of people, and a way of portraying them in literature, upon an idiosyncractic feeling about herself. And third, that she should do it so successfully. It sounds strange, to convey so much about one's characters through their hats: but it is a wonderful idea, and Jean does it with genius. Think, for example, of Sasha's search for the right hat, *her* hat in *Good Morning, Midnight*; and of the two old women who do the same thing in that novel, several stages further down the road to madness†. Once again hats betray the truth: however old and ugly they have become, these women are still searching — they are searching more frenziedly than ever —

* This is part of what has made people from Ford onwards feel she is an 'instinctive' writer.

† The first old lady is trying on hairbands, combs and feathers rather than hats; but like Stephan's sacking the principle is the same.

for beauty, happiness and pleasure. Underneath Sasha is still Marya, longing for joy. We see this in many things: but in nothing more succinct, more mysteriously convincing, than her hat.

The mention of the two old women in *Good Morning, Midnight* takes us on to a perennial device of Jean's, which she already uses consummately in *Quartet*: showing us other girls and women as mirrors of the heroine's state or her fears for the future. The two old women in *Good Morning, Midnight* do the latter. Sasha even thinks so herself, about the second one: 'Watching her, am I watching myself as I shall become?' The first girl Marya sees in *Quartet*, just after Stephan's arrest, also prefigures her own future.

> Opposite her a pale, long-faced girl sat in front of an untouched drink, watching the door. She was waiting for the gentleman with whom she had spent the preceding night to come along and pay for it, and naturally she was waiting in vain. Her mouth drooped, and her eyes were desolate and humble.

Marya, too, is penniless, she too will become desolate and humble; and Heidler too will end by refusing to pay for any more drinks.... The next girls we see mirror Marya's present: the frail little girl on the merry-go-round, and the little Spanish dancer, who is also 'like some frail and passionate child'. Both are 'the weak creature doomed', '*L'Enfant Perdu* or The Babe in the Wood', as Cairn calls Marya. But of course the little Spanish dancer sings of stabbing. And the next time Marya sees one of these girls who are really images of herself, the same ambivalence appears. It is in Cannes, after her affair is over. The girl is writing a letter, as Marya has just done to Heidler.

> Marya watched a fierce-eyed, beak-nosed girl opposite who was also writing rapidly. As she wrote, tears came to her eyes. Probably a letter of rupture.

The first girl Marya had seen had desolate and humble eyes: this one has 'fierce' eyes, and she may be making the 'rupture' herself. *Both* are images of Marya: for she has been both abject and attacking with Heidler, and she has had fantasies of being still more attacking. As she is reflected in these two mirrors, at the beginning and end of *Quartet*, Marya is still passive and innocent, but beginning to feel the 'wolf' that walks at Sasha's side in *Good Morning, Midnight*.

There are glimpses, too, of other kinds of women: Marya's opposites, even enemies. The little maid at the Hotel des Palmiers is (Jean remarks) Marya's namesake, yet her opposite: a cheerful hard-working peasant girl, who sings and mops and minds the *patronne's* baby. Jean quite often includes glimpses of such girls in her fiction. There is the goose-girl in 'Vienne', for instance, going in and out of the inn carrying pails and tubs; in *Good Morning, Midnight* there is the girl in the *tabac*, who washes the glasses in a small, stinking room no bigger than a cupboard. In 'Vienne' the heroine is thrilled by the goose-girl, seeing in her a natural beauty and pride; but Marya's attitude to the little *bonne* is unclear, and Sasha's to the *tabac*-girl is deeply ambivalent. This last girl has sturdy legs, thick curly hair, and a filthy apron. 'I know her,' Sasha says. 'This is the girl who does all the dirty work, and gets paid very little for it.' That is like Sasha herself, who was paid only four hundred francs a month and lodged in a small dark room. And at first she greets the girl like a fellow doormat: 'Salut!' But then she seems to withdraw: 'Sorry for her? Why should I be sorry for her? Hasn't she got sturdy legs and curly hair? And don't her strong hands sing the Marseillaise? And when the revolution comes, won't those be the hands to be kissed?' She ends ambivalently, perhaps sympathetic, perhaps mocking. 'Well, so Monsieur Rimbaud says, doesn't he? I hope he's right. I wonder, though, I wonder, I wonder....'

It seems to me that these strong, undaunted working girls are not *entirely* to the heroine's liking. She identifies with them because they are poor and oppressed: but really they are as different from her as the rich. They are just as tough, just as unsentimental; and she probably fears that when their chance of power comes they won't include her either. Marya has equally mixed feelings about the other prisoners' wives, for example. In her rebellious moods she feels a passion of sympathy for them: but when she waits with them under the eye of the warder she is 'full of an increasing shame at being there at all.' Other oppressed women, I think, mainly frighten her: when they are strong, because they are different from her, and she is afraid they will not understand her; when they are weak, because they are like her, and she is afraid she will have to share their 'drably terrible life of the underdog' forever.

But Marya's clearest enemies are still the rich. We glimpse them not in real women, but in an image: the 'stone ladies' in front of the Hotel Negresco in Nice. The Negresco was (and is) the most expensive hotel in Nice, the apotheosis of comfort and carelessness. Outside it smile the statues, as if to say — Jean writes — 'Think what you like, curves are charming.' They are fat, smug, perfectly self-satisfied — like most of the women, we may guess, who enter the hotel. This use of an appropriately dehumanised image for the heroine's female enemies returns in *Good Morning, Midnight*, with the dolls in Sasha's dress shop. Sasha thinks 'what a success they would have made of their lives if they had been women. Satin skin, silk hair, velvet eyes, sawdust heart — all complete.' That is the heroine's — and Jean's — image of the successful woman: a thing made of sawdust or stone. It is a perfect image, summing up everything she feels about her worst enemy, worse even than men: her smugness, hardness, inhumanity; and (in Sasha's dolls) the unnatural perfection of beauty women must have to please.

There is another whole system of images in *Quartet*, which completely expresses Jean's point of view. They are images for the four main characters: images of animals. Heidler, who has the most power over Marya, seems above the animal kingdom. But at the end, when Marya talks obsessively to Stephan about him her eyes are fixed on a big spider. And a spider renders Heidler perfectly: fat and still, waiting for his prey. Mostly, however, Jean keeps her animal imagery for the hunted rather than the hunters: for the underdogs, the dumbly oppressed. Even Lois is this with Heidler, because she is afraid to lose him. So when he speaks sharply to her she looks 'like a hurt animal', and when she must be polite to Marya she has the eyes 'of a well-trained domestic animal'. But the real animals, of course, are the Zellis.

When Marya is happy with Stephan it is because he is like an animal in a positive sense: 'vivid', 'natural', 'natural as an animal'. Then after his arrest both Zellis are animals in a negative sense: treated by society as less than human, put in a cage like Stephan, or kept as a pet or a creature to be hunted for sport, like Marya. In prison Stephan seems 'like some bright-eyed animal staring at her.' They speak in a small cubicle, through bars 'that were like the bars of an animal's cage;' when Stephan is let into this cage from the bigger cage behind, it is 'as if he had been shot out of a trap.' Every image repeats that he is a small wild creature cruelly trapped and caged.

But the main centre of this second sort of animal imagery is, of course, Marya herself. The very first time she meets the Heidlers this note is struck: they speak of her in the third person, 'as if she were a strange animal,' 'or at any rate a strayed animal — one not quite of the fold.' This is ominous and frightening, because we all know what a herd will do to a strange animal that strays into its territory: close ranks against it, as the white people do to Antoinette's family in *Wide Sargasso Sea*. Then of course Heidler falls in love with her, and in the spring she is briefly excited and expectant. Now Jean puts beside her the 'homeless cats': strayed animals too, 'furtive, aloof, but strangely proud'. This time, just before the affair begins, is Marya's moment of pride and power. Lois knows it, and she watches Marya warily, 'as if she were observing some strange animal that might be dangerous, debating the best method of dealing with it.' But Marya's moment as a dangerous animal doesn't last long. Soon she becomes as trapped and caged as Stephan. And at the end the animal we see beside her is no longer a proud, homeless cat, but the desperate young fox in the zoo at Nice. The fox is a wild animal that is usually hunted; here it is locked up for people like Miss Nicolson to stare at. And that is exactly what Miss Nicolson does to Marya. The image of the fox in the cage exactly pictures Marya's entrapment by Heidler, and the way it exposes her to the malevolent curiosity of the Montparnos. We must pity the poor young fox; and its plight tells us that we must pity Marya, and why.

When Stephan comes out of prison and seems so changed to Marya, she says, 'If anybody tried to catch me and lock me up I'd fight like a wild animal; I'd fight till they let me out or till I died.' But Stephan replies, 'Oh, no, you wouldn't, not for long, believe me. You'd do as the others do — you'd wait and be a wild animal when you came out.' This is true of him: once he is back out in the world he begins to look like a wolf to Marya. And it is true of her own imprisonment by Heidler. She cries, she abandons herself to 'futile rages', but really she has surrendered to him, and goes on trying to please him to the bitter end. Only when she is out of her prison, because Heidler has pushed her out, is she really a 'wild animal': not towards him, but towards Stephan, and ultimately only towards herself, for she is the one who is left for dead. Once again this foreshadows what will happen in a later novel. For when, in *Good Morning, Midnight*, Sasha decides to release the wolf that walks beside her, it is against the gigolo, who is none of the men who have hurt her; and when she does so, it is she and not he who is destroyed.

There is another group of images which begins in *Quartet* and grows through all four 'modern' novels. This group pictures the heroine's alienation, the fact that (as she tells us) she hates and fears other human beings. I mean the image of the stranger; and especially of the strange man, the 'unknown'.

*Quartet* both begins and ends with strange men accosting the heroine in the street. Marya does not even understand the first ones, who address her 'in unknown and spitting tongues'; the last one speaks French, but he is an 'internationalist' too. Marya goes with him 'silently', 'like a sleep-walker': as Anna will go with strangers, as Julia will be picked up by George Horsfield and Sasha by the gigolo. With each step in the heroine's life 'unknowns' take her over more and more. Anna loves Walter for half of *Voyage in the Dark*; Carl and the others are punishments she inflicts on herself. But Julia fixes her last gasps of emotional energy on strangers – not even on Mr Horsfield, but on the two 'unknowns' who bracket her story: the one who desires her at the beginning, which gives her the energy to go to London, and the one who rejects her at the end, which finishes her off completely. Then finally *Good Morning, Midnight* is entirely about the heroine's relationship with an 'unknown'. René is a stranger who picks Sasha up in a bar, a foreigner whose home she cannot even guess; a man who remains a stranger even in love, as a gigolo, and in war, as a Foreign Legionnaire. With this man Sasha has the heroine's last chance of love. She loses it, of course. But almost as significant is the fact that she could only take it in the first place with such a complete, such a *professional* alien.

*Quartet* has other techniques of alienation too, which Jean will also use in the other novels. Often the heroine does not see people, but only parts of people. The lawyers in *Quartet*, for instance, are terrifying, because they are only black robes, black beards and mouths gaping in laughter, 'showing a long pink and white tongue.' When Marya meets the Heidlers for the first time after Stephan's arrest, everyone seems broken into pieces. Lois reduces beauty to 'an angle of the eyes and mouth ... a certain angle of the eyes and mouth.' Marya notices Heidler's oddly shaped, three-cornered eyelids; of the other people in the restaurant she sees only arms, legs, feet, shoulders, backs.... Then at the end of *Quartet* the Zellis meet in Monsieur Bernadet's room in the rue Bleue, and the walls are covered with gigantic enlarged photographs of families, and of young men in their Sunday best. Marya and Stephan have their last violent quarrel here, while these dehumanised people stare down at them, well-behaved, smirking, glassy-eyed. In just this way the bust of Voltaire will sneer down at Anna on the last night that she spends with Walter.

Finally, there is in *Quartet* an anticipation of a strange and important later image: the image at the end of *Good Morning, Midnight* of the man in the dressing gown, the skeleton-thin 'ghost of the landing' whom Sasha takes into her bed in place of her lost lover. This is one of the most powerful scenes in Jean's fiction, and one of the most ambiguous. To some readers it is the triumph of Sasha's compassion for other human beings over her fear of them. To me it is the opposite, and full of horror: Sasha's final acceptance of nothingness and degradation. We must fight it out when we get to *Good Morning, Midnight*. But let's just notice this foreshadowing of the 'ghost of the landing' here in *Quartet*. As Heidler deliberately and brutally ends their affair, saying that he has a horror of Marya – that she makes him sick – someone watches them with avid curiosity:

... a little man whom she had met when she first came to Paris five years before, a little, yellow, wizened man and his name was — she couldn't remember — something like Monferrat, Monlission, Mon ... something.

It seemed to her enormously important that she should remember the name of the little man who, staring at her, was obviously also thinking 'Who is she, and where have I met her?' She couldn't see his face clearly. There was a mist around it. Her hands were so cold that she felt them through the thin stuff of her dress. Mon — Monvoisin, that was it.

That is all. Monsieur Monvoisin peers at Marya in her humiliation, as Miss Nicolson will peer a bit later. He doesn't take Marya over from Heidler, as the *commis voyageur* will take Sasha over from Rene. In *Quartet* that is done by the 'unknown', a short time later. But it *could* have been Monsieur Monvoisin. That would have been worse. The unknown is at least young, and not unkind; Monsieur Monvoisin is 'yellow' and 'wizened' — old, or ill, or both. For Marya it is still someone recognisably human who waits for her after Heidler. For Sasha it is something less than human, a ghost. But that ghost has the room next door to hers: he is her neighbour. And *this* thin yellow man is called Monvoisin: 'my neighbour'.

Marya has to struggle to remember, as though through a mist. And I think the idea came to Jean through a mist too. That is, I do not want to say that there was a conscious connection for her between 'Monsieur Monvoisin' and Sasha's ghostly neighbour: either a clairvoyant one, so to speak, when she wrote *Quartet*, or even a retrospective one when she wrote *Good Morning, Midnight*. The ending of *Good Morning, Midnight* rose up out of her subconscious, which was the way she usually wrote, and the way she always wrote best. 'I was never satisfied with the last chapters,' she said of *Good Morning, Midnight* in 1956. 'So as the book had to be finished I drank a bottle of wine. The gigolo, René, became very important, [and] the Man in the Dressing Gown appeared from Heaven knows where to supply the inevitable end....' That suggests that he was entirely invented: and so, I think, was Monsieur Monvoisin. *He* welled up from her subconscious too. Both represent something which the heroine feels is watching and waiting for her, and which Jean connects, probably unconsciously, with the idea of a neighbour. What *is* this subconscious idea? What is waiting for her, and what is her 'neighbour'?

Well, between Monsieur Monvoisin and the *commis* there are two other thin and sinister figures, in *After Leaving Mr Mackenzie*. One is the cadaverous, yellow-toothed old man in a loose grey suit who dances with Julia, clutching her tightly, 'pervading her'. The other is a figure she glimpses at the very end of the novel: 'a thin man, so thin that he was like a clothed skeleton, drooping in a doorway.' For the old dancer Julia feels intense horror. For the skeleton in the doorway she would once, she thinks, have felt pity; but now she feels nothing at all.

Now precisely this will become the question at the end of *Good Morning, Midnight*: does Sasha feel horror or pity for the *commis voyageur*? These half dead, half human figures are, I think, her 'neighbours' in a metaphorical but simple sense: other lonely, dispossessed human beings, just like her. What does she really feel for them: pity, horror, or — Julia's final state — indifference? I don't think that Jean ever looked absolutely steadily at the honest answer — not even in *Good Morning, Midnight*, her most honest novel. But through 'Monsieur Monvoisin' she had already felt the question begin to press in her very first novel.

★ ★ ★

This is one of the most important and striking things about Jean's work: that it is all of a piece, like a tapestry woven in separate parts but to the same pattern, so that when it is sewn together you can hardly see the seams. It is not that she is consciously working out the same ideas or theories. On the contrary she keeps returning to the same shapes in her tapestry because she *hasn't* worked out what they mean, or why they trouble her: she returns to them in the way you return not to an idea but to a pain. If she does return to an idea — that life is black and cruel, for instance — even this is less an idea than an overpowering feeling. The seamlessness of her tapestry comes from something much solider than an idea: it comes from an unchanging deep structure.

It is not only the London and Paris novels that are connected by their shared imagery. This deep structure (and its imagery too) connects *all* the novels, including *Wide Sargasso Sea*. Indeed, if there is one which is slightly different it is *Voyage in the Dark*. In *Voyage in the Dark* the heroine is entirely the innocent victim; she turns on no one (except in imagination, on an unknown in the street; and though she doesn't understand why, she recognises the moment as extraordinarily significant). In Jean's original intention Anna loved someone, hurt no one, and died. But the other four heroines are different. Marya, the first, acts like Sasha, the third: both turn on an innocent man (Stephan; the gigolo) to revenge themselves for what other men have done to them (Heidler; Mr Lawson, Mr Blank); but both hurt — or even kill — only themselves. Antoinette will do the same, with the difference that she will attack not a substitute but her lover himself. She will set out to destroy Rochester, his house, his friends — everything she hates about England: but like Marya and Sasha she will succeed (we know from *Jane Eyre*) only in killing herself.

This is, or suggests, the deep structure. There are other connecting threads too. We have already seen one strange and sinister one: Marya, Julia and Sasha each ends nearer and nearer a shadowy 'neighbour', on whom she tests the final degree of her alienation from the human race. There are other, fascinating ones. Several times in *Quartet* Marya prefigures Sasha at the end of *Good Morning, Midnight*, lying with her arm over her eyes to keep the world away. She prefigures Julia too, in her fear of 'nothing'. When Marya reaches the lowest point of her loneliness and degradation she writes to Heidler that she is 'nothing at all. Nothing. Nothing.' It is this 'nothing' that Julia in *After Leaving Mr Mackenzie* was afraid of as a child, that she tries to understand at her mother's funeral, and that she feels is all she has reached, despite her bursts of defiance and 'greatness'. Antoinette too is afraid 'of nothing, of everything' as a child, and less afraid of the rats than of the emptiness when they've gone; and when she tells Rochester that the servant boy is crying for love of him, Rochester says: 'Who would have thought that any boy would cry like that. For nothing. Nothing....' If love is nothing, the heroine is nothing, and this nothingness is what she fears. Anna doesn't use this word yet; when she loses Walter she speaks of dying and of drowning, but not yet of a blank of nothingness. That begins with Marya, after Heidler.

There is, indeed, a straight line between Marya, the first heroine, and Antoinette, the last. Anna only imagines violence, holding her bracelet like a knuckleduster over her hand; Julia has fits of rage, but is so afraid and distracted that she only half acts on them; and though Sasha tells herself she will take her revenge on René, she is too self-mocking, and still too in need of love, to do more than talk. But Marya and Antoinette are wild and angry women. Marya threatens — vividly — to kill Lois, she hits Heidler, and fights furiously with Stephan and screams abuse at him; Antoinette attacks Richard Mason, bites her husband, shouts abuse at him, and lifts a bottle against him with murder in her eyes. Jean tries to keep us on Marya's side, by keeping us inside her self-justifying thoughts as she attacks her innocent husband. That is a mistake, and doesn't work. In *Wide Sargasso Sea* she shows us Antoinette's rage plain, from the outside, without excuses: but we have suffered with her from childhood, and we see Rochester plainly too. Though Antoinette is further gone than Marya — madder, drunker, more destructive — we sympathise with her more. But these are differences in the degrees of skill with which Jean presents the two heroines to us. In themselves – at least, in their maddened violence – they are much the same.

And there is an extraordinary prefiguring of Antoinette's end in Marya's (as there was also of Sasha's). It comes at the turning point of the affair, when Marya has come with the Heidlers to their cottage at Brunoy. She wakes at midnight 'to a feeling of solitude and desolation'. Like Antoinette, she lies in her dark room 'up a narrow staircase', while her lover and the woman he prefers sit together in the lighted room below. Like Antoinette, she has planned nothing – as she's told Lois, she never does. But like Antoinette, she is 'brooding, nervous, waiting and hoping for the violent reaction that might free her from an impossible situation.' She lights a lamp – Antoinette picks up a candle – and leaves her room. Now, of course, the two stories diverge. Marya hears the Heidlers talking about her, bursts in and makes 'a hell of a scene'; Antoinette suddenly knows 'why I was brought here and what I have to do,' and takes her candle downstairs to set fire to Rochester's house. *But Marya almost did this too,* without consciously intending to. Just before going into the Heidlers' room, 'she realised that she was holding the lamp at a dangerous angle, and put it down on the kitchen table.' She has almost set fire to Heidler's house.... Perhaps already, as she wrote *Quartet,* the story of Bertha Rochester which she'd read as a child was stirring in Jean's subconscious. For the deep structure of so many of the heroines' stories is hers: a woman ending her impossible bondage with an act of violence, which however fails, and punishes only herself. It happens to Marya, attacking and losing first Heidler, then Stephan; it happens to Sasha, attacking and losing René; it happens too to Maidie Richards (in 'Tigers Are Better-Looking') and Selina Davis (in 'Let Them Call It Jazz'), who hit back at the world and are immediately sent to jail.* It happens most completely, of course, to Antoinette, who alone of Jean's main heroines definitely dies.† But interestingly, Marya may already have died, at the end of *Quartet.* Jean's two most violent heroines, therefore, her first and her last, are the ones who die: and how extraordinary that the dealer of Antoinette's death, the flame she herself carries, is already there forty years before, in Marya's hand as she is about to let go and hit Heidler.

*'Till September Petronella' shares this deep structure too, but this time Jean hid it *very* deeply. Petronella loses Julian in the end, but doesn't seem to have attacked him: we know that in the real event, Jean *did* attack Philip Heseltine.

†Jean originally meant Anna to die too. But that was for a different reason – self-pity rather than self-punishment. And – I will argue – Jean came to realise that her original ending wasn't right, and that Anna should live.

Jean had found her own subjects and her own style straight away, in *The Left Bank*. But it was with *Quartet* that she began to be the writer she would remain for the rest of her life. Here she first stated the pessimism and nihilism that would culminate in *After Leaving Mr Mackenzie*, and here she shakily began the sustained self-examination that would culminate in *Good Morning, Midnight*. But the last part of her long effort to understand her life had not yet begun: I mean the effort to understand her lovers, to see a man's point of view. That would not begin until *After Leaving Mr Mackenzie*. It had to wait, I shall suggest, for her second husband, with whom she began to see that men could be as vulnerable as she. That was necessary to wake her sympathy; alas, it was probably also enough to end it, at least for him. But it was this marriage that enabled her to move on from *Quartet*; that gave her not just time and a place to write in, but a steady loyalty and kindness that broke down her worst barriers of fear and suspicion against half the human race. If they had stayed as strong as they were when she wrote *Quartet* she would have been a much lesser writer than she became. Even as it is, her men remain her weakness — even in *Wide Sargasso Sea*. But the enormous journey she made towards understanding is very clear: from none at all for Heidler in *Quartet*, through reluctant beginnings with George Horsfield in *Mackenzie* and Walter in *Voyage in the Dark*, to wry sympathy (but still from the outside) with René in *Good Morning, Midnight*, to a sustained effort in her last novel at a real understanding of her opposite and enemy: the cool, rational, worldly Englishman.

*Quartet*, then was the beginning. Jean was not yet in control of two vital things, her anger against men and her presentation of her heroine. But apart from these she was already in possession of almost all the most important themes and techniques she would ever use.

She'd exposed morality and respectability as pretence, and shown the reality she saw beneath. The pace and shape of *Quartet* is as perfect as in all her novels, its imagery as powerful. And if she fails with her heroine and her heroine's lover because she is too *parti pris*, she already succeeds brilliantly with characters from whom she is naturally more detached. Her observation is wonderfully acute, perhaps especially when it is sharpened by dislike ('everything — even sin — was an affair of principle and uplift if you were an American, and of proving conclusively that you belonged to the upper classes, but were nevertheless an anarchist, if you were English'). But even better, she can *hear* people. She is masterly at capturing their surface posturing and inner meanness in the way they speak. The 'long-necked and very intelligent women', for instance, at parties: 'You know my Ting-a-Ling, Lois? Sweet thing! Well, the little woman who used to look after Ting-a-Ling writes. She writes poems. I got something of hers into our club magazine. Oh, well, then she got very careless and absent-minded and I found a flea on Ting. So I sent her off....' But one of Jean's special talents was pinning people down like butterflies through the letters they write. Two of her novels turn on letters – *Voyage in the Dark* (Vincent's to Anna) and *Wide Sargasso Sea* (Daniel's to Rochester). But in all her work she uses letters often, to make a point, or reveal character. This skill of hers was already complete in *Quartet* too. We never meet Marya's family in *Quartet*: they are absent, that is the point about them. But Jean puts in a letter from Marya's aunt: just a quick sketch, to fill in her description of them – 'respectable people, presentable people (one might even go so far as to say quite good people),' but 'poverty is the cause of many compromises.' This letter is as good as Vincent's in *Voyage in the Dark* at revealing its author: this time someone decent but distant, and determined to stay that way.

> Is your husband well? You don't mention him. You have not quarrelled with him, I hope, or he with you. As I say, your letter distressed me and I feel so powerless to offer help of any sort.
> So write soon and tell me that things are going better with you....
> P.S. Have you thought of visiting the British clergyman resident in Paris?

The worst sting, the real give-away, is, as usual, in the tail.

Although *Quartet* is stylistically astonishing for a first novel, it has of course lapses and uncertainties. Jean has, for instance, a verbal habit of hedging her bets which intrudes awkwardly into her lucid and flowing prose. For no reason at all her faith in herself suddenly slips, and she hastily inserts the phrase 'as it were ...' It happens half a dozen times in *Quartet*, and it always seems unnecessary (as in 'His sidelong, cautious glances slid over her as it were,' 'the sound of music reached them faintly, as it were with regret,' or 'Rolling down to Rio as it were'). It's surprising she didn't remove these 'as it were's thirty years later, when *Quartet* was republished. However unconfident she remained in life, in writing she very soon gained that certainty which is one of the main qualities of her prose. You can feel it: she knows exactly what she is doing. She really knew in *Quartet* too, and it's a pity that the text retains those half-dozen suggestions that she didn't.

Even in writing, however, there were things she didn't know how to do, and the other weaknesses in *Quartet* (and the other novels too) come when (only rarely) she tries to do them. These things can be collected under one term: abstractions. Jean couldn't talk, or write, in generalities. Abstraction was alien to her, and bored her; it also frightened her, because educated English people (she felt) used it against her. She never *knew* (she herself would say) about anything, not even about things she loved or liked – clothes, paintings, furniture. So she was all right – she was marvellous – as long as she stuck to what she saw and felt, but the moment she abandoned her own real experience and tried to write like *anyone* she sounded wrong: uncertain, vague. It was like the vague look she would get in her eyes if she felt bored or threatened; and then what she was saying would sound – because it was – insincere. For example, in *After Leaving Mr Mackenzie* she puts into Julia's mouth a description of a Modigliani painting which seems to me a perfect Jean Rhys description: particular, sensual, filled with her own personal imagery and feelings.

> 'This picture is of a woman lying on a couch, a woman with a lovely, lovely body. Oh, utterly lovely. Anyhow, I thought so. A sort of proud body, like an utterly lovely proud animal. And a face like a mask, a long, dark face, and very big eyes. The eyes were blank, like a mask, but when you had looked at it a bit it was as if you were looking at a real woman, a live woman. At least, that's how it was with me.'

Now compare this to the description of some drawings at the beginning of *Quartet*: 'Marya, helped by the alcohol, realised that the drawings were beautiful. Groups of women, masses of flesh arranged to form intricate and absorbing patterns.' This is general and vague: we don't know how to picture it. Marya may *think* the drawings are beautiful, but she doesn't feel or see it; and we are so used in Jean's prose to being moved along on a flow of feeling that when it suddenly disappears, we notice.

This problem can become more serious. Sometimes it threatens to enter Jean's account of her heroine's plight, so that she is tempted to explain it in terms which (however good they are) she doesn't really understand: in John's terms of political rather than personal exploitation. It is thus one of *Quartet*'s strengths – and not, as some might feel, a weakness – that, even though Marya meets the official world more than any of the other heroines, Jean does not explicitly argue that general social organisation is responsible for her troubles. *We* can draw abstract lessons from Marya's vivid and personal experience of lawyers, of prison, of the rich and corrupt. Jean wants us to; but – cleverly – she only suggests them. She knows about Marya that 'her sentimental mechanism was very simple,' and that her feelings about other underdogs are not reasoned positions, but extensions of personal passions. I think she knew it about herself too: and therefore made an excellent decision, and not a deplorable one, to leave such reasoned positions out of her novels. It is not that she entirely lacked general ideas, or failed to put them in her books: in fact *Quartet* is full of rage against corruption, immorality, the abuse of power. But this is, once again, a technical question, a question of presentation. She was bad at arguing about ideas, but good at showing us the experiences that led to them — and so at making us share them in a deeper than merely intellectual way. And mostly she knew this strength, and stayed within it. When we draw social and political lessons from Jean's novels we should remember that it is we who draw them.

This is one of the most intriguing of all the paradoxes about Jean Rhys, that she knew so little, and wrote only about herself, and yet she managed to write novels which were completely modern, full of feelings, ideas, even literary techniques that were absolutely of her time. Her preoccupation with exile was the shared obsession of thousands of newly uprooted people, and of great contemporaries like Eliot, Pound and Joyce. Her pessimism and nihilism were intensely personal — but at the same time everywhere in the postwar world, and in writers like Conrad, Kafka, Canetti, Céline. She probably never read most of these, and couldn't have said what nihilism was: but she was as sensitive to the ideas around her as to everything else. She absorbed those that fitted her own experience; and in her intense, brilliant and simple way she explored them in her fiction.

None the less she would have insisted — she always did insist — that she wasn't doing anything so grand; she was simply writing about herself. And that was the truth. As she put it: 'Not that my books are entirely my life — but almost.' When we return to her life now, therefore, we can see from *Quartet* what direction it was taking. She had lost her husband and her lover. The second was the more important: John was too beaten down now to protect her, but with Ford she had lost above all a powerful protector. And it was *the third time* she'd lost just such a safe, powerful English lover: first Lancelot, then Maxwell Macartney, now Ford. In her next novel Jean would write that the end of Julia's affair with Mr Mackenzie was a turning point in her life: it had 'destroyed some necessary illusions about herself which had enabled her to live her curious existence with a certain amount of courage and audacity.' And although she later denied that Mr Mackenzie was Ford, it's clear that the break in her life between Ford and Leslie was exactly like the heroine's between Mr Mackenzie and Mr Horsfield.

Between Marya and Julia there is a steep decline. It has two main symptoms, or takes place in two main areas. First, drink. Marya drinks more and more, to understand, to feel secure, to deaden her pain; until Jean writes 'Well, there she was. In a bad way. Hard hit. All in. And a drunkard into the bargain.' Even the youngest heroines – including Anna – turn to drink to feel strong and deaden pain; but it is Marya who first decides 'I must get so drunk that I can't walk, so drunk that I can't see,' and Marya, and Roseau of 'La Grosse Fifi', who first do so. I think the same was true of Jean. If there was a moment when she too could no longer turn back from becoming 'a drunkard into the bargain' it was now, after her affair with Ford was over.

The second symptom we've already seen: a desire to hit back at her tormentors. Once again it is there even in Anna, in her smashing the picture of the dog, in her obscure, repressed moment with the knuckleduster. But again it is Marya who turns a corner: who wants to scream, attack, hurt someone so much that it terrifies her, so much that she does. Roseau was 'suspended over a dark and terrible abyss – the abyss of absolute loss of self-control'; Marya falls into it, screaming vile words and insults at Stephan. This too, I have guessed from John's novels and Ford's, happened to Jean, at the same time and in the same manner.

The two symptoms are of course connected. The more the heroine drinks, the more she loses control of her anger. And this was simply a self-portrait. Jean too felt suspended over an abyss. She would drink as much as Marya, Julia and Sasha, and lose control of her anger even more completely then they. She would turn it against innocent bystanders too, rather than against the men who had rejected her. She never spoke a word of hate or blame against Lancelot, or Maxwell Macartney, or even – after *Quartet* – against Ford. She was, perhaps, too afraid to cut herself off from them forever. Nor did she blame herself for these losses, except for being too soft and innocent. She couldn't admit that sometimes she'd behaved like Stania, even like Lola Porter. That was what filled the abyss, that was what she was most afraid of: her own anger, hate and violence. Yet she tried to face it; she *did* face it, in her heroines. That was, therefore, where she would now find her moments of greatness, as a writer. As a woman she ran away from it, to alcohol – which of course, as it did for her heroines, only released it instead. This battle between strength and weakness, honesty and self-deception, would be the main story of the coming years. Indeed it would be the main story of the rest of her life: a battle between a great writer and a drunkard.

# PART TWO

# WORK
# 1928-1939

# CHAPTER ONE

# Leslie, 1928–1930

*The thirties — The family — Lancelot
Leslie — Maryvonne — After Leaving Mr Mackenzie*

The late 1920s and the 1930s were Jean's most concentrated writing time. That is clear just from the dates of most of her published books — 1927, 1928, 1931, 1934, 1939. Only her last novel, *Wide Sargasso Sea*, and two books of short stories came later. But a first version of *Wide Sargasso Sea* was already written before 1940; as for the stories, almost half of the new ones in *Tigers Are Better-Looking* were also written, or at least begun, in the thirties; and so were almost half of those in *Sleep It Off Lady*.* In other words, Jean conceived and probably wrote the majority of her lifetime's work, published and unpublished, between 1927 and 1939: four novels, eight stories (of which two reached novel length), a mass of autobiographical writing, and a further lost novel. Only her early diaries and her first volume of stories, written under Ford's patronage, came before; and about fifteen stories, her final version of *Wide Sargasso Sea*, her unfinished autobiography and a few commissioned pieces after.

This great burst of writing in the 1930s was natural: Jean was in her forties then, and one's forties are often a time to take stock, and still have enough energy left to write it all down. But of course *any* age can be that sort of time for a writer; there must have been other reasons. I think there was above all one: Jean's second husband, Leslie Tilden Smith.

Jean moved in with Leslie in 1928, and lived with him until his death in 1945. Or rather, until he joined the Air Force in February 1940: after that they were only sporadically together until late 1942, by which time Jean was far gone in her wartime depression. Their

---

*In *Tigers Are Better-Looking*, the title story, 'Till September Petronella', 'Outside the Machine'; in *Sleep It Off Lady*, 'Pioneers, Oh, Pioneers', Goodbye Marcus Goodbye Rose', 'Before the Deluge', 'On Not Shooting Sitting Birds', and 'Kikimora' (not counting 'Night Out 1925' and 'The Chevalier of the Place Blanche', which were old stories of the twenties).

uninterrupted life together, therefore, began in 1928 and ended in 1939: exactly the span of Jean's best writing years.

Leslie's importance in Jean's life needs to be shown and understood, for it has been much underestimated. He was a gentle, quiet, self-deprecating man; he died long before Jean's fame began to grow in the 1960s, and he never spoke or wrote about his life with her. More sadly, Jean rarely spoke or wrote of it either. She put Lancelot, John and Ford at the centre of her novels, Leslie (in the form of George Horsfield) only at the edge of one; and though she talked later of her love for Lancelot, and of her debt to John and to Ford, she hardly ever mentioned Leslie. Yet he did more for her, as a writer and as a person, than anyone. This is one of the unhappy mysteries of Jean's life; but one that, if we can understand her at all, I think we can come to understand.

This hidden relationship was the main one of her middle years. There were other important ones too: to her family, to John and Maryvonne, to Lancelot; to the literary world; to England, where she slowly and reluctantly returned. But her most important relationship of all now was to her writing. It was to this that she gave most of her time and all of her energy. She would always say that she never wanted to write, but only to be 'happy'; she would often have to be pushed to write, by a bottle of wine, by Leslie. But throughout the thirties she also felt driven to write. 'Writing was really something for which she had an enormous need at times,' Maryvonne has said, remembering her childhood. And Jean herself said: 'Writing took me over. It was all I thought of. Nothing and nobody else mattered much to me.'

Her need was to make sense of her life; to fight for the right control of her anger and self-pity, and to understand herself. She'd begun the fight in *Quartet*, but there anger and self-pity had defeated her. In her novels of the thirties she would continue the fight, and win. That was the real story of these years.

But something else was happening too. The truth was, quite literally, too painful for her to bear: yet she was forcing herself to bear it repeatedly, and each time more. She had to *live with* each of her novels for a year at least, usually longer; we mustn't forget that human fact. So her burden of guilt and self-hate grew. Each hard-won step in her battle extorted a price with equal and opposite force, like a lived-out law of motion. By 1939 she had sealed the victory over herself in writing; but in her life her dark side was left in possession.

★   ★   ★

At the end of 1927 Jean was still living in The Hague with John and Maryvonne. Perhaps she was working on *Quartet*; perhaps she was still stuck on it. But now something happened which took her away from *Quartet*, towards the next stage of her life and her next novel. She heard from London that her mother was dying.

In *After Leaving Mr Mackenzie* Julia's mother has been ill for six years, paralysed and bedridden for three, as a result of successive strokes. This was almost certainly true of Mrs Rees Williams, who was perfectly fit in the early 1920s but could only 'affix her mark' to her will (though 'with full understanding') by the end of 1924. And now she was dying. Other things in the novel were also probably true: that Jean, like Julia, hadn't seen her mother during her years of illness, for instance. She liked to see her family when she could show them success and happiness, as perhaps she'd done in 1921; but there'd been precious little of either since 1924. And that she arrived in England with very little money. She hadn't sold *Quartet* yet; all she'd earned in the last year was her *Perversity* fee, and presumably something for *The Left Bank*; John was as poor as usual. All the family's disapproval of her, all her guilt and resentment against them, would be entrenched by these facts, just as they are in the novel.

The setting was real: Jean's family, like Julia's, had a flat in Acton. It was at 28 Woodgrange Avenue. In fact it was two self-contained apartments with their own shared entrance hall, one upstairs for Minna and Aunt Mackie, and one down, for Brenda, Mrs Rees Williams and Auntie B. Woodgrange Avenue was far from fashionable, and the railway ran past the end of the road, but the house was decent, comfortable, thoroughly respectable.

The people were real too. Julia's mother looks like Jean's, with 'high cheek bones and an aquiline nose'; and Julia's sister looks like Brenda, tall and dark, 'strongly built and straight-backed', her expression 'dark and still, with something fierce underlying the stillness.' Minna and the aunts didn't fit into the shape of Jean's novel, so she left them out. But two other real people — solidly, menacingly real — she left in.

'Uncle Griffiths' is based, I'm certain, on Jean's Uncle Neville Williams, her father's brother. Uncle Griffiths comes to London from his unnamed home, as Neville Williams must have come from Harrogate; he looks 'a good ten years younger' than he is, which was almost certainly true of Neville Williams, who lived to ninety-four (he would have been seventy-eight then). Neville Williams, doctor, mayor, favourite son, would have seemed to Jean — and probably was — exactly the smug, prejudiced, establishment male she draws in Uncle Griffiths, 'laying down the law to his audience of females.'

(And yet she also tries to understand him — for he lays down the law 'as if the sound of his own voice... reassured him.' In this novel she will try to understand — a bit — her own 'good' sister; and her father's 'good' brother too.)

Secondly, 'Miss Wyatt': half nurse, half Norah's friend; thin, determined, efficient. In the flat in Acton there was someone exactly like this: a small dark woman called 'the nurse', who, however, wasn't a trained nurse, but a sort of untitled housekeeper (which explains the odd fact in the novel that a nurse is called in at the end, although there's already a perfectly good nurse there). This 'nurse' was almost certainly a Miss Woolgar, who helped Brenda when Minna became ill in the late thirties.* Jean makes Norah and Miss Wyatt go away together after Mrs Griffiths dies; she gives the friendship between the two women a lesbian closeness, with Norah relying very much on mannish, protective Wyatt. All of this Jean invented, to render the closed circle, the safety that excludes Julia. The Rees Williamses were formal, and used to taking the devotion of servants for granted: the nurse was not even allowed to sit down with them in the sitting-room. But there *was* 'a good relationship' between her and the family, and especially between her and Brenda. And years later — long after Jean wrote *Mackenzie* — Brenda and Miss Woolgar did 'go away together', for Brenda took care of Miss Woolgar till the end of her life. First she arranged a flat for her nearby in Ealing; then, when she left London in the 1960s, she moved Miss Woolgar to a nursing home near her in Suffolk. Jean's picture of this mutual loyalty and dependence in the late twenties was — as always — more an image of her own feelings than of theirs; none the less — again as always — she was being hypersensitive to what lay beneath the surface, and so (as with Philip Heseltine in 1915) almost clairvoyant.

These, then, were the 'facts' in which Jean rooted herself to write *Mackenzie*. She was seeing her family for probably the first time in years, possibly only the third or fourth time since she had left home as a girl. Her mother was dying, and she had never made her peace with her. God knows what she told them all about John and Maryvonne. She was very poor, she had become a drunkard.... If

---

*Owen's widow, Dorothy Rees Williams, only saw 'the nurse' briefly, and isn't sure if she was the same person who helped Brenda with Minna later. But the descriptions are the same — small, thin and dark, older than Brenda; and Dorothy thought the nurse's name was 'something like Annie or Alice', which is close to Miss Woolgar's name, Adelaide. Brenda treated Miss Woolgar very much like a long-standing family servant; which fits a longer time together than just the years with Minna, and also confirms a close bond of loyalty.

she tried to say that she was, however, a published writer it would only have made things worse. The Rees Williamses didn't value writing; quite the contrary. *The Left Bank* would have seemed to them merely an embarrassment, a public proof of depravity. Jean must have felt from them the usual things, the things she could least bear: disapproval and rejection. And she reacted to them as she usually did: by behaving as badly as everyone expected.

In *After Leaving Mr Mackenzie* Julia is late for the funeral; at it she abandons herself to wild sobbing; after it she has the ugly, violent quarrel with her sister she has been resisting since their first meeting. The family's story is shorter and uglier. Gwennie — as they never stopped calling Jean — almost missed the funeral service altogether. (It was held at Golders Green Crematorium, just as in the novel.) Only at the end did she come in — and then only to make 'a terrible disturbance'. She screamed at her sisters, accusing them of having stolen her mother's money. There is no word (of course) of anyone shouting back, as Norah does in the novel. Just Jean screaming, in the middle of the Crematorium.

Perhaps it wasn't exactly like this: everyone who was there is dead, no one can be asked now that it's all over. But there may already have been public scenes in Paris; there would be public scenes quite soon in England. There can be little doubt, I think, that there was some kind of painful scene now, and that Jean made it. Or that, therefore, the breach between her and her family widened still further. 'I shall never bother any of you any more after this,' Julia says. 'Really.' And when Uncle Griffiths sees her leaving he thinks 'Now what'll become of her, I wonder?' 'And, with decision, he crossed over to the other side of the street.' Jean hadn't felt that she had a family for a long time. But now her mother had died; and immediately after that, this disaster. She didn't want them, she hated them; nevertheless she put this final loss of a family at the heart of the loss-haunted emptiness of *Mackenzie*.

★     ★     ★

Another final loss in *Mackenzie* is that of Julia's first lover. 'This was the affair which had ended quietly and decently' when she was nineteen; and he has kept his promise to be her 'friend for life', giving her 'a good deal of money, first and last'. Now she goes to his rich man's house, with its servant at the door, its wood fire in the hall, its beautiful room upstairs: and in the beautiful room, waiting with a nervous headache, is W. Neil James.

It is easy to recognise Lancelot. Jean had come to 'borrow' money from him, for example, after Maryvonne was born; then again some time after the affair with Ford was over. After that she had dropped out of touch with him for a time. But when *The Left Bank* was published in 1927 she wrote and told him. He replied warmly — and now that there was no Julian to hound her, she kept his letter.

My dear kitten — I was very glad to get your letter & I shall be intensely interested to read your book — I have been often anxious about you as I've not heard a word from you — I was in Paris for a day at Easter & could so easily have come to see you. Is all well. Write & tell me. Lancey.

This was welcoming; and some time between this letter and the writing of *Mackenzie* in 1929 and '30 I think she went to see him, just as Julia goes to see Mr James in the novel. From the spring of 1928 on she was living with Leslie: quite possibly, therefore, *Mackenzie*'s timing is real, and Jean remet her first lover, as Julia does, during the brief and tense visit to her dying mother.

Walter Jeffries had been rich, cautious and kind: W. (Walter?) Neil James is richer, more cautious, and less kind. Exactly the same changes had taken place in Lancelot. By now he was nearing sixty, and he was very rich indeed. He was the main owner and inhabitant of Mount Clare; on top of that he continued to own a town house, and now a beautiful country house as well, The Old Hall at Garboldisham in Norfolk. At Garboldisham he was the complete feudal lord, with a large staff from whom he demanded old-fashioned deference ('You had to doff your cap,' one says). At Rowe and Pitman he was the same: distant and dominating, 'an absolute monarch of uncertain temper' who kept an impenetrable barrier between himself and his staff.

But behind this wall of wealth and power his insecurity was as great as ever; greater. Wealth and power merely allowed him to assuage it. For example, to avoid choice or change, to surround himself in every detail with what he already knew and loved, he had the furniture at Garboldisham specially made — as exact copies of the furniture at Mount Clare. And he chose his friends too (like Jean, but more successfully) for comfort and reassurance. He'd become a complete, a neurotic, an almost comical snob. He'd always cultivated rich and grand people: but once it had been (partly) for business, now it was for its own sake. They showed him the material and social success he'd craved, and proved that he'd achieved it; they surrounded him with beautiful manners, beautiful objects, and the comfort of avoiding anything pitiful or mean. Throughout the thirties he made grander and grander friends, up to and including the Queen. He would entertain the young Princesses at Mount Clare; he would entertain the Queen herself at Garboldisham. He was distantly related to her family; sometimes he would even refer to 'my cousin, the Queen'.

This keeping of grand company soothed him, but it unsettled him too: it made him feel 'a comparatively poor man'. To a few people whom he allowed near him, dependants and personal servants, he was generous and kind, but with others he was nervous and watchful, determined not to be taken advantage of. (And of course people did try to take advantage of him. By the time he died he had no fewer than twenty godchildren, as though people had been lining up to grab him for their children.)

All of this would make a dangerous mixture for a meeting with Jean. And it is all dangerously there in Mr James's meeting with Julia. The 'trying to be so kind' that is all that is left of his kindness; the 'My dear, don't harrow me' that is all that is left of his sensitivity to suffering. His desire to get rid of this 'tactless' resurrection of his past, which slips through his pretence (I've got loads of time − heaps of time. Nearly three-quarters of an hour...'); his safe smugness, 'so perfectly certain that all is for the best and no mistakes are ever made.' His caution, suddenly faced with someone who is bound to want something; his relief when she comes clean and asks for it; his fear of being exploited ('Everybody tried to get money out of him. By God, he was sick of it...').*

In *Mackenzie* this meeting ends as their affair had ended, sadly but decently, 'without fuss or scenes or hysteria.' Julia doesn't even cry, though she wants to. A week later he sends her twenty pounds; and he writes, firmly, 'I am afraid that after this I can do no more.'

Something like this final break must have happened, I think, for

---

*And a few kinder things as well. 'Before the war I'd always thought that I rather despised people who didn't get on,' Mr James says ('You want to get on, don't you?' Walter had said to Anna.) 'But after the war I felt differently. I've got a lot of mad friends now. I call them my mad friends.' I'm sure Lancelot said something just like this to Jean. One of his proudest recruits to Rowe and Pitman just after the war was John Bowes Lyon, brother of the future Queen (and Lancelot's connection to her). Jock Bowes Lyon had been badly wounded, drank very heavily, and died a few years later.

Just after this conversation Mr James takes Julia to see his pictures. 'Do you like that?' he asked, 'hesitating, unsure of his own opinion'; 'I wish I could get somebody who knows to tell me whether it's any good or not.' That sounds just like Lancelot. Except in business, he *was* unsure of his own opinion, uncertain (as Jean wrote about Mr James) what to love. He collected paintings too; and often brought his latest acquisition to show his partners − especially Hugo Pitman, who was a well-known connoisseur and could advise him.

Jean to put it in her novel. Like Mr James, Lancelot would think 'If I don't look out this is never going to stop'; like Mr Mackenzie he would see that 'the final stage in her descent of the social scale was inevitable, and not far off.' And he would have to stop her from coming back; he would have to stop her from threatening his social position, the friendships with dukes and duchesses he'd worked so hard for, and cherished so much. Perhaps it was like this: a polite but firm letter, after he'd glimpsed how low she'd sunk. Perhaps it was even gentler, and she merely drifted away into Leslie's care. But perhaps it wasn't.

Perhaps it was 'a fuss' after all: 'hysteria' from Jean, and a few 'scathing but truthful remarks' from Lancelot (as from Mr Mackenzie, and from Heidler before him). That would account for the difference between Lancelot's warm letter and Mr James's cold one; and it would account for Jean's knowing so well what he was thinking ('As to what *he* thinks,' she wrote about Rochester many years later, ' – it's guessing.... I can't do it the usual way – by dialogue because I'm uncertain about *that*.... I can remember. I *can* record speech. But I was not listening in 1840.') If she did make a scene with Lancelot at last she would lose him forever – the one person she could turn to for help, the one lover who still thought kindly of her, the one man she had really loved. Even *he* would have seen what she wanted to hide. It would be like Antoinette's feeling about Granbois, when Rochester stops loving her there: 'I used to think that if everything else went out of my life I would still have this, and now you have spoilt it.' Except of course that *she* would have spoilt it. If that is what happened it would make another, unseen loss to haunt *Mackenzie*, and to push Julia into the limbo she inhabits, the first circle of madness.

The next bit of the story Jean tells is selling *Quartet*. Once she said she sent it from Paris; mostly that she brought it to England herself, usually from Amsterdam. But she remained registered in The Hague for another six months. I think 'Amsterdam' was just her short-hand for 'Holland', and that what happened was this.

She went back to The Hague, but that was really over now. For soon Maryvonne was sent to Hilversum, presumably to friends, and the 'idea was' (Jean wrote) 'to sell *Quartet* and to go after to Paris, on my own.' Probably it was now, in The Hague, that she finished it, 'quickly', as she said. And sent it to Jonathan Cape, who'd published *The Left Bank*. But Cape was afraid that it libelled Ford and wouldn't take it (this Jean always said, however much the other details of her story differed). *What now?* She would have to start from scratch with other publishers. But that would mean going to

England. She'd always sworn she wouldn't go back, and the last time it had been worse than her worst fears. She was ill, she hated her novel... But John persuaded her to go.

She went back to one or both of the people she'd (probably) met in 1926, through Ford: Edward Garnett, and her agent. (Sometimes she said one, sometimes the other.) In the end Garnett sent *Quartet* to Chatto and Windus. The three met for tea, Jean, her agent and Garnett, and Garnett had good news: Chatto's would take the novel.

Jean's agent now, and probably in 1926, was Leslie Tilden Smith. So by the spring of 1928 she had not only sold her first novel; she had also, despite all her intentions, returned to England.

★   ★   ★

In *After Leaving Mr Mackenzie* George Horsfield is part of Julia's ghastly trip to London to see her dying mother; and she's met him before that, in Paris. Apart from the latter setting it was probably true of their models, Leslie and Jean, that they too had met before.

Leslie had first had a literary agency with his wife, Kathleen Millard. During that time (his daughter Anne says) he wrote to Ford, asking if Ford needed an English agent; and Ford replied that he didn't, but Jean did. He sent some of her *Left Bank* stories: and it was Kathleen Millard, according to Anne, who first saw them, and said to Leslie: 'This young woman is excellent. You must take her on.' But shortly after that their marriage ended, and they separated.

So Leslie was on his own when (still according to Anne) Jean arrived in the winter of 1926 with her *Left Bank* stories. (And it may have been he, then, who found a publisher for her first book, as well as the next four.) He was living at Boyne Terrace Mews in Holland Park – which Jean used for *Mackenzie*: 'Five rooms over a stable, which had been converted into a garage,' in 'a small dark street in the neighbourhood of Holland Park.' 'Ford had given Jean some money', Anne says, which she'd presumably used to get to England, and to buy clothes ('so much for her ticket, so much then was left for new clothes,' Julia calculates, leaving Paris). But now she was penniless ('on arriving in London, there would be about thirty shillings left. Suddenly she began to doubt the wisdom of going there with so little money'). So Leslie rescued her, it seems, for the first time in 1926. For a few weeks she stayed with him and Anne (who was with her father for the winter) at Boyne Terrace Mews; then he found a bed-sitting room for her nearby, and paid the rent for some time longer.

If this is right, then it's quite likely that she saw Leslie again when she came at the end of the next year to her mother's deathbed.

Perhaps this meeting went as badly as Julia's with Mr Horsfield: her state of mind was quite as bad as Julia's, and Leslie was still deeply shaken by the breakdown of his marriage. But then she had to come back to England to sell *Quartet*, only a few months later: and of course she would go straight back to him. He was her agent, and he had already been very kind to her. He placed *Quartet*, or helped her to; and he took her in again.

Anne was nineteen and about to be married in June. A month or so before, Leslie came to her and said that Jean could no longer afford her bed-sitting room, and 'wouldn't it be nice if we invited her to stay with us,' just temporarily? Anne didn't mind sleeping in the sitting room for a few weeks; she gave Jean her bedroom. In around May 1928, therefore, Jean moved in with Leslie: and of course it wasn't just temporarily. She stayed on after Anne was married; she stayed on, Anne says, 'forever'.

Once again Jean's life seemed to be fated, just what she needed waiting for her. In her last years she spoke deprecatingly of the start of her life with Leslie, saying they began 'a fifty-fifty affair'. But that was through the shadow cast by what happened later. At the time I think she turned to Leslie as she'd turned to John: with hope and gratitude, and for a time at least with love.

He was in many ways her perfect Englishman. He had a strikingly beautiful voice and was well-groomed and handsome. He was charming and sociable, he could deal with people for her. He'd been brought up with money — originally made from hops, just like George Horsfield's. He'd been to public school and to Oxford. But he'd seen the other side of life too: divorce, and the uncertain existence of a not very successful literary man. 'He looked rather subdued,' Jean wrote of Mr Horsfield, 'till you saw in his eyes that he was not quite subdued yet, after all.'

For Leslie the affair was much more than fifty-fifty. He was diffident, quiet, not good at showing his feelings, but he'd fallen in love with Jean. She was thirty-seven now, but said she was only thirty-three, and looked younger. She was arresting, extremely attractive: with large eyes, a beautiful figure in elegant French clothes, and a soft childlike voice. She was very silent, and had to be drawn out carefully; but when she did speak or smile it was with great charm and sweetness. She was shy and fragile; she was a unique writer; she was penniless and needed him. Perhaps he'd already seen something of her dark side. If so it had had the opposite effect from Julia's on Mr Horsfield: it had made him more anxious to rescue her.

To his children it must have seemed that Leslie too had been rescued. He had been so desperately sad when their mother had divorced him; now he had someone gentle and dependent to look after. From the start Anne noticed Jean's extreme preoccupation with her looks, her clothes, her face massages. And she didn't see much of her, for she got up late, and when Anne went occasionally to see her father in the mornings they'd be alone. But whenever she did see her, Jean was 'charming', 'gentle and nice': and quixotically generous. She wanted to thank Anne for giving up her room, but she hadn't a penny: so she gave her one of her favourite Paris treasures, a chic and expensive 'little black dress' she'd bought with money from Ford. (It was 'a beauty', Anne says: she wore it for years.)

Only weeks after she'd moved in Jean was already certain enough of Leslie to draw a line under her arrangement with John. On 19 June the Lenglets officially ended their life together in The Hague. Jean is recorded as leaving to London, John to Amsterdam. The same day John registered in Amsterdam and Maryvonne was back with him.

Jean did leave 'to London', but only reluctantly, despite Leslie. She had been so determined not to go back to England; she tried to pretend she *hadn't* gone back to England. She told Leslie that she hated London and needed to be in Paris, especially to write. Paris made her want to write; and made her feel she could, in one of its 'little cheap hotels where, rent paid, one feels so safe and not noticed and nobody cares a hoot about anybody anyway.' Throughout the thirties she went back there as often as she could, frequently paid for by Leslie.

She probably went for the first time this summer, while *Quartet* was being prepared for the presses. One of the things she did there, I think, was to sit for (or perhaps just fetch) Violet Dreschfeld's portrait bust of her. I hope that means that there was not a rift between them, as there is between Marya and Miss De Solla, and (probably) between Julia and Ruth. Violet Dreschfeld was an artist; now she knew that Jean had turned her terrible story (which perhaps she hadn't believed) into art. It was a happier ending to their relationship for Jean than she put into her novels; and that was often true.

Just once, many years later, she made that claim that she'd sent *Quartet* from Paris — 'the only copy', '*most* unwillingly, and never had it back to revise, never saw the proofs, and had to change the title at the last minute....' Perhaps she sent a last corrected typescript from Paris, this summer, a few months before the novel was published. It would be so like her not to want to let it go even now. And to complain, all those years later, that she hadn't seen the proofs. She hated reading proofs; as long as she was with Leslie she left it to him; and she knew really, if she made herself remember,

that Leslie had proof-read *Quartet*. But the moment there was any
pressure, she would feel alone and friendless, and forget all the help
she'd had. Even − no, especially − from Leslie.

★        ★        ★

In late September *Quartet* was published in London (under the title
*Postures*), and by early October the reviews began to appear. On the
whole they were very good. Almost everyone recognised the clarity
and truthfulness, the economy and power of Jean's writing. But
almost everyone also shook a nannyish head and a nannyish finger
at her characters. The *New Statesman* was the worst, saying snidely
that 'On an extended canvas one becomes more than ever conscious
of the unsatisfactoriness of getting drunk as a remedy for every trial
and trouble.' The *Manchester Guardian* was typical. 'The limitations
are the limitations of the subject, of the characters,' it said. 'Miss
Rhys is an artist ... but a great deal depends on what she does next.'
We'll accept *one* sordid book, everyone seemed to agree, because it's
undeniably well written; but you'll have to show a bit of moral uplift
next time, or you'll have gone too far.

We can be sure that Jean would hardly hear the thin melody of
praise for her art beneath the loud drum-rolls of condemnation for
her characters − that is, for *her*. But she didn't wait to hear any of
it now. The next time we see her she has retreated once again to
Paris. She is in yet another Montparnasse hotel; but this time she
has her daughter with her.

For the last six months Maryvonne had been with her father in
Amsterdam. When he was left with her care, John said, he 'wished
to bring her up in peace and quiet.' He found work as a private tutor,
teaching French and English; and he seems to have taken care of her
himself. But he cannot have earned much, and it was obviously a
struggle ('*toute la peine que je me suis donnée tous ces mois...*' he
wrote to Jean some months later). He was still living a poor,
precarious existence, only a year away from the last criminal charge
against him. While in the meantime Jean's life had changed hugely
for the better. She had a new novel published, and a new home with
Leslie; John had nothing. The one thing they both wanted was to
give Maryvonne a good home at last, 'peace and quiet'. It must have
seemed now that her best chance of that was with her mother.

In the autumn of 1928, then, Jean went to Holland to fetch her.
First she took her back to France: to Paris, where they probably
went to see Germaine Richelot; then to Bandol near Toulon for a
holiday. Jean was in a rare mood, so rare that Maryvonne has always
remembered it. She felt healthy and happy, relaxed, 'at peace with

the world. . . .' It was, I am sure, because she was taking Maryvonne home with her at last. Among the photographs she kept there are two or three, rather faded, of a little girl and a woman in a wide-brimmed hat. They are standing in front of a very white wall with a very black door in it, like a Mediterranean house in bright sunshine. The woman's face is shadowed by her hat, the little girl's bleached by the sun; and there is no date or name on the back. But they are both smiling. It is clearly a happy time that Jean wanted to remember. Perhaps it is Bandol in 1928, and what she wanted to remember was the hopeful moment when she meant to cancel the past and become a good mother.

This new life began in November: in February it was over. Maryvonne was back with John, and she had been (he said) both spoiled and neglected. 'Croyez-moi,' he wrote to Jean,

> *lorsqu'elle est revenue de Londres elle était un enfant gaté qui, si elle avait continué à ne pas sentir une certaine autorité au dessus d'elle, serait devenue une incapable dans la vie*

And a six-year-old was no longer a baby, he added, who only needed to sit quietly at one's knee: '*Elle désire jouer, courir, discuter même. . . .*' Jean's great desire to be a loving and loved mother had come up against a real child, who needed attention, a strong hand, a regular, reliable, ordinary routine. All these things were utterly beyond her. Her great hopes, her good intentions, had come to nothing.

The problem was, of course, that she had begun to think of *Mackenzie*. She'd probably even begun to write it, for she told the American publishers of *Quartet* that it would be ready by the summer. And how could she give all her attention to a child when she was writing a novel? One day she even asked Anne if she could take Maryvonne out, because she was (she said) very tired. Maryvonne spoke no English yet, and Anne had little experience of children, but of course she agreed. They went to the park, and for a long walk; they tried to speak French together. Maryvonne was quiet and well behaved, but of course it was a strain. By four o'clock Anne gave up and took her home. And now for the first time she saw Jean's temper flare. 'You are much too early!' she shouted, when she saw them on her doorstep. She had wanted some time alone, to write, or to drink, or both. And they had spoiled it.

So now Maryvonne was back with her father. He took care of her himself when he could; when he couldn't she went to a Madame van der Heyden, or to rich friends of John's (or so he planned) in the summer. She started school in Amsterdam. But then something happened, and John couldn't manage either. Perhaps he couldn't find work; perhaps, as he said himself, 'it got too much for him,' and he 'became restless again.' For the next year or more he mostly disappears from view. (His own story was that he went 'from Tokyo to New York to France', and that in France he had some sort of breakdown. But John's own stories are not to be relied on. For much of the time he seems to have been at least based in Holland, working at one point as a travel guide, taking groups of Dutch tourists to Paris.) While he was away, he said, he left his daughter with 'relatives'. One of these was (I think) once again Jean. But this time Maryvonne did not live at home with Jean and Leslie: she went to a boarding school in Norwood, in south London. And it didn't last long. By late 1931 she was back with John, or he with her; and the rest of her schooling was in Holland.

When Jean first had to let Maryvonne return to her father at the end of 1928 she was frantic with grief and worry. He couldn't take care of her — she was always with other people — with strangers.... That was terrible. And Maryvonne would forget her — that was even worse. John insisted that neither was true. Her 'voyages' would make Maryvonne independent and at ease in the world, he said; and

> ... *si tu voyais comment le soir quand je la couche elle m'embrasse pour toi, tu ne dirais pas qu'elle oublie son affection pour toi. J'espère que ce mot t'aura consolé un peu de toutes tes fausses idées. Je répète, il n'ya pas de quoi te mettre marteau en tête.*

Jean remembered this exchange all her life. When she was over eighty she said: 'I noticed how much Maryvonne was changing to me and wrote a panicky letter saying I was sure that she was forgetting me.... Of course John answered that I was quite mistaken, and of course I wasn't mistaken at all.'

When they were divorced in 1933 Maryvonne chose to stay with her father, and to see her mother only in the holidays. But really this pattern had already been established much earlier. Apart from the episode of the boarding school in London, I think that Maryvonne spent the whole decade of her childhood — from 1929 to 1939, from seven to seventeen — divided in much the same way between her parents: her daily life in Holland with John, his relatives or friends; her holidays with Jean and Leslie in England. And I think that Jean felt the same way about it all those years. When Maryvonne wasn't there she missed her daughter and longed for her return; when she *was* there she found that she needed feeding and dressing and talking to, and interfered with the twin necessities of her own life, writing and drinking. So when Maryvonne wasn't there she longed and planned to be a good mother to her; but each time she came she failed, and each time she left she had to remember another failure. The first time it happened, in early 1929, she had just got some money from the American publication of *Quartet*: with that she went to Paris and wrote (she said) the first half of *Mackenzie*. During the next two years, as she worked on the novel, it probably happened again, several times. This repeated failure to keep a child and a child's love doesn't enter *Mackenzie* (or any of the other novels). But its very absence shows that this was a subject Jean could not approach, even in fiction. Julia (like Sasha) has no living child, only a dead one. That comes, I think, not only from the fact about Jean's son, but also from her feeling about her daughter. Maryvonne's is the third, hidden loss that went into *Mackenzie*.

★   ★   ★

*Quartet* had been simple — a cry of rage at the loss of love. *Mackenzie* is very different. It asks *why* there is no love left for Julia; it begins Jean's quest for understanding. That quest will end in *Good Morning, Midnight*. Here Jean is in the state John knew so well: she really knows the truth already, but she won't face the consequences. So Julia is already an extraordinarily honest heroine, but Jean doesn't yet face the consequences. Her self-knowledge is not yet in the book, but only behind it. *Mackenzie* is no longer self-pitying and angry at other people, like *Quartet*; but it is not yet self-mocking and angry at herself, like *Good Morning, Midnight*. It is in between. Loss and failure have drained it of all emotion; in a moment of absolute emptiness and indifference it looks down on Julia from a distance, seeing her clearly, but almost without recognition. It is like Julia herself: absent and ghostlike, in the hour between dog and wolf.

While she was writing it Jean becomes, for us, the same: absent, a blank. At one point in 1928 she was in the Hôtel Henri IV just behind the Quai des Grands Augustins, writing about Julia in the 'Hôtel St Raphael' on the Quai des Grands Augustins. Julia 'read most of the time,' she wrote most of the time; otherwise they were almost the same woman. Thirty-five years later, writing *Wide Sargasso Sea*, she said, 'It's a bit risky perhaps imagining madness, but risks have to be taken.' Perhaps she first found that out now, as a ghost writing about a ghost in *Mackenzie*.

There was one other loss, or reminder of a loss, that she took with her to Paris. Throughout 1929 she worried away at the problem of *Perversity*, convinced (despite proof to the contrary) that Ford had deliberately cheated and betrayed her.* That too worked its way silently into her novel; and into the portrait of Mr Mackenzie, who only departed from his code of morals and manners 'when he was practically certain that nobody would know that he had done so.'

Yet against all these losses that fill and haunt *After Leaving Mr Mackenzie* there was one great gain: Leslie. Why wasn't that there? Why does Julia lose Mr Horsfield too, when Jean had won Leslie? Was this her self-pity again, distorting an important part of the truth about the way people treat defenceless women? Or had she, despite appearances, not won him after all?... Well, she didn't trust love, she didn't think she deserved it. Perhaps she'd already begun to destroy it. But even if she hadn't, she wouldn't believe in it. She wrote *Mackenzie* either beside Leslie in London, or knowing that he was there. Yet I'm sure that the abandonment of Julia by Mr Horsfield was more than just an artistic decision.

---

*He hadn't, over *Perversity*. But she was right none the less. For at the very same time as she was starting *Mackenzie*, Ford was finishing *When the Wicked Man*, with its cruel portrait of her as Lola Porter. (Of course Ford probably thought the betrayal was Jean's − he'd begun *When the Wicked Man* in October 1928, just after the publication of *Quartet*.)

Roseau, Dominica, at the turn of the century.

The Administrator of Dominica, Sir Henry Hesketh Bell,
with the Legislative Council in 1901. Dr Rees Williams is third from
the right in the second row down.

At Geneva: Granny
Woodcock and Great Aunt
Jane with an unidentified
woman.

Brenda Lockhart, Jean's
Auntie B.

Jean's sister Brenda, at school
in England.

Minna Rees Williams, Jean's mother.

*Top*: The Rees Williams' house on Cork Street, Roseau; lacking its verandah, which has been enclosed, and the garden at the back, which has been built over.
*Bottom*: All that was left of the Geneva garden when Jean revisited Dominica in 1936.

From a group photograph of the Perse School staff in 1908. Kind Miss Street is in black, with fierce Miss Osborn, in a spotted dress, on her right.

Lancelot Grey Hugh Smith, the love of Jean's life, in 1912 or '13.

Jean (on the right) in *Chanteclair*, 1910.

Julian Martin Smith, Lancelot's cousin, the original of Vincent in *Voyage in the Dark*.

Philip Heseltine, the original of Julian in 'Till September, Petronella', in 1915, on the verandah of the cottage described in the story.

# CHAPTER TWO

# *After Leaving Mr Mackenzie*

Towards the beginning of *After Leaving Mr Mackenzie* we hear that Julia's affair with Mr Mackenzie and its end in a lawyer's office 'had been the turning-point in her life. They had destroyed some necessary illusions about herself which had enabled her to live her curious existence with a certain amount of courage and audacity.'

That description of the heroine at this point in her life is an exact description of *After Leaving Mr Mackenzie* at this point in Jean's writing. It has lost the necessary illusion that allowed Jean to write *Quartet* 'with a certain amount of courage and audacity': the illusion that her heroine is innocent, and other people wicked. She cannot write out of that illusion any more. In this novel she sets out, therefore, to find another answer to her question: why is the heroine so unhappy, why is her life a failure? Like Julia herself she makes 'a huge effort'; 'And the effort hurt, yet it was almost successful,' but not quite. In *After Leaving Mr Mackenzie* she does not quite grasp another answer; like Julia, she gives up; she draws a blank.

*After Leaving Mr Mackenzie* itself is the blank she draws. It is the bleakest and emptiest of Jean's novels. The others all have at their centre a love affair: unhappy, and over at the end, but over *only* at the end, and filling their stories with powerful if negative feeling. At the centre of *After Leaving Mr Mackenzie* is emptiness. All the love affairs, all the human contact of any sort that Julia has had are over before it begins. And in it she is cut off from them finally, one by one: from her family, from her first lover, from her last lover, from her possible lover, from herself. At the end she is left unspeakably alienated, empty and alone. She was already so alone at the beginning that we can't imagine how she could be more alone: this novel extends the boundaries of our understanding of solitude. Already in the first chapter she has given up any attempt and any real desire for human contact. In Chapter Two she suddenly wants to survive: that means re-entering human society, and even pleasing some members of it. Very occasionally therefore she still desires approval, or 'some show of affection or at any rate of interest,' a look or a word 'that would make her feel less lonely.' But she no longer even thinks of love. She doesn't want love from George Horsfield, but only money, and his company in the dark. Even then she can hardly stir herself to get them. She forgets him completely as soon as he's gone, and cannot even believe in his reality when he is there. Other people are no longer real to her. That is the extent of her solitude.

What she wants instead is something very different from the other heroines. She wants what Jean herself sought in writing about her: 'the truth about myself and about the world and about everything that one puzzles and pains about all the time.' So I have called *Mackenzie* (fairly seriously) Jean's philosophical novel. Julia is not a philosopher, of course, because Jean was not a philosopher: she is really what Jean was, a writer. She doesn't actually write anything; but alone of all the heroines she shows us Jean's quest as a writer, rather than her quest as a woman.

This makes *After Leaving Mr Mackenzie* a crucial point in Jean's career. Without it people might have been able to overlook the real nature of what she was trying to do: to think that she just wrote 'sordid' novels, or 'women's novels' of an unusually depressing kind. Of course they would still have been wrong and blind; but without *Mackenzie* there would have been nothing in Jean's work which carried a refutation on its surface. If it were only for that reason I would argue that *Mackenzie* has been the most undervalued of all the novels. But it is not only for that.

*After Leaving Mr Mackenzie* was written only two years after *Quartet*: yet it is as though Jean had had decades of development in her control of her subject. When it first appeared critics did recognise its excellence, and praise it as enormously better than *Quartet*; but since then it has suffered the neglect of the middle child, overshadowed by its sisters. I would like to restore it to its rightful place. It is almost as tough as *Good Morning, Midnight*, almost as technically sophisticated as *Voyage in the Dark*.

It is not, in my opinion, her masterpiece: that is *Wide Sargasso Sea*, because it is the most humane. This sort of ranking is usually idle and inevitably subjective, but in Jean's case it isn't unimportant. Because all her novels attack the same question, with the same experiences and conscious beliefs: but each delivers a better answer. That is important, both about Jean's personal psychology, and especially about her struggle and achievement as a writer. *After Leaving Mr Mackenzie* is exactly at the mid-point of this development. Jean had started so high as a technician that already in her second novel she was nearly at her technical peak. But in terms of her obsessive question she was exactly midway. She thinks there *is* no answer: only nothingness ('The answer's a lemon,' as Laurie will say in *Voyage In The Dark*). *But unknown to her a new answer is breaking through.* Mackenzie is the most conscious of Jean's novels about her question, but the least conscious about the answer. It is troubled, waiting, in between.

That is why people have not loved *Mackenzie*. Julia in the novel, and Jean writing it, have been stopped and held by nothingness, by a nameless fear. The other novels are full of struggle for life, despair and anger and hatred of life: at least they are full of life. But *After Leaving Mr Mackenzie* is full of death. Its imagery and atmosphere are of stifling and stunting, of dwindling into emptiness. So it is not easy to love; but it is impossible not to admire.

★　　　★　　　★

*The truth about the world*: Julia's world is still the one that Jean met in her years alone in London: a dog-eat-dog world, an endless and merciless battle for survival. Happiness in this world is power. When Mr Horsfield first gives Julia money he feels 'powerful and dominant. Happy'. That is a man's power in the book: money. A woman's only power is beauty. So when Julia's beauty attracts a man on the street she too tastes power and is happy. First she attracts him: then she cruelly dismisses him, closing the swing-door of her hotel 'as hard as she could into his face.' And immediately:

> She could not have explained why, when she got to her room, her forebodings about the future were changed into a feeling of exultation.
> She looked at herself in the glass and thought: 'After all I'm not finished. It's all nonsense that I am. I'm not finished at all.'

Power and safety, of course, mean not caring too much about others. Pitying them, or even worse needing them, makes you vulnerable and weak. So when Julia wants affection from her sister Norah she becomes awkward; when she needs money and a kind word from Uncle Griffiths or Mr James she becomes nervous; when she allows herself to remember Mr Mackenzie's 'cool and derisory smile' she is utterly abject and miserable. George Horsfield retreats into not caring; Julia, who is still more vulnerable, must go further, and feel active anger and dislike. She regains her balance with Uncle Griffiths when she suddenly despises him: 'Because she felt such contempt her nervousness left her.' *Anger* is what gives her the courage to confront Mackenzie, to dismiss the man in the street, to forget a 'pompous and superior' waiter. When she is carried on the tide of her anger

even Mackenzie can be dominated: when she first walks in to the
Restaurant Albert *he* is speechless, nervous, 'really afraid of her'. A
moment later he sees that *she* is nervous, in a state of collapse;
immediately his own nervousness leaves him and he is on top again.
At the end of their encounter Julia remembers her anger, and so
climbs back on top once more – frightening him, saying 'I despise
you,' and flicking her glove in his face in a classic gesture of
contempt. But in the midst of the gesture her real contempt leaves
her, for she does it 'so lightly that he did not even blink.' Staring
straight at her, Mr Mackenzie gets back on top, and stays there. With
Uncle Griffiths, with Norah, with Norah's friend Miss Wyatt, she
jockeys for position: usually underneath, but occasionally on top, for
when she is not jealous of their safety she knows they are jealous
of her freedom. Even her relationship with her dying mother turns
on power: her mother's power to deliver 'an ultimate and final
judgement' on her; her own power to do the same, for in her
mother's single moment of awareness, by a horrible coincidence Julia
is laughing. With George Horsfield she hardly has a relationship, she
is so indifferent to him; but for that very reason she has a good deal
of power over him. The question between them is not so much
whether he will love and stay with her – that is only the barest and
briefest possibility; rather it is whether he will help her, whether he
will give her some comfort and some money. And this question
teeters back and forth with the balance of power between them,
which moves – since Julia feels almost nothing for him – with
the movement of his feelings for Julia. When he feels warm or
sympathetic, her power over him increases, and her chances of
survival go up; when he feels irritated or cautious she loses her hold,
and down they go again.

This dark view of human beings was of course already *Quartet*'s
('Nearly everybody will be *vache* if you give them a chance'), and
it will be Jean's to the end. Here she sums it up after Uncle Griffiths
has refused to help Julia: 'It's childish to imagine that anybody cares
what happens to anybody else,' Julia says. And Uncle Griffiths
replies: 'Of course, everybody has to sit on their own bottoms. I've
found that out all my life. You mustn't grumble if you find it out
too.'

One part of this view becomes even stronger now: the idea that
the means to survival, money, belongs to men, and that it is therefore
men who own power. Women can get it only through men, if they
are beautiful (or, more rarely, if they have something else that men
want, as Uncle Griffiths' wife has docility and companionableness).
If they are plain, and without any other marketable quality, they can
grab no power at all, and only bare survival. This is almost the first

thing we see about the world outside Julia, through Liliane the chambermaid: 'she worked without stopping from six in the morning until eleven or twelve at night, and ... being plain, she would probably have to work like that until she died.'

In *Quartet* the powerful and the powerless were not quite so exclusively divided along lines of sex. True, Heidler was the most powerful person, with Lois's power dependent on his, so that in the brief time he preferred Marya she was the more powerful of the two women. But the least powerful person in the whole story is also a man: Stephan, locked helplessly in prison while his wife betrays him and his life is ruined. In *After Leaving Mr Mackenzie* this sense that men can be poor and powerless too has almost disappeared. There are the 'unknowns', and the poor thin skeleton at the end, drooping in a doorway; but these are hardly real people, and in any case they are outnumbered by equivalent, ghostlike, unnamed women. All the main male characters have money. Mr James has been very rich ever since Julia has known him; Mr Mackenzie is 'comfortably off', and even Mr Horsfield owns a business, though it is 'small and decaying'. Mr James's riches sound inherited (that beautiful house, that gentlemen's club); and Mackenzie and Horsfield too have done without working hard, and don't work at all while Julia knows them. Mackenzie was helped by his father, and by a 'certain good luck which had always attended him'; Horsfield also inherited his business from his father, and during the six months that Julia has been alone in her hotel he has been spending a 'legacy' on a holiday. Uncle Griffiths, finally, has only irrational fears of penury, and has been 'the large and powerful male' of the family since Julia's childhood. Altogether, therefore, there is a sense in this novel that men and money belong together; that money is handed down from father to son, so that without any of them making any visible effort generations of men form a smooth wall of money, with no chink to let a woman in. (And of course, though there were many millions of poor men in 1930, where there *was* money in a family this was more or less true.)

The women, accordingly, are all poor. Life says to them all the time what London says to Julia: 'Get money, get money, get money, or be forever damned.' *After Leaving Mr Mackenzie* is full of anxious, detailed, female calculations about money. Most of all Julia's, of course. She gets three hundred francs a week from Mr Mackenzie. Her hotel costs sixteen francs a night, which means a third gone. The rest must pay for cafés, meals, her bottle every night. Mr Horsfield gives her 1,500 francs; she spends most of it on clothes, and has the equivalent of thirty shillings left for London. Her Bloomsbury hotel costs eight shillings and sixpence a night. She pays for a night, plus a shilling for the meter and a shilling to the boy. The next day she has lunch at Lyons and goes to a film, after which she has only a little over one pound left. A boarding house — bed and board for a week — will cost two pounds; she gets one pound from Uncle Griffiths and another pound from Mr Horsfield, and moves. Then she buys her mother a bunch of roses for six shillings and has only ten shillings left. Her mother dies and Norah gives her a ring worth about one pound. She gets through the next two days because Mr Horsfield buys her suppers. Then Mr James sends her twenty pounds; she pays her bill and goes back to Paris. Mr Horsfield sends her ten pounds there, which once again she spends on clothes. At the end she is completely broke again, and 'borrows' one hundred francs from Mr Mackenzie ....

Norah is almost as poor. The first thing Mr Horsfield imagines about her is 'No money. No bloody money', and he is right: 'Norah ... was labelled for all to see. She was labelled "Middle class. No money".' She has eight pounds to last a month: 'count up for yourself.' When her mother dies she cannot afford a choir at her funeral. This idea is the perfect image for Jean's poor middle-class women: they cannot even have a song sung for them when they die. Norah's being so poor must mean that Uncle Griffiths does not help her — and indeed we hear he doesn't. 'The truth is,' he says, 'that I haven't got any money' (though if he had he would not give it to Julia, certainly not, but to her sister Norah, ... because she was a fine girl and she deserved it'). Of course that isn't the truth at all; but the result is that even the good sister gets no money from the safe rich male of the family. The only money she will get will be female money, her mother's and her Aunt Sophie's. This is the usual female money — enough for the organist but not for the choir. It will be enough for Norah 'to do what she likes' or at least to go away, once they are dead; but it is not enough to pay for any help now, and free her from years of slavery.

Men have the money and the power then, and if they don't deliberately oppress and crush women with it, they don't share it either. They give women just enough to keep them alive, never enough to buy pleasure or freedom. So the family 'back their approval' of Norah, 'but not in any spectacular fashion'; and so Mr Mackenzie gives Julia not the lump sum she asks for, but only the carefully judged allowance, 'receipt of which' she must every week 'acknowledge and oblige'. Men make the decisions, which women can only accept. So Julia's and Norah's father evidently took their mother from her South American home to cold grey England, then promptly died and left her to his unhelpful brother. So Julia herself is 'let down' by all her lovers from the age of nineteen, 'five or six times over'. The ultimate image of women's state, which haunts Julia at both ends of the novel, is the old black-clad woman who lives upstairs in her Paris hotel: 'cringing' and 'malevolent', 'having neither money nor virtue', forsaken by a man who has long ago forgotten all about her. It is towards this state that Julia is moving, and where Sasha arrives.

More than in *Quartet* therefore, it is men who (like Mr Mackenzie and Maître Legros) 'perfectly represent organised society'. Julia's landladies are disapproving and mean; and Norah and Miss Wyatt also distrust and dislike her, and are her enemies. But only Mrs Atherton, the London landlady, has her own small measure of ownership and arrogance. The landlady of the Hôtel St Raphael is thin and hesitating; Norah is poor and oppressed; and Miss Wyatt, as Norah's hanger-on, is a dependant of a dependant. Women are in fact more hostile and dangerous to Julia than men; but because they are as weak as she, and fighting for the same crumbs of survival. They have, at least, the same excuses. But the men have no excuses at all.

From *Mackenzie* on there is a growing feeling that English people, and especially English men, dislike and despise women. Here, for example, the narrator looks at the audience in a London cinema:

> ... The girls were perky and pretty, but it was strange how many of the older women looked drab and hopeless, with timid, hunted expressions. They look ashamed of themselves, as if they were begging the world in general not to notice that they were women or to hold it against them.

By *Good Morning, Midnight* this will be such a familiar idea that it will become a joke — 'everybody knows England isn't a woman's country,' René says, 'you know the proverb — "Unhappy as a dog in Turkey or a woman in England."' It's already a joke in *Mackenzie*. When the page announces 'a lady' (Julia), Uncle Griffiths responds with dismay: '"A lady?" said Uncle Griffiths, in a voice which sounded alarmed and annoyed, as he might have said: "A zebra? A giraffe?"' And later Jean slips in another little 'joke', putting Julia once again in a cinema:

> After the comedy she saw young men running races and some of them collapsing exhausted. And then — strange anti-climax — young women ran races and also collapsed exhausted, at which the audience rocked with laughter.

In other words, if women try to enter the English man's world (compete in races, or perhaps write novels) they haven't a chance.

★

Julia's world is still like Marya's, full of smug cold powerful people who exclude her from the 'sacred circle' of money and security. Yet it is changing. Nobody is as gratuitously evil as Heidler: in that sense it has become more balanced. At the same time, it's not just one monster 'letting down' the heroine; everybody does. So the exclusion that she meets is both more believable and more complete. It is therefore even more frightening. Julia is more frightened, and so is Jean. They both make an immense effort to explain their terrible experience to themselves, to find some meaning and some reason. But they both fail. Julia feels threatened by madness: 'I'm going dippy, I suppose.' And so, we can guess, did Jean. That is her great achievement here (and in her last two novels too): to watch her own disintegration coolly, and to record it. For in *After Leaving Mr Mackenzie* she anatomises a break-down, a crack-up. From the beginning Julia is abstracted, incoherent, only half there; not quite in control of her attention, her voice, her laughter, the expressions on her face. At the end she says 'Do you know what I think? I think people do what they have to do, and then the time comes when they can't any more, and they crack up. And that's that.' The next night, she cracks.

Madness makes philosophers of its victims. For being mad is being outside the consensus of what is real and what is true; and once you are outside it you begin to notice that that is what it is: a consensus. If you are *barking* mad you stick to your own reality and don't even notice that it doesn't fit with other people's. But if you are only sometimes mad, or only half-mad — and that is Julia, and Jean — then when shared reality drops away, you cannot securely replace it. I think this is what happened to Jean. It had always been happening, because she had always been a secret dissident; but in the 1930s it began to show, as loss and drink broke down the mask of docility and agreement she had taught herself to wear. That is how she came to write a philosophical novel now, although she was the least abstract of writers. That is how she came to ask the philosophical question of *Mackenzie*: *What is the truth behind appearances? What is the real meaning of my experience?* And that is how she came to give the idealist's, sceptic's and solipsist's answer: she cannot know; there may be no meaning at all.

Once these metaphysical doubts are raised, philosophers are driven to question the most fundamental categories of our experience — space, time, personal identity. And Jean's living philosophy — her half-madness — drove her in exactly the same direction.

One of the biggest splits and break-downs in the heroine will be in her sense of self, in her own identity. Julia is the first to feel it. When she wants to please Uncle Griffiths, yet also to defend her husband against him, she splits in two, her 'real self' and another: 'She felt as though her real self had taken over, as though she had retired somewhere far off and was crouching warily, like an animal, watching her body in the armchair arguing with Uncle Griffiths about the man she had loved.' But even more, she splits in two when she tries to think of her past and present. On her first morning in London she imagines that she meets her own ghost, the ghost of her younger self:

> The ghost was thin and eager. It wore a long, very tight check skirt, a short dark-blue coat, and a bunch of violets bought from the old man in Woburn Square. It drifted up to her and passed her in the fog. And she had the feeling that, like the old man, it looked at her coldly, without recognising her.

At first Julia cannot decide which is her real self, the younger or the older. She finds a card among her papers, saying *'Wien, le 24 août, 1920, Menu'*.* First she thinks 'I can't believe that was me.' And then: 'No, I can't believe that this is me, now.' She develops this uncertainty into a theory: that 'Every day is a new day; every day you are a new person. What have you to do with the day before?' With this theory she chops her life up; and so, perhaps, evades guilt and grief for the past. Back in Paris, she had already done this to her visit to London: 'already it was a little blurred in Julia's memory. It had become a disconnected episode to be placed with all the other disconnected episodes which made up her life.'

But toward the end she tells us which self she chooses as her real one: the very youngest. 'When you are a child you are yourself,' she says:

> and you know and see everything prophetically. And then suddenly something happens and you stop being yourself; you become what others force you to be. You lose your wisdom and your soul.

If her real self is her childhood one, and if she stopped being that real self when she stopped being a child, then she is not responsible for what has happened to her since; indeed, *it hasn't really happened to her.* That is Julia's theory. The narrator is close to Julia throughout; but here she *becomes* Julia, moving from 'she' to 'you' – Julia addressing herself – in a simple and smooth transition. Jean, of course, holds herself at a fictional distance even from the narrator, not to speak of Julia. But (of course) I think she is both; and that she could be Julia precisely because she could hide behind the fiction

---

*The menu card which Jean kept – see Page 116.

of not being. And so (of course) I think this is her own theory: one she experiences as she breaks apart; and one she holds on to, because it allows her to feel it isn't really *herself* who has grown up, grown old, and ended alone with a bottle in a cheap hotel.

Now, splitting your present self off from your past, and denying any identity between them, naturally splits up your experience of time. It leads you, in other words, to a second philosophical question, a second philosophical challenge: to the ordinary idea of time. And that is where it leads Julia. She mixes up her pleasant memories with imagination; and her unpleasant memories move around in time, as though they too were merely imagination ('always she would remember [slapping Mr Mackenzie] as if it were yesterday – and always it would seem to have happened a long time ago'). Often she feels that time has gone in a circle or stood still, that 'the last ten years had been a dream' and she has always been where she is now, in a Bloomsbury hotel, or beside her mother in a silent room. When she cracks she feels this about the future too. After she's screamed at Norah, for instance, 'she could not imagine a future, time stood still'; and after she screams on the stairs with Mr Horsfield she tells herself that 'Every day you are a new person.'

Julia breaks up time and her self in order to break the link between cause and effect, act and consequence. If there is no single time, past present and future, through which her single self moves, then she need not regret her youth, mind her present or fear her future ... I am sure that's why she does it, and why Jean did it too. But like so many of her remedies it was too desperate. Cutting your 'real' self off from the past and future will save some present shame or fear, but soon it will produce its own torment. You will feel you *have* no real past or future, that you have no real self; and these feelings are worse than the ones you have escaped. This is just what happens to Julia. In fact it has already happened to her before the novel begins: it is another thing the novel is 'after'. It happened (she tells George Horsfield) when she first came to Paris, and went to sit to Ruth the sculptor.

One day (Julia recounts) she starts to tell Ruth why she left England. And suddenly she is telling her everything, her whole life story up to then. 'Everything I had done,' she feels, 'had always been the only possible thing to do'; and she feels she is explaining this 'as if I were before a judge.' And then it happens. She feels that Ruth, her judge, does not believe her; and she feels she doesn't believe herself either.

' ... I felt as if all my life and all myself were floating away from me like smoke and there was nothing to lay hold of – nothing.

And it was a beastly feeling, a foul feeling, like looking over the edge of the world. It was more frightening than I can ever tell you. It made me feel sick in my stomach.

'I wanted to say to Ruth: "Yes, of course you're right. I never did all that. But who am I then? Will you tell me that? Who am I, and how did I get here? ...."

'[My past] had all gone, as if it had never been. And I was there, like a ghost. And then I was frightened, and yet I knew that if I could get to the end of what I was feeling it would be the truth about myself and about the world and about everything that one puzzles and pains about all the time.'

In the course of the novel Julia returns twice to her pursuit of this vital hidden truth. First briefly, seeing her dying mother:

It seemed as if she had been sitting there for many years and that if she could go on sitting there she would learn many deep things that she had only guessed at before.

But then fully, at her mother's funeral:

... That was a dream, too, but a painful dream, because she was obsessed with the feeling that she was so close to seeing the thing that was behind all this talking and posturing, and that the talking and the posturing were there to prevent her from seeing it.

And now she names this thing: and it is what she has always been afraid of. It's the thing she'd felt with Ruth — that there was '*nothing to lay hold of — nothing*'; the thing she'd felt as a child, chasing butterflies: '*That was the first time you were afraid of nothing.*'

... she was tortured because her brain was making a huge effort to grapple with nothingness. And the effort hurt; yet it was almost successful. In another minute she would know. And then a dam inside her head burst, and she leant her head on her arms and sobbed.

She cannot get beyond this nothingness. Despite all her efforts, she has reached only *nothing*.

... She was crying now because she remembered that her life had been a long succession of humiliations and mistakes and pains and ridiculous efforts. Everybody's life was like that. At the same time, in a miraculous manner, some essence of her was shooting upwards like a flame. She was great. She was a defiant flame shooting upwards not to plead but to threaten. Then the flame sank down again, useless, having reached nothing.

This *nothing* is the end of Julia's search, the closest she can get to the truth about her life. But in *Mackenzie* all these things are connected: nothing, truth, smoke, shadows, drowning, death. Shadows and smoke are nothings, and she is afraid of them. (She feels her life drifting away like smoke, the old woman she dreads resembling is a shadow.) At the end of the book she stands watching them all: 'Shadows of smoke in the water'; they seem not to be on the surface but struggling up from the depths, and they beckon to her. This is surely death beckoning to her, though she denies it to the young policeman. It cannot be a tree, as the policeman says, for trees are friendly life to Julia,* and there is something sinister and ' without joy'. Death is linked to shadows — she sees shadows at her mother's funeral; and it is linked to what she wants to know — so she feels 'intense curiosity' as well as fear watching her mother die, and she asks her question at the funeral. *Death somehow contains the answer.* That is the deepest reason why the heroines all end — clearly or ambiguously, physically or 'really' — dead or dying. (The halfway–down reason was guilt, the shallow one self-pity). Jean really knew from the beginning that her heroines desire death, as well as fear it: that death is the ultimate solution for them, as well as the ultimate punishment.

★   ★   ★

*The truth about myself:* Even Marya knew that she was 'All in. And a drunkard into the bargain,' and of course it was Jean who told us so. But that was about all she told us. She tells it only from Marya's point of view; and with all the excuses of Heidler's inhuman cruelty, on top of open pleas for our sympathy. This changes with Julia. We hear about a great deal more than drunkenness; we hear it almost entirely from outside Julia; and we hear it with few excuses made.

This is so from the very beginning. Julia's reaction to her room shows us a sensitive and individual mind — but it also shows us that she drinks too much ('Julia was tired of striped papers. She had discovered that they made her head ache worse after she had been drinking'). We know her pain, and the reason for it, straight away ('the sore and cringing feeling, which was the legacy of Mr

---

*'When you were a child, you put your hand on the trunk of a tree and you were comforted, because you knew that the tree was alive — you felt its life when you touched it — and you knew that it was friendly to you, or, at least, not hostile.' Trees will become more and more important to the heroine, and to Jean, as images of life that is friendly 'or, at least, not hostile' to her. So the worst thing she can say of people will be that they lop or cut down trees, the best that they seem to her 'like trees walking'.

Mackenzie'): but we also know that she brings a bottle home every night. Then the narrator takes us into her room and into her mind: and instead of excuses there is — as the landlady says — a woman who is 'mad, slightly pricked'. She locks herself away for six months — she paces her room talking to herself, consumed with hatred — she lies motionless for long periods, fatigued, her mind ' a confusion of memory and imagination', like an old woman's. Julia herself knows that she is a drunk ('no place is a place to be sober in. That's what I think') and going mad ('I'm going dippy, I suppose'), and so does everyone else: the narrator, the other characters, the reader.

As time goes on we see less of drink, but more of madness. Julia's moods swing irrationally, out of her control. She walks so blindly through the streets that she bumps into people. She is so cut off, drifting in her memory and imagination, that when she tries to talk to people she is vague, abstracted, incoherent, unable to hold on to their reality or even to her own need of them. She says 'I think people do what they have to do, and then the time comes when they can't any more, and they crack up': and we see that that is true of her. As long as she can, she hides her disintegration — from Ruth ('I had just sense enough to pull myself together and not say anything so dotty'); from Mr Horsfield ('You don't suppose I'm mad, do you? To tell you what's the matter. You'd simply make some excuse to go off and leave me if I told you what was really the matter'). And as long as she can she controls her anger, especially against her sister. But at last it breaks out ('You've never once looked at me as if you care whether I lived or died. And you think I don't know why? It's because you're jealous of me, jealous, jealous, Eaten up with it'). After that Julia has cracked. She sits 'with her knees rather wide apart, her eyes fixed'; she doesn't know what she's doing or who she is ('She was certain that if a stranger were suddenly to appear before her and ask in a sharp voice: "What's your name?" she would not know what to answer'). She loses all sense of reality. She hardly takes in Mr Horsfield at all; she abandons her body first to the old dancer who terrifies her, then to him. She feels she is being touched by 'someone dead' (the old dancer; on the staircase with Mr Horsfield), and she becomes completely hysterical. She is like a 'clockwork toy that has really run down': moving 'with a rather grotesque attempt at dignity,' jerking herself from side to side like a woman 'no longer young walking on very high heels.' She drags herself back to her hiding place in Paris, but she is 'cringing and broken,' though 'she would not acknowledge it.' 'Anything puts her in a state now.' She half thinks of suicide. She doesn't do it, but she is finished. When Mr Mackenzie sees her she looks untidy; she has 'gone phut quite suddenly.' She takes a hundred francs and two pernods from him.

She is a down-and-out: a beggar, like the old man with the mandoline.

All this we see not only as Julia feels it, from the inside, but *from the outside, as it looks to others*. Again this happens from the start: with the landlady; with Mr Mackenzie: 'She was irresponsible. She had fits of melancholy when she would lose the self-control necessary to keep up appearances. He foresaw that the final stage of her descent in the social scale was inevitable, and not far off. She began to depress him.' From the moment that Julia and Mr Horsfield meet we see Julia through his eyes.* We see the loneliness and sadness, the prettiness and pluck that stir his sympathy; but we see many other, worse things too. Her 'furtive and calculating expression' as she prepares to please him, her sulkiness and silence when she imagines he doesn't believe her; her irritating vagueness and impatience; her pathetic boasting about her rich ex-lover; her 'at once too obvious and too obscure' attempts to seduce him; at the same time, an unmistakable indifference to him, so that he is sure she will forget him as soon as he is gone, and she does. It is even clearer to us than it is to him that she only wants him for company in the dark. When he seems to be about to leave, she turns on him sharply; when he wavers in front of the prim pink landlady she dismissed him, her eyes 'cold and hostile', 'as if she hates him'.

Through Julia's family we see that she has had 'practically nothing to do with us for years,' then suddenly appears, needing money. Through Miss Wyatt, and Mr Horsfield again, we see how people are sure that this will go on. And through several hotel hangers-on – a baggage boy, a page, a maid – we see that Norah is right, and Julia no longer looks 'a lady'. They all think she looks a tart, and show it.† Of course, when we see people thinking these things about Julia we are also being shown the cruelty, the quickness to judge and condemn, of other people. Sometimes that is all we are being shown: in Uncle Griffiths, for example, or Mr Mackenzie. We are mostly meant to despise them for their mean suspicions, rather than look

---

*We hardly even know how *she* sees *him* – or rather, we know that she hardly sees him at all. Only once do we overhear her thoughts about him: 'He's been taught never to give himself away. Perhaps he's had a bad time learning it, but he's learnt it now all right.'

†Even in her more 'respectable' days, to more 'respectable' people, the heroine evidently has something dubious about her, and looks more the mistress than the wife. Here Mackenzie thinks of Julia that 'perhaps she had never really been married at all'; in *Quartet* Miss De Solla muses: 'Is she really married to the Zelli man, I wonder?'

through them to any truth about Julia.* But usually, I think, things are more complicated. Whatever we're meant to conclude, we are still seeing more of what others think of her and less of what she thinks of them: and that is already an important change from *Quartet*. And very often Jean lets us know that what they say is at least partly true. It's true, for example, that Julia has not seen her family for years (she hasn't been to London for three years, she tells Horsfield; and though she talks of seeing her ex-lover then she says nothing of her family). Yet she certainly asks for money and help as soon as she arrives. It's also true that Julia asks Mr Mackenzie for money again, although a month before she'd refused to take anything from him. So we must agree: Julia *will* write to her sister (and probably to Mr Horsfield too). Jean must have known this; but she did nothing to stop us. For 'other people' are perfectly right about the facts: Julia is a beggar. It is only how one judges these facts that concerns Jean. Julia says: 'You see, a time comes in your life when, if you have any money, you can go one way. But if you have nothing at all — absolutely nothing at all — and nowhere to get anything, then you go another.' Jean wants us to understand and accept this — wholly, not just partly, like Mr Mackenzie — and so to sympathise with Julia. She does not wish to deny the *facts* at all. But given how uncomfortable the facts are, this is already rather brave.

Besides, it isn't just through hostile people that we see Julia's weaknesses. We see more of them through Mr Horsfield than anyone else, and Mr Horsfield isn't hostile, only (and not always) afraid. And large chunks of his thoughts about Julia (and Mackenzie's too) come to us as something close to free indirect speech, embedded in the narration. There is therefore a blurring of the line between how Horsfield perceives Julia, and what is true, what the narration endorses. This is carried still further by the fact that the narrator often moves from his thoughts to hers, with no suggestion that hers are uniquely privileged as true. And some things are clearly true, seen from no one in particular's point of view — that Julia takes Horsfield's money without protest, for instance; that she constantly checks her appearance and powders her face; that she starts and stops speaking as though he wasn't there (in the story of Ruth); that she forgets him as soon as he's gone. We believe Mr Horsfield, therefore,

*E.g. Uncle Griffiths' 'you were sure that ... people like her were preparing the filthy abuse they would use ...', or Mr Mackenzie's 'so you left these people alone. They would be pretty certain to tell you lies, anyhow.' We may take these suspicions to be justified too, if we are out of sympathy with Julia. Then there is a gap between what Jean wants us to think and what we do think, as there was in the case of Marya.

and his free indirect narration: we feel that his descriptions of Julia as drunk, vain, sullen, ungrateful, cold and hostile are at least half true.

Many of Julia's traits — drunkenness, indifference to anyone who can't help her — we've already seen in Marya. But not all, especially not the little shameful ones; and only from the inside. With Julia we see them from the outside, starkly, in their effect on others. Paradoxically, therefore, we can feel closer to Julia than we could to Marya: for where there was a gap between Marya's feelings and ours we recognised it alone, with a jar; while with Julia *Jean* recognises it, so that the gap is crossed, and we can see our affinity to Julia on the other side. So when we hear, for instance, that Mr Mackenzie and Maître Legros 'perfectly represented organised society, in which Julia had no place and against which she had not a dog's chance,' this could have been one of Marya's special pleadings — except that this time Jean has first written: 'When she thought of the combination of Mr Mackenzie and Maître Legros, all sense of reality deserted her and it seemed to her that....' Jean knows now that the heroine's feelings fail to fit not only 'respectable' people's, but reality.* What happens now is very interesting. For we have a radical change from *Quartet*: a clear insight within the novel that the heroine is worse than flawed — out of touch with reality, 'going dippy', grabbing at people as though they were objects, treating them with coldness, ingratitude, indifference. *And yet within the novel the conclusion is not drawn.* Julia sends Mr Horsfield away because he often falters in his sympathy for her, and withdraws from her himself ('He suddenly remembered that he was not in love with Julia; and he thought, "I am not going to be rushed into anything." ') In other words, Julia is seen, not as the maddest of Jean's heroines (that is Antoinette) but as the baddest: yet *After Leaving Mr Mackenzie* still blames Mr Horsfield in the end for the fact that he will not love her. Once again, therefore, *After Leaving Mr Mackenzie* is an in-between, a half-way novel: only half-way to the answer of *Good*

---

*There are other examples, mostly to do (interestingly) with money. When Julia first sees Mackenzie's cheque she starts to plan her future 'in an excited and confused manner, for at that moment all sense of the exact value of money had left her.' Every time she gets money this happens: she goes to London on a mere 1,500 francs; and when Mr James sends her twenty pounds she says 'in a matter-of-fact voice', 'you see I'm quite all right. I don't want any more money.' She herself knows that the first is not only hard to explain to respectable people, but objectively pretty crazy; and if she has lost all sense of reality by the second, Jean hasn't, and gives it to Mr Horsfield: 'Well,' he says, 'twenty quid won't last forever.'

*Morning, Midnight* in which Jean will both see her heroine – her fictionalised self – clearly, *and* lay the responsibility for her life on her. Here she sees her clearly, yet stops short of accepting any blame. She suddenly gives up, as Julia does at her mother's funeral; and falls back on the solution she'd used in *Quartet*, of blaming men. At the start she blames Mr Mackenzie, at the end Mr Horsfield. Well, Mr Mackenzie is mostly Ford: Jean has still not forgiven him. And Mr Horsfield is based on Leslie. Her new clarity about her heroine really begins not after leaving 'Mr Mackenzie' – that produced *Quartet* instead – but after meeting 'Mr Horsfield'. And much of this new clarity comes through 'Mr Horsfield's' eyes in the novel. This suggests another aspect of Leslie's importance for Jean. By making her see herself plain he helped to make her a great writer; but for the same reason he was fatal to her survival as a sane but self-deceiving woman.

Despite all her new clarity, Jean remains on Julia's side against the world. There are many ways in which she shows that she is, and that she wants us to be too. We learn straight away that Julia has retreated into drink and hatred of the whole world; but immediately we also learn that she is beautiful and childlike, abandoned and abused; 'a dreamer' who is 'too vulnerable ever to make a success of a career of chance.' She is utterly alone and utterly lonely; she is utterly, utterly tired.* Yet she still has enormous pluck, defiance and courage. She keeps pulling herself together and trying again, right to the end. She sees the difference between herself and Norah – and so does Mr Horsfield – in romantic and favourable terms: she has dared to rebel against poverty and conventional expectations, while Norah hasn't. She has at least 'had a shot at the life I wanted'; and she's quite right that if she'd succeeded, and been rich, 'people would have licked my boots for me.' The most reluctant reader must admit – as even Mr Mackenzie does – that there is something in what she says: that life isn't fair; that if you have absolutely nothing, and nowhere to get it, you cannot go the way of the person who has money. In trying for the life she wanted, instead of settling for the 'drug' of universal admiration, she *has* been braver than Norah; and though they have both suffered in their opposite ways, Julia remains the kinder. She makes the first move towards Norah, which Norah ignores; and she has impulses of pity towards her sister, while Norah feels only

---

* 'Tired' (fatigued' 'weary' 'sleepy' etc.) must be the feeling most often expressed by Julia, as it was by Jean in real life. I've counted fifteen uses of 'tired' and the others (mostly 'tired') in the novel, often two to a page; and I've probably not found them all.

curiosity, hate, disgust, and 'a fierce desire to hurt' Julia. Again the
yardstick, the moral measure, is imagination, not action. Julia hasn't
*done* anything for her sister: it is Norah who has done things for
people, for six years. But Julia has *felt* for her; and that, for Jean,
is what counts. It is the same with the skeletal man at the end. Julia
would never have done anything; but once she would have felt for
him. Again this is close to free indirect speech — more Julia's own
thoughts than any 'objective' narrator's. Still the sense of these last
pages is that, until the very end, Julia is kinder and better than
'sensible', 'respectable' people.

Mr Horsfield is our main window on Julia's attractiveness, as he
is on her unattractiveness. If he shows us what Jean has come to
recognise is unlovable in her heroine he also shows us what she
thinks still deserves (our) love. He is moved by her loneliness and
poverty, her recklessness and courage, her weariness and her childlike
beauty. And if Mr Mackenzie (with that 'kink in his nature', 'that
volume of youthful poems') one-eighth agrees with Julia, Mr
Horsfield agrees with her quite a bit more. He agrees that 'It's so
damned easy to despise hard-up people when in one way or another
you're as safe as houses'; when Julia cracks up he takes her side
against the horrible landlady. He imagines himself saying to her: 'I'm
not one of the others; I'm on your side ... I hate things as much
as you do, I'm just as fed up as you are.' 'The strangest understandings, the wildest plans lit up his brain — together with an overwhelming contempt for the organisation of society ...' It all fades
away when his caution reappears. But when he lets her go he feels
not only relief, but pain, 'deep down', 'Like the pain of loss'. And
the world he goes back to without her is lowered, suppressed, and
stunted.

Julia is thus an in-between heroine: bad but brave, and above all
unblamed. In particular she is bad but unblamed about her anger.

Like all the heroines she is a dependent person, a beggar and a slave.
This fills her (as it fills her sister too) with anger, hate and violence.
But at the same time it stops her from expressing them, because her
existence depends upon pleasing and attaching more powerful people.
So she must suppress and hide her violent desires: they are her most
dangerous enemies, her enemies within.

We have already seen this *impasse* in Marya: in the way that she feels
the 'will to stab' the Heidlers, but only unleashes it on Stephan, who
is as powerless as she. This indirect and safe release of her violence
satisfies her — 'a delicious relief flooded her' — and it satisfied Jean
too, as an ending to her novel. But it doesn't so easily satisfy the
reader. When the last stage of the drama inevitably follows, and

the heroine herself is punished by her violence instead of her lover, we do not react as *Quartet* intends, with pity for her impotence. Jean will never change this fundamental story: oppression – anger – indirect revenge – failure and self-destruction.* But she will find much better ways to tell it.

The first step is here with Julia. She too hates and is full of anger. She paces her room, 'consumed with hatred of the world and everybody in it.' She longs to fly at the First Unknown – she inwardly curses a girl who stares at her – even longs to curse a maid with unfriendly eyes.... Finally her anger does break out – even against people who are important to her survival. She screams at Norah and calls Uncle Griffiths 'an abominable old man'; with Mr Mackenzie and Mr Horsfield she makes scenes in restaurants, talking loudly and unstoppably, grimacing, crying. This is what she has become. She knows it: 'I'm sorry,' she says sullenly to Mr Horsfield, 'you see, that's how I am.' And Jean knows it too: these 'fits of rage,' she writes, 'were becoming part of [Julia's] character.'

But Julia still stops short of letting her full anger show to the people who are most important to her, on whom she depends for money and hope: her ex-lovers. When she sees Mr James she thinks, 'How rum if after all these years I hated him – not for any reason except that he's so damned respectable and secure.' But even to herself she answers 'I'm not even sure if I hate you'; and she continues to behave well enough so that he sends her twenty pounds. And even her main anger, with Mr Mackenzie, she contains, in a way that repeats but much improves on Jean's solution to the problem of Marya's.

It's not just that when Julia turns on an innocent man as a substitute he is less innocent than Stephan. This is an improvement too, but it's still Jean's old kind of indirectness. The real improvement is a new kind of indirectness altogether: not of the victim, but of the act itself and its description.

I mean the famous incident of Julia's slapping Mackenzie's face at the beginning. Even though she hits *him*, still the act is indirect and incomplete. It's almost as though she hardly does it at all. She hits his cheek 'so lightly that he did not even blink'; she does it not with her hand (as Marya hit Heidler, and fought with Stephan) but with a glove; and the gesture is a formal one, part of the traditional ritual of the duel, not Julia's own personal expression. She has done it, and directly, to Mackenzie: yet she's still kept the act distant, pale, alienated from herself. But even more indirect and distant is the way

---

*Except in *Voyage in the Dark*, where Anna does not seek revenge against Walter even indirectly, but goes straight to self-destruction.

that Jean describes it. She never tells it from Julia's point of view, so that we never actually know what she is feeling. First she tells it from Mackenzie's point of view: and we see only how Julia *looks*. Then she tells it again, from Mr Horsfield's point of view: and it is even more distant, more indirect, more unreal.

> ... he remembered the quarrel he had seen in the Restaurant Albert and smiled to himself ...
>
> There had been something fantastic, almost dreamlike, about seeing a thing like that reflected in a looking-glass. A bad looking-glass too. So that the actors had been slightly distorted, as in an unstill pool of water.

Moon asks what has happened: and Horsfield says 'Oh, nothing, nothing.' *Julia and her act of anger have been nullified* in every way. To impotence by Mackenzie. To a distant, distorted reflection by the narration and the looking-glass. And finally, again, to nothing. This brief scene enacts for the first time the heroine's whole journey: oppression — anger — indirect revenge — annihilation.

With her next novel Jean will begin to explore the roots of the heroine's story, in her childhood. This will be her best way of making us understand and sympathise with her: as a result Anna and Antoinette are her most attractive heroines. (She doesn't give Sasha a childhood: and that is another way in which Sasha is her bravest, least specially-pleading heroine.) In this way too Julia is exactly in between. Julia is the first heroine to have a childhood: but its bearing on her guilt or innocence is ambiguous and obscure.

We learn about it, very briefly, the night before Julia finally cracks. We hear that 'the last time she was really happy — happy about nothing' was at ten years old, or even younger: and that soon, or already (she can't remember which came first) she was 'afraid about nothing' instead. In other words, by ten at the latest her childhood was over, and she was already embarked on the heroine's journey to annihilation. That must be meant to stir our sympathy. Perhaps it does a little, but we need to know more. We will know much more about Anna and Antoinette, and that will work. But we now learn a bit more about Julia: and it doesn't.

That first time she was afraid, she remembers, she was catching butterflies. When she'd caught one she put it away in a tin, and listened to the 'fascinating sound' of its beating wings inside. It was, she says,

> a fine thing to get your hand on something that a minute before had been flying around in the sun. Of course, what always

happened was that it broke its wings ... or became so battered
that you lost all interest in it. Sometimes it was too badly hurt
to fly properly.
    'You're a horrid, cruel child and I'm surprised at you ....'

The symbolic structure of Jean's mind seems to have turned upside
down. Usually the heroine would *be* the pretty, ephemeral butterfly;
and it would be some heartless boy thinking it 'a fine thing' to
imprison a live thing and listen to it tearing itself to pieces. Usually
it's the heroine herself who fears the huge thing creeping up behind
her, who is imprisoned, who is too badly hurt to fly again .... *Yet
here she does exactly these things to another creature.* We can't help
agreeing with the parental voice – she *is* being horrid and cruel.
    Is this what Jean intended? Is this her way – indirect and distanced
once more – of admitting that Julia is not so different after all from
other people, who are 'indifferent and without pity at all?' But how
do we reconcile this with the narrative's claim that she only *ends* like
this, after a lifetime of humiliation? All the way through, I've argued,
the novel is still Julia's. Despite everything we see her *do*, the core
of her difference remains: she feels pity for others, which no one
(except very briefly Mr Horsfield) feels for her. But if this isn't an
admission of Julia's guilt, then, what is it?
    The only alternative is that it is the same kind of failure as the end
of *Quartet*. There Jean showed us Marya being cruel *without realising
she was cruel*; expecting us, therefore, to take her side. Those last
pages of *Quartet* broke the novel apart, because Jean's and Marya's
solipsism became too visible, and we dissented from their version of
the story. Perhaps the same is happening here. Perhaps Jean simply
doesn't realise how cruel Julia is being; and perhaps she doesn't
realise how false it sounds when she claims that 'If people didn't
understand' this child, she 'couldn't help it'. For 'you simply didn't
answer,' she says: and we see that she didn't *try* to make herself
understood, that she cut herself off from other people from the start.
'Don't you be so sure about what I've felt and what I haven't felt,'
Horsfield says: and perhaps that's what she has always done,
prejudged people and then blamed them for it.
    If this is so, then isn't *After Leaving Mr Mackenzie* as flawed as
*Quartet* in its presentation of the heroine?... Well, not quite. This
is a fleeting childhood memory, not a major event in the novel; much
happens after it, instead of its being the end of the story; and Stephan
is human, while this is after all only a butterfly. Besides, *the whole
novel* is divided about Julia, as we've seen, showing us her rages,
manipulativeness and parasitism as much as her suffering, courage,
and pity. And this division against itself is mostly a strength rather

than a weakness, because Jean is mostly in control of it: it is her theme. This heroine is between dog and wolf — still a victim, but beginning to rise up and strike her oppressor. Of this part of the novel, the childhood memory, I think Jean isn't in control: either she doesn't realise that it displays a lack of pity, or if she does realise it, and is telling us so, then that deeply undermines her main claim for Julia. But this lapse fits into *Mackenzie*, as the lapse at the end of *Quartet* did not. Julia *is* therefore flawed in her presentation; but nothing like as badly as Marya. And Anna, Sasha and Antoinette will in their different ways not be flawed at all. Again: Jean gets better every time.

★    ★    ★

*Other people*: *After Leaving Mr Mackenzie* is the point at which other people enter Jean's fiction. In *Quartet* there was only one living point of view, the heroine's. Occasionally we slipped into other people, and saw Marya through their eyes;* at the beginning and end of her affair with Heidler we glimpsed Lois's feelings too. But no one has a reality even approaching the heroine's. This changes with *Mackenzie*.

We seem to start as in *Quartet*, with just a glimpse of the landlady's thoughts in the middle of Julia's. But then suddenly we have three whole sections of Mr Mackenzie; the encounter in the restaurant, the climactic slap, are both told from his point of view. So is our last impression of Julia: the black specks in her eyes, the feeling of melancholy she gives him. But the other point of view on Julia is of course Mr Horsfield's: and we get his almost more than hers. Their first encounter, in Paris, is told entirely from his side. When they meet again in London we begin with Julia; but soon we hear his thoughts too, more and more. Then in their last time together we begin again briefly with Julia; but we soon settle with Horsfield, and the dance hall, their night together, her breakdown on the staircase and her departure are all told from his point of view.

*Everyone* is given a chance to speak to us about Julia, and sometimes about themselves too. Whenever Julia meets her sister we hear as much from Norah as from her. We even hear something from Uncle Griffiths, Mr James and Miss Wyatt. Our forays into these three are more like those in *Quartet*: brief, exceptional, and calculated to expose them as much as Julia. But with Mr Mackenzie, Norah, and especially Mr Horsfield it is different. Julia is no longer the only real subject in her world: she is equally, or even more, an object in theirs. And so the third person narration of *After Leaving*

*E.g. Miss De Solla; Madame Hautchamp; Cairn; Heidler.

*Mr Mackenzie* is completely appropriate to her story. It was *in*appropriate to Marya, the most solipsist heroine. We felt more and more that *Quartet* was *her* story, her partial and personal version; and that therefore the claim to wider truth that the third person implies was illegitimate. By the time we get to Anna, Sasha and Antoinette, Jean herself has come to see how much it is only one person's truth she is telling, and she writes all three novels in the first person. But with Julia she is genuinely telling much of the story from outside the heroine: that is part of what makes *Mackenzie* bleaker and deader than the others. So the novels after *Quartet* are all told in the appropriate narrative voice: *Mackenzie* from outside the heroine, the others from inside.

The first recognition of other people's existence in *Mackenzie*, therefore, is technical: a matter of how the story is told. But there are recognitions too in *what* we are told: primarily, that the heroine is not the only weak and suffering person in the world. When we get inside Norah, for instance, we don't see only that she hates and resents Julia: we see also her compunction, her struggles against herself, her sadness and despair. Uncle Griffiths *is* an abominable old man, without pity for anyone 'beyond the pale' — Dostoievsky's Idiot, the pickpocket, Julia. But even he has moments of honesty and impulse; and even he has his sadness and fears. He can feel 'old and very melancholy', he's afraid of poverty and death. The first may be unnecessary, but the second can't be; and Heidler, for instance, wasn't afraid of anything. He was completely strong, and completely cruel. After *Quartet* this easy idea drops away, and cruel men are also weak ones.* (This comes closer to home, for of course the heroine is weak: now it's at least possible that she is also cruel.) This deeper and more painful insight culminates in Rochester, in *Wide Sargasso Sea*: there Jean will clearly recognise that men are cruel not when they are safe but when they are afraid. But it began in *After Leaving Mr Mackenzie*, and it penetrates right down as far as Uncle Griffiths.

But it is, of course, in the important men, Julia's lovers, that we especially see this new willingness to recognise the reality and vulnerability of other people. It is their points of view we mostly inhabit when we are not inside Julia's; and it is their natures we are mostly shown, when we are not being shown Julia's. Even Mr James *tries* to be kind, has his 'mad friends', and is anxious and unsure in the presence of things he loves. But Jean's real effort at understanding is with Mr Mackenzie and Mr Horsfield. Mr Mackenzie is most-ly, of course, a satirical portrait, in which Jean emphasises his

---

*Except for Mr Blank in *Good Morning, Midnight* — but as his name shows, he is not a real man, only an abstract representative of exploitative society.

self-protective, Uncle Griffiths side. Yet from the very start she shows us his other side too: the vulnerability and uncertainty that have made him like this. *He hid behind* an absent-minded expression, she writes; *he had trained his smile* not to be bashful; he stuck to his code of morals and manners *in self defence*. For in fact he's drawn to emotion and impulse – to poetry, which he has written, to Paris, to reckless and unhappy women like Julia. He has a 'kink' in his nature; he too is split. 'I like Paris, but I loathe the French,' he says. He half agrees with Julia about the unfairness of life; as soon as he's no longer embarrassed or threatened by her, he pities her.

But the main locus of Jean's new attempt to understand men's caution towards her heroine, rather than just denounce it, is of course in Mr Horsfield.

Julia thinks Horsfield is like Mackenzie: someone who's had a 'bad time learning to be hard, but he's learnt it now all right,' and is only theoretically kind. *But Jean's narration shows that this isn't really fair.* First of all, Horsfield is just as close to Julia as he is to Mackenzie. He is quite alone (except for his cat), sad and lonely, 'lamentably deficient' in love of life and humanity. Yet – again like Julia – 'he was not quite subdued yet, after all.' If he is 'dried up' it is with thirst for love, or at least for human contact. He spends his legacy seeking the sun; and when he meets Julia he is stirred, briefly but repeatedly, to rebellion and escape. His attraction to Julia may have an element of the cruel kind of sexual excitement that the heroine's passivity arouses in men ('she was shivering. This added to his sensation of excitement and triumph'). But he is sensitive and kind; feeling this attraction makes him feel obliged to help her, to take care of her. In London he feels detachment and irritation with her; but when he senses her desire to keep in touch with him he obeys it, and asks her to dine with him a week later. He has far less money than Uncle Griffiths or Mr Mackenzie, but he gives more to Julia than they do, and he doesn't force her to ask. When he sleeps with her, he feels very sentimental about her and wants to cry. Of course, like Mackenzie he is split, and his cautious side always takes over. His relationship with Julia is a see-saw between impulses of kindness, pity and attraction, and cautious movements of withdrawal ('you gave way to an impulse. You did something you wanted to do – and then you were enmeshed in all sorts of complications . . .') In bed with her, despite his feelings of pity and fondness, 'Every moment his desire to get out of the room was growing stronger.' When Julia breaks down on the staircase, he first takes her side against the landlady, and 'the strangest understandings, the wildest plans lit up his brain.' But as soon as he is home he suddenly sees her 'not as a representative of the insulted and injured', but as a 'solid human being' who will need endless care; he retreats firmly, and lets her go. He feels pain at her loss (or just at the loss of his own wilder and kinder self?), but at the same time relief. Finally she makes a scene in the restaurant, and it's all over. 'He understood her, but in a cold and theoretical way'; and as he returns to his familiar, stunted world he tells himself, as cynically as Miss Wyatt tells Norah, that 'of course, she will write' for money.

Despite this end, Mr Horsfield is very different from Mr Mackenzie. Where Mr Mackenzie stifles all his sympathetic impulses towards Julia and shows her only the hostile ones, Mr Horsfield does the opposite. And Mr Horsfield actually admits straight away that he shrinks from Julia not because she is so different from himself, but *because she is so similar*. That is much further than any of the other men (Mr Mackenzie, Uncle Griffiths) can go. In response, Jean can go further with him than she can with any of the others. He is the first man she tries to see more sympathetically, just as Julia is the first heroine she tries to see more critically. And on the whole she is remarkably successful. Her picture of the see-saw of Mr Horsfield's feeling shows an absolutely clear grasp of the way that decent, ordinary men could perceive her heroine. Nothing the critics could say about her could surprise her (although of course it could still hurt). She knew it all herself: it was she who'd told them.

There is, however, one feature of Jean's sympathy for Mr Horsfield which is problematic, and intriguing. One of the ways she shows her sympathy is by making him sad and lonely, just like Julia. That works well enough. But there are other similarities, too: in fact, *Mr Horsfield sometimes seems curiously and improbably like Julia*. His thoughts about the sadness of *joie de vivre*, for example, or the illusion of art, sound just like hers. So do his thoughts about drink — his longing for it, his feeling that when he is slightly drunk 'he understood life better than he understood it as a general rule.' When Julia cries in the cinema he is cross, because 'all he wanted to do was to have a good time and not think' — which is exactly what all the heroines want to do. And when he speculates about Julia he gets it uncannily right:

> ... of course, she must have some pathetic illusions about herself or she would not be able to go on living. Did she still see herself young and slim, capable of anything, believing that, though everyone around her grew older, she — by some miracle — remained the same? Or perhaps she was just heavily indifferent. . . .

This strange similarity between the heroine and her more

sympathetic men will persist. It will recur in René – though in this case it will work, because part of the point is that the gigolo is a young, male version of what Sasha has often had to be. But it will also recur in Rochester, in *Wide Sargasso Sea*: and there it will be less appropriate, and more disturbing, as it is in Mr Horsfield. Jean's novels always feel limited but brilliant, because limited to what she knows. But sometimes they feel *too* limited, because she knows too little. We sense that there is really only one person she understands from the inside, herself: and that whenever she tries to get inside anyone, however different, she turns him into herself. In a way, therefore, her most ambitious and important characters – her understood enemies – are also her most flawed. As long as she only observes people, she never puts a foot wrong. Going into them, she shows the limits of her imagination. Yet it was worth it. It made her books less perfect, but greater.

There is another person in *Mackenzie* who is surprisingly like Julia: her sister Norah. She too, for example, is 'so tired', she too thinks of herself as a slave, and as buried alive; she too cries for her dying youth and beauty ('If this goes on for another year I'm finished. I'll be old and finished, and that's that'). Anyone would feel like this, if she were thirty-one and had spent six years as an unpaid nurse. But the more we hear the less we can escape the feeling that Norah's voice is too like Julia's.

> ... they did not help. They just stood round watching her youth die, and her soft heart grow hard and bitter. They just sat there and said: 'You're wonderful, Norah.' Beasts ... devils .... For a long time, she had just lain on her bed, thinking: 'Beasts and devils....'

Norah stops herself, and consoles herself with thoughts of money – and that is not like her sister. But soon she sounds extraordinarily like Julia again:

> And then she had felt very cold, and had pulled the bed-clothes over her. And then she had felt so tired that after all nothing mattered except sleep. And then she must have slept.*

Now Norah is also like Julia in another, very significant way: she is divided. When we first meet her we hear:

---

*Compare Julia's feeling after her mother dies ('she was filled with only one wish – a longing for sleep'); or after her quarrel with Norah: 'she felt nothing, except that she was tired and that she wished to be left alone to rest there, quietly, in a darkened room.'

She had a sweet voice, a voice with a warm and tender quality. This was strange, because her face was cold, as though warmth and tenderness were dead in her.

She is split between warm and cold, soft and hard. Once she was soft, she thinks, but now she is growing hard. After she and Julia quarrel she manages to forget her very quickly.

Norah lay back, with her eyes shut. She thought: 'My God, how hard I've got!' Her lips trembled: 'What's happened to me?' For a moment she was afraid of herself.

*Now this is just what happens to all the heroines.* Anna asks exactly the same question, when she finds herself wanting to hit the man in the street: 'What happened to me then? Something happened to me then?' (*Voyage in the Dark*). And it is of course Julia's own story: her last remaining pride is her tender heart, but she finds herself at the end of *Mackenzie* 'without any pity at all'. Sasha will spend the whole of *Good Morning, Midnight* trying to let out the wolf inside her and hurt someone; and Antoinette will set out with fire in her hand to do it. The heroines don't say that they are afraid of themselves, of their own hardness: instead they say they are afraid of other people's. But it seems to me that that is the truth: they *say* they hate and fear other people, but they really hate and fear themselves. That is why they let themselves be abused — why they expect punishment, and invite it. And that is why (of course) Jean did too. Yet the only character she ever gives this recognition to — 'For a moment she was afraid of herself' — is the hated sister, Norah. This of course suggests something rather interesting. The heroine is not only increasingly split herself: a large number of Jean's novels and stories are split in the same way. There are very often *pairs of women* in them, one soft and one hard, who are sometimes friends, more often enemies. For instance: Marya and Lois in *Quartet*; Anna and Ethel (and Maudie and Laurie) in *Voyage in the Dark*; Antoinette and Amélie in *Wide Sargasso Sea*; Roseau and Peggy Olsen in 'La Grosse Fifi', Petronella and Frankie in 'Petronella', Maudie and Heather in 'Tigers Are Better-Looking'.* And Julia and Norah in *After Leaving Mr Mackenzie*. Only *Good Morning, Midnight* seems not to pair Sasha with anyone: because both the woman and the wolf

*And other examples too. Inez and the nurses, or Mrs Murphy and Pat, in 'Outside the Machine'; the narrator and her hostess in 'At the Villa d'Or'; Lotus and Christine in 'The Lotus'; Selina Davis and her neighbour in 'Let Them Call It Jazz'; Teresa and Miss Spearman in 'A Solid House'; Rosalie and Irene in 'Pioneers, Oh, Pioneers'; Audrey and Monica in 'The Insect World'; Miss Verney and Miss Baker in 'Sleep It Off Lady'.

are located, at last, within the heroine herself. In other words, it seems to me that until *Good Morning, Midnight* (and again after it) Jean tended to separate the soft from the hard person, and to put them into two different characters. And here the two characters are the closest they will ever be until they merge: sisters.

That is, of course, typical of *After Leaving Mr Mackenzie*, the novel in which the knowledge Jean sought is already there, but only subconsciously, not yet fully seized. There is, I think, some evidence that this particular part of it — the secret identity between the two sisters, which allowed Jean to express truths about the one through the other — happened unconsciously. For at one point there is an actual *confusion* between them, so that for a moment we do not know which sister we are with. And it is at a most important point: when the key question of the novel is posed.

It happens in Chapter Nine of Part Two. The family is travelling to Mrs Griffiths' funeral. The third section ends: 'Norah was silent, looking down at her hands clasped together in her lap.' Then the fourth section begins:

> The car stopped. Everybody walked in a short procession up to the chapel of the crematorium, where a clergyman with very bright blue eyes was waiting. That was a dream, too, but a painful dream, because she was obsessed with the feeling that she was so close to seeing the thing that was behind all this talking and posturing . . .
>
> . . . In another minute she would know. And then a dam inside her head burst, and she leant her head on her arms and sobbed.

'She' must be Julia, not Norah: for Julia is the one who sobs, with her arm pressed over her eyes, while Norah watches the coffin 'with eyes wide open'. But when we first meet that *she* we can't be sure. The dream, and the question, sound like Julia — but logically it should be Norah, the last one to be named. . . . It's quite extraordinary that when Jean brings the novel to the point of asking the heroine's central question — what is behind the nothingness that her life has reached? — there should be this confusion: is it Norah or Julia who is asking? is it Norah or Julia whose life is nothing? But it is so. There is a moment when in logic and grammar Norah seems to ask what is really Julia's question. That was surely an unconscious slip: so it was probably unconscious too when at the end of the same chapter Norah also gives Julia's answer: behind the nothingness is *herself*. That is what she is afraid of.

★

Not only Julia's sister is like her, her mother is too.* She too is beautiful, unhappy in England, abandoned to a poor and lonely exile by a man. All three women are buried alive in a cold grey country; they are all poor and dependent; they are all, physically or emotionally, paralysed and dying.

This identity or similarity among the three main female characters gives us a sense of the common plight of women: such a strong sense that it emerges as one of the novel's themes. And yet − is it? Is *Mackenzie* really, as this makes it sound, a feminist novel?

Well: hardly. For there is of course no solidarity among these women, no common cause possible between Julia and the others. Obviously not between the sisters; but not between Julia and her mother either. Julia's first abandonment was by her mother; after that she was afraid of her, disliked her, became indifferent to her; now she says 'Darling' but 'her heart is dead'. Instead her mother is dangerous, the possible source of a final condemnation: 'Supposing that her mother ... with one word or glance put her outside the pale, as everybody else had done.' There *is* a portrait of female solidarity in the book − but it is a hostile one. Like the most unscrupulous anti-feminists, Jean suggests that Norah and Miss Wyatt are probably lesbians. Miss Wyatt is decidedly mannish, with her 'shirt blouse' and tie, and her gestures 'like the gestures of a man'. She behaves throughout as Norah's protector, and they will go away together at the end. So far from admiring her female pair, Jean reduces it to a pale imitation of an ordinary one. It is like the film of the young women running races and collapsing exhausted, after the young men: the same thing, but comical.

No: here, as usual, Jean's motive force was private. The 'ugly sister' and the 'beautiful mother' answer her artistic needs, of showing and of hiding aspects of her heroine. And of course they answer personal needs too. There can be no doubt that Jean hated and resented Brenda as much as Julia hates and resents Norah; at the same time she recognised that Brenda's life was terrible too, and in fiction she could show it. As for the mother, Julia's feelings are once again very close to Jean's, as she wrote of them in *Smile Please* and elsewhere. But though Jean ended as indifferent to her mother as Julia, her death would desperately upset her. The central role that the death of the mother plays in *Mackenzie* shows that it did. Her mother's dying would release her pity for her, and her earliest memories; it would push into the background − though not obliterate − her memories of the woman who preferred her sister, who was a cold English judge

*This identity between the heroine and her mother will be even stronger, and more deliberate, in *Wide Sargasso Sea*. See Part Three, Chapter Four.

and hard taskmaster. All these would enter the portrait of Julia's mother; but the 'beautiful mother' would dominate. Jean would even kill off her father, in order (I feel) to remove the lasting focus of warmth in her childhood, and concentrate her imagination on her mother.* The result in *Mackenzie* is to increase the feeling of male dereliction: with the exception of Uncle Griffiths, Julia's family is entirely female. When they set off for the funeral the voice summons only women: 'Ladies for the first carriage, please.... Ladies for the second carriage.' To some degree, perhaps, Jean deliberately emphasised this male dereliction. But mostly I think she was just sticking to her memory. For when Mrs Rees Williams died the family who came to her funeral must have been almost entirely female: Auntie B and Aunt Mackie; Minna and Brenda and Nurse Woolgar; probably Aunt Clarice and Neville Williams's wife and daughters; Owen's mother and sister-in-law. Edward was away in India, and Owen in Australia; Neville Williams's son was in South Africa. That is why there are no men except Uncle Griffiths in Acton or at Golders Green in *Mackenzie*: because there were no men except Neville Williams in Acton or at Golders Green (for Mrs Rees Williams really was buried in Golders Green) in reality. Of course, there were dozens of other facts that Jean *didn't* pick up and use, because they didn't fit into the shape of her novel. This one did: and so she used it.

★     ★     ★

*The novel*: *After Leaving Mr Mackenzie* is the novel between dog and wolf. It is about everything being over, life being empty; it is about nothingness. And every line of the writing echoes the nothingness and the negativity. There is a perfect match between the heroine's alienation and the alienation of Jean's narrative techniques.

This begins, as we've seen, with the title. It's not even *leaving* but *after leaving* Mr Mackenzie. The other titles are strong nouns, statements, orders, salutes. This one is a formal name pushed behind a gerund, behind a preposition. The formality is never lifted; we never know Mr Mackenzie's first name. We know Mr Horsfield's and Mr James's; but the narration never uses them, they remain 'Mr' too. In *Wide Sargasso Sea* Antoinette's lover will never be named at

---

*In *Voyage in the Dark* she will do the opposite: make her mother even more distant — turn her, in fact, into that other mother figure, the wicked stepmother; and concentrate on her warm and sympathetic father. In *Wide Sargasso Sea* she will remember both: the 'beautiful mother', and the dead but kind father, from whom all security had come ('my father, visitors, horses, feeling safe in bed — all belonged to the past').

all, not even as 'Mr'. This will fit Antoinette's exile, from England and from reality. *After Leaving Mr Mackenzie* is halfway there.

This novel is also constructed differently from the others. It has three parts; each part is divided into chapters; each chapter is divided into numbered sections. None of the other four novels is chopped up like this. They all flow, or rush; *Mackenzie* moves in short jerks, like Julia on her high heels. It is the only one with a table of contents, where the chapters are planned, named and numbered. These are the technical expressions of Julia's tiredness, and of her having replaced the search for love with the search for knowledge.

The second structural uniqueness of *Mackenzie* is the direction of its movement. The other novels move in straight lines. The last three have two lines each: in *Voyage in the Dark* and *Good Morning, Midnight* the heroine's past and present, in *Wide Sargasso Sea* the heroine's and her lover's. They move in a kind of cross: upwards (or less down) for the past, or the man, downwards for the heroine. *Quartet* has only one line, straight down. But *Mackenzie's* is circular. The story begins in the hotel in Paris, moves to London, returns to the hotel in Paris. It begins with Mr Mackenzie, moves to Mr Horsfield, returns to Mr Mackenzie. 'She felt that her life had moved in a circle. Predestined, she had returned to her starting point,' Jean wrote in the middle; but it is equally true at the end. Though in between Julia has also moved downwards – she has lost a few more people, her life has become still emptier. Perhaps, then, the movement of the book is a spiral: as though Julia were sliding slowly down the huge mauve corkscrew, suspended in space, which she sees at the beginning.

And the narrative stance increases the sense of alienation. For this is Julia's story: yet so often it is told from outside her, and against her. The subject of this novel, therefore, is made an object in it, whose fate we can see as clearly as Mr Mackenzie can: 'the final stage of her descent in the social scale was inevitable, and not far off.' We see almost all the crucial scenes of her story this way, without knowing from the inside how she feels: her slapping Mackenzie; her meetings with Mr Horsfield, and her sleeping with him;* her final breakdown on the staircase.† So we are distanced from her; it's

---

*Here we are explicitly reminded how little we know of Julia's side of the story: 'But the worst of it is', Horsfield thinks, 'that one can never know what the woman is really feeling.'

†The only crisis during – or rather after – which we do get inside Julia is the quarrel with Norah. And what we see in her then is only indifference: the immense indifference which always descends on her 'Just when in another moment her brain would burst.'

almost as though we are watching her in the looking-glass, like Mr Horsfield. And of course she's distanced from herself. She feels a great many things, as intensely as ever – anger and terror, excitement and hope – but they pass rapidly, and are hardly connected to reality. Her fears are irrational (of the old dancer, for instance, or on the staircase), and so are her hopes. On the rare occasions she escapes her passivity and acts, it is very strangely: without her own will (going to London) or against it (with the old dancer). A great deal of the time she is vague, indifferent, floating; anxious but absent, her eyes fixed and unseeing. When we are inside the other heroines their intense emotions and vivid, sensual perceptions fill their stories with colour, however sad or tragic they are. But even when we are *inside* Julia that colour has largely disappeared. She is like a shadow seeing shadows; she is like someone under a spell. And we feel among shadows, and under a spell, as we read the novel.

I have hesitated to say that *Mackenzie* is about the lack of communication, because that's such a hoary old chestnut. But of course it's true: *Mackenzie* is about the lack of communication between Julia and other people. From childhood, when she ' simply did not answer' misjudgements, to now, when she feels it is only 'her body' defending her husband to Uncle Griffiths, Julia has been unable to tell her real feelings or meanings to anyone. It is what she longs to do – to 'explain', to tell 'everything', to her mother, to the slim soft woman in the café, to Ruth and the lovely woman in the picture. But she does it only once, to Ruth – only to feel that what she so wants to tell isn't true, and she doesn't exist at all. The rest of the time she hides her real feelings ('You'd simply make some excuse to go off and leave me if I told you what was really the matter'). They only emerge when she loses control – breaks down, or loses her temper. Otherwise she expresses them indirectly. Thus for example she says to Mr Mackenzie 'I hate hypocrites,' when what she means is '*you* are a hypocrite, and I hate you'; or she defends the viewpoint of Dostoievsky's Idiot as an indirect way of defending her own. When Mr Horsfield offers help with obvious insincerity she checks her face in the mirror, as though she were afraid *she* was ugly, when really she is thinking that *he* is. A few moments later she says 'It's funny how you say one thing when you're thinking of quite another, isn't it?'

Now what Jean does, of course, is once more to match Julia's indirectness with her own. Her main method is the same as always, to hide her meaning in imagery. And in *Mackenzie* her meaning is more hidden than in all the rest of her fiction: for her imagery here is uniquely ambivalent and obscure.

This begins straight away: indeed the first two pages set the tone of the entire novel, and perfectly sum up its essence. In the cheap French hotel, and the thin, whispering landlady; but especially in the dominant image of Julia's horrible room.

The room is sombre and gloomy and 'one-eyed', because it has only one window, set very much to one side – and is that not a good description of Julia's view of the world? But it also has 'individuality' and 'fantasy' – as Julia's view certainly has – which Jean sites especially in 'the pattern of the wallpaper':

> A large bird, sitting on the branch of a tree, faced, with open beak, a strange wingless creature, half-bird, half-lizard, which also had its beak open and its neck stretched in a belligerent attitude. The branch on which they were perched sprouted fungus and queerly shaped leaves and fruit.

This is strange, significant, obscure. It is full of deformity – the misshapen fruit, the creature which is neither bird nor lizard: like Julia, belonging to no species. This creature's open beak is 'belligerent' – but is the other's? Might it not be, instead, about to speak? But the effect in any case is aggressive and sinister. Interestingly, Jean knows we will find it sinister, but says it isn't: 'The effect of all this was, oddly enough, not sinister but cheerful and rather stimulating.' And I think that here a feeling is stirring, which will become very important in the last two novels: the feeling that hostility and hate are not really sinister, as they may seem, but 'stimulating'. It is people's hostility that rouses Julia to resistance and defiance ('Left quite alone, you would have let go of your own accord'); Sasha and Antoinette will be kept alive only by a 'flame of hatred', like the woman on the floor above Julia. It is this idea that I think Julia's wallpaper pictures – the cheeringness of feeling 'belligerence' in a hostile world. But even Jean may not know it clearly;* and certainly we can't.

After the wallpaper Jean shows us the rest of the room. There is a big pink bed, a red plush sofa, a wardrobe, and on a ledge below a mirror, a painting. The bed is comfortable, the wardrobe and the mirror evidently neutral. But the sofa and the painting contain for Julia the sinister and depressing quality she didn't find in the wallpaper. What Jean writes about the picture we can again apply to her own imagery: 'Every object in the picture was slightly distorted and full of obscure meaning.' Every object in Julia's room is the same.

---

*She only expresses it clearly, again, through Norah: ' "I'll come to the door with you" ', said Norah. She now felt that she did not want to let Julia go. She hated her, but she felt more alive when her sister was with her.'

... really she hated the picture. It shared, with the colour of
the plush sofa, a certain depressing quality. The picture and the
sofa were linked in her mind. The picture was the more
alarming in its perversion and the sofa the more dismal. The
picture stood for the idea, the spirit, and the sofa stood for the
act.

This is sinister and striking, but again obscure. What idea does the
picture stand for, which is perverse, and what act the sofa, which
is merely dismal? Perhaps the idea of life itself, and the act of daily
living — for the objects in the picture are a meal, a bottle of wine
and a piece of cheese. But we don't know. There is something
'distorted' (again) and frightening here, but what it is is hidden. And
it will remain hidden, as we've seen. The novel's main question will
remain hidden in Norah, its answer in nothingness. And when we
return to the question left open in the wallpaper — is the 'large bird'
attacking the Julia-like creature, or is she the only 'belligerent' one?
— the answer, in Julia's childhood memory, is confused and obscure.
The key images of the novel, like all the rest of it, are only half
worked out, half conscious, in between.

As long as it stays away from its overwhelming question, however,
the rest of *Mackenzie*'s imagery is clearer, continuing *Quartet*'s but
moving it on. Julia's remaining feelings are focused on people who
are not really real at all, but images of her memories, hopes and fears.
The two 'unknowns', for instance, are just her hope and her fear
incarnate: the first gives her the energy to go to London, the second
deals her the final blow. The old violet seller is her fear of how much
she has changed, the old dancer her fear of madness and death, the
slim soft woman her hope of kindness, the skeleton in the doorway
her fear of her own hardness.... And all around her, as in *Quartet*,
are 'people' who are merely echoes of herself. Some are men this
time, like the dirty old mandoline player who tries to beg from Mr
Mackenzie just before she does. But most are women: the 'woman
on the floor above', whom Julia consciously sees as the end of her
road; the woman who passes her and Horsfield on their way to the
cinema, looking 'mournful and lost, like a dog without a master':
another old woman when she is back in Paris, who is 'transparent,
like a ghost'. At the end these images of herself seem to multiply
endlessly, and stare back at her: 'The houses opposite had rows of
long windows, and it seemed to Julia that at each window a woman
sat staring mournfully like a prisoner, straight into her bedroom.'

All the rest of Jean's permanent, obsessive imagery is here too.
There is dark and light — but now both are fearful. There are
animals: Mackenzie and Norah like horses, Julia like a dog, but

moving towards the wolf; and the idea, as in *Quartet*, that 'Animals are better than we are, aren't they? They're not all the time pretending and lying and sneering, like loathsome human beings....' Popular songs comment again – 'Roll me over on my right side', which reminds Horsfield of Julia, or '*Pars, sans te retourner, pars*', when she is about to take her last step down the 'social scale'. Flowers and trees are important again. The tulips in Mr James's hall, for instance, are 'flame-coloured' and dying like Julia, or stiff and virginal like Norah; the 'frail and drooping' roses that Julia buys for her mother are again images of herself, so that she cannot bear to enclose them in the coffin. Trees are friendly again, and comfort her; and after each loss we see a tree thin, leafless, stunted, dead. The moon is dangerous, as it will be in *Wide Sargasso Sea*; shadows beckon to death, and death awaits in water.

But with all this there is something new too: images of absurdity. Not quite new, for even Marya once thinks, in the middle of her misery, how Heidler looks like Queen Victoria. But *Mackenzie* has many such moments. There are the young women collapsing, to the laughter of the audience; there are the absurd sources of the men's money – 'a line of coastal steamers' for Mr Mackenzie, and hops for Mr Horsfield: 'I'm a decaying hop factor, damn you! My father did the growth and I'm doing the decay.' There is the fat South African, whose card Julia lets drop on to the tube-train floor: 'No one was watching. He picked the card up, brushed it, and put it back in his pocket, crossed his legs, and composed his countenance.' But best of all is Horsfield's own moment on the stairs.

In the dimness of the hall a white face glimmered at him. He started, and braced himself for an encounter. Then, relieved, he saw that it was a bust of the Duke of Wellington.

This is like a rehearsal of Julia's own terror, in the night to come: but punctured, satirised, in an absurd and comic key. And we remember the picture and the sofa at the start: one perverse and alarming, the other merely dismal.

★     ★     ★

*Between dog and wolf*: I began by saying that *Mackenzie* is Jean's most conscious, rational novel, in which the heroine pursues knowledge rather than love, and asks herself the question which in the other novels Jean only asks *about* her. Yet now we've seen that the opposite is also true: *Mackenzie* is the most subterranean and *un*conscious novel. For Julia cannot answer the question; and nor can Jean, except confusedly and obscurely. It's as though forcing herself to ask it — like Julia's forcing herself to face Mr Mackenzie — has 'left her in a state of collapse', and she can do no more.

Already in *Quartet* there was a sense of doom and foreboding. It will be in all the novels: but most of all in *Mackenzie*. The worst things that happen all signal themselves long before. Julia's and Norah's quarrel, for instance, nearly happens at their very first meeting, and comes so close at the second that Norah feels breathless. Finally, though they both try to resist it, it breaks through. And the worst thing of all, Julia's breakdown on the stairs, also struggles to surface, like the shadows under the Seine. On the day her mother dies 'all the way home she was thinking: "If I have any luck, I oughtn't to meet anybody on the stairs."' On the evening of the funeral, 'as she dressed she twice looked suddenly and fearfully over her shoulder.' Then, after their night together, Mr Horsfield writes 'I'm going, or I'll risk meeting somebody on the stairs,' and he does — he meets the Duke of Wellington, who is dead. So that when Julia stops and screams that 'someone dead' has caught hold of her hand, we are ready: Jean has secretly but steadily affected us with Julia's nameless fear.

What *is* this thing that Julia fears so? It is, I think, the very same thing as 'the truth about myself and about the world' — 'the thing that was behind all this talking and posturing' — the 'something huge' that was behind Julia when she was a child. It is all the same thing; and it is connected to the unconsciousness that hides it.

Julia is a deeply unconscious heroine. She acts always reluctantly, often without or against her will — going to London, dancing with the cadaverous old man. *And with her all the characters* act in a similarly reluctant, trance-like way, as though they are in the grip of something which threatens the conscious order of their lives. Mr Mackenzie and Mr Horsfield fall for her like this — against their wills, consciously resisting. Mr Mackenzie feels that his brief obsession with her was an 'insanity, for which he was not responsible'; Mr Horsfield tries to cancel a meeting with her but cannot: 'I felt I had to come. I wanted to see you.' Norah tries to stop herself from quarrelling with her, but cannot. They all want their lives to look decent and in control: so they all hide, and almost forget, deeper truths — Mr Mackenzie his poetry, Mr Horsfield his loneliness, Norah her longing for freedom and happiness before she is too old. It is Julia who reminds them of these suppressed truths. She arouses Mackenzie's 'insanity' and Norah's 'spirit of rebellion'; she gives Mr Horsfield back (he says) 'his youth'. Yet they all fear her, resist her and reject her; they push her away out of sight, and return with relief to their familiar, quiet, passionless worlds.

Julia is thus — as Mackenzie says — 'a dangerous person'. She is a living reminder to all 'good' people of the alternatives to self-control and respectability. She is a messenger of anarchy and licence, who destroys their rational control and releases their most secret feelings – lust, loneliness, anger, jealousy. . . . She is, in other words, herself an embodiment of all such hidden feelings: *herself an embodiment of the unconscious.*

Now of course this isn't all of Julia either: but it is the wolf in her. The wolf is her subconscious: her most primitive, most lawless, most repressed self. That is what men are so attracted to, and what at the same time they so fear: and so does she. Everyone dreads losing control. But that is especially the fear of the Jean Rhys heroine, 'suspended over a dark and terrible abyss – the abyss of absolute loss of self-control.' The death that Julia fears is the death of her conscious, controlling self: the murderer she fears is her own sub-conscious.

All this is true of the heroines because, of course, it was true of Jean. She too was suspended over an abyss, and hung on with desperation to the last shreds and appearances of self-control. She was herself divided – fractured – between a lady above and a savage below.* That was the war that tore her apart. She fought to keep the lady on top and the savage hidden; she fought to rescue the lady from the dark water of the sub-conscious. But though she feared the lady's drowning as her own annihilation, she really hated her. Especially as a writer, she came to know that the savage was her true self, the source of her real and individual vision. So her warring, divided feelings became still more warring and divided. She *had* to save her well-behaved exterior – but she hated and despised it; she desperately feared the savage inside – but really she loved and was proud of it. So part of her desired to give up and 'die' – not just out of fatigue, but because madness and death were defeat only for the lady; for the savage they were liberation and triumph. And that is, finally, the feeling behind Antoinette's suicide in the last of the novels.

But Antoinette was far in the future. What is stirring now, below the surface of *Mackenzie*, is something wholly feared. Everything in the novel shares the same movement: of something obscure and fearful beginning to shake itself free, like the shadows rising from the Seine. One last image distils this in the novel. It comes in the most obscurely titled chapter, 'It Might Have Been Anywhere'. Julia and Mr Horsfield are climbing the stairs to her room, as they will

---

*See Heidler to Marya in *Quartet*: '"Savage," he said, watching her. "Bolshevist! You'll end up in red Russia, that's what will happen to you."'

do again the next night, when she will break down. She is shivering with fear, he with excitement.

> They reached the staircase. He put his hand on the banisters, and mounted noiselessly after her. She was invisible in the darkness, but he followed the sound of her footsteps, placing his feet very carefully, so that they made no sound.
> The stairs were solid; there was not a creak.
> They mounted silently, like people in a dream.

All around them respectable English people sleep, while they climb towards Julia's bed and the slaking of a thirst they didn't know they had. It is like a dream; like the rising up of a subconscious need. But it is like something else too: the movement of the heroine through the whole of Jean's work. It is as though, in her own sub-conscious, Jean already knows the whole story; and here the image of it clairvoyantly surfaces, as the image of its end will surface in Antoinette's clairvoyant dream.

For the heroine's whole journey is just such a nightmare-like climb up a staircase. Even Anna and Marya have upstairs rooms, in Ethel's flat, and in the Heidlers' studio and cottage; both of Marya's are at the top of a 'narrow staircase'. But with Julia the staircase and the height of the heroine's room begin to hold an ominous meaning. In her Paris hotel the cringing, malevolent old woman whom she fears to become lives 'upstairs'; in the London boarding house she is upstairs herself, on the very top floor. That is where Sasha will be too, even in Paris.* And Antoinette, of course, will be highest of all: not even on the top floor, but in the attic; and finally on the roof itself, from which she will jump. And she has come here, just as Julia has, up a dark staircase, in a dream:

> ... *There are steps leading upwards. It is too dark to see the wall or the steps, but I know they are there and I think, 'It will be when I go up these steps. At the top.'*

The last time she has her dream is at the very end of *Wide Sargasso Sea*. This time the dream ends, and she thinks: '*I know now that the flight of steps leads to this room.*' Jean saw the steps first in *Mackenzie*; finally the nightmare climb ends thirty years later, in *Wide Sargasso Sea*.

Then we remember that Jean did not put Antoinette in the attic: Charlotte Brontë did, more than a hundred years before. Surely *that* is where the image came from — from Jean's reading *Jane Eyre* on

---

*See too, in *Good Morning, Midnight*, the mulatto woman in Serge Rubin's story.

the verandah of the Victoria Library at home. Surely that is how it had managed to lie in her subconscious all those years, drawing her heroines irrestibly upward. Yet this makes it more mysterious instead of less. For it is as though the image of the madwoman in the attic lay waiting not just for forty years, for the heroines, but for over a hundred, for Jean herself: so that her whole journey was mapped out in advance, and not by her. And that, of course, is what she always felt.

# CHAPTER THREE

# Leslie, 1931–1934

*Reviews – Friends – Leslie – John – Marriage and death –*
*The ending of* Voyage in the Dark

*Mackenzie* was published in England in February 1931, in America in June. It got more reviews than *Quartet*, by more august reviewers. It was, deservedly, much more highly praised, but it was just as much reviled. The *Daily Telegraph* called it 'superb', The *Observer* 'flawless'; in America the *Saturday Review* said that Jean's prose had 'the balance and beauty of verse', the *New York Post* that she'd 'produced an impressive, infinitely understanding work on the very theme she bungled in *Quartet*.' But then came the 'good' people. *The Times* and the *Times Literary Supplement* printed the same review on the same day, admiring Jean's 'clarity and economy of language', but calling *Mackenzie* 'a sordid little story', 'a waste of talent'. 'We can do without the sordid and vulgar side of life,' said the *Nottingham Journal*; and the *Boston Transcript* in America: 'Unless you are absorbingly thrilled by knowing what kind of existence ladies like Julia lead . . . you wonder where the brilliance comes in.'

This was bad enough, but it was the sort of sneer Jean was used to. She could tell herself that such people were prigs and philistines, who would never understand her art. But there was something worse: even those who praised *Mackenzie* most for its artistry found Julia supine, worthless and pitiful, and the novel unpleasant, uncomfortable, frightening, terrifying. Nobody could *like* her work, or find it pleasant to read; nobody, it seemed, could like her heroine. *But her work was her own inner world, her heroine herself.* So despite all the praise she herself was once again rejected. It must have seemed to her that people – even the most sympathetic ones – reacted to her books as they did to herself: they liked the wrought surface, upon which she spent such painful labour; but the person underneath frightened and dismayed them.

And of course it was true. Even her best friend, Germaine Richelot, had said *Quartet* was '*une oeuvre d'art*', but that 'no one can read it without wishing that the next will soon come and be different . . . that the author may adapt his or her remarquable qualities to something less depressing.' And even critics who were writers themselves, and who admired her most, said the same thing. Frank Swinnerton said *Mackenzie*'s 'theme was disagreeable', Norah Hoult that Julia was a 'pitiful and uncomfortable human being'. What Rebecca West said was typical − and also funny and true.

> It is doubtful if one ought to open this volume unless one is happily married, immensely rich, and in robust health; for if one is not entirely free from misery when one opens the book one will be at the suicide point long before one closes it. Miss Jean Rhys has already, in *The Left Bank* and *Postures*, quietly proved herself to be one of the finest writers of fiction under middle age, but she has also proved herself to be enamoured of gloom to an incredible degree.

★      ★      ★

Jean got her first fan letters for *Mackenzie*. One was from Ivan Bede, Ford's secretary on *the transatlantic review*, whom Jean had put into *Quartet* as Cairn. Now he recognised himself again: it may be 'vanity' or a 'suspicious nature', he says, but he thinks he recognises 'an imaginary American you thought you knew along about 1924 and '25 in Mr Horsfield. . . .' In fact Mr Horsfield was mostly Leslie, at least in his English incarnation: but Ivan Bede was rather like Leslie, gentle and sensitive, and he'd probably done more to try to rescue Jean in 1924 and '25 than she'd left in *Quartet*. Perhaps there *were* elements (the Parisian elements?) of him in Horsfield too. (John certainly seemed to feel the connection: he called the character he based on Leslie in his third novel 'Leslie Bead'.)

Another man also wrote to her after *Mackenzie*: the novelist and biographer Morchard Bishop, whose real name was Oliver Stoner. Oliver would write again after *Good Morning, Midnight*, and again after *Wide Sargasso Sea*; finally then, in her old age, they would become fast friends. But the two friends she made now were both women.

The first to write, only weeks after *Mackenzie*'s publication, was Peggy Kirkaldy. She was a passionate devotee of literature, already a friend of many writers − Dorothy Richardson, Elizabeth Bowen, Osbert Sitwell − and she wanted to add Jean to the list. A few weeks later they met over cocktails. The meeting was a success; by the summer Jean's letters were to 'My dear Peggy'.

Yet almost immediately there was a quarrel. It wasn't a serious one, but − together perhaps with Jean's habit of disappearing to Paris, and to different London addresses − it seems to have disrupted their friendship for many years. Their relationship would continue like this — full of gaps produced by Jean's touchiness, and by the rows that resulted. 'My dear Peggy,' she wrote now,

> You must try to forgive me. Spiteful was the wrong word — I didn't mean spiteful — I meant — It would take too long to explain — I meant that there's a lot of *Touché* — *En garde* — *Touché* — *En garde* — about one's intercourse with most human beings. And I've been so much alone that I've got out of the [words missing]. Well — hell anyway. I won't think it any more of you Peggy.

She had had only one real lasting female friendship, with Germaine Richelot. Germaine had been a perfect friend, as Lancelot had been a perfect lover: close enough to her in nature to understand, rich and kind enough to help. Yet even with Germaine she had quarrelled. How could she *not* have quarrelled with Peggy Kirkaldy? For Peggy was like her too, but in all the wrong ways. She was highly strung, brittle, very volatile; if she could be overwhelmingly kind she could also be cuttingly cruel. She too had had a preferred sister, a critical mother, a failed marriage; she was socially more adept, but secretly just as insecure. Underneath Jean's shyness lay a great need to be the centre of attention: and underneath Peggy's cultivation of her *salon* lay the same need. 'When she came into a crowded room the lights went up like obedient servants,' says one of her closest friends. Jean would want the lights to go up for *her*, or the room to remain in restful darkness. I expect she was jealous of Peggy, and also afraid of her. Peggy was clever in the English fashion, literary and knowledgeable, with a sharp wit and quick repartee. Jean wasn't clever; she was bad at conversation, and intellectuals would easily think her stupid. Peggy was an intellectual; she was even an intellectual snob. Jean would *expect* harsh judgement from her, and she thought she got it, repeatedly ('she took offence at most unsuspected things,' Peggy said).

At the same time, they admired and liked each other very much. 'Peggy you are pure eighteenth century and you are wasted in this disgusting age. I do like your gaiety and your courage so much,' Jean wrote, after yet another quarrel. During her worst times in the forties and fifties it was Peggy to whom she turned, especially in letters. That is where each could do what she was best at: Jean writing, and Peggy reading. Peggy wasn't shockable, and she took Jean's side. But even after that Jean would take offence again, and lose Peggy for another six or seven years. Luckily Peggy found her again in the end; and for the last year of her life (Peggy died of cancer in 1958) they exchanged affectionate letters.

Jean was finding it increasingly hard to keep her friends when she actually met them, and the best of many of her relationships would be in letters. Certainly that was true of the second friendship that began with *Mackenzie*. For Evelyn Scott was even more difficult a friend for her than Peggy Kirkaldy. They managed to keep going (more or less) for five years, mainly because Evelyn spent them mostly in America. When they met in New York in 1936 there was an almighty row, and the friendship was over.

Evelyn Scott was an American writer, three years younger than Jean (though as Jean was shaving four years off her age she would seem a year older). She was married to an English writer, John Metcalfe. The two were just as poor and impractical a pair as Jean and Leslie. Evelyn wrote hugely and variously — she'd already published six novels, a book of verse and an autobiographical memoir. Jack Metcalfe's style was more like Jean's. He wrote tight, macabre tales of psychic horror, and novels of failure in love set in grey English towns. He was given to drink and ill-health, extremely reticent, withdrawn and lonely. Jean liked him — perhaps better than Evelyn, who was often a tiresome person, again rather in Jean's own fashion: hysterical, quarrelsome and demanding. But she had a fine sensitivity and a real love for Jean's prose; and for Jean herself as well.

Evelyn's experience had been interestingly similar. Her family was also white gentry among black peasants, this time in the American South. She too had been a rebel and a misfit. She too lived a rackety, poverty-stricken bohemian life, taking more than the respectable number of husbands and lovers; her family, too, thought her a fallen woman. This experience of multiple exile had left her with a similarly pessimistic and paranoid world-view. The 'Evelyn Scott woman' is like the 'Jean Rhys woman': dependent and rebellious at the same time, impotently resentful of the power over her of men and of 'organised society'.

The difference is that Evelyn was a bad writer, over-prolific, undisciplined and often incomprehensible. *But she was a wonderful critic.* She was an early champion, for instance, of Joyce, D.H. Lawrence, Faulkner. And now she became a champion of Jean's.

She first wrote to Jean on the way back to America from a visit to England. Her letter was impulsive and enthusiastic in the open American way ('I am afraid this is effusive,' she said). But in fact it suited Jean very well not to have to parry the 'Touché — En garde' of English approaches. (*Would* things have been different if she'd gone to America?...) Warmed and emboldened, she replied in an unusually relaxed tone. 'I like Mackenzie better than anything I have done yet,' she said. She even confided that she was working on another novel.

For the next five years Evelyn was a great support and encouragement to Jean. She recommended *Mackenzie* all around America; later she introduced Jean to an American agent and American writers. And during the three years Jean struggled with *Voyage in the Dark* she wrote her eager, urging letters. Alas, too eager, too urging. Every word of truth is precious, she exhorted her: 'Can I be blamed for regarding it as your obligation not to withhold it?' And

> ... you have a technique, a veracity, a fund of material, a sensitivity in presenting it and a sureness and perfection that it's a CRIME to stifle — Go on!

It was well meant, and high praise. But Jean couldn't bear words like *obligation* and *crime*. They put her under pressure, they made her nervous; and she was already in a state about the novel, and missing Maryvonne.... I suspect she replied angrily, or else refused to reply at all. The next time Evelyn wrote it was to Leslie, to explain that her letter had been the 'exasperation of affection'. Leslie smoothed things over, and soon they were writing again. But it had been a warning.

In 1931 this particular row was still two or three years away. But Jean had definitely reached the stage she had described in Julia: fits of rage were becoming part of her character.

★    ★    ★

We know that Jean was struggling with guilt and grief over Maryvonne. But was anything else going wrong? I think that it was: that she was having to relive an old disappointment.

It was rather like her first marriage, or at any rate like Sasha's: 'He seemed very prosperous when I met him in London, but now no money — nix.' Leslie had never been 'very prosperous', but he was a gentleman; and when Jean met him he had, like Mr Horsfield, 'a small and decaying business,' his literary agency. After Kathleen Millard had left he had taken another partner and carried on. But Leslie was never any good at making or keeping money. His business didn't prosper: and by 1930 he had to admit defeat. He closed down the agency and became instead a freelance publisher's reader. This insecure and poorly paid job remained his only source of earnings for the rest of his life.

It was never enough, and he borrowed half his inheritance before he came into it.* Still he needed more; in the end he borrowed so much from his family that his old uncles refused to see him. Even

---

*Not all while he was with Jean. He'd already borrowed a lot of it during his first marriage.

with all this borrowing, up to the arrival of the rest of his inheritance in 1936 he and Jean were miserably poor. They moved constantly, from one fairly squalid address to another; until 1936 they never had a proper flat, only rooms with a shared bathroom and kitchen. First they moved from near Victoria Station to near Paddington; in 1933 and '34 they moved at least four times, from Hampstead to Bloomsbury to a bungalow on the Thames, which was probably a sort of holiday chalet. (Later Jean would quite often be reduced to holiday chalets, even in the winter. At least this was in the summertime.)

Jean — divided as ever — was not happy feeling completely secure either. She didn't want to be 'respectable', to trade her vision for a mess of pottage. But this was the opposite extreme. She had been so poor for so long, she needed money so badly; complete *in*security, so bad for anyone, was terrible for her. I'm sure she'd hoped, yet again, to escape it with Leslie; instead, yet again, it had caught her more tightly.

Leslie read for several publishers — Harpers, Jonathan Cape, Hodder and Stoughton, Faber and Gwyer (the original of Faber & Faber). But from 1931 his main employer was Hamish Hamilton. Hamilton himself met Leslie now; and saw how bad things had already become.

Leslie's daughter Anne had already noticed scratches on his face, once or twice a black eye, but Leslie had explained that the cat had scratched him, and he'd bumped into something, like an idiot. Anne believed him, but Hamilton didn't. He recognised 'the scars of war', and he began to feel sorry for Leslie. Finally one day he saw Leslie's face actually bleeding. He felt he must do something; and he went to call on Jean.

Jean was clearly depressed and drinking, but she pulled herself together. Hamish Hamilton was an old-fashioned gentleman, and never told anyone exactly what had passed between them: but he did say 'she didn't seem to resent my interference.' Did she promise him not to fight with Leslie any more? I'm sure she did, if he'd brought himself to make such a direct accusation. But it could make no difference. If she could have stopped herself she would have, long before. She'd go on fighting with Leslie; it would become common knowledge among his friends and family. In the end he even admitted it to his children.

But why? Why was Jean so angry at Leslie that she not only 'wanted to fly at him and strike him,' like Julia with the unknown, but *did*, repeatedly? It cannot just have been disappointment at their poverty. It cannot just have been — though of course much of it was — drink. Leslie was a remarkably, an unusually nice, kind and gentle man.* He loved her, and she loved him; that came out, like the sun, whenever they had a better moment. And it came out in the novels: for it was only after meeting Leslie that Jean began to admit that there were kind and gentle men among her heroines' lovers. *Why,* then, was she so angry with him?

Partly it was his very niceness and kindness. They deprived her of the comfort of blaming everything on men; they forced her to see that in this case at least she was the guilty one. *They showed her up,* and not only to herself. She soon began to feel that everyone preferred Leslie to her: not only friends and acquaintances, but even her own daughter. When Maryvonne came on her holidays to England, and they took her on camping trips or to the theatre, Jean feared that 'It was Leslie she thanked and liked, not me.' And it was true. Jean brought her presents from Paris and wrote stories for her; sometimes they played acting games together – Maryvonne as Jim Hawkins, Jean stumping about as Long John Silver, with a make-believe parrot on her shoulder. But these moments were rare. Jean was far more often writing or drunk or crying than ready to play ('My mother tries to be an artist and is always crying,' Jean quoted her, at six or seven). It was Leslie who was reliably kind; and in return Maryvonne loved him. 'There are a hundred small things I can remember,' she wrote to Anne many years later. 'Only he made my holidays in England bearable when I was a child.'

And then, Leslie was *too* nice and gentle: he was weak and timid. He did everything to please Jean, then apologised for not doing more, and when she was in a temper he couldn't cope with her at all. He hated any sort of violence and any sort of scene; he couldn't shout back, still less hit back. But this left him with no response to Jean's explosions except silence and withdrawal. That was so controlled, so *English,* it would only goad her more.... Perhaps if he could have been less good she could have been less bad. As it was, she could only despise him for being weak, and herself for being wicked.

---

*Everybody thought so, including Jean herself ('I did love him ... and knew all his generosity and gentleness – very well'). Not only Anne, who had of course the bias of a daughter (though there are plenty of daughters who *aren't* biased in favour of their fathers), but also her brother Anthony Tilden Smith who, it was generally recognised in the family, wasn't Leslie's son, but Hughes Massie's, the literary agent. John liked Leslie very much, and knew how much he'd helped Jean. Hamish Hamilton called him 'a nice, gentle, genuinely literary' man. Among Jean's letters there's a touching one from a writer called Michael Leigh, thanking Leslie for all he's done for him; and he was very kind and helpful too, as we'll see, to another young writer, Esmond Romilly.

At the beginning, Anne is certain, Leslie was in love with Jean. But this romantic love, at least, didn't survive her battering; whereupon — typically — Jean believed that he had never really loved her, that he had always been, and still was, in love with Kathleen. And now in his silence and withdrawal she began to see what she feared most: *disapproval*. Not a flash of anger that would pass, but a steady, cold, English disapproval, like all English people's, like her English mother's. And that she really couldn't bear.

Anne is also certain that even after Leslie fell out of love with Jean, even later, when he was most unhappy with her, he still cared for her, especially as a writer. He spent all his time encouraging her to write, trying to make her write, helping her so that she *could* write. He typed her work, took it to publishers and sold it. He took over all the domestic chores, the cooking, the laundry, the housework; he borrowed still more money, to send her on writing holidays to Paris and the countryside. When she wasn't writing he fretted; when she was writing, he was happy.

And yet, despite all this, Jean felt that *he disapproved of her writing too*. 'I am always being told that unless my work ceases being "sordid and depressing" I haven't much chance of selling,' she told Evelyn in 1931. That was many people — reviewers, publishers, everyone (and of course it was true). But it was also Leslie. I think he knew how good she was: he was, as Hamish Hamilton said, 'genuinely literary'. But he was after all her agent; it was his job to sell her work, and God knows they needed the money. And perhaps he didn't realise quite how deeply rooted in her was Jean's dark and unsellable vision; perhaps he couldn't realise it and go on living with her. Though he encouraged her writing, therefore, though indeed he sacrificed his life to it, he probably also — just sometimes, just a little — tried to change it. And to Jean that would be a dead giveaway. She would know that, at the very deepest level, he didn't really understand or approve of her.

People have always wondered how she could have spent her life, almost without a break, with husbands and lovers, yet have written only about being alone. When we realise that her main writing years were spent with helpful, dedicated Leslie, we must wonder even more. But this, I think, was the reason. It wasn't only that she returned always to earlier abandonments, though that was also true. It was that, even being with Leslie, she often felt abandoned. And often was.

★       ★       ★

Jean began *Voyage in the Dark* soon after *Mackenzie* had left her. But by the end of 1931 she was 'very down'. Her drinking was getting worse, the fighting with Leslie had begun; probably she was stuck on the novel. She needed to escape. This time she went, not to Paris, but to Amsterdam.

For the last few months John and Maryvonne had been in yet another Dutch city, Arnhem. Maryvonne stayed there with a family John had worked for, finishing the school year; but John returned to Amsterdam. Jean found him there in January 1932, 'very unhappy'. He had finished a novel in French, but found no publisher for it. 'So,' Jean said, 'I took it back to London and worked at it with rage, fury and devotion.'

This was *Sous les Verrous*, which Jean translated, cut and recast as *Barred*. Then she did what she would never do for herself: wrote to her literary admirers — Rebecca West, Frank Swinnerton, Norah Hoult — asking for their help to get the book published and reviewed. No doubt Leslie helped too: and in April Desmond Harmsworth published *Barred*. Norah Hoult reviewed it; so did J.B. Priestley, Compton Mackenzie, the *Times Literary Supplement* and the *New Statesman*. The reviews were good, the book was a success; a Dutch publisher took it the same year, and a French one the year after.

'It was a very little thing to do and it did help a bit I think,' Jean said later. In fact it helped a great deal. *Barred* made John literary friends, encouraged him to write — and publish — a second novel in the same year, and eventually helped him to return to his real profession, journalism. It was, in fact, a turning point in his life; a big thing, not a little one.

The episode was typical of the strange relationship between those two strange people, John and Jean. This must have been a time of great tension between them. Jean almost certainly wanted a divorce, in order to marry Leslie; she certainly wanted Maryvonne. And John wouldn't give her either. Yet Jean worked for him with 'rage, fury and devotion' — probably with more rage and fury, but also with devotion. She 'did leave out some of his bitter remarks about me,' but 'left some in' — indeed, left most in. Here was Jean, who could be so angry and cruel — so full of '*amour propre mal placé*', as Germaine had said — to people who offered her help and kindness; but to John, who was offering neither — if anything, the opposite — she did probably the best turn of her life. Again — *why?*

Because, I think, she often found it easier to give than to receive help. Because she saw John as a *copain*, someone in the same boat, at that moment even poorer and more friendless than she; and all her instincts of solidarity would be aroused. They had worked together like this before, when they'd been at a low personal ebb: in 1927, when their marriage was only recently over, but John had helped Jean with the translation of *Perversity*. Perhaps this was a kind of return for that help, five years later. In fact they'd first tried to make money out of a literary collaboration as far back as 1924, when Jean had translated and tried to sell John's stories; and they were still almost as poor now. I think they'd settled into a habit of helping each other and sharing the proceeds, no matter what else was happening.

This question goes beyond *Barred* and 1932, at least as far as 1934. For in that year John and his future wife Henriette van Eyk published a collection of short stories together, called *An den Loopenden Band*. John contributed twelve short stories; and *no fewer than ten are or contain almost word for word Dutch versions of stories or bits of novels by Jean*. Did Jean know? Was this part of an agreed literary collaboration, as Maryvonne believes, or part rather of John's tendency to embezzle?

He was certainly prepared to hijack Jean's works in order to swell his reputation. In a *curriculum vitae* he sent in reply to a literary survey he wrote: 'Books written in collaboration with Jean Rhys: *Left Bank, Quartet, After Leaving Mr Mackenzie* etc.' (This got in to the Dutch *Who's Who*, and proved much harder to get out again.) He claimed particularly – not only to Henriette van Eyk, but also to the critic Victor van Vriesland – that he'd had such an 'important share' in *Mackenzie* that it 'sprang from their mutual co-operation.' Even Maryvonne says this can't be true, and the most he could have done was correct, or help correct, the proofs.

In 1977, when Jean was very old and John had been dead for many years, a Dutch journalist noticed the startling similarities between *An den Loopenden Band* and her work, and asked Jean about it. She was (he reported) 'shocked and puzzled', and replied roundly: 'Mr de Nève [John's pen-name] printed my stories under his name without my knowledge.' But when Diana Athill mentioned it to Jean face to face she felt 'just a small nuance of extra vagueness in her expression of surprise and disclaimer of any knowledge.' She concluded that John *had* probably 'pinched' the stories; but that 'it *might* not have been quite as simple as that.' By then it was very clear that Jean's 'business' arrangements were never simple. In this area of selling her work she felt – and was – particularly hopeless. She would accept help from anyone who offered it, and would be quixotically grateful and generous. Only later (sometimes) would she regret it, and feel she'd been taken advantage of. By 1977 this had happened again, quite spectacularly. It was a pattern – one of the many recurring patterns of her life.

I think most people who knew both John and Jean agree. Jean would accept any help, any plan, at whatever cost. John would feel it was fair to use things they'd discussed, or to which he'd contributed ideas: and he probably *had* contributed some ideas (not to speak of his life) to *The Left Bank* and *Quartet*. He was generous to her whenever he was able – publishing some of her poems and paying for them out of his own pocket in 1935; writing about her and trying to sell *Good Morning, Midnight* in France in 1938. She in turn was generous to him, for example over *Barred*. I think it is virtually certain that at some point before *Barred* they'd come to some kind of arrangement – certainly informal, perhaps hardly discussed – that each would try to sell the other's work as well, and share whatever money was made. For Jean also had in *her* possession at least three stories by John. One, 'The Chevalier of the Place Blanche', she published in *Sleep It Off Lady* in 1975 – though unlike John she then acknowledged him as its original author. Two she never published: 'The Poet', which they'd tried to sell together in Paris in 1924, and which John put into *An den Loopenden Band*; and a story still more in his style than hers, called 'Vengeance'. *But 'Vengeance' she presented to the literary agent Hughes Massie as her own.* (This must therefore have been very early, before Leslie became her agent in – probably – 1926.) Jean never published 'Vengeance', but evidently she tried to; perhaps she tried to publish 'The Poet' and 'The Chevalier' too. It was still unfair, because she had many more stories to share with John than he had to share with her. But she wouldn't want to count; and no doubt he always meant to write more.

During the rest of the 1930s they went on helping each other. In 1935 John translated *Voyage in the Dark* into Dutch, as well as publishing Jean's poems (in a new magazine he'd co-founded); and there was a plan for his third novel, *Muziek Voorop*, to be translated into English, no doubt by Jean. This came to nothing, but instead she corrected and revised a translation of Henriette van Eyk's novel *Gabriel*. (In turn, many years later, Henriette did a second Dutch translation of *Voyage in the Dark*.) And Jean never said a word about *An den Loopenden Band*.

It is just conceivable that she didn't know about it: that John continued to lie to her as Stephan Zelli lied to Marya, and that, reckless and lazy as Marya, she never enquired. But Maryvonne was no longer a small child; and for this to work John would have had to lie to her too, or to have involved her in lying to Jean. I don't believe he would have done that. No: I think Jean knew about the book, gratefully took her share of the proceeds, and reflected philosophically that she might still be able to sell 'Vengeance', 'The Chevalier', or whatever else John had given her or might give her one day. And forgot all about it. But when she was reminded of it forty years later, things were very different: time had judged her to be a much greater writer than John. Then she would feel that the arrangement had turned out — like all such arrangements — to be very unfair. And she made her accusation: John had taken the stories without her permission. She shouldn't have done that, if they'd had the agreement I'm sure they did have; but then John shouldn't have claimed them as his own *tout court* either, and never have retracted. He was high-handed, and lied and stole when he needed to: but not from his comrades. If he had lived to know the whole story, I think he would have wanted to right the balance himself.

By the end of 1932 John had still not got over Jean. *Barred* had been full of hurt pride and unrequited love for 'Stania'; so was *Kerels*, the novel he wrote in the autumn of 1932, about his life in the poorhouse in 1927. In the first part of his next novel, *Schuwe Vogels*, Jan van Leeuwen is still obsessed with Stania, and refuses to give her the divorce she wants until he finds another partner himself. John's new partner, Henriette van Eyk, said this was true: and it clearly was. For John met her in January 1933; and five months later he and Jean were beginning divorce proceedings.

In later life Jean said (as always) many conflicting things about this painful subject. About the date, of course — sometimes suggesting it was as early as 1929 or '30, sometimes as late as 1937. And more importantly, about who divorced whom. Once at least she said she'd divorced John — 'I divorced him, me!' Usually she said that he'd divorced her, very unfairly; because (she suggested once) he'd 'found out about Leslie.' But that can't have been true; John had known about Leslie for years. Jean's vagueness, confusion, contradiction, covered up a painful memory: for she had had to be the 'guilty party'.

In their marriage the betrayals hadn't been all on her side, but the law was against her. Her marriage to John could have been nullified all the time they were together; but at the very moment she put herself in the wrong by beginning her affair with Ford, John became her irreproachable, monogamous husband. So he'd remained ever since. Legally she had no case against him; she'd had to wait until he was ready to bring a case against *her*.... She took another step towards Antoinette, who says 'There is no justice,' and who flies at Richard Mason with a knife when he says *legally*.

So here she was: the 'guilty party'. The accusations were mounting up. She'd accused herself in *Mackenzie*, John had accused her in *Barred*; now a real judge was accusing her in a real courtroom. It was the first time *that* had happened, but not the last. It would happen again — and again; until the single most painful and most honest thing she ever wrote took the form of a prosecution.

★

In September 1933 the divorce became absolute, and Jean was free to marry Leslie. But they didn't marry straight away. Perhaps Leslie was hesitating — no one would be surprised, least of all Jean herself. His father, who was an old-fashioned Victorian clergyman, disapproved of her very much; so much that when they did marry Leslie didn't tell him. But the main reason would be his own worries: especially, I'm sure, about Jean's drinking. Over the last year or so it had changed. It had been serious for a long time; now it was a disease. It was clear that she was becoming an alcoholic.

At one point this year — probably in the summer, as the divorce was proceeding — she was so 'crazy with depression' that she must have fallen into a particularly bad bout of drinking. And she evidently agreed that she *must* try to stop. Somehow Leslie scraped together enough money for her to get away to the seaside for a whole month and dry out. She managed it — 'haven't touched a drop for a month,' she wrote to Evelyn Scott. She ate and slept, and was better. But she didn't draw any conclusions; she never meant it to be more than temporary. 'I'm relying on the kick I'll get out of my first drink,' she said. To the end she couldn't give up that brief 'kick', however much it cost.

But the rest must have helped, and she finally got back to *Voyage in the Dark*. In order to write she was soon back on 'two bottles of wine a day', and for a time she plunged back into despair 'about the book and about everything'. Still somehow she managed to finish it. In February Leslie was typing it — and she, 'of course, couldn't resist fiddling about and making alterations.' None the less it was 'really', she said, 'in its last stages'. Despite all that had happened in the last three years, she had written her sweetest novel, the one that would always be her own favourite. She and Leslie were so poor that they couldn't pay the rent; but it was a triumphant, a hopeful moment. He asked her to marry him.

★     ★     ★

'When he asked me to marry him.... I was so happy I could scarcely believe it,' Jean remembered when she was old. She was so happy she even wanted to see her family. Luckily her favourite brother Owen had just returned from Australia with his wife and child. She took Leslie to meet them.*

She was forty-three now and had been drinking steadily for years. But like Dorian Gray she was quite unmarked, and she always looked

---

*It may also have been at this hopeful moment that she took Maryvonne to see her sisters. Maryvonne remembers two visits to her aunts, one just before the war, and one when she was about twelve: that is, around 1934.

ravishing when she was happy. Her skin was soft, her hair dyed, she looked *young*. And she was gay and charming. She brought Owen a bottle of whisky, four-year-old John a train; she sat down on the floor beside the little boy and chatted to him. But she hadn't brought anything for Dorothy, and I don't suppose she chatted to her very much either. Dorothy was strong, practical, very English − a natural enemy. She thought Jean 'one of the loveliest women I'd ever seen'; but she much preferred Leslie.

On 19 February they were married. This time Jean took five years off her age and said she was thirty-eight. But already, of course, her mood of exaltation had passed. One day a few years later she scrawled a note 'To Leslie' (though like Petronella in her story* she wasn't really writing to him, but to herself):

> Coming forth from my [?]
> loveless frowning bridal day
> I saw a [?]
> Behind me frowns and scowls
> Before me what?

She had hoped, in her childlike, childish way, that ... what *had* she hoped? That everything would change, that *she* would change, once they were married? In 'To Leslie' she would write

> You ran up the staircase saying
> I was waiting for you
> I thought Perhaps it's happened
> But it hadn't happened

She always waited for a miracle to happen − and of course it never did. Things did change after they were married; but not for the better.

They were extraordinarily poor. This was the year they moved at least three times, and spent the summer in what I've guessed was a holiday bungalow.† John couldn't help, because he was just as poor as they were. He was at last finding work as a freelance journalist: but in 1933 he'd been declared bankrupt, and for many years almost everything he earned went to his creditors. So Jean had to turn back

---

*'Till September Petronella', written in the thirties and published in *Tigers Are Better-Looking*.

†It was called 'Luxor'. 'Pharoah's island this place is and we've got "Rameses" and "Ishta" on one side of us and "Assouan" on the other side and "Thebes" over the way,' Jean told Evelyn Scott. (There was 'even' a picture of Osiris on the lavatory door, 'which I think disrespectful and going a bit far.')

to her own family. But 'Of course she'd write,' she'd made Miss Wyatt say, with contempt, in *Mackenzie*. She couldn't ask her sisters. There was only one alternative: Owen.

But Owen's return to England had been a rout and a defeat. His fruit farm in Australia had failed; back in Depression-ridden England he couldn't find a job. His wife had had to go back to work as a shorthand-typist; and it was she who was supporting the family. Perhaps Jean didn't know all this in detail, but she must have known that Owen was struggling. She must also have been desperate, however: for now she wrote and asked if he would lend her some money. Owen was as generous (and as feckless) about money as Leslie, and he wanted to help her. He wanted to send her something, even if it was only ' a fiver or a tenner'. But Dorothy was outraged. His own family was barely surviving – and Owen was going to give money away to Gwennie, who'd been a sponger and wastrel for years. . . . 'If you send that woman one penny I go out that door and I never come back,' she told him. I don't think Jean got her tenner.

In the end her rock-bottom poverty was relieved 'in the usual way', as she put it. First, in July 1934, Auntie B died. Jean had always felt that her aunt didn't like her, and now she didn't go to her funeral. But Auntie B was the only one of the family to remember Jean in her will. She left most of the little she had to Brenda, who'd taken care of her for the last six and a half years: but to 'Ella Gwendoline Lenglet' she left one hundred pounds. (That was perhaps the germ for Sasha's legacy in *Good Morning, Midnight*: ' "You may consider yourself very fortunate," he said, and when I saw the expression in his eyes I knew exactly why she did it. She did it to annoy the rest of the family . . . .')

A month after Auntie B Leslie's mother died. This time there was rather more money: over five thousand pounds, divided equally between Leslie and his sister Phyllis. Finally, in September 1935, his father followed; and Leslie came into the remainder of his inheritance. He and Jean would spend most of it pretty quickly; none the less after this they were never quite so poor again. Jean was pleased, of course, but also not pleased. She hated the way money only seemed to come from someone's dying. 'I always think that alone is enough to prove how rotten the whole system is,' she said. 'Never mind.'

★    ★    ★

'Well, Evelyn, I don't know if I've got away with it,' Jean wrote when *Voyage in the Dark* was being typed in early 1934.

> . . . I don't know. It's written almost entirely in words of one syllable. . . .

...I have no self-confidence — have cut too much and worried over things that were already done as well as I could do them with my one-syllable mind.

But it would turn out that she had to cut a bit more.

Leslie took the novel first to Jonathan Cape, who'd published both *Left Bank* and *Mackenzie*, and had turned down *Quartet* only because he was afraid of a libel suit. But Cape said that Jean was 'grey', that 'people would dislike it, and that 'he couldn't hope to sell it even as well as *Mackenzie*.' Leslie then thought of his main employer, Hamish Hamilton; but 'Hamish Hamilton wanted it cut so much that it would become meaningless.' Jean began to feel 'as down as hell'. Her old dilemma was returning: when she'd told her truth, people didn't like it ('I don't know whether I'm mad or everybody else is. But one of us is'). 'I've always prided myself on being more or less indifferent to what most people thought about a book once it was finished,' she said. 'Self deception obviously.' Of course it was. She couldn't be indifferent to what people thought about her books, because her books were her truest self. 'Indifference' was only an ideal, like courage.

At last, however, Michael Sadleir of Constable wrote to say that he liked *Two Tunes* (as the novel was still called) and wanted to publish it. But even he wanted one change — 'Not of course to his own taste, he explains, but to please prospective readers....' He wanted her to change the ending.

Jean was frantic. 'The worst is that it is precisely the last part which I am most certain of that will have to be mutilated' she cried to Evelyn. 'I *know* the ending is the only possible ending....'

She was at the height of her structural and stylistic powers in *Voyage in the Dark*: but I think she was wrong, and Michael Sadleir was right. For her great technical skill was only half the equation: the other half was her grip on her subject, herself. And that grip, which had steadily tightened from *The Left Bank* through to *Mackenzie*, had cracked under the pressure of these last years, and loosened in *Voyage in the Dark*. Jean had been driven back twenty years to her first affair, and even further back to her childhood, in order to find beauty and innocence in her heroine. She'd found them; and in the rest of the novel she persuades us. But in the last part she had overdone it.

For one thing, her original Part Four was almost 2,500 words longer than it is now — making the novel almost a fifth longer. And almost all those words were stream-of-consciousness memories of Anna's childhood, as her mind clouds: hard to read, often rambling. And finally: in it, *Anna dies*. That was the main change Jean so hated and resisted. Yet it was also right. She had already been led by her self-pity to bungle the end of *Quartet*: and her self-pity would have bungled this too. With Anna dying at the end *Voyage in the Dark* was a more clichéd and sentimental novel.

Jean insisted to the end of her life that she had been right and everyone else wrong about the ending of *Voyage in the Dark*. But I'm certain Diana Athill is right that this was purely *pro forma* – one of her 'automatic "anti-them" stories'. For she had the chance to restore her original ending, *twice*, and neither time did she take it. The first time was soon after it all happened, when John published his Dutch translation in 1935; the second time was in 1964, when she went over it for reissue. At that point she didn't even mention the original ending to Diana – though she'd got it out only nine months before, and had tried to use bits of it for *Wide Sargasso Sea*. That's not the sort of thing she would forget; and she was extremely thorough and tenacious when she really wanted to change something. No: I think she secretly knew very soon that the new ending was better. It's just that she enjoyed feeling – she *had* to feel – a victim; and this was a good story.

As she told it in the 1970s, Michael Sadleir called her twice to his office to ask her to change the end of the novel. The first time she refused, and rushed out 'afraid of bursting into tears'. The second time she gave in. 'So I spent several gloomy weeks trying to think of two or three paragraphs that wouldn't spoil the book,' she said. Part of this was an understatement – I'm sure 'gloomy' meant 'miserable and furious'. But part was an overstatement: to let Anna live she added only a few lines.

The last paragraph of the original ending had been:

And the concertina music stopped it was so still and lovely
　　　and it stopped　　　and there was the ray of light
along the floor like the last thrust of remembering before
everything is blotted out and blackness comes....

Instead Jean now wrote:

When their voices stopped the ray of light came in again under the door like the last thrust of remembering before everything is blotted out. I lay and watched it and thought about starting all over again. And about being new and fresh. And about mornings, and misty days, when anything might happen. And about starting all over again, all over again....

Judge for yourself.

Later on Jean always said that *Voyage in the Dark* was her best novel, her favourite and her most autobiographical. It was her favourite, she said, because it came the easiest: 'It is the only book I have ever written quickly, easily and with confidence.' But we know now that this wasn't true. Why *was Voyage in the Dark* her favourite, and the only one she admitted was autobiographical, though they all were?

The answer to both questions is the same: because the heroine was as she wished to be seen, young, loving and abused. She knew that *Voyage in the Dark* was a good novel; and at the same time these comforting things were true. That is why she liked it, and was willing to admit that it was based on her own life.

And Jonathan Cape's predictions were wrong: other people liked it too. It wasn't 'grey' — that was *Mackenzie*. *Voyage in the Dark* is full of strong, warm feelings: for Anna, controlled first by Jean's skill and then by Michael Sadleir's; for Dominica; for Lancelot; for the chorus. Despite its sadness, it is the novel which least separates Jean from the rest of humanity. That's also why she liked it best; and why many readers do too.

# CHAPTER FOUR

# Voyage in the Dark

In *Voyage in the Dark* Jean moves on in every way. Even in terms of her worst temptation, the special pleading for her heroine: for though *Voyage in the Dark* slips back to the innocent heroine, it manages a *successful* one. True, some of this is due to Michael Sadleir, who removed the most obvious bid for our sympathy, Anna's death at the end. But most of it is due to Jean. With Marya, her other victim-heroine, she protested far too much. Here she doesn't protest at all: she can't, because she doesn't let herself tell Anna's story. But she doesn't let Anna protest either. She lets us hear her self-pitying thoughts ('I'm nineteen and I have to go on living and living and living'); but more often she makes her tell everyone she is 'all right' — which leaves us to draw our own conclusions. Nor does she suggest, as she did about Marya, that Anna is really much better than her oppressors. She lends Maudie half of what she has left in the world: but apart from that she gives no one but herself a thought throughout the novel. With Walter she is humble, sweet and adoring, but rarely gay (only when she's tight) and never giving. She makes no demands on him, and fights back only once, when she knows he's going, and jams her cigarette on his hand. So she is far from the avenging furies Julia, Sasha and Antoinette became to their lovers. But that is the most we can say. Her innocence is mostly negative; all Jean pleads for her is 'not guilty'.

Nor does she overdo the extenuating circumstances. *Voyage in the Dark* takes us into the heroine's childhood, which explains so much; but the explanation is not laboured. Anna is a troubled child, especially after her father remarries; but she has many friends — her father, Francine, Aunt Jane, Uncle Bo. Perhaps we feel the opposite, then — that Anna's extreme passivity and easy collapse remain a mystery? Well, they do: but only like the true mystery of personality. Anna is a misfit and an exile, a girl who has never grown up. There are many such people, and Anna is a sympathetic, illuminating example. *Voyage in the Dark* seems to me to get this difficult balance right: to bring us as close to understanding the growth of a Jean Rhys heroine as, given our natures and histories, we can, without pushing or 'harrowing' us into resistance or dissent.

*Voyage in the Dark* is the first of the novels to move from the third to the first person: it recognises in its form, therefore, that this is only one person's point of view. But at the very same time it has the strongest sense so far of other people's separate existence. In *Quartet* other people were seen almost wholly in terms of Marya's need or fear of them, rather than in terms of their own experience. With *Mackenzie* they began to grow clearer, and to have their own needs and fears. But *Voyage in the Dark* has a dozen important and well-developed characters apart from the heroine: Walter and Vincent, Laurie and Maudie, Carl and Joe, Ethel, Germaine, Aunt Hester, Francine, Anna's father Gerald and her Uncle Bo. These not only have lives of their own, wonderfully observed; but over half of them are sympathetic to Anna, and not unkind – Walter himself, Laurie and Maudie, Germaine, Joe, Francine, Gerald and Bo. Only one, Aunt Hester, is 'respectable'; and only three – Vincent, Ethel and Carl – are really horrible.

This is a great opening out of Jean's imagination, and a vast improvement in her ideas about the cruelty of people. This wider understanding began with Mr Horsfield in *Mackenzie*. It remains with Walter in *Voyage in the Dark*: but less with Walter than with others, because Anna (and Jean) need so much from him. It's rather the secondary characters of *Voyage in the Dark* who are uniquely sympathetic in Jean's world. Laurie and Maudie, Germaine and Joe, Francine, Gerald and Bo are unlike anything else in Jean's fiction except La Grosse Fifi: ordinary people, selfish enough, but who yet can be decent and touching.* Even the villains, Vincent, Ethel and Carl, are so well drawn – their voices, habits, looks so accurately captured – that they become too vivid to be mere pawns in Jean's game. She hates them, and makes us hate them; but the attention she gives them emerges as a kind of zest very different from the blank, passive horror of Heidler. She was still too angry when she wrote about Ford, too depressed when she wrote about her mother and sister. Now she writes about the worst moment of her life, when she lost her first lover: but it is twenty years later. She has had time to quiet her despair, and to perfect her art; the result is her most balanced novel.

*With its touch of Gothic romance, *Wide Sargasso Sea* makes its sympathetic characters (Aunt Cora, Christophine, Sandi) into something else: larger-than-life heroes and heroines of tragedy.

Jean always stuck close to what she could do, and avoided what she couldn't: it was an advantage of her intensity and narrowness that she almost couldn't do otherwise. But nowhere is this more true than in *Voyage*. With its chorus girls, gas lamps and messenger boys the story is clearly Edwardian, but its real subject is so inward and eternal that it could be any time at all. Jean has cut this novel down still further than *Quartet* or *Mackenzie*. She gave Marya feelings about the other prisoners' wives, and thoughts about morality and law; she made Julia ask questions about identity, appearance and reality. But Anna does none of these things. She hardly reads, she never thinks. She likes Laurie and Maudie, but she says nothing about the lot of chorus girls. She doesn't plan, reflect or reason; she is unconscious and irrational, she lives in dreams and images, hardly at all in an external world. And the novel works exactly the same way. The unconscious which pushed up through the middle of *Mackenzie*, with Julia and Mr Horsfield on the stairs, has taken over. We are inside the stream not so much of Anna's consciousness as of her unconscious. Her fears bulge in omens and images. Memory, dream and waking experience mix and finally merge. Only people's voices, and her own sensations, impinge: heat and cold, colour and greyness, beauty and − mostly − ugliness. All connections are cut: we move from past to present, from event to feeling, without a break, without explanation. *But we need no explanation*. We understand Anna best this way; we feel for her, and with her, more strongly and immediately than any explanation could achieve. When Anna talks to Walter about her island she thinks:

> 'I wanted to make him see what it was like. And it all went through my head, but too quickly. Besides, you can never tell about things.'

That is exactly how Jean writes in *Voyage in the Dark*. She wants to make us see what it is like, but it all happens too quickly and deeply for words. And so, though her business is words, she goes beneath them. She doesn't 'tell about things' in *Voyage in the Dark*. She gives us the less-than-half-conscious stream of Anna's experience: and its meaning appears mysteriously, apparently by itself, like the champagne on Ethel's table − 'All done by kindness, as Laurie would say.' Everything else drops away, and only what Jean does best is left: the telling of her own inner, emotional story. *Voyage in the Dark* is in this way the purest of Jean's novels: her most characteristic personal expression.

★     ★     ★

*Techniques:* The first page and a half of *Voyage in the Dark* carry off the same trick as *Mackenzie*: four hundred short words and we are in the heart of the novel, possessing its main images, possessed by its special music. 'It was as if a curtain had fallen': and we have the divided, exiled heroine. 'Not just the difference between heat, cold; light, darkness; purple, grey' — and we have the main images of her division; 'But a difference in the way I was frightened and the way I was happy,' and we have its two main feelings.

From the next lines we know where, geographically, this division lies — between grey England and a bright tropical place. And the division is emphasised again: sometimes England seems real and sometimes 'back there' does, 'but I could never fit them together.' Past and present, dream and reality — Anna will never be able to fit them together. In so far as there are stateable themes in the novel, this is the main one.

Already, therefore, we have the keynote of *Voyage*'s subject, and especially of its style. Nothing is logically or chronologically explained; everything is given to us simply and dramatically, in a flow of memories and sensations, evoking, revealing, implying. This gives *Voyage in the Dark* the leaping, flashing movement of consciousness itself, or of half-consciousness like Anna's. She is always trying *not* to think, because she is afraid: it is the old business of not wanting to face consequences, not wanting to face reality. And this gives us the other characteristic quality of all Jean's writing: a sense of doom and suspense, the feeling that no escape is possible or even desired. *This must happen* is the atmosphere of all the novels: but especially of *Voyage in the Dark*, with its childlike somnambulist heroine.

All of this — the drama and immediacy, the sense of doom — are achieved by cutting. Jean cut every link, every explanation. She was afraid she'd cut too much, but she hadn't. *Voyage in the Dark* is her masterpiece of cutting.

As in *Quartet*, Jean begins by cutting unnecessary narrative information. We only guess that Anna is a chorus girl until five pages in to the novel; we only guess she's from somewhere like the Caribbean until the twelfth page — and on the fifteenth the map reference will precisely locate Dominica, *if* we go and look it up ourselves. She gives us only the main scenes of the story, barely suggesting the links between them. For example — we don't read Walter's first letter, or see Anna meet Vincent, or see Carl leaving; we don't know how many men Anna climbs the stairs with before the man with the bandaged wrist, or how long she cries after Vincent leaves, or how long she has to wait after Mrs Robinson's 'operation'. The first cuts keep the pace taut and the focus inward; but the second do more: they increase our sense of Anna's reticence and courage.

Like Julia with Mr James, she has refrained from 'harrowing' us. Her worst moments are hidden in the blank spaces after Carl leaves, after her visit to Mrs Robinson, after the end.

Other cuts reveal the characters as much as or more than what we see and hear. After Anna's night with Laurie and Joe, for instance, she wanders along Oxford Street. She thinks 'about my room at Camden Town and that I didn't want to go back to it,' and stands staring at dresses. Then a taxi passes slowly and the driver looks at her. She gets in and says '227 Bond Street' — Ethel's address. That's all: not a word about a decision, or — except 'I didn't want to go back' two paragraphs before — about reasons either. They're not there because of the tautness, the tense lassitude of the telling; but then we also feel they're simply *not there*, because Anna doesn't decide or consider reasons.

And every conversation has its real links and connections cut, its real meaning unstated. Take Anna's and Walter's exchange about Vincent and Germaine, for instance, when Anna has just learned that Walter is about to go away.

'As a matter of fact he's given her far more than he can afford,' Walter says; 'She thought she had her claws well into him. It's a very good thing he's going away.' Anna doesn't react to this last part, though it must concern her most. 'Oh, has he given her far more than he can afford?' she says. And now Walter doesn't react either. 'By the way,' he says, 'did you tell Vincent about Southsea? You shouldn't give yourself away like that.'

Everything important is unsaid here. That Walter means all he says about Vincent and Germaine also for himself and Anna, and that Anna knows it; that when he says she shouldn't give herself away what he really means is that she shouldn't have given *him* away. Just because none of these things is said we know them — like Anna — with sickening certainty. We know too that Jean has given us a horribly real picture of how people do convey such things to one another, and we are utterly persuaded: cruel fangs lurk beneath the surface of the best-loved faces.

There is simply no one better than Jean at conveying a lot by saying a little — even when it is happy. This is the key moment, for instance, when Anna falls in love with Walter.

> I got the glass out of my handbag and looked at myself every time the taxi passed a street-lamp. *It's soppy always to look sad. Funny stories — remember some, for God's sake.*
>
> But the only story I could remember was the one about the curate. He laughed and then he said, 'You've got a hairpin sticking out on this side, spoiling your otherwise perfect appearance.'

> When he pushed the hairpin back his hand touched my face and I tried to catch hold of myself and remember that the first time I had met him I hadn't liked him. But it seemed too long ago, so I stopped trying.

All Anna's loneliness and pretence, her hope and fall are here, in a few hundred simple words. Later we will see her dull despair in one paragraph ('there were never any scenes, there was nothing to make scenes about. But I stopped going out; I stopped wanting to go out. That happens very easily....'); her fear she is pregnant in a few lines ('Like seasickness, only worse, and everything heaving up and down. And vomiting. And thinking, "It can't be that, it can't be that. Oh, it can't be that...."'). This is what you remember about *Voyage in the Dark*, apart from the sad story and the sinister images: this simple, rapid, kaleidoscopic clarity.

Probably the most technically difficult thing in *Voyage in the Dark* is done in just this quick and simple way: I mean the movement back and forth in time, the interweaving of Anna's past into her present. Jean does it without any fuss at all. Sometimes she explicitly has Anna think or dream of the past. More often she just slips a memory into the stream of the present, between dots or blanks or dashes. Occasionally she gives us no warning. But the transition is always easy. Jean uses a simple and natural device, which other stream-of-consciousness writers had discovered too: the association of ideas. Her fever reminds Anna of having fever at home, Sunday reminds her of Sunday at home. Thoughts of breakfast at Bird Street take her back to Francine, thoughts of her own death slide into thoughts of her mother's (though she doesn't say it's her mother). Often the ideas that carry Anna back into her past come to her from songs, like, 'Drift, drift, Legions away from despair':

> It can't be 'legions'. 'Oceans' perhaps. 'Oceans away from despair'. But it's the sea, I thought. The Caribbean Sea. 'The Caribs indigenous to this island were a warlike tribe and their reistance to white domination, though spasmodic, was fierce ....' But they are now practically exterminated.

This captures exactly the flow of memory and association — and once again tells us about Anna without seeming to. She too has been dominated by a white Englishman (though she hardly resisted at all), and she too is now 'practically exterminated ....' Most of *Voyage in the Dark* is written in this flowing, inward, dreamlike style, in which almost everything suggests and symbolises something else. Anna's memories are just like her present thoughts, only more.

Especially Part Four, of course, which is almost all memory, almost all dreams, and which is built entirely upon the dream-principle of the association of ideas. A ticking clock connects the moment of abortion with the moment (probably) of conception. The man's white face and Anna's 'please stop' carry her back to the white masks of Masquerade and Hester saying 'it ought to be stopped' – and forward again to Mrs Polo saying the same thing. Anna's giddiness merges into the giddiness of the Masquerade dance, and 'Stop stop stop' resumes – to her white-faced lover, to Walter about going – to the horse of abortion she's riding.... The ideas of inexorable time, of being unable to stop, of falling, tie her past and present together in dread, and in the final sickening fall which is the birth of a dead baby: Anna's baby, but also Anna herself, who will have to start all over again, all over again.... It is all done with the extreme compression of poetry and dream, like the last pages of Rochester's part of *Wide Sargasso Sea*.

When Jean cuts all rational, external explanation and squeezes her novel into poetry and dream, she squeezes her meaning into one means of expression only: imagery. If *Voyage in the Dark* is all compression it is also all imagery.

Anna's voyage is completely pictured, for instance, through the images of her rooms. Before she meets Walter they all suggest oppression and entrapment. On tour the rooms are all the same, like the streets and houses ('all alike, all hideously stuck together'): 'Always a high dark wardrobe and something dirty red in the room.' In Southsea there is a limbless tree and limp washing in the walled-in garden; inside two bronze horses paw the air on either side of a big, dark clock. In Judd Street the feeling of entrapment grows. On a black table there is another clock, square-faced and stopped; and

> ...a plant made of rubber with shiny, bright red leaves, five-pointed. I couldn't take my eyes off it. It looked proud of itself, as if it knew that it was going on for ever and ever, as if it knew that it fitted in with the house and the street and the spiked iron railings....

Nothing could be more sharp, hostile, sinister; nothing could more horribly suggest that Anna herself fits in with none of these things, that they are all arrayed, smug and shiny, against her.

When her first meeting with Walter ends in disaster the Judd Street room becomes cold and close, 'like being in a small, dark box.' The next day Anna starts to be ill, and thinks of 'that story about the walls of a room getting smaller and smaller until they crush you to death.' ('I believe this damned room's getting smaller and smaller,' she thinks). But then Walter comes, with his kindness and his power, and 'The room looked different, as if it had grown bigger.' Their affair begins, and immediately she moves to a bigger room. But it isn't really safe: it's not 'cosy', but rather impersonal, like (Anna says) a restaurant. Still, the feeling of entrapment has briefly lifted. At the peak of her happiness, at Savernake, the window is open and a 'cool smell that wasn't the dead smell of London' comes in. But immediately the bubble bursts, and entrapment returns for good. The room in Camden Town is at the back of the house, without a view even of one of those small grey streets. Anna keeps the curtains drawn all the time; and 'The window was like a trap. If you wanted to open or shut it you had to call in somebody to help you.'

When Laurie and Joe try to debauch her it is in a hideous dark-brown room, with another stopped clock on a high black mantelpiece. Her room at Ethel's is big but dark, because the blinds are always pulled halfway down. The rest of the house is like Ethel — presenting a clean, conventional, lying exterior (white walls, chintz chairs, and 'the *Cries of London* in the dining room'). Finally Anna takes a flat in Langham Street with Walter's money: and it too has a ghastly conventionality, false and cloying: 'full of furniture and pink curtains and cushions and mats with fringes. Very swanky, as Maudie would say. And the *Cries of London* turned up too, but here in the bedroom.'

Anna's voyage, in other words, is very like Sasha's rise and fall, as summarised in *Good Morning, Midnight*'s extraordinary incantation:

> ...A room. A nice room. A beautiful room. A beautiful room with bath. A very beautiful room with bath. A bedroom and sitting room with bath. Up to the dizzy heights of the suite.... Swing high.... Now, slowly, down. A beautiful room with bath. A room with bath. A nice room. A room....

It is not just Sasha whom Anna points ahead to, however. For of course Antoinette's story is also of entrapment: she ends in the smallest and most inescapable room of all. *And Anna seems to rehearse this too.* After Walter has dismissed her she goes to meet him once more, to try to persuade him not to let her die ('I only want to see you sometimes, but if I never see you again I'll die'). In the taxi on the way there she remembers a flat she'd once been to on the Marylebone Road:

> ...there were three flights of stairs and then a small room and it smelt musty. The room had smelt musty and through the glass of a window that wouldn't open you saw dark green trees.

Julia had been climbing the same stairs as Antoinette; now Anna moves towards the same room.

At each stage of Anna's affair the main truth about her — that she is *afraid* — is embedded in an image. When it begins she sees a couple leaning against the railings in Brunswick Square, kissing: and rather than romantic or beautiful, they seem to her ugly and afraid: 'They stood without moving in the shadow, with their mouths glued together. They were like beetles clinging to the railings.' As it is about to end — though she doesn't know it — she watches some children playing. A little boy lets a big one tie him up with a rope. Even though he can't move he laughs: until the big boy pushes him over and starts to kick him.... Then as Anna waits for Walter to return from New York she dreams about the bathing pool at Morgan's Rest. In *Wide Sargasso Sea* a monster crab lurks there: and in *Voyage in the Dark* there are crabs under the rocks too, 'and when you throw stones at them their shells smash and soft, white stuff bubbles out.' A page after this ghoulish image of destruction Vincent's letter arrives. Before we even read it we share Anna's memory of Uncle Bo's false teeth:

> ...Uncle Bo was on the verandah lying on the sofa his mouth was a bit open.... I got up to the table where the magazine was and Uncle Bo moved and sighed and long yellow tusks like fangs came out of his mouth and protruded down to his chin — you don't scream when you are frightened because you can't and you don't move either because you can't....

Anna thinks: 'But what's the matter with me?... What's this letter got to do with false teeth?' But of course it has everything to do with a beloved face suddenly transformed into tusks and fangs. This is what she's been afraid of all along: 'all my life I had known that this was going to happen.... I'd been afraid for a long time, I'd been afraid for a long time.'

After the affair is over there is one more image, I think, of it, or rather of Anna after it. It comes in the cruelly funny moment when the massage couch collapses and the small grey man sticks his foot in the boiling water. He has come to Ethel for sex and comfort, as Anna went to Walter; like Anna with Walter he has found only hurt and humiliation. And

> he sat on the piano stool playing with one finger. But his foot kept jerking up and down, as a thing does when it has been hurt. Long after you have stopped thinking about it, it keeps jerking up and down.

After losing Walter Anna's real life is over. Everything afterwards is automatic and involuntary, just her hurt self jerking up and down.

There are many other systems of images — *Voyage in the Dark* is more or less just dialogue and imagery. And they are mostly the same as we've seen before. That is not a weakness of the novels, but a strength; it gives them each (and all together) their great power. For these images are not artificially invented or manipulated: they are the natural and permanent modes of Jean's mind. She was more conscious than Anna (a little more). Anna only has her images; Jean also uses them.

For example, the animal imagery of *Quartet* and *Mackenzie* has moved on here, to something even more horrible. Anna sees the matron of the chorus girl's hostel praying, with long moving lips and closed eyes: 'Just like a rabbit she was, like a blind rabbit.' But even worse are lower, cold-blooded, sinister animals. There are the 'beetles' who gave us such an ominous picture of love at the start of Anna's affair; and Ethel, the nastiest person in the novel, is an ant. Jean's imagination crawls with horror at this idea of Ethel as an insect: 'she had her own cunning, which would always save her, which was sufficient to her. Feelers grow when feelers are needed and claws when claws are needed and cunning when cunning is needed. . . .'* There is Uncle Bo, suddenly growing tusks and fangs like a cross between an elephant and a snake. There are the crabs lurking in the pool, and the barracudas in the sea, 'hundreds of them — swimming by the side of the boat, waiting to snap. Flat-headed, sharp-toothed, swimming along in the cold white roads the moon makes on the water.' Under every stretch of water, behind every face — lurk the teeth, claws or fangs of dangerous and vicious animals.

Like *Mackenzie*, *Voyage* uses flowers and trees to picture feeling and meaning. The shiny spiky red rubber plant distils the smug hostility of Anna's boarding house; when Walter wants to seduce her he sends red carnations, when he feels gentle and protective he sends purple violets. While Anna is living her half-life as a chorus girl we see the lopped tree in her Southsea garden, 'like a man with stumps instead of arms and legs.' When she is happy with Walter in the Savernake hotel there are pictures on the walls in which 'the placid shapes of the trees made you feel that that time must have been a good time.' She doesn't know it, but the good time is nearly over: and the tree on which she sits at her happiest moment 'had fallen down, with its roots still partly in the earth.' Then it is over; and at Ethel's the trees throw shadows like skeletons and spiders. As she

---

*People as insects is one of Jean's most frightening visions, which will have its fullest expression in the short story called 'The Insect World' (and in a draft, 'The Ant Civilisation').

waits to arrange her abortion she sees a last tree, 'perfectly still, as if it were dead', 'and the forked twigs looked like fingers point-ing. . . .'

*Voyage in the Dark* picks up much else from *Mackenzie* (and *Quartet*), and carries it forward. There is the central image of drowning which haunts all the modern heroines: Anna drowns when Walter rejects her; and when Ethel says 'Why don't you clear out?' she says 'I can't swim well enough, that's one reason.' And there is the connected image – connected, that is, to death – of shadows. When Walter is about to leave her, 'the shadows of the leaves on the wall were moving quickly'; when she goes to Ethel's she finds shadows indoors and out. And when she lies dying (or now almost dying) she thinks of the turning on the road to Constance Estate, 'where the shadow was always the same shape – shadows are ghosts you look at them and you don't see them – you look at everything and you don't see it only sometimes you see it like now I see – a cold moon looking down on a place where nobody is a place full of stones where nobody is. . . .' Once again it's almost as though Anna is looking ahead to Antoinette: as though this were *her* clairvoyant dream, of the stones that await Antoinette at the foot of Thornfield Hall.

The West Indian connection brings out a new image too, or one which was only hinted at in *Mackenzie*: the image of a slave. In *Mackenzie* Jean gave this image to Norah, who reads in *Almayer's Folly*: 'The slave had no hope and knew of no change. . . .' Here she gives it directly to the heroine; and something very interesting has happened to it. It no longer means just hopelessness and exploitation: now it carries the complex excitement of Jean's adolescent dream of Mr Howard. For in bed with Walter Anna thinks of the slave-girl her own age, Maillotte Boyd. ('*Maillotte Boyd, aged 18. Maillotte Boyd, aged 18 . . . But I like it like this. I don't want it any other way but this.*') This is what the heroine has always desired: as far back as Roseau in 'La Grosse Fifi' she has longed only to lay her life in the hands of her lover: '*Chante, chante ma vie, aux mains de mon amant!*' But of course this most desired self-surrender is also most dangerous. And in the end the excitement always disappears, and she is left only with slavery. So Roseau was left with 'I'll do anything you like, but be kind to me, won't you, won't you?' and Marya with 'I love you, I love you, I love you. Oh, please be nice to me. Oh, please say something nice to me,' quivering abjectly in Heidler's arms. So Anna is left now, when she imagines pleading with Walter: 'You think I want more than I do. I only want to see you sometimes, but if I never see you again I'll die.' Finally this slavery – without excitement, only peace, without love, merely being kept alive – is the best, the most that Sasha desires, in her brief fantasy before she loses everything:

> ...Now he ill-treats me, now he betrays me. He often brings home other women and I have to wait on them, and I don't like that. But as long as he is alive and near me I am not unhappy. If he were to die I would kill myself.

We are back in the darkest part of Mr Howard's house, where Jean the child-slave was made to wait naked at Mr Howard's table. But even this is desired; even this is better than the one intolerable thing, the complete loss of her lover. Which is, of course, what always happens.

There are two other streams of imagery in *Voyage in the Dark* which follow developing directions in Jean's mind. One will flow into *Good Morning, Midnight*, the other into *Wide Sargasso Sea*.

The first is images of England. There are many of these: images of divisiveness, for instance, like the little square fields Anna first sees, 'everywhere fenced off from everywhere else'; or images of hypocrisy, like her Judd Street room: '*This is England and I'm in a nice, clean English room with all the dirt swept under the bed.*' But most persuasive — as always — are images of *Anna's feelings about England*; and these are the ones I mean.

The main one, repeated many times, is of a high, dark wall. English people's voices are like 'high, smooth, unclimbable walls,' and the look in Vincent's eyes is like a 'high, smooth, unclimbable wall: No communication possible.' England blocks Anna and excludes her. When she tries to think of her life there without Walter's protection 'it's as if you're face to face with a high dark wall.' But Jean uses this image as she used the image of the funfair in *Quartet*: to contain both Anna's hopes and fears, and the transformation, the betrayal, of the one into the other. For the origin of this image of the high dark wall was the picture on the biscuit tin of her childhood, which contained at the same time all her most romantic expectations.

> There was a little girl in a pink dress ... and a little boy in a sailor-suit, trundling a hoop, looking back over his shoulder at the little girl. There was a tidy green tree and a shiny pale-blue sky, so close that if the little girl had stretched her arm up she could have touched it. (God is always near us. So cosy.) And a high, dark wall behind the little girl.

> Underneath the picture was written:
> The past is dear,
> The future clear,
> And, best of all, the present.

But it was the wall that mattered.
And that used to be my idea of what England was like.
'And it is like that, too,' I thought.

Once again the revelation, the betrayal, is carried by a simple, ambiguous pronoun. For *Mackenzie* 'she' hid Julia's question (possibly) in Norah; in *Good Morning, Midnight* 'he' will disguise the dreaded *commis voyageur* as the desired gigolo. And here 'that' and 'it' reveal the bright, cosy dream of English security as — for Anna — a dark, high wall.

This high English wall not only blocks and excludes her, it also judges and dismisses her. That is what is in those English voices, like Hester's ('I have spoken and I suppose you now realise that I am an English gentlewoman. I have my doubts about you'); and in Vincent's eyes ('And sure enough he raised his eyebrows, "Thank me very much? My dear child, why thank me very much?"'). Already at the end of *Quartet* there were high walls, in Monsieur Bernadet's room; and from them the 'glassy eyes' of people in their Sunday best 'smirked' down on Marya's loss of control, and on her punishment. Now in *Voyage in the Dark* more high walls sprout more glassy eyes. In the hotel at Savernake stags' heads are 'stuck up all over the dining room', looking down with 'enormous glassy eyes', just like the judgemental English gentlewomen ('This stag or whatever it is. It's exactly like your sister, Vincent, horns and all,' Germaine says). Over Anna's last time with Walter his 'damned bust of Voltaire' watches, 'stuck up on a shelf, sneering away' as she loses her lover, and almost loses control. And finally, as she dances with one of her pick-ups, 'the dog in the picture over the bed stared down at us smugly' — and she does lose control, and smashes the glass. When we get to *Good Morning, Midnight* these watching, glassy eyes will be everywhere; and just before the *commis* comes, Sasha, very drunk, will see the apotheosis of this imagery:

All that is left in the world is an enormous machine, made of white steel. It has innumerable flexible arms, made of steel.... At the end of each arm is an eye.

When she looks more closely she sees that only some of the arms have eyes, and some have lights. But that is only so that the eyes can see better: and there is no longer anywhere at all, not the smallest corner, where the heroine can hide.

The second stream of imagery runs into *Wide Sargasso Sea* instead. We've seen how Julia tried to ask her question rationally, and failed: all she reached was *nothing*. Now the feeling grows in Jean that 'words are no use,' as Antoinette will say. This begins with Anna, who feels that 'you can never tell about things,' and to whom only pictures, not words, have meaning: 'I am bad, not good any longer, bad. That has no meaning, absolutely none. Just words. But something about the darkness of the streets has a meaning.' It will culminate in Antoinette, who cannot make Rochester understand her with words ('words are no use, I know that now'), and who knows that without the right feeling behind it even the best word is 'a damn cold lie'.

If you have this feeling – that words are no use, and only pictures have meaning – naturally you will try to convey your meaning in word-pictures and not just in words. And that is what Jean does, by putting her meaning into images. But she goes further, and wants to convey this feeling about words and pictures itself: and this feeling itself, therefore, she puts into a picture and not words. In *Voyage in the Dark* she gives us a picture of how her meaning is conveyed in pictures: she gives us an image of her imagery. It comes, quite properly, right at the beginning. Anna is reading 'a book about a tart' – which is, of course, just what we are doing. And this is what Jean tells us about how Anna reads:

> ...The print was very small, and the endless procession of words gave me a curious feeling – sad, excited and frightened. It wasn't what I was reading, it was the look of the dark blurred words going on endlessly that gave me that feeling.

Jean isn't openly telling us to read her own novel this way. Yet she *is* telling us, secretly, her own feeling about meaning. This small incident of Anna reading suggests, in the end, so much: that her own story will be sad, exciting and frightening; and that these responses will come to us only if we attend to the pictures and feelings the story evokes, rather than just to the abstract meaning of its words.

Nothing, of course, could be more like Jean than this distrust of 'just words', and the sense that all that matters goes on beneath their surface. It's part of her general sense that what is important is hidden; it's part of her instinctive preference for suggestion over statement, for feeling over thought, for – in the language of the West Indian novels – black over white. Thus Christophine, the wise and warm black woman, will say to Rochester, the clever, cold Englishman: 'Read and write I don't know. Other things I know.' And *Voyage in the Dark* too suggests that in her attitude to words Anna is taking the black way. As a child she escapes her white family whenever she can and goes to talk to the black servant-girl, Francine.

> 'What do you talk about?' Aunt Hester used to say.
> 'We don't talk about anything,' I'd say. 'We just talk.'
> But she didn't believe me.

That is the difference between black and white. Jean's white people think talk is what the words say, and that this is something solid and definite. Her black people talk as they sing or laugh, to share their feelings; and they know that people, not words, mean things. So, for example, with the word 'slavery'. There is no more slavery in the Jamaica of *Wide Sargasso Sea*, white people would say: but then we hear Christophine. 'No more slavery! She had to laugh! "These new ones have Letter of the Law. Same thing."' Rochester, of course, denies it. 'Slavery was not a matter of liking or disliking,' he says. 'It was a question of justice.' But Antoinette – and Jean – agree with Christophine. Justice is a cold word, Antoinette says. 'I wrote it down and always it looked like a damn cold lie to me.' Liking and disliking *are* what matters. If there is liking slavery is just a word; if there is disliking, justice is just a word too.

This is Jean's own attitude to words, and her practice with them as a writer. She distrusts abstract nouns like slavery and justice; she sticks to concrete images and personal feeling. She will not generalise – though she has things she urgently wants to say, about her life and about life in general. Her solution is the solution of poetry: to embody the ideas in images, the abstract in the concrete and sensual. And it works. We come away from *Voyage in the Dark* with feelings of horror and pity, fed by images of Ethel-as-insect, Anna-as-slave, England as a cold dark place full of mean streets, trap-like rooms, sneering eyes and high, unclimbable walls. As long as Jean *said* things about society, or people, we could if we wished resist her: but these intense unargued images slide into our minds and stick there before we've even noticed. Her genius was to cut out everything else she did less well, and to use them.

Before moving away from the technique of this novel, I want to look at several things about language.

Jean distrusts words as much as Anna and Antoinette, I've said, as a means of expressing her truth, of making us (like Rochester) understand her. But – or rather *and therefore* – she is fascinated by other people's use of language. That is why her dialogue and letters are so good: because she listens with the acute attention of the outsider to people who have tamed words. In *Voyage in the Dark* there is a specially clear example of this: her fascination with the language of the chorus. The great point about this language is that it distils the group's code: it gives its members a ready-made phrase for every situation, an inherited worldly wisdom. Maudie is full of such phrases. '"Swank's the word", she would say,' Jean reports. If someone's mad she says he's 'up the pole', if she's depressed something 'gives her the pip', or 'God hates her and her eyes don't

fit.' 'Only three more weeks of this tour, T.G.,' she says to Anna;
and in Cockney, to Walter's friend Jones: 'I was speaking to you,
'Orace. You 'eard. You ain't got clorf ears.' Laurie too is armoured
in catch phrases. 'Never say die', she says when she hears about
Walter, and 'the answer's a lemon'. When Anna asks where Carl is
Laurie says: 'Echo answers Where?'; when Joe laughs at her long
words she says 'Long words is my middle name'. Laurie and Maudie
are only chorus girls, but they manage life much better than Anna.
Especially Laurie. She may be a tart, but she enjoys it. She can always
make men crazy about her. She introduces Anna to Carl, she finds
her an abortionist and a flat. She knows what to do, and she knows
what to say. When Anna doesn't know how to ask Walter for help,
she does. 'Don't be a fool,' she says. 'Say, Dear Flukingirons, or
whatever his bloody name is. I'm not very well. I'd like very much
to see you. You always promised to help me. Etcetera and so on....'
All of this — the toughness, the knowingness, the ability to survive
— is summed up in the laconic swank of chorus-girl language. *But
Anna never uses it.* The chorus is only a miniature of the wider
world, in which everyone knows what to say and do but she: in
which everyone knows the rules of the game but she. It is one more
club to which Anna, like Marya before her, never belongs.

There is one aspect in particular of chorus-girl language that Anna
never masters: cracking jokes. Maudie can do it: 'We're taking the
air,' she says when they meet Walter. 'Not all of it of course.' Laurie
can do it too, teasing Anna about her virginity: 'Tell him to borrow
the club tin-opener. Say "P.S. Don't forget the tin-opener."' But
Anna is no good at jokes. Already as a child she can't keep up with
Aunt Hester's funny stories, like the one about the undergraduate
who charmed lovely Aunt Fanny by quoting 'A cat may look at a
king, so why not I at a prettier thing?' Anna tries to cap this with
Judge Bryant's 'Let us pass You damned old ass': 'There's a certain
difference,' Aunt Hester says, 'but of course you can't be expected
to see that.' Then when she is falling in love with Walter she thinks
'*It's soppy always to look sad. Funny stories — remember some, for God's
sake.*' 'But the only story I could remember was the one about the
curate,' she tells us; and we don't even hear that one. Then when
her affair is over she tells herself: '"Of course, everything will be all
right. I've only got to pull myself together and make a plan." ("Have
you heard the one about....")' Anna never hears 'the one about',
and nor do we. In *Quartet* Jean had complained for Marya, in words,
that 'All the fun and sweetness of life hurt so abominably when it
was always just out of your reach.' Now she shows it instead — she
puts fun and jokes out of Anna's reach. All that's left for her are
the cruel, absurd jokes played by life: like the grotesque start to her

love affair, in the corked wine scene ('The waiter sniffed. Then Mr Jeffries sniffed. Their noses were exactly alike, their faces very solemn'); or the grotesque scene of the collapse of the massage couch, and the scalding of the small grey man's foot. Then she does want to laugh — and once she starts she can't stop. But of course this isn't fun, it isn't real laughter; it's horror and hysteria instead.

To my mind *Voyage in the Dark* is the most beautifully written of all the novels, with the exception of Part One of *Wide Sargasso Sea*. All Jean's prose has the beauty and intensity of poetry; but especially these two novels, or parts of novels — for in *Voyage in the Dark* too the most lyrical sections are Anna's memories of childhood. Like Julia, the child in Jean feels and sees 'prophetically': as soon as she returns to her childhood her writing becomes pure poetry. That first page, for instance, with its litany of smells and calls ('Salt fishcakes, all sweet an' charmin', all sweet an' charmin'); or the invocation of colours — 'red, purple, blue, gold, all shades of green' — and blue remembered mountains, with their mysterious French names: 'Morne Anglais Morne Collé Anglais Morne Trois Pitons Morne Rest — Morne Rest one was called....' Her observation is sweet and piercing, like the note of the Mountain Whistler: 'That's how the road to Constance is — green, and the smell of green, and then the smell of water and dark earth and rotting leaves and damp.... The noise the horse's hoofs make when he picks them up and puts them down in water....' The limpid observation continues in Anna's present life as well. Walter's violets 'smelt like rain', the eyes of the religious ranter at Speaker's Corner 'had a blind look, like a dog's when it sniffs something....' Some things in *Voyage in the Dark* deserve to become treasures of the language. Like: 'Money ought to be everybody's. It ought to be like water. You can tell that because you get accustomed to it so quickly.' Or: 'Of course, as soon as a thing has happened it isn't fantastic any longer, it's inevitable. The inevitable is what you are doing or have done. The fantastic is simply what you didn't do. That goes for everybody.'

This same perfection of observation is in what people say and write — Vincent's letter to Anna, Ethel's to Laurie, Bo's to Hester, Anna's to Walter which she never sends, all capture a whole person, a whole type of person in a very few words. It's in what they *don't* say too, like Anna's and Walter's conversation about Vincent and Germaine; Walter's coughing nervously as he says good-bye to Anna; Anna on her way to plead for her life, only able to think about the tip she should have given Willie.... It's even in the ending, done with such reluctance and despair. In fact this ending that was imposed on Jean became a perfect example of her method: she doesn't *tell* us of Anna having really died and ended, but of her 'starting all over again' – so we think of her having really died and ended, for ourselves. Reading *Voyage in the Dark* – reading all Jean's novels – is like this: having to guess her real meaning from hints, false scents, denials ('Nothing to kneel about. How perfectly ridiculous!' ; 'I must be crazy. This letter has nothing to do with false teeth.') It is like listening to a very shy and delicate person, who both hopes and fears we will understand her.

★   ★   ★

*Characters*: Anna is an archetypal Jean Rhys heroine. She is an exile and an orphan; none of her remaining family wants to take responsibility for her. She has felt alone, different, disapproved of since childhood. She is distracted and vague: she looks 'half-asleep', 'potty', as though she takes ether. She is always cold, sad and tired. But she is also pretty, pleasure-loving and reckless; she tries hard to be brave, and her moods change so quickly that she easily springs back from misery to hope. She needs very badly to be pretty and to have nice clothes. She is acute about people ('He's one of those people who always says much more than he means instead of the other way about,' she says about her Uncle Bo), but she doesn't 'know how to take' them. She cannot think, decide or plan; she lives in dreams and cannot connect them to reality. She too suffers from the heroine's inability to *act*, to cross the gap between dream and reality, desire and execution. In *Quartet* whatever Marya did would only make things worse, so she did nothing: she remained fixed in her nightmare of love and hate like someone in an hypnotic trance. Then Julia was *after* everything: she drifted through her story like a ghost, flicking at Mackenzie's face only in a distorting mirror, following not her own decisions but external omens. And Anna behaves in the same ways. When she does do something she feels in a dream or a fever, as though it isn't happening at all. On her first night with Walter she wants to stop, but instead she goes on, feeling 'cold and as if I were dreaming.' When he puts money in her bag she wants to stop him, but instead she says 'All right, if you like – anything you like.' When he is about to 'kill' her ('If I never see you again I'll die. I'm dying now really') she wants to stop him, but after the first moment she lets go and falls back into the water.

That is Anna's movement throughout her voyage – wanting to stop, but being carried irresistibly on, as in her dream of wanting to get off a ship on to land, but being 'very powerless and very tired, and I had to go on.' When she is a child she tries to stop living, but fails and carries on ('that would have been a better fate,' Annette says in *Wide Sargasso Sea*, 'To die and be forgotten and at peace'). At the end of the novel Anna tries to stop dying – '*Stop stop stop ... I tried to hang back but it was useless ... I'm going to fall nothing can save me now*' – but that really fails too. At the same time she doesn't want to live, but she must ('Starting all over again, all over again ...'). *Whatever she wants to do, she does the opposite.* That is even worse than the spell Marya and Julia were under, of being able to do nothing. It's a spell Sasha will be under even more.

There are two things Anna really wants to stop: time, and the recognition of her fear. These two haunt the novel namelessly, recognised only when they are inescapable. When Anna's affair nearly doesn't begin she hears 'a noise like when you hold a shell up to your ear, like something rushing past you.' Only when Walter is gone for good does this image recur, and she identifies the 'something' as *time*: 'That's when you can hear time sliding past you like water running.' In between she tells us constantly what time it is; and clocks are everywhere. But fear is even more pervasive. Even when she is happy she is afraid. She won't face it – 'Everybody says the man's bound to get tired and you read it in all books. But I never read now, so they can't get at me like that, anyway' – but everything she sees and hears is full of fear. The 'beetles', the little boy being tied up, the crabs under the rocks, Uncle Bo's fangs; and the Hyde Park Corner ranter, who shouts after her and Maudie – 'Already the fear of death and hell is in your hearts, already the fear of God is like fire in your hearts.' At the height of her happiness, at Savernake, she hides in magic: 'It's unlucky to know you're happy; it's unlucky to say you're happy. Touch wood. Cross fingers. Spit' – but on the wall the shadows of leaves move quickly.... Back in London she tries to pretend nothing has changed, without success. She has to admit she is afraid ('Being afraid is cold like ice'). But still she tries not to know: '"Afraid of what?" I thought.' Because she won't face her fear it only grips her more cruelly, and suddenly she is sick and sweating. Still she tries to tell herself there is no reason. Only when it has happened, and Walter is gone, does she use the word *fear*: 'There's fear, of course, with everybody. But now it had grown, it had grown gigantic; it filled me and it filled the whole world.' And at last she admits that she's always been afraid. 'I saw that all my life I had known that this was going to happen, and that I'd been afraid for a long time, I'd been afraid for a long time.' So had we.

All of this, of course, is one thing above all: childlike. The heroines are all childlike – fearful but evading their fear, insightful but incompetent, reckless, dreamy and dependent. But Anna is the most childlike of all. Walter calls her a baby, Vincent calls her a child

('Well, how's the child? How's my infantile Anna?'). She is utterly innocent and ignorant, she doesn't know her way around. She tries to follow the rules for success ('always say you have a previous engagement'), and pretends she's done so when she hasn't (of course Walter gave her money, she tells Laurie.) But really she can do nothing for herself, and obeys first Maudie, then Walter, then Ethel, then Laurie. Really, like Marya, she is a Babe in the Wood. But there is one important difference between Anna and Marya, and between Anna and Julia too, who is also like a lost child. Anna *is* a child. She is eighteen, and a virgin; she has only recently learned to kiss. We never see her older than nineteen, and we've seen her as young as twelve or less. If she's hopelessly childish we forgive her, and are not surprised. That is not so easy with Marya and Julia. (It's not needed with Sasha, who is the only grown-up heroine – though even in Sasha the gigolo sees a child). Only in Anna – and later in Antoinette – is the heroine's childlikeness what Jean hoped: natural and charming.

With Anna, therefore, we are coming to a new understanding of the heroine. We never saw Marya as a child; our glimpse of Julia as a child was confusing and alarming. But with Anna we see the start of the most important things about the heroine: the central split in her, and her refusal to grow up.

The central split has been between security and excitement, dog and wolf, the lady and the savage – or, we see in Anna, white and black. For Anna *is* white, but *wants* to be black ('I wanted to be black. I always wanted to be black'). The black girl Francine is the only person apart from Walter with whom she feels really happy. Francine is natural and vivid, like an animal, as Stephan was in *Quartet* (and now we know where this feeling about Stephan came from). Francine doesn't wear shoes, she isn't afraid of cockroaches, or of menstruation. She eats with noisy enjoyment; she sweats. Anna, on the other hand, must wear vests and stockings and gloves as well as shoes, in tropical weather – but when *she* sweats it is ' a disgusting and disgraceful thing to happen to a lady.' 'Being black is warm and gay, being white is cold and sad.' Anna hates being white, and spends her time with Francine. That makes Hester dislike her. But she knows that Francine dislikes her too, because she is white. Like Antoinette she is lost in the gulf between black and white, belonging to neither. Her split, her inability to belong, her exile, are – we now know – not only inner states but outer ones, geographical and cultural. We have a way in to her difference and loneliness, and some idea of their causes.

Her refusal to grow up we see very clearly, in the long childhood memory after she breaks with Aunt Hester. It is on the day she has her first period — changing from a child to a woman. When Francine explains it to her it seems 'all in the day's work', but when Hester takes over, 'her eyes wandering all over the place,' Anna wants to die. She knows 'that I'd started to grow old and nothing could stop it,' but she tries to stop it. She takes her hat off and stands in the sun, which can kill a frail white child in her island. She doesn't die; but she gets fever, and is ill for a long time. Her passage from childhood to adulthood, in other words, is desperately reluctant, a mortal struggle. So is Antoinette's, who has a long blank of illness after fire ends her childhood at Coulibri. It's extraordinarily revealing that both the heroines whose growing up we witness should experience it as a facing of death, and accomplish it only through violent, transforming illness. The truth about all the heroines comes clear: *they cannot bear to grow up*. For them leaving childhood is the first death: when 'You stop being yourself,' as Julia said, when 'you lose your wisdom and your soul.' The real death in Jean's world is always the death of the soul: it happens finally with the loss of love and the coming of madness, but it happened first with the end of childhood.

As well as the most childlike heroine Anna is, as we know, the most innocent. 'This was the affair,' as Julia says, 'which had ended quietly and decently, without fuss or scenes.' But in fact Anna is at the turning point: the point at which the innocent child begins to move towards the angry, violent woman. And delicately, but fully and honestly, Jean explores that moment. Anna relies on drink from the start; and as soon as she loses Walter she turns to it very thoroughly. By the final pages Laurie is already saying to this youngest heroine: 'Well, anyhow I should go slow on the gin if I were you. You've been taking too much lately.' And soon after she loses Walter the other thing happens too: 'slowly, slowly you feel the hate back starting.' She tries not to face the hate in her, just as she tried not to face the fear. When she slides her bracelet down over her hand she cannot remember the word for the way she wants to use it: *knuckle-duster*. She thinks: 'What happened to me then? Something happened to me then?' But soon she remembers the word and knows what has happened to her: *she wants to hit someone*.

Finally she does — and like the other heroines she picks a weak and inoffensive victim, the bleary-eyed pick-up with the bandaged wrist. This is shocking enough, because she hits him on his bandaged wrist. But it is not her most abandoned and satisfying act of violence. That she directs towards a picture which hangs over her bed. She stops dancing, hurls her shoe at it and breaks the glass. 'I've wanted to do that for weeks,' she says. The picture is called *Loyal Heart*, and it is of a begging dog. And Anna has hated dogs not only for weeks,

but all her life. On that important day with Aunt Hester her dog
Scamp 'fawned on her':

> 'I hate dogs,' I said.
> 'Well, really!' she said.
> 'Well, I do,' I said.
> 'I don't know what'll become of you if you go on like that,'
> Hester said. 'Let me tell you that you'll have a very unhappy
> life if you go on like that. People won't like you. People in
> England will dislike you very much if you say things like that.'

*It was all there from the beginning*, the heroine's inability to fit in, her
fatedness to an unhappy life, her rejection of docility. Scamp was
fawning, the dog in the picture is begging: and Anna rejects them both
violently. We remember Marya, quivering in Heidler's arms 'like some
unfortunate dog'. We remember Julia, in the hour between dog and
wolf, and Sasha, with the fierce wolf that walks by her side. Anna's
voyage towards them could never have been stopped. And it is really
she, who seems so innocent and passive, who first destroys the
fawning, begging dog, and makes way for the wolf to emerge. And that
was true of Jean. It was when *she* was 'Anna', and had lost 'Walter', that
she 'made up her mind to be selfish and cold' — that *she* decided to
destroy the dog, and become a wolf. And in the episodes of the
knuckle-duster and the picture of the loyal, begging dog she expresses
this, in her submerged, half-conscious way.

Anna, then, is not only the heroine for whom Jean and Anna herself
plead the least. She is also a real child; she's still largely innocent;
and none the less she, Jean and we all half-recognise her nascent anger
and hatred. For all these reasons she is Jean's most successful
innocent heroine. Marya, her first attempt, was a failure. Julia was
more successful, but also less innocent. Sasha will be wholly successful — but because she is guilty, not innocent at all. And if Antoinette
starts as innocent as Anna, she ends up mad and hating. Jean's noblest
heroines are the guilty ones, Sasha and Antoinette. But what she
herself most deeply desired was to draw a heroine — that is, a self
— who was young and innocent, whom people would pity and
believe. That she achieved most purely with Anna. So although it
dealt with the most painful event she could consciously remember,
Anna's was her favourite novel.

Walter is Jean's fifth portrait of an Englishman. Heidler and
Mackenzie had been based mostly on Ford, George Horsfield on
Leslie. W. Neil James was her first sketch of Lancelot: now comes
the full drawing.

Of course she changed him a great deal to suit her purposes. For instance, she made less grand than he was, perhaps to make her story more likely than the reality had been. But it's the other ways in which she changed him that give us the real insight into her idea of the English gentleman, her heroine's opposite and enemy.

First, she made Walter more secure than Lancelot. There is little trace left of Lancelot's own uncertainties – of his loneliness and shyness, his fastidiousness, his lack of success with women. Perhaps these things were not so evident at forty, or not so evident to Jean ('He was a sort of god to me,' says Julia, and Jean said 'I came to worship him'). But perhaps, too, she deliberately cut them. In any case the result is the same: Walter becomes more solid and philistine, and Anna's isolation in an uncomprehending world is more complete. In *Voyage in the Dark* someone accuses Walter of having no imagination. Lancelot *had* imagination – too much, solider men would say, for his own good. But the English officer and gentleman, like Ford's Edward Ashburnham, must have none at all: it is a weakness, and he suppresses it. Lancelot tried to, but Walter has succeeded. He is cautious and keeps his distance: he likes cold places, and says 'The tropics would be altogether too lush for me.' He is used to command, as Anna happily discovers with her landlady. But – unlike Lancelot* – he is pompous and arrogant about it. Their love affair is bracketed by the same expression on Walter's face: the shocked sniff of the 'Brothers Slick and Slack, the Brothers Pushmeofftheearth' – the eyebrow-raising disapproval of the English for anything outside the rules. That is what we remember about him. That, and the dark side of Lancelot's weakness: the role he lets Vincent play in his affair. He denies to Anna that he'd let 'Vincent or anyone else interfere with me,' but neither she nor we believe him. He clearly admires his handsome and worldly young cousin; his ideas about her 'getting on' seem to come from him; and he certainly consults him at the end. Finally he takes refuge in illness, in being busy, in going abroad, and leaves all the dirty work to Vincent. Without the rest of Lancelot's hypersensitivity, only cowardice and the easy retreat to money and safety remain.

Nevertheless Walter is a great improvement in Jean's sympathy and fairness to the English gentleman. Heidler was so much nastier, Horsfield so much weaker. For a start, unlike the gross, plump-handed Heidler (we don't know about Horsfield), Walter is attractive. And not merely in a conventional way: that is left for Vincent ('black hair and a brown face and broad shoulders and slim

* See letter to Francis Wyndham, 4 October 1973 – 'Walter was a wrong name. Quite wrong. Walter could so easily have been pompous.' (*Letters*, p.64)

hips — the whole bag of tricks, in fact'). Rather he is attractive in ways that express his character, in how he walks and talks and dresses. And from the start he *is* different. He is always with another man (first Jones, then Vincent) who is really cold and mean, and to whom he is contrasted. Mr Jones mocks Anna and Maudie about their ages, but when Walter hears that the girls call Anna 'the Hottentot' he takes her side ('I hope you call them something worse back,' he says); when Mr Jones mocks Anna's claim to be playing in London Walter defends her ('"Holloway's London, isn't it?" "Of course it is," Mr Jeffries said'). And he doesn't look at her breasts and legs 'as they usually do'. Instead he 'looked straight at me and listened to everything I said with a polite and attentive expression' (though then Anna thinks he smiles, 'as if he had sized me up'). Later he will listen to her talk of home, just as Lancelot listened to Jean.

There are even traces of Lancelot's tenderness left in Walter. He is drawn to her in the first place because she is shy and anxious: 'You looked awfully pathetic when you were choosing those horrible stockings,' he says. He sends her a little note which ends: 'Shy Anna, I love you so much. Always, Walter.' This is no merely cold and lustful brute; it is someone who has (briefly) let himself be touched, and who lets himself show it.

There is one other trait of Lancelot's which Jean has kept for Walter: his hypochondria. It turns the end of their affair to pathos and absurdity, when Walter says, in his last words ever to Anna: 'I shouldn't wonder if I got ill with all this worry.' But it has other consequences too. Walter had begun very differently, when he came to comfort Anna in her fever:

> I said, 'Take care. You'll catch my 'flu.'
> 'I expect I shall,' he said. 'It can't be helped.'

He had imagined he could manage Anna's 'fever', the disorder of love. As soon as he's learned he can't, he rapidly withdraws. But this in itself shows that he is far from the cold, rational, manipulative monster we saw in Heidler. At the very least, Walter is weak and human.

Vincent, of course, is the real villain in Anna's affair. It's hard to draw a really convincing villain: and Jean hadn't succeeded with Heidler, because she tried too hard. She's learned her lesson here. First of all, she shows us very little of Vincent. We don't even hear of him until her affair has been established for a month or two, and we don't meet him until Savernake, when it is nearly over. He is a hidden menace for us as much as for Anna; and we are hardly given the chance to form our own opinion of him.

From the moment we do see him, however, Anna's dislike and fear of him are very cleverly justified. Walter seems absurdly, suspiciously eager for her to approve of him. And as soon as his name comes up there is pain and constraint between them. Walter shows his conventional side, approving Vincent's idea that Anna should 'get on'; and he makes it clear he doesn't imagine their affair will last forever ('Oh, you'll soon get sick of me,' he says, inverting the truth, as usual). At Savernake, even before we see Vincent it's clear he is at least a philanderer. Then we meet him: and Jean manages a nasty, believable villain. He's believable just because — unlike Heidler — his evil is small and human. He is a careless, conventional, super-cilious young man, and he clearly feels that Anna is too young and too troublesome. He is smooth and successful, smug and self-satisfied. When Germaine says that Englishmen 'can't make women happy' he taunts her, his face 'smooth and smiling': 'Can't they, Germaine?'; when she leaves, upset, he mocks her: 'Going to curl your hair?' Even Walter is frightened of his inquisitiveness and his willingness to tease. Anna is so frightened that he always makes her feel she's said something stupid. 'Good-night, Vincent,' she says, 'thank you very much.' 'And sure enough he raised his eyebrows, "Thank me very much? My dear child, why thank me very much?"'

The second and last time we see him Vincent is even nastier, and even more believable. His reflections about Laurie — 'She really is pretty. But hard — a bit hard. They get like that. It's a pity' — show his shallowness and exploitativeness, quite apart from Anna. Then he asks for Walter's letters, and Anna hands them over.

> 'You're a nice girl, you really are. Now, look here, don't go getting ideas into your head. You've only got to make up your mind that things are going to be different, and they will be different.... Are you sure these are all the letters?'
> 'I've told you so,' I said.
> 'Yes, I know.' He pretended to laugh.
> 'Well, there you are. I'm trusting you.'

That is dreadfully convincing. If we've resisted Jean's portrait of Vincent before, we can't any longer. But I doubt we have much resistance left: for of course we've read his letter. Its clichés are so heartless — youth is the greatest gift, love isn't everything — its kindness so cheap and lazy: 'I am afraid I am going to upset you and I hate upsetting people....' And its careful back-tracking is a dead giveaway: 'Walter will always be your friend and he wants to arrange that you should be provided for and not have to worry about money (for a time at any rate).' The whole letter is a masterpiece of Jean's ear for falsity and carelessness, like the voices of the women at

Heidler's parties. Poor Julian Martin Smith: I'm sure he was never quite as awful as this. Jean's skill and anger have lifted him into a literary monument to safe rich selfishness. One of the things she shared with other writers of her time was the desire — and ability — to subvert the values and achievements of the imperial age. This portrait of Julian Martin Smith, war hero and golden boy, as a thoughtless exploiter of the poor and weak, is a perfect example of that breaking of the icons.

Walter and Vincent are *Voyage's* swipes at Englishmen. Walter at least was tempered by Jean's love of Lancelot, and by her growing instinct for balance and truth. But when it comes to English *women* her holds are unbarred. After Vincent the novel's meanest villains are women, who distil the English qualities Jean most feared and detested: respectability, snobbery, hypocrisy, meanness.

First Hester, Anna's stepmother. Hester is centrally based on Aunt Clarice, Dr Rees Williams's sister. She has come, like Clarice, as an outsider to the West Indies; she stands *in loco parentis* to Anna, as Clarice did to Jean; she talks of Cambridge and her clever Uncle Watts as Clarice must have talked of Cambridge and her clever Uncle Potts. But Hester also draws on all the deadly dull, disapproving Lockharts, the ultra-respectable, ultra-English members of Mrs Rees Williams's colonial family. Like them she refuses to talk — she refuses even to think — of anything not wholly proper and nice. Like them, and like all Englishwomen of the kind Jean loathed, she is a snob. She has the English lady's voice — while Anna, she says, has a 'nigger's' voice ('Exactly like a nigger you talked — and still do'). Hester has the English puritan fear of everything free, gay, beautiful: 'Don't say my goodness,' she says when Anna exclaims at Aunt Fanny's beauty, 'My badness, that's what you ought to say.' She despises blacks, and distrusts the whole West Indian world: 'This place gives me the creeps at night,' she says. Hypocrisy is her morality: it matters less what Anna does than that she not speak of it; far worse than Uncle Bo's illegitimate children is his 'flaunting' them. She is not entirely without concern for Anna — she does worry about her, and has helped her with school bills and doctor's bills in the past. But she has no real love or warmth for her. She takes responsibility for Anna because it is her duty; and when it begins to cost her too much — partly in worry, but mostly in money — she thinks only of how to get rid of her. For Hester is not only unloving; she is mean. That is true of all these cold, hypocritical English; as Antoinette will say, 'Gold is the idol they worship.' All they really love is money.

Second, Ethel. Ethel is far worse than Hester: from Jean's first description of her as short and fat and dirty, with short legs and dusty hair, the intensity of her loathing burns through her prose.* Ethel too is mean, trying to get as much money as she can out of Anna from the beginning, extorting more as soon as she dares. She too is 'respectable' – respectability is her constant cry. She is a masseuse – but she is respectable, she is a trained nurse, she is a lady. And now Anna's violence erupts into her narration: 'A lady – some words have a long thin neck that you'd like to strangle.'

Ethel, of course, is the arch hypocrite. For under this vaunted respectability she hides crude exploitation and corruption. She makes her living by exploiting English furtiveness about sex, offering 'manicure' and 'Swedish massage' and saying to Anna: 'If people do things thinking that they're going to get something that they don't get, what's it matter to you or me or anybody else?' Laurie even thinks Ethel is prepared to go further. When Anna refuses to take a client upstairs she says, 'I bet the old girl wasn't pleased. I bet you that wasn't her idea at all.' And when Anna becomes Carl's concubine Ethel happily accepts it. She looks at Anna with new respect; she gives her days off; she merely raises her rent, and takes the money.

Ethel is ready to make money out of sex, but like Hester she fears and despises it. Hester despises black people, and the whites like Uncle Bo who descended to their easy, natural level. Ethel hates men, and she hates 'foreigners'. It is foreign *masseuses*, she claims, who are less than respectable. Foreign girls have 'soft, dirty' ways, foreign men seduce English girls with flattery.... This English attitude to sex will remain the heart of the matter – in Sasha's conversations with René, in Antoinette's relationship with Rochester. Sex is something foreigners and blacks do, not good Englishmen and Englishwomen. That is what Rochester secretly thinks too: so that once he'd made Antoinette desire him he was simply waiting for Daniel's letter.

Ethel is a mean, hypocritical English enemy. But she is something else as well. She is to a surprising extent also one of those women who mirror the heroine, or echo her ideas. Ethel is lonely, like Anna; she too feels despised, she too takes refuge in drink. In fact Ethel expresses some of Jean's feelings and ideas *instead* of Anna. 'Sometimes when you do things on the spur of the moment it brings you luck. It changes your luck,' she says. And:

'...oh God, what a life I've had. Trying to keep up and

* Which makes one feel, again, that she was based on someone real. (Cf. the Minneapolis Minnesota *Journal*: 'Mrs Heidler is drawn with such maliciousness by Miss Rhys that the suspicion persists that she hated and sometimes feared this character.')

everybody else trying to push you down and everybody lying and pretending and you knowing it. And then they down you for doing the same things as they do.... '

We've seen Jean do this before, in both her previous novels – use other characters as images and echoes of the heroine. This was one thing that actually worked better in *Quartet* than in *Mackenzie*: for in *Quartet* Marya's mirrors were half-surreal, background figures, multiplied as in a dream; while in *Mackenzie* important others began to sound too like Julia. Now *Voyage in the Dark* solves the problem another way. Ethel and some of the others are quite major characters, who need independent, undreamlike lives. But this time Anna doesn't herself express the ideas, they do – for Anna, as we've seen, hardly expresses any ideas at all. Once again, therefore, the technique works. For the ideas about life we pick up from Ethel, from Joe – 'We're all crabs in a basket' – from the others, all tell us about Anna's life. But because Anna doesn't tell us them herself there is no uneasy sense that the others merely rubber-stamp and repeat her, or that they are even perhaps mere projections of her. Instead we can believe in them as themselves. And at the same time Anna's own believability is immensely enhanced. For the ideas which illuminate her life are cynical and black: however sad and lonely she is, she is too young to have them. Giving them to others is, therefore, the perfect solution. *We* still get them, but not from *her*.

Jean's other spokesmen in the novel concentrate on her growing obsessions about England. Vincent's girlfriend Germaine (who is half-French) picks up the idea that we've already met in the cinema in *Mackenzie*, and which will become comic in *Good Morning, Midnight*, tragic in *Wide Sargasso Sea*: the idea that Englishmen don't like women. 'Scorn and loathing of the female – a very common expression in this country,' Germaine says; and

> 'The women here are awful. That beaten, cringing look – or else as cruel and dried-up as they're made! *Méchantes*, that's what they are. And everybody knows why they're like that. They're like that because most Englishmen don't care a damn about women.... '

The other two spokesmen suggest more generally that England, or London, is a horrible place to live. One is the unknown man who had Anna's rooms before her, and who left some poems in a drawer. 'Horse faces, faces like horses. And grey streets, where old men wail unnoticed,' goes one; and another, rawly: 'Loathsome London, vile and stinking hole.... ' The second is Laurie's friend, d'Adhémar. He talks of the London streets:

'It's terrible,' he said, waving his hands about. 'The sadness, the hopelessness. The frustration — you can breathe it in. You can see it; you can see it as plainly as you see the fog....'

Later he suggests a Sasha-like laugh in the face of absurdity. 'Here's to the smug snobs and the prancing prigs and the hypocrites and the cowards and the pitiful fools! And then who's left?' he says, as Anna goes to swallow her words and take help from Vincent. Or when she cries, having done it:'*T'en fais pas, mon petit. C'est une vaste blague.*'

These are all, of course, Jean's own ideas; and I've no doubt the poems too were hers. The violence of 'Loathsome London' especially hints at the barely checked passion which gives *Voyage* its energy: its invisible but driving anger.

Anna, as we've seen, is already turning from soft to hard, from dog to wolf. And this opposition is mirrored, is externalised, in her two friends.

Maudie looks tougher than Anna — she handles their landladies, she talks cynically, she tells jokes, she knows who has money. But it's all talk. In fact she stays in the dead end of the chorus, unlike Laurie; and she craves marriage and respectability, first with Viv, then with Fred, her electrical engineer from Brondesbury. Like Anna, she feels demoralised and despised ('I'm so damned shabby,' she says, and 'when you're shabby you can't do anything, you don't believe in yourself'). She's a loser; we can't imagine she'll win her strait-laced Fred.*

Laurie, Jean said,† is 'poles apart, from Maudie's hopelessness. She has no doomed yearnings for marriage and respectability: she is frankly a tart, and enjoys it. Maudie only talks about using men; Laurie does it. 'I bank half of everything I get,' she tells Anna, 'and there's no friend like that.' She is, as she says herself, 'a good old cow', and fond of Anna. She's crude and careless, especially when she's drunk — in the episode with Joe in the hotel, for example, she's

---

*However, in Jean's short story 'Kismet', which is similarly set in the middle of her first affair, the chorus-girl narrator goes to visit her ex-room-mate Billie (Jean also called her room-mate Billie in *Smile Please*) 'somewhere near Belsize Park'. And Billie *is* married to someone called Fred, has a baby and expects another. I think it's very likely that there was a real model for Maudie/Billie — perhaps Mollie Cole — who probably did marry her Fred. Once again Jean would have sharpened reality with her own ideas and fears.

†For Jean's summary of Laurie and Maudie see *Letters* (to Selma vaz Dias, 12 July 1963).

pretty callous. But she is the only person who really helps Anna. Without her, we feel, Anna wouldn't have had anywhere to go, wouldn't have had her abortion, wouldn't have done anything at all. And Laurie isn't only kind to Anna. She's kind to the old woman who works for her so badly ('I'd fire the old sod tomorrow only I know she'd never get another job,' she says). The last we see of Maudie she's 'borrowed' eight pounds ten from Anna, which we can see she'll never give back. Laurie and Maudie are part of a lesson Jean was slowly learning: that it's weakness and need that make people treacherous; in a few at least strength makes room for kindness.

But there's another interesting thing about Laurie: she's very sexy. She's always making fun of Anna's virginity: 'Can't you manage to keep the keep the door shut, Virgin?' she says, 'Tell him to borrow the tin-opener. . . .' She 'can always make men crazy about her': 'I expect,' she says, 'because they feel I really like it and no kidding.' When Anna thinks of making love with Walter she remembers Laurie saying: 'Some women don't start liking it until they are getting old; that's a bit of bad luck if you like. I'd rather wear myself out when I'm young.'

When we think of the older heroines, Marya and Sasha, we wonder whether, for all their desperate need of men, they really like physical love at all. We never see Marya enjoying love with Heidler, only hating it at the end; and Enno leaves Sasha because, he says, 'You don't know how to make love. You're too passive, you're lazy, you bore me.' Julia, as ever, is absent. She has no lover; she merely spends one night with Mr Horsfield, during which Jean doesn't give us her feelings, and we feel she probably hasn't any. Even with the heroine-in-love, Anna and Antoinette, the need for safety, attention, affection seems greater than any physical desire. Yet there are hints that trapped inside her, like the desire for joy in Marya, a deep natural sexuality is fighting to get out. It's there in Anna's thoughts: '*I don't want it any other way than this*'; 'When he kisses me, shivers run up my back. I am hopeless, resigned, utterly happy'; 'You shut the door and pull the curtains over the windows and then it's as long as a thousand years and yet so soon ended.' It's there in Sasha's desire to touch René's hair — 'I've wanted to do that ever since I first saw him'; it's there in Rochester's remark about Antoinette: 'Very soon she was as eager for what's called loving as I was — more lost and drowned afterwards.' There are so many lovely girls in Jean's fiction; this, and the sense that for the heroine sex is what she pays for a man's protection, can make us wonder whether the Jean Rhys woman is not really afraid of men, and inclined to a narcissistic form of inversion. But then the multiple reflections of the heroine have, as we've seen, literary as well as narcissistic purposes. And if we pay attention to Anna and Antoinette, and to a portrait like Laurie's, I think we see a more likely explanation. It's similar to the other truths we've discovered about the heroine: that the sensuality she fears is not men's but her own. It is there, all right, especially with the lovers based on Lancelot. It is the heart of what all the Englishmen need, so that they are drawn to Marya, Julia, Anna and Antoinette like moths to flame, like the toms to Sasha's kitten. But it is also the heart of what they all fear and distrust: that foreign, tropical thing in her which is uncontrolled and uncontrollable. So it is also why they leave her. Because she feels this, and because she has her English side too, she fears it as much as they.

Sex, in other words, is part (perhaps heart) of the wolf rather than the dog: part of the heroine's *un*-English, unrespectable side. Jean explores it most in Antoinette: but also in Anna, and in distanced and thus less troubled form, in Laurie. And apart from Francine, who is black, Laurie is the most sympathetic other female in the novel.*

We meet four clients of 'sexual services' in the novel. Two are evidently Englishmen: Ethel's massage couch victim, and Anna's pick-up with the bandaged wrist. Both of these are nameless, faceless and furtive. The other two, however, are different. Carl Redman and Joe Adler are fully named and individuated; they are not furtive, and they are not English.

Carl is American. He isn't 'nervous or hesitant', but big, calm and solid. There are only hints left of his sadism in *Triple Sec*: just the way he says '"Now, what have they been doing to you?" in that voice which is just part of it.' He *is* 'part of it' — he uses Anna for his passing pleasure, and then, like all the others, dislikes her for getting hard. But he isn't (like Carl in *Triple Sec*) a bad man. He gives Anna generous amounts of money. Above all, he isn't a sneerer: he accepts the world, and doesn't judge Anna for the way she survives in it.

---

*If we're to say something about the origins of Laurie, as we did for Maudie, I suspect she's partly based on Daisy Irving, who was also the model for Daisie in 'Before the Deluge' (*Sleep It Off Lady*.) Daisy Irving was (briefly anyway) a star, rather than a mere member of the chorus: and the Misses Cohen remember Jean as someone who'd 'come in when Miss Gaynor was fitting her costume,' which sounds more like a main player than a chorus girl. Laurie also makes a remark about being briefly in a London show. Daisie in 'Before the Deluge' has a similar careless kindness, a similar flat, and a mother (Laurie calls the old woman who works for her 'Ma').

Joe, his secretary, is positively nice, and Anna likes him. He teases her, and is perfectly ready to take sexual advantage of her: but she works at Ethel's and goes around with Laurie, so we can't blame him for assuming she's a tart. When he learns she isn't he's kind. 'Don't do that, don't cry,' he says, and covers her with an eiderdown. 'D'you know, kid, I like you.' He is honest and cynical ('What's the use of lying? we're all crabs in a basket'). He is a dependant himself, and a Jew; he is essentially on Anna's side, one of the powerless. And he is no sneerer either.

Here, then, is a pretty positive pair of portraits. We've come far from the cosmic malevolence of Heidler: and Carl and Joe contribute a good deal to the saner, kinder atmosphere of *Voyage in the Dark*. Joe especially shows us that despite everything Anna – and Jean – can still like an ordinary man.

The nicest people, though, the ones Anna loves, are in another time and place altogether: in her West Indian past. And they have all the qualities the English lack. They are warm and natural, full of physicality and feeling, without snobbery or pretence. The black girl Francine – as we've seen – fits into the natural world: she's not afraid of cockroaches, she doesn't need shoes, she makes eating a celebration and menstruating perfectly ordinary. Then there is Anna's father, the planter. He too is full of feeling, and doesn't hide it. He has a terrible temper; he also, it seems, has bouts of depression ('that time I was crying about nothing,' Anna says, 'and ... he hugged me up ... and then he said, "I believe you're going to be like me, you poor devil"'). He calls the English hypocrites and prefers the French; he is 'slack' and sees nothing wrong in dancing, or in recognising Uncle Bo's illegitimate children. Finally there is Uncle Bo himself, who is not a gentleman. Instead he is a philanderer and a drinker – 'Uncle Bo!' says Hester, 'Uncle Boozy would be a better name for him.' And of course Anna likes him. 'He's nice,' she says; 'I like him much better than my other uncle.'*

In *Quartet* Jean had explicitly reversed conventional morality: and she has done it again here. 'Self-control' and 'good behaviour' are merely unnaturalness and hypocrisy; 'drunkenness' and 'philandering', 'flaunting' and 'slackness' are true naturalness, honesty and kindness. But this time no one has said anything about it. Anna simply loves her father, her uncle and Francine, and hates Hester and the smug, hypocritical English; and so do we.

★   ★   ★

*I don't know whether Uncle Bo is based on anyone in particular, but 'my other uncle' could well be a reference to 'Uncle Griffiths' again – Neville Williams, Mayor of Harrogate, and the son favoured over Jean's beloved father.

*Themes*: All Jean's fiction aims to hurl down 'the smug snobs and the prancing prigs and the hypocrites and the cowards', and to raise up in their place 'the pitiful fools'. That culminates in the last novel, where she will expose the emblematic Englishman, Rochester, and elevate that most despised creature, the mad, drunken woman. This is perhaps the heart of her modernism, the thing which makes her far more radical than such civilised sisters as Virginia Woolf or Dorothy Richardson. But here she does something else too. She shows us from the inside what it feels like to be such a subverter of values. And what it feels like to Anna – as to Raskolnikov, or Kafka's K. – is not a victory but a voyage in the dark, an abyss of doubt and uncertainty. She cannot believe in the old morality any more, but on the other hand she cannot invent a new one. She is left with nothing, only a sort of surprise – 'My God, how did this happen?' – 'Is that me?' *Morality has become meaningless*: 'I am bad, not good any longer, bad. That has no meaning, absolutely none. Just words.' In this way Anna is an absurd heroine, an existentialist heroine, like Julia. And Jean has a wonderful image for this new meaninglessness.

> There was an advertisement at the back of the newspaper: 'What is Purity? For Thirty-five Years the Answer has been Bourne's Cocoa.'

This comes, very accurately, during her meeting with Aunt Hester, guardian of the old values. And it comes again, like a chorus:

> 'What is Purity? For Thirty-five Years the Answer has been Bourne's Cocoa....' For Thirty-five Thousand Years the Answer has been....

Anna – Jean – doesn't say what the answer has been for 'thirty-five thousand years'. But in her world it means no more than Bourne's Cocoa.

*Voyage in the Dark* picks up another theme from *Quartet* too, and from *Mackenzie*: the enormous importance of money. The single greatest division in Jean's world is between people who have money and people who haven't: greater even than the division between men and women, except that (as we learned in *Mackenzie*) it's usually the same division. That is also true here, but less so. Walter and Vincent and Carl have money, Anna and Germaine and Maudie haven't. But there are people of both sexes in between. Ethel worries about money, but has more than her pathetic male clients; part of the pathos of Maudie's ambition is that her engineer from Brondesbury won't have much either. And Laurie banks half of everything she gets: she has to get it from men, but she does so very successfully. And Hester has her three hundred a year; perhaps it originally came from Anna's father, but it's hers now, and she protects it as fiercely as Uncle Bo protects his, which clearly isn't much either.

Money ought to be everybody's, Anna thinks: but it isn't. Instead 'the poor do this and the rich do that': the poor have beastly lives and grey faces and ugly clothes, and the rich have power and confidence and fun and happiness. When Anna has Walter's money on her side landladies are tamed and her rooms grow bigger, when she has Carl's money Ethel is tamed and the whole world seems to open up before her. But in the end money comes only to hard and clever girls like Laurie. For Anna it remains a fantasy, like the film about rich people she watches in a cinema that smells of poverty. This is Anna's anguish: her longing for beauty and joy and ease; her brief chance and hope of them; their utter loss and disappearance. And yet, we realise, *in a strange way she doesn't really want them*, or doesn't want them enough. Early on she thinks:

> '...It would be too awful if it were always going to be like this. It isn't possible. Something must happen to make it different.' And then I thought, 'Yes, that's right. I'm poor and my clothes are cheap and perhaps it will always be like this. And that's all right too.' It was the first time in my life I'd thought that.

Why does she think it? Why at the end, when Walter drops her, does she simply disappear — why does she behave so absurdly, so self-destructively, so unlike Laurie? Vincent can't understand it. 'You must have known that Walter would look after you,' he says. 'He was awfully worried when you went off and didn't let him know where you were.... He'd fixed everything up....' But Anna replies bitterly: 'So much every Saturday. Receipt form enclosed.' That's it: she cannot be a Laurie, not because she is too broken, but *because she is too proud*. She had rather be poor and wear cheap clothes than be rich but humiliated. Here prickly, angry Jean peeps through meek and mild Anna, and we can see why *her* dream failed. It's not so much — as we were told about Marya — that she cannot play the game: *she refuses to*. She wants money, but she wants self-respect more. We are halfway to Jean's other theme about money, which dominates *Wide Sargasso Sea*: that it is the goal of the vulgar and worthless, not of the truly noble, who put everything — kindness, loyalty, love — before it. These two ideas battled it out in Jean's work, and in her life too: the desperate need for money, and the deep despising of it. Neither ever won. Like her other inner division, this one played havoc with her life, but gave her fiction a rich, dramatic tension. It stops *Voyage in the Dark*, for instance, from being a monotone lament for the loss of love and money: for underneath all the time burn pride and anger.

A third theme of this novel is also an old one, but one which will never change: the cruelty of people. Anna tries to tell herself it is only her imagination, but she doesn't succeed. She sees horrible cruelty in the way people look at you − 'So that you know that they would see you burnt alive without even turning their heads away.' She sees the world as a conspiracy of cruelty, in which people are kept going by hope ('So much hope for each person. And damned cleverly done too.') After she has been to Mrs Robinson she is afraid of everyone she passes in the street. 'Just because I was dying, any one of them, any minute, might stop and approach me and knock me down, or put their tongues out as far as they would go.' This becomes her main image of cruelty, 'Like that time at home with Meta, when it was Masquerade and she came to see me and put out her tongue at me through the slit in her mask.' In the delirium of Part Four the mask with the poked-out tongue − like Uncle Bo's fangs − reappears twice. Finally it becomes the novel's image for life as a whole. '*A pretty useful mask that white one watch it and the slobbering tongue of an idiot will stick out − a mask Father said with an idiot behind it I believe the whole damned business is like that. . . .*' We are back with Marya and the idea of cosmic cruelty, back with Julia and the idea of meaninglessness. In her last two novels Jean will give different answers to her question, *Why does the heroine suffer?* *Voyage in the Dark* gives both *Quartet*'s and *Mackenzie*'s answer, for the last time: and does it better than either of them, because both more subtly and more concretely.

There are two slighter themes in *Voyage in the Dark*.

The first is the theme of split and division. In *Mackenzie* Julia already felt her past self so divided from her present that she lost hold of her real, continuing identity. Anna is younger than Julia, but she is, of course, the creation of the next stage of Jean's life and craft. In her, therefore, the alternation of memory with present experience is not just a device to reveal her history: it is one of the central meanings of her story.

The very first thing she tells us is that her past and present, the West Indies and England, are radically divided, as though she had not just crossed the world, but been reborn. Sometimes one is the dream, sometimes the other; 'but I could never fit them together.' Words don't move from one to the other: if this is 'beautiful' that wasn't; if those were 'flowers' what are these? From this first fracturing she slides easily into others. When she sees Maudie again after leaving the chorus she thinks, 'When I remember living with her it is like looking at an old photograph of myself and thinking, "What on earth's that got to do with me?"' Then when she has lost Walter, and her life has become hell, she feels increasingly that she is living in a dream. 'The light and the sky and the shadows and the houses and the people — all parts of the dream, all fitting in and all against me.' Even when she escapes this bad dream it's only into a good one: 'imagining that there was nothing I couldn't do, nothing I couldn't become. Imagining God knows what. Imagining Carl would say, "When I leave London I'm going to take you with me"....'

Once again, as in *Mackenzie*, the heroine has tried to make herself an escape, but has made herself a trap instead. Julia refused to recognise her young self in her old one in order to spare herself pain — only to suffer something worse, the fear that she didn't exist at all. Similarly, Anna felt as a child the wonderful relief of waking up to find that some terrible thing had only been a dream ('I only dreamt it it never happened ...'). Marya too found this a great relief: '" It's a dream," she would think; "it isn't real" — and be strangely comforted.' It seems to me that this is what Anna is trying to do again. She *wants* to believe that her life in England is only a dream, until she meets Walter; after she has lost him, she wants to believe it even more. The trouble is that it isn't true: her life in England is reality. So telling herself it's a dream doesn't make things better, it makes them worse: it loses her reality altogether. Like Julia, she has tried to avoid suffering, only to find a worse one.

Finally, this reality, this England. *Mackenzie* was already full of hatred of England, and the sense that England hates the heroine. Both are even stronger now. *Mackenzie* was already divided between Paris and London, with the long dark story of death and degradation set firmly in London. In *Voyage* this scheme is still more a part of the story. London is the dull, dark present, lit only by the single flash of the affair with Walter; the brightest past is far away in the West Indies. From the first page England is cold, dark, grey. Everything is small and mean; rooms are dirty, London is loathsome. Above all England is hypocrisy, repression and coldness. 'The place stinks of hypocrites if you've got a nose,' Anna's father says. To him and to Anna Morgan's Rest is beautiful and fertile; to Hester it is Morgan's Folly, 'nothing but rocks and stones and heat and those awful doves cooing all the time.' The strong sweet smell of West Indian flowers makes Hester faint, the stirring West Indian night makes her afraid. The dangerous, mysterious, living world is too much for the English. They want life to be as tame and unnourishing as their food: 'If it had tasted of anything they would have suspected it.'

As to England's hating the heroine, we've seen that that too is very powerfully here. Germaine Sullivan tells us that Englishmen hate women; Joe Adler tells us that Englishwomen do too ('Oh, women. How you love each other, don't you?'). And Aunt Hester tells Anna that in particular 'People in England will dislike you very much,' when she's still a child in the West Indies. This was one of Jean's deepest feelings: that it was all fated, just waiting for her, decided long long ago. That feeling will be the heart — the very shape and conception — of *Wide Sargasso Sea*.

★    ★    ★

With this third novel Jean reached the end of the first part of her journey. She had achieved what she set out to do in her first novel, and to some extent still in her second: to show us an innocent heroine, a guilty hero, a cruel world. Anna is her best innocent heroine. Walter is her best guilty hero, at least until Rochester. Vincent, Ethel and Hester are her best villains — far more convincing than Heidler at the beginning or Daniel at the end. Throughout *Voyage in the Dark* Jean sticks to what she does absolutely best: remaining inside her heroine, and observing others; letting imagery, event and dialogue speak for themselves; writing in 'words of one syllable' and cutting to the bone; using the natural, irrational rhythms of feeling, thought association and dream. When she tries something difficult and new — the vital time shifts of the novel — she manages it with perfect simplicity and lack of fuss: it is something she does best too.

*Voyage in the Dark* is thus the highest product of Jean's most natural gifts as a writer, which are the gifts of a poet — form, imagery, observation. In it she is doing what she really wants to do: excusing her heroine and blaming the world; remembering her own youth and innocence; hearing the tune of the past behind the discord of the present. It gives us the beginning of the heroine's story; and it is about the single most important event in Jean's grown-up life, which cut her off from happiness and made her a writer. If you respond to her particular genius, and want to follow wherever she leads, you must read everything she wrote. But if you will only ever read one of her novels, it probably ought to be this one.

# CHAPTER FIVE

# Leslie, 1935–1939

*After* Voyage in the Dark *– 'Till September Petronella' and*
*'Tigers Are Better-Looking' – Dominica – Paultons Square –*
*Good Morning, Midnight*

*Voyage in the Dark* was a success, Jean's biggest so far. A few critics
were still so alarmed by the 'dreadful' story and 'difficult' theme that
they felt it necessary to say these left 'no unpleasant flavour'. And
Jean must have found it hard to remember that this (from the queen
of the middle-brow reviewers, Sylvia Lynd) was praise: 'The truth
about the grotesque and ugly and wretched and contemptible side of
life could scarcely be told better than it is told here.' But now there
was universal recognition of the beauty and economy of her prose,
the intensity and truthfulness of her vision; and a recognition too
of her much greater compassion and understanding. Even *The Lady*
recommended *Voyage* to 'those well-balanced women of normal
resource who "cannot understand" how any girl ever takes to the
streets for a living, and also to those who sentimentalise over those
who do.'

Jean's old admirers, Norah Hoult and Frank Swinnerton, praised
*Voyage in the Dark* (quite rightly) still more than *Mackenzie*; and a
new one, the novelist Clemence Dane, saluted it with (I think) great
accuracy, and evident emotion:

> The book is impressive in its simplicity, its originality, and its
> power to express the emotions and bewilderments of the
> inarticulate. It is a remarkable book, a tormented book, but it
> has also subtlety and tenderness.

Even readers agreed, and *Voyage* sold a bit better than the earlier
novels. Not much better; Jean made hardly anything from any of
her books until *Wide Sargasso Sea*. But in May 1936 Constable put
out a cheap edition of *Voyage* (at two shillings and sixpence, half the
original price of five shillings). It was hardly popular, but it was at
least less *un*popular than the others had been.

1934 had really been an *annus mirabilis*. Jean was married and
respectable again; she'd written a novel she liked, and which had been

her best success so far. The literary world admired her and awaited her books with excitement. She was, surely, poised on the edge of what she'd always wanted: for her life to change, for the door to open and happiness to come in.

In 1935 she glimpsed this possibility of a different kind of life at least twice, in two new friends. One came through Leslie and his work; one through her own.

One day Leslie was given a new job: to edit a book called *Out of Bounds*, by a wild young man called Esmond Romilly and his brother Giles (who were, like Jean's uncle, relatives of Winston Churchill). The year before, when he was only fifteen, Esmond had run away from Wellington in a blaze of publicity ('Winston's "Red" Nephew: Colonel's Son Runs Away from School,' said the *Daily Mail*). He'd been living in David Archer's famous left-wing bookshop, but had been turned out for drunken behaviour, and had spent six weeks in a remand home for delinquent boys. Then he'd been in a flat with friends, but that had ended too. He was badly in need of money and of somewhere to live. *Out of Bounds* was meant to solve the first problem, and soon Leslie was working hard on that. Then he solved the second problem as well: Esmond moved in with him and Jean.

Esmond was a flamboyant, wild and witty person, extremely charming, brimful of ideas and fun. He must have seemed to Jean the son, or perhaps the self, she'd never had: rebellious and anarchic, like her, but unlike her confident and daring; a dreamer, like her, but full of resource and guile. He made an enormous impression on her; she and Leslie both loved him. Forty years later she still remembered him. He was 'quite fearless as far as one could see,' she said. 'And such fun!... He had more charm than anyone I've ever met & I still often think of him.'

For a few weeks or months while Esmond was living with them, perhaps her life opened out: perhaps she glimpsed tantalising possibilities of romance and adventure. But they were only for Esmond. In early 1936 she and Leslie left England for a long holiday, leaving Esmond in their flat. By the time they came back he had run away again, this time to the Spanish Civil War. He fought in the International Brigade, and was invalided home; when he returned he took his young cousin Jessica Mitford with him. The two were chased across Europe by the furious Mitford family, followed by the press every inch of the way. It was high romance, high farce, and in the end tragedy. Esmond married Jessica and they had a daughter; but in 1941 he was killed in action, aged only twenty-three.

Jean's second new friendship was with a woman: Rosamond

Lehmann, another novelist with a growing reputation, thirteen years younger than her.* Rosamond was at a difficult point in her own life. None the less, I think, she offered Jean a glimpse of her dream of the 'happy woman'; for she was beautiful and stylish and, compared to Jean, at home in England and the world. At the same time she was a sensitive artist and a generous woman; she might have made Jean a uniquely understanding friend. What happened instead gives us a clear and painful picture of the fate of Jean's high hopes – or ours for her.

*Voyage in the Dark* had come out in October 1934. Soon afterwards Rosamond wrote to Jean, praising it and saying how much she would like to meet her. And in January Jean accepted an invitation to meet Rosamond, her sister Beatrix and her friend Violet Hammersley for tea.†

On the appointed day the Lehmanns and Mrs Hammersley waited in some excitement for Jean to arrive. They were looking forward to meeting someone bohemian and *louche*, someone as daring and unconventional as her books. That was their first surprise. Jean was impeccably well dressed, like the ladies of Roseau at a tea-party: coat and skirt, hat and gloves, all present and correct: a perfectly respectable lady. *How could this be Jean Rhys?* But it went on. She sat down and took tea very politely. Rosamond found her very beautiful, with great charm and 'animal magnetism'. But it was all suppressed: Jean was demure, shy, distant. They could get nowhere near her. Mrs Hammersley tried; she'd been brought up in Paris, and had no patience with English reserve. She probed; she tried to dislodge Jean from tea-party banalities, to make her talk about herself and her work, about its intriguing atmosphere of lassitude and self-abandon.... But it was no good. Jean refused to talk about herself or her work at all. When she told the story later she implied that it was the others who had been 'respectable' – except for Beatrix Lehmann, who, she said, had suddenly winked at her. But the truth was exactly the opposite. It was she who had come as a Roseau lady; and a Roseau lady she had remained.

*By 1935 Rosamond Lehmann had published two novels, *Dusty Answer* (1927) and *Invitation to the Waltz* (1932), and was working on a third, *The Weather in the Streets* (published in 1936).

†Beatrix Lehmann (who died in 1979) was a well-known actress. Their brother John (d. 1987) was a writer, editor and critic, who would later publish several of Jean's stories in the *London Magazine*. Mrs Hammersley was a family friend of the Lehmanns, godmother to John. She was a friend of many writers, including for instance Jessica Mitford's sister Nancy. In her heyday, married to a rich banker, she had surrounded herself with a court of writers and artists and had been painted by Wilson Steer. Now she was a widow, and had lost all her money; she dressed in black, and enjoyed a melodramatic gloom. She died in 1964.

Nevertheless, and though Rosamond couldn't have guessed it, Jean had liked her. And when Rosamond wrote again, a sympathetic letter ('I guessed, and now am sure, that you are frightened of people'), she agreed to another meeting. But now her mood had darkened.

1935 was the year of George V's Silver Jubilee, and England was waxing sentimental. The climax would come in May; but the atmosphere of self-congratulation must have been building up for months, and Jean couldn't bear it. She appeared with a black eye, which Rosamond immediately guessed was the result of a drunken fall. And she was deeply, undisguisably despairing 'about the Jubilee and about the world.'

Rosamond was more sympathetic than ever ('I did love seeing you, although I felt terribly distressed at your sadness'). But she would see Jean only once more. She didn't turn up to their next meeting; Rosamond never knew the real reason why.* But some time after that Jean wrote herself, and asked Rosamond to tea with her and Leslie at their rooms in Bury Street. And instead of confirming their friendship, this meeting ended it.

When she arrived Leslie met her at the door instead of Jean. He said Jean wasn't well, he looked ill himself. Rosamond wondered what to do; but Leslie suggested she come up anyway.

Afterwards Rosamond couldn't understand why he'd done this, for when she entered the sitting-room Jean was lying on the sofa, drunk. She looked ill, unkempt, dishevelled; she didn't speak to Rosamond, didn't seem to know she was there. Instead she spoke, incoherently and incessantly, half to herself and half to Leslie. 'Poor Leslie,' she kept saying, 'poor, poor Leslie. He looks so miserable and wretched and ill.' And to Leslie: 'Why are you sad? Are you very sad? Why do you look so sad?' That is what everyone asks the heroine in her novels: '*Pourquoi êtes-vous triste?*' But now *she* was asking it, of Leslie – and not pityingly, or sorrowfully, but in a needling, taunting tone, challenging him, daring him to answer.

She was trying to get him to say it: *I'm sad because of you, I'm ill because of you, it's your fault.* . . . But he wouldn't say it. He wouldn't hit back, he wouldn't shout back, he wouldn't even say that he blamed her. He simply remained silent and stony-faced, and didn't speak a word. Years later Jean wrote about a husband: 'I'm not one to whine. . . . I attack. Usually, he did not answer me – just looked at me with his marble face.' When Rosamond read the words 'marble face', Leslie's face that day came back to her with ghastly clarity.

She stayed only a few minutes. There was nothing she could say or do; she could hardly bear to look at either of them. Leslie saw

*For that reason, see pages 347–48 below.

her out. He was unable to hide his despair, and Rosamond felt unbearably sorry for him. And she knew she couldn't see Jean again. She remembered the impossibly proper lady who'd come to tea: Jean wouldn't be able to face the stranger who'd seen the cruel, tormented woman beneath. She would want to forget her; and Rosamond didn't write again.

It was now the second half of 1935, at the latest early 1936. Jean and Leslie had been married for a year and a half, perhaps two years. The miracle Jean had hoped for hadn't happened. She hadn't changed, her slide had not stopped. On the contrary, she had become an irretrievable alcoholic.

She knew it herself. In her Black Exercise Book a few years later she wrote 'I've been drinking for the last six years,' and 'I've made a complete wreck of myself or rather I've certainly put the finishing touch to the wreck. . . .' And in *Good Morning, Midnight* she wrote of Sasha:

> It was then that I had the bright idea of drinking myself to death. . . .*
> . . . I've had enough of thinking, enough of remembering. Now whisky, rum, gin, sherry, vermouth, wine with the bottles labelled 'Dum vivimus, vivamus. . . .' Drink, drink, drink. . . . As soon as I sober up I start again. I have to force it down sometimes. You'd think I'd get delirium tremens. . .
> Nothing. I must be solid as an oak. Except when I cry.

Everyone else knew it too. Leslie, of course: Rosamond Lehmann had seen as he saw her out that he knew it. Leslie's family, from whom he'd managed to hide most of the bad times so far: but 'from the moment they'd married', Anne says, they became too bad to hide, and Leslie admitted to her what his bruises and scratches really were. He said openly now that he had to get away from her sometimes, because she was 'in a terrible temper'; then he would come to see Anne, or go for long walks by himself, and stay away for hours.

John knew it too, and like Jean he put it into a novel. In *Schuwe Vogels* Stephan Hale comes to London to discuss divorce with his wife Helen: and finds that she 'has become an alcoholic and is sliding

*After Sasha gets her legacy from the relative who wants 'to annoy the rest of the family' ('Thirty-five pounds of the legacy had accumulated, it seemed. That ought to do the trick.') Auntie B *had* left Jean a legacy in 1934, as we know; and perhaps there really was a connection. It was a lump sum of her own money, and if she wanted to drink every penny of it no one could stop her.

inevitably towards her final destruction.' *Schuwe Vogels* is again, of course, fiction; and John had borne a great burden of pain and bitterness against Jean for a long time. But by late 1936, when he wrote the novel, he was remarried, and he and Henriette, Jean and Leslie, were friends, on good terms. Consciously, at least, I think he was only trying to describe what he saw; but his portrait of 'Helen' is appalling.

This comes as an ironic revelation in the story, because before he arrives Stephan Hale is jealous of Leslie Bead and what he imagines to be his happiness with Helen. But he approaches him first, alone: and Leslie tells him the truth. His life with Helen is the opposite of happy; it is a living hell of drunkenness and violence. Then Stephan remeets Helen and sees the truth for himself. She becomes very drunk, and starts a violent quarrel with Leslie; finally she turns on him too, and hurls abuse at both of them. The Beads live by a river; drunk as she is Helen runs off to go swimming.

The novel's ending is horribly revealing. Bead goes after Helen but returns, saying he can't find her. Then both men go; and they find her drowned. After she is buried Bead is very distressed: and he tells Stephan that he *did* find Helen the first time, that she wouldn't get into the boat, and that trying to pull her in he accidentally hit her with an oar. He is afraid that he may have killed her; but at the same time he is relieved that she is dead. And Stephan, of course, is freed too; and the book ends with his striding into a future of happiness with his new wife, Kay.

It's just like the ending of *Quartet*, when Stephan Zelli goes off with Mademoiselle Chardin, leaving Marya (perhaps) dead on the floor....Except that this time it is not an aspect of Jean's self-pity, but rather of what she pitied herself for: the fact that people, and especially her lovers, could hate her and wish her dead. I think it is inescapably clear that they could, that at least in fiction Ford (in *When The Wicked Man*) and John (in *Schuwe Vogels*) did. And even Leslie. Of course it is in John's novel, in John's fantasy, that 'Helen' dies, that 'Leslie' is relieved she is dead, that he may even have killed her himself. But Leslie would not have been human if he had not, sometimes, felt the same. Jean thought he did. For sometimes that 'marble-faced' husband looked at her (she wrote) like a 'hanging judge'.

Leslie knew that when she was sober she was different. And she was sober often enough so that he could never give her up, or stop caring for her. But being Jean — or perhaps just being human — she couldn't forget the bad moments, when even Leslie became the man who hated her.

★      ★      ★

Between *Voyage in the Dark* and *Good Morning, Midnight*, Jean said later, she 'hadn't been able to write a word for three years.' She was exaggerating, as usual. Perhaps by now she didn't feel she was writing unless she was writing a novel. But between 1935 and 1939 I think she wrote two of her greatest short stories: 'Till September Petronella' and 'Tigers Are Better-Looking'.

These two stories locate Jean very precisely on her journey: at the high point of her art, but a very low point of her feeling. They are full of fear, full of hate, especially of women. Mr Severn in 'Tigers' sees nothing all around him but 'Threats and mockery, mockery and threats.... And desolation, desertion and crumpled newspapers in the room.' Heather is 'so sharp she cuts herself,' even the black girl in the night club is a cruel snob, and 'some men aren't so slow either,' says Mr Severn. In 'Petronella' hate is everywhere: between the country people and the Londoners ('Julian says he almost faints when he thinks of it. I say, why think of it?'), between the taxi driver and the young man, between everyone and women. 'You poor devil of a female, female, female, in a country where females are only tolerated at best,' chants Marston, and Julian is reading a book about 'the biological inferiority of women'. 'Retire under the table,' he says to his lover Frankie, 'because that's where I like you best.' He hates girls really, Frankie says; but so does she. 'They'll kick your face to bits if you let them,' she tells Petronella. 'And shriek with laughter at the damage.'

These are, of course, Jean's fears and Jean's obsessions. In the war stories they will break out of her grip and seem like madness; but here she still controls them, so that they frighten us as much as her. These stories were, in fact, the bridge on which she moved from her third to her fourth novel. For her art and craft were already complete in *Voyage in the Dark*: it was the self-exposure she'd begun in *Mackenzie* which she had to repossess and push on towards *Good Morning, Midnight*. That is what these stories do; and that is why they are so frightening. In 'Petronella' she is telling the worst truths about herself, in 'Tigers' the worst truths about her marriage, and that is what is really frightening her. She cannot yet do it openly and bravely, as in *Good Morning, Midnight*; she can only do it secretly, half-consciously, mysteriously. That yields for these stories some of her most characteristic and alarming writing.

The worst things in Jean's world — in any world — are cruelty, exploitation and rejection. She spent her whole life and much of her work accusing other people of showing them to her. But in *Good Morning, Midnight* openly, and in 'Till September Petronella' hiddenly, she recognises the truth: that she also showed these things to other people.

In the summer of 1915 she had cruelly exploited and rejected
Adrian Allinson. He had been in love with her beauty and then with
her, and she had used him (as later she would use John) to get away
from London. She wouldn't cook, walk or swim; she wouldn't sleep
with him — unless he fought; she wouldn't leave. She was not the
victim of a sexual despot who was merely using her — as *Quartet*,
for example, portrays Marya; she was the sexual despot herself, using
poor, decent, vulnerable Allinson.

All of this Jean admits in 'Petronella'. She shows us Marston's
decency and vulnerability — his flowers, his tears, his unattractiveness ('the Apotheosis of Lust. I have to laugh when I think of
that, for some reason'). And she shows us Petronella's cruelty.
Petronella lets Marston kiss her — while she gazes at Julian; she
giggles with Frankie over Marston's appearance and says 'He makes
me go cold.' When he apologises to a farmer who has been rude to
them she refuses to talk to him all the way home. And it is not just
over Marston that she has sexual power. At the height of Marston's
quarrel with Julian, Marston says 'You're letting your jealousy run
away with you': and Julian is enraged. 'Jealous of what?' he
shrieks. . . . What can Marston mean but that Julian is jealous of his
affair with Petronella, however unsuccessful? And what can we
conclude from Julian's fury but that it is probably true? In fact
Petronella is not a victim at all, like Marston: she is much more like
Julian himself. They are the sexually powerful ones of this quartet,
the most attractive and the most selfish. The real battle is not an
attack of the most powerful person — 'the great Julian' — on the
weakest, as Petronella at first seems. The underlying truth is that it
is a battle for superiority between the two most powerful. That, I'm
certain, was the truth about the battle between Philip Heseltine and
Jean. And that is the truth she left in her story, just beneath the
surface.

She put it not only into Petronella's behaviour to Marston and her
quarrel with Julian; she put it most deeply and secretly into an image.
Travelling back to London in her first-class carriage Petronella kisses
her reflection in the glass: if she's been like Julian she's now like
Marston again, telling herself 'Never mind, never mind.' Then she
turns, because

> I felt as if someone was staring at me, but it was only the girl
> on the cover of the chocolate box. She had slanting green eyes,
> but they were too close together, and she had a white, square
> face that didn't go with her slanting eyes. 'I bet you could be
> a rotten, respectable, sneering bitch too, with a face like that,
> if you had the chance,' I told her.

The train got into Paddington just before ten. As soon as I was on the platform I remembered the chocolates, but I didn't go back for them. 'Somebody will find you, somebody will look after you, you rotten, sneering, stupid, tight-mouthed bitch,' I thought.

Who is this chocolate box girl? Is she the heroine's opponent, the 'respectable' woman who always wins, and always sneers at her? She could be. 'Somebody will find you, somebody will look after you' would fit. But the slanting eyes don't — the slanting eyes Jean had herself, and which she usually gave to her heroines, or to characters she (and they) liked....* I think the chocolate box girl is partly *Petronella herself*. Her reflection in the mirror is her victim side, the side that is like Marston; and the chocolate box girl is an image of her other side, the side that is like Julian, that makes victims of other people. It can be a rotten sneering bitch if it has the chance — and Jean knows that it *had* just had the chance, and had taken it, spurning lovelorn Allinson and sneering at unfit, unfighting Heseltine. When Petronella hates the chocolate box girl, that is Jean hating the sneering half of her; when Petronella leaves the chocolate box girl behind, that is Jean wishing she could leave her sneering half behind too — cut it off and forget it had ever existed. But in writing 'Till September Petronella' she remembered it; and in this brief, mysterious image I think she put her self-hatred and self-blame themselves into the story.

That is what happened when she sat down to write: she remembered the dark, painful truth and told it. And that, I think, is what 'Tigers Are Better-Looking' is about. It is about dark, hidden truths, and how they insist on being recognised in a certain kind of writing. Alone in Jean's fiction 'Tigers' is about writing.

It begins with a piece of writing, Hans's letter. Then immediately we see Mr Severn struggling to write his 'swell article' on the Jubilee. Usually he has no trouble trotting out 'anything that anybody liked', like the tame grey mare that Hans has called him. But today he can't, perhaps because he has been shocked into real feeling by Hans's desertion. There is a new devil in him, a new voice, that insists on

---

*Thus, for example, Suzy in *Triple Sec* and Marya in *Quartet* have slanting eyes. The only comforting person in *Good Morning, Midnight*, the *sage femme*, has them, and Sasha says 'I like people with clear, slanting eyes.' In 'Learning to Be a Mother' in *The Left Bank* the narrator feels love for her baby son for the first time when she notices his eyes: 'He opened his eyes and looked straight into mine. His were set slantwise, too, and I imagined they looked sad.... Little thing! I must kiss him....'

writing not the bland, acceptable thing *but something that sounds like Jean Rhys*: uncomfortable truths in plain prose.

> ...*As the carriages came into sight some of the crowd cheered and a fat man said he couldn't see and he was going to climb a lamp-post. The figures in the carriage bowed from right to left — victims bowed to victimized. The bloodless sacrifice was being exhibited, the reminder that somewhere the sun is shining, even if it doesn't shine on everybody.*
>
> *"E looked just like a waxwork, didn't 'e?' a woman said with satisfaction....*

And Mr Severn thinks: 'No, that would never do.'
What happens in the story is that a respectable Englishman gets hurt, and drunk, and falls through to the dangerous hidden depths — public violence, policemen and prisons. For one night he is transformed, like a reverse Cinderella, from a have to a have-not; and from a slick commercial journalist to someone filled with strange wild words. He feels sick and sleeps, as usual in *rites de passage* (in Rochester's, for example, in *Wide Sargasso Sea*). When he wakes he is sober, but not yet himself: the words still whirl in his head, though they seem meaningless. But with the light of day his sanity returns. He tries to be kind, but the most he can bring himself to do for Maidie is to give her a lift home in his taxi. Like Mr Horsfield after getting rid of Julia, he returns with relief to his safe and quiet corner. And everything falls back into place at last, most of all language. The wild, sad, true Jean Rhys voice falls away, and he is the tame grey mare again, trotting out his swell article.

> ...The tormenting phrases vanished too — 'Who pays? Will you pay now, please? You don't mind if I leave you, dear? I died waiting, I died waiting. (Or was it I died hating?) That was my father speaking. Pictures, pictures, pictures. You've got to be young. But tigers are better-looking, aren't they? SOS, SOS, SOS. If I was a bird and had wings I could fly away, couldn't I? Might get shot as you went. But tigers are better-looking, aren't they? You've got to be younger than we are....' Other phrases, suave and slick, took their place.
>
> The swing's the thing, the cadence of the sentence. He had got it.
>
> He looked at his eye in the mirror, then sat down at the typewriter and with great assurance rapped out 'JUBILEE'....'

'Tigers' is one of Jean's most deceptive stories. First because it is only a little about a despised underworld, and much more about writing about it. Second because it is only a little sympathetic to Mr

Severn, and really much more hostile to him. It takes us inside him, and it shows him as Jean usually shows her heroine: rejected (by Hans) and despised (by Heather and the black girl, by the doctor and the policeman). But really, of course, he is one of them. Maidie has been here before, but he hasn't; and we feel he won't return. He has only briefly fallen through to her world of unadaptedness and violence, and to Jean's wild, true words. In the end he rejects them both sharply. '*Good*-bye,' he says to Maidie, ignoring her outstretched hand; and he dismisses the Jean Rhys voice with that pompous, patriotic word: *Jubilee*.

And there is a third reason. Mr Severn is only partly an invented, representative commercial journalist. Really he is much more Leslie. That is the sense in which 'Tigers' is secretly about Jean's marriage.

The obvious Leslie characters in Jean's fiction are all husbands or lovers of the heroine: Mr Horsfield in *Mackenzie*, Stephen in 'Kikimora', the dying husband in 'The Sound of the River'.* But Mr Severn has the same muteness, Englishness, caution and convention as both Horsfield and Stephen; the same reluctant sympathy with the Jean Rhys woman, and the same relieved retreat from her, as Horsfield. He lives in 'darkest Bloomsbury' as Leslie (and Jean) did; he takes in Hans as Leslie (and Jean) took in Esmond. Leslie even tried to do a bit of journalism in 1935. I think there can be little doubt that Mr Severn was based on him.

When Mr Horsfield turned away with relief from Julia he seemed very different from Leslie, who married Jean and lived with her until he died. Yet beneath the surface he wasn't so different after all. But could this be true of Mr Severn and Leslie, especially in relation to Jean's writing? How can Leslie, who did all he could to help Jean write and publish, who was the main reason she *could* write and publish in the richest decade of her life − how can Leslie be Mr Severn, who turns away with relief from the Jean Rhys voice to 'anything that anybody liked'?

Well, he was, at least sometimes. As early as 1931 she wrote to Evelyn Scott, 'I am always being told that until my work ceases being "sordid and depressing" I haven't much chance of selling.' This was many people − the critics, for example; but it was also Leslie. Jean told Francis Wyndham several times that he had not appreciated her work quite rightly; and in the nineteen-seventies she summed up what she meant in a way which sounds balanced and true. Her second husband, she said, 'a publisher's reader, encouraged her

---

*Mr Horsfield is the one Leslie's family recognised. His daughter Anne says 'My father was the "hero" in *After Leaving Mr Mackenzie*,' and adds that 'Horsfield' was the name of Leslie's best friend during the First World War.

writing, recognised her talent, but told her that she would never sell well.'

In the finished story the battle between Jean and Mr Severn is subtle. We may almost be tricked into hoping that he will find the cadence of his sentence — until we notice those few little words, 'suave and slick', 'anything that anybody liked'.... But in Jean's notebooks and drafts the battle is open, and almost openly with Leslie. In her Black Exercise Book, for example, she gives a 'Mr Smith' a harsh and pointed attack on everything she stood for, everything she was trying to do.

> People write to make money [he says]. They write what they're told to write, what they get paid for writing and what people expect them to write. There never has been any other sort of writing and there never will be. All these people who drink and starve and all the rest are mad. They're not only mad but very foolish.

And in the Black Exercise Book too there is a quarrel with someone called 'L' about women writers. A 'Miss L' has written a very good book of short stories, of which one of the best is about a servant girl. A certain critic, says L, claims that Miss L 'must have been a skivvy'; and that, if so, he can dismiss the story as 'merely personal reminiscence'.

> Well I said supposing he meets her & she obviously isn't a servant what then....
> Well then said L enjoying himself in his quiet way it's valueless too absolutely false a hysterical woman longing for experiences she's never had any doctor or dentist will tell you that line
> So you get her either way
> Yes he said now don't get excited he said don't use that awful language....

The self-hatred and self-condemnation which were the point of 'Petronella' Jean hid in the image of the chocolate box girl. And the hatred and condemnation of Leslie which were the point of 'Tigers' she hid in an image too. In his cell Mr Severn sees a message scratched up: 'Lord, save me; I perish', and underneath 'SOS, SOS, SOS'. This message joins the tormenting Jean Rhys-like phrases which drown out his tame cadence : and in a perfect picture of that process, Mr Severn copies it out and signs it with his own initials. Now Jean left a little private hint, even in the published story, that the usurping voice was her own. For the real name of its Jean Rhys woman, Maidie, is *Gladys Reilly*: and the initials under the original message are

*G.R.* But in a draft of the story we can see where these initials came from. For instead of *G.R.* there is *G.R.W.*, for *G*wen *R*ees *W*illiams.

From *After Leaving Mr Mackenzie* to 'Tigers Are Better-Looking' there has been a sad decline in the Leslie figure. Mr Horsfield had at least been seeking the sun, hoping that it would 'develop the love of life and humanity in which he felt he was lamentably deficient.' He had let Julia go with a pang, and with only secret relief; while Mr Severn rejects Maidie openly and rudely. In fact Mr Severn ends by openly hating Maidie; and in the drafts Jean openly hates Mr Smith/Mr Severn. He is a hypocrite ('He belonged to the Labour Party but detested anything sordid ... most of his friends had money'), a philistine (that speech about writing for money), and an exploiter of artists ('probably an amateur. No use to me').

On the other hand, when we go back from the notebooks to the finished story, we see the opposite truth too. Mr Severn is no longer any of these things; his worst traits are meanness and a mania for order. He too has suffered a rejection: and it has (however briefly) made him join Maidie in her underworld of drunkenness and violence. There are, I think, several things at work here. One is Jean's artistic control: her growing understanding that balance is truth and truth balance. Another, perhaps, is guilt: for she put herself not only into Maidie, who is Mr Severn's victim, but also into Hans, who victimised *him*. But the third thing is what most often made Jean write the way she did: she was sticking to the truth of her memory. Mr Severn joins Maidie in her underworld because Leslie did: the main event of the story really happened.

George V's Silver Jubilee was celebrated from 6-9 May 1935. There were parades, just as Mr Severn describes; there were broadcasts and articles; Britain congratulated herself even more than usual. It was just the sort of atmosphere to madden Jean — fulsome sentiment masking poverty, inequality, the shadow of war. And it did madden her. Rosamond Lehmann saw her at the time: and Jean's despair 'about the Jubilee and about the world' was acute. And now came the central event of 'Tigers'.

Rosamond arranged to meet Jean in the Café Royal on 14 June, when she was next in London. But on the night of 13 June (13 again!) Jean and Leslie were in Wardour Street — just like Maidie and Mr Severn. Like Mr Severn, Leslie got drunk; unlike Maidie, Jean got drunk too. There was a brawl, in which Leslie was battered and bruised, like Mr Severn, and Jean probably was too. At four in the morning they were both arrested. They spent the night in police cells, just like Maidie and Mr Severn; like Maidie and Mr Severn, they were both seen by a doctor. The next morning they were taken to Bow Street, just as in the story. Jean appeared first before the magistrate, as *Ella Tilden Smith (Journalist)*.* The charge was Drunk and Disorderly. She pleaded as she did for Maidie in the story: Not Guilty. But the magistrate was unimpressed. After ten other cases — other drunk and disorderlys; prostitutes up for soliciting — it was Leslie's turn. He too was accused of being 'Drunk and Disorderly at Wardour Street': and he pleaded Guilty (like Mr Severn in 'Tigers': 'It'll soon be over now, we've only got to plead guilty'). They were each fined almost exactly as in the story: thirty shillings and sixpence each, plus the doctor's fee. Perhaps they really had to wait for this to come from a friend; if so they chafed, because Rosamond Lehmann was waiting at the Café Royal. But Jean must have felt like Maidie: she looked too awful. She didn't go; Leslie did instead. 'Your poor husband limped in, chipped and bruised' (Rosamond wrote to Jean), 'to announce the disaster!' Not the real disaster, of course: Leslie said they had had a car crash.

It's interesting, and typical, that Leslie pleaded guilty, Jean not guilty. It's highly unlikely that quiet, conventional Leslie started the trouble (like Mr Severn), with Jean the innocent onlooker (like Maidie). She had already been subject to rages for years. It's much more likely to have been she who suddenly broke out, who 'screamed, shouted, cried, made a scene'. And yet, then, it would be characteristic for each to plead the way they did. Leslie would know it was a hopeless battle, and would want to get it over with quickly. Whereas Jean would be stubborn, irrational; all accusations would become one accusation in her mind, and she would refuse to accept any of them. This June morning in 1935 was her first step towards the ghastly courtroom of the Ropemakers Diary; and Leslie's, we must fear, towards the 'hanging-judge' which became her last image of him.


Jean's decline into chronic alcoholism, and its effect on her marriage, were the main facts of her life between *Voyage in the Dark* and *Good Morning, Midnight*. But of course it wasn't all gloom and anger. There were many better times, much helped by the fact that they had become a little less poor. In the late summer of 1935, for instance

*This is interesting, of course — could she have been trying to do some journalism herself; and did that too go into Mr Severn, struggling against his Jean Rhys voice to write a 'swell article'?

— despite the trough of the Jubilee in May and June — they had a lovely holiday with Maryvonne in Wales; and half of 1936 was a holiday, at least part of it lovely too.

There was also their friendship with John and Henriette. Throughout 1935 John remained so poor he couldn't marry, so poor his friends published an appeal for help for him in the Dutch papers. He was also ill; he spent six months in Italy in a vain attempt to be cured, and Jean visited him there. But in September he got a job as the London correspondent of the newspaper *Het Volk*; soon after Henriette joined him, and they were married in London in January 1936.*

John soon hated his job, and it didn't last long: he quarrelled with the editor and resigned in February. But somehow he and Henriette stayed on in London until September. Jean and Leslie were away on their holiday between February and early July; but before they left and after they returned the friendship grew. In *Schuwe Vogels* Leslie Bead asks Stephan to help him when Helen is in a rage; and so did the real Leslie ask John. John could calm Jean down; Leslie couldn't. That alone would have made things better as long as John and Henriette were in London. And besides, all four got on. Jean was kind to Henriette, and very fond of John; and the two men liked one another.

One can't help wondering, of course, how *Schuwe Vogels* affected this friendship. The portrait of Jean was so harsh, the fantasy of murder so evident.... Yet in 1940, and after, they were still friends. Perhaps John could keep the contents of his novels from Jean (it would be easier than *An Den Loopenden Band*, with its giveaway titles). She couldn't read Dutch; and if he told her that *Schuwe Vogels* was — say — about an earlier period of his life, like *Muziek Voorop*, she might well be as incurious as ever and believe him. (But by 1937 Maryvonne was fifteen, and she certainly read Dutch....) But then Jean had already accepted his portrait of her in *Barred*,

---

*Henriette later said that she'd brought Maryvonne with her from Holland, and that Maryvonne, now aged thirteen, 'was to stay with her mother. But that was impossible because she drank so much, and when she had been drinking she became aggressive. Maryvonne did not have much of a life with her, so she was brought back to Holland and put into a Catholic convent school.' This was reported in a Dutch magazine 'not known for its accuracy' (my Dutch colleagues tell me); and certainly Maryvonne has never mentioned it. But it is of course possible. Jean *was* drinking very badly now, and Maryvonne did at least once accuse her of this. But by February she was certainly in her Dutch convent school, where Jean visited her before leaving for Dominica.

which was painful enough. I suspect that she knew, or half-knew, about *Schuwe Vogels*, though she was spared from reading the novel word for word by her ignorance of Dutch; and that she and John could keep up the pretence between them that it was only fiction. But if she did know, this dark portrait of her in 1937 as a violent and vengeful alcoholic must have been one of the things that pushed her towards a peak of honesty in 1938 and '39, and a trough of depression after.

★     ★     ★

In September 1935 the Reverend Tilden Smith died, and Jean and Leslie knew there would be some real money. It didn't take them long to decide how to spend it: he would take her back to Dominica. 'I suppose going back ... is foolhardy,' Jean wrote to Evelyn Scott, 'but I want to so much — I can't help risking it. You can imagine the wild and fantastic plans and hopes....' I think we can too.

She hadn't seen her island for thirty years. But already for the last five it had haunted her. She'd poured out memories of it, which she'd put into *Voyage in the Dark* (though in the end she'd had to take half of them out again). Not all were happy; but it had made her happy to remember them. Of course she couldn't resist doing that dangerous thing — going home.

And in fact it was an extremely important experience for her: her most important new experience as a writer, which allowed her to take the new direction of her last novel. So far, in *Voyage in the Dark*, she had remembered and used Dominica in a very personal way, as the dreamlike contrast to her life in England. Now the island would strike her more than anything she'd seen since she left it: more than London, more even than Paris. It impressed itself on her mind not just as part of her story, but as itself, with its own story, its own beauty and squalor and sadness. She was a supreme egoist, for whom most places (like most people) were reflections of her own moods and feelings more than simply themselves. That is true even of London and Paris in her novels. But in *Wide Sargasso Sea* Dominica — though she calls part of it Jamaica — is *itself*. Its presence is so strong that it is almost another character in the novel; it and its people are real, separate existences, with their own histories and their own meanings. 'I feel that this place is my enemy and on your side,' Rochester says — which is just how Jean and her other heroines feel about England. But Antoinette replies: 'You are quite mistaken. It is not for you and not for me. It has nothing to do with either of us ... it is something else.' I think that is one thing Jean learned when she went home now.

First she and Leslie went to Holland, just for a few days, because Jean wanted to see Maryvonne. If what Henriette van Eyk said was true, Maryvonne had only recently returned there, after yet another failure of the hope that they might live together. In that case Jean felt guilty before they arrived; in any case she felt guilty when they left.

Maryvonne had caught measles and was in the infirmary. 'I noticed at once that she looked thin and pale,' Jean still remembered in 1971. 'But the old nun who was with her seemed kind,' and 'Because I liked my convent I imagined that a convent was a pleasant safe place to be.' But when she left she took with her a sad and anxious image: a pale girl in a convent, with a strange look in her eyes.

Was she even then remembering herself instead of her daughter, left in her Roseau convent at exactly the same age? Or was Maryvonne really unhappy in her convent, as Jean later believed? 'Then I understood why she'd looked at me as she did when I left. She must have felt utterly lonely and betrayed....' Perhaps both were true. But in any case this must have gone far beyond the convent. Jean was surely afraid that her daughter felt abandoned and betrayed by her in general, not just in her convent, but in her whole life. And deep down, this must have been true. When Maryvonne grew up she understood Jean: her strange self-obsessed nature, her overwhelming need to write. But when Jean felt during the next years more in Maryvonne than 'the usual antagonism' of an adolescent girl towards her mother, we must guess that she was right. And perhaps she felt it first now; or perhaps it was just her guilt speaking.

After this brief unhappy visit Jean and Leslie returned to England just long enough to leave it again. On 25 February they sailed from Southampton, on an old but elegant French ship called the *Cuba*. And this time their departure was unclouded delight. Anne and her husband Henry came to see them off, bearing bouquets of flowers; and not only Jean's brother Owen, but both her sisters too. Jean was radiant, excited, quite without her usual lassitude and shyness; she kissed everyone goodbye, her arms full of flowers. Anne was interested to see Jean's sisters, whom she hadn't met before. They looked very different from Jean, she remembers: 'Very nice, ordinary women.'

The *Cuba* had a French crew and a mixture of passengers, mostly French, English and South American. Jean and Leslie had a table on the French and South American side of the dining room, which suited both of them. None the less Jean took a dislike to her closest neighbour on the ship, a 'handsome but terribly strident' Italian woman with two objectionable children and a husband who looked

like a gangster (the description is Leslie's). And now we hear of
something which will later reach unmanageable proportions in Jean's
life: quarrelling with neighbours. 'Jean had words with her *bête noire*
yesterday,' Leslie wrote to Anne, 'which has subdued the young
woman but doesn't make things any pleasanter. I have not heard
any of her remarks, which include me, but she is exactly the type to
make them.' Only Jean has heard the remarks; but Leslie believes
her.... Well, as she would soon say, persecution maniacs are usually
persecuted: I'm sure the Italian woman did grumble, and dislike her.
But I'm also sure that she was beginning to magnify people's hostility
to her: picking up a real feeling, but half-imagining the dialogue, as
though they were characters in her novels.

In the last week they entered the Sargasso Sea, and Leslie wrote
of the warmer weather and the floating weed, adding 'But no
derelicts!' Jean had surely known about the Sargasso Sea before, with
its entrapping weed and becalmed wrecks. But if not, she certainly
heard of it now. And the image was fixed in her mind of a bar: a
place where sea and air conspired to stop you, to prevent passage
from the West Indies to England, from England to the West Indies.

On 6 March, about midnight, they passed Dominica, and saw it
lying in the moonlight. But they didn't go there yet. First they had
a week on Martinique; then another week on St Lucia, where Jean
had had a happy time at her Uncle Acton's wedding so long ago.

Now Acton was dead, and his widow, pretty Evelina, had come
back to St Lucia with her two daughters, Lily and Monica. (Their
son, Don, was dead too, having mysteriously shot himself at the age
of eighteen, according to Jean.) The Lockharts, at least Jean's branch
of them, seem generally to have been bad at making or keeping
money ('there's something wrong with our family. We're soft or lazy
or something,' Norah says in *Mackenzie*); and Aunt Ina and her
daughters were poor. They had taken jobs running the Hotel St
Antoine outside Castries. Intelligent Lily did the accounts, pretty,
practical Monica dealt with the guests, and Aunt Ina was the
manageress, 'for she knew a lot about real French Creole cooking.'

Jean and Leslie stayed at the hotel, of course. Jean saw more of
Monica now than of strange, awkward Lily, who went for long
lonely walks at night, and edited a little magazine in which she wrote
all the stories herself. But Lily would come to England, and would
become the member of the family with whom Jean got on best. Now
she said that she liked Lily's magazine, though Leslie could 'see no
merit' in it, and indeed it was sadly amateurish to English eyes. Jean's
mind cast a transforming glow, like this one, over most things to do
with her home, compounded of nostalgia, loyalty and self-protection.
But Lily's magazine — like the *Dominica Herald* articles Jean would

parody in 'Fishy Waters' — was a reminder of the thin and narrow soil from which she came; and out of which she somehow, single-handedly, made the narrow but rich art of her novels.

The hotel was comfortable and attractive, and Jean was happy there. One afternoon when she asked for tea the tray was brought up by a woman dressed in the old fashion — the bright long dress, the *foulard* and *madras* of the *gwan' wobe* (*grande robe*) of the French Antilles. It was, Jean said, 'the past majestically walking in.'

But even here there were too many people around, and especially too many people she knew. She couldn't work 'until we can get quite by ourselves and do what we like when we like,' Leslie said, and she was 'feeling the urge.' So 'we're off.' On a Tuesday afternoon towards the end of March they arrived at last in Roseau.

One of the first things Jean did was to write to her dear Good Mother. Things were changing: the nuns were in a new convent, and there was talk of their having to leave altogether. But Mother Mount Calvary was still there, and warmly welcoming. 'My dear Gwen,' she replied,

> What a surprise! Welcome to Dominica. Oh! yes, come at 4 o'clock this afternoon.
> How could I forget you, Gwen?
> Yours affecly
> M Mt Calvary

It was a sad meeting, Jean felt. Mother Mount Calvary kissed her very affectionately, but as soon as she stopped smiling 'her face looked old and sombre.' Almost all the other nuns Jean had known were gone. Two were dead; Mother Sacred Heart, who had influenced her so much, had fallen ill and gone back to England years before. Then suddenly in the face of one of the nuns Jean saw an expression she remembered: 'It was the little Irish nun whom I'd caught looking at herself in the barrel of water.' She would put this little nun into *Wide Sargasso Sea*: 'We have no looking-glass in the dormitory, once I saw the new young nun from Ireland looking at herself in a cask of water, smiling to see if her dimples were still there.' But there were no dimples now. 'She looked a frightened old lady.'

In the Good Mother's office there was, Jean saw, only one photograph: of her own father. (He'd been a doctor to the convent, perhaps a benefactor.) When she left, sad and relieved to get away, she walked into the Anglican graveyard nearby and found his grave. It was very neglected, overgrown with weeds, the Celtic cross her mother had so proudly put up knocked over. 'Well there I sat and wept for the past,' she wrote. Her father, she felt, was utterly forgotten, except by herself and the nuns. No hospital was named after him, not even a ward; no one remembered his kindness to the poor, no one tended his grave. Greedy new tropical life had grown up over him, as it did over everything in Dominica. His life had been, in the patois, *temps perdi*: wasted time, lost labour.

Jean was unhappy in Roseau. It seemed to her very changed from the pretty wooden town she remembered. Everything looked shrunken and shabby. She was very glad when one of her mother's friends offered them her estate on the other side of the island for a nominal rent. It was called Hampstead — the only thing about it Jean didn't like, with its reminder of England. It was very remote and hard to reach: two and a half hours by motor launch, four by fisherman's rowboat, which Jean and Leslie had to take when they missed the launch by a few minutes. But that suited her. 'The wonderful thing is to wake up and know that nobody can get at you — nobody!' she wrote to Evelyn Scott. She had been feeling 'awfully tired'; but Hampstead was 'a beautiful place to die in', and she was very happy. 'Jean is working again,' Leslie wrote to Anne. 'She is very well and is simply loving the place.'

They stayed at Hampstead for six weeks. There was little to do but read, write, sunbathe, swim — and drink rum. They were driven round: to the Falls, the Freshwater Lake, the Sulphur Spring; one day to the Carib Quarter at Salybia. They relaxed. Leslie began to look better than Jean had ever seen him. Dominica poured sun and rain on them as lavishly as ever. The Atlantic side of the island was very different from the Caribbean side where Jean had grown up: flatter, to her eyes less beautiful. But still very beautiful. And because it was different, not so painful. 'I was at home and not at home,' she said.

Yet very soon, of course, reality intruded. 'Several years steady drinking hasn't made me calm about cockroaches,' she told Evelyn. And even in the wilds of Dominica there was no escaping people. Not far from Hampstead were two other estates owned by Europeans. Naturally everyone knew of their arrival straight away; and very soon they were asked to lunch by the ladies of both places.

The lady of Pointe Baptiste Estate was the redoubtable Elma Napier, Dominica's 'first white lady' in the 1930s and long after. Everything about Elma Napier would rub Jean the wrong way. She was a famous hostess and a great organiser (in the forties she was even elected to the Caribbean legislature); she presumed to love Dominica, although she'd only arrived a few years ago. Worst of all, she was 'by way of being literary'. Over the next years she would publish two novels and two volumes of autobiography; but when Jean and Leslie met her one of her novels had just been declined — by Hamish Hamilton.

Naturally she had them both to lunch 'double quick'. She was nice to Leslie, Jean said; but very different to her. 'Tomahawk in hand, smile on face'; and 'I could see that she thought it all my fault' about her novel. . . .

This can't have been serious — not even Jean can really have thought that Elma Napier could blame *her* for the rejection of her novel. But by now this was (as Julia had said to Mr Horsfield) how she was. She couldn't bear Mrs Napier — but she couldn't bear to be ignored by her either. And I'm sure Mrs Napier did ignore her. It was Leslie she wanted to talk to, and Jean was always shy and silent in company. Very likely she wasn't even introduced as a writer: Elma Napier never mentioned meeting Jean Rhys, even later when Jean was famous, and much discussed on Dominica. Perhaps Jean feared that she hadn't heard of Jean Rhys, or would despise her books if she had (both of which were very probable). So she kept silent, perhaps about her books, at any rate in general, and left the talking to Leslie. But she hated being ignored; and so she hated Mrs Napier. When the Napiers left for a visit to England she wrote 'Thank God.'

The other couple, the Ashpittels, were slightly better: they were planters rather than writers, and Mrs Ashpittel was 'much milder' than Mrs Napier. But Jean was clearly entering a trough of insecurity ('I agreed with everything she said God help me — and was very miserable all next day'). 'Jean hasn't been very well lately,' Leslie was saying towards the end. 'The heat has been rather too much for her.' Of course it wasn't just the heat, and she wasn't just 'not very well'. The risks she had foreseen — as always — had overwhelmed her. The end of everything she remembered, the pushing out of the 'old whites' and the coming of the new: these were some more of the important lessons she learned for *Wide Sargasso Sea*, but now they plunged her into paranoia.

She became convinced, first of all, that the servants disliked her. They liked Leslie, not her, and if they were nice to her it was only for his sake. One in particular she distrusted: Dora, daughter of the estate overseer, Theodore. Leslie thought Dora was splendid: she waited at table so deftly, every morning she put little earthenware bowls of fresh flowers out on the verandah. . . But in Dora Jean saw an enemy. One day she was stung badly by something: and surprised Dora 'grinning' with delight and satisfaction.*

---

*She put Theodore into 'Temps Perdi', which she began now, as 'Nicholas', and Dora as 'Myra'. This was, perhaps, how the treacherous servant in *Wide Sargasso Sea*, who abandons Pierre to the fire, came to be called Myra.

This was mostly, but perhaps not entirely, her imagination. Her paranoia was to magnify hostility, not to invent it. She was one of the old whites, after all, and I think she behaved like one. She saw dislike not only in her own servants but in all the native people of her island; and probably some of this was true too. But now her sense of rejection began to spiral.

She wasn't allowed to remember, she felt. If she asked for a fruit she had liked or a road she had travelled as a child, people would look 'annoyed', 'offended', 'disbelieving'. 'There's no road there,' their driver would say (just as Baptiste says to Rochester in *Wide Sargasso Sea*). 'Maybe just a track a horse could follow, but no road for a car.' And Jean refused to believe him. Now this *was* paranoia. Perhaps occasionally he didn't want to bother; that was 'typical Dominica'. But everything, even tarmacadam and stone, breaks and crumbles and disappears in Dominica in a year or two — and she had been away thirty. She must have known that. But she was blocking out facts and knowledge. She couldn't bear that the road no longer be there; he must be lying.

The climax of her fight against facts came in this way, over a road. Jean suddenly had a 'splendid idea': she and Leslie would cross the island on the old Imperial Road, which she remembered being opened with such pomp and ceremony. Theodore was against it, and Leslie was very doubtful. But the more they shook their heads the more determined she was to go; and finally they gave in.

At first everything went well, and it seemed to her that they were setting out on a 'wonderful adventure which would certainly end happily.' But of course the road was soon no longer a road, but a steep mountainous track. Jean tripped and fell and could no longer walk without limping; mules had to be rented. But as soon as she climbed on to her mule it threw her off over its head. Only the guides' look of contempt roused her from crying — just as in *Wide Sargasso Sea* only the thought that the black people are laughing at her spurs Annette to leave her burning house.

There was not the smallest trace left of the Imperial Road. And now it began to rain — a proper Dominican downpour. Leslie 'didn't turn or look at me but I could see from his back what he was feeling....' Still somehow they got through: only to find that their driver had wanted to return to Roseau without them. Jean said to herself 'That's how they are. That's how they are' — just like Aunt Cora, when Myra leaves Pierre to die in the fire ('That does not surprise me at all'). And even when they were safe in bed that night she refused to believe that the Imperial Road could simply have disappeared. No: again she'd been cheated and lied to.

By now it was well known on the island that Gwen Rees Williams was home on a visit. And back in Roseau before leaving, her 'outside' relations, Owen's children, came to see her. Ena, the eldest, came twice; and the other two, Mona and Oscar, came too.

Now it was Jean's turn to be generous and understanding. Kindness to one's illegitimate half-black relations is a touchstone for her in both her West Indian novels, an infallible way of distinguishing the smug snobs and prancing hypocrites from brave and decent people. So now Leslie was impatient at their 'begging'; but she gave them presents and money, and even refused to be angry at Oscar when he was rude about the amount. She was especially kind to Ena, admiring her beautiful long hair, and making a fuss of her baby. She wanted very much, I think, to be like her father, who, when Ena had told him once that her name was Williams, had said 'Why not Rees Williams?' ('Illegitimate children wandering about all over the place, called by his name,' Aunt Hester says of Uncle Bo in *Voyage in the Dark*, '– called by his name if you please....') That was *most* un-Lockhart behaviour; and for decades after it white children were still made to cross the street when their illegitimate coloured relations were approaching.

The last thing Jean did before leaving Dominica was to visit Geneva, the old Lockhart estate, once more. Just recently, in the early thirties, the house had been burned down again; all that was left was fern- and creeper-covered ruins. It is an unlucky place, they say on the island. In this unlucky place Jean had been happy. But now? She stared at it, trying to remember 'the house, the garden, the honeysuckle and the jasmine and the tall fern trees.'

> But there was nothing, nothing. Nothing to look at. Nothing to say. Even the mounting stone had gone.

This word 'nothing' will echo and mount through *Wide Sargasso Sea* like a dirge. But in her novel Jean won't allow *nothing* this final victory. As Antoinette watches the Coulibri house burn she thinks: 'There would be nothing left but blackened walls and the mounting stone. That would always be left. That could not be stolen or burned.'

That is the last thing Jean learned, for both *Good Morning, Midnight* and *Wide Sargasso Sea*, from this return to Dominica: to wrest triumph out of disaster for her heroine in the story, and for herself in telling it. She did it by taking back the material for her last, great novel and for several stories. And she wrote about it in one of these stories, 'The Bishop's Feast'. For the narrator of 'The Bishop's Feast' hears that the nuns of her old convent are to be sent back to England, but that the old Mother Superior refuses to go. She returns to the town the day before they have to leave: and learns that Mother Mount Calvary has died that morning.

... I felt very sad, but also something like triumph, because in the end she had won. She had always done what she said she'd do. She had said she would never leave the island, and she hadn't.

This was Jean's fiction, not fact — at least in its timing, for Mother Mount Calvary died several months after her visit.* But fiction or fact, it contained an important new idea: that death itself could be a victory. That is the idea that lies behind the end of *Wide Sargasso Sea*.

From Dominica Leslie and Jean sailed to New York. They both loved New York — 'superlatively marvellous,' Leslie said; 'so alive', said Jean. They'd heard that Leslie's share of his father's estate was bigger than they'd expected — and they were being deliciously extravagant. Leslie planned a grand return home on the *Normandie*, Jean had all her teeth crowned and bought armfuls of expensive clothes. They lived in a charming 'very French' hotel near Washington Square, in a *suite* ('Up to the dizzy heights of the suite ...'). Of course it couldn't last, neither the mood nor the money. Leslie soon gave up the *Normandie* and took a cabin on the cheaper *Lafayette* instead. And Jean's gay and hectic mood moved to its inevitable crisis.

Evelyn Scott, who was back in New York, organised several parties for her. Jean said she was 'pleased and flattered', and enjoyed these parties 'more than I've enjoyed anything for years.' Perhaps, at first, that was true. But she couldn't cope with meeting so many people, and she started to drink to give herself courage. Later she would say that she hadn't been sober 'for one instant' in New York. During the last few days she knew herself that she was 'really ill', 'drinking a hell of a lot to keep me going.' Evelyn knew it too, and asked a doctor to see her; but it was too late. On her last night in New York she flew 'off the deep end', and had her almighty row with Evelyn. 'Once I got going old griefs and grievances overwhelmed me,' she wrote afterwards. 'I got that nightmare feeling of a scene which with slight variations had often happened — as it has, and I mixed it up with all the other scenes....' Evelyn had become what Stephan becomes to Marya at the end of *Quartet*: 'the symbol of everything that all her life had baffled and tortured her.'

God knows what she screamed at her; in these rages she was — like Marya with Stephan — devastatingly cruel. She apologised by

---

*Unfortunately Dominican church records don't make it clear whether or not she died on Dominica. Jean may well have made up that part too.

letter when she got home; but she was still trying to defend herself, and it was more an argument than an apology. And after a while Evelyn seems not to have replied. During the next years she had terrible troubles of her own: Jack Metcalfe had a nervous breakdown, and she had to work desperately hard to keep them afloat. Soon after her own life and career collapsed. In fact the rest of her life was uncannily like Jean's: dogged by poverty, neglect and paranoia. Some of it even happened near Jean in London, but neither of them knew it. They seem never to have met or written to one another again.

Jean spent most of the voyage home in her cabin, one foot 'the size of a house'. Evelyn apparently knew what had happened, and I think we can guess: she had injured it in a drunken fall, perhaps during their encounter. The week's rest seemed to cure it; but then it got 'suddenly worse again' (or perhaps she fell again), and she had to go to hospital and then a nursing home. This, too, would become a pattern.

She always hated nursing homes; in one of her last stories an old lady is harmed rather than cured in one, more by what happens to her there than by her age or illness. This first place was no exception. It was 'grim, clean, hard, cheerless, smug, smirking,' she said; and with her eye for the distilling detail: 'Here comes the nurse with one piece of bread and butter and a bit of cake yellow trimmed red cherry and black currant....' (like Anna's boarding-house meal, 'two slices of dark meat on one plate ... On the other plate a slice of bread and a lemon-cheese tart ...').

Clearly, she was no better. She tried to joke — 'persecution maniacs ... always have been and usually still are, the victims of persecution' — but failed. 'Of course they're called maniacs,' she said. 'It's part of the game Society plays — Let's Pretend that there is no such thing as this petty, leering, unsplendid cruelty, this damnable dropping of water in the same place for years....' And now a new idea appears: the idea that, in England especially, the most persecuted person of all is the *woman writer*. She dashed it down in the postscript of her last letter to Evelyn:

> I think that the anglo-saxon idea that you can be rude with impunity to any female who has written a book is utterly *damnable*. You come and have a look out of curiosity and then allow the freak to see what you think of her. It's only done of course to the more or less unsuccessful and only by anglo-saxons.
>
> Well my dear if it were my last breath I'd say HELL TO IT and — to the people who do it — ....

This idea – that a woman writer was a freak, and despised for her deformity – was getting very close to her most secret fears. It would become the heart of her paranoia: a sure sign, whenever it appeared, that she was in a trough of depression.

But there was another side to the pattern too, thank heaven: she sank very low, but she always shot up again. And now a better time was coming. ('So there's a good time coming for the ladies, is there?' says Petronella's landlord, ' – a good time coming for the girls? About time too.') It had (as usual) to do with money.

Jean's family were convinced that Leslie had inherited sixteen thousand pounds, perhaps even twenty thousand pounds, and that 'a year later' it was all gone. 'Never did I hear the end of *that* expensive holiday,' Jean said. Sixteen to twenty thousand pounds was probably what Leslie and his sister had inherited *together*, and his share was less than half of it. But of course even (say) eight thousand pounds was a good deal; and most of it does seem to have disappeared in Dominica and New York.

Leslie's family was through with 'lending' him any more money, as we know. But Jean's life was full of benefactors – her unusual need drew unusual help, as though by magic. There'd been Lancelot, there was Leslie himself; and now there was his sister.

Phyllis Tilden Smith had inherited much more than Leslie, because of his borrowings. She was single, self-denying, extremely tender-hearted; she was also very fond of her brother, and she felt guilty to have had more when she needed less. Leslie went straight to her when he came home: and she offered to pay his rent, his telephone, many of his expenses, as long as he needed. Jean wasn't to know; she wasn't doing it for Jean, but for Leslie. And probably Jean never did know. As with John, she probably never asked. But for the rest of their life together they were able to live slightly more comfortably. Especially now, when perhaps there was also something left of Leslie's own money. They found a beautiful flat; they bought new furniture for it; in August or September 1936 they moved in.

Number 22 Paultons House was a top flat in a pretty Chelsea square which had been a garden in the seventeenth century. At last Jean had a chance to make her surroundings beautiful, and she took it. She was good at beauty when she had some money. The furniture at Paultons Square was attractive, the beds were covered with soft pale green sheets, the walls hung with sketches of her by various artists. A daily woman came in to clean. For once Jean could have everything around her 'right', close at last to an imagined ideal; and

the boring part of it, the housework, was done by somebody else. In these — rare — circumstances she took a housewifely pride in the flat; and she was happier than she'd been for a long time.

It was in this happier mood that a new friend found her. Eliot Bliss was a novelist too, and also from the West Indies.* She'd recently published two autobiographical novels, the second, *Luminous Isle*, about Jamaica in the 1920s. Eliot had first heard of Jean in the late twenties and much admired her books. In New York in 1936 she'd met the poet Horace Gregory, who was such an admirer of Jean's that he was supposed to have read *Voyage in the Dark* to the assembled pupils of a girl's school — a daring thing to do in the thirties, and probably not easy even now. Gregory must have met Jean at one of Evelyn's parties; he gave Eliot an introduction to her.

Already in 1936 Jean kept her number out of the general telephone directory; but Eliot eventually discovered it and rang up. She was invited to visit; and after that again. 'Jean didn't like many people,' Eliot says, 'she shut herself away from them. But she liked me.' In the winter she went back to America; but during the summer of 1937 she saw Jean every fortnight. The friendship was short: she never saw her again, though they wrote occasionally until the war, and then again later. But Eliot's glimpse of Jean in 1937 is important. Without it our picture would be different, and darker.

Like many people who drink too much, Jean had times when she was fatter than usual. She hated herself fat; it was part of the depression of which her drinking was both effect and cause. (She'd had a plump period, for instance, in the bad year of 1935.) But the woman Eliot Bliss met was thin and elegant. She was always beautifully dressed; her hair was white, and fashionably 'blued'. Eliot couldn't guess how old she was. Leslie said he didn't know, because Jean didn't tell the truth about her age.

Eliot knew that Jean had very little to do with literary people — she'd gone to only one literary party in her London life, Jean said, the one where she'd met Rosamond Lehmann. But to Eliot she unbent and was friendly. She didn't talk about her life, because she'd written about that; nor about her family. But she talked about her books, and about Eliot's books, and a lot about the West Indies. 'She wasn't a bit gloomy,' Eliot says; rather she was the optimist of the two, and wrote 'Great is truth and it shall prevail' in Eliot's copy

---

*Eliot Bliss, born in Jamaica in 1903. *Sarabande* was published in 1931, *Luminous Isle* in 1934. Both have recently been republished in Virago paperback.

of *Postures*. She cooked West Indian suppers, at which they drank a great deal of wine; when they were both drunk they would write Jean's credo in Latin on the wall: *Magna est veritas et praevalet*.

Jean's capacity for drink was enormous, much larger than Eliot's, who was always ill after these sessions. Sometimes they would get so drunk they would end up on the floor, and Leslie would have to put them both to bed. Sometimes, too, in these very drunken moments Eliot would see Jean's darker side. Her infectious gaiety would pass, and she would fall into a rage. She would rail at Eliot for being an 'unfeeling aristocrat', accuse her of belonging to the snobs and prigs and respectable people. She would, Eliot says – using Jean's own words – 'go off the deep end,' much as she'd done with Evelyn. But here was the key to their friendship, and to why it ended only because Eliot left for America: *Eliot didn't mind*. 'Jean didn't mean it,' she says. 'She wasn't attacking me, she was attacking the world. I'd seen it before, in other artists.'

This was the sort of understanding Jean needed. It was always and only this sort of person who could be her friend: the sort who didn't take to heart, who didn't disapprove, who almost didn't notice her bad behaviour. Like Serge Rubin in *Good Morning, Midnight*, when Sasha tells him 'in a loud, aggressive voice' to go out and get a bottle of brandy:

> This is where he starts getting hold of me, Serge. He doesn't accept the money or refuse it – he ignores it. He blots out what I have said and the way I said it. He ignores it as if it had never been, and I know that, for him, it has never been. He is thinking of something else.

Of course this was easier to do if you were only a friend and not a lover or a husband; almost no one who was really close to Jean could preserve this loving detachment. But those who could saw the best side of her. 'Jean was really very sweet-natured,' they say. 'Except when she was drunk she had a very sweet temperament.' They saw the sweetness as the real Jean, the hatred as the drink; while others felt the hatred was real, the sweetness a mask which drink dislodged. There is no way of telling which was the truth; perhaps there was no truth. *You made the truth*: if you believed in her goodness she could be good; but if you judged her wicked – she was. Her torment was that she feared her judges were right; and that then she couldn't forgive herself, as her friends did.

Eliot Bliss was typical of these friends. She knew Jean liked her because she'd 'come to pay homage', and that 'really she wasn't interested in anyone but herself.' But she paid much more attention to the good things about her – her beauty and gaiety, her loyalty and kindness, her capacity to enjoy simple things. So the good things came out; and like the bad ones they were always the same. She wouldn't say a bad word about a friend, and wouldn't let Eliot say one either; she listened kindly and unshockably to Eliot's troubles. All the friends of her old age will recognise these qualities; just as all her judges will recognise the others.

One more thing Eliot saw very positively: Jean's marriage. During the time she knew them, she is certain, Jean and Leslie were happy together. 'They loved each other,' she says firmly. She saw them have rows — when Jean drank some wine Leslie was keeping for a special occasion, for example. But when he drove Eliot home he would speak very fondly about Jean. 'He adored her,' Eliot says, 'and understood and admired her work completely.... I think she was happier with him than with anyone she had ever known.'

She knew them only briefly, at a particularly good moment, and there was much that she did not see. *But she was also right.* Leslie did love Jean, and did everything he could for her. And Jean was sweet and loving to him when she was sober, and she *was* happier with him than with anyone she'd ever known before. It's just that she couldn't be happy with anyone, except for brief moments.

In the Paultons Square flat Jean even had a little room to write in. Later she would spend years and years longing for just such a room of her own, but when she had it, it oppressed her. 'I've even got a little room with a desk in it to write my next "masterpiece" on,' she wrote in the first days after moving in. 'All I've got to do is start it go on with it and then finish it — Nothing!' I'm sure she did work here on and off, on diaries and stories; but her 'next masterpiece' wasn't coming. Finally, in November 1937, Leslie got the money (perhaps from his sister) for the usual solution: Jean went to Paris.

I think she probably already had the main idea and the main character (other than the heroine) of *Good Morning, Midnight*: the hopeful young man who picks Sasha up, looking for money and comfort, but whom she tries to use for her plan of revenge. Part of that character was, once again, John. In the 'Chevalier of the Place Blanche' he had drawn himself as a man who lives on women; and René has John's Foreign Legion past, and Stephan Zelli's naturalness, secretiveness and certainty. But if there was another real part of René I think she had that too.

She'd been back to Paris, by herself, several times. She'd begun *Mackenzie* there between 1929 and '30; she'd rushed back from there to begin *Voyage* in early '31; I think she may have been there again in something like the English hospital which led to 'Outside the

Machine'. Perhaps after that the visits slowed down or even stopped, because there wasn't enough money; this may have been a factor in her not writing 'a word' between *Voyage* and now. Whenever she was alone in Paris she was always being approached by 'unknowns', even picked up by them; that had started even while she was still with John, and it went on even while she was with Leslie. But I think three encounters in particular went into René.

One was with someone who, when he heard the poem *Pour un coeur qui s'ennuie, oh le chant de la pluie*, said to her: 'There you are. An omen. You'll go back to London.' And yet, Jean said, he'd never been to London... (from him René's superstitiousness, and the funny, absurd conversations about 'the untapped goldmine just across the Channel'?). A second was someone she didn't know, but who told her the stories of the man whose wife shoots herself, and of the man who fails to visit his dying lover, which she used to such mysterious and chilling effect in her novel. But only the third has a name, and a definite date.

In early March 1930 Jean had a letter from someone whom she'd met in Paris, and who seems to have come to London for the first time. She has already invited him to tea 'in memory of the bottle of Chianti'; now he invites her to 'a Cocktail', 'in memory of many Pernots!...' The gaiety, the gallantry (he also invites her to dinner and a 'show'), the uncertain spelling all sound like René. And the name is foreign, perhaps Arab or North African (which I feel René may be): *A. Sawi*. Jean kept a few letters like this, from strangers who never appear again. Some are fan letters. But others, I think, she kept because they were connected to her writing.* I think she

---

*They are from three people besides Sawi. One is Simon Segal, the painter on whom she based Serge Rubin, also in *Good Morning, Midnight*; I discuss him next. Another is Toni de Boissière, a Jamaican friend of Esmond Romilly's, whom she drew on for Hans in 'Tigers Are Better-Looking'. Jean kept several of Toni's letters. One began 'Ma chérie, my dear'; another said (of Jamaica, where he had returned) 'This country has been very unlucky for me. It gave me the plague first of all and no sooner am I free of that they try to kill me....' (He'd had a car accident.) Compare Hans's letter : 'Mein Lieb, Mon Cher, My Dear, Amigo,' and 'I came to London with high hopes, but all I got out of it was a broken leg and enough sneers to last me for the next thirty years....' The third was a Hamish Hamilton colleague of Leslie's called Nigel Sligh, who wrote in 1938 praising Jean's novels ('you are a pure artist') and thanking her for dinner. Despite the praise I wonder whether Sligh wasn't at least one model for 'Baron Mumtael' in 'Kikimora'. The mood of the story is so paranoid that what he was really saying would hardly register; he was English and literary, and Jean would be afraid of him.

Finally, Jean also kept a letter she herself had written to Leslie from Paris,

kept 'A. Sawi's' because he'd given her the idea for *Good Morning, Midnight*.

Now, on this 1937 visit, she gathered up much of the novel's background. The World Exhibition was being held in Paris, for example; she'd make extraordinary use of that as part of the novel's dominating imagery — as though it had been made for her own particular obsessions, like (a little later) *Jane Eyre*. But there were a few more human encounters that would go into the book too.

The most important was with the original of 'Serge Rubin'. Jean may have met him already, but she went to see him again now. He is Sasha's only real friend in *Good Morning, Midnight*: the only person who can make her remember 'the touch of the human hand'.

The original of 'Serge Rubin' was called Simon Segal. He was a Russian Jew, eight years younger than Jean. He'd trained as an engineer, but came to France in 1925 to be a painter. He had a hard life. He was very poor, and had kept himself alive at first by working in a factory; he was given to Russian despair and Jewish melancholy. His painting was simple and sensual, like Jean's prose. He painted nothing easy or fashionable, just poor people, and scenes of war. He was an exile and a rebel, like Jean; like her he put his private vision into his art with single-minded fury, and was never likely to sell. Jean liked him as much as Sasha liked Serge Rubin; and she put every detail of their friendship into *Good Morning, Midnight*.

She bought from him the painting she describes in the novel: *Old Man with Banjo*. They arranged to meet for her to pay him, just as in *Good Morning, Midnight*, and just as in *Good Morning, Midnight*, Simon Segal didn't arrive. They did have a mutual friend: Delmar in the novel, Delmotte in reality. Jean gave him the money, just as in the novel; and just as in the novel, Simon Segal wrote her a letter of thanks and apology. He didn't get to the Gare du Nord either — but because he arrived too late, like Serge Rubin, not because he didn't come at all. He too hoped that she would like '*mon petit bonhomme jouant au banjo*': '*Peut-être vous donnera-t-il du courage. Ne désespérez pas.*' In the middle of his letter he wrote: '*Je vous serre la main,*' and signed: '*Votre ami, Simon Segal.*' In *Good Morning, Midnight*, when Sasha and Serge Rubin part, Jean wrote:

---

probably in the early 1930s. In it she says she 'can't find the prospectus', and will just go to Fontainebleau and look. There seemed no reason to have kept this letter — until I remembered the opening line of 'Outside the Machine': 'The big clinic near Versailles was run on strictly English lines. . . .' Perhaps she'd been in such a place near the other famous royal palace, and kept this letter as a reminder.

Then he gives my hand a long, hard shake and says '*Amis*'.

When he shakes my hand like that and says '*Amis*' I feel very happy....

The war, and Jean's life after it, ended that friendship. It was as brief as her other friendships of the thirties, with Evelyn Scott, Rosamond Lehmann, Eliot Bliss. But even including the chorus girls of *Voyage in the Dark* — and only excepting perhaps, La Grosse Fifi — 'Serge Rubin' is the best-loved friend in Jean's fiction. She'd put her love for her father and for Lancelot into *Voyage*; she would put her love for black people, and for her Great Aunt Jane, into *Wide Sargasso Sea*. Her feeling for Simon Segal was baulked (and perhaps ill-expressed) in life, like the others; but like the others she expressed it in a novel.*

Jean had another friend in Paris, of course, one of the few who'd lasted a long time: Germaine Richelot. But that friendship probably ended now. Jean had already quarrelled once with Germaine over money, and I fear she did so again; for in *Good Morning, Midnight* there is a glimpse of a friend called Sidonie, who lends Sasha the money to go to Paris, and Sasha is very resentful. She hates Sidonie for saying 'I can't bear to see you like this' ('Half-shutting her eyes and smiling the smile which means: "She's getting to look old. She drinks."'). Her paranoia now includes her friend: 'I can see Sidonie carefully looking round for an hotel just like this one. She imagines that it's my atmosphere. God, it's an insult when you come to think about it!' Sidonie has offered her money, and she has taken it. But she doesn't feel helped, only victimised: 'I had not seen this woman for months and then she swooped down on me.'

There is the French name; there is the lending of money and the finding of a Paris hotel; there is old and honest friendship ('We've known each other too long to stand on ceremony,' Sidonie says). And already in 1920 Germaine had 'lectured' Jean on 'the evils of alcohol'. Every detail of the 'Serge Rubin' episode happened; so did every detail of Sasha's and Enno's marriage. I'm sure 'Sidonie' was *someone*; and who else but rich, kind, candid Germaine Richelot?

It's very sad, and predictable, that Jean's longest and best friendship should end like this; and then be irretrievable, because war placed between them a vaster evil. Soon — probably during the war or just after it — Jean wrote very warmly about the first days of their friendship, but she never published 'The Richelots of Paris'. Even if

---

*Simon Segal married and went to live near Cherbourg. There, fortunately, he survived the war, though I don't know whether Jean ever knew that. His paintings hang in several French museums, including the Musée d'Art Moderne in Paris. He died before Jean, probably in the early seventies.

Germaine survived the war* she couldn't have read this grateful, debt-discharging piece. Not until 1979, in *Smile Please*, were Jean's happy memories of Paris in 1919 published. Only if Germaine outlived her — and they were (Jean said) the same age — could she have known that she was, after all, fondly remembered.


The last months in Paultons Square were no longer so happy. Jean and Leslie had one of their most spectacular rows here, when she not only hit him but threw his typewriter out of the window — from several storeys up, so that it was lucky no one was passing below. And towards the end, I think, her paranoia was raging: as she devastatingly describes in 'Kikimora'. When the 'small, fair, plump' Baron Mumtael visits, Elsa's hands shake with nervousness, she plunges 'deep into the scorn of his pale blue eyes.' When he praises her cooking she pretends she's bought it all ready-made. She has 'repeated whiskies', until she has the courage to speak to him 'belligerently' ('My *dear* Elsa...,' says her husband Stephen.) The Baron loves England and hates 'the spoilt female'; when Elsa's cat scratches him he repeats again and again 'One can't be too careful with the scratches of a she-cat' — and each time Elsa says ('breathing deeply') that Kikimora is a male. When he leaves she goes to the bedroom and cuts to pieces the dinner suit she has been wearing, saying 'I'm destroying my feminine charm.'

It's like her lie about the food — she will *not* please such a man, she will not decorate herself for him (just like Sasha in *Good Morning, Midnight* — 'A little pride, a little dignity at the end, in the name of God... I will not grimace and posture before these people any longer.') 'Kikimora' is a perfect example of the self-destructiveness of the heroine's revenges: the way that, however much she means to hurt someone else, the only person she *can* hurt is herself. And of course Baron Mumtael has mocked her 'feminine charm' and hated it; in destroying it, therefore, she is not really defying him at all, but accepting his judgement.... 'Kikimora' is a sinister little gem of a story, in which everything is the opposite of what it seems. That

---

*Jean never learned what happened to the Richelots — who were, of course, half-Jewish — apart from the ominous fact that the Nazis had taken over 3 rue Rabelais as their headquarters during the war. But she hoped they'd survived, because the last time she'd seen Germaine she'd seemed forewarned. I haven't been able to find any trace of Germaine or her family either. Happily, however, their names do not appear among those of French Jews sent to concentration camps in Germany. We too can hope that they escaped.

is perfectly pictured in Elsa's and Stephen's exchange when the Baron has gone, which is at the same time exactly observed, utterly real: 'He was so nice, wasn't he?' she says, and 'I didn't notice that he wasn't nice,' he replies.

Very likely Jean was low and drinking hard in the summer of 1938 because she was writing *Good Morning, Midnight*. She said all sorts of things about this, as usual; but she must have written this most painful of her novels between about November 1937, when she got back from Paris, and about September 1938, when she moved into other writing. Indeed these years just before the war, 1938 and '39, were years of almost compulsive writing, as though she felt the abyss of the war ahead. Maryvonne remembers her 'enormous need' to write at times; and this was one of them. She wrote mostly in the mornings; and not in that little room with its waiting desk, but mostly in bed, 'the whole bed ... strewn with pages.'

With the 'irresistible wish' to write *Good Morning, Midnight* upon her Jean began fast, and thought (as she always did) that she could do it quickly. But 'it wouldn't come right,' especially the last chapters. She wrote and rewrote; she 'really worked hard', and 'forced myself to it'. It began to obsess her, 'the words repeating themselves over and over again in my head till I thought I should go mad.' For weeks she couldn't get the ending. She had a time of such despair that she tore up the book, her contract, and even Simon Segal's painting. She drank very heavily; 'lately,' she wrote in her notebook, 'I'm drunk mostly all the time.' But when she was drunk (she said later) 'the Man in the Dressing gown appeared from Heaven knows where to supply the inevitable end.'

It was done; but of course she was 'worried' about it. All the time Leslie was typing it I'm sure she 'fiddled about' and made (minute) alterations, as she'd done with *Voyage in the Dark*. Finally, 'it was sent off while I was asleep' – that is, Leslie simply took it. And there was 'an argument' – that is, a terrible row. While that was still going on Michael Sadleir of Constable rang to say he liked it; 'so I didn't worry about it any more. I let it go.' Or rather – she felt at the time – *it* let *her* go. 'It had slipped away from me, I hope not too soon. Instead of that I was back in the West Indies living my life as a child all over again....'

At first returning to her childhood was like returning to warmth and light, as in *Voyage in the Dark*; and it relieved her very much to pour out her memories 'from the heart', without having to force them into the shape of a novel. But soon these memories became dark and painful. They led her, as we shall see, not away from self-knowledge but deeper into it.

★      ★      ★

There is little trace of Jean's life outside writing in 1938 and 1939.*

She and Leslie left Paultons Square in mid-1938 and moved to Taplow, near Maidenhead; we can only guess why — perhaps Leslie's money really did run out now, or perhaps his sister decided the rent was too high. Most of what we know is about other people.

John, for instance. As another war approached the world again found a place for his obstinate, anarchic idealism. In 1936 he had spoken at a Congress of Writers Against Fascism; that was a sign of recognition, and it brought more. He was made a correspondent for the *Daily Herald*. In 1937 he went to Spain, where he met (he said) Hemingway and La Pasionaria; in 1939 to Denmark and to Germany itself, just before the outbreak of war. There (he said) he was arrested by the Gestapo, but got away and back to Holland. The Germans would have saved themselves a lot of trouble if they'd hung on to him. He was about to turn his best and worst qualities — his restlessness, his recklessness, his contempt for any rule — to the best account of his life, in service of the Dutch Resistance.

Maryvonne, of course, was growing up. There was that 'antagonism between her and Jean — more than 'the usual', as Jean said — but they had good times together too. The last few summer holidays before the war were the best ones, because Jean and Leslie were not quite so poor. They had a car, and took Maryvonne to Scotland, Ireland and Wales; once Jean arranged a wonderful ballet party for her. Maryvonne understood something of Jean's need to write now; she even helped with *Good Morning, Midnight*, sorting out the scrambled pages, counting the number of words.

Maryvonne also remembers Jean taking her to see her sisters Minna and Brenda just before the war. She was having a little more contact with them now: perhaps because they were in almost more trouble than she, so that they had less chance to feel contempt, and she more to feel sympathy.

*She did make one friend in these years: Phyllis Shand Allfrey, who was a poet, writer, and left-wing politician, and who also came from Dominica. Phyllis was a grand-daughter of Dr Henry Nicholls, the senior doctor in Dr Rees Williams's time; Jean's childhood friend Willie Nicholls was her uncle. She was twenty-five years younger than Jean, and Jean always called her and her husband Robert 'my young friends'. She returned to Dominica in the 1950s, became (briefly) Minister of Labour, and wrote a good novel about the island, *The Orchid House*. She corresponded faithfully with Jean in her last years, and regularly sent her the Dominica *Star*, which she and Robert edited. She died in 1986.

During these years just before the war Phyllis came to know Jean well, and learned a good deal about her life and nature. But in her old-fashioned Dominican way she wouldn't talk about it. So we must do without a third novelist's glimpse of Jean in the 1930s.

What had happened was that Minna — stiff, proud Minna — had developed Parkinson's disease. It is not clear exactly when her illness began. When she came to see Jean off to Dominica in early 1936 she seemed perfectly all right, but now she was rapidly becoming bedridden, her body wasted, her limbs shaking and paralysed. Brenda's brief independent life was over, having lasted only three or four years. At one point she'd had a job and earned some money, but now she had to ask Miss Woolgar — *Mackenzie*'s Miss Wyatt — to come (or come back) and help her; and she returned to her old, hard routine of nursing a dying woman.

There were only two members of the older generation left now, Jean's Aunt Clarice ('Hester' in *Voyage in the Dark*), and her Uncle Neville Williams ('Uncle Griffiths' in *Mackenzie*). Her father had died so young, in his mid-fifties; but both his brother and sister lived to their nineties. Neville Williams would die in 1944, aged ninety-four; and now, in December 1938, Aunt Clarice died at ninety-one. She had been 'the greatest character of them all,' Dorothy Rees Williams says: clever, amusing, independent. But she lived her last years, and probably died, even more alone than Auntie B. The Rees Williamses had very little luck. Most of them seemed to sink down in the world from the false promise of ease in the West Indies, almost though not quite as utterly as Jean. The women almost all did. Owen did, working only unreliably throughout the thirties, later becoming ill with bronchitis and hardly working at all; depending upon his wife until he died. Only Edward (and finally Brenda, as we'll see) escaped genteel poverty. Jean saw herself as utterly opposite and outside her family, speaking only for herself, and they fervently agreed. But in a way she was also speaking for them — indeed for all colonials coming 'home', after years or generations, to an uncushioned, unprivileged life in England. Perhaps her father was the luckiest after all, dying young and never leaving the island.... That would become one of her leitmotifs in *Wide Sargasso Sea*: to die is a better fate, says Annette, better than to be 'abandoned, lied about, helpless'. Her family would think that exaggerated, hysterical; but in a way it was their epitaph too.

What Jean was doing in 1938 and 1939 was *writing*. Often Leslie had had to encourage her to write, often he felt she was dreaming (or drinking) her life away; but not now. She wrote *Good Morning, Midnight* in a year; as soon as that was finished she began to pour out childhood memories. She had already done this in the early thirties, and put many of them into *Voyage in the Dark*. Some of those had been bad enough — the memory of trying to die in the sun, for example, or the sense of being doomed to dislike and disapproval. But since then she had become an alcoholic; her control over her personality, like Julia's and Sasha's, had broken down. And — whether as cause or effect — the memories that flooded in now were still darker: a recurring nightmare; her many fears, of insects, of punishment, of Meta; the old man who mentally seduced her; her mother beating her, her mother stopping beating her and saying 'You'll never be like other people. . . .' Some of these she would use twenty or thirty or forty years later; some she would never use at all. But some she used straight away. For I think she tried now to write not just one but two novels about Dominica.

Later she said, of course, many different things about when she had first had the idea for *Wide Sargasso Sea*. Sometimes she spoke as thought it had never occurred to her until 1957. Sometimes she said she'd wanted to defend the 'poor Creole lunatic' when she arrived in England at sixteen and read *Jane Eyre*; sometimes that she'd read it as a child, and had had *Wide Sargasso Sea* 'lying inside me' ever since. I think this last is the nearest to the truth. But what is indisputably true is this: that in 1945 she had a novel 'half-finished', and that this was *Le Revenant*, which was a first version of *Wide Sargasso Sea*.

I think that the idea stirred in her whenever she read (or even thought of) *Jane Eyre*. And that this happened again now — and for the first time took a clear shape in her mind. One day after *Good Morning, Midnight* had been published Leslie gave her *Jane Eyre*: and suddenly — so he told Anne, and so Jean must have told him — she had 'a marvellous idea'. She was very excited. She wrote *Le Revenant*, or half of it, very quickly, and Leslie typed what she had written. He liked it; even she felt that this 'might be the one book I've written that's much use.' But then something happened. They had a furious row; and to punish Leslie she took his typescript and burned it in the grate.

The punishment worked. Usually Leslie covered up Jean's most destructive behaviour, if he could; but he was so upset by this that he told his daughter. Of course it had punished Jean herself even more. It was only the typescript she'd burned, it's true; she must still have had her handwritten version. But that was always a nightmare, a chaos; it was a great struggle and an important step to transform it into a final, tidy typescript. Later she said that the manuscript was lost 'when I was moving from somewhere to somewhere else', and that she was 'desperate'. But then she found 'two chapters' in a suitcase, and used those for *Wide Sargasso Sea*. . . . Perhaps she did also lose parts of the handwritten version (or versions) of *Le*

*Revenant.* But saying that 'The MSS was lost' was often, like her vagueness and incompetence, a disguise to cover something worse — deliberate, irrational, self-destructive violence.

That was the first novel of 1939, and she burned it. The second — she said — she simply forgot.

This is an extraordinary, a typically Jean story. She had 'every word of that book in my head', she told Francis Wyndham (she always felt that at the start). But 'just in case' she jotted down the title and outline. It was to be called *Wedding in the Carib Quarter.* There were three parts, *Preparations for the Wedding, The Wedding,* and *After the Wedding.* The chapter headings for Part One, *Preparations for the Wedding,* show all the quintessential Jean Rhys ingredients — narcissism, memory, darkness and light: *The Bridesmaids dress, The Bridesmaids terror, The Bridesmaids trapezc, The Bridesmaid a bit tight on punch....*

Then (Jean told Francis twenty-five years later) 'I pranced away to enjoy myself & get a bit tight & all that.... But when I got back to it *Gone!* And it never came back either.' It was like her 'long dream' of Mr Howard: as soon as it was over it 'went out of my memory like a stone.' And for the same reason — it was too dangerous to remember. For when, in the 1960s, she got out the piece of paper on which she'd scrawled the plan for *Wedding in the Carib Quarter,* she made a short, strange note on it.

> & a fearful warning too! that was! It went for keeps. Attention
> Miss! Or Madam. No playing around with ME (it said).

Why was this novel so dangerous it had to be forgotten — even more dangerous than Sasha's drinking, than Antoinette's madness? Is it fanciful to be reminded by some of its last chapters — *The Honeymoon Horses, The Ride to the Hills* — of Owen's story of Missy and her half-Carib lover? I think of the drunken illegible scrawls in her Orange Notebook — 'This feeling I have about the Caribs & the Carib Quarter is very old very complicated' — 'When I try to explain the feeling I find I cannot or do not wish to' — 'And it was one of the few things I'd kept intact because I never spoke of it....' I think of Sandi, and of his and Antoinette's 'life and death kiss....' But it's no good. All the forces which impelled Jean towards uncovering the truth stopped short here. *'No playing around with ME':* we will never know.

*Le Revenant* and *Wedding in the Carib Quarter* were lost, but *Good Morning, Midnight,* thank heaven, survived, though Jean had once torn it up too. It was her greatest victory over herself, her most honest and most moving achievement, but when it appeared in April 1939 it received the coldest welcome of any of her novels since *Quartet*.

Ever since then everyone — critics, her best friend, her husband — had repeated that she wrote superbly well, but in the service of a sordid and unacceptable vision. Yet in novel after novel Jean had refused to abandon that vision. The closest she'd come to something gentler was *Voyage in the Dark*, and *Voyage in the Dark* had been a success. But in *Good Morning, Midnight* she'd moved the furthest away. People can never bear much reality anyway, T.S. Eliot tells us; exhausted by the struggles of the thirties, and overwhelmed by the certainty of another war, they could bear even less. Jean had written her greatest novel so far, and no one wanted to read it.

It was sparsely and grudgingly reviewed. The *Birmingham Post* called it 'an intensely moving experience'; but the best most critics could muster was 'impressive'. Even Jean's champions deserted her. Norah Hoult was away in America; but Rebecca West didn't review *Midnight*, and Frank Swinnerton reviewed it badly. Oliver Stoner, who'd written to Jean so kindly about *Mackenzie*, wrote again now and praised *Good Morning, Midnight*; but even he found it 'hopeless' and depressing.

And if the English had hardly a good word for the novel, no one else would have it at all. The Americans wouldn't take it; the French (who were tried for the first time now) wouldn't either. In early 1940 John sent Jean a copy of a letter from the French translator he'd found, giving the reason: and it was the same. *'Malgré tous mes efforts,'* she wrote, *'Plon ne veut pas publier* Good Morning, Midnight. *Comme Stock, il admire les qualités incontestables du livre mais le sujet (en ce moment surtout) effroye tout éditeur.'* Twenty years later Jean wrote the epitaph for her last modern novel: 'The war killed it.'

She reeled under these blows. One night soon after the publication of *Good Morning, Midnight* Anne met her father and Jean at a pub. Jean sat, silent, morose, between Leslie and Anne, who tried to chat lightly. Suddenly she turned to Anne and said 'You're *exactly* like your father.' That was all; for the rest of the evening, silence.

Silence would have been her best response. I think there must have been many rages too (including the one in which she burned *Le Revenant*) in the year between April 1939 and February 1940, when Leslie rejoined the RAF and their lives changed. And this time at least, who could blame her? She had driven herself to face the truth; then she had driven herself to make it into something 'cold, empty, beautiful'. For this she had lost her hope of happiness and of her daughter. And all for what? *For nothing.* She wrote in a letter: 'I have worked hard for a long time & it's been no good at all — None.' And in a notebook: 'I will never succeed in England. Never.'

★

It was true: all the huge effort with which she had driven herself towards self-knowledge had brought her no success and no recognition. Yet it had succeeded. It had succeeded in *Good Morning, Midnight* and in 'Till September Petronella'; and it had succeeded in her notebooks of the thirties, the Green and the Black.

In them she already understood, for instance – though she wouldn't say it to anyone else for years, and then only rarely – what the real relation was for her between writing and happiness. *Writing itself could make her happy*, if she gave herself up to it completely, as though to a lover:

> ... Not for hope of heaven not for fear but for love. Was that what I've been always meant to learn?
>
> Then I think that after all I've done it. I've given myself up to something which is greater than I am. I have tried to be a good instrument. Then I'm not unhappy. I am even rather happy perhaps.

So she understood her happiness; and she understood her unhappiness too. She understood that it came from a split inside her: a split caused by her different vision. Half of her – the writer's half – was true to that vision; but the other half was afraid of it. 'I was afraid to pay the price of seeing,' she wrote:

> ... I was afraid of being laughed at – when I was lonely I could see but I was afraid of that too –
>
> Yet often I was not afraid & I paid because it was stronger than I. ...
>
> When I saw they hated me then I shut my eyes. I could make them love me. I could deny myself. Then I could make them love me & be kind to me.
>
> That has been the struggle.
>
> On the one hand love beauty peace & blindness
>
> On the other hate ridicule fear & to see
>
> That was the struggle

The price of 'seeing' was loneliness and madness ('They say madness that way to madness') and the feeling of being hated. But the price of closing her eyes, of acting and pretending ('I could act & make them like me but no one can act for ever') was madness too: 'When I let go of what I have seen I am lost in a world so black & deadly that I am crazy with fear.' That was the struggle. Accepting her vision and denying it were equally dangerous; there was nowhere to go.

Finally, in the last pages of the Green Exercise Book Jean tries to face, outside fiction, what this insoluble struggle had done to her.

She still did not want to say that she had hated first; and perhaps she hadn't. But she knew that she had, at least, been lazy, that she had wanted to take without giving. 'I longed to be kind and for the kindness of others,' she wrote. 'But I was not able to try for kindness — it must be there & I must swim in it like a fish in water. I didn't understand that one has to try terribly hard for even a little love — no it must be round me like water round a fish...'. So first 'When I met with unkindness I went back into myself & was alone'; but now 'To hate my reaction is a raving hate.' And she knew why:

> ... It is only lately that I answer unkindness with raving hate
> — because I've got weaker. My will is quite weakened because
> I drink too much.

In this notebook, and in her last novel, she had reached her goal of truth and self-knowledge. But I think this inner success was more fatal to her than any outer, visible failure (*They say madness that way to madness...*). In order to achieve it she had had to rise above 'the I you mean', as she called it here, and become 'another I who is everybody'; and she could not do that for ever. Instead it would be a long time before she could do it again. In the end she would write another great novel (and another great notebook too). But for the six years of war, and for another dozen after it, she would write only diaries and stories, with great difficulty. And most of the stories she wrote in the war were not written by the 'I who is everybody' but by an 'I' who was too close for comfort to her hated and hating self. She had answered her question; but the effort broke her.

# CHAPTER SIX

# *Good Morning, Midnight*

*Good Morning, Midnight* turns on Jean's oldest and deepest fear: that behind everything something opposite and horrible is hidden. That is what Marya feels about the Heidlers' posturing, what Julia grapples with at her mother's funeral, what Anna sees when she gets Vincent's letter. It will lie at the heart of *Wide Sargasso Sea*'s dangerous beauty: in the perfect pool hides the crab, in the handsome husband hides the man who hates you. But in *Good Morning, Midnight* this horrible reversal of surface and secrets is the dominating principle. Sasha's revenge on men reverses and reveals her own self-destruction. First with Enno: each thought the other had money, but neither had; she thought marriage would be her escape, but instead it was just another step downwards. And now the same thing happens with René. He too thinks Sasha has money — and once again she hasn't. Each time they meet there is a reversal. Sasha has always been a sex object, offering herself up to men's gaze: at their first meeting suddenly *he* is the object, exhibiting himself to *her*. At their second meeting there is a reversal which seems happy: Sasha steels herself for the man at the door to be the horrible *commis*, and it is René. But this is itself a reversal, a mockery and inversion of the last and worst one: for at the end Sasha wills the opening door to bring her René, and instead it reveals the *commis*.

The *patronne* says, 'A nice room' — and Sasha watches cockroaches crawl out from under the carpet; she and Enno pay their room's rent in advance — and wake up to see the walls covered with bugs. The hall looks clean, but the upstairs landing is full of dirty sheets; you can have your food brought up to you, but the waiter has a louse on his collar. Sasha marries, and the songs are about poverty, the news about murder. She plans 'a nice sane fortnight', and her clock 'makes a noise between a belch and a giggle'; the man outside sings of love, and she dreams of entrapment and murder.

In *Good Morning, Midnight* Jean gives the idea of horror inside promise a new twist. She makes it blackly funny. She has always been self-mocking, but this is a new kind of humour: an overwhelming sense of absurdity. Even – especially – the horrors are pathetic, laughable. The episode of the 'kise', for example, is a sustained exercise in Kafkaesque absurdity, funnily horrible, horribly funny. In it Sasha searches for she-knows-not-what, the holy grail, the 'kise' – the keys? – (which is really the *caisse*, money); and what she finds is lavatories. She tries to escape Mr Blank's office – and walks, like a slapstick comedian, straight into a lavatory. She searches frantically for the 'kise', and every passage ends in a lavatory. 'The number of lavatories in this place, *c'est inoui*....' You look for the 'kise', you are promised a room, and you get a lavatory. She learns 'what things are like underneath what people say they are,' and what they are like is lavatories. Sasha's own movement is like this – a squalid, shameful descent, as towards the lavatory ('You're always disappearing into the lavabo,' says René). 'You know what happens when you get excited and exalted, don't you?' she says to herself. 'Yes.... And then you know how you collapse like a pricked balloon?....' From hope to fact, from dream to reality, from René to the *commis*, Sasha's movement is a deflation, an ignominious collapse. 'Yes, I am sad, sad as a circus-lioness, sad as an eagle without wings,' she said – 'Or perhaps if I said "*merde*" it would do just as well.' In the painter's studio she sees a wooden chair with *merde* written on it, and thinks: 'The answer, the final answer to everything?'

A joke, appropriately, pictures this central reduction. Sasha goes to a bar whose proprietor used to be called Pecanelli: and remembers that the boy who took her there called it the Pig and Lily. These are the poles of Sasha's story. On the one side her hopes and dreams – the Lily; on the other side reality – the Pig.

This reductive opposition is also the key to Sasha herself. When she meets the two Russians she thinks, 'The short man must be the more wordly-wise; the other is like me – he has his feelings and sticks to them.' Jean's heroine, from Anna on, 'has her feelings and sticks to them'; she has very little 'worldly wisdom', very little sense of reality at all. With Julia *some* idea of reality began to creep in, and she was beginning to know how others saw her. Sasha is still, as she says, like the 'feeling' Russian and not like the 'worldly' one. Indeed, she is more cut off inside her head than any of the heroines – utterly alone, spinning a fantasy of revenge. *But at the same time* she is the most 'worldly-wise' of all the heroines: the one who wholly knows how others see her. Jean both takes us inside Sasha, where the lily hides, *and* shows us her outside, in merciless detail – the pig, laughable and squalid.

'I know about myself, you've told me so often,' Sasha says. She knows that (at least sometimes) she only imagines squalor and cruelty; she knows the sane explanations, and the sane remedy ('Human beings are struggling, and so they are egotists. But it's wrong to say that they are wholly cruel — it's a deformed view.') Jean knows even more. She knows all Sasha's weaknesses, all her sins, both tragic and comic. She knows that Sasha is tragically wrong about René, that her suspicions of him are paranoid. She knows that Sasha can be sulky, surly, loud, aggressive; she knows that she lets people down. She knows all about Sasha and drink: that she has tried to drink herself to death, and is still trying; that she goes into bars to get drunk; that drink makes her quarrelsome, that it makes her look nice only for an instant, and then makes her look awful. She knows that Sasha is cruel, that she plans revenge on an innocent person; almost worse, she knows that she is absurd. For of course her plan of revenge fails, and so does everything else she touches. Her attempt at motherhood is a tragedy, but everything else is a farce. She can't manage, she can't understand, anything. Not marriage ('He seemed very prosperous when I met him in London, but now no money — nix. What happened? He doesn't tell me'; 'Did I love Enno at the end? Did he ever love me? I don't know'). Not, certainly, her jobs — she's a receptionist who can't receive, a saleswoman who can't sell, a guide who can't guide, a teacher who can't teach. She is the biggest fool he's ever met, Mr Blank says, 'half-witted', 'hopeless': and though we are not meant to believe *him*, everything confirms what he says.

All this is worlds away from innocent and beautiful Anna, beautiful and doomed Antoinette. Here is Jean, whose whole desire is to evoke intense and exclusive pity for her heroine — and she allows us to see her drunk, humiliated, stupid. Her direction is always downwards, towards deflation and humiliation, towards the shameful, squalid truth, towards the lavatory. And she sinks 'to the accompaniment of loud laughter.' Her room laughs at her, the *commis* laughs at her, even René laughs at her. Laughter is what she dreads most: 'When you are dead to the world, the world often rescues you, if only to make a figure of fun out of you'; 'Now I am sick of being laughed at — sick, sick, sick of being laughed at.' *Yet she laughs at herself* 'till the tears come into her eyes'; and through her Jean does the same. In *Good Morning, Midnight* she was doing the hardest thing of all: letting us judge her, letting us laugh at her.

The novel is full of imagery of this central act: imagery, I mean, of exposing oneself to hostile, contemptuous eyes. We've seen these eyes already in *Voyage in the Dark*, and even in *Quartet*, watching the heroine from high up on the wall — the photographs in *Quartet*; the stags' heads, the bust of Voltaire, the picture of the dog in *Voyage*.

But eyes are *everywhere* in *Good Morning, Midnight* — 'knowing', 'arrogant', 'glassy', 'cold', 'abominable'. 'I think most human beings have cruel eyes,' Sasha says. Everywhere are looks — blank, sly, amused, pitying, severe. People look at Sasha, peer at her, 'fling themselves' at her. 'Don't let him notice me, don't let him look at me,' she prays when Mr Blank arrives. 'Isn't there something you can do so that nobody looks at you or sees you?' But there isn't. The close-set eye-holes of Serge Rubin's mask stare at her: 'That's the way they look when they are saying "Why didn't you drown yourself in the Seine?" That's the way they look when they are saying: "*Qu'est-ce qu'elle fout ici, la vieille?*"' 'Now everybody in the room is staring at me,' she thinks, at Theodore's. 'All the eyes in the room are fixed on me. It has happened.' She is only safe when no one looks at her. Looking is a challenge and an invasion, as when Sasha stares at the girl in the room opposite, and knows she will retaliate. Looking is judging: it is what men have always done to Sasha, what she can do now to René. When she is happiest, with René and with Serge Rubin, *she* is looking at *them* — watching Serge dance ('I'd rather watch you'), curious to see what René looks like. Or if these two do look, they don't judge. Serge ignores her bad behaviour. René sees her real self, Sasha the child. And finally she offers that self to him, 'simple and not afraid', saying 'He can look at me if he wants to.' But of course it's too late, he is not even there. Instead of René looking at her there is the horrible machine, all lights and eyes, and the mean, flickering eyes of the *commis voyageur*.

Sasha fears being looked at for a perfectly good reason: the looks *will* be stares and sneers and judgements. It is evident that she has often made scenes in public places, and now she cries in the first restaurant we see her in; she cries at Theodore's and 'raves' at the Deux Magots. That's why they 'don't like her' in certain cafés: *she makes an exhibition of herself.* Jean knows this about herself; and in her indirect, half-conscious way she puts it into the novel. There is a strange series of images in it which are, I think, this half-repressed, Freudianly punning knowledge.

In Sasha's nightmare at the beginning the signs, and the man's steel hand, all point 'This Way to the Exhibition'. Everyone follows them, but Sasha thinks: 'I don't want the way to the exhibition. I want the way out.' When she is a guide an old lady wants to be taken to an exhibition, which Sasha must find though she knows nothing about it; and the Pig and Lily boy takes her to another exhibition, of down-and-outs sleeping in a café ('"Would you like to go in and have a look at them?" he said, as if he were exhibiting a lot of monkeys'). Finally, it is October 1937 and the World Exhibition is on. Sasha wants to see it before she leaves Paris. René is reluctant, and dislikes it, but Sasha thinks: 'Cold, empty, beautiful – this is what I wanted, this is what I imagined.'

What *are* all these Exhibitions? They are, I suggest, a punning image of the central truth of the book: that in it Sasha, constantly and against her will, makes an exhibition of herself; and that with it Jean, half against *her* will, makes an exhibition of Sasha. The movement of exhibitions pictures the movement of Sasha's – and Jean's – feelings about this self-exhibition, this self-exposure. First the idea is a nightmare. Sasha doesn't want to go there, she wants the way out; but she can't find it, she must go to the exhibition. And the novel goes on – Jean goes on writing. Then Sasha must find it: she doesn't know what it is – like the 'kise' – but her survival depends on finding it, and showing it to two 'respectable' women. Next is the horrible and degrading glimpse of what an exhibition is: the poor sleepers, like 'a lot of monkeys'; the old man who for a few drinks will eat his glass. But at the end Sasha *wants* to go to the exhibition; and though it is cold and empty it is beautiful, it is what she wanted and imagined. So, exactly, must Jean have felt: struggling against writing this book – feeling she had to – feeling it was horrible and degrading – feeling that it, and Sasha, and she herself, were left cold and empty, but that after all it was beautiful, and what she wanted. *Good Morning, Midnight is* cold and empty, and it does leave Sasha exposed and degraded. But part of Jean – the part that wouldn't take the exit, but wrote the book – knew that it was true and beautiful. As it is.

This is a familiar movement, a familiar idea, in Jean's work: fear and the desire to escape something horrible and hidden; but then the relief of facing the worst, the peace of indifference. *Indifference* is the closest the heroines get to happiness, including Sasha: 'People talk about the happy life,' she says, 'but that's the happy life when you don't care any longer if you live or die.' Indifference, being 'dead to the world', is her heaven; indifference is 'the bitter peace that is very near to death.' And this ultimate indifference, I fear, is all that Sasha finally achieves.

I am referring to the ending of *Good Morning, Midnight* and how it should be interpreted.

Its intended ambiguity turns on the pronoun 'he'. 'It isn't such a long time since he left,' Sasha thinks – meaning René. For the next two pages 'he' remains René, as in her head she pleads with him to return, imagines him returning. Then on the last page 'he' stands there, looking down at her – but now he wears a white dressing gown, and his mean eyes flicker. The real 'he' has protruded through the 'dream' he, and the horrible truth is revealed.

This ambiguity of 'he', which unleashes the horror on us as slyly as it is unleashed on Sasha, is brilliantly controlled (though it can still elude an unwary reader). But now there is a further ambiguity. This 'he', the *commis*, is everything Sasha has most feared and hated. He is the last stage of what she fears for herself — mad, grinning, babbling to himself, never going out. He gives her 'a nightmare feeling'. He is the heroine's last and worst 'neighbour', the ultimate death figure — 'a skeleton', a 'ghost', 'something that doesn't exist'. Sasha's acceptance of him into her body, which has just so painfully come alive, is appalling. First her dream of René — 'love, youth, spring, happiness' — rebirth, as his name suggests — and now this mean, cringing madman.... It is unbearable, almost unreadable. *And yet*: there is the line, 'I look into his eyes and despise another poor devil of a human being for the last time.' *That* isn't horrible, surely? Isn't it hopeful, isn't it even good and great? Isn't it Sasha — and through her, Jean — accepting her common humanity with her neighbour at last? — forswearing hatred, and so not only sin, but her awful loneliness? So it has sometimes been read: as a triumph and a celebration, echoing Molly Bloom's great affirmation with Sasha's last words, 'Yes — yes — yes....'

Well: it remains ambiguous, and perhaps that is the best — the most effective. But I think that when we fully understand the emotional logic of the Jean Rhys heroine, we cannot rest with this hopeful interpretation.

For that logic is, as always, paradoxical. René was Sasha's last chance of love, and she threw it away. That is unambiguously bad and sad. But now the *commis* gives her her last chance of hate, and she throws that away too: *and for the Jean Rhys heroine that is also bad*. The wolf in her is her real self, better and more real than the docile dog. She has feared it and fought its rise to her surface, but it is the only part of her she truly values. We know this from the novels' contempt for the tame pale English, from their sympathy for everything 'black' and everything 'French'. We know it from Julia's feeling about the Modigliani woman, 'like an utterly lovely proud animal': 'I felt as if she were laughing at me and saying: "I am more real than you. But at the same time I *am* you. I'm all that matters of you."' We know it from the way Sasha would rather be the crazy old woman than the smug saleswoman, from the way she says 'You haven't left me one rag of illusion to clothe myself in. But by God I know what you are too, and I wouldn't change places.' The young heroine had wanted love, but that is all over. Now she wants, she needs, hatred.

When we get to *Wide Sargasso Sea* we will know it for certain: that when she reaches the end of her voyage, when she is an old, forsaken shadow like the woman above Julia, *only the flame of hatred keeps her alive*. First Rochester destroys Antoinette's chance of love: that's easy, because she's never wanted to love or even live before. But then he tries to destroy her hate, and leave her nothing. He seems to succeed: and she is mad, dead, a ghost. *That* is what happens to the Jean Rhys heroine when hate, which is all that is left to her, is taken away. But in fact Rochester doesn't succeed. Antoinette 'hasn't lost her spirit' — she's still so 'fierce' that Grace Poole doesn't dare turn her back on her. And her last act is not a *yes* but a *no*, an attempt to carry out at last all the heroines' thwarted plans of revenge. It doesn't work either, we learn in *Jane Eyre*: but the end of *Wide Sargasso Sea is* a triumph. At last the heroine escapes the prison of her madness and solitude; at last she stops uselessly, insanely willing reality to conform to her dream, and sets out instead to *do* what she has dreamed of.

*Wide Sargasso Sea* shows us that 'the real death' is not of the body but of the soul, so that once the soul is dead, the death of the body is a desirable, triumphant escape. And only hate, pride, fierceness can rouse a dead soul to that escape. That is why it is a bad thing and not a good one that Sasha gives up hate at the end of *Good Morning, Midnight*. Only hate would keep her alive, keep her *herself*. Accepting the *commis voyageur* means accepting death and nothingness. It means accepting that she is the same as all the other poor devils of human beings, all the pitiful fools, all the defeated. It means accepting she is a dog after all. For the Jean Rhys heroine that is not an affirmation; it is the ultimate negation.

This is the end of the story of the 'neighbours', then, and it's not a humane one. But we shouldn't have expected that. The heroine was never humane, after all, that wasn't the point about her. She was isolated, angry and honest. *That*'s what she tells us about from first to last, in Sasha's end as much if not more than elsewhere.

But a last word about this ending. It is not only cold and empty, but also beautiful, also what both Sasha and Jean herself wanted. *Can* that be true? I think it can. Perhaps Sasha wanted it because, like all the heroines, she wanted peace, however bitter — the 'Star of Peace', no matter how '*mesquin*'. And Jean definitely wanted it, because she wanted the truth when she wrote, however awful. So we are right to feel a welcome and a triumph in the ending too. For Sasha it's only the most despairing welcome, the sort we give to the death of someone in unbearable pain; it's wrong to imagine it anything more. But for Jean it contained a triumph, the triumph of turning her plummeting life into great writing.

★     ★     ★

*The writing: Good Morning, Midnight* contains some of Jean's most
intense and powerful writing. Like *Voyage in the Dark*, it is close to
poetry — it *is* poetry, and of a similar form. Jean has built this book
as Sasha has arranged her 'little life', on a skeleton of streets and
rooms. It opens in Sasha's room: '"Quite like old times," the room
says. "Yes? No?"' Then we see the street outside, 'going sharply
uphill and ending in a flight of steps. What they call an impasse.'
Sasha has gone up and down, up and down, like the figure in the
corkscrew in *Mackenzie*, and ended in an impasse. She is back in
Paris, remembering the past; she is back in a cheap hotel. 'Always
the same hotel. You press the button. The door opens. You go up
the stairs. Always the same stairs. Always the same room.' And now
the corkscrew again, the swing high-swing low, the going nowhere
through that spiral of rooms:

> That's the way it is, that's the way it goes, that was the way
> it went.... A room. A nice room. A beautiful room. A
> beautiful room with bath. A very beautiful room with bath. A
> bedroom and sitting room with bath. Up to the dizzy heights
> of the suite. Two bedrooms, sitting room, bath and ves-
> tibule.... Swing high.... Now, slowly, down. A beautiful
> room with bath. A room with bath. A nice room. A room....

That is the trajectory of Sasha and of all the heroines: shooting
upwards briefly, defiantly — then falling down again, 'useless, having
reached nothing.' That's the way it went with Julia; that's the way
it goes with Sasha and René; that's the way it goes even with flowers,
waving against the curtains 'like the incalculable raising its head,
uselessly and wildly, for one moment before it sinks down, beaten,
into the darkness.' The whole business is quite crazy, quite pointless.
At the beginning Sasha tries to change her room for a better one,
and her search is crazy ('I say confidentially, leaning forward: "I want
a light room"'), pointless. 'All rooms are the same. All rooms have
four walls, a door, a window or two, a bed, a chair and perhaps a
bidet. A room is a place where you hide from the wolves outside
and that's all any room is. Why should I worry about changing my
room?' Part Two ends where Part One began, in Sasha's room,
'saturated with the past'; and when she watches that past it is
'Rooms, streets, streets, rooms....' In Part Three we move with her
through the past, to end again with the chorus: 'A room? A nice
room? A beautiful room? A beautiful room with bath? Swing high,
swing low, swing to and fro....' Finally, back to Sasha's little life
— and back to the opening line:

Eat. Drink. Walk. March. Back to the hotel. To the Hotel of

Arrival, the Hotel of Departure, the Hotel of the Future, the Hotel of Martinique and the Universe.... Back to the hotel without a name in the street without a name. You press a button and the door opens. This is the Hotel-Without-a-Name in the Street-Without-a-Name, and the clients have no names, no faces. You go up the stairs. Always the same stairs, always the same room.

The room says: 'Quite like old times. Yes? ... No?.... Yes.

All that is left now is Part Four — the end of Sasha, and the echoing, three times over, of that little *Yes*. If we still have any doubts about how to read it, this 'Yes', affirming only negation, should tell us.

The whole novel thus has a perfect, circular shape. And so especially has Part Four. At the beginning René enters the room instead of the *commis*, at the end the *commis* enters instead of René; briefly Sasha comes back to life from death, only to fall back from life to a deeper death again. Within this circular, entrapping structure there are constant, poetic repetitions. Sasha's 'little life' repeats itself, becoming more and more desperate. First there is 'Planning it all out. Eating. A movie. Eating again. One drink....' Then: 'My life, which seems so simple and monotonous, is really a complicated affair of cafés where they like me and cafés where they don't, streets that are friendly, streets that aren't, rooms where I might be happy, rooms where I never shall be....' Finally, the end of Part Three we've just read — 'Eat. Drink. Walk. March. Back to the hotel. To the Hotel of Arrival, the Hotel of Departure....' The short staccato words, the tiny contrasts, the constant halts make us *feel* what they tell us: the entrapment, the barely-aliveness of Sasha's little life. The song she hears on the very first page repeats like a chorus, 'gloomy Sunday', '*sombre dimanche*'; so do other images and phrases — the sad afternoon sun, and 'spoiled, all spoiled', 'Everything all spoiled....'. And all through there is exact, evocative, incantatory prose poetry. There is Sasha's terrifying self-portrait at the beginning: 'Saved, rescued, fished-up, half-drowned, out of the deep, dark river, dry clothes, hair shampooed and set. Nobdy would know I had even been in it. Except, of course, that there always remains something. Yes, there always remains something...'. And her extraordinary prayer to money near the end:

Now, money, for the night is coming. Money for my hair, money for my teeth, money for shoes that won't deform my feet (it's not so easy now to walk around in cheap shoes with very high heels), money for good clothes, money, money. The night is coming.

There is the chanting German of '*Ja, ja, nein, nein*', like 'Yes? No?

Yes?'; and of '*aus meinen grossen Schmerzen mach ich die kleinen Lieder, homo homini lupus ...*', the first exactly true of Jean, the second exactly true of Sasha. There is the lyrical poetry of the two mannequins, one beautiful as a '*fleur de verre*', the other as a '*fleur de terre*', and of Sasha's sadness — 'sad as a circus-lioness', '*Tristesse, lointaine ...*'. There is the painful poetry of the death of Sasha's baby: 'And there I am ... without one line, without one wrinkle, without one crease'; and the self-mocking poetry of the disappearance of her lover:

> I get downstairs to the telephone. There is nobody on the line.
> 'There was a *monsieur*,' the *patronne* says.
> There was a *monsieur*, but the *monsieur* has gone.

And there are perfect little poems about places, always such strong emotional presences in Jean's writing. Serge's Martinique music evokes a lovely tropical image or memory: 'The hills look like clouds and the clouds like fantastic hills.' London, by contrast, calls out a little satirical word-picture: 'Things were always half-and-half. They changed one sheet at a time, so that the bed was never quite clean and never quite dirty....'

Like all good poetry, the telling of *Good Morning, Midnight* mirrors what is told. Sasha is trapped and divided: and so is her narrative. She is dazed by drink, besieged and battered by memories: and so is her language. Her memories flash through the narrative just as they do through her experience; so do her dreams, fantasies, fears, images, jokes. Memory takes her over more and more, despite her resistance: and so it takes over the narrative too, until Part Three is memory only. When she wakes up in the middle of the night and starts to cry, the narrative breaks into a separate small paragraph, its own brief wakening in the middle of the night. When she remembers a happy moment the narrative slips into brackets — '(But sometimes it was sunny.... Walking along in the sun in a gay dress, striped red and blue....)': its own minor exception. Jean's language is always taut and swift, short lines trimmed into paragraphs like arrows in a quiver. But here it is more so than ever. *Good Morning, Midnight* is full of clipped lines, sentences of single staccato words, sentences without a verb — 'Eat. Drink. Walk. March' — 'A room. A nice room. A beautiful room'; and descriptions like the one of Mr Blank — 'Bowler hat, majestic trousers, oh-my-God expression, ha-ha eyes' — or the English huntsmen: 'The cold clear voices, the cold, light eyes ...'. Scenes are set in a few quick words, like reminding oneself of something — '*The room at the Steens*', 'Drinking coffee very early in the morning, everything like a dream.' It's all allusive, glancing, like someone speaking to herself, who has no need of explanations.

We do not need to be told that Sasha is alone and lonely, lost in her memories and dreams. Her language shows her loneliness; it is loneliness distilled.

★    ★    ★

*The Imagery*: Through the three earlier novels we have watched the heroine's subconscious rising to her surface, consciously resisted and feared. That voyage from dog to wolf has been their subject; and it has also been Jean's style. With each step her narration has become more inner, more allusive; and with each step her meaning has become more hidden in imagery, as in a dream. I'm sure she was not in rational control (though she was always in artistic control) of much of this imagery: the ones which work out their logic from book to book, for instance — the dog and the wolf, the ghastly ghostly 'neighbour', the woman moving unstoppably up the stairs. And by the time we get to *Good Morning, Midnight* much of its individual imagery, too, bears the stamp of the unconscious. Thus, the Freudian puns on 'keys' and 'making an exhibition of oneself'; thus perhaps the deep joke of the Pig and the Lily. This is because with each book she was pushing herself closer to facing the wolf, and because in *Good Morning, Midnight* she faced it.

There is one particularly poignant example of this process in *Good Morning, Midnight* — the flight from a guilty, wolfish truth, the struggle to face it, the resolution in a hidden, half-conscious recognition. When Sasha's baby dies she refuses to think about it: 'Not to think.... Above all, not to think'; 'The cork of a champagne bottle pops. Why worry? Our luck has changed.' But then she goes on:

> The fat man and I are in a corner by ourselves.
> He says: 'Life is too awful. Do you know that story about the man who loved a woman who was married to somebody else, and she fell ill? And he didn't dare go and ask about her because the husband suspected her and hated him.... And then one day he asked and she was dead. Doesn't that make you laugh? She was dead, you see, and he had never sent one word. And he loved her and she was dying and he knew she was dying and he never sent one word.'

We don't know where Sasha was when her baby died, but we know where Jean was: drinking champagne in the rue Lamartine. She knew her son was dying, and she never sent one word. But twenty years later she puts the death of Sasha's son into her novel — and right next to it this story-within-a-story, this apparently

distracting detail. She has hidden her guilt several times over —
behind Sasha, who is fiction; behind a story which isn't even about
Sasha, or the death of a child. *And yet it is there.* On the surface Sasha
blames God ('God is very cruel.... A devil, of course. That accounts
for everything — the only possible explanation'): but then immediately comes this guilt-ridden story. This way it is more insidious,
and more powerful. This way it is part of the pattern — part of the
principle of exposure and reversal, the surface splitting open to reveal
the horrid depth. And this way it is Jean making art out of herself
once more, not just out of her experience, but out of her instincts.
One of her strongest instincts was to hide: and some of her strongest
writing, like this, is a species of hiding.

The rest of *Good Morning, Midnight*'s imagery flows in from the
other novels. Sasha's self-esteem depends as much as Julia's on
'unknowns' ('A man sitting nearby asks if he may look at my
evening paper.... Then he tries to start a conversation with me. I
think: "That's all right...".'); and René, as we've seen, is the
ultimate unknown. All the people who approach Sasha in the present
time of the novel — René, Serge, the two Russians — are as poor,
as exiled and marginal as she; and around them is a penumbra of less-
than-half-humans, the *commis* like 'a paper man, a ghost, something
that doesn't exist,' the Martiniquaise like 'something that was no
longer quite human, no longer quite alive.' Serge paints misshapen
dwarfs, two-headed men, four-breasted women; when Sasha thinks
of London she remembers 'the people passing in the street and ... a
shop window full of artificial limbs' all in one breath, as though she
can barely tell the two apart. At the beginning she dreams of a man
whose hand is made of steel; in the end, as we know, the whole world
is just such a half-human, half-metal machine, with arms and eyes,
but made of steel.

*Good Morning, Midnight* brings to a climax too the imagery of
mirroring women. There are a few who are smart and successful,
whom Sasha both envies and despises, like the girl in the grey suit
she sees when she first comes to Paris, or the *patronne* of her hotel,
who says '*Tu vas voir si je n'ose pas.*' The most perfect of these are
of course the inhuman satin-and-silk dolls of Mr Blank's shop ('what
a success they would have made of their lives if they had been
women'). Then there are many who mirror Sasha's current situation
— the girl who writes to her lover, the destitute girls at the convent,
the 'sketches of little women' on the menu, who all need money,
like her. But most numerous of all now are the warnings of what
Sasha will come to. There is the Martiniquaise, 'at the end of
everything', 'like looking down into a pit'. There are the two mad
old ladies who try, defiantly or despairingly, to find 'pretty things'

to cover their age and ugliness. And twice Sasha explicitly sees herself as a mad or drunk old woman, wandering the streets of London and Montparnasse.

Interestingly, no less than three times Sasha meets a *pair of women* – the bald old Englishwoman at Mr Blank's and her grim reluctant daughter, the placid mother and slightly less placid daughter whom she leads (or misleads) through Paris, and the American mother and daughter at her hotel, who talk so brightly about Verlaine and Rimbaud.* These pairs echo the main structural principle of the novel, the division between dog and wolf, surface and depth, present and past, dream and reality. *Everything is double*, to mirror Sasha's doubleness, as woman and wolf. The people in Serge's paintings, double-headed and double-faced; soft Lise and tough Paulette, the optimistic Russian and the pessimistic one, the nice boss and the nasty one, the *fleur de verre* and the *fleur de terre*, the old whore and the young one, the Pig and the Lily.

Songs bring out the meaning of events, as always ('Pain of love, pain of youth, walk away from me, keep away from me...'); colours render mood, blue for hope ('the long, lovely blue days'), red ('cruel red') for misery. Clothes and hair are still deeply connected to the heroine's identity. She always remembers her hats and coats of the past; it's her hat and coat now that present her (falsely) to the Russians and the gigolo. She still hopes for miracles from her hat and her hair ('Tomorrow I'll be pretty again, tomorrow I'll be happy again, tomorrow, tomorrow ...'). But her new realistic side knows this is all an illusion. 'Three hours to choose a hat; every morning an hour and a half trying to make myself look like everyone else.... And, mind you, I know that with all this I don't succeed.' And in the business of dyeing her hair *blond cendré* we see all the impossibility of Sasha's changing her own colour: 'First it must be bleached, that is to say, its own colour must be taken out of it – and then it must be dyed, that is to say, another colour must be imposed on it....' 'It is very, very rarely, Madame, that hair can be successfully dyed *blond cendré*.' Sasha tries none the less, and the hairdresser says 'Yes:' 'A success.' But we know about these *Yes*'s now; and so does Sasha. 'I succeed in flashes only too well,' she thinks – at fooling other people, like the gigolo. But she can't fool herself. She *isn't* like other people: 'Every word I say has chains

---

*This touches on the theme of the cruelty of people to artists, which Serge Rubin also suggests, with his life (until recently) in '*la crasse*'. It also adds to the atmosphere of violence and squalor of Sasha's hotel, because the poets' relationship was extremely stormy, and ended with Verlaine shooting and wounding Rimbaud.

around its ankles... Since I was born, hasn't every word I've said, every thought I've thought, everything I've done, been tied up, weighted, chained?'

There are fewer trees and flowers in *Good Morning, Midnight* than before, because there is very little life left in Sasha's world. When flowers do appear they suffer the reversal that everything does here, and contain nothing: 'A vase of sprawling tulips on the table. How they give themselves! "Perhaps it's because they know they have nothing to give," Enno says.' But animal imagery is as strong as ever. We've seen the pig — and the lily; there's still the dog for servility ('But what do you think I am — a little dog?') and the wolf for ferocity ('One day the fierce wolf that walks by my side will spring on you'). People are 'a pack of damned hyenas'; and Sasha is, as well as a wolf, like a circus-lioness, an eagle, a mare, a kitten:

> The kitten had an inferiority complex and persecution mania and *nostalgie de la boue* and all the rest. You could see it in her eyes, her terrible eyes.... Well, all the male cats in the neighbourhood were on to her like one o'clock.... She wouldn't eat, she snarled at caresses.... 'Oh, haven't you heard?' they said. 'She got run over....' Right out into the street she shot and a merciful taxi went over her.

This is Sasha's whole story — the whole story of all the heroines: her eyes that invite abasement, so attractive to the predatory male; her distrustful rejection of 'caresses'; her violent death, first feared ('I'm worried about her'), then welcomed as a mercy.

Finally, there are the central images of blockage and stasis that affect all the heroines: and they too are worst for Sasha. Time is completely blocked for her. When she tries to plan clocks stop her, by just ticking, or by giggling and belching obscenely. She cannot live in the present except in the few moments she's happy; she cannot imagine the future; she tries not to remember the past. She gets drunk in order to abolish time ('when I have had a couple of drinks I shan't know whether it's yesterday, today or tomorrow'); she refuses to believe in it: 'I don't believe things change much really, you only think they do. It seems to me that things repeat themselves over and over again.' First she stops time because she wants to ('I never think of what it will be like to have this baby or, if I think, it's as if a door shuts in my head'); finally it stops itself, to her deepest despair: 'You fall into blackness. That's the past — or perhaps the future. And you know that there is no past, no future, there is only this blackness, changing faintly, slowly, but always the same.' It's the same progression as for Julia; but Sasha is at the dead end of it.

Space is blocked for Sasha too: from the start she's in 'what they call an impasse.' And Anna's high, dark wall comes back to her. When Enno left her she saw 'a dark wall in the hot sun.' And now, when she tries to escape her sordid hotel, it comes back again. She knows what she wants: a 'light' room, that doesn't look into the courtyard — that doesn't look, that is, on to walls. But of course a wall is what she gets. The girl shows her a comfortably furnished room: but it 'looks on to a high, blank wall.' Serge Rubin tells us something of the meaning of these blocking, stifling walls. After his meeting with the Martiniquaise, he says, 'I got an astonishing hatred of the house.... Every time I went in it was as if I were walking into a wall — one of those walls where people are built in, still alive.' Sasha may be 'still alive' at the end of the novel, but only in a living death, like the Martiniquaise, trapped forever in her blank wall.

The only ways through walls, of course, are doors. Sasha sees many doors but they are mostly closed. In the passages at Mr Blank's, in the leering night-time houses, in her head when she thinks of the future. And 'the doors will always be shut, I know.' In her cheap hotels they open — but always on 'the same stairs.... the same room'. Then twice in the book she is happy. On her first day in Paris, when Enno gets some money:

> I've never been so happy in my life. I'm alive, eating ravioli and drinking wine. I've escaped. A door has opened and let me out in the sun. What more do I want? Anything might happen.

And again in Serge Rubin's studio, when she goes off into a dream: 'the dreams that you have, alone in an empty room, waiting for the door that will open, the thing that is bound to happen....'

When she is happy 'the thing that is bound to happen' seems the same to her as the 'anything' that 'might happen', the infinite promise and excitement of escape. In reality, of course, when the door finally does open, the promise of *anything that might happen* with René — 'love, youth, spring, happiness' turns into a very different *thing that is bound to happen*: the horror of the mad mean *commis*. Only for Antoinette is this resolved. 'I got up, took the keys and unlocked the door. I was outside holding my candle. Now at last I know why I was brought here and what I have to do.' Only for Antoinette is 'the thing that is bound to happen' and the 'anything that might happen' the same: death, and escape.

★     ★     ★

*Humour: Good Morning, Midnight* is the blackest of the novels, but not the deadest.* That was *Mackenzie*, in the hour between dog and wolf. In *Good Morning, Midnight* the wolf has arrived. Sasha has become the woman on the floor above Julia, kept alive – until the end – by a flame of hatred. This flame galvanises the novel, and sharpens to a razor's edge its mocking, sardonic humour.

We've seen how Jean laughs mercilessly at Sasha, in the 'kise' episode, and in her other jobs. The worse Sasha's state, the more she (Jean) mocks her(self). When she's starving, 'That was the high spot.' When she's out of practice with love, '"Would you like some whiskey?" I say.... That's original. I bet nobody's thought of that before.' And when she's lost René forever: 'Well, well, well, just think of that now. What an amusing ten days! Positively packed with thrills. The last performance of "What's-her-name And Her Boys" or "It Was All Due To An Old Fur Coat". Positively the last performance...'.

She mocks other people too. The young couple feeding each other like birds: 'At any moment you expect these two to start flapping wings and chirping.' The poor women who write to magazines: 'No, *mademoiselle*, no, *madame*, life is not easy.... But there is hope (turn to page 5), and yet more hope (turn to page 9)....' Or the rich couple based on the Hudnuts: 'I'm afraid Samuel didn't like the last story you wrote ... considering the cost of these stories, he thinks it strange that you should write them in words of one syllable.' Jean exhibits everyone; she cuts through *every* lily to the pig.

But her main vein of comedy in *Good Morning, Midnight* is not mockery: it is absurdity. Lise is absurd – feeling so old she cries, at twenty-two; Alfred is absurd, reciting 'Answer with a cold silence...' while 'sweating like hell'. René is absurd, with his ideas about England – 'the untapped gold mine just across the channel.' And of course Sasha is the most absurd of all. Her marriage, for instance, which she never planned, and which was based on a misunderstanding about money:

> ... We get a taxi and drive through the rain to the town-hall and we are married with a lot of other couples, all standing round in a circle. We come out of the town-hall and have one drink with Tonny and Hans. Then they go home to look after the shop. We go on to another place. Nobody else is there – it's too early. We have two glasses or port and then another two.
>
> 'How idiotic all that business was!' Enno says.

---

*I'm grateful to Larry Cole for making me see the humorous aspect of *Good Morning, Midnight*.

Her work when she's married is absurd — teaching English to a Russian who speaks it already. Her memories of London are absurd. Her drawers fall off at a bus stop. The man whose offer of sexual delights she refused sends her a box of Turkish Delight. 'Well, now, what is it, this Turkish Delight? Is it a comment, is it irony, is it apology? ... I'll throw it out of the window, whatever it is.' Her present is wholly absurd. Its central event, the encounter with René, is a ludicrous mismatch, misfire, mistake. And round it Jean dots scenes of small but total lunacy. In the Pig and Lily,

> the door opens. Five Chinese come in. They walk down to the end of the room in single file and stand there, talking. Then they all file solemnly out again, smiling politely.

In the Luxembourg Gardens two men look almost exactly alike, very tightly buttoned into black overcoats. One runs after a little girl calling 'You have a drop on your nose, you have a drop on your nose...'. And in the same Gardens, later:

> There are some fish in the pool of the Medicis fountain. Three are red and one gold. The four fish look so forlorn that I wonder whether they are just starting them, or whether they have had a lot, and they have died off.
>     I stand for a long time, watching the fish. And several people who pass stop and also watch them. We stand in a row, watching the fish.

★     ★     ★

*The Characters:* Sasha is the culmination of the worst truth about the heroine. Antoinette may be mad, and for one brief moment she is ugly, drunk and violent. But apart from that moment she remains young and beautiful, able to inspire love — in Christophine, in Aunt Cora, briefly and reluctantly in Rochester; even at the very end she can inspire pity and respect in Grace Poole. Above all she is a victim: of history, of fate, of a man. Sasha is none of these things. She is getting old and ugly. We only have her word for it, but no one seems to like her: her family hates her, and her only friend may despise her; her husband may never have loved her, and René may only wish to exploit her. All this, perhaps, may come down equally on the self-pity side of the scale. But not the last thing: *Sasha is not a victim.* She is the opposite.
    On the one hand, we don't see her being disastrously rejected, like the other heroines: her husband leaves her and Mr Blank exploits her, but we see nothing in her life like Anna's rejection by Walter, or

Marya's by Heidler. And on the other hand, we do see her murderous cruelty. There is her cold-blooded plan of revenge on men, through René: 'You talk to them, you pretend to sympathise, then just at the moment when they are not expecting it, you say, "Go to hell".' (We remember Anna: 'It was when I wasn't expecting it to happen — just when I wasn't expecting it' — but that's not here, in this novel.) Even more violent and shocking is her dream of revenge, on a woman, the red-headed girl at Théodore's:

> ...One day, quite suddenly, when you're not expecting it, I'll take a hammer from the folds of my dark cloak and crack your little skull like an egg-shell. Crack it will go, the egg-shell; out they will stream, the blood, the brains. One day, one day....

This violent dream, of course, she never carries out; but her plan of revenge on men she does. And in that she is not only cruel but arbitrary, because René has done nothing to harm her. She has become *just like Heidler*: motivelessly malevolent, playing God or the devil.

She is cruel: but finally her cruelty fails, like all her plans, and she is only absurd. She is also a drunk, who can no longer hide her pity for herself and her hatred of others. She is not mad, like Antoinette, but Antoinette's madness has grandeur. Sasha suffers something smaller but much worse, the thing the heroine has feared since Roseau: 'absolute loss of self-control'. She loses control of her good manners, her appearance as *une femme convenable*, frequently and shockingly, in public. And in private, with René, she loses control of her hatred. The wolf bursts out through the dog, the Pig through the Lily, the savage through the Lady. And the result is everything the earlier heroines have feared. She loses her last chance of love and hurts only herself; and the dreaded, ghostly, unexisting neighbour claims her.

In other words, Sasha works through the heroine's story — oppression, anger, indirect revenge, self-destruction — most openly and consciously of all the heroines. She knows she is doing it, and Jean knows she's doing it. There will be only one more step to go, and Jean will have the whole answer to her question.

Sasha is thus the heroine whom we see most clearly from the outside. But she is the one we see most clearly from the inside too. In her the heroine's two main psychic wounds are most severe: her 'unadaptedness', her alienation from other people; and the split within her, her alienation from herself.

Sasha's split, like the rest of her movement, is a series of ironic reversals. With their lovers the other heroines have tried to resist the wolf and remain the docile dog. With René Sasha does the opposite

— tries to resist the loving, trusting dog and be only the avenging wolf. That doesn't work, and for a second on her landing she releases the dog, 'hugging him, so terribly happy'. But that doesn't work either: as soon as she wants to be the loving dog, the hating, suspicious, cruel wolf returns. Her voice taunts René, and she thinks 'That's not me speaking.... Nothing to do with me. I swear it.' She cries when he's gone, and thinks: 'This is me, this is myself, who is crying. The other — how do I know who the other is? She isn't me.' She has split completely.

Now, this split actually leads quite directly to the other, her alienation from other people. Consciously Jean thought that it was a matter of being born adapted or not adapted: and she suggests that Sasha was born not adapted. ('What is she doing here, the stranger, the alien?.... I have seen that in people's eyes all my life'; 'Since I was born, hasn't every word I've said ... been tied up, weighted, chained?') And certainly it's true that Sasha's unadaptedness goes deep and far. Marriage, baby, jobs, friends — she's got them all wrong. She can't even fill in the hotel register. She can laugh in the right places in the cinema, and she can buy a ticket in the Luxembourg Gardens. But that's about all.

None the less this incapacity of Sasha's to fit in is what half of her chooses: 'If I must end like one or the other, may I end like the hag'; 'by God I know what you are too, and I wouldn't change places.' We are back with the girl torn between longing to be like the others, and contempt for them: between the sense of her difference as shameful, and the sense of it as special. In the end the second feeling is stronger. The fitters-in are smug, sane devils, and if the only alternative is to be a damned soul, then she chooses to be a damned soul. At least then she will not be guilty. As Delmar says: 'When you aren't rich or strong or powerful, you are not a guilty one. And you have a right to take life just as it comes and to be as happy as you can.'

The trouble is that she can't be happy. For she still has her other half, which longs to fit in and belong ('think how hard I try and how seldom I dare'). That gives her no peace. And it makes her fear and despise her fellow failures, her 'neighbours', so that she cannot belong with them either. So she is entirely alone: 'No voice, no touch, no hand.' She cannot join anyone, or do anything, because whatever she chooses will hurt half of her.

Sasha is thus the most blocked of the heroines. Marya was blocked too, covering up her impulses with opposite actions; and Julia acted only arbitrarily and palely, as though reflected in that distorting mirror. But Sasha, though she formulates the first active plan of revenge, *cannot carry out her intentions at all.* She determines not to remember, and immediately remembers; she determines not to cry and immediately cries. She tries to destroy herself and can't; she tries to destroy René and can't. She doesn't want to go back to London but does; she doesn't plan to marry but does. She wants a calm book, and gets a lurid one; she wants a new room but keeps the old one. She wants to avoid a hostile café, Théodore's, the Dôme, and 'of course' it's the hostile café, Théodore's, the Dôme she goes to. Part One ends: 'I'll lie in bed all day, pull the curtains and shut the damned world out'; Part Two begins: 'All the same, at three o'clock I am dressing to meet the Russian.' In her dream she wants to avoid the Exhibition, but goes to it. She hates Mr Lawson but she feels her mouth go soft under his; she wants the gigolo, but rejects him, loathes the *commis voyageur*, but accepts him. The only intentions she *can* carry out are to dye her hair and buy a hat; and these don't get her what she wanted either.

This tragi-comic inability to carry through her desires is the heart of Sasha's story. She cannot move from intention to act, dream to reality; whenever she tries she gets the opposite of what she wanted. It makes her the *reductio ad absurdum* of all the heroines, as Jean saw them most clearly in Julia: 'her life had been a long succession of humiliations and mistakes and pains and ridiculous efforts.... At the same time some essence of her was shooting upwards like a flame.... Then the flame sank down again, useless, having reached nothing.'

Finally, Sasha has a problem about her history similar to Julia's too. The beginning of the end for her, she says, was Enno's departure; and at just that moment this happens:

> ...There's an English *valet de chambre* at the hotel who tells the *patron* that whatever I call myself now he had known me very well in London and that I had come to Paris with a great friend of his, a jockey, and that I had treated his friend very badly and that I was the dirtiest bitch he had ever struck, which was saying something. Useless to deny all this, quite useless.... Was it hysteria, or a case of hate at first sight, or did he really mistake me for this other girl? I shall never know.

Sasha evidently has no doubts at the time about who she is and what she has done, as Julia did. Nevertheless her story has been disbelieved, as Julia's was. *And perhaps rightly*, if we think of the circular, repetitive time of the novel. For when we see Sasha ourselves, back in Paris a few years later, she *is* being a 'dirty bitch' to a young man. This is her true identity after all, clairvoyantly seen by a stranger.

★

*The Others*: It seems to me that the heroines' feelings about themselves and their feelings about the rest of the world go together. Julia and Sasha, the oldest, the most self-mocking and self-aware, are also hardest on other people: most suspicious, distrustful, even paranoid. Anna and Antoinette, the youngest, most innocent and most victimised, live in a colourful world which contains at least a few other living, even likeable people. Their lovers are tempted by love; they reject it because they are weak and afraid, not just because (like Heidler) they abuse power. The women in these two novels include several who are strong, individual, positive presences: Laurie, Maudie, Francine in *Voyage*, Christophine, Aunt Cora and Tia in *Wide Sargasso Sea*. Even the villains are allowed their own voices – Vincent and Daniel write their own letters, have their own stories. By contrast Julia and Sasha live in grey, impoverished worlds, inhabited only by passing strangers seen wholly from the outside, or (in *Mackenzie*) by other sad, blocked and dying people. This isn't just due to the 'West Indian factor' – though it's interesting that greater life should spring up in the two West Indian novels. For Laurie and Maudie aren't part of Anna's West Indian life; they belong to London and to the present, yet they have reality and vitality, they impinge upon Anna and the reader with their lively individual voices, their very different experience. And Tia, Aunt Cora, especially Christophine, do the same. It seems to me that the novels divide in this way between those written, as it were, by Jean (*Voyage in the Dark* and *Wide Sargasso Sea*) in which the heroine is the innocent victim she wanted to see – and in which, paradoxically, there is therefore some feeling left over for other people; and those (*Mackenzie* and *Good Morning, Midnight*) written by her other, mocking, self-aware self, in which the heroine is seen from the outside in all her hollowness and absurdity – but so, then, is the rest of the world. It's as though there was no clear, ordinary distinction for her between her heroine – herself – and other people: if she doubted and mocked herself, the world filled with doubt and mockery; if she could feel some pity and excuse for herself, she could find some pity and excuse for (a few) other people.*

---

*I've left out *Quartet*, because the pattern hadn't yet settled down there. Jean *wanted* to present Marya as an innocent victim like Anna and Antoinette, but failed. She also wanted to present Heidler as the ultimate villain, and failed: which suggests that the similarity I later find between her judgement of the heroine and her judgement of others was a balancing factor for her, the only way she could achieve control over unbalanced feelings of pity and fear.

*Good Morning, Midnight* is, as a result, like *Mackenzie*, and unlike
the two West Indian novels, in this way: *Voyage in the Dark* and
*Wide Sargasso Sea* open up to real worlds outside the heroine — the
worlds respectively of Edwardian chorus girls and of the nineteenth-
century Caribbean; while *Mackenzie* and *Good Morning, Midnight*
remain locked within the heroine's head, and no one else is quite as
real. Enno and his friends are only memories. Serge Rubin is present
but elusive — met only once and never seen again. Delmar 'seems
more the echo of a thing than the thing itself'; the *commis* isn't real
at all, but a nightmare figure of mysterious fear. That leaves, of
course, the gigolo, the other main character — the 'male lead', they'll
say when they make the movie. Surely *he* is powerfully there. He
is the heroine's opposite and enemy, the man; he's also everything
she doesn't want him to be — innocent, charming, irresistible. Yes;
this is all true. Yet he has a curious unreality too. We never know
what he really thinks and feels, even what he really *is*; he is as mysterious to us as to Sasha. He is Sasha's dream figure, almost as much
as the *commis* is her nightmare. Both of these — his reality and
unreality — are important for the full resonance of his role in the
story.

He seems real to Sasha, and so to us, partly because he *is* mysterious, because he withholds most of the truth about himself. The
*commis voyageur* is no more than Sasha imagines, a figure of fear. His
possible reality as a travelling salesman in a cheap hotel is the distant
background of this portrait, which we hardly feel or remember. He
is a 'lay figure', as Jean says about Bertha Mason, a symbol recognised
by his dress, like Death. About René Sasha has many and conflicting
feelings, as we have about real people. She wants and fears him, loves
and resents him; she finds him both attractive and absurd. He won't
fit into her fantasy of him, as the *commis* wholly fits into her
nightmare: he is there when she doesn't want him to be and not there
when she does; he escapes her plan of punishment. That makes him
feel quite real.

With René as a real man *Good Morning, Midnight* tells the
heroine's key outward story: she has a chance — a last chance —
of love, and through her own distrust and deliberate cruelty loses
it. It's clear there is this chance, though (and this itself is very real)
we can't be completely certain it really exists. René *seems* genuine
: he's nervous, he speaks urgently, he's really in trouble, he isn't
dressed for the Paris weather. On the other hand he is also lying.
He's not a French Canadian, as he says he is ('*Elle n'est pas si bête
que ca*'); he knows Paris, though he says he doesn't. He'd preyed
on at least one rich woman in the past — on the same rich woman
as Sasha — and claims to be preying on another now (though

Sasha says she doesn't believe in his American). Sasha's suspicions are clearly not unfounded; but neither is her hope. René is gay and natural, and makes her feel the same; he understands her — her childlikeness, her self-doubt, her fear — but doesn't use his knowledge against her. Despite herself she begins to love and trust him. If wanting to comfort someone isn't love, what is? she asks — and she wants to comfort him; 'If we're going to start believing each other it's getting serious, isn't it?' she says — and she is beginning to believe him. The truth is finally revealed by the plot: he *was* sincere. He doesn't take the money; he wanted her and not her money after all.

The story Sasha's is closest to is Marya's. This displacement of Sasha's anger on to René, his escape, and her final acceptance of the dreaded *commis* echo Marya's attack on Stephan instead of Heidler, Stephan's escape, and the closing glimpse of Marya dead or unconscious on the floor. This confirms the idea that one of the real people who went into the gigolo was John. He has not only bits of John's character and history (the Foreign Legion, the lack of papers). More importantly he has what Stephan had from Marya, what Enno had from Sasha, and what, we must surely guess, John had from Jean: an insecure love, a sympathy and pity for what they shared: for his risk-taking, his fun-loving and his anxiety. And most importantly, he reflects Jean's guilt towards John: her recognition that despite his elusiveness he had really loved her; that she had turned her anger on him unjustly; and that it was after losing him that she really 'began to go to pieces'.

But though the gigolo often feels like a real, separate person, he often doesn't. An important element of this is something we've already seen, for example in Norah and Horsfield in *After Leaving Mr Mackenzie*: a resemblance to the heroine, so that these others almost seem like mirrors or extensions of her own experience. René is, after all, a male version of Sasha — living off women as she lived off men, and unable to stop himself falling a little in love with his latest victim. He lives a dangerous hand-to-mouth life very like hers, and like her believes in luck and superstition. He too has been 'wounded', and is 'not always so fond of human beings'; he too is, or claims to be, alone in a strange city. He is sensitive and perceptive, like Sasha, but — judging from his choice of her — his commercial judgement is just as poor. Perhaps he has a better chance of success than she did: he's happier, healthier, less naive, and as soon as he's hurt he leaves. But maybe he's only younger. When he speaks of his wounds he seems to fall into a strange sad state, not so far from Sasha's black misery: perhaps no further than Sasha was herself at his age. He's not so far from it even now. 'Have you ever felt like this,' he says, ' — as if you can't bear any more, as if you must speak to someone, as if you must tell someone everything or otherwise you'll die?' He repeats this Sasha-like feeling several times. And others too; in fact he often sounds exactly like her. 'It's always when a thing sounds not true that it is true,' for instance; the heroines are always saying that. Or take the whole conversation about London. René is exactly like Anna was, and like Antoinette will be — full of absurd optimistic ideas about England, though he's never been there. Indeed their conversation about London could be the heroine (or even more, Jean) talking to herself — mocking herself for her ridiculous childhood hopes; blackly mocking the English for their dislike of sex and of women. René here is not at all like a separate person, a stranger recently met and hardly known; at most he and Sasha are like a double act, feeding each other lines from a written and rehearsed routine.

In the top line of this story, then, René is a real man, and Sasha loses her last chance of love by lashing out at him. But below this there runs a strange and intriguing under-melody, in which René feels less and less real, more and more like a figure in Sasha's fantasy, a mirror of her experience, or an aspect of her divided nature. I think he is all this, especially the last. Think back to Jean's (Anna's) first loss of love, with Lancelot (Walter), and what she told Francis Wyndham about that: she determined to perform an 'emotional operation on herself', to 'lock my heart and throw away the key,' as she wrote in one of her wartime stories. 'But of course this willed transformation was never complete,' Francis Wyndham says, 'and like a bungled sex-change operation it resulted in a confusion of identity.' Exactly; and exactly true of Sasha here. She tries to kill off in herself the need to love and trust; she tries to become cold, hard, invulnerable. But she only half succeeds: and so she breaks in two, into a cold hard self who sends René away, and a soft loving self who cries for him to return. In the under-melody, in which René is more, or less, than a real man, *that* is what he is: Sasha's own capacity for love and trust, *in fact her own younger self*, which she is consciously trying to cut off and send away. He is like the younger heroine, as we've seen — gay and optimistic, but already alone and already wounded: and the *commis voyageur* is like a nightmare vision of her future self, mad and mean, the ghost of a cheap hotel. In this sense there is no one in the novel but Sasha — or only Serge and Delmar far away, Enno and the others long ago. The main present drama between Sasha, the gigolo and the *commis voyageur* is (on this reading) an internal one: a battle between her own past and future, her own sanity and madness; between her impulse to join the human race and her impulse to stay outside it.

This means that we have two ways (at least two ways) of reading the novel's ending. On any reading the *commis voyageur* – alone, ghostlike, cringing, mean – represents a terrible, terminal condition. In so far as he is separate from Sasha he is (I've suggested) the culmination of the heroine's 'neighbour': 'another poor devil of a human being', mean and degraded. And the horror is that Sasha must finally accept him as her equal, her fate: she's tried to escape him for the gigolo, as she tried to escape her cheap hotel for a better one; but now she must accept him as she's accepted her room – 'Here I belong and here I'll stay.' On this reading her loss of the gigolo is the loss of a real chance of love through her own cruelty and suspicion; and her acceptance of the *commis* as her *semblable*, her *frère* is an acceptance, therefore, of her equality with the worst of cruel, suspicious humanity. That is why she has to give up hating them; but it is also why it is so horrible to her to have to do so. This must, I think, be our main reading. It makes sense of the tensions of the ending; it makes sense of Jean's own torment. But now if we think of the gigolo as the best, the *commis* as the darkest and meanest side of Sasha herself – that is a fruitful reading too, indeed for all the heroine's stories. It explains why they can never hurt anyone but themselves: because there's never anyone else there. And it gives us another element of the horror we feel in the ending: for Sasha's acceptance of the *commis* is now accepting suspicion and solitude as all there will be forever, with her loving, trusting side finally vanished. Such hate- and fear-filled solitude is the 'misery of utter darkness' we've just seen engulfing Sasha at the Deux Magots: so we know what swallows her up after the dots, in the empty, silent last page.

★  ★  ★

*Themes*: Just as the essential drama of *Good Morning, Midnight* has narrowed down to the heroine and two representative men, the lover and the neighbour – or perhaps just to the heroine – so its themes too have narrowed down from the earlier novels. Only one idea runs through them all, and is retained – though partly reversed – here: the cruelty of people and of 'organised society' to the weak and unprotected. *Mackenzie*'s struggle with nothingness and absurdity has also been retained; or rather it's been resolved, so that absurdity is at the heart of this novel's answer to the question of the cruelty of the world. The other themes with which *Quartet* began – the criticism of conventional morality and substitution of a morality of feeling, the key idea of pretence – have gone. In both of these the main ingredient was the superiority of the heroine: and that, of course, is what has most utterly and importantly gone. Sasha is pretending nothing to herself or to us any more; and because Sasha is or fills the world, pretence is no longer anywhere.

The main retained idea, then, is the cruelty of people. That is still there; the world is still a terrible place to the old, to the poor, to 'all the fools and all the defeated'. But it is no longer simply the blank, motiveless cruelty Marya saw in Heidler, or Anna in the woman at Oddenino's. That's still there too, in the horrible story of the Martiniquaise; in the cruelty of Sasha's family, the insensitivity of the boy from Manchester, the sudden maliciousness of Alfred the Turk, the nastiness of the fat hatshop girl and the red-haired girl at Théodore's. But *Good Morning, Midnight* doesn't leave it at that; its account doesn't end with Sasha's. First, it shows us that *she* is cruel; second, it shows us that she is wrong. She's wrong about the gigolo; she may therefore be wrong about others too. Her blanket suspicion of everyone is her worst mistake. She is like Lise: she has given up absurdly too soon.

And there's a third way in which this novel undermines the idea of people's cruelty: via the sense of absurdity which has come down from *Mackenzie*, and which now fills its world. Even the rich and powerful — especially the rich and powerful — are no longer simply cruel, but more than anything absurd. Mr Lawson, with his 'long, narrow, surprised face' and his imitation American, is so absurd that when Sasha remembers him she can't stop laughing. The Lyonnais is absurd, with his ambition to have his photo on the bands of his cigars. Even Sasha realises that her rich employer at Antibes was a ridiculous woman; and René is clear that all rich people are ridiculous, without the slightest idea how to enjoy their money. The only rich and powerful person who remains fairly straightforwardly terrifying is Mr Blank; and even here there are undermining glimpses. Sasha herself sees he's naive about how she got her job; and Jean sees that the expression on his face is as funny as Mr Lawson's: 'He looks at me as if I were a dog which had presented him with a very, very old bone.' Serge Rubin tells the worst story of cruelty in the book; but about his clients — the rich and powerful in *his* life — he just smiles, and calls them idiots.

Sasha may still believe in the cruelty of the world, then: but Jean doesn't, at least not wholly or simply. She explores it obsessively still: but as a belief, even a delusion, of her heroine's more than as a fact about the world. To her great question *Why do such terrible things happen? Good Morning, Midnight* answers, more than any of the other novels: *Because I expect, create and deserve them.*

There is, however, one way in which *Good Morning, Midnight* seems to keep its eye firmly fixed on cruelty. For it attempts to generalise from Sasha's case: to state the case of the underdog in general, not just the case of a fictional Jean Rhys. The main location of this attempt is, of course, in Sasha's tirade against Mr Blank. He represents 'society', she is 'an inefficient member' of it: her attack is therefore quite general. 'So you have the right to pay me four hundred francs a month, to lodge me in a small, dark room, to clothe me shabbily, to harass me with worry and monotony,' she mocks him. 'Let's say that you have this mystical right to cut my legs off. But the right to ridicule me afterwards because I am a cripple – no, that I think you haven't got. And that's the right you hold most dearly, isn't it? You must be able to despise the people you exploit....' This striking out into social criticism is echoed several times later: when Sasha suggests that the hardships of her confinement are shared by all poor people; when she says 'never tell the truth about this business of rooms, because it would bust the roof off everything and undermine the whole social system'; when Delmar suggests that the rich and powerful are automatically guilty. This is brief and allusive, as always. But it's more open social criticism than in any of the novels since *Quartet*: hugely more than in the last one, *Voyage in the Dark*, which had none at all, even though its plot was a classic tale of the rich getting the pleasure, the poor getting the blame. In this if nothing else *Good Morning, Midnight* is on a straight line to *Wide Sargasso Sea*, which finally roots the heroine's suffering in her social and political condition.

And yet – it's not quite true. Jean *tries* to lift this novel from the particular to the general, from Sasha to all the poor and defeated – but she's too honest to succeed. She shows us that in fact Sasha doesn't really care about the poor and exploited at all – like the curly-haired girl, who has a really nasty job, and probably gets far less than four hundred francs a month. 'What's all that to me?' she asks. 'What can I do about it? Nothing.' She was 'very much impressed' by her rich employer's house at Antibes; she only wanted to keep her job there, and still dreams about it sometimes. When René makes fun of the rich she counters by making fun of him: 'You're going to alter all that, aren't you?' No: the truth is told (again) by Delmar, speaking of Serge Rubin. 'Serge understands everybody,' and 'says he's of the extreme left,' he says: but it's all nonsense, he doesn't really care. '*Mais au fond, vous savez, il s'en fiche de tout, il s'en fiche de tout le monde.*' That's the truth about Sasha too. She even says so. 'The agitation is only on the surface. Underneath I'm indifferent.'

This aspect of the novel follows the main pattern of effort, failure and collapse. For there is something very important about Sasha's attack on Mr Blank: *she didn't really make it*. She didn't even think it. She thinks it now, and we overhear her; but to his face she said only that she was ill, and as far as we know thought nothing. In other words, Sasha's attack on the man she hates is exactly like Antoinette's: only dreamed,* years later. And the real attack she makes, at the end of the story, isn't on Mr Blank, or on Mr Lawson, who have exploited her. It's on René, one of her fellow exploited: on a brother doormat, someone who is a mirror of herself. Jean tried to lift Sasha out of herself, on to the level of the 'social system'; but she fell back, having reached nothing. Sasha cannot even *want* to attack the Mr Blanks and Mr Lawsons; she can only want to attack a René, and she can only manage to hurt herself. It's always the same: the heroine cannot escape the circle of her self. However hard she tries she remains locked inside her own head. And that was true of Jean too, even as a writer. She tried to get her most objective novel outside her heroine, to make it cry for all the fools and all the defeated. But it only cried for herself after all. Because it's so sharp and true we can take from it a more general meaning. Jean would be glad; she would want us to. But she couldn't *write* a general meaning, even here.

★    ★    ★

The first thing that strikes us when we read Jean Rhys — especially the four 'modern' novels — is how obsessive she is, how similar they are. There is always the same heroine, at different ages. There are always the same themes of isolation and rejection, of cruelty and oppression, of passive and impotent anger. There are always the same images, though some of them grow from novel to novel: Anna's and Julia's dog who becomes Sasha's wolf; Marya's 'Monsieur Monvoisin' who becomes Sasha's neighbour; the women — including the heroine — whom age and lost love push ever higher up the stairs. There is always the same stasis: the same block between intention and act, dream and reality; the same 'shooting upwards not to plead but to threaten,' and the same sinking down again, 'useless, having reached nothing.' There is always the same sense of doom, of something hidden and waiting beneath the surface. And to all this dark and hopeless lassitude there is always the same contrast — in Jean's flashing, mocking, knifelike prose.

It's almost as though all her writing from *Quartet* to *Good Morning, Midnight* was one long novel, slowly spiralling up the same circular staircase, up Julia's mauve corkscrew. Each step ends in failure,

*For the actual setting fire to Thornfield Hall occurs only in *Jane Eyre*; Antoinette only dreams it, and *sets out* to do it.

abandonment, solitude — but Anna thinks about 'starting all over again', and Julia steps into the hour between dog and wolf with another hundred francs in her handbag. Finally the whole series ends in the acceptance of utter failure, as Sasha puts her arms around the *commis*.

Each novel, and all four novels together, are about the death of love; but they are even more about the birth of hate. By *Good Morning, Midnight* Jean knows where that hate really is: not in other people, but in the heroine. 'And when I say afraid,' Sasha says, 'that's just a word I use. What I really mean is that I hate them,' 'the whole bloody human race.' When she thought of her suffering and rejection, that is what Jean felt: she hated the whole human race. But she couldn't bear to; it made her feel terribly guilty, and terribly alone. So she hid it; and it took her four novels to cut away the surface of self-pity and expose it. She began *Quartet* in hot anger and the desire for revenge; finally in *Good Morning, Midnight* she faced that, and understood it. And then she put down her pen and forgot again.

But now it's clear that our first feeling was wrong. Underneath the obsessive patterns, the echoes and repetitions, there's been huge change and growth in the four modern novels. From Marya through Julia to Sasha (with a slip back to the beginning of the spiral in Anna) Jean struggled from blindness to self-knowledge, from the rejection of blame to the acceptance of it. It cost her everything; but it was worth it. *Good Morning, Midnight* is her masterpiece of self-knowledge, and a very great novel. The only question is whether you can bear it; if you can read it at all, you must admire it. You can't feel about Sasha as you can about Marya, even about the others — simply irritated by her incompetence, her self-pity, her excuses. For she irritates herself; she takes the words out of our mouths, and is crueller to herself than we could ever be. And there's neither self-pity nor excuses left; there is no more hiding, no more pretending. Sasha is to us as she imagines being to René at the end; not indeed 'simple and unafraid', but herself. *We can look at her if we want to.* It is an extraordinary achievement, for Sasha is as awful as she fears. And yet we like her. We certainly like her infinitely more than Marya. The reason, of course, is that she *knows* she's awful, and Marya didn't. Marya told us she wasn't to blame, so we blamed her even more; she thought she was better than other people, so we knew she was worse. With Sasha it is the other way around: she accepts her guilt, so we can admire and pity her. And when I say Sasha, of course, I mean Jean too. We couldn't have pitied and admired her so much if she'd never written *Good Morning, Midnight*; and we would pity and admire her still more if her other novels had been as brave.

But she couldn't do it. She didn't want to be loved and pitied for being awful but brave, as she was; or to be admired for being a great writer, as she was. She wanted to be loved and admired for being what she wasn't: ordinary, gentle, entirely beautiful. It was an impossible desire. The only real tribute is the other one after all: the one readers of *Good Morning, Midnight* pay to Sasha; and the one I hope readers of this book will pay to Jean.

She couldn't do it, I say – but she was pushing herself towards it in all her writing, and in *Good Morning, Midnight* she got there, to the exhibition of herself. Already in *Mackenzie*, at the beginning of her great decade of writing, the heroine's brain had almost burst with the effort to know 'the thing that was behind all this talking and posturing.' For Jean the novels themselves were this effort to know. And in the last one of the decade she succeeded. At the end of *Good Morning, Midnight* she wrote:

> This is the effort, the enormous effort, under which the human brain cracks. But not before the thing is done, not before the mountain moves.

For Sasha this is the effort to will René back, to will reality to fit her dream. And the effort succeeds: a real man enters her room. But of course this real man isn't René – isn't love; he is the *commis* – meanness and madness. And Sasha says: 'I don't need to look. I know.' She knows the reality beneath the posturing at last; and it's this: meanness and madness. Her brain cracks, and she accepts them as her fate, her due.

In writing this, Jean was also writing about her own effort. In *Good Morning, Midnight* she knew the reality beneath her own posturing: and it wasn't gentleness and love, but meanness and hate. In the novel's ending she accepted them. But the effort cracked her brain, as it cracked Sasha's. I've said that Antoinette's madness awaited Sasha in the blank page at the end of the novel: of course that was fiction, because Sasha and Antoinette are fictions. But Jean was real. It was her own real madness she pulled down at the end of *Good Morning, Midnight*, and knew in the long blank page before *Wide Sargasso Sea*.

If we think of *Good Morning, Midnight* humanly, as something Jean lived with for perhaps a year of her life, we can see this madness coming. Not just in what's there – in Sasha's misery and degradation, in her inability to escape or act, in all the terrifying imagery. We can also see it in what is absent: in the way the novel lets go of what's been, so far, the heroine's world. It's never been a solid world, and it's got steadily less solid; but in *Good Morning, Midnight* it breaks up and disappears altogether. The heroine has always lived in cheap hotels, but at least other people had homes and houses in the other novels – the Heidlers in *Quartet*, Julia's family in *Mackenzie*, Walter in *Voyage in the Dark*. There are no homes left in *Good Morning, Midnight*; the whole world is cheap hotels. There are no 'respectable people' left, except at the very fringes of the novel. Mr Blank, Mr Lawson, Sasha's friend Sidonie, her family, employers and clients – they're all minor characters who've never been important to her, and who are now only memories. All her present and most of her past are filled with people as drifting and rootless as herself. René, Serge and Delmar are all lonely exiles like her, Serge an artist, René an adventurer, Delmar we don't know what ('He looks like a person who is living on a very small fixed income'). Enno was an adventurer too, a *chansonnier* and occasional journalist; all their friends were poor and raffish like themselves, and several of them (like Dickson in The Hague, Alfred in Paris) were also exiles. Even the 'respectable' ones we see in foreign countries – Mr Blank in France, Mr Lawson in Belgium, Sidonie (we guess) a Parisian in London. *No one* is at home or solid any more.

The main solid, respectable person who's missing, in fact, is the heroine's English lover. Sasha has never had – at least she never tells us she's had – a lover like Walter Jeffries or W. Neil James, Heidler or Mr Mackenzie. All the other heroines have come close to a solid world through their English lovers. Indeed that was Anna's and Marya's whole story – coming close to the solid world, and losing it. The solid English lover receded to the very edges of Julia's story, but he was still there. With Sasha he's gone altogether, forgotten perhaps, or never achieved. So the heroine is cast utterly into limbo and insecurity; she has no connection left, however tenuous, to English respectability, which, however much she hated it, was the only safe and comforting thing in her world. This suggests several interesting things. About Jean herself it suggests that by the time she wrote *Good Morning, Midnight* Lancelot was really and finally lost to her; and that Leslie – for all his respectable family, his Oxford accent and education – couldn't give her that solid feeling. About *Good Morning, Midnight* it raises a question. Without the English lover we haven't seen Sasha seriously rejected, like the other heroines. The only man we ever see her with apart from René is her husband, Enno; she doesn't hate *him*, and we wouldn't understand if she did. May we not wonder, then, quite where her desire for revenge comes from? The only lovers she can want to revenge herself on (Mr Lawson and Mr Blank are not lovers) are casual pick-ups, such as she is (she thinks) to René; these are the only other men we know she's had. And this makes her seem, surely, a little madder: that she should want such revenge for passing, anonymous failures. The big hurt which we know motivates the other angry heroines is missing.

*Good Morning, Midnight* then, is like a boat that's cut its moorings and drifted free. Real people, solid land, the possibility of both love *and* hate, all disappear. England especially disappears; even France is reduced to a few voices in a few rooms. Europe and Jean's real life there are exhausted and empty. She is turning away. To breakdown; but also to the other time and place she carried with her: the past, and the West Indies.

# PART THREE

# THE LOST YEARS
# 1939-1966

# CHAPTER ONE

# War, 1939-1945

*Norfolk — Breakdown — The Gower Peninsula*
*John and Maryvonne — Leslie's death*

The second war, like the first, was a black hole in Jean's life. She fell back into the water, and it closed over her head: only occasionally can we glimpse her white face. In the last years of the 1930s *Good Morning, Midnight* had appeared and disappeared; she had written the first version of *Wide Sargasso Sea*, and then burned it; she had touched another novel in her West Indian past — but *it* had burned *her*, and she'd dropped it; she had written notebooks full of buried memories and lacerating self-analysis. She had come closer than she ever had before, or would again, to the truths she both pursued and fled. That in itself must have unbalanced her. Then the war finished her off: taking Maryvonne from her, and Leslie, and John; isolating her in strange cold places among strange cold people; worst of all, killing her best book, adding up all her labour of twelve years and under it writing: *nothing*.

Until the summer of 1939 she and Leslie had been living in Taplow, on the Thames to the west of London. But just before war broke out they seem to have moved back into London, indeed back into Chelsea. Maryvonne was in England on her annual summer holiday, and on 3 September Leslie took them boating on the river. When they got home trenches were being dug in Hyde Park. John wrote to Jean that Maryvonne must return to Holland at once because Hitler was planning to invade England. ('He doesn't seem to have realised,' Jean said, 'that he'd invade Holland first.') She let Maryvonne decide: where did she want to be? For the second time in her life Maryvonne chose her father. 'She left on one of the last planes,' Jean said: and that was the last she would see of her for six years. In 1939 Maryvonne was still a child, a convent-educated seventeen; in 1945 she would be a woman who had survived dangers and deprivations Jean could hardly imagine.

'I didn't exactly retire to the country when war broke out,' Jean wrote in her self-mocking mode to Diana Athill. 'What happened was more complicated. Too complicated to condense. Still I'd like *someone* to know just for the record what actually happened.' When Jean says something's too complicated to tell she means she *won't* tell, for her own reasons. And despite her ringing declaration, she doesn't. 'Leslie (my husband) joined the RAF when war broke out,' she said. 'I went around with him for a time, then about buzz bomb period we came back to London.' Leslie joined up in February 1940; the buzz bombs, the first of Hitler's 'secret weapons', came at nearly the end of the war. She's left the whole time blank, from 1940 to 1944.

The parts which can be filled in show why she kept silent.

First, she said, she 'went around with Leslie for a time.' Even this doesn't seem to have been quite true. Leslie was commissioned as a Pilot Officer on 15 February 1940, and posted first to Bircham Newton in the north-west corner of Norfolk. He stayed there for a year; then in February 1941 he was promoted to Flying Officer,* and sent to an Air Ministry Experimental Station at West Beckham near Holt. Presumably Jean went with him to Bircham Newton; but by August 1940 she was already in Holt, six months before him. And when he arrived in February 1941, she soon moved on – even perhaps had already moved on – to Norwich. Much was already wrong between them; but nothing could be wrong enough to make Jean choose to live alone. Something extra must have happened to make her leave Bircham Newton around mid-1940, and again to leave Holt in early 1941.

Well, something certainly happened in May 1940: Hitler's armies invaded Holland. And the last thing Jean thought she knew about Maryvonne made things worse: she was staying with Jewish friends. Jean had been worried about her for many months, now she was terrified. And this may have been a last straw. When Laura breaks down in 'I Spy A Stranger' it was (we can calculate) in a June. Jean very often kept the timing of real events for her fiction. It is possible, therefore, that in or around June 1940 she had some sort of collapse, serious or spectacular enough to make her need to get away from Bircham Newton.

In any case we know that she did move on to Holt ahead of Leslie; and that instead of getting better there she got worse. We know this from what she wrote there – 'Temps Perdi' and its traces in her Orange Notebook; and from outside her writing too. This time we *know* that something happened. It was the same thing that

---

*Not that he ever flew. Leslie was fifty five in 1940, and all his Air Force jobs were in administration.

had happened in 1935, during the Jubilee: at the end of July she was arrested for being drunk and disorderly. But this time there was a new dimension to her humiliation: it was reported in the local papers.

> Ella Gwendoline Tilden Smith, of Holt, was fined for being drunk and disorderly on the highway at Holt.
>
> ...Police Constable Haverson stated defendant was unsteady on her feet, her appearance was dishevelled, and her breath smelt strongly of spirits. She broke out into a stream of abuse of the English race, declaring, according to one witness, 'I am a West Indian, and I hate the English. They are a b----- mean and dirty lot.' The disorderly conduct ... arose only after one of the witnesses had thrown water over her. Mrs Tilden Smith was very distressed because no news had been received of her daughter in Holland since the invasion of that country.

It's terrible to think of this — Jean on a country road, raging at England; someone throwing a bucket of water over her. And this was the woman who had already written some of the finest prose of our century. No wonder she struggled all her life to understand herself; no wonder she felt like twins, one 'accepted', 'the other lost, betrayed, forsaken, a wanderer in a very dark wood.'

This other was taking over now; and that's no wonder either. Surely this part of 'Temps Perdi' came unaltered from Jean's diary: 'I did not want to live there [in Holt] alone — especially in October, November, December and January.' (Leslie arrived in West Beckham in February). But judging from the story and its related writings, that is what she did. Why? All she left in 'Temps Perdi' is a typical acceptance of fate: 'There are times when one is helpless.' Perhaps (as I've guessed) she had made it impossible for herself to stay in Bircham Newton, with a similar sort of disaster. Or perhaps the house was offered to them early — they always longed for decent housing. 'Rolvenden' (as Jean calls it in 'Temps Perdi') was certainly decent, with three bedrooms, a garage, a lawn, a large vegetable garden. But she soon hated it, and it — she felt — hated her. It was square, red brick, on the furthest edge of the village. 'There is nothing in it that you can say is ugly,' Jean wrote, 'on the other hand there is nothing that you can say is beautiful, impulsive, impetuous or generous.' Everything in it was cheap and cold and hard — the beds, the tables and chairs, the pictures on the wall. It hid its hate under a hypocrite's mask of beige: beige paint, carpets, curtains, upholstery, bedspreads. 'Everything wears this neutral mask — the village, the people, the sky, even the trees have not escaped.'

'Even the trees have not escaped': things were getting bad. Her other allies, books, began to desert her too. 'This is my life now, books,' she scrawled in the Orange Notebook, amid things she would use for 'Temps Perdi'. 'I should die if it were not for books.' But in the story itself she wrote: 'Now I am almost as wary of books as I am of people ... when there are so many all saying the same thing they can shout you down and make you doubt, not only your memory, but your senses....' Instead she clung to her memory and senses against the world. She retreated into the past, into memories of Dominica and Vienna which she put into 'Temps Perdi', into memories of the First War which she didn't. And 'all sorts of strange things' began to happen. 'I don't fight against them any more. I've opened the door and "walk in" I say....' She *knew* things: that people were stealing from her − her coal, even her letters; where a stolen letter lay, hidden under the snow; when her cigarettes had arrived in the shop. Above all, she knew she was hated. 'I am greatly disliked,' she wrote − and then, pressing hard, she gave the last two words capital letters, for emphasis or mockery. And added, in brackets: 'That isn't a miracle either.'

Everyone knew about her, of course. She wrote of a gardener who 'has heard of my disgrace,' and who 'peeps in on me as I lie huddled on the sofa, with the curtains half drawn, reading *Martin Chuzzlewit* in very small print.' Generally she pretended to be asleep; she spoke to him once and found him 'nice', but even then she immediately retreated: 'I cut this conversation short because I like him and am nervous of something happening to spoil the liking...'. Otherwise she felt like Laura in 'I Spy a Stranger': surrounded by gossip, suspicion, cruelty, hate. And no doubt that was true too. She knew how she looked, how she behaved. When she drank, she talked like 'an old shrew', and people laughed at her ('Very cold weather, Madam,' says one of the coalmen in 'Temps Perdi', winking at the first one... and before they got to the gate... I saw that they were shaking with laughter.') She knew she had 'a *gift* for making enemies'; that people thought she was crazy, a witch, a German spy. To keep herself from cracking entirely she wrote and wrote, trying to keep on with her task of telling the truth.

> The worse things get the more I cling to it − all the big things gone, all the little things gone − the more I cling to the one thing I have left, the desire to tell the truth. 'Ah, swine!' I think, 'I have that left anyway.'

But she didn't. She was too far gone. That comes out as she went on:

> I cling to this idea obstinately, as some people cling to spite, some to anonymous letters, some to religion, some to money,

some to the idea that they are really of a very high caste indeed in spite of dirty tricks and dirty clothes....

Her swelling obsessions fill the Orange Notebook, and the other fragments that probably also date from this period. And though she tried harder than ever to cut and shape them, the stories she made from them are full of obsessions too.* We know what they are: her hatred of England, England's hatred of women (England's hatred of her). Thus, in the Orange Notebook she puts down the coalmen's conversation — ' "That's the bathroom in there." "Is there a woman in the ditch?" said the second man — In the ditch, that's what he said' — and then goes on:

> I'm sick of the woman hatred in this country. It's so mean, so stupid and so ugly that ['it is quite impossible 'scored out] it would be mean and & cowardly not to hate back....
> *Who* said England & hell, the white cliffs of Albion & of hell, or hell like England has white cliffs —

There are other resemblances....

'Temps Perdi', the most contained wartime story, to some degree controls and transforms these twin obsessions. The coalmen's conversation is expanded to reveal as much aggression in the narrator as in the men. The rest of the 'woman hatred' is distanced, given to remembered, non-English people: to Captain Yoshi, who says that only the Germans know how to treat women, and to the 'up-to-the-minute Negro' who writes 'Girls muck, girls muck' on a tree. The England-is-hell idea is distanced too, attributed to a book and made at least a bit lighter: ' "It would be a very humorous idea if England were designated as the land of the dead ... as hell. In such a form, in truth, England has appeared to many a stranger." ' (But Jean can't resist underlining it: 'To many a stranger ...,' her narrator echoes.)

Then, in 'I Spy a Stranger', the obsessions came closer. First of all, Laura's 'persecution mania' is entirely underwritten. The formal

---

*By 'What! No Trumpets?' her original title for 'Temps Perdi', she wrote in the Orange Notebook: 'Combination of [?] and Diary'. At least a dozen pages of the Orange Notebook contain material that went into 'Temps Perdi'; only three have connections to 'I Spy a Stranger', but it clearly comes out of the Holt experience too, and/or similar experiences just before (perhaps) and after. 'I Spy a Stranger' is set in a small town on the east coast, just like 'Temps Perdi'.

The Orange Notebook has a great deal more about 'women hatred', eg in an early version of 'The Insect World'. Also just on its own, eg: 'You simply cannot imagine my dear the hatred of the average man here for woman.'

distancing which is achieved by having her story told by someone else is only superficial. Mrs Hudson is not on Laura's side (though not entirely against her either); but the effect of this is to present her quite objectively, and not only in her own view, as innocent, persecuted and misunderstood. She *is* 'tactless and badly behaved', and quarrels with everyone; but Mrs Hudson's account, and Mrs Trant's and Dr Pratt's remarks, justify her. Her life has fallen to pieces through no fault of her own; her sweetheart and friends are threatened by the Gestapo; and no one in England understands. Instead they all behave much worse than she does. Ricky, Fluting, the townspeople are all monsters, with whom it *would* be mean and cowardly not to quarrel — especially, as with Fluting, in defence of others. There is no hint that this heroine (like Sasha Jensen, or the narrator of 'Temps Perdi') drinks too much, or attacks people for no reason, or does anything but keep silent as long as she can under intolerable provocation. Like Anna Morgan after Julia Martin, Laura after Sasha is a return from self-exposure to self-justification.

But the result is exposure rather than justification. 'I Spy a Stranger' makes Laura's madness — which is to say, Jean's — terribly visible. Like Marya's selfishness, we see it all the more because she doesn't: and because, therefore, she can't control it. We see it especially in Laura's exercise book. Here Jean's obsessions take over the story, unbalance it, make it mad. For she gives almost three whole pages — one-fifth of the story — to Laura's writing. For this to work they would have to support the story's claim that she *isn't* just 'a crazy old foreigner', 'as mad as a hatter', as Ricky says; they would have to make us, like Mrs Hudson, 'see what she meant'. But I fear they don't do this: I fear they make us see what Ricky meant instead.

Thus, Jean's machine obsession, which begins in 'Outside the Machine' and *Good Morning, Midnight,* flowers here: 'A mechanical quality about everything and everybody which I found frightening. When I bought a ticket for the Tube, got on a bus, went into a shop, I felt like a cog in a machine in contact with others, not like one human being associated with other human beings. The feeling that I had been drawn into a mechanism which intended to destroy me became an obsession....' And her insect obsession too, which would come out again in 'The Insect World': 'Titles of books to be written ten years hence, or twenty, or forty, or a hundred: *Woman an Obstacle to the Insect Civilisation?*' .... Above all, her twin obsessions about England and its hatred of women:

... Then, of course, England and the English. Here everybody, especially Blanca, would become acrimonious. 'Their extraordinary attitude to women.' 'They're all mad.' ... And so on....

And I began to feel that she wasn't so far wrong. There is something strange about the attitude to women as women. Not the dislike (or fear). That isn't strange of course. But it's all so completely taken for granted, and surely that is strange.... There is *no* opposition....

Titles of books to be written ten years hence, or twenty, or forty, or a hundred: *Woman an Obstacle to the Insect Civilisation? The Standardisation of Woman, the Mechanisation of Woman, Misogyny* — well, call it misogyny — *Misogyny and British Humour* will write itself ... *Misogyny and War, the Misery of Woman and the Evil in Men or the Great Revenge that Makes all other Revenges Look Silly.* My titles go all the way from the sublime to the ridiculous.

Apart from being too mad, this is also, surely, too literary. It is like Jean's list of her titles in the Orange Notebook; it is the sort of thing a writer would think of — but Laura isn't a writer. It is as though both the problems of *Quartet* have returned together: the loss of control over the heroine's anger, and the intrusion of an uncontrolled, unexplained literary element. It intrudes again later, when Laura quarrels with old Mr Roberts for pretending to kick his dog. He says 'Here's Emily Brontë' and pretends to kick it — and Laura can hardly contain her anger. This feels 'exaggerated', baffling; we can't quite understand it. For this is *Jean's* anger, a woman writer's anger at a joke against a woman writer, and again — Laura isn't a writer. It would have been better for this story if she were.

Thus, 'October, November, December and January' passed at Rolvenden. Finally loneliness drove Jean so far that even writing no longer helped, was no longer possible. So she resorted once again to her final solution: running away. By the spring of 1941 she'd run away to Norwich. But before that she'd tried to run even further. In 'A Solid House' the heroine remembers trying to kill herself:

> ... You know, there does come an afternoon when you think 'I want a rest, I want a good long sleep.' So I took two tablets, and then another two. Then I drank some whisky and it seemed quite clear. Now, my lass, now Hope, the vulture, will have to go and feed on somebody else. I thought, 'I must wear my pretty dress for this.' So I went upstairs and put on my blue dress and powdered my face. I didn't hurry, but when I came down again the hands of the clock hadn't moved at all. Which shows that it's true, what they say: 'Time is made for slaves'. Then I knew I must do it so I swallowed all the tablets in the bottle with the

whisky. Seven grains each they were — strong. And I saw some spilt on the floor. 'I must take these too,' I thought. But before I could take them I don't remember anything more.
When I woke up the first thing I saw was the blue dress on the chair. And the doctor was there. 'What are you doing here?' I said, and he answered, 'It's the afternoon I always come to see you.' So I knew it was Tuesday. A whole night and a day gone, and I shall never know what happened. And afterwards too I don't remember. I had dreams, of course. But were they dreams?...

At the very end of her life Jean said that she did once try to commit suicide. She thought the doctor would send her to an asylum, she said; but he was silent, indifferent. Perhaps that was true. Or perhaps what Teresa says in 'A Solid House' is true — *'Afterwards too I don't remember. I had dreams, of course. But were they dreams?'* — and then she tells of a dreamlike, or nightmarelike, house, which she seems to approach from a river.

> ...The paddle did not make a sound, the dead leaves slowed the punt down. Round a corner was the house — turrets and gables and balconies and green shutters all mixed up. It looked empty and dilapidated. The boards of the landing stage were broken and rotten. Two statues faced one another — the gentleman wore a cocked hat, knee-breeches and tail-coat, but the lady showed a large breast. She held up her draperies with one hand, the other was raised as if she were listening. The lawn was dark green and smooth and in the middle was a cedar tree. The rocking-horse under it was painted white with red spots. There wasn't a sound. And I knew that if I could pass the statues and touch the tree and walk into the house, I should be well again. But they wouldn't let me do that, the simple thing that always makes you well.

In the published story she goes on 'How much shall I tell her? Shall I tell her that in spite of everything they did I died then?' And in an early draft she wrote more:

> ...Shall I tell her about the four [walls?] of the room where I lay [?] I got to know the shape of each shadow; and I knew that the tree outside waved so wildly because it was trying to tear itself up by the roots, and escape.... And every night the white ship whistled — once gaily, once calling, once to say goodbye.

Perhaps Jean didn't go to Teresa's riverside asylum, or to Laura's near Newcastle, with its barred windows and its high wall. But she did go to somewhere like them, at least once.* This was in any case a time when she was close to real madness, out of which she created her maddest heroines, Teresa, Laura and Antoinette. Especially Antoinette, to whom she gave Teresa's special dress, the statue's raised draperies, and the white ship calling.

By March 1941 she was in Norwich, in dreary digs in a street in Chapelfield: the 'solid house', we may guess, in which 'Miss Spearman' lets rooms to Teresa after her illness. Teresa is at most a few weeks past her attempt to kill herself, and her stay in the other 'solid house' where they failed to help her; she's still extremely shaky. And so was Jean. She was seeing a psychiatrist – the first time that had happened, as far as we know. His name was Dr Rose, and he had a private practice in Norwich.

Her main trouble was the same as ever: she was utterly lonely. She was so lonely that she got in touch with Peggy Kirkaldy, whom she hadn't seen since their quarrel ten years before. She went – by herself – all the way to Colchester to visit her. But alas, it was no good. 'I've been alone so much and so long that talking went to my head,' she wrote to Peggy afterwards: she couldn't stop talking about herself, herself, herself.... She lay awake that night, unable to face returning to her solitude.

> I've tried to train myself to bear complete loneliness [she wrote], tried hard. But the night before I left Colchester I lay awake horrified at the thought of it. Revolted – longing to come down to you and implore you to help me out of my solitary confinement. And what it's made of me.

She didn't come down, 'for now I'm too deeply suspicious of human beings.' Instead she dwelt on her suspicions – Peggy had been irritated by her, Peggy didn't like her ... she worked herself into a volcanic state: and when Peggy said something rude (she thought) next day, she exploded. God knows what she said – something bad enough to make Peggy turn away again and not seek her out for several years. Jean was desolate; she hadn't meant to do this, quite

---

*Diana Athill, for instance, always had the impression that Jean's family had committed her, probably more than once, and that this was at the root of her intense hatred of them. And there is some proof that this may already have happened before 1950 (we will see that it happened at least once after). In Jean's Ropemakers Diary (written around 1951–52) half the pages were torn out, but some had words left on the margin. They were clearly from drafts of letters, one to Owen, one to Edward; and in the one to Edward there is the line: 'As for the other ... home ... that turn ... a looney-bin': surely 'As for the other nursing-home, that turned out to be a looney bin.'

the opposite. She tried to apologise, she said how much she admired and cared for Peggy, she pleaded brokenly:

> Please think of me kindly. I need it badly. Badly. Also *please* don't think that I contemplated hanging on to you – mentally or otherwise.
> No it was just – I wanted to be sure you were my friend and –
> How stupid this all is. Pompous and meaningless. Impossible –
> . . . .
> Oh Peggy. I can't bear much more of my hideous life. It revolts me quite simply – . . . .

It's one of the most nakedly desperate letters she ever wrote. But even in the middle of this she could see the root of her trouble: '*Dear Peggy – I meant for once to write about you and not about myself. You see – "it's stronger than I"* . . . .' She could see it; but that was all.

Two days after this letter Jean may have received another blow. For on 23 March Lancelot Hugh Smith died. For days his obituary, his funeral and memorial services, appeared in the national papers, and perhaps she saw them. If anything could have made her feel more miserable it would be this death. Lancelot had been her greatest love and best hope of happiness; and if he was dead she must be old. He had died very near her, in his house at Garboldisham and he was buried at Garboldisham a few days later. But of course for Jean it might as well have been a world away. If she knew about it, she didn't go to his funeral.

She was so low now, in any case, that she turned to someone else for help: Phyllis Shand Allfrey, her 'young friend' from Dominica. She'd already talked more openly to Phyllis Allfrey than to most people, perhaps because of their Dominica connection; and I think she did so again now. At any rate Phyllis certainly learned this spring where Jean was, and what a bad state she was in. And she determined to do something about it. A year or two before she had met a kind, idealistic clergyman who lived in Norfolk, the Reverend Willis Feast: would he help Jean? He would. Whenever she was at rock bottom, *someone* would always help. Now it was Willis Feast.

He called on Jean in her rooms, taking one of his daughters along. (Even 'Miss Spearman' can't have said anything about that – a respectable middle-aged clergyman and a child.) Bombs were falling on Norwich, as they do in 'A Solid House'. This made yet another reason to rescue Jean, and Mr Feast invited her to come and stay with his family in the village of Booton. That was how she came to be living in a country vicarage in the summer of 1941.

There were often extra people at the Rectory, partly because of Mr Feast's desire to offer refuge, and partly in order to eke out his meagre clergyman's salary. This summer, for example, there was also an elderly aunt who had come to escape the bombing in London. But Jean had the 'best bedroom': it was large and light, and she spent almost all her time there. She didn't even have to join the family for meals; all three were brought up to her on a tray. Leslie came once a week and spent the whole day with her. The weather was fine; on specially sunny days she would take a rug and cushion into the garden and lie in the shade of a large beech tree, reading *For Whom the Bell Tolls* very slowly. It was warm; she was both left alone and taken care of, and she should have been happy. But of course she wasn't. And because for once she was not alone, we can catch a rare glimpse of what she was like from the outside, through other people's eyes.

She was now fifty years old; she had her fifty-first birthday at Booton in August. Her hair was quite white, or grey, and she hated that. Also she was plump again. But she was still very attractive, and still wanted to be. To the Feasts' elder daughter she looked like Claudette Colbert. When she went into Norwich she would dress smartly (but datedly) in a suit, and a hat with a feather. When two men friends visited Mr Feast she was 'quite natural' with them, and 'really seemed to enjoy herself.' Once she even held court under the beech tree in the garden: attracting the men's eyes, because her long flowered housecoat was tight and one or two buttons were open. At such times she was 'very sweet and regal'. Sometimes she talked intently about books – including her own – to Willis Feast, who was keenly literary. But these relaxed and engaged moments were rare.

The trouble was that she was drinking, and not writing, and she thought she would never write again. Also she was terribly worried about Maryvonne. She told Willis Feast that Leslie drank, which wasn't true. Everyone knew that *she* was drinking, and that she had been ill and had tried to commit suicide. And everyone could see that she was in a very bad state. She couldn't concentrate; she had no energy; she was restless and bored. Willis Feast racked his brains to think of things to interest her, but she turned them all down. Finally she agreed that she would like to arrange flowers: but she hadn't the energy to pick them. The rector went out and picked some rhododendrons himself, appearing with them hopefully, incongruously in his arms. But no one remembers her arranging them.

Most of the time she hid away in her room, holding herself in, avoiding people, 'shamming dead' like Laura in 'I Spy a Stranger'. But everyone could see, too, that she was really 'very miserable and bad tempered.' She would 'fly off the handle on the slightest provocation.' Poor Mr Feast was no better than Leslie at these moments. At lunch in Lyons' or Woolworth's in Norwich Jean would grumble at being taken slumming and he would try vainly to soothe her. His friend Eric Griffiths* showed impatience instead – and made an enemy of her. She plainly disliked him; she told him he was 'self-satisfied'. Later she accused his wife and sister of wanting to stab her with their knitting needles – *à propos* of nothing, and perhaps half-joking; just because (Griffiths thought) she was bored with the conversation. Then one day she turned on Willis Feast himself. He heard her going out to the garden and went to the door to ask 'Are you all right?' She flew into a rage, shouting 'Why can't you leave me alone? Why do you always spy on me?' She couldn't stop; she grew more and more hysterical, until Mrs Feast slapped her face like a nurse and she calmed down.

Apart from this occasion she was quiet and polite in front of the Feast children, who were only ten and thirteen; but even with them she couldn't always keep control. One chilly evening the elder, Barbara, was sent up to ask if she wanted a hot water bottle. Perhaps, like any thirteen-year-old, she resented being sent on errands; 'perhaps,' she says, 'my tone of voice was rather truculent, I don't know.' But Jean flew at her. 'It went on and on, ridicule, sarcasm.... I don't know exactly in what terms, only remember crying and crying....' Someone must have rescued her, probably her mother. After this Jean apologised; she gave Barbara a tortoiseshell bangle, and Mrs Feast a 'little black dress'. She had to make amends, to repair the damage. For again she'd blown her 'respectable' cover; again she'd given people the chance to talk about her, to criticise her, to despise her. And of course to some extent they did.

That is all Barbara remembers, though Mr Griffiths recalls 'weeks of trouble and turmoil in Booton vicarage.' For the bombs stopped falling on Norwich in the autumn; and in September Jean went back there.

This time her circumstance were rather better – a small but pleasant flat in Thorpe, a suburb near the river, full of her beloved trees. Perhaps Leslie came to be with her there. But on the one occasion we see Jean in Thorpe there is no sign of Leslie – and no sign of any improvement in her state of mind either. It was Willis Feast's farewell visit, to which he also brought Eric Griffiths, perhaps as protection. And protection was needed: she was 'hellishly angry'. But then Feast sent his friend out for a bottle of gin. It worked. The gin soothed her, even made her gay; and 'the "party" ended,' Mr Griffiths remembers, with Jean 'pleasant to me as she had never been

---

*Rector of a neighbouring parish, a few years younger. These are Mr Griffiths's memories.

before.' For once, drink had done what she always wanted: made her *different*, made her 'as much fun as the next woman really.' If only it hadn't: such moments only gave her hope, of course, and made her go on drinking.

Jean stayed in Thorpe, with or without her husband, until early 1942. Then in mid-February Leslie suddenly left West Beckham, first to a temporary attachment 'pending posting', then to Henbury near Bristol for 'Supernumerary Admin. Duties'. Even on his bland, official RAF record this looks like a hurried demotion, and so it was. The reason, of course, was Jean. She had got into trouble again; into a fight again. It was in a pub, Leslie told his daughter (and later Jean told Francis Wyndham): some people had upset her, and she'd shouted 'Heil Hitler!' at them. It was the second public row (at least); and it was too much for the 'hush-hush' authorities — as Jean called them in 'I Spy a Stranger' — at the Air Station. Leslie was a security risk: he must leave straight away. He regretted it very much; he'd enjoyed both the work and the people at West Beckham. He must have felt, and probably looked, the hanging judge again. But they had to go.

★　　★　　★

Leslie stayed in Bristol until August. Jean told Willis Feast and Eric Griffiths that she was returning to London, and she probably did. One couldn't blame Leslie for feeling safer without her; and very likely she preferred London to yet another lonely posting. But on her own London would have been lonely too. Perhaps this was a time, then, like the one in 'The Insect World', when Audrey lives in London beside a street which has been badly bombed, and which she is sure is haunted. This story also draws on Jean's memories of the First War: for Audrey's work in a government office, and probably for the other characters, her friend Roberta and her flatmate Monica. But the Second War provides the heart of the story: its time, 1944 or '45 ('there had been the big blitz, then the uneasy lull, then the little blitz, now the fly bombs'); and the very deep disturbance of its heroine. Audrey tries to escape from life into books: 'Almost any book was better than life,' at least 'life as she was living it.' But of course she can't escape; on the contrary, she's deeply trapped in her obsessions. I suspect Jean was in a similarly extreme state now; she certainly was by the end of the war.

In the meantime, we know just a bit more. In August 1942, Leslie was moved again, this time to Ludlow in Shropshire, very near the Welsh border. This, then, was the summer that he and Jean had a holiday in the Gower Peninsula. It was a break in the gloom: one of the few positive experiences which carried enough emotion and meaning for her to want to write about it.

The first thing Jean liked about the Gower Peninsula had to do with her obsessive subject — women. She noticed several women particularly: the landlady of their small hotel; an elderly woman in a nearby cottage; and 'Lady B', who owned most of the peninsula, and certainly behaved as though she did. These women had some quality English women lacked, Jean thought: not aggressiveness, but a sort of self-confidence. Usually she suggests that the confidence that has been beaten out of English women is confidence in their sexual attractiveness. And that is part of what she means. But here we see that there is something else as well. For the confidence these Welsh women have is not sexual. Rather it is a social certainty, 'as if without trying they knew that they could command respect and authority.' This is very different, and very revealing. It shows that what Jean missed for women in England — that is to say, for herself in England — was not just being loved or desired, but having *respect and authority*, independence, power. She thought she desired slavery; but she also desired mastery.

The other thing she liked was the Gower itself. The weather was perfect; the countryside was breathtaking, and quite empty; Lady B took advantage of wartime regulations to keep everyone out. For the first time Jean began to believe that England could be beautiful.* She even went for long walks — 'which really I am not in the habit of doing.' She walked to a river and saw two kingfishers; she walked to the top of a hill and saw the sea. One day she followed a delicious smell, and came on a huge field of cowslips. 'The scent was so sweet, so strong that you simply can't imagine it,' she wrote. 'I stayed for a long time unable to leave the place. It was after this that I fell in love with the Gower Peninsula.'

I think this may have been a turning point for her. During the next dozen years and more she remained (with a few breaks) in London, but from the moment that Leslie died she hated it, and plotted and longed to escape into the countryside. Some of this was the hope of cheaper living; but more of it was an idea, a vision of the possibility of peace. And I'm sure that came from Wales: where her father came from, where she'd had happy holidays with Maryvonne, and where now she'd had this experience of dignity and beauty. Indeed, when she first got out of London it *was* to Wales: and she still thought the men were nicer to the women than in England.

The Gower Peninsula may have been a more immediate turning point as well, for a few months later Leslie resigned his commission.

*It was Wales of course, but that was how she put it.

The only official reason ever given was that he had a weak heart — though this had been discovered when he *entered* the Air Force, on both occasions, and had never kept him out of even active service. The real reason, again, was Jean. She may have asked him openly to come to London: if so, it was very likely on this holiday together. At any rate he was too worried about her to carry on. He knew now how impossible it was for her to survive alone; and any chance of a decent Air Force career for him was over anyway. At the end of October he resigned and joined Jean in London. He didn't tell his children any of this: not that he'd had to leave the Experimental Station and accept lower-grade work, not that he'd resigned his commission. He did say he was worried about Jean, and considering resignation; but not till much later did his daughter realise he had actually done so. In 1942 he let her believe that his RAF career was in excellent condition. He had come down from Norfolk to London, he said, to work at the Air Ministry. In fact he had merely gone back to work as a publisher's reader.

The rest of the war is almost a blank. 1943 is utterly so. Whenever Jean spoke of returning to London during the war she dated it by the 'fly bombs' of 1944; and of 1944 and 1945 all she said (to Leslie's daughter, when he died) was that they had been unhappy.

We know that she and Leslie found a flat in Hampstead, near Primrose Hill. Leslie's sister was still paying. He worked for Hamish Hamilton, possibly for other publishers. Jean wrote. She started 'The Insect World'; she worked on 'Temps Perdi' and 'I Spy a Stranger', and on the other stories that would go into *The Sound of the River.* Her daughter's fate continued to torment her. One day when the bombing was particularly heavy she and Leslie went up on to Primrose Hill and prayed for Maryvonne's safety.

We know that things were bad. Leslie would only meet Anne for lunch, alone. She wasn't allowed to come to the flat, and he was open about the reason. Jean was being too difficult, too impossible, 'so please don't come'. He began to be more open altogether. Now, around 1944, he admitted that he'd had to leave Norfolk and then the Air Force altogether; and that it was because of Jean.

There was just one better time, at least as far as Leslie's children knew. It seems to have been in 1944 too. Jean stopped drinking: Leslie got her to stop, his daughter believes. And the ban on the flat was lifted. Anne went, and Jean showed her around. It was on the top floor of a tall house in Steeles Road. There was a kitchen, bedroom and bathroom, and a small second bedroom which Jean was doing up for Leslie. She was doing it beautifully, in bright warm colours; and she herself was in a bright, warm mood. She was 'very sweet and charming'; she talked in a 'little' high voice about Leslie's room. It was one of her moments of hope, of 'exaltation', when she felt young again and new: she could change, her life could change, everything could be different.

But of course it couldn't. The last year of the war was the worst. Jean hated the war, she hated everything; she was so bad that Anne never saw her again. She was ill; Leslie was ill. She was 'frightened of my own loneliness, the not knowing. I did not *know* anything you see....' Even as the war drew to a close, even as it ended, things didn't improve. On the contrary, she felt (she wrote to Anne afterwards) 'a dreadful foreboding'. That was hindsight, perhaps, but it was certainly true that the war's ending didn't end her nightmare. Its climax was just coming.

★    ★    ★

Out of the war years came 'Temps Perdi', 'I Spy a Stranger', 'A Solid House' and 'The Insect World'. These stories are all too close for comfort to Jean's madness of that time, and their drafts are even closer. We hear it in the heroines' voices. 'The Universal Robots have arrived,' Laura says in 'I Spy A Stranger'; when Monica in 'The Insect World' says 'All right, old girl,' Audrey shrieks at her: 'Damn you, don't call me that. Damn your soul to everlasting hell *don't call me that* ....' Worst of all is Teresa in 'A Solid House'. 'See people,' she thinks. 'Watch the witch-hunting, witch-pricking ancestor peeping out of those close-set Nordic baby-blues....' And listen to her wondering how much to tell Miss Spearman about 'what it feels like to be dead':

> ... It's not being sad, it's quite different. It's being nothing, feeling nothing. You don't feel insults, you wouldn't feel caresses if there was anyone to caress you. It's like this — it's like walking along in a fog, knowing that you have left everything behind you.... When you start you often look back to catch them laughing or making faces in the bright lights away from the fog. Later on you don't do that; you don't care any longer. If they were to laugh until their mouths met at the back and their heads fell off like some loathsome over-ripe fruit — as they doubtless will one day — you wouldn't turn your head to see the horrible but comic sight.

Compare this to Anna Morgan about others: *you know that they would see you burnt alive without even turning their heads away.* Now the hidden truth is out — the hate is the heroine's, not other people's.

★    ★    ★

As soon as the war was over one wonderful thing happened: Jean had a long letter from Maryvonne. At last she knew she was safe, and what had happened to her during those six dreadful years.

In 1941 she'd gone to work with her father to keep the Dutch Resistance paper *Vrij Nederland* alive. This lasted for five months; then John was arrested. He'd been living as bravely and dangerously as Jean knew he would: not just on *Vrij Nederland*, but also helping stranded RAF pilots to escape and return to England. It was for this he was arrested. Maryvonne was arrested with him and sent to prison. But she was young and innocent-looking, and nothing was proved against her. She was released — and immediately joined the Resistance. She'd had 'incredible adventures'; and also met a young man, Job Moerman, with whom she'd decided to spend her life. That was the good news: she was alive and well, and about to be married. But there was bad news too. She was afraid that John was dead.

By the time he was arrested he had helped thirteen pilots to escape. He was tried, together with two other 'pilot helpers'. The other two were sentenced to death and shot. John escaped death this time, but only by accepting a very dreadful substitute: he was declared insane, and sent to an asylum.* The next three years he spent once more behind bars, first in the asylum, then in a series of Dutch prisons. But in September 1944 something even worse happened: he was deported to a concentration camp, Sachsenhausen, in Germany. There conditions were so appalling that John asked to plead guilty to the original charges against him and be shot. Obligingly, and correct as ever, the Germans sent him back to Holland, where he was tried and sentenced to death a second time. But the Allies were coming: and before the sentence could be carried out he was hurriedly shipped back to Sachsenhausen. He had escaped a quick death a second time, but surely only to meet a slow one.

This news about John must have added to the horror of the last months of the war, which had nearly finished Jean and Leslie. They decided now on another holiday in the country. They would not go to Wales this time, but to somewhere just as remote and empty. They found a cottage to rent on the edge of Dartmoor. Leslie got the money from his sister, as usual; and in late September they left London.

*There are several stories about how this happened (as usual, with John). One that he pleaded insanity; one that the Germans thought him insane, because he insisted on receiving the death sentence together with his comrades; and one (the most likely) that Henriette van Eyk's brother managed to get his sentence reduced to insanity by 'pulling strings'. (John and Henriette themselves said it had not been of his own doing.)

In 'The Sound of the River' the cottage is primitive and it rains all the time, but the woman approves of it, 'of the moor and the loneliness and the whole set-up, especially the loneliness.' Her husband likes it too. He is tired, and clearly ill: 'She saw the deep hollows under his eyes, the skin stretched taut over his cheekbones.' And she is in the grip of a dreadful, unidentified fear. They have clearly had a bad time; yet they are doggedly, self-mockingly hopeful. 'You're the sort who never knows better [than to depend on luck],' he says. 'Unfortunately we're both the sort who never know better.' He doesn't really understand her, and he can't comfort her ('My dear, really. You are an idiot.') But they're close, and they care for each other. 'Let's be happy here,' he says to her; and he is the only thing in the world she is not afraid of.

I think that this was the underlying truth between Jean and Leslie too. But — as we know — their life had been a series of violent rows for over ten years; and it didn't stop now. One night after they'd been there a week or so, they had another. It was so loud (or Jean was so loud) that, although the cottage was indeed quite isolated and hidden away, the neighbours heard it clearly. And the next day it happened.

In 'The Sound of the River' the woman wakes up to their first fine day. But when she says 'It's a lovely day' to her husband he doesn't answer. She touches his hand, and it's cold. Her heart swells and grows 'jagged claws': he is dead in the bed beside her.

It didn't happen exactly like this. But it did happen. When they first woke Leslie seemed quite well; but very soon after he came into the bedroom saying he had a terrible pain in his chest and arm. Jean gave him a hot drink, a hot water bottle, some of her pills. But the pain got worse, and Leslie seems to have half guessed it was his heart. He asked Jean to leave a note for the landlord to call a doctor.

We only have Jean's several versions of what happened next. In the story the woman runs to the landlord's house and finds the telephone room locked. She 'walks up and down for a bit,' not knowing what to do, but finally breaks open the door and telephones to a doctor. In the letter Jean wrote to Anne a week later she says she only left the note for the landlord and went back to the cottage. Then 'I sat on a sofa thing for a moment for I'd had 'flu and felt giddy. I heard a strange groaning noise but it was a few seconds before I connected it with Leslie.' She rushed into the bedroom and found him unconscious ('I believe'). Only then did she run back to the landlord's hostel and break down the door and telephone a doctor. She ran back again, she told Anne, but 'as I took Leslie's hands in mine he died.'

In the story the doctor is suspicious, interrogating the woman about why it took her so long to call him. In reality too people were suspicious. When Anne heard the news she asked the landlord if Jean had killed her father. And Jean's own family were worse. She told them herself, they said, that while her husband was dying she sat in another room, smoking and having a drink, and never went to him....Jean repeated, in the story and in her letter to Anne, that she held Leslie's hand as he died. But by then he was almost certainly unconscious, and she would have felt he was already dead. That is surely why she wrote to Peggy Kirkaldy that 'He died really while I was trying to telephone for help ..., so we didn't even say goodbye.' She must have said something like this to her family. And of course she did say to Anne that she sat on a sofa 'for a moment' before going to him when he was dying. In every version of the event time does pass, when she should have been fetching help, or being with him. She even says so, and why, in the story. 'I was late,' the woman says, 'because I had to stay there listening. I heard it then.... I heard the sound of the river.'

When we read that in the story we shiver with her, at the brush with horror and death she conveys so well. But if we heard it in reality we too might shiver at her. It was her fearfulness again, her extreme incapacity — and also her honesty, *saying* that she sat somewhere else, even for a few seconds, while her husband lay dying. Anyone might do this, in blind terror; but only Jean would tell people, and not foresee that they would be shocked and disapproving.

Yet part of her, of course, knew they would be; part of her was as shocked and disapproving as they were. That part emerged in a fragment she published near the end of her life, 'The Joey Bagstock Smile'.

When I left, I knew that I should not see him alive again. And I thought of the way he'd smiled at me — triumphantly, mockingly. Why should a man look like that when he's dying?...

'Then came the day when I kissed his forehead and it was cold,' the published piece goes on: but the draft makes it sound more immediate. 'I kissed his forehead and he was cold, so cold,' it says:

... But his smile was gone and he had his marble face, his marble face I knew so well.

When I looked at him dead I thought 'that's the marble face I know so well, the hanging judge's face.'

God knows what will happen to me now....

... I think I must be going mad, for I see it everywhere, the Joey Bagstock smile.

That is Jean's guilt speaking, the story's suspicious doctor inside her own head. To Anne she said that the last conscious thing Leslie did was to say 'Oh Jean what a terrible strain for you' – and that is probably the truth, that is the utterly characteristic thing for Leslie to say, even as he lay dying. But instead she imagined him (really or only fictionally) smiling at her like a sly old man, triumphantly, mockingly. What could that smile mean? Perhaps: *I knew you'd kill me, and now you have. You're guilty, and now everyone will know.* Jean never admitted to feeling any guilt over Leslie's death. But it came out anyway – in 'The Joey Bagstock Smile', in the suspicious doctor of 'The Sound of the River'. It couldn't come out straight; so it came out as art.

*Should* she have felt guilt? Alas – perhaps. Not so much over the day of his death: catastrophe can leave anyone frozen like a rabbit in a glare. But over something worse. Leslie was only sixty years old. He'd evidently had a heart weakness most of his life, but only a slight one. He came from a long-lived family, and should – his daughter says – 'have lived for years and years'. He smoked heavily: that was no doubt the main reason his life was cut short. But his family felt that Jean was the other. He had had so many years of hopeless battle: unable to make her comfortable or calm; battered by her anger and unable to fight back; becoming stony-faced and silent. Jean surely knew what they felt, violently resented it, and secretly feared it was true.

She was in shock. The people in a neighbouring cottage, a man and two women, took care of her. 'I thought all people were so cruel but these three were kind,' she wrote to Anne. The man telephoned Jean's elder brother Edward, who had recently returned to England. That night she stayed with the kind neighbours; and the next morning Edward came. The cottage had been booked for a month, though they'd stayed only a week. Edward paid the bill 'in full', Jean wrote. 'All was paid in full.' Then he took her home with him.

Edward must have handled everything – the inquest, post-mortem, cremation. Maryvonne was called, and Leslie's three children. His favourite daughter, Anne, couldn't come, but his son Anthony did. Anthony arrived to find Jean in bed, and despite Edward still needing help: all her clothes were dirty, Leslie had meant to take them to the laundry. . . . Time had stopped for her; she was even more helpless than usual. Anthony didn't understand, and was angry. But Jean took flowers to where Leslie's body was lying; and then went, with Edward, Maryvonne and Anthony, to the cremation service. 'It was a fine and clear day,' she wrote, 'and I had all the time the feeling that Leslie had *escaped* – from me, from everyone and was free at last.'

But now what would become of her? She was alone. Maryvonne had to return to her husband in Holland, and Jean was determined from the start 'not to hang around *their* two young necks.' She still had the Steeles Road flat, and a little money. But not for long. Leslie had left almost nothing; and almost as soon as he'd died his sister stopped paying the rent. Now Jean wrote to Peggy again, saying that she had a 'horror' of returning to London. She clung to the idea of finishing her novel, 'because Leslie liked it, . . . and because I think it might be the one book I've written that's much use.' Did Peggy know of 'a flat, rooms or a cottage' where she could live quietly and write?

Needless to say Jean found no such haven. She would return to Steeles Road, and stay till the next summer at least, probably longer, But before that she stayed on for a while longer with her brother Edward and his wife Gertrude. And here she went through the final experiences she used for 'I Spy a Stranger'.

Edward was being 'wonderfully good' to her, even though (Jean said, and it was probably true) they hadn't seen each other since she was a small girl. But the situation was impossible. Her state of shock made Jean more paranoid, more passive, more demanding than ever, and Edward and Gertrude were the wrong people for her to be with at the best of times. Even she could not exaggerate their Victorian respectability. They were formal, stiff, autocratic; with a strong sense of duty – that is why Jean was there – but with unbendingly high standards for everyone else as well. Jean was hysterical when Edward brought her back, which was a bad beginning. At first they probably forgave her; but after a bit their disapproval must have begun to show. And like Laura, Jean withdrew. She locked herself in her room and refused to eat. Edward and Gertrude tried to reason with her; they called in a doctor to reason with her – but this only made her worse. Then there were dreadful scenes, just like those in 'I Spy a Stranger'. Jean 'went mad'. She refused to get up at all; when she thought they meant to force her, she tied herself to the bed. She cried, she threw tantrums. Under his military correctness Edward hid a volatile Rees Williams temper: finally, like Ricky, he lost it. He shouted; Jean clung to the bedpost and shouted back. Gertrude must have felt – they must all have felt – like Mrs. Hudson: that they were possessed by the Devil.

The rest of the family never knew (or at least never said) how this ghastly *impasse* was resolved. Perhaps it was resolved as it is in 'I Spy a Stranger', with Jean persuaded (again?) to go to a 'nursing home' ('As for the other . . . home . . . that turn . . . a looney-bin'). Perhaps (as the family think) the police were called in. In any case Jean's briefly renewed friendship with her older brother was wrecked.

He would go on doing his duty by her, but little more; and Gertrude would refuse even to have her in the house again.

She went back now to the horror of London and of absolute solitude. It was surely the fear of this that had made her spiral down so quickly to her worst state of demonic fury. It was like the brief holiday of thirty years before, with Adrian Allinson, Philip Heseltine and Puma Channing: no matter how unwelcome she was, and how unhappy, she was still more afraid to go than to stay. But she had to go, and she did.

She was so poor now she had to sell Leslie's books. How did she live — who paid, for instance, for Steeles Road? Someone would soon come to her rescue, as always. But in the meantime the family must have paid.

Owen, as ever, had no money to spare, and by 1945 Minna was very ill. But Edward, as a retired Colonel of the Indian Army, was relatively well off; and now Brenda was even more so. Her long period of sacrifice and spinsterhood was over. During the war she had met and married a rich and generous man, Robert Powell. Robert paid for Minna to go into a nursing home nearby for her last years (she died in 1949); he was also extremely kind to Brenda's cousin Gwen Williams, who was arthritic. When Brenda told him about her other sister's plight he was willing to help again. The family, and Maryvonne too, are quite definite that between them Edward and Brenda gave Jean an allowance for many years.* That almost certainly began now, towards the end of 1945. She had lost her husband, and the support of his sister; and at the same moment Edward, the head of the family, met her again and saw what a destitute state she was in. Whatever shock and distaste he and Brenda felt for her behaviour, family loyalty would insist that they help her. Indeed, the more shock and distaste they felt the more they *wanted* to help her, in order to keep her out of trouble, and their name out of the papers. Jean had probably dropped from her family's view during the war, as she had from everyone's else's. But from 1945 she was in touch with Edward and Brenda at least, though probably only by letter; and they were giving her a weekly allowance.

This renewed connection with her family had begun terribly and continued worse. She owed them gratitude, which always made her feel and behave badly. Her sister could no longer be pitied: she had got what Jean had always wanted — a rich, kind, devoted husband

---

*And in the torn draft of her letter to Edward in the Ropemakers Diary the fragments *'llowance'* and *'wance'* appear twice in a paragraph about money.

— and must be envied instead. Jean and her family were already objects of hate and misunderstanding to one another; but in the next years these feelings took on mythical proportions, even — or especially — on the side of the ordinary,'respectable' family. Not so much for Owen, whose life and nature were closest to Jean's; but for Edward, and most of all for Brenda. Edward was a doctor, and had seen a bit of the world; but Brenda and Robert were 'respectable' through and through. Now Brenda and Robert went to Leslie's funeral in London (Jean was too distressed to go) and met Leslie's daughters, who were not unnaturally bitter about her. And horror stories were told. Leslie's daughters would have nothing to do with Jean, Brenda reported to Owen, and no doubt to Edward. When Leslie married her he'd had between sixteen and twenty thousand pounds, and a year later there wasn't a penny left.... She had killed him, she'd sat smoking and drinking in the next room and left him to die alone....

Jean was right. It wasn't only she who said wild, cruel things. Respectable people did too — and they were worse. Having experienced so little, they believed everything; and people believed *them*. When she said and wrote over and over again that everything was lies, that the truth was forgotten and only the lies survived and grew — no doubt she 'exaggerated', but essentially it was true.

# CHAPTER TWO

# Max, 1945–1957

*Seven years' bad luck: 1945-1952 — Maidstone: 1950–1952 —*
*The Ropemakers Diary — London: 1952-1955 — Bude: 1955-1957*

The war was over, but so was Jean's writing life, for many years. She had a book of short stories ready. But they were, as she knew, 'too bitter'; and without Leslie they didn't find a publisher for twenty-three years. If he had lived perhaps *The Sound of the River* would have been sold, and *Wide Sargasso Sea* finished and published ten or fifteen years earlier.

Jean often longed, and often tried, to go on writing. But in the twenty years between the end of the war and the publication of *Wide Sargasso Sea,* she produced only two new pieces of published fiction: the short stories 'The Day They Burned the Books' and 'Let Them Call It Jazz'. Sometimes she carried on working on her West Indian memories;* sometimes she wrote diaries of her current life; a few times she even tried to write a sellable article or script. But she didn't succeed. For long stretches she didn't even try.

The reason, of course, was her life, her circumstances, and particularly the man who shared them. John and Leslie had both wanted her to write, and in their different ways had helped her. But now John was — not dead, thank God, but distant and ill, and Leslie was dead. Jean often said how little she wrote after 1939; and once or twice she recognised the connection to Leslie. She 'rather smashed up after [Leslie's death] for some time', she told Oliver Stoner in 1953, and in 1966 she suggested to an interviewer that the shock of that death had begun her long 'disappearance'. But the clearest recognition came in a letter to Leslie's daughter in 1968. Anne had married an American

---

*In 1958 she told Francis Wyndham, for instance, that she'd been 'getting down all I remembered about the West Indies' for 'some time'. 'For some time' could mean anything, of course. (See e.g. *Letters,* 184, where she tells Francis in 1960 that she had just written 'Let Them Call It Jazz', whereas she'd really begun it eleven years before). It's clear that the West Indian memories in the Executor's Archive, go back to the 1930s.

and left England just after the war: because of this — and because, of course, she did blame and dislike Jean — she dropped out of touch with her. But after *Wide Sargasso Sea* she wrote to her again. And in her reply Jean said: 'Leslie's death was a terrible shock to me — perhaps the greatest shock I've ever had. I think that for a long time afterwards I didn't know what I was doing or what to do & I stopped writing for years.'

Her disappearance was not only a matter of not writing, or of not publishing. However little connection she had to London literary life, before the war she had at least been there. She and Leslie had always lived in or near London. Leslie's friends — though they grew fewer — were writers and publishers; and he knew what was happening in contemporary writing, though he didn't always like it. In other words, Jean's isolation from other writers and readers in the thirties was self-imposed, and it was not complete: as we've seen, she'd had (brief) friendships with Evelyn Scott, Peggy Kirkaldy, Eliot Bliss, Rosamond Lehmann. But now Evelyn and Rosamond had completely disappeared from her life, never to return; Eliot would return only in the late fifties; and even Peggy — whom Jean had turned to in 1941 and 1945, and would turn to again soon — lost touch with her for years at a time. In 1949 Jean made a new literary friend, but immediately lost her again until 1956. With rare exceptions, therefore, and those mostly in letters, she lost even the tenuous contact she had had in the thirties with other writers. From 1939 until 1957, when the BBC broadcast an adaptation of *Good Morning, Midnight,* and first Francis Wyndham and then Diana Athill encouraged her to return to work on her last novel, Jean lived almost entirely among completely unliterary people. She had found it hard enough to write even with Leslie pushing and supporting her, and friends praising and encouraging her. Without any of this now she might have slowed down anyway, even if nothing else had happened.

There was another literary connection that seems to have ended now too: Jean's collaboration, even her contact, with John. Up to 1939 and even beyond it had continued. A month before war broke out John had written a powerful recommendation to French readers — 'Jean Rhys, *romancière inconnue,*' published in *Les nouvelles littéraires.* In 1940 he'd still been trying to get *Good Morning, Midnight* published in France. But then he'd been caught up in the war.

Mercifully, and almost incredibly, he had survived Sachsenhausen. After his failed bid to be shot he'd been sent back, in the chaos of the times, without a dossier. And the concentration camp had this much in common with the outside world: the best way to anger authority was to be without papers. This lack of official identity had pursued John all his life, and it didn't let go now. Yet even with this added horror he survived. He also survived the next murderous onslaught of fate: the notorious death march from Sachsenhausen to Mecklenburg-Schwerin, organised by the panic-stricken Germans in the last week of April and the first week of May 1945. Nine thousand died in this infamous attempt to hide Nazi crimes, but John survived.

Not long after Maryvonne's letter to Jean he was back in Holland. He may even have come to see her at the end of the year: he wrote, full of sympathy over Leslie's death, and said he would. But if so, that was probably the last time they saw each other. John changed his life again. He divorced Henriette van Eyk. In 1946 he went to Poland for the Red Cross, wrote a pamphlet for them, and published a novel, *Glorieuzen* (*The Glorious Ones*), about his war. In Poland he met a Countess, once the wife of the head of Poland's National Bank, now reduced to penury and homelessness by the war. He paid dedicated court to her, got her and her son out of Poland, and married her. But soon after this his extraordinary resilience finally failed him.

The miracle is that it had lasted so long. For thirty years he'd been fighting chronic ill health and poverty. He had been hunted, deported, imprisoned for long years. But now the camp and the terrible march broke down his health for good. He went on writing, producing two more novels, *Polse Nachten* (*Polish Nights*) and *Bij Ons op den Heuvel* (*On Our Hill*) during the 1950s. But he was increasingly ill and wretchedly poor. Between 1947 and 1952 he and his wife lived exiled (as he felt) from Amsterdam, often with friends. Even once they returned to Amsterdam his life was very hard. Like Jean he seems to have been cut off from his former friends and completely forgotten. He'd lost almost all his books and papers, confiscated by the Germans when he was arrested. He had nothing; he was in increasing pain; his wife nursed him devotedly. The 1950s, in sum, would be as bad for him as they were for Jean; and one result was that they seem at last to have lost touch with one another. They were both too poor, too ill, too old, too busy just surviving. They corresponded with Maryvonne, but not with each other. Perhaps some constraint had grown up between them. In 1953 Jean sent John her love via Maryvonne — 'if you think he wishes to hear it;' and in 1957, congratulating Jean on the broadcast of *Good Morning, Midnight*, John wrote: 'I received your address from Maryvonne. Hoping you are well and won't be annoyed at my writing ....'

As a writer, then, Jean became even more isolated after the war than she'd been before it. And gruesomely, appropriately, everyone thought that she was dead. In 1950 the novelist Julian MacLaren Ross told Francis Wyndham that she had recently died in a sanatorium. At the BBC people said she'd died in tragic circumstances in Paris; the literary world said she'd died during the war. It seemed amazing, even unsuitable, when she turned out to have been living in squalid and obscure cicumstances in England all along. With the acuteness of someone whose best jokes are against herself, Jean picked up this feeling immediately. 'I don't know why Constable thought I was dead,' she said, when the BBC found her in 1956. 'It does seem more fitting, I know, but life is never neat and tidy.'

As a writer she was alone: but as a woman (as usual, as always) she was not. In these years, indeed, she was with the man who loved her most, or most generously, of all her men. Perhaps that is why she said that she didn't write for the twenty years of their marriage because she was happy — which certainly wasn't true. She still wanted and tried to write; and though she could feel more loved than ever before, she couldn't feel secure. On the contrary. Her third husband was even more of a gambler than her first and even more unworldly than her second; to his despair, therefore, he was even less able to give her what she needed. And unlike them he couldn't understand her need to write.

None the less, Jean knew that he gave her everything, he held nothing back, and that he did not judge her. He was as bad as she was, in some ways worse, so she could be generous to him, and grateful, and fiercely loyal. She was all those things in their twenty years together (as well as their opposites). In what she said about him afterwards too: another reason, perhaps, why she pretended she'd been happy.

George Victor Max Hamer was a cousin of Leslie's: his mother and Leslie's father were first cousins. He was born in 1882, three years before Leslie and eight before Jean. When he was seventeen he joined the Navy; he served for twenty-one years, including the whole of the First World War. In 1911 — when Jean was in the middle of her affair with Lancelot — he married. In 1914 his daughter Mary was born, and in 1918 a son, who died in infancy. In 1920 he was invalided out of the Navy on grounds of 'neurosis': probably shellshock, war fatigue. Despite this, and despite the fact that he was nearly forty, he applied himself to learn a new profession. In February 1930 he qualified as a solicitor, and soon after went to work for an uncle (who was also a relative of Leslie's). When the Second War broke out he rejoined the Navy, as Leslie rejoined the Air Force: though of course at fifty-eight, like Leslie at fifty-five, for 'admin. duties' only. In 1945 he was a Lieutenant Commander with the Balloon Barrage at Tring.

Jean always said that she met Max because he was the executor of

Leslie's will. He was just moving back into civilian life: into partnership in a firm of solicitors, William P. Webb and Co, of Gray's Inn. Poor Leslie had so little to leave that his will was not probated; Max presumably handled it on his own. And so they met.

It was a meeting with many echoes. Echoes for Jean, because Max was in many ways like Leslie: from the same family and background (Max's father was a clergyman too); small, slight, gentle, well spoken. And echoes for us too. For Max was like Lancelot, Maxwell Macartney, Ford, Leslie: a respectable, well brought up Englishman. But more like Leslie than the others – and most, perhaps, like 'Harry Benson' of *Triple Sec*: for he'd been poor, and not successful. During his solicitor's training he'd had only a Navy pension of £186 a year; then he'd practised only 'in a modest way'. But like 'Harry' he had an upright, military bearing: 'at his worst', Jean said, he looked like a reliable lawyer, 'at his best' like a naval officer. He had a strong face, dark blue eyes and sensitive hands. He *was* sensitive, even vulnerable, like Lancelot: and after six years back in the Navy he was once again mentally exhausted. He knew what it was to be a failure, poor and ill, and he sympathised with Jean. He was impulsive, even reckless, and he seems to have fallen for her very quickly and completely: rather like Mr Sims in 'Let Them Call It Jazz', who offers Selina Davis refuge when he's seen her only once or twice in a café. Indeed Mr. Sims is clearly based on Max – the only character in Jean's fiction who is.

> This man is not at all like most English people. He see very quick, and he decide very quick. English people take long time to decide – you three-quarter dead before they make up their mind about you. Too besides, he speak very matter of fact, as if it's nothing. He speak as if he realise well what it is to live like I do – that's why I accept and go.

In this way the meeting was like the one with John, thirty years before. This man wasn't big or strong or rich; she couldn't fall in love with him, as she'd done with Lancelot or Ford. But he was sympathetic, and he offered to rescue her. So she, too, accepted.

By February 1946 he was coming to see her regularly; by July he was 'still hanging around', helping her paint the flat. When Maryvonne's husband Job came to England in 1946 and knocked on the door Max answered, and it was soon clear to him that Max was living there, though to Job's amusement this was never admitted. Jean didn't appear, and Max claimed she was ill: 'You'll think it very odd I'm here,' he said, but that was why – Jean wasn't well, and he was 'helping out'. Clearly, moving from Leslie to his cousin was moving from the edge of respectability closer to the centre. Jean had found someone like her: someone who could no longer live like a Victorian, but still wished to seem to. When they could no longer pretend they weren't living together they pretended instead that they were already married. That couldn't happen, of course, until Max was divorced: so in the meantime Jean had her name changed to Hamer by deed poll.

The first two years or so of her life with Max seem to have been uneventful, perhaps even happy. The early stages of a relationship were always best for her: once again she'd been saved, rescued, fished up from the deep dark river. And Max was so good to her: she wrote and said always that he was 'sweet', 'a dear', 'very kind'. He knew — no one better — that she was penniless, yet he married her. And to do so he had had to divorce his wife of more than thirty-five years; and lose his only child too, for his daughter broke off with him when she learned that he'd left her mother. All this he did for her, and Jean was grateful.

They were married on 2 October 1947 — two years to the day since Leslie's death, and two weeks after Max's divorce became absolute. Maryvonne and Job were delighted: they liked Max very much, and they were relieved that Jean would be taken care of. They had a baby now, and in the next year they would leave Europe for Indonesia. In the summer of 1948 Maryvonne came to say goodbye, bringing the baby for Jean to see. Jean found her a 'darling': 'she has slanting eyes,' she said (like herself, like her son), and she'd fallen in love with her. Jean would never be a good grandmother in practice, as she was never a good mother, but her love was genuine; and reiterated, often heartbreakingly, over the years. Yet in a way she wasn't unhappy that Maryvonne would be on the other side of the world. Her desire was always to hide from her daughter the awfulness of her life: not to upset her, not to ask anything of her or drag her down. And that was easier (it always had been) with Maryvonne far away. In fact the years the Moermans were in Indonesia — from 1948 to 1957 — were exactly the right ones, from this point of view, exactly the years of Jean's least containable disasters. She said so herself, with characteristic understatement — half evasion, half secret self-mockery: 'As for me, I had such a — well, a trying time after the war that I was thankful that Maryvonne had her own life and wasn't involved with mine.'

At first, however, Max made things hugely better. Again like Mr Sims, he owned a house: not near Victoria, but in Beckenham, in the far south of London. Like Mr Sims, he moved Jean into it; unlike Mr Sims, of course, he came with her. They got there around the autumn of 1946. Jean was delighted. It was out of the town, nearly country; it had a garden, and plenty of trees; at last perhaps she could settle down and just 'flop' for the rest of her life. She and Max were full of enthusiastic plans. They would have the house repaired, they would live on the ground floor and rent the top two floors as flats. The builders began work. Max worked in his London office; Jean worked on the house, or wrote or thought about writing. Soon she was married and respectable again; she was in her own house, even if it *was* damp, and cold in the winter. She must have felt she'd really escaped: the war was over.

But of course she was Jean, and it wasn't. The main problem was the same as ever: money. Max had tried to have the house repaired cheaply, on the black market — and the builder absconded with several hundred pounds. Beckenham was still London, and expensive; and Max had his wife's alimony to pay. Then — or perhaps before — Max quarrelled with his partners and left his office: 'That I think was the real start,' Jean wrote to Peggy.* He set up with another partner, called (according to Jean) Yale. And now he became impatient — 'mad', she said — to make money. Perhaps it was largely for her sake, as Max himself said. In any case he now tried all sorts of schemes. In an extraordinary echo of 'Harry Benson', he invested in something to do with nightclubs; he met an inventor called Roberts who would make their fortune; he invented things himself. Jean began to get nervous. She couldn't believe in his 'music hall acts'; he was an incurable optimist, he was naive, he trusted people too much, or the wrong people. He was always out chasing the latest will-o'-the-wisp; the house was lonely and ghostly, and her small money was wasting away on 'hairdos and housecoats' to woo him back. Several times she tried to leave Beckenham, with or without Max. But each time her passivity and his optimism persuaded her to stay. They began to argue, about people, about money, like Selina and Mr Sims ('"I don't think so much of money. It don't like me and what do I care?" I was joking, but he turns around, his face quite pale, and he tells me I'm a fool.').

Then things got suddenly worse. One of his friends told Jean that Max was drinking, and so was his partner, Yale. And Yale was a crook, just out of gaol. Max was 'getting in with the worst crooks in London.' Perhaps Jean faced him with this. In any case Max and Yale quarrelled violently and parted ways. 'Then my dear,' Jean told Peggy, 'I went all of a doodah and of course I started to drink again.' The honeymoon was over.

In 'Let Them Call It Jazz' Selina Davis lives in Jean's house in Beckenham. It is run down and ghostly and the cellar is full of rats; but it has an overgrown garden with apple trees, and 'it have style.' One evening Selina sees the woman next door looking at her over the hedge. 'At first I say good evening, but she turn away her head,

---

*Although Max probably received a reasonable sum for the sale of his partnership or interest in the firm. If this had indeed happened earlier, he may have bought the Beckenham house with this money.

so afterwards I don't speak.' The woman's husband stares at her 'as if I'm a wild animal let loose'; the woman watches her, 'hating'. Bit by bit they persecute her. They complain to the police. Then they call them, and Selina is fined five pounds for being drunk and disorderly. She can't pay; and now she does drink, to drown her fears. Drunk, she sings and dances in the garden. The neighbours are horrified. 'This is a respectable neighbourhood,' the woman says, and taunts Selina in a 'sweet sugar' voice. Selina's arm 'moves of itself', and she throws a stone through their stained-glass window.

On 1 April, 1948 the following item appeared in a local paper:

> 'I lost my head and threw a brick through the window because her dog, a killer and a fighter, attacked my cat,' said Ella Gwendoline Hamer (56), a writer, of 35, Southend Road, Beckenham, accused at Bromley on Tuesday, of breaking a pane of glass, value £5, belonging to Mrs Rose Hardiman, of 37 Southend Road. Hamer was bound over and ordered to pay £5 to Mrs Hardiman.

It was just like thirteen years before, when she put the unbearable events of her first arrest and trial into 'Tigers Are Better-Looking'. On the one hand she kept the details the same, to get them right, and to write them out − the next door neighbour, the broken glass, the five pound fine. And on the other hand she added and subtracted, mixed in bits of other events before and after: and brought out their most general meaning, the humiliation of the outcast and despised.

In life too she treated this loss of control in typical ways. When the police had first arrived she had shouted, 'Yes, I threw the brick through the window and I shall do it again.' But she pleaded Not Guilty to the charge of wilful and malicious damage. Mrs Hardiman's dog had killed two of her cats, she claimed in court and ever after; so she lost her head and threw the brick through the window. She had done it: but not deliberately, and under extreme provocation.

We'll never know the truth. Perhaps it was all just Jean's paranoia; but on the other hand it's quite possible that Mrs. Hardiman's dog *had* attacked her cats, even killed them. Dogs do, after all. And reality had a terrible way of living up (or down) to her worst expectations. We read her endless accusations of people − their meanness and cruelty, especially to women, especially to *her* − and we think that she exaggerates. And of course she does. But amid the court reports in the *Bromley and West Kent Mercury* there was a nauseating little column called ' Smiles in Court', which reported the things poor desperate people had said so that readers could laugh at them. Over the next two years Jean provided them with lots of good material. So now, for instance:

Defendant (*a woman*): Did you warn me about your dog, saying it had better not see my cats, as it would kill them?
Witness (*also a woman*): No, I said that it would chase them. That is natural.
The Chairman (Mr A.W.Hurst): Yes, it is natural for a dog to chase cats. I know, I keep them.

And later:

Told she would be remanded, accused, *a woman*, said: 'Not for thirteen days — that's my unlucky number.'

Read these, and then think again of Teresa in 'A Solid House': 'all the secret hatreds that hissed from between the lines of newspapers.... A woman? Yes, a woman. A woman must, a woman shall or a woman will....' And she doesn't sound so mad after all.

Jean's feud with Mrs Hardiman and her husband Horace simmered away for months. She was sure they 'gossiped about us like jimmy-oh' — and no doubt she was right about that. But no more cats disappeared, and she threw no more bricks at their window. Her anxiety grew worse; but she focused it elsewhere.

By October she was sure that Max was heading for 'a smash', and by Christmas she had worked herself into a frenzy. She told Max that their marriage was a failure and she wanted to leave. But when he told her he couldn't give her back the fifty pounds she asked for, that was enough to stop her. As so often before (and after) she couldn't move; she just stayed, and everything collapsed around her. They 'started to quarrel — constantly. Everyone blamed me — *ça va sans dire* — I was a harridan, a drunkard, Heaven knows what. And bats of course. The more they abused me the more bitter I became, and the worse I handled the whole affair — in fact I couldn't have behaved worse or with less tact.'

That was how Jean put it afterwards to Peggy Kirkaldy. To Maryvonne at the time she said even less: just 'I haven't been well for some time and "things are getting on top of me" as they say.' But in fact she was so bad she nearly telegraphed to Maryvonne to ask her to come, all the way from Indonesia.

Something new had happened, which ought to have eased the situation, but which did the opposite instead. Around November 1948 the upper floors of the house were ready at last, and were let: the first floor to a Mr and Mrs Bezant, the top floor to a Mr and Mrs Daniell. This meant money coming in; but it also meant, of course, people in the house itself: strangers to disturb her and to be disturbed. Whatever neighbours had heard and said from next door was nothing to what tenants of the same house heard and said now. From the day they moved in, Mr Bezant said, he heard 'nothing but screaming, shouting and abuse four times week from this woman.' Jean's obsession with Mrs Hardiman faded (for the moment); this was much worse. The horror was no longer out in the street, beyond thick walls. Enemies, judges, people who hated her, had come into her own house; the wolves had entered her room.

From Christmas to the spring she tried to hang on. Max got a new legal job: not a particularly good one, only managing clerk at four hundred pounds a year; still, it was a job. But he kept up his association with Roberts the 'inventor' as well. Jean pretended to be happy ('Well Happy!'). She didn't drink so much (she said), but she didn't eat much either. She was so tired, so cold, she had 'flu; a ghastly weakness and a great indifference were taking her over. She couldn't work on *Mrs Rochester*. She tried to write something to make money, but fell asleep after two lines. Sleep was 'so *lovely* better than food or thinking or writing or anything....' She was trying to play dead: and instead of convincing others, she'd convinced herself.

It didn't work, of course. There were probably several skirmishes and angry encounters. Then one evening in April the Bezants gave a party. Jean was (she said) trying to read, and the noise was 'appalling'. She went upstairs to ask them to stop. She was angry; and when Mr Bezant made an insulting remark to her she slapped his face.

According to Sidney Bezant his party was over by eleven. As his guests left, Jean, who was in the hall below, began shouting. She came upstairs. She 'said something' about his wife; he remonstrated; and Jean punched him in the face. He called the police.

This only maddened Jean further. By the time a constable arrived she was completely out of control. She raged at everyone; she called the constable 'Dirty Gestapo', and hit *him* in the face too. He arrested her. They struggled – he twisted her arm, Jean said – and like Antoinette with Rochester, she bit him.

The next day, 12 April, she was brought to trial at Bromley Magistrates Court, charged with assaulting both Mr Bezant and the policeman. She was remanded for thirteen days on bail. (This was when she said 'No, no, no, thirteen is my unlucky number.')

None the less, thirteen days later, on the twenty-fifth, the trial proper was held. Jean told her story and Bezant his. Max gave evidence on her behalf, but her previous offfence against Mrs Hardiman was brought up against her. She pleaded – of course – Not Guilty; but to no avail. She was bound over to keep the peace for a year; fined £4 (£3 for the policeman and £1 for Mr Bezant, which I hope allowed her a momentary sardonic grin), and given twenty-eight days to pay.

This wasn't the end, alas. Jean would go all the way to Holloway, like Selina Davis. The only difference was that in reality it would take a year instead of a fortnight, five trials instead of two; and she didn't just sing and dance and break a window.

After the trial — the second, after the case brought by Mrs Hardiman — Jean went home, apparently alone. Max must have had to return to work. She was feeling — she said later — 'very distressed and worried'. Then on top of everything else she couldn't find her key. A policeman helped her to put a board up against her bedroom window and climb in. But as she did so she slipped: she either 'just escaped a bad fall,' or else 'fell fifteen feet' (she seems to have said both). By the time she got inside she was naturally extremely shaken. Then she saw her tormentors, the Bezants and Mrs Daniell, in the hall.

According to Mr Bezant they found Jean standing in the hall when they got home. She was 'in one of her awkward moods'; 'her eyes were staring and she looked fierce.' (She probably *did* look agitated, Jean said, explaining about her fall. . . .) She began to shout at them, using 'foul and violent' language. She said, 'Get out of this house. This is my property. Get out.'

According to Jean, Mr Bezant had provoked her first. He'd said, 'I see you didn't like what happened in the court today. I have got you where I want you now and I'll get you lower still.' She went up to him and said 'How dare you speak to me like that in my own house!' He told his wife and Mrs Daniell to go upstairs, but Jean followed them, saying, 'If you think I am going to pay this fine, you have made a mistake. I would sooner go to prison for life.' He lifted his arm — to protect himself, he said; or as Jean said, he knocked away her hand, which she'd put over the banister. Then — he said — she struck him on the arm and again on the face; or — Jean said — her hand fell against him, or she clutched at his arm to regain her balance (again she seems to have said both things). He said, 'Ah, another assault, I've got you. I am going for the police.' And she ran down the stairs 'as fast as she could and stood with her arms across the front door,' barring his way.

The gesture was pathetic, frightening, futile. Bezant called the police anyway. The next day Jean met Mrs Bezant and Mrs Daniell and attacked *them*. Or so they said. All three charged her, with two separate accounts of assault.

The case came up ten days later. Once again Jean pleaded Not Guilty. She complained that she had no witnesses, whereas 'he had his wife and umpteen others,' so 'they can say what they like about me.' In any case they were believed, and she was found guilty of the assault on Mr Bezant. The prosecuting counsel then withdrew the other charges, saying that they hadn't been made 'in a vindictive spirit', but only because 'the lives of my clients are being made intolerable by this woman.' And he suggested that the Bench might wish to seek some medical or psychiatric advice. The magistrate agreed. 'Having seen the defendant in court,' he said, he felt it was 'necessary in her own interests that she be given a psychiatric examination.' He adjourned the case for twenty-one days for the examination to be made.

On 27 May Jean didn't appear. A warrant was made for her arrest; the tenants made further complaints. But she didn't appear on 17 June, or on 24 June; and — as she'd threatened — she didn't pay the fine either. At the 24 June hearing it was reported that Max had telephoned to say that she was ill and could not attend.

That was on a Friday. On the Monday, 27 June, Jean finally appeared again on the charge of assaulting and beating Mr Bezant on 25 April. She had finally co-operated with the psychiatrist, and a report was made. The psychiatrist must have said that she was free of any serious mental illness, but diagnosed her as a hysteric. For Jean said in court that the doctor had been 'very fair' — but that she thought it 'rather odd to say that she was hysterical because she wrote books. It was rather English. . . .' Then she couldn't stop. People told lies about her — she wasn't rich enough to bring an action against them, so she had to suffer this persecution. She had suffered a year of torture in horrible Beckenham — she wanted desperately to leave England. 'Why don't you make a law to stop gossip?' she demanded of the magistrate. *That* 'would stop half the misery in this country. . . .'

In 'Let Them Call It Jazz' Selina Davis wants to put her case in a 'decent quiet voice', but instead she hears herself 'talking loud and I see my hands wave in the air. Too besides it's no use, they won't believe me, so I don't finish. I stop, and I feel the tears on my face. . . . They whisper, they whisper. They nod, they nod. . . .' To Peggy Jean wrote: 'I began to cry in the witness box,' and 'He asked me if I had anything to say. So I said it.' The magistrate remanded her in custody for a week for a further medical report. 'Protesting loudly' that it was not fair, that there had already been a medical report, Jean was led from the court.

She spent at least five days in the hospital wing of Holloway Prison. Selina Davis says 'Some of what happen there I forget, or perhaps better not remember'; and clearly she speaks for Jean. Holloway (she wrote to Peggy) was 'an evil and useless place' which 'does nothing but harm to everybody'. The governor and the woman doctor were smiling villains. The male doctor seemed benign, but 'I wonder whether *he* pushes all the dirty work onto *her*.' Everything was promised but nothing done: 'It takes a few days to tumble to this, and meanwhile they've had some fun.' Yet Jean also felt like Selina: 'The things they say you mind I don't mind.' Like solitude. 'When they clang the door on me [Selina says] I think, "You shut me in, but you shut all those other devils *out*. They can't reach me now."' Jean recognised humanity and intelligence in the assistant governor; even some of the warders weren't 'quite stone yet'. And for her fellow prisoners she felt what she'd felt for the chorus: 'such an affection'. She especially liked 'my old gypsy who was tough as old boots.' Others, like the 'quite young girls with no teeth and hardly any hair,' she pitied; and all she listened to eagerly, with her novelist's ear ('Of course I knew people called London the Smoke but never heard anyone do it "so natural"').* Selina clams up at first, so that 'they can't trip me up'; but later she tells the doctor 'a little of what really happen in that house. Not much. Very careful.' Jean must have done the same. And the Holloway report said again that she 'wasn't crazy.'

On 4 July she was back in front of the same magistrate. Max was shown the doctor's report. Jean was put on probation for two years, on condition that she attend a clinic for medical and psychiatric treatment. And at last she was let go.

She had had sixteen months of 'fights with one and all,' 'starting with the wretch who killed my cats and ending with … the magistrate.' During all that time she had told no one. She told Peggy only when it was all over, and on the 'astringent note so beloved of the Angliche' ('my career has been a *trifle* stormy and it all ended up in Holloway. Yes dearie – am now an old Hollowayian…'). Maryvonne, of course, she never told at all. She wrote to her as soon as she was back from Holloway, saying that she'd been ill and in hospital, but reassuring her immediately: 'Well here I am all right again, a bit "rocky" perhaps but quite all right.' She tried to imagine Maryvonne's life in Java. She tried to write about cheerful things – books she would send, the baby, the perfect summer weather, colours and scents and pretty, cool women. Complaints did slip out – a hurt wrist, hideous London, endless soul-destroying housework. But when we think what she'd just been through her bravery is heart-breaking. Just a month after Holloway she wrote: 'Still there are always moments, or weeks – or months perhaps. And you will have them too be sure. I won't bore you with mine, except to say that they always

---

*cf 'Jazz': 'one day an old woman come up and ask me for dog-ends…'; and Jean to Peggy Kirkaldy: '… such an affection for them. Especially for one old girl who looked like a gypsy, was very pally. I couldn't understand what she said very well, she talked the most fascinating lingo, cigarettes being "doggins" and London "the Smoke" etc.…'

happen when one least expects them. In between there are the little happy minutes or sensations' ('trees, shadows, a shaded light,' as she wrote to Peggy later).

In the summer after Holloway Jean must have had her medical and psychiatric treatment − 'medical' no doubt having to do with drying out. Possibly, then, she wasn't drinking, or wasn't drinking so much. At first − most understandably − she and Max tried to move away. They looked for somewhere in Shepperton, where Jean had lived with Leslie in 1934, and in London; in August they seem to have packed up and gone to a room in Holland Park, meaning to look further from there. But this all came to nothing, and by September they were back in Beckenham. Jean decided that the house itself, at least, wasn't so bad. It was built in 1840, 'one of my favourite years' (the year of Antoinette's honeymoon with Rochester, so perhaps she was thinking about her unfinished novel). She longed to write again, but couldn't − '*Pas un mot!*' She thought about Holloway: 'They have a song there that haunts me, the girls I mean. In fact the whole place haunts me. But what can I do?' No one would publish such 'unpleasant facts', especially in England. So slowly even the desire to write left her. 'It's the first time in my life,' she told Peggy, 'and is a bit like losing one's arms or even eyes, but it's not my fault and I can't do anything about it.' She 'sank into apathy'. She avoided trouble, and that was all.

In September Max found '*another* new friend who is promising heaven and earth.' Jean saw at once − at least so she said afterwards − that this one was different. Very clever, very persuasive, and utterly heartless. Also 'it stuck out five miles that he was a crook.' Max was obstinate; so she was cautious, and said she liked his new friend. But now she had a new worry.

Max and his friend, Michael Donn, first set up business together in East Ham, in Donn's part of the world. At the same time Max continued to work for Cohen and Cohen in the City. Then in late October or early November Donn joined Cohen and Cohen too. He and Max became inseparable, and Max was more optimistic than ever about 'making some money soon'. Perhaps Jean allowed herself to believe him; perhaps she only pretended to. But underneath the worry got worse. She got her 'usual November 'flu', which she often invoked to cover being drunk or hung over.

And then in the middle of all this worry and foreboding an extraordinary thing happened. She saw an advertisement in the *New Statesman*, and it was for her.

Jean Rhys (Mrs Tilden Smith) author of *Voyage in the Dark, After Leaving Mr Mackenzie, Good Morning, Midnight*, etc. Will anyone knowing her whereabouts kindly communicate with Dr H.W. Egli, 3 Chesterfield Gardens, N.W.3.

Again the last minute rescue, the magical, fateful possibility of change! She sat down straight away and wrote to the address on the advertisement. And two days later she had a reply.

The advertisement had been placed by an actress called Selma vaz Dias (Hans Egli was her husband). Selma was twenty years younger than Jean, energetic and ambitious. She had come across *Good Morning, Midnight* some years before and been struck straight away by the character of Sasha. Now she had adapted the novel into a dramatic monologue for radio. But of course she needed Jean's permission to perform it. She'd got in touch with Constable, who gave her the last address they had, and Jean's married name. But her letter had come back, marked 'name unknown'.

Typically Selma didn't give up. The BBC's enquiries came up with the story that Jean had died in Paris. Selma wrote to the British Consul there, but that of course led nowhere. She learned about Leslie and Maryvonne; but Leslie was dead and Maryvonne had disappeared. Selma couldn't find anyone who had known Jean before the war. Finally she searched the death certificates in London: but happily Jean wasn't there either. So she put the advertisement in the paper.

What happened now was typical of everyone concerned. Selma had planned 'a preliminary reading' of her *Good Morning, Midnight*. In fact this was a public performance, with admission charged, so that she needed Jean's permission for it just as much as for the BBC broadcast. But it was arranged, and the tickets printed, for 10 November, only five days after the *New Statesman* advertisement appeared: in other words, Selma would have done it anyway. That was typical of *her*. Of Jean many things were. She mocked herself and everyone: 'I am very astonished that the BBC like my work (especially *Good Morning*) but it seems they thought I was dead — which of course would make a great difference. In fact they were going to follow it up with a broadcast "Quest for Jean Rhys" and I feel rather tactless at being alive! However, I'm cheered up too for if they can make a fuss of me dead surely they can make a *little fuss* even though I'm not....' Really she was excited and exalted. She thought of the money, especially for Maryvonne and the baby; the 'numb hopeless feeling that stopped me writing for so long' disappeared, and anything seemed possible again. Two days before the reading she sat down and went through Selma's script with great concentration. She sent a few small suggestions in a modest and generous letter ('You've adapted my novel very sensitively, and seen Sasha almost as I saw her. Thank you.') But that was all she could do. Her anxiety over Max's involvement with Donn was mounting; so was her paranoia, which had reverted to the Hardimans next door; and so were her inability to face the world, her 'flu and her drinking. She didn't go to Selma's reading, or even phone to make her excuses; Max did both for her. Two days later she wrote, pleading illness and no telephone;* and she did send a telegram. 'I assure you,' she told Selma, 'that being down with 'flu in a cold flat and no telephone just at this moment is *exactly* me. It would happen just that way and no other.'

In fact it was exactly as she'd written in *Good Morning, Midnight* itself: 'You know what happens when you get excited and exalted, don't you?... Yes.... And then, you know how you collapse like a pricked balloon, don't you?... Yes, exactly....'

On 16 November, only eleven days after the *New Statesman* advertisement had appeared, she was arrested again for being drunk and disorderly. It was quarter to two in the afternoon and she was still in her nightgown and slippers. She'd clearly had an argument with her upstairs tenant. While the police were hearing Mrs Daniell's complaint Jean went out into the road. She crossed and recrossed it, talking to people; the traffic had to stop for her. She had a piece of paper in her hand which she waved around; she 'said something about the BBC.'

A week later she told Peggy that 'my bitter enemy next door is now telling everybody very loud and clear that I'm an imposter "impersonating a dead writer called Jean Rhys".'('It's a weird feeling being told you are impersonating yourself. Rather nightmarish. You think: perhaps I am!') So she must have told people now who she was. And two weeks later she was saying 'I know that's a great fault of mine. I get exalted and make people hate me....' We can guess what had happened. She had told all her enemies that the last laugh was hers: she was being rediscovered, the BBC were about to broadcast her work, she would soon be famous.... And they refused to believe her. As she so often said and wrote: truth is improbable; the simple truth is the one thing that no one will believe.

She had to appear in Bromley Court yet again. She was very agitated, claiming that before the police arrived 'garbage had been emptied over her' (presumably by Mrs Daniell). She denied being drunk; 'all she had had to drink was a little wine to warm herself.' Max conducted her defence himself. He confirmed that there was 'less than a quarter of a bottle of Algerian wine in the house,' and she

---

*She did have a telephone at Beckenham (she gave the number, Beckenham 6922, to Peggy in a letter of July 1948). But it was probably cut off now. (In early 1950 she wrote to Peggy that the phone had been cut off 'for ages'; and a week after the reading she certainly had to go out to telephone.)

couldn't have got drunk on that. And this time the magistrate (a different one) believed them. Or at least he didn't believe anyone else. He said the evidence was not satisfactory, and dismissed the charge.

That was a respite, but the only one. A week after it Selma vaz Dias came to see Jean for the first time. She was large, lively, generous and not English,* and Jean liked her. But Selma was not tactful. Jean was 'bowled over' to learn that 'my being dead is about the kindest thing she heard. The unkindest — well let's not go into that.' But she did:

> I can't resist quoting something Miss vaz Dias said: 'Dear Miss Rhys — you're so *gentle* and *quiet* — Not at all what I expected!' — I gathered afterwards that she expected a raving and not too clean maniac with straws in gruesome unwashed hair. . . .

Poor Jean. It was like the Rosamond Lehmann meeting all over again, but worse. The more Selma expected her to be mad, the more she tried to seem quiet and sane. But she couldn't. In fact she was 'awfully all of a twitter and moony': so distracted that she forgot to put the coffee in the pot, and poured Selma a cup of boiling water. She quite often did such things because she was nervous, so she drank something to calm her nerves, and ended up tipsy as well. It wasn't a good method; but in fact she usually achieved her main aim, which was to hide the fact that her nervousness was not merely neurotic and constitutional. She often had a very good real reason. This visit of Selma's is a perfect example.† For on that very day, Thursday, 24 November, the *Beckenham and Penge Advertiser* splashed her last encounter with the law across its front page. MRS HAMER AGITATED, they'd written in large letters right in the middle; and '*Only Had Algerian Wine,*' and a long account of the trial. True, they reported that the charge had been dismissed; but only at the end, and only after much humiliating detail. Jean can hardly not have known: and she must have been terrified that, passing the Beckenham shops, Selma would notice. And she must have thought again: *It would happen just that way and no other.*

In fact Selma didn't see the horrible headline. Luckily she was almost as self-obsessed as Jean, and didn't notice much at all (she came away saying Jean was 'tall and thin and Gothic', for instance — which far more accurately describes herself — and afterwards wrote to her complaining of her own depression). This of course suited Jean ('Individualists, completely wrapped up in themselves,

---

*Selma was born in Holland of Jewish parents, and educated partly in France.

†As Jean half admitted, many years later: 'I was slightly absentminded (with reason I assure you).' (To Diana Athill, 7 July 1963.)

up in themselves, thank God. It's the extrovert, prancing around, dying for a bit of fun − that's the person you've got to be wary of'). So the visit was a success. Jean began to 'wake up and make plans and come alive again': 'I wanted to do a thing about Holloway to be called Black Castle.' Perhaps Selma could do another monologue of that; and in the meantime she would talk about Jean's short stories in a broadcast she was giving on the Third Programme. Jean promised to listen.

But this flare of her flame was pathetically brief. She missed Selma's broadcast, because of a 'lightning' electricity strike, and then missed the repeat because 'the Third Programme wasn't obtainable....' She *was* unimaginably incompetent, but this was even worse than usual. Really she didn't want to listen: she couldn't pull herself together enough to be in the right place at the right time. For she was cracking up; and the new life and hope Selma had brought couldn't stop her.

Maryvonne fell ill in December, which was another worry. But the main trouble was Max. From the moment Donn had joined him at Cohen and Cohen's − at exactly the time Selma had appeared − Jean 'hadn't known one minute's peace.' Donn was a big spender, with a taste for smart restaurants. Max hardly came home any more; she even wondered if Donn had produced 'some ghastly smart girl' for him. Their money troubles got worse instead of better. In mid-November Max told Donn he'd sold the Beckenham house. He'd got six thousand pounds for it, but he wouldn't receive the money for a few weeks. Meanwhile, therefore, he began borrowing large sums through Donn against this amount. 'Every day' (Jean told Peggy) 'he'd say "Tonight Donne's* getting me two hundred or five hundred or a thousand" and always he'd get more haggard and shabby and disappointed.' Finally he disappeared for five days. When he came back he said he'd been to Paris with Donn to borrow money there. He and Donn left Cohen and Cohen and set up on their own again. 'He said they'd make all the money in the world because Donn knew all the crooks in London. (That part I believed.)' Indeed it was true, but it didn't help poor Max. On the contrary.

All this was too much for Jean. One Saturday night in January 1950 she got very drunk and clashed with her last tenant, Mr Daniell. He smacked her on the face, she said; she was hit on the head, too; it was the third time she was assaulted.... This time she was determined *she* would invoke the law. Near midnight she went to Beckenham Police Station to lay a charge against him. But she could not follow the advice Christophine (that is, she herself) gives to Antoinette in *Wide Sargasso*

*Jean usually spelt Donn's name this way.

*Sea*: 'Speak...calm and cool.... Don't bawl at the man and don't make crazy faces. Don't cry either....' Instead she did everything wrong; indeed, everything bizarre and shocking. So far her worst term of abuse had been 'Gestapo'. But in her rages she had no principles; anything would do. The Bezants and Daniells were Jewish, or she thought they were. So now Germaine, Maryvonne's friends, the concentration camps were forgotten, and Jews were her enemies. When she accused Daniell she called him a 'dirty stinking Jew'. The Inspector offered to send a policeman back with her to investigate the complaint; but she said she was too tired to walk and needed a car. He suggested she ring for a taxi from the kiosk outside. She refused to leave until Daniell was brought in and charged, and threw her coat on the floor to prove it. The Inspector ejected her, twice. Finally she stood outside the station, shouting 'You can't get justice. This country is run by rotten stinking Jews....' A crowd gathered; and she was arrested.

Two days later she appeared at Bromley Court for the eighth time in two years. She continued to behave bizarrely, with a self-destructive inappropriateness worse than any of her heroines. She arrived late; then said in explanation that she'd had to come by bus, though she usually travelled by taxi.... She denied the charge, of 'using insulting words and behaviour:' she wasn't drunk, she hadn't shouted anything about Jews. Her probation officer testified that she had been complying with the terms of her probation, but it didn't help. She was found guilty and fined one pound. 'I have such a bad reputation in Beckenham that no one will believe me,' she said. It wasn't the explanation, but it was certainly true.

That was a Monday, 16 January. On the Thursday she quarrelled with Daniell a second time, on Saturday a third time. He charged her with assault again, and put their first fight in as well, for good measure. Jean appeared at Bromley on this charge two or three weeks later.* It seems that only the first assault was considered; she was remanded on bail, and a further trial arranged for the second and third assaults. But this case was adjourned, perhaps because Jean didn't appear.

If she didn't appear she had a good reason. For in the week between her two trials Max had disappeared again. Then − through the Law Society, she said − Jean heard that on her 'unlucky number day', the thirteenth, he had been arrested. The 'smash' she'd foreseen for so long − the main cause of all *her* smashes − had finally come.

---

*The appropriate court records for this period seem to be missing, and there are only the vaguer newspaper reports to go on.

Max had been arrested — naturally — with Donn. 'Thousands were missing. Cohen's, moneylenders and some clients.' Max swore Donn had had it all: it hadn't even done him any good. They were initially charged the next day with stealing seven empty cheques, 'valued at one shilling and twopence'. Of course that was only the warning shot across the bows. Max was granted bail; and the case was adjourned for a week.

It is almost unbearable to think of Jean and Max now, in hated, hating Beckenham, waiting. They were sixty and sixty-eight years old, penniless, both facing trial. Jean would be (at the least) fined again; Max would surely get several years in prison, and she would have to spend them alone. It couldn't be worse. And yet she was better when the worst had happened. Relieved; released from the paralysis of waiting. She talked about suicide ('I really want of course to vanish for *good and all*'), but she didn't mean it. She talked about going to 'a Catholic place', and perhaps she did mean that. But mostly she tried to think of a job she could do. The trouble was, the answer was *none*. She couldn't type, cook, sew; 'in fact I'm completely useless really,' she wrote to Peggy. 'I could read to people. Do you think that would be possible? I know a woman in New York who used to earn a sort of living that way. But this is not New York — or 1936. . . .'

Max's trial was to be held in London, so now they really had to go. Jean sold their furniture and books, and for a while they lived on the proceeds. She found a home for her last remaining cat (with one of her Beckenham enemies, but at least she liked cats). The BBC finally turned down *Good Morning, Midnight,* as she'd always known they would; in the middle of all this she hardly noticed. When her trial opened in March she gave an undertaking to leave Beckenham in three weeks, and the case was adjourned until then. When it was reconvened on 30 March the magistrates were told she had left the night before: the only thing left in the flat was a divan bed. The case was adjourned *sine die*. Jean's long battle with Beckenham was over.

She and Max moved into a room in a Kensington hotel. Now *his* case ground on, through adjournments, committals, pretrials and postponements. It took over three months altogether. Poor Max was so 'smashed up' that Jean had to manage, and she did. She hid everything, of course, from Maryvonne, and probably from her family.* Her only confidante and support was Peggy Kirkaldy. Max's

---

*The most she said to Maryvonne was, at the very beginning, 'Max has got into an awful money jam. He thinks he'll get out of it but of course it's a bit nerve-racking.' Maryvonne and Job had no idea of what had happened until years later. As to Jean's family, they too knew about Max's 'smash' later, but I'm sure Jean would have kept it from them as long as possible.

family, she felt (and I'm sure it was true) blamed her as much if not more than him. No doubt they thought, as Leslie's family had too, that it was her need for money that had driven him to it ('That isn't all true but it may be a bit true,' Jean told Peggy). And aloud and often they said that she should have come and told them as soon as she suspected something was wrong. But of course she had felt they wouldn't listen to her, wouldn't believe her: 'my appearance or manner or something is *dead* against me and no one takes me seriously until it's too late.'

Jean's life really did seem to be the same few scenes re-enacted over and over. For now Max's sister stepped into the place of Leslie's. Just as her furniture money must have been running out, Jean had a solicitor's letter saying that 'a friend who wishes to remain anonymous will supply me with money to live on for the present.' She never knew for certain who it was:* but Max said it was a combination of Lord Listowel, who was a relative, and his sister. Like Phyllis Tilden Smith, then, Dorothy Norman probably gave Jean money: but in a still more reluctant spirit. She said the blow to her family would kill her; and she went away to the country, in order, Jean said, 'to avoid my arguments, prayers & tears'. She understood: 'She's old too & sick & proud & this has been an awful blow & somebody's got to be the sacrificed goat. I suppose that's me.' But of course it hurt. As with Lancelot, with Ford, with Phyllis, with Edward and Brenda, she knew she was both dependent on 'respectable' people, and despised by them.

She and Max were caught, like animals in a trap. She flew into rages 'so easily', and cried easily, and laughed and cried at the same time, 'which is a bad sign.' She thought of suicide again, but laughed at that too ('Then I thought of Max's story of the old lady who went to church with her ear trumpet. And so the stern Scotch sexton or verger or something, eyed her a bit. Then he said, "Madam one toot and you're oot." Perhaps that's what it would be like, one toot and you're oot....') Max was worse. He too had fits of violent rage. And he was still obsessed by Donn, still hypnotised by him. He kept meeting him – or trying to, because Donn never turned up. 'It's crazy,' Jean said, and surely it was.

Surely *Max* had been 'crazy', for several years. He seems to have lost all judgement, all sense of reality, even before he met Donn. Well: he

---

*'Certainly not my relatives,' she said, though presumably Edward's and Brenda's allowance continued as before. Leslie's daughter Anne thinks it may have been her Aunt Phyllis again, because she was a cousin of Max's as well. But the most reliable idea must surely be Max's at the time.

had had two breakdowns (or at least periods of great mental stress) before; he was clearly vulnerable. He loved Jean and wanted to rescue her; he'd given up everything for her; and for at least three of the five years they'd been together she had been in an acute state of anger and agitation. That had been at least partly because of him; but it must have affected him as well. Probably, in other words, they had literally driven one another mad.

And yet they stuck together. Jean thought several times that perhaps she should have left him, for his sake as well as hers ('Perhaps it would be kinder to fade out, not worry him'). But of course she couldn't abandon him now; 'and I'm so alone and such a helpless person really.' So they clung to each other. In between sessions at the Guildhall and Old Bailey they went to pubs and films, to museums, to Westminster Abbey. The anonymous friend bowed to family pressure and reduced Jean's allowance. She didn't eat properly, she still drank too much, and her paranoia burgeoned: 'I carry round letters to prove everything I say now. They bulge out of my bag and are a great nuisance, but I find it better just to plonk the evidence down....' What was she saying? That Max was innocent, that he had been used? That Jean Rhys wasn't dead; that *she* was Jean Rhys? Again, she was often right: people refused to believe the simple, improbable truth.


Max's trial finally began on 9 May, 1950. The charges were larceny and obtaining money by false pretences: from the moneylenders Donn had taken him to, via cheques stolen from Cohen and Cohen and fraudulently signed by Donn. Donn was accused on all these counts with Max, plus four more separately. Typically, Donn denied the charges; equally typically Jean tried to persuade Max to deny them too, but everyone else said he should plead guilty, and he did. As she'd predicted, Donn tried to shift the blame on to him. She felt, bitterly, that he succeeded. Donn's lawyer was 'very good (and very expensive)', while at the crucial moment Max's lawyer wasn't there. When they were convicted Max got three years — 'which is, at his age, a sentence of near death'; while Donn, who (it turned out) had two previous convictions and double the number of offences, got only four.... This was both true and not true. Donn did have more counts against him, and previous convictions (indeed he had only just got out of prison when Max met him). And Max did do less to defend himself: for instance, he seems to have called no witnesses, and to have made no statement to the police. But his lawyer put his blameless record very fully to the court; and the judge clearly found that Donn was the responsible party: 'Much of this misery, subterfuge and trickery was conceived by you. It was not Hamer who was responsible for the somewhat intricate machinery by which these frauds were accomplished. You, Donn, by your volubility and your apparent revelling in subterfuge were responsible in the main for what happened here.' Donn was the crook; Max was his stooge, under his influence. This was — as Jean recognised — clearly established. The key to the severity of Max's sentence came in these words of the judge's: 'As a solicitor you are responsible in the highest degree for your actions.'

Even if Jean had taken this in she would have thought it a mockery. How could Max have the responsibility of power when he had never had any power? And she would have thought it humbug too. In a despairing moment Donn's elderly mother claimed to her that the real crooks were the Cohens, who had taken most of the money themselves and left her son to take the rap.... I don't suppose Jean believed in Donn's innocence for a moment, but I expect she believed in the Cohens' guilt as well. 'I've never believed much in justice,' she wrote. 'Now *Nada*.' In *Wide Sargasso Sea* Christophine will say that slavery and 'Letter of the Law' are the same thing, and Antoinette will say that justice is a cold word, that there is no justice. We will hear the passion in their voices. That passion came from Bow Street, from Holt, from Beckenham; and now from poor Max at the Old Bailey.

He was convicted on 22 May and sentenced two days later. Jean's heart broke for him. 'I wish I could serve this sentence,' she wrote to Peggy. 'I wouldn't mind much. Except the cold.' He was to go to Maidstone Prison, and she prepared to follow. Like Marya Zelli when *her* husband was jailed, she tried to sell her clothes. She also tried to sell two Chinese vases brought back from the Boxer Rebellion by an uncle of Max's ('I hope he did loot them & they are worth something'). A quarter of a century later she turned this incident too into a story. 'The Chinese Vases' never quite worked, and wasn't published. But it shows once again how Jean turned every sad experience into fiction; and how each of her sad fictions is based on a real experience.

She wrote to Maryvonne that they'd left Beckenham because the house was so damp and cold. Then she said, 'Well my dear you'll be wondering what it really is all about' — and still didn't tell her. Max had 'got into money difficulties but I think all will be well now ... nothing is wrong between us. It's only dam dam money.' She gave Maryvonne Peggy's address to write to. She expected to disappear; and she did.

In one of her last letters from London she said: 'I'm lazy and hopeless Peggy but honestly I do have a rum time....' 'A rum time': that was vintage Jean.

★ ★ ★

From May 1950 to March 1951 Jean completely disappeared. She did not write to Maryvonne, or to Selma. And she broke her few other tenuous connections, or they broke with her. Her last letter to Peggy Kirkaldy was a long report of Max's trial at the end of May. In it she asked Peggy once more if she knew of a cheap room, and if any of her friends 'could say I was their companion or maid or something' (then 'I could live cheaply in this cheap room & write, & this bloody unknown would be happy thinking I was washing dishes or something'). Peggy had been responding with quick affection and support, and she surely tried to do so again: but Jean heard a false note, as she always did when she had to give up and ask for help. As soon as Peggy knew she was in trouble, she told Maryvonne, she wrote like this:

> Dear Jean, I can't let you have any money because I had a bad week at the races and am heavily in debt to the bookies. Yrs Peggy. (She had become a great racegoer and betted a lot)
> I wrote back
> Dear Peggy, I never asked you for money. Yrs Jean.
>
> And that was that. I was sorry because I liked her and had known her so long. But really!

It was Germaine Richelot all over again, and like Lancelot too: as soon as money came between them she went mad with pride and bitterness, and had to destroy everything. And did. Peggy Kirkaldy wouldn't find her again for seven years, by which time she – Peggy – was dying.

That was one break. The other was with her sister Brenda. That relationship, of course, had hardly been a success from the beginning. But since (probably) Leslie's death, Brenda had been helping Jean, together with Edward; and there does seem to have been some contact between them. By now that contact was over. Robert had told Jean she was not to write to Brenda any more. They would continue to contribute to her allowance, but from now on only Edward would see her. We have only the family's memories – or myths – about what had happened, but they agree. Brenda was too upset by Jean and her 'goings-on' to continue: that part Jean might have reported herself, bitterly. But there was more. It wasn't just that Brenda wanted to forget and deny her. She wouldn't speak about such things; but when she did, just once, to her sister-in-law, she said something rather different. She couldn't get Jean out of her mind, she said; she wished she could do more. But it was impossible, because Jean hated her.

She *would* say this, perhaps, rather than that she hated Jean — though perhaps not, for she'd have thought it only decent to despise someone who had fallen so low. In any case I am sure it was also true. Over and over again Jean made it impossible for people to help her by hating them for making her ask. It would be a miracle if she didn't do this to Brenda too, even more. For she had more reason to hate Brenda than almost anyone else in the world: for all the reasons we already know, and for a new one too. Jean never told this to anyone, and she cut it out of what she wrote — not to protect Brenda, but to protect herself. It almost certainly dates from her wildest years, the late 1940s, when she was locked in battle with her Beckenham enemies, splashing her name in the papers, and having to see psychiatrists.* For what she wrote in her Ropemakers Diary in Maidstone, and then mostly scored out was this:

> I have been accused of madness. By my brother & sister. Also by others. Not by the doctors who saw me....

*By my brother & sister.* That must be, I think, why she now hated Brenda more than ever. And Edward too, I'm sure. But she had to go on taking the money, and someone had to go on giving it. She dropped out of touch with him too for long periods; but from now on she would write, when she had to write, to him alone. She always found it easier to forgive and forget what men had done to her, anyway; her hatred of women was deeper and more tenacious. And one of its main targets and sources in her life was Brenda: the loved daughter and wife, and now also her accuser and betrayer. The force of her hatred must have been frightening. I think that Brenda was frightened; and that that was her main reason for refusing even to receive a letter from Jean for thirty years.

In March 1951 Jean surfaces in Maidstone, all ties cut. She stays for two years — and is gloriously, unpredictably, inimitably herself. For what could have been harder? — when would she have been likelier to break down altogether? She was alone in a strange provincial town. She saw only Max, ill and broken in prison, like a nightmare repetition of Paris twenty-five years before. She was dependent on money from their hated families. In cheap temporary rooms, surrounded by drab postwar strangers who never read books, who spoke another language, 'like facing a blank wall all the time.' And all

---

*Unless from before — during the war, or at Edward's just after it; or even some earlier time when doctors saw her.... But I don't think she could have kept the Beckenham years completely hidden from her family; and they would certainly have renewed their accusations then.

the time she had to keep up a façade of cheerfulness to Maryvonne.... But she did it, and more – she did it gamely, even hopefully. It is extraordinary. When she should have been happy and hopeful – when most probably she *was* happy and hopeful – in Beckenham in 1947 and '48, for instance, she couldn't do it: she made enemies, she set out to destroy it. Now, when she was at rock-bottom, when the worst had happened, she was relieved, she could rebuild, she could even do the hardest thing of all: she stopped drinking. No doubt not for the whole two years; she promised herself a lovely 'debauch' now and then, and I expect she had it. But she told Maryvonne she wasn't drinking; 'Can you credit it?' she asked, in her self-mocking way, and I do. For that must have been the key. She lived with everything she most dreaded for two years: isolation, solitude, unbelonging. And yet she didn't break down. There is no trace of her in the Maidstone court reports; when she was famous no Maidstone neighbour ever appeared, like Mr Bezant of Beckenham, to say that Jean Rhys *couldn't* be a great writer, she was just a crazy drunken woman.

Most important of all, she wanted to write again, and she did. Not fiction, but one of the bravest pieces of her life. Without the Ropemakers Diary, she wrote in Maidstone around 1952, she could not have written *Wide Sargasso Sea*. Like her poetry it put her back in touch with the deepest source of her art – the lucid honesty and self-understanding which drink drowned and degraded. Over the last fifteen years she'd sunk deeper and deeper into this degradation, until she'd reached the pit in Beckenham. And that, precisely, released her. After some of the drunkest and maddest times of her life she suddenly had some of the soberest and sanest. It was too late for a cure, and she would slip back again. She slipped back now, sometimes, especially in the first year (her first landlady, she said, was 'grand guignol' – in other words, she still hated people, and had scenes). But her letters to Maryvonne, and the Ropemakers Diary itself, make it clear: alone in *la crasse* in Maidstone she was, at least sometimes, better and healthier than she'd been through many of her years of marriage. In a way solitude suited her, if only she could have borne it. She craved dependence as she craved drink: but like drink it was bad for her. If she'd been forced to be independent, as she was in Maidstone, perhaps her whole life could have been saner and healthier. And perhaps she would have written only brave and honest books, like the Ropemakers Diary. Or perhaps, of course, she wouldn't have needed to write at all.

What did she *do* in Maidstone? She went for walks, and to the cinema. She visited Max; and though he was sad and ill she could feel she was being good to him, and useful. And, I think, she worried less about money. Her allowances can't have come to much; but she had only herself to keep now, and if on top of this she wasn't having to buy drink all the time, she would have more to spare than she'd had for years. So she could do what she'd always wanted: sit quietly in a cheap room, and write and read. And that, I think, is what she mostly did. She counted her blessings: 'books and the hope of writing again and Max.' She buried herself in books: Koestler and Sartre, H.E. Bates and Conan Doyle. She bought books for Maryvonne and her daughter, Ruth Ellen. She thought about them a lot; she sent them presents, and very loving letters: 'I don't know what else to say except (sentimentally) that I love you. Always have, always will.' Without constant drink and constant fear she even liked some of the places and people around her. Especially during her nine months at the Ropemakers Arms.

'This is a quiet place, though it's a pub,' she told Maryvonne. 'I have a tiny bedroom & sitting room & from the sitting room I can see (thank God) a chestnut.' Her rooms were 'small and dark but not without something attractive'; the sitting room felt peaceful. There was ' a row of black elephants on the mantelpiece, a table with a plate of red apples and some flowers (a present from the landlady this morning), a lot of books and an electric fire. So you see what more can I want?' Jean, who so hated landladies, said this one was ' a real dear and so is her husband.' She was very kind. She brought Jean these flowers, and a feather mattress; one day she even bought her some books from the second-hand stall in the market. 'When I speak of these rooms, and of my landlady and landlord, I touch wood all the time,' Jean wrote. Was it really these people, or was it her own mood – her soberness, the lifting of her paranoia? Probably it was a bit of both. In any case it was in this temporary haven that she was able to write again: for the first time, probably, since she'd tried to begin 'Black Castle' two years earlier.

The Ropemakers Diary came straight out of Jean's life, especially of the past few years. She had always felt accused, secretly guilty; but in these years the accusation had become open and official. She had been tried, in a real court before a real judge, and condemned not once but many times; her husband too had been accused, condemned and imprisoned. So when she cast her diary in the form of a trial, she was doing what she always did: drawing directly on her own recent experience, knowing its detail, needing to exorcise its horror. It was fiction, of course, as all her writing is fiction: no one ever asked her *these* questions. But it was also absolutely real. She knew exactly how these people spoke, and not just from books. She could have got 'Objection sustained' from books; but not the different tones of prosecution and defence, not the pounce of *So your first statement was not correct?* or the pedantry of *Did you make great efforts to, shall we say, establish contacts with other people?* ... In a paragraph which she scored through violently she wrote: 'During the last few years you have been sent to Holloway, you have spent some weeks in a mental observation ward. You have sat through an Old Bailey trial. *Enfin* — these last few years. Do you wish to write about that?' And answered herself: 'No. Not yet.' She never did write (or at least keep) anything which was openly and clearly about her trials or Max's, or about her experiences in ' a mental ward'. But she did, of course, secretly: in 'Let Them Call It Jazz'; in *Wide Sargasso Sea*; and here, in the courtroom drama of the Ropemakers Diary.

Everything else in the diary also comes out of her life in 1951 and '52: quotations from the books she was burying herself in; descriptions of her life at the Ropemakers Arms; thoughts and memories of her forty-five years in England. These too are sharp and clear. The kind landlady, but the hateful other women ('Of course, meeting these women I can see that, as women, they are much better than I'). Her hatred of England, which was disappointed love. The mistake she made in coming back to it: 'I swore that nothing would ever make me return. No hardship. No sadness. Nothing. I should have stuck to that.' But *The Trial of Jean Rhys* is its heart, and the most important thing she'd written since *Good Morning, Midnight*.

Jean tries herself very differently from the Bromley magistrates. She doesn't accuse herself just of drunkenness; indeed she puts question marks beside this charge, perhaps because she wasn't being drunk any more. She doesn't accuse herself of violence either, as the Hardimans, Bezants and Daniells had done. These things were merely facts: that is, unimportant, so that she could pass them over; and shameful, so that she would want to. She ignores facts and acts and goes straight to feelings: to her deepest feelings, to her ultimate humanity or lack of it. This is the subject of her self-accusation: *has she ever really loved, pitied, known another human being?* This was her question in the novels too, in the heroines' relationships to their 'neighbours'. But now she raises it in the open, about herself. She defends herself, she half denies the accusation, but she makes it.

'It is in myself,' she says. '*What is?*' 'All. Good, evil, love, hate, life, death, beauty, ugliness.' '*And in everyone?*' 'I do not know everyone. I only know myself.' '*And others?*' 'I do not know others. I see them as trees walking.' '*There you are!*' the Counsel for the Prosecution cries triumphantly. '*Didn't take long, did it?*'

The Counsel for the Defence tries to help her help herself. '*Did you in your youth have a great love and pity for others?'* he asks, *'especially for the poor and unfortunate?'* 'Yes,' she replies. *'Were you able to show this?'* he asks. 'I think I could not always,' she says. 'I was very clumsy. No one told me.' *'Excuse of course!'* the Prosecution shouts.... *'It is untrue,'* the Defence goes on, *'that you are cold and withdrawn?'*

It is not true.

*Did you make great efforts to, shall we say, establish contacts with other people? I mean friendships, love affairs, so on?*
Yes. Not friendships very much.

*Did you succeed?*
Sometimes. For a time

*It didn't last?*
No.

*Whose fault was that?*
Mine I suppose.

*You suppose?*
Silence.

Later, near the end, Jean wrote *Mea culpa, mea culpa, mea maxima culpa*. But also that she was guilty of all the mortal sins except one: coldness of heart. So she both accepts and denies the central charge. But her accuser also forces her to defend the main thing in her life, her writing. And in the justification she gives for this she accepts her failure and guilt as a human being.

*The phrase is not 'I do not know' but 'I have nothing to say.'*
The trouble is I have plenty to say. Not only that but I am bound to say it.

*Bound?*
I must.

*Why? Why? Why?*
I must write. If I stop writing my life will have been an abject failure. It is that already to other people. But it will be an abject failure to myself. I will not have earned death.

This phrase, *you must earn death*, came to her, she says, as though it were spoken aloud by someone else. That is, she didn't take responsibility for it, she didn't ask what it meant. In her ultimate recognition that only her writing could save her from her human failure, she fell back on her unconscious mode. And when she unearthed the Ropemakers Diary twenty-five years later this unconsciousness had spread. She hadn't known, she said, and she still didn't know, why Max was in prison. She hadn't known other things about him either: whether he'd had any children, for instance. In fact she didn't know much about any of her husbands, or about her parents. 'Perhaps,' she said, 'I wasn't curious. . . .' Mostly this cloud of unknowing was a defence, so that people wouldn't ask her any questions. But it was also another, secret admission that the accusation had been true. She *didn't* know other people, even those who were closest to her.

In a way the Ropemakers Diary was the hardest thing Jean ever wrote, because it was without the mask of fiction. But even here she could find a self-mocking humour. '*This is the way?*' the accuser asks sceptically, about her hope of earning death through writing. 'I think so,' she says. '*All right,*' he says. '*But be damned careful not to leave this book about.*'

★    ★    ★

In May 1951, after he'd been in prison a year, Max's name was struck off the Solicitors' Roll. Exactly a year later, in May 1952, he was released. He was seventy years old. He couldn't practise his profession; his health was broken. For the rest of their lives together he and Jean were bitterly poor. The Navy withdrew his pension; and he couldn't even draw a statutory old age pension, because he hadn't paid the stamps properly while he was working. Needless to say, Jean had never paid in either. She had her allowance from Edward and Brenda; and Max had some sort of 'compassionate allowance', either from the Navy or from his family. That was all. Jean would accept nothing from Maryvonne and Job. At least twice in the 1950s she and Max had Christmas dinner only because Edward sent them a chicken.

For eight years after Max left prison he and Jean wandered around London, Wales and Cornwall, trying to find somewhere they could both like and afford. Very little remains of these years: a few letters, a few memories. Perhaps things happened that left no trace, both in writing and fighting, the things that usually happened to Jean. But I don't think so. About writing she always said she lost a lot, and no doubt she did. But I think she mostly lost things she didn't want, diaries and early drafts; the last states of things she kept, even if they were old or unfinished, to sell or work on again. And as to fighting – she can't of course have stopped entirely. She'd been making scenes for over twenty years; when finally she settled for long enough for people to remember her they said that she made them again. But I think we can be sure that she never again got into the serious trouble she did at Beckenham. Even when she was ready to fight other people were less so: for she and Max were so clearly poor and old and ill, and later she was also famous. And however much she wanted to hide her bad behaviour she was no good at it. She put it into her fiction, for instance, and never thought that anyone could guess from that what had really happened. She *needed* to work out her bad behaviour in her fiction: and I think she worked it all out. By 1950 the worst was over.

'Slightly dazed', Jean and Max returned to London in 1952. They stayed somewhere near Victoria and looked for rooms. Again they had to settle for a distant suburb — indeed, not far from Beckenham: Upper Norwood, just the other side of Penge. Jean went through her usual progress from excitement to disillusion. At first she could only feel 'I like so much not being alone.' She was happy to be back in London; the tiny flat was 'awfully nice' and the neighbourhood pleasant. Their garden was lovely; and she could go for walks in the grounds of the Crystal Palace nearby. 'Ruins and some lovely trees and usually nobody there.' Two months later she still liked the flat, but no longer the neighbourhood. By October she hated it — 'this suburb and all the mean little streets around'. She saw an advertisement for a caravan near Penzance in Cornwall and was 'crazy to go'. But she met, she said, a 'storm of sarcasm and opposition'. This wasn't from Max, who also wanted to leave London. It must have been from the family: from Edward and Brenda, who were paying the bills. Of course they were being sensible and practical: a caravan in Cornwall in the winter was a terrible idea. But this only made Jean want it more. 'I intend to find somewhere like that whatever they say,' she wrote to Maryvonne. 'We will get a little fishing boat and call it the *Je m'en fous*.' This was a typical flight of Jean fancy; but underneath it lay a typical steely determination. 'Sooner or later I *will* go,' she said; and she did.

In January 1953 she had a surge of New Year's Resolution energy. She bought a new suit and coat to go up to London in, to 'persuade people that an unwritten book will be possible if I promise it.' She spoke of two or three 'horrible interviews' for the next week: but then never spoke of them again, and probably never went. Instead she wrote to Selma vaz Dias. 'Do you remember meeting me about three years ago?' she said; she still had in mind the play they'd discussed, in which there was (she suggested cunningly) 'a part you might like'. And Max wrote to Oliver Stoner ('Morchard Bishop'), the novelist who'd written to Jean so admiringly about *Mackenzie* and *Midnight*. Max's letter gives us a rare glimpse into his gentle, diffident nature, and into Jean's quest throughout the 1950s. 'Dear Morchard Bishop,' he wrote,

My wife Jean Rhys tells me that this is the proper way to address you. It is about her I want to write as at one time you corresponded with her. She has had a very difficult time since her husband died and now is most anxious to resume what she feels is the only career she is fit for i.e. writing. My own bumbling efforts have proved quite fruitless so I thought of writing to you to ask if you have any suggestions to make. Our present difficulty is accommodation and I thought that possibly you might know of somewhere in the West Country where it would be possible to rent a cottage. I am quite sure that the place we are now in is quite unsuitable for her purpose though otherwise she is most anxious to recommence. Incidentally she has a book planned out.

Yours sincerely,
G.V.M. Hamer

When Selma answered Jean's letter she mentioned that Peggy Kirkaldy had asked after her. Jean was delighted, and wrote to Peggy straight away. So now she was back in touch with all her literary friends of pre-Maidstone days. Her great burst of energy didn't last; she soon lapsed into 'flu, drink and anger. But she still tried hard to write and to sell. She corresponded with Selma about turning *Quartet* into a play; she got out all her unpublished short stories and sent them to her. Nothing came of any of this. None the less the first months of 1953 were Jean's first attempt to get back to her life as a writer since Selma had first reawakened her desire to write three years before.

She was also, as we've seen, back in touch with other literary people. To this she had a characteristic reaction. On the one hand she was very glad, for example, to be able to share her writing problems with Oliver Stoner. But she shied away like a frightened animal from the idea of meeting him. She knew herself too well by now; there would be no more Rosamond Lehmanns. 'I would like to have a meal or a drink with you very much,' she said, 'but I find it easier to write than to talk. I'm a bit afraid of people now.... "My personal relationships seem to go wrong" as somebody said.' She didn't meet him; or Peggy either, who was unwell and far away in Colchester. Even Selma she only met once or twice, though they were trying to work together. She needed the sympathy of other writers and artists: but she didn't actually want their company. She preferred the safer if less understanding presence of Max; or of her cousin Lily Lockhart, who was also now living in London.

Lily was a bit like Jean, her still sadder reflection. She was alone — really alone, having lost her mother and sister and their Martinique hotel, and never having married. She was very poor and fiercely independent − really independent, eking out a living in a series of miserable jobs. She was proud, prickly and difficult, like Jean; and she was a bit of a writer. Jean tried to help her now, sending some of her West Indian ballads to Selma in the hope that she could sell them. That plan didn't succeed either. But Jean and Lily stayed in touch; apart from her brother Owen, Lily was the only member of her family with whom Jean had any sympathy, and the one she saw most often.

The only other person Jean always wanted to see was Maryvonne. That summer she did, when Maryvonne brought Ruth Ellen to Europe. Alas, this relationship too − this relationship especially − didn't go as Jean hoped and desired. She wanted to make a good impression so much that inevitably she made a bad one. She probably drank a glass or two of wine as well, to give her courage − with the usual effect. She was 'harum scarum'; she made a dreadful mess of the food ('those *awful* cucumber sandwiches'); she could only talk nervously about the weather.... Poor Maryvonne had just seen John being poor and ill in Holland; now here was Jean being poor and ill (though pretending not to be) in England. She must have despaired.

During these months Jean never gave up her *idée fixe* of getting out of London. In the end she achieved it, just as she'd said she would. She hadn't been joking about the 'little fishing boat', either: when she and Max left Upper Norwood in September 1953, it wasn't for a caravan in Cornwall, but for a yacht moored in an estuary in Wales.

It was almost a joke, except that it wasn't funny. It was like Dominica in 1936, when she'd been so utterly determined to cross the island on the Imperial Road that she'd nearly killed Leslie and herself in the attempt. Now she and Max were old and frail; she found it almost impossible to manage the most ordinary object, and Max (it turned out) wasn't much better. Yet here they were in a boat's cabin, with a steep ladder to climb every time they went anywhere, and the simplest household chore a major battle with complicated 'gadgets'. With winter coming, and the nights getting longer and darker.... Only Jean could have dreamt up such a plan, and only Max could have agreed to it. What their families must have said doesn't bear thinking about. (No doubt that was part of what made Jean do it.) Probably that it would all end in tears; and it did. Jean and Max lasted only two months or so on the Yacht Atlast (a sadly ironic name). Then, with appalling predictability, Jean fell down the ladder and injured her face and head. Probably she'd got drunk, against the cold and disappointment; but even sober she was quite incapable of staying on a ladder. She had to go to hospital; she had to go back to London. Her first attempt at escape had been a ludicrous failure.

After that she and Max were stuck in London for another two years.

Possibly Edward simply put his foot down (and Max's sisters and brothers, too, if they were paying): no more crazy ideas, just stay quietly in London. In any case they did stay quietly in London. This time at least they managed to escape the suburbs. They lived in Bayswater, first in rooms, then in a hotel near Kensington Gardens. This suited Jean much better; hotel life, with its service and anonymity, always had. ('Oh how I detested that place,' she said of Upper Norwood, 'and the rows of peering women opposite....' Even in the Ropemakers Arms she'd hated that: 'the houses opposite are mean and women stare from the windows.')

These two years, 1954 and 1955, were very much 'on muted strings'. Life was, Jean said, a little like Mark Twain's diary: 'Monday. Got up, washed, went to bed. Tuesday. Got up, washed, went to bed. Wednesday. Got up, washed, went to bed....' They moved twice, once from their rooms to the hotel, once from one room in the hotel to another. Each time Jean fought to make a small dismal, dark room into her own. She hung yellow curtains at the windows, and craned her neck to see some trees. And from room to room she moved her few remaining ornaments, books and pictures: sketches by Maryvonne and Aunt Clarice; pictures of a parrot, of trees, of Amsterdam.

The main problem was, as ever, *'Demon Money'*. She couldn't send presents to her daughter and grand-daughter, but only hugs and kisses; she had to save carefully in order to buy them just a few books. For the Christmas of 1954 she and Max had to accept other people's charity. There were still films to go to occasionally, and museums, and walks (on which she could still manage, despite Max, to get as lost as she'd done in Paris long ago). But that was all. When they'd moved to Wales she'd lost her briefly renewed literary contacts, and she didn't seek them out again. She wrote only to Maryvonne, who didn't always reply. In early 1955 the Hotel Elizabeth was sold and the new owner put up the prices; most people left, only Jean and Max hung on. But their days there were numbered now, and this gave Jean a new determination. In March 1955 she nearly took a cottage in Wales. By May she was saying: 'I am determined to find two rooms somewhere.' By October she'd finally done it. She saw a holiday cottage advertised near Bude in Cornwall, and took it for six months, sight unseen. This wasn't much more sensible than the Yacht Atlast; none the less, she and Max would never return to London.

★    ★    ★

Bude was a strange choice for Jean. She'd made it as she made all the very few active choices of her life: as a last resort, wildly, in pursuit not of reality but of an obsessive idea. She wanted to escape England. Always she'd turned to Wales, her father's home, where the people were 'a different race' from the English. Their voices were soft and gentle; Welsh men were polite to women, and kind to them.... That is what she sought: an alleviation of her obsession, of her sense of being disliked and disapproved of. And Cornwall was like Wales — Celtic, not Anglo-Saxon. She was choosing her father over her mother; and she was trying to go home. Like Wales, like Ireland, the West Country is wilder, greener, poorer than England — nearer to Dominica; its people are slower, gentler and more imaginative. 'Everybody says "it's only on the surface",' Jean said. 'But damn it all the surface is what you see the most.' At least at the beginning.

And at the beginning, again, she was delighted. It was 'so lovely waking up to the sea and sky instead of a view of horrible houses.' 'Bellair' was large and quite nicely furnished. There were other bungalows nearby, but they were all empty; she and Max were alone, as she preferred. There was a rough road down to the sea, then the beautiful, wide and lonely sands; above them flights of birds, and sunsets with fantastic clouds. She felt she should have been happy, and sometimes, on rare lovely days, she was: when 'the usual gale of wind and rain' stopped, and she could walk by the sea.

But of course reality very quickly poked through this surface. There was a very good reason why they were alone: 'Bellair' and the others were summer houses, quite unsuitable for winter. That is why it was so cheap, too. Anyone would have frozen; Jean nearly died. The wind knifed in straight from the sea, and 'the whole place shivered and shook.' Its machinery resisted them as much as the yacht's had done. Every morning Jean wrestled with the boiler, 'dressed in ancient slacks and an ancient jumper. *Swearing!*' Bude was miles away, by bus; she never went there. There were no decent shops anyway, and no library; she was reduced to reading the ancient summer-holiday books in the house, and mystery stories Max brought her from Bude railway station. Really no life could have been less to her liking. After the pipes burst one day she took to her bed and more or less stayed there. As Leslie had done, 'Poor Max grimly kept the show going,' taking over the boiler and the cooking as well as the shopping and the coal fire. But 'the dust piled up in the six empty rooms "with loggia dining room"....' Finally in April, as spring began, cleverer and richer holiday-makers reappeared, and their six month lease was over. On the day they left 'Bellair', Jean said, the sun came out. That's how she saw things: but it's also how she *did* them, and symbolically at least it was true.

They moved briefly to another bungalow outside Bude. The weather was better now, but nothing else. Jean was 'utterly sick' of moving, of the country, of Cornwall. There were no trees, and '"The Garden Bungalow" has no garden needless to say.' There were lovely walks, and the spot was remote; but they hated the bungalow's owners, who watched them (Jean felt) until she nearly jumped out of her skin with nerves. Max still did all the shopping, and it was too much for him. This time *he* moved them on. He saw some rooms in the town; and a week or two later they were there.

Bude itself in 1956 was still a strange home for Jean: a small, cold, dull town, as far from the life of style and modernity which she also desired as it was possible to be. She put it, appropriately, in terms of books. 'All the dullest books ever written have ended their lives here,' she told Maryvonne. 'You wouldn't believe .... Nothing ever happens and nobody ever leaves Manchester and it rains always.' She'd escaped the sharp whispering voices of literary and suburban London; she was in the safe, dull, philistine provinces – and she couldn't stand them. Nevertheless she'd stay in Bude for nearly four more years. In the rooms Max found she'd have some luck at last; and in their next and last Bude home she'd achieve her greatest flight as a writer, with Part One of *Wide Sargasso Sea*.

In October 1956 Jean and Max had been in their rooms in Bude for four months. On the morning of the sixteenth Jean received a letter from 'a friend':* the BBC were looking for her again, with a plan for 'feature production' of *Good Morning, Midnight*. Immediately the last year – the last many years – receded; immediately hope began to grow in her again 'like the beanstalk', 'like the Bo tree'. She sat down and wrote three letters: to the producer, Sasha Moorsom; to Selma, who she guessed, rightly, was once again behind this interest in her novel; and to Maryvonne. 'I know quite well this may mean nothing,' she said. 'Still I am feeling so different – almost alive again – honestly I thought I was finished for good and for keeps.' On the twenty-second she could stop 'keeping a firm hand on the beanstalk': the BBC had decided to go ahead. It was seven years since Selma had first proposed her dramatisation of *Good Morning, Midnight*, seventeen since Jean had published the novel. It had taken that long for people to recover from the war; that long before they could bear her 'harrowing'. But now, perhaps, they could also begin to understand it. The world had made Jean wait; but at last it was beginning to catch up to her.

*Who could this have been, I wonder? 'A letter' suggests it wasn't just a neighbour in Bude. She'd lost touch with all her literary friends – Peggy, Selma, Oliver Stoner. The likeliest candidate, I think, is her brother-in-law, Alec Hamer, with whom she was certainly on good terms by 1959, and whom she referred to elsewhere as 'a friend'; or it could have been Edward, whom she also often called 'a friend'. Or, possibly, Lily Lockhart.

The BBC originally planned to broadcast *Good Morning, Midnight* quite soon, but as is the way with such things it was postponed, first to March, then to May. Jean kept hopeful and busy during November, 'deluging' Selma with reviews, thoughts and memories of the novel. She'd never stopped thinking of writing, trying to write, even amid the uncertainties and discomforts of Bellair and the Garden Bungalow: she'd been writing, she said, 'mostly about the vanished West Indies of my childhood.' She carried on with that now, but it was difficult. Back in touch with literary London she heard those rumours again: Jean Rhys was dead. (Indeed in an article published this year Francis Wyndham had called her 'the late Jean Rhys'.) She felt like a ghost; or like Rasputin, 'who was poisoned, stabbed in the front and shot in the back but was still alive, kicking and crowing when flung out into the snow.' In December she got her usual winter 'flu ('twice a year and regular as clockwork,' she told Selma), and lay low through the worst of the winter. Max continued to be 'indefatigable', '"all wool and a yard wide", as they say and I envy him and feel very wanting in character and courage.' She tried to 'plod away' at a novel.* But the Bude rooms, with landlady attached, weren't good for writing; now she hankered after the Garden Bungalow, where at least they'd been alone. As spring approached she determined once more to find a place of their own, where she could write properly. After a long search she found a 'minute flat' close to the sea. It was a real flat, however small: a room divided by a curtain into bedroom and sitting room, and their own tiny kitchen and bathroom. 'If all goes well I can work here,' Jean said. All wouldn't go well, of course; but she *would* work there.

At the end of February the BBC invited Jean to attend the first read-through of *Good Morning, Midnight*. She packed everything up and flung it into storage. She 'squeezed together the money', bought 'a cheap dress and A HAT and had a make-up', and went up to London with Max. At the read-through she wept with excitement. They stayed at an hotel; the BBC gave them lunch in a smart restaurant, Selma gave them supper in her warm house, and Jean felt happier than she had 'in years and weary years'. Lifted up, she felt 'brimful of ideas and enthusiastic': 'and the idea of my next book ... clicked in my head.'

So she said to Selma, and continued to say for several years: 'The idea of writing the story of the first Mrs Rochester came to me when I was with you.' Of course this wasn't really true. The idea had been

---

*Perhaps her story about Mr Ramage, which came out of her West Indian childhood, and reached novel proportions at one stage. (It ended up as 'Pioneers, Oh, Pioneers' in *Sleep It Off Lady*.)

in her head for years (as she also said); she'd even written it, or part of it, years before. But this was the generous, impulsive side of her nature, which distorted facts quite as much as the suspicious side that inevitably followed. Selma had given her the life and hope to return to her novel: so Jean felt, for a time, that she'd given her the novel. Selma was very ready to feel this; but Jean was also ready to let her. Like ill-fated lovers, their end lurked in their beginning.

After a week Jean and Max returned to Bude. Jean had her usual elation at a new beginning — 'I felt I could have spoken the whole of Mrs. Rochester . . . into one of those recording machines.' But first they had to move in to Rocket House. The flat was damp, and things were missing — no wardrobe, teapot, mop, curtains. Most of the BBC cheque disappeared. Max dashed around and knocked in nails; Jean scrubbed floors and hung curtains, 'for these are huge windows and people peer through them on their way to the cliffs. Can't *bear* that!'

She couldn't work; instead she re-read *Jane Eyre*. The BBC wanted her to come up to London again for the second reading, but no more money could be squeezed. On 3 May the *Radio Times* carried Selma's article, 'In Quest of a Missing Author', which ended: 'She is now busy writing a novel on a most exciting subject. She is full of new enthusiasm, and I hope and pray that the re-emergence of *Good Morning, Midnight* as a radio monologue will give her sufficient encouragement to write a great deal more and come out of hiding.' Characteristically, Jean didn't see it. But Francis Wyndham did. He was working now for the publishing firm of André Deutsch, and one line in particular caught his eye: *she is now busy writing a novel*. . . . He wrote to her immediately, saying how much he admired her work, and asking if it was true she was working on a new book. It *was* true, she replied (though it was more in hope than in fact, at that moment). And delightedly, without pausing to calculate, she promised Deutsch the manuscript as soon as it was finished.

On 10 and 11 May *Good Morning, Midnight* was broadcast. Needless to say Jean's radio couldn't receive the Third Programme. Max found someone whose radio could, and off they went in a taxi to listen to Selma. Jean was so grateful she was generous with praise; but secretly she feared the adaptation was 'a bit confused', and was glad to be 'nicely tucked away', knowing nothing about people's reactions. However, the reaction was good, and a great boost to Jean both personally and professionally. Personally it brought her a 'deluge' of letters: including ones from John and from Peggy Kirkaldy, so that Selma's *Good Morning, Midnight* restored two very important friendships (just in time, for John and Peggy were both ill, and hadn't very long to live). Professionally it brought her the encouragement she couldn't do without; and two more offers from publishers for her new novel. But she was, of course, already committed to Deutsch: only by a promise to Francis Wyndham, but for Jean a promise to someone who'd been kind to her would be binding; it wouldn't occur to her to break it. At the end of May her future editor, Diana Athill, wrote with Deutsch's official offer: twenty-five pounds for the option on the new novel. Twenty-five pounds was far from a fortune, even in 1957; but Jean was thrilled at the prospect of *any* money — especially for her writing, which secretly she never expected to be paid for.

> Oh how happy I will be
> When my tired eyes do see
> That beautiful joyful lovely *Fee,*

she wrote gaily and absolutely truthfully to Selma. She accepted Deutsch's offer, with her usual 'exalted' optimism. She hoped to be able to submit the finished novel, she told Diana, 'in six to nine months time', 'as a large part of it is already written'. She was thinking of *Le Revenant* and of *Creole.** But when she looked there were only two chapters of *Le Revenant* left, and she couldn't 'lift' whole passages of *Creole* as easily as she'd imagined. She had, as always, to 'torture the thing into the form of a novel.' And this one would be the hardest of all to do: it would torture *her.* It would take not nine months, but nine years.

---

*\*Creole* was the name Jean gave to her writings about the West Indies.

# CHAPTER THREE

# The Writing of
# *Wide Sargasso Sea,*
# 1957–1966

*Cornwall – Cheriton Fitzpaine*

On 1 June Jean signed her contract with Deutsch. She was 'bursting with optimism', but she was also very nervous. This book meant too much; it had to be very good or it would be no good at all. 'It is a bit of a standing jump,' she said. It had been in her head for so long, it was completely clear – but only until she tried to grasp it. Then it danced in front of her like a mirage. 'Phrases, sentences come and go', and she was too slow to catch them. It was always like that at the beginning. But she persisted: and for two months she 'tore along', catching bits of the mirage in her net.

But then she stuck fast. Cornwall was 'NOT FOR ME!' – just sand and black rock and *no trees.* Rocket House was 'an awful place, so like a public lavatory in spite of all efforts.' Then the tourist season started, and she discovered that it wasn't even secluded. On the contrary, it was 'bang on Bude's tourist fly walk'. She'd looked so long for this flat, for independence and solitude. And what had she found? Not 'a garret or an attic or anything nice like that', but a deserted tea room. That's what Rocket House had been (though of course no one had told her), and that's what people still thought it was. They peered in at the windows and they knocked at the door, until she was 'in the cursing and weeping stage.' Peggy suggested she put up a sign saying 'NO teas – NO water – NO lavatory. So b——r off.' Jean loved that. She expanded it – '*No* matches, *No* cigarettes, *No* teas, *No* sandwiches, *No* water. Don't know where *anybody* lives, Don't know *anything.* Now B——R OFF.' 'I wanted to nail it up at once,' she said, 'but Max wouldn't. . . .' Once she felt invaded like this she couldn't stop. The man upstairs tramped about all day in heavy boots, like Morse code; she was desperate to work, but all she could do was listen. Her brain 'went blank'. 'I thought I'd get drunk. First lapse for months.'

In the autumn the tourists disappeared, but before Jean could regain her equilibrium she had disturbing news from Maryvonne. Rebellion had broken out in the Outer Islands of Indonesia, on one of which, Celebes, the Moermans were living. President Sukarno was sending in troops, the situation was extremely dangerous. With very little warning Maryvonne and Job had to leave behind the life they'd built up over nine years and return to Holland. They were lucky to escape with their lives. But it was a blow; it was hard to start all over again in cold Holland. Jean knew all about that, and she worried a great deal for her daughter. 'For a while I could not write at all,' she said. 'Then I was ill. Then Max was ill. I began to feel that Charlotte Brontë was angry with me for tampering with her novel....' And she listed her difficulties, on the model of Peggy's notice for her door.

*No* privacy, *No* cash, *No* security, *No* resilience, *No* youth, *No* desk to write on, *No* table even. *No* one who understands.

In November Maryvonne visited. Though Jean had felt so much for her in the last months, she still couldn't show it face to face: she was 'stupid' with 'flu and aspirins, she said, and they didn't talk as she'd wanted. These failed meetings made her very miserable; often she would get drunk after them for days or weeks. Probably she did so now, for in December she 'stupidly' hurt her back and took to her bed.

January and February brought cold and 'flu, lethargy and depression as usual. But in March she wrote to Francis Wyndham about her book, and in conception at least it was already quite clear. She already had the title too, or nearly. One of her cousin Lily's poems, *Creole Song*, began 'Across the gold Sargasso Sea, I watch my heart come back to me'.... That had sunk into her subconscious; now she woke up one day thinking the words 'Sargasso Sea', and was pleased. Immediately she doubted the idea; she'd go on doubting it for years. As she said to Selma vaz Dias: 'I am a tormented person, and even writing is clutching at clouds and shadows.' The writing of *Wide Sargasso Sea* was almost all like this: a torment of doubt about what she had already done, as much as about what she should do. She'd written Antoinette's story once before; and already after the first six months she'd said that 'about half' the book was written. It wasn't the writing, but self-doubt, illness and age that made it take nine years.

In early 1958 Jean was surrounded by the ravages of all three. In February she had her last letter from Peggy Kirkaldy ('My dear ... You comfort me; I am so scared ...'). Peggy died of cancer soon after. In March her 'one nice brother', Owen, also died. He'd been ill with bronchitis for years; now he died suddenly and tragically, falling down the staircase of his London flats. Jean didn't mention these deaths in any of the letters we have, but they must have disturbed her. Peggy had been 'pure eighteenth century': brave and gay, briskly kind, and quite unshockable. It would be years before she found such a friend again. As for Owen, he was the only one of her brothers and sisters she liked, and who liked her. Now he was gone she would no longer have even a weak or secret defender within her family.

Perhaps these deaths of friends made her more vulnerable than ever to her third enemy, self-doubt. In any case it too attacked her now. Both Selma and the publishers wrote to ask after the progress of 'Mrs Rochester': and Jean, who had made no progress at all for months, immediately panicked. She *couldn't* do Mrs Rochester as a radio monologue, she told Maryvonne — but she didn't know how to tell Selma. 'Another "I" must talk, two others perhaps,' she managed to say — but 'I am anxious not to let you down,' 'I will not disappoint you....' Selma was not like Peggy, someone who could encourage but not require. She required: and instantly Jean felt that she should obey. All this made her 'a bit uncertain and worried,' she said to Selma: 'quite frantic,' she admitted to Maryvonne.

But Francis and Diana at Deutsch reassured her, as they would so many times in the coming years. They liked the idea for the book very much; they didn't mean to push her. She calmed down. And then summer was coming, the time of thaw. At last around May she could take the book up again. She'd had to 'get myself back in the mood with the help of very strong drink,' she'd told Selma: 'One day drunk, two days hangover as regular as clockwork.' But now she was back. During the summer and autumn of 1958 she had her second, probably longest period of work on 'Mrs Rochester'. She worked so hard that no one heard from her, even Maryvonne. Finally in January she wrote to Selma: 'I have finished the first draft of Mrs Rochester.'

The hardest part was done, 'the making of something from nothing.' Much was left, of course: 'cutting, joining up — all that patchwork'; and she would doubt and rewrite and doubt again, until in the end the patchwork would cost her as much torment as the original making. More, because her conditions would get much worse. *Wide Sargasso Sea* wouldn't appear for another eight years. None the less, only eighteen months after her contract was signed 'the skeleton was there.' And though she'd doubt and forget them all again, and have to rediscover them slowly and painfully, she saw all its most important and difficult requirements, and its most secret danger, in the first writing. The danger was putting herself into the mind of a madwoman: she wrote that to Selma as early as October 1957. Really it was putting herself into the part of her own mind which was mad: and though she didn't say this openly, she knew it. It was a devil of a book, she said in 1958 and '59. 'Sometimes I really do feel it would need a devil to write it well. I live in hope — who knows? I may qualify.'

The important and difficult requirements were also to do with madness and sanity. The characters — *all* the characters — had to be '*plausible*'. Charlotte Brontë's madwoman was not real. Jean had to make her real, had to make us understand her. 'She must be ... plausible with a past, the *reason* why Mr Rochester treats her so abominably, and feels justified, the *reason* why he thinks she is mad and why of course she goes mad.' This she knew how to do: there would be a 'tragedy in her life which she cannot forget. As a child.' 'I have got that,' she said in 1957; she'd had it since *Le Revenant*, nearly twenty years ago. The other part was much harder: to make the sane man plausible and real as well. But she knew how to do that too. 'He must have good reasons for thinking his wife mad (helped by prejudice no doubt but good),' she wrote. '*Mr Rochester wasn't a villain.*' That was the key. She would forget it again later, but she had it now; 'I have got that I think,' she said. Rochester must speak too: we must understand him too. That was her greatest insight; and she really had it from the beginning.

In early 1959 Jean had her usual winter 'flu. But from now on she wouldn't be able to take to her bed and leave everything to Max. It was the other way around: Max would be ill, especially in the winters, and *she* would have to take care of *him*. So now she spent her time going back and forth to Bude in the bitter cold, doing the shopping. She hated domestic tasks, distraction from work, anything she *had* to do; this was all three, and she was 'pretty well in despair'. She hardly wrote to anyone, just once to Selma.* Perhaps she managed to pick up her manuscript occasionally, but it's not likely. By the spring she was showing the usual signs of frustration: complaining again about the man upstairs, quarrelling again with the woman next door. She quarrelled with this woman every spring, because (she said) she dug up all the grass and flowers. It was like a first angry sign of life after the long cold winter.

But in the spring too Max was better, and she could return to the novel. She was bothered by the feeling that the two parts, Antoinette's and Rochester's, didn't link up. With extraordinary self-doubt, and extraordinary energy, she went back to square one: perhaps only one person should tell the whole story after all. But who? Antoinette? Rochester? Someone else altogether? She tried to tell it as Grace Poole,

---

*Now, however, she came clean about *Wide Sargasso Sea* for the radio: 'What does really worry me like hell is that I have not made it clear enough that it is emerging as a book. I could not do a monologue of Mrs Rochester....' To her relief, Selma accepted this, and was willing to wait.

but couldn't ('I wasn't even sure how she'd talk or think.') She tried to tell it all as Antoinette: but this was too obscure, too much 'all on one note', and 'A mad girl speaking all the time is too much!' She even thought of telling it all as Rochester. None of this worked; and she fell back again on the two first-person narrators, Rochester *and* his mad wife. She worked on Rochester's Part Two 'with bottles at hand', and put it away to be revised carefully 'when sober'. Then she struggled to make Antoinette's Part One 'clear' and 'smooth' and 'factual'. By the end of May she was writing: 'I live with [Antoinette] all day and sometimes dream of her at night. An obsession!' In June she decided she couldn't visit Selma in London because 'I must stick to this thing now until it is done . . . I *daren't* leave it.' In August she told her: 'Your part is finished and I hope I've got away with it.' In September she reread Rochester's part and thought it 'wasn't too bad' – adding immediately: 'But it wants lifting up in parts. . . .'

The summer of 1959 was a good one for work altogether. In May German radio approached her about broadcasting a dramatised version of *Good Morning, Midnight,* and a German publisher expressed interest in the same novel. In the end he didn't take it; but the Radio Bremen broadcast went ahead. This time Jean didn't bother going to her acquaintances with the radio. Despite her two years in Vienna she didn't understand German; and the project secretly struck her as absurd anyway. 'I find it strange,' she said, 'to think of . . . someone else toiling away *putting in* all the characters I so carefully *left out*.' She tried not to worry about it, and just to take the money.

She often said she couldn't connect money with writing ('though I adore money and need it badly, very'). That was true while she was actually writing: if you think about money then, she said, 'the voices go.' But once she'd finished things of course she was glad to get money for them. It was just that without Ford or John or Leslie to help her she didn't know how; and unliterary Max was no use in this area. But as soon as there *was* someone else to help she took out her 'MSS suitcase' and looked for things to sell. In 1957, for instance, she'd sent Selma *Voyage in the Dark* to turn into a play, and unearthed an early version of 'Ramage', wondering if the BBC might like it. Now she had a second London literary friend, who would help her even more than Selma: Francis Wyndham. She dug out her battered old collection of short stories, *The Sound of the River,* and sent it to him. Francis liked most of the stories very much. He sent them on to John Lehmann at the *London Magazine*; and Lehmann accepted two, 'Till September Petronella' and 'The Day They Burned the Books'.* They would

---

*'The Day They Burned the Books' was a more recent addition to Jean's stories, probably developed out of her *Creole* memories of the fifties. She'd thought of selling it to John Lehmann once before, through Selma, in 1953.

come out the next year, and alert the literary world that Jean Rhys was far from dead.

Things were going too well: I imagine Jean waiting for the trap to spring shut. In any case it did. On the very day in August that she received the money for the Bremen broadcast — so she told everyone — Max fell ill. He hadn't been well for at least a year; he'd complained of giddiness, and had had several falls since they'd been in Rocket House. But now he fell badly, and was so ill he had to stay in bed. He rallied occasionally, but spent most of the winter there. Jean didn't know what was wrong with him; and she was far too distracted and distrustful of doctors to ask. Max would probably have refused to see one anyway. It was only years later, when he was too ill to keep the doctors away any more, that Jean learned at last what had happened. Max had had a stroke that August day. He'd been having slight, warning ones before — that was the giddiness, the earlier falls. This was the first more serious one; there would be more. He would never be well again: and she, therefore, would never be able to work again without worry and interruption. It would drive her mad. She would be torn between anguish for Max and anguish for her abandoned book; between the terror of losing him and the terror of never finishing it. It would push her steadily back into a state of despair close to her worst, in Beckenham: even, in the end, equal.

At first Max seemed to get a bit better, and Jean kept trying to get back to the novel throughout the autumn. She was convinced (but then she always was) that another few months would be enough; and it nearly 'finished' her to have to drop it now. Sometimes she woke up 'with the whole thing clear' — but before she could catch the words and write them down she had to run to Max, or to the kitchen or the shops.... 'It nearly sent me round the bend,' she wrote to Selma. She'd always told herself she only wanted to be 'happy': but kept from her work, she knew how important it was. 'It is my only thing,' she said to Maryvonne. 'All I can do.' And she couldn't do it.

As winter closed in again she snatched at her favourite remedy, escape. 'I am certain that Max's real trouble is living in one room in beautiful Bude — (with me and book),' she said. If only she could get him away somewhere warmer he would improve, and the book could be finished. She found something in the south of Cornwall: a 'chalet' belonging to a hotel called Cellar Cove, 'which sounds good to me because it suggests a drink.' 'I've just got to pack and move — oh Lord,' she told Selma. 'Then' — oh Jean! — 'all will be well.'

This was the maddest of all her moves, with the possible exception of the Yacht *Atlast*. Max was too ill to help, and she had to do the hateful packing all by herself. Then when they got to the chalet it turned out to be tiny — 'like a very small horse box' — and 'not very healthy-looking to say the least.' In fact it looked appalling. Besides, as part of an hotel it was really intended (again) for holiday letting, and even Jean might have foreseen that there'd be trouble about staying on in the summer. But of course she didn't; or rather she refused to. Perranporth *was* warmer; Max *was* better; she was all right now. 'If I live it will be done,' she wrote to Selma when she arrived, in February 1960. Then she disappeared again.

Max, of course, wasn't better. In fact he was very ill in Perranporth: 'too bad to be possible. So I pretended it was not so.' She tried to work, but a few minute rooms were no better than one big one, and what little she managed was '"forced" — or done on drink.' Most of 1960 was lost for *Wide Sargasso Sea*. Only other things crept ahead. In January 'Petronella' appeared in the *London Magazine*; and Geoffrey Grigson liked it so much he put Jean into his survey of 'World Literature from 1900 to 1960'. Francis Wyndham's attempts to get the novels reissued in paperback failed; but in the summer Macmillan bought 'Outside the Machine' for their collection called *Winter's Tales*. 'It's a bit dreary, I fear,' Jean wrote to Maryvonne; 'but what does that matter . . .?'

In the meantime it had become clear even to her that the chalet was no solution to her search for a home. And now she discovered that it was let for part of July and August anyway: 'Old clients they say!' She lived as she wrote, in endlessly repeated patterns, like Julia's spiralling mauve corkscrew. After only three months in Perranporth she'd begun house-hunting again.

But now something happened that would put an end to at least this particular spiral. It's not quite clear how it happened. Jean said that Edward telephoned her, because he was coming on holiday to Cornwall; Edward said, or implied, that she wrote to him in despair. In any case he and Gertrude came and saw Jean and Max in their chalet. They were deeply shocked. They would have been shocked by all Jean's houses, but the chalet was 'absolutely terrible'. The roof leaked so badly it was hardly like being indoors at all. And Jean and Max couldn't pay the rent; they were 'absolutely down and out'. Edward paid the rent and took them out for lunch in Truro. 'He had a long talk with Max,' Jean said: and then he promised that he would buy them a cottage. It would take time, he warned; he might fail altogether. But he would try.

Jean was thrilled — worried and apprehensive, but thrilled. After lunch (she told Maryvonne) Gertrude bought her a hat: a good one, which shielded her eyes. But 'I would give anything at all, including the rest of my life (& even my new Hat) for nine months peace *real* peace to finish my book.' Edward, of course, would choose; she would have to go where he put her. She only hoped it wouldn't be London — she hated London. . . . Perhaps she said this to him. She certainly felt grateful; but equally certainly she felt trapped, once more at the mercy of someone she knew didn't really like her. Edward didn't, of course; but he did like Max; it was Max he felt sorry for. About Jean he felt dread at what she might do if she weren't safely tucked away somewhere, and a duty to her, as the head of the family. Apart from that he didn't want any more trouble about rent not being paid. As the source of what little money Jean had, that ended up at his door anyway.

Edward made his offer in May, and must have started looking straight away. He didn't go to London, but to an estate agent in Exeter, near his own home in Budleigh Salterton. Clearly he'd decided Jean must be near enough for him to keep an eye on, but not too near: on the other side of Exeter at least, I imagine him deciding. Certainly the cottage he found *was* on the opposite side of Exeter from Budleigh, setting the city between sister and brother like a shield. It was also in an almost inaccessible village, deep in the Devon countryside. Cheriton Fitzpaine (again I imagine) both satisfied Edward's sense of duty and stilled his dread: surely Jean would never find her way out of it, and the world (journalists for instance) would never find its way in. She was hidden about as far away as it's possible to be in England. As she would discover: to both (of course) her pleasure and her despair.

6 Landboat Bungalows was the last in a row of three farm-workers' bungalows on the eastern edge of the village. It was very small, though nothing could be as small as the chalet; and it wasn't much prettier, solider or more comfortable. In fact, the whole row had recently been condemned. The family that had been in it had moved to another, bigger house next door; which left only the middle cottage inhabited, by a disreputable family living in squalid conditions. Later, when despite everything the world found its way to Jean's door, people were often as shocked by this ramshackle cottage as Edward had been by the chalet. Jean wasn't at all; after her bed-sitting rooms and holiday houses her standards were not high. But Landboat Bungalows did suggest that her picture of her family's contempt for her wasn't wholly paranoid.

On the other hand Edward had his reasons. The first was money: he may have been genuinely unable to afford much better. He was already giving Jean money, after all; and Brenda and Robert may well have refused to give any more, if indeed he asked them. He had no extra money,* only his Indian Army pension. He had a big, handsome,

---

*Geneva, the family property in Dominica, had been sold years before, probably in the fifties, and would not have fetched a great deal.

old-fashioned house, but that was all. He didn't live in a grand style; he drove a battered old car and wore well-made but carefully preserved clothes. Most of the furniture at Knottsfield was Gertrude's; and if there was any disposable money it would have been Gertrude's as well. But Gertrude, we can be sure, would not want to dispose of it in Jean's direction. She disliked and disapproved of Jean even more than Owen's widow or Brenda's husband. Jean had told Maryvonne that Gertrude was there when Edward made his offer of a cottage; but Edward himself suggested that his wife so disapproved of his sister that she wasn't to know he was helping her. Perhaps he'd made the promise *sotto voce*; or perhaps they'd had a row about it afterwards – like Owen and *his* wife in the thirties – and he'd had to pretend to drop it. And then did it secretly, behind her back. That would give him another reason to spend as little as possible.

But whatever his reasons, and however small and scruffy it was, Edward did buy Jean and Max a cottage in the summer of 1960. *And* had it repaired, and repainted, and put in 'all kinds of gadgets to keep it warm.' Jean often pretended to people that she had found the cottage, or that she and Max had bought it or were paying rent for it, because charity shamed her. As so often, therefore, she backed herself into a corner, in which it was hard to express her gratitude, at least publicly. But she did sometimes, for instance to Maryvonne: 'my gratitude is boundless' – 'I do think Edward has been kind.' And to Maryvonne too she confided her hope and elation. 'At last, *at last* we may have some peace and security,' she wrote. 'I may even be able to finish my book – not too late I hope … I am so excited about it and a bit afraid I may wake up!'

The builders' work dragged on, as builders' work always does. Several times Jean thought they could go, and began to pack. The chalet filled up with half-packed trunks. Max was ill and 'extremely pessimistic'; that, and all the delay and uncertainty, meant that Jean couldn't touch the book all summer, her best time. But she kept her eye firmly fixed on 'the new Jerusalem', 'the Ark', the 'abode of peace'. 'When I get there I intend to *stay put* and never move again,' she told everyone. Finally, in September 1960, she and Max left Cornwall for Cheriton Fitzpaine. She was seventy. At long last she would stop moving.

★     ★     ★

For five miles around Cheriton Fitzpaine only steep narrow lanes lead in and out of it. There are some breathtaking vistas, but more often you feel enclosed by green hills and hedges, mud, a grey sky. The village, when you finally get to it, is surprisingly big but not beautiful.

A few months before Jean came she sent Maryvonne a postcard of an idyllic West Country cottage, with whitewashed walls and a deep, protective thatch: 'Harmony Cottage' the legend said. Jean had written: 'Just what I want — but hidden away somewhere.' Cheriton Fitzpaine was hidden away, but that was all. It had few Harmony Cottages, and 6 Landboat Bungalows wasn't one of them.

The first that Cheriton Fitzpaine heard of Jean was not encouraging. Edward called at the Rectory. He introduced himself: Colonel Williams,* Indian Army, retired. He was quiet, well spoken, a military gentleman. But he said 'I've brought trouble into your parish.' He had bought a cottage in the village, he explained, for his sister and her husband. At least he must have said 'for my sister and her husband'; but he hurried over his relationship to Jean, and always spoke of her with such dutiful distance that the Rector, the Reverend Alwynne Woodard, and his wife imagined she was only his half-sister. He said nothing about her being a writer. He merely conveyed that she was an extremely difficult person. He hadn't seen her for a long time, he said; but recently he had found her living in desperate circumstances and had decided to buy a house for her. He had helped her before, but something more permanent was needed now. Unfortunately he could not take her into his own house, because his wife had had a terrible time with her once, and wouldn't permit it: indeed, wouldn't allow him to have anything to do with her. So here she was in the village. She would have a permanent home at last, which she had wanted very badly; he hoped that would make her happier and more settled, but he doubted it, he knew it wouldn't really. That was why he had come. He wanted both to warn Mr Woodard and to ask him to help her. Mr Woodard promised, of course, to help; and promised too to keep in touch with Edward — to let him know, in particular, as soon as any 'trouble' arose.

The Woodards were kind and experienced, absolutely professional; they wouldn't have breathed a word of Edward's confidences. But there were servants, children, neighbours; somehow in country villages everyone knows everything. Cheriton Fitzpaine lay quietly in its valley and showed a calm green face. But underneath it was alert, waiting to see what would happen.

Jean of course arrived 'full of fight', bravely and optimistically determined to be brave, optimistic and determined. 'I love it here,' she told Francis Wyndham: 'very green and a lot of cows and the most splendid trees. Hardly any people. Oh it is quite lovely.' The outside of the cottage was shabby and tumbledown; but she would make the inside 'very splendid', red and gold, with 'red velvet armchairs and gilt

---

*So he called himself; not Rees Williams, like Owen.

candlesticks and old pictures'. This was of course purest fantasy. 6 Landboat Bungalows was dull and uncomfortable, without spark or style; and so it would remain until *Wide Sargasso Sea* brought her the money to buy it pretty things, and the friends to install them.

From the beginning, of course, Jean also saw the dangers and disadvantages of her new home. First of all, the damp and rain. Devon is one of the greenest parts of green England because it is one of the rainiest. In the first few months it rained so heavily that the Exe valley was flooded several times, her bathroom was 'a wreck' and her kitchen chimney leaked on to the floor. 'Landboat Bungalows' couldn't have been more appropriate: 'It feels like a boat — water all around.' The centre of the village was a good half-mile away and when she got there it felt secretive. Many of its houses turned blank backs on to the village street. Women 'crept about laden with food — otherwise darkness and silence.' There were no bookshops and no libraries for miles. Instead there were dogs and cows. We know how Jean felt about dogs; and some of Cheriton's were genuinely discomfiting, 'mongrel sheepdogs', says Diana Athill, 'with yellow eyes'. And now Jean found new animal enemies. 'The cows here moo at me in a very disapproving way,' she tried to joke to Maryvonne. 'I've always known dogs were cash-conscious but I didn't know cows were.' She kept up the acerbic note as long as possible. '*Not my cup of tea,*' she said after her first Devon Christmas. 'Needs some sugar!' 'My dream is to finish my book, get a face lift, and a bright red wig.' (This was to Maryvonne again.) 'Also a lovely fur coat. Underneath I will wear a purple dress and ropes of pearls. Or what do you say to rags?'

She had her usual winter *cafard* anyway, and something else too that always happened: a great reluctance to get back to work when she'd been kept from it for a long time. Rather than go back to the book she took out 'Let Them Call It Jazz' and worked on that instead. Max, who had at first seemed better, definitely wasn't; the floods continued; there were icicles in the bathroom. But 'Jazz' chased out everything else. She wrote and rewrote it at least six times, started promising to send it to Francis in February, in March finally did. She'd hesitated about having it typed locally because people were 'terribly narrow minded and they gossip like crazy.... For them 'I' is 'I' and not a literary device. Every *word* is autobiography!' 'Let Them Call It Jazz' wasn't, she insisted (naturally) to Maryvonne: 'It is not (repeat *not*) autobiography.' But of course it came too close to the truth, and so would the gossip. So she sent it to Francis in long-hand. He typed it and sent it to the *London Magazine*, and wrote to Jean praising it. Immediately she was lifted up: and now, in March, she finally unpacked her novel. 'If only I can be calm, and not get excited, or despairing, or any of those things it will come at last,' she wrote to him. 'I am quite well thank you and Max is better. This is a dull, peaceful place. If only it stays so!'

Immediately, of course, every hope of peace vanished. Alan Ross at the *London Magazine* accepted 'Jazz', and she probably got 'excited'; then she got despairing. Her joke about cash-conscious cows stopped being a joke. She fretted and fretted about the ones in the field behind her. They came too close to the house, *they kept watching her.* She complained to the farmer so often that one day in May he put up a barbed wire fence near her window. No doubt he wanted to stop her grumbling. Still, it was an unusual kindness — busy farmers don't usually build fences they don't need, especially for strangers. But you couldn't help Jean. No one could, not after Lancelot's allowance in 1913, probably not even before. God knows what she thought the farmer meant — a rebuke, a piece of condescension? Or perhaps she thought nothing, she was just angry. She pretended to believe (surely she didn't really believe?) that the fence was a clothes-line — 'a clothes line made of *barbed wire* just outside my sitting room window.' She got very drunk, and she made a terrible scene — a Beckenham scene — about it. She screamed and cursed; she threw milk bottles at the offending fence and the gathering neighbours, until one of them went to fetch the vicar. The 'trouble' Edward had warned him of had happened.

Mr Woodard took Jean home to the Rectory. Instead of strong words or strong coffee he gave her more whisky, until she was calmer and happier again. Over the next five years he would show her only such kindness and understanding, and the worse she behaved the kinder he became. But for most of the ordinary, 'respectable' people of Cheriton Fitzpaine this episode of the fence in the summer of 1961 meant the end of any kindness for Jean. They had *done* her a kindness, or one of them had, and she had turned on them like a fury. They wouldn't forgive her. For a long time many wouldn't speak to her; and from now on the gossip she always feared took wing. She knew it, of course. 'This is a village to end all villages,' she wrote to Francis a fortnight or so after the fracas.

> There are nice people called *Greenslade* and *Gosling* and *Betty Stennyford** but there are some nasty ones too and the grapevine works. If I say dam everyone knows in half an hour! ... One thing is certain — I ought not to have touched that barbed wire clothes line.

*Mr and Mrs Samuel Greenslade were a Cheriton Fitzpaine farmer and his wife who would become Jean's best friends in the village, apart from Mr Woodard. Soon after she arrived Mr Greenslade retired from farming and

She tried to 'rest', and resolved 'never to fuss again. Not about *anything*.' She knew perfectly well that was hopeless really; but she tried to persuade herself, or at least Francis. 'I can be silent too,' she said, 'and behave nicely though *that's* a strain.' She wrote poems to ease it:

> The silent field powdered with moonlight,
> And the low hills
> The low, meek unaspiring hills.
> And the tall trees
> The tall proud dark trees
> Leaning down to shallow water
> Looking into shallow water.

The trees were like herself — dark and proud, utterly different from the 'meek unaspiring hills'; but caught there, forced to see themselves reflected in shallow water, as she was forced to see herself reflected in the shallow eyes of the village. She was zigzagging, as she always did, between her own feelings of her difference and theirs: between fierce pride and a terror of judgement. That added itself to all her other difficulties about writing: she knew what her neighbours would say if her novel made her famous (what Mr Bezant of Beckenham *did* say, though only in a letter to her publisher). She dreaded fame for that reason. It was terrible to be forgotten, for her work to come to nothing, for people to think her dead; but on the other hand it was what she preferred. Half of her, therefore, didn't *want* to finish, and so perhaps emerge from safe (*well — safe*! she would have said) obscurity. She secretly mocked more than her slowness when she said: 'By that time I will be completely forgotten by everyone, and a good thing too.'

Perhaps she worked a bit in the summer, as she usually could; but the manuscript remained 'a muddle'. She kept hoping for 'three weeks peace' so that she could get *something* clear enough to send

---

became the village taxi driver. That is how Jean met him (she was as dependent as ever on taxis). Whenever she, or in later years her guests, went anywhere, it was in Mr Greenslade's taxi. And from about 1963 Mrs Greenslade brought Jean a cooked lunch every day; if she wasn't well she'd call again in the evening. Both Greenslades, especially Mr, were fond of Jean and on her side. We will hear their names often in the rest of her story.

Mrs Stentiford was Jean's right-hand neighbour, who had previously lived with her family in Jean's bungalow. Now she lived in first the nearer and then the further council house next door. I don't know who *Gosling* was.

Note that Jean names only the nice people, not the nasty ones. That was typical of her.

to Francis, but it didn't happen. The second winter in Cheriton Fitzpaine began to close in. Her book had not progressed and nor had Max; he was ill, and very down. His brother Alec visited them in early October and 'made us laugh', Jean said: 'so unusual these days!' As always, she managed to make light of things in letters, but not in reality. She was 'tired', she said, 'weary': which translated meant angry, depressed and drinking. She couldn't quite hide her anger even from Francis. 'I've been seeing a lot of the collective face that killed a thousand thoughts lately,' she wrote, enigmatically. 'And sometimes there is blue murder in my wicked heart....' I don't know what it was about this time. There was always something: the staring cows and barking dogs; the hideous cabbages in next door's garden; the village boys who came and banged on her door, the neighbour's girls who made a row and stared at her. She fought especially with this neighbour: Zena Raymond, then the village postmistress, a big strong woman with two daughters (later three). Mrs Raymond wasn't one of the genteel disapprovers. She was even poorer than Jean and lived in greater squalor, clinging on to an even lower rung of society. She was kinder to Jean than the disapprovers, as a result; but she was also ready to give as good as she got, and she and Jean had memorable battles for nearly twenty years. By the autumn of 1961 these — and probably others — were in full swing. Then the doctor prescribed some new pills for Jean. She called them 'pep pills', and perhaps they were; the effect she noticed was to make her feel more energetic. But the effect everyone else noticed was rather different. 'Peace up the lane at last,' they said: for a time at least her fury had subsided.

We must be as afraid, and as respectful, of the deep sources of Jean's anger as she was herself. But we know at least one immediate cause of it: her frustration that she couldn't work as she wished, that she couldn't indulge what her husband and brother-in-law called her 'obsession' — 'that's to say two or three hours time by myself,' writing. That was, of course, because she had Max with her now and not Leslie. Leslie had done everything; now she had to. Leslie had *wanted* her to write; Max didn't really. Without Leslie she had no one to start and stop her; no one to type her work, hawk it around, handle the money. These *mechanics* of writing, like all mechanics, defeated her, drove her frantic; she desperately needed someone else to do them. Of course she had Selma, and Francis; and she hoped for a great deal from them. She would soon promise Selma the earth (as we'll see) if she'd just go on trying to sell her work. And recently she'd asked Francis if it would be 'quite impossible to make some arrangement' with him, 'as I would with an agent?' Francis wouldn't take any money; but he did, with entire willingness, act very like an unpaid agent for her for years. He became the closest substitute for Leslie she ever had. But the trouble with both Francis and Selma was that they *weren't there.* She could hide too much from them; they only knew she needed help when she was *in extremis.* And even then there was a gap in time and space (and in Selma's case sometimes in attention too). Jean needed someone nearby, someone in the village. That was a pretty hopeless prospect: 'This is not book country,' as she said. But underneath all her bad luck there was always some good: someone did always appear, suddenly and at the last moment, to save her. So, for example, had John appeared in 1919, the 'anonymous donor' in 1950, Selma in 1956. Now it was the vicar of Cheriton Fitzpaine. When Edward had entrusted his troublesome sister to Mr Woodard he had thought only of pastoral, not literary, care. But without knowing it had chosen the perfect person to care for a writer. There it was again: Jean's invisible, improbable, last-chance luck.

Not all churchmen would have been able to help her even in the pastoral way Edward had intended: here too Jean — and Edward himself — were lucky. Mr Woodard was what such men are meant to be, and being men, only rarely are: all-accepting and all-forgiving, Christian not just in belief but in his deepest responses. He was unworldly and abstracted, almost to a fault; he didn't notice if people were 'eccentric', and if he noticed he didn't care. He was an extreme, old-fashioned idealist. Of thieves he would merely say 'If they take something they need it more than we do'; and his favourite text was St Luke: 'Consider the lilies of the field, how they grow; they toil not, neither do they spin....' Before Cheriton Fitzpaine he had been in Surrey for twenty-one years, where apart from being a vicar, and then Rural Dean of Woking, he had been Chaplain to a large mental hospital. He was no stranger, therefore, to desperate disturbance; he had seen many far worse than Jean, and had been calm and gentle with them too. He didn't watch, gossip or judge; instead he hardly noticed, then forgot and forgave. There were very few people like that in Jean's life: Germaine Richelot in the twenties; Eliot Bliss and Simon Segal briefly in the thirties; the Stoners later, in the seventies.* But this was, above all, what she needed.

To be fair to clergymen, Mr Woodard's humane Christianity was perhaps not absolutely remarkable. But the other part of Jean's luck was more so. For Alwynne Woodard was also a scholar, and in particular a lover of literature. He'd gone to Lancing College (one of the Woodard schools, founded by his own grandfather). He then read Classics at Cambridge, was ordained, and became a schoolmaster. Before he took his first parish he taught Classics and English at

---

*Francis Wyndham and Sonia Orwell then too; but again, these friendships were conducted largely by letter.

Lancing for fifteen years, to Evelyn Waugh among others. He couldn't have wanted to help Jean more; but if Edward had told him she was a writer he might have known how to do so sooner.

As it was he came to know her first in Edward's terms, as 'trouble'. There was the barbed wire row; soon there were others. He began to call on her; and she must have trusted him straight away. For very soon *she* told him she was a writer. That was what was making her miserable: not being a writer, but being unable to write. For she was stuck, she said. Because of Max's illness, because of poverty; but also because she was just stuck. The first part of the book had been all right (well – all right); it was close to her own life, and she'd known what she was doing. But 'the man's part' defeated her. She couldn't do it. *She couldn't do it....* She hinted at this despair to Maryvonne too – but only lightly, and only when it was over. 'I have been very down about my book,' she wrote in December, 'as if it had no meaning.' But from Mr Woodard, before her in the flesh, she couldn't hide her misery: she told him that she'd thrown the book away.

Now Mr Woodard was a classicist; he hadn't heard of Jean Rhys, and hadn't read her novels. Perhaps she was writing some dreadful, garrulous old woman's book – perhaps she wasn't really writing a book at all. But he was very worried about her; if she found no interest in life soon he was afraid that 'something awful' would happen. One day news came of another wild scene, and he hurried to Landboat Bungalows. At least the worst hadn't happened: Jean was alive, just drunk and ill, huddled in bed. Well, he was inside; he made up his mind to look for her book. At first he must have thought there wasn't one after all, or that she'd thrown it away as she'd said, for there was no normal pile of notebooks or paper on any of the tables. But then he must have seen a piece of paper sticking out somewhere; and suddenly he saw pieces of paper everywhere, covered with squiggles and scrawls. He retrieved them – from plastic bags and hat-boxes, from under the bed and the sofa, from on top of wardrobes and inside kitchen cupboards. He put them all together and took them home. He asked his daughter Helen to help him: together they spread out all the bits of paper they could on the big Rectory table. Luckily some pages at least were numbered, and a core of order began to emerge. Finally Helen went to bed; when she looked back her father was still bent over the table.

Jean had despaired of her book, but even she had said 'the material is all there – more so than I thought.' She would add and subtract and rewrite during seven and a half more years: but much of this was just *worry*, and later at least her labours were often only to relocate a paragraph, to change a line or even a word here or there. We can be sure that most of Part One, and the essence of Parts Two and Three, were already there. That night, sometime in the autumn of 1961, Alwynne Woodard was the first person to read *Wide Sargasso Sea*.

And now Jean's good luck flowered. For Mr Woodard loved the clear and beautiful use of language; he knew it in the classical authors, and he was open enough to recognise it elsewhere. Without any of the usual clues — hard covers, a known reputation — he recognised it now, in the ragged bits of paper spread out on his table. When his family came downstairs in the morning they found him in a state of high excitement. 'It's wonderful!' he told them, 'it's *beautifully* written.' The problem of finding Jean an interest in life was solved. He had a different job now: to encourage her to finish this book. No one else knew or cared about it — so he believed, for so Jean believed when she was in her despairing mood. This was his new mission: he would help her to finish it, and so not only help *her* — and her brother — but also help the world to get a good, perhaps a great, new novel.

He started straight away. For the next weeks he went to see Jean almost every afternoon. He understood her perfectly. 'She needs endless supplies of whisky, and endless praise,' he told his wife, 'so that is what she must have.' The village was shocked to the core about the whisky, but he didn't mind, he probably didn't notice. (Jean did both, of course. '*He* could hide behind his Greek or whatever and the rectory and so on. I had nowhere to hide.') He bought her a bed-table, the sort one eats on in hospital: Jean still liked to write in bed, as she'd done in the thirties. He probably persuaded her to let the doctor in: which resulted in the 'pep pills' for her, and a first 'rest and a check-up' in hospital for Max. With Max away she could concentrate on the novel. Mr Woodward would say 'I must go and get her on'; take a bottle of whisky and go up to Landboat Bungalows. She left the back door open for him — never the front, which was kept locked, with a chair propped under the handle. He would let himself in, and sit on the edge of her bed, sometimes for hours. They would talk about the novel, of course — she fretting, he praising. But also about other things. He learned about her other books; he took one home and read it to his family. He told her stories of his school life, which had not been without incident.* Jean was intrigued — and also reminded, perhaps of Arthur Fox Strangways' tales of Wellington, long ago. (She said she wanted to write a short story about one of Mr Woodward's vignettes, but she never did; a boy's school was too far from her experience.)

---

*In the mid-thirties, for instance, he had been involved in a great public row at Lancing, which started with his own dismissal (and another senior master's) and ended with the dismissal of the Headmaster. The story is told in Basil W. Handford's *Lancing College: History and Memories*.

Because he couldn't be shocked or disapproving she didn't try to hide from him, or on the other hand to shock him; she could *relax* with him, as she almost never could. So he saw the best of her. He loved her talk; she was so intelligent, he told his wife – almost without education, but with a wonderful mind. He had, in fact, found the only possible way of encouraging her, as he'd intended: by liking and admiring her, genuinely, without reservation. And it worked. In December she wrote to Maryvonne: 'My book has come to life again. (Hurray!) Also a Mrs Morris Brown who lives near is going to type a bit for me, from dictation.' It had to be from dictation: 'It is so corrected and rewritten that no typist could make it out.'

There'd been signs of this renewal of her energy and hope throughout the autumn: 'With a little will power and so on I'll be able to manage to fix the book up,' to Francis in October; 'It's just a matter of stubborn work now for I still have some well wishers' to Maryvonne in November. But there was one sad blow too. The news came from Maryvonne in early November: John had died.

He had been ill since the early fifties. By 1958 he was very bad. In 1959 the Dutch journalist Bibeb, who had come to interview him for his old magazine *Vrij Nederland*, ended her article with an appeal for contributions to a fund for sending him to the Riviera for his seventieth birthday. By January 1960 he was in constant pain, and on morphine. On 27 October 1961 he died.

So often Jean's 'personal relations went wrong' and stayed wrong, so that she could only put them right (if at all) in fiction. A great deal had gone wrong between her and John: their marriage; the murky business of their collaboration. But happily she did get this most important relationship right, just before he died. For a long time she'd been sending her care and concern through Maryvonne ('Will you tell him I think of him a lot, and send him my best love'). But when she knew he was dying she wrote to him herself, and told him that he 'counted for so much in my life.' 'Thank you,' John replied, 'for telling me how much I was for you in your life. You know what you have been for me and I always am still thankful for it, especially because you gave me Maryvonne.'

Jean had, I think, been the great love of John's life. Of course she had made him very unhappy; she wasn't capable of kindness, steadiness, perhaps even of real love. But for moments she *had* loved him, generously and impulsively, for his gaiety and anxiety. And now she'd managed to tell him so. It was as though she'd remembered – just in time – the *Trial of Jean Rhys*:

> *Did you in your youth have a great love and pity for others?*
> Yes.

*Were you able to show this?*
I think I could not always. I was very clumsy....

For once she hadn't been clumsy. She had acknowledged her debt
to him and to others. To Maryvonne, two years before he died: 'You
know of all the things I *might* say I will risk saying this: If I had never
met John there would have been no books, no "aliveness" and above
all, no you.' And to Francis, two and a half years after:

... he influenced me greatly and for keeps.... Far more than
anyone else has ever done, or will do.

I was such a hunted haunted creature when I left London long
ago and I became almost alive and self-confident for a time. Well.
Self confident! Alive! Nearly.

He'd 'saved her from smashing' once, as Max did later; and like Max
he had really needed her. To these two, therefore, she was always
grateful, and always loyal.

Even getting on with the book couldn't stop Jean becoming cold and
miserable in the pit of winter. She had 'flu, and a 'chill' that lasted
from Christmas to spring; she felt surrounded by sinister gossip
('"That Mrs Hamer bought a *red dress*!",' though it hung unseen in
her wardrobe). In January she was quite silent. Then in February 'Let
Them Call It Jazz' finally appeared in the *London Magazine*; that may
have cheered her up. She wrote to Francis: Mrs Brown was typing her
novel! She was delighted not to have to rewrite yet again, but to be
able to dictate ('isn't it kind?'); and Mrs Brown, whose husband was
a playwright, shared Mr Woodard's excitement about this improbably
excellent manuscript.* By the first week of February Part One was
done, and Jean promised to send it to Francis. A fortnight passed; she
wrote again. Please would he be patient – it was *far too long* – Part
One especially was 'a huge monster –' 'oh dear –'.... In the end she
didn't send Mrs Brown's typescript for another six months; by which
time it was revised and rewritten beyond recognition.
　　What had happened (of course) was that things had gone very
wrong. Part One had got typed all right; perhaps because it was the
clearest in Jean's mind, and on her scraps of paper. But then she'd
begun to feel under impossible pressure. She blamed it (of course) on
the Browns: Mrs Brown had said she couldn't spare much more time,

---

*In fact she typed for Jean *gratis*: 'as an act of charity', says Olwyn Hughes
(who became one of Jean's agents); 'for Mr Woodard and the church',
according to Mrs Woodard.

as her husband was writing a new play; Mr Brown had 'started pacing up and down, and banging on doors and finally made a bookshelf – it was really a tense afternoon.' So she, Jean, had 'got desperate, and said any old thing.' When she got home she didn't dare to look at the typescript for some time. 'When I did I dam near fainted.' It was full of errors, Mrs Brown's and her own. . . .

That was Jean's account – though immediately she felt rather guilty about it, saying that Mr Brown was 'a very nice man,' who had 'made us endless cups of tea until that fatal afternoon.' It was so typical: the initial gratitude and excitement; then beginning to feel unwanted, resented; taking refuge in vagueness; and ending up hysterically angry. That bit of the story she cut from her letters: but in fact she'd made such a furious row – either that 'fatal afternoon' itself or later – that Mrs Brown refused to do any more typing for her. That is why Jean had to return to writing out her fair copies; and why, when they *had* to be typed again the next year, someone had to come down from London to do it.

In the spring of 1962 Jean may have worked on Mrs Brown's typescript – or she may not. The row with that rarest of creatures, a local typist, had depressed her; and Mr Woodard was unhappy because he had made the arrangement with Mrs Brown, and felt responsible. It was 'some time before I could try again,' she said later. In the meantime 'Nothing happens and every day is the same and goes quickly.' But then she sold another story – 'Tigers Are Better-Looking' – to Alan Ross. Max was a bit better. Edward visited her – and *measured the gate*, which had been hanging off its hinges for months, 'so I have hopes.' Maryvonne talked of coming in the summer. And in July and August Jean was definitely back at work. She corrected the proofs of 'Tigers'; she revised Part One of the novel, writing all over the typescript. She didn't revise Part Two, but made additions in handwriting. This time she agonised not over the end – Charlotte Brontë had settled that – but over the beginning. She marked different beginnings in red pencil: 'the first "start"', 'the "wrong" start'. She kept back the 'last two chapters' of Part Two and all of Part Three. But the rest – even the new handwritten bits she had no copies of – she sent, at last, to Francis. Before the parcel, and with it, she bombarded him with explanations, doubts ('This is much too long of course'), courtesies ('Read it when you wish and have time'), thanks ('You don't know how grateful I am to you for not giving me up as a bad job'). But in September 1962, five years after she'd first told him that yes, she was working on a new novel, Francis finally saw *Wide Sargasso Sea*.

'I shall be longing to hear if you think anything right in it,' Jean had written: but of course he found almost everything right in it. He was

To the Crabtree Club: an illustration by Dorothea St-John George for
*London's Latin Quarter* by Kenneth Hare (The Bodley Head, 1926).

Monsieur and Madame Lenglet in Vienna, 1920: the 'spending phase.'

Ford Madox Ford in 1917,
by Wolmark.

Stella Bowen.

Jean in Paris, with Germaine Richelot.

Mrs Adam, who introduced
Jean to Ford.

Self-portrait of Simon Segal,
the original of Serge Rubin
in *Good Morning, Midnight*.

Selma Vaz Dias.

Leslie Tilden Smith in 1921,
aged thirty-six.

Maryvonne aged about seven.

Maryvonne at sixteen:
Jean's favourite photograph of her.

Max Hamer as a young naval officer.

The Rev. Alwynne Woodard.

Mr and Mrs Samuel Greenslade.

Jean: *top left* in Vienna; *top right* visiting Peggy Kirkaldy in 1929 or '30;

*bottom left* at Cheriton Fitzpaine in her mid-seventies; *bottom right* in Venice with Diana Melly.

Jean in old age.

thrilled by it, just as Mr Woodard had been, and he wrote straight away to say so. She was enormously lifted up by his praise.

> I can't tell you how much good your letter has done [she wrote] better than bottle after bottle of champagne. I "see" this long delayed book at last and will have the courage to finish it, I trust. Touch wood.

Francis did see some problems, and discussed them with her. For instance, Daniel's letter was perhaps a bit long. Jean agreed — she'd seen all the faults he mentioned, and more — Part Two *bristled* with them. Part Two was the real difficulty. It could — perhaps it should — be cut by half. Was the poetry at the beginning awful? Was the timing wrong? Was the whole thing wrong — should it be, perhaps, a diary or a letter, something written long afterwards to exorcise a memory? . . . It was her very first letter after receiving his, and already doubt was dislodging his praise. Two days later she added a postscript: and doubt had spread from Part Two to the whole novel. 'It should have been a dream I know with start and finish present day. Or not?' That was mid-September. Then — silence.

It was her usual pattern, exaltation to despair without drawing breath. And it had happened for the usual reason: because she had exposed herself to someone (she felt) unmasked, unbeautified, unprepared. That feeling came over her if she couldn't don her best clothes, make-up and manner to meet people; and it come over her when she had to show her work to someone. Then she felt, *always*, that it wasn't ready. No matter how long and hard she'd worked, how much she'd cut and polished, when another person first read what she'd written she panicked. He would see it was ugly — phoney — bad. 'I hate everything I write when it's finished, and cannot bear to touch it,' she'd told Francis when she finally let him see 'Jazz', a year after her first promise. It was bad enough with stories; but with her novels it was an obsession, it was sheer terror. That's why Leslie had to steal them from her, and why she'd nearly killed him for it. That's why after Leslie she had such trouble finding (and keeping!) typists — because she didn't want them. Once her work was typed there were no more excuses: it looked ready to be seen. But it wasn't; that is to say, *she* wasn't. She was never ready enough to be seen.

It was this terror of being seen which made her keep *Wide Sargasso Sea* back for nine years, though its essence was there after four, perhaps even after one and a half. But she couldn't keep it back entirely. She had to let it be seen several times before it was published in 1966: by Francis Wyndham now in September 1962; by Diana Athill and others at Deutsch in August 1963; by Sonia Orwell, and then by all the readers of *Art & Literature* in January 1964. And each time it was the same: doubt, terror, drink, anger. At the end of this year Jean wrote to Selma: 'A few months ago I nearly collapsed. Then November was so dark and howling gales....' In late November Francis did get one letter, written on vodka. It was so *dark*, dark and damp. She had had 'persistent flu'; the doctor wanted her to go to hospital. Alan Ross had asked for a piece, Chapman and Hall were after her novel, Harper's and a Hungarian magazine wanted 'Jazz'; she was taking quantities of bright red pills to face them all. As to the book – 'it is so bad in parts, isn't it? ... it wants rethinking rewriting and all – especially Part Two – *very* bad....'

> I wish I had not sent you something unfinished – better finish it first and hate it afterwards – Poor thing! – I'm leaving it alone for a bit – but it does not leave me.
> ... Unless I can do this book *a little* as I want to I don't want anybody (any publisher) to see it at all. I'd rather scrap it.

After that, apart from the letter to Selma just before Christmas, and a brief one to Maryvonne in January, no one had a word from Jean until the middle of March 1963. Later that year she wrote to Selma: 'When I was really down I did not write to anyone.'

Two things had come together: the book's being seen for the first time,* and Max's entering the last stage of his illness. In her December letter Jean had told Selma that he might be 'going for a short rest': but it was she who needed the rest. She tried to take care of him entirely by herself – refusing Meals on Wheels, not allowing the district nurse to enter the bungalow. But Max needed a great deal of care now – washing, feeding, exercise; he needed, really, a full-time nurse. And Jean couldn't even be a part-time one. 'It's a little too much for me,' she wrote, very carefully, to Maryvonne in March; 'my writing does not get done.' That was the worst part. Not because of the money she could make, 'though that is urgent'; 'It's ... the feeling that I'm losing my chance gets me down so much.' It had made her 'so awfully tired and worried' that winter that she had thought they would have to leave. She had even thought of asking Maryvonne to come. *That* only happened when she was at rock-bottom.

We have to face something very painful now, to understand what was happening. Leslie had taken her novels away before they were ready, he had judged her, he had loved his first wife better: and she had unleashed her anger on him. Max did none of these things. He was

---

*Mr Woodard had seen it, but she completely trusted him – and anyway he'd 'stolen' it much as Leslie used to do. Mrs Brown had seen it too (and of course a row had ended *that*). But Francis was the first person from literary London, from the publishers, to see it: its first empowered judge.

old and ill and broken; he loved her, depended on her, was abject before her. But just because of all this, he was an intolerable burden on her. And he needed care she longed to provide, but couldn't; he never reproached her, but she reproached herself unceasingly. *And he stopped her from working.* Sometimes, therefore, she neglected him; she left him unfed or unwashed and withdrew into her obsession. And sometimes she snapped. Then she hit him as she'd hit Leslie; and like Leslie he pretended that something else had happened.

Once at least he couldn't pretend, because Jean had attacked him so loudly that the neighbours heard her. That may have been this terrible winter, for after it Max was more in hospital than out of it. The Woodards took over; together with the doctor they had Max removed and taken to hospital. Then Jean turned on them, running wildly to their house, followed by the village. As always, Mr Woodard could calm her down. He calmed down the village too, not for the first or last time: persuading neighbours not to call the police, persuading doctors (and probably Edward) not to drag her off to a different sort of hospital.

Jean did an even better cutting job on her letters than on her novels, and no one outside the village ever heard of this terrible event, or of any others like it. But later on, when journalists, students, friends and admirers came to Cheriton to see her, she always plunged into a state of extreme agitation. They thought this was just Jean, and it partly was. But she had good reason, too: as she'd had in Beckenham long ago, when Selma only missed seeing the headline in the local paper by a miracle. Every time someone came to Landboat Bungalows and passed one of her neighbours Jean had to hope for another.

1963 was an important year. *Wide Sargasso Sea* took another major step towards completion; and Jean took a major step towards the complete breakdown she knew was coming.* Or rather Max took it for her. He'd begun to have 'rests' in hospital in 1961; the one he'd (probably) had this last dark winter was his third or fourth. But in the spring of 1963 he was back in again: and it was the beginning of the end. Jean fought to keep him with her as long as she could, and occasionally she succeeded. But this summer he would become much worse; and from then on he would be in hospital until he died. It was a long, hard death, and one's heart breaks for him. But for Jean too. For it left her to face the one thing she couldn't face: loneliness. That had broken her in Norfolk in the forties, and it would break her in Devon now. Already in September 1963 she was saying that the years in Cheriton Fitzpaine were 'the worst time of my life'; and it would get worse. It would come near to killing her.

* 'I know I've got to fall to pieces some time but there are one or two things I want to do first,' she wrote to both Selma and Maryvonne on 8 August.

In April Max was in a convalescent home in Seaton, on the Devon coast. It was too far for Jean to see him often. Instead she wrote to him, and enclosed pre-addressed envelopes so that he would reply. One of his replies she kept. It is one of the very rare occasions on which we can hear Max's voice, and glimpse something of his feeling for her. They must have quarrelled; perhaps it was now that Jean had attacked him so wildly. He was so ill he could hardly write. Yet he writes like a young and trembling lover:

> I was so relieved and heartened by your letters. Whatever you call me I love you and only you and always shall. You can bet I shall come back as soon as the [illegible] is made. I am very well, they feed you well here but it is rather an astonishing place. You deserve something better than me. I wish you had it.
> Your very loving
> 
> Max.

*Whatever you call me I love you and only you and always shall.* Of course she needed him; of course he stood between her and breakdown. He didn't understand books and writing as Leslie had done; nevertheless he was more to her than Leslie, because he loved her entirely for herself. He didn't blame her: he blamed himself. *You deserve something better than me....* He was ashamed that he hadn't been able to give her the life she needed, and deserved. She had stuck with him in Maidstone; she'd moved with him from the Yacht *Atlast* to seaside bungalows — half for her book, yes, but half for his health too. She told Selma she'd come to Cheriton Fitzpaine 'for Max'; and I expect he felt this was true. He felt he'd let her down, he'd brought her low, he owed her his life.... And when *he* felt these things she didn't need to; she couldn't be angry with him any more. Instead she could be loving and loyal. Not always: often there was a struggle in her between Max and her book, and the book won. But she felt his love and gentleness very deeply; she needed them very much; and when they weren't there any more she fell apart.

Now, in May, however, she cheered up. Max came home; Maryvonne and Ellen visited, and Diana Athill liked *Wide Sargasso Sea*. Jean hadn't realised that Francis had passed on her manuscript — which was by far the best way. No waiting, nor worry; just the good news. But of course they wanted to see the revised Part Two now, and Part Three; so it was back to the old trouble — find another typist? Write out a fair copy herself? She temporised about Mrs Brown to Francis and Diana: she was away a lot, there was trouble with Mr Brown — 'I think (fear) I have shocked Mr Brown — that very tame love affair with the coloured girl.... Or maybe it all got on his nerves because *he's* writing a thing — about Jesus Christ (I gather) ...'.

This wasn't very kind, and she immediately regretted it ('Mr Brown ... is a very nice man. Delete and forget.') It was just the sort of thing that happened to her. She couldn't admit she'd shouted at her typist, so she made up some other story; then it ran away with her, and she ended up feeling doubly guilty. But then Diana Athill saved the day. She suggested that someone come down from André Deutsch to help Jean get her book in order. Esther Whitby, a new young editor, would bring a typewriter, a tape-recorder, support and advice. Jean was delighted. She'd been let off the Mrs Brown hook, and she'd have a clean new typescript to work on. Esther Whitby's visit was arranged for early August.

First, though, two other important things happened. The first we already know: in June Max suddenly became much worse. Almost certainly he had another, more serious stroke. He had to return to hospital, this time nearby in Tiverton. Jean panicked, probably because she could see how bad he was, and feared the doctors wouldn't let him home again; but also because Max himself was very unhappy, and wrote her 'frantic letters' every day. She'd begged him not to go – she'd told the doctor she didn't approve – but 'it was arranged when I was out and without my consent,' she said. (The Cheriton Fitzpaine doctor no doubt knew she'd fight; and at that point Max had wanted to go.) The nurses were *beastly* – they didn't treat him – they didn't let him smoke – they just let him lie there, 'fretting' ... Jean couldn't bear it; she burst into tears.

Soon Max was calmer, and the worst of her panic was over. But only for the moment, and only on the surface. For now the second event happened. Max was still away in the hospital, and that, no doubt, was a factor. In the same week Jean wrote a letter to the Matron, demanding politely but firmly that he be allowed to come home ('I have thought the matter over very carefully and this is what I wish'). She must have been close to the edge of panic to assert herself like this – and then, out of the same or a different panic, to forget to send the letter. She always felt friendless and unprotected; but in this first week of July 1963 she was especially afraid that her best friend (if not protector – 'Max is not the protector type') was slipping away.

The thing that happened now was at first a great pleasure for Jean. Selma vaz Dias came to see her; and Max's brother Alec Hamer too. They were two of the very few people whom she really liked, whom she didn't fear. Alec was very like Max himself: 'A sweet man with a sense of humour.' He called Cheriton Fitzpaine 'Cheriton Fitzcowpat', and said things like 'Pray, what is the weather like at Cheriton Fitz? Very inclement I presume.' And he was slightly more literary (or less unliterary) than Max; he was writing his memoirs, and he gave Jean the White King's advice to Alice about writing: '"Begin at the beginning. Go on to the end. And then stop."' She would like that too. Indeed she'd shown him the manuscript of *Wide Sargasso Sea* very early on, in the autumn of 1961; he may even have read bits of it before Mr Woodard.

Selma, of course, was one of Jean's most important friends. Jean wholly liked and trusted very few women in her life: Germaine Richelot, Peggy Kirkaldy, later Sonia Orwell; that's about all. And Selma vaz Dias. Selma had rescued her twice, in 1949 and 1956; she'd twice restored her desire to write, even (therefore) to live. Selma lifted her up, gave her energy and hope; Selma took her work to the outside world. And Jean trusted her, confided in her: not always (not that 1949 headline, for instance), but more than most people. Selma would be fun, like Alec; and they could talk about work too, for Selma was turning *Voyage in the Dark* into a play. 'It'll be lovely seeing you,' Jean wrote to her just before she came; and for once she really meant it.

They came on 3 or 4 July, and indeed it *was* a good time. 'You did so cheer me up and I simply loved seeing you,' Jean wrote to Selma afterwards – and went on writing for months, even years. But something had happened on that visit that would finally destroy this friendship more thoroughly than any other, and that would confirm forever Jean's paranoia ('persecution maniacs always have been and still are the victims of persecution'). We only have Jean's story; and it's one of her self-defensive ones, cut to the bone. But we have at least that bare outline, polished by repetition. Selma brought a bottle of whisky (Jean said). The both drank a lot, or at least she did; they were gay and laughing. (No mention of Alec: he can't have been there at the time, or it wouldn't have happened.) Then Selma brought out 'a rough piece of paper covered with writing.' Sometimes Jean said this piece of paper was about the broadcasting rights of *Voyage in the Dark*, *Good Morning, Midnight* and 'The First Mrs Rochester'; sometimes she said 'I asked Selma what it was and she said "A joke".' In any case Jean *thought* it was a joke – she said that always. She didn't think it was serious; she thought it was a joke.

It was not a joke. It was an agreement giving Selma fifty per cent of all proceeds from any dramatic adaptation of any work by Jean – not just the ones she mentioned – anywhere in the world, *and* granting Selma sole artistic control of all such adaptations. It was, in fact, a most extraordinary document. But Jean 'scarcely read it'. When she saw the words 'all over the world' she was more convinced than ever (she said) that it was a joke. She 'didn't think twice about it'; if she thought at all (and that was later) she thought that 'Selma was a friend, that the whole thing could be talked over and "arranged".' She sipped her whisky, picked up a pen and signed.

As anyone but Jean might have guessed, this 'rough piece of paper' with her signature at the bottom would affect her for the rest of her life — and her family and her work beyond it. Eighteen months later Selma sent a more formal document containing the same terms, and Jean signed that too. It was only eighteen months after *that*, when *Wide Sargasso Sea* was about to be published, that she began to reflect on the practical consequences of what she'd done. Then of course she became worried, anxious, angry. Deutsch took legal advice and tried repeatedly to persuade Selma to withdraw the agreement, or at least to modify it; but now she too began to feel persecuted and angry, and she refused. Then, in early 1967, the dramatic agent Margaret Ramsay was brought in because Diana Athill learnt that she had once been Selma's agent, and knew her well. She finally got Selma to change the agreement, though not to cancel it altogether. Selma agreed to waive her claim to artistic control, and to reduce her share of the proceeds from a half to a third. The amended agreement was drawn up by a lawyer. It was not perfect, but in the circumstances it was a minor miracle, and everyone heaved a sigh of relief and of gratitude to Peggy Ramsay.

Jean herself gave several reasons for signing half her life's work away so gaily. Only one blamed Selma: she always insisted that Selma had presented her piece of paper as 'a joke', lightly and unseriously. That was why she felt in the end that Selma had deliberately tricked her; and if her description is fair, it was true. Selma, Alec and Jean herself are all dead now, and we'll never know. But Jean's other reasons in any case move the blame (or at least the explanation) to herself. First, she always admitted that she'd had 'several whiskies', even half the bottle: that in plain English she was drunk. And second, she always said that at the time she was obsessed with *Wide Sargasso Sea*: she couldn't really pay much attention to anything else; the novel's characters were far more real to her than anyone in the real world.

Both these explanations were clearly true. To them can be added another: she was in a state of panic about Max, seeing the threat of complete solitude approaching. Selma wouldn't seem just a friend: more than ever she would seem a saviour, a godsend, an eleventh-hour rescuer — as after all she'd been before. Jean was (to put it mildly) an extremist. Most people she feared and distrusted beyond all reason; the few she liked she gave herself up to entirely ('I can still give myself up to people I like,' Sasha says, and so Anna, Marya, Antoinette give themselves up to their lovers).

And there's another factor. Jean had impossibly high ideals of trust and confidence between people. She was ashamed of perfectly ordinary reservations and self-protection; she thought them ugly and base, and didn't want to have them. Whenever she could, or thought she could, therefore, she put them away from her, and trusted absolutely. It was a form of courtesy, of good manners, like an Edwardian gentleman's — like Lancelot's, or like her father's. (And then, of course, if they let her down there would be the other extreme: absolute distrust and absolute hatred.) There was another, similar thing too: her attitude to money, which was also an extension of an old-fashioned, aristocratic code. She adored money and needed it badly, as she always admitted: but it too was base and ugly, and she didn't like to think about it. She felt she should be above money, as a person and especially as a writer. She *wouldn't* connect money to writing, more than couldn't; and again she was an extremist, so that thinking even a little about money in connection to writing seemed to her selling her soul for a mess of pottage. It would, therefore, have been low in her, and rude to Selma, to hesitate for a moment, even to read the agreement carefully. Her sense of both her own honour and Selma's would require her to sign quickly and gaily, as though nothing could possibly be wrong, as though this sort of thing couldn't possibly matter.

These reasons deep in her nature combined with others closer to the surface. With her desire for pleasure and fun, for example, like Marya's longing 'for any joy, any pleasure': here were Selma and Alec for only a few days, or a few hours, and she mustn't spoil it. With her impatience and panic the moment any form of 'business' appeared: she'd do anything to get rid of the worry as quickly as possible, and the quickest way was to sign now and worry later. With, finally, what was after all quite a reasonable and practical attitude. She needed money and help in getting it; Selma was offering both, and had succeeded before. Fifty per cent of everything was pretty stiff; but Jean didn't rate herself highly, she knew she couldn't do the adaptation herself, and half was better than nothing, which was what there might be without Selma. Indeed, five years later she would offer Oliver Stoner the same proportion, fifty per cent, of whatever he could get for a *Wide Sargasso Sea* manuscript. As she didn't read the paper properly she thought Selma was interested only in *Good Morning, Midnight, Voyage in the Dark,* and *The First Mrs Rochester,* which were the ones she'd been involved in so far; for the same reason she assumed it was only a question of radio. If these assumptions had been right the agreement would indeed have been much more reasonable.

Given all this, it's perhaps not so surprising after all that Jean signed Selma's first piece of paper, in the summer of 1963 (though one still wonders about Selma). It's the second signature, in March 1965, that is the mystery. Her then agent asked her — in some surprise — if she really wanted to sign, and she could have said no then. But the agent, who had never met her and had no idea of her incompetence, did not spell out his surprise, and Jean did not say no. She was in a bad physical and mental state; she had had a heart attack, had spent four months in hospital and nursing homes, and was about to return to solitary confinement in Cheriton Fitzpaine. Even so, *surely* she could have refused.... But no: being Jean, she could not. She was too weak to fight. She had already signed once – *she had promised*, as she said many times. And she would repeat that she would gladly share the money if only Selma continued to sell her work, as no one else (she felt) would.... Loneliness, need, panic, honour – they all came together again, I think, and again she signed.

Well, that's the story of Selma vaz Dias, her whisky bottle and her piece of paper. She had been one of the best things in Jean's life for the last fourteen years – finding her and reintroducing her to the world, encouraging and inspiring her. But over the next years she became one of the worst things instead. And Jean treated all this in an utterly typical way. She allowed it to destroy every vestige of enjoyment she might have had in the success of *Wide Sargasso Sea*. For several years she alternated between anger and attempts at reconciliation, then she tormented herself with her own stupidity and Selma's treachery for the rest of her life. But she allowed only her closest friends to see the worst of this mess. In front of others she kept up a Sasha-like front of black comedy. When she told the story to her agent Olwyn Hughes, for instance, she called it 'The Adventure of the Drunken Signature'.

A few days later Selma came back again, with a tape-recorder this time, and recorded Jean singing some West Indian songs for their play of *Voyage in the Dark*. She sang several, including a rude one in which a woman boasts to a man '*Woman sweeter dan man, Woman sweeter dan man, If you t'ink you sweet like me, Go t'row yourself down de W.C.*' And two or three pretty patois songs, including the whole of 'Ma belle ka di maman li', which Antoinette sings to Rochester in *Wide Sargasso Sea*:

> *Ma belle ka di maman li*
> *Pourquoi les fleurs si jolis*
> *Sont morts d'un jour, sont morts d'un instant*

> *Maman li a di Ti-moun*
> *Tu connais rien*
> *Un jour et mille ans*
> *C'est la même chose*
> *Pour le bon dieu.*

The recording is astonishing to hear.* Jean was seventy-three, but her voice is sweet, light, slightly trembling, the voice of a very young girl. Her West Indian accent is delicate but distinct: she says 'dahn' for 'down' ('Go t'row yourself dahn de W.C.'), and when she explains how one of the songs should sound she says, 'It sinks and rahses.' There's something else too. She starts 'Ma belle ka' several times, but keeps confusing or forgetting the words. You can hear in her voice that she's getting very nervous. Selma asks if she'd like to leave the song out. Jean says, 'No, I can manage it all right'; but her next attempts are no more successful, and she grows more agitated. There's a click where the machine was turned off. When it comes on again Jean speaks the lines: and her voice has a catch in it, as though she's been crying. It is so like her — the nervousness, the forced bravery, the tears. Again it's hard to remember this is an old woman; it's much more like a child.

Although she never sent her letter to Max's hospital she got him home on the day she'd specified, 11 July. 'Everyone — except Alec perhaps — was dead against my bringing him back,' she said: 'everyone' being, no doubt, Edward, the Woodards, the doctors, even Selma. But as usual when she was desperate, she prevailed. Max stayed with her for two or three weeks. It was his last time at home. Jean tried frantically to persuade herself that it was best for him there. 'I've thought of several things to make him more comfortable,' she said; he was 'much better and more cheerful,' 'not so down and bewildered and despairing and neglected.' Perhaps that was true, for a short time. Max hated hospitals as much as anyone, and had certainly wanted to come home the last time. But the trouble was that Jean couldn't manage.

She tried to, she pretended to, but she couldn't. He had got much worse. 'He moaned and seemed afraid and much weaker'; she couldn't lift him. 'Last night and again this morning there was nearly an almighty crash — and a broken back would be a sad end,' she admitted to Selma. Also (though she told no one this) for some time now he had been incontinent, and the struggle to keep him clean and dry was added to all the others. She had a 'plan', she told Maryvonne; but if she had one it didn't work.

Mr Woodard, who still visited faithfully, must have told his wife how bad things were. She and her daily woman, Mrs Stentiford, came as often as they dared, cleaning and tidying the house when Jean was in bed, drunk or asleep; even once or twice bathing Max and changing his clothes. The village nurse came to see him too, still resisted by Jean. But it wasn't enough, and by the end poor Max's state was pitiable. It was fortunate (everyone must have thought) that Mrs Whitby was coming, and that Jean *wanted* Max to go back to the hospital while she was there. They might have had to remove him forcibly, otherwise.

*It is in the Jean Rhys collection at Tulsa.

He went back at the end of July, and Jean did a few days' hard work getting the manuscript ready for Esther Whitby. Or rather a few nights: she worked until dawn, and one early morning 'in a frenzy of tidying' tore up a whole chapter, no doubt thinking she'd done a fair copy when she hadn't.

Esther Whitby arrived on 2 August and stayed for three days. She lived at the Rectory and returned there for meals; but the rest of the time she worked with Jean. They didn't take any breaks. Despite all the preparations the manuscript was still 'all over the place', scrawled in notebooks, on typed and hand-written sheets. Jean sorted them out; Esther helped her, then typed the passages Jean said were ready in the right order. She found Jean chaotic and distressed by her chaos; she also found her frail and ill, so much 'on her last legs' that Esther was continually astonished over the next years that she went on living. But that was all. Jean sipped from a glass occasionally but was never drunk. She was reserved and formal, but not at all 'difficult'; on the contrary she was very nice, concerned that Esther should be comfortable and not bored.

Above all, despite being so old and ill and agitated about her hopeless manuscript, Jean worked with extraordinary lucidity and concentration. About her strangely ugly home, so unlike her stylish self, she was as passive and defeatist as ever. But about her work — about every single word — she was decisive and determined. Esther's impression was of an impossibly frail old woman, who was yet remarkably clear and in control. She saw nothing of Jean's other side at all. They finished typing *Wide Sargasso Sea* and recorded the last state of 'Leaving School'.* Esther left thinking the job was done: *Wide Sargasso Sea* was ready to publish, or very close to it.

For two days afterwards Jean slept, and her eyes, which had swollen painfully, returned to normal. But then she too began to return to normal: and unlike her eyes this did not mean a healing. The clear, controlled person Esther Whitby had met started to recede. She'd had to let Esther take a typescript back to Deutsch, though she'd been visibly reluctant. And now she began the inevitable slide into panic and self-doubt. 'Please remember that it was done quickly, without revision,' she wrote to Diana on 8 August. 'Do not criticise it as it is at all — It's a "till ready" ad lib!'

At the same time she was trying desperately to get Max home from hospital. She'd said this stay would be brief, just for Esther Whitby's

---

* Alan Ross of the *London Magazine* had commissioned this from her, as part of a series. That was in 1962. He never got it. Jean worked on it on and off for fourteen years, writing dozens of versions of each page. It finally went into *Sleep It Off Lady* as 'Overture and Beginners Please'.

visit, and she wanted very much to keep her word. 'He knows now that I am here and on his side, and that he is *not* forsaken,' she'd told Maryvonne the last time. She knew all about feeling forsaken; and was very concerned that Max shouldn't. 'Even if he has to go back for a bit he will know I do not forsake people,' she'd said. 'Not ever. *I never have* and can't start now. Too late.' It wasn't true. She'd forsaken John in his prison, Maryvonne herself in her convent, even all her life. But that only made her more desperate not to do it to poor Max now.

And yet she had to; he was not allowed home again. Anyone but Jean would have known it was hopeless. When Alec heard his brother was in hospital again he wrote to her: 'I thought he would have to as looking after him in his present state is obviously impossible for you.' And he tried to console and thank her – 'you have made a gallant effort.' But she was not consoled. Her guilt and pain for Max mounted; her terror of solitude sharpened. She'd pulled herself together into the clear and almost calm Jean for the book, for Esther Whitby; now the dark and desperate Jean would snap back with a vengeance.

Diana's response to the typescript staved this off briefly. It was prompt, enthusiastic, thoughtful. She was 'very moved and excited,' she wrote, and so was Francis. The ending was perfect, the whole novel wonderful. But she understood it was not finished: she assured Jean of her '*clear understanding* that what I have read is unrevised.' Then she made a few editorial comments, all in support of judgements Jean had already made. For instance, at this stage Grace Poole's bit of Part Three was longer: a little too long, perhaps; and yes, Grace's voice sometimes faltered. And Daniel had a whole first-person chapter to himself. It was *absolutely right* for Part Two to be told by Rochester, Diana said; but perhaps a third first-person narrator was too much. But Jean's suggestion that Antoinette might find a diary of his, or some letters, wouldn't be right: Rochester's ambivalence was very important, Antoinette shouldn't know too clearly what he feels. (This was, I think, excellent advice.) She would consult Francis about the problem of Daniel.

Jean replied to this in a long letter – encouraged, but not as lifted as she'd been by their first praise for the novel a year before. She admitted to feeling 'a bit uneasy,' because 'I don't like anyone seeing unfinished work (indeed it's a great struggle to let anyone see it at all – finished or not!!).' But she made light of having given up writing this letter the day before; and she added a postscript (or pre-script, since she put it at the beginning) of extreme politeness and modesty. 'It strikes me that I'm rather taking your interest for granted. I don't mean to do that ... read this when you want to read it.... No hurry.' She was putting her best self forward, her tea-party self, gloved and hatted. She was sober, her handwriting was strong and clear. She was still in control.

And it's a fascinating letter. She tells Diana that she'd first thought of the whole novel ('and did a bit of it') like the original ending of *Voyage in the Dark*: beginning and ending with the dream, and the rest a long, mad or half-mad monologue. But then she thought 'A mad girl speaking all the time is too much!'; and she made the decision which cost her so much, but which was I think the right one: to tell it all as 'a romance', 'a *story*', 'working up to the madness' on a solid and smooth foundation. She told Diana that Part Two had always been 'so much the worst and most difficult'. She discussed her troubles with Grace Poole, with Daniel, with Antoinette's visit to Christophine. She ran through the plot on the way — and it *does* sound finished, eveything more or less as it is today, including indeed the solution to the Daniel problem (first his letter, then Rochester's visit).

It was 'not yet a finished book' on paper, but it was 'finished in my head. At last and thank God.' Except for one thing. In Esther Whitby's typescript there seems to have been no happy time at all for the lovers before the arrival of Daniel's letter. Jean knew one was needed, and she was planning to add it. *But all she was going to give them at this point was a week*. It wasn't much; it wasn't enough. There'd be no contrast, there'd be no tragedy if Antoinette lost so little.... Something had gone wrong. Jean disliked Rochester too much now: she'd forgotten her first insight, that he was 'not a villain'. He was a 'Dreadful man' now; she 'tried to be fair and all that', but the effort showed. That was the one thing that really wasn't right yet, that really wasn't finished.

Alec was supposed to come and spend a week with her from 18 August, and that kept Jean going. But then he couldn't come. Devon was so lonely, so rainy, she wasn't well. And now Selma was putting pressure on her: she wanted 'a short extract which will give "the essence of the book"' for the radio. But it wasn't finished, or even finally accepted, and besides — 'The essence!' Still, 'Selma is my friend,' and she would try to send something.... She didn't. She tried to keep Selma occupied with *Voyage in the Dark* instead. And she tried to occupy herself with *Leaving School*, writing goodness knows how many of the fifty-odd pages of it in her Orange Notebook, and perhaps many more she cut and threw away. But by September she couldn't hide it any more. The desperate dark Jean was taking over.

She was, she told Selma, 'getting worried about too many things. *Too worried!*' She was worried about the BBC. ('It does seem to me that they scramble madly for "popularity" at one end and at the other there is this cursed snobbish hypocrite half lie — that is almost worse.') She was worried (as always) about typing and business. And she was desperately worried about Max. It cost a pound a time in Mr Greenslade's taxi to go and see him ('Buses few and impossible'), so that not only had she left him in hospital against her will and word, she couldn't even visit him. And he was getting worse – '*much* worse than he has ever been with me....' Physically that was hardly possible, and indeed she soon admitted he was looking better. But most of the time she was convinced that he was terribly unhappy, that the hospital was a '*horrible* place' and he hated it there, that he kept imploring her to take him away. Poor Max – it may well have been true. Or it may have been her own guilt and loneliness speaking. For she simply could not face these things: that she had 'forsaken' him after all; and that she had to be alone.

'This is not a place to be alone in,' she wrote to Selma. The moment Max had gone – she felt – people had begun to let their hate and envy of her show. 'While Max was with me they didn't attack openly. Now they are attacking. And how!' There was black magic in the village, the rector's wife had told her so. She'd said 'Of course my husband got rid of it. At once.' Jean wanted to believe that, but couldn't. It was still there. The 'black-eyed Susan next door' – that was Zena Raymond – was clearly a witch: why else did she borrow Jean's books, *when she couldn't read*? But *she* accused *Jean* of being a witch, and half the villiage believed it.... This was not just paranoia; they did. Because (they said) she went into her garden late at night 'and did strange things'; because she 'rushed out at night with broken bottles and shrieked'; because she threatened to cut Zena Raymond's daughters up into little pieces. Jean told David Plante about some of this much later – that alone and drunk she would pin on Max's medals, go out of doors, and shout, 'Wings up! Wings up!', taunted by the village boys. 'I think I must have been pretty nearly crazy at this time,' she said, and shuddered. But she didn't want to think that people might have such good reason; besides, she didn't believe that was their reason. They hated *her*, not bits of her behaviour. (That was her real mistake always.) It was back to that: to the sense of her deepest difference, the different vision that both debased and exalted her. They thought she was a witch, she believed, *because she was a writer*.

'I would rather do any work, or bear any hardship than have these onslaughts on something so rooted in me,' she said. But of course she couldn't do any other work, or bear any hardship; instead she attacked back, as she always did. She fought with Zena, she fought with the boys. She couldn't write. She was – she said herself – 'wild and desolate and angry'. She felt surrounded by fear and hate. Her only friends were Mr Greenslade and the Rector. Often Mr Greenslade came and drove her somewhere, anywhere, just to get away; and Mr Woodard came often too, telling her over and over that there was nothing to fear. It wasn't enough. She gave in and sent for Maryvonne. Maryvonne came, but of course she couldn't stay long, and when she had gone it was worse than before. 'Oh God,' Jean said to Selma at the end of September, 'the stupidity, the ugliness, the darkness, the loneliness and the cruelty of this *beastly* little place. This evil place.' And she turned to her last solution: escape. 'If you think of a way out, *however crazy*, tell me.'

But now Selma began to fail her as a friend. She was as much of an egotist as Jean. She was obsessed with her own troubles and didn't really listen to Jean's; she pressed and chivvied her for her 'extract'. And she didn't reply to this 'heart cry' until two months later. Jean needed a friend too badly to give Selma up, but she began to worry. In October she told Francis about the agreement she had signed. It was only about *Voyage in the Dark*, she suggested at first – but she knew really: 'The agreement covered all my books.... We were to share fifty-fifty.' She didn't accuse Selma of anything. 'But, I think, she *forgets*. Also she thinks that writing is easy.' And she hadn't replied, perhaps she was annoyed.... Really *Jean* was 'annoyed'; but she wasn't yet ready to admit it.

October was worse. November was worse still. Her mind went round and round: what to do? Go to Amsterdam? – no money. Ask Maryvonne to return? That would be breaking her vow twice in a row. Go to a nursing home and 'rest'? That was the doctor's idea, and Edward's. He had heard what a bad state she was in, perhaps from the Woodards, perhaps from the Greenslades, who were instructed to ring him if she wasn't well. And once or twice he'd seen for himself how lost and desperate she could get, so that she'd just sit in a corner, drinking. He 'hauled her off to *two* specialists': both said she was 'quite sane' (like the Holloway doctor), but that she 'might break down under her present existence'. After that he was 'convinced and kind', Jean told Francis, and proposed the 'rest' solution.... But originally she'd written only 'quite kind'; and to Selma, more openly, 'My brother is not always as kind as he seems, you know.' According to Mrs Woodard it wasn't so much a nursing home as a home for alcoholics that Edward had had in mind.

Of course Jean did none of these things anyway. She just stayed. By mid-October she was 'spending hours building up a barrier of wood and stones' against the mice – she was terrified of mice. She told Francis she wouldn't ask Maryvonne to come back; then she told Maryvonne she wouldn't ask, which was of course a way of asking. And she complained while pretending not to – 'If I can fight down the panic it'll be all right and maybe I only feel ill because of the loneliness.... So I'll do my best.' She didn't want to burden

Maryvonne: she genuinely, desperately didn't. But she couldn't help herself. And Maryvonne *was* burdened. She was about to move house; she knew how hard — how impossible — it was to help Jean. She felt dread and guilt whenever a letter arrived from England; but she didn't come.

Mr Woodard visited, he took Jean home several times for a drink and a good meal, but that was all he could do. Francis couldn't leave his London life and job: he sent a hundred pounds. Then finally Selma sent her reply to Jean's September letter, and it was belatedly generous. She invited Jean to come and stay with her for a few weeks. Again Jean felt saved in the last minute. She was hugely grateful. 'I will not forget,' she wrote: and no doubt she once more put from her mind as unworthy her suspicions of Selma's agreement.

But this invitation didn't, in the end, stop the decline of their friendship, for Jean never got to Selma's. Several things happened to stop her. Back in October Francis had written to say that a new magazine, *Art & Literature*, was interested in publishing Part One of *Wide Sargasso Sea*. Jean was too depressed to take much in, but she'd tried to sound pleased, and said she would tell Christy and Moore (who'd started to act for her) to get in touch with Diana. Perhaps she did, or more likely Francis did for her; a month later, anyway, she'd forgotten. So that when she heard now — only a few days after Selma's invitation — that Sonia Orwell of *Art & Literature* had already *had* Part One from Christy and Moore, she panicked. How *could* an 'unfinished, unrevised' manuscript have been sent to them? ('*Not by me.*') And how could she go to Selma's? She had to revise the copy sent by the agents — though she was really too worried to do it, too ill and unhappy. She couldn't understand why this had happened, when she'd said '*repeatedly*' that the work was unfinished. . . . It was a classic Jean disaster produced by her own chaos, by her need to use, yet inability to trust other people. Produced, in fact, by herself, like all her disasters — which only made it more painful.

This first delay came from Jean, then. But the next came from Selma. She'd had a film offer, she'd have to concentrate on that — a visit now was impossible, but Jean could come at Christmas. 'Of course I understand, my dear,' Jean said, and of course she did. But she didn't forget it either. She *needed* to be in London — to clear things up with Selma, to find out how many copies of her unrevised manuscript were wandering around. . . . And she needed to get away from 'Nightmare Cottage'. The pipes had burst, the roof was leaking, workmen would have to come in. That was the last straw. She couldn't wait till Christmas: she booked a room in Crediton for the week they'd be there. Then of course Selma wrote to say there was a hitch on the film and she could come after all. After Crediton, then

— say a week before Christmas — but would Selma perhaps prefer to put everything off 'till the Christmas fuss is over?' That was Jean's polite, thoughtful, well-mannered voice. She meant it — she *wanted* to be polite and thoughtful and well-mannered. But then came a nasty surprise: Selma accepted the suggestion. She was ill, there were great upheavals, Christmas wasn't a good time after all. Jean wrote a second understanding reply, but this was a very serious blow. She hadn't gone to Crediton; she'd hung on because of the prospect of Selma's, and now it was snatched away. In desperation she arranged to go to a guest house in Tiverton instead: but on the day of departure she 'burst into tears and could not stop'. She was trapped, she would never get away.

It may have been now that Mr Woodard once again rescued her. For she was 'really frightened', 'dam nearly sunk'; and then suddenly she was better. 'I will be okay and all right,' she wrote to Selma. 'I'll swim long enough now to finish the book and get away from the nightmare of Cheriton Fitzpaine.' She doesn't say why. Later, when she told Diana about a breakthrough some time after Christmas, she said it came 'out of the blue'. But this is the story she told David Plante in 1977.

Week after week Mr Woodard came to see her, telling her 'over and over that there was nothing to fear':

> . . . . Now this is what I never told you before, what I've never told anyone. He asked me one day would I take Communion. I said I didn't know if I believed. He said, 'You were baptized, weren't you?' I said yes. So the next time he came, he came with Holy Communion, with the host, and I got down on my knees, stuck out my tongue, and he placed the host on it. And then, you know, I started to write, and I finished the novel.

She didn't, of course, finish it now: but she did embark on the longest and most important period of work on it since 1958–59, when she'd finished the first draft in Bude. She was in much better heart, and for the first two months of 1964 she worked hard on Parts One and Two. Throughout January she worked on the proofs of Part One for *Art & Literature*, doing a good deal of rewriting in the process. February was tougher, with the workmen doing the roof at last, and Selma pressing her for 'her part' of *Wide Sargasso Sea*. But she was in one of her good times with whisky, when it mostly did what she wanted it to do — cheer her up and give her energy. She visited Max every week, and even allowed herself to hope that he might come home when the roof was done. By the end of February she was telling Diana that Part One was finished — 'excepting a sentence or two'; Part Two would be finished in a week; and Part Three would be easy and quick. 'I am getting along with the rest of the book fairly quickly, and don't want to be discouraged,' she wrote to Francis.

But she *was* now discouraged, briefly but badly. She forced herself to go on working, endlessly promised to send the rest of the novel, and never did. She returned to dithering over the title; she apologised, defended herself and joked over how long she'd been: 'Like Algernon in "The Importance of Being Earnest" saying "I never knew anybody take so long to dress, and with such little result".'

Several things had gone wrong. First of all, her corrected proofs of Part One hadn't got to *Art & Literature* in time, and they'd printed the unrevised version she'd been so unhappy they'd seen in the first place.... This was a classic Jean nightmare, and followed a classic Jean pattern. First she tried, and pretended, not to mind, and seemed to forget about it, working obsessively on the clean proofs. But this didn't last, and soon there was — as she put it — 'a fearful shindy.' She was furious with everyone — with Sonia Orwell, who had asked 'everybody excepting me' for the extract, with the agents for sending it, with Deutsch for letting them. And why was everyone annoyed with *her*, who was the wronged and innocent party? ... Of course she wasn't innocent. She had let John Smith of Christy and Moore feel he could act for her, and Deutsch that they could release Part One. The late arrival of the corrections was probably her fault too. She wrote on the proofs 'I had written longer additions & they had to be cut a lot. This caused delay.'

Then there was a second business fiasco at the same time, again very typical. Alan Ross, who was patiently waiting for 'Leaving School', was thinking of setting up in publishing and had asked Jean if any of her early novels were free for reissue. She could never find her contracts, or understand them if she did. Deutsch *had* said something about republishing *Midnight*, but that was long ago, and she'd never heard any more. Alan Ross's offer came just at the moment of her Christmas disappointment; she grabbed at the hope, and gave him *Voyage in the Dark* and *Good Morning, Midnight*. But now, in March, a contract arrived from André Deutsch formalising those vaguely remembered discussions: and of course Deutsch wanted the option of republishing all the earlier novels. As she'd done with Selma's contract, Jean hardly read it (did she read it at all?), and agreed. And now there was another appalling muddle. Who had the right to reissue *Midnight* and the others — Deutsch? Ross? their original publishers? Jean panicked as always, though this time she saw she wasn't entirely innocent ('I made the great mistake of not reading the Deutsch contract carefully enough'). Diana told her not to worry, Alan Ross withdrew his claim, Cape and Chatto released *Mackenzie* and *Quartet* to Deutsch in 1966, and it all got sorted out in the end. But Jean would very quickly get into the same trouble with agents, and that would be harder to get out of.

She was perfectly intelligent, and nowhere near as ignorant as she pretended in order to explain how she got into these muddles, but she was simply unable to turn down any offer of help or hope of money; and simply unable to read, understand or remember any legal or financial document. It's a common feeling – the deep reluctance that overcomes one at the sight of an official form: what amazes is the extreme Jean took it to.

Amid this chaos and anger her relationship with Selma took a precipitous step downward. Each blamed the other for the Christmas disaster, and they'd exchanged a few preliminary recriminations about that. Then in February Selma sent a renewed invitation to come 'any time', 'the sooner the better'. Jean was delighted, and said perhaps a day very soon; but of course nothing happened. Selma was an impatient person; she had little understanding for Jean's neurotic indecision. She wrote – 'quite angrily', Jean felt – saying that Jean had already promised to come several times and not arrived, and suggesting a date, perhaps rather peremptorily. Jean was already damping down suspicion and anger against Selma, and this released them. She sent back a stiff, self-pitying letter. She couldn't come, she was 'struggling against illness and a terrible *cafard*.' She couldn't possibly have given an exact date and broken it, she would have wired – it was Selma who gave exact dates and then cancelled them, *twice*. It was useless to repeat this, but it was true. . . . And now she behaved as she had during Max's trial, when she'd had the same problem ('People *always* believe a lie. They *never* believe the truth'): she sent Selma copies of her own letters and wires – 'just landed film . . . therefore advisable postpone your visit' – 'Visit over Christmas ill-advised. . . .' It was pathetic. In an absurd and minor key it was like Antoinette's hopeless attempts to tell Rochester the truth about her mother. That is how Jean made art out of herself: with the beauty of her language transforming her sad obsessions into tragedy.

By late March she was in the pit of this *cafard*. She felt utterly abandoned – no one answered her letters, or even read them – things were going on *without her knowledge* – people were pawing at her unfinished work, accusing her of things. . . . The village hated her, and she hated them – 'My pin-up boy is now – *Stalin*!! who machine-gunned those country characters like anything. . . .' Then it got particularly cold, and she got a bad dose of her usual 'flu to add to her *cafard*. And once again Mr Woodard came to the rescue: he took her home to the Rectory.

It was her second time with a clergyman's family – which shows, I suppose, how much the rectory in an English village still functioned (still functions?) as a back-up to the local hospital. Jean behaved almost exactly as she had in Booton Rectory in 1941. She had her meals alone in her room: 'she hated having the family and children around her,'

Mrs Woodard says. She was 'absolutely beastly' – wouldn't stay in bed, wouldn't eat, was entirely ungrateful. One day she suddenly said she was better – though she clearly wasn't – and went home, saying to Mrs Woodard as she left 'You must feel a great glow for having been so good.' But – as in Booton again – she did want to talk to the Rector. She sat in an armchair in his study, wrapped in rugs, in front of a good fire, and talked to him about her book, about herself and her memories. She talked a great deal (Mrs Woodard remembers) about the prison hospital: Holloway in 1949. With someone she trusted, like Mr Woodard, she talked very openly (Max did too – the Woodards knew all about both Hamers' experiences of prison). She stayed for some time, probably a week or two (Mrs Woodard says a month, but I expect it only felt like that). Afterwards Edward came to thank them. He knew that her health, both physical and mental, was deteriorating rapidly, and he worried very much about what to do.

This break from 'solitary confinement' must have helped; and now Jean did something to help herself too. It was the only thing she ever *could* do to help herself, the thing she'd learnt to do when she was a child of twelve: to write out her sadness, especially in poems. Prose had become work; she felt like Lotus Heath, 'Poetry's what I really like.' In early April she wrote four poems. One was about Max; two were writer's poems, one 'about words', the other about a young acrobat doing what looks an 'easy trick', but falling and breaking his neck (just like her, writing what must look like an 'easy' novel). But it was the fourth poem that was important.

It was called 'Obeah Night'. In it Jean became Edward Rochester: and when she did that her long battle with the novel was won. The thing that had set her against it, especially in the last year, melted and loosened. The book 'clicked': 'all was there and always had been,' 'It must have been in my mind all the time.' And she was released to rewrite Rochester's story: not much, but to change the 'slant', and to do much of it in poetry – the last, poetic pages of Part Two.

This time it was something Diana said which had sparked off the breakthrough. Even Jean had seen that Antoinette and Rochester must have a *bit* of happiness together: but Diana had said that they should have more, a few weeks. 'As soon as I wrote that bit I realised that he must have fallen for her – and violently too,' Jean wrote to Francis. She flew to poetry, 'my first & last love & my refuge,' and wrote 'Obeah Night' (*'Lost, lovely Antoinette.... I'll never see you now, I'll never know, For you left me – my truest Love, Long ago'*). Then she knew what was wrong: *'Mr Rochester was.'*

He was *all wrong.* So *cold.* . . . Also a *heel.* First he coldly marries the girl for her dough, then believes everything he's told about her, finally he drags her to England, shuts her up in a cold dark room for *years* and brings sweet little Janey to look at the result – this noble character! Noble!! My God! As soon as I saw that it all came to life. It had always been there. Mr Rochester is *not* a heel. He is a fierce and violent (Heathcliff) man who marries an alien creature, partly because his father arranged it, partly because he has had a bad attack of fever, partly no doubt for *lovely* mun, but most of all because he is *curious* about this girl – already half in love.

Then (this is good old Part Two) they get to this lovely lonely magic place and there is no "half" at all. My Mr Rochester as I see him becomes as fierce as Heathcliff and as jealous as Othello. He is also a bit uneasy (not used to strong magic at all). *Suspicious – (Why do I feel like this?)* (That you see is where I went so wrong.)

*That is where I went wrong*: she'd come to concentrate too much on his suspicion, his coldness, his caution, and had forgotten about his other side – his own passion, his ability to be tempted *and to fall* for Antoinette and her island. It was not love: Rochester does not love Antoinette, steadily, for herself, as she is. He doesn't understand her, or himself, enough for that. Not love: but passion, intoxication, the desire to possess and to understand something he's never met before – something beautiful and mysterious, but also disturbing and violent. It is in that place, and in Antoinette. The two are the same, 'mixed up perhaps to bewildered English gent, Mr R'; he is 'magicked' by both together. He is himself 'a fierce and passionate creature', 'violently in love with the place and the girl'. *And also* cautious, suspicious, afraid. So the tragedy is inevitable: but that is why it is a tragedy. Now we can understand and sympathise with Antoinette for falling in love with him, now we can understand and sympathise with *him*; now there is drama and tension, not just a single note of suffering and a single point of view. '*Romance* is back,' Jean wrote gaily on May Day 1964. *Wide Sargasso Sea* would be all right now. 'It is *there* and *okay.*'

When Esther Whitby typed it in 1963 it was only half a great novel – Part One great, but Part Two a failure. What Jean had done now was what she always had to do to reach greatness: break out of the prison of her egotism. She had done it in *Good Morning, Midnight*, enough to see herself clear; now she did it more, enough to see another person. And I think (as I've said) that the person she saw then was Lancelot. It was his vulnerability and passion she drew on for Rochester; and her love for him she drew on for Antoinette. *Wide Sargasso Sea* therefore pulls together all the connections for Jean between love and death. It explores (again) the heroine's loss of herself when she loses love; and it also explores her desire to lose herself *in* love ('*Chante, chante ma vie, aux mains de mon amant*').

What both intoxicates and terrifies Rochester about Antoinette and her island is the secret he feels they know, which is surely love – but also death ('"Die then! Die!" I watched her die many times. In my way, not in hers.') *For they are the same for Antoinette.* Her desire is to give up her self to him, and for him to give up his self to her: that they should do nothing but love, merge, be one. That is the first, pure desire of all lovers, but perhaps especially of women; and it is what all 'sane' people – but perhaps especially men – fear in extreme romantic love. This is not a manageable feminist question about inequality (thought that is here too – the law, especially property law, is again on the side of the men). It is a question – this is always Jean's question – of psychological death, of the complete self-surrender of either or both people. That is why *Wide Sargasso Sea* is not just a Gothic romance, or a study in colonial alienation, but a frightening exploration of the intimate connections between love, death and madness.

This was almost Jean's last push on the novel, and her last major one. She wrote so much through April and May – 'write write all night' – that she got writer's cramp ('must be the only person in the world who has it – what with typists, tape recorders and so on'). Apart from the novel she wrote huge long letters to Francis and Diana, often late at night, wildly scrawled and full of additions like the manuscript. She wrote about the West Indies, about Cheriton Fitzpaine and the horrible present: 'Birds in the Attic – at least I'm told they are birds,' which of course would get turned into a story too.* She wrote about Max, and money, and Mr Woodard, who was helping again, bringing whisky, sitting and talking. But most of all she wrote about *Wide Sargasso Sea*.

Usually she didn't like to talk or even think about her writing, afraid that it would stop her doing it. But in this 'exalted' mood she could. These letters of April and May 1964 are full of wonderful things about the writing of her last novel. They show, with her own directness and immediacy, her perfectionism, her hope and doubt, her great dependence on writing.

Last night I sat up very late – another bad habit – and got what I thought four or five lines right, fixed inevitable and not to be changed

---

*'Who Knows What's Up in the Attic?' 'An albatross must have got in,' Jean said. 'I'm the sort of person an albatross would like very much.'

and as they were the last lines of part II I was pleased — because four right lines can mean a lot.

*Then* I got this idea of making the last chapter partly 'poetry' ... it would be fun to do a whole *book* like that wouldn't it? I rather think someone sometime will ... I wonder ... if I am terribly excited about something that has been done ages ago —

Never say or think — 'I wish I'd left this terrible creature alone.' Really! .... Because you see if I had not had this book, this hope — *Of what? Not dough* — these years would have been very tough. Too tough I think. Even for me.

As Jean approached the end of her revised Part Two she began to lose confidence. She carried on for another two weeks, probably changing a line her or there. Finally she packed up what she'd done: the longer, happier honeymoon for the lovers, on loose ruled paper, and two red exercise books containing the last, poetic chapter of Part Two. At the end of the second she wrote

The rest of the book can be dictated.
I will get it done somehow. It is finished.

On 21 May she sent the package to Francis. She was very tired. And her exaltation had quite gone. 'I can see already that Mr R's poetry will have to be cut or turned into prose I *think*. It's all only a *sketch* as it were....'

Well, we know what will happen. '*I will not crack*' she'd written to Francis — 'if I can help it,' she'd added to Maryvonne. She couldn't help it. Really this last burst of energy for the book was only a brief break in the depression that had begun when Max had left her alone for good the previous autumn. It had itself drained her. And now the wildest and riskiest part of her novel was out in the world for anyone to see. She'd finally released it, to Francis; but of course he'd passed it on to Diana again — and Diana was going away, and 'three weeks is so long to wait....' Jean tried not to say anything to Francis, just to be grateful for his praise, and by the end of a long letter she managed it — 'Thank you again a thousand times.' But then she added a poem, a Calypso she'd written the night before, on whisky ('a lot'): and in her unconscious or half-conscious way ('A real calypso is not thought out') she expressed her sense of betrayal after all.

> *I dreamt about Judas*
> *Last night, last night*

> *I dreamt about Judas*
> *Kissing. . . .**

She felt, as always when she'd let a manuscript go, 'such a *haunt* that they may publish the *skeleton* as my finished book.' Diana reassured her: *Wide Sargasso Sea* was a masterpiece, but she agreed that some of the poetry needed cutting. But Jean was beginning to suspect Diana too: 'You said you read my letters. . . .' She tried to stave off collapse by keeping busy – she corrected *Voyage in the Dark* and *Good Morning, Midnight* for their reissue, she dug out *Barred* for Francis, she promised to get the novel ready for typing ('I will do that. I'm starting tomorrow. It's done.') But it was no good. By mid-June she admitted to Francis she was in 'a very blue mood'; by the end of June she was really ill. Mr Woodard began to pray for her; so did a new friend, a Sikh who came to her door selling bright tinsel scarves and blouses (later he and his offer of prayer went into the same story as the 'birds' in her attic). She was drinking, of course ('if one drinks a lot alone it cannot be helped'). And finally the crisis came: an attack on a neighbour, probably Zena Raymond. Someone called Edward. She had fought him before; I expect she fought him again now. But to no avail. Hospital was the only place for her when she was so bad; even Mr Woodard must have agreed. Towards the end of July she was admitted to the Belvedere Clinic of Exe Vale Hospital, near Exeter.

She was in the hospital for a month. Maryvonne was in a family crisis, and Jean managed to say: 'It will help if you come – but if too much upset of plans – Don't.' Francis sent books. One day she went back to the cottage and thought '*did* it look desolate – No wonder I was ill.' None the less, and though the doctors were against it, she was determined to leave. On her seventy-fourth birthday she returned to Cheriton Fitzpaine.

She had five or six weeks now back in her small, dark cottage. Nothing had really changed: she was still ill, still drinking. But however much she'd resisted it, the rest in hospital had helped. She could work. Diana sent her the address of a typist Deutsch often used, Mrs Kloegman; and Jean sent her the corrections and additions as she went along. She even decided now that she would go up to London

---

*Thus too, for example, in her letter to Francis the week before, in which she was so excited about her prose poetry chapter, but worried it had been done before, she says she'd been trying to remember a Jean Harlow song of the thirties: and the title is 'Everything's been done before' (She remembers one line too: 'But it's new to me, it's new to me. . .'). Clearly her mind worked this way, making unconscious or half-conscious connections all the time, not just in her fiction.

herself, to explain some of the more complicated changes to Mrs Kloegman in person.

This was always a great struggle for her – the longing to be somewhere else versus the dread of getting there. But the book pulled her on. In October she packed, grabbed the papers with the last two or three small changes she wanted to give Mrs Kloegman, and left for London.

She hadn't been there for seven years, not since Selma's readthrough of *Good Morning, Midnight*. That had been the beginning of *Wide Sargasso Sea*: now finally it was nearly done. She went to her hotel. The next day she and Diana were to have a celebration lunch complete with champagne. It would be the first time they'd met, after seven years' correspondence..... Was she pleased, excited? Terrified, probably; but those too.

They never had their champagne lunch. When Diana rang the hotel in the morning she was told 'Please come at once, the lady is ill.' She rushed over and saw at once that it was serious. She packed Jean's bag, called an ambulance and took her off to hospital.

Jean was in a terrible state – so agitated that the nurses thought she was psychotic, and put her in a bed with bars. But the real trouble was physical. She had had a heart attack.*

Maryvonne came straight away. Diana visited every day, and so did Lily Lockhart. Francis came, and Edward, and Selma once or twice, and Esther Whitby. Jean was very weak and ill. Afterwards she felt she'd wept all the time and wished her friends hadn't seen her so low. But it was drink that robbed her of control, not illness. In the intervals of worrying about her book, Diana says, she was 'sweet and grateful', and fully in possession of her beautiful manners.

But she was worrying very badly. The last few changes she'd wanted to make had grown in her mind, as always, until she was convinced that the book was far from finished, was a 'skeleton'. She made Diana 'swear a solemn oath' that it would not be published: not until she'd given her permission, if she lived, and not at all, if she died.

She lived, and the promise was kept. But for a time Diana had feared that the second part of it might have to be broken. It seemed quite possible that Jean would die; and the novel really was finished, was 'perfect'. So now she did something she never told Jean. One day when Edward was coming to London to visit his sister she rang him and asked if he could bring her the plastic bags full of paper under Jean's bed. He did; and Diana looked to see if she could work out Jean's last few corrections without her. But it was quite impossible.

---

*Edward was told it was a stroke; but she was on pills for her heart for the rest of her life.

There were the same lines, the same paragraphs, with very slight variations, written over and over again in different notebooks, on different pieces of paper: only Jean would know which one she wanted. Diana put everything back in the bags, and Edward put the bags back under the bed.

After about a month in hospital Jean was moved to a convalescent home in Surrey, and then to a small nursing home Edward found in Exmouth. This was a disaster ('three people to one room'), so she moved again. The Caroline Nursing Home was much better, but now there was another problem. Diana had offered to set the novel in galleys so that Jean could have a clean new copy to work on. Unfortunately this convinced Jean that Deutsch were pressing ahead with publication after all; and no matter how often Diana reassured her she slipped back into her fear a moment later. Then they lost touch for a few weeks, because Jean had forgotten to tell Diana about her last move. She lay in the Caroline Nursing Home until the end of February, fretting that Deutsch would publish the 'skeleton' of her novel, and agitated by pressure from Selma ('when oh when will I be able to get my part of Saragossa Sea to do on radio, they are so keen to have it'). She was in no fit state to return alone to her cottage anyway, and this made it worse. Again Edward and the doctors were against it, again Maryvonne couldn't come to take care of her for the first few weeks. But 'I am *free* there — and I've always had "Give me Liberty or give me Death" as my slogan. . . .' She could go to bed and get up when she liked, she could eat — or not eat — when she liked, she could drink when she liked. So against everyone's advice, and against her own fears, on 1 March she went home.

It was a crazy thing to do of course — but she couldn't have stayed in the nursing home either. There was no solution to the conflict of her needs, for company *and* solitude, safety *and* freedom. There never had been. Simply, it got worse now, like everything else. Like her health, for instance — from now on she was not just chronically ailing but chronically ill, with a heart condition kept under control by medication. And like her loneliness.

For the next many months, she said, from March to October, she heard from no one.* And she saw almost no one: Mr Greenslade when he drove her somewhere, Mrs Greenslade when she brought lunch; Mr Woodard only occasionally; Edward never, because his wife

---

*This was probably an exaggeration, but it's true that there are only a few letters from 1965 in her archive. The problem was that she was impossible to help. She wouldn't let anyone come down and help her, she took queries as harassments, she hid the depths of her desperation as long as possible. Her friends were trying to respect the privacy she so fiercely protected, and to wait patiently for her to recover.

was dying. She did see Max, as often as she could when she first came back; but that of course meant only greater sadness. The truth was that he was incurable, just waiting to die. When he did die, a year later, Jean wrote to Selma, 'He saved me from so much, but I could not save him from the last years in hospital which he hated.' As the months crept on she stopped mentioning him in her letters; he was so ill, *she* was so ill, she probably stopped going.

And the worst trouble, of course, was the book. Deutsch were expecting it by the end of April, but *she could not touch it.* This drove her frantic. She sent Diana paranoid letters, promising to send back her advance straight away ('please please stop imagining us as fierce and cross,' Diana replied, and of course they wouldn't take her money). Jean said she was calmer, but she wasn't. She *hated* her novel, 'for I told myself if I hadn't tried so hard I wouldn't have collapsed.' Every time she looked at a blank piece of paper she felt sick. She spent days 'walking up and down the passage, afraid of the spiders and the mice, and all the people in the village,' reading the same few books over and over. Then the summer came, when she should have felt better, and she realised she would never be well again.

> Every morning three bogies stood round my bed.
> 1) The book needed rewriting parts I & II
> 2) I'd never be well again
> 3) Here I was & here I'd stay except for a miracle.

By August she was sending Maryvonne naked pleas for help — 'I am very lonely bewildered and unhappy ... too unhappy to write which is perhaps the worst thing that has happened.... It's as if for the time being my courage has gone, and how do I know when it will come back.' But Maryvonne had had to learn to protect herself and her family from emotional blackmail, and she didn't come. The only thing to do was to wait for the spell to be broken.

Finally, in October, it was. This was the rescue Jean attributed to a new treatment, some new pills the doctor had given her. She began to feel better. She went for walks, and for rides in Mr Greenslade's taxi. She sent Maryvonne much better letters, full of memories and plans. She slept from eight o'clock to three or four in the morning, then went to the kitchen for tea. She drank cup after cup, and smoked one cigarette after another, and 'watched the light, if any, appear at last.'

Then in November she could write again. That she attributed to something less practical than pills: to 'a cheap pretty dress in a window....' 'I forced myself to go in & buy it. It didn't last but it did its job. I was able to rewrite parts II & III of the book!' At the end of the month Diana received the new Part Two. Jean had cut and smoothed the poetry she'd written for Rochester in early 1964 into the charged poetic prose we have now. Diana had thought the novel beautiful before. Now she wrote to Jean: 'I have never said this to anyone else, but you are a perfect writer.'

In mid-December 1965 Jean also broke her long silence to her friends. She'd nearly finished her rewriting, she told Francis: and 'I will never forget how very kind and encouraging you were, or how you helped me.' At Christmas she sold four stories to *Art & Literature*. In January the literary agent Olwyn Hughes called on her – and immediately Jean asked her to act for her uncollected stories. She now had two literary agents, she'd soon have more.

In February she learned that Diana, André Deutsch and Hamish Hamilton had proposed her to the Royal Literary Fund for an award, and that they'd been successful. She would get three hundred pounds a year from the Fund, for five years. She was very grateful – and also very worried. The Royal Literary Society was so *respectable*, and they wanted to know so much about her. . . . So she was pleased, but also 'dazed' and 'bewildered'. There'd be much more of such success in the next years, and she'd have this double reaction to all of it. Because it had come too late to enjoy, she usually said. That was true. But she didn't (of course) add the rest of the truth: that by the time it came she had too much to hide.

Now she was working on Part Three. Most of the work was cutting. 'I have this idea that all difficulties can be solved, and all put right by *cutting*,' she told Diana – 'in fact I nearly wrote to you and suggested cutting all Part Three. . . .' Luckily she didn't do that. She cut the house party Rochester gives in *Jane Eyre* as part of her new sense of his (limited) decency. She cut Grace Poole's speech to the bone, because she still didn't know how she'd talk (that was true). Again she actually changed very little. The Part Three Deutsch already had 'was beautiful and convincing', Diana said. But she *thought* about the most radical changes; and the small changes she did make she brooded about with agonised intensity. They didn't take long to do; 'it's casting about – trying this way and that – takes the time,' she said. 'And the worry.' Mr Woodard was helping again, listening to her worries, taking her home for warmth and meals. 'When this book dies I will die,' she said to him; and she talked so obsessively about the ending of her novel that his family were half afraid she would try to live it out, and burn down the Rectory.

On 24 February Jean wrote to Diana that the book was finished, and she would post Part Three to be typed early the next week. For once she did – though she did still have a few more changes, and would Diana please send a copy of the typescript when it was ready, so that she could do them?

But on 2 March the hospital telephoned: Max had had a relapse. She (or perhaps Edward) called Alec and Maryvonne. 'There was never any hope but I hoped,' Jean said. And indeed he could go on like this, no one could tell. On the seventh she wrote to Diana that she 'wanted to use any strength I have left' to do the last few deletions to Part Two, the last few additions to Part One. Alec even prepared to leave. But that day, without gaining consciousness, Max died.

Early in the morning two days later he was cremated at Exeter. Jean was prostrated with grief; Alec and Edward made all the arrangements. When they came home Jean wrote to Diana.

> ... I feel that I've been walking a tightrope for a long, long time and have finally fallen off. I can't believe that I am so alone, and that there is no Max.
>
> I've dreamt several times that I was going to have a baby — then I woke with relief.
>
> Finally I dreamt that I was looking at the baby in a cradle — such a puny weak thing.
>
> So the book must be finished, and that must be what I think about it really. I don't dream about it any more.
>
> I am sorry for a sad letter and I send you my love.
>
> Jean.

She never made those 'last' few additions and deletions. *Wide Sargasso Sea* simply slipped away from her now, as *Good Morning, Midnight* had nearly thirty years before. Leslie had released her from her other novels by taking them away; Max released her from this one by dying. It was the last thing he could do for her.

Max was a sociable man, much as Leslie had been; Jean felt guilty about drawing them both into her solitude. With all their moves, with prison and his illness, Max was drawn in very deeply. He was Jean's husband for nearly twenty years, but he remains a shadowy figure.

A few people in Cheriton Fitzpaine remember a small, pale old man in a beret (Harry Martin the builder was sure he was French because of that beret). He wasn't sociable any more; he was too bitter and ashamed to want to talk to people. But when he did talk he was quiet, kind, well spoken. He loved Jean; and she always said he was sweet and kind, a dear, 'all wool and a yard wide.' She'd grabbed at him when she was down, as she'd grabbed at John; and she'd come to love him as she'd come to love John. But she dragged him down. He couldn't take care of her; she had to take care of him, and that she couldn't do. Then she would feel so worthless she would hate him. In those moods at the start she ignored him and wouldn't speak to him; at the end she didn't feed or wash him. *But I'm trying to write a book*, she would say, *how can you expect me to*? Sometimes she would refuse to go and visit him in hospital, even if someone took her. 'Why should I trouble with that old bundle of rags?' she would rage — then the next day she'd write a desperate letter about how he had saved her long ago, and say 'Max is not a rag doll ... to me. He is Max.'

It's hard to think of how much Max suffered, and how little he, or Jean, could do to help. For months, for example, he had great pain in his feet — just because neither of them had thought to cut his toenails. And once, in hospital, he asked his visitors what the weather was like outside. It was raining, they said: and he took the umbrella by his bed and put it up, lying flat on his back in bed. It was because it had rained so badly in the chalet, and that's what he'd done then: patiently, resignedly put up an umbrella indoors.

It was Max to whom Jean should have dedicated *Wide Sargasso Sea*, for its writing cost him even more than it cost her. So Mrs Woodard thinks, who knew them together. 'Jean was very lonely,' she says, 'but she had what Max called her obsession, her writing. He was the lonely one.'

At the end of March Diana came to Cheriton Fitzpaine to go through the last typescript with Jean. Two days later she wrote that she had read the whole book through again, and it was marvellous. She sent Jean a writer's praise.

> ... No one is ever going to know what labour and torment has gone into the years of writing this book. It's going to alight in their hands as complete and natural as a bird on a bough, as though it had just come into existence by itself. Does that make you feel better, after all the blood sweat toil and tears? It ought to make you feel so proud — a rare and splendid creator.

# CHAPTER FOUR

# Wide Sargasso Sea

*Introduction — The meaning of* Wide Sargasso Sea *—*
*Structure and style — Conclusion*

*Wide Sargasso Sea* is Jean Rhys's masterpiece of revenge and self-pity. It is the expression of the whole of her: of her artistic strength and her psychic weakness, of her literary genius and her personal despair. The first four novels are extraordinarily convincing: we cannot deny that they must be true. But they retain — even *Good Morning, Midnight* retains — some important weaknesses: and these are triumphantly set right in *Wide Sargasso Sea*.

First, the aloneness and lack of background of the heroine, from Anna to Sasha, leave us with no sense of how she came to be so vulnerable, so self-destructive, so half-dead already. We feel that we have not been given the whole story; or if this *is* the whole story, we can't quite understand it. We are left in need of an explanation.

And that is what *Wide Sargasso Sea* gives us. It tells us the whole story, not just of Antoinette, but by extension of Anna, Marya, Julia and Sasha as well. Of course it did not begin and end with unhappy love affairs; it is a far deeper and far older story than that. *Wide Sargasso Sea* shows us the destruction of a personality from its real beginnings, in childhood; and it locates the personal destruction as part of the destruction of a family and of a whole society. That is why it is Jean's masterwork: it completes her other novels; and it is in itself more complete and more satisfying, and therefore — despite its distancing in space and time — even more believable than they are.

And yet, as we know, *Wide Sargasso Sea* is also 'incomplete'. We need *Jane Eyre* to fill out its meaning, just as we need *Wide Sargasso Sea* to fill out the meaning of the earlier novels: *Jane Eyre* tells us the end of Antoinette's story, as *Wide Sargasso Sea* tells us the beginning of Anna's and Marya's, Julia's and Sasha's. Has *Wide Sargasso Sea*, then, not exactly the same weakness?

No, because there is a vital difference. The incompleteness of *Wide Sargasso Sea* is a deliberate, and a brilliantly successful, device. In the earlier novels Jean has assumed that we will recognise her heroine in our own experience; if we do not, our sympathy fails. But *Wide Sargasso Sea* poses no such problem. We learn in its last Part that Antoinette is Bertha Rochester; and Bertha Rochester is not like us, she is mad. It is, however, *absolutely appropriate to leave this judgement that she is mad outside her own story*: to leave it to *Jane Eyre*. This 'incompleteness' of Wide Sargasso Sea's identification of its heroine, far from being a weakness, works perfectly: it allows us to understand that she is aberrant, and yet, within the book itself, to identify ourselves imaginatively with her 'aberrant' point of view.

This, then, is the first way in which *Wide Sargasso Sea* goes beyond the achievement of the earlier novels: it tells the whole story and the whole truth. The second lies in the way the story is told. Jean's main demon has always been self-pity and special pleading: too uncritical an identification with her heroine, and too little sympathy with anyone else. She has fought against this in two ways: an inner and an outer way, a way of the lily and a way of the pig. The way of the pig began in *After Leaving Mr Mackenzie* and reached its peak in *Good Morning, Midnight*: showing us the heroine from the outside, in all her failure and squalor. The way of the lily began in *Voyage in the Dark*: leaving the heroine innocent and abused, but never *saying* she is, and telling her story so well that we believe it, and sympathise. This way reaches its peak in *Wide Sargasso Sea*. *Good Morning, Midnight* was the masterpiece Jean didn't really want to write, or only half of her wanted to write; *Wide Sargasso Sea* is the masterpiece she did want to write, the highest expression of all of her.

Like Anna, Antoinette never expresses pity for herself, and no one expresses it for her. She tells us at the start that she and her family are poor, marooned and mocked: but she tells us so in a clear and uncomplaining child's voice, without comment or judgement: 'I got used to a solitary life.' Later she tells Christophine that she is afraid, and asks for help; but she speaks simply and directly out of her pain, without describing or dwelling on it, and we believe her. Christophine expects her to 'have spunks' and fight for herself; the closest she comes to offering Antoinette excuses is to say that 'people fasten bad words on you and your mother.'

There is one character, however, who does openly express self-pity: the embittered half-caste, Daniel Cosway. That it is he and not the heroine is crucial in several ways.

Christophine is scornful of Daniel's claim to be Antoinette's half-brother. But whether or not it is factually true, it is true in all the ways that matter in Jean's world: metaphorically, emotionally, spiritually. For he is an extreme embodiment of the heroine's condition: the condition of the oppressed and despised person, rejected by all, belonging nowhere. And by putting this condition into *someone else as well as the heroine* Jean solved her most intractable problems.

The truth she struggled to see and to tell us was that instead of ennobling, suffering often corrupts; that people are turned cruel by cruelty, unjust by injustice; that oppressed people are dangerous people, obsessively aggrieved and vengeful ('Yes, they've got to be watched,' Rochester says, 'for the time comes when they try to kill'). But exploring this truth through the heroines alone alienated our sympathy from them – aggrieved and angry people are hard to like, no matter how well we understand their point of view. And it made her explanations of them seem like excuses, like self-pity. By sharing this central insight between Antoinette and Daniel, Jean triumphantly avoided both traps. We understand how Daniel came to be as he is, and condemn his society more than him: he is Jean's most powerful portrait of social injustice. But because he is not the heroine this explanation does not feel like self-pity or making excuses. At the same time we do condemn and dislike him; and again, because he is not the heroine, we can do so without damaging our faith in the novel. The difficult combination of sympathy and condemnation is made possible because he is not Antoinette; and feeling it for him leaves intact a purer sympathy for her.

Daniel is exactly as close to and as far away from Antoinette as he needs to be in order to solve perfectly the problem of the heroine's *alter ego* in both its forms. He is, first, the culmination of the 'twin' who has been pushing up through the heroine since *Mackenzie*: the hurt and despised, angry and cruel wolf, whose hatred and vengefulness he crystallises, while leaving the other primitive passions, for sex and self-surrender, to Antoinette. And he is the culmination, too, of all the nightmare 'neighbours' since Monsieur Monvoisin of *Quartet*: thin, yellow-faced, with flickering eyes, a little yellow rat in a little dark room. He is the darkest side of human failure, hated and despised by all, hating and despising all: mean, cruel, malicious. That is what the heroine could not bear to identify herself with; and in *Wide Sargasso Sea* Antoinette is not identified with it, but contrasted to it. Even in her worst moments of madness and hatred she is not mean or cruel, but open, violent, self-forgetful. If we see Daniel as the heroine's last 'neighbour', we see starkly dramatised what Jean hated most in herself and wanted most to leave behind: self-pity and bitterness, malice and cruelty. In *Good Morning, Midnight* she expected us to sympathise with Sasha although she is bitter and cruel. Now she no longer expects this. She has recognised that self-pity and bitterness are undignified and despicable, and among the army of impulses which destroy our hopes of love.

With the help of her *alter ego* Daniel, then, Antoinette is freed of the malice and sterility which he embodies. She is also freed of envy, especially of other women, which too often surfaces in the other heroines and the other novels. In them, if another woman wins the love and approval desired by the heroine – as Lois does in *Quartet*, or Norah in *After Leaving Mr Mackenzie* – she is punished by being exposed as cruel or malicious or stupid, or merely respectable. In other words, Jean does not only tell us, in the earlier novels, that women are rivals, but she also betrays the fact that that is what she feels. With a few exceptions, such as the chorus girls in *Voyage in the Dark*, we are not allowed to like or admire any other woman. But in *Wide Sargasso Sea* Antoinette, and we, love and admire not only kind older women such as Aunt Cora and Christophine, but also the young and beautiful de Plana sisters. Hélène does not lord it over Antoinette because of having prettier hair; she is 'polite', tactful and like all the sisters, 'never seemed vain'. This licence Jean gives her heroine and her readers to like and admire other characters paradoxically but predictably means that we like the heroine better. She doesn't require us to pity her for others' better fortune: and so, at last, we do.

Jean also gives Antoinette a magnanimity that the earlier, more self-obsessed heroines lacked. What a contrast, for example, between the endings of *Quartet* and of Rochester's section of *Wide Sargasso Sea*. Marya rails against Stephan, blames him, humiliates and taunts him, asks him for love and pity and gives none back. Antoinette, already so destroyed that she speaks in 'a doll's voice', asks Rochester for love and pity too, but for *someone else* – the servant boy; and when he roughly refuses she says only, 'I don't understand you.'

And this touch – that she thinks of someone else when she is losing herself – helps not only the heroine but the whole novel. That the boy too loves Rochester, and that Rochester shuts his heart to him too, gives Antoinette's plight resonance and significance beyond one unhappy love affair. It shows us that 'terrible things happen' to many – to all – who need love, not just to Antoinette; and that Rochester is lost to love, not just to Antoinette. And it identifies Antoinette once more with 'black' against 'white', with those who feel simply and truly against those who think cleverly but falsely.

But let us return again to the question of self-pity, since it is at the heart of what I want to say about *Wide Sargasso Sea*. It is this: that by achieving complete artistic control over her demon of self-pity, Jean produced her masterpiece. For, first, *Wide Sargasso Sea* is still driven and informed by self-pity: it was still that which drove her to write, and it is the genuineness and strength of her self-pity that give *Wide Sargasso Sea*, like all her books, its extraordinary power and undeniability. But, second, it is in *Wide Sargasso Sea* alone that she has her powerful emotion under complete artistic control: here alone *it is refined not only out of the heroine but ultimately out of the book itself,* so that we feel the pity instead of her. Here at last she achieved what she had never so completely achieved before: to stop asking for love, and to stop complaining that she did not receive it: so at last, for *Wide Sargasso Sea,* it came.

There are two crucial ways in which Jean refines Antoinette's self-pity not only out of her (and, as I have argued, into Daniel), but finally out of the book itself. Both are subtle but very simple, as all really good ideas are.

First, there is the important fact that the most unbearable part of Antoinette's story, the last and worst rejection of all, *is not told by Antoinette herself* (except in one small section), but by Rochester. This is a wonderful leap of Jean's imagination. It is not just that it was extraordinarily daring of her to move into a man's mind, to try to see the world from the enemy's point of view; it is not even that she succeeded so well in conveying the alien feel of Rochester's conventional and logical male mind. But *in itself* the move expresses and displays this greatest lifting of her self-obsession: it is the clearest recognition, among all her books, that there *is* a male point of view that can be inhabited: that men too have fears and feelings, seek love and — in their way — are destroyed by its loss. And even more: she reminds us of this fact *just when Antoinette is suffering most;* just when it would be most easy and natural for her to slip back into pointing out her pain, and calling out for our pity.

Thus, on the first sudden descent of Antoinette's suffering, when Rochester has received Daniel's letter, and so has left her bed by night and is 'scornful and silent' by day, she briefly takes over her own story again. But this brief section is a fine example of the total absence of a plea for our pity in Antoinette's narrative: the pain is so pure and so clear; it is only in what she says has happened and in what she asks Christophine to do; it needs and receives no description from her. Then, when the second and final climax of the loss of her brief love comes, after Rochester has been 'poisoned' by the love potion and takes Amélie in revenge — then we do not hear Antoinette's voice at all. We hear Rochester's: all he tells us about Antoinette is that she is asleep, and then that she leaves — in fact, he doesn't even tell us that, only that 'I knew I should hear her horse's hooves' when she leaves the house. We hear Christophine's voice: it is she who tells us about the week or so of Antoinette's most acute suffering and attempted cure, after which she returns to Granbois transformed into Bertha Mason. Antoinette speaks only after these events, and then only as perceived and reported by Rochester. She has done the crossing of the border between sadness and madness outside our sight and hearing: that is to say, outside the book. And so there *can* be no self-pity expressed for it. But of course that was Jean's decision: when she decided to let Rochester tell this part of the story, she decided to leave the self-pity outside the book.

But she decided it long before that, in the very germ of the idea for *Wide Sargasso Sea*: and here we come, I think, to the single most brilliant source of *Wide Sargasso Sea*'s greatness. It is, I believe, a great paean of self-justification, revenge and self-pity: but the conception itself of the story, the extraordinary idea for it — that it should have its ending *in another book* — puts our realisation of this truth outside what Jean herself wrote. This idea seems to me to have the simplicity and perfection of genius: by this one stroke she satisfied both neurosis and art, and turned the first into the second.

Everyone knows, of course, that the end of Antoinette's story, previsioned only in part and only in dream in *Wide Sargasso Sea*, is in *Jane Eyre*. But some very simple things have not been said about the end of the story in *Jane Eyre*, and what it tells us about the meaning of *Wide Sargasso Sea*. For what happens in *Jane Eyre*, when Bertha Mason sets fire to Thornfield Hall? She — who is, in *Jane Eyre*, grotesquely lunatic — kills herself; Rochester escapes death only by chance, and is badly mutilated; then, after much suffering, he is finally restored to health, happiness, and marriage to Jane Eyre. Now, what would all this mean from Jean's point of view, as we know it from all her books and stories, from everything she ever wrote or said?

First: that the poor alienated white West Indian outcast has been labelled a villain and a murderess, and represented as grotesque and inhuman, a mere 'lunatic' seen crudely from the outside. Second: that her alienation and maltreatment drive her to suicide. Third: that in killing herself she also takes revenge upon the man who (Jean tells us in *Wide Sargasso Sea*) has been so largely responsible for her state; she destroys the prison he has kept her in, and nearly destroys him. But fourth: that fate cheats her of the revenge appropriate to his crime against her, namely his death. And in the end the truth is worse still: her whole effort of revenge against him has been in vain. He recovers from his injuries — even regains his sight! — and ends happy: not only with another woman, but with a woman whom Jean and her heroine would surely find threatening and antipathetic: independent and competent, decisive and rather bossy. Perhaps worst of all, Jane Eyre is plain and not at all chic, but she gets Rochester because she is better at handling men. She knows what to do, as Antoinette does not, when Rochester misuses her: she knows she must, in Christophine's words 'pack up and go' — and she does. Charlotte Brontë, of course, doesn't present Jane Eyre as a controlled, manipulative Lois Heidler — but we can guess that that is how Jean saw her.

That is why I say that when we see it, as we must, in relation to

*Jane Eyre*, *Wide Sargasso Sea* is a great work of self-justification, revenge and self-pity. But only the self-justification is here, showing us Antoinette inhumanly abused in her family, her society and her search for love. The rest, the revenge and the self-pity, are both left out of the book, both left to *another* book. For it is *Jane Eyre* which tells us that 'Bertha' dies: Antoinette is still alive on the last page of *Wide Sargasso Sea*, and we only know that her dream is enacted in reality (as it were) if we read *Jane Eyre*. In an extended but accurate sense, therefore, it is *Jane Eyre* and not *Wide Sargasso Sea* which tells us that the suicide which every Jean Rhys heroine, including Antoinette, stops short of, is the logical outcome of such treatment. Telling us this, of course, is a classic bid for sympathy: 'If you hurt me,' or 'If you leave me, I shall kill myself' is a classic piece of emotional blackmail. *Wide Sargasso Sea* plus *Jane Eyre*, therefore, *is* a bid for sympathy, a piece of emotional blackmail; at the same time, because it transfers that bid to another book, *Wide Sargasso Sea* in itself can remain an unblemished work of art.

And the revenge too is left out of *Wide Sargasso Sea*, is left to *Jane Eyre*. For remember: in *Wide Sargasso Sea* itself all that Antoinette does is dream of her revenge and set out on it: in the last line of the book she is still upstairs in her attic. It is only in *Jane Eyre*, which Jean Rhys did not write, that she leaves her prison at last and commits her violent act. Therefore, when we see *Wide Sargasso Sea* and *Jane Eyre* together we realise that the story as a whole is a fantasy of revenge: but the *Wide Sargasso Sea* section of it (if we can speak this way) is innocent. Jean Rhys's Antoinette is not a murderess, though she has enough cause to be, and though she dreams of murder; it is Bertha, who is Rochester's and Charlotte Brontë's creation, who is the murderess.

I have been suggesting that Antoinette is different from the other heroines: that she unties the Gordian knot that has bound them — that she wakes up and *acts*. And in an important sense this is true: she does at least start out to act. Anna lies still, reluctant to start again; Julia is in the hour between dog and wolf; Sasha lies in bed willing love and spring to return and accepting her neighbour instead; only Marya has (indirectly) taken her revenge, and been punished for it. But in fact Antoinette does not act either. In fact her vivid picture of fire, of Rochester calling, of her leap, is only a dream; and only *Jane Eyre* shows us that this time there was no failure, no reversal, and a Jean Rhys heroine has managed to carry out an intention at last. But of course that was no Jean Rhys heroine, but a Charlotte Brontë villain. Antoinette *only* starts out to cross the gap from dream to reality, from intention to act; in *Wide Sargasso Sea* she does not cross it. She is not, after all, the resolution of the Jean Rhys heroine, but her archetype. Her oppression and anger are the worst; and her revenge and self-destruction are the most indirect, because they are not in the book at all.

This shows us two things, I think, one about Jean and one about her last novel. It proves that what really made life intolerable to her, what drove her to drink and to write, was not other people's cruelty but her own. The great drama of all the novels is the heroine's attempt to be cruel, her failure, and her punishment anyway. The very first heroine, Marya, lashes out cruelly, but at the wrong man – and straight away she is punished and left for dead. Julia can only take her revenge through a glass darkly; Anna doesn't do so at all; Sasha fails utterly and absurdly, but is hideously punished anyway; and now, we see, Antoinette can't do it, in her own name and her own book, either.

It all goes back to the moment when Jean lost Lancelot, and made up her mind to be cold and hard forever – the moment she gave to Anna, when she feels her bracelet like a knuckleduster and knows something irrevocable has happened. That resolution, to allow the wolf in her to come out, split Jean in two and ended all possibility of action for her. From then on whatever she did would be intolerable to half of her: if she did not hate and take revenge she would seem to herself a coward; but if she did she would seem to herself a damned soul. Her cure had been, like her heroines', worse than the disease; her magic formula had run away with her, like that of the sorcerer's apprentice. She ended up almost permanently in the grip of the damned soul, yet at the same time almost unable to act at all. This dilemma she gave to her heroines: and most dramatically to Antoinette, who dreams so ferociously, who sets out, but whose act was only committed in someone else's fiction.

And about the last novel we now see this: that read together, *Wide Sargasso Sea* and *Jane Eyre* make more of a plea for our pity than any other single novel of Jean's. For read together they show us that the heroine is driven to suicide; that Antoinette cannot kill Rochester, cannot even, in the end, hurt him; that in the end she is *dead,* and Heidler/Rochester and Lois/Jane have won again. And from Jean's point of view this has all been decided, already written, a hundred years before. She has proved that the heroine never had a dog's chance: her fate is out of her own hands, and even out of her creator's. In other words, when we read *Wide Sargasso Sea* and *Jane Eyre* together we see Jean's hidden message: her heroine – her self – is a doomed and innocent victim. *But this is not the message of* Wide Sargasso Sea *taken by itself,* because the death of Antoinette and the marriage of Rochester and Jane are not there. Again, therefore, *Wide Sargasso Sea* is the supreme stroke of Jean's genius, which always lay in choosing what to leave out. It leaves out not only the things which are psychologically repellent to her — the violent revenge, the responsibility for action — but the things which are artistically repellent to us — the threat of suicide, the plea for our pity — and hands them all over, so to speak, to Charlotte Brontë.

Jean thus finds in *Jane Eyre* the way out of her *impasse* at last. Antoinette can preserve her innocence and passivity, while Bertha Mason acts. Bertha Mason's fate can encode the claim on our pity, leaving only the best features of the Jean Rhys heroine for Antoinette: her dignity and courage in adversity, her steady gaze at hell, her simple, compelling description of what it is like to be there. And Antoinette and Jean can remain in their natural element, dream, while Bertha Mason and Charlotte Brontë inhabit reality. Typically, appropriately, that is where the heroine dies: not in Jean's book, or therefore by Jean's hand, but in Charlotte's book, killed by Charlotte, who despised Bertha Mason. Again this contains a message — Jean's old message, that reality is cruel and hostile to the heroine; but again it is not in *Wide Sargasso Sea* itself, but only in *Jane Eyre*. As soon as Antoinette leaves Jean's book — which is a nightmare, but at least her own, and in which at least her creator (herself) can cherish and understand her — the cruelty of other people awaits, and long-deferred death closes in.

Finally, the key idea of *Wide Sargasso Sea* — its ending in *Jane Eyre* — solves not only the problems of responsibility and self-pity, but also the problem of time. Ever since Julia we have watched the split in the heroine loosening her hold on time. Anna lives in a kaleidoscope of past and present which finally blurs, Sasha ends in 'the No time region', in her attic Antoinette thinks 'Time has no meaning.' This dissolution of time accurately renders the heroine's disordered experience. But it is also a perfect artistic device for Jean, allowing her to transform an unnoticed receptacle into a dramatic expression of one of her major themes. The fact that *Jane Eyre* was written before *Wide Sargasso Sea*, so that the end came literally before the beginning, is a perfect image of her vision: *her heroine's suffering is inevitable and predestined.* Antoinette's story is a perfect image of all the heroines' stories: she lives painfully and without plan from day to day, while all the time her fate has been sealed by someone hostile to her, long ago.

★   ★   ★

The meaning of *Wide Sargasso Sea* is simple: the world is a terrible place. In it, especially, frail and fearful young girls, who long for love and happiness, are fated instead to rejection, persecution, madness and death. This young girl, Antoinette, is as though mesmerised from the start by her fate. She meets hatred and rejection without surprise or defence; and she glimpses their inexorable increase in her dreams, in which, though 'sick with fear',

> I make no effort to save myself; if anyone were to try to save me, I would refuse. This must happen.

Her terrible fate *must* happen: and it *has already happened* – to her mother and, in another book, to herself. Our sense of its inevitability is therefore, this time, as overpowering as hers. The murderous secret hidden just beneath the more or less pleasant surface of things, which almost revealed its name to Julia, and which finally invaded Sasha, hangs over Antoinette in everything she sees: in flowers and forests, in past and future, especially in people. The terrible fear which haunted the earlier heroines becomes Antoinette's whole world: this time she and we will have to face and understand it completely.

Part One does not shirk this task: indeed, it tells the dreadful truth clearly, both beginning and ending with swift and direct statements of it, spoken in the genuine voice of that place. Only one and a half pages into the Penguin edition of *Wide Sargasso Sea*, Godfrey says: 'The devil prince of this world, but this world don't last so long for mortal man'; and at the end we hear:

> 'Such terrible things happen,' I said. 'Why? Why?'
> 'You must not concern yourself with that mystery,' said Sister Maria Augustine. 'We do not know why the devil must have his little day. Not yet.'

Godfrey is a link with Antoinette's past, where all good things belong; and Sister Maria Augustine is the guardian of Antoinette's brief peace at the convent ('my refuge'): she tells Antoinette, truly, 'You will not be frightened of me.' They are among the very few, therefore, who will not lie or mock, and we can trust them to tell us the truth of *Wide Sargasso Sea*. It is, accordingly, that the world is a place where the devil reigns, and terrible things happen; a place from which it is therefore a deliverance to escape, even into death.

The 'terrible things that happen' are ('Isn't it quick to say. And isn't it long to live,' says Antoinette) rejection, hatred and isolation. Love, trust, and giving oneself up to someone without reserve or fear: these surely are 'the magic and the loveliness' which Rochester senses in Granbois and in Antoinette, which he loses before he has found them, and which he believes at the end to be the secret which Antoinette knows and will not tell. But the true secret of Antoinette's world is *not* love and trust – for when she gives herself up to love she is destroyed. Rather, 'the devil prince of this world', and so its secret is exactly the opposite: that self-surrender is met by rejection, trust by betrayal, and love by hate. Love does not exist in *Wide Sargasso Sea*: its 'more or less pleasant surface' slips, like a mask, like Uncle Bo's remembered face, and reveals the horror beneath: the murderous fangs, *a man who hates you.* Antoinette has been tricked into love, as she was tricked into marriage. All along its true nature has been waiting to reveal itself: as the 'nothing. Nothing. . . .' that has pursued the heroines since Julia, and which echoes in Rochester's voice at the end of Part Two. This is the fear that has always pursued Anna and Marya, the 'something huge' which pursued Julia as a child, but eluded her at her mother's funeral; this is the secret that Rochester thinks is 'not nothing', hiding beneath the surface of the world, which 'is nothing'. And it is a *Good Morning, Midnight* reversal once more: because the secret *is* nothing. Where the heroine – where even this hero – hoped to find love there is *nothing* ('Who would have thought any boy would cry like that. For nothing. Nothing.'). There is only betrayal, hatred, isolation; Sasha's slowly revolving blackness, 'No voice, no touch, no hand'.

But Antoinette, of course, has already learned this secret, and this time we have learned it with her. For *Wide Sargasso Sea* is the novel which shows us how and why the heroine is so afraid, so convinced of betrayal and hate, even before she meets them finally and fatally in 'the man who hates her' of her dream. Here we see how she has already met them: in her family, and in her society.

First of all, we see that Antoinette has lost her father to death, and her mother to alienation, poverty, and an anxious and hopeless love for Antoinette's brain-damaged brother Pierre.* Before Cosway's death, and before the doctor tells Annette the verdict on Pierre which makes her suddenly grow thin and silent, Antoinette has felt her mother could 'cover me, hide me, keep me safe. But not any longer. Not any more.' And when she tries to touch her, Annette

> pushed me away, not roughly, but calmly, coldly, without a word, as if she had decided once and for all that I was useless to her. She wanted to sit with Pierre or walk where she pleased without being pestered, she wanted peace and quiet. 'Oh, let me

---

*Dennis Porter calls Pierre a 'half wit'; Wally Look Lai calls him a 'congenital idiot'. But they are simply swallowing what Charlotte Brontë says, or what Antoinette tells Rochester that people say – and what people say in Jean's novels is never true or fair. The most reasonable conclusion from the description given by Antoinette ('Pierre . . . staggered when he walked and couldn't speak distinctly') is surely that he was (not very severely – after all, he can walk and talk) spastic, or brain-damaged at birth.

alone,' she would say, 'let me alone,' and after I knew that she talked aloud to herself I was a little afraid of her.

When she has a nightmare, her mother worries only that she has woken Pierre; when the final disaster comes, Annette thinks only of saving Pierre from the fire. Finally, Antoinette returns to her after the fire, when Annette is already half mad, and Pierre is dead:

> 'But I am here. I am here,' I said, and she said, 'No' quietly. Then 'no no no' very loudly and flung me from her. I fell against the partition and hurt myself.

Next of course, black and white society equally reject her. She is already torn between them, because although she knows she is white she prefers the warm, gay blacks; her dilemma is ironically solved when neither will accept her anyway. Most readers have concentrated on Antoinette's rejection by black people, especially in the person of Tia. And this *is* vitally important. Antoinette's first trauma is her encounter with a little black girl who follows her, singing '*Go away white cockroach, go away, go away*': it is after this that she retreats for the first time into her characteristic defence of immobility:

> When I was safely home I sat close to the old wall at the end of the garden. It was covered with green moss soft as velvet and I never wanted to move again. Everything would be worse if I moved.*

The importance of this rejection is emphasised by the repetition of its motif, exactly like a chorus, when as a young bride at Granbois Antoinette is taunted by Amélie's song:

> *The white cockroach she marry*
> *The white cockroach she marry*
> *The white cockroach she buy young man*
> *The white cockroach she marry.*

Directly after Antoinette's first experience of hatred and rejection by a black girl her own age, Christophine tries to cure her (she will always try to cure her) by introducing her to Tia. Antoinette and Tia become friends: it may be for days or for weeks, it is not clear; but it is for only one page of *Wide Sargasso Sea*. Money comes between them, as money always does throughout this and all Jean Rhys's books, and as money is a theme too in Amélie's song. The pennies that Christophine has given Antoinette shine 'like gold': and if gold

*Compare *Voyage in the Dark*: 'It's funny how you think, "It won't hurt until I move," so you sit perfectly still.'

is the idol the English worship, as Antoinette says, the black people too 'know about money.' Tia covets the pennies; she takes them when Antoinette comes up choking, after the underwater somersault Tia has bet her she couldn't do. This brief scene synthesises perennial Jean Rhys themes and images in a startlingly complete way: the 'gold in the sun' that sows envy even between children; the heroine's failure to perform quite perfectly, which is instantly met by betrayal — for Tia cheats, taking the money just because Antoinette 'hadn't done it good'; the rise of hate and self-protective lies in the heroine: 'Keep them then, you cheating nigger.... I can get more if I want to'; above all, the identification of losing money and beautiful clothes with the loss of status and self-respect. By taking her money and her dress Tia changes places with Antoinette, indeed leaves her lower than she herself had ever been:

> Real white people, they got money.... Old time white people nothing but white nigger now, and black nigger better than white nigger.

It is interesting that at this low point, when Antoinette has become the 'white nigger' that the Luttrells will laugh at, the imagery of drowning reappears: 'it certainly look like I drown dead that time.'* Antoinette's deaths, spiritual and (in *Jane Eyre*) physical, will be by fire — active, flamboyant, her spirit leaping to meet its fate: here, in her shameful social abasement, she reverts to the cold, wet, ugly death that dogged the earlier heroines.

The other scenes in which Antoinette is subjected to cruelty and rejection by the blacks to whom she feels so close are also important. There is the terrible attack on the house; the famous scene in which Antoinette runs to Tia, thinking 'I will live with Tia and I will be like her,' only to be met by the stone Tia throws; the encounter with the black girl and the half-caste boy, in which they taunt her with being crazy, the zombie daughter of a zombie mother; and later, the taunts of Amélie, which culminate in a dreadful echo of the 'changing places' Antoinette rehearsed with Tia, when Amélie takes her place in Rochester's bed. After each rejection she suffers some form of traumatic reaction. After the fire and the final rejection by Tia, she is ill for six weeks; after the encounter outside the convent she cries hysterically; after Amélie sings '*White cockroach*' she seems to imagine she's back at Coulibri during the fire, and tears her sheet into strips as Aunt Cora tore her petticoat for Pierre; and of course after she has to listen to Rochester's night with Amélie, she begins in earnest her retreat into madness.

*Antoinette is quoting Tia's words.

There is no doubt, therefore, that the steps of Antoinette's rejection and suffering at the hands of black people are crucial to her loss of self and sanity. The scene with Tia, in particular, is rightly read as a dramatic picture of Antoinette's fundamental identification of herself with black rather than white society:

> As I ran, I thought, I will live with Tia and I will be like her. Not to leave Coulibri. Not to go. Not. When I was close I saw the jagged stone in her hand but I did not see her throw it. I did not feel it either, only something wet, running down my face. I looked at her and I saw her face crumple up as she began to cry. We stared at each other, blood on my face, tears on hers. It was as if I saw myself. Like in a looking-glass.

It's as though Tia was her good 'twin', her good 'dark' side: not a hating wolf, but a warm gay girl who fits into the natural world. This split in the heroine came first, therefore (for Antoinette here is years younger than Anna, when she split into dog and wolf at nineteen). The split which destroys her is between her conscious controlled self and her dark impulses to anger and cruelty. But there has been this earlier split, between her conscious, controlled 'white' self and the gay, natural — and socially inferior — 'black' self identified with Tia. It has happened at the same point as Anna's attempt to die in *Voyage in the Dark* — on the edge of adolescence: clearly it is linked to the heroine's disturbed and disturbing sexuality. At her only moments of sexual happiness she becomes again like a black slave — '*Maillotte Boyd, aged 18*', and a bare-legged girl in a hot country. It is this lost or suppressed Tia in the heroine to whom the Englishmen from Heidler to Rochester are so irresistibly but reluctantly, and finally fatally, drawn ('She is Creole girl,' says Christophine, 'and she have the sun in her').

It is true, therefore, that Antoinette's experiences of rejection from black people are important, more numerous and often more dramatic than her sufferings at the hands of other whites. But it seems to me that in the end they are not *more* important. Whether she likes it or not Antoinette is white, and her future is with white people; she would have been happier and wholer if it could have been with the blacks — or, even better, with those metaphorically and otherwise in between, like herself. But part of what Jean is showing us is that, in this devil's world, that is impossible. As Amélie says,

> 'I hear one time that Miss Antoinette and ... Mr Sandi get married, but that all foolishness. Miss Antoinette a white girl with a lot of money, she won't marry with a coloured man even though he don't look like a coloured man.'

Amélie's intentions are malicious, but she is telling the truth about a divided society.

Despite her feelings for black people, therefore, it is inevitably Antoinette's expulsion from white society that leaves her homeless, and that moves her inexorably towards her future and her destruction. Thus, it is after her first experience of alienation from *white* society that she has her first clairvoyant dream, in which, in chilling hallucinatory images, she glimpses her death by hate. She comes home wearing Tia's dress, only to find that for the first time in years her mother has smart white visitors.

> They were very beautiful I thought and they wore such beautiful clothes that I looked away down at the flagstones and when they laughed — the gentleman laughed the loudest — I ran into the house, into my bedroom. There I stood with my back against the door and I could feel my heart all through me.

Antoinette's wearing Tia's dress — again that symbolism of clothes — is the visible sign that she is already different from other white people, already, because of her poverty and exile, a 'white nigger', unable to 'fit in'. The scene is, indeed, a seminal Jean Rhys experience: the poor outcast white girl, half black or worse than black; mocked and laughed at by the 'beautiful' and beautifully dressed white people, and especially by the white 'gentleman'. This shame at being poor, badly dressed, and so unable to be attractive to 'gentlemen' unbearably haunts every Jean Rhys heroine. Its terrible effect on Antoinette is not stated openly, as it sometimes is in the earlier novels ('About clothes, it's awful'); instead, it emerges from the structure of her descent into hell. For immediately after this terrible experience of shame she has her first clairvoyant dream:

> All that evening my mother didn't speak to me or look at me and I thought, 'She is ashamed of me, what Tia said is true.' I went to bed early and slept at once. I dreamed that I was walking in the forest. Not alone. Someone who hated me was with me, out of sight. I could hear heavy footsteps coming closer and though I struggled and screamed I could not move. I woke crying.

The experience of betrayal and loss with Tia is terrible, and makes her feel sick and cold. But it is the experience of social shame in front of her own, white society — and her belief that her mother feels that shame too — that makes her drop through to another level of experience altogether: to a clairvoyant insight into her future of hatred and fear. 'I woke next morning knowing that nothing would be the same. It would change and go on changing.' From now on she is unstoppably on the road to Thornfield Hall.

The second time she has the dream is similar to the first. It is not, as we might perhaps expect, after the climactic attack by the black people on her family at Coulibri. Rather, it is at the very end of Part One, after Antoinette's eighteen months' refuge at Mount Calvary Convent; it happens after Mr Mason tells her 'You can't be hidden away all your life,' and says that he has 'asked some English friends to spend next winter here':

> It may have been the way he smiled, but again a feeling of dismay, sadness, loss almost choked me. This time I did not let him see it.... The girls were very curious but I would not answer their questions and for the first time I resented the nuns' cheerful faces.
> They are safe. How can they know what it can be like *outside*?
> This was the second time I had my dream.

Once again what has happened is that white society has refused to let her stay 'inside'; she cannot, like the nuns and the other girls, remain inside the convent, or inside all the other 'thick walls' which will protect them from the things she will have to fight — that is, the strange and hostile world. She is pushed out, into the arms of Rochester, who will hate her. And that is when she has her dream, her vision of where, inexorably, this will lead her.

This truth — that it is her expulsion from white society, even more than from black, which makes Antoinette feel most alone and afraid — sums up Jean's ambivalent attitude to 'white' people — that is, English people — in her writing.

They are quintessentially cold, judging, cruel and hypocritical; but on the other hand they are also safe, peaceful and calm. Thus, for example, at the end Antoinette thinks:

> That afternoon we went to England. There was grass and olive green water and tall trees looking into the water. This, I thought, is England. If I could be here I could be well again and the sound in my head would stop.

This calmness and security of England makes her 'glad to be an English girl' when Mr Mason rescues them ('but I missed the taste of Christophine's cooking'); it is the reason why 'The Miller's Daughter' is her favourite picture ('a lovely English girl with brown curls and blue eyes and a dress slipping off her shoulders'). In fact, if she could only *be* English, be accepted by the English, perhaps the Jean Rhys heroine would have been content — perhaps Jean would have been happy, and would never have become a writer. Perhaps neither would have hated England, if only it had accepted and returned her love. Even as it is, it remains a haven of envied security and ease — and in the Englishmen she meets she keeps falling back in love with it, and trying to find, through them, her way back in. Why else on earth does the sharp, honest, and ironic heroine keep falling for these conventional, self-contained and self-deceiving Walters, Hughs and Georges? Because she is not drawn only to black life: instead, as always, she is torn between two equal and opposite desires, for excitement, but also for safety. She loves 'black' life, passion, openness and adventure. But this way is dangerous − if you gamble, you may lose. She desires what we all secretly desire: the excitement of the gamble, without the risk of loss. As Cairn says in *Quartet*: 'You've got to be either an *arriviste* or a *je m'en fichiste* in this world. But if you're a *je m'en fichiste* you've got to be able to stand the racket afterwards.' The Jean Rhys heroine is a *je m'en fichiste* who can't stand the racket afterwards. And so she is drawn back to the white way. It is sane and safe; it risks nothing and loses nothing. And so she both despises and desires it. She despises it for its cowardice and self-induced stupidity, and for the ruthlessness with which it protects itself from those who threaten it: that is, from those like her. But when she is at her most desperate, she allows 'white' people − even the Heidlers! − to close ranks around her, with a sigh of a relief.

It is wrong, though, to imagine that this could last forever either. Her honesty and irony, her restlessness and self-distrust will soon combine to drive her out again. They always did.

We come then to Antoinette's final experience of rejection, in Part Two of *Wide Sargasso Sea*. Rochester has married Antoinette without love, in cold blood; he has briefly surrendered to desire and even to the beginnings of love; but his 'little love' has died under the blows of jealousy, suspicion and humiliation delivered by Daniel − and perhaps too because Antoinette is really too far gone in fear and withdrawal to change him. She has tried in the end to do so through *obeah*, and Rochester has taken his revenge through Amélie ('Yes, that didn't just happen. I meant it'). By the end of this, Antoinette's transformation into Bertha Mason is complete:

> Her hair hung uncombed and dull into her eyes which were inflamed and staring, her face was very flushed and looked swollen.

She drinks, she bites, she is full of hate and murder; and then she is quite empty, a ghost. This final rejection has made her mad.

A central exploration of the connection for the Jean Rhys heroine between the last gamble of romantic love and final psychic death occurs at the height of their happiness, when Rochester has come as close as he can to self-forgetfulness and love ('... I have forgotten caution'). The heroine has of course only the briefest taste of this happiness: almost immediately the mask of the world slips, and Daniel's letter arrives. But at the height of their 'short youth' Jean compresses her view of the fate of her heroine into a characteristic metaphor. For her, love is life itself; without love, existence is merely 'a long time to wait before it's over': 'I never wished to live before I knew you,' Antoinette says. 'I always thought it would be better if I died. Such a long time to wait before it's over.' And yet, in this world where the devil is prince, love is, secretly, also death: because when you think you are offering yourself up to love, in fact you are offering yourself up to death by denial and rejection. As Rochester says: 'Desire, Hatred, Life, Death come very close in the darkness. . . . Not close. The same. . .'. Antoinette, characteristically, does not say or even think this: but she and Jean express it in the metaphor of her game of dying.

She has been afraid from the start that Rochester's love will be the last and worst 'pleasant surface' to hide cruel fangs beneath: 'I am afraid of what may happen,' she has said, when he asked her why she did not wish to marry him. She is still afraid, or even more afraid, now.

> 'Why did you make me want to live? Why did you do that to me?'
>
> 'Because I wished it. Isn't that enough?'
>
> 'Yes, it is enough. But if one day you didn't wish it. What should I do then? Suppose you took this happiness away when I wasn't looking. . . .'
>
> 'And lose my own? Who'd be so foolish?'
>
> 'I am not used to happiness,' she said. 'It makes me afraid.'

And so she plays at cheating this real, emotional death by dying 'Now, when I am happy.' 'Say die,' she tells Rochester, 'and I will die.' This game of death is one of Jean's central images, expressing one of her most powerful ideas: that 'There are always two deaths, the real one and the one people know about'; and that the real one is emotional or spiritual death, which comes with the end of all hope of love. Compared to that, physical death ('the one people know about') is unimportant. Thus, at the beginning of her writing life, in *The Left Bank*, she drew Carlo, who has missed the chance to die with her lover at the height of their love:

> Oh God, what a fool I was — what a fool! To have been so close to a sweet death and to have pushed it away! Because I was frightened. And went on living — to be a wreck! And to grow old — and to be the butt of a lot of thick fools — I clung on to mean, silly life.'*

*'The Blue Bird', *The Left Bank*.

It was a moment of aberration for Carlo to fear physical death; she already knows, and later tastes that knowledge to the dregs, that the fear of life without love is far more rational. It is far better to die happy than to exist without love. This is not, of course, an original idea; Colette, for example, writes brilliantly of women who so fear the loss of love that they try to throw it away, so as to forestall its being taken from them. But the Jean Rhys heroine – so 'intense', so 'unbalanced', so damaged by her earlier deaths – goes as always a step further than a whole woman would go. Renée in Colette's *The Vagabond,* for instance, merely tries not to love Maxime, and to stop him from loving her; Antoinette dreams of dying. At the same time, of course, she only *dreams* of dying, and at her lover's command. In other words, however negatively and fearfully, Renée acts; Antoinette, even in her deepest intuitions of what she will not be able to bear, only play-acts. And yet this inability to act is at the same time a measure of how the endorsement of love really is a matter of life and death for her: without the love she needs she is already half dead, a ghost, unable to act on the living.

This sense of the death-dealingness of the loss of love, then, though not unique to Jean's fiction, is uniquely intense and 'unbalanced' there. And since to love in her world is always to lose, love, at Granbois, *is* death. This is behind the metaphor of Antoinette's game, and it is confirmed by Rochester, when he wonders what the secret of Granbois is:

> ... always this talk of death. (Is she trying to tell me that is the secret of this place? ...)

'She knows, she knows,' he tells himself, just as at the end he repeats that Antoinette is among those who 'know the secret and will not tell it'. At the end the secret is 'magic and loveliness', which he has 'lost before I found it': love and happiness. Now he thinks it may be death. And it *is* also death: they are, as he says, not close, but the same.

Of course, what Rochester himself identifies with death at Granbois is not love but *desire*: 'Desire, Hatred, Life, Death came very close in the darkness.' With wonderful economy Jean distils here her idea of men – of Englishmen – and the way they cheat and betray her heroines' offer of love. Again, it is not an original or even rare idea; but it is presented so originally and subtly that its truth transcends cliché and reservation. It is that men rob love with sex; that they respond to a woman's offer of her self with the offer of their bodies. It is presented in a brief sketch: in the scene in which Rochester agrees to play Antoinette's 'game', but turns it into quite a different game, his own.

'Die then! Die!' I watched her die many times. In my way, not hers. In sunlight, in shadow, by moonlight, by candlelight. In the long afternoons when the house was empty. Only the sun was there to keep us company. We shut him out. And why not? Very soon she was as eager for what's called loving as I was — more lost and drowned afterwards.

In these few short words Rochester transforms her way into his. He turns death into orgasm, the little death — he can only die a little because he can only love a little; he turns love into sex — 'what's called loving'. Poor Antoinette: to her love and sex are surely inextricable; in any case, the only love she's ever had from Rochester has been sexual. It is natural, therefore, that she should try to win back his love through sex — and, of course, it is doomed. For as Christophine says, 'If the man don't love you I can't make him love you.... Even if I can make him come to your bed, I cannot make him love you; afterward he hate you.' Antoinette cannot afford to believe that. At last she rouses herself to act, and gives him Christophine's potion: and, as always in Jean Rhys, achieves only her own destruction.

These deep and fateful differences between Jean Rhys men and Jean Rhys women are perfectly treated in *Wide Sargasso Sea*: glancingly and without emphasis, through compression and metaphor. So she treats them here, in Rochester's and Antoinette's love-making; and again later, in the final confrontation between Rochester and Christophine. In the middle of their fierce battle of wills Christophine suddenly laughs — 'a hearty, merry laugh'. For, she says, when she undressed Antoinette she saw that Rochester had been 'very rough with her': and, in an extraordinarily contrasted mood of relaxed humour and digression, she tells him of the man who chopped off his wife's nose with a machete.

'I hold it on, I send a boy running for the doctor and the doctor came galloping at dead of night to sew up the woman.... By this time the man crying like a baby. He says, "Doctor, I didn't mean it. It just happened." "I know, Rupert," the doctor says, "but it mustn't happen again. Why don't you keep the damn machete in the other room?" he says. They have two small rooms only so I say, "No, doctor — it much worse near the bed. They chop each other up in no time at all." The doctor he laugh and laugh.'

'All that is a little thing,' she says, ' — it's nothing.' In other words, for her and for Antoinette physical injury, even physical death, is little, is nothing, as long as there is love. For Rochester it is love itself which is little, and which is nothing. That is surely the point of this digression, this striking change of pace and tone: that pain and death are matters of the spirit, not the body, because the body can neither give love nor take it away. The fiercest of love's fierce play will not break Antoinette: 'It's not for that she have the look of death on her face.' Only hate can do that: not a man's body, but his hating self. This truth comes out in the man's own words, in the middle of the most compressed and poetic passage of the novel:

> I could not touch her. Excepting as the hurricane will touch that tree — and break it. You say I did? No. That was love's fierce play. Now I'll do it.

The central insight of *Wide Sargasso Sea* is, therefore, into the death of the soul or self. This death is, from the outside, madness: and the central insight of *Wide Sargasso Sea* is, accordingly, into the genesis and nature of madness. Its genesis lies in the repeated unmasking of the world's secret cruelty and hate; and especially its last unmasking, in the person of a man whom the heroine loves, but who hates her. Its nature is once again best expressed by Jean in a metaphor, this time one quite brilliantly borrowed from *obeah* superstitions: the idea of a *zombie*.

The black children who torment Antoinette on her way to school explicitly identify madness with the idea of a zombie:

> 'Look the crazy girl, you crazy like your mother ... she have eyes like zombie, and you have eyes like zombie too.'

And the day Antoinette goes to Christophine in despair at losing Rochester, Christophine evokes the same image:

> 'Your face is like a dead woman and your eyes like a soucriant.'

(A soucriant is another word for a zombie.)

This is the definition of a zombie which Rochester finds in his book, *The Glittering Coronet of Isles*:

> A zombie is a dead person who seems to be alive, or a living person who is dead.

And that is a precise picture of Jean Rhys's idea of madness: a live body containing a dead soul; a person who has not yet suffered 'the death people know about', but who has suffered the real death, perhaps more than once. The European version of a zombie is of course a ghost: and a ghost is what Rochester calls Antoinette after he has deprived her of all feeling, even hate:

> ... she was only a ghost. A ghost in the grey daylight.... Say die and I will die.... She lifted her eyes. Blank lovely eyes. Mad eyes. A mad girl.

The zombie, or the ghost — the living dead — sums up Jean's main point about madness, or emotional death: that it is the real death, so that after it, the sooner physical death comes the better. Even Rochester seems to understand this, for when Antoinette says her piece about there always being two deaths, he replies: 'Two at least.... for the fortunate.' That is, if you are fortunate you will die only twice, once in the spirit and once in the flesh; the flesh *can* only die once, but the spirit can die many times. Antoinette is not one of the fortunate: she has already died in spirit several times before she met Rochester, and she will die this way several times more. He reduces her to a zombie; but she will still be able to seize a brief respite with Sandi, an even briefer attempt at escape, a long imprisonment and two acts of hatred and revenge before her final immolation. That is to say, she spends many years *mad*, before the liberation of death. That is why physical death *is* a liberation from living death, which is worse than mere burial. We can now understand the full meaning of Godfrey's words at the start of the novel: 'The devil prince of this world,' he'd said, 'but this world don't last so long for mortal man.' That 'but' shows that the world's not lasting long for mortal man is not a consequence but a consolation. Once you have died the real death, the less long the world lasts for you the more fortunate you are. Antoinette has no true autonomous death wish, but only a desperate desire for life and love; once that is beyond hope, however, she does wish for burial. (And for the heroine, as always, we can read Jean.)

Being mad, then, for the Jean Rhys heroine, is being a zombie: physically alive, but really dead. Now, there is something which keeps the zombie physically alive — and yet at the same time also spiritually dead. It is what we have seen before, in *After Leaving Mr Mackenzie* and *Good Morning, Midnight*: *hatred*, the return of the hate, rejection and murder which she has suffered. This is terribly clear in *Wide Sargasso Sea*. When we first see Antoinette as Bertha Mason, flushed, swollen and rambling, she is, for the first time, filled not with fear or pain but hate:

> 'I hate Granbois now like I hate you and before I die I will show you how much I hate you....'
> She smashed another bottle against the wall and stood with the broken glass in her hand and murder in her eyes.
> 'Just you touch me once. You'll soon see if I'm a dam' coward like you are....'

In just the same way, and in almost the same words, had Annette screamed at Mr Mason, after he had killed what she loved, Coulibri and Pierre: 'Don't touch me. I'll kill you if you touch me. Coward. Hypocrite. I'll kill you.'

Once again the echo and parallel between the two stories, Antoinette's and her mother's, make a pattern in our minds which convinces us that this is how madness is, not just for Antoinette, but for anyone at all like her.

When the madwoman is deprived of her fuel of hate, she is utterly dead, reduced to nothing, her 'zombie' state complete.

> You hate me and I hate you [says Rochester]. We'll see who hates best. But first, first I will destroy your hatred. Now. My hate is colder, stronger, and you'll have no hate to warm yourself. You will have nothing.
>
> I did it too. I saw the hate go out of her eyes. I forced it out. And with the hate her beauty. She was only a ghost. A ghost in the grey daylight.

This is the final step in the enfeeblement and death of the self: a sort of catatonia, a state of utter indifference and alienation. Without her hate to warm her, Antoinette falls into this state. And yet Rochester can never finally murder her: always her hate slowly returns, to 'warm' her again, to bring her back from catatonia to a living death, kept alive by a flame of hatred, like the woman on the floor above Julia. Thus, even after years at Thornfield Hall, Grace Poole tells us, 'she hasn't lost her spirit' − which is clearly the spirit of murder and revenge:

> She's still fierce. I don't turn my back when her eyes have that look. I know it.

And of course Grace Poole is right: she lets her vigilance lapse only rarely, but when she does Antoinette tries to kill Richard Mason, and then Rochester. Her hatred and desire for revenge end only with 'the death people know about' − that is, with her actual physical death, in the inferno of Thornfield Hall.

One of my aims in this book has been − however reluctantly − to take issue with the optimistic reading of the direction of Jean's work as a whole. Many critics have argued that in both form and content the novels move through a positive progression, from rejection and despair to a final reassertion of the possibility of love and compassion between men and women.* The form of the last novel, they argue, with its dedication of a whole third to Rochester's point of view, shows the final triumph of Jean's own compassion for the other, the hostile male

*E.g. Elizabeth Abel, Louis James, Elgin Mellown, Thomas Staley.

stranger. I have already argued that this interpretation of *Good Morning, Midnight* is wrong-headed; that it is blind and deaf to the *feeling* of that novel, and in particular to the horror of its ending. I agree that the form of *Wide Sargasso Sea* demonstrates an increased willingness in Jean to try to see the other's, the man's, point of view. But first of all this attempt shows characteristic limitations. Second and more importantly, it is still an attempt to see the point of view of someone who is defined, *vis à vis* the heroine, not as husband, lover, friend or even enemy – but simply and starkly as either destroyer or destroyed. And even without *Jane Eyre* it is clear that he is the destroyer, Antoinette the destroyed. She is, again, the archetypal Jean Rhys heroine: not different, but the same. Her voyage is as much in the dark as Anna's, as much towards nothing as Julia's, as much towards failed revenge and death as Marya's and Sasha's. It is the same voyage, from oppression and rejection to intolerable anger and hate; from failed revenge to self-punishment and death. It's true that there is a fierce triumph in her end – but only because her imprisonment has been worse. She welcomes death, because she is really, spiritually, dead already.

There are really four stages of this voyage in the dark towards death, and only *Wide Sargasso Sea* clearly and thoroughly explores them all. First, the child's natural love and trust are met with hate and rejection: we've glimpsed this in *Voyage in the Dark*, but see it plain in Part One here. Second, from her deep hurt she starts to hate back (again also in *Voyage in the Dark*). Third, because rejection has half killed her already, she takes refuge in indifference and passivity (rehearsed especially in *After Leaving Mr Mackenzie*). And fourth, she receives the final and worst rejection of all, in love (rehearsed especially in *Quartet*). At last she returns hate and rejection (rehearsed in *Good Morning, Midnight*). But for her hatred is destructive, intolerable, one of the things which split her in two: it keeps her alive, but it also keeps her mad. The only way out for her is final, physical death.

The first stage, Antoinette's rejection by her family and her community, we have already followed. The second stage follows immediately that rejection is complete: she withdraws from people, and begins to hate.

> ... I went to parts of Coulibri that I had not seen, where there was no road, no path, no track. And if the razor grass cut my legs and arms I would think 'It's better than people.' Black ants or red ones, tall nests swarming with white ants, rain that soaked me to the skin – once I saw a snake. All better than people. Better. Better, better than people.

Like the other heroines – like Anna with her knuckle-duster – the moment she begins to hate is also the moment she begins to split.

Better. Better, better than people. Watching the red and yellow flowers in the sun thinking of nothing, it was as if a door opened and I was somewhere else, something else. Not myself any longer.

I knew the time of day when though it is hot and blue and there are no clouds, the sky can have a very black look.

The third stage afflicts Antoinette in her refuge, the convent — which is therefore both a peaceful haven and yet also a place of death. Life becomes a series of tricks she can learn, to hide and detach herself: the trick of saying her prayers without meaning them, the trick of washing and dressing without touching, or others seeing, her body. In these simple and precise images we see Antoinette losing touch with her real thinking and feeling self: so that when that self asks, 'But what about happiness.... is there no happiness?', the new protective, indifferent self answers: 'Oh happiness of course, happiness, well ... I soon forgot about happiness.'

One cannot imagine how her growing passivity and impassivity could be more poignantly expressed, but it is. In the scene just before this, Aunt Cora, whose love and protection have been so vital for her, tells her she is leaving:

> One hot afternoon in July my aunt told me that she was going to England for a year. Her health was not good and she needed a change. As she talked she was working at a patchwork counterpane. The diamond-shaped pieces of silk melted one into the other, red, blue, purple, green, yellow, all one shimmering colour. Hours and hours she had spent on it and it was nearly finished. Would I be lonely? she asked and I said 'No,' looking at the colours. Hours and hours and hours I thought.

This is extraordinarily fine: nothing is said, but all is conveyed. The colours, which are the colours of her home and herself,* melt into one undifferentiated shimmer; her response to her aunt's 'Will you be lonely?' is lifeless, indifferent; she dwells on the 'hours and hours and hours' Cora has spent on the counterpane as a substitute for the months and months and months she will have to be alone. In other words: she distracts herself, and she will not feel.

Together with detachment and indifference comes a growing sense of inevitability, of fate: the pattern of her destiny, like the pattern of the counterpane, is nearly finished. Very soon she cannot feel at all, even if she wants to:

*'We can colour the roses as we choose and mine are green, blue and purple. Underneath I will write my name in fire red....'

My mother died last year, no one told me how, and I didn't ask ... Christophine cried bitterly but I could not. I prayed, but the words fell to the ground meaning nothing.

After this she tries to remain safe, if alone and alienated, behind her wall of indifference, to meet Rochester 'with silence and a blank face', 'silence and coldness'. But these 'poor weapons' do not last long; and soon she is plunged into the fourth and final stage of her spiritual death, which we have already explored: surrender and loss; hatred, madness, and self-destruction.

This end has been fated and previsioned many times over, in many books. In *Wide Sargasso Sea* itself, in Antoinette's dream; in *Jane Eyre*; and obsessively, in detail, in Jean's earlier novels. Julia is the exception here, because she never comes to life at all. But Anna, Marya and Sasha all rehearse exactly the last part of Antoinette's story. All are half-dead already when their lovers meet them (with an air of 'fatigue, disillusion and extreme youth, ... shadowed eyes, ... pathetic and unconscious lapses into helplessness.') All are briefly brought to life by love. But finally all are abandoned again to a death-in-life made even more intolerable by their brief glimpse of escape ('But if one day you didn't wish it. What should I do then?'). Anna has many, Marya several, months with their lovers; but Sasha's return to life has been reduced to a few moments. Antoinette, we know, was to have had only a week, and has only a few. It has thus got steadily worse, but it has always been the same story: the sleeping beauty is brought back to life by the prince's kiss, only to lose him, and life, again.

Sasha, the oldest heroine, and the apotheosis of the pig, is the furthest away from Antoinette, the apotheosis of the lily. Yet their love stories are the closest of all. Both try to hold back, try not to love and trust 'a beautiful young man'. Both succumb to the temptation of love and are — painfully — brought back to life. Then both lose him again; and both try to call him back to their beds by a kind of magic. Sasha's mental magic brings her not René but the *commis*; and Antoinette's *obeah* magic doesn't really bring her Rochester either. He is drugged, 'not himself' ('I remember saying in a voice that was not like my own that it was too light. I remember putting out the candles on the table near the bed and that is all I remember. All I will remember of the night.') If he gave her little enough love before, what he gives her that night is much closer to hate, and soon becomes hate forever. Both Antoinette and Sasha, when they will their lovers to come back, live out Antoinette's clairvoyant dream: they receive instead a hating stranger. That terrible fate is also, once again, like that of Antoinette's mother, who is at the end of her story the sexual prey of several hating strangers. Antoinette explicitly draws the parallel

between her mother and the black man, and Rochester and herself:
'. . . a black devil kissing her sad mouth. Like you kissed mine,' she
says. Rochester making love to Antoinette when he hates her, the
black man debauching Annette, and the *commis* entering Sasha's room
and bed, are all part of the same horrifying vision: the final rape of
the heroine's humanity and soul, the final surrender to psychic death,
as she accepts into herself hate and nothingness, madness and
degradation, forever. *That*, Jean tells us not once but over and over,
is the end of her story.

★　　★　　★

*The problem of Part Two:* The most important point about the design
of *Wide Sargasso Sea* is that its middle part is told, not by the heroine,
but by the 'hating stranger', Rochester. This is, of course, the most
significant new departure in Jean's method, which has always − with
the exception of a few lines or a few pages − focused on the heroine's
point of view. The question which must arise, therefore, is: how
successful is Part Two of *Wide Sargasso Sea?*

The *principle* of giving this section to Rochester to tell makes vital
sense: first, because it relieves Antoinette of the burden of 'harrowing'
us with the worst suffering of her life; and second, because this
structure itself shows that rejectors as well as rejected have a point of
view. But how successful is Jean at fulfilling her promise − that is, at
actually giving us Rochester's point of view?

The answer is, I think, both very successful, and yet not quite. She
does for the first time show that men too, even Englishmen, need love
and are hurt by its loss. At the end of the novel 'Mrs Eff' tells us that
Rochester is not a mere archetypal Jean Rhys Englishman, rich, smug,
and cold; and Part Two shows us convincingly that this is true. He
learned to hide his feelings when he was a small child, Rochester says:
but he still *has* them. Despite himself he listens to music he has 'never
heard before.' It is utterly strange to him, but *he wants the secret* of this
place and of this girl. He tells us and he tells Antoinette that he does
not love her; but he admits to himself just once, when it is safely past,
that he did: '*Love her as I did − oh yes I did. . . .*'

He does what Jean Rhys men can do: he divides desire from love,
and mostly admits to one but not the other. But there are 'blanks in
his mind that cannot be filled up,' things he cannot remember or
admit. And what Jean allows him to tell us shows that he came closer
to love with Antoinette than he will ever afterwards want to think.
At the end, for instance, he thinks 'Antoinetta − I can be gentle too.
Hide your face. Hide yourself but in my arms. You'll soon see how
gentle. . . .' He feels that 'Only the magic and the dream are true,'

and he says to her, 'I have made a terrible mistake. Forgive me.'* Even when she answers him with hate, and he returns it so well that she goes mad for good — even then he thinks, 'Give not one-third but everything.... Keep nothing back,' and 'I don't know what I would have said or done. In the balance — everything.'

*Rochester could have loved Antoinette*: what stopped him was nothing simply mean or cold, but rather fear. Fear of passion, and of the loss of control and independence which that would unleash; fear of being drowned in Antoinette's world of boundless 'black' self-surrender. To that extent his fear is 'English' and opposed to the Jean Rhys heroine's. But otherwise it is just like hers. He fears, for example, betrayal and humiliation, just as she does ('You deceived me, you betrayed me'). He fears and suspects people, just as she does ('I thought I saw the same expression on all their faces. Curiosity? Pity? Ridicule?'; 'Wherever I went I would be talked about'). In fact he makes the same mistake as the previous Jean Rhys heroine. He doesn't let himself trust Antoinette, as Sasha doesn't let herself trust René; he will not believe in her love for him, as Sasha will not believe in René's ('she thirsts for *anyone* — not for me'). He does want her: 'What will I care for gods or devils or for Fate itself. If she smiles or weeps or both. *For me.*' He wants her so much he can't let anyone else have her ('A pang of rage and jealousy shot through me'; 'she'll have no lover, for I don't want her and she'll see no other'). But he is like her, or like Sasha: they both lose their chance of love, because neither will trust the other.

And isn't Antoinette, indeed, like this too? I think there is a suggestion that she is: that their love fails because they are *both* too afraid, neither really given up to the secret of love and trust. This may be the meaning of the cryptic thought we overhear in Rochester's last conversation with Christophine. She has said: '... all you want is to break her up':

> (*Not the way you mean, I thought*)
> 'But she hold out, eh? She hold out.'
> (*Yes, she held out. A pity*)....

Could this not mean that it was Antoinette's *coldness and silence* Rochester wished would not hold out: that he had wished she would entirely give up her attempt to resist love and trust, and that he felt she had not? Could it not mean, in fact, that, like Sasha, Antoinette herself is partly responsible for the loss of love, because she herself will not take the chance of betrayal, any more than Rochester will?

---

*He does seem actually to say it to her: 'I knew what I would say. "I have made a terrible mistake. Forgive me." *I said it*, looking at her, seeing the hatred in her eyes....'

This lone elliptical remark of Rochester's may seem slim evidence to go on. But consider too that Jean does tell us that Antoinette betrays him, when she tries to trick him into loving her ('Nearby a cock crowed and I thought, "That is for betrayal ..."'); and add these points to the other evidence of his temptations to let go and love Antoinette: then I think the possibility is at least intriguing that it is partly Antoinette herself who has lost the chance of real love with Rochester. It is true that Rochester becomes a monster to her at the end — but then so (in *Jane Eyre*) does she to him: it is a battle (as the Jean Rhys woman's battles always are) to the death. But Part Two, supported by the rest of the text, shows us that Rochester does not destroy Antoinette out of inhumanity and the abuse of power, but out of human weakness; and *perhaps*, if she had been more — and not less — open to love, it need never have happened.

So far, then, Part Two is successful at putting before us, with a good deal of sympathy, Rochester's point of view. But it's already clear that the sympathy moves along lines familiar to us: Jean has given us an Englishman who is sympathetic because he is *like the heroine*. He is weak and afraid, like her; and for the same reason as her: because he has been hurt before, and in the same way. Both are rejected children, rejected by a parent in favour of a brother. Note, too, that the same is true — at least in his own mind — of Daniel Cosway, rejected by his father in favour of his half-brother Alexander. Partly we may see in these parallels between Antoinette and her destroyers the corollary of the greater kindness in Jean's world, in Christophine and Aunt Cora: the understanding that the strong more often sustain than destroy, and that it is the weak and already damaged who pass on hate and pain.* But partly it may be the other thing as well: Jean's characteristic inability to inhabit any sympathetic point of view but her own.

If the only similarity between Antoinette and Rochester were in their histories and sufferings we could believe that it was only and entirely a deliberate, and successful, artistic device. But it extends beyond that. Rochester may not be the archetypal Jean Rhys Englishman, but he is still meant to be a typical Jean Rhys male: conventional in his thinking ('Of course, of course I believe in the power and wisdom of my creator'); materialist in his ambitions ('Your husband certainly love money ... money have pretty face for

---

*This may not always work: Rochester's favoured brother, we hear, has 'round conceited eyes', and may indeed be a Heidler. But it could be confirmed by Sandi, son of Alexander: Alexander, we know, was loved by his father, and Alexander prospered; now his son Sandi is strong, protective and loving to Antoinette.

everybody: but for that man money pretty like pretty self'); above all, rational and 'clever' in an abstract, non-intuitive way ('Slavery was not a matter of liking or disliking . . .'). *But far too often his experience sounds like Antoinette's*, or Jean's own, rather than that of such a man. Thus, for example, on the morning they set out for Granbois, he tells us that he

> got up very early and saw the women with trays covered with white cloths on their heads going to the kitchen. The woman with small hot loaves for sale, the woman with cakes, the woman with sweets. In the street another called *Bon sirop, Bon sirop*, and I felt peaceful.

This sudden, sensuous and unexplained sweep of feeling across the mind is so like Antoinette, so unlike what we know of Rochester. And why should the strange black voice in a strange language soothe him? – while of course it *would* soothe Antoinette, with its associations of black women in the kitchen: that is, with Christophine, in her safe childhood past. Then a few pages later Rochester tells us how he feels his room 'A refuge,' until Baptiste suddenly appears, and 'the feeling of security . . . left me.' Once again the feelings themselves, and the way they are experienced and expressed, seem Antoinette's, not Rochester's at all.*

This limitation on Jean's ability to draw sympathetic but different enemies affected characters in other novels, as we know – Norah and Horsfield in *Mackenzie*, for instance; and it also affects other characters here. Listen to Grace Poole, for example:

> *After all the house is big and safe, a shelter from the world outside which, say what you like, can be a black and cruel world to a woman. . . .*
>
> *The thick walls, she thought . . . above all the thick walls, keeping away all the things that you have fought till you can fight no more. . . .*

Once again this close parallel between the thoughts of gaoler and gaoled, oppressor and victim, has two equal and opposite results. On the one hand it displays Jean's recognition that the gaoler has acted not out of power but out of need, so that – perhaps – only a trick of fate has made Grace the wardress and Antoinette the poor madwoman. At last, in other words, the Jean Rhys heroine – and Jean Rhys – can look at her tormentor and say: there but for the grace of God go I. But on the other hand it suggests not so much an insight

---

*Rochester is even clairvoyant, like Antoinette: drunk, he draws 'an English house' with a woman standing in a third-floor room.

into common human weakness as a limited grasp of its sorts and varieties. Jean seems able to describe and to pity only people who are weak *in her way*, not in any other.

However fine her effort to understand Rochester, therefore (or for that matter, Grace Poole), it does not finally *quite* succeed. 'People have always been shadows to me,' she said. 'I never have known other people. I have only ever written about myself.' That was true. It made Part Two of *Wide Sargasso Sea* her greatest humane effort; but also left it slightly, and characteristically, flawed.

If *Wide Sargasso Sea* seems to me the greatest triumph of Jean's art, it is mostly because of this: that without abandoning her main task of justifying her heroine – indeed, while bringing that to its fullest completion – she also extends her sympathy most widely and humanely to others, especially to her old enemy, the Englishman. It is, in other words, because of *what* she does in it. But it is also because of *how*.

Despite her age, despite her wretched circumstances, there is no falling off in her powers here – quite the contrary. Her last two novels, *Voyage in the Dark* and *Good Morning, Midnight,* had been almost pure poetry: and so is *Wide Sargasso Sea*. Indeed, Jean's style reaches its peak of appropriateness and effectiveness in this novel. Her writing 'in words of one syllable', for example. The clear simplicity of her narrative helps to give all the novels what Francis Wyndham calls their 'quivering immediacy'. But when the heroines were between the ages of nineteen and forty-two this simplicity carried the danger that we might feel them to be unreasonably childish, intellectually as well as emotionally immature. In this way *Wide Sargasso Sea* once again goes beyond the earlier novels, and provides an artistic solution to a psychological problem. For when we first meet her here the heroine *is* a child, under twelve years old. We enter her mind then, when her simplicity, her intensity, and her failure to reflect on her situation, or to take a 'wider' (moral, political or social) view, are all natural and right. Again the wider reflections are left almost entirely to us: and here, where the heroine is first a child and then a madwoman, this technique is most effective and appropriate of all. She goes straight from the unexplained certainties and taboos, wonders and fears of childhood, to the unexplained certainties, taboos, wonders and fears of madness: and perhaps for the first time we can follow this movement entirely without reservation.

In much the same way, *Wide Sargasso Sea* of all the novels makes the best use of Jean's 'quivering' pace. The stories of Anna, Marya, Julia and Sasha are all tautly and economically told: but with each of the early novels that economy can come to feel closer and closer to the economy of death and emptiness it describes. *Voyage in the Dark* pauses for glimpses of childhood, sunshine, even play; but the other three novels concentrate without a break on the cold and cruelty of Europe. There is a coiled and controlled energy in them, very different from the heroine's lassitude; but the feeling they may give is of a growing emptiness inside, an internalisation of this cold and dark into their own voices. But even at the end of the *Wide Sargasso Sea* there is no cold or dark inside Antoinette, but only outside her, in Thornfield Hall: and the same is true of the book itself. Inside both is a hell: but not, this time, a hell that freezes: rather, a hell that burns. The change in the imagery of death is exactly appropriate: by falling and drowning in the earlier novels, but here by leaping and by fire.

Some readers may feel, on the contrary, that *Wide Sargasso Sea* is too full of incident, that it is a Caribbean 'Gothic novel', too close for comfort to melodrama. But if one *is* gripped by the purity and intensity of Jean's belief in these events and their significance, then their piling rapidly upon one another in the way they do adds to the brilliance and fascination of the novel.

The most striking and perfect, however, of all the aspects of the style of *Wide Sargasso Sea* is its poetry: its use of echo and imagery as the main vehicle of its meaning. It is perfect, because it so precisely expresses one of the main ideas we have found at the heart of all the novels: that truth is hidden beneath the surface, and particularly beneath the surface of words. The heroine is always trying to pierce through the surface of what she hears and sees to the truth that lies beneath; and words, more than ever now, are 'no use' for learning or conveying truth: 'I know that now,' says Antoinette. Her husband's words to her — 'You are safe' — are worse than no use, because they are the opposite of truth. They are, as he says himself, 'less than nothing'. Yet Antoinette is always surrounded by words, by voices and whispers, in the garden at Coulibri, on the night of the fire, and with Grace Poole and Leah at Thornfield Hall: 'So there is still the sound of whispering that I have heard all my life, but these are different voices.' And it is not just she who faces the necessity and impossibility of sorting out truth from falsity in words. That is Rochester's trouble with Daniel's story, and with the stories all around: '. . . he hear so many stories he don't know what to believe.' It is at the heart of his final doubts about what he has done to Antoinette: '. . . suddenly, bewilderingly, I was certain that everything I had imagined to be truth was false.' And most of all, it afflicts us too. How much of what Daniel says is true? How much of what Rochester says is true? Grace Poole, for example, says that 'he was a wealthy man' even *before* he inherited his father's and brother's property on their deaths: while Rochester's excuse for entering his loveless marriage is clearly financial ('Dear Father ... I will never be a disgrace to you or to my dear brother the son you love. No begging letters, no mean requests. None of the furtive shabby manoeuvres of a younger son. I have sold my soul or you have sold it....'). Then again, how much of what Antoinette and Christophine say about him is true? They feel that he has calculatedly cheated her not just of his love but of her money: but did he really mean to? He says, again in the letter he imagines writing to his father, 'The thirty thousand pounds have been paid to me without question or condition. No provision made for her. (That must be seen to)....'; and at the end, about Granbois, 'I had meant to give it back to her. Now — what's the use?'

What *is* the truth? We know as little as Antoinette: like her we become 'undecided, uncertain about facts — any fact'. The main modes of understanding the world and her fate to which she resorts are subconscious ones: dream, emotion and image. And so in *Wide Sargasso Sea* they become our modes of understanding as well. Unlike Christophine, we may know how to read and write: but in *Wide Sargasso Sea* everything we know comes not through the rational use of words, but through 'other things'.

The first 'other thing' is dream. Antoinette, and we, gain our chief insight into her fate through her clairvoyant dream. And her mode of perceiving the world even when she is awake is continuous with the world of dreams. She slips (one critic says) 'from the real to the unreal almost imperceptibly'; she is wholly guided by emotion and instinct; she sees the world — and especially people — as unpredictable, shifting, deceptive, and almost wholly closed off from any effort she might make to affect or change them. The whole of her life is like a dream, and in particular like *her* dream: she is sick with fear, but she knows it must happen. And when we have finished her story we learn that what the dream told us and her was true: it *did* have to happen. For even if we have not read *Jane Eyre*, the story turns out to have been told in retrospect by Antoinette; and if we have read *Jane Eyre* (or even just heard of it), we know that it is the story of Bertha Rochester, whose fate has been known since 1847. This is of course the perfect image of the novelist's and the heroine's fatalism; it also confirms our sense that dreams, more than waking life, will tell us what is true.

Like all Jean's heroines, Antoinette lives almost entirely in *feeling*, and relies on her feelings to get at the truth. This is expressed most strikingly, as we've seen, in her battle with Rochester, after his night with Amélie and her return from her refuge with Christophine. 'I thought you liked the black people so much,' she says, 'but that's just a lie like everything else':

> 'You abused the planters and made up stories about them, but you do the same thing. You send the girl away quicker, and with no money or less money, and that's all the difference.'
> 'Slavery was not a matter of liking or disliking,' I said trying to speak calmly. 'It was a question of justice.'
> 'Justice,' she said. 'I've heard that word. It's a cold word....'

For Antoinette, words are always turning cold; slavery — which is just a word too — *is* a question of liking and disliking, *because everything is.* This is what all Jean's novels tell us, but *Wide Sargasso Sea*, in its attitude to the real insitution of slavery, shows it to us most sharply of all. The white people here who live in the closest and most human feeling — positive *and* negative — with black people are the old slave owners: Antoinette's father, who (like Uncle Bo in *Voyage in the Dark*) has black children, and gives 'Presents and smiles for the bastards every Christmas'; her mother, who understands the worst and the best of black people ('They are more alive than you are, lazy or not, and they can be cruel and dangerous for reasons you wouldn't understand'); and her Aunt Cora, who doesn't trust Myra, but who sings the slaves' songs. The Cosways may own slaves, but they live with them as people; the new English, for all their 'justice', are cold and hard, and care less for black *or* white than for money. Rochester has become one of them by the end, and proves Christophine right by using the law as brute power against her. As always, the cold and rational Englishman crushes the world of feeling — that is, the world of the heroine — beneath his feet.

After dream and feeling comes the most important mode of Antoinette's way of understanding the world, and of communicating it to us: imagery, and particularly the echo and repetition of images. At Granbois, for instance, Antoinette tells Rochester, 'I was always happy in the morning, not always in the afternoon, and never after sunset.' Then, when we read that the white ship that takes her away to England

> ... whistled three times, once gaily, once calling, once to say goodbye

we hear the echo, and know that the time after sunset is coming for her.

So much of the meaning of the novel is conveyed to us in this way: that is, on the principle of echo and repetition — which is, in relation to *Jane Eyre*, the originating principle of the book as a whole. Thus,

Antoinette's story echoes and repeats her mother's; and it does so down to the most haunting details. After she has finally lost Rochester, 'the frown between her thick eyebrows, deep as if it had been cut with a knife', echoes her mother's frown after the death of her father: 'a frown ... between her black eyebrows, deep — it might have been cut with a knife'. Even more striking is the echo of the mother in the daughter's characteristic retreat into passivity and immobility. After Pierre dies and Annette is left to the black man who abuses her, Antoinette sees her 'with her head bent so low that I couldn't see her face. But I recognised her hair, one plait shorter than the other.' Then when Antoinette herself is afraid to marry Rochester, he sees her in the same way:

> She was sitting in a rocking chair with her head bent. Her hair was in two plaits over her shoulders. . . .

This principle of echo also works in the three rejected children (Antoinette, Rochester, Daniel) and the three clairvoyant dreams. It works in the repetition and echo of names: Antoinette's echoes her mother's, 'Annette',* and Sandi's is a diminutive of his father's, 'Alexander'. There is a suggestion therefore that from the start Antoinette's fate will be like her mother's, destruction; and that Sandi, like his father, will prosper. Once again Jean has suggested, but not said, that people's fates are decided from *before* the beginning, before they are even born.

This principle of echo works most importantly in the repetition, and variations on the theme, of the word *nothing* throughout the novel: the word which is Jean's final name for love. Almost the first thing Antoinette tells Rochester is that she is afraid of everything and of nothing; but she is much more afraid of nothing, because when the rats come and sit on her windowsill she is not frightened, but when she wakes again and there is *nothing* there she is. After this it is Rochester who rings the changes on 'nothing'. Her tears, he says, are

---

*Indeed, Antoinette says her name *is* her mother's. Names are altogether very important in *Wide Sargasso Sea*. So many characters have two names, or else none. Rochester is never named; and Antoinette, Christophine and Daniel have two each: Antoinette of course is also Bertha, Christophine is also Josephine, and Daniel is also Esau (who was, of course, the brother cheated of his heritage). Antoinette and Daniel both have two surnames as well: Antoinette both Cosway and Mason, Daniel both Cosway and Boyd. This absence, multiplication and uncertainty of names increases the dream or nightmare-like atmosphere, in which people's identities can no more be known than any other fact, and the important question '*Qui est là?*' can never be certainly answered.

'nothing', his words to her 'less than nothing', and 'the happiness I gave her worse than nothing'. After Daniel's letter all there is around him is 'Nothing. Silence. Heat'. And while for Antoinette it is money which is nothing ('she don't care for money — it's nothing to her'), for Rochester it is love. This is expressed, we remember — and the contrast with *money* echoed — in the last scene of Part Two. Rochester, in a cold fury, asks what 'the nameless boy' is crying about, and Antoinette answers:

> 'He asked me when we first came if we — if you — would take him with you when we left. He doesn't want any money. Just to be with you. Because —' she stopped and ran her tongue over her lips, 'he loves you very much....'

And this is Rochester's verdict on love:

> That stupid boy followed us, the basket balanced on his head. He used the back of his hand to wipe away his tears. Who would have thought that any boy would cry like that. For nothing. Nothing....

Here the key images and ideas of the novel — of all the novels — come together. Inside the heroine all that matters is love, but outside her, in her lover, all that matters is money ('of course, that is what all the rigmarole is about'; 'Gold is the idol they worship'). In the world love is not *all*, but *nothing*: that is the secret she discovers. So her love becomes her death, as in her game; her lover becomes the man who hates her, as in her dream. The secret is out; the reversal is complete; the story is over.

Apart from this dominating principle of echo and repetition, the novel teems with all sorts of imagery. Jean has used all the images before: they are her constant vehicles. But here in the natural and especially sensuous world of the West Indies they reach a new pitch of vividness and power.

*Light and dark*: The imagery of light and dark in *Wide Sargasso Sea* is both pervasive and (as before) ambiguous. There are occasions when light and dark carry their traditional charges of positive and negative respectively — for example, when Antoinette, knowing that she has not made Rochester understand her, says, 'I wish to stay here in the dark ... where I belong.' But mostly, like everything else, they reverse and change places. 'Black' and 'white' do, of course — black is mostly warm and gay (Tia, Christophine), white mostly cold and sad (Mr Mason, Rochester). Night and the dark are connected to

Antoinette, they are her natural element. Rochester at first longs for the night and the night flowers, as he longs for Antoinette; but at the same time he fears the night, and he ends by disliking the scent of the night flowers as much as Hester in *Voyage in the Dark*. For the darkness represents the 'primitive', and passion, with all their attraction, but also all their fear: their bringing together of love and hate, life and death, in the risk of self-surrender, which Antoinette fears too, with good reason. At the same time, the sun too can mean passion (Antoinette has 'the sun in her', says Christophine); and it too can be fearful and death-dealing, as easily as the night. Antoinette is afraid of *obeah* in the sunlight, as Julia was afraid in the sunlight rather than the shadow. Anna went out into the sun when she wanted to die; and when Antoinette takes refuge in the non-life of the convent she finds it at the same time 'a place of sunshine and of death'.

> Everything was brightness, or dark. The walls, the blazing colours of the flowers in the garden, the nuns' habits were bright, but their veils, the Crucifix hanging from their waists, the shadow of the trees, were black. That was how it was, light and dark, sun and shadow, Heaven and Hell....

This is, it seems to me, a very precise image of the ambiguity for Antoinette of her tropical paradise. Brightness and dark, heaven and hell, come as close – are as much the same – as love and death, everything and nothing. In this nightmare world the one constantly changes into the other: the bright moon brings madness, the bright sun brings fear. The ambiguity reaches its peak in Antoinette herself. Rochester sings to her:

> *Hail to the queen of the silent night,*
> *Shine bright, shine bright Robin as you die....*

– and she will. Antoinette herself is the queen of night, who will shine brightest as she dies: for the brightness of the fire at the end, though it brings death, is a way out of hell.

*Nature*: In *Wide Sargasso Sea*, even more than in the urban, European novels, Jean makes particularly powerful use of the natural world around her heroine to express her feelings and meanings. That is why we feel both that the physical world is especially strongly present in this novel; and yet that in it we are locked especially firmly in the heroine's world of dream.

Birds, for example, carry much significance at crucial moments of the story. There is the parrot, Coco, for whom Annette turns back to her burning house, and the sight of whose burning body slows and stops the black mob, because 'it was very unlucky to kill a parrot, or even to see a parrot die.' This is because the parrot is associated, in many myths and perhaps in *obeah*, with the soul: so that Coco here is an image of the imprisoned soul which is first Annette's (so of course she must go back for it) and finally Antoinette's. Antoinette's own burning plunge to death echoes Coco's; and Coco's call, '*Qui est là? Qui est là?*' expresses her fear of the hating stranger: when she herself is about to die, she

> ... heard the parrot call as he did when he saw a stranger, *Qui est là? Qui est là?* and the man who hated me was calling too, Bertha! Bertha!

In between, and continuing the echoes between Antoinette and her mother, Annette had screamed the same words at the start of her madness: '*Qui est là? Qui est là?*....' The parrot, therefore, is the image of the Jean Rhys woman's dying soul: which is trapped, which meets the hating stranger, and which is destroyed in a holocaust of fire.

Then there is the 'solitaire' or mountain bird, whom Rochester hears twice, once at the beginning and once at the end of the love which turns into nothing. Its call is 'a long sad note ... shrill and sweet. A very lonely sound.' For a brief moment, when he feels that he has found the secret, 'the magic and the dream', in Granbois and in Antoinette, he determines to listen to the solitaire. Again, the bird is an image of Antoinette herself, to whom he listens only so briefly:

> ... I will listen to the mountain bird. Oh, a heartstopper is the solitaire's one note — high, sweet, lonely, magic. You hold your breath to listen.... No.... Gone.

Then there are the cocks, who crow 'for betrayal';* and the crab in the pool, an image of the cruelty hidden under the surface of things. And the moths. On their first night at Granbois Antoinette and Rochester sit and eat by candlelight, and 'A great many moths and beetles found their way into the room, and flew into the candles and fell dead on the tablecloth.' Later on Antoinette explicitly identifies both herself and Rochester with the dead moths: 'It doesn't matter what I believe or what you believe, because we can do nothing about it, we are like these.' But here she is mistakenly extending her own passivity and fatalism to him. For in the earlier scene one of the moths which blunders into the flame is picked up and saved by Rochester,

---

*This happens three times. The first is when Rochester has betrayed Antoinette into a loveless marriage; the second when Antoinette betrays him by trying to trick him into loving her; the third when Rochester writes to arrange the first stages of Antoinette's imprisonment.

who then lets it fly away, saying, 'I hope that gay gentleman will be safe.' Nothing could be more clearly contrasted to Antoinette's self-abandonment and death by fire than this extraordinary image of Rochester's self-preservation and escape.

Flowers and trees are among the most common and permanent of Jean's images. The heroine, with her frailty and her brief happiness, is always identified with flowers, and especially with roses. Here, for example, Rochester says to Antoinette, '*Rose elle a vécu. . . .* Have all beautiful things sad destinies?'; and there are always two pink roses on their tray. Rochester tells Antoinette that she is like the orchid that grows 'long sprays of golden brown flowers': then, when he has read Daniel's letter, he breaks off a spray of that orchid, and tramples it into the mud. This reminds us (an echo again) of the frangipani wreaths which awaited them on their marriage bed, and which Rochester had trodden on, filling the room with the scent of crushed flowers. This powerfully sensuous image conveys once again the connection for the heroine between sexual love, and cruelty and death at the hands of her lover, which we see too in her dangerous game of 'Say die', and finally in her clairvoyant dream.

The frangipani is the flower of the red jasmine tree, so that by extension Antoinette is identified with that tree as well. And so she is, at the end, with the flamboyant tree, which lifts up the buried soul when it flowers: the flamboyant tree is the flame tree, and its flowers are 'the colour of fire and sunset', the colours of Antoinette's death. And there is the bamboo, which is the emblem of her passive bending to the cruelty of her fate:

> The hurricane months are not so far away. . . . Some of the royal palms stand . . . stripped of their branches, like tall brown pillars, still they stand − defiant. Not for nothing are they called royal. The bamboos take an easier way, they bend to the earth and lie there, creaking, groaning, crying for mercy. The contemptuous wind passes, not caring for these abject things.*

Rochester is the wind, and for a moment he does think of pity; but the moment passes, her abject plea fails, and he becomes the hurricane which will break the tree.

Rochester is also − in contrast to Antoinette's living flowers and trees − a stone. 'That's how you are,' Antoinette says, 'a stone.' Stone is everything opposed to Antoinette, everything cold and dead: it is a stone, thrown by Tia, which spoils her for her wedding day and all

---

*Compare this with 'La Grosse Fifi' in *The Left Bank*: ' "I love your name anyway," he said . . . − "It suits you." "Yes, it suits me − it means a reed," said Roseau . . . − "A reed shaken by the wind. That's my motto, that is".'

other days; and Rochester's world, into which she must go, is full of stone. After Daniel's letter, and again after she has drugged Rochester, he flees to the forest, and finds the strange road and the strange priest's house, of which all but he are afraid: the road and the house are built of stone. In the way of nightmare, this forest is, surely, the forest of Antoinette's dream: the forest which, the second time she dreams it, is transformed into 'a garden surrounded by a stone wall', and a flight of steps; the third time, of course, she knows that the flight of steps leads to the attic at Thornfield Hall. Thus, Rochester's stone road has become the flight of steps leading Antoinette to her prison. Finally, her last act (dreamed in *Wide Sargasso Sea*, performed in *Jane Eyre*) is to fling herself down upon the stone of Rochester's home — 'a place full of stones where nobody is' (*Voyage in the Dark*). Like flowers and trees, Antoinette dies; only stone survives, like the mounting stone at Coulibri, which Antoinette is sure will be the only thing to survive the first terrible fire. And, of course, as *Jane Eyre* tells us, Rochester, the stone, does survive.

*Colours*: Like flowers, colours are always very important to Jean. Antoinette here is all bright colours ('green, blue and purple'), but mostly red ('Underneath, I will write my name in fire red'); she is also white, for innocence, like the white of Rochester's favourite dress.* The flowers with which she is identified are shades of red — the red frangipani, the pink roses, the golden-brown orchid, the flame-red flamboyant tree. And she identifies herself particularly with her flame-red dress: 'If I had been wearing my red dress Richard would have known me,' she insists. When she is afraid that she has been robbed of her red dress she is fearing the loss of her identity, her self:

> ... I held the dress in my hand wondering if they had done the last and worst thing. If they had *changed* it when I wasn't looking. If they had changed it and it wasn't my dress at all....

But she has not entirely lost her soul, even now; and when she sees her red dress she remembers her home and Sandi, she remembers who she is and what she must do.

Rochester, of course, rejects her in her red dress ('Does it make me look intemperate and unchaste?' I said. 'That man told me so.') He rejects her emotion and passion, and he is moved to his own little love and little death only by her *white* dress, which makes him 'savage with desire'. This imagery of the red and white dresses shows us (as the

*Rochester does not say at the time that the dress which arouses his desire is white; but immediately after their love-making Antoinette says, 'I'll wear the dress you like tonight,' and later he says 'She was wearing the white dress I admired.'

image of the kitten shows us in *Good Morning, Midnight*) that the Englishman's sexuality is not loving but cruel, called forth not by whole women,* who can respond with their own passion, but by passive innocent girls, whom they can imagine, and then turn into, the sad victims of men. Antoinette's true red is turned into the dead redness of Thornfield Hall, which is 'brown or dark red or yellow that has no light in it'; and covered over, by Grace Poole, by a grey English wrapper.

Blue, green and yellow are also significant colours for the Jean Rhys heroine. Blue is most often for happiness – the blue air at Granbois, the blue sofa on which Annette lay when Antoinette still wanted to be near her; or the 'blue cup and saucer and the silver teapot' of Anna's 'lovely life' as a child, the blue skies of Sasha's fine days. Yellow is for danger and hostility – the colour of Daniel's skin and the goat's eyes, the colour of Antoinette's shawl on the night she gives Rochester the *obeah* potion, and of the blanket on his bed which helps him to vomit it up the next morning. Green is for the natural world of growth which menaces Rochester ('the green menace – I had felt it ever since I saw this place'). But all bright colours menace him:

Everything is too much.... Too much blue, too much purple, too much green.

These bright colours, of course, are Antoinette's element, and she identifies them all with herself ('We can colour the roses as we choose and mine are green, blue and purple'). To him, at best, they seem unreal, a dream; while to her it is cities, houses and streets which seem unreal. If Antoinette had ever gone to London or Paris, they would always have seemed grey and unreal to her. They do, of course, to the other heroines: and now that we have seen, in the last novel, the bright world which is natural to her, we understand that too.

★　　★　　★

*Wide Sargasso Sea* poses what has been Jean's question all along: 'Such terrible things happen. Why? Why?' To earn death with her answer she has had to do what is hardest for any human being, but especially for her: to examine her own conscience, and to try to understand her enemy's point of view. *Good Morning, Midnight* was the highest achievement of the first effort, *Wide Sargasso Sea* of the second. Its strength and its weakness lie in the same thing: the similarity that Jean constructs between her heroine and her enemy, the Englishman. In

---

*It is not even *Antoinette in her white dress* which so attracts Rochester, but the dress alone, lying on the floor.

some of its details this similarity is a failure of her imagination; but at its heart it is a success, saying *He is just as weak, just as afraid, as me.* The success was much greater than the failure – especially when we remember that the Englishman whom Jean loved most, and who hurt her most, was Lancelot, of whom exactly this was secretly true.

At the same time there is only the smallest suggestion that this heroine is at all like Sasha: also responsible herself for her loss of love. It's in Rochester's brief line, and in the idea that resentful revengeful Daniel is, symbolically, a part of Antoinette – the broken off, wolf-like twin. Mostly, and on its surface, *Wide Sargasso Sea* gave the answer Jean wanted to give to her question: the terrible things are not done by the heroine, she is the victim of an inexorable and hostile fate, she is the apotheosis of the lily. *And yet that works here too,* because of the connection to *Jane Eyre.* For we know that Antoinette Cosway is Bertha Mason: and so we already know about the pig. We've already seen Antoinette from the outside; we've seen her from the outside for a hundred years. So the fact that the whole point of this novel is to show her to us from the inside only is more than fair and reasonable – it is welcome, it is overdue.

*Wide Sargasso Sea* is Jean's masterpiece because it is her most complete expression, the point where her own split, between the strong artist and the weak woman, is most triumphantly healed. It contains her greatest humanity, rooted in the loves of her life: the black people of her island; her father and her Great-Aunt Jane; Lancelot. It accomplishes the justification of her heroine at last, by showing us her beginnings, and by that stroke of genius – allowing us to know that the innocent, abused girl of this book is also the destructive, lunatic villain of another. It solves the problems of self-pity (for us) and revenge (for Jean) by the same stroke of genius – leaving them both to another book, or to the relation between that book and this one. It resolves all Jean's main themes and questions. It shows us the original world of visible beauty and invisible menace. It grapples with that hidden menace, the unnamed thing that pursued, caught and filled Anna, Marya and Julia, and fully names it: it is Julia's nothingness, but in the place where love should have been; it is the collapse of everything ('love, youth, spring, happiness') into nothing, love into death, trust into betrayal. It completes the heroine's dream, her voyage in the dark, taking her to the top of the stairs and to her last room; making her the ghost kept alive by a flame of hatred. And in Tia and Daniel Cosway it explores the two different meanings of darkness, the two different dark sides of the heroine. Tia is the strength and gaiety (and also the treachery) of the primitive. Daniel the half-breed, neither black nor white but yellow, is the heroine's last neighbour and last twin: the wolf-like other who destroys her chance of love, because 'the hate in that man Daniel — he can't rest with it.'

*Wide Sargasso Sea* is, finally, Jean's poetic masterpiece. To me Part One of this novel is the single greatest flight of her particular genius — extraordinarily young and fresh, full of energy and conviction, simple, lucid and beautiful. And the last pages of Rochester's Part Two — the remnants of Jean's poetic breakthrough to him — attain a controlled wildness even more haunting than the last pages of *Voyage in the Dark.*

... The tree shivers. Shivers and gathers all its strength. And waits.

(There is a cool wind blowing now — a cold wind. Does it carry the babe born to stride the blast of hurricanes?)

She said she loved this place. This is the last she'll see of it. I'll watch for one tear, one human tear. Not that blank hating moonstruck face. I'll listen.... If she says goodbye perhaps adieu. *Adieu* — like those old-time songs she sang. Always *adieu* (and all songs say it). If she too says it, or weeps, I'll take her in my arms, my lunatic. She's mad but *mine, mine.* What will I care for gods or devils or for Fate itself. If she smiles or weeps or both. *For me.*

Antoinetta — I can be gentle too. Hide your face. Hide yourself but in my arms. You'll soon see how gentle. My lunatic. My mad girl.

Here's a cloudy day to help you. No brazen sun.

No sun.... No sun. The weather's changed.

*Wide Sargasso Sea* is a dark triumph, just as *Good Morning, Midnight* was: the partial triumph of the heroine's escape (but only to death), and the whole triumph of Jean's art. It is the final apotheosis of her identity with her heroine — and also of their difference. For like Antoinette she roused herself, after long 'nights and days and days and nights' of defeat and despair, to a huge effort of memory (and that is like Sasha too) and to a last, fiery act. Like Antoinette, therefore, she triumphantly transformed and escaped her prison. But of course Antoinette did so in an act of destruction, which brought her only death: while Jean did it in an act of creation, which will bring her her share of literary immortality. We cannot, therefore, feel for her the pity we feel for her heroine. Their 'flame sank down again, useless, having reached nothing'; hers reached up to one of the finest novels of the century.

# PART FOUR

---

# LAST YEARS
# 1966-1979

---

# CHAPTER ONE

# Life, 1966–1975

In March 1966 Jean's life suddenly changed. It would soon be for the better, but at first it felt worse. Everyone had left her: Max, Antoinette and Rochester, Christophine, everyone. Now that the great struggle with her novel was over even Mr Woodard began to fade away. He would still come to see her when he was needed, but there were others who needed him more now. The Greenslades remained, being 'dears and terribly kind' to her: 'I couldn't live here without them,' Jean said. But 'it wouldn't be true to say we have much to talk about.' Sometimes she saw no one but Mrs Greenslade all day, and sometimes not even Mrs Greenslade. Then the solitude became 'really too much for me. It is making me dull and stupid so that I feel '*a quoi bon*?' to everything. . . .' The only companion who remained, faithful as ever, was whisky. She leaned heavily on it, she told Francis; and even confessed to Maryvonne: 'Whisky is now a must for me.'

But whisky wasn't enough. There always had to be someone to pick her up – nameless men after Lancelot, Ford after John, Leslie after Ford, Max after Leslie. When she was young it was men; from now on it would be mostly women.

The first woman she turned to was her daughter. She'd been moving towards more and more open need of Maryvonne ever since Max had gone away to hospital and left her alone. Now it was quite naked. 'I feel very lonely,' she wrote to her ten days after he died: 'I long for a miracle; perhaps you will be the miracle that will bring me to life.' From now until she died Jean went on longing for that miracle: that Maryvonne would love her as much as she needed to be loved. But no one could do that; and especially not Maryvonne. Jean had not put her first when she was young. Maryvonne didn't want to punish Jean, but she *did* put her daughter first, and her husband; and she continued to refuse to sacrifice the peace of her family and home to her mother. After the success of *Wide Sargasso Sea* there were other people who were willing and eager to care for Jean: people from the world of her books, which she had chosen, however reluctantly. Maryvonne came to see her several times this year, and at least twice a year from then on. But – as everyone who knew Jean understood very well – she could not share her home with her.

Immediately, therefore, Jean attached herself to the first of the people from the world of books who appeared: Diana Athill. 'When I told Mrs Greenslade that you might come she said "It's as if God sent someone to you!",' she wrote. Diana came at the end of March and took away with her not just *Wide Sargasso Sea* but Jean's problems.

Money was the first of them: apart from Edward's allowance Jean had only her three hundred pounds a year from the Royal Literary Fund. And housing: could she find an alternative to Cheriton Fitzpaine? Diana tackled both of them straight away, writing to the Royal Naval Benevolent Society about money, and to a housing association at Chingford in Essex about a flat for Jean. Neither of these would come to anything – the Royal Naval Benevolent Society could only offer Jean sixty pounds a year, and she would die in Cheriton Fitzpaine. But Diana would try again; she remained one of the leaders of those who helped Jean to survive, practically and emotionally, during her last years.

Not all were women. Edward, for example, reappeared this year. His wife had died; he had gone away to recover. But now he was back. He brought Jean a cake for her birthday; he visited again at the end of September, and offered to pay her fare and Maryvonne's to London for the launch of *Wide Sargasso Sea*. The next spring he offered her a thousand pounds towards the flat at Chingford, and went to look at it when Jean couldn't. Sometimes – talking to the Woodards about her, for instance – he was as unkind as Jean feared; but now, when they were both bereaved and sad, he was generous to her. Her other male friends, Alec Hamer and Francis Wyndham, always were. Alec sent her funny letters, books, helpful advice.* Francis suggested that André Deutsch propose Jean to the Arts Council for a bursary. This

---

*There are only four or five of his letters left in Jean's archive, but there may have been more (they had 'a correspondence', Jean told Francis). Unfortunately her letters too have been lost.

Immediately after Max's death Alec was thinking of moving to the country, Jean told Selma vaz Dias: is it over-imaginative to hear a note of hope in her voice that he might think of moving to, or near, Cheriton Fitzpaine? See Jean to Selma, 18 March 1966: 'Alec was awfully good to me & helped me tremendously. He *is* a brick.... Some miracle will save me perhaps but are there any miracles left for me?'

worked, and she was awarded £1,200 the next year. It was one of the first examples of an important and happy change in her life: from *Wide Sargasso Sea* on she would have a little more money.

But these, of course, were all old friends and supporters. The first new ones arrived now: both women, and both also brought to her by *Wide Sargasso Sea*.

As the novel was about to appear Jean agreed to her first interview, with Hunter Davies of the *Sunday Times*. 'She's a strange, shy, very dignified lady who lives alone in a remote part of Devon,' Davies wrote. 'She has no telephone and few friends....' In that remote part of Devon Joan Butler read the article, and thought immediately of the strange woman in the wide felt hat who walked the streets of Cheriton Fitzpaine without speaking a word to anyone. *She* was a writer, people said; it must be the same one. She sounded so lonely, and as though she felt Devon was unfriendly. Both these ideas upset Joan. So she wrote to Jean, saying she would like to meet her.

This was the beginning of an important friendship for Jean, in spite of the fact that Joan Butler was not a natural, congenial friend: almost no one could be that, certainly not Joan. She was — is — as different from Jean as anyone could be. She is steady, rational, down-to-earth: what Jean would call (not intending it as a compliment) *sane*. She loves England and dislikes France; she loves the countryside, especially Devon. She is interested in reality, especially political reality, and she is very left-wing. ('Jean said I was a communist — well, I am, almost.') She admires Jean's writing, but can't like the books; she is irritated by the heroine's passivity ('Why can't she just *do* something?'), and even more by the political passiveness the books as a whole imply. In turn Jean would often be irritated by her. She put her into 'Sleep it Off Lady' as Letty Baker, of whom Miss Verney says 'She'll know exactly the sensible thing to do.' And in a draft which was cut from *Smile Please* she wrote of a woman who was, she knew, 'very intelligent in some ways'. 'If Jesus Christ was only a man,' she makes the woman say,

> 'a very good man but a man, everything will get much clearer. It's the other thing that worries me because I can't understand it, and I don't like things that I can't understand.'
> 'But you can't understand everything,' I said. 'The whole thing is a mystery.'
> 'And I don't like mysteries,' she said.

Typically, Jean stops there, leaving her dissent hanging in the air. But in life she would argue. She and Joan argued often, about everything — about religion and politics, France and England — and Jean would get (Joan says) 'very heated'. Yet she wanted her to come, every Sunday from five to six as they'd agreed; she was angry if Joan was late, and didn't want her to leave. Even when they argued she seemed to say *Talk to me*. And so Joan did: about events in the village and in her family, about music and books (but not Jean's own books), about Jean's happy memories of Paris (but only rarely, when she was drunk, about the sad ones). For that, of course, was why Jean needed her. She needed someone to talk to. The Greenslades were so good, but they didn't talk much. 'They are both kind,' Jean wrote, 'and I am grateful, but *far apart*.' They – especially Mr Greenslade – satisfied the part of her that enjoyed servants, being taken care of, made a fuss of. But she also needed conversation. And as Mr Woodard came less often – and later became ill, and moved away – that would come more and more from Joan Butler. And the other things Mr Woodard had done too: helping her with shopping, taking her into a warm home and family – at Christmas, for example – offering an alternative to the Ring o'Bells pub when people came to visit her. Because Joan was a woman, because she was 'sane', but mostly, of course, because Joan didn't love *her*, as Mr Woodard had, Jean didn't love and trust Joan as she'd loved Mr Woodard. But she did need her; and her London friends came to rely very much on Joan Butler to watch over Jean for them while she was in Cheriton Fitzpaine.

It was the second woman who came now who took over the other side of Mr Woodard's friendship. *Wide Sargasso Sea* brought her Sonia Orwell too, for it was Sonia's publishing Part One in *Art & Literature* that had first brought them together. Jean had found her letters very kind from the beginning. And as *Wide Sargasso Sea* was about to come out Sonia wrote to Diana Athill, offering her help with Jean 'in any way'. And she meant it. She used George Orwell's estate to help other writers and artists, and over the next dozen years she used it most generously to help Jean, beginning now as she meant to go on. She sent Jean a present of whisky, and asked how she could help with her Cheriton isolation. As soon as anyone suggested a real alternative Jean panicked (at least she could *afford* Cheriton Fitzpaine, she replied). She didn't really want to move; she always preferred a known unhappiness to an unknown and possibly worse one. What she wanted was a break, a holiday: to 'just FLOP, be taken care of for two weeks or so.' And that is exactly what Sonia gave her. She arranged everything, like a fairy godmother. She and Francis went to Brighton and chose a hotel. She arranged for Mr Greenslade to drive Jean down, for Diana Athill to settle her in, for the hotel to give her a table to herself, so that she wouldn't have to speak 'to a single soul except kind waiters'. She bought her a pretty pink dress. And last but not least she paid for it all – the hotel, restaurants, hairdressers, everything; she even tipped everyone in advance, so that Jean wouldn't have to. And she went on giving Jean such presents for the rest of her life: clothes, make-up, bottles of whisky and champagne sent regularly by post; and months of winter holidays throughout the 1970s, in London flats and hotels, every penny paid and every detail thought out in advance. Jean thrived under such generosity like a plant under sun, and like a child she partly loved Sonia for her presents. But it was mostly for the other reason: that like Mr Woodard, and unlike kind but cool Joan Butler, Sonia *approved of her*. She sympathised with her longing for pretty clothes (without wholly sharing it: Diana Athill re-members her groaning at the prospect of shopping for a dress with Jean because, she said, nothing bored her more than dress-shopping. But she never gave any hint of this boredom to Jean); and with her need for drink too (Sonia did share that). So Jean could come out of hiding with her. She trusted Sonia with more of herself — her memories, her real feelings — than she had ever trusted anyone, I think, since Germaine Richelot: more than Peggy Kirkaldy, much more than Selma vaz Dias. As much as she could love another woman she loved Sonia; and was, therefore, at her best with her: relaxed, happy, enchanting. She had *fun* with Sonia. Then her friends would see her as she must have been as a young girl, and with Lancelot: giggling and laughing, singing songs, telling funny stories — 'being,' Diana Athill says, 'perfectly charming in a comically frivolous way.' Only those who really liked or loved her saw this side for more than the most fleeting moments. Max (I hope) and Alec Hamer, Alwynne Woodard, Sonia Orwell and Francis Wyndham, Oliver and Mollie Stoner; Diana Athill sometimes ('but Jean didn't quite trust me, I know' — she was too English). A few others, too, towards the end of her life: kind young men like Larry Cole, who wrote to her after *Wide Sargasso Sea*, or Michael Schwab and David Plante, who helped her write *Smile Please*; kind women like Antonia Fraser and Diana Melly. And Maryvonne, who could make her laugh ('which is something a lot of her friends can't manage'). These moments never lasted long; they fled at the slightest hint of disapproval — which came often enough, and when it didn't come Jean imagined it. But at least she had them.

Most of what *Wide Sargasso Sea* brought her was good — new friends, more money, greater comfort. But some was bad, especially for her: interviewers and photographers, the invasion of her privacy. That wouldn't start until publication day. But something else did: the looming of the question *What now?* Long before its public success Jean's friends, and Jean herself, recognised that *Wide Sargasso Sea* was the climax of her career. It was a great, a crowning achievement; it had cost her so much for so long; she was seventy-six years old, and tired out. Couldn't she stop now, couldn't she have a rest at last? Francis, for instance, thought she could and should. She'd done enough, why should she write any more? Sonia thought she was only happy when she was writing; but of course she was often fiercely *un*happy then as well, and that would be especially true after *Wide Sargasso Sea*. She was, to a large extent, written out; her wonderful memory was deteriorating; in the end she wouldn't be able to hold a pen.

After the great success of *Wide Sargasso Sea* her publishers were naturally pleased at any prospect of more Jean Rhys, but Diana felt she'd done enough too, and told her she shouldn't bother to go on if she didn't feel like it. But she did go on. She worked on old stories and wrote new ones, and published them when she was eighty-five; even then she went on, and was still working on her autobiography when she died. We must be glad she did. Half the stories of 'Sleep it Off Lady' are excellent; and though *Smile Please* was scrappy and unfinished, we would have far less insight into Jean without it. But she'd written out the last and worst thing, her madness; there was nothing really pressing on her after *Wide Sargasso Sea*. Wouldn't *she* have been happier if she could have stopped writing?

Well, perhaps. But if there's one thing we know now it's that happiness wasn't possible for Jean. She'd never really had any choice about whether to write, and she still didn't. Before it had been a need, now it was a habit; and it was still the only way she could feel she was earning death. What was there in her life apart from writing? She couldn't live in a settled communion with herself, with her daughter or friends. Now that she was old, and (for the first time) as truly alone as her heroines, it was harder than ever to get from moment to moment, from day to day. If she had lived to be a hundred she would have gone on writing.

She felt this straight away. Only weeks after Diana had taken away *Wide Sargasso Sea* she told Maryvonne that 'to write again . . . is what I want and ought to do.' By the summer she was saying: 'There is one more book I want to write if I can.' She'd tried 'to fill the gap' with *Leaving School*, which had got up to ten thousand words – a small autobiography. And this gave her, I think, the idea of what her 'one more book' should be. She would write her autobiography – or rather, being Jean, her autobiography as a novel. She told Diana that she was 'trying very hard to start writing again,' and that the 'poor and gloomy title' for these attempts was *'Death before the fact'*, a quotation from St Teresa of Avila. In the end these autobiographical writings would become the 'fictions' of *Sleep It Off Lady* and the 'facts' of *Smile Please*.

★

Even before *Wide Sargasso Sea* came out it was clear that it was going to be a success of a different order from Jean's earlier novels. Ten days before Diana wrote: 'Now you've got hard-back, paperback, book club and America lined up. Overcome your native pessimism, dear Jean, and face the fact that *Wide Sargasso Sea* is already being a *success*! Oh I do hope there is some pleasure in this for you.' But we know what happened: there would be no pleasure. It wasn't just her usual nerves, though there was that too — about getting up to London, about publicity. (She 'funked' an interview on BBC 2, for instance, even though it would have been with Francis.) It was something else: the Selma problem.

Jean had been working herself up to worry about this since the moment — probably the second — after she'd signed the first agreement. But now it was coming to a parting of the ways. Of course she had never produced a 'radio version' of *Wide Sargasso Sea*, and in September the BBC said that the novel couldn't be used for broadcast as it was. With all the hope and praise she was getting for it this will not have bothered Jean; but it must have been a blow to Selma. Then someone else wanted to adapt *Mackenzie* for television, and Jean wanted to let her. She told Selma, repeating as she always did 'We can go shares' (although this time of course there'd have to be three). Selma didn't reply, and she began to worry. She saw Selma in London on launch day; but Selma said nothing about it, so nor did Jean.

Now came the next turn of the screw: 'Woman's Hour' decided to broadcast *Wide Sargasso Sea*, but they didn't want to use Selma. Selma 'went mad with rage': she wrote a furious letter to the BBC. She insisted that she had to be the adaptor. She told everyone that she alone had discovered and nurtured Jean through the lost years — and now she was being betrayed. Jean had more or less written *Wide Sargasso Sea* for her — and she wasn't even mentioned in Francis Wyndham's introduction. The vipers and jackals were descending, after all the work had been done — by Selma, who alone had any integrity, who alone really valued Jean's work. . . . She'd become as paranoid as Jean. According to Jean she now took her adaptation of *Voyage in the Dark* to the BBC without showing it to her — as though 'sole artistic control' meant just that, that she had the right not even to consult Jean herself. 'This right she has not got,' Jean wrote furiously. 'I refuse point blank to give it to her.'

Now she *was* worried; she was frantic. 'I know how easily my books could be utterly spoiled,' she told Diana. She fretted so much she couldn't work. Olwyn Hughes tried to persuade her that this sadness was a small detail in the great happiness of *Wide Sargasso Sea*; Mr Woodard spent hours trying to console her, in vain. The Selma affair obsessed her more instead of less as time went on — and not, for once, unreasonably. In December the BBC cancelled the 'Woman's Hour' reading; in February the *Mackenzie* adaptation was dropped. Deutsch took legal advice, and began to consider a case against Selma. Jean's friendship with her had 'flown right out of the window.' She no longer simply distrusted her; she felt that 'Selma is trying all she can to harm me.' Selma felt much the same about her, or about her friends and protectors. Their long battle had begun.

But let's get back now to the main thing: *Wide Sargasso Sea*. It came out on 27 October; on the twenty-eighth the reactions began, and they were wonderful. Everyone noticed *Wide Sargasso Sea*, almost everyone praised it. It was a 'magnificent comeback' said the *Spectator*, 'astonishingly convincing' (*London Magazine*), 'a rare synthesis of the baroque and the precise' (*The Times Literary Supplement*). Only a few critics dissented slightly, saying that *Wide Sargasso Sea* was too close to melodrama, to Gothic romance. But *The Times Literary Supplement*, the premier forum of establishment literary opinion, dedicated to it a long, serious, enthusiastic essay. *Wide Sargasso Sea* was, it said, the culmination of Jean's art. 'The earlier heroines existed in a social vacuum, whereas Antoinette's tragedy is in part at least the tragedy of the society to which she belongs. Also Mr Rochester is the only one of the men in her novels who is "presented live".' These were indeed the crucial points, the ways in which *Wide Sargasso Sea* both enhanced and surpassed the earlier novels. In saluting the last one in this way the *doyen* of literary London by implication recognised the stature of Jean's work as a whole.

So did the *doyen* of literary New York the next summer. In the *New York Times Book Review* Walter Allen set *Wide Sargasso Sea* and its heroine in the context of Jean's whole career, and exclaimed at the extraordinary aptness with which she could complete Anna, Marya, Julia and Sasha with a character from nineteenth-century fiction. In the end he found the same weakness as the English critic of *Books and Bookmen* — Rochester, 'damned old Part Two'. Well, they were right, as the *The Times Literary Supplement* critic was also right: Rochester *was* Jean's most living hero, yet even he is not quite as sure and clear and right as the heroine. The Other, the Man, remained by comparison a shadow. But it hardly mattered. *Wide Sargasso Sea* was a work of genius: flawed genius, perhaps, but everyone felt the unmistakable touch of the wing. At last Jean had everyone's attention, and almost everyone's admiration.

I say 'Jean' and not just '*Wide Sargasso Sea*', and I mean it. Her work is so personal that reading it is like being alone with her in a locked and shuttered room. Everyone who loves her work — or even hates it — feels a need to reply, to agree or argue, to *meet* her. Her publishers knew that, I think; and they knew too that her personal story was extraordinary enough to attract even those who hadn't read her yet – who perhaps, indeed, never would. The West Indies, and Paris in the twenties, were romantic and exotic; her long disappearance was tragic and mysterious, her final triumph a fairy tale. Publishers, press and public all felt the drama of her rediscovery. Even several early reviews picked it up; after *Wide Sargasso Sea* won the W.H. Smith Prize all the interviews told and retold the tale of her return from the dead. Jean hated this concentration on *her* instead of her novel, of course; once again her fate had made inevitable what she least desired.

Selma didn't like it either. Not a single review mentioned her; and the most complete early account (in *Books and Bookmen*, in December) gave Francis Wyndham the sole credit for Jean's rediscovery. But then Diana Athill suggested that it would be 'fair and right' to acknowledge Selma's role somewhere, and Jean agreed. A 'Publisher's Note' was inserted in the 1967 reissue of *Good Morning, Midnight*, thanking Miss vaz Dias for her part in the rediscovery of Jean Rhys.

Despite the best reviews of her life Jean was very low at the end of 1966, mostly because of the Selma anxiety. But thankfully she could still be lifted up: and Sonia's Brighton holiday lifted her greatly. 'The whole point of the holiday' (Sonia said) 'is to have every form of service you need,' and she did. She stayed in bed as long as she liked and rang down for whatever she wanted. Sonia, Francis and Diana, Alan and Jennifer Ross, visited; every evening there were champagne cocktails with someone sympathetic. Jean loved it. It was exactly her idea of a lovely time; 'It was heaven!'

Coming back to Cheriton Fitzpaine was a shock. She was so used to it she didn't normally notice; but now she had tasted comfort, and she did. Despite Edward's occasional efforts 6 Landboat Bungalows was still pretty grim. Outside it looked mean and bleak, with its low walls and corrugated iron roof; at worst almost derelict, with empty window panes from Jean's fights with the village boys, the broken glass strewn over the weed-filled grass behind the hedge. Inside it was cramped and poor. The floors were still covered with wartime lino, the bathroom was unheated, the electric cooker in the kitchen was ancient, there was no telephone, record player or radio. The rooms were very small, the sitting room bleak and bare, the bedroom and tiny 'spare room' crammed with cheap furniture. In the wall of the narrow corridor, opposite the bedroom, an orange light bulb was plugged into a socket and left bare. Later, when friends were redoing the cottage for Jean, they learned why it was there: to give her the feeling of sunshine. Of course a heater would have been more expensive, but that was not the real reason for the orange bulb. It was that Jean preferred illusion to reality: heat on her body was less important than heat in her imagination, because that is where she lived.

Some months earlier she had made another characteristic resolution: not to 'doll up' the cottage, 'for that would be too much as if I were here for keeps.' But now she broke it. She had Sonia, and good reviews; in the spring she heard that she'd won a two hundred pound prize from the Royal Society of Literature; and soon *Wide Sargasso Sea* came out in America, and *Voyage in the Dark* and *Good Morning, Midnight* were reprinted in England. So she went on a few small 'spending sprees' to 'make this place less grim.' Among other things she bought a flower painting from Selma – perhaps in a spirit of reconciliation, after Selma had agreed to relinquish her claim to artistic control over adaptations. On a summer visit Maryvonne painted the sitting room yellow. At last one room looked pretty now, Jean told her: 'I'm so pleased with it.'

Even so, of course, she still thought about moving. She went round in circles about this, like a record stuck in a groove. She'd been alone in Cheriton from the beginning (this wasn't true, Max had been with her for the first three years). It was the coldest rainiest windiest place in England, her solitude and isolation there were unimaginable, she couldn't survive another winter. And yet – she could do as she liked (especially drink as much as she liked) there; she was used to it; it would be such an uprooting to leave, 'and how do I know where or whether I'll get rooted again?' She summed up her obsessive round better than anyone else could, as always. 'On fine days . . . I make up my mind to stay. On dark days to go.'

So it went now about Chingford. In the spring she was decorating the flat in her mind – a grey or beige carpet, old rose curtains, 'a desk, a lamp with a pink shade'. But it was in a 'Housing and Community Association', and 'the word community rather alarms me.' When someone told her that Chingford was horrid and she'd hate it she believed it immediately. Edward wanted her to go and see for herself what it was like; but she'd never done such a sensible thing in all her years of moving, and she wouldn't start now. In the end everyone went and looked at it *but* Jean – Francis, Diana, Sonia, Edward. And they all agreed: Chingford was expensive, it still wasn't ready, and above all it wasn't right for Jean. Much emphasis was put by its organisers on how members of the community would look after each other, and her friends could envisage only too clearly how much Jean would hate *that*. So they consoled themselves with the knowledge that for all her complaints she really meant it when she said, as she often did 'Better the devil you know'. No one ever seriously tried to move her again. Instead all efforts would go into making her cottage more comfortable, her holidays from it longer.

Now Deutsch wanted to publish her book of short stories, *The Sound of the River*, and to include some of *The Left Bank* as well. Jean agreed to drop 'I Spy a Stranger' and 'Temps Perdi' as too 'sad and bitter', and to change the title of the collection to *Tigers Are Better-Looking:* to emphasise her 'disaster-defying humour' over her sadness, Diana said. No one knew that Mr Severn was closely based on Leslie, so no one understood that in accepting this suggestion Jean was also accepting an emphasis on her division from him, instead of on her love. Perhaps she felt that if she rejected it she would be asked why, a question impossible to answer without lying.

She herself decided that changes must be made to the *Left Bank* stories. She cut 'Fifi' to make it 'less self-pitying', and 'Vienne' to make it tighter and less 'naive'; she thought about cutting 'Tea with an Artist' to make it less 'sentimental'. In other words she listened to her young voice with her mature ear, and unerringly caught and cut her natural weaknesses: self-pity, naivety, sentimentality.

The rest of her time, in the year after *Wide Sargasso Sea*, was taken up with what many writers prefer to the agony of actually writing: parties, prizes, personal publicity. In June the reissues of *Voyage in the Dark* and *Good Morning, Midnight* brought her more reviews, more attention, more praise. In July there was the Royal Society of Literature presentation ceremony. Jean refused to go. Diana and Sonia went for her; Diana accepted the cheque, Sonia sent a welcome description: 'all round the room people were saying *what* a marvellous writer you were.' (And an even more welcome one: 'You would have been far the most attractive woman there.') Then in October came news of another, even greater accolade: *Wide Sargasso Sea* had been awarded the W.H. Smith Prize for 1966. Even Jean had to be pleased: 'how wonderful,' she wrote to Sonia – but also 'A bit terrifying.' Immediately she begged off this award ceremony as well. Her health was bad, was the official story; but her friends got the real reason. 'The idea of a huge cocktail party at the Savoy alarms me. And a speech. No No!' As to the reception, 'I really can't face that. *Can't.*' ('Supposing I burst into tears – what a thing!') In the end she went up to London and saw the few people she wanted to, while Maryvonne went to the prize dinner and accepted the cheque for her. That was in December; in the same month Jean heard that she'd got the Arts Council bursary for which she had been proposed. The W.H. Smith Prize was one thousand pounds, the bursary £1,200. Suddenly there was more money than she had had in many years. *That* part of her success even she enjoyed.

What she didn't enjoy, of course – what she loathed and feared –

was the publicity: talking about her life, *being seen*. She refused outright to be interviewed on television, even by Francis,*. But she reluctantly agreed to be interviewed by journalists; and in 1967 it happened many times. Especially after the W.H. Smith Prize there was a rash of articles about her, complete with photographs.

She bore it because she had to, to sell the books. But each interview threw her into a state of anxiety before and depression after. It was, of course, because she was afraid that something she would say or do, or something they would discover, would flush her out of hiding. She would have to lie, or at least keep silent, about so much in her life and nature, and she hated lying. It was wrong, and it was dangerous – in life as in writing she was nervous cut off from the 'facts', aware that she knew too little of the world outside her head to invent convincingly. It was like this in ordinary life too; but in ordinary life people didn't ask such direct questions or expect direct answers. Interviews meant probing, analysis, understanding. She didn't *want*, in life, to be understood; she didn't want, in life, to understand herself. She couldn't. She could only do it in writing, behind the mask of fiction – and even then it was hard enough.

Almost always, however, interviewers were too charmed by her, and too careful of her frailty, to press her. So she did not fear questions so much – or at least she didn't say so. She shifted anxiety from what *she had said* to how *she had looked*. She had always obsessively beautified her face, her body, her hair, because that was as close as she could get to beautifying the self inside; and that is what she tried to do now.

In the spring and summer of 1967 she thought and wrote constantly about being photographed. Showing people her face would help to sell her books, they said – though she was sure a picture of *her* face couldn't help at all (seeing a picture of George Eliot's, for example, had put her off her books forever). But they insisted, and all she had was a passport photo and an old photograph from Vienna. Even Jean could see that something nearly fifty years out of date wouldn't do, and of course the passport picture was ghastly. Anything was better than that – even having new ones taken. First Mrs Woodard found her a commercial photographer in Exeter, who produced some retouched studio pictures in which she looked very pretty and quite unreal. She was rather pleased with them ... but alas, it was no longer the 1910s or 1920s; people were not content with artificiality. (Except

---

*In 1970 she did agree to a French television interview, and in 1974 finally to an English one, with Tristram Powell (shown on *Omnibus*, 24 November).

Sonia, kind as ever, who said they were 'absolutely lovely'.) So Olwyn Hughes put Jean in touch with Faber's photographer, Ander Gunn. He took seven photographs, and Jean waited many agonising weeks for the results. When they came she realised that they were very good; but they depressed her terribly. 'I am a sad and lonely person & I *hate* Cheriton Fitz — but I do not wish to give that away to all & sundry for a few pence!' she wrote to Olwyn. She hated the ones that showed her sad and old, and sad was worse than old. But she hated even more the ones that made her look 'smug' and 'plump': 'exactly like the type of woman I most detest,' 'the plump lady saying tally-ho type. . . .' This is just like the hidden imagery of the girl on the chocolate box in 'Petronella', with her 'square, smug face that didn't go with her slanting eyes.' Unconsciously and unerringly — just as when she'd written that story twenty, thirty and more years before — Jean had struck straight to the heart of her fear: that however much she tried to make herself look like a chocolate box beauty, the 'rotten, sneering bitch' would come through. She liked only one of Ander Gunn's photos: the last one, which 'has a bit of defiance and "in spite of it all" about it.' This is her plucky side, the gallant, disaster-defying side that also lifts her writing. She wanted the photographs to hide her ugliness: but also to hide her despair. She couldn't be brave, but at least she could look it; that was her form of courage.

The image of the photograph — of being caught forever failing to be beautiful — became a main image of her last years. She used it in her autobiography: *Smile Please.* That begins with Jean as a child of six, having her photograph taken. She is prettily, perfectly dressed; she'll never look so pretty again. But already something is wrong: already the same things are wrong that will always be. She is too sad, and she cannot behave.

'Smile please,' the man said. 'Not quite so serious.'. . . .
I looked down at my white dress, the one I had got for my birthday, and my legs and the white socks coming half way up my legs, and the black shiny shoes with the strap over the instep.
'Now,' the man said.
'Keep still,' my mother said.
I tried but my arm shot up of its own accord.
'Oh what a pity, she moved.'
'You must keep still,' my mother said, frowning.

*Wide Sargasso Sea* continued to bring her friends, old as well as new. Leslie's first wife, Kathleen, was still alive, and when she heard about the success of *Sargasso Sea* she immediately wrote and told Anne in

America. Anne was astounded — like everyone else she had been sure Jean was dead. But she was also thrilled that her father's long faith and sacrifice were vindicated. She got Jean's address from Deutsch, and from now on they were back in touch again.

Then in early 1968 another old acquaintance reappeared: Oliver Stoner, who had first written to her in the thirties. He and his wife Mollie lived in Devon: that was why Jean had asked for his advice when she and Max had first wanted to move to the country. Now of course he read and admired *Wide Sargasso Sea*; and after its great success he learned from a local paper that Jean had not only managed to get to the country, but was actually living not very far away. He sent her 'greetings and congratulations', and their friendship was renewed.

It was an important one for Jean. Oliver and Mollie loved and approved of her as unreservedly as Francis and Sonia did, but they lived much closer. They couldn't call every day or every week, as Mr Woodard had; but they could and did visit her often, especially in the early years, when all three were still relatively fit.* In this first summer of their reacquaintance, for instance, the Stoners came to Jean at least twice, and Jean went to them once and stayed the night — an effort for her, and a monument to their appeal.

Oliver Stoner was like Francis Wyndham, or Alwynne Woodard: a literary man, who loved and admired her books, she knew, but loved and admired *her* even more. He was gallant, old-worldly and generous: this autumn, for instance, he spent much time and energy doing Francis's job as unpaid agent, negotiating for Jean with people who wanted to buy her manuscripts. And he collected, he loved, he lived for books. Books filled every room, every corridor of his house; it was as though they were the owners, and Oliver and Mollie their guardians. Oliver had read *everything*, and known everyone in the thirties and forties literary world. He and Jean could talk for hours. And Mollie would let them: providing the drinks, stoking the fire, 'creating' (she says) 'the atmosphere.' Jean would have loved that: receiving this kind, clever man's attention, and being taken care of by his generous wife. Indeed, Mollie was just as congenial a friend as Oliver — perhaps even more. Oliver was a rationalist and an intellectual; Mollie was a Catholic and a painter (which Jean always admired). She had known poverty, and was the opposite of smug; she had a wonderful zest and humour, and an intuitive understanding.

---

*In the late 1960s Jean was in her late seventies, Oliver in his late sixties and Mollie in her fifties. Jean was already very frail, but would, of course, become more so. The Stoners remained agile; but Oliver would become very deaf, and Mollie developed cataracts and lost much of her sight.

Jean talked to Oliver; but with Mollie she often didn't need to. Both the Stoners loved and approved of her — but Oliver with a courtly reserve, Mollie with open warmth. Neither thought the 'unrespectable' things about her mattered — but Mollie hardly noticed them. For instance, she *liked* 6 Landboat Bungalows, even when she first saw it in 1968, when it was still very squalid. Jean never ceased moaning about her home herself; but she was like someone with a smelly old dog — she didn't like anyone else to criticise it. Both Stoners made her feel *better* about everything; and that's what she needed.

Two new people appeared this year. Neither would become a close friend; but just for that reason perhaps they saw Jean vividly and clearly.

The first was a woman: a journalist and writer called Joan Forman. She felt what so many did, reading *Wide Sargasso Sea* — 'I must meet this person'. But unlike most, she acted. She wrote to Jean early in the year; and in the summer she came to Cheriton Fitzpaine to see her.

She had to come all the way from Norfolk, so she travelled down the night before and stayed in the pub in the village. Here she had a first strange experience. When she said she was going to see Jean Rhys, the people in the bar made (as she puts it) 'derogatory remarks'. But, she said, Jean was a great writer! There was silence then; but filled with sceptical and knowing looks louder than accusations.

The next day Joan knocked on Jean's door at exactly the moment they'd agreed. And now something even stranger happened. The door opened only the tiniest fraction; through the crack Jean's frightened eyes peered at her. Joan said who she was, she reminded Jean of their appointment, she tried to explain; but Jean didn't seem able to understand. For a long moment she wouldn't let her in. Finally, reluctantly, she did; but when they sat down in the bleak sitting room she was silent. For the first quarter of an hour she sat stiffly, answering only in monosyllables, as though she still didn't understand who Joan was, as though she still thought she was an enemy. At last it got a little better, and she agreed that Joan could come again the next day.

This time Joan brought a present — a bottle of whisky — because Jean had mentioned it was her birthday. Even so, and even though she'd agreed to this visit only the day before, the same thing happened. She was wary and afraid; she didn't want to let Joan in; and at first she sat stiff and silent. But finally she began to relax (perhaps they'd opened that bottle of whisky). She talked about Dominica, and about Paris, where she'd been young and beautiful.

She even talked a bit about Cheriton Fitzpaine — such a cold place, such cold people. She had had very great difficulties in this village.... She laughed; but underneath the laughter you heard the pain.

Jean was, I suspect, less dismayed by this rocky start than Joan. After all, it was how she very often behaved. They continued to correspond, and to see one another occasionally, mostly when Jean was in London. She went on talking to Joan as she talked to everyone: most of the time skilfully hiding what she wanted to hide, but occasionally succumbing to her writer's taste for truth — telling Joan once, for instance, the story of John's arrest for embezzlement in Paris. Now it was Joan who held back. She felt very strongly and clearly Jean's cavernous need; she knew if she came too close she would be swallowed up. So she remained distant: in a cowardly way, she thought, but it was not really cowardly. Quite a few people would remain this sort of friend to Jean — a bit distant, on the periphery. They often got the best of her; and often this sort of friendship suited her too. It didn't promise so much as others, but then it didn't disappoint so much either — not only Jean herself, but the other person.

The next new friend would also remain mostly a correspondent. This time it was a man: Herbert Ronson, a friend of the Stoners. Jean's relationships with men, even now, had to turn on dependence even more than her relationships with women. Oliver, Francis, Alec — all had to *help* her in some way. Ronson's special subject for her was travel. Over the next seven years he sent her information about Morocco, Portugal, Holland, Dominica — for all of which she was very grateful, and none of which she ever used. Now he came to give her some of this information in person: and wrote a touching and amusing account of Jean at seventy-eight.*

Mr Greenslade met him in Tiverton and drove him along the tortuous roads to Cheriton Fitzpaine. (And now we can see why Jean liked Mr Greenslade so much: he was 'large and genial', 'an armchair driver' who met each hazard with the utmost placidity. He was, in fact, exactly the sort of man Jean liked, 'a comfortable man', 'a "don't worry leave it all to me" man'.) Mr Greenslade left Ronson in front of Jean's gate — or rather 'where the gate is judged to be, the approach to Landboat Bungalows being considerably obscured by tangles of overgrown weeds and festoons of bright nasturtiums.' Now he too has trouble getting in. There is a long pause before Jean appears at her door; then she clings to it, 'supporting herself or protecting her

---

*'Meeting Jean', in London Magazine, July 1986. All quotations are from this piece.

solitude.' She is tiny, frail, quivering; she has 'a pale face, white hair waved and tinted heliotrope and large dreamy eyes.' She looks to him like 'an ancient nun'; or like 'the deposed and forgotten queen' of a country that no longer exists.

Somehow he gets inside. Mr Greenslade reappears with a bowl of ice-cubes, and Jean mixes gin-and-vermouth, twice, 'with shivery clashes and tinkles'. She tells Ronson 'in a delicate near-whisper that she *must* get away next winter, away from the *cold* (the mellow October sun pours in through the window).' He brings out his holiday brochures and starts to talk. This is why he has come; but Jean doesn't seem to be listening. Her eyes 'become deeper and darker pools,' she grows 'ethereal, detached.' Then she leans towards him and 'in a ravishing undertone' asks, 'Will you take me to Holland?' '*Of course* I will!' Ronson replies – he's been 'entirely captivated,' 'robbed of volition,' from the start. But he never will. Jean pushes the brochures away with a despairing gesture. She has given up all hope of travel; she'd given it up before he came.

They talk: about writing, about money ('She has none'), about the press ('the photographer swore blind I had approved the photos but I hadn't, and the man wrote lies, all lies'). All along Jean has been fumbling surreptitiously at her belt, which her crippled fingers have been unable to buckle. At last she pulls it away and drops it under her chair. 'It is as if she is putting away some small part of an illusionist's equipment, abandoning a trick which, in any case, would not have come off.'

They walk in the garden ('a rough-and-tumble plot'); Jean signs Ronson's copy of *Wide Sargasso Sea*. She has only allowed him an hour, with the 'veiled implication' that any more would make her 'disintegrate, melt away or otherwise vanish.' After exactly an hour there's a rap on the door: Mr Greenslade to take him away. He looks back at Jean's tiny cottage; and it seems to him she *has* vanished.

When I went to see her seven years later it was exactly the same. The reluctance to let you in – much worse again, as it had been with Joan Forman (was this because we were women?) The determination, seductively murmured but steely, to bend you to her current need – yet the sense that she'd despaired of succeeding from the start; the complaints about the cold, about money, about the papers ('all lies'); the sudden and certain feeling that she had withdrawn, that you were already forgotten. Ronson leaves out her sense of humour, and a certain wickedness. But otherwise it's all there. She didn't change – not from one time to another, not from one person to another. She was like this with Adrian Allinson in 1915 and with me in 1975. She was – as she said – a record, always playing the same tune.

★

After the long struggle of writing *Wide Sargasso Sea* and watching Max die she had hoped for 'a miracle': it might be Alec, it might be Maryvonne, but in her mind it was always a person. Of course when it came it wasn't a person at all, but her own book. *Wide Sargasso Sea* was the miracle which changed her fortunes, which brought her the company and attention she longed for, and also dreaded. It had already rescued *Voyage in the Dark* and *Good Morning, Midnight*; now it also rescued her rejected book of short stories. Nine of *The Left Bank* stories were added to it; and 'Let Them Call It Jazz' and 'The Day They Burned the Books' substituted for 'I Spy a Stranger' and 'Temps Perdi'. As we know, the title was changed from *The Sound of the River* to *Tigers Are Better-Looking*. As we also know, Diana didn't realise that this emphasised Jean's differences with Leslie over her love for him, and Jean didn't tell her.

*Tigers* was almost unanimously praised. The few reservations that were expressed were fair, and always the same: that Jean's writing sometimes stayed too close to 'paranoid case history'. But even for these critics her prose was moving, her vision truthful, the core of her art the opposite of self-indulgent. That was especially clear in this collection, in which people could compare early work with late. This art did not console (said the *Observer*), it was the result (said the *London Magazine*) of 'considerable self-denial.' It had become increasingly sophisticated (said *The Times Literary Supplement*): but in pursuit of her own aims, untouched by literary fashion. And so she had not dated: she was (said *The Times*) 'a twentieth century master'.

This new step in her fame and praise meant – of course – more requests for interviews. She gave her first big one now, to the journalist Hannah Carter. It appeared in *The Guardian* in August, under the title 'Fated to be Sad'. And Jean, of course, hated it.

All interviewers, she wrote towards the end of her life, 'gently pushed' her

> ... into my pre-destined role, the role of victim. I have never had any good times, never laughed, never got my own back, never dared, never worn pretty clothes, never been happy, never known wild hopes or wilder despairs. In short I have never been young, or if I was, I've forgotten all about it.

This was almost entirely unfair. It was *she* who gave people the idea that she was a victim: she who talked about the sadness of her life, about its having been fated. She also talked – a bit – about the happy moments, and when she did they were reported. But she didn't write about them, as she said; and nor therefore (except in passing) did her interviewers. She wrote about the storms and not the (brief) calms of her life because she needed to write them out — but also because they were dramatic, they were interesting; they fascinated her, and they fascinate us. The worst that can be said about the journalists who interviewed her was that they worked on the same principle.

And in fact Jean almost always ended up talking quite openly about herself to people who asked her. There were, of course, parts of her life which (as Joan Forman noticed) she kept hidden: especially the worst times, during and after the two wars. But even these she'd briefly and occasionally mention; and then she wouldn't hide that they were bad, though self-protection required a great deal of understatement. Now, for instance, she told Hannah Carter that the years after *Good Morning, Midnight* were 'very troublesome indeed'. And she told her much more — about writing, about coming to England, about Cheriton Fitzpaine ('They said I was a witch ... In the evenings, reinforced with wine, I used to shout defiance at them from the window'). She was, after all, addicted to the truth, though it too might harm her. She hated lying and did it badly. So she took refuge mostly in silence and vagueness, and denials afterwards. But at the time, faced with a new, live, interested human being, she found herself talking. She was just like Antoinette, trying to protect herself from Rochester 'with silence and a blank face': 'Poor weapons, and they had not served well or lasted long.' She'd ended up talking to Joan Forman; she ended up talking to me. 'Well,' she said, with her sudden, disarming smile, half an hour after barring her door to me, 'I'm talking to you after all, aren't I?'

By the end of 1968 she had taken several more steps along the road to wider fame. *Wide Sargasso Sea* had come out as a Penguin paperback. Penguin had bought *Voyage in the Dark* and *Good Morning, Midnight* too; they would appear the next year. *Wide Sargasso Sea* was going to be translated into French, and so were *Good Morning, Midnight* and *Tigers Are Better-Looking*. It was beginning to be clear that this rescue from oblivion would last: that life wouldn't turn around and say 'Where are you?' this time, that this time she wouldn't be thrown back into the deep dark river. She would never be rich, but she would have some money at last; she would never be a bestseller, but she didn't want to be. She would have, in fact, what she'd always wanted: appreciation for her work, and security for herself. And yet (of course, *of course*) she could never just relax and enjoy it. It had come too late, as she always said. Not the appreciation, perhaps: I think she could and did value that. But the security — that she couldn't value, because she couldn't feel it. Insecurity was a habit she couldn't break. Insecurity, loneliness and persecution: however much her life improved, she still felt them. They went too deep to change.

She was saying now that she'd always been alone in Cheriton: that Max had died soon after they'd moved there, and she'd been alone ever since. It wasn't true, but it was how she was feeling. In early 1968 she wrote down her solitary routine. It remained much the same for the next seven or eight years, until she had to have a nurse to take care of her.

She woke very early, got up around seven, lit the electric heater in the kitchen and the cooker as well, and sat smoking until the post came. If there was no post she waited for the papers instead. Then breakfast, reading the papers 'as slowly as possible'. By the time she'd done that, it was half past ten or eleven o'clock. Slowly she tidied up, bathed, dressed. That took till a quarter to one, and Mrs Greenslade bringing lunch. After lunch she smoked again. Then it was time to work, or to try to work, until five. At five a short walk. At seven bread and cheese; at eight or half-past eight whisky, a book, bed. 'If it's a good book I'm happy lying there a bit drunk & reading. If not — I drink more whisky. It's like that day after day & has been for a long time.'

She had a new fear now: that Maryvonne might take Selma's side against her. 'I do think it would be rather sad,' she wrote to Diana, 'if Maryvonne got it into her head that I'd behaved badly or unkindly to Selma when it's the other way around.' I don't know what put this idea into her head; perhaps she knew that Maryvonne and Selma were (briefly) exchanging letters. But at the same time Maryvonne was beginning to be more open about her feelings towards her; and they weren't happy. Mostly she felt that 'I've never been able to see my mother as a real person. What I've seen is her likeness in a looking-glass.' This was of course Jean's doing: she hid her real life and her real feelings from Maryvonne as much as she could, because they were too bad, she was too ashamed of them. But then Maryvonne felt rejected, and accused her of 'pretending' ('I am sorry you think I "pretend" about everything,' Jean wrote to her. 'But really if I faced the exact truth about myself, that I am old, sick, alone & loathe Cheriton Fitz I could not go on living at all').

This was her tragedy. She hid from people because she feared their disapproval: and of course she hid most from those she loved most, whose approval she most needed. So where she wanted most closeness she put most distance; and both she and the other person ended up feeling like Julia Martin — that she was pretending, that she wasn't real, that under the careful mask there was nothing there.

At the end of the year Maryvonne came to see her while she was staying with Sonia in London, and asked some direct questions about her birth and her childhood. Perhaps Jean tried to answer, perhaps she tried not to. When she got home she tried again in a letter. She told Maryvonne about fetching her from the clinic and taking her to Mrs Adam; she told her that when at last she had no money, 'not a sou', she still refused to part with her: 'I simply said *No* I will *not*. I don't care what *anybody* says. I did my best & doubtless others did too....' This 'doubtless others' must have sounded very grudging to Maryvonne — what about her father, who had always been so good to her? But really Jean was trying *not* to accuse John, by keeping silent. To others she would say that the collapse of her first marriage wasn't just her fault, it was 'more complicated than that'; to Sonia she said now that Maryvonne's relationship with her father '*was* very close and I can't disturb it.' Of course she was trying to protect herself from Maryvonne's disappointment and disapproval; but she was also trying to protect John. As usual her conflicting desires pulled in opposite directions, and she achieved neither. Maryvonne must have been left with a greater sense of mystification and mutual distrust than ever.

During 1969 Jean's reputation grew steadily. *Voyage in the Dark* and *Good Morning, Midnight* came out in paperback, and *Quartet* and *Mackenzie* were reprinted, all in May, and all to superb reviews. She was beginning to be translated into Dutch, French, German, Norwegian. She was particularly pleased to be read in France, and praised the French translations with delight. 'Better than the original sometimes,' she said.

Immediately after the four reissues in May, the *Observer* published another big interview with her. It was called 'The Inscrutable Miss Jean Rhys': but once again Jean wasn't really so inscrutable. She told the young interviewer, Marcelle Bernstein, a good deal — about writing, about her early life, about being suspected of being a witch in Cheriton Fitzpaine. In the photograph (which of course she loathed) she looks wary: but again she couldn't carry through her intention. Out of this interview, like the others, comes a sense of intimacy which we recognise: it's the same sense of a mask slipped or stripped away that we find in the novels.

And this interview in particular had the same effect as the novels: large numbers of readers felt as though Jean had addressed *them* personally, and wanted to reply. After it she received floods of letters from people: rarely about books or writing, but about themselves, their troubles and sadness. That is what reading a Jean Rhys novel, story or interview is like: you recognise this pain, you are consoled to know it shared, and you want to console her in turn. But Jean wasn't consoled. She did her best, she answered all the letters carefully, but they were a burden to her. She didn't know what to say — especially, she told Sonia, 'when they offer to come here and "take care of me."' Two people did that. She wasn't touched, or (much) amused; 'horrible idea!' she said.

None the less she made several new friends now, and at least one came as a result of this interview. Larry Cole, a young teacher who was living not far away in Cornwall, wrote to her after he'd read it and asked if they could meet. As he neither poured out his woes nor asked her to read his first long novel, she replied very graciously. And for the next several years, until he moved away, Larry visited Jean quite often.

Everyone who knew her was struck by Jean's extreme incompetence, her apparent inability to manage the simplest objects — telephones, typewriters, parcels, radios. Larry saw some remarkable examples of this. She still had no telephone or television, but when he first met her she did have a new red gramophone, a present from Maryvonne. But she had a terrible problem with her long-playing records (she told him). There was always only one song on them she wanted to hear, but it was never at the beginning: she had to endure all the ones she *didn't* want before getting to the one she did.... Larry showed her how to move the arm until the needle began with the track she wanted, in the middle or at the end of the record. She refused to believe it was possible; she watched him, anxious and alarmed, while he did it; when 'La Vie en Rose' began she exclaimed with childlike wonder. It was the same when she wanted to listen to a programme of readings on the radio. 'All I ever get is music,' she said hopelessly. 'I don't know where the talking can be.' Larry said all she had to do was adjust the dial. Once again she wouldn't believe him until he demonstrated, found Radio Four, and told her not to move anything except the On/Off switch at the required time. 'She was so thankful and appreciative I felt as if I'd showered her with all the perfumes of Arabia,' Larry says. (But of course when the time came she couldn't manage the simple switching on either.)

It was an extraordinary thing, this incompetence of Jean's — so profound that in all practical matters she 'needed as much looking after as a child of ten,' as Diana Athill says. What was it? What was happening, as she stood helplessly in front of a simple radio or record player, unable to hear the one thing she wanted?

Partly, Larry felt (like Maryvonne), it was a pretence: something exaggerated if not invented, a game. But why did she play such an uncomfortable, such a sometimes disastrous game? Larry's feeling was that she did it, at least partly, to annoy. She had a wicked, teasing side, like a child with grown-ups: pushing them to see how far they will go. And like a child who could really do things perfectly well if she tried, she preferred to have them done for her: that is how badly she needed the smallest sign of attention and care. She had stuck emotionally (Diana says) in childhood: she felt happiest when she was treated as a child.

But I think there were other reasons too. If it was possible to manage things she'd have to try. She preferred to think it wasn't possible, that whatever happened was her trap, her fate. Then she could be angry at objects instead of at herself, which she could only ever do in writing. She *liked* being incompetent about typewriters, wrapping paper, radios. It was safe. Besides, like her general 'vagueness', it was good camouflage. If she couldn't type, and couldn't find typists, people couldn't see her writing; if she couldn't manage the radio she couldn't hear the programmes. In fact she never managed to hear anyone's radio performances — not Selma's in the past, for example, and now not a new friend's, Antonia Fraser's. She was surely afraid of what they might do to her books (Antonia Fraser was reading an extract from *Good Morning, Midnight*); and like many deep and narrow artists she wasn't really interested in other people's work. But all this, she knew, was untrusting and unkind, and she wouldn't want to admit it. It was easier to pretend that she'd simply missed the broadcast — that her clock was wrong, her radio was wrong, she couldn't find the station. And not just to pretend, but *really* to miss it, really to be unable to find the station.

She ought to have heard Antonia Fraser's broadcast, because Antonia too had become a friend. She was a great admirer of Jean's; and when her *Mary Queen of Scots* came out in 1969 she gave Francis a signed copy of it for her. Jean thanked her; they corresponded, eventually they met. Antonia remained a more distant friend, like Joan Forman, and saw Jean only occasionally. But in this more distant mode she was the same sort of friend as Sonia: generous, un-judging, *fun*. She was a writer too; more important to Jean, she was a beautiful woman, and she enjoyed it and thought about it, as Jean did. Not as obsessively as Jean — that would be hard; more healthily and happily. But she too loved clothes, scent, make-up, hairdressers, all the pleasures of feminine allure. She *liked* Jean's preoccupation with such things; she admired her extraordinary complexion, her never-say-die clothes and wigs and manicures. And again Jean bloomed in the warmth of approval and understanding. When she was in London they would meet in expensive restaurants, and have a lovely time. If Jean burst into tears in the middle of lunch for no reason she would say 'It was just one of those things', Antonia must forgive her; and Antonia did. Jean never raged at her (though she sometimes raged *to* her, about other people): partly because they weren't close enough, but mostly because Jean wasn't angry at her.

She was too generous and approving. She didn't think Jean ill-read, just because she couldn't read Balzac, Fielding, George Eliot, Joyce. She listened to Jean's superstitions without contempt. She gave her beautiful presents — Miss Dior scent, clothes, flowers. And she gave her a glimpse of her dream: the life of a happy woman.

Jean was nearly eighty, but she still had that dream. She wrote about it now to Diana Athill. She'd met another woman who embodied it, and she sent Diana a long, passionate description of her — which is really, I think, a description of how she would have liked to be herself, as an older (never an *old*) woman.

> ... She was not young hardly made up, but very small and slim. Beautifully dressed in black. *Such* a nice thing to see a beautiful dress after utilitarian Cheriton Fitz.
>
> Well, her face was wrinkled but charming, her eyes brown & small but very bright & lively, she had small hands and feet and wore very very pretty shoes. She talked of Paris & 'St Petersburg' which she'd known well in her youth. Not too much. Her voice was low but clear & her hair perfectly done.
>
> Well my dear I was dismayed when this apparition from a vanished world went on to say: 'I wish so much that I had been a writer.'(!!)
>
> I thought volumes but only said that it was a lonely job sometimes. I also said that I envied her which was true. But imagine! She doesn't know....

She too still had a small slim body and a charming (if wrinkled) face. But all the rest — the perfect clothes and hair and voice, the knowledge of how not to talk 'too much' — these she could only envy. Instead, she was a writer.... She never got to know this woman. But just for that reason their encounter shot straight through to her permanent obsession: the mutual exclusion between being beautiful and happy, and being a writer. That wound wouldn't heal.

She was trying to write her autobiography now: that must have opened it up again. It wasn't going well. During both wintry ends of 1969 she was ill as usual and could work only very slowly. She tried to help this with whisky, which made her slower. The trouble was that she was asking herself the old hard questions. And this was autobiography, not fiction; *she couldn't hide.* She had more strongly than ever, therefore, the sense that she was writing the Trial of Jean Rhys: and the jury were hostile. 'I've a very strong feeling that if I write truthfully of the West Indies as I knew them no one will believe me,' she told Sonia; and Francis: 'I don't remember what I'm expected to remember or feel what I'm expected to feel. Indeed I remember & feel exactly the opposite.' Partly this was a political feeling. Like many who have lived on the right side of a feudal arrangement, Jean was inclined to defend the colonialists of her father's generation; and she knew that this would be deeply unfashionable. But it was also, as always, a personal feeling. Digging out *Creole* to use for the autobiography, she was rediscovering how far back her unbelonging went. *It went back to the beginning.* To her mother saying to her, aged perhaps ten, 'I've done my best, it's no use. You'll never learn to be like other people.' And to her feeling then — 'that went straight as an arrow to the heart, straight as the truth. I saw the long road of isolation and loneliness stretching in front of me as far as the eye could see, and farther.' She'd been right; she was still on it.

She had friends now, good kind ones, more than she'd ever had before. They wrote to her; she saw them in Cheriton in the summer and in London in the winter. Alec cheered her up very much when he visited in July; in August she stayed at the Stoners' again; in September Mr Woodard, Sonia and Francis, and a cheerful Dutch journalist called Hans Roest all visited and lifted her. At Christmas she was fêted with cards and presents — chocolates, scent, whisky, champagne — most generously of course by Sonia, whom she sent a little necklace in return. When presents arrived she wrote 'Gloom vanished' — '*Pas de cafard*' — 'Instant euphoria!' But she needed this all the time — constant presents, constant lifting. The moment it stopped she fell back into her usual darkness, waiting for six o'clock and her only ever-present pal, whisky.

Despite everything, therefore — her old novels rescued, her good reviews, her good friends — 1969 was full of the old feelings. Even the baby next door looked like 'a real old village gossip';* one of her first full sentences was 'Oo the bloody 'ell is she?' Things were going on in London which she, 'in prison here', knew nothing about. No one was on her side, and she understood no one. The *Observer* photograph was awful, a 'dreadful gaga tortured expression' — if they publish it 'no one will want to read anything I write.' The interviewer 'was Selma's friend. So all the talk about frailty, trembling hands etc. was just what was wanted. . . .' This was of course in a pit of paranoia, which centred again on Selma.

The Selma affair had raised its ugly head again because Margaret Ramsay had sold an option on the film rights of *Wide Sargasso Sea.* That meant a chance of real money. But also, of course, it didn't — because half of it would go to Selma.

---

*Zena Raymond's youngest daughter, Saskia. Several people in Cheriton Fitzpaine suggested to me that despite all the trouble between them this rather exotic name came from something of Jean's — a version of 'Sasha', perhaps?

But now, in fact, Selma was anxious for a reconciliation. Knowing this, Peggy Ramsay and Diana Athill suggested to Jean that she personally ask Selma to reduce her claim from half to a third. (However much Selma wanted to make things up, this was as far as she would go.) Jean did, and Selma agreed. Peggy Ramsay prepared a new contract which reached Jean in early August. And now the improbable (but inevitable) happened. The contract contained the new, more favourable terms: but it was 'business', and she couldn't understand it. Her panic at anything legal flared ('It was when he said "legally" that you flew at him,' Grace Poole says to Antoinette.) She became convinced that this was an attempt to tighten Selma's hold instead of loosen it; that Selma was trying to seize — *had* seized — the copyright on all her novels.... Diana calmed her down and persuaded her to sign the contract.

Now Jean understood that it wasn't a trap, but as much as possible the release from one. But her relief didn't really touch her paranoia about Selma. It drove her, despite her dread of the law and of death, to face both and make a will, in order to keep all she could out of Selma's grasping hands.

It was so typical of her not to have made a will until now — though she was seventy-nine, had felt physically weak all her life, and had been kept alive by pills for the last half a dozen years. Now, naturally, her health was worse than ever. The previous spring she'd had a bad attack of colitis; in the summer of 1970 she would have another heart attack, though only a slight one this time. But it was her fear of Selma, not such 'facts', which had driven her to act. When she was young she never expected to live beyond thirty or forty: when she was old she never expected to die. That was Jean all over — perverse, reality-denying. Yet in a strange way it was also true. She *was* closer to dying in her youth, by suicide or inanition; the longer she survived the more attached she became to surviving. Perhaps because when she was young she always expected to be happier, so that she was constantly disappointed; when she was old she didn't really expect any more than the few good moments she had. In this way, too, the end of her life was better than its beginning.

In 1970 *Good Morning, Midnight* was published for the first time in the United States. America was ready now for this 'fiercely unforgiving book': especially American women. No sooner had one critic suggested that *Good Morning, Midnight* might become 'a strong weapon in the current and growing movement towards women's liberation' than another used it exactly that way.

Now the only thing Jean liked about feminists was teasing them ('"I didn't like the suffragettes much", I say. "Didn't you," she says, shocked'). She stood outside the women's movement as she stood outside everything. Nevertheless they were right to hail her as a champion. Her novels explored the pain (and pleasures) of female dependency with great insight and honesty — with greater insight and honesty, often, than was achieved later, in books written to a self-conscious polemical plan. From now on the women's movement would increasingly appropriate her and misinterpret her intentions. But though she meant only to explore her own alienation and oppression, not women's in general, despite herself she did have a great deal to contribute to that wider question. She and the women's movement had nothing whatever in common; yet they helped one another. Jean gave them some of their greatest literature, and they gave her recognition. It was the coincidence of *Wide Sargasso Sea* with the beginnings of 'women's lib' in the mid-sixties, and the reissue of her early novels with its growth in the seventies, which more than anything else ensured that she was 'rediscovered', and stayed that way. It's still true today, with her novels more often on Women's Studies courses than any other. But it is changing. The other concept through which critics look at her work now is colonialism: recognising, in other words, the extent to which she writes out of other kinds of oppression than women's. And at last another term is being brought in too — modernism. At last, that is, she is being studied not just as a woman, or as a colonial, but as a figure in twentieth-century literature: not just as a victim, but as a writer. That would have pleased her.

Now, however, her writing was not going well. She was doubting the autobiography, restlessly rehearsing titles for it, thinking it 'dull and factual'. She left it for another attempt to adapt *Quartet* for the stage; then she got out some short stories to work on. By the summer she'd promised to do 'a short story or two'. The autobiography was getting pushed into the background — though (she lamented) it was what she really wanted to do. Really, I think, she *didn't* want to do it, and was turning to stories for relief. She would often do this when she couldn't get on with longer work; and now longer work was becoming more difficult. But she was right, this time, to worry about it. The stories would lead her away from the autobiography until they were published in 1976. And she didn't have enough time left for that. She never did finish the autobiography, and wouldn't live to see it published.

Other things were distracting her from work too. In February, for example, a team came to interview her for French television. This was a revealing little episode. First, of course, that she'd agreed to be on French television at all, when she'd categorically refused to be on English — 'Too nervous!' (though she seems to have managed to forget it was television, in order to face doing it). Then second, that she reported it to Francis and Sonia, who loved and indulged her, in her helpless mode: as soon as the interview began, she said, every word of French 'flew out of my head'. (Just like Sasha, when she thinks Mr Blank wants to test her German: 'All the little German I know flies out of my head'.) Yet Maryvonne, who was there, was '*astonished* at how she could say exactly what she wanted in French....' It was like Larry Cole's feeling about the incident of the gramophone: she wasn't really as helpless as she appeared. It's as though she put on helplessness like a pretty dress, because it was feminine, because it brought her attention and service. But then it also became real, like the frown one's mother said would stay on one's face forever.

To explain this paradox — that she was as helpless as a ten-year old, and also she wasn't — she fell back on the vocabulary of inspiration and possession. Now she admitted to Oliver Stoner that she'd managed to speak French — but only because one of the interviewers was such a 'charmer', she'd been 'hypnotised'. So she managed *never* to take responsibility, either for achievements or for failures; not even for her writing ('I'm a pen. I'm nothing but a pen.') Her self-distrust ran too deep. If she'd faced the fact that *she* was writing, or speaking French, she couldn't do it.

Another distracting (to Jean) and revealing (to us) event of 1970 also had a French connection. At the end of March a letter arrived for her from her French publishers, Denoël. It came from a prison in Lyon: from a man accused of murder. He was innocent, he said, but no one would defend him. Would Jean help him to find a lawyer? '*Je suis seul, isolé, abandonné de tous,*' he wrote. '*Je mets tout mon espoir en vous, en votre humanité....*') He had read her very acutely: these were exactly the words to touch Jean's heart. She became 'extremely anxious to do something — anything — for him.' She replied straight away — '*Courage', 'Je ferai mon possible*'; then she wrote to the French translator of *Tigers*, Pierre Leyris, and asked him to help. Leyris found a lawyer, and Jean had a message of thanks via Denoël. She was happy; but also very worried and anxious. The man was 'so lost and alone'; very likely his case was hopeless; she didn't know what to do.... The incident had brought back painful memories. The stranger was partly John to her, whom she should have helped more than she did, long ago. And partly Max too perhaps, though she didn't say so — who had also been innocent, or at least a pawn in someone else's game. And he was, of course, partly herself. All her trials must have come back to her, the real ones, the imaginary one in her Ropemakers Diary. 'It's not true that you're innocent until proven guilty,' she wrote fiercely to Oliver. 'Not in France or England or anywhere else. You are guilty until you can damn well prove you are innocent. Sometimes you can't.'

Like so many of her readers, the prisoner in Lyon had looked straight through her books to *her*. It was as though she'd reached out through the books and touched him, and he'd reached back and touched her. This hardly ever happened in life; there she never really escaped the prison of herself to touch another person. She could only do it through her books. But through them, of course, she touched many thousand times more people than could any ordinary 'happy woman'.*

Soon after this meeting-through-books Jean had one of her rare meetings-in-life which hinted at the possibility, at least, of some real communion. It too was with a man; a young man, for Jean: a fifty-year-old Dutch poet and teacher called Jan van Houts.

Van Houts had made an appointment to see her while he was on holiday in England. But when he arrived in Exeter he was offered his rented car a day early. So he did something which no one who knew Jean would have dared to do: he drove to Cheriton Fitzpaine a day early, and knocked on her door.

It opened a little and she asked what he wanted. 'She was very shy and wary,' van Houts has written — a vast understatement, I'm sure, and a key to the kindness that endeared him to her. But when he said he was Jan from Holland and had an appointment with her for the next day, she let him in. They drank some whisky from his duty-free bottle; and she told him 'the three words of Dutch she knew.' One of them was *verdomme*: *damn*.

That was the beginning. The next day they drove to Tiverton, because J.D. Salinger had been stationed there and they both admired *The Catcher in the Rye*. After that they went for more drives, around the Devon hills and to the seaside; or they sat in her sitting room or kitchen and talked. Thus they spent five days: five days of perfect weather, five days of happiness for Jean. She wore her entire wardrobe in one week. In the car they sang songs together, although he said he couldn't sing. (In the story Jean wrote about him he has a good voice, and she thinks 'How long was it since she had sat by a man driving fast and singing?') Their last day of all was by the sea. Jean sat in a deck chair in the sun, Jan stood behind her, and together they watched a man in a white shirt feeding the white gulls. They

---

*Jean went on thinking about the prisoner in Lyon for months. In 1971 Amnesty said they would try to help him, and he wrote to thank her again, sending her a pair of miniature *sabots* he'd whittled. She kept these; but I don't think she ever knew the end of his story.

had lunch in a restaurant in a cellar, which Jean loved because she had 'more than a touch' of agoraphobia. Then they drove home to Jacques Brel on the radio. It was glorious, Jean said; and she wrote to Maryvonne: 'I shall not forget it.'

*What had happened?* Here was a stranger, who had done everything wrong — arrived without warning, suggested sightseeing, asked about her life, wanted to film her — and she went along with it all happily, even the filming (after a day or two's hesitation). He filmed her at the seaside, and standing by her front door; she went on talking naturally to him, saying she liked to see him work — and indeed in his pictures she looks relaxed and happy, not wary and frightened as usual. It must have been him. There must have been something about him which comforted her, as there was about Mr Greenslade (and it must have been a perfect moment when the one handed her over to the other saying 'Look after her — that's my girl'). He was Dutch, which she liked, and he was a poet, which she liked very much; but most of all she just liked *him*. She felt they understood each other, as though they were the same sort of person, even the same person. In Jan's account she says to him, 'We know what we think of each other,' and 'It's as if I've known you a long time.' In her own short story she wrote:

> At the door he turned. 'We recognised each other, didn't we?'
> She didn't answer. She thought: yes, I recognised you almost at once. But I never imagined that you recognised me.

Of course she doesn't say *what* they recognised. But Jan does. Jean gave him a copy of *Voyage in the Dark*, in which she'd written 'To Jan from Jean Rhys — Outside the machine': 'Because,' she said, 'you're outside the machine too.' He nodded, so perhaps it was true. In any case that was what she felt; that was what made her happy. *They were the same, she wasn't alone.*

But soon, of course, she was. 'Will you write to me please,' she begged Francis, 'for I have a bad *cafard*. A friend came to see me, it was sunny and we went driving around. It was fun but after he went back to Holland I got this sad & *à quoi bon* feeling....' And to Sonia: 'I've given up trying to make sense of the muddle that is life,' 'always "here you are" & then "where are you?".' When she came to write the story of Jan's visit it was in the shadow of this feeling. True, the elderly narrator feels safe and happy with the young man; they recognise each other and laugh together. But it's against an overwhelming background of fear and despair. In reality Jean and Jan had sung popular songs together like 'The Man of la Mancha'. In the story 'Jan' sings alone: operatic arias 'not in any language she knew,' and the heroine says 'They always sing when they are dying.' She only *tries* to sound welcoming when he appears on the wrong day, and she won't let him photograph her; when they talk of going to Italy she knows it is only fantasy, but doesn't know if he knows: 'How few people understood what a tightrope she walked ... The abyss. Despair.' They have only one outing, to the sea, and he is gone; she is left alone, to think of her real escape – not Italy, but suicide. At the end of the story the wind is up and it has turned cold. The heroine has made a fool of herself buying nightgowns meant for women a fraction of her age; Mr Singh has said he will pray for her; and she has 'locked the door', closing off all hope, shutting herself in with the unnameable thing in her attic. All through Jean's fiction we have watched her heroines climbing towards the attic and what was waiting there. Finally Antoinette was shut in with it, and it was madness. Now an old woman is shut in with it too, and even without the opening arias we know what it is. In the next story it will come down from the attic and get her: the 'Super Rat', death.

Through most of the autumn of 1970, she was 'blue' and ill, hardly working, trying not to think about being old and close to death. But she didn't die. Instead someone else did: her brother Edward.

He had reached a venerable eighty-seven, but he had never really recovered from his wife's death four years before. In mid-1969 he'd had a spell in hospital. Jean visited him there, and once or twice at home – which was no longer Knottsfield, but 'nice rooms & a nice landlady'. But sometimes she didn't go, either because he was too ill, or because she was. At Christmas *he* visited *her*, and she determined to return his visit 'as soon as I feel well enough.' So she told Maryvonne. But after that she doesn't mention him again: until a year later, to say that he has died.

Probably, then, she didn't see him during the last year of his life. So the family certainly believed: and of course they blamed her for it. Brenda was ill too, and lived far away in Suffolk. Jean lived close by, and owed him so much – yet during all the months he was alone and dying (they say) she never once went to see him....

Well, she was old and ill herself, afraid of hospitals, afraid of dying. She had found it hard enough to visit Max when he was in hospital, and she had loved Max. She didn't even like Edward, and he didn't like her. He had done his best by her – but dutifully, with severity. She wasn't able to do things because they were her duty; quite the contrary. There was so much between them, years of distrust, resentment, obligation. The whole family disapproved of her books: but Edward said so. He had seen her when she was quite broken down, after Leslie's death and in Cheriton Fitzpaine. He had accused her of alcoholism and of madness; he had wanted to lock her up. He was ashamed of her and wanted to hide her away. These were her own worst feelings, the ones she drank to forget and wrote to exorcise. And he embodied them. She should have gone to see him; but we can understand it if she didn't.

Still, once he had died she was sad. He couldn't hurt her any more; and with him — as she'd broken so completely with Brenda — her last link with the past had gone. 'I was fond of him & will miss him,' she wrote to Sonia; and to Oliver: 'He was a friend.' She hadn't gone to any family funerals since her mother's; not to Minna's, not even to Owen's. I'm sure she had felt (quite rightly) that she would be unwelcome. But this was different. Edward had come to Leslie's funeral, and to Max's; he would have come to hers if she had died first. She knew from his lawyer that Brenda and her husband wouldn't be there: so she both could and should be. She decided to go to Edward's funeral.

Alas, it was a classically appalling occasion. It was also a sad one. There were of course no wife or children, no other brothers or sisters, few friends. The arrangements had been made by Edward's solicitor, who appeared to be the chief mourner. Owen's widow came, his son and daughter-in-law, and Brenda's adoptive son Robin Beck. Apart from Jean and Maryvonne that was all that was left of the family. A few of Gertrude's relatives came too; perhaps a friend or two. There weren't (Dorothy Rees Williams says) a dozen people there altogether. It was a harsh image of decline: the proud Rees Williamses reduced to a handful, burying the last head of the family, and seeing from the empty pews that he had been a lonely old man.

But the worst, of course, was the atmosphere between this remnant of the family and Jean. The family was her most hostile jury of all, and she must have spent hours and days on her clothes and hair and make-up. Which they, of course, would see as showing-off, as outrageous indulgence. 'For years we'd heard about the destitution of Gwennie,' Dorothy Rees Williams says; for years Edward, whom they'd come to mourn, had lost money like blood to keep her alive. And now here she came, beautifully turned out, in a chauffeur-driven limousine.... Of course this was only Mr Greenslade and his taxi; and John Rees Williams, for example, knew it. None the less Mr Greenslade would have polished his car and looked the part; and Jean certainly made an entrance, leaning on his arm, looking (John says) handsome and imperious. Now came the next false step, the next widening of the gap. 'That woman,' Dorothy says — and I'm sure she speaks as usual for the whole family — 'That woman had led my poor brother-in-law a hell of a life, and out of his Christian spirit and his bringing-up he did what he could for her.' She had shown him no gratitude, and she'd left him to die alone. But now, during the service, she cried as though her heart were broken, as though she'd lost her dearest friend. 'You couldn't hear the man speak for her sobs,' Dorothy says. And she was 'enraged', because 'I knew what hypocrisy it was.'

We can be sure Jean did cry like this — we've only to think of Julia Martin at her mother's funeral, abandoning herself to sobbing like a child. It *would* seem hypocrisy, as Dorothy says; and attention-seeking, like the arrival in the 'limousine'. Maybe it was this, too; Jean always did need to be the centre of attention. But it wasn't hypocrisy: that was their sort of sin, not hers. Perhaps, like Julia, she was crying for herself; or perhaps she was crying for her real sins towards Edward, which the family (as of course she knew) were at that very moment blaming her for. She cried so easily for no reason at all; how could she *not* cry now?

But even this wasn't the end. Jean said afterwards that she knew no one there: and of course she didn't know Gertrude's relations, or John* and his wife, or Robin Beck. But she *had* met Dorothy, though it was long ago; and Dorothy says she introduced Jean to the others before the service began. In any case, when it was over Dorothy asked if she would like to come to tea. And now of course accounts differ. The family say that Jean 'cut us absolutely dead.' She said 'No, thank you,' and (in Dorothy's words) 'stepped away.... She was right-down rude.' Jean said to Maryvonne:

> After the service they came up & spoke to me but all the strange faces bewildered me & I didn't know what to say. One woman asked me if I'd like some tea & I remembered having met her once years & years ago but it was very vague.
> The others I didn't know at all ... so as I was feeling rather ill I asked Mr Greenslade to take me away & he did.

And to Sonia: 'I felt so sad & awful that I left the crematorium as soon as I could.'

It's a microcosm of all her disastrous social experience. She feels 'bewildered', sad and ill; she 'doesn't know what to say,' and she runs away. But to others her 'vagueness' and her disappearance seem rude; they feel that it is deliberate (Dorothy, for example, wondered if this was Jean's revenge for the money she'd stopped Owen from sending in 1934 ....) On her side, Jean felt their disapproval and anger. They didn't *want* her to come to tea; *they* were rejecting *her*, really. Both sides were right. The family certainly did reject her; but her 'vagueness' was a rejection too, and insulting. Despite all explanations she still mixed up Robin Beck and John Rees Williams, and still said 'I *think* the woman who offered me tea is a friend of Lily's....' Of

---

*She'd met John as a small boy, but now he was a man of forty.

course she was old, and upset. But she was often like this, and she always had been ('You are a very peculiar child,' her mother had said when she had behaved exactly like this with 'Mr Hesketh'.) Often she'd fail to greet or thank people, she'd give them the wrong present or no present at all, and take refuge in 'bewilderment' or 'vagueness'. Faced with social responsibilities she did genuinely panic. But it was also, at least a little, an excuse and a cover. She would drift into 'vagueness' when she didn't want to listen, when she was bored or felt a duty looming. The truth is that she simply couldn't care about anyone else, and people felt this selfishness as rudeness. Now, for example, she'd been to her brother's funeral, and the thing that upset her most, that she kept repeating, was that all the people there had called her 'Gwennie'. It was a detestable name, she'd always hated it. 'They all called me Gwennie & it was like a horribly sad dream.'

I think that to her her name was magically important. 'Gwennie' was what they had tried to make her, 'Jean' was what she'd made herself. And her grasp of 'Jean' was weak — if she didn't get away from them quickly they could turn her into 'Gwennie' again ... Perhaps that was why. But the fact is that this — *herself* — was her preoccupation and her prison. It turned everything into her own sad dream, even someone else's funeral.

Nothing was worse for Jean than being old. Her desire was unchanged: to be beautiful. But she wasn't any more. She continued to play with boxes of make-up, to sit in front of the glass for hours, just as Adrian Allinson had seen her do in 1915. But now there was no reassurance. There was only searching for the face she'd always known and not finding it; there was only her favourite theme, 'death before the fact', made visible. Once, for instance, Diana Melly* watched her preparing for a visit from her accountant. She gazed at herself in the glass for so long that Di lost all patience, just as Adrian Allinson did. But then Jean turned her lost look on her, gave a twisted smile and said: 'Found drowned.' That's what the coroner says at inquests on drowned persons; that's what she'd always said about her heroine — 'Saved, rescued, fished-up, half-drowned, out of the deep, dark river....' Di's anger disappeared. It wasn't vanity but despair that sent Jean to her looking-glass, and kept her there.

What life took away with one hand, however, it gave her with the other. Just when she couldn't really use it any more it gave her the one thing she'd always needed as much as beauty: money.

*A close friend of Jean's last years, as we shall see.

She had an old-fashioned attitude to money: a Rees Williams attitude, which for once chimed with her own feeling as artist and rebel. Money wasn't important; it was low to talk about it and even lower to think about it. Usually this attitude is a luxury: you can despise money because you have it. Jean, of course, didn't have it; but she continued to despise it. She wrote without regard to it, and chose truth to her vision over it. In fact she feared it – 'LOST, LOST, ENDLESSLY, FINALLY AND FOR THE FIRST TIME, LOST,' as she wrote when she was more comfortable: 'Like Esau, who sold his birthright for a mess of pottage.' But on the other hand she worshipped it. 'Oh, great god money – you make possible all that's nice in life. Youth and beauty, the envy of women, and the love of men....' She never resolved this contradiction, any more than any of the others. In 1972 she still wrote (to Maryvonne):

> I know that money has nothing to do with happiness – one thinks. And yet – it can help very much believe me....
> Of course now that I have a little I can't make much use of it. Still on fine days & when I feel well I'm not unhappy.

By the time she died all her books except the first and last were available in paperback in Britain, America and France. Three were under option to be made into films: *Quartet*, which *was* made (rather well) by Merchant-Ivory, and appeared in 1981; and *Good Morning, Midnight*, and *Wide Sargasso Sea*, which in the way of that world have still not been made, but which have continued to bring in option money for twenty years. Several of the novels and stories were adapted for television – 'I Spy a Stranger' in 1972, for instance; in 1973 *Voyage in the Dark*, 'The Lotus', 'Outside the Machine' and 'Tigers Are Better-Looking'. It was easy now to sell stories and articles: 'The Insect World' in 1973, 'Sleep It Off Lady' and 'Fifi' in 1974, 'My Day' and 'Mrs Pearce' in 1975, five of the *Sleep It Off Lady* stories to *The New Yorker* in 1976. Under Edward's will she also continued in effect to receive an allowance from him, in the form of the income from one-third of his estate; and he left her Landboat Bungalows for her lifetime.* All of this meant that when the Royal Literary Fund asked in 1972 if Jean needed any more help Diana Athill was able to say that she was no longer indigent. None the less she did receive other awards, for which indigence was not a condition: from 1974 a Civil List pension of five hundred pounds

---

*Evidently (and quite reasonably) Edward still distrusted her capacity for practical management, and left the bungalow and one-third of his estate outright to Maryvonne on Jean's death, Jean only the use of them during her lifetime. From now on, therefore, Jean referred decisions on the bungalow to Maryvonne as its real owner.

a year 'recognition of her services to literature', in 1977 an Arts Council award of three thousand pounds to write *Smile Please*, and several grants throughout the seventies, to help pay for literary assistants.

The result of all this was that in the last decade of her life, for the first time since the 'Spending Phase' of the early twenties, Jean was *not poor*. She was not rich either, though her family was convinced she was. In 1976, for example, the year in which *Sleep It Off Lady* appeared and was very widely and enthusiastically reviewed, her income was £5,352. And her accountant assures me that she never earned very much more. But she was of course living rent-free; she still ate little, drank less towards the end, and could only dream of travel. In other words, her expenses were very low; and when they were higher – decorating her cottage, or paying for her London holidays – she still had generous help from her friends. Even if she didn't make large sums, therefore, it all added up: at one point in 1977, for example, she had over eleven thousand pounds in the bank. That isn't a fortune, and it didn't stay there long. But it was unheard-of riches for Jean, far more than her husbands had ever managed to provide. By then she was having to pay a retinue of helpers – nurse, cleaning woman, literary aide, agent, typist, gardener, driver; *but she could*. She could also buy lovely clothes, *expensive* clothes, like a beautiful Jean Muir wool caftan for hundreds of pounds; and she could go to expensive beauty clinics for elaborate treatments.

Of course it was quite crazy, quite pointless, to do this all *now*, when she was in her eighties. But it's what she'd always wanted to do with money, and it was too late to change. Sometimes she could laugh about it: 'I am a fool,' she said, when she came out of a clinic looking exactly as she did when she went in. But mostly, of course, she was closer to crying than laughing. *It had all come too late*: that was her constant lament. The prizes, the fame, the money, they were all too late, she couldn't enjoy any of them. And of course it was true. If she'd had the money she had in her eighties when she was in her twenties and thirties she could have made herself as beautiful and desirable as she'd dreamed.... But then she *was* beautiful and desirable in her twenties and thirties; she was even briefly rich, and it hadn't stopped the black moods, the loneliness. No: it was cruel of life to give her what she wanted only when it was too late for her to enjoy it; but it had always been too late. At least she did have it, a bit, at the end. And she did enjoy it: in the first half of this last decade, before she became too old and ill, she was often excited, lifted up, happy. Several people who knew her through the sixties and seventies felt that there was 'an amazing change' in her with money, beautiful clothes, London visits. And with recognition too, from people she admired, like V.S. Naipaul and Al Alvarez; and from people the Rees Williamses admired, like the Queen. She was thrilled to be invited to a Royal Garden Party in 1975, and to be awarded a CBE in 1978. Perhaps it was her last triumph over the true-blue Rees Williamses; or perhaps it pleased the part of her that was still secretly a Rees Williams. In any case she lived just long enough to know of her success, and even savour it. She couldn't be happy; neither she nor we could expect that any more. But her end was better than her beginning. She was happi*er*.

From early January to the end of March 1971 Jean was in London, at a hotel in Eaton Place Sonia had found for her. This first London winter holiday was the best. She saw all her friends. She had long talks with Francis; she went on lovely outings — to restaurants and the ballet, to *The Mousetrap* with Antonia Fraser, to Biba's with Diana Melly. To dozens of shops, of course: shopping was to the end her greatest pleasure. Shoes were a necessity, hats an obsession, jewellery pure pleasure. The only trouble was that she could never choose. She tried on as many hats as Sasha — and the next day sent back the one she'd finally chosen. But still her beauty could save her. Once, after she'd taken hours to decide between two cheap but pretty rings, the stall-holder ran after her and pressed the other, blue, one into her hand. 'You have such beautiful eyes,' he said, 'I want to give you this one too.'

But the happier the holiday the more trouble she was storing up for its end. She didn't want the fun to stop; more than ever she dreaded the return to solitude. So as the time to go home approached she became angry. (When she was happy, David Plante noted, 'she allowed herself to be, at least a little, sad. When she was really unhappy, she was angry.') She fought, no doubt with others too, but most sadly with Maryvonne.

'I was a bit sad at leaving London, facing solitude again,' she wrote to her afterwards, 'so I talked a lot of rot. But it was all on the surface — I'm not really a prejudiced person. . . .' Her rage must have poured out — old rage against 'respectable people', and new rage against black people. What she said was true: she had no racial prejudice at all, in the ordinary sense: on the contrary, as we know, she'd always preferred blacks to whites. But this was part of her latest obsession, the feeling that her world had disappeared, and was being forgotten and lied about. Black people were claiming now to have been oppressed by her father's generation, when in fact — she felt — they'd been helped and respected. And white people — at least English people, who knew nothing about it — believed them, beat their breasts, attacked her father. . . . Jean didn't dislike blacks; but she did dislike armchair liberals, and she loved her father. So she poured out her 'prejudice', and quarrelled with Maryvonne.

But her older and realer prejudice came between them even more. Maryvonne felt she'd been assigned the part of the 'sensible daughter, not to be told much'; and when Jean raged against 'respectable people' she took it personally. 'I never know whether she really likes me or not,' she wrote, with Jean-like understatement. In their bad moments, like this one, Jean seemed to despise her. But when she got home there was a desperate letter, saying that that was 'all on the surface', and that there was 'one thing you must understand': 'I love you, have always loved you, always will.' That was the truth. But it was Jean's last, most tragic failure — like a punishment for a lifetime of such failures — that she couldn't show it.

It wasn't only Maryvonne who felt despised by Jean, of course: Jean also felt despised by Maryvonne. Maryvonne disapproved, she felt, of her addiction to clothes and make-up. This time, for instance, she had hated Jean's new pink suit: she'd said it was badly made, and meant (no doubt) that it was embarrassing. But she'd also made — or Jean had felt — more serious accusations: that things hadn't been right between them from the beginning, that Jean had been drunk; that she had been a bad mother.

Now, at eighty, Jean faced these things clearly for the first time. She *had* been a bad mother, she admitted to Sonia Orwell. She had hung on to Maryvonne when she was a baby, but 'that was partly obstinacy and partly instinct,' and she still didn't know if she'd been right or wrong. Then she'd let John have her, because she'd had no choice. But later she had let her down — when she didn't realise how unhappy she was in her convent; really throughout the thirties, when she was so obsessed with writing that 'everything else was a bit vague.' Then came the war, and after the war Indonesia; so that instead of becoming closer they'd grown still further apart — and Jean had welcomed this, because her own life was so difficult. So of course Maryvonne felt abandoned, even angry; Jean understood perfectly. Maryvonne was so admirable: she bore no malice, she was very intelligent, trustworthy and thoughtful; and all Jean wanted to do was to make it up to her. So she wrote, without sparing herself, to Sonia.

But to Maryvonne herself she could not be so honest; the impulse to defend herself took over. Her divorce had been 'very unfair', she said ('but I'm not going into that'). If Maryvonne had begun to find its arrangements 'rather funny' as she grew older — well, 'me too perhaps'. Then came the books, which she *had* to do, so that 'I daresay I was often very tiresome.' But not drunk. She was not able to admit that. 'I really was mostly drunk from frustration and worry,' she said. She'd just found a poem she'd written to Maryvonne on her ninth birthday: it was very bad, but she must have felt all was well between them (she said) or she wouldn't have written it. She sent it to her now:

*TREES. On Maryvonne's ninth birthday.*
Trees rooted in the earth,
Their trunks strength,
Their branches spreading widely —
The branches giving themselves.
Forked they give themselves.
The leaves dance in unknown rhythms
An ancient pattern against the sky.
Fantastic the moonshadows on the ground.
Gay-patterned the sun shadows,
Sweet the sound of wind in the leaves....

This is sad and strange. The question was not what *she'd* felt but what Maryvonne had; and what did this poem have to do with that? There's not one line to or about her; its only connection to another living soul is in its dedication. It is almost a caricature of Jean's isolation; and of how her best intentions to break out of it and express her love failed.

Back in Cheriton Fitzpaine, she returned to work. She looked at the autobiography: it wasn't bad, but 'how shall I say — it's not connected.' Instead, stories were buzzing around in her head (one would become 'Who Knows What's Up in the Attic?', another 'Rapunzel, Rapunzel', another 'Sleep It Off Lady'.) They pushed aside the autobiography again: she began to work on them. She called them 'horror stories' — 'Sleep It Off Lady' might not frighten anyone else, she told Antonia Fraser, but it frightened *her*. ('I say with great relief "You've done enough for today — you can stop now."') But by October she'd finished the first draft. By November, of course, she'd decided she wasn't satisfied with it, or with any of them. It was really the autobiography she wanted to do. But *that* felt so 'long ago and far away', she got the feeling it was quite useless.... So she would go back and forth for the next few years, feeling whenever she tried to write a story that it was the autobiography she really wanted to do, whenever she tried to write the autobiography that it was really the stories. The real trouble was that she couldn't 'finish things' now; she seemed to be able to write only in short disconnected bursts. That was all right for the stories; short and sharp was their proper feeling. But the autobiography needed a more connected memory, a smoother flow. She could only hope its parts would fall into place. 'A lot to hope perhaps' she wrote to Francis; and it was. *Sleep It Off Lady* would be a collection any writer could be proud of; but in *Smile Please* she would show her age.

Age was beginning to take its toll all around her. Of the

Greenslades, for example. Mrs Greenslade's arthritis had become too bad now for her to bring Jean's lunch every day, and her neighbour Gladys Raymond took over. And Mr Greenslade would only have one more year as her 'chauffeur'. At the end of 1972 he had an eye operation; after that he was never well enough to drive again. One of Jean's most unclouded friendships was drawing to a close.

Mr Woodard too was beginning to fail. He was a year and a half older than Jean, and had advanced arterial disease. Still he insisted on walking around the village; his daughter had to follow him in a car and pick him up whenever he collapsed. This he did more often than necessary, because his clerical collar pressed on his neck, regularly delivering the *coup de grace* to his frail circulation. But he refused to wear anything else. The doctor was furious – 'He's childish,' he said, 'absolutely *childish*.' No wonder Jean loved him. He still came to visit her, and cheered her up immensely. 'He really is a dear,' she wrote to Sonia. 'He told me a long story about setting his cassock on fire without noticing it. . . .' He was even vaguer than she was. 'He had a brilliant intellect, but couldn't take the top off a milk bottle,' his younger daughter says. He didn't know how to turn off the bath; he didn't know how to make a cup of tea. To him Jean's extravagant incompetence would have seemed perfectly normal.

Finally, there was a friend who died this year, though she was a whole decade younger than Jean: her cousin Lily Lockhart. Jean had liked Lily, and Lily had liked Jean. She didn't mention this death to anyone; but five years later she sat down to write about Lily, and as she wrote she cried.

She first called this story 'Liliane' – transforming plain and dumpy English Lily into something exotic, feminine and French. When it was published it had moved still further from reality: it was now 'The Whistling Bird', identifying Liliane with the rare and beautiful *siffleur montagne*, the solitaire who'd also stood for Antoinette in *Wide Sargasso Sea*. Jean had turned Lily into a version of herself: into her most unreal and sentimental self, the lovely, lonely, innocent girl. She had to, I think. For Lily's story was like a caricature of her own; and as soon as Jean felt that parallel she had to rewrite it.

Lily's life in England had been even greyer and poorer than hers. She had never married; she had survived (barely) in a series of mean office jobs and dreary London bedsitters. She was still more isolated than Jean. 'I have never known anyone who kept her contacts with other people so formal,' Jean wrote of 'Liliane'. She would make an appointment with you for exactly an hour and three quarters, and leave after exactly an hour and three quarters. She was even more hidden away than Jean, but behind a no-nonsense cheerfulness, and an even more perverse pride. She refused any attempt to help her, and insisted on 'paying her way' even if she had to starve herself to do so. When Jean tried to give her a bit of money for a holiday she reacted as Jean had so often done herself — with a stiff, insulted pride, returning the money and saying she didn't need a holiday. She was a reader and even a writer, like Jean; and like Jean she was a misfit in her family, in the world. But unlike Jean she had no genius to sustain her and earn her death. Jean had made five splendid and unique novels out of her suffering. Lily had only a few letters and photographs, and a few copies of the little magazine she and her sister had produced during their time in St Lucia. 'Oh such a sad little thing,' says Diana Athill, who saw it. 'It would be impossible to imagine a sadder little "treasure".'

Underneath all this Jean, at least, saw real gaiety and vivacity. But perhaps she simply had to. And she gave 'Liliane' the same desire for death as Antoinette, as all her heroines. If the mountain whistler were caught it would probably die, she says to Liliane: 'Not at once,' Liliane replies; and adds, in a draft, 'You can't always die when you want to.' This longing for death wasn't mere fiction for Jean. Perhaps it wasn't for poor Lily either.

Ill health kept Jean in Cheriton Fitzpaine until mid-January of 1972, and much diminished her pleasure in her second London winter. She fell and damaged a rib; then she had toothache and gastric 'flu. Still she tried to do too much. When she got back in March she felt, I think, as one often does after a holiday — that she needed a holiday. She worked during the summer, but only slowly and 'in snatches', veering from the autobiography, to stories, to an article on old age. This, she told Maryvonne, would be like the story of the vicar's attitude to sin: 'He was agin it.'

More important than what she was writing now was what was being written about her. She was beginning to be accepted as an important twentieth-century writer. In 1971 she'd appeared for the first time in a standard American reference work; this year she appeared in her third English one. In 1973 she'd be in *Who's Who*. Scholars of West Indian literature had begun to study *Wide Sargasso Sea* as soon as it was published, but in 1972 the first scholarly article on the whole of her work appeared in an academic journal. During the next two years there were several more; from 1975 on there were many; since her death in 1979 she's become an industry.

She didn't care about academic analyses, she would hardly be aware of their existence. But ordinary newspaper articles were different. These continued to affect her — almost always badly. A *Guardian* interview with her in January upset her: 'No more interviews for me,' she said (and promptly gave half a dozen more before she died). The photograph, of course, was hideous, and the interview was so *personal.* . . . Once she'd told so much truth her only defence was to deny it, and attack. 'My answers got wilder and wilder,' she said. 'The French who interviewed me did not ask a single personal question. Only about my books. But the English seem determined to present me as a complete fool with a lurid past. . . .' Naturally this was quite unfair. There was a great deal about her books in the *Guardian* too; and both this and the portrait of her — lonely and bitter, preserving a façade of elegance and resignation — were insightful. But she didn't want insight; or anyway, no one else's.

Another article now, however, she liked more than anything anyone had ever written about her except Francis. 'I was touched and moved to tears and of course enormously pleased,' she wrote to him about it. 'I'll read it whenever I feel discouraged and it will cheer me up.'

It was by V.S. Naipaul — a novelist, a West Indian and an outsider, like herself. It was an account of all her novels; of the way they 'modify one another and make a whole.' And now something interesting happened. The article concentrated on the heroines, relating them only generally to her: yet she said 'it's marvellous, and a nearly complete understanding of my life.' She couldn't bear the connection to be explicitly made; when it was, she denied it. But so long as people were kind and polite — so long as no one rudely ripped away the mask of fiction, but left her beside her shaded lamp, in the shadow — then she felt the connection simply and deeply, and in her natural honesty blurted it out.

What did Naipaul say about the heroines? That they were outsiders, 'appearing to come from no society, having roots in no society,' coming 'from a background of nothing to an organised world with which they could never come to terms.' That they were isolated from time too, Julia having no past at all, the others being cut off from it by 'the journey from an unknown island' and the break in their lives. That even in the West Indian novels there is no happiness, no innocence, but only ever loss. The journey was 'not . . . from innocence to darkness, but from one void to another'; there was never any 'real relishing of the world,' but 'at the centre . . . always something like withdrawal.' All this, then, Jean recognised as true, not just of the heroines but of herself. And the rest, presumably, too: that the men in the novels are not only predators but prey; that the heroines become steadily less passive and more aggressive. Naipaul set these insights within the highest evaluation of Jean's art, saying that she'd been thirty or forty years ahead of her time. It was, perhaps, easier to accept insight when it was accompanied by such genuine admiration. And even more by sympathy — the sympathy of another pessimistic, perfectionist writer. 'What a stoic thing she makes the act of writing appear,' Naipaul wrote. That's just what it was. Jean was right to be 'touched and moved to tears.'

The last piece she read about herself this year, by contrast, moved her to fury. It was a book, or rather it was in a book: Arthur Mizener's biography of Ford, *The Saddest Story.*

*The Saddest Story* had actually appeared in 1971. It was typical of Jean that she didn't read it for a whole year. (She had known it was coming for much longer, for Mizener had written to ask her some questions for it in 1965.) But then Stella Bowen's *Drawn From Life* had been published in 1940, and she'd never read that at all. Her ability to block things out had been at work again. And when she did finally get Ford's biography now and read it, it was as though by accident: as though, even, against her will.

She was in Crediton library, she said, looking for something to read, when the young librarian came up and asked if there was anything she particularly wanted. She knew him by sight, but he'd never spoken to her, 'or as far as I know looked at me before'; so she felt her usual flood of shyness and 'bewilderment': 'I was rather startled by his friendliness, and titles, writers and publishers flew out of my head. The only book I could remember was *The Saddest Story* by Arthur Mizener....' She'd asked for it at last – but not really; she hadn't meant or decided to, it had just happened.

Reading it similarly leapt out of her control. 'I felt more and more that I didn't want to open it' – but she did. Then 'I made up my mind to read it carefully and no skipping' – and she didn't. She skipped until she saw bits from *Drawn From Life*. She read about Ford's 'unfortunate affair with Jean Rhys', larded with quotations from Stella. She 'shut the book and flung it to the end of the bed,' determined not to read any more. But soon that resolution was broken too. She looked up her name in the index, and 'read about my fictitious daughter by Ford, my hysterical attacks on him in the street, the allowance paid to me for a long time by Ford and Stella....' 'I got up in a furious rage and when I thought but there's no one, no one to say "But these are obvious lies" tears came into my eyes.'

She was in a frenzy of rage and self-pity for days. Sonia, Francis and another friend came on a visit, but she couldn't enjoy it. She brooded on Stella's undying enmity, and on Mizener's. She couldn't sleep. She felt back in that time and place, but in someone else's version. Finally she determined to write about it to make it go away. In the back of an old notebook she dashed down her own version, which she called *'L'Affaire Ford'*. It began in Crediton library; then went back to the beginning, to meeting Ford through Mrs Adam.

'*L'Affaire Ford*' is a strange, unfocused document which doesn't answer any of Mizener's 'lies'. The worst accusation it makes against Stella is that she forced Jean to sit on the *strapontin* in taxis, while she sat comfortably, gossiping with friends. Then it dashes off to Juan les Pins, and spends the rest of the time recalling the absurd but happy summer with the Hudnuts.

At first I thought: she was old. She couldn't fix her mind even on self-defence any more; she'd got stuck in the groove of those few memories – the *strapontin* and Juan les Pins, which she told over and over again. But then I thought of Antoinette trying to defend herself to Rochester, and the awful mess she makes of it. And Selina Davis trying to defend herself to the magistrate, and Jean herself, doing the same. . . . *She'd always done it.* She would get 'bewildered'; everything she ought to say would 'fly out of her head.' *It was because there really was nothing to say.* She couldn't defend herself, because she really knew there was no defence.

In fact Mizener hadn't told the story entirely unfairly. He'd quoted from *Quartet* too, and allowed the quotations to show that Heidler/Ford was cold, egotistical and evasive, that Lois/Stella sniped nastily at Marya/Jean whenever he wasn't there. If he also said that Jean's portrait of Marya rather confirmed Stella's of Jean – well, despite Jean's intentions, it did. She had to go all the way to the notes at the back of the book to find better reasons for her anger – the 'fictitious daughter', the 'hysterical attacks', the allowance, only appear there, not in the main text. And again her paranoia distorted what Mizener had done. For he didn't 'quote all the lies & gossip as fact,' as Jean told Sonia: he quoted them as gossip. Some of the gossip – the 'fictitious daughter' – was certainly not true; some of it – the 'hysterical attacks' – was possibly not true,* and Mizener should have said so. But he didn't say it *was* true either. The only thing he said was true was that 'Ford and Stella provided an allowance for Miss Rhys at least until the end of 1926.' Jean always furiously denied this too, as we know. But in essence it was probably true.

'*L'Affaire Ford*' followed the old, old pattern: 'She was a defiant flame shooting upwards not to plead but to threaten. Then the flame sank down again, useless, having reached nothing.' She could only call

---

*Though when we consider all the fiction everyone wrote, we must wonder. Not just Lola Porter's behaviour to Notterdam in *When the Wicked Man*, which is of course Ford's creation; but Julia's slapping Mr Mackenzie in *After Leaving Mr Mackenzie*, Houdia's shooting Steiner in 'Houdia', and Stefan's wanting to shoot Heidler in *Quartet* (and John and Henriette van Eyk said he'd tried. . .). There was certainly a lot of violence in the air, at the very least.

Mizener a liar after drink, in conversation: in writing she'd told the truth for too long to change. The most she could do was put up the smokescreen of the *strapontin* and Juan les Pins; and on every point she'd been so eager to challenge, remain silent.

There was more trouble this year, which Jean put into fiction this time: into her 'horror story', 'Sleep It Off Lady'. The trouble was with the children next door, and especially with the girl whom she called Deena.

This was Viv, one of the daughters of Zena Raymond, her old enemy. In 1972 Viv was about twelve years old, like Deena in the story. And she did indeed hang around Jean's house, and stare, and make loud noises. She'd been doing it for years; when Jan van Houts came in 1970 he saw her, and Jean already said 'She watches all the time.' But she was altogether sadder than Deena, whom Jean makes 'plump', 'with a pretty, healthy but rather bovine face.' Viv was fat rather than plump; and she was retarded. For her story Jean removed these handicaps: Miss Verney was the outsider, the one with the handicaps; the child had to be a perfectly safe, healthy, sinister person. Of course the fact that Viv was abnormal didn't make her constant stare more comfortable; but it did change its meaning. In 'Sleep It Off Lady' Deena is exactly like the little girl in *Good Morning, Midnight*, who tells the Martiniquaise that she has no right in the house, that she hates her and wishes she were dead. In other words, Deena wasn't really like Viv at all, but a paranoid fantasy child who'd inhabited Jean's mind for at least thirty years. The real child was like her mother, Zena — quite ready to join battle with Jean, but underneath not unkind. When Jean went into hospital at the end, for example, Viv picked a bunch of flowers and asked for them to be taken to her. This is very different from the horrible child of 'Sleep It Off Lady', who leaves Miss Verney to die.

But Jean's paranoia about children was bad now. 'For the last few months there's been the sound of children shrieking, and banging dustbins until I've been distracted,' she told Diana. 'It's one child really....' It was so bad that for a time she talked again of moving. All children began to look sinister to her. One visitor brought a grandson: 'never have I seen a child with such a cynical expression,' Jean said. It's also Deena's 'cynical eyes' which depress Miss Verney in the story. Jean told Mr Woodard that her distrust of children came out of memories of their cruelty to her in her own childhood, and that may well have been so. But I wonder if it wasn't also Sasha's fear of being seen that was bothering her again: her fear that being *seen* was being *seen through*. Children's eyes can have that penetrating quality: they don't yet see only what they're expected to see, or say it either.

Finally, 1972 brought losses. They were sad ones for Jean, because they were among her greatest friends and supporters. First Mr Woodard, who after twenty-five years in Cheriton Fitzpaine retired and moved away. They didn't keep in touch. It had always been easy to lose touch with Jean; and in his own way that was also true of Alwynne Woodard. He was a rescuer, and Jean had been rescued; he'd left her to her London friends with a clear conscience. Nor did she mention his departure now. But he'd loved and helped her, he was gentle and kind, and she didn't forget him. Two years later he died, and Jean told a significant story about his death. One day (she said) after she hadn't seen him for some time, she felt him standing behind her in her kitchen. She turned round, but there was no one there: and two weeks later someone told her he was dead.

This is a very West Indian story; Owen's daughter Ena Williams tells a similar one about sensing the moment her father died. But that's the point: you only feel the death of someone close to you, someone to whom you have had a special tie. Jean's story tells us that she felt such a special tie to Mr Woodard, as Jean's stories always do — indirectly, in an image.

We know the second important man who disappeared from her life this year: Mr Greenslade. He had his operation in December; for some time he hoped he'd be able to return to his taxi, but he never did. From now on Jean was driven by his replacement, Mr Pike. Mr Pike was nice, but it wasn't the same; and Jean missed her oldest Cheriton friend very much. He'd been so reassuring, she wrote, so gallant.

> ... For so long he's carried my parcels, waited patiently while I buy this and that, helped me over difficult places. Once when I forgot my keys he managed to climb in through a difficult window.... He always knows when it's going to rain; when he puts up a fence it stays put; when he plants anything it grows. How can I pay him for all that?

She couldn't, of course. All she could do was remain loyal to him. This she did: she refused to register Mr Pike in the same way, and always called him, vaguely (though I hope not to his face) 'Mr Fish'.

Her last loss of 1972 was the saddest: her brother-in-law Alec died. Until the year before she'd seen him regularly. She liked him very much; he was kind and funny, and he reminded her of Max. The literary friends she had now understood her rather better; but Max's and Alec's lack of literary interest had been part of their charm for her, holding out the hope that with them she might be, at last, an ordinary, happy woman. Alec's death touched this side of her, the side that wanted to believe in simple goodness. 'He called himself "a simple soldier",' she wrote, 'and I believe he was.'

★

As a result of these deaths and disappearances, Jean's carers from now on became even more exclusively female. Not that men completely disappeared from her life, of course. Francis Wyndham and Oliver Stoner remained close friends, and there would be other male helpers and admirers. Indeed men remained supremely important to her: however much she liked a woman she would turn away the moment a man entered the room. She still needed to seduce men, and she still did. She flirted with the poet Al Alvarez; she so charmed an elderly American that he pressed her to come to New York. She couldn't, of course, but she liked to think about it. And then he died. Diana Melly remembers Jean's fathomless sadness when she heard the news: 'The last lover gone,' she said.

But men had never managed to care for her in the way she needed. She needed *limitlessness*, both of love and of money. Even if they'd been much better providers than they were her poor husbands couldn't have supplied that. When she was younger and stronger her need must have been overwhelming, and of course it stretched ahead of them for endless years. But she was so old now it couldn't go on forever: and this limited limitlessness seemed possible to several women. To Sonia Orwell, as we've seen, whose generosity continued to flow — chocolate eggs at Easter, partridges and *marrons glacés* at Christmas, a flood of presents whenever she came to Cheriton Fitzpaine — 'a toothbrush marked J, several pots of African violets, a cushion wastepaper basket, gay boxes of matches, cigarettes and a lovely little ashtray, nice things to eat and drink....' To Diana Melly, especially in the last few years. And now to two other women as well.

Gini Stevens and Jo Batterham were young, kind and extraordinarily energetic. They admired her work so much that they ventured to call on her one autumn evening at Landboat Bungalows. She invited them to visit her in London in the winter, which they did. They became regular shopping companions. Then Jean bought three paintings, and one turned out to be by Jo's father. Perhaps that strange coincidence sealed the friendship, giving Jean her familiar feeling of fate and predestination.

1973 was a better year than 1972 had been, largely because of them. Jean stopped complaining about the child-noise next door, and even managed a bit of work. By the summer she'd finished two or three stories, and told Francis and Sonia that she was going back to the 'crawling' autobiography (she didn't of course, but got out two very old stories and worked on them instead). One of the stories she'd finished was 'The Insect World', which Francis promptly sold to the *Sunday Times*.

What Gini and Jo did — after Jean had been there for thirteen years

— was to make Landboat Bungalows really comfortable at last. With great reluctance Jean had accepted first a telephone and then a television, just in the last two years. Now the rest of her home was brought into the twentieth century. Heating was put in, a new cooker, a new fridge. It was enlarged, cleaned, freshly furnished and painted. The outside never looked much more than a temporary lean-to; but inside Jean's cottage became pretty, warm and welcoming.

Originally the idea had come — naturally — from Sonia. The first plan had been to build an extension, evidently so that Jean could have a live-in companion if necessary. (She accepted that part of the idea very reluctantly, as we might guess, and indeed it never happened.) In the end Sonia advised against this plan, and Jo agreed. Instead they decided to enlarge the sitting room by combining it with the spare bedroom, and to create a new, separate spare room by building a new shed in the garden. The horrible old shed — which Miss Verney cannot destroy in 'Sleep It Off Lady', but which hides the 'Super Rat' that will destroy *her* — that horrible old shed Gini knocked down single-handed, and Mr Muggeridge the gardener carted it away. Gini and Jo did as much as they could themselves; then they made all the arrangements for the heavy work with Mr Martin the builder, and took Jean off to Jo's house in Putney, to give her a rest and a splendid party while he did it.

In December she returned to a transformed cottage. The new cedar hut smelled delicious and looked warm and summery, with an Indian bedspread and cushions. The house was bigger, warmer, lighter. The sitting room was painted white and filled with white chairs and a white carpet. There were new curtains from Sonia, and new Habitat chairs and rugs installed by Di Melly. 'It's no longer a bit melancholy here,' Jean wrote to Sonia, 'but the reverse. Jo has lined the kitchen curtains with pink. It's like living inside a shell. I'm so delighted and happy with it all.'

This first great change Gini and Jo made to Jean's life was so successful that it immediately led to a second. Their talents were not only domestic: Jo sculpted and Gini wrote. Despite her dream of the 'happy woman', Jean admired creativity very much; art was an escape from herself in this way too, and she was generous to people about their work. This was especially true of visual artists, whom she found romantic and exciting — it was an important part of her friendship for Jo. But it was Gini's literary skills that were directly useful. Jean was always looking for literary assistance — for a typist, and more and more for someone to dictate to, as her hands grew shakier and stiffer. Gini got on so well with her, and had already organised her life so that she could give a good deal of time to her. She was the obvious solution. In October 1973 Diana Athill wrote to the Arts Council asking for a grant to enable Gini to work with Jean for ten days a month. At long last, at eighty-three years old, she'd evidently achieved acceptance: within a month the grant was made.

At long last too, therefore, she achieved something she hadn't had for nearly thirteen years: she was *taken care of.* Mrs Raymond, Mrs Lee and Mr Muggeridge, helped and overseen by Gini and Jo, Sonia and the two Diana's, had taken over most of the boring, distracting domestic burdens — the shopping, the laundry, the garden, the cooking and cleaning. And now the practical side of writing, the typing and posting and keeping copies and filing which Jean could never bear, and which she'd left entirely to Leslie — now *that* boring and distracting burden was being taken over too. *Wide Sargasso Sea* had taken nine years and nearly killed her because of all these things. But that was now transformed. Half of 'the "treatment" which has proved so marvellously successful,' Diana Athill told the Arts Council, 'is Gini's taking every kind of worry or imaginary worry off Jean so that she gets up of a morning straight "into" the story she's working on.'

Jean was moving towards a new book: not the autobiography, but a book of stories. Now that Gini was there to help it was made official, and at the beginning of 1974 she signed the contract with Deutsch. She was 'really very anxious to work,' and she did. *Sleep It Off Lady* would take another two years. But in that time she would rework six more old stories and write six more new ones — in her mid-eighties. There can be little doubt that a main difference between *Wide Sargasso Sea* and *Sleep It Off Lady* — between nine years and two — was Gini. Though in the end Jean's new Leslie could make her no happier than the old.

The first new stories were begun in the spring of 1974. 'Fishy Waters' (Jean told Diana Athill) was 'not about myself for once,' but about a man called Jimmy Longa who had come to Roseau when she was a child. But it *was* really about herself. For Jimmy Longa is, like Ramage, a substitute for herself — an outcast, stoned by children, accused of turning on one and harming it (as she'd often threatened to harm the children next door, especially Viv). And for another reason too: because Matthew Penrice, like Dr Cox of 'Pioneers', was based on her father.*

---

*In early drafts — as always — this autobiographical connection was much clearer. One, for example, was told from the point of view of 'a little girl (ME of course) who liked Jimmy,' just as 'Pioneers, Oh, Pioneers' is (partly) told from the point of view of Rosalie, who liked Ramage. And in many the Matthew Penrice character had come to the island at

But it was true, therefore, that there were several competing centres for her sympathy in 'Fishy Waters': Jimmy, the underdog on trial; Matthew, who can't escape the 'envy, malice, hatred' he finds everywhere; Maggie, who like Annette Mason understands black people but not her white husband. That was very unlike Jean's usual narrow focus. Perhaps that's what made it especially hard for her — she toiled at it for ages, wrote about sixteen different versions, and still wanted to tear it up. But it also made it the success it is, which is an unusual one for her. The several voices telling the story (the letter writers, Maggie, the neutral voice in the middle) give it a variety of tone that usually eludes her. And the unusual spread of her sympathy draws us in: so that the abrupt yawning of the opposite possibility — that *everyone* may be horribly, inexplicably cruel — is more shocking and believable than ever.

Jean of course, had doubts about all the stories ('Too long & glib. Or too short & unfinished'; 'they are *all* unfinished.') None the less, about half the collection was done a year before the deadline.

In the meantime her reputation was steadily growing. 1973 had been a good year in England, with *Voyage in the Dark* and *Tigers Are Better-Looking* coming out in paperback, and *Voyage, Tigers*, 'The Lotus' and 'Outside the Machine' all being performed on television. Now 1974 was the year of America. *Tigers* was published there, and *Mackenzie, Good Morning, Midnight* and *Quartet* were all issued for the first time in paperback. The reviews were almost all excellent — unreservedly admiring, accepting her importance without question. But one stood out from all the others. It was by Al Alvarez, and it appeared on 17 March in the *New York Times Sunday Book Review*.

Alvarez's claim was made boldly in his title: 'The Best Living English Novelist'. And he argued it irresistibly, with a poet's ear for the accurate and unforgettable phrase. Her heroines 'have no one to fall back on, no money, no will to get on, and one skin too few,' he wrote; her prose is 'reticent, unemphatic, precise, and yet supple, alive with feeling.' 'Although her range is narrow, sometimes to the point of obsession, there is no one else now writing who combines such emotional penetration and formal artistry or approaches her unemphatic, unblinking truthfulness.'

This article had a huge and lasting impact on both sides of the

---

twenty-seven, like Dr Rees Williams (in the final version he has only retired there); his routine of bridge and the Club is Dr Rees Williams's; in one draft he'd even had fever, like Dr Rees Williams.

As to the story of Jimmy Longa, it, like Ramage's, was a real Dominica legend; 'Jimmy Longa', like 'Ramage', was the man's real name.

Atlantic. *The best living English novelist* set the seal on Jean's acceptance. That was its most important, long-term effect; and it had a very
welcome short-term effect too. The next week *The New York Times*
gave its whole 'Book of the Times' column to another enthusiastic
review (of *Good Morning, Midnight*, by Anatole Bruyard); and
suddenly there was (reported the *Publishers' Weekly*) a 'rush on Jean
Rhys.' The paperback publishers of *Mackenzie* and *Good Morning,
Midnight* rushed out a second and then a third printing; the (different)
publishers of *Wide Sargasso Sea* ordered a reprint of twenty thousand
so urgently that they didn't stop to replace the cheap bodice-ripping
cover. The first publishers grabbed *Quartet*, the second *Voyage in the
Dark*, and both brought them out too as fast as they could, printing
as many as one hundred thousand copies of *Voyage*. Briefly, for the
first time in her life, Jean was a best-seller.

Alvarez sent her a copy of his article. She liked it very much, and
was very grateful for the help it had given her. She invited him to
Cheriton Fitzpaine straight away. And now came the occasion when,
aged eighty-three, she flirted with him like a young girl.

They sat in her sitting room, Alvarez says, and had an entirely
unliterary conversation. Of course that was just what Jean liked, and
slowly her shyness and nervousness disappeared. She was beautifully
and elaborately dressed, as always, in a bright dirndl skirt over a full
petticoat. Alvarez noticed that she was crossing and recrossing her
legs a good deal, giving her full skirts a saucy little kick each time.
She was an old lady and a great writer, but for the moment that was
hard to remember. Mesmerically his eyes were drawn to her legs, and
as her petticoat lifted again he saw that they were as slim as a girl's.
For a second or two he stared at Jean's legs in frank male admiration.
Then he looked up, guiltily, to meet her eyes.

To his amazement she wasn't embarrassed or angry at all – rather
she was secretly, transparently delighted. After that, he says, he could
do no wrong; they were friends for life. He saw her on her visits
to London: only rarely, and remaining rather formal, paying gallant
flirtatious court to her from a certain distance. He did this to save
himself: because (like Joan Forman, and others too) he saw very
clearly in her books and her 'wonderful violet eyes' her rage and
destructiveness, her need for a victim. What perhaps he didn't see
was that Jean was saved too. She knew all about herself; and I'm sure
she was glad for the distance he kept, in which she could enjoy her
power without abusing it.

Altogether this was a good year for new young men. Another was
Charles Cox, a friend of the Stoners. He wrote to Jean offering help
– lifts in his car, occasional typing. He was married, with a new
baby, so he couldn't (Jean said) 'be at my beck & call'; but 'he comes

when he can and is really sweet & very capable.' And there was a third: Tristram Powell, who was directing a series of films for the BBC. He was a great admirer of Jean's work, and had asked if she would be willing to be one of his subjects. We know Jean's horror of being photographed, and her shyness even in private conversation ('I was always silent,' she told Sonia now, 'except when drunk or otherwise excited. Now it's difficult for me to talk at all except to a few people.') But Tristram won her over, and she agreed for the one and only time of her life to be interviewed on English television.

Tristram questioned her very gently; and she allowed herself her usual confusion (she thought that only her voice would be heard, and she wouldn't be seen). Thus protected by both Tristram and herself she actually enjoyed the fuss and excitement of the interview. But then of course she awaited its showing with dread. 'My face is all wrong,' she wrote to Francis, '[and] I invariably talk the most awful nonsense. I hear myself doing it & can't stop. . . .' Neither was true. She looked beautiful, and what she said in her soft, light voice was intelligent, modest, and mostly true. But when Tristram showed her the film she had the inevitable reaction. While she'd been so nervously waiting she'd hoped he would cut the interview ruthlessly, but now she felt 'They cut so much it makes no sense.' Besides — and this was of course the real reason — 'as usual I look awful & on the verge of nervous collapse.' When the programme was broadcast she asked Joan Butler to watch it with her, because she couldn't face it alone. But when the interview began she couldn't face it anyway. She left the room, tears streaming down her face, and refused to talk about it afterwards.

But things had been going very well. She had her nice new house, and was even getting trees from the council to plant around it. ('I've always wanted to live in a forest,' she wrote to Francis). She had her old friends and her new friends and plenty of visits. She had her American fame — which meant interviews, but in chic magazines like *Mademoiselle* and the famous *Women's Wear Daily*. She even had money and recognition from England, which gave her her Civil List pension this year. . . . In fact things had been going *too* well. Something had to go wrong.

Typically, it was the thing that had been most right that went most wrong: the arrangement with Gini Stevens.

It had started so well. 'Gini is such a help. So patient, understanding & very tidy indeed, so I daresay I'll soon stop looking frantically for things that aren't there,' Jean had written to Francis in the spring. And she *had* changed since the days when rage had threatened even her best friendships, with Germaine Richelot, Evelyn Scott or Peggy Kirkaldy: for she never simply blamed Gini for what happened. On the contrary she behaved very generously towards her, making her the agent for the stories she'd helped with (*another agent!*), and wanting her to share in the profits of *Sleep It Off Lady*. 'Nothing is Gini's fault,' she said, even when it had all fallen apart. Gini had been patient and kind and cheering, she had done so much work and 'put up with a lot'.... – '*when she could be here.*'

That was the rub. Gini had a full, even a fraught life; she couldn't be at Jean's beck and call much more than Charles Cox. She could stay in Cheriton Fitzpaine only for ten days or so at a time (which had after all been the arrangement); and she could never say exactly when she would return. While she was away she hardly ever wrote, or answered Jean's letters, or telephoned – or so it felt to Jean. This was the mood she always got into ('I hear nothing at all from anybody at all'), so it's quite possible that Gini stayed in touch more than Jean remembered. But it's also quite possible she didn't. 'She doesn't quite understand,' Jean said, 'But who could?' – and both were true. Gini couldn't guess how much reassurance Jean needed, because no one could; and if she guessed she couldn't give it, because no one could. She couldn't understand how ordinary open-endedness or changes of plan would obsess Jean and stop her from working. 'Poverty doesn't matter & unhappiness can be a spur,' Jean wrote – 'But uncertainty can be the very devil.' It went right off her scale of awfulness; it was 'worse than cold'. It made her so frantic that she imagined abandonment all the time. If Gini went out for a few minutes and Jean noticed her car gone, she immediately thought she'd driven off and left her.

The arrangement had begun in November 1973. By June 1974 Jean was already worrying. She did what she'd always done: she told no one. People were trying to help her, she didn't want to complain. And the more she needed someone the less she dared to be a 'nuisance' – 'The more precious the friendship the more lightly I feel I must go,' as she put it to Sonia. Later on she said that she knew 'almost at once' the arrangement wouldn't work, and this seems to have been true, for she let little hints drop, especially to Maryvonne. But she said nothing clearly to anyone, so the usual happened. Her anxiety turned inwards, and fastened on everything but its real object: especially (of course) on 'business'. 'Letters and articles from America' arrived telling of her new best-sellerdom: *but where was the money?* It was all so slow, and no one explained ('I get vague letters but always they mean nothing real...'). She was 'bewildered', then 'puzzled', finally 'utterly at sea'. Then of course she got ill and couldn't work, only 'moon around & sneeze & watch the rain & listen to *dam* wind'. At last it became 'too much to endure,' and she was 'well on the way to cracking up.' No wonder she couldn't face herself on television by November. In December she was in a nursing home.

Now there was a brief respite, for Sonia and Francis found her a new hotel, the Portobello, which became her favourite. 'I loved the Portobello & my London holiday,' she wrote to Francis when she got home in early 1975. But the trouble was that she hadn't said anything about Gini. Because 'seeing people and feeling better makes me optimistic,' she explained later, to Diana. 'Also I wasn't sure you'd be interested....'

So nothing was solved, and the uneasy arrangement continued. Her agitation grew, but somehow she managed to work again. Still the May deadline passed. In June Gini went down for a fortnight. In July Jean was writing an 'extra' story ('I Used to Live Here Once'?); in August she was still tinkering with 'Fishy Waters'. Finally in the autumn she let her last book go.

She had done it, and of course she was relieved. But two years of bottled-up uncertainty had taken their toll. They'd turned her against the stories, which were 'wearisome' and a 'burden' in the summer, 'a curse from first to last', 'two years wasted' by the autumn ('*Tant pis*'). And they'd pushed her again into business paranoia. Deutsch were being 'evasive' about the money from her American sales, she was expected to stay alone and work and be 'a penny in the slot machine not worth a stamp or a telephone call,' while 'these people are making money out of me....' None of this did she say to Diana, or to André Deutsch — she never did confront the doer of the deed, real or imagined, until it was too late. It wouldn't have helped if she had; she wouldn't have believed what they said, and a minute later would have forgotten it. Her paranoia was too deep now. She became convinced that she was in such trouble with the Inland Revenue that they were about to 'distrain' her bungalow. A taxman came to the house to 'harass' her very early one morning, 'almost before the break of day,' she said, and she was so upset by this that she fell and cracked a rib. 'I was so worried I fell,' she said. 'I've been dying ever since....' When Diana complained to the Devon Tax Inspector on Jean's behalf he said, very firmly, that his department never made personal visits. If he'd read Jean's letter he could have added: particularly not before the break of day.

Finishing a book was always a bad time for Jean: giving it up, letting it be seen, often unleashed a bout of paranoia. But 1975, her eighty-fifth year, had been a turning point for her. In the two short pieces that she published this year, 'My Day' and 'Mrs Pearce', she recognised that she was irretrievably old, irretrievably dying. Mr Greenslade, her best and oldest friend in Cheriton Fitzpaine, died in October. And by then she herself was as low as she had ever been.

She was utterly weary, she fell, she cried when she saw a spider. She was angry and paranoid, she felt threatened and cheated. She hadn't much time left now, yet two years had been wasted. *She* had never wanted to write those stories, but only the autobiography. *Sleep It Off Lady* wasn't her idea, and nor was the arrangement with Gini; that had been made by Deutsch and the Arts Council while she was in a nursing home, and they hadn't consulted her at all ... she'd scrap the stories, and return Deutsch's advance if they wanted. They were no good, she didn't want to publish them. Her work was mediocre, it was nothing. 'Nothing! Nothing!'.

Her friends realised that 'a rescue operation was a matter of desperate urgency.' But Jean wasn't well enough for an hotel. Someone offered her a flat, but it fell through. Finally an hotel was found in Kensington which catered to elderly people, and so might be able to manage Jean. But she loathed it. Her room was gloomy and the place was full of 'old people, all alone'. Of course she knew she was old — 'only a lunatic wouldn't be convinced' — but she wasn't like *them*.... She still refused to recognise her neighbour. Here, in December 1975, at one of her lowest points in years, David Plante came to see her.

The many many years of fear and lies and drink and anger had twisted her. 'Her body seemed bent in many ways,' Plante wrote, 'she had to grab one leg and heft it across the other, and, once crossed, you thought she could never uncross them': and he also meant this, I think, as a picture of her mind. As they talk her face — already distorted by the make-up she's scrawled on it with shaking hands — twists in a sneer or contorts in tears. She talks as she did to Peggy Kirkaldy in 1941: about herself, Ford, Paris, herself, herself.... As she gets drunker her moods and expressions begin to change as fast as Dominican weather; unpredictably she laughs, cries, shouts, talks to herself. Sometimes she is sweet and gentle; sometimes she's like a hard old whore, spewing out hate against all her old targets — women haters, people in power, England. Her make-up smears, her eyes swell, her nose reddens; she lurches from wall to wall as she walks, and her cane gets caught between her legs. Finally she gets stuck in the toilet, because Plante has forgotten to lower the seat; and he has to lift her out and carry her, sobbing, moaning, utterly drunk, to the bed.

This is what happens to Jean: she falls through the safety net of ordinary tidy life to an ugly, abandoned hell — *and someone is always there to record it.* Up to now it has been herself: and in *Mackenzie* or *Good Morning, Midnight* or 'Jazz' or 'The Lotus' she's been no less hard on herself than Plante is. But she lifts her own books, and his, by her celebration of absurdity, her 'acerbic note' of self-mocking laughter. The next time she saw him she said: 'Now, David, if that ever happens to you with a lady again, don't get into a panic':

You put the lady on her bed, cover her, put a glass of water and a sleeping pill on the bedside table, turn the lights down very low, adjust your tie before you leave so you'll look smart, say at reception that the lady is resting, and when you tell the story afterwards you make it funny.

# CHAPTER TWO

# Death, 1976–1979

From childhood Jean had seemed physically feeble. Her brothers and sisters were big and strong and dark, while she was delicate and fair. In her teens in Dominica, swinging languidly in her hammock, in her twenties in England, taking taxis in London, refusing to totter more than ten minutes in the country, she already showed the lassitude and exhaustion of her middle and old age. But this too was a pretence; or else she was instinctively and successfully husbanding her resources. For she abused her body for a long lifetime, giving it far too little food and far too much alcohol, battering it with cold, poverty, discomfort, depression, drunken falls and violent rages. From her early seventies on she looked as though she was dying. And yet she didn't die. Physically as well as mentally she was 'twins', weak and faint on the surface, tenaciously strong beneath.

At last, however, her secretly strong body began to fail. In her last three years she aged rapidly. She could no longer manage daily life alone, either in London or in Cheriton, and had to give up her precious privacy. The two things she lived for, pleasure and writing, became still harder to attain. She became more and more housebound. London could no longer be a constant 'round of treats', and Cheriton Fitzpaine of course she hated more than ever. She did still write; she wrote to the end, and here she was still often and amazingly herself. Her concentration was astonishing. She couldn't read proofs any more, so they would be read to her; she would sit quite still, and remember every word, saying 'the third line down, change this for that.' Sometimes she would dictate a whole perfect paragraph, quickly and it seemed without thinking. But these shafts of light were rare. She needed, as always, a drink to start and several to continue; but now she would quickly become tired and muddled and have to stop. The last straw was that she had to dictate everything. There was no alternative; she could hardly hold a pen any more, her fingers were too bent and her hand shook too badly. But dictation drove her mad.

She would weep, or 'beat her breast and gesticulate' with frustration that she could no longer put her own words on paper. And being Jean, she was afraid of betrayal. A non-writer wouldn't understand, wouldn't be able to make sense of her jumble of words; but a writer was even worse, he would rewrite her, he would quite unconsciously change her voice for his. She had sacrificed her happiness, her whole life, for the demon of her different vision; it would be too much to bear if in the end that too was taken from her.... There was no possibility of this happening — she was underestimating both herself and her helpers — but the fear lay behind some of the worst moments of her final years.

The first of these came very soon. After the débâcle of the Kensington hotel Sonia moved Jean back to the Portobello, where she'd been so happy the year before, and at first she was happy there again. David Plante returned, and they worked together on the story she told him he should write about their lavatory misadventure, which she called 'Shades of Pink'. Then one day she complained that nobody was interested in the one thing she wanted to do: her autobiography. David said that if she needed help with dictation he would gladly give it. So they began to work together on *Smile Please.*

She began with a passage which followed straight on from *Voyage in the Dark*: 'After what was then called an illegal operation, I stayed in a flat in Langham Street.... I didn't see him, but he sent me a big rose plant in a pot and a very beautiful Persian kitten.' David went to see her three or four days a week. Sometimes she was too tired to work, and though she talked about her life he didn't write down what she said. At other times they worked, Jean propped up in her chair on a large cushion, her brief bouts of dictating punctuated by drink and conversation, mostly about writing. Thus they began to build up *Smile Please* piece by small piece, very differently from Jean's usual cutting and chiselling-down operation.

Despite this, all went well for several weeks. By the end of March they had many parts of her life recorded on pieces of paper. But then (no doubt because Jean was about to go home, and David wouldn't be able to help for many months) they tried to organise the pieces chronologically. This was of course a sensible, indeed a necessary, idea — but one that was utterly foreign to Jean. She simply had no idea of ordinary time; and of course she'd lied and covered up so much, which would or might be uncovered by accurate dating. She rubbed her hand over her face as David pressed her to remember. She became more and more muddled; she slumped back vacantly in her chair, as though she had lost interest. Finally, she held her head in her hands and said, 'I can't go on, I can't. This isn't the way I work.' That was all — this time. But her will was steel as, underneath the 'vagueness', it always was. 'We never again,' Plante says, 'attempted to make a chronology.'

By now Jean had become too old and ill to enjoy her London holiday. And in the middle of it, at the end of February, she fell and broke several ribs. She went to a nursing home in Ladbroke Terrace, where an X-ray showed that her heart was much enlarged, so that nothing could be done about the ribs. This decided her friends: she couldn't live alone any more. Diana Athill wrote to Joan Butler in Cheriton Fitzpaine, asking her advice about finding Jean a housekeeper.

Help had always been there when she needed it, and it still was. Only a short time before a young woman had come to the village who was exactly what was needed: a trained nurse, intelligent and capable, who was looking for part-time employment. Joan Butler put her in touch with Diana, and Diana explained what Jean needed: someone to come in for about four hours every day, in the morning. She needed help to get up, bathe and dress; her lunch had to be cooked and a light meal left for her supper. That was all; Mrs Raymond would continue with the washing and cleaning. The young nurse, Janet Bridger, accepted.

In early April Diana collected Jean and, with Sonia, drove her home. Jean made a scene, dismayed at having to return to her isolation — and at the same time, no doubt, at its disruption by a new and unknown person. But in fact her new life began well. She liked Janet: she was nice, she said, very efficient, and interesting too. Janet had spent several years working in the Arctic, so 'knew all about the Esquimaux.' They could talk, and Jean was not quite so lonely. Of course there were problems. Janet would tidy things away and Jean couldn't find them — a new version of her old problem of losing things. ('That's my life,' she said, thinking of *Smile Please* too — 'always bits missing.') When Janet was there Jean fretted that it was hard to write, however helpful her interruptions; when she wasn't there she fretted about *that*, because she was 'so expensive'. But that was just Jean. For their first six months together the arrangement with Janet worked well.

So did the other that was set up for her now. A young writer, Michael Schwab, briefly took over David Plante's role as her literary assistant on *Smile Please*. Gini still came down to Cheriton Fitzpaine for the odd week, but now that *Sleep It Off Lady* was with the publishers her main work with Jean was done. They remained friends; but her new assistant suited Jean better.

Michael Schwab lived nearby and came in regularly, once a week, so there was none of the uncertainty that had ruined her relationship with Gini. She always preferred the company of men anyway, and he was a congenial man. 'He is so relaxed & calming & if there's not a thought in my head we just have a drink & a cigarette & he goes home peacefully,' she told Francis. David Plante worked very hard for her, and he was indeed her chief support on *Smile Please*; but he had his own ways and his own voice, of which she was afraid. Also he had volunteered to help her as a friend, whereas Schwab's work was paid for by South West Arts. Altogether, therefore, this relationship was clearer and easier. Schwab took dictation, typed, occasionally drove her somewhere or made phone calls for her ('as I seem to be getting worse & worse at the thing'). She liked him; and – the key, as always – he liked her and took her side. Especially after her death he felt that she had been victimised as she'd feared, and he defended her. The second half of *Smile Please* was unfinished and shouldn't have been published, he said (getting at Deutsch); and Jean wasn't just a 'helpless, thoroughly unreasonable, gin-soaked *miserable*' (getting at Plante and his memoir). I think he was right about both these things; and that his response to Jean – wholly positive and protective, like Francis's and Sonia's, the Stoners', Jo's, Mr Woodard's – is an important balance to the others. 'My experience of her was altogether different,' he says.

> ... Her perception was astonishingly clear, cool, private and touching. Despite injustice, she remained compassionate. And despite the chilling isolation of her old age she could be intensely sociable.

David Plante (or Joan Forman or Al Alvarez) wasn't wrong in seeing a darker view. But if even physical objects are changed by being observed – as we're told – how much more so are people? Nothing was more likely to make a negative judgement of Jean come true than thinking it. If someone let her fool him a bit, or was simply too nice to see her dark side, it wouldn't have to come out. Not that Michael Schwab was entirely blind to it. He too often felt anxiety approaching her house, and exhaustion leaving it, as though Jean were 'a witch ... a siren, beckoning with an inner sensuality, beautiful and terrifyingly dangerous.' But when he speaks of her compassion, or Sonia Orwell of her selflessness ('there's no describing how selfless she could be when she thought about her friends or other people, or indeed, people in general'), we know that with people who were compassionate and selfless to *her*, she could be compassionate and selfless in return.

She started to work with Schwab as soon as she got back in April, and carried on through to November. She began with a poem about death, and with memories of going to church in Dominica. She often returned now to thoughts of death and religion, though she refused to believe she must soon die. 'I can't believe it's going to happen. I never could,' she said; and 'The funny thing is I feel as though my life was just starting.' She was saying the same to Sonia — 'But darling I'm not old *inside*'; and to David Plante, with typical abandon: 'It's unfair. I'm dying, my body's dying, and inside I think: it's unfair, it's unfair, I've never lived, I've never lived. . . .' During May and June she was low, and didn't work very much. Her doubts about *Smile Please* returned. She was writing about something that didn't exist any more, 'perhaps never did'; and it was all too disjointed to be any good. The bits of her life wouldn't join, wouldn't flow. 'There's Dominica, and that's completely separate from London, and then there's Vienna and Paris. My obsession is to fit it all together.' Then she was better again. One day in July she dictated memories of her nurse Meta to Schwab for two and a half hours without a break. Later, rested after the summer and excited by the prospect of London, she dictated to him drafts of 'The Imperial Road', 'Bricks Without Straw' and 'The Whistling Bird', as well as *Smile Please*. By now she had a bundle of her Dominica stories very like the bundle of *Wide Sargasso Sea* drafts of a dozen years before: 'Some she has dictated several times, each without reference to the one before, yet most of it identical, word for word,' Schwab wrote.

On 21 October *Sleep It Off Lady* was published, and reviewed splendidly, everywhere. But Jean was not convinced. You know when you've done something worthwhile, she said, and the stories weren't; except for one or two they were 'no damned good.' She was far too hard on them: about half *were* damned good. But even at eighty-six she was doing what she'd always done, what all artists, perhaps, have to do: forgetting the last book, and fixing her hopes and eyes firmly on the next. If she could only finish the autobiography, she told Sonia, 'I'll like it better than anything I've done.'

Because of *Sleep It Off Lady* there was a lot of publicity this year — four of the stories in the *New Yorker*, interviews and articles about her in the papers and on the radio. It was some of these that spurred her into writing her 'Declaration of Rights' against interviewers. They always got things wrong, she complained to Diana Athill.

> Poor John did not 'walk out on me because I had a baby.' It's the last thing he would have done. On the contrary we went to Vienna.
> I am not an ardent Women's Libber
> Or a Lesbian
> Or a Victim (eternally)
> Or a darned Fool.

She put all this into 'Making Bricks Without Straw' ('Wailing, I have gone from tyrant to tyrant, each letdown worse than the last.

All this, of course, leads straight to Women's Lib ...'). It ends: 'Inaccuracies occur, for people must be entertained. So now I can read calmly of my dark dreadful life, extraordinary versions of my first marriage, that I worked on the stage for ten bob a week (this last annoys me), but as a rule I don't turn a hair.'

This was hardly true, of course — though it did show that her ability to strike the 'acerbic' note was undiminished. In fact when she began 'Making Bricks Without Straw' she was in one of her panics about 'business', and turning hairs everywhere. The bank had written to say she was over one hundred pounds overdrawn, she told Schwab; she wanted to dictate a reply. Schwab got out her financial papers for her: and saw she had thousands of pounds in the bank.... She was worrying about agents too, saying she didn't have one, when her problem was still that she had too many. (That, at least, was sorted out now: apart from stage and screen, which remained with Peggy Ramsay, Anthony Sheil took over as her sole literary agent in November.)

It was the time of year, once again, when she must be allowed to escape Cheriton and come to London. But now her friends were seriously worried. She really could no longer manage an hotel, getting up and down to the dining-room, seeing herself to bed. They met at Sonia's and discussed what to do. The best thing, they decided, would be a flat, where they could shop and cook for her, keep her entertained, take care of her entirely. Sonia found just what was needed, a ground-floor flat near Sloane Square; and after a week or two's delay because she had 'flu, Schwab drove Jean up to London.

The horrors of packing, travel and upheaval put her into a state of high tension. Sonia was waiting for her in the flat, but she couldn't be grateful. The sitting-room walls were green: *bad luck*. The bathroom door didn't lock. 'This is the sort of place where ever-one knows where everyone is,' she said sourly. It was an ominous beginning.

And indeed this London holiday went even less well than the one before. Jean now needed more care than she wanted. At their meeting her friends had devised a very careful and complete rota. Every day they took turns to help her with getting up (by half past ten or eleven); with her bath, dressing, lunch, light supper; with getting to bed (by nine). There was a notebook in the flat called the 'Jean Book', written by Di Melly, which contained the rota; and very full, tragi-comic instructions about how to ensure peace of mind for Jean, and so for everyone else, as far as possible. Avoid argumentative subjects like politics (Di wrote), and emotional ones like age. Let her do what she likes about her looks. When helping with dressing remember she is very modest. Don't give her a drink unless she asks, and don't drink something else in front of her or she'll want it too. At night leave a small light on, give her two sleeping pills, and make sure that the bottle is *tightly* closed.

The rota included Jean's inner circle of friends — the two Diana's, Athill and Melly, Jo Batterham, David Plante — plus other friends and helpers, such as the actor Peter Eyre and the writers Bernice Rubens, Diana Petre and Shusha Guppy.* All these came to take care of her; on top of this there was a constant flow of other visitors and 'servicing crew', as Schwab called them, to help and entertain her — 'publisher, accountant, agent, agent's partner, hairdresser, doctor, attendant friends, admirers, and myself.' Jean could hardly cope with Janet's single, slender interruptions in Cheriton Fitzpaine; now her whole life was interruptions. It was all meant most kindly, but it was too much for her. And she became morose; she complained. She hadn't a moment to herself, they treated her like a puppet, she said. And Schwab at least agreed: sometimes people shouted at her, or spoke across her as if she wasn't there.

There were just too many people, and too much drink. And then the opposite would happen. By the evening she would be drunk and miserable; the nights were long; and now she would complain instead that she was always left alone. On bad days, Di Melly wrote, 'one arrived panting at five o'clock to be greeted with tears and moans.' 'She was quite sure it was a mistake to have come up to London,' David Plante said; and Diana Athill: 'There were days when she complained that it was not much better than being at Cheriton.' By mid-November she was in her gramophone-groove of drunken self-pity. No one understood; everything was 'lies, damned lies'.

> She falls on the floor [Schwab wrote] ugly and angry, flecked with foam. I try to pick her up, but the limp body is heavy. She crawls slowly to the settee like a dog. I feel immensely for her vulnerability and lift her onto the soft cushions, this hollow-eyed bag of flesh and bones.

Schwab now returned to Devon, and Plante took over again. Working with her was extremely difficult now. She was too quickly drunk, too forgetful, she would repeat the same often pointless story over and over. Her many different versions of the same part or

---

*Francis couldn't help very much, because his own mother was ill and dying at the same time (she died a few months before Jean). Sonia helped all the time, from finding the flat to washing Jean's clothes; but she wasn't on the regular rota. (The amount she none the less did is clear from Jean's letter to her after this holiday: 'Thank you for all you've done for me, the big things and the little ones which count so much.')

paragraph confused her. She would choose the best and tell David to tear up the others; but even after he'd torn up 'waste-paper baskets full' it was still a jumble. They spent days trying to fit the pieces together in their minds, to find the all-important 'shape' of the autobiography. But Jean despaired. 'It can't be done. It's too jumbled,' she'd say. Finally David felt that something had to be done; and he suggested to her that he do a paste-up.

'A paste-up?' she asked. He tried to explain, but 'it was like trying to explain a computer system to her.' Nevertheless, she agreed. 'Please put it all in chronological order and cut out the repetitions,' she said. David took the autobiography home and spread it out on the floor. He cut it up into pages, paragraphs, sometimes single sentences, and pasted them in what he hoped was the right order on to large sheets. The next day he read it through to her. She listened in silence. When he asked what she thought she said, in a weak voice, 'Fine.' And David went home to type it.

This was the second and far worse disaster of her enforced collaboration on *Smile Please*. By the time Diana Athill arrived to help her to bed she had worked herself into a terrifying state. 'It's David's book now, not mine,' she raged; he had taken over her work and destroyed it. She was drunk, swearing, more frantic than Diana had ever seen her; more frantic than Diana hoped to see anyone ever again.

Plante typed out the paste-up and gave it to Jean, saying 'This is *your* book, not mine or anyone else's.' ('Of course it is, and if I don't like it I'll tear it up and throw it away,' she answered.) Diana gave him a cheque for five hundred pounds, and David decided sadly that he had been paid off. He saw Jean often over the holiday season, but they didn't mention the autobiography. On New Year's Eve she had a champagne party. She sat amid her friends and raised her glass. 'Oh well,' she said, sadly. 'Another year.'

In fact the collaboration wasn't over. In the end, Diana says, Jean realised that Plante hadn't harmed *Smile Please* but helped it: and I suspect she really knew this from the start. For the five hundred pounds he received only two days after her wild fury hadn't come from the publishers, as he thought, but from Jean herself. She'd told Diana to say it came from them. Just possibly this was meant to be a curt dismissal with money, like the one Lancelot had delivered to her; but it looks more like a confession and a restitution, a way of recognising that Plante had helped her without actually saying so. And soon after the New Year's Eve party she asked him, rather timidly, to go on working with her.

He did, of course. And very occasionally, over the next month, she still suddenly dictated something clear and beautiful. But sometimes whole paragraphs seemed worthless to him — and perhaps also to her, for the more banal they were, the more she wept as she dictated them. Often she didn't want to work at all now, but just talked, easily and movingly, about writing, about herself, about her family. But all too often she fell back into her gramophone-groove — yelling her hatred of people, moaning and crying that she was utterly alone and no one helped her, when in fact her friends were turning their lives upside down for her. Plante wondered how much of the loneliness she complained of was a self-imposed silence, in which she waited and hoped for 'one or two good sentences'. I think he was at least partly right, and that even now 'one or two good sentences' were what mattered most to her. Once she dictated, weeping, a sentence which included the words 'a sort of despair'. She listened to him reading it back to her, then said: 'Cut the "sort of" and leave just "despair".'

Her increasing dependence was depressing her very badly. She felt a prisoner, as though her nightmare of Antoinette in the attic had come true. And now her stubborn sameness was almost sublime. She was eighty-six years old, 'more hunched and twisted than ever,' unable to do anything for herself, almost unable to move — and all she could think of was escape. 'I want to go away,' she told David. 'I want to do something really wild, really really wild.'

It was crazy, of course. But in fact she was, at last, quite rich and famous and well-loved enough to press reality into the shape she desired. Despite all the obvious and appalling difficulties two of her kindest friends decided that she should have her dream of escape, as wild as she wanted. They would take her wherever she'd like to go. They thought first of her beloved Paris — but it would be so changed, she would hate it and be unhappy. Jean herself came up with the answer. She'd always longed to see Venice, she said, and never had. Could they go to Venice?

In late February 1977 Jean and David put her unfinished autobiography into two huge envelopes and sealed them with sealing wax. David wrote on them 'TO BE DESTROYED UNOPENED IF ANYTHING SHOULD HAPPEN TO ME'; and Jean signed, twice, both 'Jean Rhys' and 'E.G. Hamer'. Jo Batterham and Di Melly — the two who'd undertaken to 'magic' this dream into reality — slaved away at the details. Despite this, of course, during the last days Jean panicked. She got a cold and said she couldn't go, though the doctor said she could. She'd read in a guide book, she told David, that Venice was full of rats. She looked at him triumphantly, accusingly, 'as if,' he says, 'she had found out something everyone had deliberately kept from her.' 'They're taking me to a place full of *rats*,' she said. When David tried to turn this into a joke — 'But there are a lot of cats' — she refused to laugh, and only raised her eyebrows.

Nevertheless she went, and it was wonderful that she did, for this was to be the very last moment she could still enjoy such a 'treat': Venice came just in time. Drinking champagne in the aeroplane she was elated. The splendour of the Hotel Danieli was what she'd always dreamed of, and she swept into its marble hall as though she were coming home. The gondola rides were perfect. Charmed by the gondolier, she completely forgot her fear of water; she loved the sound of it, and if it was 'a bit stinky', as Jo said, she didn't notice. She lay back gracefully on the cushions, seeing sky and beautiful buildings for the first time in years — for she was so bent now that sitting in her wheelchair she could rarely see above the shop windows.

For two weeks her routine was pure pleasure. All morning Di would help her choose clothes, make-up and a hat for the day; or else she'd be at the hairdresser having everything done, her hands, her hair, her wig. At lunchtime all three would set out together to a restaurant, the more bohemian the better. After lunch an excursion, gondolas or shopping. Then back to the Danieli for a rest. Finally, the best part of the day for Jean: sitting at the bar with cocktails, 'making up imaginary stories about the other guests while a coat-tailed pianist strummed out nostalgia.' (Di and Jo loathed this loud, sentimental music; but that only amused Jean more.) At these moments she was relaxed and giggly. She even wrote a gay, true little poem.

> *They twig*
> *It's a wig*
> *What care I?*
> *I am shy*
> *And it helps.*

Of course it wasn't all perfect, especially for the two helpers. Jean was as demanding as ever; one of them had always to be on call, and she wanted whatever anyone else had. Also they knew very well that the better she was now, the worse she'd be when the holiday was over. Pushing her in her wheelchair beside the canals, they debated whether to tip her in, now that she was happy. . . . But really they knew they'd given her something very rare. Thanking Di afterwards, Jean said 'I'll never forget Venice.' She talked about it often, and in her memory it became more and more perfect.

Back in England the return to Cheriton Fitzpaine was staved off for a few days while Jean stayed at the Mellys'. Finally, however, it could be put off no longer, and she began her usual six months or so, April to October, at home.

It was a bad time, as Di and Jo had foreseen. The honeymoon with Janet was over. Already at the end of their first six months Jean had begun to say that Janet was only 'quite kind'. And Janet was beginning to see that the 'gentle and charming' old lady whom Diana Athill had described, and whom she had first met, was something rather more complicated. She *was* sometimes gentle; but she was also many other things. She was very tense and nervous, and for a week before an interviewer or photographer came she would be in a turmoil, impossible to live with. She didn't understand anyone's point of view but her own. Janet would type out poems for her, for example (Jean always recruited *everyone* for typing). Janet was no typist, and this was quite a labour for her. But though she asked Jean many times to point out the few words or lines she wanted to change, so that just those could be retyped, Jean would always strike the whole poem through, so that it would all have to be redone from start to finish. She was a 'user', Janet decided: because of the things that had happened to her, but none the less a user. Her excuse was always that she 'didn't understand' – about machines, typewriters, correcting fluid. But that was what it was, an excuse; she didn't *want* to understand.

Worse than any of this, however, was something which we'll recognise, but which Janet, of course, was not prepared for: Jean's rage. She was so *full* of rage, Janet says; she was enraged with everyone. It was unpredictable, irrational rage, and it seemed to be directed against her. Everything would be calm and peaceful – and suddenly out of nowhere Jean would fly at her. She would say 'awful things', so awful that sometimes Janet was reduced to tears. Later, when she'd calmed down, she'd say that it wasn't Janet's fault, that her anger wasn't meant for her. But this was hard to remember. And when Janet asked who it *was* meant for, Jean wouldn't say. Janet didn't have the advantage of having 'met this before, in other artists,' like Eliot Bliss or (perhaps) David Plante, who understood it too: when Jean turned her rage on him he guessed that it was for 'a very general "you": people.'

Sensibly Janet turned for advice to the person who knew Jean best: Maryvonne. What should she do, she asked, when Jean was angry, impossible, abusive? 'Just walk out and leave her alone,' Maryvonne replied. But she couldn't do that, Janet protested, she was a nurse. 'Yes,' Maryvonne said, firmly. 'It's the only thing to do.' And so Janet tried. The next time Jean flew at her, she turned away as calmly as she could and walked to the door. But then an extraordinary thing happened. Jean, who was so crippled, so immovable, was out of her chair 'in a flash'. Janet, her spaniel Katie and Jean all raced to the door – and Jean won. She slammed the door shut. It half-caught Katie, and as Janet bent to snatch her out of the way Jean locked the door and pulled out the key. Janet looked up: and there was Jean, backing away, laughing at her, waving the key tauntingly in the air. Janet felt absurdly threatened, caught in a nightmare just like Jean's own ('He smiles slyly,' 'his face black with hatred'). But how could this be happening? — this was her *patient*, a little, crippled, old lady.... At last she remembered that a spare key was kept in a kitchen drawer. She fetched it, and let herself and Katie out.

It's a horrible story, but I'm sure it is true. Edward and Gertrude would have recognised this devilish Jean; so would the Bezants and Daniells of Beckenham; so would others, even now. It was like Julia Martin slamming the door in the unknown's face and feeling exuberant; or like Marya Zelli screaming at Stephan, laughing insultingly, and feeling a delicious relief flood her.

Perhaps — it would have been natural enough — Janet had done something like the unknown in *Mackenzie* ('he caught hold of her arm, and squeezed it as hard as he could'); doubtless too, it was not Janet Jean was mocking but 'them', 'the others', 'people'. But in these moods she was sinister, witchlike; as cruel as her own most frightening creations, the small-skulled redhead in *Good Morning, Midnight*, or the *commis voyageur*. Janet had 'never been so frightened,' she'd 'never wanted to get out of anywhere more.' As though by black magic, Jean had transferred her own worst feelings of terror and entrapment to another person. She had made someone suffer *like her*.

The rest of 1977 was fairly disastrous. On top of everything else it was full of deaths: Mrs Greenslade's, for example, which wasn't unexpected; but soon after that Selma vaz Dias's, which was. There'd been no communication between Jean and Selma for years, and Jean wouldn't have been saddened by this death, as I'm sure she was by Mrs Greenslade's. But it brought her something worse than sadness; it brought her trouble.

Selma died of cancer on 31 August. In her will she'd left all her literary rights to her children: and ever since the Adventure of the Drunken Signature her literary rights had apparently included her share of Jean's adaptations. *Did they still?*

The answer, it seems, is that they did. When the final contract had been drawn up, in 1969, everyone had concentrated on getting Selma's signature to the vital reduction of her claims which Peggy Ramsay had won. Selma was only in her mid-fifties then: no one thought of her dying, or therefore of limiting her claims to her own lifetime. It was a fatal oversight. Legally, it appears, Selma's rights were *what was written*, and in the contract it was not written that they were to end when she died. So they did not end when she died. Selma may not have meant to turn herself into a vampire, sucking Jean's blood even after she'd died: she didn't name her third of Jean's adaptation income among her rights, and she may not have intended to include it. None the less, since it is not excepted, it is included. The law made Selma into a vampire, whatever she intended. ('Justice,' Antoinette had said, 'is a damn cold lie'.) The only people who could release her – and Jean – are her children, by voluntarily renouncing their legal rights. But they didn't do this during Jean's lifetime, and they still haven't done it. Jean saw that stretching away ahead of her forever. All her life she had wanted to make money for Maryvonne; when she was old it became an obsession. But this last desire was deprived of action, like so many others. Jean's resentment and regret, especially for Maryvonne's sake, were boundless.

There was yet another death this year, which must in some ways have meant even more to Jean than Selma's. She didn't write to anyone about it, I don't think she ever talked about it. However, I am sure she noticed it, and thought about it. For it was that of her oldest and greatest enemy: her sister Brenda.

This unhappy relationship had of course ended long before the one with Selma: Brenda's husband had stopped Jean even writing to her by the early fifties. The Greenslades had vaguely known that there was a sister, and some trouble between them; but Mrs Woodard, for instance, had no idea that Jean had any family apart from Edward. In other words, Jean hardly ever mentioned Brenda; she just tried to forget she existed. And Brenda did exactly the same about her. This lasted for years, right through the sixties. Then one day a change nearly happened. Brenda's husband Robert Powell came to see Diana Athill at Deutsch. He said that Brenda was old and ill now, and very worried about the breach. Could they not get together with Jean somehow and make it up? Diana hoped they could, and she gave Robert Powell Jean's address.

What happened, I wonder? For nothing ever came of this overture. Was it just a brief obsession of Brenda's, which Robert happily forgot as soon as she did? (Robert heartily disliked Jean, and did what he did only for Brenda.) Or did Jean perhaps tear up a letter, or never reply? In any case there was no healing of the breach. When Edward died in 1970 Brenda was too ill to come to the funeral; but Robert could have come, and as a stickler for propriety would have felt he should. Instead he sent his adopted son: at least partly, I'm sure, because he didn't want to meet Jean. Then in 1975, when Brenda's will was made, it didn't contain the one gesture it could have: a token bequest, at least, for Jean. By now Brenda was very ill, and had almost lost her memory; so that once again this must have been mostly Robert's decision. But Robert, whatever he felt about Jean, was a kind and decent man, and dedicated to fulfilling every one of his wife's whims. If there'd ever been even a hint of reconciliation it would have come out *somewhere*. Brenda had clearly managed really to forget Jean, along with everything else, at last.

The story of Brenda's decline is a very sad one: but it is also strangely illuminating, when we think of Jean. For the main feeling that Jean's life and nature give us (and certainly gave her) is one of being apart and alone: different, isolated, unlike anyone else, especially her own family. And this is true. And yet at the same time it isn't true. Many of her characteristics were family ones, shared by her sisters and brothers. If anyone was different it was Minna – who was brought up apart from them, and then became ill. But Edward, Owen and Brenda had several traits in common with Jean. All four had a kind of family reserve and unapproachability, but also great charm, and a dry sense of humour. They all had high standards of behaviour, especially, for instance, about loyalty and discretion – which however they all, not just Jean, had difficulty in living up to, because they all had volatile tempers. And they were all, not just Jean, quite difficult and demanding. Partly, perhaps, this was as much a colonial characteristic as a family one; but they all assumed that they were in some way special and ought to be served, and if they weren't they were all – not just Jean – inclined to sulk.

But beyond this, in her decline and death Brenda became *more and more like her rejected sister*. It was as though Jean had been the scapegoat, the one who bore the family curse for all to see: while it took disease and death to wear down Brenda's better-fitting mask, and reveal the same face beneath.

Brenda's illness had begun around the mid-1960s, when she was approaching her seventies. It sounds like a form of early senile dementia – perhaps Alzheimer's disease, though it was not diagnosed as such. She became confused and forgetful; she began to wander around Richmond near her home, not knowing who or where she was. Robert retired early to take care of her, and they moved to Southwold in Suffolk. But there she grew worse: and as she grew worse she grew more like Jean. She became depressed and agitated, getting worse as night approached. If you attended to someone or something else she would grow frantic; if her husband disappeared for a moment she was convinced he had abandoned her forever. When she was at her worst she wouldn't eat or talk to people; she would repeat incessantly 'Oh God what shall I do?', and cry and tear her hair. Only music would soothe her a bit, or a book; like Jean, she would read the same one over and over again.

All of this – the anxiety and uncertainty, the fear of being abandoned – was like Jean: it had merely come out in Jean sooner and more often, had been closer to her surface all her life. But these things, alas, are universal — below all our surfaces somewhere; which is why Jean speaks to us all in the end. But there was something else, too, that came out in Brenda as disease wore away her 'respectable' side: and this was, perhaps, less universal. It was Jean's demon of rage and aggression.

The very first signs of change that Brenda's family had noticed were sudden, irrational outbursts of anger. Then one day she screamed at her charwoman for no reason at all — Brenda, who was normally so well behaved and fair. After that she began to hit out unpredictably at people; finally she stopped recognising Robert, and attacked him as well. The 'good' sister was now the same as the 'bad': lashing out at the one person who loved and served her most, just as Jean had done with John and Leslie and Max. At this point, of course, 'respectable society' did to Brenda what it had several times done to Jean — put her away in a hospital, and filled her with drugs. She spent a year in St Andrew's Hospital, Northampton; then her last year in a small hospital near her home in Suffolk. Finally she died. Soon afterwards Robert had a long-delayed nervous breakdown.*

Anger and anxiety, aggression and the fear of abandonment: these were the poles of the 'bad' sister's torment — and also, when her defences were destroyed, of the 'good'. It's the anger that is the engine of this infernal machine, because great anger makes us afraid: afraid that we'll lose control and attack, afraid therefore that we'll be hated and abandoned. Such great anger, I think, is bred by oppression and injustice: by a sense of having been denied, ill-used, unloved. We'll never really know why Jean felt these things so deeply; or why Brenda must have done so too, despite her (probably) happier childhood and her far more secure and successful later life. The family's explanations centre on her long years of caring for her mother, her aunt and her sister, and on one of their results — the fact that she never had children, though she longed for them. And as far as it goes this must be right. But one can't help wondering if it didn't go further. Why were these sisters, so different in every other way, both secretly so angry? Was there something in their shared background to make them so — as women, as white West Indians, as (most closely shared of all) daughters of Minna Rees Williams? We'll never know, especially about this last; but we must guess, I think, that there was something.

We'll never know, either, what Jean felt when she learned that her

---

*He recovered, however (unlike, one can't help thinking, poor Leslie), and outlived Brenda by seven years, dying in 1984.

hated younger sister had died, that she'd outlived them all now, that she was the last survivor. We don't know how much she'd heard over the years about Brenda's sufferings; or whether it might have softened her heart to know that of all the people in the world, Brenda's torments were close to her own. But I doubt it. Jean didn't forgive women as easily as men. She never forgave Stella Bowen; 'she died hating Stella,' Francis Wyndham says. I'm sure she died hating Brenda too.

As autumn approached her need to escape Cheriton was as strong as ever, but her ability to survive anywhere else had been reduced to zero. She was 'terribly tired' and had been 'falling about', 'as usual'. She returned to her old refrain — 'if I could have a week's real rest I'd be alright again, or almost'; and also to her oldest idea of peace, a Catholic convent. She asked Sonia for the address of the 'Blue Nuns' in London: 'somehow I feel I'll be able to relax there better than elsewhere.' But the Blue Nuns were full up; and one more dream of escape and safety disappeared.

Several years before she had written about 'old Mrs Pearce', who, people said, was now 'perfectly happy in an old people's home. "Perfectly happy, they're *so* kind."' 'Mrs Pearce' was already then a prevision of herself; but now the reality had arrived. She was too incapable and too often senile now to go anywhere but to an old people's home. In the autumn of 1977 Di Melly looked at several. They were all private, and all expensive, but she couldn't imagine Jean in any of them. Finally however, she found one which everyone felt even Jean might take to. It *was* an old people's home, with nurses available; but it looked like an hotel, with large separate rooms, an elegant dining room and a bar. Hoping against hope, Jean's friends booked her into this very expensive 'hotel', and in late October Janet brought her up to Surrey.

As long as Janet stayed with her and saw to her every need, Jean managed. But on the very first weekend Janet went into London to see her parents: and Jean collapsed instantly. Janet had deserted her without warning (not true, for the plan had been carefully discussed in advance). The corridors were too long, the room too big, the looking-glass too high.... But worst of all were the people. They were *old*, and crippled, and dying, and 'the mere sight of them' (Diana Athill told Sonia) 'filled Jean with horror.' She wasn't like them, she refused to be like them. She couldn't, alas, refuse to be old and crippled; but she could refuse to be docile and sociable, as they were, making the best of it, fitting in. She was furious; she plunged into paranoia and depression.

There was nothing for it but to take her away. But where could she go? There was the possibility of a room in a house near Jo, but that wouldn't be ready for three weeks. Sonia couldn't help this time, because she was still in Paris. So once again Di Melly came to the rescue. For three weeks, or even until the school holidays in December, Jean could stay with her. The other Diana packed Jean's case; and Di and Jo fetched her and brought her home.

That was how it happened that Jean spent her last London winter at the Mellys'. For of course she didn't just stay for three weeks, or until the Christmas holidays: she stayed for three months and more. Di gave Jean her bedroom and bathroom, her husband George gave her his box mattress; Di's lodger had to move out, and when her children came home they shared a room or slept on the landing. It was a last example of something Jean had done all her life: depend so helplessly on other people that they had to rearrange their whole lives to rescue her. Of course she was old and ill now; but it had always been the same. She knew it better than anyone. She had described it perfectly in *Mackenzie*, nearly fifty years before.

> Suddenly Mr Horsfield saw Julia not as a representative of the insulted and injured, but as a solid human being. She must be taken somewhere – not later than the next morning. She must have a bed to sleep in, food, clothes, companionship – or she would be lonely; understanding of her own peculiar point of view – or she would be aggrieved.
>
> He saw all this with great clarity, and felt appalled.

The difference was that in the end Mr Horsfield – like Jean's family, like Lancelot, like Ford, Like Maxwell Macartney – turned away and closed his door; whereas in life many of Jean's friends, and all her husbands, almost endlessly tried to give her what she needed. She remembered the former more than the latter: because, inevitably, these failed. Of this process too this winter of 1977-78 was a last example.

Di Melly felt sure that she knew what Jean wanted, and that if she dedicated all her time and energy to supplying it, she could make Jean happy. What Jean wanted was comfort and company, warmth, beauty and freedom from worry. So she got Di's bedroom, the best and biggest in the house: divided in two, to make a bedroom and a sitting room, 'one part blue lit and the other pink lit,' Jean said, and both with pink-carpeted floors. And Di took on herself the organisation of Jean's life. She handled her money, so that Jean never had to think about it at all. She organised her meals and bedtimes, her constant stream of visitors, her outings and entertainments, her calls from doctors and hairdressers, her sessions with David Plante. After she'd been there for a week Di made a list of what had to be done in the course of a day to keep her happy — and it was, Diana Athill says, a 'hell of a lot.' But Di was glad to do it. Jean was so very old it couldn't go on for long; at last, for once she should have exactly what she wanted. (But 'How often have we said this?' Diana worried.)

For a long time — a quite astonishingly long time — it worked. Di — 'extraordinary and adorable girl,' Diana wrote to Sonia in Paris — ministered to Jean 'exquisitely but without fuss'; and even after a month Jean still had not 'moaned once about anything (except occasionally in a ritual way the State of the Nation ...). Being comfortable and *not lonely* has made her a different being, poor old love.' During that first month she was drunk only twice; 'ninety per cent of the time she's great and fairly sober,' Di reported, also to Sonia. It was true that she frequently burst into tears, but they were, she insisted, tears of relief. Di found this hard to remember; but Sonia thought it was true. 'Oddly enough,' she told Di,

> I absolutely believe Jean when she says her outbursts of tears are of relief — though, naturally, other things come in, but you see she has, at last, achieved exactly what she wanted always i.e. total dependence on someone else, and affection and warmth and prettiness.

'Now my drenched handkerchief is hanging out to dry,' Jean wrote to Sonia herself, in December, 'and I'm as happy as Larry.' 'She's bound to have fits of woe,' Sonia repeated after reading this letter, 'because she's Jean.... But I'm inclined to think she's probably never been as happy in her life as she is now, and if you can stand it, that's marvellous!'

Di stood it for many weeks, with strain and effort of course, but also with enjoyment. She took Jean on 'orgies of clothes-buying' — satin knickers, a lilac kaftan, a pink lurex blouse — and noted in her diary: 'Great joy from clothes.' She invited people to lunch and tea — familiar friends like Francis Wyndham and Al Alvarez; and also new people who wanted to meet Jean, like Penelope Mortimer, and Dee Wells and her husband Sir Alfred Ayer. It was usually the women who wanted to meet her, but the men whom she enjoyed.

She also got on very well with Di's husband George Melly, the writer and jazz singer. He read poetry to her in his deep rich voice; and one day she gave him a poem of hers which John Chiltern, the bandleader, set to music. It was a satirical little *jeu d'esprit* which much appealed to George. 'It's the rain Without the roses', one verse went,

> *It's the sky*
> *That's never blue*
> *It's nuts*

*Without the chocolate*
*It's life*
*(Pause)*
*With you.*

Jean and George were very funny together, because George was deaf and Jean spoke in a whisper, so that their conversations were full of misunderstandings. Di enjoyed listening to them. And like Mr Woodard, or Francis, she herself very much enjoyed talking to Jean. Often people didn't; they would feel bored and frustrated because Jean was so secretive and formal. But Di was happy to respect her embargo on questions about her life; and perhaps as a result Jean quite often talked about it anyway. Not about her childhood, or her affairs or marriages; but about the Crabtree Club, or Paris, or how she'd 'once slit her wrists in a hot bath, but someone walked in.' She liked to listen to Di's problems, and was always very sympathetic and unjudging. And there were still some perfect moments. She loved going to Ronnie Scott's jazz club in Soho, where George Melly often sang, or to bad films with Di's mother, or – the last 'treat' of all – to Buckingham Palace to receive her CBE. But most of all, as Sonia had said, she enjoyed being taken care of. Everyone buzzed round to serve her, like a queen bee: friends and admirers, hairdressers and aromatherapists; above all, of course, Di herself. Di brought her everything: food, drink, make-up, clothes, friends, music. She massaged her feet, she dried her bed, she even cleaned up daytime accidents before anyone had noticed. And this time Jean *was* grateful. 'You have "magics",' she said; and spoke 'so sweetly and sincerely' to her, Di says, that 'of course I was quite charmed.'

What went wrong was what always went wrong: drink and paranoia, paranoia and drink. After the first month Jean's 'ninety per cent of the time' sobriety began to lapse. When David Plante had first returned to write with her she'd been able to work a bit, and very slowly they'd finished the first part of the autobiography. But as December darkened into January their work sessions degenerated. Jean quickly became drunk, and in desperation David became drunk with her. She began to cut too much, to cut passages David thought should stay in. The best of her was no longer in her writing now, he thought, but only in her talk about writing. With one drink she started shouting, 'Lies, lies!'

and when we tried to work her dictation was incoherent. I took down sentences, sometimes words, to compose at home scrappy paragraphs. We were meant to be working on her later life. I was determined to finish at least a first draft. But the deeper she got into her later life, the more incoherent she became. After half an hour, she couldn't work.

The 'later life' never would be written.

Perhaps it was partly this trying to face the unfaceable that ended Jean's peace. But it would have ended anyway; it always did. As it receded from her she became a centre of destruction, like a small storm mowing down everything in its path. She returned to her old paranoid trick of refusing to see people, and then complaining 'No one ever comes to see me.' She became abusive. She began 'falling about' again; once she pulled a whole lavatory cistern down with her. One night she fell so badly she couldn't move at all, and Di had to roll her on to a blanket and drag her back to bed like a dog.

It was exhausting and discouraging, and once or twice people found Di in tears. But for several weeks she didn't despair. After all, it was nothing new; the friends all knew that Jean drank as much if not more in Devon, and that her complaints and accidents there were mostly due to drink. George helped by seeing the funny side: he began to call Jean 'Johnny Rotten', after the bad-boy lead singer of the Sex Pistols, who shared (among other things) her initials.

By now, however, it was February, which meant that there was only a month of the winter holiday left, and the return to solitude was looming. We know what this always did to Jean; and so did Di. Things duly got worse. But then, quite suddenly, they got impossible.

In early February Di organised a careful rota of Sarah, her ex-lodger, and various friends, because she had to be away for a weekend. Immediately Jean regressed to 'an anxious toddler with endless tantrums'. She told Sarah that Di's house was 'a hell-hole', in which 'she'd been incarcerated for three weeks without having seen a soul.' On Saturday night she kept Sarah up 'from two till five a.m. ringing the bell and falling about,' until she bruised herself badly again. When Di returned poor Sarah was white and trembling, and Jean was 'a Fuseli monster' complaining of heart pains. When Di refused to give her more than two drinks on top of her pain killers she raged at her: '"Balls, balls, balls!" says the Fuseli monster.'

From then on the sweet and grateful Jean was completely lost, and the mad, bad, dangerous Jean was in full possession. She began to drink wildly and uninterruptedly. If Di tried to dissuade her she would say, 'I think I'd better go back to Devon.' Sometimes she just shouted for more, and once when Di said no she spat at her. Like Janet, then, Di left the room: and Jean fell and gashed her head.

She was witchlike with everyone. David Plante would come down from her room grey with fatigue and despair. She refused to see her grand-daughter, Ellen; once she was 'so awful' to Maryvonne – who'd come over three or four times in the last months – that Di says 'Maryvonne actually fainted.' It was as though she was punishing everyone for Di's imagined abandonment.

And clearly it was this she couldn't bear: the smallest withdrawal by someone she'd let herself trust, which for Jean meant someone to whom she had given herself up entirely. Thus, for example, when Di turned her attention and sympathy to a friend who'd suffered a tragedy, Jean became drunk and furious. And once, when Di went out briefly — but only a few days after that first fatal 'abandonment' — Jean 'threatened to slash all the paintings if Maryvonne left before I came back.' Maryvonne said she'd never known Jean 'so vicious and monstrous'; yet when Di went in to her she found her 'very meek and pathetic,' begging her to stay and talk, because 'I'm so lonely....' Di's image of the 'toddler' was right. Like a very small child, Jean's need of people she depended on was so great that it left her only the most extreme alternatives if she felt they'd abandoned her: to punish them violently, or to placate them abjectly.

For the rest of her stay she swung from one extreme to the other every day, almost every hour. It was hair-raising, quite impossible, and it made them both ill. Even Jean's favourite routines of dress, wig and make-up became an intolerable effort for her; she was so miserable that Cheriton Fitzpaine seemed a haven. As for Di, her decline was steep and visible. She became grey and ground down, as though she had been emptied of everything, sucked dry. She no longer knew what to do, she'd lost all her certainty. Only one thing was clear, to her and to everyone: Jean had to leave. It was settled that she would go home at the end of February. In the last week things were so bad that Di phoned Sonia in Paris for advice. Sonia knew Jean's worst witchlike mood very well. You mustn't take her back to Cheriton yourself, she told Di; above all, don't stay alone with her there. 'You must, must, must protect yourself now,' she said.

Di was preparing to ignore this advice and drive Jean home when — disaster. A snowstorm hit Devon, leaving the roads impassable; and Jean's return had to be postponed. Di could hardly believe it. Jean *didn't* believe it — it was all lies, a plot, a trick to keep her prisoner.... That was the last straw. One of them would have to go, preferably into a hospital. Di was just as ready as Jean; but in the end of course it was Jean whom Diana Athill carried off, furious and screaming, to a nursing home.

A few days later they'd both recovered enough for Di to drive Jean home as planned. All the way down Jean looked round grimly: there was no sign of snow. It had (freakish but true) *only snowed in Devon*, Di explained: but when they got to Devon there was no snow there either. Di was furious; Jean's small smile of triumph became a sneer. But then — at last — there was proof: just outside Cheriton itself the narrow road was completely blocked by a wall of snow. Di reversed and found another entrance. Nothing was said; but at some level at least, Di hoped, Jean must know she hadn't lied.

At some level, of course, she did: but we know how good she was at burying what didn't fit her obsessions. Soon she had 'embroidered a wicked version of the winter': 'everything was lovely until Di and George and the whole family *went away* and left her in that house all alone.' Not only that, but Di had made her spend far too much money; and *'they' had even stolen her manuscripts....* This story she told to anyone who would listen. She expressed no gratitude to Di; instead (says Al Alvarez) 'she crucified her.'

Thus ended the last and (as Sonia Orwell said) probably the most successful attempt to make Jean happy. It had of course been doomed from the start. Di knew that now. 'In the end I realise one can't make her happy, or even alright,' she wrote sadly to Sonia.

And yet, just as her dream of happiness vanished again, Jean remembered her best vision of it. She talked about it often, Di remembers, and David Plante wrote it down. It had happened in France in the thirties, she said; one hot August day as she was walking along the road between Théoule and Cannes. She had stopped by the sea at a place called La Napoule. And suddenly, for the first and only time in her life, she was purely, intensely happy. For (as she had scrawled, close to the time),

> ... I existed no longer ... I was the wind the trees the sea the warm earth & I left behind a prison a horrible dream of prison ... – Do you see now oh then it was just a dream of prison....

This was her best, her truest idea of escape; not from anyone or anything else, but *from herself.* It was what she'd really longed for all her life – to escape this prison of self and join the world. Especially, she knew at that moment, to join other people. 'It's this feeling of being one with human beings,' she'd written, 'but I cannot – only through books sometimes I can get it.' And telling it to David now she said 'I thought: why do I hate people? They're not hateful.' Telling it now she felt it was something larger – a vision of happiness which wasn't just for her. There were no words to describe it, she said,

> except perhaps in a still unknown language. I felt a *certainty* of joy, and terrific terrific happiness, not only for me, but for everyone. I knew that the end would be joy.

Again she was being just like Antoinette. For Antoinette was also immured in a room in someone else's house; and she also lost all control, attacking her step-brother with a knife ('Blood all over the place,' says Grace Poole.) And the very next day she too had a vision, which was also of a (fearful but) joyous escape. For Antoinette that escape was death. I think it was for Jean too; and that in remembering now that 'the end would be joy' she was feeling her escape approaching.

★     ★     ★

On 1 March Jean was back in her bungalow. She wouldn't leave it again, except to go into nursing homes and hospitals. After only a few weeks at home she'd already had at least one fall; and at the end of March she went into a nursing home in Exeter. She remained weak and shaky and went on falling. Or so her friends heard: Jean denied it. 'I *haven't* fallen since I've been here,' she wrote angrily to Di. 'Please don't believe all the gossip you hear about me as I'm afraid it gets rather exaggerated en route.' However, she certainly had a bad fall in May, and when her friends went to see her that month they found her pretty low. Diana spent a weekend with her in late May. Saturday was fine (she reported to Di), Jean was quite clear-headed and even 'giggly':

> ... But Sunday I was leaving, so grievance set in at crack of dawn and she was soon doing her gramophone-needle-stuck-in-a-groove thing of going over and over miseries of one sort and another.... She is back, God help us, on the theme of how Cheriton can only be endured if she can feel sure that she'll be able to escape to London for the winter! When reminded of how she mopped and mowed in London she says 'I know I was miserable in London, but it's better to feel miserable than to feel dead.'

She was 'desperately scared' about money, and she was complaining about everyone. In London Di had abandoned her, in Cheriton no one ever visited her, and now Jo had made her buy a chaise longue she didn't want, and what was she going to do? ... 'Really, what is the point' — wrote Diana, reduced to Jean's own helpless fury — 'of everyone helping her when she ends up miserable and blaming her misery on whoever it was who did whatever it was?' David Plante found her in the same angry, miserable mood. When they tried to work a bit she could do nothing but cut — she cut words, sentences, whole paragraphs. She couldn't see the point of *Smile Please*, of writing, of life. She said 'I want to take a pill and die.' (To Diana she'd said, more colourfully, that she would starve herself, then lie down in the garden on a rainy night.) There was one big change, which should have made a difference: she could no longer drink, or very little. But it didn't make any difference. The habit of anger was too ingrained now; she no longer needed drink to release it. 'Without drink, she raged,' David wrote in his memoir: 'It means nothing, it means nothing, writing, nothing, nothing!' Finally she caught herself, saying, 'Don't listen to me, I'll depress you.' And Joan Butler said to him: 'Go back to London. You really can't do much for Jean now.'

But if the storms didn't change, nor did the breaks between them. The last summer of her life brought Jean fairer weather, as summer had always done. During June and July especially she was better. She fired off a spate of letters, some of them even 'business'. She went into Exeter. She had visitors – Maryvonne and Job, Di, her agent Anthony Sheil – and went to the Stoners as usual for her birthday. She even worked. She put the finishing touches to 'Making Bricks Without Straw', which appeared in *Harper's* in July, and corrected the proofs of 'The Whistling Bird' for the September *New Yorker*. She worked on her last two stories, 'Chinese Vases' and 'The Imperial Road'.* And she 'toiled away' at *Smile Please*, adding 'a few frills' and then immediately cutting them out again. At the height of the summer she was so optimistic that she promised to surrender the first part of the autobiography by September. She didn't, of course; in the end she was never happy with even Part One of *Smile Please*.

In this last summer she was so much stronger that – despite everything she'd said in 'Bricks Without Straw' – she agreed to several more interviews and meetings with strangers. She was always doing this, of course: letting hope triumph over experience. At Di's in London she'd let a young woman from the *New York Times* interview her; now three more came. She got into her usual state beforehand, so that one was almost not let in, then quizzed about her tape-recorder, and another Jean seemed to have forgotten about altogether. But with all three she settled down quite quickly into friendly conversation. One, Elaine Campbell, asked straightforward biographical questions and received no answers; but Jean still talked happily to her about the West Indies, where they both came from. Another, Madeleine Slade, didn't attempt to ask any questions; she and Jean just chatted – about spiders and mice, London prices, the letters Jean received from all over the world, such as one that day from Japan, entirely in Japanese. The third, Elizabeth Vreeland, got the most out of Jean about her life and her books, and the way she used the one for the other. Jean also used this interview well, to do something she'd wanted to do for a long time: make up for the hate she'd poured out against Ford in *Quartet*,

---

*Neither ever published. They can be read in the Jean Rhys Collection at the University of Tulsa.

and express her gratitude to him. 'Ford helped me more than any-body else,' she said.

Elizabeth Vreeland was a veteran journalist, which is why she got so much out of Jean. But it's also why she missed something. This Jean told instead to Madeleine Slade, who was not a journalist, but someone who loved her writing and felt it spoke for her.

To the end Jean insisted that she would rather 'be happy' than write; that she wrote because 'I was fated to write ... which is horrible.' The most she would usually say was that it was the one thing that could earn her death (so now, to Elizabeth Vreeland: 'I'm rather useless, but perhaps not as useless as everyone thinks'). But she let the truth slip out to Madeleine: 'I really like it you know!' she said. It sounded, Madeleine thought, 'as though she were betraying a secret.'

I think it *was* a secret, and one she could only tell a stranger, when she was close to death: that she'd spent her life writing – had sacrificed everyone and everything to writing – not just because she had to, but because *she wanted to*. This was the last, most deeply buried truth beneath her passivity and belief in fate. Of course she'd drifted and been driven. But in fact, against enormous odds of poverty and neglect, she had determined, she had insisted on writing.

In the late autumn of 1978 Jean finished the first part of *Smile Please*. Deutsch had decided to publish this separately: so that she could work on the second part without pressure, they said; but really because they knew it would never be done. In mid-November Jean had a happy day when a letter came from Diana praising the new little book. But otherwise her letting go of *Smile Please* was no easier than any of the others. Despite Diana's praise she wasn't happy with it, and kept wanting to revise it to the end. Despite her dread of galley proofs some were produced for *Smile Please*; then Diana couldn't come and help her with them. With all these worries she couldn't get on with Part Two: 'I haven't the heart,' she wrote to Anthony Sheil. But the truth was she didn't really want to.

Instead her thoughts remained in Dominica, though not happily. In the summer she'd cut out an article from the *Dominica Star*, which Phyllis Allfrey was sending her. It was about a twenty-one-year-old girl who was lost in the tropical forest for days. It ended: 'WARNING: Visitors should realise that the terrain of Dominica, though a pinprick on the map, is as vast as an African jungle when you get lost....' What she said about Dominica to Elizabeth Vreeland in October was similarly dark. Her childhood there had been lonely and 'peopled with fears', she said; that was one reason why she didn't go back. And when she *had* gone back once she'd hated it. 'No,' she said, 'I think "Never Go Back" is a good motto.' Instead she dreamed of places she'd never been to: Morocco, California.

Of course she couldn't really go anywhere; London was just as impossible as Morocco. Yet she fervently planned to go up to London all that winter, no matter how weak and ill she got. Escape was the one drug she couldn't give up.

October and November were still all right; she was sending letters, receiving visitors, finishing *Smile Please*. But her last year was like every year since she'd come to England: *cold* was the enemy. 'Cold has a dreadful way of freezing me up, body and soul,' she wrote to Di in December. She grew weaker. In January she wrote to Maryvonne: 'It's been a bit of a nightmare here. We were snowed up, Mrs Raymond is ill and I'm afraid I collapsed too and have spent about a week in bed....' She had pleurisy – though she only admitted to 'a touch', so as not to have to give up the rooms she'd booked in Blake's Hotel. But she got worse, and the rooms had to be cancelled after all. Finally in February she 'cracked up' completely and had to be admitted into a nursing home. When she arrived there she weighed only six stone; when she left she was still so thin her clothes hung on her. She'd always denied her strength, and felt and behaved as weak as a kitten; but now that her strength was really leaving her she denied that too. 'The nursing home I stayed in was rather nice and did me a lot of good,' she said, on the one occasion when it couldn't really be true. She *liked* being thin, and she *was* going up to London soon. 'I've only got to go onward and upward,' she wrote with absurd and touching bravado to Oliver Stoner. And with a characteristic hope: 'perhaps when summer comes.'

In early March she signed her last contract, very shakily. It was for 'Outside the Machine' to go into a new edition of *Winter's Tales*; she got one hundred pounds for it. In early April she wrote to several London friends that she had rebooked Blake's Hotel, and would be there on the twenty-first. She and Diana could then go through *Smile Please* together.

Two days before she was to leave Cheriton for London Diana's phone rang. It was Janet: Jean had had another fall. She had fractured a hip and could no longer avoid hospital.

That last year had been so wretched that even those who loved her most hoped she would die. But she had survived so much that it seemed possible she would survive this too. 'Oh dear,' Diana scrawled to Di, 'I have a feeling that being Jean she will miraculously get over this....' Perhaps even now she could have, but her hip had been broken in such a way that she had to undergo an operation, and after it she had a series of small strokes. She lay in the hospital for three weeks, her consciousness mercifully shrinking. She didn't speak, she didn't eat: none the less she hung on, she survived. Friends from both Cheriton Fitzpaine and London visited her, but after the first few days she hardly seemed aware of them. George Melly noticed a last change of her name: the card on the end of her bed said 'Joan' instead of Jean, as though even now people wouldn't believe her; or as though even dying she was, mysteriously, 'twins'.

On 14 May Jo Batterham was in Dorset visiting her youngest son at school. People had said that Jean did not recognise anyone; but she felt she must go to see her. There was no flesh left on her; one eye was rolled upwards. But one of her hands moved, and Jo took it. Softly she sang some of Jean's favourite songs, *Je ne regrette rien* and *La vie en rose*; she said 'You'll go to a happy place, you'll be with the nuns.'

She asked the doctor how long Jean could live. Oh, he said, it could be weeks. But when Jo came back from lunch Jean was colder and more restless. A nurse tried to give her some medicine on a spoon, but she refused it.

When Jean started to die, Jo says, she felt a moment of fear. But then 'she just went peacefully into a realm of colours.' To the end she was unpredictable, defiant. She had had such a terrible fear of death. For nearly seventy years, ever since Lancelot had left her, she had talked often of suicide: but she had never let go of life, not even in this last awful year. She was too afraid of nothingness. Yet what Jo felt now was neither fear nor nothingness: it was happiness. It came from Jean and it filled the room. Like Antoinette she had woken up, walked down the dark passage and escaped at last.

# CHAPTER THREE

# Jean

Jean was always the same: passive, narcissistic and paranoid; charming, seductive and full of fun, but also unreachable, unhappy, and full of rage. When she was old it became worse. She longed as much as ever to love and be loved, especially now by her daughter and grand-daughter; but she failed as much as ever. She was more terrified than ever, especially of people. She lived even more in the moment, and was more intensely sensitive for herself and more quickly forgetful of others than ever. 'Poor Sonia,' she would say, 'Poor Francis,' when her dearest friends were ill or overburdened and couldn't come to see her: but she spoke vaguely, and really she felt betrayed. She cried as easily as ever, she flew into rages as easily as ever; no one could give her the degree of attention and service she needed just to stop her pain.

She was also as dedicated as ever to the surface of things. She didn't like analysing or explaining books or people; she preferred them to remain a mystery. This was because *she* preferred to remain a mystery, to herself and to everyone else. Her books all plumb the mystery; but that is why she could only write them instinctively, unconsciously, behind the masks of fate, fiction, drink, a pretty dress. Again her feeling seemed to her the whole truth, and she thought that all analysis must be destruction. But again I think she was wrong, and that we must at least wonder what could have made her what she was: such an extraordinary and paradoxical person and writer.

Dominica first and certainly, 'the only home I ever had', as mys-terious as she and as perverse; so creative and so destructive, so rich and so poor. The story of her novels is Dominica's story: slavery, revenge, failure; but also defiance, self-mockery and irrepressible renewal. Their atmosphere is Dominica's, 'beauty and violence, beauty and decay'; and the atmosphere of her life was too, 'Here you are, and then immediately afterwards, Where are you?'

Certainly, too, her ancestry, her genes. Directly, on both sides: her father was vivid and moody, a rebel and given to drink; and not only her sister Brenda but also her mother and Auntie B suffered at the ends of their lives from dementing illness. Add to this Minna's 'shaking paralysis', and Edward's much milder version; and Jean's family begins to seem like Antoinette's in Daniel's dark hints. Not tainted with madness and idiocy, of course; none the less with some neurological weakness, which the Dominican voices in Jean's head built and brooded on, to make her identification with Bertha Mason still stronger and more fated.

Her ancestry further back too. For she was split, divided against herself, 'twins': half of her longing to belong, to be liked, to be a safe and happy 'ordinary woman'; the other half determined on risk and difference, and to be truthful to that difference in her writing. It was like a war in her between the Lockharts and the Rees Williamses, between the conventional, conformist, colonial English and the dark, subversive, romantic Celt. Between light and dark, in fact; and perhaps in another way too.

Her attitude to black people was ambivalent — half admiration and identification, half fear. But her attitude to any suggestion that there might be black blood in *her* was especially so. Sometimes she quoted her father — 'Who's white? Damned few'; sometimes she said 'The English legend that there is always a black grandmother tucked away is only a legend.' She had always wondered about her own great-grandmother ('Spanish? I wonder'). When she was a child she often hoped that the legend was true of her. When she was a young woman she denied it, angrily. When she was old she said it was probably true. And it may have been. Several people felt there was black blood in her: Ford when she was young, Rosamond Lehmann in her middle age, Mollie Stoner when she was old. It showed especially in her eyes, which looked huge even though they weren't, and as frightened as a deer's even when she wasn't, because you sometimes saw the whites all around them, like a black person's eyes in a white face. It was part of her mystery and her difference, both as a woman and as a writer. It gave her writing a special note, Rosamond Lehmann said to me: 'plangent, like a horn'; like 'a different bloodstream' running under the other.

How she came to be as she was is one question. The other is: what was she? In particular: was she mad?

She was afraid she was. In her wartime notebook she scrawled a conversation with a policeman. The policeman says: *If the law says you're dangerous you're dangerous, if the law says you're mad you're mad. Then God help me*, she replies.

*Wide Sargasso Sea* doesn't deny that Antoinette is mad, it shows us why: because first her childhood, and then an Englishman, have driven her mad.

But the answer of the doctors at Holloway in 1949 and in Devon in 1964 was that she was not mad. And recently I've asked again. I took a summary of Jean's character and life to several analysts of different schools, and they all agreed. She was not mad, they said, because (apart perhaps from a few episodes) she never really lost touch with reality. And that was true. At the ghastly old people's 'hotel' in Surrey, for instance, an old lady, chatting about the weather, said to her, 'But I always say that we need winter, it kills the germs.' Later Jean said, 'She meant *me*, you know.' 'How *can* you be so paranoid?' Diana Athill asked. Jean giggled and replied: 'Oh I am, I am, I'm terribly paranoid. If I were rich I'd see a shrink every week, not that it would do me any good.'

The analysts all agreed too on what she was. I put in my list all her most permanent and most painful feelings. Her sense of being nothing, a ghost, already dead; or else twins, one docile, the other lost in a dark wood. Her constant anxiety ('The insecure feeling, that prevents you from being happy and living from day to day'); her constant battle against depression, which was what the make-up, the clothes, the treats, the drink were all for. Her absolute inability to be alone: 'You know I can't be alone. I can't,' she wrote in the very beginning, in *The Left Bank*. Her inability none the less ever to feel anything *but* alone: ever to feel any real connection to or understanding of another human being. Her wild changes of mood, hope to despair, exaltation to abasement. Her attempt to hide her real feelings, saying 'You must always pretend, never let yourself go in front of other people.' Yet her immediate and intense expression of her feelings in her face; so that sometimes people felt she covered up, and sometimes that she put things on, and that either way 'You never knew where you were with her.' Her inability to contain her very worst feelings, so that her rage and violence burst out even against those she most needed, even to the extent of public humiliation. Her extreme passivity, and her extreme incompetence, so that she 'never understood more than half the world'. And her extreme emotional need and dependence – which could suddenly change to extreme opposition and independence, so that at one moment she was 'a bit of rather battered ivy', and the next 'a savage, a Bolshevist', convinced that everything bad that ever happened to her came from giving in to other people, and not following her own wish, her own vision.

They recognised it all. Jean suffered, they said, from what is now called a borderline personality disorder. This disorder goes back to infancy, to a failure of the relation between mother and child. The child's needs are not met; from the start, therefore, it feels what Jean felt: hostility from the world, and deep, unassuagable rage towards it. And it fails to develop a complete, autonomous self. That is the key: the nothingness where the self should be. That is the nothingness Jean always felt. That is why she could not be alone, or control her rage, or accept any responsibility whatsoever. That is why she had to fill the void with extreme experience, and at the same time block off everything that threatened to overwhelm it. That is why she had such a voracious, insatiable need for dependence — and then suddenly such a fear of being taken over. All this, all Jean's suffering and all her awfulness, came from the emptiness inside her that was her unfinished self. She wrote: *Just this hollow feeling I get sometimes which sounds nothing but can be quite bad.*

I think this must be true. It must go back to her mother, who mourned her dead sister and preferred the living one to her. She said it herself, in *Wide Sargasso Sea*; and in the one absolutely clear thing she said about her childhood: that she loved her father, but hated her mother. So she *was* fated, as she felt. From the beginning she was unhealable, a stranger on the face of the earth, and full of rage.

But now I think she was right about the folly of seeking explanations, because they work only for what goes wrong; we can't explain what, despite everything, is right, but can only be thankful for it. The doctors' explanation of her personality is surely true; it is illuminating; but it doesn't touch the real mystery. If Jean was a borderline personality *of course* she couldn't be alone, of course she couldn't control herself or accept control, couldn't act or decide, couldn't do what was hard, above all couldn't accept the evil inside her. And yet she did.

She should have been only a cripple, only a drunkard. But she was not. That was the mystery: that she lived for nearly ninety years in such pain; that she escaped her fate after all; that she wrote her books. The *nothing* that she so feared, and saw behind and under everything, was her own self. But in her writing she herself made it whole.

# NOTES

In order to keep these Notes within manageable proportions, sources are not given in the literary critical chapters, except where there seemed a particular need.

To the same end, sources are given in the biographical chapters *per paragraph*. Paragraphs are identified by their opening words, and the sources which follow are for the whole paragraph. Where a paragraph runs over two pages the sources are listed, after the identifying words, under the initial page number. If a paragraph does not appear, nothing in it comes from or refers to any other source.

Again in order to save space, abbreviations have been used for all regularly recurring sources. Names and titles have been abbreviated as in the key below.

JEAN RHYS'S PUBLISHED BOOKS

*The Left Bank* (LB), Cape, 1927; *Quartet* (Q), *After Leaving Mr Mackenzie* (ALMM), *Voyage in the Dark* (VID), *Good Morning, Midnight* (GMM), *Wide Sargasso Sea* (WSS): page references to all the novels are to the Penguin editions; *Tigers Are Better-Looking* (TABL), André Deutsch, 1968; *Sleep It Off Lady* (SIOL), André Deutsch, 1976; *Collected Stories* (CS), W.W. Norton, 1987; *Smile Please* (SP), André Deutsch, 1979; *Jean Rhys, Letters, 1931*–1966, ed. Francis Wyndham and Diana Melly (L), André Deutsch, 1984.

Also: *Penguin Modern Stories* I, 1969 (PMS), in which 'Temps Perdi' and 'I Spy a Stranger' were first published.

JEAN RHYS'S PUBLISHED STORIES
(in order of their occurrence in the Notes)
'Temps Perdi' (TP); 'Pioneers, Oh, Pioneers' (POP); 'The Day They Burned the Books' (TDTBTB); 'Goodbye Marcus, Goodbye Rose' (GMGR); 'Invitation to the Dance' (ID); 'The Sound of the River' (The S of the R); 'The Bishop's Feast' (BF); 'Overture and Beginners Please' (OBP); 'Mixing Cocktails' (MC); 'The Blue Bird' (BB); 'Before the Deluge' (B the D); 'Kismet' (Kis); 'Till September Petronella' (TSP); 'La Grosse Fifi' (LGF); 'Vienne' (V); 'On Not Shooting Sitting Birds' (ONSSB); 'Learning to be a Mother' (LM); 'Illusion' (Ill); 'Mannequin' (Mann); 'Let Them Call It Jazz' (LTCIJ); 'Tout Montparnasse and a Lady' (Tout M); 'The Chevalier of the Place Blanche' (Chevalier); 'At the Villa d'Or' (V d'Or); 'In the Rue de l'Arrivée' (R de l'A); 'Hunger' (Hunger); 'A Night' (A Night); 'Discourse of a Lady Standing a Dinner to a Down-and-Out Friend' (Discourse); 'A Solid House' (ASH); 'Tigers Are Better-Looking' (TABL); 'Outside the Machine' (OM); 'The Lotus' (The L); 'Night Out 1925' (NO 1925); 'Heat' (H); 'Fishy Waters' (FW); 'The Insect World' (TIW); 'Rapunzel, Rapunzel' (Rap Rap); 'Who Knows What's Up in the Attic?' (WKWUITA); 'Sleep It Off Lady' (SIOL); 'I Used to Live Here Once' (IUTLHO); 'I Spy A Stranger' (ISAS); 'The Whistling Bird' (TWB); and 'My dear darling Mr Ramage' (Ramage), the first title for POP.

(These are not all Jean Rhys's published stories, but only those referred to in the Notes.)

Jean Rhys's unpublished work is held in three places: The Special Collections department of the McFarlin Library, University of Tulsa (Tulsa); The Manuscript Department of the British Library (BL); Jean Rhys's Executor's Archive (EA).

I wish to express my thanks to all three for permission to quote from the materials they hold.

JEAN RHYS'S UNPUBLISHED WORK
(in order of its occurrence in the Notes)
Black Exercise Book, Tulsa Item 1:1 (Bk Ex Bk); 'Mr Howard's House', dated
4–12–38, EA (Mr H H); Red Exercise Books, Tulsa Item 1:1 (Red Ex Bks); Green
Exercise Book, Tulsa Item 1:1 (Gr Ex Bk); 'The Birthday', Tulsa Item 1:5 (Bday); 'The
Cardboard Doll's House', Tulsa Item 1:7 (CDH); 'Lost Island' or 'Down Along',
'Fragments of an Autobiography' (LI); 'The Imperial Road', Tulsa Item 1:24 (Imp Rd);
Ropemakers' Diary, EA (RD); Orange Notebook, EA (O Nbk); 'Essay on England',
EA (E on E); 'L'Affaire Ford', EA (L'Aff Ford); 'Leaving School', Tulsa Item 1:28, also
drafts in EA (LS); *Triple Sec*, EA (TS); 'And Paris, Sinister', Tulsa Item 1:8, two versions
(APS); *Wedding in the Carib Quarter*, lost novel (WCQ); 'Music & Words', EA (M &
W); 'The Chinese Vases', Tulsa Item 1:27 (Ch V); 'The Forlorn Hope', EA (FH).
(These are not all Jean Rhys's unpublished works, but only those referred to here.
Also, not all works referred to are listed here, but only those for which abbreviations
are used.)

OTHERS' WORKS
(in order of their occurrence in the Notes)
David Plante, *Difficult Women*, Gollancz, 1983 (DW) (I wish to thank David Plante for
permission to quote from this book); Louis James, *Jean Rhys*, Longman, 1978 (James);
*The Persean Magazine*, Vol V, 1906–1909 (Persean) (I wish to thank the Perse School
for Girls for permission to quote from this book); Stella Bowen, *Drawn From Life*,
Collins, 1941 (DFL) (reissued by Virago Press, 1984, but references are to the 1941
edition); Adrian Allinson, *Painter's Pilgrimage*, unpublished autobiography, 1941 (PP)
(I wish to thank the Executors of the late Mollie Mitchell Smith for permission to
quote from this book); Edouard de Nève, *Barred*, translated by Jean Rhys, Desmond
Harmsworth, 1932 (B); Edouard de Nève, *Sous les Verrous*, Paris, Librairie Stock, 1933
(S les V); David Plante, 'Jean Rhys: A Remembrance', *Paris Review*, Fall 1979, pages
238–284 (P Rev); Emile van der Wilk, *Ed. de Nève*, Uitgeverij De Schaduw, Tilburg,
1989 (Ed. de N); *transatlantic review* (tr); Thomas Staley, *Jean Rhys, A Critical Study*,
MacMillan, 1979 (Staley); Arthur Mizener, *The Saddest Story, A Biography of Ford
Madox Ford*, Bodley Head, 1971 (Mizener); David Dow Harvey, *Ford Madox Ford,
1873–1939, A Bibliography of Works and Criticism*, Princeton University Press, 1962
(DDH); Bernard J. Poli, *Ford Madox Ford and the Transatlantic Review*, Syracuse
University Press, 1967 (Poli); Alan Judd, *Ford Madox Ford*, Collins, 1990 (Judd);
Thomas C. Moser, *The Life in the Fiction of Ford Madox Ford*, Princeton University
Press, 1980 (Moser); Paul Delany, 'Jean Rhys and Ford Madox Ford: What "Really"
Happened?', *Mosaic*, Vol XVI, No 4, Fall 1983, pages 15–24 (Delany); Frank
MacShane, *The Life and Work of Ford Madox Ford*, Routledge & Kegan Paul, 1965
(MacShane); Sondra J. Stang, ed., *The Presence of Ford Madox Ford*, University of
Pennsylvania Press, 1981 (Stang); Violet Hunt, *The Flurried Years*, Hurst & Blackett,
London (Hunt); Douglas Goldring, *South Lodge*, Constable, 1943 (SL), and *The Last
Pre-Raphaelite*, Macdonald, 1948 (LPR); Ford Madox Ford, *The Good Soldier*, Bodley
Head, 1915 (all references are to the Penguin Modern Classics edition) (GS), and *When
the Wicked Man*, Cape, 1932 (WWM); Richard M. Ludwig, *The Letters of Ford Madox
Ford*, Princeton University Press, 1965 (Ludwig); Edouard de Nève, *Kerels*,
Amsterdam, Querido, 1932 (Kerels); Elgin W. Mellown, *Jean Rhys, A Descriptive and
Annotated Bibliography of Works and Criticism*, Garland, 1984 (Mellown); Jan van
Houts, 'The Hole in the Curtain', translation by John Rudge of 'Het Gaatje in het
Gordijn', Zaandam, October 1981 (H in C); Paul Bailey, 'Jean Rhys: "I'll have to go
on living ..." ', BBC Radio 3 programme, broadcast 15 August 1981 and 16 March
1982 (Bailey radio); Edouard de Nève, *Schuwe Vogels*, Amsterdam, Querido, 1937 (Sch

V); D. A. Callard, *Pretty Good for a Woman: The Enigmas of Evelyn Scott*, Cape, 1985 (Callard); Jean Bouret, *Simon Segal*, Collection Artistes de nos temps, Paris, 1950 (Bouret).

NAMES OF SOURCES, CORRESPONDENTS, ETC.
(in order of occurrence in the Notes)
Jean Beck (JB); Daphne Agar (D Ag); Elizabeth Varvill (EV); John Rees Williams (JRW); Jean Rhys (J); Dorothy Rees Williams (DRW); Diana Athill (DA); Selma vaz Dias (SvD); Maryvonne Moerman (MM); Megs Frampton (MF); Elsie Gale (EG); Eva Abraham (EA); Janet Bridger (J Br); Ena Williams (EW); Lennox Honychurch (LH); David Plante (DP); Francis Wyndham (FW); Richard O'Donoghue (R O'D); Anne Smyser (AS); Aubrey Baring (AB); Stella Bowen (SB); Faith Raven (FR); Lancelot Hugh Smith (LHS); Julian Martin Smith (JMS); Bill Corney (BC); L.E. Robins (LER); Oliver Baring (OB); Michael Schwab (MS); Peggy Kirkaldy (PK); Adrian Allinson (AA); Gerald Brenan (GB); Diana Melly (DM); George Melly (GM); Maxwell (Henry Hayes) Macartney (MHHM); Sonia Orwell (SO); Arthur Henry Fox Strangways (AHFS); Tony Gould (TG); Phyllis Shand Allfrey (PSA); Leslie Tilden Smith (LTS); Emile van der Wilk (E vd W); Martien Kappers (MK); Jean (John) Lenglet (JL); Henriette van Eyk (HvE); Germaine Richelot (GR); Al Alvarez (A Alv); Ford Madox Ford (FMF); Violet Hunt (VH); Olwyn Hughes (OH); Oliver Stoner (OS); Maude Ehrenstein (ME); Muriel (Sue) Ramsay, formerly Tilden Smith (MR); Jan van Houts (JvH); Evelyn Scott (ES); Eliot Bliss (EB); Hamish Hamilton (HH); Diana Petre (D Pet); Anthony Tilden Smith (ATS); Robin Waterfield (RW); Rosamond Lehmann (RL); Polly Pattullo (PP); Simon Segal (SS); Eric Griffiths (EGr); Barbara Campbell (B Ca); Willis Feast (WF); Jo Hill (JH); Job Moerman (JM); Max Hamer (MH); Mary Woodard (MW); Alec Hamer (AH); Michael Donn (MD); Peggy Ramsay (PR); Joan Forman (JF); Esther Whitby (E Whit); Pauline Thomas (PT); Basil Handford (BH); Joan Lee (J Lee); Joan Butler (J But); John Smith (JS); Alan Ross (AR); Yvonne Davet (YD); Antonia Fraser (AF): Herbert Ronson (HR); Larry Cole (LC); Marc Varney (MV); Ellen Moerman (EM); Anthony Sheil (Ant S); Charles Cox (CC); Tristram Powell (TP); Elaine Campbell (EC).

(These are not all the sources, correspondents etc. referred to, but only those who occurred several times, and whose names have therefore been abbreviated.)

NOTE ON LETTERS
Letters consulted and/or quoted are in:
*L:* J's letters between 1931 and 1966, chosen and edited by FW and DM.
*Tulsa:* J's letters to SvD, OS, AS and OH, and a few others (eg J to HR, LTS to AS, MM to AS.)
*EA:* J's letters to PK, SO, EB, AF, DM, Ant S and others given to FW for *L.* Others' letters to J, friends and business.
*Personal possession:* J's letters to MM, DA, FW, JF and LC. I wish to express my thanks to their owners for allowing me to see them.
*Other:* ES's and GB's letters to and from J are in the Humanities Research Centre at Austin, Texas.

NOTE ON TS (EA)

The typescript of TS in EA consists of 226 typewritten pages numbered from 4 to 230. It begins at the height of the affair with 'Tony' (Lancelot) and ends with the meeting with 'Michel' (John).

Clearly this is only part of the original TS. That went on to at least Vienna and Budapest, since V was described in tr (Dec 1924) as 'from the novel called Triple Sec' (p 639). Also J wrote that in it Mrs Adam had left out a lot 'about the F__ strasse' — ie about the Favoritenstrasse in Vienna (SP draft in EA.)

J's attitude to TS is typical of her relationship to the truth about her life, eg in interviews when she was old: her natural honesty made her tell it, but later her fear made her try to take it back again. Thus, she kept TS — through all her travels — and gave it into the safe-keeping of her Literary Executor; every time he asked her what he should do with it — give it back to her, or destroy it — she hesitated, and asked him to keep it a bit longer. But on the other hand, (a) she claimed that Mrs Adam had changed it (SP 155), often a great deal (even saying to SO and FW 'It's not by me, it's by Mrs Adam [J to SO 16 Aug 1976, and J to FW in conversation]); and (b) she always denied it was a diary, saying she'd just written it 'in diary form' (see SP 128–30 and 155, and J to FW 7 Nov 1968), the Lancelot affair and its aftermath, eg, all in one 'spurt' in January 1914.

Both of these denials were, I believe, false, and I have used TS as something close to a 'record of facts' (as J called her first stab at Q).

(1) It is clear that Mrs Adam did *not* change very much. I'm sure SP 155 is the truth: she cut J's ms and arranged it into Parts and chapters. The direct, naive voice is J's alone, patently an early version of the narrative voice of the novels, and utterly foreign to Mrs Adam's heavier, more conventional and more 'educated' tone.

(2) TS was, I'm certain, a diary, though some sections may well have been written retrospectively (eg the account of the MHHM engagement, vide p 177: 'Never was able to stand up against pity or understanding. And I imagined he gave convincing proof of his. *Didn't know him.*' (My emphasis.) My reasons are:

(a) All the details I've been able to check — about LHS and JMS, about MHHM, about the central event of TPS, about JL — have proved to be minutely accurate.

(b) One of the first people to see it — FMF's secretary Ivan Bede, who read it in 1924 — called it a diary (Ivan Bede to J, 2 Feb 1931.)

(c) It often reads like a diary. Events are given arbitrary weights, as one would do in a diary, rather than fitted in to a 'shape', as J would do in her novels. Real names slip in several times ('Lancey' and 'Julian', 'Adrian' and 'Phil', 'Shirley' and 'Mabel'), and remain in the tr version ('John' and 'Ella'). Sometimes 'Suzy' breaks off when someone walks in (eg pp 110, 114) — and surely J didn't set out to write 'in diary form' *that* self-consciously. Finally, there is this, on p16:

'It's a funny thing that when I first started this diary I thought it was going to be a bore — and that I'd have to force myself to write in it. Instead of that it's my friend. — I mean like my friend. I don't write in it. I talk to it and tell it everything — just how my dear always looks & what he says & what I think & do. Perhaps if I tell it about the thought that spoils things it may help. — The worst of it is, diary, that it's not a thought but a fact ...'

Again I can't believe that J would have set out to write this artificially; the whole book has far too rushed and ingenuous a tone. I'm sure that some parts of TS at least were a day-to-day diary; and some were 'spurts' written after (probably soon after) the events they describe. And all stick close to the facts, as J always did in her first versions.


## NOTE ON DATING OF THE BK EX BK (TULSA ITEM 1:1)

The Bk Ex Bk was almost certainly mostly written in late 1938.

Pages 1–18 contain an early version of TABL and may date from earlier, perhaps as early as 1935, when the central event of the story happened.

Pages 19–68 are memories of childhood, including Mr H H. These are established as 1938 by:

(1) Page 36, about Mother Mount Calvary: 'I saw her again two years [ago].'

(2) Page 69: 'I've been working for a year at a book about Paris.' This is established as GMM by p 74: 're book: I meant it to be the last adventure love adventure of a woman who is growing old.' J began GMM during or after a trip to Paris in Nov 1937 (L 137 nl).

(3) Page 70: 'I woke up two days ago with the thing wiped clean out. It had slipped away from me . . . . Instead of that I was back in the West Indies . . . . I began to write it.'

(4) Page 71: 'I went for a walk along the towing path [and note that in late 1938 J and LTS were living in 'River Court', Taplow, on the Thames near Maidenhead]. It was a foggy day. I had such a [strong? strange?] feeling that I was on the edge of something . . . . And do you know where I was sure I would find myself? – In Mr Howard's house. It has relieved me to write . . . .'

(5) The typed versions of some of these sections of the Bk Ex Bk ('Start of a short story', 'Mr H H' and 'Fears') in EA are all dated to the end of 1938 (14 Sept, 4 Dec and 6 Dec 1938 respectively).

Pages 75–92 continue with childhood memories; pages 73–75 are 'The Forlorn Hope'; and pages 94–101 are the conversations with 'L' (see Part Two, Chapter 5) and thoughts about women hatred. I feel certain these all carry straight on, and were written at the same time.

# NOTES

PART ONE, CHAPTER ONE
Information about Dominica taken from the following books, which will be referred to in their abbreviated form:
Thomas Atwood, *The History of the Island of Dominica*, 1791 (Atwood); Sir Henry Hesketh Bell, *Glimpses of a Governor's Life*, 1946, and *Obeah*, 1889 (Bell, GGL and O); Basil E. Cracknell, *Dominica*, 1973 (Cracknell); J.A. Froude, *The English in the West Indies*, 1888 (Froude); Lennox Honychurch, *The Caribbean People*, 1979, *The Dominica Story*, 1984, and *Caribbean Landmarks*, 1986 (Honychurch, CP, DS, CL); Patrick Leigh Fermor, *The Traveller's Tree*, 1950 (Leigh Fermor); James Pope Hennessy, *The Baths of Absalom*, 1954 (Pope Hennessy); Anthony Trollope, *The West Indies and the Spanish Main*, 1859 (Trollope); Alec Waugh, 'Typical Dominica', in *The Sugar Islands*, 1958 (Waugh); Owen Rees Williams's unpublished book of Dominican memories, copy given to author by DRW (Owen).

*Page*
3 Nothing brings ... WSS 16-17
The rain forest ... Cracknell 11; Waugh 311; Bell GGL 7; VID 15; Colonial Office List, History of Dominica.
The sun shines ... Bell, GGL 77, 0 120; Froude 137.
All this careless ... Pope Hennessy 41; PSA, The Orchid House, 75; Froude 137; WSS 17, 139; VID 77.
The beauty is ... Froude 141, Honychurch CP 52; Owen 115; Bell GGL 10-12; Atwood 20.
4 Violence lurks ... Honychurch CP 58-63; Leigh Fermor 107n; History from Cracknell, Froude, Honychurch and Colonial Office List.
Even after ... Froude 134; WSS 22-3.
On top of ... Atwood 7; Bell GGL.
Quotation TP, PMS, 81; CS 267-8.
Nothing ever ... Waugh 281, 283; Pope Hennessy 44; Cracknell 20, 77, 79, 84-87, 95; Honychurch CP 80, DS 209; *Daily Telegraph*, 1 Sept. 1979; Q 70-71.
5 All this has ... Pope Hennessy 40; Colonial Office List 1891, 157, 164; Bell GGL 8; Cracknell 85; Trollope 159.
And it showed ... Froude 145, 153, 167; Bell O 45-6; JB, interview with author 18 June 1985; Emma Gale and Nicole Stott, interview with author, 11 April 1988; Cracknell 11. In the end it was 1958 before the Imperial Road was finished.
Perhaps it goes ... Pope Hennessy 45.
Footnote: D Ag and EV, to author, 11 July 1990.
6 This elusiveness ... Leigh Fermor 79, 93-4; Waugh 283, 285, 287, 290; Pope Hennessy 17, 57; interviews D Ag and EV, 13 June 1986, and Emma Gale and Nicole Stott, 11 April 1988; WSS 58-9, 141.
On both sides ... JRW, interview with author 11 May 1985 and Letters; Owen 2; Ned Thomas to J, EA; SP 69-70; VID 59-60.
William went ... Same sources. A first daughter, Hannah Sophia, died in childhood.
7 From this side ... SP 20, 67-8; VID 81. 'Bod Gwilym' was given as J's Roseau address when she registered at the Academy of Dramatic Art (letter to author from R O'D, 9 Oct 1984).
On her mother's ... SP 33-8; Owen 12-16; JB interview and family tree;

James, 45, 47, 63; Bk Ex Bk 30-31. 'Geneva' was initially a Swiss religious foundation, which gave it its name (D Ag and EV); Owen gave its size as 1400 acres (12).

Parliament passed the Act of Abolition of Slavery on 31 July 1834. In practice freedom came to the slaves of the British West Indies in two stages: from 1834-1838 they held the intermediate status of 'apprentice'; then on 31 July 1838 complete freedom came at last. Thus when Antoinette and Rochester begin their honeymoon in 1840 slavery has only been fully abolished for two years. This great-grandmother ... SP 33-4; WSS 19-25; VID 56; Bk Ex Bk 30; DW 17, 54; Froude 147; James 47.

When her husband ... JB interview and family tree; Owen 13.

Footnote: Mr H H, 2.

8  She and Edward ... JB family tree; SP 33; Owen 14. Edward died of appendicitis.

This was ... Owen 15-16. J says in SP that the twins (her mother and Auntie B) managed the estate after their father's death; but Owen's version is much more likely to be true. Later the elder son, Norman, ran Geneva, while Acton worked in Government service, and lived on several of the islands (JB). In TWB J says that Acton 'died suddenly, leaving very little money, and his widow and three children were obliged to give up the estate.' (CS 396). Acton's children were J's cousins Lily (Emily) and Monica whom she met again in the 1930s and (in Lily's case) later.

What made ... SP 68, 72; DRW interview 19 March 1985; JRW letter to author 9 June 1985.

At fourteen ... SP 67, 68, 71; DA, 'Notes for a biography which will never be written', 'The father'. Information about Dr Rees Williams' early career from SP, 'My Father' and Owen, Chaps. 1 and 3. Again I follow Owen when they differ.

9  From Manchester ... Letters to author from Univ. of Manchester Medical School, 16 June 1986, and Royal College of Surgeons of England 2 Sept. 1986: also Register of St George's Hospital Medical School, copy to author from St George's Library, 25 Sept. 1986. Information about Dr Rees Williams' later career from Owen, Chaps. 4 and 5, and SP 'My Father' and 'My Mother'.

Stowe is ... Owen, Chaps. 4 and 5.

William worked ... Ibid.; SP 68. J also made the story of her father's fever part of Dr Cox's story in early drafts of POP (see BL, ADD57859).

Minna was ... Owen 24-26; SP 46.

William and Minna ... JRW interview; Owen; VID 7; James 2. (D Ag tells me that it is not St Mary Street, as Professor James has it, but Queen Mary Street.)

Dates of birth of the Rees Williams' children could not be established in the usual way because all birth and death records for the period were lost in a fire (D Ag to author, 23 July 1986). Sources therefore were: Indian Army List 1939 (Edward); DRW and JRW (Owen); Death certificates and Baptismal information (Minna and Brenda; D Ag 23 July 1986). J was only baptised in September 1893, and began to lower her age very early (e.g. on her first marriage); but her birth date is established as 1890 by three factors. (1) she said she arrived in England at nearly 17 (SP 168-9) in an August (OBP, CS 317), and she entered the Perse School in the autumn of 1907 (Perse School records); (2) when she entered the ADA in January 1909 her age was given as 18 (letter to author 9 Oct. 1984); (3) her cousin Lily told DA: 'Jean was ten years older than the century'.

10  Much later ... LI; Original Ending of VID, Tulsa Item 1: 11; Bk, Red and Gr Ex Bks passim; Bday; CDH; 'Start of a Short Story', dated 14-9-38; New Story; 'Fears', dated 6.12.38 (all EA).

Not completely ... DA has repeatedly made the point to me that J would only lie if it was absolutely necessary (e.g. letters to author 5 Aug. 1983 and 30 June 1986).

But did she ... J to SvD, 5 Oct 1957 (Tulsa 2: 6).

In 'Heat' ... H, SIOL 39, CS 295; Bell GGL 46.

Brenda Gwenith ... D Ag to author, 23 July 1986; JB family tree; DRW letter to author 4 Apr. 1986; *Dominica Dial*, 4 Jan 1890; Owen 47-8 and Introduction. Owen gives the older girl's age as 3, which would have been Minna's age in 1889, and the younger's as 9 months. He says the epidemic was of diphtheria rather than dysentery.

11 Jean was born ... SP 42 (on mother loving babies).

Often ... Interview with Dr Joan Schachter and Jan Wiener, MSAP, 2 Mar 1986.

Like her heroines ... L 12, 61, 135, 170; Bk Ex Bk 48; WSS 147.

Quotation: Autograph ms, Queen's Velvet notebook, EA. See also SP 42 and 'Fears' 4.

In the next ... SP 19-23. Originally J had written that it was 'my fifth birthday or perhaps my sixth' (Red Ex Bk No.1, page 3.) She settled for 'sixth' (SP 23), perhaps because that's what she had written in ALMM (ALMM 77). So she then said that Brenda was born when she was seven (SP 26). But this was wrong. Brenda was born on 30 Dec 1895, when J was five years and four months old.

12 Four months ... SP 42; 'Fears' 4; ALMM 77; WSS 19; MM interview with author 7 Dec 1984.

By the time ... SP 20, 26; Red Ex Bk No. 1, page 3; 'Fears'; 2 LI6.

After her mother ... 'Meta', SP 29-32; Bk Ex Bk 20.

Meta played ... 'Meta', SP; SP52; 'Fears' 9-10; VID 151, 156.

Meta taught ... 'Meta', SP; 'Fears' 2; VID 27; L 28; Bk Ex Bk 22-3.

13 She never ... 'Meta', SP.

Whether it was ... 'Fears' 1-3; Bday 3; SP 77; WSS 41; Bk Ex Bk 26.

She already had ... VID 27, 58; WSS 20; SP 'Black/White' and drafts for it in EA; Queen's Velvet Notebook No 1, page 2, EA; Bday 4; SP 31, 50.

On the other ... SP 47-8; WSS 30.

14 And there was ... Imp Rd; TDTBTB, TABL, 41, 44, CS 152, 154-5.

Quotation: SP 49.

On one side ... SP 21, 66.

15 This perversity ... 'The Doll', SP 39-41.

Quotation: SP 40.

There was a ... 'The Doll', SP 39-41.

But there were ... I date these pleasures to about this age because the end of J's visits to Geneva came a short time after her uncle Acton's marriage (see SP 55-6). She says (SP54) that this happened when she was 'about twelve years old', but it must have been earlier : Acton's first child, J's cousin Lily, was born in 1901. I'm guessing, therefore, that his marriage was around 1900, when J was ten.

Her mother ... SP 36, 37, 40, 41; Queen's Velvet Notebook No 2, EA, page 6; L 176.

Jean would suffer ... Gr Ex Bk, 39-40; L 176; 'Geneva', SP 33-38; CDH; Queen's Velvet No 2, EA, 6; WSS 122.

16 Great-Aunt Jane ... 'Geneva', SP 33-38; CDH; Owen 14-15; VID 45.

Not only ... SP 34, 45; CDH; WSS 35, 47, 94-5.

17 At about ten ... 'St Lucia', SP 54-57; SP 168.

Several other things ... SP 26; JRW letter to author, 17 Apr 1985. Edward and

Owen went to Wellingborough School in Northamptonshire from 1900–1902 (Edward possibly longer). J says that she never saw either of them again for many years (SP26), but I think that was only true of Edward, who stayed on in England to train as a doctor, and then went out to India. Owen returned to Dominica (see below, page 29.)

Minna went to her uncle and aunt while they were in St Kitts (SP 26), which was in the years 1889–1895 (David P Henige, *Colonial Governors*, and Colonial Office List 1900, page 399). John Kemys George Spencer Churchill, a grandson of the 5th Duke of Marlborough, married J's aunt Edith Maxwell Lockhart in 1884. He was Acting President of Dominica between 1882 and 1887; Commissioner of Montserrat 1888–9; Commissioner of St Kitts, Nevis and Anguilla, 1889–1895; finally Colonial Secretary of the Bahamas, 1895–1905. He died in 1913. (Henige; Colonial Office Lists 1900 and 1912; *The Times* obituary, 11 Aug 1913.)
And at much . . . SP 36, 41, 46, 55–57.
Footnote: SP 44, 46; DRW interviews; Owen 208. John Spencer Churchill was born in 1835, his wife in 1854.

18  At Bod Gwilym . . . SP 56; 'Fears' 3a; MF, reported to author by D Ag, 22 Oct 1986.
Whatever Mr Kennaway . . . MF and EG to D Ag, letters to author 22 Oct and 5 Dec 1986; MF interview with EA, sent to author March 1989; SP 26, 59, 60, 64–6; D Ag to author, letter 21 Aug 1986; JB interview.
MF and EG, née Grell, were born in 1894 and 1890 or '92 respectively. MF died in 1990, EG a year or two before. (D Ag to author, 16 May 1990.)
As she grew . . . DRW and JRW interviews; Queen's Velvet No 2, EA, 5; SP 42–3, 59, 65, 71–2; DA, Notes for a biography, 'The mother' and 'The father'; VID 36, 44, 81; LI; Mr H H; Owen 62, 137, 176, 211; MC, TABL 176, CS 38; James 2; typed drafts for SP 'Poetry', EA; O Nbk, 7 and 96.

19  Now that Jean . . . 'Fears' 3a; SP51.
Quotation: GMGR, SIOL 30, CS 289.
She also . . . Untitled Sketch, Tulsa Item 1:6; Bk Ex Bk 75–7. See also TDTBTB, TABL 42, CS 153.
Then, of course . . . D Ag letters to author, 2 Dec 1986 and 21 Jan 1987; LI 4; SP 26; VID 37.
That was before . . . ID, CS 401–3.

20  At the edge . . . Bk Ex Bk 29; draft for SP 'Black/White' dated 9 Oct 1978, EA; E on E 2; SP 56, 80, 84ff.
She had tried . . . Bk Ex Bk 42.
After the socialist . . . 'The Religious Fit', SP 77–87; D Ag to author, 2 Dec 1986; Owen 149; Bk Ex Bk 33–6, 38; SP draft for 'Poetry', EA; SP 79; POP, SIOL 21, CS 284. I take the order 'socialist fit' then 'religious fit' from Mr H H, page 1.
There is some confusion about the name of Dr Rees Williams's second estate, after Bona Vista. LH, who is Dominica's historian, suggested to me that it was an estate called 'Curry's Rest'. But Dr Rees Williams names 'Amelia Estate' in his will, and Owen's 'outside' daughter EW remembers visiting him and an 'Auntie' at 'Amalia' (EW to author, Aug 1985, and to D Ag, D Ag to author 2 Dec 1986).

21  Jean told . . . Bk Ex Bk 38; SP 79; LI 9.
Quotation: Bk Ex Bk 38.
Of course it . . . SP 81; Bk Ex Bk 39–40; Mr H H 1; LI 9.
It had been . . . LI 8–9; Bk Ex Bk 38, 40–1; SP 81. See also WSS 48.
She lived in . . . SP 47, 62, 171; James 7–8; TDTBTB, TABL 42, CS 153; TP, PMS 71, CS 258.

Words were ... Bk Ex Bk 47-8; WSS 137, 149; SP 58-60, 63.
22 Quotation SP 59.
By the time ... SP 36, 92; MC, TABL 174-5, CS 37; DA, Notes for a biography, 'The mother'; J Br, interview with author, 24 Nov 1984; CDH 3; Owen 137-8; Bk Ex Bk 28-30; 'New Story', EA, page A3.
She wanted ... SP 81-2; Bk Ex Bk 27; 'New Story' A3; WSS 107.
23 Her family ... DW 37; DRW interviews; Mr H H; Bk Ex Bk 27-8.
But one day ... Bk Ex Bk 28, 48; SP 62; O Nbk 94; Mr H H.
There were only ... Bk Ex Bk 22, 25, 41.
Most of all ... 'Fears' 1a; Bk Ex Bk 19, 43; SP 44-5, 57.
Quotation: The S of the R, TABL 140, CS 237.
Now Mrs Rees ... Owen 176; DRW interviews; JRW interview; Mr H H 1; ALMM 77; Bk Ex Bk 22, 45; 'Fears' 3.
24 In Mackenzie ... ALMM 77; WSS 17, 19, 40; Bk Ex Bk 24.
Quotation 1: GMM 113.
We cannot know ... Bk Ex Bk 24, 64; GMM 112; 'Fears' 4.
Quotation 2: 'Fears' 3. See also Bk Ex Bk 21-2 and 44-5.
From May ... Official Gazette for 20 May 1904 (information from LH, sent to author by D Ag 23 July 1986); *Dominica Guardian* 12 May 1904, page 4; SP 79.
25 This convent ... WSS 45, 47, 48; SP 79; Mr H H 3.
Besides, happiness ... SP 49-50; VID 46. 'Beatrice Agostini' from Venezuela was surely based on one of these sisters too (no doubt the main one, 'Louise'). That must be why J connected them with angostura bitters, 'though I'm sure their name wasn't Angostura' (SP 49-50). (Perhaps Louise was the girl's real name, for it's her name in BF and its drafts too.)
The trip ... Owen 160; VID 53; SP 67-9; OBP, SIOL 77, CS 322. Sophia Rees Williams had died in 1896, William Rees Williams in 1900 (JRW).
26 One day ... SP 82, 86; Bk Ex Bk 48; WSS 109.
There was ... SP 61-2; and see VID 59-63, where Anna tries to die on the day she has her first period.
But now ... Mr H H 1; SP 62, 86-7; MC, TABL 175, CS 38; 'New Story' A5; and see GMGR, SIOL 30, CS 290.
In Goodbye ... GMGR, SIOL 25, 27, CS 285-6; Bk Ex Bk 49-68; SP 62. I quote 'record of facts' from J's description of the first state of Q, in L'Aff Ford.
27 Mr Howard ... The story of Mr H here (to page 29) is taken from : Bk Ex Bk 49-68; Mr H H; Bday; Tulsa Item 1:16 (an early draft of GMGR); and GMGR itself (for people and events already established in the others). Where discrepancies occur I follow the Bk Ex Bk account, which is clearly an attempt to remember a long-suppressed experience as accurately as possible.
They walked ... WSS quotation from page 20, VID from page 44.
29 Mr Howard died ... SP 62 for 'I became very good at blotting things out.'
Does that sound ... VID quotation from page 48. J claims very strongly in the Bk Ex Bk (59) that the experience with Mr H was no invention, but really happened. Nonetheless she uses the word 'dream' several times, in the Bk Ex Bk and the Tulsa draft of GMGR : 'the long strange dream'. I repeat it because it conveys so well the sense of an intense experience, which may yet have been partly, at least, imagined.
Quotation: GMM 147.
Jean's brother ... Information here, in footnote and on page 30 from DRW and JRW interviews; also from EW letter to author 14 December 1985 and D Ag to author 2 Dec 1986.
30 Missy had grown ... The story of Missy from here to page 32 from Owen 132-155.

They couldn't get ... DRW interviews; MC, TABL 174, CS 36; SP 62-3 and 82.

She did only ... SP 62-3; Bk Ex Bk 68; Owen 137.

The other thing ... Owen 137; LS Tulsa draft No 49; O Nbk 24.

31 Missy's secret ... Bk Ex Bk 51, 64.

32 If I could die ... WSS 19, 77. See also Carlo in BB, CS 64.

If it did ... Pope Hennessy 44; D Ag interview 1986; WSS 134; Owen 156. For Dr Rees Williams's being loved, *Dominica Guardian* 24 June and 1 July 1910, pages 2-3 in both; and LH and MF, reported to author by EA, March 1989.

33 Where did this ... Plan of WCQ kindly shown me by DP (see DW 57); O Nbk 52; WSS 152. The only other explanation, that Owen based Missy's behaviour on a reading of J's books, I think we can rule out. WSS, which was her main love story, was not published until eight years after he died.

Of affairs like ... L 263.

She had just ... D Ag interview; JB interview; LS drafts (Red Ex Bk in EA, 8; O Nbk in EA, 83-5, 94, 116; Tulsa Item 1:28, Nos 48 & 51); SP drafts of 'Leaving Dominica' in EA; OBP, SIOL 70-1, CS 316-7.

J's eighteen months at home after boarding at the convent were from Jan 1905 to Aug 1907. Dr Rees Williams's leave was from May to Dec 1904 (Official Gazette); and J arrived in England in August 1907 (see Notes to page 9 above.)

He told her ... OBP and drafts as above.

34 Quotation: OBP, SIOL 70-1, CS 317.

After that ... LS and 'Leaving Dominica' drafts as Notes for page 33 above.

Soon she began ... LS drafts (Red Ex Bk, EA, 2-4; O Nbk, EA, 96); VID 157.

Her Aunt ... SP 69, 93; Bday 2; VID 59-60; O Nbk 84-5; Gr Ex Bk 37-8.

Her mother ... SP 45, 93.

Jean's father ... O Nbk 70, 84, 85, 96; VID 28; SP 93-4.

PART ONE, CHAPTER TWO

37 All her life ... O Nbk 96; draft for SP 'First Steps', EA; SP 97.

But her moods ... Same sources; also O Nbk 72; RD, SP 168 and EA.

The bewildering ... See LS drafts and OBP.

It started with ... SP 97-8.

38 At home she ... E on E 3; MC, TABL 174, CS 36; SP 98-9.

Over the next ... SP 100, 169; O Nbk 66, 73.

She was at ... O Nbk 67, 68, 72; SP 169; OBP, SIOL 71, CS 317.

So it began ... E on E; typescript draft of SP, 'First Steps', EA.

39 Still, she ... E on E; Queen's Velvet Notebook No 2, page 7, EA; SP 170.

The first thing ... E on E; O Nbk 74, 119; OBP, SIOL 71, CS 317-8.

In 1907 ... *The Perse School for Girls, 1881-1981*, by M.A. Scott (1981); interviews with Old Perseans. That J entered the Perse School in 1907 is proved by the Register in the School Archive; and by the *Persean Magazine*, Vol V, 1906-1909:

Autumn Term, 1907

The girls who entered this term are as follows:

VIb K Harbord

Va H Johnson, M Newton, G Williams and G Watson.

40 But the Perse ... Interviews with Old Perseans; J to FW, 23 Sept 1968.

What really happened ... O Nbk 91.

What she remembered ... O Nbk 77, 93, 97; VID 56; OBP, SIOL 67-72, CS 314-318.

41 Miss Street ... OBP, SIOL 66, 68, CS 313, 315; SP 101; Persean 321; O Nbk 76; interviews with Old Perseans.

But far far ... OBP, SIOL 66, CS 313; Scott op. cit.; LS draft, Red Ex Bk, EA, 17; interviews with Old Perseans.

Unluckily ... Scott, Chapter Five, 'Boarding Houses'; *The Perse School for Girls, 1881-1956*, M.H. Cattley, page 13; O Nbk 87, 97, 100, 109, 111; LS draft, Red Ex Bk, EA, 17; LS draft Tulsa No 48; OBP, SIOL 66, CS 313.

42 Miss Osborn ... LS draft Red Ex Bk, EA, 18-19; Persean 237; OBP, SIOL 68, CS314.

Still, Autolycus ... Persean 279-80.

At the end ... Ibid. 314; LS draft Red Ex Bk EA, 22-3.

43 Jean's explanation ... and footnote LS draft Red Ex Bk EA, 22-4.

And in ... Ibid. 24; Persean 361.

She'd now ... LS draft Red Ex Bk EA, 24, 26; Tulsa No 49.

First ... Persean 370.

Quotation: OBP, SIOL 66-7, CS 313-4.

44 She'd always ... LS draft EA 12.

She Stoops ... Persean 321, 370; OBP, SIOL 73-4, CS 319-20; LS draft EA, 19; Tulsa No 48.

Quotation: OBP, SIOL 73, CS 319.

Suddenly ... OBP, SIOL 74, CS 319; LS draft EA, 21-2; Tulsa No 49.

Since she'd left ... 'The RADA', in Tulsa Red Ex Bk No 1, at end; Bk Ex Bk 79; 'New Story' A4; OBP, SIOL73, CS 319; 'The Inscrutable Miss Jean Rhys', Marcelle Bernstein, *The Observer*, 1 June 1969, page 40.

When the answer ... OBP, SIOL 74, CS 320; LS draft EA, 25; E on E.

I was happier ... Same sources.

45 Her lessons ... Same sources.

He taught her ... E on E; OBP, SIOL 74, CS 320; LS draft EA, 26; Tulsa No 49.

Miss Wilkinson ... LS draft EA, 26.

Aunt Clarice ... OBP, same page; SP 102; LS draft EA, 26. J wrote 'Upper Bedford Place' in SP and OBP, and 'Lower' in some drafts (eg 'The RADA'). There is no Upper or Lower today, but Bedford Place is off Russell Square.

Tree's School ... RADA letterhead; SP 101-2; list of students, sent to author by R O'D, 17 Oct 1984; 'The RADA'; LS drafts in Tulsa (No 53 for Juliet); LS draft EA, 29 (Lady MacBeth); letters from ADA to Dr Rees Williams and Clarice Rees Williams, sent to author 18 Feb 1986. 'Miss Gertrude' was Gertrude Burnett (see *The Stage*, 28 Dec 1909, page 18).

46 But Tree's ... SP 103; draft of SP 'First Steps', EA; ADA student list. About friends, however – in one draft of LS (Tulsa No 52), after her account of telling tall stories to the other girls, J had written 'stopping disliking them and even making some friends'. But then she'd scored it out.

Her name ... SP 103; draft of 'First Steps', EA 2; *Burke's Peerage and Baronetage* 1970, 1186; ADA list.

The lesson ... LS draft EA, 22 ('They'll teach me how to drop my voice').

47 On this occasion ... and quotation: SP 103.

She was made ... SP 103; letter to author from R O'D, 10 Feb 1986; *Burke's Peerage*, 1186.

It went far ... SP 103; *Who Was Who, 1916-28*, 441-2.

In The Social ... *The Social Fetich*, 2-5, 11, 28-9.

All these ... SP 103.

48 She said it ... Draft of 'First Steps', EA; DA to author in several conversations; SP 165.

And during ... SP 102-4; Tulsa drafts of LS Nos 48 and 54 ('Tubby' and 'Tuppy Bewes'); ADA list; *Burke's Landed Gentry*, 18th ed., Vol III (1972), page 65; OBP, SIOL 76, CS 321; O Nbk 123; Tulsa LS draft No 53; letter to author 23 Jan 1986.

Jean always ... SP 101.

Later ... SP 104-5; OBP, SIOL 75,. CS 320-1.

Footnote: *Who Was Who, 1916-28*, 441-2.

49 It wasn't ... Dr Rees Williams died on June 19, 1910. See eg his will (sent to author by D Ag); *Dominica Guardian* 24 June and 1 July 1910. J was at Tree's School from 16 Jan to 28 July 1909 (letter to author from R O'D, 9 Oct 1984.)

At the end ... Letter from Geo P Bancroft, Administrator, to Miss Clarice Rees Williams, 31 Mar 1909; copy sent to author by R O'D, 18 Feb 1986.

No doubt ... See Q 15.

Quotation: Letter from Geo P Bancroft to William Rees Williams Esq., 1 July 1909, sent to author 18 Feb 1986.

No reason ... Letter to author from R O'D, 21 July 1986.

When she ... OBP, SIOL 75, CS 321.

50 The social ... LS draft EA, 26.

It was her ... Everyone who remembers her in old age remarks on J's whisper. In her mid-twenties (as we'll see) her voice still grated on some people; but by her mid-thirties her second husband's daughter noticed its soft, childlike quality (AS interviews).

For days ... OBP, SIOL 75, CS 321. The Perse School Registry gives Clarice's address as 'Minafour', St Asaph.

Clarice was ... OBP, SIOL 77, CS322; DRW interviews; LS draft EA, 30, 32; Tulsa No 49.

Jean's first ... LS draft EA, 10 and 30.

Jean replied ... Ibid. 30-1; Tulsa No 49; OBP, SIOL 75, CS 321.

Would she have ... LS draft EA, 32.

51 If they did ... SP 105; Tulsa LS draft No 49.

Marya had ... and quotation Q 14-15. Blackmore's was the oldest theatrical agency in London, dating from 1868. It was owned by Herbert Blackmore and his partner Lionel Wallace. (*The Era*, 13 Aug 1910, page 13.)

Clarice must have ... OBP and Tulsa draft No 53.

In Jean's ... OBP; Tulsa draft No 53, page 5. In OBP J puts her threat to marry Harry Bewes here. This may have been right; or she may have moved it from an earlier point, since Harry had left the ADA the term before.

52 Sometimes she ... and quotation Q 15.

Perhaps this ... Information about 'Ladies of the chorus' from AB, Nov 1984.

Surely this ... SP 112.

53 I was astonished ... OBP, SIOL 76-7, CS 321-2.

Well: she was ... SB, DFL, 166-168.

But not yet ... OBP, SIOL 77, CS 322; untitled fragment in EA, beginning 'My sad métier', 2.

Jean joined ... L 235.

54 Quotation: SP110.

*Our Miss Gibbs* ... *Oxford Companion to the Theatre*, 3rd ed., ed Phyllis Hartnoll (1967), page 360; *Who's Who in the Theatre*, 2nd ed., (1914), ed John Parker, page xiii; *The Gaiety Years*, page 162. *The Era* for 1910 lists two George Dance companies and one George Edwardes, all doing OMG. For *Floradora, The King of Cadonia* and *Cingalee*, see *The Era* for 1909 and 1910, passim.

The story ... The plot of OMG is described in *The Play Pictorial*, Vol XIII, No 80 (seen in the Gaiety file for 1909, The Theatre Museum.) Titles of shows from *The Era*, Aug 1909, and from Allardyce Nicoll, *English Drama 1900-1930*, page 182.

The melodramas ... Titles from *The Era*, 1909, passim.

Of course ... VID 64; typed drafts of 'Chorus Girls' and 'The Interval' for SP,

EA; Hartnoll op. cit. page 116 (for Rosie Boote); *The Gaiety Years* 177 (for Lily Elsie); SP 116 and FW to author (for Nancy Erwin).

The summer tour ... Sir George Dance's principal production of OMG was on the road by the first week in Aug (see *The Era* for 5 Aug 1909) – too early for J to have joined it, having only left the ADA on July 23rd. In any case the No 2 company was the more likely place for a beginner. *The Era* for Aug 19 and 26 shows the No 2 company beginning its tour at The Pavilion, Ramsgate, on Aug 23 and going to The Royal, Worthing, on Aug 30.

55 In Voyage ... VID 31.

First she had ... SP 106; VID 18-19.

In Quartet ... Q14; Tulsa LS draft No 54; SP 106; *The Era*, 1910, passim (for places toured). It never becomes certain whether J was in George Dance's No 1 or No 2 company : some of the places she says she played in were visited by both, some by neither. Nor are the companies identified in the theatrical press as No 1 or No 2, but only as 'N' and 'S' (which does not seem to mean North and South). On the whole the greater consistency and likelihood lie with the No 2 company, except for the summer tour of 1910, in which only the No 1 company visited Cork, which J definitely remembered (*The Era*, 24 Sept, page 18, and B the D, SIOL 83, CS 324). Also, at least for J's second tour, the No 2 company contained (as we'll see) an 'Olga Gray'.

At best ... *The Era* and *The Stage*, 1909 and 1910; VID 8; SP 110; Q14.

Then it was ... VID 8.

There were good ... SP 63, 110-111; VID 8-9, 128; Q 14; 'My sad métier' 2.

56 On this winter ... VID 8, 15, 31; Kis; SP112, 171; LS Tulsa draft No 53 and EA draft page 33; Bernstein article (for J's getting pleurisy like Anna. Did Aunt Clarice pay the doctor's bills, as Hester does in VID 55? ...)

But it didn't ... *The Era*, 13 Apr 1910 shows the tour ending on 7 May in the Grand Theatre, Fulham, London; SP 106.

A man called ... *The Era* for 4 June 1910 (page 26) shows Joe Peterman as the producer of sketches called 'The Pawnbroker' and 'The Belle of the Orient'. *The Stage Yearbook* for 1911 lists among 'Principal Sketches' of 1910 'Chanteclair or Hi Cockalorum' etc (page 201); also 'Chicks in the Wood' by Peterman in December.

For Rostand see *The Era*, 29 Jan 1910, page 15 and 5 Feb, page 21. A 'Chanteclair' craze : see *The Era*, 4 June 1910, page 6.

Jean never said ... For second photo of Liska's Troupe, see SP. SP 107, 112; L 13; DP interview with author, 29 Oct 1984; *Monna Vanna* programme, Queen's Theatre, 1914, file, Theatre Museum; Hunter Davies, 'Rip van Rhys', *Sunday Times*, 6 Nov 1966, page 13; John Hall, 'Jean Rhys', *The Guardian*, 10 Jan 1972, page 8; *The Era*, 9 Oct 1909, page 11, 22 Jan 1910 and 16 Apr 1910, page 7; TSP, TABL 37, CS 148-9.

J describes Maudie in VID as tall and thin, with a long white face and a nose which 'made a straight line with her forehead' (VID 9). This sounds very like the tall girl next to J in the Chanteclair picture, and in the Liska's Troupe picture as well (second from left). Perhaps she was Mollie, which would easily become Maudie (and Billie in SP too.) It's interesting that the part of Chanteclair himself in Joe Peterman's production was played by an actor called Eustace Burnaby, who was Hughie Pierrepoint in one of George Dance's OMG companies (see *The Era*, 18 June 1910 and *The Stage*, 23 June 1910). This suggests that Peterman may have come to OMG to recruit for Chanteclair; and provides another reason to think that this was the company J was in.

57 According to Jean ... SP106; *The Era*, 18 June 1910, page 5, 25 June 1910, page 19; *The Stage*, 23 June 1910, page 10.

What happened ... and quotation SP 106-7. *The Stage*, 16 June 1910, page 13 said that Chanteclair had been touring for 'the last few weeks', so it probably opened in May.

Before she left ... SP 107, 123.

But Joe ... SP 107; L225.

Jean always ... SP 108.

58 I have forgotten ... Ibid.

Aunt Clarice ... Kis; *The Gaiety Years*, 163; DRW interviews; VID 55; LS draft EA, 34.

This was ... Kis; LS draft EA; SP 107-11.

In fact ... SP 171-2.

59 She wouldn't ... Barbara Bocardo, 'Notes by a Oxford Lady', *Oxford Journal Illustrated*, 12 Oct 1910, page 11.

Chorus girls ... SP draft of 'Black/White' in EA.

She was ... Kis; SP111; VID 39; B the D, SIOL 82, CS 323-4.

But she wasn't ... SP 112, 170-1; *The Era*, 1 Oct 1910, page 15; Q 15.

60 Quotation: Q15.

Marya learned ... Q 15; SP 170.

The chorus ... Kis; Q 14; B the D; SP 111; VID 80.

In the Forest ... *The Forest Lovers*, by Maurice Hewlett. Quotation from Chapter VI, *The Virgin Marriage* (Thomas Nelson & Sons, 1939 ed., page 63.).

I got sick ... SP 112.

It was December ... SP 112; James, 13; *The Era*, 24 Dec 1910, page 10 and 31 Dec, page 15; Lyceum 1910 folder in Theatre Museum.

61 In Voyage ... VID 8, 10, 73; TS 6. The 'N' company of OMG played Portsmouth (of which Southsea is the port) in early November, then ended in Hammersmith at the end of the month (*The Era*, 5 Nov 1910, page 18 and 19 Nov, page 18.) J remembered playing The King's Theatre, Hammersmith (L 235), and Holloway (VID 13) is characteristically close in sound to Hammersmith.

The first thing ... VID 14, 40; AB interview with author, 6 Nov 1984; Bday 6; SP 114.

Quotation 1: VID 12.

That was just ... VID 12, 19.

Quotation 2: VID 11.

Soon all her ... SP 114-5; VID 30, 35; TS 10, 19; AB interview; FR interview with author, 30 Oct 1985.

LHS was initially identified by his office address on one of only two letters from him which J kept. His identity as her lover was confirmed by many things: (1) AB recognised his handwriting; (2) he was a stock-broker, like Walter in VID; (3) he owned a bust of Voltaire just like the one J describes in VID (75, 77); (4) he lived in Roehampton, like Tony in TS; (5) J (or Mrs Adam) slipped up once in TS and wrote 'Lancey' for 'Tony'; (6) his relationship with his cousin JMS was very like Walter's with Vincent in VID – and J identifies his cousin as 'Julian' in SP; (7) he'd spoken to friends of a girlfriend in the theatre, of whom his cousin said, 'That girl is getting too fond of you.' (Peter Chance to JMS; JMS interview with author, 14 Nov 1984; AB interview.)

62- 3 LHS : Interviews 1984 and 1985 with AB, JMS, BC, FR; LHS, 'Rowe and Pitman', sent to author by LER; letters and telephone conversations with LER; *Burke's Complete Peerage*, Vol XII (1953), pages 252-7; *Burke's Landed Gentry* (1939), page 2080; *Alumni Cantabrigienses*, Part II, 1752-1900; *The Hambros*, 1779-1977, by Bo Bramsen and Kathleen Wain (1979); 'The "old boy" brokers', *The Observer* Business Section, 27 March 1983; *The Times* obituary, 25 Mar 1941, page 8 and 27 Mar 1941, page 7.

John Hugh Smith : *Alumni Cantabrigienses*; FR interview.

Mount Clare is now a teachers' training college, and much of its parkland has been built over by high-rise council housing. A monument still stands in front of the house, inscribed with the names of Lancelot and his sisters and brothers.

63 By 1910 ... LHS had shared 30 Charles Street with his cousin Everard Martin Smith until Everard's marriage to Violet Hambro in 1906 (JMS interview.) Whether it was love ... TS 17; and see VID 44 : 'Your predecessor ...'. In Voyage ... VID 32, 48, 49, 64, 68.

64 In Triple Sec ... TS 4, 12, 14; VID 48, 67-8.

And Lancelot ... SP 114, 116; DW 17; VID 45-8.

And he loved her ... TS 10-18; VID 148.

Freedom and ... Untitled fragment, Tulsa Item 1:6, beginning 'It had always been like that. "You're a worrier," Aunt Jane said', page 2.

These were ... Information about LHS on pages 64-66 from interviews AB, JMS, BC, FR, OB; *The Hambros* by Bramsen and Wain; LHS will.

66 When she knew ... VID 23, 33, 44, 148. See J in MS, *Recollections*, page 9 (sent to author, 6 Dec 1985) : 'he was quite a sensitive man. He wouldn't have been interested in me if he hadn't been sensitive.'

Like real dreams ... TS 6, 14, 16; VID 34, 43, 51, 135; SP 113.

Quotation: *The Play Pictorial*, Vol XIII No 80, in The Gaiety folder, Theatre Museum.

At night ... TS 14; VID 25, 82.

67 At the height ... *Who's Who in the Theatre* 2nd ed., 1914, ed Parker, page 777; TS 11, 17; VID 73; *The Gaiety Years*, 176; Daly's 1911 file, Theatre Museum. J often spoke of being in *The Count of Luxembourg* (eg to DA and FW, and see L 235). She never said it was George Edwardes' own production at Daly's Theatre (in B the D the 'Guv'nor' promises her she should be in his next show at Daly's, but she never says she is.) Yet I think it must have been. There was a touring company of *The C of L*, in which J's friend Daisie played Angèle Didier (see *Who's Who in the Theatre*, 3rd ed., 1916, page 328); but J only ever spoke of touring in OMG, and said in B the D that she first met Daisie when she took over from Lily Elsie. Vincent says in VID (73) that he and Walter are trying to get Anna into the new show at Daly's in the autumn; and in TS Tony plans to 'put Suzy on at the Gaiety' (11). Also J remembered royalty coming to a first night (SP 133) : she thought it was to *Monna Vanna* in 1914, but The Stage Yearbook doesn't list *Monna Vanna* as visited by royalty, while it does list *The C of L*. (See also *The Gaiety Years*, 176.)

By now of course ... TS 16, 18, 20; SP draft for 'The Interval', EA.

All her life ... B, pages 85-6.

So it was ... TS 4, 11, 12, 15; VID 44.

68 But of course ... VID 64; TS 6, 17.

She didn't meet ... TS 15; VID 43, 68-9.

Julian Martin ... Information on JMS from the present JMS, phone call, 29 Oct 1984; TS 15.

Julian was ... JMS; BC, letters and phone conversations, 1984; LHS, 'Rowe & Pitman'.

69 Lancelot did not ... AB interview.

The summer ... VID 64, 67, 69.

Some time ... SP 117; TS 17-18, 21; VID 72; AB interview.

Anna is ... VID 76-7; TS 21-4.

According to ... VID 72; TS 20, 25.

70 In Voyage ... VID 78, 99, 100; Q 70.

Letter from Guy ... TS 26; VID 79-81; GMM 36.

I'm so damn ... TS 27.

Jean saw ... VID 82, 86; TS 27.

*Note on the timing of the affair with LHS*

Jean left Tree's School on 23 July 1909 (R O'D letter). She does three tours (SP drafts in EA). These are approximately:

Aug – Dec 1909

Jan – May 1910

Chanteclair in this break, May/June 1910

Aug – Dec 1910

Dec 1910 she is in *Cinderella*, and has met LHS (SP 112). So the affair begins in the late autumn of 1910.

Daisie Irving took over from Lily Elsie in *The C of L* in autumn 1911, and evidently J knew her for some time (B the D). Judging from VID and TS the affair ended in an autumn; but probably not, therefore, in this one.

This is confirmed by Mme Faber beginning to advertise in the autumn of 1912, not 1911. (See Chapter Three below.)

Jean always said her affair lasted 18 months; and in TS Suzy says 'Not two years yet' just before the end (17). So the Savernake summer was 1912, and the end of the affair autumn 1912. The 18 months were Nov/Dec 1910 to the summer of 1912, when LHS left for America.

PART ONE, CHAPTER THREE

71 It was as though ... WSS 19, 106.

But now ... Q96; L10–11.

She had already ... LGF, TABL 201, CS 93; V, TABL 221, CS 111; POP draft in BL (ADD 57859), No 2, page 6 verso.

72 Now she wrote ... TS 30; VID 89–90; SP 114 (poem).

In the boarding ... VID 91–96; TS 28 & 50.

There is no ... and quotation: *Daily Telegraph*, 9 Nov 1912 (most readable, 21 Nov, page 18); TS 50.

Ethel of course ... VID 119; *Daily Tel*, 26 Feb 1913, page 18, column 5.

First ... TS 33, 39, 47–8, 57, 66 ('Shirley' for 'Alison'); L 227; VID 109.

73 One night ... TS 38ff; VID 104ff.

Once again ... TS 50–57; VID 113, 119–21.

Jean was a ... TS 52, 56, 63–5; VID 123; GMM 132.

And yet Jean ... TS 16, 43, 55. See note about timing at the end of this chapter.

74 That was why ... TS 29–33, 36, 43, 48; VID 120–1.

Quotation: TS 48–9.

That too ... GMM 158–9.

In both Triple Sec ... , quotation and When he touched ... TS 62, 66, 68–70; VID 131–2.

Carl is ugly ... TS 66, 72, 75, 79, 80, 82, 99. And see VID 133–136.

Jean's situation ... TS 76.

75 Quotation 1: VID 134–5.

In Triple Sec ... TS 84.

Quotation 2: ONSSB draft in EA.

Either by Carl ... TS 85, VID 140.

In her ignorance ... TS 82, 83, 87, 88.

In Voyage ... VID 141–7; TS 90–1.

This is what ... TS 92–4. (See note on TS.)

76 He wouldn't ... TS 90, 97–9.

But this dream ... TS 97–8, 103–4; VID 79; LHS, 'Rowe & Pitman'; AB interview; SP 118.

The moment ... TS 98-9.

By now ... TS 101-2; VID 143, 150.

Anna gets only ... VID 150; TS 101, 109.

Afterwards Jean ... TS 101, 103, 105, 108; SP 118.

At last she ... TS 108-9.

At this time ... TS 111; SP 118. For identification of Jennie in TS with Mabel Hampshire, see SP draft of 'Christmas Day', EA, and TS11 ('Mabel' written for 'Jennie'.) Jennie's surname in TS is Kent — a typical J substitution for Hampshire; and Jennie is an artist's model too. By 1968 J had forgotten who 'Jennie Kent' was (J to FW, 7 Nov 1968.).

77  One day ... TS 112.

Her love affair ... TS 112-3; SP 172.

But on her ... TS 116; SP 121 (including quotation).

Even when ... SP 121.

She saw ... TS 118.

Now came ... TS 119-20; SP 122-3.

78  Now she did ... TS 120-1; SP 120-3.

It grew colder ... SP 123-4; DW 15; SP draft for 'Christmas Day', EA.

Quotation SP 124.

She ate ... SP 125-6.

Then there was ... SP draft for 'Xmas Day', EA; DW 16-17; SP 126.

79  So Jean ... SP draft for 'Xmas Day', EA; SP 126-7; BB, CS 64.

1913 was ... J to PK, 5 July 1957; interviews passim.

The room Mabel ... to end of quotation: SP 128-9; DW 23.

For a week ... SP 129-30; SP draft for 'Xmas Day', EA; DW 23-4.

80  This is such ... Elizabeth Vreeland, 'Jean Rhys', *Paris Rev*, Fall 1979, page 224 (for writing only in 'spurts'). J always told the story this way, eg to FW, 7 Nov 1968. But FW is also sure that she started writing about her experience in 'spurts' before 1914 (see L 65); and she certainly went on doing so after. See note on TS.

Now she sat ... TS 132-40, Timing as in TS. Identification of Tonks with 'Mr Davids' from FW. Sir Edward Poynter was nearly 80 in 1914 (1836-1919.)

This painter ... TS 128, 131, 136; Bruce Arnold, *Orpen : Mirror to an Age*, 1981, pages 172 and 405; letter to author from Bruce Arnold, 25 Mar 1990 : 'On balance the portrait of Tommie would seem to be a fictionalised version of Orpen.' Orpen's dates were 1878-1931.

81  Well, she did ... TS139-40. 'Harry Benson's' real name appears to have been Jimmy (see SP drafts for 'Paris Again', EA.)

Harry had been ... TS 142-5.

Harry, like ... TS 146-156.

Harry actually ... TS 157-165.

81  She rings ... TS 167-170.

In Suzy's ... TS 140, 151; SP 131; SP draft for 'Xmas Day', EA; *Who's Who* 1928, page 301; Michael Holroyd, *Augustus John*, Penguin 1976, p 354 (for date of opening of Crabtree Club).

Alan Bott (1893-1952) became a writer too, though a very different one from J. His books were *An Airman's Outings* (1917), *Eastern Flights* (1920); two well-known books of social history, *Our Fathers* (1931) and *Our Mothers* (1932); and *The Londoner's England* (1947). He was also editor of *The Graphic*, Chairman of The Book Society and the Reprint Society, and a publisher with Avalon Press and Pan Books. (*Who was Who*, 1951-60, p 120.)

82  Anything went ... *Augustus John*, 534-5; SP 131; TSP, TABL 35, CS 147.

The Crabtree ... and next four paras on the Crabtree Club from: *Augustus John*, 485 and 534-5; Kenneth Hare, *London's Latin Quarter*, 1926, pp 40-42; C.R.W.

Nevinson, *Paint and Prejudice*, 1937, pp 62-3; PP, p 90; TS 173; SP 131-2; J to
GB, 30 Sept 1967; DM and GM interview, 3 Oct 1984.

83  But now she did ... Maxwell Macartney was born 13 Dec 1880 (*Times* obituary,
    8 Nov 1954).
    TS 174, 177; SP draft for 'Leaving England', EA.
    In Triple Sec ... TS 172-4; ONSSB draft in EA.
    Ronald was ... TS 174-7, 187-8; SP 132.
    And then ... TS 176-7; SP 132.

84  Suzy lies ... and quotation TS 178.
    Jean hardly ever ... MHHM was first identified because he both lived on Kings
    Bench Walk and was a war correspondent for *The Times (Kelly's Directory* 1915,
    p 637; SP draft for 'The Interval', EA, p 5; *The Times* marked copies, war reports,
    eg Oct 1914 – Mar 1915 passim.) His identity was confirmed in phone
    conversation with Miss S Maberley Smith, 29 June 1990, and letter from Dr
    Barbara Coventry, 6 July 1990 : all details of 'Ronald's' family and character in
    TS were true of him. J did speak of 'the first Max' at least once to SO (DA to
    author.)
        Information on MHHM from phone call and letter above; *The Times* obituary
    8 Nov 1954, p 8; TS 174.
    She must have ... TS 178.
    But ... SP 132.
    First they were ... TS 174, 178-9.

85  Their real lives ... TS 191; see Q43, B86, S les V, 85-6.
    She had several ... TS, 'Hebertson', pp 180-186 (AA); TS 188 (Alastair); Tulsa
    LS draft No 53 (Freddy).
    He too ... and next five paras on AHFS: *Burke's Peerage and Baronetage* (1970)
    p 1408; *Music & Letters* July 1948 pp 229-237; *The Times* obituary and 'In
    Memoriam AHFS' by Richard Capell (sent to author by Times Archive); letters
    from Times Archive to author Feb – Mar 1985; letter from TG to author 10
    Mar 1985; Wellington College Yearbook 1910, pp 52-3; *History of Wellington
    College*, 1859-1959 by Basil Newsome, p 264; Wellington College Yearbook
    1948, p 16; Exhibition of Wellington College Archives, June 1977, by Mark
    Baker; 'An Englishman, and ardently so', by Mary Lago; conversations FW with
    author, eg 27 Nov 1985 and 17 Oct 1989.

86  Now, after ... SP 133; *Monna Vanna* programme, in Queen's Theatre 1914
    folder, Theatre Museum.

87  *Monna Vanna* ... *Monna Vanna* programme; SP 133.
    On August ... JMS and BC interviews; letter from Francis Grenfell to Mrs
    Martin Smith, 12 Sept 1914 (copy sent to author by JMS.)
    The man ... SP draft for 'The Interval', EA.
    Maxwell Macartney ... *The Times* marked copies, Oct – Dec 1914; TS 179.
    Suzy spends ... TS 180; SP draft for 'The Interval', EA.
    I hated ... SP draft above; TS 179a.

88  What could she ... TS 179a; SP 133-5.
    The younger men ... SP 135.
    Adrian Allinson ... PP, Chapters 16-18, 'War Years', Chapter 21, 'Peter
    Warlock', and pp 30 and 124; Peyton Skipwith, 'Adrian Allinson : A Restless
    Talent', *Connoisseur*, Vol 198, No 798, Aug 1978, pp 264-273; *Adrian Paul
    Allinson, 1890-1959*, account for Fine Arts Society exhibition, sent to author by
    Peyton Skipwith.
    But he was ... PP 145, 149, 352-3; TS 180; Skipwith 267; John Rosenberg,
    *Dorothy Richardson : The Genius They Forgot* (1973), p 61.
    Now it was ... From this para to the end of this part, p 93, the J–Philip

Heseltine encounter, information from : PP 149-153; TSP, TABL 11-39, CS
125-150; TS 179-186, 'Hebertson'; Gr Ex Bk 18-20. Also, on Philip
Heseltine : Cecil Gray, *Peter Warlock* (1934); F Tomlinson, *Peter Warlock
Handbook* and *Warlock and Van Dieren* (1978); I.A. Copley, *The Music of Peter
Warlock* (1979) and 'Warlock in Novels', *Musical Times*, Vol 105, No 1460,
Oct 1964.

91 As he grew ... Though his friend Van Dieren, eg, claimed it wasn't suicide
(Tomlinson, *Warlock and Van Dieren*, 35.)
Heseltine had ... I've heard somewhere too that gloomy Maclintick in
Anthony Powell's *Dance to the Music of Time* is based on Heseltine.
His effect ... Both DA and FW are clear that J fell for Heseltine (FW to author
in several conversations; DA interview 25 Oct 1984.)

92 This short ... PP 151 ('a streak of hard determination').
She would often ... Eg in the Chateau Juan-les-Pins in 1925, or at her brother
Edward's in 1945.

93 Petronella returns ... TS 33, 209; TSP, TABL 26ff and 33ff, CS 139ff and 145ff;
Q 118-19; ALMM Part One Chapters 3 and 4, Part Two Chapter 2; GMM
60ff; ONSSB draft, EA; PSA, 'Jean Rhys : A Tribute', *Kunapipi*, Vol 1, No 2,
1979, p 23; SP135.
By the spring ... TS 187.
She always said ... Eg SP111; TS187-8.
She felt ... TS 187, 195-6, 215.

94 After three ... TS 196-8, 221 (my emphasis.)
Jean's odd ... TS 190-3.
All my life ... TS 195.
Quotation 1: TS 201.
Suzy cannot ... TS 200.
Quotation 2: TS 201.

95 She starts ... TS 201.
Jean's rage ... TS 82, 87-8, 118, 169, 176-7, 183, 202.
For a week ... TS 206.
Maxwell Macartney ... Miss S Maberley Smith; Dr Barbara Coventry; *Times*
obituary.
After Suzy's ... and quotation: TS 203.
As always ... TS 205.
Quotation 2: TS 205.
But then someone ... TS 202-8.

96 There are air-raids ... TS 209-12.
Suzy doesn't ... TS 213.
She goes ... TS 214-15, 218.
Torrington Square ... *Orpen : Mirror to an Age*, p 48 and DA, conversation
with author; TS 216, 219.
Jean paid ... TS 216-19, 222; SP 138.

97 The house ... TS 216-228; SP 135-6.
She never forgot ... SP 136, 139; L 267; TS 216, 230; SP draft of 'Leaving
England', EA.
Then one day ... TS 222; SP 136-7.
The next day ... and quotation TS 223.
After lunch ... TS 223; SP 137-8.

98 Night after ... TS 225-6.
Quotation and following line: TS 226.
He must be ... TS 223-5.
Marya ... Q 16.

99 A few weeks ... TS 224, 228; SP 138-9.

Almost immediately ... SP 139. (SP draft in EA, 'Autobiography', says JL left 'a few days later'.

She never ... SP 139; SP draft for 'Leaving England', EA. In a letter written in 1936 J's then husband LTS mentions that J had met her cousins Lily and Monica 18 years before, ie in 1918 (LTS to AS, 19 Mar 1936, Tulsa Item 3:1.) In 1918 Lily would have been 17 and Monica only 13, ie both still at school; it seems more likely that they would have met at a whole family gathering than that J would have sought them out at school.

But she held ... TS 224; SP 138-9; SP drafts for 'Leaving Eng', EA.

She'd been ... TS 230; BL ADD 57858, pp 144-146 (BL pagination; typescript pagination 2-4.)

'... she seems to have escaped the sack' : her next memory is of the autumn and the Armistice.

100 In November ... SP 139; P Rev 258-9.

A week before ... SP 139.

Lancelot had ... Information on LHS's war from LER, 16 Nov 1984 and 19 Nov 1984; *The Hambros* by Bramsen and Wain.

This was ... SP 140; SP draft for 'Leaving Eng', EA.

He should have ... SP 140.

At last, at last ... SP draft entitled 'Songs My Mother Didn't Teach Me', EA, p. 3; SP draft for 'Leaving Eng', EA; SP140-1, 172.

*Note on timing of events from the end of the affair to leaving England*

VID says Nov (p 119) or Dec (p 125) to Mar (p 140), though it puts the Mar in 1914.

Mme Faber advertised at Bird Street from Nov 1912–Feb 1913 (after that at other addresses).

TS says three months at Ethel's (p 95) and four months from the last meeting with Tony to seeing him again (p 97). (TS suggests different years, eg 1911 for Ethel's; then on p 66 1911 is changed in pen to 1913 [for the meeting with Carl].) Generally TS is unreliable about dates, though I think its date for the end of the MHHM engagement, eg, is correct. Vide SP 135 saying that J no longer worked at the soldiers' canteen after mid-1917, which would fit with the big break with MHHM, leaving the Temple, going to Mme Zara, etc (though J attributes this to the closing of the canteen, not to her own decision.)

So : circa Nov 1912 – Feb/Mar 1913 at Ethel's.

Leaving Ethel's and discovering she was pregnant, the same, ie, circa Feb/Mar 1913.

Then the gap at Jan's; it's evidently summer while she awaits her abortion, and the abortion is late. So at circa 4 or 5 months, ie June/July 1913.

Then the holiday at Ramsgate.

Finally the sad Christmas, dated as 1913 in P Rev.

The Crabtree Club time dated by its opening : April 1914.

J engaged to MHHM by June (SP 133).

They remain on-and-off engaged until mid-1917.

J meets JL Christmas 1917.

1918, the Ministry of Pensions job (BL ADD 57859).

J leaves for Holland in early 1919 (SP 139).

PART ONE, CHAPTER FOUR

103 Willem Johan ... Marriage certificate, copy sent to author by E vd W; information on previous marriage and divorce from E vd W, letter to author 20 Dec 1988.

John Lenglet ... Letters MK to author 12 Dec 1986 and 18 Jan 1987; letter E vd W to author 28 Dec 1986; E vd W, *Ed. de Nève* (1989), information from MK, Aug 1988. All information from *Ed. de Nève* hereafter subsumed under MK meeting.

His mother ... MM interview with author, 7 Dec 1984; MK mtg and letter to author 18 Jan 1987; Robert-Henk Zuidinga, 'Een Literair Raadsel', *De Haagsche Post*, 19 Mar 1977 ('A Literary Enigma', EA), hereafter referred to as Zuidinga; Bibeb, Interview with Jean Lenglet, *Vrij Nederland*, 27 June 1959, account in MK, 'Jean Rhys in the Netherlands : An Annotated Bibliography', 1986, pp 10–11 (kindly sent to author by MK).

The Lenglets ... MM to author in conversation; MM interview; Q 15.

As he grew ... Bibeb interview with JL in MK bibliography; MK letter to author 11 Nov 1986; Zuidinga.

104 From seventeen ... MM interview with author.

By the time ... MM interview; L 282, 284; 'Vengeance', short story by JL adapted by J, Tulsa Item 1:4; Bk Ex Bk, p 6 at back; DW 14. It's just possible that J's 'G.K. Chesterton socialism' came from MHHM as well or instead; he may have been rather left wing, and had a portrait of GKC in his flat (TS 175; Miss Maberley Smith.)

John's story ... Letters E vd W 20 Dec 1988 and 11 Jan 1989; MK mtg.

Now he was ... Same letters; marriage certificate, copy sent to author by E vd W, 14 Apr 1989.

Though there were ... Letters E vd W 2 Nov 1988, 20 Dec 1988, 11 Jan 1989 and 19 Mar 1989; Bibeb interview with JL in MK bibliog.

105 According to Dutch ... Letter E vd W 11 Nov 1989; SP140.

Did she know ... Q 14; letter E vd W same date; DW 54; and see eg 'Jean Rhys' by John Hall, *The Guardian*, 10 Jan 1972, p 8 (never asking JL where money came from); MK mtg.

A year after ... MM interview; letter to E vd W from the Commandement de la Légion Etrangère, 10 Jan 1989, copy sent to author by E vd W 14 Apr 1989.

This was a ... MM interview; MK mtg.

For this sacrifice ... Bibeb interview with JL in MK bibliog; H v E, *Dierbare Wereld*; MK mtg and 'Jean Rhys and the Dutch Connection', *Journal of Modern Literature*, Vol 11, No 1, Mar 1984, p 160; letter to E vd W from Légion Etrangère; E vd W letter to author, 11 Feb 1989.

What happened ... E vd W letter to author, 11 Feb 1989; MK mtg.

106 Sasha in Good ... GMM 95–7; Gr Ex Bk 13.

I think it ... P Rev 259; JL/J marriage certificate; GMM 95–6.

Sasha and Enno ... GMM 101.

Jean must have ... MK mtg and 'Dutch Connection' p 159; SP 137, 141–2; Gr Ex Bk 4–7; MM interview.

Sasha cries ... GMM 101.

Quotation: Gr Ex Bk 4–7.

107 It was a ... Gr Ex Bk 9–13; GMM 102.

All my life ... Gr Ex Bk 12; GMM 101; J to PK, 18 Jan 1953; J to SO, 17 Nov 1966; L 112 (to MM, 1953); Polly Devlin, 'Reflections on an Interview', *Vogue*, Dec 1979, p 116; Bernstein article p 49; J to GB, 2 Aug 1967.

It was a ... SP 142; SP draft for 'Paris', EA; Bk Ex Bk 14.

Quotation: GMM 104.

108 She'd escaped ... SP 142; L284; Nan Robertson, 'Jean Rhys : Voyage of a writer', *NY Times*, 25 Jan 1978; Vreeland 234; GMM 39; ALMM 65.

This love ... L 284; SP 169, 172; SP draft for 'Paris', EA; VID 32.

John was different ... J to SO, 3 May 1971; SP 142; SP draft for 'Paris', EA. No

10 rue Lamartine is still a hotel today, with the same little iron balconies J
describes (SP 146, GMM 105).

She never knew ... Gr Ex Bk 26-9; SP draft for 'Paris', EA; GMM 105; SP 146.
109 John found ... SP 146; SP draft for 'Paris', EA.

She went ... SP 142-3; SP draft for 'Paris', EA; 'Clouds in Stone : The
Richelots of Paris', typescript in EA, p 2.

As soon as ... SP 143; 'Clouds' p3, 8; SP draft for 'Paris', EA.

It was October ... SP 142, 146-7; letters and interviews as in notes to p 107,
'All my life ...'.

She would wake ... SP draft for 'Paris', EA; Gr Ex Bk 25; SP 144; GMM 110.
110 After this ... SP 144-6; SP drafts for 'Paris', EA; 'Clouds' 2-7.

After lunch ... SP 145-6; SP drafts for 'Paris', EA; 'Clouds' 3.

She loved and ... 'Clouds' 1-9; SP 142-3; SP drafts for 'Paris', EA.
111 Freedom and ... SP 146; 'Clouds' 3-4.

She could never ... SP 146; SP draft for 'Paris', EA; 'Clouds' 2.

But soon it ... SP 146-7; SP draft for 'Paris', EA.

Sasha has her ... GMM 49-50, 116.
112 When her baby ... LM, CS 57-59; GMM 50.

Jean took them ... SP draft for 'Paris', EA; DP interview with author, 29 Oct
1984.

He was a ... GMM 52; DA, Notes for a biography; SP draft for 'Paris', EA;
documents on death of William Owen Lenglet in EA; SP 147; DP interview. The
building which was the Hospice des Enfants Assistés still exists; it is now the
Hôpital St Vincent de Paul.

At first Jean ... SP draft for 'Paris', EA; SP 147-8; DP interview. Colette also
appears in LM (CS 56) and in the Gr Ex Bk (25). I suspect she was the model
for Paulette in GMM (125ff).

The next day ... SP 148; DP interview.
113 When she told ... DP interview.

I think the ... DW 18 (see also SP draft for 'Paris', EA : 'I was an inexperienced
mother'); DA, Notes for a biography (and see GMM 116: 'God is very cruel,'
I said, 'very cruel'); DA interview with author, 24 May 1979.

William Owen ... Documents on death of William Owen Lenglet in EA;
ALMM 81.

But now this ... GR to JL, undated; MK mtg and 'Dutch connection' p 160;
V, in tr, Vol 11 No 6, Dec 1924, p 643 and in TABL 213, CS 104; TS 222;
'Clouds' 1; SP 148; Vreeland 225.
114 The Commission ... SP 148; P Rev 259; 'Clouds' 4.

Then they were ... SP 151-2; 'Clouds' 1-5. I have left out the story of the
little boy called Jacques which J put here in SP (148-151), because in an earlier
version (and J's earlier versions are always closer to the facts) JL was still with
her when it happened; indeed he, not she, writes to apologise to the child's
parents. Given J's and JL's natures, I think this was the likelier story.

Jean arrived ... Passeport à l'Etranger issued to J on 30 Mar 1920 'pour se
rendre de Paris en Autriche', and stamped 16 Apr 1920 in Vienna (EA); 'Clouds'
1; TP, PMS 74 and 78, CS 261, 264; V, TABL 209 and 210, CS 100 and 101.

The atmosphere ... SP draft for 'Paris', EA; V, TABL 204, CS 95; J to FW, 1
May 1964; L 284; J to DA, 1 Dec 1966.

J told Vreeland (225) that JL was Col Miyake's English secretary. But in her
draft for SP she said he was the French secretary, and this seems more likely.
115 When she arrived ... J to DA, 1 Dec 1966; menu card addressed to 'Mme John
Lenglet, Favoritenstrasse 48, Wien IV' in EA; V, TABL 209, CS 100; TP, PMS
73-4, CS 260-1; APS, p N3.

The house belonged ... J to DA, 1 Dec 1966; APS; V, TABL 208, CS 99-100.
They stayed ... V, TABL 215, CS 106; TP, PMS 74, CS 261; V, TABL 207-215, CS 98-105 (André).
Footnote: Signature on menu card, EA.

116 That first year ... SP23; menu card in EA; TP, PMS 76, 78, CS 263, 264; V, TABL 203-6, CS 95-8; letter to author from Azusa Tanaka, National Diet Library, Tokyo, 28 Nov 1985. According to the biographical records kindly sent to me by Mr Tanaka, Mitsuharu Miyake's dates were 1871-1945, Hiroshi Oshima's 1886-1975.
In the spring ... V, TABL 215, CS 105-6; *transatlantic review* p 642 (for title, 'The Spending Phase').
Jean didn't like ... SP draft for 'Paris', EA; John Hall article; MS, *Recollections*, p 23.
It all happened ... L 294; V, TABL 215, 217, CS 105, 107; DA interview with author, 24 May 1979; P Rev 259.

117 They'd been poor ... Interviews with DRW and AS; SP 44; VID 82.
Quotation: V, TABL 215-16, CS 105.
I was cracky ... V, TABL 202-3, 210, 218-19, CS 94-5, 101, 108; Zuidinga; TP, PMS 80-1, CS 266-67.

118 Well : almost ... V, TABL 210, 216-20, CS 101, 106-109.
In the high ... V, TABL 222-3, 229, CS 111, 118; L 284; Zuidinga; J to MM, 7 Oct 1972. The only time J tried to date events in her life (with DP in P Rev 258-265) she put this move in 1922. But that wasn't right. She must have been in Budapest by Aug 1921, because she told MM she was conceived there, and MM was born in May 1922 (J to MM, 26 Nov 1968). Also the 'flight' from Budapest almost certainly began in Oct 1921 (see p 121 below). In my interview with J in 1975 she said she'd spent two years in Vienna and a few months in Budapest. In fact it was about 15 months in Vienna and three in Budapest.
There was so ... P Rev 259; Staley 9.
And she had ... Same sources; TS 225.
And she may ... DRW interviews.

119 Quotation 1: V, TABL 223, CS 112-13.
I was very ... J to MM, 16 Nov 1968.
Quotation 2: V, TABL 223-4, CS 113.
Ten days ... V, TABL 224, CS 113.
In the first ... *tr* Vol II No 6, Dec 1924, p 639; V, TABL 224-5, CS 114.

120 You aren't ... V, TABL 225-7, CS 115-6.
Even so ... and In the middle ... V, TABL 227, CS 116.
As soon as ... to A minute later ... p 121 V, TABL 228-35, CS 116-23; *Encyclopedia of World History* ed. W.L. Langer (1948), p 1014; *The Times* obituary of Zita of Bourbon-Parma, 15 Mar 1989.

121 Vienne ends ... V, TABL 231, 235, CS 120, 123; Passeport à l'Etranger, EA; Zuidinga.
I was a ... TS 97; J to MM, 16 Nov 1968; P Rev 258-9; SP 153; SP draft for 'Paris Again', EA.

122 When Jean and ... Extrait du Registre d'Immatriculation, 28 Aug 1922, EA; letter E vd W to author, 19 Mar 1989; ALMM 48, 94-5; GMM 29.
They hadn't even ... P Rev 259 (Japanese passport).
On 17 October ... Letter E vd W to author, 19 Mar 1989 and divorce document enclosed.
The questions ... MK mtg; E vd W letter, 11 Jan 1989.
We'll never ... P Rev 259-60.

123 But Jean couldn't ... J to MM, 16 Nov 1968.

Mrs Adam is ... Tulsa draft of LS, No 53; SP 154; P Rev 259; Bibeb interview with JL in MK bibliog; letters to author from Times Archive, 15 and 21 Nov 1984.

Footnote: *Who Was Who, 1929–40* and *1949–60*; letter to author from *Times* Archive, 21 Nov 1984; papers and documents in Mrs Adam's Nachlass, kindly shown me by her Executor, Hubert M. Sturges. Staley (10) and FW (L 65, n.1) put J's first meeting with Mrs Adam in London during the War, but that is unlikely, as the Adams spent the war in Paris, and there wouldn't have been much travel once it had begun.

Staley (who evidently based his account on interviews with J in 1977) says that she had met Mrs Adam 'a few times' before their encounter over JL's articles (ie before 1924). There is also some tenuous evidence in EA that the Lenglets and Adams may have met during the formers' first stay in Paris : a letter of condolence on the death of William Owen, dated 21 Jan 1920 and signed with what looks like 'H. Tobey' and an illegible surname. Mrs Adam always signed herself 'H. Pearl Adam' (for Helen), and called her husband 'Toby' (see papers in Nachlass); so the letter may have been from them, signed in a friendly shorthand.

124 When John went ... J to MM, 16 Nov 1968; photograph in EA. In her next letter J suggested that this happened almost immediately after MM's birth, rather than six months later ('You were in Paris before you were three weeks old'.) But this was almost certainly not true. Staley (again no doubt from his interviews with J) says MM remained in the Brussels clinic until she was six months old (9); and MM herself gives this timing (MM interview with author.)

But now ... J to MM, 16 Nov 1968; P Rev 260 and 264; FW conversations with author, 4 Oct 1984 (re GR's help); MM interview with author (MM said she was in her Brussels clinic for six months, then in a French one until the age of three.) And see Staley, p 9 : 'After Jean and de Nève were able to earn a bit of money ... their friend Germaine Richelot found a place in Paris for Maryvonne to stay until she was three.'

The rest ... J to MM, 16 Nov 1968; J to SO, 2 Dec 1968 and 4 June 1971; P Rev 264; JL to J, 11 Sept 1961; MK mtg. For GR and/or one of her sisters wanting to adopt MM, see below.

When she talked ... SP 153; P Rev 259–60; DA, Introduction to SP, 9–10; interviews DA and FW.

125 In 1923 and ... And see Staley p 9; GMM 16.

Sasha is not ... GMM 26–28, 110; Vreeland 227; SP 148–51.

There was only ... A Alv, 'The Best Living English Novelist', *NY Times Book Review*, 17 Mar 1974, p 7.

In After Leaving ... ALMM 39; *Dictionnaire des peintres, sculpteurs, dessinateurs et graveurs*, ed. Benézit, 1976; *Eve*, 26 Sept 1928, clipping in EA.

126 There are several ... Q 7, 11, 22; ALMM 38–40; I11, TABL 151–5, CS 1–5. Violet Dreschfeld was the daughter of Dr Julius Dreschfeld of Manchester and Selina Gaspary of Berlin (information from Manchester Art Gallery.)

Being a mannequin ... GMM 18; Mann, TABL 160, 164, CS 20, 23 (and see GMM 16 : Madame Perron); A Alv, interview with author, 11 July 1985; TS; Bk Ex Bk 72.

And the atmosphere ... Mann, TABL 161–2, CS 21–2; 'Songs My Mother Didn't Teach Me', EA; ALMM 34; TS 207.

127 And the language ... Mann, TABL 163, CS 22–3; GMM 21.

Even this job ... GMM 19; Mann, TABL 166, CS 25–6.

And what about ... ALMM 39; GMM 20, 114, 118.

In reality ... Bibeb interview with JL in MK bibliog, p 11; MK mtg; Q 143. And see Q 20 : 'Sometimes, without warning or explanation, he would go away for two or three days.' And BB (CS 61) about Paul : 'The Bad Man stayed over on the other side of the river, but he would swoop down and carry her off at intervals.'

PART ONE, CHAPTER FIVE

129   Whatever their jobs ... SP 153.
      John wrote ... SP draft for 'Paris Again', EA; 'The Poet' by Edouard de Nève, EA. What J says about 'The Poet' in SP (153) is a confusion; Aristide Briand was Premier of France while she was there (1925-6).
      I had brought ... SP 153.
      It seems odd ... DW 24; SP 154.
130   However, it happened ... SP 154-5; DW 24. See note about TS.
      And hers ... SP 155; SB, DFL p 166; Mrs Adam books and papers in Nachlass.
131   Jean had never ... L'Aff Ford, EA, 3; P Rev 250; Tulsa LS draft No 53; SP 155-6; L 65. As MK points out in a recent article ('Measure for Measure : Quartet and When the Wicked Man', *Jean Rhys Review*, Vol II No 2, Spring 1988, pp 2-17), there are some conflicting stories about how TS got its title, and how it came to FMF (Note 58). Thus DP in P Rev (249-50) says that Mrs Adam called it TS; and Vreeland (225) quotes J as saying that 'someone in John's office' in Vienna had shown her 'stories' to FMF. J's stories were often repeated, and often differed slightly; but she always told the diary-*Suzy Tells*-TS story to FW the same way, and he is sure that that is the correct version. As to the 'someone in John's office', J never said this to anyone else, and I think we can dismiss it.
      In April Ford ... Mizener 334; DDH 95; DFL 116-7; Poli 125; Judd 348, 356.
      Stella Bowen ... DFL 109 (and see Moser, 118-9 : 'For Ford the courage to start every new, serious novel about modern love had to come from a new woman', quoted in MK, 'Q and WWM', Note 41); Mizener 345; Poli 125; Judd 357. Everyone agrees that J and FMF met in the autumn of 1924; see also Staley 10, Moser 235.
      It was Beauty ... Judd 350; Mizener 330; MacShane 162.
      Quotation: MacShane 149; Judd 2.
      In fact ... V, TABL 227, CS 116; LTCIJ, TABL 51, 161-2; Q 10, 35, 66; Mizener xix and 263; Judd 43, 128, 191, 284-5.
132   He was older ... Alan Tate and Edward Crankshaw in Stang; P Rev 260; Mizener xiv.
      No wonder ... ALMM 13, 48, 94; Delany 16; Q 53.
      Ford would ... Delany 18; Hunt 50-1.
      Gertrud Schlabowsky ... Hunt 50-1, 65, 85-6; SL 54; LPR 156-7; Judd 188-9; Q102. The Kalmucks are a Mongol people living in the western USSR (Concise Oxford).
133   Ten years ... Judd agrees with Goldring that there may not have been a sexual relationship between FMF and Gertrud, but this seems to me naive (Judd 188).
      Some scholars have argued that GS was part of the literary genesis of Q : see• eg Peter Wolfe, *Jean Rhys* (1980), 79-81; Judith Kegan Gardiner, 'Rhys Recalls Ford : Quartet and The Good Soldier', *Tulsa Studies in Women's Literature*, Vol I, No 1, Spring 1982, 67-81. However I agree with MK (Q and WWM, Note 19) that J had most probably never read GS; and that the explanation of the similarities between Edward Ashburnham's love affairs and H.J. Heidler's is that they were both based on FMF's. GS 32, 131; SB, quoted in Delany, 18.
      Then at last ... GS 116.
      Ford's first ... VH had not been a Leonora to FMF but a (indeed the) Florence

(Judd 255, Mizener 253). FMF had met SB in the spring of 1918 (see eg Judd 313). DFL 73; Delany 17; Mizener 253, 328 and Note 10; Moser 185-195; Hunt 244. Of the question ... GS 108; Hunt 155; Q 92. And see Mizener 259-60; Judd 241-3; and Judd 37, quoting Tietjens in *Parades End* : 'You seduced a woman in order to be able to finish your talks with her.'

134 Quotation: GS 109.
There is one ... Stang 6.
Jean wasn't ... FMF's Preface to LB, TABL 148 ('I was immensely struck ... with her singular instinct for form'); V, TABL 220, CS 110.
Ford set her ... SP draft for 'Paris Again', EA; Gini Stevens, 'Every day is a new day', *Radio Times*, 23-29 Nov 1974, p 6; Ruth Gorb interview with DA, 'Powers of a Weak Person', *Hampstead & Highgate Express*, 9 Nov 1984, p 15 (hereafter referred to as 'DA, *Ham & High*'); DDH 169; Vreeland 226; L'Aff Ford.

135 Quotation: SP draft for 'Paris Again', EA.
By the time ... Poli 117, 119, 125; Judd 122, 322, 342, 353-4; 394; Mizener 327, 332, 343; DFL 117, 129; Q 11, 49-50, 54-5, 66-7; MacShane 162-4; DDH 455; Hemingway, *The Sun Also Rises*, Chapter 3.
Stella thought ... DFL 129-30; Q 34, 54-6; and see Tout M, CS 16-17.
Ford said ... MacShane 163; SP 168; P Rev 260; J to TG, 29 Nov 1973; FW interview with author; Peter Burton, 'Jean Rhys', *Transatlantic Review*, No 36, Summer 1970, p 107; Q 50; DFL 130; Judd 355.

136 Yet Stella's ... DFL 13, 32, 87-8, 131, 167; Poli 132; Stang passim (on FMF's generosity); Delany 16.
And yet ... Q 41-3, 48; DFL 49, 73, 119, 166-7; Judd 313, 343-4, 360.
Footnote See Poli 59; MacShane 223; Q 59, 71-5; FMF, *Memories and Impressions*, 338-9; APS; Ivan Bede to J, 2 Feb 1931.

137 Earlier in the ... DFL 123-5, 150; Poli 109; Mizener 341; Judd 352-3, 357, 363; Q41.
This was ... Q Chapter 14; DFL 123-4; MacShane 193; Q 54.
In December ... *tr* Dec 1924; L65.

138 Jean was free ... Letter to author from Direction des Services d'Archives, Préfecture de Paris, 28 Nov 1985, and accompanying trial record; letter to author from Chambre de Commerce et d'Industrie de Paris, 2 July 1986.
In the Chevalier ... and quotation Chevalier, SIOL 116-7, CS 343-5.
But something ... Chevalier, SIOL 217, CS 345; S les V 13.
On 28 December ... Letter from Préfecture de Paris and trial record.
In Quartet ... Q 21, 23, 27; S les V 13, 15, 28; B 19, 44.

139 Everyone blamed ... MK, 'Q and WWM', loc. cit., 5-6, 9-10; Q 40, 46; S les V 43, 93, 99, 113; B 96, 99, 103; DFL 166-8. For Lola Porter as a portrait of J, see: Moser 258-9; Delany 21; MK, 'Q and WWM'.
Now Ford ... FMF : See MacShane 223; Poli 143-4; DDH 439; Stang xix-xx; Mizener xvi, xviii. Judd tries to defend FMF on this charge, not (to me) very successfully (see Judd passim, eg 2, 6-7, 18, 60-1, 333.) JL : E vd W letters to author 28 Dec 1986, 21 June 1988; MK mtg; S les V 119 and 154 (sentence exactly as in reality). SB: e.g. Delany 17; MK, 'Q and WWM', 1; Mizener xx and 346 (quoted in MK, loc. cit., Note 2, p 10).

140 What happens ... S les V 93, 95, 100 (and B 95, 103). Note that even in Q nearly a month passes before Marya gets the Heidlers' invitation (Q 39).
Surely this ... MacShane 194; Mizener 357; letter and trial record from Préfecture de Paris.
In Sous les ... S les V 123; Q 36, 39, 43; WWM 51-2, 148-9, 160, 162.

141 According to Stella ... DFL 166.

For the first ... Q 47, 49, 50; WWM 180–1; DFL 166.

They continue ... S les V 84–6, 93, 98; Q 59–60; B 85–6.

The fifth ... On Henrietta Felise : Moser 258–9; Mizener 361–2. On J : DFL 168; Judd 363.

142 Henrietta ... WWM 78–80, 84, 87, 102, 114, 118, 202–3. Henrietta Felise also tells Notterdam the correct, West Indian definition of a Creole (WWM 171–2).
In Quartet ... Q 56; WWM 214.
Immediately ... WWM 221–2, 225; Q 57.
And Henrietta ... WWM 227.

143 But now ... Q 61–2, 66.
Quotation 1: Q 67.
Of course ... Q 71.
Jean was ... P Rev 260–1; DFL 166; Q 66–70.
But of course ... WWM 181, 187; Q 48–9, 67–9, 73–4; P Rev 260; L'Aff Ford 3–4.
Quotation 2: DFL 167.
Peace and ... DFL 167–8; Q 72, 78–9, 82, 91, 94; BB, CS 65.

144 When Heidler ... Q 36–7, 50, 74–5, 85–6.
Sous les ... S les V 90–5, 113–6, 122–4, 140–1, 149, 157.

145 Well : John ... SP 15; MK, 'A Gloomy Child and its Devoted Godmother : Jean Rhys, *Barred, Sous les Verrous* and *In de Strik*', *Autobiographical and Biographical Writing in the Commonwealth*, 1984, 126–8; B, eg pp 44, 60, 76, 85–6, 95–6, 99, 103, 118, 127, 139–41. 172–4, 240, 242; FW letter to author 27 Oct 1988 and conversations; L 283.
In Quartet ... Q 85; S les V 201–3.
John left Fresnes ... Letter to author from Préfecture de Paris; Q 103–6, 110, 115; S les V 158, 165; B 157. And see P Rev 263.

146 In Sous les ... S les V 141, 171, 173–4, 177, 181, 183–4, 189. Compare B 172–182: J left out only Stania's refusal to stay with Jan because of her fear of deportation.
On their last ... Q 110–3; S les V 196; and see B 193.
Jan goes ... Q 111, 114; S les V 198, 210; MK mtg.

147 But she couldn't ... L'Aff Ford 4; P Rev 261; and see DFL 166.
This would be ... P Rev 263; GMM 139–41.
The American lady ... P Rev 261; L'Aff Ford 4–5; J to TG, 29 Nov 1973.
Quotation GMM 139–40.

148 The lady isn't ... V d'Or, CS 73; MM to MK, Nov 1981; J to DA, 1 Apr 1966; P Rev 261; L'Aff Ford 4–5; Judd 362.
The Chateau ... P Rev 261; L'Aff Ford 4–5; V d'Or, CS 73, 75–6; GMM 141.
For the first ... L'Aff Ford 4–5; Q 94; GMM 139, 141; P Rev 261–2; CS 78; DA conversations with author.
MM told MK that she remembered being in Juan les Pins with her mother during this period (MK mtg). But this must be a confusion with a later visit to the Riviera, probably in 1928 (see below); J could hardly have had a three-year-old with her at the Chateau Juan les Pins. I'm sure what she told DP is the truth: that she *intended* to bring MM to Juan les Pins, as part of a future plan.

149 She stayed ... MM suggests J may have been with the Hudnuts for up to six months, but J often confused the length of an episode with its importance to her. Certainly she was in Paris before Christmas, because at that point the Fords left Paris for Toulon (Mizener 349). GMM 139; L'Aff Ford 5; P Rev 262.
But then ... L'Aff Ford 5–6; P Rev 262.
Jean was ... L'Aff Ford 6–7; P Rev 263; J to TG 29 Nov 1973; Stang 236–7; MK mtg.

H.G Wells (according to Crankshaw in Stang 237; according to Judd 62 it was Stephen Crane) said : 'One day Hueffer will patronise the good God himself, but God won't mind, because Hueffer is all right.'

150 Jean behaved ... L'Aff Ford 6; P Rev 262.

Mrs Hudnut ... Same sources.

Jean was back ... L'Aff Ford 7; Mizener 348; Judd 367; P Rev 262; Q 87, 93, 99. DP calls J's hotel the Hotel de Rive; but she'd probably said *de l'Arrivée* (see R de l'A, LB; and GMM 120 : 'The Hotel of Arrival, the Hotel of Departure ...'.)

Now, Jean ... J to TG, 29 Nov 1973.

John was gone ... Q 88, 92.

151 But now ... L'Aff Ford 7; P Rev 263; Q 88, 92-3.

Heidler also ... Q 88-94. And see P Rev 263 : 'Stella was completely hostile.'

This went on ... Ludwig, FMF to R.A. Scott James, 3 Feb 1925; Mizener 349-52; Judd 367.

And Jean? ... This para is slightly tentative because AS, who is the source of it, did not tell me the story of J's and LTS's meeting in this way. However she did tell it this way to MK, in a letter of 1987; and MK kindly passed it on to me (letters 20 Aug and 16 Oct 1988). I think this timing for J's first meeting with LTS is very probably accurate; it makes sense, eg, of the otherwise rather mysterious letter to Edward Garnett (J to EG, April 1) if it was sent in 1926 rather than in 1928. The letter implies that J has already approached Garnett about a 'story'; she explains she's had to put it aside for three months 'while Stella was ill', and asks if he would still care to see it. A 'story' fits a LB story better than Q; and in 1926, but not in 1928, J was close enough to the Fords to use an illness of SB's as an excuse for delay.

Garnet : see *The Readers' Encyclopedia*, 383; Judd 46; P Rev 264.

152 And this wasn't ... DW 26, 36; Vreeland 224; Robertson; Burton 107; J to FW, 7 Nov 1968.

Jean cut ... and She stayed ... J to EG, 'April 1'; Mizener 350; Judd 368.

She moved back ... GMM 120; Q 87, 93, 106; S les V 238; ALMM 7-8. This must have been the room described in S les V, because it was in 1926 that JL returned to Paris (see below).

In the spring ... Mizener 351; Judd 369; Q 96.

Jean knew ... VID 83.

153 Jean was desperate ... VID 35; ALMM 78-9.

It's all ... Q 91-2.

Quotation 1: Q 94.

When she cries ... Q 101.

Quotation 2: Q 101.

Jean had struggled ... LGF, TABL 198, CS 90.

154 The main reason ... Q20, 95-6; S les V 184; B 182.

Drink did ... GMM 102-3.

That is what ... Q 96, 101-2.

All this ... DFL 166-8. See MK, 'Q and WMM' 10-11 for a similar argument about FMF failing to revenge himself on J with his portrait of her as Lola because it was simply too bad. See eg MacShane (216-7) too on WWM's weakness.

From the beginning ... WWM 171, 211, 257, 263. And see TS 225 on JL's sharp repartee, MM interview and MK mtg on his pride.

155 That is at ... WWM 206-8, 216-7, 243, 284; WSS 122, 128; Q 82.

Lola's behaviour ... WWM 189, 208-11, 247, 249, 255, 263, 266-7, Q 102.

Notterdam admits ... WWM 153, 184, 190, 211, 234, 245, 247, 249, 275.
156 Quotation: Q 114-5.
Usually falling ... ALMM 24.
157 Marya's affair ... Q 99.
John had ... S les V 205-6, 209-14; B 209-12; records of the Santé prison, 5-10 Aug, 17-22 Sept 1926, sent to author by the Service d'Archives, Préfecture de Paris, 21 May 1986.
And sooner ... Q 100; S les V 215-6; prison records.
Jan now finds ... S les V 228-237; B 226-236; MK mtg; MM interview.
Jan finds Stania ... and quotation: S les V 238.
Stania denies ... S les V 239-243; B 240-242.
158 It was probably ... P Rev 263.
In the Hotel ... Q 124-6.
Roseau ... LGF, TABL 189-193, CS 83-86; Q 124-6.
Marya is alone ... LGF, TABL 187, 197-8, CS 81, 89-90; P Rev 263; *Augustus John* 535; Casino card in the name of Ella Lenglet, dated Sept 1926, EA. The suggestion that Mr Wheeler is based on Mr Hudnut was made to me by MK.
I'll move ... LGF, TABL 186-8, CS 79-81; SP 129; WWM 51-2, 263.
159 In Quartet ... Q 127-8.
Jean said ... P Rev 263-4; Santé records, Préfecture letter 21 May 1986; LGF, TABL 201, CS 93; Q 128.
When Marya ... Q 128, 131, 133, 136.
John's story ... S les V 243-5; B 242-5.
Of herself ... P Rev 264; Staley 14. And see *Kerels*: 'Stania had not had the courage to share his fate.'
160 Marya is ... Q 137, 141; S les V 245-7 (left out of B.)
Both Stephan ... See *Kerels*, and MK mtg.
At the end ... S les V 247.
161 Now Jean ... DA to author, 5 Aug 1983, and to Francis Pagan, 1978 (quoted in Judd 363); J to TG, 29 Nov 1973; Mizener 583; SB to FMF, 29 Oct 1926 and FMF to SB, Jan 1927, quoted in Judd 362.
For Maître Legrand see : S les V 94; ALMM 10, 14, 17, 23-4; Poli 23; FMF, *It Was the Nightingale* (1934), 290, 330.
Her life went ... ALMM 10, 14, 26; SP 120-1; GMM 72. J's time of starving and contemplating suicide was probably now, because this was the moment (I think) at which she was abandoned by both FMF and JL.
That was the high ... quotation, and After the first ... GMM 72, 74, 119-20. J had let LHS pay her hotel bill too (TS 118).
As always ... Hunger, CS 44; P Rev 258; A Night, CS 47-8.
162 Quotation 1: A Night, CS 147-8.
Quotation 2: R de l'A, CS 50, 52.
In September ... Judd 369; Mizener 352; DFL 168; P Rev 264; H. Pearl Adam to J, 13 Dec 1926 (which suggests that J was out of Paris at that date).
Footnote: GMM 36, 118.
163 She had already ... P Rev 263-4; L'Aff Ford 2; L 62, 100, 104; J to SvD, 3 Feb 1957; J interview with author, 29 Sept 1975. The short story was 'Houdia'.
Jean said later ... J to OH, 2 Feb 1966 (Tulsa Item 3:4); L 100; SP 129; 'The daughter about the mother', Zuidinga p 8; DW 15, 36.
We have one ... H. Pearl Adam to J, 13 Dec 1926.
Houdia ... L 104; MK mtg.
A bit melodramatic ... L 104.
164 Nonetheless he ... Telegram FMF to GR, 4 Jan 1927; letter FMF to Pascal Covici, 5 Jan 1927 (copy sent to LTS); P Rev 264; 'The Dividing Line', unused

draft for SP, EA; GR to J, 18 Nov 1929; Staley 14. J's and JL's working on *Perversity* together in Amsterdam must have been Jan 1927, because by early Feb JL was in The Hague (MK mtg).

This last kindness ... P Rev 264; SP 15; GR to J, 18 Nov 1929; FMF and LTS correspondence, Feb – Apr 1929; DDH 97; Mellown 143-4; Ludwig 177 (5 Mar 1928 to Isobel Patterson).

By the time ... Stang xxix, xxxiii, 214, 225, 232-3; DDH 96; Judd 1, 167; Q 41.

Jean of course ... Letters FMF to LTS, Feb – Apr 1929; Mellown 4-5; P Rev 263.

In the meantime ... MK mtg.

165 Now that he ... MK mtg and letters 20 Aug and 18 Oct 1988.

It was like ... MK mtg.

In his second ... MK mtg; Victor van Vriesland, review of *Kerels, Kroniek van het Proza*, 25 Nov 1933, and E. Elias, review of *Kerels, Groene Amsterdammer*, 27 July 1934, both in MK bibliography.

Jan hopes ... Ibid; *Kerels*, quoted by Bibeb, Interview with J, *Vrij Nederland*, 28 Feb 1976 (in MK bibliog.)

I don't think ... L 101.

She was as ... L 101, 171; J to FW, 14 Sept 1959; J to DA, 14 Oct 1968; J to MM, 24 Nov 1969; P Rev 263 (though the geography is slightly wrong here.)

166 Now Jan's question ... Not even FMF or his biographers suggest that he went on giving J money after early 1927.

In fact Germaine ... Valentine Williams to GR, 19 Jan 1927; FW to author, 4 Oct 1984; GR to J, 12 Sept 1927; convents etc in Alençon, Dreux and Montigny-sur-Loing to GR, July 1926; Judd 362 ('the Richelot cheque'.)

In Jean's story ... J sent 'Susan and Suzanne', along with 'Houdia', to SvD in 1953. Both have subsequently disappeared, except for Part III of 'Susan and Suzanne', which is in the BL (ADD 57859, on versos of pages numbered 3 and 4 by BL.) The full story of 'Susan and Suzanne', like 'Houdia''s, was told me by MK from JL's Dutch translation (MK mtg and letters 20 Aug and 18 Oct 1988.)

Footnote 1: L 105; BL, ADD 57859.

168 But Susan and ... Envelope addressed to GR from 'Le Berceau', 160 Rue St Martin, Dreux, Eure et Loire, dated 5 July 1926.

And Mme Brega ... SP 143; SP draft for 'Paris', EA; Discourse, CS 46; ALMM 129.

But Mme Brega ... 'Clouds', EA.

169 In the final ... and quotation: GR to J, 12 Sept 1927.

Happily, they ... See letters GR to J, 1929 and 1931; but also see below, eg the portrait of Sidonie in GMM.

There are two ... Letter to GR from Maison Ste Marie, La Genevraye par Montigny-sur-Loing, Seine et Marne, 5 July 1926 (there is also a letter from the Institute Ste Marie at Alençon); GR to J, 12 Sept 1927; MK mtg.

   J and MM registered in The Hague on 12 Oct 1927. Thus J's account to DP ('Her husband went to Paris to take their daughter back to Holland' P Rev 264) is probably wrong, unless JL came to fetch them both. But note the connection to the idea of adoption at this point.

170 This was a ... to From Oct 1927 ... (page 171) MK mtg.

He was thrown ... Also L 61 (1949.)

171 From October... Also MM interview; P Rev 264; Staley 14.

Did I love ... GMM 108-9, 119. DA reports J saying : 'I married my first husband to get away from London'. (DA to author.)

It wasn't ... DA interview with author, 25 Oct 1984. Note that in the draft for

GMM called 'The Fugitive' (Gr Ex Bk, 21-31) The Enno figure is called Paul. Montparnasse calls . . . BB, CS 60-65. Both Sasha and Carlo feel that they 'go to pieces' after the JL figure has left them (GMM 119, CS 65).

172 Did he ever . . . MM interview; MK mtg; DA interview 25 October 1984; S les V 84, 86.

Quotation 1: S les V 85.

At the same time . . . B 86-7.

Quotation 2: S les V 85. Cf Q 9.

So Jan . . . S les V 85; B 86; GMM 107.

Que j'ai grimacé . . . S les V 86, 115-6; B 87; MK mtg.

Ford's and Stella's . . . Mizener 362-3, 384; DDH 125; DFL 169; Judd 376, 386.

173 Did they ever . . . Mizener 357, 362, 583; ALMM 8, 17, 26.

When she read . . . L'Aff Ford 2; interviews and conversations with DA, eg 17 Aug 1983; Mizener 583.

But when they . . . WWM 317; DFL 109.

Towards the end . . . Vreeland 226; Burton 106-7; Stang 214; P Rev 260; DDH 267; Judd 358; L'Aff Ford 3; 'The daughter about the mother' in Zuidinga p 9.

174 She gave him . . . L'Aff Ford 3; Stang 16, 214, 227; DDH 154, 250; Judd 54-5, 196-7; FMF Introduction to LB, TABL 149; conversations with DA and FW. See also Judd 358 : 'What [FMF] taught [J] was not so much *how* to write, though there was some of that, as that she *was* a writer.' On J's Frenchness as a writer, see Wyndham Lewis's review of LB, in the *Saturday Review*, 23 Apr 1927 (Mellown 5) : 'The form of Miss Rhys's studies is purely French . . . in [their] balance . . . economy . . . poise, directness and clarity.' On FMF's, see also John Rodker's comment on GS : 'The finest French novel in the English language.'(Quoted in FMF's Introduction to GS, 8.)

She generously . . . DA letter to author 5 Aug 1983 and interview 17 Aug 1983; J Br interview.

Quotation: P Rev 263; DA interview 24 May 1979.

But this wasn't . . . ALMM 24; Q 114. On J's being in love with FMF, see FW, quoted in Judd, 361. Judd suggests (365) that J was less important to FMF, but the fact that their affair ended his relationship with SB shows that this was, at least briefly, not true.

FMF died at Deauville on 26 June 1939 (Judd 441) and SB in England in 1947, aged only 52. Their daughter Julie married a writer, Roland Loewe, with whom she had a son, Julian. Julie has also recently died.

PART ONE, CHAPTER SIX

177 When Postures . . . Reviews from clippings in EA : *New Dominion*, W. Virginia, 12 Feb 1929; *The Observer*, 7 Oct 1928; *Daily News*, 8 Oct 1928; *Manchester Guardian*, 26 Oct 1928; *New York Telegram*, 28 Jan 1929.

Footnote: See Mellown 7-11.

179 The key to all . . . For Stephan meeting Marya four or so years before, see Q 15-16 and 29 : they met when she was 24, and she is now 28.

185 Footnote: For getting inside Lois see Q 40, 64, 110; for Heidler see 101, 102. For Stephan see 17, 143, 144.

191 Like all subversive . . . For Marya's remorse towards Lois, see Q 73; towards Stephan, see 105 and 138. For her pity towards Stephen see eg 37 and 136. For his towards her, see eg 31 : 'It is you I am worring about', and 36 : 'I have such a cafard when I think of you, Mado.' Also his great kindness to her once he is out of prison, which I mentioned earlier (eg 104, 110, 138, 141). For Heidler, see 78-9, 100, especially 115 : 'I'm not being treacherous; I'm being cruel

perhaps ... but I'm not being treacherous. I've never shared a woman in my life, not knowingly anyhow, and I'm not going to start now.' Marya accuses him of having forced her to share him, of using Lois to torture him with : 'He answered coldly, "I don't know what you mean." And she saw that it was true.' For Lois, see eg 44 and 49. Marya sums up both Heidlers (48) as 'plump, sleek, satisfied, smiling and hard-eyed' people.

197  Footnote: Minneapolis, *Minn Journal*, 17 Feb 1929 (clipping in EA).

198  Economy and pace ... 'A jumble of facts' is J's description of the 'notes' (ie the exercise books) from which she'd written VID (Vreeland 223). In *L'Aff Ford* she referred to her first version of Q as 'a record of facts' (p 2).

202  When Ford tried ... For imagery of streets like water reflecting lights, and tall dark houses, see eg : 22: 'People hurried along cowering beneath their umbrellas, and the pavements were slippery and glistening, with pools of water here and there, sad little mirrors which the reflections of the lights tinted with a dull point of red.' 38: 'Every time that the door of the café swung open to admit a customer she saw the crimson lights of the tobacco shop opposite and the crimson reflection on the asphalt and she began to picture the endless labyrinth of the Paris streets, glistening hardly ... ' 57-8: 'The street was quite empty, a long street glistening with light like a sheet of water.' For the tall dark shuttered houses, see eg 29 and 96.

215  She'd exposed ... For J's skill in using letters, see eg the lawyers' notes in ALMM and Mr Fraser's letter in WSS, both conveying the cold and cruel power of the law. In VID Ethel's long letter (191-3), Uncle Bo's shorter one (52-3) and Anna's postcard (53) ('This is a very windy place') all convey their characters as powerfully as Vincent's. George Horsfield and W. Neil James in ALMM write revealing letters to Julia (103, 112, 124, 130); Rochester's letters to his father in WSS give us crucial insights into him (63, 133); and in Q, apart from Marya's aunt's letter, three others show us people's natures : Marya's letter of abject despair to Heidler (121), Heidler's cold and controlling reply (127), and Stephan's impulsive and optimistic note to Marya (127-8). In the stories too letters play an important role. TABL begins with Hans's letter to Mr Severn, and POP ends with Rosalie's to Ramage; Myrtle's letter is the turning point of OBP; and the irrational, hate-filled voices of a small West Indian island leap out of the letters of 'Again the Antilles' (LB) and FW (SIOL).

216  Although Quartet ... For eg's of as it were's, apart from the ones given, see Q 82, 85, 99.


PART TWO, CHAPTER ONE

223  The late 1920s ... For J's stories being largely written or begun in the 30s: TABL: There are 8 new stories (plus 9 reprinted from LB). ASH and The S of the R date from the war and LTCIJ from the late '40s and after.
      This leaves 5 new stories, TSP, TDTBTB, TABL, OM and The L. TDTBTB is based on a childhood memory, so is perhaps drawn from the autobiographical writings begun in the '30s and used eg for VID; but J claimed to go on with these into the '50s, and may have done so (see L 153). She first refers to TDTBTB in 1953 (L 100); so I do not count this one. But the other 4 were almost certainly during the '30s. The first 3, at least, were in The S of the R (L 40).
      SIOL: NO 1925 is about Paris in the '20s and was originally written there (J to SO, 7 Oct 1973). Chevalier was originally a story of JL's, as J notes on the title page; he'd written it in the '20s and she'd 'tinkered about' with it 'now and then' ever since (J to DA, 8 Sept 1976). These two belong essentially, therefore, to the '20s.

'Kikimora' is set in J's life of the '30s (Stephen is based on LTS, and Kikimora was a real cat they had in the '30s — see L 209); most probably it was at least begun then, probably around 1938 (see Chapter 5 below). B the D and ONSSB are about the time just after the end of J's first affair, as TSP is too; most likely early drafts of them formed part of the novel-length version of that story (see L 185, 207). These three, therefore, were probably at least begun in the '30s.

Five stories are based on J's writings about her childhood, which she began in the '30s: POP, GMGR, BF, H and FW. The latter three she may have worked up into stories only later (BF became part of one of her last stories, Imp Rd, though part of it definitely dates from the '30s — a typescript of it in EA is dated 14-9-38). But POP and GMGR were worked on much earlier. An early version of POP, called 'The Martyr', is in the Gr Ex Bk, which Tulsa dates to 1920-35; and parts of the handwritten versions in the BL are in J's very firm early hand (BL ADD 57859), under titles ('The Price of Peace', 'A Candle in the Sun') which appear in the list in her wartime O Nbk (pp 25-6), evidently for inclusion in her planned book of stories. And the early version of GMGR, Bday, is typed on the same machine as other childhood memories dated in the late '30s; bits of it appear in one of these (New Story, dated 1938, in EA) and in the Bk Ex Bk, written in the late '30s. Only 9 of the 16 stories in SIOL, therefore, were begun or mostly written after the '30s: TIW (during the war — drafts of it appear in the O Nbk); OBP, which began as LS in the early '60s; BF (probably and partly), H and FW; and 4 stories of J's old age, Rap, Rap, WKWUITA, SIOL and IUTLHO.

Finally, TP and ISAS, which were published separately, are wartime stories, written during the war (bits of both appear in the O Nbk, and both were ready for inclusion in The S of the R in 1945). (Parts of TP go back earlier: J told FW, 1 May 1964, that she'd begun it on her Dominica holiday in 1936.)

The 'about 15 stories' which came after the '30s were therefore, to sum up: TP, ISAS, ASH, TIW, and possibly The L, from the war; LTCIJ, from the late '40s and after; TDTBTB perhaps from the '50s; and OBP, BF (partly), H, FW, Rap Rap, WKWUITA, SIOL and IUTLHO from the '60s and '70s.

The two stories which reached novel length were TSP (L 185, 207) and POP (J to OS, 25 Feb 1970, Tulsa Item 3:19) and OS interview with author, 24 Nov 1984.

The lost novel was WCQ (see Chapter 5 below.)

224 Leslie's importance ... I tried to start doing justice to LTS in my first short study of J, *Jean Rhys*, Penguin Lives of Modern Women, 1985.

This hidden ... J to SO, 3 May 1971; AS interviews with author, 20 and 24 Aug 1984; 'The daughter about the mother' in Zuidinga, 9; 'The Dividing Line', unused draft for SP, EA.

On J's not wanting to write but only to be 'happy': See eg FW's Introduction to L, 10: 'In old age J often said that, could the choice have been offered her, she would have preferred a life of only average happiness to the greatest literary triumphs.' Also eg L65, J to PK, 6 Dec 1949: 'I never wanted to write. I wished to be happy and peaceful and obscure'; to DP (P Rev 251): 'I never wanted to be a writer. Never. I couldn't help it. All I wanted was to be happy.' Also eg to TP in their interview in 'The Jean Rhys Woman', Omnibus, BBC, broadcast Nov 1974.

225 At the end of 1927 ... MK mtg.

The only thing we know for certain about J's mother's death, from outside her fiction, is that she came to the funeral (DRW interviews, 19 Mar and 11 Apr 1985). But we must surely guess that she saw her mother before she died, as Julia does — though J denied it (DW 44). She was more in touch with her family than the novels (or she) suggest; and she had good reason to want to forget and deny the funeral experience. Watching the mother die is the central emotional experience of ALMM, and J always stuck close to that. She certainly stuck close to many other facts there, as in all her novels.

The family were usually able to reach her. In WWI, eg, they sent her their warnings about marrying JL; in 1928 Auntie B put 'Ella Gwendoline Lenglet, now living in Paris' into her will (immediately after this disastrous experience!); and once J was back in England, and then Edward too, she remained in touch with all her sisters and brothers (see below).

In After Leaving ... ALMM 44, 52, 76; DRW interviews.

Re J visiting her family when she could show them success and happiness : eg visiting Owen in 1934; seeing her sisters when leaving for Dominica in 1936. She said (in DW 44) that she 'had hardly seen' her mother in England.

The setting was ... DRW interviews; JRW interview 11 May 1985. Address shown in both Mrs Rees Williams and Brenda Lockhart wills.

The people were ... ALMM 51, 53, 70.

Uncle Griffiths ... ALMM 52, 57, 96.

226 Secondly ... DRW interviews; JB interview; ALMM eg 69, 88.

These, then ... Re the Rees Williams's attitude to J's writing : see L 109, 'They all say I have written feelthy books': and JB told me that Brenda and Robert Powell did have several of J's novels — but kept them in brown paper wrappers.

227 In After Leaving ... ALMM 92-99; DRW interviews.

There wouldn't have been much for anyone to steal. Mrs RW had presumably sold the family house in Roseau, and Amalia Estate, which however would have brought in very little. Aunt Hester says of Morgan's Rest in VID (53) : 'a place that lost money and always has done and always will do ...'. Compare this to Dr RW's request in his will that every effort be made 'to make my estate Amelia a paying concern, as it will keep my family from want': and D Ag's comment (4 Oct 1986) : 'It is rather pathetic, his belief that Amelia would keep the family from want. Alas, this is rarely the case, estates usually gobble up money rather than provide it.'

Perhaps it wasn't ... Owen and Dorothy were still in Australia, and so couldn't come to the funeral. DRW's mother and sisters went in her place; it was from them that she got this story. They too are dead now. ALMM 101.

Another final ... ALMM 78-80.

It is easy ... P Rev 259; Bibeb interview with J in *Vrij Nederland* (transcription of translation in MM to DA), 1 Mar 1976; LHS to J, 4 May 1927.

228 Quotation LHS to J, 4 May 1927.

Walter Jeffries ... Lawson Knights, conversation with author, 30 Oct 1984; ME letter to BC, 12 June 1985 and letter to author 20 Sept 1985; BC letters to author, 1 Dec 1986 and 12 Dec 1986; LER to author, phone conversation 16 Nov 1984; OB interview with author, 25 Oct 1984.

But behind this ... Interviews and letters AB, OB, BC, JMS, FR.

229 This keeping ... AB interview; ME letter 12 June 1985; JMS interview; LHS will.

All of this ... ALMM 79-82.

In Mackenzie ... ALMM 78, 124.

Something like ... ALMM 21, 81-2.

Footnote: Lindsay Vincent, 'The "old boy" brokers', *Observer*, 27 Mar 1983; LER phone conversion; AB interview; ME letter 12 June 1985.

230 Perhaps it was ... ALMM 21; Q 14; L 281; WSS 121.

The next ... L 255; J to DA, 14 Oct 1968; P Rev 264; 'The Dividing Line'; MK mtg.

She went back ... MK mtg; 'The Dividing Line'; L 171; J to DA, 14 Oct 1968; FW chronology in L 13; FW letter to author 27 Oct 1988 and meeting with author 29 Oct 1988; P Rev 264; SP 172; J curriculum vitae in EA.

231 She went back ... 'The Dividing Line'; L 13; P Rev 264.

Leslie had ... AS interview 17 Dec 1985; P Rev 264.

So Leslie was ... AS to MK, MK to author in letters 20 Aug and 18 Oct 1988; ALMM 44 and 68. See Part One, Chapter 5, pp 151-2.

If this is ... AS interview 17 Dec 1985. MK suggested to me that Julia's remeeting with Mr Horsfield during her visit to her mother's deathbed may have been a reflection of reality (MK letter 20 Aug 1988.)

232 Anne was nineteen ... AS interviews 20 and 24 Aug 1984.

Once again Jean's ... 'The Dividing Line'; P Rev 264. For J's romantic time with LTS, see the letter which must be to him beginning 'Dear — dear'.

He was in ... AS interviews 24 Aug 1984 and 17 Dec 1985; AS letter to author 7 Aug 1985; MR letter to author, 18 July 1985; ALMM 31-2, 63.

For Leslie ... AS interviews.

To his children ... AS interviews.

233 Only weeks after ... MK mtg.

Jean did leave ... AS interviews; L 171, 226. Re pretending she hadn't gone back: she often spoke as though she'd spent all ten years between 1919 and 1929 in Paris : eg in her cv; Burton interview; to JvH in 1970 (see H in C, 4).

She probably ... Re J going to Paris this summer : see letter LTS to J, 16 July 1928, which suggests she was away from home; and the portrait bust by Dreschfeld, who was based in Paris.

Just once ... L 255; DA note on letter to J, 2 Mar 1965; J to DA, 14 Oct 1968.

234 In late September ... Reviews sent to J by cutting agencies, EA; *New Statesman* 6 Oct 1928; *Manchester Guardian* 26 Oct 1928.

We can be sure ... Envelope addressed to J at the Hotel de Brest et de Rennes, 124 rue de Rennes, 8 Oct 1928.

For the last six ... Bibeb interview with JL: (in MK bibliog); JL to J, 21 Feb 1929. JL said he was 'left with the care' of MM when she was two : but of course when she was two he was about to enter prison in France. After that he was on the road, in the poorhouse, etc. The time that he alluded to, therefore, must have been early 1928, when MM was five. Indeed the photographs he sent to J of MM with him in Holland are clearly of a five to six-year-old child (see SP and *Ed. de Nève*. The *Ed. de Nève* one (p 69) is dated 4 April 1929.)

In the autumn ... GR to J in Bandol, 15 Nov 1928; MM interview; photographs in EA. This was the occasion I think MM confused with J's summer at the Chateau Juan les Pins.

235 This new life ..., quotation, and And a six-year-old ... JL to J, 21 Feb 1929. The problem was ... Simon & Schuster to J, 21 Feb 1929; MK mtg; Bibeb interview with JL; MM interview with author. That now was the time of MM's stay at a South London boarding school is only a guess, but a good one : she thinks it was at about six; and after 1931 her schooling was all in Holland.

236 When Jean first ... and quotation JL to J, 21 Feb 1929. I am guessing that MM returned in late 1928 because JL refers in Feb 1929 to '*toute la peine que je me suis donnée tous ces mois.*'

Jean remembered ... J to SO, 3 May 1971 (though J dates it to after her divorce.)

When they were ... MM interview; ES to LTS, 29 Sept [1933]; MM to AS, 30 July 1968 (Tulsa Item 3:1) ('Only [Leslie] made my holidays in England bearable when I was a child'); MM and J correspondence May 1971; Burton interview; 'The Dividing Line'; P Rev 264; ALMM 19, 80-81. For MM's absence from the novels, see Bailey radio : MM said, 'I've tried to find out whether there is a character like me in her books. I'm never mentioned.'

237 While she was . . . Envelope addressed to Mrs Lenglet, Hotel Henri IV, 25 Place Dauphine, Paris, dated 1929; ALMM 9; L 277.

238 There was one . . . JL to J, 21 Feb 1929; GR to J, 18 Nov 1929; FMF and LTS correspondence, Mar to June 1929; ALMM 18.
Footnote: Mizener 388; Mellown 7.


PART TWO, CHAPTER TWO

250 Footnote: See L 107 and SP 162.

251 As times goes on . . . For Julia's irrational swings of mood, see 45, 49; bumping into people, 16; vague, 38; abstracted, 42; incoherent, 32, 54; unable to hold on to their reality or her need, 63.

252 All this we see . . . For Julia's sulkiness and silence, see 31; vagueness, 38; boasting, 42, 67; attempts to seduce Horsfield, 67; indifference to him, 68, 103, 114; hostility to him, 112, 120.

253 Besides, it isn't . . . For egs of Mr Horsfield's thoughts about Julia, see 29–43, 63–8, 103–13, 118–27. For egs of Mr Horsfield's thoughts about Julia being embedded in the narration, see 31 (her sulkiness and indifference), 38 (her vagueness and impatience), 42, 67 (her vanity and boasting). For egs of places where the narration moves from Horsfield's thoughts to Julia's, with no suggestion that hers are privileged, see 38, 42, 63–65, 103, 104, 120. For Julia's taking Horsfield's money without protest, 36; constantly checking her appearance, 31, 35, 65, 66; drunk, 37; vain, 42; sullen, 134; ungrateful, 36; cold and hostile, 120.

255 Despite all her . . . For Julia's pulling herself together, see 31, 124, 130; for her impulses of pity towards Norah, 73, 98; for Norah's curiosity, 52; hate, 77; disgust, 98; desire to hurt, 74.

257 The first step . . . For Julia's talking loudly, grimacing and crying, see 23, 25, 126.

260 Everyone is given . . . In their first meeting we are first inside Julia (51) then Norah (52–3) then both (53–5). In the second it's first Julia (73) then Norah (74), and we stay with Norah's most private feelings (74–6) until we return to both equally at the end (77). In the third (the mother's death) we are with both (87–90). In the fourth too (91 with Julia, 92 with Norah). In the fifth (the funeral) we are first with Norah, then with Julia (92; 93 on); in their quarrel we are with both equally.

261 The first recognition . . . For Norah's compunction, see 54; struggles, 74, 97; sadness and despair, 74–6. Mr Mackenzie's : 17–23.

262 Julia thinks Horsfield . . . For points about Horsfield, see eg 63 (sad but not subdued); 27, 31 (lonely); 28 (deficient in the love of humanity); 111 (desiring human contact); 110 (sensitive); 66–7 (feels detachment and irritation but asks her to dine); 36, 64 (gives her money); 117 (sentimental); 112 (wants to cry).

263 Despite this end . . . For Mr Horsfield recognising his similarity to Julia, see 31. There are, however . . . For important similarities between Mr Horsfield and Julia, see 28, 34 (joie de vivre, illusion of art); 32, 35 (longing for drink and feeling of understanding).

267 Not only Julia's . . . For similarities between Julia and her mother, see eg 70 (beautiful), 76 (unhappy in England).

269 And the narrative . . . For Julia's irrational hopes, see 45, 131; vague, fixed and unseeing eyes, 37, 42, 63, 99, 120; under a spell, 84.

272 All the rest ... For friendly trees, see 9, 76, 115; for thin, stunted etc see 89, 93, 127, 135.

273 I began by ... For Julia's and Norah's meetings, see 51-5, 74, 97.

276 For the heroine's ... For Anna's room, see VID 113; Marya's in the studio, Q 44, in the cottage, Q 77. The old woman who lives upstairs in ALMM, 11, 137; Julia on the top floor, 109-110. Sasha on the top floor in Paris, GMM 125; the mulatto woman in London, GMM 80.

PART TWO, CHAPTER THREE

279 Mackenzie was published ... Mellown 23-4; reviews in EA. (*Daily Telegraph* 30 Jan 1931; *Observer* 8 Feb 1931; *Saturday Review of Literature* 25 July 1931; *NY Evening Post* 26 June 1931; *The Times* and *TLS* 5 Mar 1931; *Nottingham Journal & Express* 27 Feb 1931; *Boston Transcript* 29 Aug 1931.)
This was bad ... *Sat Rev of Lit, Daily Tel, NY Eve Post, Observer* reviews cited; also *Yorkshire Evening Post* 20 Feb 1931 and *Evening News* 6 Feb 1931.
And of course ... GR to J, 15 Nov 1928; *Evening News* 6 Feb 1931 (Swinnerton); *Yorks Eve Post* 20 Feb 1931 (Hoult).

280 Quotation: *Daily Tel* 30 Jan 1931.
Jean got her ... Ivan Bede to J, 2 Feb 1931; AS interviews; L 20, n1; Sch V. I deduce that J's fan letters for ALMM were her first from the fact that there are no earlier ones in EA.
Another man ... Note on the Jean Rhys letters by OS, Tulsa Item 3:13.
The first ... L 19; EB interview with author, 29 Oct 1984.
Yet almost ... J and PK had another row in 1941 (see L 35) after which there are again no letters until 1945 (see L 39, which suggests that their last meeting 'wasn't too happy', and that J will now seem a stranger to PK.) From 1945 to the early 50s they remained in touch, though there were quarrels here too (see L 245); but then there was another big row, this time over money (see L 92-3). Finally PK found J again in 1957, and they wrote affectionately to each other in the last year of PK's life.

281 Quotation: J to PK, 'Monday' [1931].
She had had only ... L 19n1; EB interview with author; L 45, 93.
At the same time ... L 45, 55-6, 70-82; note as previous para.
Jean was finding ... Callard, Chapter 23; L 32-4. ES was in America during most of 1932-3 and 1935-6; even when she was in England she was often in Suffolk (Callard).

282 Evelyn Scott ... L 21, n1; Callard 97-8, 126, 189. On ES's quarrelsomeness, see Callard passim, eg 70.
Evelyn's experience ... Callard 1, 5, 36, 57, 121, 125.
The difference ... Callard 39, 83, 116. Callard doesn't say ES was a bad writer, but everything he does say shows it.
She first ... L 21.
For the next ... Callard 125; L 34; ES to LTS, 29 Sept, probably 1934; Carole Hill (agent) to LTS, 18 Oct 1934; undated letter ES to J, probably 1932.

283 Quotation: ES to J, 22 Jan, probably 1934 (because ES was correcting proofs of *Breathe Upon Those Slain*, published in 1934.)
It was well ... ES to LTS, 29 Sept [1934].
In 1931 ... ALMM 45.
It was rather like ... GMM 96; ALMM 31; AS interview 24 Aug 1984.
It was never ... AS interviews; HH to 'Pauline', 2 May 1985 (copy sent to author by D Pet, by kind permission of HH); addresses on J's letters of the '30s; L 24-5.

Footnote: AS interviews; Rev Tilden Smith will (after the death of his wife half his property should go, he says, to LTS, 'except what has already been given which will not count').

284 Jean — divided ... See M & W.

Leslie read ... AS interviews; HH letter to 'Pauline'.

Leslie's daughter ... AS interviews; HH letter to 'Pauline'; HH letters to ATS, 19 and 22 Nov 1980 (copies sent to author by D Pet, by kind permission of HH.) Jean was clearly ... Ibid.; RW to author, 29 Feb 1987.

But why? ... ALMM 45. EB, eg, is quite adamant that J and LTS loved each other and were, in their good moments, very happy together (EB interview and letter 11 Nov 1984.)

285 Partly it was ... AS interviews; L 29, 152, 261; Imp Rd 11; J to SO, 3 May 1971; MM in Bailey radio and interview with author; MM to AS, 30 July 1968.

And then, Leslie ... AS interviews; MM interview; AS letter to author, 9 July 1985. ATS said LTS was 'too kind by half' (HH letter, 27 Nov 1980.)

Footnote: L 38; AS interviews; HH to ATS, 27 Nov 1980; Michael Leigh to LTS, 16 July 1945; EB to author, 11 Nov 1984 ('he was a very sweet man, subtle and clever himself'.) Michael Leigh wrote half a dozen novels in the 40s and 50s, one of which he intended to dedicate to LTS (but in the event didn't). He died in the US in 1965 (letter to author from his agent, David Higham, 4 Dec 1985).

286 At the beginning ... AS interviews; 'JBS'.

Anne is also ... AS interviews.

And yet ... L 21; Gini Stevens article, p 6; HH to ATS, 27 Nov 1980; FW to author in several conversations, eg 29 Oct 1988.

People have always ... See eg Phyllis Rose, 'Jean Rhys in Fact and Fiction', *Yale Review*, Summer 1980, pages 596-602 : 'Which is the real "fact" — that she was married three times, or the loneliness which permeates the novels? ... if she was almost continually married in her adult life, why does she always portray herself in her fiction as alone?' (p 600).

Jean began Voyage ... L 21-2, n2; L 281. In Tulsa LS draft No 53 J wrote that she rushed back to London from a visit to Paris to begin VID. In the Bk Ex Bk, p 69, she wrote : 'I've been working for a year at a book about Paris' (GMM), and 'I have been drinking heavily — Well I've been drinking for the last six years.' She wrote GMM from 1937-1938; going back six years means that by 1932 her drinking had become 'heavy' in her own admission.

287 For the last few ... MK mtg; JL Preface to B; L 283. J said that JL hadn't tried to find a publisher, and JL that she insisted it be published.

This was ... Frank Swinnerton to J, 9 Jan and 21 Jan 1932; Norah Hoult to J, 5 Apr 1932; Rebecca West to J, 8 Apr 1932; LTS to JL, 1 May 1932 (copy sent to author by E vd W); Mellown 145, 147-8.

It was a very ... L 283; MK mtg.

The episode ... L 283; SP 15; GR to J, 12 Sept 1927.

Because, I think ... MK pointed out to me this previous co-operation at a difficult point (MK to author, 26 June 1986.)

288 This question goes ... MK, 'Dutch Connection', 165-6; MK letter to author 26 June 1986. Five stories from LB appear more or less complete in *Aan Den Loopenden Band* : R de l'A as 'Dolly', BB as 'Carlo', LGF as 'Fifi', and 'From a French Prison' as 'Gevangenisbezoek'. 'Een Schrijver' combines 'The Grey Day', the first few pages of V, and Hunger. 'Mado' combines various episodes from Q, and 'Nocturne' draws heavily on it. 'Suzanne' is a translation of 'Susan and Suzanne', and 'Houdia' a version of 'Houdia'. (Information from MK, Dutch Connection 165, mtg and letter 18 Jan 1987.)

He was certainly ... MK mtg; MK 'Dutch Connection' 165; HvE to Bibeb in interview with JL (MK bibliog 12); Victor van Vriesland, review of ALMM in *Kroniek van het Proza* II, *Nieuwe Rotterdamsche Courant*, 24 Sept 1932 (MK bibliog 1); MM unpublished interview with MK, 3 Nov 1981, reported in MK bibliog (12).

In 1977 ... Zuidinga; DA to author, 20 Dec 1985.

I think most ... MK mtg; DA to author, 20 Dec 1985; 'Jean Rhys, Romancière Inconnue', *Les Nouvelles Littéraires*, No 880, 26 Aug 1939, p 8, by Edouard de Néve; JL to J, 17 Jan 1940; MM in MK, 'Dutch Connection', 166; MK to author, 26 June 1986; 'The Poet' and 'Vengeance' in EA. 'Vengeance' is Tulsa Item 1:4. J mentions that Hughes Massie was once her agent, 'ages ago' (L 105).

289 During the rest ... Mellown 50; MK mtg; MK letters to author, 14 Jan 1987, 18 Jan 1987, 20 Aug 1988; MK 'Dutch Connection' 163-4.

It is just ... MM interview; MK mtg. (Re JL being high-handed, lying and stealing when he needed to, but not from his comrades.)

290 By the end ... MK mtg; MK letter to author, 11 Nov 1986; E vd W to author, 11 Jan 1989; Zuidinga p 4.

In later life ... 'The Dividing Line'; P Rev 265; DA in SP 11; FW in L 20 n1; JvH, H in C, p 3; J to MM, 7 May 1971.

In their marriage ... WSS 121, 150. JL's decree of divorce from his second wife was made absolute on 16 Jan 1925, just as J was beginning her affair with FMF. (Date from E vd W, 20 Dec 1988.)

291 In September 1933 ... MK mtg; AS interviews; Bk Ex Bk 69, 71. JL would put all this into Sch V : Leslie Bead's family's disapproval of Helen; Helen's much increased drinking, so that when Jan comes to discuss divorce with her he finds she has 'become an alcoholic, and is sliding irrevocably towards her final destruction.' (Quoted in MK bibliog, 8.)

At one point ... L 22. The letter is undated, but sounds like spring or summer, with larks and foals on the downs. And see L 27, to ES in Dec 1935 : 'As to the drawbacks of trying to stop drinking – well I know a little about that too!!' But the rest ... L 23. I am guessing that the depression J refers to in her Feb 1934 letter is a different one from the one she mentions in the undated letter of the year before. This one sounds like a winter depression (one reason was the weather – 'a yellow fog, very cold'), whereas the 1933 one sounds (see note above) a spring or summer one. Clearly a good deal of time has elapsed between the two letters, and I doubt J would refer to a long-past bout of depression to the same person (ES) again.

Re VID being J's favourite novel : see eg H in C, Vreeland and Robertson interviews.

When he asked ... 'JBS'; DRW interviews.

She was forty-three ... DRW interviews.

Footnote: MM interview.

292 On 19 February ... Marriage certificate; 'To Leslie', written on old, yellowing paper in pencil in J's early middle hand ('30s –'40s would by my guess), EA; 'JBS'; AS interviews.

They were extraordinarily ... J's letters, L, Tulsa and EA, 1934; L 25; MK mtg; AS interviews; ALMM 101.

Footnote 2: L 25.

293 But Owen's return ... DRW interviews.

Perhaps Jean ... Ibid. J certainly knew that Owen was struggling in the '50s : 'I've *one* nice brother but he is poor,' she wrote to SvD in 1953 (L 109).

In the end ... L 27; SP 36, 41; DRW interviews; Brenda Lockhart death certificate and will; GMM 36.

A month after ... Fanny Smith and Rev Tilden Smith wills; L 27.

Well, Evelyn ... and quotation L 24.

294 Leslie took ... L 22, 24–5. In 'The Dividing Line' J says that 'Chatto & Windus turned it down' and doesn't mention the others. LTS may well have tried Chatto's too, as they'd published *Postures*. But J's contemporary account is more likely to be accurate than her memory forty years later.

Nancy Hemond Brown, who has made a valuable study of the changes J made to VID, believes that Cape reluctantly accepted, and advertised, the novel (as *Two Tunes*) before there was the dispute about the ending and 'Cape withdrew from the contract' (see Nancy Hemond Brown, 'An Edition of the Original Ending of Jean Rhys's Voyage in the Dark', p2). But she bases this on the letter to ES of Feb 1934 (L 24), which doesn't seem to me to imply acceptance, but rather rejection; and on a letter to SvD written in 1963. But J's memory is notoriously fallible, especially after so many years. There is a contract for *Two Tunes* with Constable in EA, and it was with Constable that J had the dispute about the ending. I know of no evidence that there was ever any other contract for the novel.

At last ... L 25; 'The Dividing Line'.

Jean was frantic ... L 25.

For one thing ... VID Part IV, Tulsa Item 1:11; 'Dividing Line'.

295 Jean insisted ... DA interviews; L 233, 236, 279; DA to Nancy Hemond Brown, 6 July 1984, in Brown, 'An Edition ...' p 4. J sent the original ending of VID to SvD, who was adapting the novel to a play (L 238). Bits of the original ending J used for WSS were eg the mother brushing her hair (p 209, WSS 119) and Père Lilièvre's house (p 211 and WSS 86). For an argument that J continued to prefer the original ending, see Brown p 4. FW, however, agrees with DA that she did not (Brown, same p.)

As she told it ... 'Dividing Line'.

Quotation 1: Tulsa 1:1, p 226.

Quotation 2: VID 159.

296 Later on ... H in C; Vreeland and Robertson interviews; draft for SP dated 14 Mar 1974, EA.

PART TWO, CHAPTER FOUR

315 There are two things ... For Anna constantly telling us what time it is, see 43, 81, 82, 111, 122, 130, 133, 145, 155.

For clocks, see 11 (Southsea); 30 (Judd Street); 76 (Anna's last night with Walter); 104 (Ritz Plaza Hotel); 156 (on the night with the white-faced man, and on the night of the abortion.)

319 First, she made ... For Walter's disapproving expression bracketing the affair, see 17 and 85.

328 The nicest people ... For Uncle Bo's not being a gentleman, see 55. The person we know had several illegitimate children was, of course, J's brother Owen. I came across no suggestions that Owen drank; but apart from this I wonder whether J may have based Uncle Bo on him (and 'He's nice, I like him much better than my other brother' would fit too. See L 109 : 'I've *one* nice brother'.)

PART TWO, CHAPTER FIVE

335 VID was a success ... *Sunday Times*, 11 Nov 1934; *Yorkshire Post*, 31 Oct 1934; *Women's Weekly*, 12 Jan 1935; *Harper's Bazaar*, Nov 1934; *Times Literary Supplement*, 1 Nov 1934; *NY Times*, 17 Mar 1935; *Saturday Review*, 1 Dec 1934; *NY Herald Tribune Books* 17 Mar 1935; *The Lady*, 8 Nov 1934; Other clippings and reviews in EA.

Jean's old admirers ... and quotation: *Dublin Magazine*, Jan 1935; *Observer*

advertisement, 4 Nov 1934; *Book Society News*, undated clipping in EA, 1934.
Even readers agreed ... Staley 16, Callard 126, Mellown 42.
1934 had really ... RL interview (for 'The literary world admired her ...')

336 One day Leslie ... Jessica Mitford, *Hons and Rebels* (Penguin) 74-5, 81ff, 88,
91; RW conversation with author 21 Feb 1987; AS interview 20 August 1984;
FW to author, 24 Aug 1984; J to AS, 27 May 1973 (Tulsa 3:1).
For a few weeks ... *Hons and Rebels*, 108, 141, 145, 150, 245.
Jean's second ... RL interview (for 'a difficult point ...').

337 VID had come out ... Mellown 37; RL to J 21 Jan 1935 (EA); FW to author.
On the appointed day ... RL interview, letter to author 16 Feb 1986 and
telephone conversations 23 Feb and 14 Mar 1986; FW to author (for 'Beatrix
Lehmann ... had suddenly winked at her').
Footnote: Information on Violet Hammersley from Harold Acton, *Nancy
Mitford : A Memoir*, 67-69, 160.

338 Nonetheless, and though ... EB interview with author; RL letter to author; RL
to J, 21 Jan 1935 (EA).
1935 was the year ... RL interview; RL to J, 'Monday' (EA).
Rosamond was ... RL to J, Ibid; RL interview.
When she arrived ... and Afterwards ... RL interview and letter.
She was trying ... 'JBS'; RL interview.
She stayed only ... RL interview.

339 It was now ... The meeting in the Café Royal had been in June 1935; in Feb
1936 J and LTS left Bury Street.
She knew it ... Bk Ex Bk 69, 71.
Quotation: GMM 37.
Everyone else ... RL interview; AS interviews; DA interviews.
John knew it ... Victor van Vriesland review of Sch V (quoted in MK
bibliography, 8); Bibeb interview with Jean, quoted in MK bibliography 12.
Footnote: GMM 37.

340 This comes ... and The novel's ... The story of Sch V told to author by MK.
See also MK, 'Q and WWM', loc. cit., 8, for Helen in Sch V as 'a devastating,
but probably realistic portrait' of J.
It's just like ... 'JBS'.
Leslie knew ... AS interviews.

341 Between VID and ... Bk Ex Bk 69.
These two stories ... As in the literary critical chapters, page references are not
given for the two stories under discussion.

343 Footnote: TS 207; Q7; GMM 51; 'LM', CS 58-9.

345 The obvious Leslie ... JL had intended to publish an article by LTS in his
*Chronicle of Contemporary Art and Culture* in 1935, but didn't do so. (MK to
author, 20 Aug 1988.)
Well, he was ... J to ES, 23 June 1931, L 21; FW to author; Gini Stevens article,
6.
Footnote: AS to DA, 27 Jan 1967; AS to author.

346 Quotation 1: ('People write ...') Bk Ex Bk 12.
And in the Black ... and quotation 2: Bk Ex Bk 96-99.
The self-hatred ... Bk Ex Bk 1 for original initials. It looks as though
underneath 'GRW' Jean had first written 'L' (for Leslie').

347 From ALMM ... O Nbk (EA) 15; Bk Ex Bk 12.
Rosamond arranged ... Bow Street Police Court records, 14 June 1935, Greater
London Record Office and History Library; RL interview; RL to J, 'Sat.
morning', EA; FW to author, 29 Oct 1988.
Jean's decline ... L 26-7.

349 There was also ... MK mtg; L 284. The appeal for help for JL was published
on 8 May 1935.
John soon hated ... Ibid; LTS to AS, 11 June 1936 (Tulsa 3:1); AS interview;
Bibeb interview with Jean (in Kappers bibliography 12); JL to J, 9 Nov. 1945.
One can't help ... See MK, 'Q and WWM', loc. cit, 9, for the suggestion that
Jean would not have known about the contents of Sch V because she could not
read Dutch.
Footnote: MK 'Dutch Connection' 161; Zuidinga, quoted in MK bibliography
13; MM to J, 7 May 1971; L 28.

350 In September ... L 27.
And in fact ... WSS 107. For Dominica striking J more than anything she'd
seen since she left it, see the photographs in EA: she kept over 100 from this trip.

351 First she and Leslie ... L 28; J to SO, 3 May 1971.
Maryvonne had ... LTS to AS, 21 Feb 1936 (copy sent to author); J to SO, 3
May 1971.
Was she even ... J to SO, same letter; MM to AS, 30 July 1968. (Tulsa 3:1); MM
interview; 'The daughter about the mother', Zuidinga. J had been just under and
just over fourteen when her father got his leave between May and December
1904; in February 1936 MM was three months short of fourteen.
After this brief ... AS interviews. Anne placed this animated family farewell at
the earlier point (J and LTS flying to Paris and Holland); but this sort of detail
is very easy to confuse, and I think it was more likely to have been at the second
departure, to the West Indies.
The Cuba ... and next three paras: LTS to AS, 29 Feb 1936 (copy sent to author).

352 Now Acton ... 'TWB', CS 396-397; ALMM 74; L 28.
Jean and Leslie ... 'TWB'; LTS to AS, 29 Feb 1936 and 19 Mar 1936 (Tulsa 3;1);
DA to author, 16 Jan 1986.

353 The hotel was ... 'TWB'; LTS to AS, 19 Mar 1936; Leigh Fermor 99.
But even here ... LTS to AS, 19 Mar 1936.
One of the first ... 'BF', SIOL 33, CS 291; Imp Rd (EA) 5; D Ag interview with
author.
Quotation: Mother Mount Calvary to Jean, 31 Mar 1936, E.A. And see 'BF',
SIOL 33, CS 291.
It was a sad ... 'BF', SIOL 33-4, CS 291-2; 'Imp Rd' (E.A.) 7; WSS 46.
In the Good Mother's ... 'Imp Rd' 7; SP 71, 73; D Ag interview; 'TP', PMS 81,
CS 268.

354 Jean was unhappy ... L 28; LTS to AS, 22 Apr 1936 (copy sent to author).
Hampstead was also the name of a nearby village (information from PP). But
there is still an estate called Hampstead there, which is now owned by the
government (D Ag.). Similarly, LTS refers to the Ashpittels' estate as Melville
Hall, which was also the name of its village (and the present site of the island's
airport). Hampstead used to belong to the MacIntyre family, friends and indeed
relatives of the Lockharts (D Ag).
They stayed ... 'Imp Rd' 9-10; 'TP'; LTS to AS, 22 Apr and 25 May 1936
(copies sent to author); photographs in EA.
Yet very soon ... L 28-29; AS interviews.
The lady of ... PP; D Ag; L 29. Elma Napier settled in Dominica in 1932 (D
Ag, who is her daughter).

355 Naturally she ... L29.
This can't have been ... D Ag interview; LTS to AS, 22 Apr 1936; L 29.
The other couple ... LTS to AS, 22 Apr and 25 May 1936; L 29.
She became convinced ... 'Imp Rd' 5, 10, 11; 'TP' 82, CS 268; LTS to AS, 1 June
1936 (Tulsa 3:1).

Footnote: See 'TP' 82 (CS 268) and WSS 30-3. J told FW and DA that she began 'TP' in Dominica (J to FW, 1 May 1964, to DA 3 May 1967).

356 This was mostly ... 'Imp Rd' 1.

She wasn't allowed ... WSS 87-8; 'Imp Rd', 9.

The climax ... and next two paras: 'Imp Rd'. WSS quotation from page 33.

By now it was ... Oscar was born around 1916, and died around 1980; Mona died early, in her thirties (Information from EW, letter to author Dec 1985).

357 Now it was Jean's ... VID 55; WSS 24-5; LTS to AS, 1 June 1936; EW letters to author, Aug 1985; D Ag and Rosalind Smith interview, Dec 1986.

The last thing ... LTS to AS, 1 June; D Ag interview; SP 38; photographs in EA.

Quotation: SP 38.

The word 'nothing' ... WSS 38.

358 Quotation: 'BF', SIOL 36, CS 294.

This was Jean's ... Bk Ex Bk 36-7.

From Dominica ... LTS to AS, 25 May and 11 June 1936; L 31; AS interviews; GMM 29.

Evelyn Scott ... Callard 150; J to SvD, 25 Aug 1963 (Tulsa 2:7); L 32, 33: J to DA, 29 May 1964; ES to Dr Lewin, 'Saturday' [1936] (EA); Q 143.

God knows ... L 32, 34; Callard 168, 173, 179-80; Callard to FW, 25 Jan 1982.

Footnote: D Ag letter to author 2 Dec 1986.

359 Jean spent most ... L 30-1. J's pattern of falling and hurting herself had probably already started the year before, if not earlier. Rosamond Lehmann had noticed a black eye at their second meeting, around Jubilee time; and later that summer J would hurt a wrist (L 26). But August 1936 is the first time a hospital is mentioned.

She always hated ... L 30-1; VID 89. The story set in a nursing home is 'Rap Rap'.

Clearly, she was ... L 31.

Quotation: L 32.

360 But there was ... 'TSP', TABL 13, CS 126.

Jean's family ... DRW interviews; J to FW, 1 May 1964; AS interviews. Rev Tilden Smith's will mentions a sum around £10,000; but then there was that 'more' that was discovered later. Staley (who presumably got it from Jean) mentions £8,000 (page 16).

Phyllis Tilden Smith ... AS interviews, and letter to author, 29 Sept 1984; L 31.

Number 22 ... L 31; EB interview with author 29 Oct 1984; estate agent's advertisement ('a garden in the seventeenth century').

361 It was in this happier ... EB interview; L 26 and 255.

Already in 1936 ... EB interview and letter to author, 11 Nov 1984.

Like many people ... L 177; Bk Ex Bk 72-3; RW telephone conversation, 21 Feb 1987; EB interview and letter.

Eliot knew ... EB interview; J to EB, 20 Dec 1978 (copy in EA).

362 Jean's capacity ... EB interview.

Quotation GMM 78.

Of course this was ... EB interview; OS and Mollie Stoner interview, 24 Nov 1984; FW, L 12.

Eliot Bliss ... EB interview.

363 One more thing ... EB interview and letter.

She knew them ... AS interviews; JL to J, 1945 (EA).

In the Paultons ... L 33, 137 n.1.

She'd been back ... 'The Dividing Line', SP draft, EA; 'LS' draft, Tulsa No. 53; L 22; S les V 85; J to LTS, 'Dear-dear', undated, from Paris, EA.

364 One was with ... 'LS' draft, Tulsa No. 53; GMM 131; 'APS', No. 1.
In early March 1930 ... A. Sawi to J, 6 Mar 1930. Judith Thurman ('The Mistress and the Mask', *MS*, Jan 1976, pages 50–52 and 81) also guesses that René is Moroccan.
Footnote: Letters in EA; RW to author (on Toni de Boissière).

365 The most important ... L 137. J kept a card advertising SS's Dec 1936 exhibition (now in EA): this may mean she'd met him then (or even before), but of course he could also have given it to her later.
The original of 'Serge' ... and She bought ... Benézit (1976), 499–500; Bouret; letters SS to J, EA; GMM 83–4, 90.

366 Quotation: GMM 84.
Jean had another ... GMM 11, 12.
Footnote: Bouret; letter to author from M Bouret's publisher, Editions Ides et Calendes, Neuchâtel, Switzerland, 10 July 1986.

367 The last months ... AS interviews; letter to author from MR, 15 July 1985; 'Kikimora', SIOL 93–99, CS 331–334.
It's like her lie ... GMM 128.
Footnote: SP 147; SP draft for 'Paris', EA; letter to author from Centre de documentation juive, Paris, 9 Dec 1985.

368 Very likely Jean ... 'The Dividing Line', SP draft, EA; Phyllis Rose in *Yale Review*, page 598; Bk Ex Bk 69, 72; 'Start of a short story' (EA), dated 14.9.38; L 137; Zuidinga, 'The daughter about the mother.' In the Bk Ex Bk J says that she has worked on GMM for 'a year'; then slips into memories of childhood, of part of which 'Start of a short story' is a typed version. See Note on dating of the Bk Ex Bk.
With the irresistible ... Bk Ex Bk 69,70,74; L 137–8.
It was done ... L 23, 138, 277; Bk Ex Bk 70; DA interview with author, 17 Aug 1983: MM told her, when J was refusing to let go of WSS: 'You must just take it. That's what Leslie did. There'd be a dreadful row and she would nearly kill him, but it would be done, and next day she would be quite happy and have forgotten all about it. That's how several of her earlier books were "finished".'
At first ... Bk Ex Bk 70–1.

369 She and Leslie left ... Nigel Sligh to J, 7 May 1938; LTS driving licence for Oct. 1938-October 1939, EA.
John, for instance ... MK mtg; Bibeb interview with JL, MK bibliography 11.
Maryvonne of course ... J to SO, 3 May 1971; PSA, 'Jean Rhys: A tribute', *Kunapipi* Vol 1, No. 2, 1979, page 24; MM in Zuidinga; MM interview with author.
Maryvonne also ... MM interview.
Footnote: PSA in *Kunapipi*; PSA letter to author, 25 Mar 1983; LH, DS, 176–7.

370 What had happened ... Minna Rees Williams death certificate; DRW interviews; JRW interview; MM interview; AS interviews; LTS to AS, 22 Apr 1936 (copy sent to author).
There were only two ... DRW interviews; JB interviews; Clarice Rees Williams and Neville Williams death records. Clarice died on 5 Dec 1938, Neville on 11 Jan 1944. Clarice had been living on the south coast for some years before her death; Owen and Dorothy didn't go to her funeral, so it's very likely no one else of the family did either.
Owen worked in an office for some time, but was often reduced to part-time work, for example selling vacuum cleaners at the Ideal Home Exhibition; his last job was as a museum porter at £2.10 a week. Dorothy became a shorthand writer on Hansard (DRW interviews; LTS to AS, 22 Apr 1936).
What Jean was ... AS interviews; Bk Ex Bk.

Thus eg the nightmare became Antoinette's in almost every word. 'Mr HH' became 'Bday' and then 'GMGR'. Her lists of children's names and clothes for her trousseau went into 'GMGR'; memories of children, especially their dislike and cruelty, went into 'TDTBTB'; her fears of Meta and of insects went into SP. She never published her memories of her mother beating her — except, as I've suggested, in Lise in GMM.

371 Later she said ... L 39, 40n, 153, 213; DA in Bailey radio; Vreeland 235; Polly Devlin, 116; MM in Zuidinga.

I think that ... AS interviews; L 213. This is evidently what happened in 1957 with SvD — the idea came back to J. See L 143, 213.

The punishment ... L 213. And see eg L 239 for the struggle of transforming J's pieces of paper into a tidy typescript.

372 That was the first ... 4 Jan 1957 to SvD (Tulsa 2:6): '... the plan of a new novel carefully drawn up in 1939'... It was to be called *Wedding in the Carib Quarter*. See also L 213, where Jean recalls *Le Revenant* and WCQ together.

This is an extraordinary ... J to FW, 1 May 1964; plan for WCQ, copy given to author by DP.

Then (Jean told FW ...) J to FW, Ibid; Bk Ex Bk 68. She took out the plan for WCQ at least twice, once in July 1962 (see L 213) and once in May 1964. Quotation: Plan for WCQ.

Why was this ... O Nbk (EA) 48, 52; WSS 152.

373 It was only sparsely ... L 34; reviews in EA (and see Mellown 53–55). Quotations from advertisement in *Sunday Times*, 14 May 1939; *Sunday Times* 11 June 1939. Frank Swinnerton's review was in the *Observer*, 23 Apr 1939.

And if the English ... L 171, 277; Thérèse Aubray to JL, 12 Jan 1940 (EA). John Lehmann tried to find a French publisher for GMM too (see L 59, 138). It was finally published in France in 1969, and in the United States in 1970 (Mellown 8, 64).

She reeled ... AS interviews. And see L 66, 97, 138, 277.

Silence would have ... GMM 137; L 44; Bk Ex Bk 73.

374 Quotation: 1 ( ... Not for hope ...): Bk Ex Bk 72–3.

Quotation: 2 ( ... I was afraid ...): Gr Ex Bk 32–36.

The price of ... Gr Ex Bk 32, 33, 40–1.

Finally, in the last ... Gr Ex Bk 34, 37–8, 39.

375 Quotation: Gr Ex Bk 39.

In this notebook ... Gr Ex Bk 35. The other great notebook is the RD, published in SP (pages 157–173).

PART TWO, CHAPTER SIX

378 'I know about myself ...' For Sasha imagining squalor and cruelty, see 33, 45; for her knowing the sane explanations, 41, 47–8, 56–7; for her being sulky, loud, surly, aggressive, 52, 59, 78; for her letting people down, 54; for her drinking herself to death, 30, 37; for her still trying, 89; for her going into bars to get drunk, 89; for drink making her quarrelsome, 102; for its making her look nice only for an instant, 150, and then awful, 142.

379 The novel is full of ... For eyes being everywhere, 'arrogant', 'glassy', etc. see 13, 17, 19, 22, 35; for 'most human beings have cruel eyes', 81; for looks being everywhere etc., 11, 87, 133; for people looking at Sasha, 43, 76.

388 GMM brings to a climax ... For Sasha twice seeing herself in mad or drunk old women, see 36, 37–8.

390 Finally, there are the central images ... For clocks stopping Sasha, see 29, 95; for Sasha's not being able to live in the present, see 84; except when she's happy, 96; not being able to imagine the future, 114; trying not to remember the past,

14; getting drunk to abolish time, 121; not believing in change, 56; stopping things because she wants to; falling into blackness, 144. See also the image of the whirlpool, 38.

392 We've seen how Jean ... See also, for J laughing at Sasha, her identification with the 'good young man' in the film, 90.

395 Now, this split ... For Sasha being unable to fill in the hotel register, see 13; for laughing in the right places in the cinema, see 15; for buying a ticket in the Luxembourg Gardens, see 46.
Sasha is thus the most blocked ... For Sasha determining not to remember and immediately remembering, see 14–15; determining not to cry and immediately crying, 24; trying to destroy herself, can't, 37; not wanting to go back to London but does, 36; not planning to marry but does, 96; wanting a calm book and getting a lurid one, 111; wanting a new room but keeping the old one, 31ff; wanting to avoid hostile cafés and going to them, 40, 42, 60.

403 This aspect of the novel ... For Sasha's attack on Mr Blank, see 26: 'Did I say all this? Of course not. I didn't even think it.'


PART THREE, CHAPTER ONE

411 Until the summer ... See L 34, 99; J to SO, 3 May 1971; JL to J, 17 Jan 1940 (EA); JvH, 'H in C'. J dated MM's return wrongly to JvH ('May 1940'); she was already back in Holland in January as JL's letter shows.
'I didn't exactly ... J to DA, 3 Jan 1967. She gave exactly the same abridged account of the war to OS in 1953: 'I was living in Chelsea when the war broke out, then Leslie my husband joined up – the RAF. We wandered about the country a bit, but were back in London for the fly bombs, and those other horrible affairs the V2s. Leslie died suddenly in 1945 ...' (L 99).

412 First, she said ... Record of service of Flying Officer Leslie Tilden Smith MA (77703), sent to author from MOD RAF PMC 26 July 1985. J's being in Holt by August 1940 is established by the newspaper report quoted on page 413; her having moved on to Norwich by spring 1941 is established by her letter to PK of 21 March.
Well, something ... PSA in *Kunapipi* (for MM). For J keeping the time of real events, eg beginning Anna's affair at the end of a tour, in the autumn, ending it in an autumn, and ending the stay at Ethel's in a spring; ending Marya's affair, and Stephan's prison sentence in the summer. In these cases J kaleidoscoped years: it was the weather in the background of events which she kept rather than their duration. But that is what she would have done here, with 'June'. For Laura breaking down in a June: alternative titles for 'ISAS' in the O Nbk were 'There Were Roses That June' and 'Wonderful Roses That June'.
In any case we know ... That 'TP' dates from J's time in Holt is clear from internal evidence: the evacuated small east coast public school was Gresham's in Holt ('TP' PMS 69, CS 256.)

413 Quotation: *Norwich Mercury and People's Weekly Journal*, Sat 1 Aug 1940, page 6. This time J pleaded Guilty.
It's terrible ... Quotation from 'TIW', SIOL 126, CS 351.
This other was ... 'TP' 69–73, CS 256–260.
'Even the trees ...' O Nbk 57–59; 'TP' 70, 72, CS 257, 258; BL ADD 57858, pages 144–146. See also 'ISAS' PMS 61, CS 249: 'I am very unpopular in this town', in Laura's exercise book.

414 Everyone knew ... BL ADD 57858, page 147; 'ISAS' 53–5, 62, 64–5, CS 242–4, 250–4; 'TP' 72, CS 259.
Quotations: BL ADD 57858, page 149.

415 Her swelling obsessions ... BL ADD 57858, pages 147-156; O Nbk 56.
Quotation: O Nbk 56, 57.
'Temps Perdi' ... 'TP' 70-1, 78, 88, CS 257, 264, 274.
Then, in 'ISAS'... 'ISAS' 56, CS 245.
Footnote O Nbk 25 ('What! No Trumpets?'), 26, 42, 61 (connections to 'ISAS'),
60 ('you simply cannot imagine ...'); 'ISAS' 53-54, CS 242-3.

416 But the result ... 'ISAS' 53, 60, 64, CS 242, 249, 252.
Thus, Jean's machine ... 'ISAS' 58, 60, CS 247, 249.
Quotation: 'ISAS' 59-60, CS 248-9.

417 Apart from being ... 'ISAS' 62, CS 250-1 ('Here's Emily Brontë ...').
Thus 'October ...' 'TP' 70, CS 257. E Gr remembers that Jean had made a
suicide attempt before coming to the Feasts in the summer of 1941 (E Gr to
author, 19 July and 12 Aug 1985).
Quotation: 'ASH', TABL 129-30, CS 229.

418 At the very end ... PRev 271.
Quotation 1: ('The paddle ...') ASH, TABL 130, CS 230.
Quotation 2: ('Shall I tell ...') BL ADD 57858, page 86 (page 11 of J's typescript
of 'ASH').
Perhaps Jean... See 'ISAS' 66, CS 255.

419 By March 1941 ... L 35; BCa to author, 3 June 1985; E Gr to author 19 July
and 12 Aug 1985; 'ASH', TABL 130-1, CS 230-1.
'Her main trouble ...' to 'It's one of the most ...' (420): L 35, J referred to
what she had said as 'my quite unforgivable reaction'... The next letter in their
correspondence was from J to PK in 1945 (L 39). When EB asked PK for J's
address during the war, PK was silent: EB thought she was trying to keep J to
herself, but more likely PK simply didn't have it (and was, perhaps, still
smarting). (EB interview with author.)
Footnote: DA interviews with author; SP drafts (EA); DW 53-55.

420 Two days after... LHS obituaries and funeral notice in *The Times*, eg 25 Mar
1941, page 8, 27 Mar 1941, page 7, 28 Mar 1941, page 7, 2 Apr 1941 page 7;
Funeral Service Programme, Church of St John the Baptist, Garboldisham, 26
Mar 1941, sent to author by Lady Alethea Eliot; AB interview and letters.
She was so low ... PSA to author, 25 Mar 1983; BCa and E Gr, letters to author;
WF letters to JH, 15 Sept 1979 and 31 Oct 1980. The Rev Willis Mansfield Feast
(b.1902) was Rector of Booton with Brandiston from 1935 to 1971 (*Crockford's
Clerical Directory*).
He called on Jean ... WF to JH (sent to author by JH).
There were often ... BCa to author; WF to JH.

421 She was now fifty ... to end of section (423): BCa, E Gr and WF letters.

422 This time her circumstances ... See also PSA to J, 19 Sept 1941 (EA): 'I imagine
the new flat must be rather nice'; L 106 ('as much fun as the next woman really').

423 Jean stayed in Thorpe ... Record of Service, LTS; letter to author from the
Librarian of the RAF Museum, 14 Feb 1986; AS interviews; 'ISAS' 53, CS 242.
Leslie stayed ... Record of Service; E Gr to author; 'TIW', SIOL 125, 133, CS
350, 357. Audrey's visit to Roberta in TIW is very like Norry's visit to her ex-
chorus girl friend Billie in 'Kismet', set during Jean's first affair (Kis 102, 104).
Monica is rather like the girl or girls J knew in London when she was young,
Jenny of TS or Estelle of TSP: 'an optimist' (TIW 126, CS 351), a fitter-in. Jean
wrote about the Pensions Office where she worked in 1918 in what was
probably an earlier version of TIW (see BL ADD 57858, pages 144-146).
In the meantime ... Record of Service; 'Cowslips' (EA)

424 The first thing... and The other thing ... 'Cowslips', EA.
I think this... L 39 (for hating London from the moment LTS died); L113.

The Gower Peninsula ... Record of Service; AS interviews; AS letters to author, 7 and 22 Aug 1985. AS is definite about LTS and J's return to London in 1942, because it coincided with her move to the headquarters of the 8th American Air Force (letter to author, 9 July 1985).

425 The rest of the war... L38, 99; J to DA 3 Jan 1967.
We know that she ... AS letters to author, 7 and 22 Aug 1985; L38; J to OH, 23 Nov 1968 ('TIW' was written 'at the time... or very soon after'); MM interview.
We know that things... AS interviews and letter 22 Aug.
There was just... AS interview 17 Dec 1985; L43.

426 But of course... AS interview 24 Aug 1984; L 38.
Out of the war years ... And see DA to J, 28 Feb 1967; she suggests leaving 'ISAS'out of TABL because it is 'so sad and bitter'.
Quotation: 'ASH', TABL 131, CS 230.

427 As soon as the war ... J to SO, 3 May 1971. J must have heard from MM before July 1945, because in his letter of 16 July Michael Leigh refers to MM's marriage (Michael Leigh to LTS, 16 July 1945, EA).
In 1941, she'd ... L 39-40, 284; Bibeb interview with JL, in MK bibliography, 10; J to SO, 3 May 1971; MM to AS, 30 July 1968 (Tulsa 3:1).
By the time ... Bibeb, *loc. cit*; L 284; MK mtg; EvdW, letter to author 2 Nov 1988; JM to author, 20 Apr 1989.
This news about John... L 39; AS interview 24 Aug 1984.
Footnote: Bibeb, *loc. cit.*; MK mtg.

428 In 'The Sound of the River'... 'The S of the R', TABL 138-144, CS 236-241.
I think that this... AS interview 24 Aug 1984.
It didn't happen ... L 36.
We only have... L37.
In the story... AS interview; DRW interview 11 Apr 1985; L 39.

429 Quotation: 'JBS'.

430 That is Jean's... and Should she have felt ... AS interviews.
She was in... AS interview 24 Aug 1984; L 37. Edward had been due to end his service with the Indian Medical Service in 1940, but stayed on until 1945. (Indian Army Lists; JRW interview.)
Edward must have ... AS interviews; L 37.

431 But now what... L 39-40, 71; AS interviews; AS to DA, 27 Jan 1967.
Needless to say... J stayed at Steele's Road until at least July 1946 (see L 44); DRW interview 19 Mar 1985, suggested that J stayed with Edward and Gertrude for 'a week or two'.
Edward was being ... DRW interviews; JB interview; L 38.
The rest of the family ... RD, EA; DRW interview 11 Apr 1985. For Edward's and Gertrude's future behaviour see Part Four, Chapter One.

432 She was so poor ... AS to MM, 30 July 1968 (Tulsa 3:1); J to MM, 16 May 1970.
Owen, as ever... DRW interviews; JRW to author, 9 June 1985; JB interview; MM interview. DRW put the allowance at £3-£4 per week (interview 11 Apr), but at this distance in time that may of course not be accurate.
This renewed connection ... DRW, JRW, JB interviews; L 39, 82; J interview with author, 1975.

PART THREE, CHAPTER TWO

435 The war was... L 40.

Jean often longed... Hannah Carter, 'Fated to be sad', *The Guardian*, Aug 1968; AS interview 24 Aug 1984. 'TDTBTB' and 'LTCIJ' appeared first in the *London Magazine*, in 1960 and 1962 respectively (see Mellown 136). The RD was written c 1951 or 1952, while MH was in prison (not in the 1940s, as J says in SP 159); on and off throughout the fifties she tried to write 'English Harbour' as a sellable article or film script (see eg J to JM, 1 May 1950, EA; L 49-50 (1949) and L 144 (1957); J to FW, 14 Oct 1960).

The reason... L 99; Hunter Davies article; J to AS, 29 May 1968 (Tulsa 3:1); AS interviews; EB is also certain that LTS's death was a terrible blow to J (letter to author, 11 Nov 1984).

Footnote: L 66, 153.

436 Her disappearance ... AS interviews; EB interview; LTS to J, 16 July 1928. (LTS calls T.S. Eliot a 'very high-brow writer', and says he is 'exceedingly obscure'). Of J's isolation JL wrote in *Jean Rhys: Romancière Inconnue*: 'cette solitude imposée à elle-même'. See also J to GB, 30 Sept 1967 (EA) 'The few friends I made seemed to disappear after the second war.'

There was another... *Les nouvelles littéraires*, 26 Aug 1939; JL to J, 17 Jan 1940 (EA).

Mercifully, and almost... MK mtg; Bibeb interview with JL (MK bibliography page 11); JM to author, Apr 1989.

437 Not long after ... MK mtg; JL to J, 9 Nov 1945 (EA); Bibeb interview.

The miracle is... MK mtg; Bibeb interview; letters MK (20 Aug 1988) and EvdW to author; L 109, 284; J to OS, 14 June 1968 (Tulsa 3:14); JL to J, 12 May 1957 (EA). There is also negative evidence of a break between J and JL in the fifties: see L 90 (J getting JL's news via MM in 1951), L 92 (J not knowing JL's address in 1952).

As a writer... L 150 n.; SvD 'In Quest of a Missing Author', *Radio Times* 3-11 May 1957; DA, 'Jean Rhys and *Wide Sargasso Sea*', Introduction to 'Texts Plus' Edition of WSS (Hodder & Stoughton, 1989); L 136.

438 As a writer... and Nonetheless, Jean... MM interview; MW, interview with author, 5 Dec 1985; L 74, 75, 155.

George Victor Max Hamer... Hamer family tree by AH, copy given to author by AS; MM interview; birth and death records, St Catherine's House; *Beckenham Journal*, 27 May 1950; Law Society letter to FW, 23 Mar 1982; AS to author, 19 Sept 1984; L 43.

Jean always said... AS, 29 Sept 1984, and interviews; L 74, 75; MD statement to police, 2 Mar 1950, sent to author by Lord Chancellor's Department, 21 Nov 1985; probate records, Somerset House.

439 It was a meeting... AS interviews; marriage certificate J and MH, 2 Oct 1947; *Beckenham Journal*, 27 May 1950; MM interview; L 80.

Quotation: 'LTCIJ', TABL 48, CS 158-9.

By February 1946 ... L 43, 45; JM in MM interview; J and MH marriage certificate. J had gone on being 'Mme Lenglet' while living with LTS, certainly for several years, perhaps until they were married (see eg A Sawi letter to J, 1930).

440 The first two years ... DA interviews; 'The Dividing Line', EA; J to PK, Jan 1953; J to DA, 3 Jan 1967; L 74; MM interview. MH had married Dorothea Gumbleton in January 1911 and divorced her in 1947 (marriage and divorce records, St Catherine's and Somerset House). AS suggested that the break between MH and his daughter came with MH's 'smash' rather than with his leaving her mother.

They were married... J and MH marriage certificate; JM to MH, 23 Feb 1948; J to PK, 'Friday', 1949; L 46, 47; J to SO, 3 May 1971.

At first, however ... L 48, 49, 50, 57, 74. J and MH were certainly in Beckenham by July 1947 (see JM to MH, 23 Feb 1948); in late 1949 J spoke of having been there for three years (see L 44).

441 But of course... L 46-47, 75, 77; MM interview; 'LTCIJ', TABL 52, CS 162. Then things got... L 75.

In 'LTCIJ'... TABL 49-50, 54-5, 57-8; CS 160, 164-5, 167.

Footnote: MD, statement to police.

442 Quotation: *Beckenham and Penge Advertiser*, 1 Apr 1948, page 5. See also Bromley Court Registers, Minute Book 15, 788/8/6, 30 Nov 1948 — 25 Apr 1950, Court 5, 30 Mar 1948, page 40.

In life too ... *Beckenham Journal*, 3 Apr 1948, page 2 ('Broke Neighbour's Window'); L 48.

443 Quotation 1 (Defendant (a woman) ... ): *Bromley and West Kent Mercury*, 2 Apr 1948, page 1.

Quotation 2: (Told she would ... ): Ibid., 14 Apr 1949, page 1. The emphases on *a woman* throughout are mine.

Read these... 'ASH', TABL 120, CS 221. Think of Laura's exercise book too, which contained 'headlines and articles and advertisements and reports of cases in court and jokes ...' ('ISAS', PMS 58, CS 247).

Jean's feud... L 48. Mr Hardiman is named as Horace in the Bromley Electoral Register, 1948.

By October... L 70, 75. J writes in March and Apr 1950 that she's seen MH 'riding for a fall' since 'last October' (L 73), and been 'certain' since what sounds like Christmas 1949. But in the account to PK (L74-78, 1950) she puts this suspicion and certainty before her own 'smash' in the summer of 1949, which moves them back to 1948. And I think this is right. It explains the frantic state that led to her smash; and it fits with her letter to MM of Jan 1949 (L 47-48), which identifies Christmas 1948 as a particularly bad time.

That was how... L 47.

Something new... *Bromley & West Kent Mercury*, 29 Apr 1949, page 7. Mr. Bezant said here that he lived in the Hamers' house 'since last November', i.e. Nov 1948. Both the Bezants and the Daniells are registered as 'newly qualified electors' in 1949, so I am assuming they arrived at approximately the same time.

444 From Christmas ... *Beckenham Journal*, 27 May 1950; L 48-50, 75.

It didn't work ... *Bromley & West Kent Mercury*, 29 Apr 1949, page 7; L 76.

According to Sidney ... Ibid. same page; *Beckenham & Penge Advertiser*, 28 Apr 1949, page 9.

This only maddened ... *Bromley & West Kent Mercury*, 14 Apr 1949, page 3, 29 Apr 1949, page 7; *Beckenham & Penge Advertiser*, 28 Apr 1949, page 9.

The next day ... Bromley Court Registers, Minute Book 15, Court 5, 12 Apr 1949, No 788/5/13; *Bromley & West Kent Mercury*, 14 Apr 1949, pages 1 and 3; *Beckenham Journal*, 16 Apr 1949, page 5.

Nonetheless, thirteen days ... *Bromley & West Kent Mercury*, 29 Apr 1949, page 7 and 13 May 1949, page 3; *Bromley & Kentish Times*, 29 Apr 1949, page 2; *Beckenham & Penge Advertiser*, 28 Apr 1949, page 9; Bromley Court Registers, Minute Book 15, Court 1, 25 Apr 1949, page 55.

445 This wasn't the end... The five trials over fifteen months were on 30 Mar 1948, 12 Apr 1949, 25 Apr 1949, 6 May 1949, 27 June 1949.

After the trial... *Beckenham & Penge Advertiser*, 12 May 1949, front page; *Bromley & West Kent Mercury*, 13 May 1949, page 3; *Beckenham Journal*, 14 May 1949, page 11.

The gesture . . . Ibid.; also Bromley Court Registers, Minute Book 15, Court 3, 6 May 1949, page 68, which puts the assaults on Mrs Bezant and Mrs Daniell on 26 Apr 1949.

The case came up . . . *Bromley & West Kent Mercury*, 12 May 1949, page 3; *Beckenham Journal*, 14 May 1949, page 11; *Bromley & Kentish Times*, 13 May 1949, page 2; *Beckenham & Penge Advertiser*, 12 May 1949, front page; Bromley Court Registers as previous note; L 76.

446 On 27 May . . . *Bromley & West Kent Mercury*, 24 June 1949, page 3; *Beckenham Journal*, 4 June 1949, page 6, and 2 July 1949, page 3; *Bromley & Kentish Times*, 1 July 1949, page 2.

That was on . . . *Bromley & West Kent Mercury*, 1 July 1949, page 3; *Beckenham Journal*, 2 July 1949, page 3; *Bromley & Kentish Times*, 1 July 1949, page 2.

In 'LTCIJ' . . . 'LTCIJ', TABL 61, CS 170; L 76; J to PK, 'Friday', 1949; *Beckenham Journal*, 2 July 1949, page 3.

She spent at least . . . L 55-57, 76; J to PK 'Friday' 1949; JH to SO, undated letter from Venice 1977 (first page missing), EA ('Jean suddenly told us she'd been in Holloway once for two weeks. . . she'd loved being there as she was shut up all alone and it was so peaceful'); 'LTCIJ', TABL 61-64, CS 170-173.

447 On 4 July . . . *Bromley & Kentish Times*, 8 July 1949, page 2; *Beckenham Journal*, 9 July 1949, page 11; Bromley Court Registers, Minute Book 15, Court 1, 4 July 1949, page 77.

She had had . . . J to PK, 'Friday', 1949; L 50-55; L 80.

Footnote: 'LTCIJ', TABL 63, CS 172; J to PK 'Friday' 1949.

448 In the summer . . . L 51, 52, 54, 55, 56, 76; J to PK, 'Friday' 1949.

In September . . . MD statement to police; L 52, 76, 77.

Max and his friend . . . MD statement; LK 57, 59; DA interviews.

Quotation: *New Statesman*, No. 38, 5 Nov 1949, page 533; L 59.

449 The advertisement . . . and Typically, Selma . . . L 64; PR to author, 10 Oct 1985; SvD, 'In Quest of a Missing Author'. This is SvD's 1957 *Radio Times* article, and by this point she'd naturally forgotten a good deal, and dramatised the rest. Thus e.g. she says that Constable hadn't heard from J since 1939, whereas in fact they'd had *The Sound of the River* from her — and turned it down — in 1946, only three years before (see L 43-4). (Presumably the address they gave SvD, therefore, was Steele's Road.) The account evidently combines SvD's searches of 1949 and 1957. But the main work must have been done the first time.

What happened now . . . L 58-62, 64, 76; SvD to J, 14 Nov 1949 (EA).

450 On 16 Nov . . . *Beckenham & Penge Advertiser*, 24 Nov 1949, front page.

A week later . . . L 64-5.

She had to appear . . . *Beckenham & Penge Advertiser*, 24 Nov 1949, front page; Bromley Court Registers, Minute Book 15, Court 3, 18 Nov 1949, page 77.

Footnote: L 46, 68; *Beckenham & Penge Advertiser* as above ('she . . . went out to telephone her husband').

451 That was a . . . and Quotation: L 64, 65.

Poor Jean . . . L 66-7; *Beckenham & Penge Advertiser* as above.

In fact, Selma . . . L 66-7, 76, 226n.; GMM 43.

Footnote 1: (Selma was . . . ): L 59 n.1.

Footnote 2: (as Jean . . . ) L 226.

452 But this flare . . . L 67; J to MM; 11 Feb 1950.

Maryvonne fell ill . . . L 67, 76; MD statement to police.

All this was . . . *Beckenham Journal*, 21 Jan 1950, page 6; *Bromley & Kent Mercury*, 20 Jan 1950, page 5; *Bromley & Kentish Times*, 20 Jan 1950; Bromley Court Registers, Minute Book 15, Court 1, 16 Jan 1950; WSS 96; DA interviews.

453 Two days later . . . Reports as previous note. She had been to court five times

before going to Holloway, and now three after (4 July 1949, 18 Nov 1949, 16 Jan 1950).

That was a Monday ... *Beckenham Journal*, 11 Feb 1950, page 7; *Bromley & Kentish Times*, 24 Feb 1950.

If she didn't ... L 77; MD statement.

454 Max had been ... L 69 n, 77; *Beckenham Journal*, 18 Feb 1950, page 16; *Beckenham & Penge Advertiser*, 16 Feb 1950, page 1.

It is almost unbearable ... L 70–71, 73, 77.

Max's trial ... L 64, 69, 70, 73, 74; *Beckenham Journal*, 11 Mar 1950, page 7, and 1 Apr 1950, page 3; *Bromley & Kentish Times*, 10 Mar 1950, page 2, and 31 Mar 1950, page 2.

She and Max ... L 70, 72, 73, 77, 78, 80, 81; letter from Guildhall Justice Room to FW, 25 Mar 1982 (MH first appeared in the Justice Room on 14 Feb 1950, was remanded on bail of £500 until 22 Feb; on 22 Feb the case was adjourned until 6 Mar; committal proceedings took place on 13, 14 and 22 Mar; the trial was set for 18 Apr then postponed to 9 May. MH was finally sentenced on 24 May.)

Footnote: J to MM, 11 Feb 1950; DRW and JRW interviews.

455 Jean's life ... L 70, 77, 81; J to PK, 22 May and 28 May 1950. MH had another sister, Violet. But J only mentions Dorothy Norman (named in her letter to PK, 28 May); so I think she must have meant her. Besides, Dorothy, at seventy-five, was definitely 'old' ('She's old too and sick ... ').

She and Max ... L 71, 77, 79; J to PK 28 May 1950.

Footnote: L 77; AS interviews.

456 And yet they ... L 73, 74, 79, 82; J to PK, 28 May 1950; PK to J, 22 Apr 1950.

Max's trial ... L 82; Copy of Indictment, the King v George Hamer and Michael Donn, sent to FW by the Lord Chancellor's Dept, Mar/Apr 1982; *Beckenham Journal* 27 May 1950, front page; J to PK, 28 May 1950; letter to author, Lord Chancellor's Dept, 13 Dec 1985.

457 Even if Jean ... J to PK, 28 May 1950; WSS 22, 121.

He was convicted ... L 82; Lord Chancellor's Dept to FW, Mar/Apr 1982; J to PK, 28 May 1950; 'ChV'.

She wrote ... and In one ... L 78, 80–1.

458 From May ... J to PK, 28 May 1950; PK to J, 22 Apr 1950; L 82. There is no reason to think that PK's or SvD's, or MM's collections of J's letters is incomplete.

Quotation: L 93.

That was one break ... DRW interview 19 Mar 1985; JB interview. JB remembers that when she arrived in England in 1951 J's contact with Brenda was already over. (Evidently J had at least occasionally written to her, or Robert Powell could not have told her to stop.)

459 Quotation: RD, EA. See SP 164, top. 'By my brother and sister ...' etc. was already removed from the typewritten draft of 24 June 1976 (EA).

By my brother ... For J's dropping out of touch with Edward for long periods: when Edward bought Landboat Bungalows for her in 1960 he told Mr and Mrs Woodard that he had not been in touch with her for a long time (MW interview).

In March 1951 ... L 86, 89; DA interviews.

Footnote: DRW interviews.

460 Most important ... J to MM, 19 Aug 1951; L 89; SP 165.

What did she do ... SP 160, 167; L 86, 88, 89, 91, 92, 97; DW 54; MW interview.

461 'This is a quiet ...' J to MM, 19 Aug 1951; L 88; SP 164, 165, 167. And see SP 163; 'I have not written for so long that all I can force myself to do is to write, to write.'

The Ropemakers Diary ... SP 159, 162; RD, EA. This was cut from the same place (second speech, SP 164 top) as 'By my brother and sister ... etc.

462 Everything else ... SP 166, 168, 172. (In the published version J changed 'these women' to 'this woman'.)
Jean tries herself ... SP 173.
'It is in myself ...' SP 161-2.
The Counsel ... SP 162.

463 Quotation 1 ('It is not true ...'): SP 162-3.
Later, near ... SP 173. In the published version 'coldness of heart' is reduced to 'coolness'.
Quotation 2 (The phrase is not ... ): SP 163. In the published version 'will be an abject failure to myself' is reduced to 'could be an abject failure to myself'.
This phrase ... SP 163; P Rev, 280-1; DW 54.

464 In a way ... SP 164.
In May 151 ... Letter to FW from Law Society, 23 Mar 1982; L 93, 119, 124; MM interview; MW interview; J to DA, 3 May 1966.
For eight years ... For J keeping the last states of things to work on, see her references to her 'Mss suitcase', eg to SvD, 4 Jan 1957: 'I've gone through my Mss suitcase hauled about all these years.' She was always 'finding' things, eg 'Houdia' and 'Susan and Suzanne' in the 1950s (see L 104-5), 'Ramage', 'TIW' and early Paris stories in the 60s (see J to OH, 24 Feb and 28 June 1968, Tulsa 3:6); also the (or an) original ending of VID, and several old stories, galleys and notebooks in the 60s (see J to OS, 6 Dec and 15 Dec 1969, Tulsa 3:18). See also eg DP's finding the RD in her 'black file', among 'yellow scraps of earlier stories', in the 1970s (DW53). J's papers were always in great confusion (see eg J to DA, 3 Mar 1967); in Cheriton Fitzpaine she kept them in a cupboard where they got soaked (see J to OS, 15 Dec 1969); but she did keep them. (Think of TS).

465 'Slightly dazed' ... J to PK, 18 Jan 1953; L 94, 95, 96, 99.
In January ... J to PK, Ibid.; L 96-7.

466 Quotation MH to 'Morchard Bishop' (OS), 29 Dec 1952, L 98 n 2.
When Selma ... J to PK, 11 Jan 1953; L 99-108; J to PK, 18 Jan 1953; J to SvD, 6 Apr 1953 (Tulsa 2:5).
She was also ... L 97, 98, 104, 106; J to PK, 18 Jan 1953; J to SvD, 23 Jan 1953 (Tulsa 2:5) (shows a meeting). J had already refused to meet Eric Ambler in 1950 (see L 77).
Lily was a bit ... DRW and JB interviews; L 108-109; J to SvD, 'Sunday' 3?, 1953 (Tulsa 2:5).

467 The only other ... L 109-111.
During these months ... L 111.
It was almost ... L112-113.
After that ... L 115; RD, EA (cut from published version).

468 These two years ... L 95, 116-118, 122.
The main problem ... L 117-123. For losing literary contacts on moving to Wales and not renewing them, see L 107 n 2 (OS), and PK and SvD correspondence.
Bude was ... L 113.

469 And at the beginning ... L 123-5.
But of course ... L 123, 125, 133, 136.
They moved briefly ... L 126-129.

470 Bude itself ... L 127.
In October 1956 ... L 133-136; *New Statesman* No 52, 6 Oct 1956, page 435 (see Mellown 171); J to SvD, 4 Jan 1957 (Tulsa 2:6).
Footnote: For friendship with AH by 1959, see L 165. For calling both AH and

Edward 'a friend', see eg L 199 (Alec); and 'The Cottage' (unused draft for SP, EA), and J to FW, 5 July and 27 Sept 1960 (Edward).

471    The BBC ... J to MM, 16 Dec 1956; Mellown 151, 171; L 133–136, 140-1, 145, 153, 167; J to SvD, 4 Jan 1957 and 3 Feb 1957 (Tulsa 2:6). For J's 'lying low' during the worst of the winter, see L: very few letters between Dec and Feb (only one to SvD, eg. which is not in L).
At the end ... and So she said ... L 140, 142-146, 149; J to SvD 5 Oct, 1957. For her also telling SvD it had been in her head for years, see L 143. She summarised it to FW in July 1962: ' "Le Revenant" came to life *or back* again (in a way) when I met Selma and was talking to her' (L 213).

472    After a week ... J to MM, 21 Feb 1957; L 142-147; J to SvD, 5 Oct 1957; SvD article, page 25.
On 10 and 11 May ... Mellown 151; J to MM, 14 Apr 1957 (left out of L 144-5), 17 May 1957; JL to J, 12 May 1957 (EA); PK to J, 4 May 1957; L 147-8.

473    Quotation and following paragraph: L 147-148, 167, 213; J to SvD, 5 Oct 1957; Bk Ex Bk 70.

PART THREE, CHAPTER THREE

475    On 1 June ... L 149, 152, 156, 158, 159, 162, 224; J to PK 16 June, 5 and 11 July 1957.
But then ... L 151, 152, 158; J to PK Ibid, and 30 July; PK to J, 1 Aug 1957; J to SvD, 5 Oct 1957; J to MM, 27 Sept 1957.
In the autumn ... L 115, 149; J to SvD, 5 Oct; J to MM, 27 Sept; MM to AS, 30 July 1968.

476    Quotation: J to SvD, 5 Oct.
In November ... L 150, 156; J to MM 24 Nov 1957; MW interview with author, 5 Dec 1985.
January and February ... L 149-154; 'Creole Song' by Lily Lockhart, Tulsa Item 1:14; J to PK, 30 July 1957; J to SvD, 5 Oct 1957. J also told DA that the title of WSS came from a poem by her cousin Lily (DA to author).
In early 1958 ... PK to J, 4 Feb 1958; L 19 n 1, 45, 109; DRW interviews; death and will records, St Catherine's and Somerset House.

477    Perhaps these deaths ... L 155, 157.
But Francis and Diana ... L 158, 159; J to MM, 21 May and 14 Dec 1958.
The hardest part ... L 158-160; J to MM, 14 Dec 1958; J to SvD, 5 Oct 1957.

478    The important and ... L 156, 159; J to SvD, 5 Oct 1957.
The early 1959 ... L 154-5, 160, 162, 164, 168, 189; J to MM, 17 Feb/16 Mar (sent together) and 17 May 1959.
But in the spring ... L 161, 162, 164, 168, 172, 180, 184, 186, 233, 234; J to MM, 17 Feb/16 Mar 1959; J to SvD, 25 May and 11 Aug 1959.
Footnote: L 160-1.

479    The summer ... L 163, 166, 167, 294; J to SvD, undated, 1959; Mellown 65. The Radio Bremen broadcast of GMM went out on 5 June 1959 (Wolfgang Kruger Verlag to J, 29 June 1959, EA).
She often said ... L 149-50, 169-171; DW 36; J to SvD, 4 Jan 1957, 11 Aug 1959; J to FW, 1 Sept 1959; Mellown 135-6.
Footnote: L 100, 105.

480    Things were going ... L 172-3, 182, 229; J to SvD, 21 Jan and 24 Feb 1960; J to EB, 2 Feb 1960; MW interview (on J's and MH's distrust of doctors).
At first Max ... L 173, 175, 176, 178; J to SvD, 21 Jan 1960.
As winter ... L 175, 179, 180.
This was the maddest ... L 182-184; J to MM, 30 May 1960; DRW interviews.

481    Max, of course ... L 184, 186, 187, 189, 196; Mellown 135; letters from

publishers (e.g. Penguin, Ace Books) to FW, July 1960. (Tony Godwin of Penguin wrote to FW on 12 July, 'Jean Rhys is, I'm afraid, completely unknown.')

In the meantime ... J to MM, 30 May 1960; L 186.

But now... J to MM, Ibid; 'my sad métier', SP draft in EA; MW interview; DRW interviews; J to DA, 3 Jan 1967. See also J to MM, 19 May 1960, in which she says that Edward is coming to Looe, so that she will be seeing him.

Jean was ... J to MM, Ibid; MW and DRW interviews; MW letter to author, 15 Dec 1985.

482 Edward made ... MW interview. Edward must have started looking very soon, because he found the cottage by June (L 187).

6 Landboat Bungalows... MW interview; MS, *Recollections*, page 8; author's visit, Sept 1975.

On the other hand ... DRW, JRW and JB interviews; MW interview.

Footnote: JB interview.

483 But whatever ... L 187, 188, 191, 192, 195; J to FW, 5 July 1960; J to SvD, 20 Oct 1960; JvH, 'H in C', page 4; J also seems to have told several people that it was her brother-in-law AH who'd bought the cottage, or left it to them (Michael Henshaw to author; JF interview, 26 Nov 1985).

The builders' work ... L 189-192; J to MM, 21 July 1960.

For five miles ... J to MM, 22 May 1960.

484 The first that ... MW interview; MW letters to author 15 Dec 1985 and 8 Jan 1986. Edward's hopes and doubts are mostly my interpretations of MW's account, based also on my knowledge of what had happened before and would happen later.

The Woodards were ... For Cheriton Fitzpaine knowing everything, see e.g. L 203, 209, 231.

Jean of course ... J to SvD, 20 Oct 1960; L 195-197; on Landboat Bungalows, e.g. E Whit interview, 15 Oct 1985; and 'Jean by Jo' (JH), page 3.

Footnote: MW interview.

485 From the beginning ... L 195-201; J to SvD, 20 Oct and 28 Dec 1960; DA to author.

She had her usual ... L 187, 196, 197, 200, 201; J to FW, 14 Oct, 19 Feb, 6 Mar, 7 Mar, 20 Mar, 1960. For J's reluctance to get back to work after a long time, see also L 98 (1953) and J to DA, 15 Dec 1965. Her reluctance to have 'LTCIJ' typed locally, which is quoted here, actually refers to Perranporth; but she certainly felt the same about Cheriton Fitzpaine.

486 Immediately ... L 202; MW letter to author, 31 Jan 1986.

Mr Woodard ... MW interview.

Quotation: L 203.

Footnote: PT (the Greenslades' granddaughter), interview with author, 4 Dec 1985. In 1963 MW stopped doing Meals on Wheels, so that was probably the point when Mrs Greenslade took over.

487 She tried ... L 203.

Quotation: L 204.

The trees were ... DA interview with author, 25 Oct 1984 (for Mr Bezant's letter); L 203.

Perhaps she worked ... L 202, 204, 205, 207; MW interview; PT interview; MW letter to author, 31 Jan 1986.

488 We must be ... L 199; MW letter 31 Jan 1986; J to FW, 5 July 1960; J to DA, 6 Apr 1964 (left out of L 259). For MH not really wanting her to write, see e.g. L 75, 155. These were low points, so that she probably exaggerated; nonetheless, as he got worse he no doubt did begrudge her time and attention. And see e.g.

J to MM, 12 Jan 1959: 'Max gets bored with endless conversations about this poor limping book.' For SvD's attention sometimes lapsing, see the fracas over Christmas 1963 (pages 509–513 below).

489 Not all churchmen ... MW and Helen Howitt (daughter) interview; Jesus College, Cambridge, records; obituary, *Church Times*, 6 Sept 1974; BH to author, 21 Jan 1986; E Whit interview and letter to author, 8 Feb 1986. See also rear Admiral Robert Woodard (son) to author, 22 July 1990: 'Your description of my father is accurate, he was a most caring man with a depth of compassion and very high moral standards — he was also blessed with a most marvellous sense of humour and fun ... he could not bear pompous people and delighted in "popping their balloons"!

To be fair ... Jesus College, Cambridge, records; obituary; BH letter.

490 As it was ... MW interview; L 210.

Now Mr Woodard ... MW and Helen Howitt in interview; MW to author, 6 Jan 1986.

Jean had despaired ... L 201. For J's writing practice, e.g. DA interview, 17 Aug 1983, and her account of J's saying WSS was not finished because it contained 'two unneccessary words. One was "then", the other "quite"'. (SP 8). See also her dozens of versions of 'LS' in Tulsa 1:28 and her O Nbk.

For the timing of this event ('Sometime in the autumn of 1961'): MW was uncertain whether it was 1961 or 1962. But she was certain that her husband now introduced J to Mrs Brown, a young woman in Cheriton Fitzpaine who could type her novel (MW to author, 6 Jan 1986): and J began to mention Mrs Brown in mid-October 1961 (L 207, 208). Mrs Brown began typing for her in early 1962 (L 210).

The letter in which J says she's been 'very down about the book' was written in Dec (28 Dec 1961, to MM, L 210), and in it she says 'it has come to life again'.

And now Jean... MW interview and letter, 6 Jan 1986.

He started... L 209, 271, 275; MW interview and letter 6 Jan 1986.

Footnote: BH, *Lancing College History and Memories*, Phillimore, 1986.

492 Because he... MW interview; L 210.

There'd been... L 207–208.

He had... L 90, 182; J to MM (Oct 1957) and 14 Dec 1958; JL to J, 11 Sept 1961; Bibeb interview with JL (in MK bibliography, page 11).

So often Jean's... L 106, 109, 182; JL to J, 11 Sept 1961.

Jean had... MK agrees that J had been the love of JL's life. (MK mtg).

Quotation SP 162.

493 For once ... L 182.

Quotation: L 282, 284.

He'd saved her ... L 227.

Even getting on ... L 209, 210, 214; J to FW, 5 Feb and 20 Feb 1962; Mellown 136; MW interview.

What had happened ... L 216, 220; J to FW, 20 Feb 1962 and 30 Mar 1964.

Footnote: 'Jean Rhys' by OH, description of the J — OH correspondence, Tulsa Item 3:3; MW interview.

494 That was Jean's L 220; MW interview.

In the spring ... L 211–216; J to SvD, 12 Mar 1962; J to FW, 15 July and 22 Aug 1962 (left out of L 214); MW interview; Mellown 136. Edward visited quite often in the winter of 1961-2 and the summer of 1962: see L 210–212.

Re the selling of the short stories to the *London Magazine*, FW adds: 'John Lehmann chose "TSP" and "TABL" — then added "TDTBTB" as an afterthought. "TABL" was lost by Charles Osborne, and found by him long afterwards, when Alan Ross had become the Editor. Everyone (except me!) was

very insouciant about the loss, including Jean – although it was her only copy.'
'I shall be . . .' L 215.

495 Quotation: L 215.
    Francis did see . . . L 215–216.
    It was this . . . L 217; J to SvD, 21 Dec 1962. For the essence of WSS being there after four years, I'm thinking of the autumn of 1961, when Mr Woodard read it; for 'even probably after one and a half' I'm thinking of Jan 1959 ('I have finished the first draft of Mrs Rochester,' to SvD, L 159).

496 'I wish I . . .' L 217.
    After that . . .' J to MM, 4 Jan 1963; L 242.
    Two things . . . MW interview; J to MM, 15 Mar 1963.
    We have to face . . . MM interview; MW interview.

497 Once at least . . . MW interview. And see L 245 for Edward 'hauling' J off to two specialists.
    This account is based on MW's memories only. But I think they are reliable. She would have known nothing of Jean's behaviour with Leslie, or in Beckenham, but her descriptions match what we know of those times. Her daughter Helen supported them. And the Woodards knew J and MH better than anyone in Cheriton Fitzpaine except the Greenslades. No one else, indeed, knew them at all: 'They kept themselves to themselves very much,' says Harry Martin the builder. Sadly the Greenslades died long before I got to the village. Zena Raymond was ill and I couldn't speak to her. Mrs Stentiford had moved away; and J Lee, J's other neighbour, is an easy-going, motherly woman who indulged J in life, and to whom a few rows would seem of no account. She didn't mention them, and nor did I.
    The Cheriton Fitzpaine doctors, quite properly, would tell me nothing, though it was clear that J had been a handful. My only informants apart from MW and her daughter, therefore, were the Greenslades' grand-daughter PT, and J's best friend in the village in later years, J But. PT remembered the terrible rows with Zena Raymond, and did say that the Greenslades would 'hear terrible tales'. But she said no more. J But only knew J after WSS in 1966 – that is, after MH's death; and didn't live in Cheriton Fitzpaine itself until 1977. She did however say that there were stories that J had murdered MH; and that when she herself first met J, alone and at night, the doctor's wife rang to check that J hadn't murdered *her*. (Interviews with J Lee and PT, 4 Dec 1985, and with J But, 24 Nov 1984.)
    Jean did . . . Interview with J Br (for J's extreme agitation over visitors.)
    1963 was . . . J to SvD, 21 Dec 1962; L 209 (first mention of a 'rest' in hospital for MH, in Dec 1961), 222, 223, 229, 238.

498 In April Max . . . and Quotation: MH to J, 5 Apr 1963, EA.
    Whatever you call me . . . MW interview; J to DA, 3 Jan 1967; J to SvD, 19 Dec 1963.
    Now, in May . . . L 219–221. J to MM, 23 May 1963, shows that MM and her daughter had just visited; MH went back to hospital in June (L 222), so he must have come home from Seaton.

499 First, though . . . L 222–228; 'My sad métier', SP draft in EA.
    Soon Max . . . L 225, 228; J to Matron, Belmont Hospital, Belmont Road, Tiverton, 4 July 1963 (typed original, in EA); 'My sad métier'.
    The thing . . . L 205, 225; 'The Dividing Line', SP draft in EA; AH to J, 31 Jan 1959, and 1 Dec 1966 (EA).

500 Selma, of course . . . L 222–3.
    They came . . . L 31 ('persecution maniacs) and 228 ('You did so cheer me up').
    All J's letters of late 1966 and early 1967 (and many later too) repeat the SvD

story in similar ways — to FW, DA, MM, OS, OH and others. I have taken my account (pages 500 to 503) from: J to DA, 27 Dec 1966; J to OS, 9 Aug 1969; J to SO, 21 Aug 1969; J to PR, 6 Oct 1978; and FW's summary in L 289 n 1. J almost always said SvD had *said* her piece of paper was 'a joke'; once (to OS, 9 Aug 1969) she said she'd only implied it.

It was not a joke ... Sources as above; FW conversations with author.

501  As anyone ... DA to J, 9 and 15 Feb 1967; DA to author; J to SvD, 11 June and 14 June 1969.

Jean herself ... Sources as before; plus eg J to SO, 31 Aug 1979; J to OH 17 Oct 1969; L 271.

Both these ... GMM 51.

And there's another ... DA and FW conversations with author; L 171; 'M & W' ('Dedicated to all those who, having miraculously weathered the storms of a mis-spent life, come safely to haven in a comfortable flat in Kensington and while stuffing themselves with food, respectable voices bleating on the north, south, east and west sides of them, seeing through a half-open door the street outside calm and tamed (one more effort and the whole thing will eat out of my hand) hear a voice crying "LOST, LOST, ENDLESSLY, FINALLY AND FOR THE FIRST TIME, LOST." Like Esau, who sold his birthright for a mess of pottage.')

503  These reasons ... Q 59; J But interview; J to OS, 24 Sept 1968 (Tulsa 3:15). Given all this ... L 289, n 1; DA to author. JS of Christy and Moore was briefly J's agent as well as SvD's. (See JS correspondence with J, 1964–1969, in EA.) For J repeating that she would gladly share the money if only SvD continued to sell her work, see eg J to SvD, 26 Feb and 16 Sept 1966.

502  Well, that's ... J to OH, 17 Oct 1969.

A few days ... L 226; Tape recordings, Tulsa Item 4:22; WSS 76.

Quotation: Author's version, from tapes. See also Tulsa Item 1:14, 'Songs for Voyage', music and words for this song and the others, including 'Women sweeter dan man'. (Transcribed by Clifton Garter.)

504  Although she never ... L 225, 227-9; J to SvD, 15 July 1963. I've guessed that this was MH's last time at home, because by 8 Aug AH wrote that he was back in hospital, and 'looking after him in his present state is obviously impossible for you' (AH to J, 8 Aug 1963, EA.) There are no further references to MH at home in J's letters.

She tried to ... 'My sad métier'; L 228-9; J Br interview.

Mr Woodard ... MW interview.

505  He went back ... L 230; J to E Whit, 27 and 31 July 1963.

Esther Whitby ... and Above all ... E Whit interview with author, 15 Oct 1985; J to SvD, 8 Aug 1963.

For two days ... L 231-2; J to MM, 8 Aug 1963; J to DA, 8 Aug 1963; E Whit interview.

At the same time ... L 229, 231.

Footnote: J to AR, 5 Nov 1962; L 217. For versions, see O Nbk 65-125, and Tulsa Item 1:28.

506  And yet ... AH to J, 8 Aug 1963.

Diana's response ... DA to J, 12 Aug 1963.

Jean replied ... L 232-4. See also L 238 and 239, in late Aug and early Sept: she hasn't ' a drop' of whisky; 'a life without drink or books ...'

507  And it's ... L 232-4; J to SvD, 25 Aug 1963 (left out of L 235). Daniel had been very troublesome. J had discussed him with Mr Woodard too. As MW remembers, J had thought of Daniel as the answer to another problem: how to bring Rochester the news of Antoinette's mother's insanity. MW thinks her

husband suggested a letter. J never said his help was so detailed; but of course it may have been. She discussed the book with several people – FW, DA, AH, as well as Mr Woodard; and she took DA's advice on the important point of the length of Antoinette's happiness. 'Whatever we came up with,' DA says, 'was sort of stirred into the brew, and then finally she saw a way. It is possible that something Mr W said was stirred into the brew, too.' (DA to author, 22 Jan 1986).

It was ... L 233-5; DA to J, 12 Aug 1963; J to SvD, 5 Oct 1957.

Alex was supposed ... AH to J, 8 Aug 1963; L 235-240; J to FW, 26 Aug 1963; O Nbk 65-125.

She was ... L 238-240, 248; J to FW, 26 Aug and 6 Sept 1963.

508 'This is not ...' L 238-241; PT interview; MW interview; J But interview; DW 48. J sets this after MH's death; but as we know, her dating is hopeless. I am guessing that the time she was remembering was this very bad one, when she was first alone.

Re 'black magic in the village': this was certainly not J's imagination. MW said very much the same to me twenty years later; and Mr Woodard talked about it quite calmly and openly to E Whit (DA to author).

'I would ...' L 240-242, 245; DW 49.

509 But now Selma ... L 242-5.

October was ... L 245-248; PT interview; DRW interviews; J to FW, 11 Oct 1963; J to SvD, 3 Dec 1963; MW interview.

Of course Jean ... L 246-248; J to MM, 30 Nov 1963; FW conversation to author.

510 Mr Woodard ... MW interview; L 247-8; J to SvD, 19 Nov 1963; J to FW, 21 Nov 1963.

But this invitation ... L 243, 249; J to SvD, 21 Nov and 3 Dec 1963; J to FW, 21 Nov and 27 Nov 1963.

The first delay ... L 249, 257-259; J to SvD, undated (Dec), 3 Dec, 6 Dec, 12 Dec, and 19 Dec 1963, 'Wednesday' Jan and 'Wednesday' Mar 1964; SvD to J, 27 Feb 1964; J to FW, 27 Nov 1963; AH to J, 20 Dec 1963. I'm guessing that J hadn't gone to Crediton, because she'd hardly go to both Crediton and Tiverton within a week or two. Re Christmas 1963 as a very low point, see J to FW, 27 May 1964 (left out of L 280-2): 'I was very lonely about Christmas, and had fearful warnings about the booksy world and so on ... as I was alone and cold, as usual I started worrying. I wrote letters like this: "I am on the brink of cracking up." But always tore them up ... So you see I got into this panic and couldn't work well.'

511 It may have been ... J to SvD, undated (Dec) 1963; L 260; DW 49-50. J dated this event to DP in a very confused way – to after her heart attack, which she puts after MH's death, which it wasn't (again suggesting that she simply identified being alone with Max's being dead, forgetting that she had three years without him before he died). She also suggested (if DP renders her faithfully) that she'd only got to know Mr Woodard in the final stages of writing WSS. This is false, as we know – and of course WSS was finished when MH died. In other words, J was collapsing her whole friendship with Mr Woodard into one blur, and we can only guess when this event happened. But it was during one of her lowest times in the writing of WSS (she felt, she said, that 'it would be impossible ever to write again', DW 49). There were three: the winter of 1961-2, the autumn of 1963, and Mar to Oct 1965. From the first Mr Woodard rescued her in the way we've seen; from the last J always said she was rescued by a new treatment, better pills (see eg L 293; J to SvD, 15 Dec 1965; J to MM, 22 Oct 1965). That leaves now, the autumn of 1963, as the most likely time for this rescue.

Week after week ... and Quotation: DW 49-50.

She didn't ... L 253-4, 263; J to FW, Jan and 5 Feb 1964; J to DA, 12 Jan and 23 Feb 1964; J to SvD, Jan and 18 Feb 1964; SvD to J, 27 Feb 1964; J to MM, 18 Feb 1964. Re 'one of her good times with whisky': Helen Howitt noticed that this could happen — whisky could (briefly) do J good (MW interview).

512   But she was ... L 253-257; J to DA, 23 Feb 1964. For better working days see J to FW, 21 Mar 1964; J to SvD, same day.

Several things ... J to SO, 1 Mar 1964; L 242, 254, 261; J to SvD, Mar 1964 (left out of L 257-9); J to DA, 27 Mar and 6 Apr 1964 (left out of L 256-7 and L 259-60); J to FW, 30 Mar 1964; *Art and Literature* proofs of Part One. WSS.

Then there was ... J to FW, 21 Mar, 30 Mar, and 27 May 1964; J to AR, 4 Jan, 21 Mar, and 6 Apr 1964 (EA); J to DA, 27 Mar and 6 Apr 1964) (Left out of L); DA to J, 3 Apr 1964; JS to J, 22 Apr 1964 and 11 Nov 1966; Norah Smallwood (Chatto and Windus) to DA, 22 Nov 1966. Constable had released their option on GMM in 1957 (letter 12 June 1957, EA.) There is not documentation of AR's withdrawing his claim, but he must have done so.

513   Amid this ... J to SvD, 'Wednesday' (Jan 1964), 'Monday' (end Feb 1964); 'Wednesday' (early Mar 1964); SvD to J, 27 Feb 1964; L 82, 257, 260.

By late March ... L 258-260, 271; J to FW, 8 Apr 1964 (left out of L 260-1); MW to author, 15 Dec 1985. For the village hating J, see L 258, 263; for her hating them, see L 267, 268.

It was her ... MW interview and letter 15 Dec 1985; L 286 n 1.

514   This break ... L 260, 261, 262, 267, 268, 271; 'The L', TABL 110, CS 213. The other poems were 'The Old Man's Home', later changed to 'The Cut of His Jib' (about MH); 'The Forgotten Word', and 'The Easy Trick' (all in EA).

It was called ... L 261-2, 264-266, 267, 269, 271, 277.

This time ... L 234, 262, 266; J to FW, 1 May 1964.

Quotation L 269. ('So cold' comes from later on in the letter.)

515   That is where ... L 262, 269, 274; J to FW, 1 May 1964; WSS 138, 141.

516   What both ... WSS 77, 91.

This was almost ... L 261, 266, 270-5, 274-5, 279. For writing about WSS, L 261-282; and J to FW, 1 May and 27 May 1964.

Usually she didn't ... Re J not liking to talk about her writing, see eg: J to SO, 'Saturday' (Jan 1967, from Brighton); DA in Bailey radio; J But interview.

Quotations: L 276; L 277 (and see J to DA, 29 May 1964 and J to SO, late Apr 1964); L 272.

Footnote: L 268.

517   As Jean approached ... L 274, 277, 278, 279; J to FW, 5 June 1964 (left out of L 282-3); BL ADD 57857, last two items.

Quotation ... BL ADD 57847, page 140 (BL pagination).

On 21 May ... L 278.

Well, we know ... L 272, 281, J to MM, 18 May 1964 ('It is hard to work for so long and against such difficulties, only to crash at the end — So there is only one answer I must not crash — and *will not* if I can help it.')

Quotation L 281.

518   She felt ... L 278-285; J to DA, 28 May 1964; DA, Introduction to 'Texts *Plus*' edition of WSS; DA interview 25 Oct 1984; J to FW, 28 June and 5 July 1964. Re J drinking see also, eg, J to FW, 5 June 1964 (left out of L 282-3); 'I'll see what whisky will do — *may* exalt me again' .... She was admitting it now — 'If one drinks a lot alone it cannot be helped. It'll only be living up to my reputation' (to FW, 5 July). Compare this to Feb when she was still saying 'I have to be careful not to give myself a reputation as boozer plus witch' (to SvD, 18 Feb), though she did say, 'I've taken to whisky in a big way ...' Of course

she'd had a reputation as 'boozer plus witch' for several years.

She was in ... L 285, 286; J to MM, 6, 14, 23 Aug 1964; J to FW, 1 and 5 Aug 1964; J to SvD, 'Aug' 1964, from Belvedere Clinic; J to DA, 30 Aug 1964.

She had five or six ... L 286; DA to J, 1 Sept 1964; J to Mrs Kloegman, 15, 23, 30 Nov 1964; SP 13; DA, Introduction to 'Texts *Plus*' edition of WSS.

Footnote: L 276.

519 This was always ... Eg J interview with author, 29 Sept 1975, re going away: 'I often funk it'; L 298; SP 13.

She hadn't been ... and next two paragraphs: SP 13; DA, 'Jean Rhys and the Writing of "WSS"', *Bookseller*, No 3165, 20 Aug 1966, pages 1378-9; DA in *Ham & High*, 15.

Maryvonne came ... DA to author; L 287, 289; J to FW, 15 Dec 1965.

But she was ... DA to author; L 287-8; DA interview 25 Oct 1984; DA in *Bookseller*, page 1379.

She lived ... DA interview and conversations with author; DA in Bailey radio.

520 After about ... L 287-290 and 287 n; J to DA, 24 and 27 Feb 1965; DA to J, 1 and 2 Mar 1965; DA to author; L 287-8 and J to DA, 17 Feb 1965 (re J and DA being out of touch); J to SvD, 22 Feb 1965; J interview with author; 'Mrs Pearce'; J to MM, 28 Apr 1965.

It was a crazy ... L 297, 298.

For the next ... J to SvD, 15 Dec 1965, 27 Feb 1966, 18 Mar 1966; J to DA, 24 Mar 1965, 20 Feb 1966; J to MM, 28 Apr 1965, 22 Oct 1965; L 291, 298; DRW interviews. Gertrude died of cancer in Aug 1966.

Footnote: DA conversations with author; DA Introduction to 'Texts *Plus*' edition of WSS; DA to the Royal Literary Society, 20 Jan 1966.

521 And the worst ... L 288, 290; J to DA, 15 Dec 1965, 3 May 1966; DA to J, 19 Mar 1965; J to SvD, 15 Dec 1965 and 26 Feb 1966; J to MM, 28 Apr 1965 and 22 Oct 1965; J to SO 'Saturday' (Jan 1967); Hannah Carter, page 5; DW 49.

Quotation: J to DA, 3 Jan 1967.

By August ... L 291-2; J to MM, 22 June, 1, 10, 15, Sept 1965. She often said this period from March to October 1965 was the worst time in her life. See eg J to JF, 6 Sept 1968; J to OH, 25 Feb 1966; DW 49.

Finally, in October ... L 293-4, 298; J to MM, 22 Oct 1965; J to FW, 15 Dec 1965; J to SvD, 15 Dec 1965; J to OH, 23 Jan 1966.

Then in November ... J to SO, 'Saturday' (Jan 1967, from Brighton); DA to J, 26 Nov 1965; J to DA, 20 Feb 1966; L 297; MW interview. On 22 Oct she was still writing to MM, 'I do not believe I will be able to write a word here'; On 9 Nov 'I still find it difficult to concentrate on my book' (L 293). But on 11 Nov she told DA she was going ahead (J to DA 11 Nov 1965, DA to J, 15 Nov 1965).

522 In mid-December ... See notes to previous page ('Finally, in October ....'); J to FW, 15 Dec 1965, 14 Jan 1966; J to MM, 31 Dec 1965; OH note on correspondence, Tulsa Item 3:3. The four stories were 'TP' and 'ISAS', 'The L' and 'The S of the R' (see L 295 n 2). OH (sister of Ted Hughes) had heard of Jean through the Browns, and they'd exchanged letters some months before (see J to OH, 23 Nov 1965). Christy and Moore had been concentrating on getting the best-received novels, VID and GMM, republished, and hadn't said much about the others. J had therefore asked OH to act for them too (see L 295 n 1).

In February ... L 295-6, 298 n 1; J to DA, 14, 23, 29 Jan and 20 Feb 1966; Marcelle Bernstein 50.

Now she was ... L 296-297; J to DA, 29 Jan 1966, 20 Feb 1966; MW interview.

On 25 February ... L 298; J to DA, 24 Feb 1966, 7 Mar 1966.

523 But on 2 March ... L 300-1; AH to DA, 7 and 10 Mar 1966; J to SvD, 11 Mar

1966. Edward and AH were in touch (see AH to J, 20 Dec 1963). AH came to the funeral, and so did MM (L 300-1).
Early in the morning ... L 301; AH to DA, 10 Mar 1966; J to SvD, 11 Mar 1966; J to MM, 4 Mar 1966 (re Edward making the arrangements).
Quotation: L 301.
Max was ... J to PK, 24 June 1957; L 195. Eg Sasha Moorsom doesn't mention MH at the BBC lunch in 1957, nor does J mention him at SvD's (Bailey radio; L 142). Perhaps J didn't come; or perhaps J ignored him, as she sometimes did (see page 524), and he just sat so quietly that no one noticed or remembered him.
A few people ... MW interview and letter 6 Jan 1986; PT interview; J Lee interview, 4 Dec 1985; MM interview; J to PK, 18 Jan 1953; J to DA, 3 Jan 1967; L 134, 149, 178, 228.

524 It's hard ... MW interview and letter 31 Jan 1986; J to DA, 12 Mar 1966; DA to J, 11 and 28 Mar 1966.

Re 'the last typescript' of WSS; DA sent all the versions of WSS back to J (see DA to J, 15 Nov 1965, 9 Mar and 10 Mar 1966), presumably including the handwritten revisions which went to Mrs Kloegman. In 1968 J told OS that she'd destroyed her handwritten manuscript, though she'd since found one chapter of it (J to OS, 21 Aug 1968). This was presumably the last 'chapter' of Part Two, which is now in the BL (BL ADD 57857). Sadly, therefore, nothing else remains. That is of course what J wanted − 'I do think that one's struggles to get the thing right ought to be private − not seen and if possible not known or even guessed. Certainly not' (L 255). She wanted people to see only the finished product − the finished book, the finished self. She couldn't believe that people would admire her more for the struggle instead of less. I do believe that: hence this chapter, and this book.
Quotation: DA to J, 9 Mar 1966.

PART THREE, CHAPTER FOUR

533 Finally, the key ... For Sasha entering 'the No time region', See L 138.
534 The 'terrible things ...' John Hearne, 'Wide Sargasso Sea: A West Indian Reflection', *Cornhill Magazine*, Vol 180-1, Summer 1974 (pages 323-333), page 328, also argues that love is the secret that Rochester desires.
535 Footnote: Dennis Porter, 'Of Heroines and Victims: Jean Rhys and Jane Eyre', *Massachusetts Review*, Vol. 17, 1976 (pages 540-552), page 543: Wally Look Lai, 'The Road to Thornfield Hall', *New Beacon Reviews*, Collection One, 1968 (ed. John La Rose), pages 38-52, on page 45.
546 The zombie, or ... Several critics argue that physical death is a liberation for Antoinette. See eg Elizabeth Abel, 'Women and Schizophrenia: The Fiction of Jean Rhys', *Contemporary Literature*, Vol. 20, No 2, Spring 1979, pages 155-177, on page 174; John Thieme, 'Apparitions of Disaster', *Journal of Commonwealth Lit.*, Vol 14, No 1, pages 116-132, on page 123; Angela Williams, 'The Flamboyant Tree', *Planet*, Vol 33, Aug 1976, pages 35-41, on page 41.
Shirley Hazzard, Review of Q, *New York Times*, 11 Apr 1971, page 6, also argues that the heroines 'embody not so much a capacity for suffering as a thwarted capacity for joy.'
547 Footnote: See Elizabeth Abel, *loc. cit.* pages 167 and 176-177; Louis James, *Jean Rhys* (1978), page 29; Elgin Mellown, 'Character and Themes in the Novels of Jean Rhys', *Contemporary Literature*, Vol 13, No 4, Autumn 1972, pages 458-475, on page 462; Thomas Staley, *Jean Rhys* (1979), page 97.
548 Rochester could have ... I am indebted to Jan Sharp for the point that Rochester especially fears being drowned in Antoinette's idea of love as boundless self-surrender.

555 Despite her age ... FW refers to J's 'quivering immediacy' in his Introduction to WSS (Penguin edition page 6).

In much the same way ... Re the feeling of growing emptiness the early novels may give, see V.S. Naipaul, 'Without a Dog's Chance', *New York Review of Books*, 18 May 1972, page 30; 'at the centre there is always something like withdrawal.'

556 Some readers may ... See eg Kay Dick, 'Wife to Mr Rochester', *Sunday Times*, 30 Oct 1966, page 50;'Only Jean Rhys's intrinsic grip on basic tragedy saves *Wide Sargasso Sea* from melodrama'.

PART FOUR, CHAPTER ONE

571 In March 1966 ... MW interview; J to MM, 18 May, 'Thursday' (July), 9 July 1966; J to FW, 8 Apr 1966.

But whisky wasn't ... DA in *Ham & High*.

The first woman ... J to MM, 18 Mar, 15 Aug, 15 Sept, 9 and 11 Oct 1966; J to SO, 3 May 1971; J to FW, 8 Apr 1966; J to DA, 14 Apr 1966; MM to AS, 30 July 1968; DA to author, interviews and conversations.

572 Immediately ... J to DA, 10 Mar and 3 May 1966; DA to Royal Naval Benevolent Society and to Housing and Community Association, Chingford, both 12 May 1966; Royal Naval Benevolent Society to DA, 18 May 1966.

Not all were ... J to MM, 10 May, 15 Aug, 26 Aug, 21 Sept, 1 Oct 1966; J to DA, 12 Apr and 7 Oct 1967; AH to J, 1 Dec 1966; FW to André Deutsch, 4 Dec 1966; Arts Council to J, 15 Dec 1967 (EA).

Footnote: FW to author.

573 As the novel ... Hunter Davies, page 13; J But interview with author, 24 Nov 1984.

This was ... J But interview; 'SIOL', SIOL 169, CS 383.

Quotation: Typescript draft for SP (marked 'MGS', i.e. MS).

Typically ... J But interview; 'MGS' typescript draft for SP; PT interview with author, 4 Dec 1985. Both MM and DP stayed with J But, for instance.

J had exactly the same conversation about 'mystery' with DA (DA to author, 13 Mar 1990).

574 It was ... L 254, 274; SO to J, 1 Mar and 2 May 1964, 2 and 5 Jan 1967; SO to DA, 13 Oct 1966, 5 Jan 1967; J to SO, 17 Nov and 21 Dec 1966, 'Sunday' (Jan 1967), 'Sunday' (Jan 1967) and 18 Feb 1967; J to MM, 'Sunday' (Jan 1967); DA in *Ham & High*; DA to author 24 and 30 June 1986, 13 Mar 1990; DA to J, 2 Jan 1967; DA interviews and conversations; FW to author, 4 Oct 1984; JH, 'Jean by Jo', page 3; MM to AS, 27 Nov 1972 (copy sent to author by AS).

575 Most of what ... L 12; FW to author 17 Oct 1984; J to SO, 2 May 1967.

576 After the great ... DA interview, 17 Aug 1983.

She felt this ... J to MM, 10 May and 9 July 1966; J to SvD, 15 June 1966; J to DA, 1 Apr and 26 Apr 1966; J to AR, 19 June 1963; SO to J, 28 Apr 1968; GB to J, 11 Aug 1967; YD to J, 18 Dec 1968; W.L. Webb, 'Lately Prized', *The Guardian*, 14 Dec 1967.

577 Even before ... DA to J, 17 Oct 1966; J to DA, 11 Oct 1966; J to MM, 1 Oct, 17 Oct, 21 Oct 1966; J to OH, 22 Oct 1966; J to SvD, 15 June 1966; J to FW, 8 Apr 1966.

Jean had been ... L 243-4; J to SvD, 16 Sept 1966; J to DA, 1 Dec 1966; J to MM, 24 Sept 1966. The person who wanted to adapt Mackenzie was a Mrs Elizabeth Hart (see JS to J, 14 September 1966, EA). For an account of the J-SvD fiasco told more from SvD's side (but without, it seems to me, justifying her behaviour), see Donna Marie Nudd, 'The Uneasy Voyage of Jean Rhys and Selma vaz Dias', *Literature in Performance*, pages 20-32.

Now she was ... J to DA, 1, 6 and 27 Dec 1966; OH to J, 6 Dec 1966; MW interview; J to MM, 5 Dec and 29 Dec 1966; DA to J, 28 Feb 1967; JS to J, 15 Nov 1966.

578 But let's ... and So did ... Mellown 17, 70–74; *Times Literary Supplement*, 17 Nov 1966, page 1039; L 269.

I say ... For early reviews, see eg Neville Braybrooke in the *Spectator*, 28 Oct 1966; John Knowler, *Books and Bookmen*, 12 Dec 1966; Francis Hope, *New Statesman*, 28 Oct 1966.

579 Selma didn't ... Mellown 71; DA to J, 21 Dec 1966.

Despite the best ... SO to J, 2 Jan 1967; J to SO, 'Sunday' (Jan 1967); J to MM, 'Sunday' (Jan 1967) and 4 Oct 1967; J to JF, 24 Sept 1968.

Coming back ... J to MM, 15 Feb and 24 Mar 1967; 'The Cottage', draft for SP: DA, *Ham & High*; JH, 'Jean by Jo', pages 3–5; DRW interviews; J But interview; OS + Mollie Stoner interview, 24 Nov 1984; JF interview, 26 Nov 1985.

580 Some months ... J to OH, 30 July 1966; Royal Literary Society to J, 5 Apr 1967; Mellown 43, 56, 72; J to MM, 24 Mar and 26 July 1967; J to SO, 14 and 24 July 1967; OH to J, 19 Feb 1967.

Even so ... J to DA, 12 Nov 1966 and 7 Feb 1967; J to SO, 2 Sept 1968; J to FW, 11 Sept 1967 and 19 Feb 1968; J to GB, 20 Sept 1967. Almost all J's letters repeated plaints about the cold, wind, rain and isolation of Cheriton Fitzpaine.

So it went ... J to DA, 29 May and 7 Oct 1967; J to FW, 12 May and 18 Oct 1967; J to SO, 29 Apr and 20 Oct 1967; J to MM, 3 Aug, 29 and 30 Oct 1967; DA to Chingford Housing and Community Association, 12 May 1966; DA to author, 24 June 1986.

581 Now Deutsch ... DA to J, 28 Feb and 21 Mar 1967; J to DA, 3 Mar 1967.

She herself ... J to DA, 6 Mar 1967.

The rest of her time ... SO to J, 21 July 1967; J to SO, 20 Oct and 29 Dec 1967; J to FW, 14 Oct, 18 Oct, 24 Oct 1967; Webb article; Arts Council to J, 15 Dec 1967; Mellown 175; DA, Note on Jean Rhys's 'hibernations' (her regular winter visits to London).

582 What she didn't ... Judy Froshaug came in May (J to OH, 22 May 1967) and her interview with J appeared in *Nova* in September; in June Sally Williams interviewed her (J to OH, 2 June), and this appeared in the *Evening Standard* on 12 and 21 June. Other interviews were planned with 'a Sunday Times man' in April (J to SO, 29 Apr), the poet Dom Moraes in May (OH to J, 3 May), an American in June (J to OH, 24 June), and a Dutch journalist in October (J to MM, 4 Oct).

She bore it ... J Br interview, 24 Nov 1984; DA to author, 5 Aug 1983, 30 June 1986.

Almost always ... Eg J to MM, 27 May 1967.

In the spring ... J to DA, 16 Mar, 5 May 1967; SO to J, 2 May 1967; J to OH, 22 Apr, 1, 5, 12 May, 3, 5, 7, 10 and 13 June 1967; (OH note on Jean Rhys correspondence, Tulsa 3:3).

Footnote: *Radio Times*, 23–27 Nov 1974, page 38.

583 Quotation: SP 19.

WSS was ... AS interviews; AS to DA, 19 Jan 1967; Tulsa Items 3:1.

584 Then in early ... OS Note on the Jean Rhys letters, Tulsa 3:13.

It was an important ... and Oliver Stoner ... J to OS, 27 May, 3 June, 28 June, 14 Aug 1968 (Tulsa 3:14 − 3:15); J to MM, 17 June, 9 Aug 1968; Tulsa Items 3:15 − 3:16; OS interview with author, 24 Nov 1984; J to SO, 2 Sept and 14 Nov 1968; J to FW, 7 Nov 1968.

585 The first was ... to This time ... JF interview with author, 26 Nov 1985; J to JF, 23 Feb 1968. See J to SO, 28 Aug 1968; 'I'm not going to give any more interviews except to friends!'

586 Jean was ... JF interview with author and correspondence with J.
  The next new ... Tulsa Items 4:3 – 4:5.
  Mr Greenslade ... to They walk ... (page 587): HR, 'Meeting Jean', *London Magazine*, July 1986, pages 75-78. By kind permission of Mr Ronson.
  The 'comfortable man' quotations come from J to SO, 11 Nov 1967, and are actually about Laurence Cottrell, whom she met over the W.H. Smith prize.
587 When I went ... J interview with author, 29 Sept 1975.
588 After the long ... and Tigers was almost ... Mellown 45, 82-4.
  This new step ... Hannah Carter article, 5.
  Quotation: 'Bricks Without Straw'.
589 And in fact ... See eg Mellown 175-176; Hannah Carter; DA to author, 5 Aug 1983 and 30 June 1986; WSS 76; JF interview with author; J interview with author.
  By the end ... Mellown 47, 57, 64, 75, 79, 92; YD to J, 18 Dec 1968. Re Jean's success coming too late, see eg Marcelle Bernstein, page 50; JF interview with author; Al Alv interview with author, 11 July 1985; D Pet interview with author, 12 Oct 1984.
590 She was saying ... J to SO, 15 Jan 1968; Hannah Carter; J to DA, 11 Nov 1966. For J's routine remaining much the same for the next seven years, see 'My Day' and 'Mrs Pearce'.
  She woke ... J to SO, 22 Feb 1968.
  She had a new ... J to DA, 7 Feb 1968; MM to SvD, 6 Dec 1967 and 16 Jan 1968, SvD to MM, 9 Feb 1968 (Tulsa 2:13); MM to AS, 30 July 1968; J to MM, 15 Jan and 9 Aug 1968.
  At the end ... J to MM, 16 Nov 1968; J to SO, 2 Dec 1968; FW to author.
591 During 1969 ... Mellown 12-13, 28-9, 47, 57-8; J to FW, 20 Oct 1969. J to MM, 29 Jan 1970; J to OS, 5 Sept 1969; J to AF, 21 Nov 1969.
  Immediately after ... Marcelle Bernstein; J to DA, 11 June 1969.
  And this interview ... J to DA, 24 July 1969; J to MM, 25 June 1969; J to JF, 26 June 1969; J to OS, 26 June 1969; J to SO, 2 July 1969.
592 Nonetheless she made ... LC to author, 7 Nov l985; J to LC, 27 Oct 1969; Two people actually sent Jean manuscripts (see J to SO, 20 June 1969).
  Everyone who knew ... LC to author, 7 Nov 1985; Marcelle Bernstein; J to FW, 6 July 1970.
  It was an extraordinary ... DA to LC, 18 Aug 1981; JF interview with author.
  Partly, Larry ... LC conversation with author, 29 May 1987; DA interviews and conversations with author.
593 She ought to have ... J to AF, 14 July 1970, 6 Apr and 19 Oct 1971 (see also J to HR, 'Monday', 1970 (Tulsa 4:4), 'Isn't that *just* like me?'); AF interview with author, 5 Nov 1984; J to MM, 10 July 1969; DW page 45. For AF's presents to J, see their correspondence in EA.
594 Quotation: J to DA, 6 Aug 1969. The woman was Maerie Hume McKinney, a friend of the Stoners (see Ibid., and Maerie Hume McKinney to J, 8 May 1969, in EA.)
  She was trying ... J to MM, 13 Jan, 14 Feb and 27 Dec 1969; J to SO, 2 July, 29 Oct, 21 Dec, 27 Dec 1969; J to FW, 30 Sept and 15 Oct 1969; J to OS, 15 Dec 1969; 'Fears', 6-12-38, in EA.
595 She had friends ... J to MM, 10 July 1969; J to OS, 14 July 1969; J to FW, 23 Sept 1969; J to SO, 25 Sept, 21 Dec, 27 Dec 1969, 7 Jan 1970. See also AF, LC and JF correspondence. For waiting for and relying on whisky, see (eg) J to SO, 15 Feb 1969 ('I try to keep off whisky and soda until such and such a time. Then watch the clock anxiously'), and J to FW, 23 Sept 1969 ('That's the great snag and temptation down here – the whisky bottle.')

Despite everything ... J to SO, 4 Apr and 23 Apr 1969; J to MM, 24 Aug 1969; J to OS, 7 Aug, 9 Aug, 19 Aug, 30 Aug, 5 Sept 1969; J to FW, 27 Nov 1969; J to DA, 11 June, 24 July, 2 Aug 1969.

The Selma affair. ... J to MM, 5 June 1969; J to DA, 11 June 1969; J to FW, 27 July 1969; J to OS, 5 Sept 1969.

596 But now ... DA to J, 9 June, 31 July, 5 Aug 1969; J to DA, 6 Aug 1969; J to OS, 4 Aug, 7 Aug, 9 Aug 1969; J to SvD, 11 June and 14 June 1969.

Now Jean ... J to DA, 6 Aug 1969; J to OS, 9 Aug 1969; J to MM, 24 Aug and 6 Oct 1969.

It was so ... For J's bad health in the winter of 1969-1970, see her letters at the time to MM, FW and SO. For colitis, see J to MM, 2 Apr 1969; for heart attack, J to OS, 10 June 1970.

In 1970 ... Mellown 58-61.

Now the only ... 'Bricks Without Straw'. See also DW 39.

597 Now, however ... J to FW, 4 Dec 1969, 15 Jan, 21 Jan, 19 May, 24 May, 14 Aug 1970; J to OH, 17 Oct and 19 Nov 1969, 26 Feb and 20 Mar 1970; J to MM, 4 Aug 1970. For J turning to shorter pieces when stuck on longer work, see eg L 50 and 144 ('English Harbour' when stuck on WSS), and L 184 ('LTCIJ' when stuck on WSS).

Other things ... J to SO, 28 Feb and 21 Mar 1970; J to FW, 14 Mar 1970; MM interview with author.

598 To explain ... J to OS, 6 Mar 1970; DW 31. See also SP 61; 'I believe that sometimes human beings can be greater than themselves', 'can be taken over, possessed by something outside, something greater.'

Another distracting ... J to SO, 21 May 1970; J to FW, 27 Mar, 2 Apr, 10 Apr, 15 Apr, 21 Apr 1970; J to MM, 14 Apr 1970; J to OS, 6 Apr 1970. J copied MV's letter to FW in her letter of 27 March.

599 Soon after this ... to Of course she ... (page 600): JvH, 'H in C'. By kind permission of Mr van Houts. See also J to SO, 21 May 1970, and J to MM, 16 May 1970. The story J wrote about JvH is 'WKWUITA'.

Footnote: J to SO, 21 May 1970; MV to J, 3 July 1971; Amnesty International to J, 1 Apr 1971 (both in EA).

600 What had happened? ... MK, 'A Little Learning', *Maatstaf* No. 3, 1983 has several of JvH's photographs of J (on pages 70-71).

Quotation: 'WKWUITA', SIOL 152, CS 371.

But soon ... J to FW, 12 May 1970; J to SO, 3 June 1970; 'WKWUITA' and 'H in C', *passim*.

601 Through most ... Eg J to SO, 27 Oct, 5 Nov, 9 Dec 1970; J to MM, 2 Nov 1970.

He had reached ... J to SO, 9 Dec 1970; J to MM, 2 Apr, 12 June, 25 June, 28 Oct, 17 Nov 1969, 29 Jan and 26 Nov 1970.

Probably, then ... DRW interviews, JB interview.

Well, she was ... DRW interviews; MW interview and letter to author, 15 Dec 1985; PT interview.

602 Still, once ... J to OS, 21 Nov 1970; J to HR, 18 Dec 1970; J to SO, 9 Dec 1970; J to MM, 26 Nov 1970.

Alas, it was ... to But even this ... (page 603): DRW interviews; JRW interview and letter to author, 9 June 1985.

By Christmas Mr Greenslade had a new, very smart car (see J to MM, Christmas Day 1970 and J to SO, 24 Dec 1970): he may very well have had it already.

For J's saying she knew no one at Edward's funeral, see J to MM, 26 Nov 1970.

603 Quotation: J to MM, 26 Nov 1970.

And to Sonia ... J to SO, 9 Dec 1970.

It's a microcosm ... DRW and JRW interviews; J to MM, Ibid.; SP 92; MM interview with author; JF interview with author; DA interviews with author.

Re mixing up Robin Beck and JRW; she wrote to MM 'One of the young men had a very nice face and seemed a bit disturbed. I *think* he was my brother Owen's son, but I can't be sure.' I'm certain this was Robin Beck: everyone felt that way about him.

604 Nothing was worse ... DM diary notes, 9 Nov 1977 (EA); DM interview with author, 3 Oct 1984; DW 39; 'Possible end to the autobiography', draft for SP in EA, marked 'MGS' (MS): 'I have only one object in my mind, that somehow when I look in the glass the face I always had known will look back at me.'

605 She had an ... 'M & W', 'V'.

Quotation: J to MM, 7 Oct 1972. See also eg J to EM (grand-daughter), 12 July 1977 (EA).

By the time ... Mellown, appropriate pages (for paperback editions of the novels), 152 (for film of Q), 137–149 for stories and articles; Edward's will; Royal Literary Fund to DA, 15 Aug 1972; J to DA, 19 Aug 1972; 10 Downing Street to J, 25 Jan 1974; Arts Council to J, 8 Mar 1977; Arts Council to DA, 11 Nov 1973; J to SO, 4 Oct 1976 (South West Arts providing MS.) Glenda Jackson bought the film rights of GMM in 1976. WSS has been under option to someone more or less since it came out; in 1990 the rights were bought by an Australian producer, Jan Sharp.

Footnote: Edward's will.

606 The result ... DRW interviews; tax submission to Inland Revenue, 1976 (EA); Michael Henshaw to author, 1985; bank statements for 1977 (EA); DM interview with author; DW 43.

J's nurse was J Br; her cleaning woman was first Mrs Raymond, then Mrs Lee; her typist Mary Stephenson (see DA to SO, 1 Nov 1977); her gardener Mr Muggridge; her driver Mr Greenslade, and then Mr Pike. Gini Stevens and MS ('literary aides') were paid for out of grants, and DP offered his help free; J did however give him £500 in 1976 (DW 30 and 36). She had, of course, many agents – JS, OH, Gini Stevens, PR, Ant S ... But after 1976 Ant S became her sole literary agent (see Ant S to J, 29 Nov 1976, in EA), and PR her sole dramatic agent. Apart from these, of course, there was always her one-third to SvD.

Of course ... DW 43; A Alv, D Pet and JF interviews; OH description of Jean Rhys correspondence (Tulsa 3:3); MW interview; Lord Chamberlain's office to J, 23 July 1975; Central Chancery of the Orders of Knighthood to J, 11 Jan 1978.

From early ... J to MM, 2 Dec and 30 Dec 1970; J to SO, 14 Nov and 7 Apr 1970; J to JF, 12 Sept 1971; SO to DM, 16 Aug 1977; J to FW, 7 Apr 1971; 'Jean by Jo' page 2; AF interview with author; DM interview with author; JH to author, March 1990.

But the happier ... DW 28.

I was a bit ... J to MM, 7 May 1971; For J's 'prejudices', see J to FW 9 and 27 July 1975, MS *Recollections*, page 29, and DW 17, 50. Certainly J often defended her father's generation in old age (FW to author).

608 But her older ... MM to AS, 30 July 1968 and 27 Nov 1972; J to MM, 7 May 1971. And see DA to author, phone conversation 16 Aug 1988; 'Jean really loved Maryvonne, though they couldn't get on. They always quarrelled within two days, and Jean started it.'

It wasn't only ... J to SO, 7 Apr 1971; J to MM, 17 Nov 1969, 7 May 1971.

Now, at eighty ... J to SO, 3 May, 14 May, 4 June 1971.

But to Maryvonne J to MM, 7 May 1971.

609 Quotation: J to MM, 11 May 1971.

Back in Cheriton ... J to FW, 7, 11, 30 Apr, 24 Nov 1971, 11 Sept 1972; J to

AF, 15 July, 19 Oct 1971; J to SO, 19, 24, 30 Nov1971. This problem about not being able to finish things was at least a year old (see J to SO, 27 Oct 1970).
Age was beginning ... J to SO, 24 Nov 1971, 20 Dec 1972; PT interview; J to OS, 14 July 1974.

J only ever had one quarrel with the Greenslades; now, towards the end. Like so many of her quarrels, it was about money. She thought she'd paid for something; the Greenslades knew she hadn't (this happened with J But too). It was very quickly smoothed over by SO, who was fortunately there at the time. There were no hard feelings on either side, and the friendship was saved. (J to SO, 23 Aug 1971: PT interview: J But interview.)

610 Mr Woodard too ... MW and Helen Howitt in interview; J to SO, 24 Nov 1971.

Finally, there was ... Death records, St Catherine's House; DRW interviews; MS, *Recollections*, page 32. Lily died in the autumn.

She first called ... MS, page 32; *New Yorker*, 11 Sept 1978, pages 38-9, CS 396-400. J writes *siffleur de montagne*, but Leigh Fermor, eg writes it without the *de* (page 125), and LH agrees (DS, page 14).

Lily's life ... DRW interviews; LTS to AS, 29 Feb 1936; DA letter to author, 16 Jan 1986; JB interview; 'TWB'.

611 Underneath all this ... 'TWB'; MS, 34.

Ill health ... J to MM, 28 Dec 1971, 6, 12 Jan, 20 Feb, 5 May, 28 June 1972; J to SO, 13 Jan, 11 May, 30 June 1972; J to AF, 30 Jan 1972; J to OS, (?) Feb and 22 Mar 1972; J to FW, 11 May and 11 Sept 1972.

More important ... Mellown 176-181 for up to 1972, 181-186 for 1973-1974, 186-202 for 1975-1982.

She didn't care ... John Hall, page 8; J to SO, 13 Jan 1972.

612 Another article ... J to FW, 15 May 1972.

It was by ... V.S. Naipaul, 'Without a Dog's Chance', *NY Review of Books*, 18 May 1972, pages 29-31; J to FW, 12 May 1972. The article was written on the occasion of the reissue of ALMM in America.

What did Naipaul ... Naipaul, *op.cit.*; J to FW, same letter.

613 The last piece ... L'Aff Ford is dated to 1972 by (1) '1972' appearing on the draft in the Gr Ex Bk (Tulsa 1:1, at the back); (2) J's letter to FW about it, and his reply, are dated 28 and 29 Dec 1972; (3) FW's *Trotsky*, to which he refers as recently published, appeared in 1972.

The saddest story ... Mizener to J, 26 Nov and 2 Dec 1965 (EA); L'Aff Ford.

She was in Crediton ... and Reading it ... L'Aff Ford.

She was in a frenzy ... J to SO, 7 Dec 1972; J to FW, 28 Dec 1972; Gr Ex Bk. J's letter to SO is misdated to 1973.

614 L'Affaire Ford ... L'Aff Ford.

In fact, Mizener ... Mizener, 345, 583; J to SO, 7 Dec 1972. For the question of FMF's 'allowance', and J's 'hysterical attacks', see Part One, Chapter Five.

615 This was Viv ... PT interview; JvH, 'H in C', pages 3 and 7; 'SIOL', SIOL 168, CS 383; J But interview; MW interview.

But Jean's paranoia ... J to MM, 7 Oct 1972, 9 Oct 1973; J to DA, 19 Aug, 12 Sept 1972; J to SO, 1 Sept 1972; J to FW, 11 Sept 1972; J to SvD, 25 Sept 1972; 'SIOL', SIOL 168, CS 383; MW interview.

Finally, 1972 ... MW interview; 'In Memoriam Rev. F.A. Woodard', *Church Times*, 6 Sept 1974; DW 49-50; MS, *Recollections*, 14-15; 'Possible end to the autobiography', pages 4-5 (EA).

616 This is a very ... EW to author, Aug 1985.

We know ... J to SO, 20 Dec 1972, 15 Mar, 29 May, 24 Aug 1973.

Quotation: 'My Day'.

She couldn't ... J to OS, 3 May 1973.

Her last ... Death records; J to SvD, 25 Sept 1972; FW to author, 21 Aug 1984.
For J's seeing AH and liking him, see eg J to OS, 14 June and 3 Aug 1968; J to
MM, 10 July 1969; J to SO, 14 Aug 1970.

617 As a result ... JH interview with author, 25 Oct 1984; A Alv interview with
author, 11 July 1985; DM interview with author, 3 Oct 1984.

But men ... J to MM, 31 Mar, 4 Sept 1972; J to SO, 1 Sept, 20 Dec 1972, 14
Apr 1973.

Gini Stevens ... JH interview with author; 'Jean by Jo', page 1.

1973 was ... J to MM, 7 June, 9 Oct 1973; J to SO, 29 May, 29 July, 24 Aug
1973; J to FW, 27 June, 3 July, 9 July 1973. The 'two or three' stories J finished
were (it's clear from these letters) 'SIOL', 'TIW' and possibly still or again
'WKWUITA'; the two very old ones were 'Kikimora' and 'NO 1925'.

This year J also had a much shorter London holiday, February only, which
also perhaps helped to conserve her energy. This was because she'd cracked a rib
in a fall; also Eaton Place was being sold for flats, and SO had to find her a new
hotel. Certainly she enjoyed the winter break in 1973 much more than the
previous year. (Information from J to SO, 21 Jan, 5 Mar 1972; J to MM, 30 Nov
1972; J to AF, 7 Dec 1972; DA, Note on Jean Rhys's hibernations.)

For the importance of Gini and Jo to the improvement in Jean's life see eg.
OH's description of her Jean Rhys correspondence in Tulsa: 'Then in 72-3 she
befriended two women who "took her over" for a few years, making her life
easier in the ways she most needed – fairly constant company, driving her
around, taking her shopping for the lovely clothes she still craved, organising
refurnishing of her cottage and typing her work.'

What Gini and Jo ... J to MM, 15 June 1971, 11 Aug 1972; 'Jean by Jo', pages
4-5; my own observations, 1975; MS *Recollections*, 31.

618 Originally the idea ... J to SO, 3 Apr, 29 Oct 1973, 2 Apr 1974; J to MM, 15
Mar, 28 Mar, 12 July, 11 Sept, 9 Oct, 22 Oct, 11 Dec 1973; 'Jean by Jo', pages
3-5; JH to author, 10 Mar 1990.

In December ... J to SO, 3 Apr, 29 May, 27 Dec 1973; J to DM, 7 Oct 1973;
'Jean by Jo', pages 4-5.

This first ... L 53 and J to MM, 14 Apr 1957 (in these letters J encourages MM
to write and paint); FW to author; JH to author, 10 Mar 1990; DA to Charles
Osborne (Arts Council), 7 Oct 1973; Arts Council to DA, 16 Nov 1973.

619 At long last ... DA to Charles Osborne, 7 Oct 1973.

Jean was moving ... DA to J, 10 Jan 1974; J to FW, 30 Dec 1973; J to SO, 10
Sept and 27 Dec 1973.

The first new ... J to SO, 2 Apr 1974; J to FW, 11 Apr, 20 May 1974; J to DA,
4 Feb 1974; Cheriton Fitzpaine interviews.

Footnote: J to FW, 20 May 1974; Red Ex Bk No 2, pages 1-7 (Tulsa 1:1).

620 But it was true ... 'FW', SIOL 43-62, CS 298-311; J to SO, 24 May 1974; J to
FW, 20 May 1974, 9 July, 29 July, 27 Aug 1975; DA to Charles Osborne, 7 Oct
1973.

Jean, of course ... J to SO, 14 May 1974; J to FW, 29 Mar, 20 May 1974; J to
MM, 27 Mar, 8 June 1974, 14 Apr 1975.

In the meantime ... Mellown 16-18, 34, 61-2, 84-87, 152; BBC to J, 14 Aug
1973 (EA). 'ISAS' had been televised in 1972 (see J to DA, 12 Sept 1972).

WSS had been paperbacked in America in 1973 (Mellown 76). This left only
VID, paperbacked in 1975 (Mellown 48), *Tigers,* paperbacked in 1976 (Mellown
90), and SIOL, paperbacked in 1978 (Mellown 106).

Alvarez's claim ... A Alv, 'The Best Living English Novelist', pages 6-7.

This article ... Alice K. Turner, 'Jean Rhys Rediscovered: How It Happened',

*Publishers' Weekly*, 1 July 1974, pages 56 and 58; Mellown 62–3, 184.

621  Alvarez sent ... A Alv interview; DA interview, 25 Oct 1984; *Publishers' Weekly* article; J to OS, 17 Apr 1975 ('My books had no sale in New York until Alvarez wrote his article'); J to FW, 11 Apr 1974; J to LC, 22 Sept 1975.
They sat ... and To his amazement ... A Alv interview. For J liking A Alv, see eg J to FW, 11 Apr 1974, J to LC, 22 Sept 1975.
Altogether it was ... CC to Jean [?] 1974 (EA); J to SO, 24 May 1974, 'Friday' [1975].

622  Tristram questioned her ... J to FW, 29 Mar 1974; J to SO, 2 Apr 1974; TP to J, 30 Oct 1974 (EA); J to OS, 21 June 1975; J But interview.
But things ... 'Jean by Jo', page 3; 'My Day'; J to FW, 30 Dec 1973; J to MM, 2, 27 Mar, 11 Apr 1974; J to SO, 14 May 1974; Mellown 185; DA to J, 18 Sept 1974 and J to DA, 19 Sept 1974 (*Women's Wear Daily*); 10 Downing Street to J, 25 Jan 1974.
It had started ... J to FW, 20 May 1974 and 9 July 1975; DA to J, 3 July 1974; OH description of Jean Rhys correspondence (Tulsa 3:3); J to OS, 17 Apr 1975; J to SO, 'Friday' [1975]; J to MM, 8 June 1974.

623  That was the rub ... J to SO, 29 Aug 1974, 24 Oct 1975, and 'Friday' [1975]; J to OS, 7 and 17 Apr 1975; J to DA, 12 May 1975; DA to Charles Osborne, 7 Oct 1973; DA to J, 16 May 1975; J to FW, 7 Nov 1974.
The arrangement ... Arts Council to DA, 11 Nov 1973; DA to Gini Stevens, 20 Nov 1973; J to SO, 16 June, 11 Aug, 23 Sept, 11 Oct 1974; J to MM, 8 June and 21 Sept 1974; J to FW, 7 Nov 1974; J to OS, 7 Apr 1975; Gini Stevens to OS, 11 Dec 1974; J to Michael Henshaw, 25 Nov 1974.

624  Now there was ... DA to J, 7 Nov 1974; DA, *Ham & High*; J to FW, 27 Feb 1975; J to DA, 12 May 1975.
So nothing ... DA to MM, 16 May 1975; DA to J, 16 May 1975; J to MM, 14 Apr and 11 July 1975; FW to DA, 25 May 1975; J to SO, 2 Aug and [?] Oct 1975; J to FW, 27 Aug 1975; J to DA, 2 Oct 1975.
She had done it ... J to MM, 8 Mar, 14 Apr, 15 June, 20 Nov 1975; J to OS, 29 Mar, 7 Apr, 17 Apr 1975; J to SO, 14 Mar, [?] Oct, 24 Oct, and'Friday', 1975; J to FW, 7 Mar and 9 July 1975; DP interview; DA to Tax Inspector, 13 Apr 1976 (enclosed in DA to J, same date); Tax Inspector to DA, 5 May 1976.
Finishing a book ... Mellown 137; PT interview; J to SO, 24 Oct, 'Friday', and 10 Nov 1975; J to FW, 9 and 27 July 1975; J to OS, 17 Apr 1975; J to MM, 8 June 1974; DW 19, 30.

625  Her friends realised ... DA to DM, 6 Sept 1976; DA, Note on Jean Rhys's hibernations; 'Mrs Pearce'; DW 10ff,66.
The many many years ... DW 9–28.

626  Quotation: DW 28.

PART FOUR, CHAPTER TWO

627  At last however ... SO in DW 66; SO to DM, 16 Aug 1977, 5 Dec 1977; J to SO, 29 Sept 1976; J to OS, 17 Apr 1975; DA to MM, 20 Dec 1976; DA *Ham & High*; DA in Bailey radio; JH to DM, undated; DM interview; DW 30, 33, 41, 50.

628  The first ... DW 28–30.
She began ... DW 30–33; DA to author, 5 Aug 1983. The line 'After what was then called ...' now opens the second paragraph of 'Christmas Day' in SP (page 118).
Despite this ... DW 32.

629  By now Jean ... DA to J, 17 Apr 1976; DA to J But, 1 Mar 1976; J to DA, May 1976; CC to OS, 25 Mar 1976 (Tulsa 4:2).

Help had always ... J But to DA, 3 and 6 Mar 1976; DA to J Br, 1 Apr 1976; J Br to DA, 3 Apr 1976. J Br had recently injured her back and could no longer work full time (J Br interview with author, 24 Nov 1984).

In early April ... DA to J, 17 Apr 1976; J to DA, 17 Apr and 'May' 1976; J to SO, 17 Apr and 16 Oct 1976; J to MM, 14 May 1976; MS, *Recollections*, 20, 23; J Br interview. J Br said: 'We had three and a half years together, of which the first one was fine.' It was just over three years altogether (April 1976 to May 1979), with long winter breaks when Jean was in London. I'm taking it (with help from Jean's letters) that the first 'fine' year was from April 1976 to April 1977, of which in fact J Br and J spent only April to October 1976 together. So did the other ... DW 33; J to SO, 21 June 1976.

Michael Schwab ... J to FW, 27 Aug 1976; J to DA, 25 Aug 1976; J to SO, 4 Oct, 16 Oct, 21 Oct 1976; DW; MS, pages 1-2.

630 Quotation: MS, 1.
David Plante ... MS 31, 35; DW 66.
She started ... DW 23, 66; MS 7-11, 13-14, 16-18, 21, 23, 26-28, 30, 32, 35.

631 On 21 October ... J to SO, 21 Oct 1976; Mellown 96-100; DW 38; MS 8; J to OS, 15 Sept 1976; J to FW, 25 Oct 1976; J to DA, 25 Aug 1976 ('[I feel] it is my business to live so that I've a chance of finishing [SP]').
Because of ... Mellown 138; Bibeb, interview with J; Ned Thomas, 'Meeting Jean Rhys', *Planet*, Aug 1976, pages 29-31; Anna Petschek, 'The shy lady novelist who went missing for 20 years', *Daily Express*, 1 Sept 1976; Barry Pree, 'Meet ... Sargasso Lady', *Observer Magazine*, 3 Oct 1976; Angus Wilson and Milton Shulman discuss SIOL, 28 Oct 1976, BBC (Mellown 152).
Quotation: J to DA, 8 Sept 1976.
She put all this ... 'Bricks Without Straw'.

632 This was hardly ... MS 28 (also 13, 23, 32, 35); J to SO, 29 Sept 1976; J to MM, Oct 1976; J to DA, 8 Sept 1976; J to FW, 25 Oct 1976; Ant S to J, 29 Nov 1976.
It was the time ... DM interview; DA interviews; DA, Note on Jean Rhys's hibernations; MS 30, 33, 38; J to FW, 25 Oct 1976; J to MM, 30 Oct 1976.
The horrors ... MS 39; DW 33.
And indeed ... DW 33, 37; DM interview; 'Jean Book', in EA.

633 The rota ... 'Jean Book', EA; MS 39-40.
There were just ... DM interview; DA, Note on Jean Rhys's hibernations; DW 33, 42; DM to SO, begun in Wotton-under-Edge [1978], EA; MS 41.
Quotation: MS 41.
Schwab now returned ... DW 33-4.
Footnote: DA interviews; FW interviews; J to SO, Apr 1977.

634 'A paste up?' ... DW 35.
This was ... DW 35; DA interview 17 Aug 1983.
Plante typed ... and In fact ... DW 36; DA interview. DA also points out that J left SP 'in more or less the chronological form he devised for it'.
He did ... DW 36-7, 41-46.

635 Her increasing ... DW 36-8; 'Jean by Jo' 7.
It was crazy ... 'Jean by Jo' 7.
In late February ... DW 44, 46; DP interview with author.

636 Nevertheless she went ... DA to DM, 24 May 1978; 'Jean by Jo' 7-8; JH to SO, undated, from Venice, EA.
For two weeks ... JH to SO, same letter; 'Jean by Jo' 8; JH interview with author, 25 Oct 1984.
Quotation: 'Jean by Jo' 9.
Of course ... JH to SO from Venice, 10 March 1977, and undated; JH to GM from Venice, 12 Mar 1977; J to DM, 29 Mar 1977; J But interview.

Back in England ... DM interview.

It was a bad ... J to SO, 16 Oct 1976; DA to J Br, 1 Apr 1976; J Br interview with author.

637 Worse than any ... J Br interview; DW 50.

Sensibly Janet ... J Br interview.

638 It's a horrible story ... Judging by WWM, FMF would have recognised this devilish J too; and the actress Anna Massey, who went to the Chelsea flat once to help with J, and saw her 'scoot along like nobody's business when she wanted to' (Anna Massey to author, 1985).

Perhaps ... J Br interview.

The rest of 1977 ... The last Tulsa letter between J and SvD is from 1973.

Selma died ... Death records.

The answer ... Information on the legal position from FW in many conversations, most recently 17 Oct 1989; also from PR, telephone conversations 27 Nov 1984. Legal advice has often been taken over the twenty-one years since the final contract between J and SvD was signed, and it has always been concluded that this would be the likely verdict in a court of law.

Almost all J's letters about the SvD affair reiterate her despair that it was reducing her money for MM. Just as one example, see her summary to PR, 6 Oct 1978 (EA).

There was yet ... Death records.

This unhappy ... JB interview; PT interview; MW letter to author, 6 Jan 1986; DA interviews.

What happened ... JB interview; DRW interviews; DA interviews; Brenda Powell will; Brenda Powell clinical record, St Andrew's Hospital, Northampton; JRW letter to author, 9 June 1985.

640 The story of Brenda's ... DRW interviews; JRW interview and letter to author, 9 June 1985; JB interview.

Brenda's illness ... DRW interviews; JB interviews; St Andrew's Hospital, Northampton, clinical record and correspondence; J to SO, 27 June 1977.

641 The very first ... DRW interviews; JB interview; clinical record and correspondence.

Anger and anxiety ... JB interview (for family's explanations).

We'll never know ... FW interviews.

Footnote: Death records.

642 As autumn ... J to MM, 8 Aug 1977; J to SO, 4, 17 and 26 Aug 1977; FW to author.

Several years before ... 'Mrs Pearce'; SO to DM, 16 Aug 1977; SO in DW 65; DM interview with author; DA, Note on Jean Rhys's hibernations; J to MM, 8 Aug 1977; J to SO, 12 Oct 1977; DA to SO, 1 Nov 1977.

As long as ... DA to SO, 1 Nov 1977; DM interview.

There was nothing for it ... DA to SO, 1 Nov 1977.

643 That was how ... DA to SO, 21 Nov 1977. J stayed at the Mellys' from Nov until late Feb, when she went into a nursing home. She was back in Cheriton Fitzpaine by 1 March 1978 (see DM to SO, 1 Mar 1978).

Quotation: ALMM 122.

Di Melly felt sure ... DM interview; D Pet interview; DA to SO, 1 and 21 Nov 1977; J to SO, Dec 1977; DW 46.

644 For a long time ... DA to SO, 21 Nov 1977; DM to SO, undated letters, 1977/8.

Quotation: SO to DM, 21 Nov 1977.

'Now my drenched ...' J to SO, Dec 1977; SO to DM, 5 Dec 1977.

Di stood it ... DA to SO, 21 Nov 1977; DM interview; DM diary notes, 9 Nov 1977; A Alv interview.

She also got on ... DM interview; DM to SO, undated letter, 1977/8.

Quotation: DM interview; 'Life with You', EA. This has now been set to music, and is sung by GM on 'Anything Goes', record album by GM and John Chilton's Feetwarmers.

645 Jean and George ... DM interview; DM undated letters to SO, 1977/8; DM diary note, 9 Nov 1977; DA to SO, 21 Nov 1977; Central Chancery of the Orders of Knighthood to J, 11 Jan 1978 (investiture at Buckingham Palace, 7 Feb 1978).

Some of the people who found J's conversation frustrating, because so secretive and formal (though often they didn't mind) were PR (to author, 27 Nov 1984), D Pet and A Alv (interviews). Occasionally J told DM about the more hidden events of her past as well. In Venice, for instance, she told her and JH about having been in Holloway once, 'for shouting Heil Hitler at her neighbours' (JH to SO, from Venice 1977). She told this to Francis too, and no doubt to SO. Indeed I'm sure she told most to SO, about whom she once said to DP: 'She is the only woman I trust'. (DW 68). (And see eg J to SO, 1 Sept 1972, which shows that she'd talked to SO about MH's 'smash': 'I don't know quite why I ended up speaking about a part of my rum life that I've bottled up for years.'

What went wrong ... DM interview; DM to SO, undated letters 1977-8; DW 46-7, 50-53.

Quotation: DW 53.

646 Perhaps it was ... DM undated letters to SO, 1977/8; DW 46, 52; DM interview.

It was exhausting ... DW 57; SO to DM, 23 Dec 1977; GM in DM undated letters to SO, 1977/8 and in DM interview with author.

By now ... DM dated the real troubles of J's stay to the last three weeks and J was back in Cheriton Fitzpaine, as we know, by 1 Mar.

In early February ... DM interview; DM undated letters to SO, 1977/8; DA to SO, 23 June 1978.

The phrase 'a Fuseli monster' must have come from GM, the art expert of the family. Henry Fuseli was an Anglo-Swiss artist, contemporary of Blake, who was famous for his 'Gothic horror' paintings, eg *The Nightmare*.

From then on ... DM interview and letters to SO. See also DW 56.

She was witchlike ... DM interview and letters to SO.

647 And clearly ... Ibid.

For the rest ... Ibid.; D Pet interview; DW 56; SO to DM, 21 Feb 1978.

Di was preparing ... and A few days ... DM interview.

648 At some level ... DA to SO, 23 June 1978; DA interviews; DM interview; A Alv interview.

Thus ended ... DM to SO, undated letter 1977/8.

And yet ... DM interview; DW 56, 61; 'FH'.

Quotation: Bk Ex Bk 93 (Tulsa 1:1); DW 61.

This was her best ... Bk Ex Bk 95, DW 61. DP omits the line I quote here, perhaps because he couldn't read it. See also the typescript of 'FH' in EA:

'One day to set against all this. It happened when I was sitting in the hot sun thinking and then not thinking and then being intensely happy, for I no longer existed. I was the wind and the blue sea. The "I" was left behind – a horrible dream of prison. Everything was laughing with joy. Do you see now? I knew that my life on earth had been just a dream of prison.

... Perhaps if one could have this feeling of being merged with other human beings it would be salvation but I cannot get it. I can get it partially with books. I can get the feeling that "I" "you" "he" "she" "they" are all the same – technical distinctions not real ones. Books can do this. They can abolish one's individuality, just as they can abolish time or place. People cannot do it, not with me.'

Quotation: DW 56.

Again she was . . . WSS 150, 153.

649 On 1 March . . . J to Ant S, 18 Mar 1978; DA to J, 31 Mar and 22 May 1978; J to DM undated, 1978; J to FW, 17 Apr 1978.

Quotation: DA to DM, 24 May 1978.

She was 'desperately . . .' DA to DM, same letter; DA to SO, 23 June 1978; DW 58-9; J to DM, 4 Nov 1978.

650 But if the storms . . . J to FW, 2, 3, 10, 20, 26 July 1978; J to Ant S, 1 June, 14, 19, 24 July 1978; J to Michael Henshaw, 26, 28 July, 8, 23 Aug 1978; J to MM, 15, 30 June 1978; J to DM, 24 July, 4 Aug 1978; J to OS, 14 July 1978; Mellown 139; DA to SO, 23 June 1978; J to PSA, 28 Oct 1978, 3 Mar 1979.

In this last summer . . . MM to AS, 30 July 1968 ('hopeful about kind strangers'); Nan Robertson to J, 1 Dec and 19 Dec 1977, and *NY Times* article; J to Ant S, 11 Oct 1978; EC, 'From Dominica to Devonshire: A Memento of Jean Rhys', *Kunapipi* 1, No 2, 1979, pages 6-22; Vreeland article; Madeleine Slade, 'The Visit: Autumn 1978', *Women Live*, Winter 1988, pages 19-20; J Br interview; FW to author. J had also expressed her gratitude to FMF in eg her interview with Peter Burton, to DP (P Rev 1979, page 260), and to Stang.

Footnote: 'Imp Rd' and 'Ch V' are Tulsa Items 1:24 and 1:27 respectively.

651 To the end . . . Vreeland, 224, 232; 'The Visit', 16. Quotation from 'The Visit' by kind permission of Madeleine Slade.

In the late . . . J to PSA, 28 Oct 1978 and 3 Mar 1979; J to Ant S, 13 Nov and 12 Dec 1978; DA to J, 10 Nov 1978; DA, Introduction to SP, page 7; J to DA, 22 May 1978; DA to SO, 23 June 1978; J to OS, 12 Dec 1978. J only managed to produce two tiny, scrappy bits about her later life, 'The Dividing Line' and 'The Cottage', which DA quite rightly left out of SP (they are in EA). For J's dread of galley proofs, see note made by DA, June 1980, on DA to J, 2 Mar 1965.

Instead her thoughts . . . J to FW, 20 July 1978 (*Dominica Star* clipping enclosed, dated 7 July 1978); Vreeland, 228, 236; J to DM, 25 Sept, 4 Nov, 20 Dec 1978; Ann Kilbride to J, 6 Sept 1978. J's thoughts also remained with PSA: she was planning to take *The Orchid House* to London with her, to look for a publisher for it, but never got there (J to EC, 4 and 21 Nov 1978 and 15 Jan 1979).

652 Of course she . . . DM interview.

October and November . . . Ibid.; J to DM, 4 Nov, 7 and 20 Dec 1978, 'Monday' (Jan), 23 Jan and 5 Apr 1979; J to Ant S, 11, 18 Oct, 13, 29 Nov 1978, 3 Mar 1979; J to PSA, 28 Oct 1978 and 3 Mar 1979; J to EC, 4 and 21 Nov 1978; J to MM, 15 Jan 1979; DA, Introduction to SP, page 8; J to OS, 11 Mar 1979.

In early March . . . Contract for *Winters Tales*, signed 9 Mar 1979, EA; Mellown 129; J to Ant S, 5 Apr 1979; J to DM, 5 Apr 1979; DA, Introduction to SP, page 7.

Two days . . . DA to DM, undated (1979).

The last year . . . DA to DM, Ibid.; SO to DM, 20 Jan 1978; DA interview with author, 24 May 1979; DA to LC, 7 June 1979; J But interview; JH interview; GM in DM interview; J Lee interview, 4 Dec 1985; JH to author, 10 Mar 1990.

On 14 May . . . and She asked . . . JH interview; JH to author, 10 Mar 1990.

When Jean started to die . . . Ibid.; SO to DM, 5 and 23 Dec 1978.

PART FOUR, CHAPTER THREE

655 Jean was always . . . DA interviews (re 'Poor Sonia', 'Poor Francis . . .').

She was also . . . DA interviews; DA in Bailey radio. And see J to SO, 14 Nov

1968: 'What makes him *tick* they say and proceed to destroy the very thing that perhaps made him tick because that is always elusive and in fact the real mystery.'

Certainly, too ... DRW and JRW interviews (re Mrs Rees Williams's and Auntie B's dementia at the end, and Edward's mild version of Aunt Minna's 'shaking palsy'.)

656 Her attitude to black ... 'TDTBTB', TABL 46, CS 156; J to Alan Plater, 2 Jan 1971 (EA); Bk Ex Bk 28–30; MR to author, 18 July and 2 Oct 1985; J to SO, 7 Oct 1973; DW 17; FMF, WWM, 73 and 249; RL interview and telephone conversation, 14 Mar 1986; OS interview. See also MS *Recollections*, 29: 'You have black blood in you, don't you, Jean?'

How she came to be ... On the question of Jean's madness, see also DA in Bailey radio.

She was afraid ... O Nbk 44–5.

657 But the answer ... Interviews and conversations with Hansi Kennedy, 9 Feb 1986, Dr Joan Schachter and Jan Wiener, MSAP, 2 Mar 1986, Dr Jack Klein and Susan Baxt, M. Ed., M.A., Nov 1988; DA to SO, 1 Nov 1977; DA to author, 30 Apr 1990.

The analysts all ... L 86, 172, 275; J to DA, 30 Sept 1972; 'A Night', CS 48; MM interview; MM in Bailey radio; MM to AS, 30 July 1968; FMF, WWM, 86–88, 227, 249, 265, 309; DW 11; J to OS, 27 Sept 1972 ('Do you think the trouble is that I'm *much too meek!*')

They recognised ... Interviews with analysts as above; 'Calypso', dated 4 May 1975, verso, in EA.

658 I think this must ... DA interview, 25 Oct 1984.

# BIBLIOGRAPHY

*Books by Jean Rhys*
*The Left Bank*, Cape 1927 (US : Harper & Bros, 1927; photo reprint ed. New York: Books for Libraries Press, 1970).
*Postures*, Chatto & Windus, 1928.
*Quartet*, André Deutsch, 1969, Penguin 1973 (US : Simon & Schuster, 1929; Harper & Row Perennial Library paperback, 1981.)
*After Leaving Mr Mackenzie*, Cape, 1931, republished by André Deutsch, 1969; Penguin 1971 (US : Alfred A Knopf, 1931; Harper & Row Perennial Library paperback, 1982.)
*Voyage in the Dark*, Constable, 1934, republished by André Deutsch, 1967; Penguin 1969 (US : William Morrow & Co, 1935; W.W. Norton paperback, 1982.)
*Good Morning, Midnight*, Constable, 1939, republished by André Deutsch, 1967; Penguin 1969 (US : Harper & Row, 1970, Perennial Library paperback, 1982.)
*Wide Sargasso Sea*, André Deutsch, 1966, Penguin 1968 (US : W.W. Norton, 1967, W.W. Norton paperback 1982.)
*Tigers Are Better-Looking*, André Deutsch, 1968; Penguin 1973 (US : Harper & Row, 1974; Popular Library paperback, 1976.)
*My Day*, published by Frank Hallman, 1975 (US) : contains 'My Day', 'Invitation to the Dance' and 'Close Season for the Old?' (US title for 'Whatever Became of Old Mrs Pearce?').
*Sleep It Off Lady*, André Deutsch, 1976; Penguin 1981 (US : Harper & Row, 1976.)
*Smile Please*, André Deutsch, 1979; Penguin 1981 (US : Harper & Row, 1980.)
*Letters, 1931-1966*, ed. Francis Wyndham and Diana Melly, André Deutsch, 1984; Penguin 1985 (US: Viking, 1984.)
*The Early Novels*, André Deutsch, 1984.
*The Complete Novels*, W.W. Norton, 1985.
*The Collected Short Stories*, W.W. Norton, 1987.


*Other works by Jean Rhys*
'Vienne', *Transatlantic Review*, Vol II, No 2, December 1924, pages 639-645.
'The Christmas Presents of Mynheer Van Rooz', *Time and Tide*, 12, 28 November 1931, pages 1360-1361.
'My dear darling Mr Ramage', *The Times*, No 57598, 28 June 1969, page 19.
'My Day', *Vogue*, 165, February 1975, pages 186-7.
'Whatever Became of Old Mrs Pearce?', *The Times*, No 59401, 21 May 1975, page 16.
'The Joey Bagstock Smile', *New Statesman*, 94, 23-30 December 1977, page 890.
'Making Bricks Without Straw', *Harper's*, 257, July 1978, pages 70-1.


*Translations by Jean Rhys*
*Perversity*, by Francis Carco, translated by Ford Madox Ford, Pascal Covici, Chicago, 1928; paperback by Black Lizard Books, Berkeley, California, 1987, translation credited to Jean Rhys.
*Barred*, by Edouard de Nève, translated by Jean Rhys, Desmond Harmsworth, 1932.

*Books about Jean Rhys*
Louis James, *Jean Rhys*, Longman, 1978.
Thomas F. Staley, *Jean Rhys, A Critical Study*, Macmillan, 1979.
Peter Wolfe, *Jean Rhys*, Twayne, Boston, 1980.
Helen Nebeker, *Jean Rhys, Woman in Passage*, Eden Press, Montreal, Canada, 1981.
David Plante, *Difficult Women*, Gollancz, 1983.
Elgin W. Mellown, *Jean Rhys, A Descriptive and Annotated Bibliography of Works and Criticism*, Garland Publishing Inc., 1984.
Carole Angier, *Jean Rhys*, Penguin Lives of Modern Women, 1985.
Arnold E. Davidson, *Jean Rhys*, Frederick Ungar, New York, 1985.
Teresa F. O'Connor, *Jean Rhys : The West Indian Novels*, New York University Press, 1986.
Kristien Hemmerechts, *A Plausible Story and a Plausible Way of Telling It, A Structuralist Analysis of Jean Rhys's Novels*, Peter Lang, Berne, 1986.
Nancy R. Harrison, *Jean Rhys and the Novel as Women's Text*, University of North Carolina Press, 1988.
Paula Le Gallez, *The Rhys Woman*, Macmillan, 1990.
Coral Ann Howells, *Jean Rhys*, Harvester Wheatsheaf, 1991.

*Other books consulted*
DOMINICA:
Phyllis Shand Allfrey, *The Orchid House*, Virago, 1982.
Thomas Attwood, *The History of the Island of Dominica*, J. Johnson, London, 1791. (Reprint ed., Frank Cass, London, 1971.)
Sir Henry Hesketh Bell, *Glimpses of a Governor's Life*, Sampson Low, Marston & Co, London, 1946; and *Obeah, Witchcraft in the West Indies*, Sampson Low, Marston, Searle and Rivington, London, 1889.
Basil E. Cracknell, *Dominica*, David & Charles, 1973.
Patrick Leigh Fermor, *The Traveller's Tree*, John Murray, 1950.
James Anthony Froude, *The English in the West Indies*, Longmans, Green & Co, London, 1888.
David P. Henige, *Colonial Governors from the Fifteenth Century to the Present*, Madison & Co, 1970.
Lennox Honychurch, *The Caribbean People*, Thomas Nelson & Sons, 1979; *The Dominica Story*, published by the Dominica Institute, 1984; and *Caribbean Landmarks*, Thomas Nelson & Sons, 1986.
James Pope Hennessy, *The Baths of Absalom, A Footnote to Froude*, Allan Wingate 1954.
Anthony Trollope, *The West Indies and the Spanish Main*, Chapman & Hall, 1859.
Alec Waugh, *The Sugar Islands*, Cassell, 1958.
Owen Rees Williams, memoir, unpublished.
Colonial Office Lists, HMSO.

THE PERSE SCHOOL:
*The Persean Magazine*, Vol V, 1906–1909, and Vol VI, 1909–1912.
M.H. Cattley, *The Perse School for Girls, 1881–1956*, Cambridge 1956.
M.A. Scott, *The Perse School for Girls, The First Hundred Years, 1881–1981*, Cambridge, 1981.

TREE'S SCHOOL:
*Burke's Peerage and Baronetage*, 1970.
*Burke's Landed Gentry*, 18th ed., Vol III, 1972.
*Who Was Who, 1916–1928*.
Lady Grove, *The Social Fetich*, Smith, Elder & Co., 1907.

THE STAGE:
Maurice Hewlett, *The Forest Lovers*, Thomas Nelson & Sons, 1939.
Phyllis Hartnoll ed., *Oxford Companion to the Theatre*, 3rd ed., OUP, 1967
Alan Hyman, *The Gaiety Years*, Cassell, London, 1975.
Allardyce Nicoll, *English Drama 1900-1930*.
John Parker, ed., *Who's Who in the Theatre*, 2nd ed., 1914, and 3rd ed., 1916.
*The Stage Yearbook*, 1910 and 1911.

LANCELOT HUGH SMITH:
*Alumni Cantabrigienses*, compiled by J.A. Venn, Part II, 1752-1900, CUP, 1953.
Bo Bramsen and Kathleen Wain, *The Hambros, 1779-1979*, Michael Joseph, 1979.
M. & E. Brock, eds., *H.H. Asquith, Letters to Venetia Stanley*, OUP, 1982.
*Burke's Complete Peerage*, Vol XII, 1953.
*Burke's Landed Gentry*, 1939.
Lancelot Hugh Smith, *History of Rowe & Pitman*, unpublished, circa 1937.

THE CRABTREE CLUB:
Bruce Arnold, *Orpen : Mirror to an Age*, Cape, 1981.
Kenneth Hare, *London's Latin Quarter*, Bodley Head, 1926.
Michael Holroyd, *Augustus John*, Penguin, 1976.
C.R.W. Nevinson, *Paint and Prejudice*, 1937.
*Kelly's Directory*, 1915.

ARTHUR HENRY FOX STRANGWAYS:
Wellington College Yearbooks, 1910, 1948.
Basil Newsome, *History of Wellington College, 1859-1959*.

ADRIAN ALLINSON:
Adrian Allinson, *Painter's Pilgrimage*, unpublished autobiography, 1941.
John Rosenberg, *Dorothy Richardson : The Genius They Forgot*, Duckworth, 1973.

PHILIP HESELTINE:
I.A. Copley, *The Music of Peter Warlock*, Dennis Dobson, 1979.
Cecil Gray, *Peter Warlock : A Memoir of Philip Heseltine*, Cape, 1934.
F. Tomlinson, *Peter Warlock Handbook* and *Warlock and Van Dieren*, Thames
   Publishing, 1978.

JEAN LENGLET:
E. Benézit ed., *Dictionnaire des peintres, sculpteurs, dessinateurs et graveurs*, Librairie
   Gründ, 1976.
Henriette van Eyk, *Dierbare Wereld*, Amsterdam, De Bezige Bij, 1973.
Martien Kappers, *Jean Rhys in the Netherlands, an Annotated Bibliography*.
William K. Langer, *Encyclopedia of World History*, 3rd ed., 1952.
Edouard de Nève :
   *In de Strik*, Amsterdam, Andries Blitz,1932.
   *Barred*, tr. Jean Rhys, Desmond Harmsworth, 1932.
   *Sous les Verrous*, Paris, Librairie Stock, 1933.
   *Kerels*, Amsterdam, Querido, 1932.
   *Aan den Loopenden Band*, (with Henriette van Eyk), Amsterdam, Querido, 1934.
   *Muziek Voorop*, Amsterdam, Querido, 1935.
   *Schuwe Vogels*, Amsterdam, Querido, 1937.
   *Glorieuzen*, Van der Loeff, Enschede, 1946.
   *Poolse Nachten*, Van der Loeff, Enschede, 1948.

*Bij ons op den Heuvel*, Van der Loeff, Enschede, 1948.
Emile van der Wilk, *Ed. de Nève*, Uitgeverij De Schaduw, Tilburg, 1989.
*Who Was Who, 1929–1940* and *1949–1960*.

FORD MADOX FORD:
See list of *Others' works*, see p. 660.
    Also : Ford Madox Ford, *It Was the Nightingale*, Heinemann, 1934, and *Memories and Impressions*, Penguin Classics; and Ernest Hemingway, *The Sun Also Rises*.

LESLIE TILDEN SMITH:
Harold Acton, *Nancy Mitford : A Memoir*, Hamish Hamilton, 1975.
D.A. Callard, *Pretty Good for a Woman : The Enigmas of Evelyn Scott*, Cape, 1985.
Jessica Mitford, *Hons and Rebels*, Penguin, 1962.
Jean Bouret, *Simon Segal*, Collection Artistes de nos temps, 1950.

CHERITON FITZPAINE:
Basil W. Handford, *Lancing College, History and Memories*, Phillimore, 1986.
Jean Rhys, 'Texts *Plus*' edition of *Wide Sargasso Sea*, 1989.
Michael Schwab, *Recollections*, unpublished.


*Books consulted in which Jean Rhys is mentioned*:

Shari Benstock, *Women of the Left Bank, Paris, 1900–1940*, Virago Press, 1987.
Elizabeth Hardwick, *Seduction and Betrayal*, 1974.
Jeremy Hawthorn, *Multiple Personality and the Disintegration of Literary Character*, Edward Arnold, 1983.
Sandra Gilbert and Susan Gubar, *The Madwoman in the Attic*, Yale University Press, 1979.
David Leon Higdon, *Shadows of the Past in Contemporary British Fiction*, Macmillan, 1984.
Selma James, *The Ladies and the Mammies : Jane Austen and Jean Rhys*, Falling Wall Press, 1983.
Rosalind Miles, *The Fiction of Sex*, Vision Press, 1974.
Ellen Moers, *Literary Women*, The Women's Press, 1978.
Kenneth Ramchand, *The West Indian Novel and its Background*, Faber paperback, 1970, and *An Introduction to the Study of West Indian Literature*, Nelson Caribbean paperback, 1976.
Elaine Showalter, *A Literature of Their Own*, Virago Press, 1978.


*Articles consulted*:

Abel, Elizabeth, 'Women and Schizophrenia : The Fiction of Jean Rhys', *Comtemporary Literature* 20, Spring 1979, 155–177.
Allen, Walter, 'Bertha the Doomed', *NY Times Book Review*, 18 June 1967, 5.
Allfrey, Phyllis Shand, 'Jean Rhys : A Tribute', *Kunapipi* 1, No 2, 1979, 11–12.
Alvarez, Al, 'The Best Living English Novelist', *NY Times Book Review*, 17 Mar 1974, 6–7.
'Against The Odds', *The Observer*, 20 May 1979, 34.
Angier, Carole, 'Jean Rhys : An Appreciation' (review of SP and Staley), *British Book News*, Feb 1980; and 'Weekend in Gloucestershire : Jean Rhys, Adrian Allinson and "Till September Petronella"', *London Magazine*, Vol 27, No 3, 1987, 30–46.
Annan, Gabriele, 'Turned Away by the Tropics' (review of SP and Staley), *TLS* No 4005, 21 Dec 1979, 154.

Athill, Diana, 'Jean Rhys and the Writing of WSS', *Bookseller*, No 3165, 20 Aug 1966, 212-213; and Introductions to SP, *The Early Novels*, *The Complete Novels*, *The Collected Short Stories*, and the 'Texts *Plus*' edition of *WSS*; and *Dictionary of National Biography* 1971-80.

Baer, Elizabeth R., 'The Sisterhood of Jane Eyre and Antoinette Cosway', in *The Voyage In*, ed. Elizabeth Abel, University Press of New England, 1983, 131-148.

Bailey, Paul 'True romance' (review of SIOL), *TLS* 22 Oct 1976, 1321; and 'Art from chaos' (review of L), *Observer*, 13 May 1984.

Baker, Mark, 'A.H. Fox Strangways', in Guide to Exhibition of Archives, Wellington College, June 1971.

Bamber, Linda, 'Jean Rhys', *Partisan Review*, 49, 1982, 91-100.

Bender, Todd K., 'Jean Rhys and the Genius of Impressionism', *Studies in the Literary Imagination*, II, 2, Fall 1978, 43-53.

Bernstein, Marcelle, 'The Inscrutable Miss Jean Rhys', *Observer Magazine*, 1 June 1969, 40-2 and 49-50.

Bibeb, Interview with Jean Lenglet, *Vrij Nederland*, 27 June 1959; and 'I Have Always Used Myself as Material and I Have Been as Honest as I Could', Interview with Jean Rhys, *Vrij Nederland*, 28 Feb 1976, 7-8.

Blodgett, Harriet, 'Enduring Ties : Daughters and Mothers in Contemporary English Fiction by Women', *South Atlantic Quarterly*, 80, Autumn 1981, 441-53.

Blythe, Ronald, 'A girl from Dominica' (review of SP), *Listener*, 6 Dec 1979.

Borinsky, Alicia, 'Jean Rhys : Poses of a Woman as Guest', in *The Female Body in Western Culture*, ed. Susan Rubin Suleiman, Harvard University Press, 1986.

Braybrooke, Neville, 'Between Dog and Wolf', *Spectator*, 21 July 1967, 77-8; and 'Shadow and Substance', *Spectator*, 28 Oct 1966, 560-1; and 'The Return of Jean Rhys', *Caribbean Quarterly*, Vol 15-16, 1969-70, Dec 1970, 43-6.

Brown, Nancy Hemond, 'Jean Rhys and VID', *London Magazine*, Vol 25, Nos 1/2, 1985, 40-59 (examination of the original ending of VID.)

Broyard, Anatole, 'A Difficult Year for Hats' (review of GMM), *New York Times*, 26 Mar 1974, 39.

Bruner, Charlotte H., 'A Caribbean Madness, Half Slave and Half Free', *Canadian Review of Comparative Literature*, Vol XI, No 2, June 1984, 236-248.

Burton, Peter, 'Jean Rhys', *Transatlantic Review*, No 36, Summer 1970, 105-9.

Byatt, A.S., 'Trapped' (review of TABL), *New Statesman*, 29 Mar 1968.

Campbell, Elaine, 'A Report from Dominica, BWI', *World Literature Written in English*, 17 April 1978, 305-16; and 'From Dominica to Devonshire : A Memento of Jean Rhys', *Kunapipi*, Vol 1, No 2, 1979, 6-22; and 'Reflections of Obeah in Jean Rhys's Fiction', *Kunapipi*,, Vol IV, No 2, 1982.

Cantwell, Mary, 'I'm a Person Without a Mask', *Mademoiselle*, 79, Oct 1974, 170-1.

Capell, Richard, 'In Memoriam AHFS', *The Observer*, 9 May 1948.

Carter, Hannah, 'Fated to be Sad', *The Guardian*, 8 Aug 1968, 5.

Casey, Nancy J (later Fulton), 'Study in the Alienation of a Creole Woman : Jean Rhys's VID', *Caribbean Quarterly*, 19, Sept 1973, 95-102; and 'The "Liberated" Woman in Jean Rhys's Later Short Fiction', *Revista Interamericana Review* 4, Summer 1974, 264-272; and 'Jean Rhys's WSS : Exterminating the White Cockroach', *Revista Interamericana Review*, Vol 4, No 3, 1974, 340-9.

Chartier, Delphine, 'Jean Rhys : L'Auto-censure créatrice, Analyse des versions successives de la nouvelle "Rap Rap"', *Jean Rhys Review*, Vol One, No One, Fall 1986, 15-29.

Codaccioni, Marie-José, 'L'Erreur chez Jean Rhys', in *L'Erreur dans la littérature et la pensée anglaise*: Actes du Centre Aixois de Recherches Anglaises. Festschrift, Université de Provence, 1980, 127-141.

Cole, Larry, 'Jean Rhys', *Books and Bookmen*, 17 Jan 1972, 20-1; and 'Jean Rhys : Some literary affinities', unpublished.

Cooke, Michael, 'Recent Fiction' (ALMM), *Yale Review* 61, No 4, June 1972, 607-9.

Copley, I.A., 'Warlock in Novels', *Musical Times*, Vol 105, No 1460, Oct 1964.

Dash, Cheryl M.L., 'Jean Rhys', in *West Indian Literature*, ed. Bruce King, Macmillan, 1979, 196-209.

Davies, Hunter, 'Rip van Rhys', *Sunday Times* No 7485, 6 Nov 1966, 13.

Delany, Paul, 'Jean Rhys and FMF: What "Really' Happened?", *Mosaic*, Vol XVI, No 4, Fall 1983, 15-24.

Devlin, Polly, 'Polly Devlin on Jean Rhys', *Vogue*, Dec 1979, 114.

Dias, Selma vaz, 'In Quest of a Missing Author', *Radio Times*, 3-11 May 1957.

Dick, Kay, 'Wife to Mr Rochester' (review of WSS), *Sunday Times*, 30 Oct 1966, 50.

Elias, E, review of *Kerels, Groene Amsterdammer*, 27 Jan 1934.

Emery, Mary Lou, 'The Politics of Form : Jean Rhys's Social Vision in VID and WSS', *Twentieth Century Literature* 28, 1982, 418-30.

Fabre-Luce, Anne, 'Incandescences', *Critique* (Paris), 29 July 1973, 674-675.

Fenton, James, 'A story of how a work of art was brought to life' (review of L), *The Times*, 17 May 1984, 11.

Fromm, Gloria G., 'Making Up Jean Rhys', *The New Criterion*, Vol 4, No 4, 1985, 47-50.

Froshaug, Judy, 'The Book-makers' (Jean Rhys and Anna Kavan), *Nova*, Sept 1967, 45.

Gardiner, Ruth Kegan, 'Rhys Recalls Ford : Q and GS', *Tulsa Studies in Women's Literature* 1, 1982, 67-81.

Gorb, Ruth, 'Powers of a Weak Person', *Ham & High*, 9 Nov 1984, 15.

Gornick, Vivien, 'Making the most of her miseries', *NY Times Book Review*, 30 Oct 1984 (review of L).

Guppy, Shusha, 'WSS by Jean Rhys', Novel Choice, *Observer Magazine*, 4 Nov 1979, 130.

Hall, John, 'Jean Rhys', *Guardian*, 10 Jan 1972, 8.

Hampson, John, 'Movements in the Underground – I', *Penguin New Writing 27* 1946, ed. John Lehmann, 133-151, on pp 149-51.

Harris, Wilson, 'Carnival of Psyche : Jean Rhys's WSS', *Kunapipi* 2, No 2, 1980, 142-50.

Hazzard, Shirley, 'Marya knew her fate and couldn't avoid it', (review of Q), *NY Times Book Review*, 11 Apr 1971, 6.

Hearne, John, 'The WSS : A West Indian Reflection', *Cornhill Magazine*, No 1080, Summer 1974, 323-33.

Heppenstall, Rayner, 'Bitter Sweet' (review of TABL), *Spectator*, 5 Apr 1968 (Jan-June 1968 vol., 446-7).

Hill, Susan, 'A foreign lustre to Jane Eyre', *Daily Telegraph*, 25 Aug 1979, 9.

Honychurch, Lennox, 'The Jean Rhys house', Historic Roseau No 5, *The New Chronicle* (Dominica), 6 June 1986, 9.

Hope, Francis, 'The First Mrs Rochester', *New Statesman*, 28 Oct 1966 (Vol 92, 638-9); and 'Women Beware Everyone', *Observer*, 11 June 1967, 26.

Houts, Jan van, 'The Hole in the Curtain', translation by John Rudge of 'Het Gaatje in het Gordijn', Zaandam, Oct 1981.

James, Louis, 'Sun Fire – Painted Fire : Jean Rhys as a Caribbean Novelist', *Ariel*, Vol 8, No 3, July 1977, 111-27; and 'Jean Rhys : Obituary', *Journal of Commonwealth Literature*, Vol 14, No 1, 5-6.

*Jean Rhys Review*, published biennially at Columbia University, New York, editor Nora Gaines.

Jones, Angela, 'Voodoo and Apocalypse in the Work of Jean Rhys', *Journal of Commonwealth Literature*, Vol 16, No 1, Aug 1981, 126-31.

Jong, A.M. de, review of *Schuwe Vogels, Het Volk*, 2 Dec 1937.

Jordis, Christine, 'Jean Rhys ou la perspective de l'exil', *Nouvelle Revue Française*, nos 366-7, juillet-aôut 1983, 156-67.

Kappers-den Hollander, Martien : 'Jean Rhys and the Dutch Connection', *Journal of Modern Literature*, Vol XI, No 1, Mar 1984, 159-73; and 'A Gloomy Child and its Devoted Godmother : Jean Rhys, *Barred, Sous les Verrous* and *In de Strik*', *Autobiographical and Biographical Writing in the Commonwealth*, 1984, 123-30; and 'A Little Learning', *Maatstaf*, 1985, No 3, 62-73; and 'Jean Rhys, het leven tussen twee werelden', *Literair Paspoort*, No 285, 1980, 661-679; and 'Een Ondoorzichtige Biographie', *Vrij Nederland Boekenbijlage*, 5 July 1986, 10-11 (review of *Jean Rhys* by Carole Angier); and 'Measure for Measure : *Quartet* and *When the Wicked Man*', *Jean Rhys Review*, Vol 2, no 2, 1988, 2-17.

Kavanagh, Julie, 'Rhys-cycled', *Women's Wear Daily*, 15 Nov 1974, 6.

Kemp, Peter, 'Deep beneath the cosmetics' (review of *Woman in Passage* by Helen Nebeker), *TLS*, 28 Aug 1981, 972.

Kersh, Gerald, 'The Second Time Around', *Saturday Review of Literature*, 50, 1 July 1967, 23.

Lai, Wally Look, 'The Road to Thornfield Hall', *New Beacon Reviews*, ed. John la Rose, New Beacon Books, 1968, 38-52.

Lane, Margaret, 'Life and hard times', (review of Q and ALMM), *Spectator*, 16 May 1969 (Vol 222, 649-50.)

Leonard, John, 'What Men Don't Know About Women' (review GMM), *New York Times*, 12 May 1970, 37.

Levi, Peter, 'The butterfly's wing', (review of *The Early Novels*), *Spectator*, 8 Dec 1984, 30.

Levin, Martin, Review of GMM, *NY Times Book Review*, 22 Mar 1970, 39.

Lewis, Wyndham, 'Hinterland of Bohemia', *The Saturday Review*, 23 Apr 1927, 637 (review of LB.)

Luengo, Anthony E., 'WSS and the Gothic Mode', *World Literature Written in English*, 15 Apr 1976, 230-45.

Macauley, Robbie, Review of SIOL, *NY Times Book Review*, 21 Nov 1976, 7.

Mellown, Elgin W.,'Character and Themes in the Novels of Jean Rhys', *Contemporary Literature*, 13, 1972, 458-75.

Mezei, Kathy, 'And it Kept its Secret : Narration, Memory and Madness in Jean Rhys's WSS', *Critique*, Vol XXVIII, No 4, Summer 1987, 195-209.

Mitgang, Herbert, 'Jean Rhys, British Novelist, Dies', *New York Times*, 128, 17 May 1979, B12.

Moorehead, Caroline, 'Spirit and the letter' (review of L), *The Times*, 21 May 1984, 17.

Morell, A.C., 'The World of Jean Rhys's Short Stories', *World Literature Written in English*, 18 Apr 1979, 235-44.

Moss, Howard, 'Going to Pieces', *New Yorker* 50, 16 Sept 1974, 161-2.

Naipaul, V.S., 'Without a Dog's Chance', *NY Review of Books*, 18 May 1972, 29-31.

Nève, Edouard de, 'Jean Rhys : Romancière Inconnue', *Les Nouvelles Littéraires*, 26 Aug 1939, No 880, 8.

*New Statesman* No 38, 5 Nov 1949, 533 and No 52, 6 Oct 1956, 435 (for Selma vaz Dias's and Sasha Moorsom's advertisements for Jean.)

Nudd, Donna Marie, 'The Uneasy Voyage of Jean Rhys and Selma vaz Dias', *Literature in Performance*, vol 4, no 2, 1984, 20-32.

Nunez-Harrell, E., 'The Paradoxes of Belonging : The White West Indian Woman in Fiction', *Modern Fiction Studies*, vol 31, no 2, Summer 1985, 281-93.

Oates, Joyce Carol, 'Romance and Anti-Romance : Jane Eyre to Rhys' WSS', *Virginia Quarterly Review*, vol 61, no 1, Winter 1985, 44-58.

Packer, P.A., 'The Four Early Novels of Jean Rhys', *Durham University Journal*, 71, June 1979, 252-65.

Petschek, Anna, 'The shy lady novelist who went missing for 20 years', *Daily Express*, 1 Sept 1976.

Piazza, Paul, 'The World of Jean Rhys', *Chronicle of Higher Education*, 14, 7 Mar 1977, 19.

Plante, David, 'Jean Rhys : A Remembrance', *Paris Review* 21, Fall 1979, 238-84.

Pool, Gail, 'Jean Rhys : Life's Unfinished Form', *Chicago Review*, vol 32, No 4, Spring 1981, 68-74.

Porter, Dennis, 'Of Heroines and Victims : Jean Rhys and Jane Eyre', *Massachusetts Review*, vol 17, 1976, 540-52.

Pree, Barry, 'Meet ... Sargasso lady', *Observer Magazine*, 3 Oct 1976, 8-9.

Pritchett, V.S., 'Displaced Person' (review SP), *NY Review of Books*, 14 Aug 1980, 8-10.

*Review of Contemporary Fiction*, Summer 1985 (vol 5, no 2) was dedicated to Jean Rhys and B.S. Johnson.

Ricks, Christopher, 'Female and Other Impersonators' (review of GMM), *NY Review of Books*, 23 July 1970, 12-13.

Robertson, Nan, 'Jean Rhys : the Voyage of a Writer', *New York Times*, 25 Jan 1978.

Rose, Phyllis, 'Jean Rhys in Fact and Fiction', *Yale Review*, Summer 1980, 596-602; and 'An Obscure Life' (review of L), *Atlantic Monthly*, Aug 1984, 109-10.

Ross, Alan, *London Magazine*, 6 Nov 1966, 99 and 101.

Sarraute, Anne, 'Une femme à la dérive', Quinzaine/Littéraire (s), 296, 1979, 11-12.

Scharfman, Ronnie, 'Mirroring and Mothering in Simone Schwartz-Bart's *Pluie et vent sur Telumée-Miracle* and Jean Rhys's WSS', *Yale French Studies*, no 62, 1981, 88-106.

Skipwith, Peyton, 'Adrian Allinson : A Restless Talent', *Connoisseur*, vol 198, no 798, Aug 1978, 264-73.

Smilowitz, Erika, 'Childlike Women and Paternal Men : Colonialism in Jean Rhys's Fiction', *Ariel*, vol 17, no 4, Oct 1986, 93-103.

Stade, George, Review of TABL, *NY Times Book Review*, 20 Oct 1974, 5-6.

Staley, Thomas F., 'The Emergence of a Form: Style and Consciousness in Jean Rhys's Q', *Twentieth Century Literature*, 24, Summer 1978, 202-24.

Stevens, Gini, 'Every day is a new day', *Radio Times*, 23-29 Nov 1974, 6.

Sullivan, Mary, 'All Underdogs' (review TABL), *Listener*, 25 Apr 1968, 549.

Thieme, John, 'Apparitions of Disaster : Brontëan Parallels in WSS and Guerillas', *Journal of Commonwealth Literature*, vol 14, No 1, Aug 1979, 116-32.

Thomas, Ned, 'Meeting Jean Rhys', *Planet*, vol 33, Aug 1976, 29-31.

Thorpe, Michael, 'The Other Side : WSS and Jane Eyre', *Ariel*, 8, No 3, July 1977, 99-110.

Thurman, Judith, 'The Mistress and the Mask : Jean Rhys's Fiction', *MS*, 4 Jan 1976, 50-2 and 91.

Tiffin, Helen, 'Mirror and Mask : Colonial Motifs in the Novels of Jean Rhys', *World Literature Written in English*, 17 Apr 1978, 328-41.

*Times Literary Supplement*, anonymous reviews of LB, 5 May 1927, 320; of *Postures*, 4 Oct 1928, 706; of ALMM, 5 Mar 1931, 180; of GMM, 22 Apr 1939, 231; of VID, 1 Nov 1934, 752; of WSS, 17 Nov 1966, 1039; of VID and GMM, 20 July 1967, 644; of TABL, 2 May 1968, 466.

Trevor, William, 'Voyager in the Dark' (review of L), *Guardian*, 17 May 1984, 18.

Trilling, Diana, 'The Odd Career of Jean Rhys' (review of SP), *NY Times Book Review*, 25 May 1980, 1 and 17.

Turner, Alice K., 'Jean Rhys Rediscovered : How It Happened', Paperbacks in the News, *Publishers Weekly*, 206, 1 July 1974, 56 and 58.

Updike, John, 'Dark Smile, Devilish Saints' (review of SP), *New Yorker*, 11 Aug 1980, 82-9.

Vincent, Lindsay, 'The "old boy" brokers', *Observer* Business Section, 27 Mar 1983.

Vreeland, Elizabeth, 'Jean Rhys', *Paris Review*, 21, Fall 1979, 219–237.

Vriesland, Victor van, Preface to Jean Rhys, *Melodie in Mineur*, tr. Edouard de Nève, de Steenuil, 1935; and Kroniek van het Proza (Prose Chronicle) reviews in *Nieuwe Rotterdamsche Courant* of ALMM, 24 Sept 1932; of VID, 20 Nov 1934; of *Kerels*, 25 Nov 1933; of *Muziek Voorop*, 20 Apr 1935; of *Schuwe Vogels*, 16 Dec 1937 ('Boekaankondigingen'); and 'Niet Bang van Bijziendheid' (Not Afraid of Myopia), *Onderzoeg en Vertoog* (Research and Representation, collected critical essays), Amsterdam, Querido, 1958, 294–301.

Warner, Marina, 'The art of survival' (review of L), *Sunday Times*, 13 May 1984.

Webb, W.L., 'Lately prized', *Guardian*, 14 Dec 1967, 6.

Williams, Angela, 'The Flamboyant Tree : The World of the Jean Rhys Heroine', *Planet*, vol 33, Aug 1976, 35–41.

Williams, Sally, 'Londoner's Diary', *Evening Standard*, 12 June and 21 June 1967, both 6.

Wilson, Lucy, 'Women Must Have Spunks : Jean Rhys's West Indian Outcasts', *Modern Fiction Studies*, vol 32, No 3, Autumn 1986, 439–448.

Wilson, Steuart, Obituary of AHFS, *Music & Letters*, Vol XXIX, No 3, July 1948, 236–7.

Wood, Michael, 'Endangered Species', (review of SIOL), *NY Review of Books*, 11 Nov 1976 (vol 23, 30–1.)

Wyndham, Francis, 'An Inconvenient Novelist', *Tribune*, no 721, 15 Dec 1950, 16, 18; and 'Introduction to Jean Rhys', *London Magazine*, 7 Jan 1960, 15–18; and 'Introduction', *Art & Literature*, No 1, Mar 1964, 173–177; and Biographical Note, *Art & Literature*, No 8, Spring 1966, 212–213; and Introduction, WSS, André Deutsch, 1966 and all subsequent editions; and 'Jean Rhys', in *Concise Encyclopedia of Modern World Literature*, ed. Geoffrey Grigson, Hawthorn Books, New York, 1963, 369–70.

Zuidinga, Robert-Henk, 'Een Literair Raadsel', *De Haagsche Post*, 19 Mar 1977, 6–8 ('A Literary Enigma').

# INDEX